COLLECTED WORKS OF ERASMUS

VOLUME 12

THE CORRESPONDENCE OF
ERASMUS

LETTERS 1658 TO 1801

January 1526–March 1527

translated by Alexander Dalzell

annotated by Charles G. Nauert jr

University of Toronto Press

Toronto / Buffalo / London

The research and publication costs of the
Collected Works of Erasmus are supported by
University of Toronto Press.

© University of Toronto Press 2003
Toronto / Buffalo / London
Printed in Canada

ISBN 0-8020-4831-5

Printed on acid-free paper

National Library of Canada Cataloguing in Publication Data

Erasmus, Desiderius, d. 1536
[Works]
Collected works of Erasmus

Translation of: Opus epistolarum Des. Erasmi Roterdami.
Includes bibliographical references and index.
Contents: v. 12. Correspondence of Erasmus,
letters 1658 to 1801, January 1526–March 1527 /
translated by Alexander Dalzell; annotated by Charles G. Nauert.
ISBN 0-8020-4831-5 (v. 12)

1. Erasmus, Desiderius, d. 1536 – Collected works. I. Title.

PA8500 1974   199′.492   C74-006326-x rev

University of Toronto Press acknowledges the financial assistance to its
publishing program of the Canada Council and the Ontario Arts Council.

University of Toronto Press acknowledges the financial support for its
publishing activities of the Government of Canada through the Book Publishing
Industry Development Program (BPIDP).

Collected Works of Erasmus

The aim of the Collected Works of Erasmus
is to make available an accurate, readable English text
of Erasmus' correspondence and his
other principal writings. The edition is planned
and directed by an Editorial Board, an Executive Committee,
and an Advisory Committee.

This book was published with the financial assistance of
George S. Dembroski.

Contents

Illustrations

Preface

The present volume includes Erasmus' surviving correspondence for the year 1526 and nearly all of the first quarter of 1527. During this time, Erasmus apparently never set foot outside the city of Basel. The urgency of his scholarly work was one reason he stayed close to home, but ill health was the major reason. During the late summer and early autumn of 1526, and again at the turn of the year from 1526 to 1527, he was far more seriously ill than usual even for a man who was chronically unwell. The ailment in the first period seems to have been a severe infection of the urinary tract, complicated by his chronic suffering from calculus.[1] In the second period, he complained of severe stomach pains[2] and looked so feeble that on Christmas day his close friend Bonifacius Amerbach, in a letter thanking the Avignon physician Hieronymus Lopis for sending medical advice that had relieved the pain, described Erasmus as a person 'than whom you have never seen a man more emaciated or more feeble.'[3] The threat of impending death probably explains why on 22 January 1527 Erasmus made the first of his three wills, a step he had long considered and for which he had made careful legal preparations since, on account of his irregular canonical status, he needed a papal brief explicitly authorizing him to dispose of his property by will.[4] During his second bout of acute illness, he seems not even to have left the house he rented from Johann Froben. In a letter of 26 January 1527, he expresses uncertainty whether the plague was still active in Basel,

* * * * *

1 Epp 1729, 1735
2 Ep 1780 n5; cf 538 below, the introductory note to Erasmus' First Will.
3 AK III 228 Ep 1170
4 See Ep 1588, a dispensation granted by Pope Clement VII on 8 July 1525. Since Erasmus was technically still under a religious vow, there was a possibility that the prior of his monastery at Steyn might have a legal claim to all his property upon his death. The text of this first will appears at 540–50 below.

something he presumably would have known if he had gone about in the city.[5]

Although Erasmus remained in Basel and pursued his scholarly work for the Froben press, he was uneasy about residing there on account of the growing strength of the Reformation party, led by his former associates Johannes Oecolampadius and Conradus Pellicanus, from whom he had become bitterly estranged because he believed that they were trying to create a public impression that he privately sympathized with their heretical views on the Eucharist.[6] In fact he had become an outspoken critic of the Sacramentarian eucharistic doctrine put forward at Zürich by Huldrych Zwingli and at Basel by Oecolampadius and Pellicanus. In 1525 he had been one of four scholars who advised the city council against permitting the publication of Sacramentarian books in Basel, advice that explains why Oecolampadius published his first two eucharistic treatises at Strasbourg and Zürich rather than at Basel. By March of 1527, however, the religious balance on the city council had begun to change, so that Oecolampadius' third eucharistic tract could be safely printed at Basel by Andreas Cratander. In a letter to Pellicanus,[7] Erasmus' assumption that the city council 'will not be silly enough to expel everyone who disagrees with Oecolampadius' was still valid (Ep 1792A:41–2); but the fact that he would even raise such a hypothetical possibility reflects a significant shift. When he formally advised the council against allowing Sacramentarian books to be published locally in 1525,[8] the council was inclined to favour such advice, even though it also allowed Oecolampadius to preach and had granted him both an ecclesiastical appointment and a theological professorship. But though the Reformers were gaining in influence, Erasmus was an open foe of the Sacramentarian cause. In May 1526, when the Catholic party within the Swiss Confederation arranged an open debate on religious issues at a meeting of the Confederation held at Baden under ground rules favourable to the Catholic cause, Erasmus declined an invitation to appear in person, citing his own poor health as an excuse; but he did send an open letter, composed in Latin but translated into German for the lay delegates, denouncing an anonymous treatise that tried to associate him with the Reformers' opinions. This letter firmly declared his opposition to a eucharistic doctrine that had already been con-

* * * * *

5 Ep 1780 introduction and lines 25–6. There is evidence of a serious outbreak of plague in October and November 1526; see Ep 1777 n1.
6 CWE 11 xii–xiv, xvii–xviii; cf Epp 1739, 1792A.
7 Allen Ep 1644 has been redated to mid-March 1527. See Ep 1792A introduction.
8 Epp 1539, 1636

demned by the church and affirmed his own refusal 'to depart from the doctrine laid down by the church.'[9] The German version was also read to the city council of Basel, doubtless at the initiative of the Catholic members; the Latin original was published by the controversialist Thomas Murner in 1527, as an annex to his edition of the acts of the Baden disputation, and again by Erasmus himself in his *Opus epistolarum* in 1529. When the Reformation party finally gained full control of religious policy in Basel, Erasmus felt bound in conscience to move to the safely Catholic university town of Freiburg im Breisgau, where he resided for six years before returning to Basel in 1535.

Although Erasmus' troubles with the Swiss Reformers took up much of his time and energy in 1526 and early 1527, the earlier year began with a crisis involving a far more famous Reformation figure, Martin Luther himself. On the very last day of 1525, Luther finally published his long-awaited reply to the treatise *De libero arbitrio* διατριβή *sive collatio* (1524), in which Erasmus had openly declared his opposition to a central doctrine of Luther, the bondage of the human will. Luther's response, *De servo arbitrio*, was shocking. It shocked not because he reaffirmed his belief that the sin of Adam had destroyed free will and had left the human will enslaved to sin, for that could have been expected. What dismayed Erasmus was Luther's contemptuous dismissal of him as an unbelieving infidel who deliberately mocked and scorned all genuine Christian belief, a cynical, sneering 'Lucian, or some other pig from Epicurus' sty.'[10] His spiritual and moral integrity was attacked, not just his theological competence. Since Erasmus was habitually suspicious, he concluded that the long interval of silence (about fifteen months) between his *De libero arbitrio* and the appearance of Luther's reply was part of a plot against him, and that the late-December publication of *De servo arbitrio* was deliberately timed to make it impossible for him to publish a reply until after the spring book fair at Frankfurt, the principal centre for diffusion of books throughout all of northwestern and central Europe. Thus the Lutherans would have a virtual monopoly on discussion of Erasmus' doctrines and moral character for more than half a year, and it would be impossible to get a reply into the hands of readers before the autumn session of the Frankfurt market.

There is little evidence to support this conspiracy theory. Luther deferred his harsh reply because he faced many other more pressing problems, and also because his contempt for Erasmus was so profound that he

* * * * *

9 Ep 1708:44–6
10 See Ep 1667 introduction.

was reluctant to respond at all, even though he knew that eventually he must. On the other hand, it is true that neither Luther nor any other person in Wittenberg made the slightest effort to provide Erasmus with a copy of *De servo arbitrio*. In the early weeks of 1526 Erasmus tried in vain to get the book, and he eventually saw it only because an unidentified friend in Leipzig sent him a copy. He probably did not receive this book until sometime in early February. Galvanized by the scurrilous nature of Luther's attack, he strained every nerve to produce a short preliminary reply (published as *Hyperaspistes* part one) and to get it into print in time for the spring book fair. Backed by Froben's willingness to devote virtually his whole printing capacity to setting and printing the rebuttal, Erasmus wrote *Hyperaspistes 1* in a mere ten days; and the publisher devoted five or six presses (probably all that he owned) to production of the book, succeeding in getting this hurried response onto the market at the March fair, in time to compete with Luther's attack.[11] It was a remarkable achievement for both author and publisher. Eventually Luther did write directly to Erasmus in justification of his book. That letter has perished, but the repressed fury evident in Erasmus' reply of 11 April 1526 suggests that Luther's letter was even more patronizing and contemptuous than *De servo arbitrio* had been.[12] Erasmus did not publish the promised (and much longer) second part of *Hyperaspistes* until September 1527. Luther simply dismissed Erasmus' rebuttal from his mind and never bothered to reply to either part of the work.

Erasmus excused the long delay in completion of the second part of *Hyperaspistes* by complaining of the distraction caused by attacks from conservative Catholic theologians who continued to be totally unimpressed by his public break with both Luther and the Swiss Reformers. These attacks came chiefly from individuals at the universities of Paris and Louvain, especially from the syndic of the Paris faculty of theology, Noël Béda. Erasmus had attempted to approach Béda directly and win him over.[13] His initial letter in April 1525 led to a lengthy exchange that began with formal civility and protestations of good will on both sides but soon degenerated into a thinly veiled hostility that continued to manifest itself in the period covered by the present volume.[14] Béda was implacable, pressing forward towards the formal condemnation of Erasmus' publications adopted by the

* * * * *

11 See Epp 1667 introduction and 1683 n5.
12 Ep 1688
13 See CWE 11 xv–xvii and the letters there cited, especially Epp 1571 and 1581.
14 Epp 1679, 1685

faculty in December 1527. A low point in this relationship came with publication of Béda's hostile *Annotationes* (Paris: Josse Bade, 25 May 1526) listing alleged errors and impieties in the works of both the French humanist Lefèvre d'Etaples and Erasmus.[15] Erasmus' letters are full of vehement complaints about these attacks by Béda and his associate, the French Carthusian Pierre Cousturier.

In February 1526 he addressed a relatively mild protest to the Paris faculty of theology itself,[16] a complaint somewhat restrained in tone because King Francis I, the principal defender of humanists in France, was still being held as a prisoner of war in Spain. After publication of Béda's *Annotationes*, however, Erasmus' appeals for fair treatment became more assertive, since he knew that the king was back in France. In three letters written in June 1526 to the supreme judicial authority (the Parlement of Paris), to King Francis himself, and to the faculty of theology, he complained bitterly that Béda and Cousturier were attacking him at the very time when he was actively defending the Catholic faith against Luther and the Swiss Sacramentarians.[17] His appeals to the Parlement and the faculty, both of which were eager to repress heresy and were generally unwilling to draw any distinction between humanist critics of abuses in the church and outright Protestant heretics, had no success, but the appeal to the king brought results. In August 1526 Francis I ordered the Parlement to stop further sale of Béda's book; according to an exultant letter written by a friend of Erasmus (who, however, was not in Paris at the time), Béda himself was forced to go from bookstore to bookstore, accompanied by a royal official, to seize unsold copies of his own book for destruction.[18] There is no independent confirmation of the story about the personal humiliation of Béda, but the confiscation itself is thoroughly documented. In any event, little seems to have been accomplished: most of the copies of Béda's book had already been sold, and in August the book was republished at Cologne, safely beyond the reach of French law. The incident also did nothing to deter the indomitable Béda, who pressed ahead with his efforts to secure formal condemnation of Erasmus' books by his faculty. Erasmus' direct appeal to external authority – the Parlement and the king – was not unique. He also wrote directly to the general of the Carthusian order, of which his critic Cousturier was a member, and urged him to restrain Cousturier's

* * * * *

15 Ep 1721 introduction
16 Ep 1664
17 Epp 1721, 1722, 1723
18 Epp 1722 introduction, 1763

excessive zeal. Here also, however, he gained fair words but no lasting success.[19]

Erasmus also had enemies at Louvain. While his past association with the College of the Lily and his role in the creation of the Collegium Trilingue left him with many admirers (including several with whom he remained in close touch, such as the humanists Adrianus Barlandus and Conradus Goclenius), his relations with his fellow theologians at Louvain had varied from open hostility to great tension even while he resided there. The death of Maarten van Dorp in 1525 removed the one Louvain theologian who had become actively supportive of Erasmus' scholarship. In the mid-1520s he did not face the kind of openly hostile publications that emanated from Paris theologians like Béda and Cousturier, but the most active scholar among the Louvain theologians, Jacobus Latomus, had indirectly challenged the Erasmian programme of church reform and theological study as early as 1519. In 1525 Latomus published three works that avoided mentioning Erasmus by name but were recognizably critical of him.[20] In March of the same year, a group of Dominican friars with connections to the Louvain faculty had published under a pseudonym a work directly attacking his book on confession, *Exomologesis*, as heretical.[21] In addition, the friars' practice of preaching sermons denouncing Erasmus, which he had already experienced while residing at Louvain from 1517 to 1521, continued through the 1520s. The Carmelite Nicolaas Baechem of Egmond was the most frequent object of Erasmus' complaints. In 1525 these complaints had moved Pope Clement VII to send an informal letter (in lieu of a formal brief) and a special emissary to admonish the Louvain theologians to avoid open attacks on Erasmus at a time when he was defending the church against Luther; and when the papal emissary, Theodoricus Hezius, passed over to the side of the theologians after reaching Louvain, the papal datary, Gian Matteo Giberti, wrote, admonishing him to fulfil his mission. In private, however, Hezius encouraged Erasmus' critics.[22] Though Erasmus continued to direct complaints to Rome,[23] papal authority was simply too remote to overcome the unremitting hostility of his critics among the friars and theologians at Louvain. The authority of the emperor Charles V, hereditary prince of the Netherlands, was closer at hand and had more direct

*****

19 Epp 1687, 1804
20 Epp 1571 n5, 1581 n58
21 Ep 1581A introduction
22 Epp 1589, 1589A
23 Ep 1716

control over the university even though the imperial court itself was far away in Spain, and Erasmus turned to his numerous and highly placed friends both at the court in Spain and at the court of the governor of the Netherlands, Margaret of Austria (the same friends to whom he continued to appeal for help in obtaining payment of the pension promised to him as an imperial councillor).[24] They obtained for him a letter from the emperor himself warmly approving his scholarship and encouraging him to continue his efforts to defend the church from the heretics. They even obtained from Charles v a direct order (well attested though the document itself has been lost) commanding the theologians to stop their attacks.[25] And the most powerful of Erasmus' supporters at court, the imperial chancellor Mercurino Gattinara, finally wrote his own letter to the University of Louvain, castigating the university authorities for their efforts to evade the imperial command and threatening not very subtly that if they did not silence attacks by their members, he would no longer exert his authority to promote the interests of the university. There is some evidence that Gattinara's intervention, unlike all other attempts, did cause the theologians to be more cautious in what they said and published about Erasmus.[26] But Erasmus' critics would not be silenced, and Louvain remained a centre of opposition.

Although Erasmus' controversies with the German and Swiss Reformers may have done nothing to mollify his Catholic critics in Paris and Louvain, they warmed the hearts of many leaders of the Catholic cause in Germany. This group included two close advisers of Archduke Ferdinand of Hapsburg: the chancellor, Bernhard von Cles, prince-bishop of Trent,[27] and his close associate Johannes Fabri, suffragan bishop of Constance, a man whose eagerness to cite Erasmus against the Lutherans made Erasmus uncomfortable.[28]

Even more important was Duke George of Saxony, who until his death in 1539 held his half of the Saxon lands firmly in the Catholic camp. For years he had kept after Erasmus to prove his orthodoxy by breaking openly with Luther; and while he welcomed the publication of *De libero arbitrio* in 1524, he thought it rather tardy and vainly attempted to transform Erasmus into

* * * * *

24 See Epp 1700 n3, Ep 1703 introduction.
25 The emperor's letter is Ep 1731; on the imperial order see Ep 1643 and cf Ep 1784A introduction.
26 Ep 1784A
27 Epp 1689, 1710, 1730, 1738, 1755, 1793
28 Ep 1690; cf Epp 1715, 1739, 1771.

a full-time controversialist engaged in refuting one by one each book published by Luther and his supporters. Publication of *Hyperaspistes 1*, which clearly demonstrated a deterioration in Erasmus' relations with Luther, delighted Duke George; and in the face of continuing pressure from Saxony for additional controversial tracts, Erasmus sent to Dresden a detailed list showing that many of his publications had in fact contradicted the Lutheran cause even though he had not engaged in a tit-for-tat refutation of each Lutheran publication.[29] Although this list seems to have impressed the duke and made him somewhat less impatient, he and his court officials Hieronymus Emser and Simon Pistoris continued to press for more books against the heretics and especially for speedy completion of the second part of *Hyperaspistes*, which did not come off the press until September 1527. Although Erasmus welcomed the endorsement of the Saxon duke and his servants, the constant nagging obviously irritated him. On one occasion when even in praising him Emser rather condescendingly informed him that he had assured the duke that Erasmus had 'never willingly departed from the decrees of the church,' Erasmus retorted sharply, 'I have never departed from the decrees of the church either willingly or unwillingly'[30] and then launched into a lengthy demonstration that there were many so-called 'decrees of the church,' and that while some of them were eternally valid and binding on all Christian consciences, many others dealt with special circumstances of a particular time and place and might indeed be amended or even abolished, provided it was done by lawful authority. In general, his relations with the authorities at Dresden remained friendly; and when Duke George became active in distributing Latin and German editions of a privately published letter that Henry VIII of England circulated among European rulers in reply to a rude letter that Luther sent to him in 1522, the Saxon court took care to keep Erasmus informed. The duke himself sent Erasmus a copy of the king's new book, probably one of the privately published copies sent directly from London to Dresden.[31] The good will of the Saxon court was not sufficient to preserve the tenure of Jacobus Ceratinus, the professor whom Erasmus had recommended for the chair of Greek at the duke's university in Leipzig, but the recommendation itself had been welcomed and accepted; Ceratinus' dismissal (which resulted from the duke's unfounded suspicions that he was a secret Lutheran) did

* * * * *

29 Ep 1773 introduction
30 Ep 1744:16–17; cf Ep 1773 n5 on the efforts of Emser and Pistoris to mollify Erasmus.
31 Ep 1773 nn7, 10; cf Ep 1776.

not upset the generally cordial relationship between Erasmus and Duke George.[32]

In the period covered by this volume, Erasmus continued his friendly relations with influential people in eastern Europe, such as Jan Antonin, Hieronim Łaski, Jan (II) Łaski, Krzysztof Szydłowiecki, and Andrzej Krzycki in Poland and Jacobus Piso and Johann Henckel in Hungary; with friends whom he cultivated as sources of information and influence in Italy, such as Francesco Chierigati at the Roman curia, the jurist Andrea Alciati (then living in Milan), the humanist Giambattista Egnazio and the publisher Gianfrancesco Torresani at Venice, and Francesco Cigalini, a physician and antiquarian at Como. In England, he continued to enjoy the favour of influential people, as reflected in his correspondence with Cuthbert Tunstall, bishop of London; the Italian-born Tudor court historian Polidoro Virgilio; John Longland, bishop of Lincoln; and Stephen Gardiner, who subsequently became bishop of Winchester and who even at this period, though still a junior figure, was well placed as secretary to the man who administered England in the name of the king, Cardinal Thomas Wolsey.[33] Although only one letter from Thomas More, Erasmus' closest English friend, survives from this period, there is evidence of other letters that were lost,[34] and Erasmus' correspondence with Robert Aldridge about manuscripts of Seneca shows that Erasmus and More remained in close touch and that Erasmus felt free to commit More to the task of forwarding letters and books to and from Cambridge.[35] Erasmus' contacts with England remained strong and friendly even though he seems never to have considered England as a place to live if the continued growth of Protestantism in Basel forced him to leave that city.

Erasmus knew virtually nothing about the Iberian kingdoms. He had declined an opportunity to accompany the household of Charles of Hapsburg in 1516 when Charles went to Spain to claim the Spanish throne. Yet the numerous Burgundian and Netherlandish courtiers who did go to Spain helped to stimulate an explosion of interest in Erasmus' programme of Christian humanism and in his publications, not only among the intellectual classes of Spain but also among spiritually sensitive Spaniards who could read only the Spanish translations of Erasmian works such as the *Enchiridion*. Between the mid-1520s and the early 1530s, Erasmus gained an enthusiastic following

* * * * *

32 Ep 1693:35–8 and nn6, 7
33 Epp 1669, 1745; cf Ep 1697 to Wolsey, who always gave Erasmus fair words but never actually translated his words into acts of patronage.
34 Ep 1770 n1
35 Epp 1656, 1766, 1797

in Spain. At the same time, however, some members of monastic orders and some theologians became convinced that his ideas were dangerous. Erasmus learned of his growing fame in Spain as early as 1517, when Cardinal Jiménes de Cisneros, impressed by his edition of the New Testament, invited him to that country.[36] In the autumn of 1526 he received a lengthy description of his standing among Spaniards in a letter from the humanist Juan Maldonado, a member of the household of the primate of Spain, Alonso de Fonseca, archbishop of Toledo. This letter described the positive response by many Spaniards to his works but also warned him of the hostility of some monks and theologians and suggested that in future publications Erasmus should avoid bold, challenging statements that might drive moderate readers into the camp of the opposition.[37] Even earlier, Erasmus had received from a Benedictine monk, Alonso Ruiz de Virués, a set of manuscript notes pointing out passages in his works that might be misconstrued to seem offensive to the religious orders and urging him to be more cautious in expressing his ideas.[38] Virués was in fact a sincere admirer of Erasmus, a friendly critic concerned only that Erasmus avoid offending timid souls who otherwise might be won over to the Erasmian programme of spiritual renewal. But Erasmus was suspicious of apparently friendly monks whose criticisms might be an entering wedge for the same kind of attacks he had faced in France, the Netherlands, and England. Only after his friend Vergara had investigated the identity of Virués and a number of Spanish friends had written to assure him of the man's benign intentions did Erasmus drop his suspicion that Virués' list of comments might be the prelude to an underhanded attack.[39]

Erasmus did have unfriendly critics in Spain, and these became more active as his works – especially the *Enchiridion*, which expressed his ideal of a spiritually regenerated Christendom – began to appear in vernacular translations. Although many of his friends at the imperial court were Netherlanders, he had also attracted highly placed Spanish admirers. Some were influential functionaries like Vergara, secretary to the primate; Pedro Juan Olivar, a humanist who was a close friend of the chancellor, Gattinara; and Alfonso de Valdés, secretary to the emperor. But they also included the primate himself, Archbishop Fonseca, and (of special value) the inquisitor-general of Spain, Alonso Manrique de Lara, archbishop of Seville. In the late summer

* * * * *

36 Ep 582; cf Bataillon (1991) I 82–3, and the admiration expressed in Ep 1277 (1522) from Juan de Vergara, a former secretary to Cardinal Jiménez.
37 Ep 1742
38 Ep 1684 introduction
39 Ep 1684 introduction; cf Ep 1786 and Allen Ep 1838 from Virués himself.

of 1526, the inquisitor-general acted to forestall attacks on the orthodoxy of the Spanish translation of the *Enchiridion* by having the book reviewed by an inquisitorial commission which determined that it was 'very profitable and highly edifying.'[40] In September the second edition appeared, bearing the inquisitor's official coat of arms, quoting the words of his commissioners, and dedicated to Manrique by the translator. Not long afterwards, Archbishop Manrique acted to silence preaching and other agitation against Erasmus by the mendicant orders, and early in 1527 he reminded the superiors of the orders that he had forbidden attacks on Erasmus, instructing them that if they found serious errors in Erasmus' books, they should write down the errors and refer them to the Inquisition. The mendicants took Manrique at his word and on 5 April 1527 presented their charges to the Suprema (council) of the Inquisition. Since there were many duplications and inconsistencies in the lists of alleged errors, Manrique ordered the mendicants to compile a single list, promising that he would submit this set of articles to a conference of theologians from the universities of Salamanca and Alcalá. After some delays, this conference began meeting at Valladolid on 27 June and continued to meet and debate the charges until 13 August, when, even though only part of the charges had been discussed and no formal decisions had been made, the inquisitor-general dismissed the conference. Thus Erasmus was not convicted on any charge of heresy, though he also was not formally cleared. Erasmus received details of the original charges brought before the Inquisition in a letter of 13 March 1527 from Pedro Juan Olivar. For the time being, Erasmus seemed vindicated by these results, but in the years following 1530, one by one the leading Spanish Erasmians were charged with heresy and subjected to imprisonment or acts of penance. The correspondence informing Erasmus of the outcome of the conference will appear in the next volume in the present series, and the later fate of Spanish Erasmianism will be reflected in subsequent volumes.

The longest single series of letters in this volume was exchanged with the Antwerp merchant Erasmus Schets, who early in 1525 had offered to take charge of the collection of Erasmus' revenues from pensions drawn from ecclesiastical benefices in England and the Netherlands. Erasmus had experienced difficulty securing regular payment of the income and even greater difficulty in getting the money transferred from northern Europe to Basel without considerable loss from the costs of exchange. His friend Pieter Gillis had handled his financial matters for a number of years; but though he was

* * * * *

40 Ep 1742 n4

a reliable friend, he was often busy with his duties as secretary to the city
of Antwerp and was not very efficient in managing financial affairs. Schets,
who had business correspondents in London, replaced Gillis as Erasmus'
financial agent within less than a year and proved remarkably loyal and efficient in transmitting funds, forwarding letters, and purchasing and shipping merchandise requested by Erasmus. By early 1526 he had arranged the
transfer to Basel of the considerable sums of Erasmus' money formerly deposited with Gillis.[41] Although he venerated Erasmus for his learning and
piety, Schets was very much the man of business, and nearly all of their correspondence deals with financial matters. For this reason, Erasmus did not
publish any of this correspondence.

But Schets was responsible for one literary action. He had valuable contacts with the court of King John III of Portugal and with merchants in that
country, and he was eager to secure for his friend Erasmus the patronage of
this young king by having Erasmus dedicate some significant work to King
John. Although at first Erasmus seems to have been cool to the plan, eventually he agreed to dedicate his forthcoming Latin edition of several works by
St John Chrysostom, which appeared in March 1527 from the Froben press.
Unfortunately for his and Schets' hopes, his dedicatory preface included
criticisms of alleged profiteering by the Portuguese in their overseas empire. Thus the epistle of dedication gave offence to the courtiers in Lisbon,
who decided not to present the edition to the king for fear it might anger
him. Instead of securing a valuable gift and establishing relations with a future patron, Erasmus received no acknowledgment and no reward. He did
not discover that the dedication had not even reached the king until 1530,
when a Portuguese visitor told him what had happened.[42]

Despite the troubles with Luther, the Swiss Reformed pastors, and his
Catholic critics, Erasmus refused to allow controversies to draw him away
from his scholarly work and his books of spiritual counsel. The edition of
Chrysostomi lucubrationes in March 1527, which failed to attract favour in
Portugal, had been preceded by publication of other works of this influential Greek church Father in the preceding year: Erasmus dedicated an edition of six sermons to his English friend John Claymond and two homilies on the Epistle to the Philippians to Polidoro Virgilio, the Tudor court
historiographer.[43] In addition, he produced an edition of several works of

* * * * *

41 Ep 1696
42 Epp 1681, 1769. The letter of dedication to John III is Ep 1800. The reasons for
    the king's failure to reply to it are revealed in Ep 2370.
43 Epp 1661 and 1734 respectively

St Athanasius, *Athanasii lucubrationes*, which was published in March 1527 as an annex to the *Lucubrationes* of Chrysostom and dedicated to another English friend, John Longland, bishop of Lincoln.[44] One of Erasmus' most important patristic editions in this period was *Adversus haereses* (Basel: Froben August 1526) of St Irenaeus, bishop of Lyon, whose work is especially important for its detailed description of early Gnostic heresies. Erasmus dedicated this edition to Bernhard von Cles, prince-bishop of Trent, a trusted adviser to the emperor's brother, Archduke Ferdinand.[45] An even more important scholarly work of this period was the fourth edition of his *Novum Testamentum*, published by Froben in late February or early March 1527. It did not carry a new dedicatory epistle but included an address 'to the pious reader' prefixed to some supplementary material.[46] Although there was one more edition of the New Testament during Erasmus' lifetime, the fourth edition was the last to undergo significant revision at his hand, and the letters of the preceding year reflect his steady occupation with this editorial task.

Closely related to Erasmus' patristic and scriptural studies were his works of spiritual counsel, one of which appeared during this period. It was *Institutio christiani matrimonii* (Basel: Froben, August 1527), dedicated to Catherine of Aragon, queen of England. Like the dedication of his Chrysostom to the king of Portugal, the dedication to the English queen failed to elicit a gift or even a prompt acknowledgment. It was not a propitious time to seek the favour of Queen Catherine, who had learned only a month earlier that King Henry intended to dissolve their marriage. This news did not become generally known even at court until July, and since Erasmus' dedication was dated from Basel on 15 July, it is certain that he knew nothing of the queen's serious trouble at the time.[47]

In the period covered by the present volume, Erasmus also published several works of classical scholarship: a Latin translation of Plutarch's *De vitiosa verecundia*, annexed to a new edition of his own *Lingua* and dedicated to a former secretary and courier, Frans van der Dilft, then living in Louvain;[48] three philosophical treatises by Galen, also in Latin translation, dedicated to his Hungarian-born friend Jan Antonin, then settled in Cracow as physician to the king of Poland and other people at court;[49] and two republications

* * * * *

44 Ep 1790
45 The dedication to Archbishop Bernhard is Ep 1738; cf Ep 1771 introduction.
46 Ep 1789
47 Ep 1727 and introduction
48 Ep 1663
49 Ep 1698

bearing only general prefaces addressed to the reader: an expanded edition
of his popular collection of classical proverbs, *Adagiorum chiliades*,[50] and a
reissue of his commercially successful 1514 edition of the widely used school
textbook *Disticha moralia*, traditionally though incorrectly (as Erasmus knew)
attributed to the famous Roman moralist M. Porcius Cato.[51]

Erasmus' active pursuit of manuscript sources for his patristic and classical scholarship is reflected in a letter to the Venetian humanist Giambattista
Egnazio, soliciting his assistance for Hieronymus Froben, who had travelled
to Italy searching for patristic and classical manuscripts;[52] in his correspondence with Robert Aldridge about manuscripts of Seneca that he had seen at
Cambridge;[53] and in his pursuit of permission to have Hieronymus Froben
search for manuscripts in the valuable library left to the diocese of Worms
two decades earlier by Johann von Dalberg, bishop of Worms, which were
currently housed in the castle of Ladenburg on the Neckar river.[54] Erasmus
also sought and received an important Italian manuscript needed for his
edition of St Irenaeus' *Adversus haereses* through the good offices of his correspondent Johannes Fabri, who originally had hoped to edit the work himself but rather reluctantly turned it over to Erasmus at the request of his
own patron, Bernhard von Cles.[55]

Other letters found in the present volume include one from the contentious French humanist and aristocrat Louis de Berquin, for whose protection from his enemies Erasmus pleaded in his letter of June 1526 to Francis I
(a passage dropped from the text that Erasmus himself published in his *Opus
epistolarum* in 1529, the year of Berquin's execution as a lapsed heretic);[56] and
letters to his French humanist acquaintances Lefèvre d'Etaples[57] and Guillaume Budé. The letter to Budé contains an interesting request that Budé
should take care to include a friendly reference to Erasmus in some of his
major publications in order to silence rumours that he was hostile to Erasmus.[58] The letters from this period also show that Erasmus continued to be

* * * * *

50 Ep 1659
51 Ep 1725
52 Ep 1707, to Giambattista Egnazio
53 Epp 1766, 1797
54 Epp 1767, 1774
55 Epp 1715, 1738, 1771
56 Ep 1692 from Berquin; for the plea to Francis I on Berquin's behalf, see Ep
    1722.
57 Ep 1795
58 Ep 1794. Erasmus felt no awkwardness about making this request; indeed, he
    himself published the letter in 1529.

troubled by the association between the deceased humanist Christophe de Longueil and the group of curial humanists whom he regarded as his sworn enemies and whom he would openly attack in 1528 in his *Ciceronianus*.[59] Also in this period Erasmus continued the correspondence he had begun in 1525 with the English humanist Reginald Pole, a kinsman of King Henry VIII, who was then studying in Padua and acting as patron to a number of young humanists from England and other countries.[60]

There are 148 letters in the main series contained in this volume, numbered 1658 through 1801 in Allen VI, plus Epp 1739A (published by Allen in the preliminary matter of volume VIII), 1784A (published in regular sequence in Allen VI 459–61), 1790A (published in regular sequence in Allen VI 470–1), and 1792A (redated from 1525 and moved to the present volume from Allen's location as Ep 1644). Of these letters, 54 are addressed to Erasmus; 86 are from him to individuals or groups (Epp 1664 and 1723 to the Paris faculty of theology, 1708 to the delegates of the Swiss Confederation meeting at Baden, and 1721 to the Parlement of Paris). Three are letters about Erasmus exchanged between other parties (Epp 1726, 1763, and 1784A), of which the most noteworthy is the last, from the imperial chancellor Mercurino Gattinara to the leaders of the University of Louvain. Five of the letters are general prefaces addressed by Erasmus to readers and printed in works published during the period covered by this volume (Epp 1659, 1667, 1725, 1789, 1801). Seven are prefaces or dedications for texts that he edited during this period (Epp 1661, 1698, 1727, 1734, 1738, 1790, 1800). Three were first printed in publications by other authors: two of these (Epp 1679 and 1685) were included by Noël Béda in his *Apologia adversus clandestinos Lutheranos*, 1529 (cf Ep 1581 introduction), and the third (Ep 1708, Erasmus' open letter to the assembly of the Swiss Confederation that met at Baden in May 1526) was edited with the acts of that assembly by Thomas Murner in 1527. Three letters (Epp 1721, 1722, 1723), addressed by Erasmus to French authorities (the Parlement of Paris, King Francis I, and the Paris faculty of theology), were printed in a clandestine pamphlet, *Epistolae tres*, that probably appeared at Paris in 1526. By far the largest group of letters in the present volume, 52 in all, were first published by Erasmus himself in his *Opus epistolarum* (Basel: Froben 1529). In summary, nearly half of the letters here translated were in print before 1530 (72 of the total 148), some of them in fugitive publications like *Epistolae tres* but others in volumes widely circulated

* * * * *

59 Ep 1706 to Andrea Alciati, then living in Milan; cf Ep 1713 to Jacques Toussain, a protégé of Budé.
60 Ep 1675; cf Ep 1627.

and widely read by contemporaries, such as *Opus epistolarum*. Others in the present volume were published after Erasmus' death in 1536 but in the lifetime of his contemporaries: Ep 1785 in the first volume to appear as part of the posthumous collection of his *Opera*, planned by Erasmus himself, supervised by his executor Bonifacius Amerbach, and published by the successors of Froben in 1538; 3 letters (Epp 1665, 1732, 1792) first appeared in the *Opera* of Juan Luis Vives (1555).

Several of the letters in the present volume first appeared in print during the seventeenth and eighteenth centuries: Epp 1717 and 1729, published by Melchior Goldast in his edition of the *Opera* of Willibald Pirckheimer (1610); five (Epp 1692, 1693, 1742, 1770, 1791) by Jean Leclerc in LB III (*Desiderii Erasmi Roterodami Opera omnia* [Leiden 1703]); Ep 1799 by Johann Christoph Wolff in 1736; Ep 1718 by Johann Heumann in 1758; Ep 1737 by Salomon Hess in 1790.

The rise of professional historical and literary scholarship in the nineteenth and twentieth centuries brought many previously unprinted letters to light and also provided new sources for improving the text of letters that had appeared earlier. Single additions to the *corpus* of Erasmian letters included: Ep 1691 by J.K. Seidemann in 1849; part of Ep 1748 by A[dolph] Helfferich in 1859 and the whole text by Eduardus Böcking in 1861; Ep 1748, with an incorrect addressee, by Helfferich, and with a correct attribution by Adolfo Bonilla y San Martín in 1907; Ep 1670 by C.A.H. Burkhardt in 1883; Ep 1757 by Hermann Baumgarten in 1888; Ep 1780 by Preserved Smith in 1918; Ep 1790A by Marcel Bataillon in 1924; and Ep 1724 by Henry de Vocht in 1928. Far more extensive contributions to the published correspondence of Erasmus were the collection edited by Joseph Förstemann and Otto Günther in 1904, which included seventeen of the letters here translated, and the collection edited by L.K. Enthoven in 1906, which provided ten. The year 1906 was also the date when the first volume of Allen's *Opus epistolarum* was published, providing the textual foundation for the great majority of letters translated in the CWE series. Allen VI drew on (and cited) all of the earlier editions, but in many cases he also succeeded in finding the original manuscript letters or contemporary manuscript copies that provided a more authoritative Latin text. Twenty-six of the letters in the present volume were first printed in Allen VI. In order to inform readers of the earliest date at which any particular letter became available to the Latin-reading public, the introduction of each letter records the earliest publication known.

Appended to the main body of letters is a group of six letters and extracts from letters exchanged between Spanish admirers of Erasmus between September 1522 and August 1527, of which the Latin text appears as Appendix 18 in Allen VI 494–502. These letters reflect the growth of Spanish

Erasmianism during the mid-1520s, stimulated by the publication of both Latin and Spanish editions of his works. But like a number of letters in the main body of the correspondence, they also reflect growing concern among conservative theologians and clergy that Erasmus' influence was undermining orthodox faith. These letters therefore supplement references in the main series to the first formal charges made against Erasmus' publications in the winter and spring of 1527 and document the preliminaries of the Valladolid Conference of theologians that met in the summer of 1527.

Also translated from Allen (vi 503–6 Appendix 19) is the text of Erasmus' first will, signed in January 1527 in order to provide for the orderly disposition of the substantial personal property that he had acquired. Although Erasmus made two additional wills, this document is significant as evidence of where and with whom he felt the closest personal ties and also as the only one of his wills that sets out the plan for the production of a collected edition of his works after his death. Even though the third will does not mention this plan (the second will is lost), Erasmus' executor Bonifacius Amerbach did carry it out, publishing the *Opera omnia* of Erasmus at Basel in 1540. Erasmus' detailed instructions for the distribution of specially bound presentation copies of this edition show how he perceived his personal, spiritual, and cultural affinities at this time; notable especially is the absence of French friends and patrons and the almost total omission of Italy and Italians from his list of intended recipients.[61]

The annotator of this volume is under obligation to many friends and colleagues who have made his own work possible. The place of honour goes to Alexander Dalzell, whose insights and meticulous care as a translator are present in every line of the text. In addition, he provided the raw materials, and often the actual wording, of most notes on classical, patristic, and scriptural matters. John H. Munro of the University of Toronto provided all notes both in the present volume and in CWE 11 that deal with monetary and financial questions. Most of the notes on these topics appear exactly as he wrote them. Because significant changes in the value of coins and precious metals occurred during the period covered by this volume, Professor Munro has also provided an appendix on money and coinage. The annotator of the next volume in this series, James Farge CSB of the Pontifical Institute

* * * * *

61 This distribution is discussed in Charles G. Nauert 'Erasmus' Spiritual Homeland: The Evidence of His 1527 Will' in *Habent sua fata libelli / Books Have Their Own Destiny: Essays in Honor of Robert V. Schnucker* ed Robin B. Barnes, Robert A. Kolb, and Paula L. Presley, Sixteenth Century Essays and Studies 50 (Kirksville, MO 1998) 103–10.

of Mediaeval Studies in Toronto, has provided friendly encouragement and valuable cautions against the temptation to view reality solely through the eyes of Erasmus. At the University of Toronto Press, Ron Schoeffel, as chair of the Executive Committee of CWE, has provided enthusiastic but patient encouragement for completion of this volume. Mary Baldwin as copyeditor watched carefully for blunders that I let slip through. The book was typeset by Lynn Burdon and Philippa Matheson. The index, as in all CWE correspondence volumes, contains references to the persons, places, and works mentioned. Nearer home, I must express appreciation to Martha Alexander, director of the University of Missouri Libraries, for permitting me to retain, beyond the usual time limit, a library study in which I could collect an Erasmian library in close proximity to my notes and my translator's manuscript. I am also beholden to the reference and interlibrary loan staffs of my university library. My wife Jean has encouraged my work and has tolerated my spending many weekends and evenings in the company of our friend Erasmus.

CGN

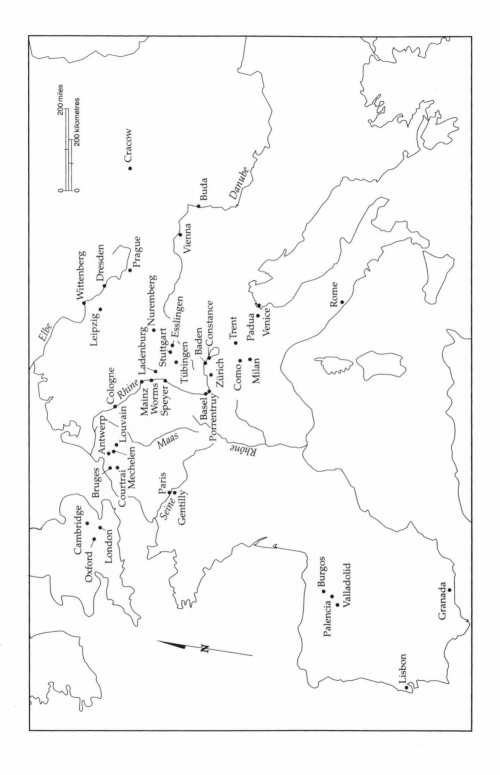

200 miles

200 kilometres

Cracow

Buda

Danube

Vienna

Wittenberg

Dresden

Prague

Elbe

Leipzig

Nuremberg

Ladenburg

Esslingen

Stuttgart

Baden

Constance

Rome

Trent

Padua

Venice

Cologne

Tübingen

Rhine

Mainz

Worms

Speyer

Zürich

Como

Milan

Basel

Porrentruy

Antwerp

Louvain

Maas

Rhône

Bruges

Mechelen

Courtrai

Paris

Seine

Gentilly

Cambridge

Oxford

London

Burgos

Valladolid

Palencia

Granada

N

Lisbon

THE CORRESPONDENCE OF ERASMUS
LETTERS 1658 TO 1801

1658 / From Erasmus Schets   Antwerp, 16 January 1526

On Erasmus Schets, the Antwerp merchant and banker who took over management and transfer of Erasmus' revenues from England and the Netherlands,
see Ep 1541 introduction. This letter clearly illustrates Schets' painstaking care
to provide rapid and inexpensive transfer of Erasmus' money to Basel, as well
as his admiration for Erasmus' publications. Like most of this private business correspondence, this letter remained unpublished until the appearance of
Allen VI in 1926; Allen based his text on the autograph letter preserved among
Erasmus' papers in Basel. Erasmus' reply is Ep 1676.

Cordial greetings. A month ago[1] I wrote to tell you how things were going.
I hope you received my letter and the little jar of imported fruit that I sent
you as a gift.

With regard to the money I received on your behalf from England, I
was anxious that it reach you quickly and with less risk of loss, so I made the   5
following arrangements: I handed over to Martin Lompart of Basel[2] 138 1/2
écus d'or au soleil[3] to send on to you. In exchange he gave me a receipt, which

* * * * *

1658
1 Ep 1651, dated 3 December 1525
2 On this rather obscure Basel merchant, who apparently was residing at Antwerp as an agent of Jakob Lompart, see Ep 1651 n6 and the other letters there
cited. Here Schets identifies Martin as a brother of Jakob, but in Ep 1676:3 he
is identified as a son of Jakob. Ep 1651 describes Martin as 'a businessman
from Basel,' suggesting that while he did business in Antwerp, he was not
permanently resident there. Whatever the family relationship, it is clear that
Schets intended to use Martin Lompart to carry gifts from Antwerp to Basel.
3 Latin *centum triginta octo cum dimidio scuta aurea solis*, the current French gold
coin. In July 1519, it had been debased from 23.125 to 23.0 carats and in
weight from a *taille* or cut of 70 per *marc de Troyes* (244.753g) to a *taille* of
71.167, to contain 3.296g fine gold; at the same time, its official value was
raised from 36s 3d to 40s 0d tournois. In the Hapsburg Netherlands, it was
given an official value of 6s 4d or 76d or groot Flemish (ordinance of August 1521; CWE 8 350); in England, a royal proclamation of 22 May 1522 (the
first to accept any foreign coins as legal tender) granted this 'crown soleil' a
rate of 4s 4d or 52d sterling, a rate fully in accordance with its gold contents.
See A. Blanchet and A. Dieudonné *Manuel de numismatique française* II (Paris
1915) chapters 19–20; *Tudor and Stuart Proclamations, 1485–1714* I: *England and
Wales* ed Robert Steele (Oxford 1910) 9 no 82, 10 no 88 (24 November 1522).
This sum would then have been worth exactly £277 tournois, or £30 0s 2d
sterling, equivalent to 1,200 days' wages for a master carpenter at Oxford or
Cambridge (6d sterling per day), about 5 years and 5 months' wage income;

I am enclosing with this letter. This is an acknowledgment that he received
the money in cash from me and an undertaking to have it delivered to you
without delay by his brother Jakob Lompart.[4] On the strength of this docu-   10
ment you may claim the sum from the said Jakob. I expect he will pay all
right; but if he does not, you should make a statement before a notary and in
the presence of witnesses testifying that he refuses to pay. Have this document sent to me along with the enclosed receipt, for in that event I shall have
to claim the money from Martin himself. I could not find any quicker way   15
of having the money sent to you or any way less subject to special charges.

Please remember to send me your receipt, for Alvaro de Castro[5] has
promised to deliver it to Canterbury, and I in turn have guaranteed indem-
nity to Alvaro. So see that both of us are discharged of our responsibilities.

I greatly enjoyed reading your *Lingua*[6] and the *Apologia* against Cous-   20
turier.[7] If Cousturier had studied your *Lingua* before he began ranting about

* * * * *

or officially £43 17s 2d groot Flemish, equivalent to 1,053 days' wages or 4
years and 9 months' wage income for an Antwerp master carpenter. In the
1520s, a master carpenter at Antwerp-Lier, earning 15d groot Brabant = 10d
groot Flemish per day, was employed an average of 221.4 days per year (230
days in 1526). See Herman Van der Wee *The Growth of the Antwerp Market and
the European Economy, Fourteenth–Sixteenth Centuries* 3 vols (The Hague 1963)
I 461, 542 Appendix 48.

4 This Basel banker is more fully documented in the records of the city than
his brother (or son) Martin. He appears again in Epp 1671, 1676, and 2193 as
a reliable and helpful intermediary in Schets' transfer of money and gifts to
Erasmus.

5 Schets' agent in London; this Spanish merchant of Burgos was resident in London and represented an important business connection for Schets, facilitating
his plan to make the collection of Erasmus' revenues from England and their
transfer to Basel by way of Antwerp more rapid and reliable and also to reduce the costs of exchange. In this case he had received from the archbishop
of Canterbury a payment of the annual pension that Erasmus received from
the revenues of the parish of Aldington in Kent. On the pension, see Epp 1583
n1, 1671 n9. On Castro and his brother Luis, who appear frequently in the
correspondence between Schets and Erasmus, see Ep 1590 n2.

6 Erasmus published this work in August 1525 (Ep 1593). Schets was aware of
the publication and apparently had received a copy by December 1525, but
at that time he had not found time to read it (Ep 1651). *Lingua / The Tongue*
appears in CWE 29 249–412, translated by Elaine Fantham.

7 The full title of Erasmus' *Apologia* is *Adversus Petri Sutoris, quondam theologi
Sorbonici, nunc monachi Cartusiani, debacchationem apologia* (Basel: Froben, August 1525), a rebuttal of the charges made by the conservative Carthusian
monk and Paris doctor of theology Pierre Cousturier in *De tralatione Bibliae*
(Paris: Pierre Vidoue for Jean Petit 1525), which was directed against Jacques

you, perhaps he would not have been so intemperate in his attacks on you
and on the humanities, for in the opinion of all the most respected and
learned men you have never produced anything except sound teaching and
good advice. No one will be surprised, however, that there are 'scourges   25
of Erasmus' when we know that there were several 'scourges of Jerome'[8]
in his own lifetime.[9] Even the gods have their enemies, and the humanities
have their detractors. Such men on account of their innate and ineradicable

* * * * *

Lefèvre d'Etaples and other reformist humanists as well as against Erasmus.
Sutor is the Latin equivalent of the vernacular Cousturier ('shoemaker,' 'cobbler'). Erasmus' dedication of his *Apologia* to Jean de Selve, first president of
the Parlement of Paris, is Ep 1591, and he briefly summarizes the main accusations levelled by Cousturier in Ep 1614. On Cousturier's background see
Ep 1571 n10; cf Ep 1687 n11. Erasmus' letters from 1525 and 1526 are full of
complaints about Cousturier, whom he regarded as one of the most malevolent and most grossly incompetent of his theological critics; see for example Epp 1571:30–63 and n10; 1581:473–9, 569–78, 910–11; 1591:29–53; 1687:50–
122. Ep 1687 is a complaint addressed to Willem Bibaut, prior of the Grande
Chartreuse and hence Cousturier's monastic superior. The exchange of hostile
tracts between Erasmus and Cousturier lasted until 1529, even though Erasmus at times regretted his initial decision to respond to the attack; see Ep 1679
n2. On Cousturier's next move in the pamphlet war see Ep 1687 n12.
8 The Latin words here translated 'scourges of Erasmus' and 'scourges of Jerome'
are *Erasmiomastiges* and *Ieronimiomastiges*, terms coined on the model of *Ver-
giliomastix* used to designate certain ancient literary critics who were harshly
critical of authors who were almost universally revered. An example of such
a critic would be the cynic philosopher Zoilus referred to by Ludwig Baer in
Ep 1741, whose nickname came to be *Homeromastix*. The Greek noun μάστιξ
means 'whip,' 'scourge.'
9 The 'scourges of Jerome' in his own lifetime included especially his former
friend Rufinus. Schets' point here is that even St Jerome, whom he and Erasmus regarded as the greatest and most consistently orthodox of the ancient
church Fathers, was unjustly subjected to attacks that impugned his orthodoxy.
On this point see Eugene F. Rice jr *Saint Jerome in the Renaissance* (Baltimore
1985) 12, 18–20, who points out that Jerome was no passive victim of Rufinus' attacks but a fierce controversialist who 'gave as good as he got' (18). In
fact Erasmus had carefully shaped the image of Jerome presented in his own
publications in order to present him as the kind of ideal Christian scholar that
Erasmus himself aspired to be. See Tracy *Erasmus* (1996) 132 and also Lisa Jardine *Erasmus, Man of Letters* (Princeton 1993) 5, 60–79. Jardine demonstrates
that this reshaping of the traditional image of Jerome was linked not only to
Erasmus' deliberate invention of his own public identity but also to an agenda
of promoting Christian humanism. Schets' use of the terms discussed in n8
above is a good example of how an admirer of Erasmus naturally associates
him with St Jerome.

ignorance and because they are driven by hidden resentment are constantly
disparaging the glory of the gods and casting their own filth into the limpid 30
pools of languages and letters. But I think your *Apologia* was all that was
needed to shut Cousturier's mouth; like Zúñiga,[10] he has had enough and
will not dare to attack you again.

I hope, dear Erasmus, that these words will cheer you up. As for myself
and your many friends, we shall be cheered if we hear more frequently how 35
you are keeping.

Antwerp, 16 January 1526

Your most devoted servant, Erasmus Schets

To the learned and incomparable Master Erasmus of Rotterdam. In
Basel 40

1659 / To the Reader   Basel, 17 January 1526

This letter is the preface to yet another expanded edition of one of Erasmus'
most successful books, the *Adagiorum chiliades* (Basel: Froben, 1526), which
added yet another 52 proverbs (with Erasmus' comments and notes on sources)
to the contents of the previous edition of 1523. On the *Adages*, first published as
a collection of only 818 proverbs in 1500 under the title *Adagiorum collectanea*,
vastly expanded in the great Aldine edition of 1508 (3260 adages) under the
present title (which emphasizes the 'thousands' of proverbs included), and
then increased by additions in revised editions issued every few years down

* * * * *

10 On this Spanish critic of Erasmus' biblical scholarship, whose harsh attacks
drew upon a mastery of Greek and Hebrew unmatched by any of Erasmus'
French critics, see CWE 8 336–46, 454–61, the correspondence between him and
Juan de Vergara in 1521–3, and Ep 1579 n25; see also Rummel I 145–77 and
H.J. de Jonge's introduction to ASD IX-2. Erasmus published his first *Apologia* against Diego López Zúñiga in 1521 and his second in 1522, but Zúñiga
was persistent despite discouragement by his patron Cardinal Jiménes de Cisneros, prohibition by Pope Leo X of his attempt to publish one of his attacks
at Rome, and explicit imposition of silence (issued in response to complaints
from Erasmus) by Popes Adrian VI and Clement VII. Yet Schets' statement
here proved to be correct: Zúñiga issued his last publication against Erasmus
in 1524; while he continued to note down Erasmian 'errors,' he did not publish
these notes and at his death in 1531 arranged for his critical notes to be sent to
Erasmus. Allen IV 622 publishes a list of the ten tracts exchanged by Erasmus
and Zúñiga. For additional information on their clash, see Epp 1260 n36, 1277
n1, 1290. Erasmus' own summary of the controversy appears in Ep 1341A, his
autobiographical letter of 1523 to Johann von Botzheim, which includes a list
of all his publications.

to the year of Erasmus' death, see Phillips *Adages*, especially xii–xiii, a summary of all the textually significant editions. See also the introductions to the
letters used as prefaces or dedications to some of the earlier editions, Epp 126,
211, 269, Ep 313 introduction, and n1 below. A full English translation of the
Adages is in course of publication. Available to date are I i 1–III iii 100 in CWE
31–4.

ERASMUS OF ROTTERDAM TO ALL WHO ARE EAGER TO LEARN,
GREETING

I was beginning to feel embarrassed, good reader, at the frequent rebirth of
this work[1] and to think that there was some justice in the complaints of the
critics that the practice of producing new editions was emptying the pockets   5
of scholars. Moreover, I was coming to the conclusion that I had laboured
long enough on this enterprise. Then suddenly I chanced on something that
might otherwise have escaped me for ever. I noticed a great number of careless mistakes in the numbering of books and chapters and likewise in the
letters used by the Greeks to denote the various books of Homer. It was   10
easy enough for such mistakes to slip in, for since there is much drudgery
involved in work of this sort, I generally indicate numbers in short form;
moreover, some Greek letters resemble Latin letters in shape, though they
represent different sounds. For example, Greek *rho* [ρ] looks like Latin *p* and
Latin *x* closely resembles the Greek *chi* [χ]. This kind of error is not easily de-   15
tected by a proofreader, however learned he may be – it may even escape the
only-begetter of the work himself! Since a monumental work like this consists almost entirely in references to authors, books, and chapters, where can
one find a reader with such a prodigious memory that he can detect a false

* * * * *

1659
1 Erasmus had brought out two editions of his early *Adagiorum collectanea* (1500
and 1506–7, with twenty new proverbs added to the second one), the vastly
expanded and significantly reconceived Aldine edition, *Adagiorum chiliades*, in
1508, and five further expansions and revisions (1515, 1517–18, 1528, 1533,
and 1536) of the Aldine edition, all first published at Basel by Froben, some
with a few and some with many proverbs added. Many of these editions were
reprinted by other publishers, even after they had been 'superseded' by more
complete editions revised by Erasmus himself. The 1508 Aldine and the 1515
Froben editions are important landmarks in the transformation of the work
from a simple collection of classical proverbs to an elaborate combination of
profound scholarship and personal opinions. Erasmus himself described this
transformation in his *Catalogus lucubrationum* of 1523 (Ep 1341A:575–621) and
also in a letter of 1520 to Polidoro Virgilio, Ep 1175.

reference at once, or is there anyone with enough leisure and patience to look   20
up every passage in the works of the authors themselves, especially when a
single misplaced letter may involve reading through the whole of Homer's
Iliad and *Odyssey*? Nevertheless, I had to face up to this disagreeable task if
I did not want the reader to be led astray or perplexed by many passages.

    The printing of the volume was already half complete before I recog-   25
nized the seriousness of the problem. So wherever an error had gone unde-
tected in the preceding pages, I added a separate note, and I have done the
same elsewhere when something escaped me or the proofreaders, though
there were very few cases of this sort. If a letter was upside down or out
of line or indistinct, I did not think it worth while to draw attention to it,   30
since this happens rarely and does not trouble a knowledgeable reader. I
have also enlarged the work by the addition of a considerable number of
adages;[2] I have not, however, burdened the volume with silly irrelevancies
but have provided essential information to make it more complete.

    In a work of this sort there is no limit to the corrections one could   35
make or to the additional material with which it could be enriched. If I am
granted a longer life and if I encounter something in one of the new authors
who are constantly being published these days, I shall not alter my text but
will add a welcome supplement. So the reader will not be burdened with expense or cheated of the fruits of scholarship. But if God takes me from this   40
world, I earnestly implore those who come after me to preserve unchanged
what I have put into shape at the cost of so much labour; and if they have
other or better things to say than those that I have handed on, I hope they
will not treat another man's work as we see the lexicons being treated in our
day[3]and as we know the collections of decreta and theological sentences were   45
treated in the past, where the last person to revise someone else's work is
given credit for the whole. Instead let anyone who wishes to produce a new

    * * * * *

2 Fifty-two entries more than the most recent edition of 1523; Phillips *Adages*
   xii
3 Compilers padded their lexicons by making additions that had no purpose
   except to increase the number of new terms that the compiler claimed to
   have added to materials borrowed from earlier lexicons. On this problem
   see Ep 1460, Erasmus' preface to an edition of the *Dictionarius graecus* (Basel:
   Froben 1524) of the fifteenth-century Carmelite friar and humanist Johannes
   Crastonus (Giovanni Crastone); see also Allen's introduction to that letter.
   Crastonus' work was first printed at Milan in 1478 and often reprinted. On
   Crastonus, see DBI 30 578–80. Erasmus' complaint was against the tendency of
   the most recent compiler to take credit for a lexicon that was largely the work
   of others.

work under his own name do so, or if he has some corrections to suggest or
new information to add, let him follow my example and treat the matter in
an appendix. I write this, not because it matters greatly to me who gets the   50
credit for the work or whose name appears on the title-page, but because
scholarship too has its meddlers, and the greater their ignorance, the read-
ier they are to lay their sacrilegious hands on the works of others. So it is
not so much my own reputation that is at stake as the contribution which
learning can make to the common good.   55

I would like the same scrupulous care to be shown to the two indexes
to my work.[4] In both, the printers had been grossly careless, with much in-
convenience to the reader, but now we have made a correspondingly strong
effort to free scholars from this annoyance. This sort of thing, whether we
put it down to haste or carelessness, has caused havoc and confusion in   60
the best of studies. I have complained of it elsewhere at sufficient length,
and the problem is only too familiar. If someone is responsible for harming a private individual, one may take an action for the loss and injury sustained. But when it is the public interest that is involved by, for example,
polluting the public wells, or diverting streams, or ruining the highways,   65
then the culprit deserves to be publicly execrated. If, then, all public possessions – all those things which the ancients regarded as sacrosanct[5] – ought
to be treated with such respect that anyone who violates them is held to
be accursed, should we not be especially respectful of books, since they are
produced at the cost of much effort and for the general benefit of schol-   70
ars everywhere? Indeed scholarship is entitled to special reverence, since
any harm done to it affects not just one city, but the whole world. So just
as we condemn those who, for a trifling profit, corrupt and adulterate the
works of writers, so we should commend those printers who, with much
effort and at great cost to themselves, ensure that the works of the best au-   75
thors see the light of day in the most accurate form possible. And in fact the
world has not been entirely grudging in its support of the Aldine press,[6]

* * * * *

4 Erasmus provided an alphabetical index (*secundum ordinem alphabeti*) and an
  index according to topics (*iuxta locos et materias*).
5 *Adagia* III x 15
6 The famous Venetian press established in 1495 by the humanist Aldo Manuzio
  (commonly called Aldus), noted for its many first editions of Greek authors
  and its relatively inexpensive editions of classical Latin and modern Italian
  authors, as well as for its handsome typefaces. Erasmus spent much of 1508
  working in the shop of Aldus, benefiting from the presence of the expert Hellenists who were associated with the press. Aside from deepening his command of Greek language and Greek sources, this period produced the vastly
  expanded Aldine edition of the *Adagia* (1508). After Aldus' death in 1515, the

which, besides giving us so many fine writers, is now producing the complete works of Galen in Greek.[7] Johann Froben is attempting the same thing in Germany with equal enthusiasm if not with equal success, but he does not reap the same profit from his labours – only a measure of fame spoiled by envy.

There is another circumstance that should encourage us to treat good literature with greater respect. On both sides of us we see men springing up who, however different their views, have the same deadly purpose: to destroy the humanities root and branch. The old enemies of literature,[8] who have long been waging an unremitting war[9] against this kind of study, have now come forward with a new theory, that all the present troubles in the world have their origin in the knowledge of languages and of polite letters. Meanwhile the opposing faction[10] insists that all secular learning should yield place to the gospel. I only wish that gospel piety had flourished so powerfully that the lamps of humane learning faded before the brilliance of its light! But while I see learning in decline, I do not see a vigorous piety taking its place. Everywhere there is much written about grace and peace, but in practice these virtues are not easy to find. How much better it would be if we were to strive with all our might, first, to put aside the madness of dissension and come together in Christian concord, and then to reconcile theology, the queen of sciences, with her old handmaidens, the knowledge of languages and the understanding of the humanities! Farewell, dear reader. May you find pleasure in what follows.

Basel, 17 January AD 1526

* * * * *

press was continued by his business partner and father-in-law Andrea Torresani, with whom Erasmus maintained polite but not warm relations, being put off by Torresani's reputation for putting commercial considerations ahead of scholarly ones. See Epp 1592 introduction, 1736 n18.

7 This important first edition of the Greek text of the ancient medical authority was a landmark in classical and scientific publishing, as Erasmus warmly declared in a letter of 1525 to Gianfrancesco Torresani, son of the publisher (Ep 1628). See also Ep 1594 nn3, 4.

8 Erasmus habitually defined his conservative critics as unalterably opposed to the humanist programme of classical literary studies. He viewed their charges that he was the source of the heresies of Luther, Zwingli, and other heretics as just another move in a campaign that was directed against humanistic learning at least as much as against the Reformers.

9 Erasmus here used a Greek phrase, as he frequently did when he wanted either to conceal his meaning from non-humanists or (as here) to attain a stylistic effect.

10 That is, the Reformers, or at least the more radical ones, some of whom denounced 'worldly' learning

1660 / From Jan Antonin   Cracow, 21 January 1526

On the Hungarian physician Jan Antonin of Košice, who received a doctorate in medicine from Padua and subsequently spent several months in Basel,
where he treated Erasmus, see Ep 1602 introduction. After returning briefly
to his native Hungary, he settled in Cracow, where he became physician to
the king and to two bishops, and where he also did much to promote Erasmus' reputation. This is a reply to Ep 1602. It remained unpublished until it
was printed by Gustav Bauch in 1885 and again by C. Miaskowski in 1900 (see
Allen's introduction). Allen also used the original manuscript in the Rehdiger
collection at Wrocław (formerly Breslau). Ep 1698 is Erasmus' reply.

If I have not hitherto addressed a single word to your Excellency, the reason,
my dear father, lay in the uncertain state of my affairs, as you will learn
from a letter that will follow shortly;[1] it will be a weighty letter, designed to
make a persuasive case. At present I cannot do more than send you a brief
summa summarum, as the expression goes, since I was informed too late of   5
the time of the courier's departure.

I saw Plutarch's *De non irascendo* for the first time at Cracow on the
third of December.[2] The choicest things are always in other people's hands
before they reach me. At the first opportunity I passed the book on to the
illustrious Master Alexius,[3] embellished in both gold and silver. I cannot tell   10
you how delighted he is with the book – or rather with the mind of Erasmus
which it reveals. He plans to send your Excellency some splendid gifts, but
they cannot be dispatched to you before the next Frankfurt fair.[4]

* * * * *

1660
1 No such letter is known.
2 In 1525 Erasmus had dedicated his Greek edition (with Latin translation) of
   Plutarch's *De non irascendo* and *De curiositate* to Alexius Thurzo, acting at the
   instance of Jan Antonin. See Ep 1572 introduction.
3 See preceding note. Alexius Thurzo, whose brothers Johannes (II) and Stanislaus were bishops and like him became admirers and correspondents of Erasmus, acquired wealth and power as a mining contractor and as secretary and
   treasurer to King Louis II of Hungary.
4 The two annual trade fairs at Frankfurt (St Bartholomew's in August and the
   Lenten fair about Easter) had become the most important commercial events
   in Germany by the later Middle Ages and attracted merchants not only from
   Germany but also from other parts of Europe. After the development of printing, the semi-annual Frankfurt fairs became the principal centre for the distribution of books, and Erasmus' publications were often timed to the dates
   of these fairs. Since the fair also retained its earlier importance as a centre

The distinguished Johann Henckel,[5] chaplain to her sacred Majesty the
queen of Hungary,[6] left a gift with me to be delivered to your Excellency   15
along with a letter.[7] I was reluctant to separate the letter and the gift, and the
courier refused to carry presents. The next best thing was to hold them here
until our merchants set out for Frankfurt. I have seen no one in Hungary
among the associates of the queen or the king or the other princes of the
realm whom I like better than Henckel, nor have I met anyone who showed   20
a keener appreciation of the great Erasmus, as he has demonstrated in the
pulpit, in private, and in public, and whenever the occasion offered. There is
no work of Erasmus that does not have a privileged place in his library, and
if a work is published in ten editions, he thinks nothing of buying them all.
Whatever he says from the pulpit, whatever lessons he teaches the people,   25
all show the influence of the Paraphrases of Erasmus.[8]

* * * * *

for trade in many commodities, for settling commercial accounts, and for currency exchange, Erasmus often sent and received not only books but also
money and gifts, transported by printers like Froben and by other merchants
who attended the fair (see for example Epp 1611, 1612, 1654, 1698, 1728).
Erasmus' efficient financial agent, Erasmus Schets, relied on the attendance
of Antwerp and Basel merchants (including the printer Johann Froben) at the
Frankfurt fairs in order to make safe and inexpensive transfer of Erasmus' revenues from England and the Netherlands to him in Basel; see Epp 1654:10–12,
1681 n5, 1682 n2, 1696 n2, 1750 n4, 1758 n2. Frankfurt's fairs remained the
centre of the German and also the international book trade through the sixteenth and even much of the seventeenth century, but the efforts of the imperial government from 1579 to impose religious censorship of books offered
at the fair caused a gradual eclipse of the Frankfurt market, to the advantage of the rival fairs at Leipzig, where after the conversion of the dukes to
Lutheranism in 1539 the distribution of books was comparatively free of censorship. See Lucien Febvre and Henri-Jean Martin L'apparition du livre (Paris
1958) 348–56, 2nd ed (1971) 323–30, and the introduction by James Westfall
Thompson to his edition and English translation of The Frankfort Book Fair: The
Francofordense Emporium of Henri Estienne (Chicago 1911; repr New York 1968)
41–123.
5 See Ep 1672 introduction.
6 Mary of Hungary (1505–58), sister of the emperor Charles v and at this time
  the recently widowed queen of King Louis ii, was an admirer of Erasmus. He
  dedicated his short treatise De vidua christiana to her in 1529 at the urging of
  Henckel; there is a translation in cwe 66.
7 Not extant. On the gift see Ep 1698 n7.
8 Both Henckel and his employer were keenly interested in Scripture, and particularly in Erasmus' Paraphrases, which Queen Mary read in German translation and then in the Latin original. See Henckel's report to Erasmus in Allen
  Ep 2011:32–9.

From what I hear, Hungary has produced a lot of scandalmongers who, whenever there are no other Hungarians present, pour out the venom they imbibed at Rome at every favourable mention of Erasmus' name.[9] Johann

* * * * *

9 On the anti-Erasmian sentiment prevalent among curial humanists, especially the informal group known as the Roman Academy, see Epp 1341A:527–63, 1479:22–4 and nn10, 12, 13, 1482:34–67, 1488:13–15, 1496:202–6. On two leading members of this group, Angelo Colocci and Battista Casali, see Epp 1479 nn12, 13 and 1270A introduction. Erasmus knew that some member of the group (he thought that it was Colocci, but it was probably his associate Battista Casali: cf Epp 1270A, 1597 n4) was the author of an unpublished 'Invectiva in Erasmum Roterodamum' that in 1524 was circulating in curial circles. A letter of 1522 (Ep 1260) from his friend Jakob Ziegler in Rome, though primarily concerned with describing the activities of Erasmus' Spanish critic Diego López Zúñiga, also confirmed the undercurrent of hostility to Erasmus and to German scholars in general within curial society, even though Ziegler also reported the outspoken defence of Erasmus' orthodoxy and character by his friend Paolo Bombace. In addition, Erasmus had learned that when Girolamo Aleandro was papal legate to Germany in 1520–1, he had denounced Erasmus in dispatches to Rome and continued to do so in private conversations after he returned to the curia. Aleandro seems to have been ambivalent about Erasmus for some time (cf Epp 1256 n11, 1324 and introduction, 1324A, 1481), but by 1525 Erasmus had concluded (correctly) that even though Aleandro did not attack him publicly, he was the probable author of an unprinted tract (called *Racha*) that attacked Erasmus as a heretic and circulated privately at the curia. See Epp 1553 n9, 1717 nn3, 18. What particularly worried Erasmus was that Aleandro was becoming a powerful person at the curia, a development evident not only from his being selected to proclaim and enforce the papal bull *Exsurge Domine* against Luther in 1520–1 but also from his being made archbishop of Brindisi in 1524 and being sent promptly thereafter as legate to the French court, a mission ended by the defeat and capture of Francis I at Pavia on 24 February 1525. Another dangerous enemy in the inner circles of curial society was Alberto Pio, prince of Carpi. Erasmus' effort to forestall an open attack from this quarter by writing directly to him, reporting the rumours he had heard about Pio's criticism of him and strongly asserting his own orthodoxy, merely led to the prince's composition of an attack on Erasmus that produced an exchange of hostile publications. On the danger posed by Pio's close connections with the humanist intellectuals of the curia, see Epp 1634 introduction, 1717 n3. In addition, Erasmus' unrelenting Spanish critic, Diego López Zúñiga, had settled at Rome in 1520 and from 1521 had been teaching Greek at the Sapienza, the papal university.
Erasmus had long been suspicious of the curial humanists as a group, though admiring certain individuals who were outstanding for their learning and piety, such as Jacopo Sadoleto; and his main complaint was not their hostility to him but their narrow and (in his opinion) fundamentally secular and un-Christian classicism (cf Ep 1717 n2). The eventual product of this tension was Erasmus' *Ciceronianus* (1528), a work sharply critical of much of Italian

Henckel, single-handed, silenced them so effectively that they are now afraid 30
to open their mouths. Your Excellency could find no one more appropriate
to whom to dedicate your book on preaching,[10] both because of his special
support of your reputation and because he would not exchange a single letter of yours for any benefice, however rich and permanent – so he said in a
crowded gathering of distinguished people. If he sets such store by a single 35
letter of Erasmus, think how he would value, not just a letter, but a huge
volume. If what I hope for should come to pass, I warrant you he will not
take second place to any bishop or abbot. There is no limit to the man's generosity. His kindness even to scholars of moderate learning is a wonder to
all. He is not just preacher to the queen; he is also parish priest at Košice and 40
archdeacon of Torna.[11] Had he wished, he could have been a bishop long
ago, but he is a man of small ambition, whose learning is the envy of many.

But I leave these matters for another occasion. The eminent palatine
of Cracow, Master Krzysztof,[12] asked me, both personally and by letter, to
mention his name to your Excellency. At the next Frankfurt fair he will 45
send you a valuable present, some gold work from the hand of my father-
in-law.[13] The same request was made recently by the right reverend Bishop

* * * * *

humanism. A bitter and enduring controversy ensued. On his relations with
the curialists, see CWE 11 xix–xxi, Epp 1701 n6 (on their linguistic purism),
1717 n2 (on their 'pagan' spirit). Erasmus had good reason to think that there
were influential people at Rome who would poison the minds of foreign visitors and the princes of the church against him. What is not clear is precisely
which Hungarian persons, indoctrinated at Rome, were the 'scandalmongers'
who would 'pour out the venom they imbibed at Rome.'

10 The *Ecclesiastes*, a book on which Erasmus had begun work (or at least so
he claimed) as early as 1519 but did not actually publish until 1535, despite
repeated encouragement from friends and patrons. Apparently he had done
some work on it in 1523 (Ep 1332:41), and he referred to it (and to Bishop John
Fisher's repeated requests for its completion) in his long letter of June 1525 to
Noël Béda (Ep 1581:743). So Antonin probably had some reason to think that
it might be near completion and ready to be dedicated to a loyal supporter
such as Henckel.

11 Košice, where Henckel became parish priest in 1522, and Torna, where he
became archdeacon about 1526, were in the kingdom of Hungary (modern
Slovakia). Torna (German Turnau), a small community, was the capital of the
smallest county of the Hungarian kingdom (also named Torna), most of which
was transferred administratively to the Hungarian county of Abauj'Torna in
1882, and the northern half of which became part of Czechoslovakia in 1920.

12 On Krzysztof Szydłowiecki, see Ep 1593 introduction.

13 Jan Zimmermann of Cracow, a prominent goldsmith and city councillor who
had produced works for the queen of Poland, the Italian-born Bona Sforza,
and other people of high rank. He was a natural choice to fabricate the gift

Andrzej Krzycki,[14] whose learning your Excellency can see from the little
book that he published recently.[15] Although he is critical of certain things
in Poland, his criticisms are not of the kind that leave the problem where   50
it was; rather, like a doctor, he points out remedies by which problems can
be prevented if they show signs of developing. I mention this because I do
not want you to draw unfavourable conclusions from the book and to use
these as an excuse for not coming to visit us. I hope my friend Krzycki's letter will persuade your Excellency to pay us a visit – what joy that would   55
bring to your humble servant! But even if you do not come, it is something to be invited by our most Christian king and to receive such generous
promises.

A short time ago Justus Decius,[16] secretary to his sacred Majesty the
king, while sitting on a horse which was a bit too lively for him, fell while   60
it was going at full gallop (such is the lot of mortal men!) and broke a bone
in his arm (known to physicians as the 'adjutory bone'). He wanted your
Excellency to have something in his own hand, so he wrote these few lines
with the other hand while his good wife held the page. He too wants to
be commended to your Excellency. These gallant persons, my dear father,   65
certainly offer considerable scope for commendation, but because the time at
my disposal is limited, I cannot fulfil the promise I made to them, as I would
like, by providing a fuller résumé of their careers. So imagine that I have
commended all these people to your Excellency in the strongest possible
terms. They certainly deserve such commendation.   70

The publication of your immortal *Lingua* has made the illustrious palatine[17] your friend for ever. The right reverend Bishop Krzycki has become

* * * * *

that Chancellor Szydłowiecki gave in response to Erasmus' dedication to him
of *Lingua*. The gift or gifts are also mentioned in Ep 1698, Erasmus' response
to this letter, and more fully in Ep 1752, a letter of acknowledgment to the
donor.
14 Bishop of Przemyśl in Poland; see Ep 1629 introduction.
15 There are several possibilities, but the reference may be to Krzycki's *De negotio
Prutenico*, a defence of his role in the negotiations that led to the secularization
of the East Prussian principality of the Teutonic Knights and so to the triumph
of Lutheranism in that region. See Ep 1629 n3.
16 Following experience in banking, finance, and mining, this native of Wissem-
bourg in Alsace settled in Cracow and since 1520 had been secretary to King
Sigismund I of Poland. See Epp 1341A n210, 1393.
17 Krzysztof Szydłowiecki, who held the title palatine of Cracow as well as chancellor of the realm, was the recipient of the dedication of Erasmus' *Lingua* when
it was first published in 1525. He promptly arranged for its republication at
Cracow by the press of Hieronymus Vietor.

devoted to you since he received your letter along with the book on arithmetic:[18] he will gladly support your Excellency whenever and wherever you
wish and as often as you wish. Justus and I ask only to do your bidding, for   75
when you issue the word of command, we know for certain that your Excellency truly loves us; in our eyes you have the status of a god. We look up to
you, we venerate and honour you, our love for you will never be surpassed
by that of any of your friends.

Luther is not well thought of at Cracow.[19]   80

Our best wishes to your Excellency, and may the Lord Jesus keep you
safe.

Written at Cracow when my eyes were sore and inflamed, on the feast
of St Agnes 1526

Your Excellency's devoted servant and son Antonin, physician   85

Please let the palatine and Krzycki and Justus know that I did what
they wished; I do not want them to make some remark to me later that it
would embarrass me to hear. I too have acquired a gift for your Excellency,
although I am afraid it is not as valuable as your kindness to me deserved,
for you were good enough to commend me a second time to posterity. It   90
will be sent to your Excellency at Lent along with the other things. My dear
wife sends her best wishes to your Excellency. Please convey my kindest regards to my distinguished friends, Master Ludwig Baer, Master Bonifacius
Amerbach, the Frobens and Master Froben's wife, also to Master Glareanus
and to Sichard and Lieven.[20]   95

To that great ornament of our age, the celebrated Master Erasmus of
Rotterdam, incomparable champion of the humanities, my respected master
and patron

* * * * *

18 *De arte supputandi* by the English humanist Cuthbert Tunstall, which Erasmus
   sent to Bishop Krzycki in 1525. See Ep 1629 n4.
19 Despite his own sympathies for some type of moderate reform, Bishop Andrzej Krzycki had published books sharply critical of Luther and his followers,
   an attitude shared by most of the circle of humanists at the Polish court.
20 Antonin had visited Basel in 1524 after completing his doctorate in medicine
   in Padua and had established friendly relations not only with Erasmus, who
   found his medical treatment helpful and regretted his decision not to settle
   there permanently, but also with several of Erasmus' close friends, including
   the theologian Ludwig Baer (see Epp 488 introduction, 1571 n6, 1674 n17);
   the jurist Bonifacius Amerbach, scion of the publishing family (Ep 408 introduction); the printer Johann Froben (Ep 419 introduction) and his wife; the
   humanist schoolmaster Henricus Glareanus (Ep 440 introduction); the humanist and jurist Johann Sichard; and Erasmus' trusted courier Lieven Algoet (Ep
   1091 introduction). There are biographical sketches of all of this group in CEBR.

1661 / To John Claymond   Basel, 30 January 1526

This letter is the dedication prefixed to Erasmus' edition of the Greek text of a collection of six sermons, *Conciunculae perquam elegantes sex de fato et providentia Dei* (Basel: Froben, February 1526), by the Greek church Father John Chrysostom. The recipient, John Claymond, was an acquaintance of long standing and since 1517 had been the first president of Corpus Christi College, Oxford, founded by Richard Foxe, bishop of Winchester, for the promotion of humanistic studies. On Claymond see Ep 990 introduction.

ERASMUS OF ROTTERDAM TO JOHN CLAYMOND, THEOLOGIAN AND PRESIDENT OF THE COLLEGE OF THE BEES AT OXFORD,[1] GREETING Flowers are attractive to bees, so I am sending you six little flowers plucked from the blooming and health-giving gardens of blessed Chrysostom.[2] From

* * * * *

1661
1 In his original statutes, the founder of Corpus Christi College, Bishop Foxe, expressed his hopes that its scholars, 'like clever bees, day and night will produce beeswax to the glory of God and sweet honeys for the use of themselves and all Christians.' See Thomas Fowler *The History of Corpus Christi College* Publications of the Oxford Historical Society 25 (Oxford 1893) 2 for the Latin text of the preface to the statutes. In his note on the salutation Allen observes that in his *Apologia* against the Paris theologian Pierre Cousturier, Erasmus seems to confuse the real 'college of the bees,' Corpus Christi, with the even more ambitious new Cardinal College projected by Thomas Wolsey, cardinal-archbishop of York, a foundation which after many vicissitudes became Christ Church, Oxford.
2 St John Chrysostom (c 350–407), patriarch of Constantinople, was one of the most highly regarded Greek church Fathers, famous as a preacher and biblical exegete, and hence representative of the type of theology that Erasmus favoured in contrast to the speculative theology of the scholastics. As a bishop who preached eloquently and in his sermons expounded a theology that was firmly rooted in Scripture and expressed pastoral concern rather than abstruse theology, Chrysostom exemplified qualities that Erasmus found lacking in most of the bishops and theologians of his own time; cf Ep 1649 n7. Erasmus focused much of his scholarly effort on Chrysostom at this period and published several of his works. In 1525 he published the Greek text of a major work, *De sacerdotio*, dedicated to the Nuremberg humanist Willibald Pirckheimer (Ep 1558), and also a Latin translation (accompanied by the Greek text) of *De orando Deum libri duo*, dedicated to Maximilian of Burgundy (Ep 1563). In May 1526 he sent Hieronymus Froben to Italy to search for classical and patristic manuscripts (Epp 1705 n3, 1720 n2), and his translation of several works of Chrysostom, *Chrysostomi lucubrationes* (Basel: Froben, March 1527), dedicated to King John III of Portugal (Ep 1800), was based in part on

these your busy and industrious swarm may collect nectar that will be as   5
beneficial to the mind as it is pleasing to the palate; with this they can perform their sacred task of making honey. I realize that for purity of Greek the
best nectar comes from the meadows of Demosthenes, Aristophanes, and Lucian,[3] for it always seems that the children of this world are superior in their
generation to the children of light.[4] Yet I must commend the judgment of   10
those who, out of love for religion, prefer the modest polish that is acquired
from the writings of the saints to the superior elegance that comes from the
books of the pagans, for the one is accompanied by a gain in piety, while the
other carries a risk to one's moral character. Honey derived from the yew
is poisonous: hardly anything is sweeter than it, yet it contains a deadly   15
venom.[5] Those who are of this opinion should thumb the pages of Chrysostom, whose style is pure and flows with remarkable ease and eloquence.
I do not want you to think that I am taking the easy course by presenting
you with someone else's work, so let me tell you that I have had to struggle
with a manuscript that is very old and has not been corrected throughout.[6]   20
    If I hear that you like this small gift, I shall send you more for the use
of your little hive of bees.[7] You must defend the hive, my dear Claymond,

* * * * *

a manuscript brought back by Froben. Several publications of other works of
Chrysostom followed, culminating in a nearly complete edition of the works
in Latin, the five-volume *Opera* of 1530, for which Erasmus served as general
editor and as translator of some of the texts. His hopes for a complete Greek
edition of Chrysostom's works were not fulfilled until the appearance of the
edition by Sir Henry Savile (8 vols, Eton 1610–12).

3 These three Greek authors are offered as examples of classical Greek eloquence in its purest (but pre-Christian) form, including (in order) the greatest Athenian orator (384–322 BC), the greatest Athenian comic poet (c 450–388
BC), and a special favourite of Erasmus, the witty satirist Lucian of Samosata
(c 120–c 180 AD).

4 Luke 16:8

5 For the poisonous nature of the yew see Virgil *Eclogues* 9.30 and *Georgics* 4.47.
Both poems advise against allowing one's bees to be placed in proximity to
yew. Cf Wendell Clauser *A Commentary on Virgil, Eclogues* (Oxford 1994) 276–7,
and R.A.B. Mynors *Virgil, Georgics* (Oxford 1990) 264.

6 The manuscript from which Erasmus drew his Greek text has not been identified, though it seems that with the aid of Hieronymus Froben he subsequently
acquired a manuscript of Chrysostom's homilies that entered the Bodleian Library in 1604 and was used by Sir Henry Savile, editor of the first full edition of Chrysostom in Greek; see n2 above. Allen Ep 1661:16n indicates that
the homilies found in this 'very old' manuscript and printed in the present
collection of *Conciunculae* are not in the Bodleian manuscript.

7 That is, Corpus Christi College; see n1 above.

all the more vigorously, the more you are beset with enemies who rise to
thwart you in the making of honey. Bees in the fields have stings and use
them to kill the drones. Christian bees have no stings, or if they have, they   25
prefer succour to attack. But even drones share the work with bees; these
men, on the other hand, are hornets, not drones, and they do nothing except
hamper those who are busy making honey. Farewell.

Basel, 30 January AD 1526

1662 / From Jacobus Piso   Buda, 1 February 1526

On this much-admired Hungarian humanist and poet, who met Erasmus at
Rome in 1509 while serving as Hungarian ambassador there, see the introductions to Epp 215, 1297. At this period he was one of the most trusted advisers to the young King Louis II of Hungary, whom he had tutored from 1516
and for whom he had also served as diplomatic representative. In this letter
he refers to Ep 1297, written in 1522 in reply to a lost letter from Erasmus
but mislaid and now finally dispatched as an enclosure. After the death of his
royal pupil in the disastrous battle of Mohács later this same year, Piso lived
at the court of the widowed Queen Mary at Bratislava until his own death in
1527. The Latin text rests on the autograph preserved at Leipzig and was first
published in the collection of Erasmus' correspondence edited by Förstemann
and Günther in 1904.

Greetings. Ursinus[1] is here again and his complaints about my tardiness are
as severe as they are just. I encouraged him to come, and he arrived in Hungary under what I hope will be happy auspices. Soon after his arrival we
had our first conversation about your good self – for you are continually
with us whether we are at lunch or at dinner, sitting or standing, riding or   5
walking. In brief, you are always present and we are always with you despite our physical separation. Since there is no better way of repairing this
misfortune than by a letter, Ursinus easily persuaded me to make this long-
delayed reply, for he would listen to no excuse for my protracted silence
until I undertook to do what he asked. Although my affection for you was   10
a strong incentive to write, the embarrassment I felt over my long neglect
of you held me back. I do not know if I have been guilty of such thought-
lessness towards any of my friends, but, in maintaining for so many years a

* * * * *

1662
1 On the Silesian humanist and poet Caspar Ursinus Velius see Epp 548:5n, 851
   introduction, 1280A introduction, 1557 introduction.

long unbroken silence, I have treated you much worse than any of the others. Far from finding an excuse in my own conscience for such a fault, I am   15
ready to acknowledge the gravity of my sin, a sin so grave in fact that it
will be no easy task to expiate it. For although you yourself, with characteristic charity, may absolve me from my sin, I am certainly not excused in the
eyes of the many distinguished people who know your feelings towards me
and mine towards you. What I feel for you is particularly evident to those   20
in whose presence I have constantly sung your praises from the moment
when your name – your divine name – was first known to me right up to
the present day, though my lofty compliments were less than you deserved
for your sterling qualities and your services to the cause of Christ.

What compounds the earlier fault of my neglect of you (for why should   25
I conceal the truth?) is the fact that I did not even reply to the letter that was
delivered to me four years ago[2] in Prague by Stanislaus, the right reverend
bishop of Olomouc.[3] I did prepare a reply at the time, but it was never sent,
because about that time I was ordered to go as a delegate to Nürnberg[4] to
his serene Highness, Prince Ferdinand;[5] I could conveniently have written to   30
you from there, but this possibility was ruled out by the unexpectedly rapid
departure of the prince. Soon afterwards another obligation was thrust upon
me, a legation to his serene Majesty, the king of Poland.[6] In packing my bags
in a hurry, it happened that the reply I had prepared to your letter got lost
among other papers and remained lost until now; and perhaps it would have   35
continued to be lost if my friend Ursinus had not urged me to look for it and
to add these lines as a sort of compensation or interest on the debt. I acted on
both counts gladly and was all the more willing to do so because the same

* * * * *

2 Erasmus' letter, probably written from Basel in November 1521 and dispatched
   together with Epp 1242–3, hence received about April 1522 (cf Ep 1272), is
   now lost. On Piso's reply, see the introduction to this letter and Ep 1297
   introduction.
3 Bishop Stanislaus Thurzo was a member of a prominent family active in mining, politics, and church administration in the kingdoms of Poland and Hungary and had become an active patron of humanistic learning. In 1525 Erasmus dedicated to him his edition of Pliny's *Naturalis historia* (Ep 1544). See
   also Ep 1242 introduction.
4 In the period here referred to, Piso was repeatedly employed on diplomatic
   missions for the king of Hungary.
5 Archduke of Austria, younger brother of the emperor Charles v. Since 1522
   he had been acting as regent in the hereditary Hapsburg lands; at this period
   he administered the dynasty's policy in central and eastern Europe.
6 This diplomatic mission to the court of Sigismund i took place in January and
   February 1523.

course was being urged with some force by the right reverend Stanislaus
Thurzo, bishop of Olomouc, a man equally distinguished for his knowledge   40
of literature and for the purity of his life. Recently, when he was spending
several days with the prince here at Buda,[7] we had a long talk about you, as
we have frequently had in the past. Far from subtracting anything from my
own time-honoured stock of Erasmian eulogies, he always adds a great new
pile of his own. The sheer force of his panegyrics does not make me feel   45
uneasy; on the contrary, I am delighted to see my own opinion confirmed
and spread abroad through the influence of so distinguished a man, for a
bishop takes precedence over a provost in dignity of rank and a Thurzo
far surpasses a Piso[8] in the splendour of his name and, I may add, in his
knowledge of literature.   50

I feel such little jealousy in this matter that I think I can rightly congratulate myself on being responsible at one and the same time for persuading the two brothers Thurzo, both bishops, to write to you, one the bishop of
Wrocław of pious memory, the other the bishop of Olomouc.[9] It was perhaps
eight years ago when they were kind enough to pay me a visit while I was   55
living at the court of the prince.[10] They began to open and examine some
books of yours that were lying on the table (I don't remember which), and
then suddenly, and with one voice, they asked me what I thought of Erasmus; they pressed me for an answer, because they knew that I was close to
you and that we had enjoyed a long-standing friendship. They were aware   60
of our friendship partly from my own account and partly from the letter
you sent from Siena to Rome, which I have guarded as carefully as if it were
gold.[11] These two saintly bishops took the letter in their hands and began to
scan it and to read it and reread it with the most lively interest. So it was
not difficult for me to persuade them to write to you, as indeed they did   65
soon afterwards and much more generously than I could have suggested,
for they thought fit to honour you not just with a letter but with gifts and

* * * * *

7 Louis II, the young king of Hungary; Bishop Stanislaus Thurzo was a trusted
  adviser and frequently visited the royal court at Buda.
8 Both as a bishop, outranking a mere provost of Pécs (Fünfkirchen), and as the
  son of an influential courtier who had been ennobled, outranking the son of
  a respectable but non-noble family.
9 In addition to Stanislaus, who became bishop of Olomouc in 1497, an elder
  brother, Johannes, had held the bishopric of Wrocław from 1506 to his death
  in 1520. Both became fervent admirers of Erasmus.
10 That is, at the court of Louis II in Buda
11 The lost letter from Erasmus to Piso referred to in the introduction to this
   letter

presents as well. This was a lesson that their excellent father,[12] of happy memory, had instilled into them: clearly he made them heirs not only of a considerable fortune but of his exceptional generosity as well.   70

I have included these remarks because of what I owe to the two bishops Thurzo and most of all to their father, who besides the good fortune he enjoyed from position, good health, children, and material possessions was unexcelled, in my experience, in piety, discretion, courtesy, fidelity, and staunchness of character. When his death was announced at Rome to   75 the most reverend Father Pietro, formerly cardinal of Reggio,[13] who had become a close friend of Thurzo's when he was legate in Hungary, he turned to me and, taking my hand as though he were about to seal a new agreement, said, 'I know, Piso, that you always had the highest regard for Thurzo. But I want you to remember this, that of all the great men I have met in   80 Europe no one was Thurzo's equal in every kind of virtue.' So on the spot we produced this eulogy[14] of a great and remarkably wise man: 'Even in Rome's opinion Thurzo shone / as virtue's model, Europe's paragon.' I have been sidetracked into making these irrelevant observations not just by my memory of a revered old man, but also by the great kindness this excellent   85 bishop showed towards you, which I have hardly ever seen equalled in men of his rank. If other bishops imitated his generosity towards men of letters, each in proportion to his fortune, the present position of the humanities would be considerably improved.

So here is my letter, my dear Erasmus, a hodgepodge which you can   90 blame partly on Velius and partly on the bishop.[15] I shall be satisfied if I have atoned in some way for my shameful neglect of you, though it may not be possible to make amends for the prolonged indolence of many years by the efforts of an hour or two; perhaps my lethargy is in some measure excused by the fact that, whether I write to you or remain silent, I have always been   95 your loyal and devoted friend. All men may match me in their devotion, but that anyone should surpass me, that I shall not allow, not even from those who have proved the strength of their friendship by their generosity and

* * * * *

12 The elder Johannes Thurzo (1437–1508), founder of the family fortune, who also established the family's close ties to the rulers of Poland and Hungary
13 On Pietro Isvales (or Isvaglies), archbishop of Reggio in Calabria, archbishop of Messina, and cardinal, see Ep 236:51n.
14 Piso was a noted Latin poet and had been crowned poet laureate by Emperor Maximilian I.
15 Because these two friends had pressed him to end his embarrassed silence and to reply after so long an interval to Erasmus' (lost) letter of 1521

their support and so have earned the right to be more appreciated than I. I am not in the least envious of them on this score: rather I am immensely 100 grateful to all who not only confirm my opinion of you, but outdo me with gifts of every kind.

Since I do not want my letter to be delivered at the beginning of a new year without a gift, I am sending you a gold coin stamped with the name of the emperor Gratian and a second coin, made of silver, dedicated 105 to Hercules.[16] I hope you will value them not for their worth but for the sentiments behind them. May Christ long preserve you in good health for the increase of his glory!

Buda, 1 February 1526
Your friend, Jacobus Piso   110

1663 / To Frans van der Dilft   Basel, 3 February 1526

Frans van der Dilft (d 14 June 1550) was the son of a wealthy family of Antwerp. He matriculated at the University of Louvain on 30 October 1514 and studied with Conradus Goclenius, who about the same time had become professor of Latin in the humanistic Collegium Trilingue, with which Erasmus had close connections. Dilft came to Basel and matriculated in the university at the beginning of the 1524–5 winter term but resided in Erasmus' household until December 1525. During this year he served Erasmus as a secretarial assistant and courier, carrying Erasmus' letters to and from distant correspondents. When he moved back to Louvain at the end of 1525 he carried warm letters of recommendation from Erasmus (Epp 1653, 1655). In the present letter Erasmus dedicates to him his Latin translation of Plutarch's essay περὶ δυσωπίας, which was printed as annex to a republication of Erasmus' *Lingua* (Basel: Froben, February 1526; reprinted again in July 1526); on the title, see n1 below. To receive the dedication of even a minor work from Erasmus was a feather in the cap of an ambitious young humanist. Dilft later returned to live with Erasmus for several months in 1527–8. Armed

* * * * *

16 The collecting of ancient coins had become a favourite hobby of admirers of antiquity, not only among the princes and the very rich, but also among humanists. For the origins of this interest in quattrocento Italy, see Roberto Weiss *The Renaissance Discovery of Classical Antiquity* (New York 1969) 167–79. The gold coins of Flavius Gratianus, Roman emperor (AD 367–83) are not now classed as particularly rare; see for example Seth William Stevenson and others *A Dictionary of Roman Coins, Republican and Imperial* (London 1889) 440–1 and Robert Friedberg and others *Gold Coins of the World, from Ancient Times to the Present* 6th ed (Clifton, NJ 1992) 78.

with a fresh set of recommendations from Erasmus (Allen Epp 2013, 2109), in 1528 he travelled to the imperial court in Spain but failed to secure an appointment there. Hence he rejoined Erasmus, who had moved to Freiburg im Breisgau in 1529. A second effort in Spain, again assisted by recommendations from Erasmus (Allen Epp 2251–5, 2481, 2523), was more successful, securing for him a position with Alonso de Fonseca, archbishop of Toledo, in 1530 (Allen Ep 2348). He was also rewarded with a knighthood for an oration delivered in 1533 at Barcelona in the presence of the emperor. In 1534 he returned to the Low Countries to marry a wealthy bride secured for him by his family. He eventually returned to imperial service in Spain in 1536 and in 1544–50 served as imperial ambassador in London, succeeding the experienced Eustache Chapuys. He retained this difficult position until he was called back to the Low Countries to help plan an abortive attempt to move Princess Mary Tudor (the emperor's cousin) from England to the Netherlands. On him see Franz Bierlaire *La Familia d'Erasme* (Paris 1968) 64–7.

ERASMUS OF ROTTERDAM TO FRANS VAN DER DILFT, A MOST
DISTINGUISHED YOUNG MAN, GREETING

No faults are more dangerous, my dear Frans, than those that masquerade as virtues. To this class belongs excessive shyness, which the Greeks call δυσωπία.[1] This noxious plant is most likely to grow in all the best and ablest 5 minds. If you try to pluck it out by force, something worse takes its place; if you let it alone, it brings with it a whole host of evils. But if you keep it on the right path with prudent moderation, it becomes the best protector of innocence and an ornament to every virtue. Aristotle rightly held that shyness was not a virtue but a condition in the young denoting an honest 10 character that is full of promise.[2] Thus the old man in the comedy said: 'He blushed; it's all right.'[3] But if modesty is carried too far, it covers up faults

* * * * *

1663
1 Plutarch's essay is known by the Latin title *De vitiosa verecundia* or, more commonly, *De vitioso pudore*. There is no exact English equivalent for either the Greek or the Latin terms, which cover loss of face, shyness, timidity, diffidence, a sense of shame, modesty, and embarrassment. Plutarch's essay is concerned mainly with an embarrassed timidity that prevents a person from saying no to an improper proposal out of consideration for a friend or fear of losing face. Erasmus translated the title as *De immodica verecundia* 'On Excessive Diffidence.'
2 *Nicomachean Ethics* 2.7.14 1108a 30–5, 4.9.1–3 1128b 10–21
3 Micio in Terence *Adelphi* 643

and prevents them from being corrected, as Flaccus wrote: 'Misplaced embarrassment conceals the unhealed sores.'[4] Plato thinks the problem should
be treated by convivial drinking.[5] Shyness blunts the edge of the mind. For   15
this reason the ancients gave the name *lusus pudoris* [the comedy of bash-
fulness] to that initial stage of madness which is said to be induced by a
potion made from a few grams of *strychnum*.[6] It is not unusual to see some
people so possessed by shyness that they seem to be out of their mind. In
brief, shyness undermines our ability not just to study and to judge but to   20
speak and to discharge all the proper functions of life.

What made me particularly interested in translating this little work of
Plutarch's, which I intended as an appendix to my *Lingua*,[7] was my realiza-
tion, when I reviewed the course of my past life, that nothing had got me
into greater trouble than diffidence and timidity, and that my worst disas-   25
ters came about when, against my better judgment, I gave in to the relentless badgering of my friends. I noticed too that the excellent qualities you
possess are joined to a singularly modest and obliging nature, so I thought
you needed the protection of this little book so that a natural modesty does
not turn into timidity. I do not know whether this has harmed you already,   30
but it was responsible, I am sure, for the fact that I was so slow to recognize your considerable ability and friendly disposition. It would have been a

* * * * *

4 Horace *Epistles* 1.16.24
5 Gerlo's French translation (VI 316) refers to *Republic* 539A–C, but Erasmus is
  really using Gellius 15.2.4, which depends on Plato *Laws* 637A and 647E.
6 Erasmus' source is Pliny *Naturalis historia* 21.177–8 (cf Theophrastus *Historia
  plantarum* 7.15.4, 9.11.6). Pliny's cryptic phrase *lusus pudoris* probably means
  something like 'having comic effects on one's modesty' / 'the loss of modesty.'
  The genus *strychnos* or *strychnon* includes various plants of the nightshade family, especially black nightshade (*Solanum nigrum*) and winter cherry (*Physalis
  alkekengi*), but the plant in question here seem to be *strychnon manikon*, that
  is, *Datura stramonium* or thorn apple. According to Pliny, 'Greek writers have
  said that a dose of one drachma plays tricks with the sense of shame, speaking of hallucinations and realistic visions; that a double dose causes down-
  right insanity' (Loeb translation). Celsus *De medicina* 2.33.2 merely identifies
  '*solanus*, which the Greeks call *strychnos*,' as among the plants that have medici-
  nal uses. In any case, the reference here, obviously derived from Pliny (whom
  Erasmus had edited the preceding year), is to some type of *strychnon* with
  hallucinogenic effects.
7 The title-page of the February 1526 edition reads *Lingua. Libellus elegans, nec
  minus utilis Plutarhi* [corrected to *Plutarchi* in the edition of July 1526] *Chaeronei
  de immodica uerecundia, recens opus, nec antehac usquam excusum. Quoniam autem
  argumentum cum Linga conuenit, adiunximus.*

blessing if I had recognized this earlier, and unless I am mistaken, a blessing for you too.

But I shall not keep you any longer from Plutarch, who will explain 35 all this better than I can. Farewell.

Basel, the morrow of the feast of the Purification AD 1526

1664 / To the Faculty of Theology at Paris   Basel, 6 February 1526

This letter was printed with Erasmus' *Prologus in supputationem calumniarum Bedae* (Basel: Froben, August 1526; reprinted with one textual change by Froben in March 1527), a rebuttal of Noël Béda's *Annotationes* directed against Lefèvre d'Etaples and Erasmus. It is part of Erasmus' effort to thwart the attempt of the anti-humanist syndic of the Paris faculty of theology, Béda, to procure formal condemnation of the theological works of both Lefèvre and Erasmus (in the latter case, specifically Erasmus' Paraphrase on Luke). Erasmus opened this campaign in 1525 by writing a letter of complaint directly to Béda himself (Ep 1571). After writing this letter to the faculty of theology, he wrote to the Parlement of Paris (Ep 1721), to King Francis I (Ep 1722), and again to the faculty (Ep 1723). On this dispute and the recent literature see Ep 1571; see also the subsequent correspondence between Erasmus and Béda, which remained formally polite but became increasingly laden with thinly veiled hostility: Epp 1579, 1581, 1596, 1609, 1610, 1620, and 1642, all dating from 1525.

Erasmus' complaint that Béda should have written directly to him rather than circulating his concerns about the Paraphrases among the Paris theologians was somewhat weakened by the fact that the two men had corresponded about Béda's articles criticizing them. Nevertheless, it remains true that Erasmus had first received the text of Béda's criticism of his work on the Gospel according to Luke not from Béda but from his recently deceased friend François Deloynes. Deloynes had received them from Béda because as a member of the Parlement of Paris he had sought the opinion of the faculty on an edition of the Paraphrase on Luke planned by the Paris printer Konrad Resch. French law required a printer (in this case, Resch) to secure a copyright (*privilège du roi*) before publication, and since March 1521 the Parlement could grant such a *privilège* for a book concerning religion only after receiving an opinion (a *nihil obstat*) from the faculty of theology. Hence it was appropriate for Deloynes to refer the proposed publication to the faculty and for Béda as syndic of the faculty to inform Deloynes of his own opinion. In addition, Erasmus, not Béda, had initiated the preceding correspondence, in which the two scholars debated the orthodoxy of Erasmus' publications. In this letter Erasmus omits any mention of this correspondence and complains that the notes extracted from his Paraphrases were circulated without his knowledge; he fails to mention that

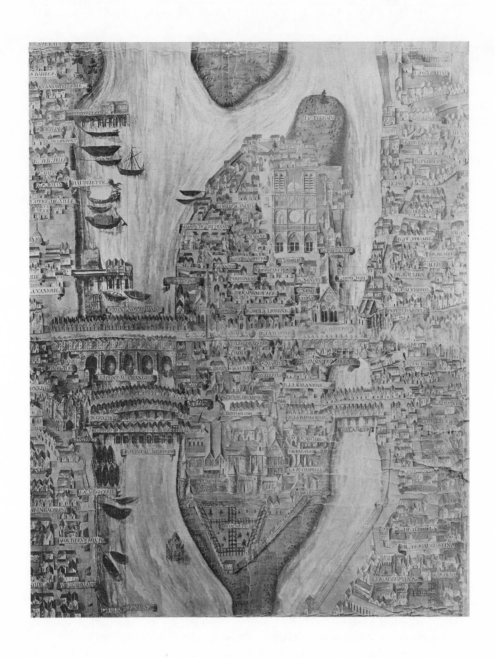

Paris in the sixteenth century
Two sections of a seventeenth-century gouache copy
of a plan of Paris done as a tapestry c 1540
Préfecture de Paris, Direction de l'Urbanisme et du Logement

he had already received them indirectly. Rummel II 33 is correct in suggesting that when the present letter was read before the faculty on 15 March 1526 (Farge *Registre* 146B page 132), Béda was able to 'put things into perspective' by reading some of the letters he had received from Erasmus, thus weakening the credibility of Erasmus' complaint.

ERASMUS OF ROTTERDAM TO THE MOST SACRED FACULTY
OF THEOLOGY AT PARIS, GREETING
Venerable fathers and sirs, I have received from Paris two documents of censure, one of which was produced jointly by two doctors of divinity, Noël Béda and Guillaume Duchesne, the other by Béda alone, who presented it   5
to the Parlement; it deals exclusively with my work on Luke.[1] The former

* * * * *

1664
1 Béda began making critical annotations on Erasmus' Paraphrase on the Gospel of Luke / *Paraphrasis in evangelium Lucae* within a few months of that work's publication by the Froben press in August 1523. His own account in the preface to his *Apologia adversus clandestinos Lutheranos* (Paris: Josse Bade, 1 February 1529), reprinted in Charles Duplessis d'Argentré *Collectio judiciorum de novis erroribus* 3 vols (Paris 1725–36; reprinted Brussels 1963) III-2 67–8 indicates that his critical evaluation began when the Paris printer Konrad Resch sought an informal theological evaluation of Erasmus' Paraphrase on Luke in order to satisfy the legal formalities necessary for republication of this work at Paris (Epp 1571 introduction and nn1, 2, 1579 n12). Béda extracted some fifty passages that he judged to be erroneous or suspect and communicated this list to Resch's intermediary François Deloynes. At a later date and without Béda's knowledge Deloynes sent a copy of these articles to Erasmus. Béda guessed that this occurred about a year after he had compiled the articles, hence in late 1524 or early 1525 (Duplessis d'Argentré *Collectio judiciorum* III-2 67); in any case, Erasmus had the articles in hand when he wrote his letter of 28 April 1525 to Béda (Ep 1571). At this period, Béda was acting on his own initiative. Although the Paris faculty of theology had begun some preliminary inquiry into the orthodoxy of Erasmus, in November 1523, when it was informed that this activity had angered King Francis I, the faculty assured him that it had not been investigating Erasmus but that its syndic, Noël Béda, was doing so on his own account (Farge *Orthodoxy* 176; Rummel II 29), apparently because of the request made indirectly by Resch through their mutual friend Deloynes. Béda probably had given his critical annotations to Deloynes before 18 January 1524, when the faculty's records show that Resch had abandoned private channels and had made a request for formal approval of his proposed edition by the faculty (Farge *Registre* 6; Rummel II 30; Farge *Orthodoxy* 177). After several sessions at which it was discussed, the matter seems to have been dropped from consideration; thus the printer's request was effectively denied by lack of formal action. Béda himself continued to regard Erasmus'

document, which later received additions, has a preface containing certain
formulae from the courts: 'I, Noël Béda' and 'having in consideration the
fear of God alone.' There follow a number of odious remarks to the effect
that my teaching on many points is 'erroneous,' that it is 'shamelessly con-   10
trary to good morals,' that it is also frequently 'schismatic,' that it 'impiously
detracts from the dignity of the religious,' that it offers a 'poisoned cup,'
and so on. Whatever may be said about these imputations, had he communicated them to me privately, I would have been grateful for his criticisms,
whether well founded or not. But instead these censures circulate in your   15

* * * * *

publications as a danger to orthodoxy and pursued his private evaluation not
only of the Paraphrase on Luke but also of Erasmus' other New Testament
paraphrases and perhaps of other works. At a date that cannot now be determined but that must be towards the end of 1524 or in the early months of
1525, Béda received from a group of Carthusian monks another request for
his opinion of Erasmus' works (Duplessis d'Argentré Collectio judiciorum III-2
68). He responded with a memorandum dated 7 April 1525 in which he declared that he did find in Erasmus' writings on Scripture and theology numerous passages that were not only erroneous or contrary to good morals
but also schismatic and impiously hostile to the monastic life. His advice was
that professed religious should be protected from reading these works lest
they be misled into error by the elegant literary style. He refers readers of
this memorandum to the articles he has excerpted from Erasmus' works. The
document (printed in LB IX 451) is signed by Béda and by another conservative theologian, Guillaume Duchesne. It is likely that the articles referred to
in this memorandum included passages from other publications of Erasmus
in addition to the Paraphrase on Luke, for in his reply to Erasmus' letter of
28 April Béda informed Erasmus that he had also made notes identifying errors in other paraphrases – on Mark, John, and Matthew and on the epistles of
Paul (Ep 1579:139–43, dated 21 May 1525). He claimed (not quite accurately)
that he had compiled these new articles in response to a request made under
the authority of Deloynes, who was président aux enquêtes in the Parlement of
Paris (Ep 1579 n1). Béda sent these additional articles to Erasmus along with
his letter of 12 September 1525 (Ep 1609:54). Despite Erasmus' protests (Epp
1620, 1664), Béda received the faculty's permission to publish his criticisms of
Erasmus' paraphrases (Farge Registre 137, session of 16 May 1526), and they
were published, together with his more extensive notes attacking the biblical
scholarship of the humanist Jacques Lefèvre d'Etaples, in his Annotationum ...
in Jacobum Fabrum Stapulensem libri duo: et in Desiderium Erasmum Roterodamum
liber unus (Paris: Josse Bade, 28 May 1526). On the failure of Erasmus' efforts
to resolve the conflict either by persuasion or by appeals for intervention by
the king, see Ep 1666 n5. Cf Erasmus' direct appeals and protests to the faculty of theology (this letter and Ep 1723), the Parlement of Paris (Ep 1721),
and King Francis I (Ep 1722).

part of the world without my knowledge. Many believe they were issued with the consent of your university, although this is not the case. I would have thought that Guillaume Duchesne did not have enough time to spend on reading my work or enough patience to stick to the task. I imagine he put his name to these strictures to please his friend.   20

But Guillaume has gone to his appointed place[2] and, as the proverb says, one should think of the living.[3] I doubt if even Béda has read everything; I rather think he farmed out the work to others, as is suggested by the different numbers used to indicate the pages. But this does not matter, since Béda now accepts responsibility for all the annotations. I have replied 25
briefly to a few of the points raised, though I have had to guess what it was that he objected to. I wanted you to be able to judge whether the ideas criticized justify the savage invective which you will find in the preface to the *censura*.

In my opinion Béda is a good man. But good men too have their preju- 30
dices. They are too inclined to favour their own enthusiasms, too unsympathetic to those of others; they follow blindly those who give a lead and give credence to false witnesses. In short, good men are human too. There is no doubt that Béda harbours a deadly prejudice against the study of languages and literature, and perhaps for this reason he is not a fair critic of my work. 35
I make no claim for myself except that when I wrote these works I did so in all sincerity and with a serious desire to advance the Christian faith. If at times I have gone astray, the mistake is due to ignorance or ordinary human carelessness.

I shall not argue against any of Béda's strictures except to say that 40
in contentious issues of doctrine, where someone has expressed an opinion contrary to a decree of the church, he has no right to tell me that I may not deal with Scripture as the orthodox Fathers did in times past, always remaining faithful to the interpretation of the church. Nor, if something in my writings seems close to a mistaken position taken by someone else, should 45
he immediately be seized with suspicion, especially when it is clear from other passages in my work what my own views are. Again, I should not be accused of schism if I criticize immoral bishops, especially if the criticism is expressed in general terms; the world is full of bishops, and we could wish that they were all such as St Paul describes.[4] Nor should he object 50

* * * * *

2 Duchesne had died the preceding September. Cf Acts 1:25, a reference Judas Iscariot.
3 *Adagia* I ii 52; cf Cicero *De finibus* 5.1.3.
4 1 Tim 3:1–7

that I am detracting from the dignity of the religious when I tell monks where true piety lies. Nowhere do I condemn any estate, only those who do not live up to its obligations. He should not imply that I was speaking of all theologians when I mentioned some of their number who hardly deserve the name.[5] I wish it could be said that there were no such theolo- 55
gians in the world! Certainly I respect the profession as a whole, and I shall continue to respect it as long as I live. Finally, he should not assert that I shamelessly threaten sound morality when I speak out against superstition and against practices that have surreptitiously crept into common use. The greater the authority that theologians wield, the more essential it 60
is for their judgments to be not just sensible and fair but free from bias as well.

Although the censure was not issued with the consent of your university, nevertheless, since Guillaume Duchesne and Noël Béda are among the most prominent of your members, many people are inferring your opinion 65
from theirs. As far as languages and the humanities are concerned, I know that experts like yourselves have no need of advice from me. It seems to me, however, that your profession would gain in dignity and distinction if theology, the queen of sciences, graciously accepted its old retainers back into its service. What our critics claim to be new is in fact old, this mating 70
of the practice of theology with the study of languages and polite letters. If there are some experts in literature who turn to impious doctrines, it is not fair to blame the sins of individuals on disciplines that are by nature good and have in the past brought no small benefit to the Catholic church.

I write this because some of your more senior members are unsympa- 75
thetic to these studies, not having been introduced to them when they were young. May the Lord keep you all safe, reverend fathers and teachers, for whom I have the highest regard. It is my fervent wish to be commended to your Reverences' favour.

Basel, the day following the feast of St Agatha AD 1526   80

1665 / From Juan Luis Vives   Bruges, 14 February 1526

On this Spanish-born humanist, whose ability Erasmus regarded highly, see Epp 927 introduction, 1613 introduction. The difficulty involving the bookseller Franz Birckmann and Johann Froben referred to in line 1 had to do

* * * * *

5 Erasmus regularly insisted that his criticism of theologians, like his criticism of bishops and monks, was always directed against specific unworthy individuals and not against bishops, monks, or theologians in general.

with a proposal by Birckmann for an edition of various works by Vives which would be printed by Froben at Basel. Although Froben as well as Erasmus and Vives had business dealings with Birckmann frequently because of his lead-ing role in the international book trade, neither Erasmus nor Vives trusted him. In Ep 1513:46–54 Vives made it clear that while he would be happy to have his *Opuscula* published by Froben, he wanted nothing to do with such an undertaking if Birckmann were involved. A further complication was that Vives' edition of St Augustine's *De civitate Dei*, produced with Erasmus' en-couragement and published by Froben in 1522, had sold poorly – in Erasmus' opinion because of the excessive length of Vives' commentary. Apparently the projected Froben edition of the *Opuscula* fell through. See Ep 1613 nn2, 3. This letter was first published in Vives' *Opera* (1555).

VIVES TO ERASMUS
That's enough about Franz;[1] he isn't worth it. It would be unfair to ask some-thing of Froben that would involve him in financial loss. It is not surprising that my works do not sell. Not only do they lack genius, but neither are they ingenious or distinguished by erudition or the celebrity of the author's   5
name – in short by any of the things that generally make books successful. I shall look for another printer whom I should be less sorry to impose on than Froben, who has earned the respect of the world of letters by publish-ing your enduring works. I feel I have reached the height of fame if what you say in your letter[2] is sincerely meant and not just written to tickle my   10
ears. Nor do I seek any other glory than to find favour with you and with men like you (if indeed there are any men like you). For what greater glory could a man obtain, what higher distinction? 'Plato alone is worth the whole

* * * * *

1665
1 Franz Birckmann, a bookseller based in Antwerp but active throughout north-western Europe, who had acquired a reputation for dishonesty. See Epp 258:14n, 1362 n1, 1388 n23, 1507, 1560 n6, 1606 n2. Erasmus made no secret of his opinion of Birckmann. Craig Thompson in the introduction to *Pseudochei et Philetymi* 'The Liar and the Man of Honour' in *Colloquies* CWE 39 344 notes that the cheat in the dialogue is intended to be identified as Birckmann; Thompson gives a number of references to letters of Erasmus that confirm this. Vives, who shared Erasmus' opinion of Birckmann's business ethics, recognized the character Pseudocheus as Birckmann (Ep 1513:49–50), and Erasmus confirms the identification in Epp 1531:49, 1560:16–19. Cf also Epp 1666:26–9, 35–43, 1778:1–3 and n1, 1781:9–10.
2 Not extant. Allen (8n) suggests that it must have been written about 25 De-cember 1525.

population of Athens,' said the poet;[3] and the musician wrote, 'Sing for me
and for the Muses.'[4] To whom could one apply these words more appro-   15
priately in our time than to you? So the advice at the end of your letter
was superfluous: 'Let us preserve our friendship for ever with the blessing of the Muses and the Graces.' I am not so careless as to lose a friendship that brings me such honour and distinction. I shall hold on to it with
all my might, as the expression goes.[5] For I have no hesitations whatever   20
about you.

Within three days, Lord willing, I shall set out for Britain.[6] I shall write
you a longer letter from there, for I have nothing worth writing about at
present. I imagine news has already reached you about the peace[7] – if by
peace we mean a period of calm and quiet so that men may return to all   25
those evils that were stopped or interrupted by the exigencies of the war.
Would that the peace of Christ, that peace which the world cannot give,[8]

* * * * *

3 Antimachus of Colophon. Cicero tells the story (in not quite the same words)
  in *Brutus* 191.
4 Antigenidas, speaking to a pupil who failed to impress the public; Cicero
  Brutus 187
5 *Adagia* v ii 15
6 At this period Vives divided his time between Bruges, where he had married
  a local woman in 1524, and England; his wife remained in Bruges. He was in
  Bruges from 10 May 1525 to February 1526, and the announced visit to Britain
  was short: he returned to Bruges in May 1526 and remained there until April
  1527, partly because of his wife's residence there but also because an anti-
  Spanish turn in English foreign policy, combined with his many expressions
  of anti-war sentiment, made him less welcome at court than in the past. See
  Carlos G. Noreña *Juan Luís Vives* (Madrid 1978) 122–8.
7 Probably the negotiations surrounding the release of Francis I from captivity in Spain (17 March 1526). The treaty between France and Spain providing for Francis' release was sworn to on 14 January and was supposed to be
  published on 15 February 1526, arrangements that the well-connected Vives
  would likely have known. Less likely would be a reference to the Treaty of
  the More (30 August 1525) by which England made peace with the French regent, Louise of Savoy. The next treaty of importance, the League of Cognac,
  which united France, Florence, Venice, and Milan in an effort to block the
  ambitions of Charles v, with Henry viii as protector of the league, was not
  formed until 22 May 1526. See J.D. Mackie *The Earlier Tudors* (Oxford 1952)
  315–17.
8 *Sacramentarium Gelasianum* 3.56; *The Gelasian Sacramentary: Liber sacramentorum
  Romanae ecclesiae* ed H.A. Wilson (Oxford 1894) 271 item 56: 'Deus, a quo
  sancta desideria, et recta consilia et iusta sunt opera, da servis tuis illam,
  quam mundus dare non potest, pacem; ut et corda mandatis tuis dedita, et,

would descend upon our hearts and upon the church. The whole world is
torn apart by factions, but we must look to Christ for the turning point;
from him alone we should seek applause. To write along these lines is not   30
without danger[9] – and what is more remarkable, the danger comes from
both sides. My friend van Fevijn[10] sends you his most respectful greetings.

Best wishes, most eminent of teachers.

Bruges, 14 February, 1526

1666 / From Polidoro Virgilio   London, 17 February [1526]

On this prominent Italian humanist, author of several influential works of reference as well as of an epoch-making history of England, who was one of the
leading scholars at the court of Henry VIII, see Epp 531:456n, 1175 introduction
and the lengthy article by Brian P. Copenhaver in CEBR III 397–9. The autograph letter survived at Leipzig and was first printed in Förstemann/Günther
in 1904. The date given at the end of the letter reflects the English practice of
counting 25 March (the feast of the Annunciation) rather than 1 January as the
beginning of the new year. Erasmus' reply is Ep 1702.

Lately a rumour has spread throughout the whole of England that you have
gone to Flanders.[1] I even heard it myself from friends. It was so convincing
that I began to write to you there and had just taken up my pen when who
should appear but your man Karl[2] with a letter from you, from which I

* * * * *

hostium sublata formidine, tempora sint tua protectione tranquilla'; also PL
74 1217; Joseph Aloysius Assemanus *Codex liturgicus ecclesiae universae* 15 vols
(Rome 1749–66; reprinted Farnborough, Hants 1968) IV-2 193.
9 Vives wrote these somewhat bold comment words in Greek, a language that
Erasmus could read but most people, even well educated ones, could not.
10 See Ep 1012 introduction.

1666
1 Juan Luis Vives, writing from Antwerp on 20 September 1525, had heard the
same false rumour. See Ep 1613:2–6.
2 Karl Harst was Erasmus' secretary and trusted confidential courier; on him
see Epp 1215 introduction, 1575 n2. He met Erasmus while a student at Louvain and in the autumn of 1521 escorted him part of the way on his move
from the Low Countries to Basel. He seems to have carried an important
letter for Erasmus at least once at that time (Ep 1241 n2) but was not in
Erasmus' employ then. He moved to Basel as *famulus* (secretary and general factotum) to Erasmus in April 1524 and served until June 1526. He then

learned that you had not set foot outside the boundaries of Basel. I was   5
pleased to hear that you are well; your letter also gave me some grounds for
hope of a future meeting between us. For peace has at last been concluded
between the emperor and the king of France³ and is almost certain to hold
for several years; so the situation has turned out so well for us that you
owe it to yourself not to stay any longer in Basel. You have English and   10
French friends all ready to help and devoted Flemish friends too: you would
be quite entitled to stay with them. A visit from you will be profitable to
yourself and will give great pleasure to your friends, for it will be easier for
them to write you a note of greeting every day and to delight and gladden
you with their gifts. Think it over, and if this does not have any effect on   15
you, remember what your enemies are always saying, that you are living in
Basel as a refugee.⁴

* * * * *

settled in Louvain, where he married in January 1527 (Ep 1778) and worked
as a teacher before entering the service of the duke of Cleves in 1530. In
1525 he undertook two delicate and confidential missions to Italy (negotiations in Rome for a papal dispensation authorizing Erasmus to dispose of his
personal property by will, and in Venice with the publisher Gianfrancesco
Torresani about an abortive plan for a new Venetian edition of the *Adagia*).
On the second of these trips to Italy, he also had the task of purchasing a
Greek manuscript of St John Chrysostom at Padua that Erasmus hoped would
contain commentaries by Chrysostom on the Acts of the Apostles; see Epp
1623, 1675 n4. This manuscript disappointed Erasmus' hopes and is distinct
from the valuable manuscript of Chrysostom brought back from Italy in 1526
by Hieronymus Froben (Epp 1661 nn2, 6, 1705 n3). Just a few weeks after
his return from Italy to Basel in November 1525, Erasmus sent him on another confidential mission to the Netherlands and England, dealing with Erasmus' literary work and private financial affairs. Erasmus trusted his discretion fully and authorized him to communicate oral reports on highly sensitive matters to recipients of the letters he brought, for example Erasmus' assessment of the religious situation in Germany in 1525, reported to a close
adviser of Pope Clement VII (Ep 1575), or providing Erasmus' friend Polidoro Virgilio with examples of the dishonesty of the prominent bookseller
Franz Birckmann, mentioned in the postscript to this letter (lines 35–41; cf n9
below).
3 The treaty providing for the release of King Francis I from captivity at Madrid
was formally concluded on 14 January, and the English ambassadors then in
Spain kept their king and Cardinal Wolsey informed on such important diplomatic news. See LP IV-1 610–856.
4 A reference chiefly to Erasmus' enemies at Louvain and elsewhere in the Low
Countries, where Erasmus as an honorary imperial councillor was expected to
reside

Your opponents have spread a rumour throughout England that you
and your writings have recently been condemned in Paris.[5] It is so persistent that everywhere people have been approaching our friend More[6] and   20
Zacharias[7] and myself, along with other friends of yours, to ask if there was
any truth in this distressing tale. Your man Karl will tell you all about it.
Since I, more than anyone else, am anxious to have you settle near here, I have
given Karl sixteen crowns[8] to buy a little horse to carry you wherever you
want to go. I write this in all sincerity and with your best interests at heart.   25

* * * * *

5 In fact Noël Béda and other conservative theologians at Paris had been working since at least 1523 to compile evidence from Erasmus' publications that
he was a heretic and favoured Luther; see Ep 1664 introduction and n1. Neither his publication of *De libero arbitrio* against Luther in 1524 nor repeated
efforts by the French court to head off a formal condemnation stopped this
effort. The defeat and captivity of the French king in February 1525 had emboldened these enemies by removing the principal protector of the humanists
from the scene, and Erasmus' effort to silence the attacks by opening direct
correspondence with their principal author, Béda, had failed (see Epp 1571,
1579, 1581, 1596, 1609, 1620, 1642). See Rummel II 30–55 for a narrative account extending to the faculty's final success in 1532 in publishing its censures
against Erasmus' publications, a decision formally voted in 1527 but much
delayed in publication, probably because of the king's opposition.
6 Thomas More had repeatedly defended Erasmus' scholarship against conservative critics, including Maarten van Dorp in 1515 (More CW XV xxiii–xxiv, 2–
149; Rummel I 8–10), Edward Lee in 1520 (More CW XV xxxi–xli, 152–95; Rummel I 111–12), John Batmanson in 1520 (More CW X xli–xlv, 198–311; Rummel
I 118–19), and Henry Standish (Rummel I 122–6; cf Ep 1126 and nn5–6, 10).
Hence people in England may well have sought news of renewed attacks on
Erasmus from him, even though Erasmus and his great English friend had not
remained in close touch after Erasmus moved to Basel in 1521. Although no
letters between them survive between June 1521 (Ep 1220) and December 1526
(Ep 1770), indirect references show that there were letters, now lost, during
that period. See Epp 1271 n21, 1385 n1, 1656 n2, 1766 n10.
7 On Zacharias Deiotarius, a Frisian long settled in England and a helpful friend,
see Ep 1205 n1. He was a servant of Archbishop William Warham.
8 Latin *xvi coronatos*. For reasons noted in Ep 1434 n3 and 1545 n6, these 'crowns'
were *écus d'or au soleil*, which had displaced the *écu à la couronne* in November
1475 and were now officially worth 40s tournois in France, 76d groot in the
Hapsburg Netherlands, and 52d sterling in England (CWE 8 350; Ep 1658 n3).
Both of these French coins displayed an emblem of a crown surmounting a
shield; but the latter also had a blazing sun placed above the crown. The sum
mentioned was then officially worth £32 0s 0d tournois, or £5 1s 4d groot
Flemish, or £3 9s 4d sterling.

I shall have nothing more to do with the notorious Franz,[9] who lauds you to the skies, induced, I imagine, by your thirteen florins.[10] He considers it tantamount to death to admit that you and he are not on the best of terms – so skilful is he at pretending.

Out of his charity and to please you, More has become my very good friend. Farewell.

London, 17 February 1525

Yours, Polidoro Virgilio

To the erudite Erasmus, my very dear friend

PS I did not know, I admit, the reason you complained so much about Franz, until your man Karl showed him for what he is – a putrefying sore exuding every kind of deceit; such a fellow would justify not just complaints but a whole torrent of blows. I wonder at your patience in putting up with his wickedness so long – to say nothing of the innocence you showed when you decided to trust his good faith time and time again in spite of being so frequently let down by his dishonesty. I even envy the man's success, for his misdeeds caused a writer of your distinction to turn from important business and write the story of the whole affair. But such is Erasmus' kindness that he always returns good for evil. From now on I shall take to heart that line from Plautus: 'Happy is the man who learns wisdom at another's cost.'[11] I am sure that was why you sent me your account of the affair. Farewell.

1667 / To the Reader

Basel, 20 February 1526

This letter was printed as the preface to the first part of Erasmus' *Hyperaspistes diatribae adversus servum arbitrium Martini Lutheri* (Basel: Froben 1526, probably

* * * * *

9 On Franz Birckmann see Epp 1665 introduction and n1. Allen (38n) is probably correct in concluding that the 'story of the whole affair' referred to in the postscript to this letter was a confidential exposé by Erasmus of Birckmann's dishonest business practices described to Virgilio by Erasmus' courier Karl Harst.

10 Latin *xiii florenis*. These are probably the debased Rhenish florins, the Rheingulden of 18.5 carats, currently worth 30s tournois and 57d to 59d groot Flemish (see Ep 1651 n5), a value that corresponds precisely to the rate of 39d sterling given to the 'Floraine of base gold' in Henry VIII's royal proclamation of 24 November 1522 (Ep 1658 n3). If so, this was a sum worth £3 3s 11d groot Flemish (at the higher rate), or £2 2s 3d sterling, or £19 10s 0d tournois.

11 A spurious line from the *Mercator* (4.7.40), not printed in modern texts. See *Adagia* I i 31 and II ix 71.

about the beginning of March). After publishing his treatise *De libero arbitrio* διατριβή *sive collatio* (Basel: Froben 1524) challenging Luther's teaching that the human will is unfree and that no human act can contribute in even the slightest way to salvation, Erasmus had a long wait before Luther issued a rebuttal – from the beginning of September 1524 until the publication of Luther's *De servo arbitrio* at the very end of 1525. Philippus Melanchthon, to whom in 1524 Erasmus sent a copy of *De libero arbitrio* together with a long and complex letter (Ep 1496) justifying his decision to oppose Luther openly, had promptly acknowledged the letter and the book and reported that Erasmus' book 'had a very mild reception here' (Ep 1500:45–6, dated 30 September 1524).

Luther himself seems to have been reluctant to reply or even to read beyond the opening pages of Erasmus' tract, but by the end of 1524 and early 1525 his sermons and his commentary on Deuteronomy show that he was pondering the question of free will. Yet he was distracted by other matters he regarded as far more urgent, such as the challenge to his leadership by Andreas Karlstadt and other evangelical radicals and the great Peasant War, which reached its peak in the spring and early summer of 1525. Although in April 1525 Melanchthon wrote to a friend that Luther would soon complete a rebuttal of Erasmus' book (*Melanchthons Briefwechsel* [Stuttgart-Bad Cannstatt 1977–] *Texte* II [1995] 279 Ep 387; *Corpus Reformatorum* I [Berlin 1834] 736 Ep 328), on 19 July he reported to the same person that Luther had not followed through (*Briefwechsel* II 336 Ep 412; *Corpus Reformatorum* I 752 Ep 343). Luther must have known that because of Erasmus' fame and large following he would eventually have to reply, but he obviously was disinclined to do so. Only in the autumn of 1525, after repeated urging from his friends and even his wife, did he set to work. He probably completed the manuscript of *De servo arbitrio* in mid-November, and it came off the press of Hans Lufft at Wittenberg on the last day of 1525. This work is a major theological statement of Luther's opinions on free will, human nature, and grace, as well as a powerful reiteration of his views on the authority and interpretation of the Bible. Yet what is most striking about it is its contemptuous dismissal of Erasmus as a secret atheist who not only failed to understand Scripture but in fact had no real religious faith at all. Focusing his attack on Erasmus' plea for undogmatic open-mindedness on difficult and abstruse doctrines like free will and predestination, Luther compared the humanist to 'Lucian, or some other pig from Epicurus' sty' (WA 18 605; see Ep 1688 introduction, where the passage is quoted, and Brecht II 226).

Although Erasmus probably expected a sharp rejoinder to what he had intended as a mild but firm rejection of the central doctrine in Luther's theology, he was shocked by the savage assault not only on his theological competence but also on his religious commitment and moral integrity. Inclined as

The Raising of Lazarus, a painting by Lucas Cranach the Younger (1515–86),
which formed part of an epitaph monument, now destroyed, for
Michael Meyenburg. For the detail showing Erasmus among the Reformers,
see opposite. Staatliche Museen, Berlin

With the publication of his *De libero arbitrio* διατριβή *sive collatio /
A Discussion of Free Will* and the two books of *Hyperaspistes*, Erasmus hoped
to make clear his opposition to Luther, but some continued to see him as one
of the Reformers, as in this detail from *The Raising of Lazarus* (opposite),
which was painted in 1558. The figures in the group have been identified
(from right to left) as Philippus Melanchthon, Kaspar Cruciger, Justus Jonas,
Erasmus, Johann Bugenhagen, and (behind Luther) Georgius Spalatinus
and Johann Foerster, who is bearded.

he was to suspect devious conspiracies, and influenced by rumours as early as April 1525 that Luther would publish his reply soon, Erasmus concluded that Luther's publication was deliberately delayed so that it would be impossible for Erasmus to produce a reply in time for the spring book fair at Frankfurt, the principal centre for diffusion of books throughout Germany. Thus he decided to issue his reply in two parts. Determined not to let Luther and his supporters have the long interval between 31 December 1525 and the opening of the autumn book fair to circulate their attacks without any response from himself, Erasmus strained every nerve to complete the first part of his rebuttal in time for the spring fair in March. *Hyperaspistes 1* was produced in about two weeks of intensive labour; indeed, Erasmus claimed that the writing took just ten days. In it Erasmus devoted much of his attention to a defence against Luther's charges of atheism and immoral scepticism, though he also clearly affirmed the authority of both Scripture and tradition and restated his belief that a simple, ethically sound Christian faith was more important than theological correctness on abstruse theoretical issues.

We now know that the delay in Luther's response to *De libero arbitrio* was not due to a deliberate plot to monopolize the discussion for nearly nine months but to Luther's preoccupation with other matters and to his reluctance to plunge into the details of Erasmus' book. But it is true that *De servo arbitrio* was translated and printed in German early in 1526 and that the Latin text was reprinted several times that year, so that Erasmus' concern to publish a timely reply before the spring fair at Frankfurt had some justification. Erasmus' sense of urgency was reflected in the special efforts that his printer, Johann Froben, made to complete the printing of *Hyperaspistes 1*, setting twenty-four leaves of type per day and employing six presses to speed production (see Ep 1683 n5 for a discussion of the efforts put forth by the press, and cf Allen's introduction to Ep 1667). Erasmus felt further aggrieved, and confirmed in his suspicion that the Lutherans were engaged in a deliberate plot to make it impossible for him to reply promptly, because he was unable for many weeks to secure a copy of Luther's attack. Indeed, he managed to produce this short and partial reply in time for the March book fair only because a friend at Leipzig sent him a copy – something that no one at Wittenberg had cared to do (Epp 1678, 1679, 1683). Even Luther's own letter (now lost) justifying *De servo arbitrio* reached him tardily. Its date is unknown, but Erasmus' chilly acknowledgment and reply (Ep 1688) is dated 11 April 1526. Although Erasmus announced in part 1 that more would follow, his lengthy *Hyperaspistes 2* did not appear until September 1527. Luther seems to have done little more than glance through *Hyperaspistes 1*, and he never wrote a response to either part. For a succinct narrative of the whole affair, see Brecht II 213–38 and, for a different perspective, Schoeck (1993) 298–309. More extensive are Georges Chantraine *Erasme et Luther: Libre et serf arbitre* (Paris 1981) and Harry J. McSorley *Luther: Right or Wrong?* (New York 1968).

ERASMUS OF ROTTERDAM TO THE READER, GREETING
The *Servum arbitrium* has come out under the name of Martin Luther, but it is the work of many people produced over a long period of time – in fact, as we were told by those who claimed to have seen a few pages, printing began a year ago[1] and the work was evidently prepared with the greatest   5 care. It took a long time for a copy to reach me, and then it was by pure chance; for it was not just Luther's followers who tried to keep it from me so as to have a few months at least in which to enjoy their triumph, but our common enemies, who dislike me for my interest in the humanities and Luther for his erroneous doctrine, did the same.[2]   10

The amount of time that I could spare for rereading my *Diatribe*,[3] working through Luther's book (which is not just lengthy, but long-winded), and composing my reply was no more than ten days, and the book reached me when I was already exhausted and still trying to finish my preparations for the forthcoming fair. If anyone doubts my word, there are reliable witnesses   15 at Basel who will testify to what I say.

Despite the difficulties, however, when I observed the insolent delight with which certain people greeted the book as soon as they got wind of it,

* * * * *

1667
1 A highly unlikely story. In any case, Luther's *De servo arbitrio* was not published until 31 December 1525. As early as 25 May 1525 Erasmus reported that Luther had written and published a reply but that he had not yet seen it (Ep 1576). See also Ep 1624 n11 on Luther's tardiness in replying, and cf the introduction to this letter.
2 Erasmus means that his conservative Catholic enemies, just as much as Luther and his supporters, wanted to prevent him from getting a copy of Luther's *De servo arbitrio* so that he could not make a timely reply to it and thus demonstrate his determination to oppose Luther and to uphold the Catholic faith. He viewed these conservatives as equally hostile to Luther and to himself; hence they were the 'common enemies' of both Luther and the proponents of humanistic learning and moderate Catholic reform. Cf Ep 1672:85–6 and n13.
3 *De libero arbitrio diatribe*. Modern readers should note that the Greek word δι- ατριβή in Erasmus' title means only 'a learned discussion,' not a violent criticism, a meaning that seems to date only from the early nineteenth century. See A *Discussion of Free Will* CWE 76 5 n1 and Schoeck (1993) 303, 308 n14, citing OED.

I decided to produce a partial reply in time for the Frankfurt fair, however
hurried the result might be. I wanted to take some of the smugness out of   20
the triumph they were preparing to celebrate before the victory was won.
My reply deals with the passage in which Luther attacks the preface to my
Diatribe; the rest I must leave for a fuller discussion when time permits. In
several places I have added in the margin the chapter numbers of Luther's
disputation to facilitate reference to the points against which I am arguing,   25
but you will first have to number the chapters of Luther's work. Farewell.
You will soon have more decisive evidence of victory in this debate.

    Basel, 20 February 1526

1668 / From Jan Oem   Louvain, 28 February 1526

> This letter, of which the autograph survived in the Rehdiger collection at
> Wrocław, was first published by Enthoven in 1906. It could hardly have de-
> lighted Erasmus, since it identifies the writer's father as the author of an anony-
> mous letter or pamphlet that was sharply critical of Erasmus' spiritual and
> scholarly publications. That pamphlet was not printed but did circulate in
> manuscript among Erasmus' enemies at Louvain. He had attributed its inspi-
> ration to the personal influence of one of his harshest critics among the Lou-
> vain theologians, the Carmelite prior Nicolaas Baechem of Egmond. See Ep
> 1469 for Erasmus' reply to it.
>   Jan Oem (d 4 May 1567), like his father, was educated in civil and canon law
> at Louvain, where he matriculated in 1523 and became licentiate in both laws
> in 1526. His father, Floris, had been a classmate and close friend of Adriaan
> Floriszoon of Utrecht, who after becoming Pope Adrian vi in 1522 not only
> personally informed Floris of his election but also nominated his son Jan to
> the prebend he himself had held. Jan was obviously well connected, which is
> probably why Erasmus replied to this letter (Ep 1699).

Most learned Master Erasmus, in the year of our Lord 1523, on the twelfth
of September, you received a letter in Dutch from an unknown friend,[1] who

* * * * *

1668
1 Erasmus in Ep 1469 all but openly stated that the anonymous letter was in
   Dutch because its author was too poorly educated (despite his doctorate) to
   write it in Latin, the appropriate language for such a discussion. In Ep 1699
   Erasmus told Jan Oem that he had not replied to the father's letter (which he
   called a *libellus*, that is, a pamphlet) because it seemed inappropriate to reply
   in Latin to criticisms made and circulated in Dutch.

concealed his name under a veil of anonymity, not to prevent you from knowing it, but for a different reason, which he explained at the end of the letter. I am his son and I live at Louvain. He suggested that, when I wrote to you (for it is not so difficult to find couriers here who are travelling in your direction), I should frankly confess that the man who sent you that letter was my father, Floris Oem van Wijngaarden,[2] a doctor of civil and canon law; he also asked me to paint as good a verbal portrait of himself as I could manage so that you would know him – at least so far as such a description would allow. He is a man with a very deep interest in Greek and Latin; he supported the establishment here in Louvain of the College of the Three Tongues,[3] and he regrets more and more every day that it was not in operation when he was still a young man living here. Nevertheless, at the age of fifty-five he began to apply himself to the elements of the Greek language, and last year he sent his son, my younger brother (who, if I am not mistaken, has not yet reached his thirteenth year), to study both Greek and Latin with Jan Beren, an excellent scholar and rector of the gymnasium at Rotterdam.[4] Moreover, my father and Pope Adrian VI (May God have mercy on his soul!), when they were both young students together at this university, developed a remarkable association, and although Adrian's move to Spain caused them to be separated from one another, nevertheless their mutual friendship continued and developed through an exchange of letters. And when Adrian was advanced to greater heights, in fact to the pontificate, he did not forget his friend Floris, to whom he wrote a personal letter to inform him of

                    * * * * *

2 On the father see Ep 1469 introduction.
3 On the famous Collegium Trilingue, established at Louvain under the terms of a legacy left by Erasmus' friend Jérôme de Busleyden, see Ep 691 and the work of Henry de Vocht there cited. Allen (13n) observes that Jan's claim that his father was associated with the founding of the college was not very tactful, since Erasmus himself had been one of the executors of Busleyden's will and had played a leading role in founding the new institution.
4 Jan Arentszoon Beren (Johannes Berius or Ursus) was a priest of Amsterdam and seems to be the Johannes Beren de Amsterdammis who matriculated at Louvain on 19 January 1521 (*Matricule de l'Université de Louvain* III-1 ed A. Schillings [Brussels 1958] 640 no 82), and in the Collège du Porc on 27 February (ibidem 640 no 114). He seems to have been close to Erasmus' old friend Cornelis Gerard, who dedicated to him for use in his school an edition of Cornelis Croock's *Farrago sordidorum verborum*, printed together in one volume with Erasmus' paraphrase of Lorenzo Valla's *Elegantiae* (Cologne: J. Gymnich 1529). Alaard of Amsterdam included verses by Jan Beren in his edition of Erasmus' *Carmen bucolicum* (Leiden: P. Balenus 1538; NK 786). Beren died before 9 April 1559.

his election to the Roman pontificate. Nor did he forget their former friendship; for without being urged by anyone, he sent me a letter *motu proprio* (as
the phrase goes),[5] assigning to me the prebend that he himself had held in
the cathedral church of St Lambert in Liège.

So, most learned Master Erasmus, I urge you as strongly as I can to be   30
kind enough to write to me and let me know if you are willing to reply to
my father's Dutch letter. But if you are reluctant to write to someone whom
you do not know, then at least write to Jodocus Gaverius[6] or to Conradus
Goclenius,[7] both close friends of mine, or at any rate to Adrianus Barlandus,[8]
with whom I am on very intimate terms, and let him know if you received   35
my letter and the letter from my father, who, I almost forgot to say, sends
you his best wishes. Farewell, most learned Master Erasmus.

Louvain, from the home of Master Jan Vullinck,[9] master of St Peter's
school and secretary to the university, in whose house I reside, 28 Febru-

* * * * *

5 OED2 IX 1139 defines such a letter as 'an edict issued by the pope personally to
   the R.C. Church, or to part of it.' Here it is a document issued to a particular
   individual, undertaken at the pontiff's own initiative, conferring a benefice
   that was at the pontiff's personal disposal (*Enciclopedia cattolica* 12 vols [Vatican
   city 1948–54] VIII 1487). In the practice of the papal chancery at the time, it
   was a simple and informal document of a type developed in the fifteenth
   century, personally signed by the pope with the formula *Placet motu proprio*
   and employing his baptismal name (in the case of Adrian VI, the same as his
   pontifical name); see *Dizionario ecclesiastico* ed Angelo Mercati and Augusto
   Pelzer II (Turin 1955) 1075.
6 On Joost Vroye of Gavere see Ep 717:22n. He not only was a professor of law
   at Louvain and a supporter of Erasmus but also, during his years in the faculty
   of arts, had been deeply interested in Greek lexicography and the syntax of
   Homer, so that he was a credible reference in a letter in which Oem emphasizes
   his father's recent conversion to enthusiasm for the study of Greek.
7 On this distinguished professor of Latin in the Collegium Trilingue at Louvain, see Ep 1209 introduction. Although Erasmus initially had not favoured
   Goclenius' appointment to the professorship in 1519, he soon came to admire his talent both as a scholar and as a teacher. He was (and was known
   to be) Erasmus' most trusted friend at Louvain, and hence another effective
   reference for the author of this letter.
8 Adriaan of Baarland was another distinguished Louvain humanist and friend
   of Erasmus, well known as one of Erasmus' defenders in that university; see
   Ep 492 introduction.
9 Also known as Jan de Winkele (d 1530). He matriculated in the University
   of Louvain in 1478, and had been secretary of the faculty since 1494 and notary of the rector's court since 1496 and of the conservator's court since 1503.
   As master of St Peter's chapter school, like many schoolmasters he boarded
   students in his house.

ary in the fifteen-hundredth and twenty-sixth year since the birth of the   40
Saviour

Your sincere friend and servant and disciple, Jan Oem van Wijngaarden

To the most learned and eloquent Master Erasmus of Rotterdam, eminent doctor of sacred letters, who holds unchallenged the first place for eloquence, my friend and much respected mentor. In Basel   45

1669 / From Stephen Gardiner   London, 28 February [1526]

This is the first letter to Erasmus from a young Englishman who was just beginning his rise to prominence in church and state. Stephen Gardiner (c 1497–12 November 1555) eventually became bishop of Winchester (1531), chancellor of Cambridge University (1540), and lord high chancellor under Queen Mary I (1553). He is best remembered as one of the conservative Anglo-Catholic bishops who supported Henry VIII on the royal divorce and the break with Rome, as a trusted diplomat under Henry, as the author of an important treatise justifying the king's break with the papacy (*De vera obedientia ratio*), and finally, after losing favour and undergoing deprivation from office and imprisonment under Edward VI, as a leader in restoring papal authority over the English church. As chancellor of Cambridge, he expressed his conservative outlook and his opposition to the spread of Protestant ideas in the university by forbidding the introduction of the new (Erasmian) way of pronouncing Greek, which he viewed as an expression of Protestant disrespect for long-standing tradition. At the time of this letter, however, and for many years thereafter, he was a warm sympathizer with Erasmus' scholarship. After the youthful encounter (1511) with Erasmus at Paris that he describes, Gardiner studied civil and canon law, obtaining doctorates (1521 and 1522) in both fields at Cambridge and then lecturing in the law faculty from 1521 to 1524. From the latter year he was secretary to the king's chief minister, Cardinal Thomas Wolsey. His acknowledged mastery of canon law made his support of the king's divorce and break with Rome extremely valuable to the government, and this usefulness was the basis of his many important diplomatic missions and his rise to the episcopate and to high political office. His background in canon law also goes far to explain his religious conservatism, his opposition to the sharp Protestant religious turn taken by Edward VI's government, and his eventual reconciliation with Rome.

The autograph original of this letter survived in the Rehdiger manuscript collection at Wrocław. Allen himself first published it (*The Academy* no 1224, 19 October 1895, 317–18); Enthoven published a critical edition in 1906. Allen's determination of the unspecified year-date rests on Erasmus' reply in Ep 1745.

STEPHEN GARDINER TO ERASMUS OF ROTTERDAM,
CORDIAL GREETINGS

However much my lack of eloquence[1] makes me hesitate to write to someone as distinguished in every branch of learning as yourself, it has not been
able to silence me altogether. On other occasions it was so powerful and   5
overwhelming that its very imperiousness kept me silent. Sometimes it does
not allow me to express what I feel, and now it is telling my feelings (which
refuse to listen) not to reveal themselves to you at all despite the splendid
opportunity which has been offered me of writing to you and of having
my letter delivered by courier. But when other people in England are tum-   10
bling over one another to write to you, why should I alone be silent? I am
the Stephen who, every time Erasmus' name comes up, makes the proud
boast that he was once Erasmus' cook![2] It is my way, you see, of making my
hearers believe in my erudition, much like those who wish to be thought
holy simply because they once set foot in the Holy Land. Of course I had to   15
write to you, so that my friends would not think me ungrateful if I failed
to thank the person whose writings I have been perusing with considerable
profit to myself; moreover, I do not want others to think that I lied when I
claimed that I was once on close and intimate terms with you.

I do not know if I ought to ask you to recall some trifling incident from   20
the past when the gift of memory was given you for the careful retention of
important things; but let me ask you if you can cast your mind back sixteen
years when you were a guest of an Englishman called Eden[3] who was living at the time in Paris in the rue Saint-Jean.[4] If I remember correctly, you

* * * * *

1669
1 Although literary modesty may be involved here, Gardiner's admission of a
  lack of eloquence (*infancia*) may also reflect his awareness that his education
  had been in law, not in humanistic subjects.
2 See lines 26–9, 43–5 below.
3 At the death of Gardiner's father, John Gardiner of Bury St Edmunds, in 1507,
  his will named John and Richard Eden as trustees of his children, and it is
  likely that young Stephen accompanied one of them to Paris as a member of his
  household. There he met Erasmus when the humanist became his guardian's
  lodger. His reference to the recent first publication of the *Praise of Folly* (1511),
  if accurate, would date their meeting to 1511 and would mean that it occurred
  fifteen years previously, not sixteen. Allen notes (21n) that someone named
  Eden was a student of law at Cambridge in 1499 and in 1506–7 and received
  a doctorate in canon law there in 1520. Allen also observes that Richard Eden
  became clerk to the King's Council in 1512 and archdeacon of Middlesex in
  1516; like Gardiner, he was later employed by Cardinal Wolsey.
4 On the location of the rue Saint-Jean-de Beauvais (now rue Jean-de-Beauvais),
  see Farge *Parti conservateur* 54 n6.

had just published the first edition of the *Moria* and had already composed a   25
large number of books, both Greek and Latin. Do you remember the young
lad[5] who was living with Eden at the time and whom you used to ask every
day to prepare a dish of lettuce cooked in butter and oil? You used to say
that no one made that dish as well as he. Well, I am that lad, Stephen Gardiner, and from that time to the present my affection for you and my loy-   30
alty have remained unchanged despite our separation. My duties at court[6]
keep us apart, but they have not prevented me from maintaining my devotion to you, although sometimes, I fear, I cannot enjoy that communion with
your writings which I find so very delightful. What a real misfortune it was
for me to have been unable to accept the offer that you made me through   35
Garret, the Cambridge bookseller![7] If he was telling the truth, you wanted
me to enter your service. Then I would have had the force of your living
presence to instruct me instead of just that silent letter, which I could only
glance at.

But it is foolish to complain of something that cannot be undone. And   40
now, when I would like to say more, that lack of eloquence which I mentioned is taking hold of me and refusing to let me go on at greater length.
So farewell, Erasmus, my learned friend, and please remember that Stephen
who was once not a bad cook – at least he could cook lettuce to suit your
taste – is ready to be your faithful friend if any opportunity arises where   45
he could be useful to you. Again farewell.

From the home of the most reverend cardinal,[8] 28 February

Your most devoted friend, Stephen Gardiner

1670 / To Duke John of Saxony   Basel, 2 March 1526

Some indication of Erasmus' shock at the bitter personal attack on his spiritual and moral integrity made in Luther's *De servo arbitrio* is this letter to
Luther's ruler and chief defender, the electoral prince of Saxony. Duke John
(1468–1532) had succeeded his brother Frederick III on the electoral throne

* * * * *

5 Gardiner describes himself as *puellum quendam* at the time. If the conjectural
   birth-date of 1497 for Gardiner is correct, he would have been about fourteen
   when he met Erasmus in 1511.
6 As secretary to Cardinal Wolsey he would have been deeply involved in the
   business of the royal court. In 1527 he accompanied Wolsey on a diplomatic
   mission to France in connection with the royal divorce, and that was the beginning of his active diplomatic career.
7 On the Dutch-born Cambridge bookseller Garret Godfrey see Epp 248:55n,
   456:313n, 777:30–1.
8 Thomas Wolsey, to whom Gardiner was secretary

on 5 May 1525. Even before his accession he had been a firm supporter of Luther. The elector's reaction to this letter, which was accompanied by a German translation signed (like the Latin original) by Erasmus, was cautious. On 21 April he wrote Luther (wa-Br 4 57–8 Ep 1000), enclosing a copy of Erasmus' Latin letter and asking him and Melanchthon to consider the matter and advise him how to reply. He also cautioned Luther not to let Erasmus' letter fall into other people's hands, lest it be printed and thus give Erasmus an excuse for a more vehement protest. Luther replied on 23 April (wa-Br 4 61–2 Ep 1002), advising the elector to inform Erasmus that since the issue involved a spiritual matter, it would not be appropriate for him as a secular ruler to get involved. There is no evidence that the elector sent Erasmus a reply of any kind. Erasmus' letter remained unpublished in the archive at Weimar until the nineteenth century, when J.K. Seidemann published it in German in *Die Reformation in Sachsen* 1 (1846) 205. The Latin text was first printed by C.A.H. Burkhardt in *Zeitschrift für kirchliche Wissenschaft* (1883) 10.

Most illustrious prince elector, although I have not enjoyed your Highness' friendship, nevertheless, since I am convinced from what I hear that you are a true and worthy successor to your brother, whose goodness I have experienced in the past, and that in fact you resemble that excellent prince in every quality, I have not hesitated to address your most illustrious Highness 5 in this letter. I was led to this by something that is important not just for myself and for your realm but for the whole cause of the gospel and for the tranquillity of all Christendom.

A year ago I published my *Diatribe on the Freedom of the Will*, in which I took particular care to avoid making a personal attack on anyone. I gave my 10 work a moderate title, calling it a 'discussion' or 'disputation.'[1] I did not assume the role of judge, but of inquirer or communicator, dispensing with all authority except that of Holy Scripture. A more courteous opponent Luther could not have hoped for. If his teaching was true, he had an opportunity to support his point of view, but if it was not, he could not have been admon- 15 ished in a more civil manner. Need I say more? There was nothing in the book to offend anyone, however sensitive to criticism. In fact, my courteous tone earned me considerable ill will from some theologians and princes, who thought I was not answering Luther but colluding with him. Although

* * * * *

1670
1 The word *Diatribe* in Erasmus' title only meant a learned discussion and did not imply violent criticism; see Ep 1667 n3.

I was pushed into the ring, against my will and despite my protests, by   20
princes of the highest rank, I swear before God that I wrote nothing in the
book that was contrary to my innermost beliefs, nor have I received a cent
from any living person for my opposition to Luther. But he has countered
with an overweight volume,[2] so full of sneers, witticisms, abuse, threats,
and allegations that there is more malice in this single book than in all the   25
works he has published to this day.

If he had called me a drunken, ignorant fool, a blockhead, a ninny, or
a dolt, I could have put up with that. These are human weaknesses and I
am human. But he goes further and repeatedly makes me out to be an atheist,[3] like Lucian,[4] affirming that I do not believe in the existence of God;   30

* * * * *

2 Erasmus' *De libero arbitrio* was rather short. Bibliographic records in *The National Union Catalog, Pre-1956 Imprints* 754 vols (London 1968–81) indicate that
the first edition (Basel: Froben 1524) contained ninety-four pages in octavo
format (thirty-four columns in LB IX, a folio format). Similar records show that
Luther's *De servo arbitrio* (Wittenberg: Hans Lufft 1525) contained 383 pages
in octavo. This comparison is not precise, but the relative length of the opposing treatises is indicated by the texts in the modern English translation of the
two works by E. Gordon Rupp and Philip S. Watson in the Library of Christian Classics, vol 17: *Luther and Erasmus: Free Will and Salvation* (Philadelphia
1969). Erasmus' book fills pages 35–97; Luther's, pages 101–334. Erasmus more
than made up for his earlier brevity in his two-part rebuttal of Luther. *Hyperaspistes* book 1 (see Ep 1667) is more than twice as long as *De libero arbitrio*,
occupying 240 octavo pages in the edition of March 1526 according to the bibliographic record in NUC (LB X 1249–1336); book 2 is even longer, 575 octavo
pages according to NUC (LB X 1338–1536).
3 Erasmus has in mind the harsh passage in which Luther accuses him of having
no religious faith at all: 'You only succeed in showing that you foster in your
heart a Lucian, or some other pig from Epicurus' sty who, having no belief
in God himself, secretly ridicules all who have a belief and confess it'; WA 18
605; see Ep 1688 introduction, where the translation is quoted more fully.
4 Lucian of Samosata (b about 120 AD, d after 180), Hellenistic satirist whose
essays and dialogues were sharply critical of human vanity and popular religion and superstition. His works were not known to the medieval West but
were discovered by Italian humanists in the early fifteenth century and were
widely admired among Renaissance humanists for their lively humour, mor-
dant wit, cynicism, and boldness and aptness of expression. A number of his
dialogues were translated into Latin by various hands during the fifteenth
century, and a few of these were printed at Rome as early as 1470. The Greek
text of Lucian was first published at Florence in 1496, and there was a second
edition from the press of Aldo Manuzio at Venice in 1503, the edition most
likely used by Erasmus, though Erasmus also cited one of Lucian's works in a
letter of 1499 (Ep 88). While perfecting his newly acquired mastery of Greek

or he calls me 'a pig from Epicurus' sty'[5] because I am supposed to hold
that God takes no interest in human affairs; or I am said to be a despiser
of Holy Writ, a subverter of the Christian religion, an enemy of Christendom, and an unconscionable hypocrite. He thinks that every pious statement in my works is insincere and that I conceal in my heart a deep hostility   35
to religion. And there are many other charges in his book, charges which
no reasonable man would make about a Turk or a Mohammedan. He acts
like this under the influence of men of no consequence and does not realize what an impression he is making. If what he teaches is true religion,
he does not see how many thousands he is alienating by the viciousness   40
of his pen. Are these jeering insults, fatuous jests, barbed taunts, false accusations, threats, and subterfuges appropriate to such a grave and serious
business, which has convulsed nearly all the world? Had he demolished my
arguments openly and vigorously by the use of reason or the Scriptures, he
would have strengthened his cause and won many supporters, but instead   45

* * * * *

in the years immediately following 1500, Erasmus began making translations
from Greek authors. During his second visit to England (1505–6), while he
resided in the home of Thomas More, he and More, who was also master-
ing Greek, competed at translating some of Lucian's works into Latin. These
texts were printed in November 1506 at Paris by Josse Bade, four texts by
More, five by Erasmus, and one by both. Erasmus sent additional translations to Bade from Florence, but these arrived so late that they were added
to only some copies of the 1506 edition. Erasmus' new additions were separately printed at Louvain by Dirk Martens in 1512, as *Complures dialogi* (NK
3434). The two sets of translations were frequently printed by important printers (not only Bade but also Aldo Manuzio and Johannes Froben), so that both
translators, but especially Erasmus, came to be associated with Lucian. Modern critics have traced the influence of Lucian on both the details and the
general spirit of their works, especially satirical works like *The Praise of Folly*,
Julius Exclusus, and *Utopia*. Although Erasmus regarded Lucian's attacks on
popular religion as superb examples of exposing hypocrisy and fraud, fully
justified since the religion attacked was pagan, Lucian was often referred to
as an atheist, an irreverent mocker at all religion. This reputation was the basis for Luther's association of Erasmus with Lucian in *De servo arbitrio*. On
the translations, see Epp 187, 191, 193, 197, 199, 205, 246, 261, and 267. Cf
Erika Rummel *Erasmus as a Translator of the Classics* (Toronto 1985), and Craig
R. Thompson's introduction to his edition of More's translations in CW III
xvii–lxxii.
5 Luther's insulting phrase (WA 18 605) had been used by the poet Horace of
himself in *Epistles* 1.4.16. On the habit of regarding both Lucian and Epicurus
as immoral and atheistic, see Thompson in Thomas More CW III xxiv n3.

he is alienating them, and not just in regard to this particular dogma, but to the whole doctrine that he asserts. He claims the inspiration of the spirit, but who can believe that the spirit of Christ dwells in a heart from which flow words of such arrogance, bitterness, savagery, malice, and abuse? I have told him this time and again, but far from mending his ways, he grows steadily 50 worse.

I have done everything in my power to assist theology and the humanities. Everyone has received from God his own special gift, and each man advances the cause of religion in his own way. If Luther must attack everyone who disagrees with him, he has plenty of opponents who have rejected 55 his views in print and who do not argue courteously as I do but attack him with savage invective. He ought to turn his sharp pen against them. There are in his own circle many who have gone into print with views that oppose his teaching on the most important points of doctrine, such as the Eucharist,[6] yet he does not allow me, who was never a member of his church, 60 to argue my case in a calm and moderate way. What, I ask you, is the point of those sneers and gibes and imprecations? All they do is stir up trouble in the world and bring the name of the gospel and the reputation of the humanities into complete disrespect – even if we suppose they could cause no difficulties for your illustrious Highness. If it is the gospel that he teaches, 65 the gospel gives us no warrant to sin as we wish but forbids us to sin at all, even if it were possible to do so with impunity. Nor does the gospel remove the authority of the civil laws but supports it. The law punishes anyone who calls another a thief or a liar or a perjurer and prescribes the death penalty for the authors of defamatory libels. 70

* * * * *

6 The conflict concerning the Eucharist between Luther and Zwingli and his followers was becoming increasingly heated at this period. The Zwinglian or Sacramentarian interpretation was already dominant among the Reformers at Basel, such as Oecolampadius and Pellicanus, whose tendency to use Erasmus' ideas as justification for their beliefs (on the Eucharist and other matters) had already led to bitter alienation of Erasmus from these former friends and colleagues. See Epp 1523, 1538, 1559, 1616:22–37 and nn2, 4–6, 1618:9–15 and nn3–4, 1620:94–102 and nn13, 14, 1621:19–30 and nn12–13, 1624:33–40, 1636 (a memorandum to the city council of Basel on the opinions of Oecolampadius), and Erasmus' bitter exchange of letters with Conradus Pellicanus, Epp 1637–40. See also Epp 1679 nn4, 11–15, and 22, 1737 introduction, 1792A introduction, and the discussion in the prefaces of CWE 11 (xvii–xviii) and this volume (xii–xiii above). Like many other Catholic opponents of the Reformation, Erasmus regarded the doctrinal quarrels and schisms among its leaders as a sign of its lack of authenticity.

In a work which is now circulating in up to twelve thousand copies,[7] he says that I do not believe in the existence of God and that I mock the Scriptures. When he writes like this, he is passing judgment on another man's conscience, which is the prerogative of God alone. This villainous precedent is followed by his disciples. I am sure that the rule of law has not 75 yet been extinguished among you; if your laws provide for the punishment of thieves and perjurers, then surely to destroy another man's reputation by telling the most dreadful lies about him is worse than any kind of theft; for good men value reputation more highly than life itself.

I write these things, distinguished prince, not because I am out for re- 80 venge, but because it is in the interest of all that Luther be warned by your authority and the authority of the laws that he must not attack anyone in such a violent way, for this brings no benefit to anyone and threatens to destroy everything that is good. He must either renounce the role of slanderer or renounce the gospel. For God has no dealings with Belial. 85

I wish your serene Highness lasting happiness, and I offer you whatever service a humble but loyal and faithful servant can provide.

Basel, 2 March AD 1526

Your serene Highness' most humble servant, Erasmus of Rotterdam

I sign this in my own hand. 90

To the most serene Duke John of Saxony, prince elector

1671 / From Erasmus Schets   Antwerp, 7 March 1526

A reply to Ep 1654. On this merchant-banker, who in 1525 had become Erasmus' financial agent in the Low Countries, see Ep 1541 introduction. Like nearly all of the correspondence with Schets concerning Erasmus' business

* * * * *

7 While it is impossible to confirm this figure, there can be no doubt that Luther's response to *De libero arbitrio* was widely and rapidly circulated, in German as well as the original Latin. First printed in Latin (Wittenberg: Hans Lufft) on the last day of 1525, it was reprinted there in April 1526, at Augsburg in March 1526, and that same year at Tübingen (with a false Wittenberg imprint), at Nürnberg, twice at Strasbourg, and in one edition without indication of place. The German translation by Justus Jonas came out at Wittenberg early in 1526 and was reprinted at Augsburg (with a false Wittenberg imprint) sometime that same year. Thus at least one Latin and one German edition, and perhaps one reprint of each, had appeared by the date of this letter. There is no way of determining the size of each press run, though twelve thousand for a single edition would be remarkably high. See WA 18 597–9.

affairs, this letter remained unpublished until 1926; Allen based his edition on the autograph manuscript found at Basel.

I wrote you recently on 10 February.[1] I sent my letter to Nürnberg, to be redirected to Basel and then on to you. I don't know if you received it or not. In my letter I told you that I had written earlier, on 16 January, enclosing a receipt from Martin Lompart, a merchant from Basel. I paid him the money that I had received from England through the efforts of Alvaro de Castro.[2] 5 You should receive it in turn from Jakob Lompart, Martin's brother.[3] I am anxious to hear from you how the business turned out.

On the day after I had made these arrangements, I set off for the fair at Bergen,[4] where shortly afterwards I got a letter from you, which had been delivered by Karl Harst.[5] When he did not find me at home, he expressed his 10 regrets to the members of my household. He made it clear he could neither go to see me at Bergen nor await my return because of the urgent necessity of his leaving for England. He said, however, that he would put off until his return the matter of business that you wished him to discuss with me. Returning from the fair, Pieter Gillis[6] explained the whole thing to me on 15

* * * * *

1671
1 This letter has not been found.
2 Castro was the agent used by Schets to collect and transmit the revenues from Erasmus' English benefice. See Epp 1590 n2, 1658 n5.
3 On Martin and Jakob Lompart see Epp 1651 n6, 1658 nn2, 4.
4 There were several places named Bergen in what was then known as the Low Countries, but the one most likely here is Bergen op Zoom, a port of considerable importance in the fifteenth and early sixteenth centuries, and convenient to Antwerp, where Schets resided. The city had two well-established fairs, at Easter and St Martin's day, though the Easter date of the spring fair does not harmonize with the dates implied by this letter unless the 'Easter' fair actually took place before the beginning of Lent.
5 See Ep 1666 n2 and the earlier letters there cited.
6 Although Gillis had served as Erasmus' financial agent in the Netherlands and was a trustworthy friend, his background was legal rather than mercantile; this and his duties as town clerk of Antwerp made him far less effective than Schets in collecting and transferring funds. From 1525 Schets gradually took over from Gillis the management of Erasmus' financial relations with England and the Netherlands. See CWE 11 xxi–xxii, Epp 1541 introduction, 1548 n7, 1654 n5. Despite some awkwardness, the change did not break his friendship with Erasmus (on which see Ep 184 introduction), and this letter appears to depict cordial relations between Gillis and Schets as well; cf Epp 1682 n2, 1750 n4, 1781:7–8.

Karl's behalf.[7] We cannot help wondering why he has been away so long, since we have heard nothing from him from the day he left, nor have we had a word from my friend Alvaro. I would not like to think that anything had happened to him.

I got the receipt that you sent me for the thirty-eight pounds sterling[8]   20
you received through Alvaro de Castro. I shall see that it is sent on to him so that he will be free of his obligation and will be able to complete the undertaking he gave to Canterbury.[9]

As for the request in your earlier letter, that I accompany your man Karl Harst to check the sum which Karl is to receive on your behalf from   25
Pieter Gillis, I shall gladly do so once Harst returns and asks for my assistance. I have had no contact on this subject with Pieter Gillis. It is sufficient for me to know your intentions in this matter.

So far I have done nothing about the bolt of linen.[10] I put the matter off, pending Harst's return, though because of his long delay I have almost   30
given up hope. Before making the purchase I wanted to find out from him how fine or coarse the linen should be to meet your needs and satisfy your requirements. I do not want to make a mistake while acting on your behalf.

Your thanks for the little jar of fruit syrup were more than the gift deserves.[11] I was glad to know you received it, but sorry it cost you so many   35

* * * * *

7 The grammar of this sentence is shaky, to say the least. The Latin clearly implies that Gillis returned from the fair to Antwerp with Schets, but the latter may well be guilty of using a dangling participle (his Latin was not very sound), and it may be that Gillis explained the matter to Schets after the latter got back to Antwerp. The present translator, while surmising that this is what really happened, has translated the sentence literally.
8 Latin *libris triginta octo sterlingis*. In equivalent silver values, this was a sum worth about £57 16s 3d groot Flemish or £363 4s 9d tournois, and also the equivalent of 1,520 days' wages (almost seven years' wage income) for a master carpenter at Oxford and Cambridge or 1,338 days' wages for an Antwerp master carpenter (6 years and 6 months' wage income).
9 In 1512 the archbishop of Canterbury, William Warham, had granted Erasmus a pension charged against the revenues of the parish of Aldington in Kent. One of Schets' principal services to Erasmus was that through his business connections in England he was able to arrange for regular collection of this income from the archbishop's officers and for prompt, cost-free transmission of these funds to Basel by way of Antwerp. See Epp 255 introduction, 1583 n1.
10 For Erasmus' request that Schets purchase linen at Antwerp and ship it to him in Basel, see Ep 1654:28–34.
11 Mentioned in Epp 1651:21 and 1658:2 and evidently in an intervening letter from Erasmus that is now lost

plappards.[12] Martin Lompart will hear from me about this, for he promised to deliver it to you free of charge. I shall try to procure some dried fruit and send it to you. I shall make inquiries from my friends, for I have none at home or elsewhere.

What you tell me about Birckmann surprises me.[13] What has got into   40
him to make him ready to lose your good will? It is always the same with these bold and impudent liars.

I shall see that the letter is delivered that you want sent to Pierre Barbier in Spain.[14]

My wife was delighted to receive the ring blessed by the king of Eng-   45
land and she sends you her sincere thanks for it. Whenever your name is mentioned, she never fails to express her unhappiness over the loss of the unicorn. She will take greater care of the ring, I am sure.[15] Farewell, dear Erasmus. I wish you every happiness and prosperity.

From Antwerp, 7 March 1526   50
Your devoted servant, Erasmus Schets

To that great scholar, the incomparable Master Erasmus of Rotterdam. In Basel

1672 / To Johann Henckel   Basel, 7 March 1526

Erasmus had learned about Johann Henckel from his friend Jan Antonin (cf Epp 1602, 1660), and this letter was written at his urging. Henckel (d 1539)

* * * * *

12 Latin *totidem flapardorum*. On this South German-Austrian silver coin, also known as a blaffert, a plafard, or a schilling, see Ep 1543 n2.
13 On this bookseller and publisher, whom Erasmus and several of his friends regarded as dishonest, see Ep 1665 n1 and the other letters cited there.
14 This reference is puzzling because Erasmus knew that his friend Barbier had left Spain in the service of Adriaan of Utrecht when that prelate was elected pope in 1522 and that after the pope's death he had entered the service of Giro- lamo Aleandro, accompanying him on a diplomatic mission to France. As of 3 October 1525 (Ep 1621 n6) Erasmus did not yet know that Barbier had left Ale- andro (April 1525) to enter the service of Charles de Lannoy, imperial viceroy of Naples. Perhaps Barbier went to Naples by way of Spain or accompanied his new patron on a trip to the Spanish court. In any case, the letter to Barbier men- tioned here is not extant. See Epp 1548 n4, 1605 introduction and n1, 1621 nn3, 6.
15 A gold ring consecrated (and hence supposedly endued with talismanic power) by King Henry VIII, one of two such rings given to Erasmus by Thomas Lupset, had been a Christmas present for Schets' wife. It was also given to console her for losing an even rarer gift, a supposed unicorn horn. See Epp 1595:120–3 and n14, 1654:35–6 and n8.

was born to an ethnic German family at Levoča, then part of the kingdom of Hungary and now in the Slovak Republic. He may have studied at Cracow but received BA (1499) and MA (1503) degrees at Vienna before going to Italy, where he studied at Padua in 1508 and Bologna in 1509. Though he was later referred to as a doctor of laws, the source of his law degrees is not documented. He had received ecclesiastical appointments as archdeacon of Békes and canon of Oradea (Várad) and the Spiš (Szepes). Back in Hungary by 1513, he became parish priest in Levoča, and his presence was probably what attracted the English humanist Leonard Cox to become headmaster of the municipal school. By 1520 Henckel had become parish priest at Košice and Cox headmaster of that town's school. In 1524 Henckel became chaplain to Queen Mary, wife of King Louis II of Hungary and sister of the Emperor Charles V. He was also made archdeacon of Torna. In the court at Buda he became a member of an Erasmian circle headed by Jacobus Piso, and his connections with this group and with Jan Antonin led to his sending Erasmus the gift and the letter (now lost) that occasioned the present letter. After the Hungarian military disaster and the death of King Louis in battle in August 1526, Henckel accompanied the queen to Bratislava but soon left court service and went back to his parish at Košice, resigning his commendatory benefices. But in 1528 the queen called him back as her confessor, and he remained in her service until she was appointed regent of the Netherlands in 1531, when, because of rumours (based on his personal friendship with Philippus Melanchthon, Wolfgang Capito, and Martin Bucer) that he favoured the Protestants, the emperor forced Mary to dismiss him. Her influence secured for him a canonry in the cathedral of Wrocław in Silesia, where he spent the rest of his life. Though never a supporter of Protestantism, Henckel was a moderate strongly associated with the reform ideas of Erasmus; and his clash at the Diet of Augsburg (1530) with the combative Johann Maier of Eck probably explains the suspicions of heresy that compelled Queen Mary to dismiss him. Erasmus included this letter in his *Opus epistolarum* (1529).

ERASMUS OF ROTTERDAM TO JOHANN HENCKEL,
PREACHER TO QUEEN MARY OF HUNGARY, GREETING

The true Christian must grieve in his heart when he considers how far the morals of those who profess the name of Christ have sunk, how close we have come to rejecting the gospel, how almost nothing remains of faith and 5 charity except the name and title, and how desperate the state to which our religion has been brought; so, by the same token, the Christian cannot but rejoice when he hears that God is renewing his blessed spirit in good and learned men who hold some position in the world, for that, like the sudden shining of a light, dispels the darkness of despair and gives us hope that the 10 righteous anger of heaven will turn to pity, and that new evangelists will arise to lead the scattered and wandering sheep back to the saving pastures of Christ and to the fold of peace within the church. Often, according to the prophets, God is angered by the sins of his people and threatens to send children to rule over them,[1] priests no better than themselves, and prophets who are not inspired with the spirit of truth. But then his anger cools and he promises the greatest of blessings, sensible rulers who uphold religion and the laws, faithful pastors, and prophets who speak the truth.

This, I believe, is why, in several places, we see Christians who are Christians in name only, so ignorant and untutored in their faith that they do not even know the Apostles' Creed or comprehend what they professed at baptism.[2] We have closed our ears to the truth, and so God has sent us teachers whose aim is not to treat our sores with healing words[3] but to scratch agreeably the itching scab of our desires. And yet our age is testimony to the power and beauty of the gospel, for at the very mention of the gospel we see the world rise from its slumbers and shake off its lethargy. But what if the world were to see in those who preach the gospel the true mind and spirit of the gospel? Now we see new prophets arising in many regions of the world,[4] humble men for the most part, despised and even disreputable in the world's eyes, who, by loud cries and lavish promises, have roused a world that had fallen into a drugged sleep[5] over human ordinances and ceremonies that are of the flesh, and having roused it, have won it over largely to themselves.

* * * * *

1672
1 Isaiah 3:4
2 In effect, two references to the Apostles' Creed, which developed in the early church from at least as far back as the second century as a statement of belief used for the instruction and testing of candidates for baptism. By the early sixteenth century, all Christians except adult converts from other religions would have been baptized in infancy, and the profession of the Apostles' Creed would have been made on their behalf by their godparents.
3 Cf *Adagia* III i 100.
4 The following description of the 'new prophets,' that is, popular preachers of various sects, especially the Anabaptists, reflects Erasmus' ambivalent attitude towards the Reformation, which, despite the excesses implied by his description, had succeeded in arousing Christians from an unthinking reliance on ceremonial acts that he, too, was trying to challenge.
5 Literally, 'as though sleeping on the mandrake.' Celsus (3.18.12) reports that sleep can be induced by placing mandrake apples under the pillow. Pliny the Elder (*Naturalis historia* 25.150) also writes about the sleep-inducing properties of the mandrake. Cf *Adagia* IV v 64.

At the beginning, when the drama first came on the stage, even good men applauded, as long as sermons dealt with the incomparable majesty and 35 authority of Holy Scripture, and we were taught not to trust in our human resources but to place all our confidence in God, and the applause continued so long as the welcome cry of evangelical freedom rang in our ears. All the abusive rhetoric[6] – about the Roman curia, the insufferable tyranny of monks, worldly bishops, and sophistical theologians whose learning left no 40 place for Christ - was received with repeated cheers. The fearless courage of the man[7] in attacking those who are venerated like gods was interpreted as proof of a good conscience.

Even Luther's name seemed a happy omen, since in German it means 'refiner.' He got it from the occupation of his father, who refines lumps of 45 copper ore in his workshop.[8] Public support was increased by the silly opposition of those who tried at the outset to hiss the play off the stage by making loud public protests, issuing censures, listing controversial passages, and making wild denunciations of the study of languages and the humanities. Since these people were already unpopular with good and learned men, 50 they made Luther's cause all the more attractive. Moreover, what made this affair look like the work of heaven was the fact that the stronger the opposition from militant schemers and from the monks who supported them, the further the mischief spread. The idea was touted that if a few were burned at the stake, that would put an end to the whole trouble. This was the plan 55 put forward by the monks. But clearly our situation was more like that of

* * * * *

6 Literally, 'as though from the cart,' a proverbial expression that Erasmus explained as referring to the licence of Athenian Old Comedy, when actors performed from carts. See *Adagia* i vii 73.
7 That is, of Luther. Erasmus never retracted his admiration of Luther's courage in speaking out against genuine abuses in the church, though he had early begun to criticize the intemperance of Luther's attacks, as reflected in the preceding sentence.
8 Erasmus must have in mind a German word such as *Läuterer*, derived from the verb *läutern* 'to purify.' This derivation is purely imaginary. The Luther family were peasants, not miners and refiners of ore. Martin Luther's father's entry into the business of mining was caused by Thuringian inheritance law: in order to prevent the excessive subdivision of farmsteads, the whole farm passed to the youngest son. Thus Hans Luder, as one of the older sons, had no land to inherit and had to find a new occupation. He attained modest prosperity as a mining contractor in the copper mines near Mansfeld and as owner of a smelting furnace. The family name itself 'may be derived from the given name of Lothar.' See Brecht i 2.

Hercules and the hydra.[9] The infection spread with every blow and took
strength and courage from our cruelty.

Caught between those who applauded and those who hissed, I guessed
the business would end in public disorder. The prophet was not mistaken in   60
his prophecy; in fact the evils we have witnessed are greater than I feared.
Both parties were engaged in a bitter tug-of-war.[10] One put papal constitutions on a level with the gospel; the other loudly maintained that these were
a plague upon the Christian faith. So five years ago I warned Luther in a
private letter that, if he was relying on the inspiration of his own spirit, he   65
should see to it that he brought to so perilous a task a mind free from any
taint of corruption.[11] At my urging he wrote several works that have great
claims on our respect, such as his commentaries on several of the psalms and
on the Lord's Prayer and his *De quatuordecim spectris*.[12] He completed these
with remarkable speed, but then volume after volume flowed from his pen,   70
each more violent than the one before. I found these deeply offensive, not
just for the arrogance of the man, but for his insatiable love of argument,
which descends sometimes into scurrilous abuse. He is encouraged in this,
I have discovered, by certain nonentities whose opinion even on the cook-
ing of vegetables would not be worth having. On the mutterings of people   75

* * * * *

9 Horace *Odes* 4.4.59–62; cf *Adagia* i x 9.
10 *Adagia* i v 67
11 Erasmus was often in touch with Luther, directly or indirectly, during the summer and autumn of 1520, even though only one letter (Ep 1127A) addressed
directly to him is known from that period. See also Ep 1113, to Philippus
Melanchthon, and Ep 1119, to Georgius Spalatinus. In all of these communications, Erasmus commended Luther for good intentions but urged him to
be more prudent and more moderate, and also more willing to seek reform
gradually: 'Hair by hair gets the tail off the mare' (Ep 1127A).
12 Ep 1127A complimented Luther on his commentary on the Psalter, of which the
second part had appeared earlier that year (see Ep 1127A n27). Luther had published his *Auslegung deutsch des Vaterunsers für die einfältigen Laien* in 1519, and
a Latin version, the form in which Erasmus must have known the work, appeared in 1520 under the title *Explanatio dominicae orationis ... pro simplicioribus
laicis composita, et aedita* (WA 2 74–130). The formal title of *De quatuordecim spectris* was *Tessaradecas consolatoria pro laborantibus et oneratis*, published simultaneously in Latin and in a German translation made by Spalatinus in February
1520 (WA 6 99–134). Though they were by no means the result of Erasmus' advice, these works were pastoral and non-polemical, precisely the sort of writings that Erasmus had urged Luther to produce instead of polemics and controversial tracts; cf his words praising *De quatuordecim spectris* in a letter of
1523 to Christoph von Utenheim, bishop of Basel (Ep 1332:62–7 and n13).

like this he takes out his insolent pen and attacks kings and men whose only desire is to serve the public good. He seems to forget what theatre he is playing in, what part he is playing, and what play he has undertaken to perform.

The man's lack of moderation is such that I began to be seriously wor-   80
ried about the spirit that animates him and to congratulate myself for not being enticed into his sect by flattery or driven there by bitterness. In spite of everything, however, I shall not cease to hope for a happy ending to the tragedy, whatever the source of the trouble may be or however it reached its present state. For I saw that if victory gave some people their way, Luther's   85
ruin would drag down with him much that was excellent,[13] just as now we see a general neglect of languages and the humanities, which he has saddled with an intolerable weight of enmity. The ancient writers lie neglected. Scholastic philosophy, which I wished to see reformed, not eliminated, is in decline.[14] Almost all liberal studies are dying. The very name of the gospel is   90

* * * * *

13 Erasmus frequently expressed this fear even when he was being critical of Luther, since he was convinced that the attack on Luther was being led by the same individuals and groups, chiefly ultra-conservative monks and theologians, who had been attacking his own works as impious or heretical. For examples, see Epp 93:49–59, 948:76–97, 967:76, 980:4–15 (addressed to Luther himself), 1033:210–31, 1119:41–3, 1126:241–5, 1141:14–35, 1143:74–6, 1144:18– 23, 1156:20–31, 1156:39–46, 1167:82–99, 1168:30–5, 1186:1–12, 1192A:14–16, 1195:107–9, 1202:211–28, 1203:14–20, 1205:31–7, 1216:80–5, 1218:8–17 and 31–43, 1228:43–9, 1238:63–104, 1244:15–22, 1263:29–31, 1274:57–60, 1275:62–5, 1299:10– 14 and 108–114, 1300:7–9, 1302:88–95, 1348:27–9, 1418:19–21 (to Pope Clement VII), 1445:13–14, 1624:55–8, 1634:102–15. Before his open break with Luther, Erasmus explicitly urged him not to bring his own name or that of his friends into his controversial writings (Ep 1127A:77–9).

14 Erasmus' disdain for scholastic philosophy and theology, at least as represented by most of the recent scholastics, is a recurrent theme in his writings. He was somewhat more respectful of the great figures of the thirteenth century, notably St Thomas Aquinas, but in his most sharply critical letter to his Paris antagonist Noël Béda (Ep 1581:640–57), he noted that some errors had been found in the works of even the greatest of them, and that each had passed in and out of fashion according to changing fads in the universities; cf Epp 809:92–90, 1581:643–57 and nn79, 82, 83, 1679 n5, 1687 nn17, 19. His criticisms are pungently expressed, though supposedly directed only against a narrow-minded few, in his widely-circulated letter to Maarten van Dorp (Ep 337). Erasmus' opinion of scholastic philosophy was affected by his humanistic tendency to belittle the Middle Ages in general, as shown by his remark that Aquinas was indeed an intelligent and industrious theologian but had the misfortune to live in a rude and barbarous age (Epp 1126:289–97 and n38, 1196:45–51, 1211:467–83), sentiments reminiscent of the judgment passed by

hated by many – so much so that we can scarcely repeat those words which St Paul taught us. The tyranny of those whom Luther thought he could vanquish with the sword of the spirit, that is, with the word of God,[15] has been made worse, not ended. The liberty we hoped for has not appeared; on the contrary good men must bear a heavier yoke, and evil men are being 95 allowed a looser rein.

One hope still remains. What is it, you ask. Let me give you the benefit of the little wisdom I possess. If the impiety of the world deserved to be treated by such men as these and by such a cruel surgeon (for no healing could come from drugs, poultices, and plasters), I hope that those whom 100 God chastised when they rebelled will be comforted by him when they come to their senses. For sometimes he corrects the sins of his people by sending the Philistines or a Holophernes or a Nebuchadnezzar and, since he is the all-powerful master of the world, he makes the wickedness of evil men redound to his glory and to the good of the church. So on occasion 105 a dose of poison has turned out to be a cure, and sometimes, when the doctors have given up in despair, the enemy's sword that caused the wound has provided the remedy. I have read how the embrace of a snake cured a long-standing and desperate case of gout.[16] The goodness of God is stronger

* * * * *

Lorenzo Valla in his *Encomium sancti Thomae Aquinatis*. Despite his coolness to the scholastics, even to Aquinas, Erasmus knew the works of Aquinas and other scholastic authorities well and was influenced by them. See Christian Dolfen *Die Stellung des Erasmus von Rotterdam zur scholastischen Methode* (Osnabrück 1936), who also argues that his attitude was not wholly negative and was influenced by a tendency within later scholasticism to bring theology back to its scriptural and patristic sources, as typified by Jean Gerson. Rudolf Padberg *Erasmus als Katechet* (Freiburg im Breisgau 1956) 124–30 has demonstrated a direct influence of two catechetical works by Aquinas on the two catechisms (1514, 1533) composed by Erasmus.

15 Eph 6:17
16 Although the wording here implies physical contact with a live snake, the reference may be to theriac. There was much debate in sixteenth-century pharmacology about the ingredients and technique of preparing an effective theriac. Theriac, a rare and costly medicament thought to be a panacea or cure for all human diseases, was compounded from viper's flesh and many other substances (sixty-four in all, according to pseudo-Galen), and supposedly mirrored the complex make-up of the human body. It was known to antiquity, since it is dealt with in three treatises attributed (falsely, it seems) to Galen, and was also discussed in Arabic and medieval Western medicine. See Thomas Holste *Der Theriakkrämer* Würzburger medizinhistorische Forschungen 5 (Hannover 1976) 18–38; Gilbert Watson *Theriac and Mithridatium: A Study in Therapeutics* (London 1966); and, for efforts during the later sixteenth century to rediscover

than adversity. The disease that afflicted us was serious and chronic, and   110
the simple and common remedies had little effect. For a long time we have
been dosed with hellebore, and it has caused such torment in the world's gut
that the remedy threatens to cause the patient's death. This indeed has been
the fate of many. May the Heavenly Physician rescue his people from their
present afflictions and restore them to some measure of health! Charity,   115
according to Paul, hopes for all things.[17]

I have not yet given up hope entirely, for I trust in the well-known
mercy of the Lord, who will not be angry with his people for ever; when he
tries us, he also gives us a way of escape so that we can bear the burden.[18]
As for the scurrilous attack that Luther made on me recently[19] – and without   120
cause too, since the argument in my *Diatribe* was courteous and free from
abuse – I shall bear the personal insult lightly, provided the public cause
of the Christian faith prospers as we would wish, and the gospel of Christ
reigns truly in the hearts of men, and though I win no glory among men,
the precious name of our Lord Jesus Christ is glorified, praised, and exalted   125
throughout the world. What gives me greater cause to hope is the appearance in several places of new evangelists[20] who preach the gospel calmly,
wisely, and in the true spirit of the gospel, turning neither to the left nor
to the right;[21] who find such satisfaction in the truth of the gospel that they
recoil from the turmoil and chaos of our disintegrating world; and who com-   130

* * * * *

the true ancient formulation, Paula Findlen *Possessing Nature: Museums, Collecting, and Scientific Culture in Early Modern Italy* (Berkeley 1994) 241–5, 247,
251, 267–86. The pseudo-Galen treatises on theriac appear in Galen *Opera omnia* ed C.G. Kühn, 20 vols in 22 (Leipzig 1821–33; repr Hildesheim 1964–5)
XIV. The author of *Ad Pisonem de theriaca* cap XV (XIV 274) reports having successfully treated gout with theriac. The two other pseudo-Galenic treatises are
called *De theriaca ad Pamphilianum* (XIV 295–310) and *De antidotis* (in two books)
(XIV 1–105, 106–209).
17 1 Cor 13:7
18 Ps 102:9 (Vulgate); 1 Cor 10:13
19 That is, *De servo arbitrio*
20 It is not clear just whom Erasmus had in mind, since he was now at odds
   not only with the followers of Luther but also with former friends and associates such as Zwingli, Oecolampadius, and Pellicanus, who had adopted
   the eucharistic doctrine that was becoming known as Sacramentarianism and
   who were also promoting religious changes far more extreme than those introduced by the Wittenberg Reformers. Perhaps he was thinking of moderately reformist Catholic clergy, often supporters of his own reform programme, such
   as Georg Witzel, Fridericus Nausea, and Johann Gropper; less probably, more
   moderate Protestant leaders such as Philippus Melanchthon and Martin Bucer.
21 Prov 4:27

mend their teaching by the purity of their lives and the gentleness of their
character and do not confuse the role of evangelist with that of a scurrilous
buffoon.

I am not writing this to compliment you, dear sir, but to give thanks to
our merciful God for the abundant talents with which he has endowed you   135
and by which he works his will in you;[22] and I sincerely congratulate the
illustrious Queen Mary, a woman who, I am told, is as pious as she is wise –
or rather, I congratulate all Hungary, and I pray that Christianity will grow
there all the stronger, the more it is exposed to attack from men who are ill
disposed towards the authority of the Christian church. As for your strong   140
support of my work, which I have learned about in a letter from my friend
Antonin,[23] I warmly appreciate your generous nature, which leads you to
support all who (as he puts it) show promise of good fruit.

I began some time ago, inspired I don't know how, to use the small
measure of grace that was given me[24] to restore the theology of the schools   145
to its origins, for it had been degenerating step by step into merely human
sophistries. To this end I produced my New Testament and editions of several distinguished authors. Then I added the Paraphrases to help the less
energetic and encourage the hesitant reader with something easy and accessible. My efforts were not altogether unsuccessful – if only this fateful   150
storm had not blown up. If it was God's will that the storm should come,
even though it was brought upon us by evil men, then I hope that Christ
will be our deus ex machina and bring a happy ending to this affair beyond
anything we expect. I am sure this would happen sooner if there were more
evangelists like you and if rulers placed the glory of the gospel above their   155
personal desires. In the Paraphrases (since you think them worth your attention) I have detected several errors that had crept in through the carelessness
of the typesetters. These have been partly corrected, that is to say, those in
Matthew, Luke, and John, for these three books have now been reprinted.[25]

* * * * *

22 Phil 2:13. Here Erasmus uses a Greek expression, ἐνεργοῦντι, which is common
    in the New Testament.
23 See Ep 1660.
24 Eph 3:8
25 *Paraphrasis in Matthaeum* was first published in a folio edition by Froben on
    15 March 1522 and included some corrections when it was reprinted in oc-
    tavo format later that month and again in 1523 (octavo) and 1524 (folio). *Para-
    phrasis in Lucam* was first printed by Froben on 30 August 1523 and reprinted
    'with the author's corrections' in 1523 or 1524 and again in 1524 and 1526.
    Paraphrasis in evangelium Ioannis was published in mid-January 1523 (in folio),
    again in March and in April 1523 (octavo), and yet again in folio in 1524, 're-
    vised by the author.' *Paraphrasis in evangelium Marci* was published in a folio

I am enclosing a list of errors which I found in these Paraphrases and in the   160
other books as well, though I have passed over unimportant details.

This is all I can say for the present, distinguished sir. When your letter
reaches me, I shall try my best to prove to you that you have not sought
the friendship of a discourteous and ungrateful fellow. May the Lord Jesus
have you in his keeping always.   165

Basel, 7 March AD 1526

1673 / To Fridericus Nausea   Basel, 8 March 1526

> On this humanistic and strongly anti-Lutheran admirer of Erasmus see Epp
> 1577 introduction and n1, 1632 introduction and nn1, 3. Erasmus published
> this letter in *Opus epistolarum*.

ERASMUS OF ROTTERDAM TO FRIDERICUS NAUSEA, GREETING

Bankrupts are in no position to help financially, but they can be of use to
others by advising them not to be too free with their money; and those
who have battled long against a stubborn illness are best qualified to show
others how to avoid the trouble or find a cure; and sailors who have suf-   5
fered shipwreck point out to those who are setting sail the dangers they
must avoid. So my dear Nausea, since I know so well what a dangerous
disease this itch to write[1] is, my advice to you is to spend several years
reading and rereading the best authors. When, with their help, you have
developed a mature style, you will be better able to take the stage in the   10
captious and haughty theatre of the world. And don't seize on the first subject, but choose something suited to your temperament and your powers.
In this way you will gain renown – a little later perhaps, but more solid
and lasting. If you follow my advice, some day you will thank me for having given it, and I shall congratulate you on having taken it. But if you   15
don't, you will at least appreciate the deep interest which I take in your
success.

* * * * *

edition in February or March 1524 (though an advance presentation copy was
dispatched to Francis I on 1 December 1523); although there was an octavo edition of Mark in 1534, not till the octavo edition of all four gospel paraphrases
in 1534 did this text also claim to have been 'revised most carefully by the
author.'

1673
1 Juvenal 7.52. This reference and the following passage constitute a polite but
  unmistakable warning that Erasmus judged Nausea's literary style and learning, as shown in his previous writings, to be defective.

I deliberately did not write, as you wished, to the magistrates at Frankfurt,[2] partly because, with the death of Crato's father,[3] there was no one
there whom I knew, but also because I did not have even a flimsy pretext 20
for writing to commend you to them. It does not make sense to perform
this kind of service when there is no point to be gained; it is better to wait
until the effort is worth while. When such an occasion arises, you will find
that I shall refuse nothing that might advance my friend Nausea's cause. I
look forward to your letter and to hearing how Cardinal Campeggi is doing 25
at Rome.[4] Floriano has left on a mission to Muscovy.[5] Farewell.

Basel, 8 March 1526

* * * * *

2 Nausea had been appointed cathedral preacher at Frankfurt am Main in 1525
  but had been prevented from discharging this function by pressures from the
  reform party because of his known opposition to the Reformation and his
  active role in organizing German prelates and princes to enforce the imperial
  edict outlawing Luther and his supporters. His attempt to persuade Erasmus
  to intercede with the city magistrates probably was related to this problem,
  though in the meantime he had accepted a similar position in safely Catholic
  Mainz.
3 Crato Stalburg of Frankfurt (1502–72), along with his brother Nikolaus, had
  received a humanistic education, studying under Wilhelm Nesen at Basel and
  then moving with him to Paris and Louvain. The two brothers had received
  the dedication of Beatus Rhenanus' unauthorized edition of Erasmus' *Famili-
  arum colloquiorum formulae* in 1518 because of their interest in classical literature (BRE Ep 80). In 1522–3 Crato resided in Erasmus' household at Basel (AK
  II Ep 902; Allen Ep 1818:3–4), and his name appears as one of the characters
  in Erasmus' colloquy *Convivium poeticum* 'The Poetic Feast' (ASD I-3 344–59 /
  CWE 39 390–418), first published in 1523. Unlike his brother he did not proceed
  to the study of law at Bologna but became an international merchant like his
  father Nikolaus. At the date of this letter the elder Nikolaus (1469–1524), who
  had become wealthy and had been a city councillor and a three-term mayor,
  was dead. Hence Erasmus is claiming that he no longer had a contact in Frankfurt through whom he might influence the ruling group. Though Crato himself may have returned to Frankfurt by then, he was still a young man: Erasmus' letter of 1527 (Ep 1818) introducing him to a Genoese merchant who had
  visited Basel explicitly refers to him as *iuvenis*, that is, 'a young man.'
4 Nausea had entered the service of Lorenzo Campeggi, who was one of Erasmus' most reliable friends at the curia, during the cardinal's service as legate
  to Germany, Hungary, and Bohemia in 1524–5 and had received his abortive
  appointment at Frankfurt in recognition of his service. On Campeggi see Ep
  961 introduction.
5 Floriano Montini served as secretary to Cardinal Campeggi during his diplomatic missions to Germany, Hungary, and Bohemia and hence had been a close
  associate of Nausea. See Epp 1552 introduction, 1578. In 1525 Montini was de-
  puted to accompany Francesco de Potentia on a papal mission to Muscovy
  (Pastor x 366).

1674 / To Jan (II) Łaski Basel, 8 March 1526

On Łaski's residence and friendship with Erasmus, see Epp 1593 n18, 1604 n1, 1615 n3. Erasmus frequently expressed regret at his departure, as in Epp 1622, 1629. This letter was first published in Erasmus' *Opus epistolarum*.

ERASMUS OF ROTTERDAM TO JAN ŁASKI, BARON OF POLAND, GREETING

If your journey, distinguished count, has turned out well, that is good reason for me to bear my grief more lightly. Your departure[1] was certainly unpropitious for me and for many reasons: to pass over the rest, I had to 5 struggle for months to restore my household to its former frugality, for you had corrupted it by your grand ways! Then throughout the whole autumn and winter I had to do battle with the stone. And as if that was not enough, I encountered so much trouble from other quarters that I soon came to the conclusion that my guardian angel had deserted me. I did not dare to hold 10 you back, since you were summoned on important business by command of the king;[2] I suspected, however, that things would turn out as they did. Certainly you would have caused yourself less trouble if you had waited here for more definite instructions.

Karl[3] has returned, bringing preserved fruit, though it had already 15 dried up. He complained that the journey robbed him of so much time for study. You see how sparing he has become of his time! I sent him off to England so that he would not go to seed from idleness. We have no news of the return of your messenger;[4] all I know was contained in a letter from Antonin, the physician, who tells me that my *Lingua* and the book on arithmetic 20

* * * * *

1674
1 Łaski had left Basel in October 1525 on orders of his uncle Jan (1) Łaski, archbishop of Gniezno and primate of Poland, who had financed his education and promoted his career in the church, grooming him to become his own successor. After spending time in Venice and Bologna, he returned to Poland in April 1526, just about a month after the date of this letter.
2 More directly, on orders of his uncle. The king was Sigismund I of Poland, an active patron of Renaissance culture. Erasmus' words in the following clause suggest that young Łaski's visit to Italy may have disappointed some hopes not now discoverable.
3 Karl Harst, Erasmus' confidential secretary and courier, had accompanied Łaski from Basel to Italy and after discharging important business for Erasmus at Venice and Rome had left for Basel about 26 November 1525. See Ep 1666 n2.
4 Cf the reference to Łaski's courier in line 91. Evidently he had perished on the way from Italy.

reached their intended destinations.[5] As for your suggestion that I write to
the king of Poland, I have not yet decided if that would be a good idea. Here
not so much as a fly[6] is going to Venice. Moreover, I did not know what part
of the world you were in, whether it was Spain or France or Poland. So I
was afraid that a letter which arrived too late would be no more welcome   25
to the king than those words of consolation which came too late to Caesar.[7]
I shall write, however, if I can find a spare moment, since the suggestion
comes from such an auspicious source.

By temperament I have always been reluctant to enter the arena. I have
never wanted the role of gladiator. But now fate has decided that I must do   30
battle against wild beasts.[8] Paris has sent me a book by Pierre Cousturier, formerly a theologian at the Sorbonne and now a Carthusian monk.[9] The work
is nothing but a long harangue about heresies, heresiarchs, blasphemies, and
schisms. I have written a reply,[10] though I found it difficult to preserve my
usual courtesy. The printing of the book had received official authoriza-   35
tion. Béda's *censura*[11] came out at the same time. This was preceded by three
pieces from Latomus,[12] and shortly afterwards a libellous pamphlet from

* * * * *

5 See Ep 1660:71–4, which mentions the safe arrival of copies of Erasmus' *Lingua*
   and Cuthbert Tunstall's *De arte supputandi* for potential patrons in Poland.
6 *Adagia* II i 84. No one was going from Basel to Venice, on account of military
   activity in northern Italy that rendered the roads dangerous.
7 When the emperor Nero was dying, a centurion placed a cloak over him in
   a false gesture of assistance. Nero said, 'Too late.' See Suetonius *Nero* 49; cf
   Erasmus *Apophthegmata* LB IV 277C.
8 As he often does when saying something rather shocking, Erasmus uses a
   Greek word, θηριομαχεῖν 'to fight against wild beasts.' Erasmus often compares
   himself to a gladiator, sometimes fighting as a *murmillo* equipped with sword
   and helmet, at other times fighting as a *retiarius* equipped with a net, but
   always reluctantly abandoning cultivation of the Muses to repel attacks by
   enemies who act like wild beasts. See also Epp 1675:35–6, 1677:10–12, 1678:28–
   31, 1687:35–6, 39–40, 1707:33–4, 1734:26.
9 On this conservative French critic of Erasmus, Lefèvre d'Etaples, and other
   reformist humanists, see Ep 1658 n7 and the further references given there.
10 Erasmus' *Apologia adversus Petrum Sutorem*; cf Ep 1658 n7.
11 Not a published work but a set of propositions extracted from Erasmus' New
   Testament Paraphrases in 1524–5 and informally communicated to Erasmus
   at Basel by a friend, François Deloynes. See Epp 1571 introduction, 1579 n29,
   1664 introduction and n1.
12 On Latomus (Jacques Masson), professor of theology at Louvain, see Epp
   934 introduction and 4n, 1571 n5, 1581 n58. He had attacked Erasmus indirectly in *De trium linguarum et studii theologici ratione* (1519) while Erasmus
   was still residing in Louvain, though this publication was overtly a response

four buffoons of the Dominican order.[13] Finally, and unexpectedly, Luther
charged forth with a work in which he has surpassed himself in imperti-

* * * * *

to a tract by the Leipzig humanist Petrus Mosellanus and did not mention
Erasmus by name. By 1520 Erasmus regarded Latomus as the ablest and
most persistent of his critics at Louvain (see Epp 1088, 1113, 1123). Latomus also criticized Erasmus in letters addressed to powerful individuals at
the Roman curia and the imperial court, and the preface of his work defending the condemnation of Luther's doctrines by the Louvain faculty of theology, *Articulorum doctrinae fratris Martini Lutheri per theologos Lovanienses damna-
torum ratio* (Antwerp: Michaël Hillen 8 May 1521; NK 1329), contained a passage that Erasmus regarded as a surreptitious attack on himself (Ep 1582:79–
84 and n12). Allen Ep 1585:80n argues plausibly that the 'three pieces' here
mentioned do not include Latomus' *De trium linguarum* ... or the treatise
of 1521 against Luther but refer to three later treatises ostensibly directed
against Johannes Oecolampadius and the Lutherans but implicitly critical of
Erasmus. These three treatises, published together at Antwerp in 1525 by
Michaël Hillen (NK 1325), were *De confessione secreta*, *De quaestionum generi-
bus quibus ecclesia certat intus et foris*, and *De ecclesiae et humanae legis obliga-
tione*. Although issued as a single volume with a common title-page, the three
tracts have separate registers, and the copies described in some modern library catalogues indicate that they were also issued as three separate publications. The first of them, *De confessione secreta*, though it attacked the doctrines of Oecolampadius, was obviously also aimed at Erasmus' *Exomologesis
sive modus confitendi* (1524). In 1526, Latomus published three additional tracts,
joined together in a single volume and directed mainly against Luther and
Oecolampadius but again implicitly critical of Erasmus. These were *De primatu Romani pontificis, adversus Lutherum*, *Responsio ad Elleboron Ioannis Oecolampadii*, and *Responsio ad Lutherum* (Antwerp: Michaël Hillen 1526; NK 1328).
Even in the last year of his life (1544), after Erasmus had been dead for
nearly a decade, Latomus was working on a tract, left unfinished at his
death but posthumously published, attacking Erasmus' *De sarcienda ecclesiae
concordia*.

13 A reference to a pseudonymous publication of 1525, *Apologia in eum librum quem ab anno Erasmus Roterodamus de confessione edidit*, attacking Erasmus' book on confession, *Exomologesis sive modus confitendi* (1524), which
bore the obviously fictitious name Godefridus Ruysius Taxander as author.
From the very beginning, Erasmus attributed it to one or more members
of the Dominican order associated with the University of Louvain. With
the aid of well-placed friends he eventually uncovered the identity of the
four perpetrators. See Ep 1571 n14 for a summary account of the publication and the subsequent solution of the mystery of its authorship. The
work by 'Taxander' also accused Erasmus of being an apostate monk, a
charge to which Erasmus replied in a letter that he never published; a fragment of that letter was discovered in 1906 and first published by Allen
(Ep 1436), who conjecturally dated it in April 1524. That fragment has

nence of every sort. [14] I have now written a partial reply; for I had scarcely   40
twelve days before the fair. I think I can divine from Luther's writings that
Pellicanus has been in touch with him and passed on some points from our
conversation.[15]

Pellicanus almost caused another uproar here. He had spread the rumour that his ideas about the Eucharist were the same as mine. I wrote   45
him a letter of protest on the subject, but without mentioning his name.[16]

* * * * *

now been redated to 1525 and translated as CWE Ep 1581A. Erasmus also
wrote a short tract replying to 'Taxander' but never published it. Erika
Rummel found it in a manuscript at Copenhagen and edited it (see Ep
1581A n1), and an annotated English translation by her appears in CWE 71
113–31.

14 A reference to Luther's *De servo arbitrio*, which, however, had hardly been
rushed into print, since sixteen months elapsed between publication of Erasmus' *De libero arbitrio* and publication of this rebuttal. See Ep 1667 introduction.
Ep 1667 is the preface to Erasmus' 'partial reply' mentioned just below, part
1 of *Hyperaspistes*, which he hurriedly composed in order to have a response
to Luther available quickly.

15 Conradus Pellicanus, a Hebrew scholar and former editorial collaborator at
the Froben press; see Ep 1637 introduction. By this time Pellicanus' open support of the Reformation and his efforts to associate Erasmus with his own
support of Johannes Oecolampadius' Sacramentarian doctrines on the Eucharist had led Erasmus to become bitterly estranged from him. In the af-
termath of Erasmus' quarrel with Ulrich von Hutten and publication of his
Spongia adversus aspergines Hutteni, Luther wrote a letter to Pellicanus (1 October 1523; WA-Br 3 158–62 Ep 661), but the growing rift between Luther
and those Swiss and South German reformers who adopted the Sacramentarian eucharistic opinions of Zwingli and Oecolampadius makes confidential,
intimate communication between Luther and Pellicanus at this period seem
unlikely. On Pellicanus see, in addition to the bibliography cited in CEBR,
Oxford Encyclopedia of the Reformation (1996) IV 241–2 and the literature there
cited.

16 Ep 1637, which reflects Erasmus' fury at what he interpreted as Pellicanus'
effort to insinuate that Erasmus privately agreed with his Sacramentarian views. Although Allen's edition provides a conventional Latin salutation identifying Pellicanus as the recipient, the two pamphlets in which it
was first printed (probably not long after it was written and probably at
Basel) as well as Erasmus' *Opus epistolarum* (1529) identify the addressee
only as 'a certain friend,' and the text of the letter likewise does not reveal Pellicanus' name; cf Allen's introduction and textual note on the salutation. See also Epp 1638 (Pellicanus' reply), 1639, 1640. For an account of
the alienation of Erasmus from this close friend because of the eucharist
controversy, see introductions to Epp 1637, 1638 and, more generally, Ep
1670 n6.

Pellicanus' letter was shown to several people by Baer[17] and Cantiuncula;[18] it was even read in the council; and in the end it was translated into German and distributed far and wide to my considerable embarrassment. Pellicanus wrote a letter in reply to mine. I wrote back and suggested he should 50 stop writing and come to see me if there was something on his mind. He came. I asked him what he meant by his letter. He kept evading the question. I began to press him. Finally, he more or less confessed that he had said that his ideas coincided with mine. I asked him what opinion he held that we shared in common. After much shuffling he replied, that the body 55 and blood of the Lord are present in the Eucharist. 'The same,' he added, 'as you believe.' 'Just that?' I said. 'Do you believe they are present only in the form of symbols?' 'No,' he replied, 'but I think the power of Christ is present.' I continued, 'Do you believe that the substance of Christ's body is present?' He admitted that he did not. After this I asked him if he had 60 ever professed these views before in my presence. He confessed that he had never done so, which was the truth. Then I asked him if he had ever heard such views from me. He said he had not. In fact, far from having heard any such thing, he had frequently heard the opposite. 'You openly declare in the presence of others,' I said, 'that you and I are in agreement; and whenever 65 you say this, you understand the statement to mean no more than that you and I agree that the body of our Lord is present, but your hearers imagine that, like you, I accept the teaching of Oecolampadius.' Now I am told that two particularly silly letters of Pellicanus' are in circulation.[19] He has been

* * * * *

17 Ludwig Baer was professor of theology at the University of Basel, a close and trusted friend whom Erasmus consulted on theological issues and whose authority he often cited as evidence of his own orthodoxy. See Ep 488 and, for Erasmus' more recent reliance on his reputation as a theologian, Epp 1539 n1, 1571 n6, 1581 (especially lines 257–62, 335, 798–803 and n100), 1609 n2, 1620:40–3, 1636 introduction, 1741, and 1744:62–5 and n10. Baer was one of the experts (Erasmus and Claudius Cantiuncula were the others) whom the Basel city council consulted in 1525 about the Sacramentarian opinions of Oecolampadius, which Pellicanus endorsed; see Ep 1636.

18 About the end of summer 1525, this humanist and jurist, then in the service of the bishop of Metz, had written a letter urging Erasmus to write in opposition to Oecolampadius' views on the Eucharist, a proposal that Erasmus politely but definitely rejected. See Ep 1616 and introduction. On Cantiuncula's earlier career, see Ep 852:85n.

19 Epp 1638 and 1639, which not only circulated in manuscript but were also printed. See introductions to those letters in CWE 11, and also Ep 1637 introduction.

invited to Zürich to teach Hebrew there.[20] He is the last of the Evangelicals 70
that I shall trust.

When Oecolampadius' book *On the Eucharist* appeared, the council, being somewhat perplexed by the unusual nature of the work, consulted me
privately,[21] along with Provost Baer, Bonifacius,[22] and Cantiuncula. When
word of this got around – for the subject was very close to the hearts of 75
Zwingli,[23] Oecolampadius, Capito,[24] and Pellicanus – before long there appeared a letter from Capito whose purpose was to challenge my competence
in the matter.[25] A libellous pamphlet was then prepared and has now been
printed; some suspected that this was also the work of Capito.[26] Such are the

* * * * *

20 In fact Pellicanus had moved to Zürich in February and spent the rest of his
   career as a pastor and teacher of Greek and Hebrew there.
21 See Epp 1616 n4, 1636 introduction, 1637 introduction, 1792A introduction.
22 Bonifacius Amerbach, humanist, professor of law in the local university, and
   close friend of Erasmus
23 Huldrych Zwingli, leader of the Reformation at Zürich, and from about
   1523 the first major proponent of the 'Zwinglian' or Sacramentarian interpretation of the Eucharist, which caused much uneasiness at Basel in 1525
   and eventually led to an enduring split between Lutheran and 'Zwinglian'
   Protestants
24 On Wolfgang Faber Capito and his earlier relations with Erasmus, see Ep 459
   introduction. His conversion in the summer of 1523 to a clearly Lutheran
   theology (except for his sympathy for Zwingli's interpretation of the Eucharist, which Erasmus found equally unacceptable) and his emergence as
   one of the leaders of the Reformation at Strasbourg led to estrangement between him and Erasmus. See Epp 1374, 1477B:72–97. Erasmus accused Capito
   of instigating the attacks on him by Heinrich Eppendorf and Otto Brunfels (Ep 1485) and believed that Capito was an inciter of unrest and ill will
   (Epp 1496:120–5, 1497:17–18). The break became so bitter that Erasmus signed
   his last letter to Capito on 2 September 1524 (Ep 1485) 'Erasmus, formerly
   yours in Christ.' Erasmus continued to suspect him of conspiracy; see n26
   below.
25 This anonymous letter, widely circulated in manuscript as *Franci cuiusdam
   epistola ad quendam ciuem Basiliensem* 'Letter from a certain Franconian [or
   Frenchman] to a certain citizen of Basel,' was actually written by Zwingli,
   not Capito, and was addressed to Oecolampadius. See Allen Ep 1644:6n. The
   letter, dated 28 October 1525, is in Zwingli *Sämtliche Werke* ed Emil Egli and
   others VIII: *Briefwechsel* II, 1523–1526 (Leipzig 1914; repr Zürich 1982) 407–13
   Ep 401.
26 Erasmus may be referring to the anonymous pamphlet *Maynung vom Nachtmal vnnsers herren Ihesu Christi* comparing Erasmus' opinions on the Eucharist
   with Luther's. Although it probably was not published until April, Erasmus

defences on which the gospel now relies! Lefèvre d'Etaples has fled from   80
France and is now living in Strasbourg,[27] but under an assumed name, like
the old man in the comedy[28] who was called Chremes in Athens and Stilpo
in Lemnos.

But why do I trouble your Highness with this weary tale? Beatus
Rhenanus has published some sort of commentary on Pliny.[29] I think he   85
intends to dedicate it to you. As soon as I find out where you have settled, I shall be in touch and shall send you longer letters than this. I am
entrusting this to the winds in the hope that it will reach you one way or
another.

Before I could seal this, I got the letter you wrote on the first of Febru-   90
ary, informing me of the loss of your courier and of your rapid return to

* * * * *

may have received some advance information that a publication associating him with Evangelical rather than Catholic theological opinions was in
preparation. The pamphlet was actually the work of Leo Jud, who in a
later pamphlet, *Vf entdeckung* (see Ep 1708 n1) acknowledged his authorship; but Erasmus suspected both Capito and Pellicanus of authorship of both
pamphlets.

27 This French humanist had fled to Strasbourg in October 1525 because of the
threat of prosecution by the official guardians of orthodoxy, the judges delegate (*juges délégués*) and the Parlement of Paris, during the extended captivity of King Francis I, the most effective protector of humanists. King
Francis was a prisoner for more than a year after his disastrous defeat
at the battle of Pavia (24 February 1525), leaving the Parlement free to
act against those they defined as 'heretics' without the king's interference.
Only after the king's return to France (17 March 1526) did Lefèvre leave
his refuge at Strasbourg, returning home indirectly by way of Basel (Ep
1713, dated 16 May 1526) and joining the royal court at Blois. On Lefèvre
see, in addition to the bibliography cited in CEBR, Philip Edgcumbe Hughes
Lefèvre, Pioneer of Ecclesiastical Renewal in France (Grand Rapids, MI 1984)
171–3.

28 The *Phormio* of Terence

29 On the earlier career of this Alsatian humanist, a close collaborator in Erasmus' editorial work for the Froben press, see Ep 327 introduction. He had
played an important role in work on the 1525 edition of the *Naturalis historia*
of Pliny the Elder, for which Erasmus was the editor of record; and in 1526
the Froben press published his commentary on Pliny. Although he lived and
worked in Basel for many years, Beatus retained close ties to his native city of
Sélestat and sometime in the mid-1520s decided to relocate there permanently.
In 1526–7 he alternated his place of residence between Basel and Sélestat and
definitively moved back to his home town in September 1528, though he still
made frequent trips to Basel.

your native land.[30] I only wish the letters you expected from home, when
you were staying with me, had been as slow and unpredictable! I have had
nothing else from you or from Pole[31] except that letter of yours which my
man Karl brought me[32] and this more recent one.   95

I am making two copies of this; one I am sending to Frankfurt, the
other to Constance. This is a trick I learned from the cardinals,[33] when there
is something important to communicate. Farewell.

Basel, 8 March 1526

Give my greetings to the palatine[34] and to your brother[35] and the rest   100
of our friends.

1675 / To Reginald Pole   Basel, 8 March 1526

On this second cousin of King Henry VIII, currently studying at Padua and
acting as patron to a number of young humanists from several nations, see
Ep 1627 introduction. The man who established contact between Erasmus and
Pole, Thomas Lupset, informed Erasmus in Ep 1595 about Pole's ancestry,
virtue, education, and admiration for Erasmus. Erasmus included this letter
in his *Opus epistolarum*.

* * * * *

30 Not extant, but Łaski's letter of 1 February 1526 to Bonifacius Amerbach,
   written from Venice, contains what was probably an identical report of the
   disappearance of Łaski's courier and the letters he was carrying to Erasmus
   and Amerbach. That letter is printed in *Lasciana* ed Hermann Dalton, Beiträge zur Geschichte der evangelischen Kirche in Russland 3 (Berlin 1898;
   repr Nieuwkoop 1973) 95–6 no 8, and it is summarized, but not printed, in
   AK III 122 Ep 1091.
31 On this second cousin of King Henry VIII, see Ep 1675 introduction.
32 Not extant, though it must have accompanied Epp 1648–50, written by other
   admirers of Erasmus who were then studying in Padua.
33 Just which cardinals taught Erasmus this practice of sending duplicate copies of
   important letters by different routes is uncertain, but he enjoyed friendly relations with several cardinals who travelled widely as papal diplomats, and also
   with their secretaries and other assistants – for example, Cardinal Campeggi,
   his servant Fridericus Nausea, and his secretary Floriano Montini; see Ep 1673
   introduction and nn4 and 5.
34 Krzysztof Szydłowiecki, to whom Erasmus had dedicated his *Lingua* in 1525,
   was palatine and prefect of Cracow and chancellor of the kingdom of Poland.
   See Ep 1593 introduction.
35 Erasmus knew two brothers of Jan Łaski, Hieronim and Stanisław, but since
   Stanisław was then in France and Hieronim in Poland, where Jan was now
   returning, Hieronim is probably the one greeted here.

ERASMUS OF ROTTERDAM TO REGINALD POLE, ENGLISHMAN,
GREETING

Reginald, my distinguished friend, a letter from the Polish count[1] informs
me that he wrote to me some time ago, enclosing a letter of yours with his
own. Whatever evil genius it was that prevented your letter from being de-   5
livered robbed me of a great treat. Nothing has come from your part of
the world except the letter that Karl Harst[2] brought from my Polish friend
and the one that I received from him today, written on the first of February. If Lupset[3] has already returned, please tell him that I got the Greek
Chrysostom, though it is Chrysostom only in name.[4] As the proverb goes,   10
I expected a treasure and got lumps of coal![5] Tell him also that I finished
Jerome by the first of March, though it was a struggle.[6] I gathered from his

* * * * *

1675
1 Jan Łaski. See Ep 1674. Presumably the letter from Pole that Erasmus never
  received was a reply to Ep 1627, and Allen (2n) shows from internal evidence
  that both it and Łaski's letter, which was delivered but is now lost, must have
  been written between 23 November 1525 and 1 February 1526.
2 Erasmus' confidential courier, who had just returned from Italy (Ep 1674 n3).
  On him see Ep 1666 n2.
3 See Epp 1595 introduction, 1594 n3. Allen observes (7n) that there is no other
  record of this unexplained, and surely brief, trip from Padua to Paris. Lupset
  had studied in Paris from 1517 to 1519 and may have visited there again when
  he returned from Padua to England in the autumn of 1526. He certainly lived
  in the French capital in 1528–9 and again for a time in 1530.
4 Erasmus had an abiding interest in the works of the greatest preacher among
  the Greek church Fathers, St John Chrysostom, and had published two of his
  works the preceding year. See Ep 1661 n2. One of Karl Harst's duties in Italy
  the preceding year was to locate and purchase this manuscript (Ep 1623:11–
  15 and n3). Exactly what the manuscript contained, and why Erasmus found
  it disappointing, is not clear. Chrysostom wrote no commentaries, but he did
  preach a sequence of sixty-five homilies on the Acts of the Apostles that Quasten *Patrology* III 440 calls 'the only complete commentary on Acts that has survived from the first ten centuries.' Many of Chrysostom's series of homilies
  expounded a particular book of the Bible; the surviving text of his homilies
  on Galatians, for example, is a verse-by-verse elucidation of the text that is referred to as a 'commentary' even though the text shows clear evidence of its
  origin as a series of sermons (Quasten III 446).
5 *Adagia* I ix 30
6 This publication was the last of the nine volumes of a revised edition of the
  greatest of Erasmus' many editions of patristic authors. Froben published the
  first edition of Jerome's *Opera* in 1516, and the same press had published the
  first of the revised volumes in 1524. See Epp 396 and introduction, 1465 and
  introduction, Ep 1623 n5.

letter that he did not plan to stay long in Paris. I shall do what he wants, only I must first find out where on earth he is.

Longueil[7] and Leonico[8] are on sale here. I am sorry that premature 15 death has taken Longueil from the world of learning; he was no great friend of mine, though I gave him no cause. I entertained him at Louvain as hospitably as my obligations and my health would allow. The ambassador of the king of France had sent me a letter of his.[9] Far from being offended by it, I had the letter published in his honour (May Christ 20 not love me if this is untrue!).[10] His works show what pains he took to imitate the style of Cicero.[11] But occasionally from the odd overblown phrase one catches a hint of youthful ambition. I would have preferred to see his commentaries in print,[12] although stylistically they have less

* * * * *

7 On Christophe de Longueil see Epp 914 introduction, 935, 1011:5–8 and n1, 1026:5–8 and n1, 1347:326–31, 1595 and n22, 1597 n5, 1603 n26, 1706 nn2, 4, 5, 6, 9. The work of Longueil on sale in Basel at this time would probably be his *Orationes duae pro defensione sua in crimen lesae majestatis ... Oratio una ad Luterianos ... Eiusdem Epistolarum libri quatuor ... Longolii vita ... ab ipsius amicissimo [Reginaldo Polo] exarata ...* (Florence, heirs of Filippo Giunta, December 1524; repr Farnborough, Hants 1967); cf Allen line 13n. Evidence that this collection of texts attracted attention in the northern book market at this time is the appearance of another edition published at Paris by Josse Bade on 13 June 1526. Longueil had been a close friend of Pole at Padua (Ep 1627 introduction). As a leading 'Ciceronian' humanist, Longueil had been critical of Erasmus (Epp 914, 935) and later became a principal target of criticism in Erasmus' *Ciceronianus* (1528); see Ep 1701 n6.
8 On Niccolò Leonico Tomeo see Epp 1479 n70, 1595 n8. The book reported on sale at Basel is probably his *Dialogi* (Venice: G. de Gregoriis, September 1524); cf Allen line 13n; but it could also have been his *Opuscula* (Venice 1525).
9 Louis Ruzé. On him see Epp 926, 928. The letter that he sent (Ep 914) was written by Longueil in 1519 and compared the literary qualities of Erasmus and Guillaume Budé, with an obvious undercurrent of coolness to Erasmus and preference for Budé. At that earlier time, Ruzé had been on a diplomatic mission to the prince-bishop of Liège.
10 He included it in his *Farrago nova epistolarum* (Basel: Froben 1519), and it appeared in subsequent collections of his correspondence. See Ep 914 introduction.
11 Not really a compliment, since Longueil was a target of Erasmus' criticism of Ciceronian stylistic purism in the *Ciceronianus*. See the references in Epp 1596 n22, 1701 n6.
12 According to the anonymous author (generally presumed to be Reginald Pole) of the biography of Longueil prefixed to an edition of his orations and letters published in 1524, among the works that Longueil wrote but never published were commentaries on the civil law and on eleven books of Pliny's

of Cicero about them. If you will see to this, believe me you will earn 25
the gratitude of the whole scholarly world, its leaders and its rank and
file.

I commend Leonard Casembroot to you.[13] Give my friend Marmaduke
my greetings in return for his.[14] I am sending this letter to Frankfurt, trust-
ing it to the winds. When I have someone more reliable, I shall write at 30
greater length. Farewell, my dearest Pole, great ornament of learning.

Luther was offended by my *Diatribe* despite its very moderate tone. So
he has attacked me in a great tome that no one would write against a Turk.
I have made a partial reply; for his work reached me late.[15] I have always
been a lover of peace and quiet, but now I am being forced to enter the 35
arena, not just as a gladiator, but as a fighter against wild beasts.[16] More of
this at another time.

Basel, 8 March AD 1526

1676 / To Erasmus Schets   Basel, 11 March 1526

This reply to Ep 1658 shows how completely, within little more than a year,
the Antwerp merchant-banker Schets had taken charge of the collection and
transfer of Erasmus' revenues from England and the Netherlands. Cf Ep 1541

* * * * *

Naturalis historia. See his *Orationes* (n7 above) folio 5. Longueil was a great
admirer of Pliny and was one of several humanists (including Erasmus) who
contributed notes to the commentary on Pliny published at Paris in 1516 by
Nicolas Bérault.
13 See Ep 1594 introduction. Between 1525 and 1527 Casembroot was studying
law in Padua.
14 Marmaduke Waldby (documented 1505–40), a graduate of Cambridge University (BA 1505), had already received several benefices in England and by 1524
was a member of the household of Pole, whom he may have accompanied to
Padua in 1521. Erasmus may have met him at Cambridge in 1505–6. He probably accompanied Pole back to England in 1527, having apparently received
a doctorate in theology while in Italy. He then served as chaplain to Cardinal Wolsey, returned to Italy for a time, and continued to gain ecclesiastical
preferment until his involvement in the Northern Rebellion of 1536–7 led to
his imprisonment in the Tower for four months and probably to forfeiture of
his benefices.
15 Luther's *De servo arbitrio* treated Erasmus as an unbelieving sceptic; see Ep
1667.
16 An example of Erasmus' custom of using Greek terms (in this case, θηριομαχεῖν)
to express outrageous or risqué sentiments. This is another of Erasmus' gladiatorial images; see Ep 1674 n8.

introduction. Like nearly all of Erasmus' correspondence with Schets, this letter remained unpublished until it was edited by Allen in 1926. Allen's source
was Erasmus' original autograph letter, which survived in the British Library.

Cordial greetings. There is no need for me to reply to all your points individually, since I believe Karl[1] has been with you. Lompart, on being handed
the receipt from his son,[2] paid over the 138$^{1}/_{2}$ crowns at once;[3] there was no
need, however, for such speed. If any money comes into your hands in future, hold on to it and send it when it is convenient. I have already sent a   5
receipt to clear Alvaro of his obligations.[4] I do not think a second receipt is
necessary. Give my thanks to Martin Lompart's son[5] for his kindness and
promise my assistance in turn if there is anything I can do for him. I hope
it will not be too much trouble to send these two letters to Alvaro. Perhaps
he will not find them unwelcome since they contain friendly references to   10
himself.

Dear Schets, if there is ever any way in which I can repay you for all
your kindness to me, you will find me an appreciative friend; I shall not
forget. Best wishes to you and to your wife and children, who are very dear
to you.   15

Basel, 11 March AD 1526

In my letter to Canterbury I confirmed that the money was duly paid
to me. This was all that Alvaro needed, even without the receipt.[6]

You will recognize the hand of your true friend.

To the honourable Erasmus Schets, merchant. In Antwerp   20

* * * * *

1676
1 Karl Harst, Erasmus' confidential courier. See Ep 1675 n2.
2 On Jakob Lompart see Ep 1658 n4. The earlier letter identifies the issuer of the
   receipt as Jakob's brother; see n2 there.
3 Latin *centum triginta octo coronatos et dimidiatum*; see Ep 1658 n3.
4 On Alvaro de Castro, an agent for Schets in England, see Epp 1590 n2, 1658
   n5. The letters for Castro mentioned just below are not extant.
5 Martin Lompart (and, evidently, his son) resided at Antwerp and acted as
   agents of Martin's brother Jakob. See Ep 1658 nn2, 4.
6 William Warham, archbishop of Canterbury, was Erasmus' most reliable English patron, and the revenues from the pension that Erasmus received from
   the parish of Aldington in Kent were regularly collected by an agent for Erasmus (in this case, Alvaro de Castro) and transmitted to him at Basel by way of
   Schets at Antwerp; cf Ep 1671 n9. The letter (not extant) to Warham acknowledging receipt constituted a release of Castro from his financial responsibility,
   though it is not clear how Erasmus thought that Castro himself would learn
   that the acknowledgment of receipt had been sent and received.

Katharina von Bora
Portrait from the workshop of Lucas Cranach, 1529
Kunstmuseum, Bern

1677 / To François Dubois Basel, 13 March 1526

Erasmus thought highly of the Paris humanist François Dubois and included this letter in *Opus epistolarum*. On the recipient see Ep 1600 introduction.

ERASMUS OF ROTTERDAM TO FRANÇOIS DUBOIS, GREETING
There is no doubt about Luther's marriage, but the rumour about his wife's early confinement is false;[1] she is said, however, to be pregnant now. If there is truth in the popular legend, that Antichrist will be born from a monk and a nun (which is the story these people keep putting about),[2] how many 5 thousands of Antichrists the world must have already! I was hoping that Luther's wife would calm her husband down. Instead, quite unexpectedly, he has published a book against me,[3] composed with meticulous care but so violent that it surpasses anything he has written about anyone before. What has happened to the peace-loving Erasmus? At a time of life when 10

* * * * *

1677
1 Luther married the former nun Katharina von Bora on 13 June 1525, and the wedding was publicly celebrated on 27 June. This was titillating personal gossip throughout western and central Europe, and Erasmus knew some details about the marriage and the bride by early October 1525, when he passed the news on in a letter to his English friend Thomas Lupset at Venice (Ep 1624). A few days later, in a letter to Daniel Mauch (Ep 1633), he added the still juicier gossip that the recently married bride had already given birth to a child; here he corrects the false rumour that the bride was pregnant at the time of the wedding.
2 See Richard Kenneth Emmerson *Antichrist in the Middle Ages* (Seattle 1981) 81 and nn22, 23 (page 267); Bernard McGinn *Antichrist* (New York 1994) 131. Hildegard of Bingen associates the Antichrist with sexual evil and has him born from an unchaste woman but does not attribute his birth to the union of a monk and a nun. See, however, McGinn's discussion (167–9) of sexuality and the Antichrist in the *Romance of the Rose*, where a personage associated with Antichrist disguises himself as a friar and is accompanied by a female figure named 'Constrained Abstinence,' who is disguised as a beguine. Hans Preus *Die Vorstellungen vom Antichrist im späteren Mittelalter* (Leipzig 1906) 15 indicates that in any case, Antichrist's mother is a whore, or an evil Jewish woman, or both parents are elderly, or he is begotten by a bastard father on his daughter, or by a monk and a nun. Julius Köstlin *Martin Luther* 5th ed, 2 vols (Berlin 1903) I 838 describes the story about the parentage of the Antichrist as a common belief among uneducated folk of Catholic sympathies, but he cites no source and may depend on this letter, to which he refers a few lines later concerning the false story that Luther's bride was already pregnant at the time of the wedding.
3 *De servo arbitrio*

gladiators usually retire, I am compelled to enter the arena with sword and helmet[4] and, what is worse, to do battle against wild beasts.[5] How very, very fortunate you are, to be able to commune quietly with the Muses![6]

Basel, 13 March 1526

1678 / To Michel Boudet   Basel, 13 March 1526

On this prelate, bishop of Langres and a patron of humanists at the French court, see Ep 1612 introduction. Erasmus published this letter in *Opus epistolarum*.

ERASMUS OF ROTTERDAM TO MICHEL BOUDET,
BISHOP OF LANGRES, GREETING

Reverend bishop, I have no news to tell you, but the bearer of this letter,[1] who is well acquainted, I believe, with your generosity, insisted that I write something. I have nothing to send you except a few short pieces 5 translated from Plutarch[2] and my reply to Luther.[3] The Jerome has now

* * * * *

4 The equipment of the class of gladiators known as *murmillones*. Erasmus is fond of the gladiatorial image; see Ep 1674 n8.
5 Erasmus uses the Greek word θηριομαχεῖν to express 'to do battle against wild beasts'; see Ep 1674 n8.
6 Erasmus' Latin is the punning, alliterative phrase *mussitare cum Musis*. For *cum Musis* cf *Adagia* III vi 89.

1678
1 Further described in line 52 as 'this young man.' Allen (43n) suggests that he may have been Hilarius Bertholf. See Epp 1257, 1712 introduction. This young humanist probably had accompanied Erasmus from Louvain to Basel in 1521 and continued to serve him as secretary and courier until late in 1524, when he moved to France, soon entering the service of Margaret of Angoulême. There is no independent evidence that he visited Erasmus in Basel at this time and could have been the bearer of this letter on his return to France. About two months later (Ep 1712) Erasmus wrote asking him for advice on how to phrase a letter congratulating Francis I on his release from captivity in Spain.
2 In May of 1525 Froben's press had published two short treatises of Plutarch, *De non irascendo* and *De curiositate*, with the Greek text accompanied by Erasmus' Latin translation (Ep 1572 introduction); Erasmus' translation of Plutarch's *De vitiosa verecundia* had appeared even more recently (February 1526) from the same press, as an annex (but with separate pagination) to his *Lingua* (see Ep 1663 introduction and n1). These are probably the Plutarch pieces referred to here. Allen (3n) notes that the Basel library contains the Plutarch translations of May 1525 bound together with *Hyperaspistes* book 1, each edition bearing a dedication to Bishop Boudet in Erasmus' own hand.
3 *Hyperaspistes* book 1. See Ep 1667 introduction.

been completed fairly satisfactorily,[4] and the *Adagia* have been added to
and corrected at the cost of much sweat.[5] I had begun to write the *Precepts
of Marriage*,[6] which was commissioned by the queen of England, a woman
as pious as she is learned, but my labours were interrupted by the sud-   10
den and unexpected appearance of a work of Luther's in which he replies
to my *Diatribe*, but in so violent and scurrilous and even vicious a fashion
that it surpasses in savagery anything he has written previously about anyone – and this in spite of the fact that my *Diatribe* was moderate in tone
and did not resort to personal abuse. He has packed into the book every-   15
thing we could expect by way of scholarship and abuse from the church
at Wittenberg. The volume is of more than average size and is being translated into German[7] so as to prejudice every labourer and peasant against
me; for in that world the voice of Erasmus is silent. They took remarkable care to see that the work would not reach me before the Frankfurt   20
fair, so that, by distributing Luther's book without a reply from me, they
could enjoy a few months' triumph with no price to pay.[8] As it happened,
a friend sent me a copy from Leipzig, but it came so late that I had scarcely
twelve days in which to read it, write a reply, and have it printed.[9] I know
you will not believe this, but the people here who witnessed it believe   25
it. I shall produce a more considered reply to the remainder of Luther's
work.

* * * * *

4 On the revised second edition of the *Opera* of Jerome, see Epp 1465, 1675 n6.
  The final volume of this edition came off the press about two weeks before
  the date of this letter.
5 See Ep 1659, the preface of that revised edition, dated 17 January 1526.
6 See Ep 1727, the dedication of his *Institutio christiani matrimonii* to Catherine
  of Aragon, queen of England. For earlier mention of the queen's request for
  such a work, see Epp 1581 n93, 1624 nn23, 24.
7 After publication of *De servo arbitrio* at Wittenberg on the last day of 1525,
  Luther's associate Justus Jonas, with the author's approval, prepared a German
  translation; it was published by the same Wittenberg printer, Hans Lufft, early
  in the new year.
8 On Erasmus' insistence on getting some response to Luther's *De servo arbitrio*
  into print before the spring session of the Frankfurt fair, and his suspicion
  (almost certainly unjustified) that Luther and his supporters had deliberately
  timed publication of Luther's book so that it would be impossible for him to
  do so, see Ep 1667 introduction.
9 The mediating role of Simon Pistoris at the court of Luther's enemy Duke
  George of Saxony, reflected in Ep 1693, suggests that Pistoris himself may
  have been the friend at Leipzig who got a copy of *De servo arbitrio* into Erasmus' hands in time to allow him to produce his hurried *Hyperaspistes 1* in time
  for the Frankfurt fair. Cf Allen 19n.

Simon Pistoris
Engraving by a Saxon artist, 1535
Berlin-Dahlem, Staatliche Museen, Kupferstichkabinett

I was not born for this sort of thing. But Fate decreed that, at an age
when gladiators are usually sent into retirement, I am compelled not just to
enter the arena with my net,[10] but to engage in θηριομαχία, that is, to do battle   30
with wild beasts.[11] For can you think of anyone madder than that dreadful
Cousturier?[12] And in the case of Luther I am at a loss to understand how two
such different personalities can exist in the same person. Sometimes, when
he writes, he seems to breathe the very spirit of an apostle; at other times
there is no scurrilous buffoon whom he does not surpass with his sneering,   35
abusive, and sarcastic wit. He has spirit enough to condemn emperors and
popes; yet at a mere whisper from some mean and worthless persons he
turns his furious temper against anyone he pleases, forgetting the kind of
drama in which he is involved and the role he has taken on.

Some books have just been published here telling us that the body   40
and blood of Christ are not substantially present in the Eucharist.[13] When I
was asked my opinion by the magistrates, I replied that I believed precisely

* * * * *

10 Another of Erasmus' gladiatorial references; cf Ep 1674 n8.
11 On Erasmus' use of Greek here Ep 1674 n8.
12 A rhetorical question consistent with Erasmus' opinion of Cousturier; see Ep
   1658 n7.
13 Principally Oecolampadius' *De genuina verborum Domini 'Hoc est corpus meum'*
   iuxta vetustissimos authores expositione liber (1525), which, however, was not published at Basel on account of the hostility of the city council to Sacramentarian opinions at that period. Cf Epp 1616 (especially n4), 1636 introduction,
   1792A introduction; also Ernst Staehelin, 'Oekolampad-Bibliographie' *Basler
   Zeitschrift für Geschichte und Altertumskunde* 17 (1918) 55 (no 113), 58–60 (nos
   123, 124). Oecolampadius' vernacular *Billiche antwurt Joan. Ecolampadij auff D.
   Martin Luthers bericht des Sacraments halb*, a defence of Sacramentarian views
   against Luther, was, however, printed at Basel by Thomas Wolff in 1526; see
   Staehelin 61–2 (no 129). But while Oecolampadius cautiously had his principal work on the Eucharist printed elsewhere, probably at Strasbourg, Andreas
   Bodenstein von Karlstadt, shortly after his expulsion from Saxony in September 1524, had a series of seven short tracts, five of them direct defences of the
   Sacramentarian position, published secretly in Basel in the autumn of 1524.
   Erasmus himself reported in letters of 10 December 1524 to Heinrich Stromer
   and Philippus Melanchthon (Epp 1522, 1523) that the city council had imprisoned two printers involved in these clandestine publications, Thomas Wolff
   and Johann Bebel. On the latter point, see Ep 1523 n21 and Hermann Barge
   'Zur Chronologie und Drucklegung der Abendmahlstraktate Karlstadts' *Zentralblatt für Bibliothekswesen* 21 (1904) 323–31. The Basel publications in question are listed and described in Ernst Freys and Hermann Barge 'Verzeichnis
   der gedruckten Schriften des Andreas Bodenstein von Karlstadt' *Zentralblatt
   für Bibliothekswesen* 21 (1904) 305–11 (nos 124, 126, 129, 131, 135, 139).

what the Catholic church had laid down.[14] That reply annoyed these new Evangelicals,[15] who were desperately eager for their view to prevail. At this point, although I was on the same side as Luther, who in this mat-   45 ter takes a different view from theirs, they incited him to attack me with all the venom at his command. Such are the tactics these Evangelicals employ. And yet, while I am locked in battle with ogres of this sort, I am attacked by Béda[16] and Cousturier[17] and men like that. Evidently both sides are playing their part in the drama as though they do not want a happy   50 ending.

If I have bored you with this letter, put the blame on this young man; he was inspired by your generosity to insist that I write it, unnecessary though it is. I wish your lordship well.

Basel, 13 March AD 1526   55

1679 / To Noël Béda   Basel, 13 March 1526

> This letter, a reply to Ep 1642 from the arch-conservative syndic of the faculty of theology at Paris, continues a correspondence that Erasmus had initiated the preceding April (Ep 1571). Although Erasmus opened the correspondence partly in order to protest against both open and veiled attacks on him by some Paris theologians, he had hoped to persuade the powerful Béda to desist from his efforts to have the faculty condemn propositions that he had extracted from Erasmus' Paraphrases on the New Testament. By this time, however, the original veneer of cordiality had worn very thin. On Béda see Epp 1571 introduction, 1664 introduction and n1. Erasmus never published this letter, but Béda did, in his Apologia adversus clandestinos Lutheranos (1529). Béda's reply is Ep 1685.

* * * * *

14 See Ep 1636, and cf his more general, but equally moderate and cautious, reply to the city council's earlier request for advice about policy towards the Reformers in general, Ep 1539.

15 Allen (36n) observes that Erasmus used the same phrase, 'these new Evangelicals,' in his Epistola ad fratres Inferioris Germaniae (1530) to express his disdain for the radical Reformers' assumption that only they can understand the meaning of Scripture.

16 See Ep 1571 introduction, 1664 introduction and n1. At this point, unlike his colleague Cousturier, Béda had not yet published an open attack on Erasmus, but his Annotationes, a work criticizing the works of both Lefèvre and Erasmus, was published late in May of 1526. See Ep 1642 n5.

17 See Epp 1571 n10, 1591, the dedication of Erasmus' Apologia directed against Cousturier's De tralatione Bibliae, and 1658 n7.

TO THE MOST HONOURED MASTER NOËL BÉDA,
CORDIAL GREETINGS

My honourable friend, certain remarks in your last letter smacked more of
the arrogance of some grand despot than the gentleness of a theologian. For
example, in one passage you tell me not to concern myself overmuch with   5
the reputation of the theologians.[1] I thought that our friendship entitled me
to exchange ideas with you on any matter that seemed relevant to the Christian faith. Then you beat me until I am black and blue for my supposed
opposition to the theologians of the Sorbonne. But the fact is that there is
no one whom I respect more than a true theologian, and there has never   10
been the least disagreement between me and a good theologian. If I complain about bad theologians who are unworthy of the name, that is not intended as an affront to the profession as a whole any more than remarks
about Christians who are usurers and adulterers are an insult to all Christian people. Your words sound as if I wanted to see the destruction of the   15
profession of theology as a whole. I am delighted that the title of theologian is highly honoured in France. I only wish you were equally respected
throughout the world. If this is not the case, it is not theology that is to blame,
but the biased judgments and censorious character of certain theologians.
And, as generally happens, the iniquities of the few are what counts.   20

    Could anything have been less appropriate than for the Carthusian
Cousturier to compose such a violent attack upon me, when he ought to have
been calming the fury of others with his own gentleness? Whatever I do, I
do conscientiously. Cousturier should have used his pen against Luther and
his friends, not against me – though I have regretted more than once that I   25
answered his attack.[2] I do not care for his style, although he has with him an
ungrateful ne'er-do-well whom I once educated and supported when he was
a starving student and whose help he employs to achieve a more polished
diction.[3] But I am at a loss to identify those ideas of Cousturier's which have

* * * * *

1679
1 Cf Ep 1642:33–4. In Ep 1620:76–7) Erasmus had stated that the unfair and incompetent attacks on him by Josse Clichtove and Pierre Cousturier had undermined his own trust in the judgment of the Paris theologians.
2 See Ep 1658 n7. Erasmus may have regretted his decision to reply to Cousturier's initial attack by publishing his *Apologia in Petrum Sutorem*, but he continued to exchange controversial tracts with this despised antagonist until
  1529.
3 The identity of this 'ne'er-do-well' (*nebulo*) is obscure. Allen (23n) suggests that
  this former friend may have been the Swiss-born humanist Ludovicus Carinus, but judging from what is known of Carinus' religious views, personal

found favour with theologians. I believe the whole work was fabricated by   30
one or two people without the knowledge of the theologians. For there are
always people who delight in such melodramas and find pleasure in the
folly of others.

As for Oecolampadius, you write as though his departure from true
religion is to be blamed on languages and letters.[4] Those who are inter-   35
ested in these subjects are now indicted as revolutionaries, although the notion that a knowledge of languages and literature is part of the discipline
of theology is very ancient. What is new is the application to theology of
the logic-chopping of sophists like Aristotle and Averroes and Scotus (who
added some thorny subtleties of his own to the system of the pagans).[5] It is   40

* * * * *

relationships, and movements during this period, this identification seems
doubtful. See Peter Bietenholz 'Carinus' in CEBR I 266–8. Since Cousturier was
evidently no longer prior of the Carthusian house of Preize (near Troyes),
which he administered in 1523–5, and did not become prior of Notre-Dame-
du-Parc in Maine until 1531, even the phrase 'whom he has with him' is not a
very helpful clue to the person's identity. It seems plausible that some Carthusian with a humanistic background was meant, but even this is by no means
certain, since Cousturier was in close touch with secular theologians like Béda.

4 Though not mentioning Oecolampadius by name, Béda's letter of 21 October
1525 (Ep 1642) does directly charge that the study of Greek and other 'liberal studies' had led directly to the eucharistic heresies of Oecolampadius,
Zwingli, and other Swiss and south German humanists. These men openly
admired Erasmus' biblical and patristic scholarship, and Oecolampadius and
Conradus Pellicanus had assisted in his research in the preceding decade. This
put Erasmus in a difficult position, which no doubt helps to explain the hostility to both Oecolampadius and Pellicanus expressed in his published correspondence of this period. Erasmus' opinion of Oecolampadius was complex.
He acknowledged his great learning and even the persuasive power of his arguments in favour of his eucharistic views, but he consistently held that the
prior decision of the church on this question must outweigh them. On Erasmus' relations with both men see the references to many letters of 1525 in Ep
1670 n6.

5 In other words, the rationalism of 'sophists' like Aristotle, the Arabic commentator Averroës, and the scholastic theologian John Duns Scotus represents
unsound innovation in theology, while the humanist biblical scholars, though
accused of being revolutionary innovators, are merely returning to the sound
old theology of the Latin and Greek Fathers. Cf Erasmus' negative judgment
of the scholastics in an earlier letter to Béda, Ep 1581:92–5, 590–1, 646–7, 651–
7. The last-mentioned passage presents them not only as unsound innovators
but also as ephemeral authorities whose reputation varied according to current academic fashion, especially at the University of Paris itself. On his general hostility to scholasticism, see Epp 1672 n14, 1687 n17. Erasmus' special

a fine principle indeed if a man renders himself liable to a charge of heresy because he complains about a theologian who has injured him and takes pleasure in the knowledge of languages and polite letters!

I would never have been offended by your annotations,[6] whether they were fair or not, if you had sent them to me. But instead you circulated them 45 in Paris with a nasty preface, which read like the report of a censor. Your labours would have been no help to me but for the fact that a chance copy was delivered to me here. Nevertheless, even this I took in good part, for I thought your intentions were sincere, even if your language was barbaric, and I would rather be struck by a friend than flattered by an enemy. I do not 50 understand what you mean when you talk about vile friendships that make the judgment blind.[7] For I count Baer among my regular friends.[8] That my little book *De esu carnium interdicto* is not as profane as some people think is proved by the fact that it caused a great commotion among the Lutherans.[9]

* * * * *

animus against Duns Scotus probably reflects his being taught in the Scotist tradition during his unhappy (and brief) period of theological study at Paris in the late 1490s. See Ep 64 and introduction.

6 On Béda's compilation of annotations identifying passages in Erasmus Para- phrases that he found doctrinally suspect, and on the ensuing conflict, see Epp 1664 introduction and n1, 1666 n5.

7 A reference to Béda's letter of 21 October 1525 (Ep 1642:50). The Latin text of Béda that was translated as 'thoughtless lover' in CWE 11 reads *improbe aman- tium*. Erasmus has here taken *improbe* as implying a moral flaw rather than a more general lapse of good judgment on the part of the friend blinded by affection. Béda's point is not that there is something morally wrong about the mutual regard between Erasmus and friends like Ludwig Baer, whose approval of his publications Erasmus cites against critics, but that because friends like Baer are favourably disposed towards Erasmus they fail to detect the dangerous meanings that Béda himself finds in Erasmus' publications.

8 See Ep 1674 n17.

9 This short work suggesting that the church hierarchy might be wise to re- lax the laws on fasting and other disciplinary requirements gravely offended traditionalists like Béda and Cousturier, despite Erasmus' insistence that any relaxation of discipline should come about only by authority of the hierar- chy and not through open defiance and popular agitation (as was currently happening at Basel, Zürich, and other places). On the background, purpose, and nature of Erasmus' treatise, see the introduction by Cornelis Augustijn to his critical edition of the text in ASD IX-1 3–12. There is no evidence of pub- lications by 'Lutherans' (a group that at this period would include the Swiss and south German Reformers whom Luther and his associates were begin- ning to denounce as 'Sacramentarians') on the issue of abolishing traditional observances that had no foundation in Scripture. Erasmus' admonitions to avoid open violations of these observances and disciplinary rules were not

I have read it again and I cannot help wondering what points you and your 55
friends found so offensive. That I am not one of those who accept nothing
unless it is stated expressly in Holy Scripture should be clear enough from
my writings – if you could find the time to read them.

Berquin sent me one or two books translated into French. He took some
extracts from my work and made additions of his own, which have nothing 60
to do with me.[10] There is strong support in these parts for Karlstadt's views
on the Eucharist.[11] Capito wrote a book in German.[12] Zwingli has defended

* * * * *

wholly contrary to the position that Luther himself took in the *Invocavit* sermons preached after his return to Wittenberg from exile at the Wartburg castle
in 1522, in which he criticized the effort of his more radical followers to carry
through an abrupt break with traditional practices and instead argued for a
policy of preparing the common people for gradual abandonment of unscriptural practices through teaching and preaching; cf *The Protestant Reformation*
ed Hans J. Hillerbrand (New York 1968) 29. Nevertheless, Erasmus' admonitions against a radical break with traditional observances disappointed and
even angered people active in the agitation for reform at Basel. Hermannus
Buschius, Otto Brunfels, and Erasmus Alber expressed hostility towards Erasmus on account of his moderation and his warnings against disorderly and
drastic change; for Erasmus' reaction, see Ep 1496:87–113. Buschius, who had
been deeply involved in the defiant violation of the Lenten fast at Zürich in
1522, was reported the following summer to be at work on a tract directed
principally against Erasmus' friend and fellow moderate Ludwig Baer, according to a letter of 6 July 1522 from Claudius Cantiuncula to Bonifacius Amerbach reporting on conditions in Basel (AK II 386–7 Ep 878). Augustijn thinks it
probable that Zwingli's criticism of Erasmus' excessive mildness was directed
against *Epistola de esu carnium* (ASD IX-1 12).
10 On this injudicious young French nobleman, whose vernacular translations of
works of Erasmus sometimes interpolated passages from Lefèvre d'Etaples
and even Martin Luther and caused the judges delegate and the Parlement of
Paris to pursue him relentlessly on charges of heresy, see Epp 925:17n, 1579
n44, 1599 introduction and n1, 1692 n1.
11 Ever since Karlstadt's brief visit to Basel in October 1524 following his expulsion from Saxony on account of his radicalism, Erasmus had identified him
(not entirely accurately) as a principal source of Sacramentarian opinions on
the Eucharist. See Epp 1522:60, 1523:102–4, 1616 nn5–6, 1618 n3, 1620:94–6 and
n13, 1637 introduction, 1678 n13.
12 On Capito see Epp 459 introduction, 1674 n24. Although his Sacramentarian
preference was formed very early in his career and he was publicly known
to hold that opinion, Erasmus seems to be mistaken in asserting that he had
written a book on the topic at this early stage of the eucharistic controversy.
James M. Kittelson *Wolfgang Capito* (Leiden 1975) 148 shows, however, that in
the summer of 1525 he did send with a delegation from Strasbourg to Wittenberg a letter refuting a published letter by Luther's colleague Johann Bugen-

his position in a number of works.[13] Oecolampadius has now written on
the subject twice.[14] When his work first appeared, the magistrates ordered
it suppressed. They consulted Baer, Cantiuncula, Bonifacius Amerbach, and   65
myself individually.[15] I read the book and replied as an orthodox believer
should. So the book is not on sale here; at the same time the magistrates
forbade anything of Oecolampadius' to be printed. There is every reason
to hope that this city will stand fast for the faith. A year ago when the
magistrates were dithering over the question of the marriage of priests and   70
monks and over other matters, I gave, when I was consulted, good Christian
counsel. If you were here and could witness the growls and threats of this
sect, which has more influence than you could imagine, you would admit
that Erasmus suffers considerably for the defence of the Christian faith and

* * * * *

hagen that attacked Zwingli's Sacramentarian opinions. Although this letter
seems not to have been published, it may have circulated in manuscript, or at
least reports of its general tenor may have reached Erasmus at Basel.

13 Although Erasmus identified Karlstadt as the source of the Sacramentarian interpretation of the Eucharist, Huldrych Zwingli, the reformer of Zürich, was
its first major supporter, in close collaboration with the Basel preachers Johannes Oecolampadius and Conradus Pellicanus. Erasmus himself, who had
been very close to all three of these men, was an important source of their eucharistic doctrine (much to his embarrassment and chagrin). On the eucharistic controversy and Zwingli's role in it, see Potter 287–315; W.P. Stephens *The
Theology of Huldrych Zwingli* (Oxford 1986) 218–59; and Gottfried W. Locher
Die Zwinglische Reformation (Göttingen 1979) 283–343. These books form only a
tiny part of the enormous literature on this controversy, which led to a lasting
division among the Protestants. See also Ep 1620 n14.

14 Oecolampadius' influential statement of his eucharistic doctrines, *De genuina
verborum Domini 'Hoc est corpus meum,'* had been published the preceding year,
probably by mid-September (Ep 1616 n4). The second work here mentioned is
probably his *Antisyngramma*, published in a collection of his essays, *Apologetica
Joannis Oecolampadii* (Zürich: Christoph Froschauer, March 1526), a refutation
of the *Syngramma Suevicum* by a group of Luther's followers led by Johannes
Brenz. Erasmus must have known of its existence by the date of this letter,
even if he had not seen it. His wording, 'now ... twice,' implies that he has in
mind a very recent second work. Cf Gottfried Wilhelm Locher *Die Zwinglische
Reformation* (Göttingen 1979) 302–3. On Oecolampadius and Erasmus' opinion
of him see n4 above.

15 See Ep 1636 introduction. Baer, Cantiuncula, and Amerbach were close friends
of Erasmus and shared both his reformist goals and his doubts about the direction taken by Luther, Oecolampadius, and other Protestant leaders. In addition, Baer and Amerbach were sons of prominent local families. As a result of this advice (as Erasmus notes below), the city council forbade sale of
Oecolampadius' *De genuina verborum domini*.

that it is unfair that he should be stabbed at the same time both by the 75
Cousturiers of this world and by the followers of Luther. And you would
be all the more ready to accept this point of view if you had read the book
that Luther has just written against me, full of venom, sarcasm, sneers, and
scurrilous abuse, more violent than anything he has written about anyone
before. I am sending you part of my reply; for only one copy of Luther's 80
work was sent to me from Leipzig, and it came so late that I had scarcely
twelve days in which to read it, write my reply, and have it printed. I know
it is hurried work. But they wanted their few months of triumph before the
autumn fair.[16] Luther's book is now being translated into German[17] to make
weavers and peasants prejudiced against me. 85

I would like to be with your faculty now, for the subject is scholastic
and Luther has deliberately reduced the whole question to scholastic subtleties because he knows I am less expert in that field.[18] Baer is busy with his
own affairs, and in any case he is no longer au courant with the topics discussed in the schools. I bought myself the works of Gerson and have begun 90
to read some of them.[19] With regard to the passage in the writings of Clichtove to which you draw my attention,[20] even if I had read it a thousand times,
I would not have come to the conclusion that it had anything to do with me;
for there is nothing there that is not totally foreign to my way of thinking. I

* * * * *

16 On Erasmus' reaction to Luther's *De servo arbitrio* and his effort to produce a
speedy reply, see Ep 1667 introduction.
17 This translation, *Das der freie wille nichts sey, Antwort D. Martini Lutheri an Erasmum Roterdam*, made by Luther's disciple Justus Jonas, appeared early in 1526
(Wittenberg: Hans Lufft).
18 On Luther's dissection of Erasmus' concept of free will, see Brecht II 230–1.
19 Béda in his initial letter to Erasmus had urged Erasmus to read the works of
this influential Paris theologian of the early fifteenth century (Ep 1579:185–90).
Although Erasmus had initially made light of this suggestion (Ep 1581:90–8),
he later promised to obtain a copy and read it (Ep 1596:20–1). Gerson was still
a living presence among Paris theologians, and an edition of his works had
appeared there in 1521 (Ep 1579 n42).
20 Ep 1642:8–10; on Josse Clichtove cf also Epp 1609 and n8, 1620 n10. His book,
published at Paris in 1524, was called *Antilutherus* but had openly criticized
Erasmus' doubts about the authenticity and apostolic origin of the works of
Dionysius the Areopagite. It had also criticized Erasmus' views on mandatory
fasting, clerical celibacy, and monastic vows, though without mentioning Erasmus by name. In his later *Propugnaculum ecclesiae*, which Béda expected to be
published by February but which was in fact delayed until May 1526, Clichtove directly attacked Erasmus for publishing *De esu carnium* and *Encomium
matrimonii* (Ep 1642 n4).

realize that in this matter your testimony must be taken seriously, since, I am   95
told, you collaborate with the writer.[21] And yet I cannot bring myself to believe that he was aiming such shafts at me; if he did aim them at me, I pray he
may bring his thoughts more into line with that sobriety which is proper for a
Christian. But I am sure there is not a syllable in that work that applies to me.

I have been compelled by various reasons to put off writing about   100
the Eucharist;[22] and besides I realize how dangerous it is to write anything
at present. With regard to 'the blessed womb of the Virgin Mary,' here is
what happened.[23] The archdeacon's proctor had invited me to dinner. We
sat for two full hours. That was very unpleasant for me, for I hardly ever
sit for more than half an hour. A long-winded grace was said, padded out   105
with fragments from various sources, the *Kyrie eleison*, the *Pater noster*, the
De profundis and much else, prayers that would perhaps be more suitable
for another occasion. When I thought it had ended, I covered my head and
began to say 'Farewell' to the other guests, when quite unexpectedly the
boy added the *Et beata viscera*. I said jokingly, 'That was all we needed!' to   110
excuse myself because I had not waited and at the same time as a criticism
of the long litany. No one hates more than I those yapping critics who attack
the Virgin. You should also be aware that at that time the mass that I was
asked to compose in honour of the Virgin of Loreto[24] had just received the
approval of the archbishop of Besançon.[25]   115

* * * * *

21 This may be a reference to Béda's own claim (Ep 1609:63–70 and n8) that
   on questions involving faith, Clichtove 'will not publish the slightest thing,
   unless it has first received my scrutiny ...' But Erasmus' words here seem
   to imply an even more active role for Béda in the composition of Clichtove's
   theological works.
22 Cf Ep 1616:21 and n2. Erasmus in 1525 referred several times to his intention to write a work on the Eucharist opposing the Sacramentarian views of
   Oecolampadius, but there is no evidence that he carried this project very far
   before abandoning it, an abandonment that he almost admits here in this letter. Cf Epp 1618 introduction and lines 13–15, 1620:100–3 (addressed to Béda
   himself), 1621:31–4, 1624:33–44. He referred to the uncompleted tract again at
   Ep 1708:55–7 and n6. Cf n4 above and Ep 1670 n6.
23 This incident occurred during a visit that Erasmus made to his friend Ferry
   de Carondelet, archdeacon of Besançon, in the spring of 1524. See his lengthy
   account in Ep 1610. Béda's aloof reply (Ep 1642:73–9) implied that he had
   heard reports that Erasmus had reacted irreverently to a prayer invoking 'the
   blessed womb of the Virgin Mary.'
24 On this mass see Ep 1573.
25 The archbishop, Antoine de Vergy, granted an indulgence to anyone who made
   use of Erasmus' new liturgy within his archdiocese. Vergy belonged to one of

So much on that subject; nor is there anything more to say. Farewell.
Basel, 13 March 1526

Your sincere friend, Erasmus of Rotterdam, signed with my own
hand

1680 / To Francesco Cigalini   Basel, 15 March 1526

The recipient of this letter, Francesco Cigalini of Como, had evidently written
to Erasmus a letter (now lost) criticizing his translation of Luke 2:14, where his
Latin had departed from the traditional Vulgate text. Erasmus included this letter in his *Opus epistolarum*, no doubt because it provided a calm and reasoned
defence of his principles of translation, written in reply to a friendly critic.
Cigalini (1489–1551) was a learned physician who had a knowledge of the
biblical languages, Greek and Hebrew. He was a friend of the Como lawyer
and local antiquarian Benedetto Giovio, who several months previously had
written to Erasmus expressing his admiration but raising several questions
about the Greek text of the New Testament. See his letter (Ep 1634A) and Erasmus' reply (Ep 1635). Cigalini shared Giovio's interest in antiquarian studies
dealing with their native Como and left in manuscript a history of the town.

ERASMUS OF ROTTERDAM TO FRANCESCO CIGALINI, PHYSICIAN,
GREETING

I think good literature and the sacred texts are fortunate that physicians
too are beginning to take an interest in them. This will make you dearer
to me, although in the long list of my friends the place I have marked out   5
for you is by no means at the end. But the overwhelming demands of my
work explain why I must reply to your long disputation summarily and
with Spartan brevity.[1]

* * * * *

the highest-ranking families of the Burgundian nobility and had been elected
archbishop in 1502 at the age of fourteen. Erasmus was not personally close to
the archbishop, who did not reside in Besançon because of a dispute with the
officials of the city; but the friend at whose urging he wrote the mass, Thiébaut
Biétry, called the archbishop's attention to it and obtained the charter granting
an indulgence. Erasmus liked to cite the mass and the grant of indulgence in
order to demonstrate his reverence for the Virgin and the approval of his pious
act by a high-ranking prelate.

1680
1 Erasmus wrote this expression in Greek (λακωνικῶς).

First of all, to translate something differently is not necessarily a criticism of an earlier standard version;[2] one might as well complain of orthodox   10
commentators who introduce a different reading into a text. This is something they frequently do, commenting on both readings without characterizing one as inferior. Secondly, I had undertaken in the work in question to translate the Greek manuscripts, not to correct them, and in fact in not a few
places I prefer the Latin translation to the reading in the Greek. It would   15
have been an impertinence on my part, however, to put myself forward as

* * * * *

2 This is the general line of defence frequently adopted by Erasmus when anyone questioned his departure from the traditional Latin text. Allen notes in his introduction to this letter that Erasmus' treatment of Luke 2:14 had already been challenged by Edward Lee, a far less friendly critic (cf n6 below); that his notes on this particular passage grew with every edition of the Annotations to the New Testament; and that the explanation given here was similar to his discussion in the edition of 1527, on which he was working at the date of this letter. Erasmus' humanistic predecessors had been critical of the tendency of medieval translators from Greek into Latin to translate word for word, a procedure which, they contended, often obscured the real meaning of the text. Translating for sense rather than literally had ancient antecedents, including Cicero and St Jerome; but Jerome made an exception for translations of Scripture, and from the time of Boethius (sixth century) medieval Christian translators overwhelmingly favoured a strictly literal procedure, at least for theological and philosophical texts, largely out of fear of transforming their translations of biblical and other religious texts from simple translations into interpretive commentaries. The great teacher who first established the study of Greek securely in Renaissance Italy, Manuel Chrysoloras, was critical of this method and favoured reformulating the original author's idea in a way that suited the new language; Leonardo Bruni, his most talented pupil, also championed a less literal procedure in his treatise *De recta interpretatione* (published in Leonardo Bruni *Humanistisch-philosophische Schriften* ed Hans Baron [Leipzig 1928; repr Wiesbaden 1969] 81–96). The same viewpoint appears in the (unpublished) works of the mid-fifteenth-century Italian humanist and biblical translator Giannozzo Manetti, who upheld the humanistic method of translating *ad sensum* (according to the meaning) rather than the medieval practice of translating *ad verbum* (word for word), though he hedged his statement in order to avoid the appearance of attacking traditional scriptural translations. On Chrysoloras and Bruni see L.D. Reynolds and N.G. Wilson *Scribes and Scholars: A Guide to the Transmission of Greek and Latin Literature*, 2nd ed (Oxford 1974) 131, and Charles Trinkaus *In Our Image and Likeness: Humanity and Divinity in Humanist Thought* (Chicago 1970) II 595–8. On the development of Erasmus' concept of a more free, less literal, type of translation, see Erika Rummel *Erasmus as Translator of the Classics* (Toronto 1985), especially 23–8.

a translator and then to translate something other than the Greek text, especially when there was agreement among the manuscripts; and it would have been more impertinent still if I had done this while placing the Greek text side by side with the Latin. This would immediately have shown me up, even if my interpretation of the Greek had not done so. You will see this confusion frequently in the translation of the commentaries on the Epistles of Paul that are falsely attributed to Athanasius, though they are the work of Theophylact.[3] Here the translator uses the text of the Latin Vulgate,[4] but the interpretation does not always square with it.

With regard to the passage in question, I admit that the preposition ἐν is missing from some of the Greek manuscripts, though the better ones have it.[5] But in a translation I could give only one version. So of the two I

* * * * *

3 In the notes to the first (1516) and second (1518–19) editions of his New Testament Erasmus had accepted the traditional misattribution of these commentaries to Athanasius but usually referred to its author as 'Vulgarius' (that is, the Bulgarian). In 1518, however, he found decisive proof that the attribution to Athanasius was incorrect and that the true author of the commentary was the Bulgarian patriarch Theophylact (died c 1108), archbishop of Ochrida, who of course used the Greek text as the basis for his commentary. See CWE 56 15 n25, and cf Erika Rummel *Erasmus' Annotations on the New Testament* (Toronto 1986) 36. Although references to 'Vulgarius' (and even to Athanasius, an attribution he already suspected) still appeared in the second edition of his New Testament (1519), from the third edition (1522) on, Erasmus systematically changed all references to the commentary so that it was correctly attributed to Theophylact.

4 The context confirms that *vulgatam aeditionem Latinorum* refers to the traditional Latin Bible, not to a Latin edition of Theophylact's commentary. Erasmus justifies his departure from the Vulgate text of Paul's Epistles by pointing out that if the Vulgate text were used, there would be an obvious discrepancy between it and the accompanying Greek text. He finds exactly such discord between the biblical quotations used in the Latin translation of Theophylact's commentary by Christopher Porsena and the interpretation given by the commentator, the Greek-speaking bishop Theophylact.

5 The passage is Luke 2:14. AV translates the disputed portion 'Glory to God in the highest, and on earth peace, good will towards men.' The Vulgate reads: *Gloria in altissimis Deo et in terra pax hominibus bonae voluntatis* 'Glory to God in the highest and peace on earth to men of good will.' The Greek manuscripts have: Δόξα ἐν ὑψίστοις Θεῷ, καὶ ἐπὶ γῆς εἰρήνη ἀνθρώποις (variant reading ἐν ἀνθρώποις) εὐδοκία (variant reading εὐδοκίας). Modern New Testament editions confirm Erasmus' statement that some manuscripts omit the ἐν before ἀνθρώποις but show that the preposition appears in the best textual witnesses; see, for example, *The Gospel According to St Luke* edited by the American and British Committees of the International Greek New Testament (Oxford 1984) part 1 (chapters 1–12) 40n (at Luke 2:14).

chose the one that appealed to me more and was supported by the better
manuscripts and the Greek commentators. Other matters had to be left for   30
discussion in the Annotations. If you had read the response which I made
to the critics of this passage five years ago,[6] you would have found either a
satisfactory answer to your question or more material to support your own
interpretation.

As for your remarks about the peace of the righteous, which is the   35
handmaiden of justice, you and I are at peace on this – except that the word
for 'peace' in the apostolic letters generally means 'reconciliation.' When
people are received into the communion of the church, one speaks of the
'giving of peace.' It is in this sense that we interpret Paul's salutations, which
call repeatedly for 'grace and peace.'[7] If you read my Paraphrase on Luke,   40
you will see that I had already reached the same conclusion as you.[8] Since
there was no sin in heaven that could destroy friendship, but only praise
and thanksgiving, the angels sing 'Glory to God in the highest,' but because
he who brings peace to all, both in heaven and on earth, came down among
men to abolish the sin of the world, they sing of 'peace on earth.'   45

Up to this point you and I are in agreement. But two difficulties remain, one about the reading of the text, which makes three clauses out of
two, and the other about the preposition $\dot{\epsilon}\nu$. You prove nothing by citing
the rather poor Latin translation of Origen,[9] except that it is clear from the

* * * * *

6 In his second *Responsio* to his critic Edward Lee (Antwerp: Michaël Hillen,
   April 1520) LB IX 146–50.
7 This formulaic bidding of 'grace and peace' as a salutation appears in all of the
   letters attributed to Paul (Rom 1:7, 1 Cor 1:3, 2 Cor 1:3, Gal 1:3, Eph 1:2, Phil
   1:2, Col 1:2, 1 Thess 1:1, 2 Thess 1:2, 1 Tim 2 ['Grace, mercy, and peace'], 2 Tim
   2 ['Grace, mercy, and peace'], Titus 1:4, Philem 3) but not in Hebrews, which
   Erasmus, in accord with modern textual critics, did not attribute to Paul (but
   cf Heb 13:20). The same formula appears in nearly all of the other apostolic
   letters: 1 Pet 1:2, 2 Pet 1:2; in variant form ('Grace, mercy, and peace') in 2
   John and Jude, as a closing benediction in 3 John 15, and even in Rev 1:4.
8 See LB VII 299.
9 The surviving Latin translation is by St Jerome, who appears to have selected
   thirty-nine of Origen's Greek homilies on the Gospel of St Luke (the original number of homilies is unknown) and to have translated them into Latin
   in response to a request from his female disciples Paula and Eustochium.
   Only fragments of the original Greek text survive, including some homilies
   that Jerome did not translate. Origen also produced a commentary on Luke,
   but only a few fragments in Greek survive. Thus Erasmus must be referring
   to Jerome's translation of the homilies on St Luke, though his negative comment on the quality of the translation runs contrary to his usual high opinion

interpretation itself what he read in his text. There is nothing relevant in the   50
passage cited from the first book of Origen *Against Celsus*.[10] I do not know
where you found the passage you quoted from Origen, for we have nothing
of Origen's on the tenth chapter of Matthew.[11] The homilies on Luke that
go under his name seem to be the work of someone else.[12] In any case the
passage you cite tells in my favour in so far as it reads 'towards men' with   55
the addition of the preposition and once uses the phrase 'the peace of good
will.' You should take note of this point.

   Now let me consider the conclusions you draw from Chrysostom, however the passage is translated. Nothing about the division of phrases is to be
found there, and you are responsible for the reading 'to men of good will.'   60
But you ought to know that these words were added by the translator. The
Greek codex has the following: 'How was it that the angels said, "Glory to
God in the highest and on earth peace"? And how did all the prophets proclaim the same good news etc?'[13] So much for relying on books translated
into another language! But to show that Chrysostom had the same reading   65
as that in my version, I shall cite a passage from his comments on the Epistle
to the Colossians, in which he explains the words of Paul 'Whether they be
things on earth or things in heaven': 'For this reason, when we give thanks,

* * * * *

of Jerome. On the homilies and commentary and their translation by Jerome
see the introduction by Max Rauer to his edition of the Latin homilies and
Greek fragments in *Die griechischen christlichen Schriftsteller der ersten Jahrhunderte* 49 *Origenes Werke* 9, 2nd ed (Berlin 1959) vii–xx. The first edition of
Jerome's translation of these homilies had been published by the Paris theologian Jacques Merlin (Paris: Jean Petit and Josse Bade 1512). The passage here
under discussion (Luke 2:14) reads, in Jerome's Latin, 'Gloria in excelsis Deo,
et super terram pax in hominibus bonae voluntatis' (homily 13 ed Rauer 77:8–
10). A Greek fragment of this text survives (ibidem) but would not have been
known to Erasmus. The Latin text of the homilies is also in PG 13 1799–1902.
10 Since the letter to which Erasmus is replying is lost, it is impossible to identify
   which passage of *Against Celsus* he had cited.
11 Only eight books from the middle of Origen's commentary on St Matthew
   survive from the original twenty-five. The surviving Greek commentary begins at Matt 13:36, and the ancient Latin commentary (except for a few fragments) begins at Matt 16:13. See *Die griechischen christlichen Schriftsteller der
   ersten Jahrhunderte* 40 *Origenes Werke* ed Erich Klostermann and Ernst Benz
   (Berlin 1935) vii, 1, 80. The text is also in PG 13 836–1600.
12 This is not the opinion of modern patristic scholarship, which does attribute
   the homilies to Origen and the surviving Latin translation to Jerome (see n9
   above).
13 *Commentarius in sanctum Matthaeum evangelistam* 35.1 (on Matt 10:34) PG 57 405

we say, "Glory to God in the highest and on earth peace, good will towards
men." "Behold," he says, "henceforth even men appeared well pleasing to   70
him." What is "good will"? It is "reconciliation." The heavens are no longer
a dividing wall.'[14] Moreover, Theophylact's reading and interpretation are
the same as mine; for he wishes the peace that is spoken of to be understood as the Son of God, of whom Paul writes in Ephesians 2: 'He himself
is our peace who hath made both one,' and he adds these words: 'The Son   75
of God, then, has become this peace upon the earth and good will among
men; that is the reconciliation of God.'[15] I have no doubt that I could produce further supporting evidence if there were more Greek books here. But
I think I have satisfied you on the reading and punctuation of the Greek,
from which, as a conscientious translator, I could not depart, especially since   80
my version is no criticism of the standard Latin text.

I must now say something about the difficulties that remain. 'How is
it,' you ask, 'that none of the old Latin Fathers mentioned this reading?' I
believe they read the passage the same way as I do and that their opinion
does not differ from mine, however different their words may sound. Here   85
I shall not introduce any forced or far-fetched argument: common sense
will support what I am going to say. There is no need for your suggestion
that εὐδοκία is used in the dative corresponding to the genitive of the Latin
text, which has the same sense as an ablative: we say, for example, *mulier
egregia forma* ['a woman with great beauty'] and *mulier egregiae formae* ['a   90
woman of great beauty']. But there is no similar construction in Greek.[16]
The Greek dative corresponds to a use of the Latin ablative that some people
wish to define as the seventh case, signifying manner or instrument, as in
the expressions ἐπάταξέ με ξίφει, that is, 'he struck me with a sword' and
ἐδέξατό με μεγάλῃ εὐφροσύνῃ, that is, 'he received me with great kindness.' So   95
your suggestion cannot stand. First, I have demonstrated on this passage that
εὐδοκία is not the same as ἀγαθὸν θέλημα ['kindly intent']; so it does not refer
to man, but to God. Jerome thinks the word was an innovation of the authors

* * * * *

14 *In epistolam ad Colossenses commentarius* 3.4 (on Col 1:20) PG 62 322. Cf Eph 2:14,
   cited also by Theophylact in his commentary on Luke 2:14 (see next note).
15 *Enarratio in evangelium Lucae* (on Luke 2:14) PG 123 724. Cf nn3, 4 above. Theophylact cites Eph 2:14.
16 Presumably Cigalini's letter had suggested that we should read εὐδοκίᾳ (with
   a subscript) as the equivalent of a Latin descriptive ablative having the same
   sense as the descriptive genitive of the Vulgate (*bonae voluntatis*) in the biblical text. Erasmus correctly points out that there is no such construction as a
   descriptive dative in Greek; the dative in Greek, when it corresponds to the
   Latin ablative, has an instrumental or modal sense.

of the Septuagint to express their meaning more precisely, namely the freely
given favour of God towards us.[17] This concept is sometimes expressed by   100
the Latin translator with the word *beneplacitum*, as at 1 Corinthians 10: 'But
to many of them God did not show his favour' [εὐδόκησεν][18] and Psalm 68: 'It
is the time of thy favour [εὐδοκίας], O Lord.'[19] But why cite these examples
when this expression is to be found everywhere in the Bible?

So the three clauses all refer to the same idea. When Christ was born   105
on the earth, the time had come when God had decided to reconcile the
world to himself through his Son. In recognition of the wondrous goodness
of God the angels sang 'Glory to God in the highest,' for nothing revealed
more clearly the benevolence of God than his giving his Son for our redemption. And since the sins of the world would be taken away by his free gift,   110
the angels added 'and peace on earth,' for the barrier that separated heaven
and earth had now been torn down. But lest anyone should think that it
was a human peace that was being promised or a peace earned by human
efforts, they added 'good will among men.' This clause must be taken in
apposition to the preceding, as though someone had asked, 'Whence comes   115
this new peace on earth?' and the reply was given: 'This is no ordinary
peace, nor is it a reward for human merit. This peace, which frees us from
our sins, is nothing less than the favour of God, freely offered, towards his
chosen people.' Christ is given the name of 'peace,' just as he is called our
'righteousness' and our 'sin,' since he is the bringer of peace, and our jus-   120
tifier, and the victim offered for our sin.[20] The Hebrews seem to like this
idiom, although Latin also says, *hic est mea mors* ['he is the death of me'] and
hic est mea vita ['he is my life']. The phrase *in hominibus* ['among men'] does
not refer to 'peace,' but should be taken with εὐδοκία in the sense 'favour
towards men.' So in another passage the Father seems to be offering a com-   125

* * * * *

17 *Commentariorum in epistolam ad Ephesios libri tres* 1.5 PL 26 478–9
18 1 Cor 10:5. The Vulgate text of this verse is: *sed non in pluribus eorum benepla-*
citum est Deo; AV has 'for with many of them God was not well pleased.'
19 Ps 68:14 Vulg / 69:13 AV. Erasmus' quotations from both Corinthians and
Psalms show that the Greek text used εὐδοκία for 'favour.'
20 1 Cor 1:30 ('our righteousness'); 2 Cor 5:21 ('our sin'). For 1 Cor 1:30, AV reads:
'But of him are ye in Christ Jesus, who of God is made unto us wisdom,
and righteousness, and sanctification, and redemption'; Vulgate reads: 'Ex ipso
autem vos estis in Christo Jesu, qui factus est nobis sapientia a Deo, et justitia,
et sanctificatio, et redemptio.' For 2 Cor 5:21, AV reads: 'For he hath made him
to be sin for us, who knew no sin; that we might be made the righteousness
of God in him'; Vulgate reads: 'Eum qui non noverat peccatum, pro nobis
peccatum fecit, ut nos efficeremur justitia Dei in ipso.'

mentary on the song of the angels²¹ when he says 'This is my beloved Son in whom I have shown favour' (ἐν ᾧ εὐδόκησα),²² for through him he begins to show favour [εὐδοκεῖν] towards us when we are grafted on to Christ by means of baptism and become with him the sons of God and brothers of Jesus Christ. The expressions 'in whom I have shown favour' and 'good will   130 towards men' are similar in meaning.

I have shown that the division into three clauses is found in the Greek and I have pointed out that the preposition ἐν is added. But even if it were not in the text, the meaning would be the same, though the style would be less smooth. I have made it clear that the peace of God is different from the   135 peace of the world, and I have shown that we get the same sense whether we read *pax bonae voluntatis* ['the peace of good will'] or *pax bona voluntas* ['peace, good will'], just as we say *urbs Roma* ['the city Rome'] and *urbs Romae* ['the city of Rome']. From which it follows that in all probability the orthodox Latin Fathers read the passage as we do and did not differ from   140 the Greek in sense, but only in the words they used.

If the clear and ample evidence that I have presented does not satisfy the brawling critics, let them follow the Vulgate, which it is not my intention to revile. Let them follow the interpretation of Bede, Lyra, and Hugo,²³

* * * * *

21 That is, the song sung by the angels to the shepherds at Christ's nativity; Luke
    2:14
22 Matt 3:17
23 Three of the most influential biblical commentators of the Middle Ages. The
    Venerable Bede, a Benedictine monk of Jarrow (b 672–3, d c 735), is best
    known for his *Ecclesiastical History of the English Nation* but wrote on many
    topics, including biblical exegesis. These exegetical works are published in
    Corpus Christianorum 118–21 and in PL 91–3. Hugo (or Hugh) of St Cher
    OP (d 1263) produced a commentary on the whole Bible, *Postilla seu com-
    mentariola iuxta quadruplicem sensum*, which was still being printed in Eras-
    mus' lifetime. Nicholas of Lyra OFM (c 1270–c 1349) was probably the most
    widely known biblical commentator of the later Middle Ages. His *Postillae
    perpetuae* were especially valuable because he had mastered the Hebrew lan-
    guage and drew on the works of Jewish commentators. Erasmus cited Bede
    as one of the standard authorities in the third edition of his New Testa-
    ment (Ep 373:38n), but in the dedication of his Paraphrase on the Epistles
    of Peter and Jude (Ep 1112:48) in 1521 he was critical of Bede's commen-
    tary. In 1501 he sought a copy of Lyra (Ep 165:13) and in 1505, though
    not wholly favourable to Lyra, cited his use of Hebrew texts of the Bible
    as justification for Lorenzo Valla's use of the Greek text in his *Annotationes
    in Novum Testamentum* (Ep 182:128–44). On Bede and Hugh of St Cher see
    Beryl Smalley *The Study of the Bible in the Middle Ages* 3rd ed (Oxford 1983)
    35–6 (on Bede), and 269–74, 295–6, 301–2, 325–6, 333–5, 357 (on Hugh).

who because of their ignorance of Greek did not understand what the word   145
εὐδοκία meant. But they should not hold it against me if I have set out the
views of Chrysostom and Theophylact, which are both reverent and well
founded, and have left everyone free to make up his own mind. I acknowledge that I am indebted to you on two counts, first, because your objections provoked me to look at the problem more carefully, and secondly, be-   150
cause you have added to the list of my friends a name that I have no reason to regret. It remains for you to place the name of Erasmus among those
whom you consider your true friends. This letter is perhaps shorter than
you would have wished, but if you knew how little spare time I have, you
would consider it prolix.   155

Basel, 15 March 1526

1681 / From Erasmus Schets   Antwerp, 17 March 1526

This letter from the Antwerp merchant who during the preceding year had become Erasmus' business agent in the Netherlands and England (Ep 1541 introduction), like virtually all correspondence concerning Erasmus' financial business, remained unprinted until the twentieth century (1904, in Förstemann /
Günther). On Schets' effort to win the favour of King John III of Portugal for
Erasmus and the reasons why Erasmus' dedication of his edition of some homilies of St John Chrysostom to the Portuguese king failed to win royal favour,
see n8 below, Ep 1800 intro, and Allen Ep 2370.

Cordial greetings, dear Master Erasmus. I wrote to you some time ago to
express my surprise at the long time your man Harst was spending in England.[1] But he has finally returned safe and sound with a letter from Alvaro
de Castro[2] advising me that I am receiving in your name from the aforementioned Harst the sum of thirty-nine *écus* and ten English nobles.[3] I shall   5

* * * * *

Smalley mentions Nicholas of Lyra, but his career came after the termi-
nal date for her study. On Lyra see *Cambridge History of the Bible* II 219,
261, 304.

1681
1 See Ep 1671:16–19, 29–31, dated 7 March. On Harst see Epp 1215 introduction,
   1575 n2, 1666 n2. His current trip to the Netherlands and England had begun
   about Christmas 1525 (Epp 1654–6).
2 Schets' agent in London; see Epp 1590 n2, 1658 n5.
3 Latin *scutatos triginta nouem cum nobilis anglicis decem.* Thirty-nine French *écus*
   au soleil were then worth £78 tournois, or £8 9s 0d sterling or £12 7s 0d groot

see to it that this money is transferred to you at the best possible rates; and to ensure that it reaches you more quickly and with the least trouble, I have already instructed my agents at Frankfurt to hand over to Froben at the next fair seventy-two gold florins for your account.[4] This is the legal equivalent of the sum in question. Harst reported to me that he had spoken to   10 Pieter Gillis about your money deposited with him.[5] Gillis said that he had arranged through his brother Frans for 600 gold florins[6] to be handed over to Froben on your behalf at the forthcoming Frankfurt fair. Pieter himself mentioned the same figure to me and explained that he could not arrange for payment of the rest of the money because of the shortness of the time   15 before the Frankfurt fair, for he had no one who could conveniently pick up and deliver the money in so short a time. I told Pieter that, if he had any money he wished delivered to you, he should give it to me as soon as possible; I promised to look after it and have it delivered to you at Basel or anywhere else that suited your convenience. He agreed to do so. If he does,   20 I too shall do what I said.

Karl Harst has gone to Mechelen – for the court is there – but he did not tell me his business. He promised to return before setting off home.

* * * * *

Flemish; ten English gold nobles, presumably angel-nobles (6s 8d), were worth £3 6s 8d sterling, or £4 16s 8d groot Flemish, or £30 10s 0d tournois (at 61s per noble). See Richet 377–96. Together, therefore, these two lots of gold coins were worth £11 15s 8d sterling, or £17 3s 8d groot Flemish, or £108 10s 0d tournois. If the latter were English rose-nobles or 'ryals,' then worth 10s 0d sterling each, this sum would have amounted to £13 9s 0d sterling in total; but the monetary conversions in the following note indicate that they were indeed angel-nobles.

4 Latin *septuaginta duo florenos aureos*, Rhenish gold florins (Rheingulden). This sum was then worth £11 14s 0d sterling, or £17 14s 0d groot Flemish, or £108 tournois. Thus, taking into account foreign exchange costs, Schets was commendably accurate and just in calculating that these 72 Rhenish florins were equivalent to the sum of 39 *écus au soleil* and 10 angel-nobles.

5 Gillis had managed Erasmus' financial affairs in the Netherlands until Schets replaced him in 1525. The present letter and Ep 1654 represent the effective closing of Erasmus' account with Gillis and arrangements for the transfer of the rather substantial balance due to Erasmus, using the Lenten fair at Frankfurt and the travel of Gillis' brother Frans to effect the delivery of funds. See Epp 1654 nn5, 6, 1671 n6.

6 Latin *sexcentos florenos aureos*, Rhenish gold florins. This sum was worth about £97 10s 0d sterling (the equivalent of 3,900 days' wages for an Oxford master carpenter, or 17 years and 7 months' wage income), £147 10s 0d groot Flemish (the equivalent of 3,540 days' wages or 16 years and 1 month's wage income for an Antwerp master carpenter), or £900 tournois.

With regard to the linen cloth,[7] the business was attended to by Pieter Gillis without my knowledge. If he had not done so, I should have been glad to do what I could to get the best price for the purchase.

I was upset to hear there is some doubt about the payment of your pension. I wish the princes of this world were as interested in learning and good literature as they are in buffooneries and follies of every kind! If they were, you would have pensions flowing in from all sides without threat of loss.

A thought has just occurred to me which you ought to reflect on. You have dedicated several of your works to kings and to many of the princes of this world. I wonder why you have not dedicated anything so far to the king of Portugal,[8] who is an outstanding Christian prince and a man of exceptional benevolence and kindness, most generous towards those who serve him, and particularly generous to those who are able, by their words and writings, to make known the blessings of the gospel, for respect for religion is deeply rooted in that country. The king, who is still a young man, has made these qualities his own, as is natural for the son of so excellent a father as Manuel.[9] In the past I had many intimate conversations with his

* * * * *

7 Erasmus had requested purchase of a specific type of Dutch linen in his letter of 24 December 1525 to Schets (Ep 1654). In Ep 1671 Schets reported that he had deferred making the purchase because of Karl Harst's absence in England since he wanted to discuss with Harst precisely what sort of linen Erasmus wanted.

8 Schets was eager to use not only his business connections with Portugal but also his connections at the court of King John III (1521–57) in order to promote Erasmus' reputation and prosperity, since the young king, like his father Manuel I, was favourable to humanistic studies. A year later, Erasmus did dedicate to him *Chrysostomi lucubrationes*, a collection of Latin translations of St John Chrysostom's works. The dedication is Ep 1800. Contrary to Schets' assurances, there was no response from the king. In fact, though Schets had the presentation copy bound and dispatched to Portugal (Ep 1849), Erasmus eventually learned that the volume had never been presented, apparently because courtiers feared that the criticism of the Portuguese spice monopoly in Erasmus' dedicatory epistle might offend the king. Cf Elizabeth Feist Hirst in CEBR II 240–1; Marcel Bataillon 'Erasme et la cour du Portugal' in his *Etudes sur le Portugal au temps de l'humanisme* (Coimbra 1952) 48–99; and Allen Ep 2370.

9 Manuel I, king of Portugal 1495–1521, father of John III, had presided over the foundation of his country's colonial empire in Africa and Asia and had also become an enthusiastic patron of humanistic learning and the fine arts. There is no evidence showing just how Schets gained the intimate personal contact with him that he claims in the following sentence.

late Majesty and I know that every year he spent large sums of money in pursuit of his love of learning, particularly theological learning. King John has his court filled with eminent scholars;[10] he has a learned council and a

* * * * *

10 King Manuel I had developed an interest in history but in general had been attracted more strongly to the arts than to humanistic studies. The identity of the 'eminent scholars' at the court of his son John III in 1526 is not very clear, since the most famous Portuguese humanist of this generation, Damião de Gois (1502–74), was still a young courtier active in diplomatic and other work for the king, principally in northern Europe as secretary of the Portuguese factory (the India House) in Antwerp from 1523. Though he became friendly with the Flemish humanist Cornelis Grapheus there and probably developed a genuine interest in humanistic learning, he did not abandon his political career for scholarship until 1531, when he became a student, first at the University of Louvain, and then, after extensive travels in eastern and central Europe (during which he visited Erasmus at Freiburg in 1533 and again in 1534), at the University of Bologna. Thus at the date of this letter Gois was neither at the Portuguese court nor in any real sense a scholar, though since he was in Antwerp he could have known Schets. In 1527, King John did begin a long series of actions to stimulate scholarship in Portugal, beginning with the endowment of fifty scholarships for Portuguese students at the Collège de Sainte-Barbe in Paris, and culminating in the foundation at Coimbra of a College of the arts modelled on the humanistic Trilingual College at Louvain. He appointed a group of humanist masters recruited from the distinguished Collège de Guyenne at Bordeaux, led by another Portuguese humanist, André de Gouveia, to the faculty of this new institution. But these steps did not take place until 1546, a decade after Erasmus' death. Hence although it is clear that under Manuel I and John III humanist influences were affecting education and literature in Portugal, the identity of these 'eminent scholars' at the court of John III remains vague. Most of King John's decisive moves as a patron of humanist learning came only after Erasmus' death, and most of the Portuguese humanists whose names are known were still studying abroad in Italy, Spain, France, or at Louvain, at the date of this letter. In 1521, the king did employ Ayres Barbosa, a humanist who had studied with the Florentine humanist Angelo Poliziano and then had spent twenty years teaching Latin and Greek at Salamanca, as tutor to the princes Afonso and Henrique, younger brothers of the king. Perhaps this appointment shaped Schets' idea of humanism at the court, or perhaps he had some advance word of the decision to found the fellowships at Paris. But until the 1530s there is not much evidence that the Portuguese ruler was particularly interested in humanism; and while there were some significant actions at that later date, by mid-century the king had come under the influence of conservative critics of humanism who feared Erasmian influence as a possible source of heresy. On Portuguese humanism in general, see A.H. de Oliveira Marques *History of Portugal* 2nd ed (New York 1976) 190–200, and in greater detail, *História de Portugal* eds Damião Peres and Eleutério Cerdeira IV (Barcelos 1932) 263–74; Theophilo Braga *Historia da Universidade de*

younger brother, Master Fernando,[11] whose only delight is in learning and   45
the humanities. I know that nothing you do for the king and his people will
go unrewarded. So what I am suggesting is in your own interest. I have
very close friends and intimate acquaintances at court who belong to the
inner circle of the king's confidants. If any opportunity arises to forward
your interests there, I am always at your disposal, whether in that country   50
or here at home.

There is an ambassador of the king of Portugal at the Roman curia, a
most distinguished and scholarly man, a member of the king's family, by
name Dom Martinho of Portugal,[12] who has expectations that two bishoprics
will soon be vacant in that kingdom. Some time ago he sent a letter to Dom   55
Rui Fernandes,[13] the king's agent and representative in these parts, asking
for information about your place of residence. At the time when he left his
country, he remarked that he was more interested in seeing you than the
sacred basilica of the apostles. He is a good scholar with a deep love for
the humanities and has such a high regard for you that he will not permit   60
anyone to be preferred to you. He feels he will be unlucky indeed if he
does not see you before he returns home, and he will count himself the
most fortunate man from all of Portugal if, when he arrives home, he is able

* * * * *

Coimbra 4 vols (Lisbon 1892–1902) I 335–6; and Joseph A. Klucas 'Erasmus and
Erasmians on Education in Sixteenth-Century Portugal' *Erasmus of Rotterdam
Society Yearbook* 1 (1981) 69–88.

11 Fernando (1507–34), third surviving son of Manuel I and brother of the reign-
ing monarch, was duke of Guarda and Francoso and was known for his interest
in letters, especially history and early chronicles.

12 Dom Martinho (d 1547) was Portuguese ambassador at Rome in 1525–7, endured along with other members of the diplomatic community the looting of
the city by the Spanish army in 1527, returned to Portugal and represented
his king on a mission to Spain in 1528, also bearing a message from the pope
to the emperor. Later in his career he became archbishop of Funchal in the
Madeiras and, later still, bishop of Silva. Bataillon 'Erasme et la cour du Portugal' (n8 above) 60–70 identifies him as an illegitimate son of Dom Alonso
de Portugal, bishop of Evora. At this period he was known as a strong advocate of a peaceful settlement between the pope and the emperor, with a private inclination to favour the imperialist-Spanish side. His reluctance in 1535
to pursue John III's order to secure papal authorization of an inquisition in
Portugal frustrated his hopes of becoming a cardinal and left him politically
out of favour after his return from Rome.

13 Portuguese factor and consul at Antwerp. The painter Albrecht Dürer received
several presents from him during his journey to the Netherlands in 1520–1; cf
Albrecht Dürer: Diary of His Journey to the Netherlands, 1520–1521, trans William
Martin Conway (Cambridge 1889; repr Greenwich, CT 1971).

to say that he saw and spoke with you. So please, try to find the time to write
him a note, say something nice about him, and tell him that you heard of his   65
reputation from Rui and me; for in this way you will win the friendship of
a most distinguished and learned man who is in a position to do you a good
turn and to be very helpful to you in the kingdom of Portugal. Please send
me a letter to be forwarded to him from here. I shall urge Rui Fernandes
to write to Dom Martinho to add wings to your reputation.[14] Farewell, dear   70
Erasmus. I wish you every success and good fortune.

> Antwerp, 17 March 1526
> Your most devoted servant, Erasmus Schets
> To that incomparable scholar, Master Erasmus of Rotterdam. In Basel

1682 / From Erasmus Schets   Antwerp, 18 March 1526

This letter was written shortly after the preceding one, largely to add the bad
news that Karl Harst's visit to the Burgundian court at Mechelen had failed to
secure payment of Erasmus' pension as an imperial councillor. On the unpaid
pension, see n1 below. It repeats news of Schets' effort to arrange transfer to
Basel of a large sum of Erasmus' money left in the custody of Pieter Gillis,
who had managed Erasmus' financial affairs until Schets took over in 1525.
It also repeats Schets' advice that Erasmus should seek the favour of the king
of Portugal by dedicating a work to him. The letter survived in manuscript
among Erasmus' papers at Basel and was first published by Allen in 1926.

Cordial greetings. I wrote you all my news, Master Erasmus, in another
letter. Karl Harst has now returned from the court. He told me unhappily
that he had not been able to make any progress with your affairs. They
are reluctant to pay the pension, although they do not scruple to scatter
money around in all directions on expenditures that perhaps will prove less   5
valuable. Unless you come yourself, I am afraid you will slip from the list.
The emperor gives orders from Spain for many things to be done here, but
his orders are not obeyed or are obeyed late.[1]

* * * * *

14 *Adagia* IV viii 86

1682
1 Erasmus and those who looked after his interests at court in the Netherlands
  were often frustrated by the tendency of officials there to delay indefinitely
  their compliance with orders favouring Erasmus sent from the distant imperial court in Spain, not only regarding the arrears that Erasmus claimed on

You will get a verbal report from Harst of my suspicions of Pieter Gillis.[2] He assures me that he ordered his brother Frans to pay 600 florins to Froben at Frankfurt.[3] I am afraid it may not happen. But you will find out from Froben. If he has not done what he says, you could write Pieter a stern letter and tell him that you and I have made an arrangement whereby all monies are to be paid to me, and I am to receive them in your name; he should, therefore, pay the money to me. In this way I shall be able to put pressure on him to pay.

Farewell, Erasmus, and please reply to my earlier letter. I shall be happy if only you will give me hope that you will dedicate something to the king of Portugal.[4] He is not afraid to pursue and conquer barbarian peoples, advancing with his arms as far as the Indies and spreading the Christian faith before the eyes of the conquered. We know that among the Indians many thousands of heathen barbarians have embraced the faith of Christ.[5] I mention this again so as to fix more firmly in your mind the point I made in my earlier letter. Farewell again.

From Antwerp, 18 March 1526

Your friend Erasmus Schets, who is ready to help you in whatever way he can

To that eminent scholar in sacred letters, Erasmus of Rotterdam. In Basel

1683 / To Hieronymus Emser   Basel, [c 19 March 1526]

Emser, secretary and chaplain to the strongly Catholic Duke George of Saxony, was widely known both as a humanist and as an antiLutheran controver-

* * * * *

his pension but also regarding efforts to silence attacks on Erasmus by conservative theologians and monks at Louvain and elsewhere. On the difficulties over the pension, see Epp 1380 introduction, 1700 n3.

2 Although Schets' taking charge of Erasmus' financial affairs relieved Gillis of responsibilities he had found burdensome and was carried out amicably, a certain tension between the new agent and the old is evident, especially when transfer of funds held in Gillis' custody was in question, as in this case. Cf Epp 1541, 1654, 1681, 1696, the last of which shows that during his trip to Frankfurt Frans Gillis paid over only four hundred florins of the amount in question. For the final clearing of Gillis' account with Erasmus, see Epp 1681 n5, 1750 n4.

3 Latin *sexcentos florenos*, Rhenish gold florins; see Ep 1681 n6.

4 See Ep 1681 nn8, 10.

5 A reference to Portuguese missionary efforts in India

sialist. See Epp 553, 1551, 1561 n6, 1566. Erasmus published this letter in *Opus epistolarum.*

ERASMUS OF ROTTERDAM TO HIERONYMUS EMSER, GREETING
I am happy that you accepted my excuses for declining your invitation, but happier still to have received it in the first place. It distresses me that we share, you and I, the same problems of old age and illness, though the stone is a much crueller disease than gout. About the omission of your name, I   5
thought I had already cleared that matter up. The situation is as I described in my letter. When I was writing the *Spongia*, I knew absolutely nothing about any attack on Luther by you.[1] But even if I had known it, you should not rush to the conclusion that I dislike everyone whom I fail to mention. In any case, we live in such an age that it is sometimes quite unsafe for me   10
to set down the names of even my closest friends, so malicious are men's tongues. I wonder where your relative has been lurking all this time, for the book you sent me, along with the letter written on 10 January,[2] was delivered on 19 March.

Luther's book reached me by chance, but it came so late that I had   15
scarcely twelve days before the fair to read through all that long-winded rubbish,[3] review my own *Diatribe*,[4] write a reply, correct the fair copies, and

* * * * *

1683
1 Although Emser had been actively opposing Luther since 1519 and had probably published as many works against him as any of his other critics, Erasmus'
polemic against Ulrich von Hutten, *Spongia adversus aspergines Hutteni* (1523)
had omitted Emser's name from the list of those who had written against the
Wittenberg reformer (LB x 1652B–C / ASD IX-1, 166–70. Emser's most widely
known anti-Lutheran works were directed to a popular audience and published in German; hence it is possible that Erasmus knew nothing (or at least
little) about them.
2 This letter is lost, but Allen Ep 1683 introduction noted that the correspondence of Philippus Melanchthon contains a reference to a letter from Erasmus
to Emser. Allen surmises that the missing letter of 10 January may have been
a reply to an earlier letter from Erasmus (the one referred to here), which is
also missing. Apparently the unidentified relative of Emser mentioned here
had been the bearer of a letter of invitation from Emser written before the
letter of 10 January but delivered to Erasmus after it. The book that accompanied the letter of 10 January is probably identical to the 'poem' identified in
n8 below.
3 For discussion of Erasmus' difficulty in getting a copy of *De servo arbitrio* in
time to write a prompt rebuttal, see Ep 1667 and its introduction.
4 His initial direct attack on Luther's doctrines, *De libero arbitrio diatribe*, published in 1524

have the work printed and proofread. The story sounds incredible, but it took place in the presence of a host of witnesses. Froben used six presses, turning out three gatherings of sixteen pages every day.[5] Luther's book de-   20
scended on me when I was already in a state of exhaustion from overwork and weakened besides by an illness that scarcely ever let up. For the weather, which has hardly changed from the end of July to the present, could not have been worse for a constitution like mine. Although Luther's work was printed simultaneously at Augsburg, Strasbourg, and Nürnberg, they took   25
incredible pains to ensure that nothing fell into my hands. Hence the need for haste on my part. Clearly their aim was to secure a triumph for themselves with no prospect of my replying before the next fair. To prevent that from happening, I countered with half a reply. The rest is now under way.[6]
I am sending what I have completed so far. You will find your name there,[7]   30
but with no special titles of respect. No one receives such titles in this work, and for good reason. If you measure friendship by the degree of mutual affection, I shall not let myself be surpassed by you; and if you gauge it by the presence of a complimentary address, I shall not prove remiss in this department either, when a suitable opportunity arises.   35

* * * * *

5 Erasmus' Latin phrase is *tres ogdoadas paginarum*, literally 'three eights of pages.' Since *Hyperaspistes 1* was published in octavo format, each quire or gathering of the book would have contained eight leaves (or folios), that is, sixteen pages. Thus Erasmus is saying that Froben's six presses turned out a total of forty-eight pages each day. The copy of *Hyperaspistes 1* at the Centre for Reformation and Renaissance Studies, Victoria University, University of Toronto, contains 118 folios (that is, 236 pages), according to Professor Dalzell's inspection of their catalogue. This figure is confirmed by the description printed in *The National Union Catalog, Pre-1956 Imprints* 754 vols (London 1968–81) 161 139, indicating a book of 240 pages and 15 gatherings of 8 pages apiece, though these data describe Froben's second edition, published in July 1526. Erasmus claimed (Ep 1667) to have written *Hyperaspistes 1* in only ten days, and this letter makes clear that Froben supported his determination to get this initial response to Luther printed in time for the spring (March) book fair at Frankfurt. Froben at various times in his career had between four and seven presses available (Carl B. Lorck *Handbuch der Geschichte der Buchdruckerkunst* I [Leipzig 1882] 136). Thus the completion of the printing by six presses within a period of five days means that the printer was deploying all or nearly all the resources of his shop in order to get the book printed in time for the spring fair. Cf Epp 1667 introduction, 1688.
6 That is, the more detailed rebuttal of Luther now known as *Hyperaspistes 2*, not published until September 1527
7 Erasmus did mention Emser in *Hyperaspistes 1* (LB X 1249) as one who had attacked Luther far more vigorously than he had.

With regard to your poem,[8] what I found attractive in it was its clarity and the brilliance and vigour of the writing. You take great liberties in your use of Greek words, shortening the final syllable in *disdiapason* and lengthening the first in *catholicus* (although this same licence is found several times in Prudentius).[9] But we shall not advance our cause by books of this kind or by fierce invective. Someday events will show that I was a true prophet. I commend the princes, however, for their energetic repression of the troublemakers. Could anything have been more courteous than my *Diatribe*? But what has it accomplished apart from stirring up the Lutherans to greater madness? I knew that this would happen; nevertheless, I gave in to the king of England, the English cardinal, the pope, and several of my learned friends, though I did not fail to point out what the consequences would be.[10] I did not expect a moderate reply from Luther, but I was not prepared for such a torrent of malicious abuse. Everywhere these people claim the humanities for themselves, presumably as a smokescreen behind which to establish their sect; yet in the end they will bring ruin to these studies too. The *Apologia* in which I reply to Cousturier[11] will show you what madness has taken hold of Paris. And Noël Béda has criticized more than two hundred passages in my

* * * * *

8 The poem mentioned is *In Euricii Cordi medici Antilutheromastigos calumnias expurgatio pro Catholicis*, published in an edition of 12 leaves without date or place of publication, a retort to a poem published in 1525 by Euricius Cordus, *Antilutheromastix*. On Emser's poem see Gustav Kawerau *Hieronymus Emser* (Halle 1898) 83–5, n127 (page 168). Although Emser was becoming known primarily as a vernacular controversialist, since his youth he had acquired a reputation as a talented Latin poet. See Heribert Smolinsky *Augustin von Alveldt und Hieronymus Emser* (Münster / Westfalen 1983) 26–7, 29.

9 Greatest of the Christian Latin poets (348–after 405). He was deeply learned in the classical poetic tradition and adapted it skilfully for treatment of Christian themes. Since he spent nearly his whole life in Spain, his exclusively western orientation may explain his frequent errors in the prosody of Greek words, a characteristic still noted by modern classical philologists, for example Max Manitius in *Rheinisches Museum* 45 (1890) 491, who notes similar flaws in Juvencus and other Christian Latin poets. On the other hand, the frequent use of a lengthened first syllable in *catholicus* was needed to make the word fit into Latin hexameter verse.

10 Erasmus had faced pressure from highly placed persons to write against Luther: from Henry VIII of England (cf Epp 1408:25–7, 1416:63–4, 1419 introduction, and further correspondence cited there), from Cardinal Thomas Wolsey (Ep 1486), from Pope Clement VII (Ep 1443B), and repeatedly and urgently from Duke George of Saxony.

11 See Ep 1658 n7.

Paraphrases,[12] of which the most damning was my comment on the words   55
of the angel 'You have found favour';[13] here I wrote, 'This does not imply
any merit on your part, but is a mark of the divine favour.'

I am sending you a poem by Andrzej Krzycki, the bishop of Hungary.[14]
I am surprised that you say nothing about Ceratinus.[15] I hear that the duke
did not like him as much as I was hoping. He is a good man with an excellent   60
command of languages, and the invitation he received involved me in some
expense. I would certainly not have acted if the prince had not insisted on
it. There is more that I would like to say to you, but I must return to my
quarrel with Luther. May it bring him no joy! I cannot understand what he
meant by combining at the same time the roles of evangelist and scurrilous   65
buffoon.

Basel, [1527]

1684 / To Juan de Vergara   Basel, 29 March 1526

This is a fragment of what must have been a considerably longer letter, addressed to the leading figure among Spanish admirers of Erasmus, concerning
a series of seven manuscript *Collationes ad Erasmum*, commentaries on points
found in Erasmus' writings that Alonso (or Alfonso) Ruiz de Virués suggested
might have been expressed more carefully so as not to incite the wrath of the
monks. On Vergara see Ep 1277 introduction. Virués (1493–1545), who was a
Benedictine monk at Burgos and had studied theology in the Benedictine college at Salamanca, was generally sympathetic to Erasmus' scholarship. About
the same time as the date of this letter, he wrote to a Franciscan of Alcalá
a letter defending Erasmus that circulated in manuscript and was eventually

* * * * *

12 See Ep 1571 introduction and nn1–2, and cf Epp 1579:140–51 and n29, 1664
   introduction and n1.
13 Luke 1:30
14 At this point in his career, Krzycki was bishop of Przemyśl and a close adviser to King Sigismund I of Poland. See Epp 1629 introduction, 1652. He
   was a highly regarded Latin poet and a pronounced opponent of Luther. The
   poem here mentioned is very likely one of his satirical anti-Lutheran verses,
   especially considering that the anti-Lutheran Emser is the addressee of this
   letter.
15 In 1525, Erasmus had successfully promoted the candidacy of Ceratinus (Jacobus Teyng of Hoorn) for the chair of Greek at Leipzig. For reasons that are
   not quite clear but may include unfounded suspicions of Lutheran sympathies,
   the university's patron, Duke George of Saxony, was not pleased with him,
   and he left Leipzig a few weeks after his arrival. See Epp 1561 (especially n3),
   1564, 1565, 1566, 1567, 1568.

printed; but Erasmus knew nothing of this at the date of the present letter and expressed irritation, fearing that even these mild criticisms might encourage 'tricksters' to attack him; see Epp 1701:33–4, 1717:48–9, and especially Allen Ep 1804:260–77 (the latter addressed to Thomas More, acknowledging but discounting as hypocrisy the laudatory words addressed to him by Virués). In order to be sure that his commentaries reached Erasmus, Virués sent two copies by different routes; it is clear from Ep 1804 that this strategy struck Erasmus as unfriendly. Eventually, Juan Luis Vives sent Erasmus a Latin translation of the defence of Erasmus addressed to the Franciscan of Alcalá (Allen Ep 1847:110–25, 136–40, written in July 1527) as proof of Virués' good will; and other letters from Vergara (Ep 1814), Vives (Ep 1836), and Alfonso de Valdés (Ep 1839), as well as from Virués himself (Epp 1786, 1838) finally convinced Erasmus that Virués was a trustworthy friend and that his notes (*collationes*) had not been a prelude to an underhanded attack.

Throughout this period, Virués at his monastery in Burgos was actively defending Erasmus' good name, and he spoke in defence of Erasmus at the well-known conference of theologians convened at Valladolid (27 June–13 August 1527) to investigate the orthodoxy of Erasmus' writings. Virués also published (in 1529) his own Spanish translation, with his own commentary, of eight of Erasmus' colloquies. Virués moved from Burgos to Valladolid and in 1531 became prior of the Benedictine community of San Vicente at Salamanca. He also became court preacher to Charles v and in 1531–2 accompanied the imperial court to Germany, probably attending the imperial diet of Regensburg (1532) and witnessing negotiations with the German Protestants at Nürnberg. He returned to Spain in 1533 and in subsequent years became involved with the Inquisition, first as a witness at the trial of Vergara in 1534 and then as the subject of trial himself. He was under detention until 1538; then, although sentenced to two years' imprisonment in a monastery, he was promptly released by authority of a papal bull absolving him obtained by the emperor, who later the same year appointed him bishop of the Canary Islands. He moved there in 1540 and died there in 1545. That the original letter of which this forms a part was considerably longer appears from Vergara's reply, where he refers to it as 'such a long and splendid' letter (Allen Ep 1814:4–5). The contents of the missing portion are probably reflected in Vergara's letter of 31 July 1526 to Virués; see The Letters of Juan de Vergara and Others, Letter 2:1–5, 64–7, 74 below. On Virués see Bataillon (1991), especially I 236–40, 319–35, 505, 519–20. Bataillon should now be modified on the Valladolid conference by Homza; see Ep 1742 introduction.

This fragmentary letter is part of a collection of manuscript copies (eighteenth and early nineteenth centuries) of twenty-four letters involving Spanish humanists that P.S. Allen found in Munich; it is known as the Heine collection after the German scholar who gathered them at Madrid in 1846–7. On this collection, see Ep 1277 introduction and also CWE 8 336, the introduction to the Vergara-Zúñiga correspondence translated in that volume by Alexander Dalzell and Erika Rummel. The present location of the Heine collection is unknown. Allen was the first to edit this fragment, in 1926.

... I have just read a work by a certain Alonso of Olmedo. He says he wrote it with your encouragement to give me the benefit of his advice ... Please tell the man to change the tone of his remarks and turn his pen against those who misinterpret my works. Let us join hands rather than start up a new quarrel. There is no shortage of tricksters who are ready to sharpen   5
their pens and attack Erasmus. I send my warmest congratulations to the University of Alcalá, in fact to the whole of Spain; it gave me great pleasure to read the laudatory remarks that Alonso made on this subject. Please give him my kindest regards. I shall write him as soon as I can. At present I cannot find even a brief moment for myself. Let Alonso think, however, that   10
this letter was written for him too.

Vives has married.[1] He enjoys the high regard of the cardinal of England.[2] Farewell.

Basel, 28 March 1526

Erasmus of Rotterdam wrote this in haste with his own hand. I hope   15
you can read it.

1685 / From Noël Béda   Paris, 29 March [1526]

This reply to Erasmus' letter of 13 March marks the continuing decline of personal relations between Erasmus and the syndic of the Paris faculty of theol-

* * * * *

1684
1 This could hardly be called new news, since the wedding took place at Bruges on 24 May 1524 and was reported to Erasmus in a letter from Vives himself dated 16 June of that year. See Ep 1455. Perhaps, however, Erasmus thought that Vives' friends in Spain had not learned of it.
2 Thomas Wolsey, cardinal and archbishop of York. Vives had sought preferment at the court of Henry VIII since 1521 and from 1523 spent some time as a lecturer in Greek at Oxford under the patronage of Wolsey. His patrons also included King Henry and especially the Spanish-born queen, Catherine of Aragon. He became tutor to Princess Mary. But his support of the queen after the royal divorce became an issue cost him the support of both King Henry and Wolsey. For a time in 1528 Wolsey held him under house arrest but in April allowed him to return to Bruges (where his wife had continued to reside), and he spent most of the rest of his life there.

ogy. Like the letter to which it replies, it was first published by Béda himself in his *Apologia adversus clandestinos Lutheranos* (1529). Open hostility and disdain for Erasmus were already evident in Ep 1642, written the previous October, and there had also been at least latent threats of a formal condemnation of Erasmus' works by the faculty of theology. Here, however, the hostility is both defiant and palpable. On the entire series of letters between Erasmus and Béda, see Epp 1571 introduction, 1664 introduction and n1.

TO THE MOST ERUDITE AND DISTINGUISHED SCHOLAR, MASTER
ERASMUS OF ROTTERDAM, MY BELOVED FRIEND IN CHRIST
Greetings, most learned sir! As is quite clear from your letter,[1] no one will be a good theologian in your eyes unless he swears an oath of allegiance to you.[2] I take exactly the opposite view, that you will not find a good the- 5
ologian anywhere who is not offended by your writings and who does not oppose with all the force at his command the errors you have spread abroad in these same writings. If you had not taken the initiative in writing to me, I would never have been bold enough even to think of writing to you. In fact, I did not write to you: I only replied to what you wrote; and I did not 10
keep silent when I judged I had something to say that was useful for your salvation. For this I am called a despot and a brawler. It is remarkable what fine words you use about the need for gentleness in theological debate – when you speak with reference to others; but I think Cousturier will show the world in his *Antapologia*, which is now in the press, that you practise that 15
virtue only with tongue and pen.[3] Whether or not Cousturier has someone to polish his work, I do not know.[4] But tell me, what did you have in mind when you addressed me recently in a letter with these words:[5] 'I would

* * * * *

1685
1 Ep 1679
2 Horace *Ep* 1.14; *Epodes* 15.4
3 This Paris theologian regarded all humanists of the Erasmian type as heretics. On his conflict with Erasmus, see Epp 1571 n10, 1658 n7. The work here discussed in a positive light by Béda, *Adversus insanam Erasmi apologiam Petri Sutoris antapologia*, was published at Paris in June 1526. See Ep 1714.
4 Erasmus had expressed dislike for the Latin style of Cousturier even though he had his works polished by 'an ungrateful ne'er-do-well' whom Erasmus had supported and educated when he was an impoverished student. The identity of this person is unknown. See Ep 1679 n3.
5 A direct quotation of Erasmus' words at Ep 1679:44–8, in apparent contradiction to his words in Ep 1620:12–15, which Béda also quotes directly and accurately. While Erasmus' complaints about Béda's compilation of articles extracted from Erasmus' publications are to some extent disingenuous and self-

never have been offended by your annotations, whether they were fair or
not, if you had sent them to me. But instead you circulated them in Paris   20
with a nasty preface, which read like the report of a censor. Your labours
would have been no help to me but for the fact that a chance copy was delivered to me here.' These are your words, and these too are yours: 'I am
delighted to have the annotations that you were kind enough to send. I wish
you had also sent me a list of the points which you found so offensive in   25
my letter to the bishop of Basel.'[6] This was written in your own hand in a
letter from Basel dated 2 October 1525.

So there is no doubt whatever that I sent you my annotations because
you insisted so strongly on seeing them. It was no accident that they made
their way to Germany. But it is completely untrue that I circulated them   30
there. If Master Bérault[7] kept a copy for himself and circulated it widely,
or if some of your other intermediaries did so, that happened without my
knowing anything about it. Be careful, therefore, what words you choose.
But what you guessed had happened, or believed had happened because
of a false rumour, I am now trying to bring about. I tell you, as God is my   35
witness, that good men wish you well, as I do myself. When they saw in
that second letter you sent me,[8] written in your own hand, that you were

* * * * *

serving, his real point in Ep 1679 was that if Béda detected dangerous errors in his works, he should have approached him directly instead of aiming first at formal condemnation by the faculty of theology and the Parlement
of Paris, and only subsequently acting to inform Erasmus of those criticisms
that Erasmus had not already received through the good offices of a friend
in the Parlement, François Deloynes. On Béda's critical notes and the ensuing
controversy, see Epp 1571 introduction, 1664 introduction and n1, 1666 n5.
6 Erasmus' permissive views on the Lenten fast, published in his *Epistola apologetica de interdicto esu carnium* (1522), a work which had the approval of
  Christoph von Utenheim, bishop of Basel, to whom it was dedicated, scan-
  dalized Béda, Cousturier, and other conservative theologians. See Epp 1539
  n4, 1581 n100. Béda had already obliquely criticized Erasmus' views on fasting in Ep 1579:104–8 and had continued to insist that Erasmus' opinions on
  fasting were wholly unacceptable and that any theologian who endorsed them,
  as Ludwig Baer of Basel had done, should be reprimanded: Epp 1609:20–42,
  1642:6–16.
7 See Ep 1571 n15 on Nicolas Bérault's role in transmitting texts and communications between Erasmus and several Paris theologians; cf Ep 1687 n13.
8 A reference to Erasmus' letter of 24 August 1525, Ep 1596, which was far
  more conciliatory than his blunt and combative letter of 15 June 1525, Ep 1581,
  which had miscarried and was returned to the sender. Erasmus dispatched it
  a second time, along with Ep 1596, the 'second letter.' Béda's quotation from
  this letter here (lines 39–41) is accurate.

promising to purge your books of error and were expressing your gratitude
to anyone who would assist you in the task (your actual words were: 'I
am ready to be a harsher judge of my own work than Augustine was of   40
his'),[9] they were delighted and gave thanks to the Lord on your account
and offered their congratulations to you and to myself as well, because my
advice had been partly responsible for the progress you had made. Because
of your fine words they hoped, as I did, for a good result.

Then they began to press me and continued to press me, even to insist,   45
that I send a warning letter in the same vein to Jacques Lefèvre.[10] I finally
did so, and with true Christian frankness I pointed out to the man what a
dangerous position he was in because of the unhealthy character of his theology. I made various offers suggesting that, if he wanted to cure himself,
I would send him copies of his commentaries on the Letters of St Paul and   50
on the Gospels, in the margins of which I had marked a number of errors;
from these he could discover what I thought.[11] He wrote back and thanked

* * * * *

9 A reference to St Augustine's *Retractationes*, written near the end of his life
(426–7) in order to qualify or retract statements made in his earlier works.
Béda's point here is that Erasmus should systematically review all of his publications and specifically retract all the incorrect and offensive statements (that
is, all statements that Béda regarded as incorrect and offensive).

10 This correspondence with Lefèvre d'Etaples does not survive, but Béda was
as much alarmed by his ideas as by those of Erasmus. Lefèvre received even
more attention than Erasmus in Béda's first general attack on humanist innovations in theology, *Annotationum Natalis Bedae ... in Jacobum Fabrum Stapulensem libri duo, et in Desiderium Erasmum Roterodamum liber unus* (Paris: Josse
Bade, 25 May 1526). In this edition, Béda's *Annotationes* against Lefèvre fill folios 1–183; those directed against Erasmus fill folios 184–229; thus the relative
lengths are 183 versus 46 folios. James Farge in a letter to the editors reports
that in the second edition (Cologne, August 1526) of his book, Béda's articles
against Lefèvre fill 234 folios, against 63 folios devoted to the notes on Erasmus. This book attacking Lefèvre and Erasmus was already in press at the
date of this letter and would be completed only a few days after Pentecost
(which fell on 20 May in 1526), the date predicted at the end of this paragraph.

11 Lefèvre's commentaries on the Epistles of St Paul (Paris: Henri Estienne, 15 December 1512), together with his earlier *Quincuplex Psalterium* (Paris: Henri Estienne, 1509), were the first major publications of what modern historians have
labelled biblical humanism. They attracted sympathetic attention from many
humanists, especially before the publication of Erasmus' *Novum instrumentum* in 1516 focused even greater attention on Erasmus. Reaction was strongly
positive among those open to humanist influence but was vehemently hostile
on the part of conservative scholastic theologians like Béda. The exact time
of Béda's offer to send Lefèvre his critical comments on the Pauline commentaries is unclear, but he does not seem to have been very active as a theologian

me warmly but refused my offer; instead he asked me to explain why I considered the passages in question deserving of censure. On hearing this, I spent several days in a state of worry without lifting my pen at all. Finally, 55 I collected my thoughts, and on 13 June 1525 I began to write something that might prove helpful to him, though I had no clear idea how far I would pursue the matter. But I persevered with the task and finally, by the middle of the month of June, two books of annotations were completed. Josse[12] began printing around the beginning of March; he is expected to finish by 60 the Feast of Pentecost.

When I realized, however, that you and Lefèvre had many types of error in common, I decided to add a short appendix to the two volumes to

* * * * *

until his growing concern about Martin Luther and about Lefèvre's criticism of traditions concerning Mary Magdalene and the marriages of St Anne led him to attack Lefèvre on these questions in 1519–20 (on these controversies see Farge *Biographical Register* 35). In 1520 Béda became syndic of the Paris faculty of theology and rapidly transformed himself into its most powerful member. It is probable that his offer occurred only shortly before he began work on the two books of annotations currently in press, and highly unlikely that he approached Lefèvre before concern about Luther and about Lefèvre's views on Mary Magdalene and St Anne led to his publications of 1519–20. For the full title and contemporary editions of Lefèvre's Pauline commentaries, see Eugene F. Rice jr *The Prefatory Epistles of Jacques Lefèvre d'Etaples and Related Texts* (New York 1972) 558–9. The original Paris edition of Lefèvre's Pauline commentaries (1512) was followed by two new editions at Paris in 1515 and another in 1517. In the original Paris edition, Béda's *Annotationes* on the Pauline commentaries filled 97 folios (plus 4 folios criticizing Lefèvre's prefatory materials), and his *Annotationes* on a more recent work of Lefèvre, *Commentarii initiatorii in quatuor evangelia* (Meaux: Simon de Colines, 1523) filled an additional 50 folios (plus 4 folios attacking Lefèvre's preface). At the request of the faculty of theology, the Parlement in 1523 acted to prevent sale of Lefèvre's commentary on the Gospels, sending its *huissier* to seize copies from the Paris bookseller Simon de Colines. See Farge *Parti conservateur* 53–7. This seizure of copies is reminiscent of the Parlement's action in August 1526, taken on order of the king, to suppress Béda's *Annotationes* against Lefèvre and Erasmus, as reported in a letter of Levinus Ammonius to Johannes de Molendino; see Ep 1763.

12 Josse Bade of Assche near Ghent (in Latin, Jodocus Badius Ascensius) was a leading Paris printer. His production included a number of works by Erasmus and other humanists, but some of his other publications, including the *Annotationes* of Béda against Lefèvre and Erasmus, reflected the views of the conservatives of the Paris faculty. On his career see Ep 183 introduction and CEBR.

Prelum Ascensianum
Title-page of Guillaume Budé *Commentarii linguae Graecae* Paris: Bade 1529
The central figure pulling the bar of the press is believed to be
Josse Bade (Ascensius), the scholarly printer of Paris,
who was a friend, correspondent, and publisher of Erasmus.
Reproduced by permission of the Thomas Fisher Rare Book Library,
University of Toronto

warn you of your errors, with brief criticisms of the points at issue.[13] You
see I did not want to appear as a respecter of persons[14] to the prejudice of   65
the truth, as might appear if I passed you by without saying a word when
the reason for speaking out in your case is almost as strong. I deal with
you, however, in very few words. Neither you nor Lefèvre should think
it unfair if, at the prompting of my conscience, I am doing what I can to
defend the truth, which both of you have injured in so many ways. Just how   70
necessary this is is clear from the fact that you are still satisfied with the
letter you wrote to the lord bishop of Basel,[15] especially since Augustine,
when discussing the Aerian heresy in his *De haeresibus* (in volume 11 of
his works),[16] demonstrates that the argument you used in that letter was
condemned long ago. And are we really to believe that that letter provoked   75
a snort of disapproval from the Lutheran faction, when it clearly supports
their side? I do not think it was this that started all the commotion among
that godless crew. It was other causes that provoked them, from which you
will hardly be able to clear yourself, however necessary that may be, unless
you retract the errors in your writings. For since these people are very clever   80
at deceiving others, they will not easily be stopped by words. I am pleased,
however, that you have taken up your pen against them.[17] May the Lord
give you the grace to carry out this task, from which you may win true
glory.

That is all I want to say on this subject. There is nothing unusual or   85
impertinent about the occasional use of strong language when the situation
demands it. You are most certainly no stranger to this yourself. So please
allow me to enjoy the same licence in defence of the truth. I only wish no

* * * * *

13 That is, the third part of Béda's *Annotationes*, directed at reproving the alleged
theological errors in Erasmus' publications
14 Acts 10:34, following the Vulgate wording and the English text in AV and
Douai (which is not reflected in recent translations such as RSV, NEB, and the
Jerusalem Bible)
15 Cf n6 above.
16 *De haeresibus* 53 (on the heresy of not fasting) concerns the errors of Aerius
of Sebaste in Pontus, who fell into the Arian heresy and, among other things,
taught that the established fasts need not be observed but that each person should fast when he wished, lest people seem to be subject to the Law.
See PL 42 39–40. Béda's reference is to volume 11 of Amerbach's edition of
Augustine.
17 A reference, presumably, to Erasmus' *De libero arbitrio* and to his more recent
Hyperaspistes 1 (Basel: Froben 1526). In Ep 1679 Erasmus promised to send
Béda a copy of the latter work, perhaps accompanying that letter, but Béda
reports at the end of the present letter that he has not received it.

one would use such language to defend what is false. And pray to the Lord
with me that he may turn all things to our salvation.   90

I do not know what is going to happen to Berquin.[18] Certainly on the
twenty-third of this month he was pronounced, by the most solemn judgment of the church, to be a relapsed heretic and handed over to the power of
the Parlement, that is to the secular arm.[19] If you read the first book of Augustine's *Contra Cresconium grammaticum*, you will no longer claim, I think,   95
that scholastic theology is less ancient or less valuable than any other.[20] Anyone who is ignorant of scholastic theology and attempts to explain theological questions exposes himself to truly horrendous dangers. In these dreadful times, when Christendom is enveloped in dark mists of error, surely
everyone must see the absolute necessity for this kind of theology? As for   100
your complaint that you are hounded by Lutherans and Catholics alike, I
admit that you must suffer for your beliefs. Those who act honourably in
all things suffer only at the hands of the wicked, which is judged a truly
glorious fate. I pray all may turn out well for you.

Thanks for sending me the Office of the Blessed Virgin.[21] But I have   105
not yet received or seen the first part of your reply to Luther. Farewell.

* * * * *

18 On Berquin's translations of Erasmian works and the efforts of the faculty
   of theology and the Parlement to prosecute him as a heretic, see Epp 1579
   n44, 1599 introduction and n1. In Ep 1679, to which the present letter is
   a reply, Erasmus correctly pointed out (lines 59–61) that Berquin's 'translations' of his works included interpolated material from other authors (including Guillaume Farel and Martin Luther, though Erasmus did not say so)
   for which Erasmus was not responsible; but this defence did not derail the
   efforts of Béda and the faculty to condemn not only Berquin but Erasmus
   as well.
19 Béda is referring to the formal condemnation of Berquin as a relapsed heretic
   by the special commission of judges delegate appointed by the pope at the
   request of the regent, Louise of Savoy (CEBR I 136–7).
20 In book 1 of this work (PL 43 445–68) against the Donatist Cresconius, Augustine does indeed uphold the use of rhetoric and dialectic in order to oppose error and uphold the truth and the unity of the church, though it is a
   rather long stretch to transform this point into a direct source of the scholastic
   method of the medieval theologians.
21 Erasmus' mass in honour of Our Lady of Loreto was written at the request of
   his friend Thiébaut Biétry, parish priest at Porrentruy, first published at Basel
   in 1523, and reissued in an enlarged edition in May 1525. See introductions
   to Epp 1391 and 1573. The second edition, almost certainly the one sent to
   Béda, also included a diploma from the archbishop of Besançon, Antoine de
   Vergy, granting an indulgence to all who made use of this mass within the
   archbishop's diocese; cf Ep 1679 n25.

From Montaigu. On the fifth day of Holy Week, 29 March 1525 according to the style of Paris[22]

Your brother who remembers you in his prayers, Noël Béda

1686 / To Francesco Chierigati   Basel, 1 April 1526

> On this well-placed bishop and curial diplomat, see Epp 639 introduction, 1336
> introduction and n2, 1344 nn4, 6. The primary purpose of this letter was to get
> a copy of Erasmus' reply to Luther's *De servo arbitrio* into the hands of a person
> in the papal curia who was personally well disposed to Erasmus and who also,
> having himself experienced German hostility to Rome while serving as papal
> legate at the Diet of Nürnberg in 1522–3, might have a realistic sense of the
> chaotic conditions prevailing in Germany. Erasmus believed that many curial
> officials lacked any understanding of the true religious situation in Germany.
> He published this letter in *Opus epistolarum*.

TO FRANCESCO CHIERIGATI, BISHOP OF TERAMO,
FROM ERASMUS OF ROTTERDAM, GREETING

I received the letter you sent from the Vatican on 13 January,[1] but it had
been opened. This happens to almost all correspondence nowadays. I keep
hearing that it is the work of Spaniards, those, I believe, who have seized   5
some sort of stronghold in the Alps.[2] The letter you sent excusing your long

* * * * *

22 Until 1566–7, much of France, including Paris, observed Easter, not 1 January,
as the beginning of the new year. Since Easter fell on 1 April in 1526, for
Béda at Paris, 29 March was still 1525, though of course he knew that in many
other regions it was already 1526. Hence his care to specify that his date was
expressed in the style of Paris.

1686
1 Not extant
2 The Latin is *iuxta Rhetos* 'among the Rhaetians.' Ancient Rhaetia was an Alpine
region corresponding roughly to the modern Grisons, the Tirol, and northern
Lombardy, though sometimes the term included also the Roman province of
Vindelicia (sometimes known as Rhaetia Secunda), extending as far north as
the Danube and the chain of forts that marked the Roman frontier between
the upper Danube valley and the upper Rhine. However it might have been
defined in Erasmus' mind, it certainly meant mountainous Alpine country
through which roads connecting southern Germany to Italy ran. The St Got-
thard pass, for example, lay on a route that passed through the Grisons (or
Grey League) from Milan via Luzern to Basel; and the Tirol was traversed by
the route from Verona via the Brenner Pass to Innsbruck and thence to Basel.

silence pleased me greatly. It was not that I ever found you lacking in kindness, for you go out of your way to shower this poor specimen of a man
with every sort of kindness far beyond anything that he deserves; rather it
was that your letter showed a great affection for me and much good will,   10
for, even amid a flood of obligations, you did not let me slip from your
mind. As for the worldwide calamities that your Reverence deplores, no
one who has maintained any respect for religion or any human feeling can
avoid being pained by these events. We have long hoped that peace would
be patched up between the kings, but the lingering postponement of our   15
hopes torments my mind.[3] I see that we are suffering what often happens
to an ulcerated body: when we have recovered from one or two sores, the
trouble breaks out somewhere else. I can tell you nothing about the business of the kings that you do not know and, if I could, it would not be safe
to write it here. There is a long road between us, nobody can be trusted,   20
and people have different interests.

The peasant rising is almost settled, but the remedy was cruel.[4] The seriousness of the trouble demanded such measures. But that plague is always
threatening to break out again. However, steps have been taken, I think, to 25

* * * * *

3 In theory, the release of King Francis I from captivity in Spain (17 March 1526)
was part of a comprehensive peace between the French king and the emperor
Charles V, though the harsh terms imposed on France virtually guaranteed   30
that war would soon break out again. Aside from Francis' shortage of money
for war, the chief impediment to speedy resumption of hostilities was that
his young sons, the dauphin François and Henry, duke of Orleans (the future
Henry II), were held in Spain as hostages to guarantee their father's fulfilment
of the treaty that provided for his release. In 1529 the Treaty of Cambrai (popularly known as the Paix des Dames), negotiated between the king's mother, 35
Louise of Savoy, and the emperor's aunt, Margaret of Austria, moderated the
harsh terms of 1526 and laid the foundation for the eventual release of the
princes upon payment of a heavy ransom. This release took place on 1 July
1530. On the captivity of the two princes and efforts to effect their release, see
Knecht *Renaissance Warrior* 247–8, 255–7, 284–6. The underlying hostility remained, and after several years of indirect conflict carried on through allies of 40
the French king, open war between Francis I and Charles V resumed in 1536.
In any case, Erasmus at Basel did not know of the king's liberation at the date
of this letter. He knew only that the negotiations for his release had been long
and difficult. Erasmus was his generation's leading advocate of peace and had
published repeatedly on that subject, notably his adage *Dulce bellum inexpertis*
(1515; *Adagia* IV i 1) and *Querela pacis* (1517).
4 The German Peasant War had begun in June 1524 and reached its peak in
May and June 1525, with southwestern Germany (very close to Basel, whose
city government vainly sought a peaceful settlement) and the province of

prevent the revolutionaries from doing again what they were allowed to do before. But there is another kind of infection that has spread through almost the whole of Europe[5] and it is much more serious than the insanity of war. For war attacks men's fortunes and their bodies; this, by destroying religion and banishing peace, condemns the whole man to the depths of Hades. The illness, however, seems less grave than it was, many are coming to their senses, and people are generally less partisan in their enthusiasms. I take no credit for this myself, even if I am the target of savage abuse from the staunchest supporters of that movement, as though I were principally responsible.

To say nothing of other matters, Luther recently attacked me in a great tome which he had worked over long and zealously; it is so steeped in bitter, sneering calumnies that for sheer acerbity it outdoes anything he has written about anyone before. I am sending you part of my reply. I shall send you his volume also if I find someone willing to shoulder such a trifling burden.[6] The bitter dissension on their side raises our hopes of seeing an end to the tragedy. Luther and some of his adherents defend the position that the real body of Christ is present in the Eucharist; many others deny this strenuously.[7] The argument goes on in an exchange of barbed pamphlets. The

* * * * *

Thuringia farther east being the scenes of the worst violence. But the uprising occurred later in some regions, such as East Prussia, the archbishopric of Salzburg, and the Hapsburg provinces of Tirol, Styria, and Austria, where disorder prevailed for several months after the repression had succeeded in the southwest and Thuringia. In the archbishopric of Salzburg, where the archbishop was perceived to be particularly oppressive, a second uprising occurred in March 1526, just weeks before the date of this letter. See the introduction to CWE 11 xi–xii.

5 That is, heresy

6 Luther's *De servo arbitrio*, his harsh response to Erasmus' *De libero arbitrio*, appeared in December 1525 at Wittenberg. It was a substantial but not a huge book, an octavo of 192 leaves (383 pages), considerably longer than part 1 of Erasmus' *Hyperaspistes*, which was little more than half as long. Although overburdening his courier with a second book may have been a concern, it is also probable that Erasmus had only one copy of *De servo arbitrio* available, since he had been unable until February to secure a copy as the basis for his hurried reply in *Hyperaspistes*. The 'other' part of Erasmus' response to Luther, part 2 of *Hyperaspistes*, was six times as long as part 1 but was not published until September 1527. Cf Ep 1667 introduction, 1670 n2.

7 Erasmus is referring to the increasingly open split between Luther and the other Wittenberg Reformers, on the one hand, and Zwingli and other Reform leaders at Basel, Strasbourg, and elsewhere in Switzerland and southwestern Germany, on the other hand. The major and most obvious issue was the nature

Swiss have decided on a public debate to be held at Pentecost in the town of
Baden,[8] which takes its name from its baths. What we may expect from that   45
I do not know. A few hapless people, who are convinced that they bear on
their shoulders the whole burden of the church, will make sure that it does
not succeed. Under the pretext of defending religion they are merely gratifying their own desires. They hate languages and letters more than they hate
Luther and all he stands for, and so they will go to any lengths to damage,   50
by whatever means they can, those who promote such studies.

In the meantime while I was doing battle with this powerful sect at
some risk to my own life, a man at Louvain released three tracts against me,
though he did not mention me by name.[9] Shortly afterwards four buffoons
from the Dominican order published a book filled with scandalous lies and   55
insults of a scurrility you would not believe; they revealed my name, but
concealed their own.[10] After perpetrating this outrage, they scattered in different directions. Then a Dominican at Paris produced a travesty of my *Colloquies* and added a preface under my name, in which I am made to condemn myself.[11] At Lyon this fool showed the world what a godly man he   60
was. I learned from a letter that he made off with 300 gold crowns belonging to his patron.[12] He was caught while having a merry time drinking in

* * * * *

of Christ's presence in the Eucharist. Erasmus himself had been alarmed by
the spread of Zwinglian or Sacramentarian views of the Eucharist in Basel.
See Ep 1670 n6 and the numerous other letters there cited.
8 Pentecost in 1526 fell on 20 May. This important disputation between defenders of traditional religious doctrines and practices led by Johann Maier of Eck,
Johannes Fabri of Leutkirch, and Thomas Murner, and a pro-Reformation delegation led by Johannes Oecolampadius of Basel and Berthtold Haller of Bern
(Zwingli did not attend) took place in the Swiss town of Baden from 19 May
to 8 June 1526, in connection with a meeting of the diet of the Swiss Confederation. The majority of the Swiss cantons endorsed Eck's propositions on 9
June, and the refusal of Basel and Bern (and of course Zürich) to accept the
decision of the diet led to the first formal split within the Swiss Confederation
over religious differences. See Ep 1708 introduction on the disputation and its
background.
9 On the Louvain theologian Jacobus Latomus and his persistent though thinly
veiled attacks on Erasmus, see Ep 1674 n12.
10 On this pseudonymous book, see Ep 1674 n13.
11 On this forged or falsely expurgated edition of the *Colloquies* and on Lambertus Campester, the Dominican friar who produced it, see Ep 1581 n59 and
CEBR.
12 Latin *trecentos coronatos aureos*, undoubtedly 300 French *écus d'or au soleil* (see
Epp 1434 n3, 1545 n6, 1658 n3). If so, this was a sum amounting to £600
tournois, or £65 sterling (the equivalent of 2,600 days' wages or 11 years and

the company of harlots.[13] Recently, also at Paris, Pierre Cousturier, a theologian and a Carthusian, devoted a full-length book to an attack on me,
which makes a lot of noise about heresies and blasphemies and unfounded   65
opinions. The only reason for all this is that I translated the New Testament
for private reading only. He is now producing a book, of which I have seen
only the beginning, but it exhibits all the fury of his ranting invective.[14] And
yet the things about which he makes such a song and dance are the merest
of trifles.   70
    Because of these people I have no time to do what I would like and
what your Reverence is urging me to do. Although it is very difficult to do
battle with such a powerful sect and more difficult still to fight on two fronts
and be assailed on both sides at once, nevertheless I am ready to die from
these woes rather than defect from the fellowship of the church. Christ will   75
give me strength and he will provide the reward. If we could talk face to
face, there is much I would like to pour into your private ear. I hope this
may be possible some day. I suffered all autumn and winter from catarrh
and the stone; only with the approach of spring did I begin to breathe again.
I pray, reverend bishop, my most respected friend, that you may enjoy all   80
the blessings your kindly nature deserves.
    Basel, on Easter day itself AD 1526

1687 / To Willem Bibaut   Basel, 7 April 1526

Erasmus was never bashful about appealing to ecclesiastical superiors in order to silence his critics, as is shown by his urging papal authority to impose
silence on his critic Diego López Zúñiga, (see Ep 1581 n9 and the earlier letters there cited) or his partial success in persuading Pope Clement VII to order
the Louvain theologians to desist from their attacks on him (Epp 1589, 1589A).
This letter reflects a similar effort to silence his French critic Pierre Cousturier
by appealing to the head of his religious order. Willem Bibaut (c 1475–1535),

* * * * *

9 months' wage income for an Oxford master carpenter), or £95 groot Flemish
(the equivalent of 2,280 days' wages or 10 years and 4 months' wage income
for an Antwerp master carpenter).
13 In Ep 1655:13–18 Erasmus claims that after returning to his friary at Lyon,
   Campester had embezzled money and squandered it on whores, though there
   is no independent confirmation of this charge.
14 See Ep 1658 n7. The book that Cousturier supposedly was 'now producing,'
   Adversus insanam Erasmi apologiam Petri Sutoris antapologia (Paris: Pierre Vidoue,
   June 1527), had already been approved for publication by the Paris faculty of
   theology without even the pretence of a formal review; see Ep 1714 n1.

a native of Flanders, had studied at Louvain (apparently without taking a degree or even matriculating). He entered a Carthusian monastery about 1499, was elected prior-general of the order in 1521, and now resided at the Grande Chartreuse near Grenoble. The point of this letter is that Cousturier's attacks on Erasmus were not only inappropriate at a time when Erasmus was engaged in defending the Catholic faith by opposing Luther but also so painfully inept that they brought discredit upon both the Paris theologians and the Carthusian order. Erasmus published this letter in his *Opus epistolarum*. His letter of 30 March 1527 to Thomas More (Allen Ep 1804) indicates that the prior-general had intervened but had not succeeded in silencing Cousturier.

ERASMUS OF ROTTERDAM TO THE REVEREND WILLEM,
PRIOR OF THE GRANDE CHARTREUSE, GREETING

I hear your Reverence thinks my little works worth reading. The less deserving they are of such attention, the more impressed I am by the generosity of your nature, a quality that always goes with true integrity. I owe you 5
a great deal for this, and considerably more because when this poor mortal attempts more than his strength can bear you sustain him before God in your prayers. But my debt to you will be greatest if you will take the trouble to point out anything in my writings that you find offensive. I am not one to fade away before the insults of my critics or to be puffed up by the applause 10
of my supporters. And yet in the past those bravos ringing in my ears from every quarter, while they could not make me forget myself, nevertheless made me somewhat more complacent and less vigilant.[1] The whole theatre of Germany rose eagerly to applaud everything Erasmus said, whether good or bad. Two or three honest mentors would have done me much more good 15
than many thousands of eulogists. I cannot think what benefit their excessive approbation brought me except to make me an object of envy; and now that the curtain has risen on a new scene in human history, men who once thought me a god now vilify my name in fanatical tracts, simply because I refused to lend my name to the Lutheran faction or agree with those who 20
disagree among themselves.[2] They were already preparing a triumph to cel-

* * * * *

1687
1 Erasmus is conceding that in his earlier works (before the Reformation crisis) he had sometimes expressed himself more freely and less cautiously than he ought to have done, though still insisting ('while they could not make me forget myself') that the plaudits of his admirers had never led him to uphold serious error.
2 A reference to the way in which the religious crisis, and especially Erasmus'

ebrate my arrival as leader of their camp; now whatever misfortunes they suffer, they attribute principally to me as the one who slowed the progress of the gospel, although I have always worked – and am still working when- 25 ever the opportunity arises – so that the present storm in human affairs, which has shaken almost the whole of Europe, may with Christ's help bring us to peace and tranquillity. For the omnipotent creator knows how to turn our madness into something good. In the meantime I pay the price for my temerity. 30

I have taken so much pains with St Jerome that I think there is very little that even an ungenerous reader would find wanting.[3] I have done the same for the *Adagia* more than once,[4] and have now begun work on the Paraphrases;[5] the rest will be dealt with in the same way. If I could have concen-

* * * * *

open break with Luther, had alienated many who a few years previously had sung his praises.

3 A reference to Erasmus' famous edition of the complete works of St Jerome (9 vols in folio; Basel: Johann Froben 1516), one of his major achievements in patristic scholarship. Erasmus had become the general editor of the whole work, which had been planned by Johann Amerbach and his successor Froben before Erasmus had any connection with that press, but his special personal responsibility was the first four volumes, comprising the letters of Jerome. In the summer of 1524 he dedicated the first four volumes of the revised edition to his patron Archbishop William Warham of Canterbury (Ep 1488), to whom he had also dedicated the earlier edition (Ep 396). The final volumes of the new edition were completed in the summer of 1526.

4 On the many editions of the *Adagia* between the first slender volume of 1500 and the final edition in 1536, the year of Erasmus' death, see Phillips *Adages* xii–xiii. Since 1515 Froben had brought out all of the revised editions, including one in 1526, though these were frequently reprinted by other publishers. In 1525 Erasmus tried in vain to interest the Venetian publisher Andrea Torresani of Asola, successor to Aldo Manuzio, in publishing the revised manuscript that Froben eventually issued in 1526. The Aldine press in 1508, during Erasmus' residence in Venice, had published the first major revision of the original work, far richer in classical sources, especially Greek ones, than its predecessors, and also far more bold in its critical judgments. On his failure to win Torresani's agreement, see Epp 1592, 1594, 1595, 1624, 1626, 1628.

5 Erasmus began his New Testament Paraphrases with Paul's Epistle to the Romans (1517), continued with paraphrases on the other epistles conventionally ascribed to one of the apostles (1519–21), and then proceeded to the Gospels, each of which was dedicated to a major contemporary ruler: St Matthew to Emperor Charles v (Ep 1255, in January 1522); St John to Archduke Ferdinand, brother of the emperor (Ep 1333, in January 1523); St Luke to Henry viii of England (Ep 1381, in August 1523); and finally St Mark to Francis i of France

trated all my efforts on this, I would still have had more than enough to do. But kings and prelates are pushing me into the gladiatorial arena at an age 35 when most gladiators have retired.[6] I made many excuses – old age, poor health, powers unequal to the task – but it was no use. I told them I would accomplish nothing except to stir up a hornets' nest.[7] For how could it be otherwise? But all was useless. I was forced to take up the gladiator's net and advance into the arena, although I was born for other things. I began 40 the fight in as civil a manner as I could with the publication of my *Diatribe*.[8] What success I had is shown by Luther's reply, in which he surpasses himself by a wide margin; for he never wrote anything that was more bilious or polemical.[9] And I gained no points from the opposing party for bringing down on my head the hostility of a formidable sect which is as much 45 to be feared for its violence as for its tongue and its pen. On the contrary, there are times when I engage the enemy in support of the theologians only to be attacked more viciously by those I am defending than by the enemy I oppose.

Although no one had less cause to attack me than Pierre Cousturier, 50 yet no one on the Catholic side has railed so violently against me. If you have read the fellow's book, I need say no more. I recognized at once a man hungry for notoriety who had sought the tranquillity of your order for no other reason than that. I wish I had followed my first instinct and not taken the advice of a man whose learning and good sense I valued so highly that 55 I could not imagine he would urge anything that would not be important for me personally or for the church generally. I had hardly completed the *Apologia* when I began to have qualms about thinking the fellow worthy of

* * * * *

(Ep 1400, in December 1523). Each of the Gospel paraphrases was published at Basel by Froben a month or two after the date of the royal dedication. His final paraphrase, on the Acts of the Apostles, was dedicated to Pope Clement VII (Ep 1414, in January 1524). He did not paraphrase the Apocalypse, of which he said in his *Catalogus lucubrationum* (Ep 1341A:772–3) that it 'on no account admits of a paraphrase.'

6 Erasmus frequently used the Roman gladiatorial contests as a figure representing his reluctant involvement in religious and other controversies; see Ep 1674 n8. He uses the figure again in lines 83–4 below.

7 *Adagia* I i 60

8 *De libero arbitrio diatribe* (1524), marking his first public break with Luther

9 The treatise *De servo arbitrio*, published on 31 December 1525. See Ep 1667 on Erasmus' shock at the savage tone of Luther's reply, which not only rejected his views on free will but also scorned him as an unbelieving infidel. Cf Ep 1688.

a reply.[10] On no other occasion did I ever feel so angry with myself. Would anyone of consequence or critical ability have considered his book worth 60 reading, since it had nothing to teach us and was simply a long- winded and scurrilous diatribe? Now he had gained the one thing he wanted: the name of Pierre Cousturier, which had meant nothing before even in Paris, was now winging its way across the world.[11]

Since this first success had turned out as he wished, he wrote an *An-* 65 *tapologia*,[12] which was so scurrilous and violent that by comparison one might judge the author of the earlier book sober and well behaved. I have not yet seen all of it, just four quaternions sent me by a friend, who had whee-dled them out of the printer while the work was being set.[13] From this sam-

* * * * *

10 On Cousturier's attack and Erasmus' reply, *Apologia adversus Petrum Sutorem*, see Epp 1571 n10, 1591 introduction, 1658 n7. On his doubts about the wisdom of publishing any reply to Cousturier, see also Ep 1679:25–6 and n2.

11 Erasmus' comment about Cousturier's standing in Paris is accurate, but not quite in the sense he intended. Cousturier was not totally unknown at Paris. During his study of theology there, he had been a regent at the Collège de Sainte-Barbe, and after becoming a fellow (*socius*) of the Collège de Sorbonne (by 1502) he served there as procurator, librarian, and prior. But a few months after receiving his doctorate in theology (16 April 1516), he entered the Carthusian order (28 January 1511). This step removed him from active participation in university affairs. He spent most of the period from 1511 down to publication of his *De tralatione Bibliae* (1525) away from Paris, serving as prior of four different Carthusian communities between 1514 and 1531. Of these houses, only Vauvert (where he served from 1517 to at least 1519), located just outside Paris, was compatible with direct involvement in university business. Even in that period, his contacts with the academic world would have been limited, since the Carthusians were a cloistered order. So his name probably had 'meant nothing at Paris,' but only because of his extended absences from the city and his official duties in a cloistered order, not (as Erasmus implies) because he was judged incompetent. On his career and publications, see Farge *Biographical Register* 119–21 (no 123).

12 Cousturier's *Adversus insanam Erasmi apologiam Petri Sutoris antapologia* (Paris: Pierre Vidoue for Jean Petit, June 1526). The Paris faculty of theology had approved this book at a meeting on 15 February, 'one of the rare occasions on which the faculty approved a book on the very day it was received' (Farge *Registre* 127 n13). Erasmus was particularly offended by the faculty's immediate and official approval of the manuscript; cf Ep 1714 n1.

13 The identity of the friend who managed to secure four gatherings (quaternions) for Erasmus during the printing is unknown. At this period, however, the theologian Gervasius Wain, who had been present at the session of the faculty that approved publication of Cousturier's *Antapologia*, might have been in a position to secure such material. He certainly was a source of information from inside the faculty, and in October 1527 sent to Erasmus not only news

ple it is not difficult to judge the rest: one knows the lion by his claws, as   70
the saying goes.[14] There is a long preface, arguing that he should not be
blamed if, in treating the subject, he resorts to ridicule and harsh words,

* * * * *

of Béda's campaign to secure formal condemnation of Erasmus' publications
but even the text of articles already condemned and those currently under discussion (Allen Ep 1884:21–5). After the faculty formally condemned Erasmus'
works on 17 December 1527, Wain tried to secure a full text of the censures but
in August 1528 reported that he had been unsuccessful (Allen Ep 2027:34–5).
Probably because of royal opposition to this action, the faculty did not record
the censures in its official register, nor did it publish them until 1531 (Rummel
II 49, Farge *Orthodoxy* 194–6). Although most historians, including Rummel,
have assumed that royal action blocked publication of the censures during
the period between 1527 and 1531, James Farge has pointed out to the editor that Béda (despite the royal inhibition of his *Annotationes* against Lefèvre
and Erasmus in 1526) had no difficulty obtaining a *privilège* authorizing publication of his *Apologia adversus clandestinos Lutheranos* (1529), in which he accused Erasmus of heresy. Thus the failure of the faculty to publish the censures adopted in December 1527 may not have resulted from prohibition by
royal authority but rather from a collective judgment that immediate publication was not in the best interests of the faculty. No one could have been
unaware that publication at the time of the censure would have infuriated the
king. The question was whether there would be any gain adequate to offset
the loss of royal favour. Not all members – indeed, very few members – were
so single-minded in their opposition to Erasmus or so courageous in defying
the royal will as Béda. He might be willing to denounce Erasmus in his own
anti-Lutheran book, and the faculty might be (and indeed was) willing to approve that book for publication; but publication of a corporate act denouncing
a scholar favoured by the king was another matter, one that required deliber-
ation. Not until 1531, when the political and religious situation in France had
changed, did the faculty judge the moment favourable for publishing its censures. Another possible inside source of information for Erasmus was Nicolas
Bérault, who served as an intermediary between Erasmus and Noël Béda in
1525 (Epp 1571:75 and n15; 1579:132–5 and n28, 1581:16–17 and n2). Bérault
himself may have been a *conseiller* in the Parlement. (Marie-Madeleine de la
Garanderie in CEBR I 126–8 attributes that office to him, though James Farge in
a letter to the editors questions whether there is documentary evidence to support this claim. Bérault seems to have been in royal service intermittently and
in 1529 was appointed royal orator and historiographer.) He was a humanist,
a friend of Erasmus, and a man close to the printing trades: when the printer
Jean Barbier died during the printing of his edition of Pliny's *Naturalis historia*
in 1514, Bérault took charge of the press, married Barbier's widow, headed the
firm for a short time, and remained an active bookseller until 1518. Furthermore, he was the person who suggested to Erasmus that he dedicate his initial
Apologia against Cousturier to Jean de Selve, first president of the Parlement
of Paris (Epp 1591 introduction, 1598:2).

14 *Adagia* I ix 34

that is, if he acts like a buffoon and a backbiter. Then he begins by denying me any credit for theological learning: he made his disputation before
the most learned scholars and received their approval, while I, according to 75
him, never obtained any degree in that subject.[15] He seems to think that the

* * * * *

15 The insinuation (or outright statement) that Erasmus lacked a doctoral degree
in theology and hence as a mere grammarian was unqualified to engage in
theological discussion was a common move by some of his scholastic antagonists. In 1525, in his reply to the letter that initiated their correspondence,
Béda addressed Erasmus as his 'beloved brother in Christ and fellow priest'
(Ep 1579:1) but pointedly made no mention of his being also a fellow theologian. Erasmus promptly challenged this omission and firmly asserted his
claim to that status (Ep 1581:21–5 and n3), precisely because being a professional theologian gave him a legal right to discuss debatable theological questions. Cousturier had explicitly denied – or at least jeered at – Erasmus' claim
to a doctorate (Rummel II 68). Béda also had charged that neither Erasmus nor
Lefèvre d'Etaples had any right to deal with Scripture or other religious texts
since they had professional competence only in languages and the humanities
and were licensed to teach only those subjects (Rummel II 33). Erasmus' earliest Spanish critic, López Zúñiga (Stunica), did call into doubt whether Erasmus had a degree in theology, and he wrote explicitly of Erasmus' suddenly
turning from a grammarian into a theologian (Rummel I 170 and n51 [pages
240–1]), but his main emphasis was on the alleged blasphemies contained in
Erasmus' writings and on parallels between the opinions of Erasmus and those
of Luther. Erasmus did, in fact, have a genuine doctorate from a real university; but he was always vague about it, partly because it was a degree *per
saltum* (conferred on the basis of his acknowledged learning as confirmed by a
special examination, but without having to satisfy the usual requirements of
years of residence, attendance at specified classes, and participation in disputations), partly because of the obscurity of the granting university, Turin, and
partly no doubt because, except in certain circumstances, he put little stock in
academic degrees, especially those in theology. It is not accurate to describe
his doctorate as an honorary degree, for it constituted a formal institutional
recognition of professional competence, but it is true that many of the more
prestigious universities refused to grant full recognition to such exceptional
degrees. For evidence that Erasmus was recognized as a qualified theologian,
see Ep 1581 n3. When he moved to Louvain in 1517, he was evidently accepted
as a qualified theologian; at least the record of his matriculation on 30 August
1517 describes him as 'Master Erasmus of Rotterdam, professor of sacred theology'; *Matricule de l'Université de Louvain* III-1 ed A. Schillings (Brussels 1958)
566 no 264. A month after his matriculation, he was co-opted into membership
in the faculty, an honour rarely given to people with a doctorate from another
university; Henry de Vocht *Monumenta Humanistica Lovaniensia* (Louvain 1934)
IV 190; cf Epp 694:4–6, 695:20–2. This recognition at Louvain did not involve
his teaching classes, nor did it make him a member of the eight member *Collegium Strictum* which governed the faculty, but he probably was a member

men who examined me[16] were not theologians or that the only theologians who deserve the name are those who follow the 'way,' as they call it, of the Nominalists and exercise their wits on certain problems that are tradition-ally discussed in the schools – and more to show off than to promote piety.[17]   80

* * * * *

of the *Collegium Largum*, which gave advice to the controlling group and at-tended formal academic convocations. Rather exceptionally, during the formal investigation of Erasmus' orthodoxy conducted by a commission of Spanish theologians at Valladolid in the summer of 1527, neither those who defended him nor his most outspoken critics raised any question about his professional qualifications to deal with scriptural and theological issues. See Homza, espe-cially page 114. On the granting of Erasmus' doctorate at Turin and the mean-ing of the degree, see Paul F. Grendler 'How to Get a Degree in Fifteen Days: Erasmus' Doctorate of Theology from the University of Turin' *Erasmus of Rot-terdam Society Yearbook* 18 (1998) 40–69. As Grendler observes, late-medieval Italian universities did not have theological faculties in the manner of north-ern universities. Instruction took place chiefly within local monasteries, and the only requirement for the doctorate was a decision by the local *collegium* of theologians to confer the degree on the basis of competence as established by examination.

16 As always, Erasmus is vague about the identity of those who examined him for the doctorate and where the examination occurred. From the very begin-ning, Erasmus was studiedly reticent and even misleading about the name of the university that conferred his degree; see Epp 200–1, 203, letters writ-ten from Florence and Bologna, implying though never stating that the doc-torate was from Bologna, a much more distinguished university than Turin, which these letters never mention. His rapid promotion to the doctorate after his arrival at Turin in August 1506 was to some extent an acknowledgment of his reputation for learning but also a result of his having connections with one or more persons influential at Turin. One possible patron was Francesco Stefano de Ferreriis (or Giovanni Stefano Ferreri), cardinal of Bologna, who was conservator of the university's privileges. He had visited Paris in 1496 and was one of those who warmly greeted Erasmus when he visited Rome in 1509. The diploma, which Erasmus preserved and which still exists at Basel, identifies the vicar-general of Giovanni Luigi della Rovere, bishop of Turin, as the person who examined Erasmus and found him sufficient. See Schoeck (1993) 72 n6. Bishop della Rovere was probably a kinsman of Pope Julius II. Early in 1506, that pope had favoured Erasmus by granting a brief (Ep 187A) dispensing him from any canonical impediments arising from his illegitimate birth that might make him ineligible to hold ecclesiastical benefices (that is, incomes).

17 A reference to the division of late-medieval philosophers and theologians, es-pecially in the German universities but also at Paris, into rival schools of in-terpretation: the *via antiqua* of the high-scholastic doctors such as Albertus Magnus, Thomas Aquinas, and Duns Scotus and the *via moderna*. Most of the

By that ruling neither Cyprian nor Ambrose would be entitled to the honour of the name![18] He should realize that it was a conscious decision on my
part and not any lack of ability that kept me from engaging in gladiatorial
contests of that sort. But I would be content to resign the honour of the title, which I never sought but which was thrust upon me. Certainly I ought   85
to be a theologian in Cousturier's eyes, since I have explained many things
that had escaped the most subtle theologians and I point out many passages
where Augustine and Ambrose, the greatest of the ancients, went astray, to
say nothing of other writers of more recent vintage, Thomas, Lyra, Hugo of
Saint Cher etc.[19]   90

But these are mere trifles. Wherever I criticize him, he tries to undermine my credibility, as if the book he published would not reveal the mind
and character of its author well enough, even if I were silent. Here are the
arguments he uses. He calls Erasmus a blasphemer who maligns not only
every class of men but also the saints and even God himself. Now listen   95
to the proof of this outrageous charge. Folly (for he scratches that old sore,
which healed long ago) says somewhere jokingly that Chance, whom the
ancients regarded as a god, was the founder of the arts. But where Chance
is, wisdom cannot exist. From this Folly draws the conclusion that she is

* * * * *

'moderns,' often called Nominalists, were to some extent direct or indirect
philosophical disciples of the fourteenth-century English Franciscan theologian William of Ockham. Erasmus disliked both traditions but particularly
objected to the highly sophisticated (and in his opinion sophistic) pursuit of
logical studies by the Nominalists. He was well aware of the conflicts between
contending 'ways' that had raged in the University of Paris just a few years
before Béda himself came there as a student. These conflicts would have been
fairly recent events, probably still discussed during Béda's years of study. Obviously Erasmus, whose stay at Paris was much shorter and whose status as
a member of the university community was irregular if not nonexistent, had
learned about the earlier conflicts within the academic community. Cf Epp
1581:651–7 and nn82, 83; 1672 n14, 1679 n5.
18 That is, great patristic authorities like the sainted Cyprian and Ambrose would
   fail to pass the test of having been schooled in the tradition of the Nominalists,
   whom changing fashion had recently made the dominant group at Paris.
19 Erasmus had already clearly expressed his judgment that even the greatest
   doctors of the scholastic tradition, while sometimes useful, were not reliable
   guides to the understanding of Scripture or of doctrine in general. Béda had
   urged him to study the scholastic theologians and to be more respectful of
   their authority (Ep 1579:24–34, 185–90), but Erasmus in response strongly expressed his distaste for them and his mistrust of them as guides in theology
   (Ep 1581:90–100, 134–6, 601–11, 645–68).

largely responsible for the discovery of the arts.[20] Cousturier uses this to ar-   100
gue as follows: 'God is the master of all knowledge, and Erasmus attributes
to Folly the discovery of knowledge; he is, therefore, a blasphemer against
God.'

Then in his thundering prose he attacks me with any evidence that
can be stretched to look like a real case of blasphemy. And what nonsense   105
he writes! Besides twisting the words of the mystic song[21] to apply to human arts, when the meaning is that nothing is hidden from God and there is
nothing that escapes his knowledge, he accuses me of blasphemy against the
Virgin Mother. For I said somewhere that there was a kind of 'intercourse'
[*coitus*] between God and the Virgin,[22] and that Gabriel was the 'grooms-   110
man' [*pronubus*] for this marriage.[23] First, Cousturier did not understand
my meaning, for I am not speaking about the union of the divine and human nature in one hypostasis or of the marriage of the bridegroom Christ

* * * * *

20 Allen's note here refers to *Moriae encomium* LB IV 427B, 434A–B, 435A (ASD IV-
   3 102, 110, 111–12 / CWE 27 102, 107, 108), but the parallels are not close. All
   three references show Folly to be the source of the arts and sciences, but none
   of them refers to Chance (*Casus*). Although his *Folly* expressed religious ideas
   that he held very firmly, Erasmus was always somewhat defensive about its
   jocular tone and conceded that it was a work written in more stable times and
   that he would not have written it, at least not in the same way, under the
   troubled circumstances of religious upheaval; see, for example, *Praestigiarum
   libelli cuiusdam detectio* LB X 1559F: 'I wrote the *Folly* when things were quiet,
   when the world was sunken in ceremonies and the rules of men, and I definitely would not have written it if I had known then that the disorders of the
   present times would arise'). See also Clarence Miller's introduction to *Moriae
   encomium* in ASD IV-3 24–8.
21 Erasmus refers to the Song of Hannah in 1 Sam 2:10, in which Hannah glo-
   rifies God in thankfulness for the birth of her son Samuel in response to her
   prayer. Cf Erasmus *Appendix respondens ad quaedam Antapologiae Petri Sutoris*
   LB IX 805E).
22 Paraphrase on Matthew 1:18 LB VII 6B. The Latin text reads: 'Verum is foe-
   tus non erat profectus e complexu viri, quemadmodum reliquae foeminae so-
   lent juxta communem naturae legem concipere, sed a Spiritu Sancto, qui per
   Gabrielem Angelum internuncium, coelitus illapsus in sacratissimum tem-
   plum uteri virginei, paterni Numinis invisibili virtute, sanctissimae virginis
   totum corpus et animum ceu complexu quodam obumbrante, citra nullum pudoris detrimentum gravidam reddiderat.' Cf Paraphrase on Luke 1:26 LB VII
   288F and on 1:35 LB VII 290B–C. In his *Appendix respondens* (cited in previous
   note), Erasmus demonstrates at some length that his phrase 'a kind of "intercourse"' is in no sense blasphemous but comes from the New Testament
   accounts of the Annunciation (LB IX 806E–807B).
23 Luke 1:19, 26

with his bride the church; I mean what Hilary means when he says that God
the Father in some way caused his Son to be born from the Virgin.[24] I say   115
that Gabriel is introduced here as the *paranymphus*, which in Latin I call the
pronubus, and that the Holy Spirit fulfilled the role that is generally performed in other cases by the action of the seed. He claims that *coitus* is not
used in Scripture except to refer to carnal intercourse between the man and
the woman. Granted; but so that no one could think of ordinary intercourse,   120
I said 'a sort of coitus.' This stupid slander he lays before the saints and
men of every class.

So much I have seen; the opening pages show what he is likely to say
as he warms to his subject. I see no good reason, however, for wanting you
to know these things. For it is too late for me to protest against his treatment   125
of me and pointless for your community to complain of the effect on you.
The work is already on sale, and he will not be influenced by your authority
since he has already shown his contempt twice for the authority of the theologians. When he published the earlier volume, Noël Béda tried to restrain
him from writing so intemperately, not because he cared for my reputation,   130
but because he realized the disgrace that would follow if the world knew
that such a writer had come from the Sorbonne. What I am telling you about
Béda is not something I imagined: he himself told me in a letter.[25] Nor is he
the only one who is upset by Cousturier's manner. There are many among
the ranks of the theologians who are deeply offended by him and ashamed   135
to have such a colleague. Theologians like Cousturier do nothing to cure
heresy; on the contrary, they turn the orthodox into heretics – though this is
something he will never be able to do to me, even if he rails against me in
a thousand volumes. Do you think he will yield to your authority when he
attacks a work that I undertook under the sponsorship of the Roman pon-   140
tiff and completed with his approval and for which I am thanked by many
bishops and theologians? Nevertheless, whatever the case may be, I did not
want you to be left in the dark, so that, if you are not able to do anything
for my reputation, you may at least, with your usual good sense, take some
thought for the honour of the profession and the redemption of the man   145

* * * * *

24 *In Matthaeum* 1:3, but not a very close match to Erasmus' text. See PL 9 920 or
   Hilaire de Poitiers sur Matthieu ed Jean Doignon, 2 vols (Paris 1978–9) I 94.
25 Ep 1642:53–60, in which Béda concedes that Cousturier's treatment of Erasmus and Lefèvre in his *Antapologia* was 'excessively arrogant and sarcastic'
   and claims to have reproved him, but still essentially dismisses Erasmus'
   complaint against him. Béda's letter does not suggest that he was as upset by
   Cousturier's extreme tone as Erasmus here suggests.

himself. As for me, since the thing has clearly reached the point of madness, I shall not be provoked in future into a reply.

Farewell, and please commend this poor sinner in your prayers to our most merciful Lord.

Basel, 7 April 1526

150

1688 / To Martin Luther   Basel, 11 April 1526

The chilly and distant tone of this reply to a lost letter from Luther reflects Erasmus' fury at Luther's manner of treating him not just as an incompetent theologian but as a person with no religious belief at all, a mere sceptic and Epicurean. Erasmus took care to include it (but not the letter to which it replies) in his *Opus epistolarum*. Luther in *De servo arbitrio* passed brutally harsh judgments on Erasmus. Perhaps the most extreme (and best-known) of these passages (WA 18 605) is translated by Philip S. Watson in *Luther's Works* ed Jaroslav Pelikan, Helmut T. Lehman, and others 33 (Philadelphia 1972) 24 as follows: 'By such tactics you only succeed in showing that you foster in your heart a Lucian, or some other pig from Epicurus' sty who, having no belief in God himself, secretly ridicules all who have a belief and confess it. Permit us to be assertors, to be devoted to assertions and delight in them, while you stick to your Skeptics and Academics till Christ calls you too. The Holy Spirit is no Skeptic, and it is not doubts or mere opinions that he has written on our hearts, but assertions more sure and certain than life itself and all experience.' Luther's tone in the missing letter seems to have been at least as contemptuous and condescending as this passage, expressing pity for Erasmus as an unbelieving soul and adding that Erasmus should be thankful that his response to *De libero arbitrio* was so mild. See Epp 1690:21–8, 1697:14–18, 1717:51–2, 1753:32–6; also a letter from More to Erasmus, Ep 1770:63–5, and *Hyperaspistes* 2 LB X 1486B–C / CWE 77 641–2. Cf Erasmus' preface to *Hyperaspistes 1*, Ep 1667.

ERASMUS OF ROTTERDAM TO MARTIN LUTHER, GREETING
Your letter[1] arrived too late; but even if it had come earlier, it would have had no effect on me. I am not such a child that after suffering so many deadly wounds I can be placated by one or two little jokes and soothed by a flattering pat on the head. The whole world now knows what kind   5 of man you are. So you restrained your pen! Well, you were so restrained that you never attacked anyone before with such ferocity or, what is more

* * * * *

1688
1 Not extant; see the introduction above.

contemptible, with such malice! Now you want to claim that you are a weak sinner, though at other times you only ask not to be treated as a god. You are, as you say, a man with a passionate temper – and you are   10 delighted to have such a remarkable excuse. Why, then, did you not use this wonderful δείνωσις² long ago when you attacked Cochlaeus³ and the bishop of Rochester?⁴ They mention you by name and resort to provocative and abusive language, while in my *Diatribe* I made my arguments in a civil manner. What is the point of all those scurrilous insults and   15 the false charges that I am an atheist, an Epicurean, a sceptic in matters belonging to the Christian faith, a blasphemer, and whatever else comes into your head – to say nothing of the many other accusations you claim to pass over in silence? These insults I take the more lightly because in no case do I suffer the sting of conscience. If my ideas about God and   20 the Scriptures were not those of a true Christian, I would not wish my life prolonged for a single day. If you had made your case with all your usual intensity but without those raving insults, you would have stirred up fewer people against you. But you chose instead to give in to your

* * * * *

2 The Greek word Erasmus uses here means 'vehemence,' 'intensity,' 'indignation' (as in Aristotle *Rhetoric* 3.16 1417a13, 3.19 1419b26). In rhetoric the word is used for intensity of style, especially when it is employed to cause hatred of a person or disgust at something (Aristotle *Rhetoric* 2.24 1401b3; Quintilian 6.2.24 and 9.2.104; Cicero *De inventione* 1.100). For discussion of this expression, see G.M.A. Grube *A Greek Critic: Demetrius on Style* (Toronto 1961) 136–7.
3 Johannes Cochlaeus (Dobnek) was one of the most extreme and persistent Roman Catholic critics of Luther from 1521, when personal interviews with Luther confirmed his belief that the Reformer was a threat to the unity of the church. Erasmus had corresponded with him since at least 1525 (Ep 1577 n2), though his first surviving letter is of the summer of 1527 (Ep 1863). The connection persisted to the end of Erasmus' life even though he was critical of the violent tone of Cochlaeus' polemics.
4 John Fisher, one of Erasmus' closest English friends and patrons (Ep 229), had become active in controversy against both Luther and Oecolampadius – against Luther in a famous vernacular sermon of 1521 and in two learned Latin treatises; against Oecolampadius in a Latin treatise focused directly on Oecolampadius' Sacramentarian interpretation of the presence of Christ's body in the Eucharist, though the latter work had not been published, and perhaps not yet finished, at the date of this letter. All three of the Latin treatises were widely regarded as major English contributions to attack on the new heresies. See Edward Surtz *The Works and Days of John Fisher (1469–1535)* (Cambridge, MA 1967), chapters 16–18.

nature[5] and devote more than a third of the book to this sort of abuse. As   25
for treating me gently, the facts speak for themselves: your work is filled
with undisguised invective, while in my *Diatribe* I refused to raise even
those matters of which the world is aware.

You imagine, I suppose, that Erasmus has no supporters. He has more
than you think. But it does not matter greatly what happens to the two of us,   30
especially not to me, since, even if the whole world applauded me, I must
soon depart this life. What distresses me, as it distresses all decent people,
is the fact that because of your arrogant, insolent, and turbulent personality
you cause a fatal dissension that unsettles the whole world, you expose good
men and lovers of the humanities to the fury of the Pharisees,[6] and you arm   35
wicked and rebellious men for revolution[7] – in a word you treat the cause
of the gospel in such a way as to throw everything into confusion, both
sacred and profane; it is as if you did not want the present turmoil ever
to have a happy ending, something that has always been my most earnest
wish. I do not ask what you owe to me, what profit you have reaped. That,   40
whatever it is, is a private matter between us. It is the calamity affecting
us all that troubles me, the universal confusion for which there seems no
remedy; this we owe to no one but you with your headstrong nature, which
is impervious to the good advice of friends but open on any subject to the
influence of a few scheming nonentities. I do not know whom you rescued   45

* * * * *

5 Erasmus' initial judgment of Luther, expressed in letters of 1519–20, was that
  he was a good man who meant well, even if he was somewhat too outspoken.
  But beginning about 1521 (Ep 1218), Erasmus began questioning the underlying spirit of Luther and commenting on his bitterness, even suggesting in a
  letter to Luther himself (Ep 1445, dated 8 May 1524) a Satanic spirit (lines 6–
  8). The question of the spirit behind Luther's words and deeds also appeared
  in a letter of 1523 to Zwingli (Ep 1384:16–22). Even in letters to vehemently
  Catholic princes, however, Erasmus still regarded Luther as 'a kind of necessary evil,' as 'violent and bitter medicine'; see Epp 1495:9–11 (6 September
  1524, to Duke George of Saxony), 1515:64 (20 November 1524, to Archduke
  Ferdinand). Thus by the time he published *De libero arbitrio*, he was ambivalent
  about Luther's character and offended by his 'arrogant, insolent, and turbulent
  personality' (line 29), yet not totally negative.
6 That is, the anti-humanistic monks and theologians who encouraged the kind of
  materialistic and externalized piety that Erasmus had denounced years before
  Luther had been heard from
7 An allusion to the Peasant War of 1524–5, for which Erasmus, like many more
  conservative Catholics, held Luther at least partly responsible. See Ep 1686
  n4 and CWE 11 xi–xii and Mark U. Edwards *Printing, Propaganda, and Martin
  Luther* (Berkeley 1994) 149–62.

from the powers of darkness; you should have turned the sharp point of
your pen against them for their ingratitude instead of attacking a treatise
that was written in a moderate tone. If you did not find your present attitude
so much to your liking, I might hope you would come to a better frame of
mind. You can wish for me whatever you please as long as you do not wish   50
that I have your attitude – unless the Lord will change it for you.

Basel, 11 April 1526, the day on which your letter was delivered

1689 / To Bernhard von Cles   Basel, 16 April 1526

On the recipient, who was bishop of Trent and the most influential adviser
to Archduke Ferdinand, see Epp 1357 introduction, 1738 introduction. Bishop
Bernhard was active as a patron of scholars, including several of the German
controversialists who wrote against Luther. He was consistently favourable to
Erasmus, who in 1523 had relied on him to give to Archduke Ferdinand the
presentation copy of Erasmus' Paraphrase on the Gospel of St Matthew, which
he had dedicated to the archduke. From 1524 he repeatedly invited Erasmus to
become his permanent guest at Trent (Ep 1409, an invitation repeated in Epp
1771, 2159, 2295, 2299, and 2383). Erasmus published this letter in his *Opus
epistolarum*.

ERASMUS OF ROTTERDAM TO BERNHARD, BISHOP OF TRENT,
GREETING
Reverend bishop, when I reflect that my obligation to you would be no less
even if I had accepted the many generous gifts that despite my unworthi-
ness you are kind enough to offer me, and when you add every day to your   5
favour towards me by new acts of kindness, I do not worry about finding
words to thank you, for that would be too commonplace a way of recognizing your generosity; I would prefer to find an opportunity to show you clear
proof of my gratitude. If you do not give me such an opportunity or if fortune does not cast one in my way, I shall create an opening for myself – and,   10
I hope, before too long.[1] In the meantime, if it is not too much trouble, please
encourage our illustrious prince[2] in the affection and good will that he shows
towards me and remind him of me frequently. The bearer of this letter is a

* * * * *

1689
1 A promise fulfilled the following summer with the dedication of Erasmus'
  edition of the works of St Irenaeus to Bishop Bernhard
2 Archduke Ferdinand, who ruled the Hapsburgs' Austrian duchies and acted as
  deputy for his brother the emperor while the latter was absent from imperial
  territory

young man of known and proven honesty. He is defending himself in a most just case, which makes me confident that you will not fail him.[3] I shall not give you an account of the case until I first tell you a story that I read recently in Seneca,[4] an author whose trustworthiness is beyond question. Perhaps this is not the only circumstance in which you will find it useful to recall the story.

Philip, king of Macedon, takes his place in the ranks of virtuous princes. He was the father of Alexander the Great, though he himself was greater than his celebrated son in those qualities of character that truly matter.[5] His fame rests first and foremost on his fairness and courtesy. He had a soldier who was stout of arm but warped in mind, whose support he had found useful on many campaigns and to whom he had often given a piece of the booty in recognition of his valour. By frequent gifts he kindled in the man's venal heart an appetite for plunder; it was like throwing the guts of an animal to a dog to make it keener for the hunt. The soldier's ship was wrecked in a storm and he was driven ashore on the property of a certain Macedonian. When the Macedonian learned of this, he fetched the man, revived him from his half-conscious state, and looked after him with great kindness for several days. Finally, when he was ready to leave, he supplied him with money for the journey. All this time the soldier kept saying to his host: 'If ever I am fortunate enough to see my commander again, I'll show you how grateful I am.' And he did as he promised. He went to the king and told him of the shipwreck, but said nothing about the help he had received. Then he proceeded to trump up a case against his benefactor and asked the king for the estate of his Macedonian host, who had taken him in, revived him, restored him to health, and assisted him with money for the journey. This was how he showed his gratitude. The king was fond of the stalwart soldier, was sorry about the shipwreck, and trusted the ungrateful wretch. In short, he gave him what he asked. This shows how even just princes make mistakes, especially in time of war.

* * * * *

3 This person, identified as Heinrich in Ep 1690, was Heinrich Schürer of Waldshut. Because the Hapsburg authorities believed that he was associated with both the Anabaptist movement and the peasant uprising, two of his estates were confiscated – through no fault of his own, according to Erasmus. He was now seeking redress from the Hapsburg government. Both Bishop Bernhard and Johannes Fabri, recipient of the following letter, were leading advisers of the Hapsburg ruler, Archduke Ferdinand. Occasional later mention of him in Erasmus' correspondence (Epp 2326, 2331, 2344) suggests that in 1529 and 1530 he was still petitioning in vain for restoration of his properties.
4 *De beneficiis* 4.37–8
5 This comparison between King Philip and his son Alexander the Great depends on Cicero *De officiis* 1.90.

I shall not finish my story without mentioning some of the moral aphorisms that Seneca inserted into the passage. 'Kings,' he said, 'give many gifts
with their eyes closed, especially in time of war. A just man is no match for 45
avarice equipped with arms. No one can be at the same time a good man
and a good leader. How will he satisfy so much insatiable greed? What will
a man have, if he has nothing but his own?'[6] The Macedonian was evicted,
but he did not accept the treachery of his ungrateful guest without a protest.
He explained the whole episode to the king in a brief, but frank, letter. The 50
good king was as much upset as the man who had been evicted. He acted at
once and ordered Pausanias – for that was the soldier's name[7] – to restore
the man immediately to his former property. What was the proper recompense for a disloyal soldier, an ungrateful guest, a greedy castaway, and a
shameless claimant? He should have carried a brand on his brow marking 55
him out as an ungrateful guest.

Perhaps this cautionary tale is not altogether parallel to the present
case. Nevertheless, there is a warning here for our excellent prince Ferdinand not to let anyone take a similar advantage of his good nature.
Punishment for the incorrigibly wicked is perfectly justified – although 60
where the disease is mild I think the sufferer should be treated rather than
punished. In the present case our prudent prince should be careful that
under the guise of justice an injustice is not done to the innocent. Many
people will appear who, under the banner of religion, will try to take revenge on those whom they dislike; more are on the lookout for what they 65
can get; and no one who has anything will escape their slanders. The whole
of Basel knows that this young man[8] has not only had nothing to do with
these factions (something that is rare and remarkable in this place), but
has always given such people a wide berth. In spite of this he is robbed
of two estates. He himself will tell you the rest of the story. He has no 70
fear about pleading his case before any judge you wish to name. Such is
the confidence of an innocent mind. You can easily learn the other facts
of the case either from that distinguished man, Johannes Fabri,[9] or from
the victim himself. May the good Lord Jesus keep your lordship safe and
well. 75

Basel, 16 April 1526

* * * * *

6 Seneca *De beneficiis* 4.37.2. The aphorisms are joined in a continuous sequence
in Seneca's text, just as Erasmus cites them.
7 *De beneficiis* 4.37.3
8 That is, Heinrich Schürer, the bearer of the letter
9 See the following letter.

1690 / To Johannes Fabri   Basel, [c 16 April] 1526

The recipient, an ardent admirer of Erasmus, was a firm and rather harsh opponent of Luther and Zwingli. As a close adviser of Archduke Ferdinand, he
was one of the major influences behind the repressive religious policy that the
Hapsburg administration adopted in the territories subject to the dynasty's direct rule in Austria and in the Vorland (or Vorderösterreich) in the far southwest of Germany. Thus Erasmus is writing to a powerful friend. At the same
time he wants to put a certain distance between himself and Fabri and, above
all, to discourage overzealous use of his own name in Fabri's writings against
the Lutherans. On earlier contact with Fabri see Ep 386 introduction; cf Epp
953, 976. Erasmus included this letter in his *Opus epistolarum*.

ERASMUS OF ROTTERDAM TO JOHANNES FABRI, GREETING
I cannot take it amiss when a good friend acts with the best of intentions.
Even if my protest has arrived too late, the advice may perhaps be useful in
the future. No doubt it is because of your devotion to me that you praise me
to the skies and brandish my name to frighten off the zealous supporters of   5
these new sects. But this brings with it problems of two sorts: first, you stir
up a hornets' nest,[1] when the hornets are mad enough by themselves, and
secondly you throw me, naked and unarmed, against a powerful faction that
has strong forces on its side and is particularly formidable because of the
scurrility of its writings. You see the hostility with which Luther attacked   10
me, though provoked by no insults from me. What would he do if he were
truly roiled? He deliberately took great pains with the book; he wanted it
to succeed and hoped my crimes would live on in its pages. The work has
already been published ten times in different places.[2]
     I know you will say one should pay no attention to accusations from   15
people like that. But since the leaders of the church, who enjoy great authority and good fortune, do not have the courage to do this, why do you bid
me do it, when I have neither the prestige to deter the slanderer nor a life so
pure that no suspicion about the truth of their charges will cling to me? Can

* * * * *

1690
1 *Adagia* I i 60
2 Erasmus was not far off in his count. The editor of *De servo arbitrio* for the
  Weimar edition lists the first edition of December 1525 and eight Latin and
  two German editions (in a vernacular translation by Justus Jonas) for the year
  1526, though it is not certain that all of these had appeared by the date of this
  letter.

you imagine the abuse Luther would hurl at my head if he were seriously   20
provoked, when, in a treatise written in what he considers a friendly and
conciliatory manner, he did not scruple to fire accusation after accusation
at me, charging that, like Lucian, I do not believe in the existence of God,
that, like Epicurus, I believe that God takes no interest in human affairs,
that I mock the Holy Scriptures, and that I am an enemy of the Christian re-   25
ligion?³ And yet he himself in a letter, a copy of which I am sending you,
comes close to demanding my gratitude for showing unwonted and unchar-
acteristic restraint when he took up his pen against me.⁴ In fact, his friends
seem genuinely surprised at the moderate tone of his reply when he was so
dreadfully provoked! They refer, doubtless, to my *Diatribe*, which contains   30
no insulting language about anyone.

I think a good man should be concerned about slander, even if the slander is without foundation. Can you imagine anything more charming than
these worthies? No conceivable charge is so horrible that this crew would
be reluctant to approve it. They are highly skilled at making their calum-   35
nies seem credible. No one can ever completely clear himself of a serious
charge: some trace of suspicion always lingers in the minds of men, and the
more serious and shameless the invention, the more readily it is believed.
Many people imagine there must be something in it since the accuser dared
to make such a serious charge. Even if one's behaviour disarms suspicion,   40
what will posterity think when it reads the indictment but has no personal
knowledge of us? These people understand the situation they are in: they
know that if they do not press on, they cannot be safe; as a result they will
do anything to avoid losing ground. Moreover, although they act as though
they are not interested in winning, yet every day we see the infection spread   45
far and wide; so if I have to flee from here, I can think of no place where I
would be safe.

* * * * *

3 See Ep 1667 introduction and Ep 1688 introduction for the blunt denunciations in *De servo arbitrio* charging that Erasmus had no religious faith at all
   and despised all religion like the Greek satirist Lucian of Samosata (second
   century AD) and the Greek philosopher Epicurus. In fact Erasmus was a great
   admirer of Lucian and early in his career had collaborated with Thomas More
   to translate several of Lucian's *Epigrammata* from Greek into Latin; cf Epp
   1670 nn4, 5; 1697 n14. But it was Lucian's wit and sense of humour that attracted both Erasmus and More, who excused his disdain for religion by noting that it was aimed at the fables of pagan religion, which Christians also
   opposed.
4 Not extant; see Ep 1688 introduction for reference to other letters in which
   Erasmus describes the patronizing tone of Luther's letter.

But supposing I could find someone to protect my person, what defence is there against fanatical books? At first Luther decided to disregard my *Diatribe*, as he himself admits, but some of his friends were upset by   50
the crowing of certain of their opponents and wrote to persuade him that, if he wanted their sect to survive, he should rub my nose in the dust. Among these, I am told, was a man who had once been a very close friend of yours and benefited from your generosity.[5] Nevertheless, if this storm could be stilled by the loss of a single Carian,[6] I would not refuse to sacrifice myself   55
for the common weal, and I would consider it gain if by my private suffering I might cure the public ill. My actions have brought me suffering to be sure, but, far from curing the public ill, they have made things worse. I wrote the *Diatribe* simply to please the princes and to leave no one in any doubt of my antipathy towards the Lutheran faction. That was what was im-   60
portant for me and for everyone else. But I knew that I would succeed only in impelling Luther to take up his pen in support of the doctrine under attack. At the very beginning I warned that the monks and theologians were assisting Luther's cause; I was not listened to. Shortly afterwards I showed how the trouble could be ended; my plan was rejected. Thirdly I raised the   65
subject in a letter to Pope Adrian;[7] I infer that my advice did not please him, for he did not reply. Now we see where things have got to. In France some of Béda's followers are on a mad rampage with censures, propositions, imprisonments, burnings, and pamphlets. I wish the plague could be controlled by such measures, but time will show that these only make the   70
problem worse.

Let me point out the strategies on which the Lutheran faction mainly relies. Sermons are preached to attract people to the cause and hold them there. Young people and those who are interested in such things are won over by support for the study of languages and letters. For the common   75

* * * * *

5 Allen (48n) suggests that this former friend was Urbanus Rhegius, who had also been an admirer of Erasmus but beginning in 1521 had become a follower first of Luther and then of Zwingli. At this period he was a preacher in Augsburg. As early as 21 October 1524, Rhegius had written to Johannes Oecolampadius sharply criticizing Fabri's activities in Hungary and Styria as a misuse of authority in order to persecute the true church, reporting that he was responsible for the burning of an innocent man. See WA-Br III 369 Ep 789 n8. See also Allen Ep 1678:36n for a much later (1530) reference to an Augsburg preacher who vehemently urged Luther to attack Erasmus. This may have been Rhegius.
6 That is, a worthless person; see *Adagia* I vi 14.
7 Ep 1352

people the bait is their love of liberty. The printing press, too, plays no small role. In addition to all this the Lutherans are greatly assisted by the almost universal hatred of bad monks, pleasure-loving[8] priests and hare-brained theologians (I am not referring to the honest ones among them). Many of the nobility, especially the lower nobility, are inclined to support 80 them, because they covet the church's wealth. Perhaps a few princes will be ready to turn the public turmoil to their personal advantage, like men who make a profit at the expense of others from a shipwreck or a fire. But if we continue to make things worse by barbed tracts, imprisonments, and executions, the painful result, I am afraid, will be total anarchy. 85

What we have seen is the beginning. The pope has restrained his people from pointing their pens at Luther, and he is wise. The Italians will leave us to battle with one another – and they will rejoice at our folly. It is time we came to our senses and, putting aside all concern for private advantage, gave our sincere attention to the interests of the nation.[9] We should 90 remember that we are all in the same boat and that it cannot sink without taking all of us to destruction with it. The disease is too serious and too widespread to be cured by ordinary remedies.

If you ask what measures I think should be taken, that question calls for a greater brain than mine; and yet, if kings seriously want my advice, I 95 shall be glad to give it, for what it is worth, provided our discussions are kept secret. We know the sort of books with which the Lutherans are flooding the world; and the stuff that is written in reply by some of our theologians is not much better. What is achieved by this battle of the books except to make the fire spread? It is the same with sermons from both sides: fierce 100 insults are traded by both parties, and the rope of controversy[10] is pulled tighter. If troublemakers are removed from the schools only to be succeeded by men whose aim is to undo the study of good and useful literature, nothing will be accomplished. The controversy goes on without end. Irresponsible preachers should be removed, especially some of the most prominent 105 ones. In their place we should appoint honest men, who will steer clear of

* * * * *

8 In Latin *Epicureos*, literally 'Epicurean'
9 The Latin is *reip[ublicae]*. The closest translation is probably 'nation,' or even 'German nation' or 'German people,' with the proviso that one must recall that in the sixteenth century, especially for the cosmopolitan Erasmus, 'nation' did not have the connotations or the emotional power of 'nation-state' that the word acquired during and after the French Revolution. A more guarded though less literal translation might be 'commonwealth,' or even 'society.'
10 Latin *contentionis funiculus*, a reference to *Adagia* III iii 77, where the word is *filum* 'thread' rather than *funiculus*.

controversial doctrines and impart only those ideas that promote piety and good morals without raising contentious issues. The elementary schools and the teaching of languages should be entrusted to those who are free from bias and who are willing to teach what children need to know. Some people are now so obsessed with hatred of Luther that they are ready to destroy the humanities and all who study them, thus driving into Luther's camp those they should be wooing. Meanwhile in the name of piety even the innocent are being cruelly treated. Those who foment sedition should be punished severely, but in such a way that the least possible harm is done to the inno- cent, that those who are capable of redemption are not driven away, and that the people are spared. Perhaps in those cities where the evil has taken root the best course will be to make room for both parties and to leave every man to his own conscience until the time comes when there is some hope of peace. Meanwhile those who incite rebellion should face stern penalties, and we ourselves should immediately correct those faults that help the evil to flourish. All the rest should be left to a general council.

But I shall have more to say about this later if I see the subject interests you – or, better still, we can discuss it face to face. In the meantime I beg you, for the sake of our friendship, to cease stirring up those hornets against me, unless you want to put an end to my life. I know you are well disposed to me and I do not deny that I am in your debt. But there is one more service you can add to those you have already done me in the past: see that the enthusiasm of a friend does not accomplish what my enemies would dearly like to accomplish. Some supporters of mine have been ill-advised enough to ask the emperor for a stern and threatening edict against the hotheads at Louvain.[11] Nothing would be better calculated to provoke them against me. Now that I have entered the fray, I cannot stand my ground without the strong and evident support of the kings. Things can no longer continue in the dark.

* * * * *

11 While no formal law was enacted, the emperor did send to the University of Louvain a direct command to silence the theologians who were attacking Erasmus. Its text does not survive. Erasmus' conclusion that it was met with successful obstruction and merely confirmed their hostility to him is well doc- umented (see also Ep 1747 and introduction and Allen Ep 1815:26–31), even though his most powerful advocate at the imperial court, the chancellor Mer- curino Gattinara, wrote in his own name (Ep 1784A) demanding that the lead- ers of the university suppress attacks on Erasmus. Erasmus had sought in- tervention by the court (see Ep 1554 to Jean Lalemand, secretary to Charles v, and Ep 1643, from Gattinara to Erasmus), but perhaps not intervention so blunt that it was bound to deepen the hostility of the faculty to him.

You will say: 'How can they help when you always refuse positions of distinction?' I am right to refuse these burdens, since I am scarcely strong enough to support myself. Let me tell you a story.[12] A certain Ruffus, who belonged to the senatorial order, having drunk too much at a dinner party, prayed that the emperor Augustus would not return safely from a journey he was planning; then he added something only a drunk man would say, that all the bulls and calves wished for the same thing. A slave who was standing at his side told his master the next morning what he had said in his cups and advised him to get to Caesar first and confess. He met Caesar on his way to the forum and confessed the malicious thoughts he had had the night before; he now wished, he said, that the curse would fall on his own head and on his children. Caesar, with his remarkable clemency, forgave the man. Then Ruffus said, 'But no one will believe that you and I are friends again unless you give me a present.' And he asked for a sum of money that one might hardly expect to get from a close friend. Caesar gave him the money and added, 'I shall make sure in future that I never fall out with you again!' Nor was this all; the slave who had warned his master was set free, and Caesar paid for his manumission.

The story ended happily for Ruffus, for Caesar piled kindness on top of clemency. So I do not think it would be immodest of me to hope for some show of favour from our generous prince that I can show off to everyone to prove how close I am to Ferdinand. I have no doubt that, given the kindness of his nature, he will be glad to do this if you suggest it to him. First, the reason behind the gift should be evident and secondly, it should be something that can be used every day. I have several gifts from princes that I prize very highly, not so much for their value as because they are proof of their affection for me. I consider it no small achievement to have won their favour.

Heinrich, who carries this letter, hangs all his hopes on you.[13] I know you will see he is not disappointed. Give my greetings to Master Lukas,[14]

* * * * *

12 Seneca *De beneficiis* 3.27
13 Ep 1689 n3.
14 Lukas Klett, also known as Paliurus, a jurist whom Erasmus met at Basel on his first visit there in 1514. He had succeeded Fabri as chancellor to the bishop of Basel, Christoph von Utenheim, and at this time was meeting with Fabri and Archduke Ferdinand at Tübingen, probably to discuss nomination of a successor to Bishop Christoph, who had indicated his intention of resigning (he did so on 19 February 1527, less than a month before his death at Porrentruy). As Klett's predecessor as chancellor to the bishop and as a councillor to Archduke Ferdinand, Fabri was naturally involved in discussions about

and to Cantiuncula[15] if he is there, and to Jakob Spiegel.[16] I pray for every blessing on our most illustrious prince, as his talents deserve. Farewell.

Basel, 1526

1691 / From Duke George of Saxony   Leipzig, 16 April 1526

> Duke George, one of the most resolutely Catholic of the German princes, had pressed Erasmus to write against Luther from the summer of 1522 (Ep 1298) and had been delighted by publication of *De libero arbitrio* in 1524, though he thought it long overdue (Epp 1503, 1520, 1550). The Saxon ruler repeatedly sent Erasmus copies of Luther's publications, trying to commit the unwilling humanist to refuting each of Luther's works. An almost comical series of letters pitted the aggressive prince against the elusive scholar, but Erasmus found excuses (including the unlikely claim that he could not read books published in High German) and refused to become a full-time pamphleteer; see Epp 1298, 1313, 1325, 1340, 1499, 1503, 1520, 1526, 1550. The further deterioration of his relations with Luther marked by publication of *De servo arbitrio* and *Hyperaspistes 1* pleased Duke George. This letter was first published by J.K. Seidemann in *Zeitschrift für historische Theologie* 13 (1849) 203–4 and again by Adalbert Horawitz in *Sitzungsberichte der kaiserlichen Akademie der Wissenschaften, philosophisch-historische Classe* 90 1 (Vienna 1878) 435–6. Horawitz used a manuscript copy made by a ducal secretary and preserved in the state archives at Dresden. Both Allen and Horawitz also printed a less elegantly phrased Latin draft in Duke George's own hand, demonstrating that he drafted the letter himself in Latin and then had a secretary rework it into a more suitable Latin style.

* * * * *

naming a new bishop for a city that was in danger of falling wholly into the hands of the Protestants, as it did in 1529.

15 See Ep 852:85n. Cantiuncula had received a doctorate in law at Basel and had served as professor of civil law and also as syndic to the city council there, but in 1524, distressed by the growing influence of the Reformation, he resigned his offices and returned to his native city of Metz. By 1525 he had become chancellor to Cardinal Jean de Lorraine, bishop of Metz, who was not only bishop of an imperial city but also an influential figure at the court of Francis I of France. Thus it is likely that he was present as the cardinal's representative at the political and religious consultations conducted by Archduke Ferdinand at Tübingen in the spring of 1526, probably in preparation for the meeting of the imperial Reichstag at Speyer the following summer. In any case, Cantiuncula was the cardinal's representative at the Reichstag.

16 On this well-connected jurist, who at this period was in the service of Archduke Ferdinand, see Ep 323:13n.

GEORGE BY THE GRACE OF GOD DUKE OF SAXONY ETC
Greetings and best wishes, most learned Erasmus. Three months ago there
came into my hands the *Servum arbitrium* of Martin Luther in which he attacks both you and your *Diatribe*. What a fine triumph for the supporters
of the Lutheran faction! How proud they were of the book! They were con-   5
vinced that Luther had outdone himself with this work, that no one had
ever produced anything like it before or ever could do so in the future,
since it was the product of a true and noble inspiration. They were sure that
the man from Rotterdam would not dare to open his mouth in reply; they
thought him completely muzzled and struck dumb. Then out came your   10
Hyperaspistes diatribae, completed in ten days, in which, with great civility,
you demolish Luther's crafty arguments and false charges and stoutly defend your own position.[1] You also point out how one day Christendom can
be rescued from these novel heresies and restored to its former peace. The
Lutherans more than once have wished you dead, but you seem to have risen   15
from the dead and are alive and well again to the benefit of us all. That old
verse about Fabius suddenly came into my head: 'By delaying you will restore the state.'[2] Everyone was convinced that you would succeed, and our
hopes never faltered. The Lutherans have shot their bolt and have nothing
to fight with but the bow, while your quiver is still full of arrows. With the   20
help of the spirit of God and of mother church you will dash Achilles[3] to
the ground and silence him for ever.

So that you do not suffer the hostility of tanners and cobblers, I shall
see to it that your book is made available in German and understood by
them. I have no doubt that many will abandon Luther's views not just   25
on this subject, but on all those other ideas of his that have been condemned. They will realize that it was not for nothing that you kept silent
up to now.

* * * * *

1691
1 Duke George learned of the rapidity of Erasmus' response to Luther's *De servo
   arbitrio* from the letter to the reader prefixed to the first edition of *Hyperaspistes
   1*, printed in March 1526: Ep 1667.
2 Ennius *Annales* 360. Duke George's quotation, *Cunctando restitues rem*, present
   in his own personal draft as well as in the polished letter, is closer to Virgil's
   adaptation of the Ennian line in *Aeneid* 6.846.
3 Symbol of anger and of determination in battle. An Achillean argument is
   one that cannot be refuted; cf *Adagia* I vii 41. In *Hyperaspistes* 1 Erasmus had
   described Luther's arguments against the will's ability to co-operate with grace
   as 'your Achillean and invincible reasons' (CWE 76 185).

Farewell, and press on as you have begun. As evidence of my feelings
for you I am sending you this cup.[4] Another gift would be more appropriate,   30
but I am a Saxon, and the cobbler must stick to his last.[5] Be assured of my
kindest regards.

Given at Leipzig, AD 16 April 1526

To that sound and erudite theologian, Master Erasmus of Rotterdam,
my faithful friend   35

1692 / From Louis de Berquin   Paris, 17 April 1526

On the author of this letter, famous in large part because he was eventually
executed as a heretic in 1529, see Epp 925:17n, 1579:200–19 and nn44, 45, and
1599 introduction and n1, also the substantial article in CEBR. The autograph
letter survived in the Rehdiger collection at Wrocław, which is Allen's main
source, but the text had been printed previously in LB III-2 1712–14 *Appendix
epistolarum* no 335.

BERQUIN TO ERASMUS

The hornets are angry again! They have accused me of heresy before the
Parlement and the pope's delegates.[1] Their only reason for doing so is that I

* * * * *

4 Allen (26n) suggests that this is the cup identified as a gift from Duke George
  in Erasmus' inventory of 1534 and bequeathed to Bonifacius Amerbach in
  Erasmus' will of January 1527 (see Erasmus' First Will, 540 below).
5 The Latin, *tractant fabrilia fabri* (literally, 'workmen handle workmen's tools'),
  is from Horace *Epistles* 2.1.116; cf *Adagia* I vi 15; II ii 82.

1692
1 The reference is to the accusations that Berquin possessed Lutheran books in
  violation of an edict of the Parlement, and that his own works and translations
  were heretical. His difficulties, which involved hearings by the Parlement, the
  faculty, and the new commission of four judges delegate appointed in 1525
  (see Ep 1717 n13), went back to 1523. CEBR I 135–40 provides a concise but
  detailed account of Berquin's several trials: in 1523, when his books were
  burned; again in 1526, when he was formally declared to be a relapsed heretic
  and was released only after the king sent an official supported by a band of
  archers to take physical custody of him; and finally in April 1529, when he was
  rearrested and executed as an unrepentant and relapsed heretic. Only King
  Francis I's repeated and direct intervention, encouraged by his sister Margaret
  of Angoulême, had saved his life in 1523 and 1526. The execution occurred
  during the king's absence from Paris in April 1529, though it is possible that

translated several of your works,[2] which, so they have the effrontery to assert, contain the most serious heresies. I scented at once what they were up   5
to – they wanted, if you please, to have Erasmus' books burned as heretical and myself along with them unless I acknowledged their heretical character.[3] If I did so, they thought it would be punishment enough to have
branded my name with deep and lasting infamy. Being convinced in my
mind that there is nothing in your books that needed to be disavowed as   10
heretical, and valuing my reputation above my life, not only did I not re-
cant, but I insisted you were the sort of person about whom there could not
be the slightest suspicion of heresy. I pointed out that your works were approved by Pope Leo x[4] and that Pope Adrian issued the most cordial invitation to you to go to Rome, not just in one or two letters in his own hand, but   15
also through his legate.[5] I told them that cardinals and princes thought and
spoke well of you, that in a letter Pope Clement made it abundantly clear
how much he liked your Paraphrase on the Acts of the Apostles and proved

* * * * *

Berquin's stubborn insistence on pursuing his complex legal appeals rather
than accepting the judgment had irritated even the king and emboldened his
accusers to act with great speed before the royal court could intervene again.
See, in addition to CEBR, Ep 1599 n1 and Ep 2188, a letter in which Erasmus
reports the execution and summarizes the case.
2 For the titles of the works translated by Berquin and details of their condemnation by the faculty of theology in May 1525, see Ep 1599 n1.
3 Berquin was convinced that the true object of the attack on him was defama-
tion and ultimately condemnation of Erasmus. That is one reason why even
when he faced execution in 1529 he refused to acknowledge as erroneous doctrinal statements that he had derived from Erasmus' works. And because Erasmus perceived such a connection, in Ep 1599, while admitting Berquin's good
intentions, he deplored Berquin's efforts to translate and publish his works in
French.
4 Erasmus had dedicated the first edition of his *Novum instrumentum* (the Greek
New Testament) to Pope Leo in 1516 (Ep 384) and had worked assiduously to
secure the papal brief of 10 September 1518 endorsing his studies of the New
Testament (Ep 864), a brief that was proudly printed on the reverse of the title-
page of the revised second edition in 1518. Erasmus had also obtained from
Pope Leo a valuable favour in the form of a brief authorizing him to hold
ecclesiastical benefices despite the legal impediment caused by his illegitimate
birth (Ep 518; cf Ep 517). He kept the texts of these communications private,
while carefully preserving the brief because of the legal privilege it conferred.
He did, however, publish Ep 519, which accompanied the dispensations and
showed the pope's favour and willingness to grant his request but made no
specific mention of the embarrassing personal details of Erasmus' parentage.
5 Epp 1324:119–32, 1338:49–64

his sincerity by sending you a most generous gift;[6] Erasmus, in his opinion, was the only person capable of refuting Johannes Oecolampadius' teaching 20 on the Eucharist.[7] I happened to hear this story somewhere – please let me know if it is true. I added that when I was translating your works, I never came upon anything unworthy of a Christian, if one took all your works together and read them, not in a captious spirit, but with a fair and open mind. If one encounters anything in your books that is contrary to Christian 25 doctrine, one can only conclude that the text is corrupt or has been tampered with. I mentioned that you had complained of this more than once, most recently in a letter to Béda.[8] I did not want them to think I had made the story up.

As for the translation, I showed them how patently false their accu- 30 sations were, that there was as much difference between my style and the style of the translation they were using as between a fox and a camel. The title was wrong, the name was wrong, there were many additions and more omissions, and many passages had been distorted by the incompetence of the translator. And in case they thought I was saying this to provide a loop- 35 hole for myself, I offered to produce my manuscript to show whether or not I was telling the truth.

The delegates had received two letters from the king's mother, order-ing them to hold the case over until the king arrived,[9] because his most

* * * * *

6 Ep 1443B; cf Epp 1414 and introduction, 1416.
7 For Erasmus' opposition to Oecolampadius' Sacramentarian interpretation of the Eucharist, see Ep 1670 n6 and the references given there; on his plan (never brought to completion) to write a work against the Sacramentarian opinions of Oecolampadius, Zwingli, and others, see especially Ep 1679 n22.
8 In Epp 1581:841–2 and 1679:59–61, addressed to Béda himself, Erasmus com-plained that in some of his translations Berquin had inserted additions of his own that had no connection with what Erasmus had written and for which Erasmus could not be held responsible.
9 Louise of Savoy, regent for King Francis I until he was released from cap-tivity in Spain on 18 March 1526. Although she had permitted the conserva-tives at Paris to pursue more vigorously than before charges of heresy against Berquin, Lefèvre d'Etaples, and others accused of heresy, she did carry out her son's written instructions to order the special commission in the case, the judges delegate, to release Berquin and suspend proceedings against him un-til the king returned to Paris. The Parlement of Paris, however, on being asked by the judges delegate for advice, instructed them to proceed with the trial, as they did, finding Berquin to be a relapsed heretic. After the king was back in France, however, he castigated the Parlement for its failure to obey his mother's order, and the Parlement did not dare to proceed to an execution.

Autograph letter from Louis de Berquin to Erasmus, Ep 1692
MS Rehdiger 254.25, folio 75
Wrocław (Breslau) University Library
Lines 60–88 of the translation correspond to this page of the autograph.

Christian Majesty intended to consult some eminent and judicious men of 40
learning about my case and Lefèvre's [10] and about similar cases involving
other people, and to have them act as judges; in spite of this, not being able
to control their anger, or anxious to please the theologians, or fearful of losing their tyrannical powers, they launched a bitter attack on the reputation
of Erasmus, referring to him constantly as a heretic and an apostate and to 45
myself as his supporter. Finally, they produced certain passages that they
claimed had been selected by the theologians from your book, though they
had been mangled and tampered with; these they asserted were heretical,
schismatic, scandalous, reeking of heresy – that is to say, they did not like
what they read. 50

It would take too long, Erasmus my learned friend, to recount the
whole of my reply; you will have to be content with this, that I did not agree
with them in even a single article. Yet I did not act in a pig-headed way:
I expounded the meaning to them, or I showed how a passage was clarified by the context, or I explained that your intention was different from the 55
way the words sounded, or that something was missing, or that the copy
was corrupt; in a word I took particular care not to submit to their malevolent purpose or give them an excuse for venting their rage against me or
against your books. Nor did I fail to mention the countless 'protestations,'
as they called them.[11] But they took no notice of these or of the edict from 60
the king's mother. But after they had brought in three monks whom I had
previously objected to, especially a Carthusian prior,[12] on the ground that

* * * * *

Thus Berquin was alive and able to send the present letter, though the Parlement refused the king's order to release him and he remained in custody
until October 1526, when royal officers released him from prison by force; see
Ep 1735 n16.
10 See Ep 1674 n27.
11 Apparently a reference to the common practice of writers on religious and theological questions, including Erasmus, of declaring their willingness to submit to the judgment of the church on all controversial questions. The problem,
of course, was who spoke for 'the church.' Unlike Béda, Erasmus obviously
did not assume that it was the faculty of theology at Paris. Indeed, his usual
substitute for the conventional form of protestation was to point out that the
pope, or an appropriate bishop, or a sound theologian (John Fisher or Ludwig Baer, for example, rather than one of his critics at Paris or Louvain) had
already endorsed a specific work that had come under attack.
12 The identity of these monks who participated in the judicial process against
Berquin in the winter of 1526 is not clear. All of the theologians who had been
named to the special committee appointed during his earlier legal process
in 1523 were secular priests (Farge *Orthodoxy* 174). Perhaps the Carthusian

they were prejudiced against you and kept applying to the whole order criticisms which you had made of certain silly individuals like Cousturier, they
did not hesitate to pronounce me a heretic and a supporter of heretics, al-   65
though I had not uttered a word contrary to the Christian faith. At other
times the Parlement has been very prompt in dealing with matters of this
sort, but in this one case it made it very clear indeed that it disapproved of
such hasty and, so to speak, summary justice; for it decided to hear my case
from A to z,[13] which made both the delegates and the theologians fume. Our   70
most Christian king, on the day on which he returned to the country, was
informed of the affair by his mother.[14] Immediately he sent a representative to the Parlement with a letter; he ordered them to wait for his arrival,
and in a second letter he instructed the presidents of the Parlement to take
care of Berquin; he said he would hold them responsible for the man's life   75
or death.

This in a few words is Berquin's sad tale. There is one point I must not
pass over: they marked no passages in the Paraphrase that you dedicated
to the king – you can guess the reason why; they did, however, carry off a
copy of my translation of it along with several other books. In the meantime,   80
while we wait for his royal Majesty, I thought it useful to send you a list
of passages marked by them. I am sending everything they singled out,
but the most important passages, that is, those they attacked most strongly,
I have indicated with a finger sign in the margin. Perhaps you would be
kind enough to reply to their calumnies, and not just in a cursory manner,   85
as you did to Béda, but with a full response backed up by argument and
the authority of Scripture. The king holds you in high regard: he says that
the theologians, although they are ready enough to attack everyone else,
have always been afraid to lay a hand on you. Now that they have begun
the attack, let him see that this time they do not come out on top. He has   90
always been a great admirer of your teaching, and his admiration will be
all the greater when he learns more about the ineptitude of the theologians.

* * * * *

prior was Pierre Cousturier, assuming that he was in Paris during the winter
of 1526 (on the uncertainty of his whereabouts at this period, see Ep 1687
n11). At least he was a Carthusian and a prior, and he was notably hostile to
reformist humanists such as Erasmus and Lefèvre. But this identification is
speculative at best, especially since Berquin mentions Cousturier by name in
a different context just a few lines below.
13 Literally, 'from the egg to the apples,' a proverbial expression referring to the
stages of a dinner party. Cf *Adagia* II iv 86.
14 The proceedings against Berquin in 1525–6 occurred while King Francis I,
Berquin's most powerful defender at this time and throughout his troubles,
was held captive in Spain. See n9 above.

People often say here that for years the theologians of the Sorbonne have not understood a single word in your writings and that they will never understand them until someone comes along to translate them into French. 95 Please send a full reply; whatever is done will be communicated to the king. The courier will wait as long as you wish, nor, I hope, will he complain that his travelling money has run out. If you would like to send a congratulatory eulogy to our prince on his return home, as I suggested some time ago, please do so; the courier will wait. Or if you prefer the courier to return 100 to me after delivering the articles and to send us the panegyric by another messenger, do as you wish. Any courier whom you send will not return without an honorarium; I give you my word on that. He will find out at the Ecu de Bâle[15] or at Bérault's house where I shall be staying, although nowadays Bérault is often absent from the city.[16]   105

* * * * *

15 This famous Paris bookstore and a related one in Lyon were established in 1504 and about 1483, respectively, by Johann Schabler, commonly called Wattenschnee, who had studied at the University of Basel. Schabler used the Basel coat of arms, *l'écu de Bâle* or *scutum Basiliense*, as the ensign for his shops. He acquired citizenship in Basel and eventually moved there and bought that city's principal bookstore. From about 1515 the Paris shop gradually came under the direction of his nephew Konrad Resch, and in 1526 Resch sold it to Chrétien Wechel, a native of Brabant who had become his manager. The shop in the rue Saint-Jacques was a centre for Baslers, especially students, in the French capital, and was an outlet for the publishers of Basel (including Amerbach and his successor, Froben) and other German printing centres. It collaborated with several Paris printers (including Josse Bade and Pierre Vidoue) as a publisher, but only in 1529 did Wechel purchase control of a print-shop at Paris. See Peter G. Bietenholz *Basle and France in the Sixteenth Century* (Geneva 1971) 27–34. Eventually the firm became an independent publisher, operating under the traditional name into the early seventeenth century.

16 On Bérault, a humanist, jurist, courtier, and trusted friend of both Berquin and Erasmus, see Epp 925 introduction, 1571:75 and n15, 1579:132–4 and n28, 1581 n2, 1591 introduction, 1598:2. It is obvious that when he wrote this letter, Berquin was confident that support from the king would lead to his early release from the prison used by the Parlement, the Conciergerie. Just eight days earlier, royal pressure had caused the Parlement to postpone execution of the sentence against Berquin (as a relapsed heretic, he was subject to the death penalty); but the Parlement stubbornly refused royal orders to release him from prison. Finally on 19 November the king sent the provost of Paris with a company of archers to secure delivery of the prisoner. Even then, the Parlement did not agree to his release but allowed the provost to take him away to the Louvre. Technically, he was then regarded as a prisoner held directly by the king, though in reality he was soon free and entered the service of the king's sister, Margaret of Angoulême.

Farewell, most learned Erasmus. As always, count me among your most faithful admirers.

Paris, 17 April 1526

Please excuse my awkward handwriting, especially in the transcript of the articles. I was sick when I wrote, but did not want to disclose these   110 matters to anyone.

1693 / From Simon Pistoris   Leipzig, 19 April 1526

> On the author, chancellor to Duke George of Saxony and a frequent corre-
> spondent of Erasmus, see Ep 1125 n6. The autograph letter became part of the
> Rehdiger collection of manuscripts at Wrocław and was first published in LB
> III-2 1714 *Appendix epistolarum* no 336.

Greetings. I cannot express in words, most learned Erasmus, the regard you have earned from prince George, duke of Saxony, by your *Hyperaspistes*. All your criticisms of Luther accord so well with his own opinion that he could not have hoped for anything better. He never grows weary of read-ing and rereading the book. You have cleared yourself of all the suspicions   5 that weighed against you with him.[1] It was because of your attack, so pow-erful and justified, on Luther's fondness for insults and distortions, that the prince has had several of the man's works translated from German into Latin;[2] these show him heaping praise on an artist for his impudent carica-tures of the different orders;[3] they also show him inciting others to defame   10

* * * * *

1693
1 Duke George had suspected Erasmus of heresy or at least softness on the
  Luther question, and even after the publication of *De libero arbitrio* in 1524 he
  was eager for Erasmus to do more. Thus the bitter tone evident in *Hyperaspistes*
  1 pleased him greatly. See Ep 1691 introduction.
2 Duke George was eager to keep Erasmus busy writing refutations to each of
  the works of Luther as they came off the press, and when Erasmus excused
  his failure to do so by claiming that he could not read High German, the duke
  ordered Latin translations to be made. The real reason for Erasmus' refusal
  was that he despised the niggling polemics on petty issues that marked much
  of the Reformation controversy. See Ep 1691 introduction, and cf Ep 1499:32–4
  for Erasmus' doubts about the usefulness of anti-Lutheran polemical tracts.
3 Many of the vernacular books and pamphlets supporting Luther were illus-
  trated with biting caricatures. An important study of the role of vernacular
  literature and of the visual propaganda that accompanied the printed texts
  is R.W. Scribner *For the Sake of Simple Folk: Popular Propaganda for the German
  Reformation* (Cambridge 1981). Many of the artists are anonymous, though
  important ones like Lucas Cranach, Hans Baldung Grien, Hans Holbein the

and vilify their opponents – and all this, if you please, in the name of Holy Scripture. I enclose these so that you can see again how right you were to make this case against him.

There are many other works of this sort in the vernacular of so shock- 15 ing a character that it is surprising there is a single Christian to applaud them. But who could bear to translate all these works with their brazen insolence into Latin? Three months ago he gave the prince the benefit of his advice in a letter which was more courteous than usual, although not entirely free of his monumental arrogance and regal threats. The prince replied in such a manner that many had to admit, however biased they may have 20 been, that none of the qualities attributed to him were unjustified. I enclose the exchange of letters between the two men, translated into Latin;[4] you will see clearly that the prince views the whole situation as you do.

We await not only a brilliant defence of free will, but a refutation of all those other ideas with which Luther invests the issue, especially his reduc- 25 tion of the church to nothing, his Hussite pronouncements, inspired by the bad behaviour of a few, on the doctrine and religious orders of the church, and his contention that the word of God cannot be spread abroad without turmoil.[5] If you prove these notions false (and of this I have no doubt), you will not just win a victory on the issue of free will but will demolish all 30 those other dogmas with which he blinds the eyes of the people, and you will bring back into the unity of the church those who have thoughtlessly abandoned it. I pray that Jesus Christ will give you the grace to press on boldly to the end along the course you have begun.

I could not keep Ceratinus here.[6] The reason he left, as I found out later, 35 was that he discovered the prince cannot tolerate people who break a vow once made.[7] For I am told he is a priest but did not want to be recognized

* * * * *

Younger, Matthias Gerung, Hans Sebald Beheim, and even Albrecht Dürer were involved.
4 Luther's vernacular letter of 21 December 1525 to Duke George is WA-Br III 637–44 Ep 954; the duke's reply, dated 28 December 1525, is WA-Br III 646–53 Ep 956. Allen (17n) points out that in Ep 1743:63–4 Erasmus reported to Duke George that he had forwarded a copy of these letters, translated into Latin, 'to the English court,' not further specifying the recipient.
5 See n2 above.
6 Erasmus had recommended Jacobus Ceratinus as professor of Greek at Leipzig, but the Saxon government soon regretted the appointment, and he departed after a few weeks. See Ep 1561 n3 and cf Epp 1564–6, and concerning his dismissal, Ep 1611 n2.
7 Ceratinus was suspected at Leipzig of favouring Luther and also of trying to conceal his status as a priest. In fact he was not yet ordained but did become a

as such. A year ago I sent you a confidential letter from Esslingen on a certain subject;[8] although I have not yet received a reply, I see you have partly done what I wanted, and I hope you will deal with the matter more fully in   40
the treatise you have begun. I wish you all the best for the future.

Leipzig, 19 April 1526

Simon Pistoris, doctor etc

1694 / To Adrianus Cornelii Barlandus   Basel, 20 April 1526

On this Louvain humanist see the introductions to Epp 492 and 1584. Barlandus had known Erasmus for many years and had been one of his principal supporters at Louvain. The letter congratulates him on his election as professor of eloquence at Louvain, the day after the death of his predecessor Paludanus (Jean Desmarez) on 20 February 1526. Erasmus published it in his *Opus epistolarum*.

ERASMUS OF ROTTERDAM TO ADRIANUS BARLANDUS, GREETING
Barlandus, my learned friend, there are two considerations that lessen my feelings of regret at the death of Paludanus:[1] first, he had reached the age at which nothing agreeable could be expected from life, and secondly, he has been taken from a world that deals harshly with the best of men. As   5
for your succeeding to the dead man's place, my congratulations go not so much to you for whatever honour and stipend the position may bring as to the cause of learning itself. For some time now not much was added to that cause by Paludanus; it will fare better in your hands, since you were made for such work.   10

There is a matter on which I would like your help. It is something that calls for good faith rather than a lot of trouble and effort. There are people

* * * * *

priest in the Netherlands in 1527. His later career suggests that the suspicions of the Saxons, expressed here by Pistoris, were unjust – or else that soon after leaving Leipzig he changed his opinions on religion. Cf Ep 1611 n2.
8 Not extant, but in Ep 1744 to Pistoris Erasmus may be providing a tardy answer to some of the confidential questions raised in the missing letter.

1694
1 Paludanus (Jean Desmarez) had been professor of eloquence at the University of Louvain and canon of St Peter's church since 1490; he had befriended Erasmus as early as 1502 and in 1517 took him as a guest into the college of which he was president, St Donatian's. He was a fine Latin scholar and a close friend of Maarten van Dorp, Erasmus' most loyal friend on the Louvain faculty of theology. See Ep 180 introduction.

at Louvain who have very great influence with the bishop to whom I am writing;[2] but I do not know how well disposed he is towards me, because of some close friends of his. You can guess, I imagine, whom I mean. Please keep this business a secret from them. I am sending my letter unsealed so that you can understand the situation from it. Please seal it and hand it to the bishop of Tournai, and when you do so, encourage him to deal with the matter as quickly as possible. If there is anything you would like me to do for you in exchange, just say the word.

Basel, 20 April 1526

1695 / To Jan de Hondt   Basel, 20 April [1526]

> This letter was first printed by Allen in 1926 from the autograph preserved at Ghent; it had lost some text at the right-hand margin, which Allen conjec-turally restored. Like Ep 1694 and the missing letter to the bishop of Tournai mentioned there, it deals with Erasmus' persistent but unsuccessful attempts to secure payment of the pension due him as an imperial councillor; cf Ep 1700 n3. On Jan de Hondt and his role in the payment of the annuity that Erasmus did receive regularly from a prebend at Courtrai, see Epp 751 introduction, 1548 introduction, 1605 n1, 1621 n3.

Cordial greetings. There is no reason, good sir, to fear for our friendship. Even if I lost my pension entirely, I have had too much evidence of your great regard for me and too much experience of your loyalty to suspect

* * * * *

2 Charles (II) de Croy (1507–64), a younger son of one of the most influential families of the Netherlandish aristocracy, had become a Benedictine monk at age nine, an abbot of two abbeys at age fourteen, and bishop of Tournai at age eighteen. He studied in the arts faculty at Louvain, from 1519 under Ja-cobus Latomus and then from 1523 under Adrianus Barlandus. About 1523 he also took up the study of theology under Latomus and Jan Driedo. Croy later continued his education in Italy at Pavia and Bologna. He was ordained to the priesthood at Rome in 1533 and finally took control of his diocese in 1539. At the date of this letter, he would have been strongly influenced by various people at Louvain, as Erasmus here suggests, some of them (such as Barlan-dus) favourably disposed to Erasmus but others (such as the conservative the-ologians Latomus and Driedo) decidedly not. No doubt this is why Erasmus arranged for his letter to the bishop (which has not survived) to be delivered personally by the sympathetic Barlandus, who was still the young bishop's tu-tor, and also why he urged Barlandus to keep it secret from those whose good will he did not trust. As this letter makes plain, Erasmus' purpose in writing was to mobilize support for payment of his imperial pension; cf Ep 1700 n3.

you of behaviour unworthy of a good and honest man. I feel fairly confident about Barbier's attitude towards me; I do not think he would do any-   5
thing to dishonour our friendship.[1] Karl's tarrying in England has proved
most inconvenient.[2] I have written to the persons you suggested so as not
to appear remiss on my own behalf.[3] Your letter to Pieter Gillis about my
affairs was wasted effort: he is more attached to me than almost any of
my friends. But in business matters of this sort he is inexperienced – and   10
also slow.[4] For the moment I am not sending a blank form of receipt,[5] for
I have doubts about the courier. If our business succeeds, either hold on
to the money or get a receipt from the man to whom you pay it, that is,
from Erasmus Schets the merchant, or Pieter Gillis, or Marcus Laurinus.[6]
Meanwhile, I hope you will continue to be my friend, as you have always   15
been. I am thinking about returning, but have not yet made up my mind.

* * * * *

1695
1 On Pierre Barbier see Ep 1605 introduction; on his assistance in facilitating
  payment of Erasmus' annuity from a prebend at Courtrai, Ep 1621 n3; on
  his past involvement in Erasmus' repeated efforts to secure payment of his
  imperial pension, Ep 1621 n4. Erasmus' slight uneasiness about his attitude
  was the result of Barbier's recent service to Girolamo Aleandro (Ep 1548 nn4–
  5), but Erasmus was aware that Barbier had openly expressed admiration for
  him (see Ep 1581 n32 and references to earlier correspondence cited there).
  By this period, Erasmus was convinced (and justifiably so) that Aleandro had
  become a dangerous enemy.
2 Karl Harst, Erasmus' trusted courier, had been in England and the Netherlands on business for Erasmus. He had just returned to Basel the day before
  this letter was written (see line 19); cf Epp 1654 n1, 1666 n2.
3 No message from de Hondt suggesting such persons survives, but probably
  Barbier and the bishop of Tournai were among those suggested. See Ep 1694.
4 Pieter Gillis had gradually turned over the management of Erasmus' financial
  affairs in England and the Netherlands to the merchant Erasmus Schets. See
  Ep 1671 n6.
5 As he had done, for example, in an earlier letter to de Hondt in 1525, Ep
  1548:27–8. The identity of the present courier is unknown.
6 Laurinus (Mark Lauerwijns) had been a member of the chapter of St Donatian
  at Bruges since 1512 and dean since 1519. Erasmus seems to have known Laurinus since the latter was a boy studying at Louvain and to have encountered
  him again at Bologna, where he received a doctorate in both civil and canon
  law before returning to the Netherlands to take up his career in the clergy.
  See Epp 201:3n, 651 introduction, 1342 and introduction, 1548 introduction
  and nn4, 6, 8. Erasmus corresponded with him frequently and repeatedly acknowledged his good will and his help. He was one those involved in the
  complicated arrangements that permitted Erasmus to draw an annual income
  from the prebend at Courtrai. He had for a time managed financial affairs for
  Erasmus as he was now doing for Leonard Casembroot (see Ep 1720:36–9).

Please give my greetings to all my friends, in particular to Johannes de
Molendino.[7]

Basel, 20 April. Karl got in here yesterday.

There is one uncertain factor in this matter – Charles de Croy,[8] who   20
was formerly, I think, bishop of Cambrai. He is a pupil of Jacobus Latomus.[9] I do not know what his attitude is towards me – not very favourable,
I imagine, if the report of friends is true. But, as a youth he always seemed
devoted to me. Farewell again.

To the honourable Master Jan de Hondt, canon of Courtrai   25

1696 / To Pieter Gillis   Basel, 21 April 1526

This letter concerning the high cost of exchange on funds that Gillis had held
for Erasmus in the Netherlands and had recently transferred to him in Basel
through his brother Frans Gillis is a rare exception to Erasmus' practice of
keeping private all correspondence concerning his financial affairs, for he
published it in *Opus epistolarum*. It also confirms the supposition that Pieter
Gillis had been somewhat offended by Erasmus' decision the preceding year
to turn the management of his financial affairs in the Netherlands over to the
far more efficient merchant-banker Erasmus Schets. See Epp 1541 introduction,
1654 nn5–6, 1671 n6.

ERASMUS OF ROTTERDAM TO PIETER GILLIS, GREETING
Johann Froben handed me 400 gold crowns[1] from your brother – no more
than that.[2] The losses on this coinage are ruinous, and will be worse if I go

* * * * *

7 On this canon of Tournai, yet another person involved in the arrangements
   for payment of Erasmus' Courtrai pension, see Ep 371.
8 See Ep 1694 n2.
9 On Latomus' hostility to the Erasmian programme of biblical humanism, see
   Ep 934 introduction. Although the possibility of open conflict had been reduced by the cautious moderation of Erasmus' *Apologia contra Latomi dialogum*
   (1519), Latomus returned to the attack, still without naming Erasmus openly,
   in three controversial tracts published in 1525; cf Ep 1674 n12.

1696
1 Latin *quadringentos coronatos aureos*, undoubtedly 400 French *écus d'or au soleil*
   (see Epp 1434 n3, 1545 n6, 1658 n3). If so, this was a sum amounting officially
   to £800 tournois, £86 13s 4d sterling (the equivalent to 3,467 days' wages or
   15 years and 8 months' wage income for an Oxford master carpenter), or £126
   13s 4d groot Flemish (the equivalent of 3,040 days' wages or 13 years and 9
   months' wage income for an Antwerp master carpenter).
2 As Ep 1654 indicates, Erasmus planned to transfer the balance of funds that

to live elsewhere. These days money never changes hands without profit to
the businessmen and loss to us.³ As for the remaining sum, do as you say   5
you intend to do. I had nothing else in mind when I removed the deposit
from your charge except to relieve you of a burden that you always seemed
to find onerous, for you are not particularly adept at dealing with business
of this sort; I was also concerned for the harmony and continuation of our
friendship. It was not that I greatly feared that something would happen to   10
destroy it – although all human affairs are as brittle as glass, and nothing is
more fragile than friendship – but I thought I should do nothing that might
allow a tiny cloud to darken the happiness of our association. So please do
not interpret my actions in any other way than I intended.

I am sorry that many people have read my letter on that case of double-   15
dealing;⁴ I had given orders to the contrary, and the story was not likely to
emerge in the form in which I sent it. But supposing it had, what discredit
would it have brought on you if the reader discovered that your good nature
was imposed on by someone who imposes on everybody?

You say you were not given a Tertullian except the one you paid for,   20
but your memory fails you.⁵ When I dined at your house shortly before
leaving for Basel,⁶ Pseudocheus⁷ brought in a case stuffed with delights.

* * * * *

Pieter Gillis had been holding for him at Antwerp by having Pieter's brother
Frans Gillis deliver the money to the Basel publisher Johann Froben while both
men were attending the spring fair at Frankfurt am Main. Cf Ep 1681 n5.
3 The cost of exchange and the delays and shrinkage involved in transferring
  money from the Netherlands to Basel were an annoyance to Erasmus, but a
  glaring exception to his generalized complaint was his good-hearted friend
  Erasmus Schets, who after taking charge of Erasmus' financial affairs in 1525
  seems to have transferred money promptly, efficiently, and entirely without
  profit to himself. See Ep 1541 introduction and the article by Eckhard Bernstein
  there cited.
4 The letter mentioned here is lost, but it undoubtedly concerned the business
  practices of the bookseller Franz Birckmann, whom Erasmus repeatedly refers
  to as dishonest. See Ep 1665 n1.
5 Presumably the edition of Tertullian by Beatus Rhenanus (Basel: Froben, July
  1521) mentioned in Erasmus' affidavit of 13 October 1524, annexed to Ep 1507.
6 Erasmus' dinner at Gillis' home in Antwerp probably took place during a brief
  visit he made to that city in the second half of October 1521, not long before
  he set out from Louvain on 28 October on a trip to Basel that turned out to be
  a permanent change of residence. See Ep 1241A introduction. Erasmus' visits
  to Antwerp earlier in 1521, when he met Albrecht Dürer at Gillis' table, would
  have been too early for him to have had a copy of the Tertullian edition to
  give to Gillis. Cf Ep 1199 introduction.
7 The name of a character in Erasmus' colloquy *Pseudochei et Philetymi* 'The Liar
  and the Man of Honour' CWE 39 344–50. The note to the translation (348 n1)

There was one copy of Tertullian – he would say nothing about the rest.
Since both you and Nicolaas of 's Hertogenbosch[8] were keen to have it (for
he was present too), I was sorry there was only one copy so that it was not   25
possible to please both of you. But I gave it to you – unless you chose to
share the book between you.

Your reply to the other complaints follows much the same lines. So I
beg you, my dear Pieter, put away all this nonsense, bury it in deep oblivion, and let us think thoughts that will nourish and promote good will be-   30
tween us. I shall take special care to give you no reason to be angry with
me. You in turn should clear your mind completely of all these silly suspicions. I do not oppose your being friends with Polidoro;[9] so far he has
always shown himself well disposed towards me. 'But stay sober and remember to be on your guard.'[10] Whatever our fate may be, I pray that you   35
and yours will enjoy great happiness. I wish all of you every blessing for
the future.

Basel, 21 April 1526

* * * * *

suggests that the name may be an adaptation of Lucian's Philopseudes ('lover
of lies') in the dialogue *Philopseudes*. The person referred to is probably the
bookseller Franz Birckmann, whom Erasmus regarded as dishonest and to
whom he and his friends sometimes applied this nickname; cf Epp 1513:48–50
and n18, 1531 n17, 1560:16–19 and n7.

8 Nicolaas van Broeckhoven, a humanist friend of both men, at the time of the
dinner party headmaster of a Latin school at Antwerp. See Epp 616:15n, 1232
introduction.

9 Polidoro Virgilio, the Italian historiographer of the Tudor court. See introductions to Epp 1175 and 1666, also Ep 1702. There had been some
tension between Erasmus and Virgilio over suggestions (mainly by other
people) that the first edition of Erasmus' *Adagia* (Paris 1500) had been pla-
giarized from Virgilio's *Proverbiorum libellus* (Venice: C. de Pensis, 1498),
but that issue had been smoothed over by the date of this letter. Late in
1520, while not conceding the priority of Virgilio's collection of proverbs,
Erasmus assured him of his own good will and reported that he had
urged Johannes Froben to bring out a reprint of Virgilio's collection, now
retitled *Adagiorum liber* (Basel: Froben, July 1521). A few days after writing the present letter, Erasmus wrote to Virgilio (Ep 1702) expressing
his own and Froben's regrets that Virgilio was dissatisfied with the quality of Froben's reprint of his *De inventoribus rerum* (Basel: Froben, June
1525). But the tenor of Virgilio's letter of 17 February 1526 (Ep 1666) confirms Erasmus' statement here that he could be regarded as a friendly figure – subject, of course, to the caution expressed in Greek immediately
afterward.

10 Erasmus' text is in Greek. The line is adapted from the comic poet Epicharmus,
cited by Cicero (*Ad Atticum* 1.19.8) and Polybius (18.40.4).

1697 / To Thomas Wolsey　　　　　　　　　　　　　Basel, 25 April 1526

Cardinal Wolsey had known and encouraged Erasmus since 1514 at the latest and together with his master Henry VIII had urged him to write against Luther. Erasmus had originally intended to dedicate *De libero arbitrio* to Wolsey but eventually thought it best not to dedicate that work to any individual (cf Ep 1419 introduction). Wolsey was sympathetic to humanist learning and at this period was engaged in the founding of Cardinal College (eventually reorganized and renamed Christ Church after Wolsey's fall from power) as a centre for humanistic studies at Oxford. Erasmus published this letter in his *Opus epistolarum*, at a time when Wolsey's fall from power could not have been foreseen, at least not far away in Basel.

TO THOMAS, CARDINAL OF ENGLAND, FROM ERASMUS
OF ROTTERDAM, GREETING

When my spirits were flagging under the weight of controversy and because of all those fanatical pamphlets (the most poisonous of which came not from the Lutherans but from those whose cause I am defending), I was given new 5
life by your Eminence's letter,[1] which was so friendly that it revealed not just your good will and support, which I have known from long experience, but your loyal devotion as well.

I imagine that the book Luther wrote in answer to my *Diatribe* has already reached you.[2] It is such a hostile work that it surpasses anything 10 he has written against anyone before. I once said there was no creature too wild for a wife to tame.[3] But I was very much mistaken. At the very time of his marriage he produced a work that showed not a hint of tenderness. Yet he is under the impression that he has restrained his pen – so much so that, immediately after the book's publication, he wrote me a letter in which he 15 virtually demanded that I thank him because in a number of passages he had been easy on me out of consideration for our friendship, and he swears on oath, and wishes me to believe, that Luther is Erasmus' friend.[4] This is

* * * * *

1697
1 Not extant, but probably brought back by Erasmus' courier Karl Harst, who had been in England in February and March and had returned to Basel by way of the Netherlands on 19 April (Ep 1695 n2).
2 His *De servo arbitrio* (1525); cf Ep 1667 introduction.
3 Ep 1653:10
4 Not extant, but the chilly tone of Erasmus' reply (Ep 1688) shows that he found the letter, as well as the treatise itself, deeply offensive.

how his wife has broken him in! I believe the first part of my rejoinder
also has reached you. I had to produce it in a hurry so that they could not   20
gloat over Erasmus' defeat without fear of reprisal.[5] Anyone who does battle
with this faction is dealing with a serpent. But I have more trouble from the
other side, which was put under a ban of silence by Pope Adrian and later
by Clement[6] and to which the emperor sent a severe and threatening letter
to the same intent[7] – all to no purpose.   25

   I am told that my *Colloquies* have been banned in your country, something which no one has attempted in Louvain or Paris,[8] although the bitterest

* * * * *

5 The preface to part one of Erasmus' *Hyperaspistes* is dated 20 February 1526,
   and the reasons for his sense of urgency in bringing out a preliminary reply
   in time for distribution at the spring book fair at Frankfurt are discussed in
   the introduction to that letter, Ep 1667. Since *Hyperaspistes* 1 had been published at an uncertain but quite early date in March, and since the book was
   rushed to the international market at Frankfurt later that month, it was not unreasonable for Erasmus to assume that Wolsey, who had followed the Luther
   affair closely, had already seen his work.
6 On Adrian vi's action to silence Erasmus' critics at Louvain, see Epp 1359 n1,
   1553 n5, 1554:33–6, 1581:417–19, 1582 n1, 1585 n14. For the efforts to silence
   the Spanish theologian Diego López Zúñiga (Stunica) by three popes and by
   the college of cardinals during a papal interregnum, see Ep 1581 n19; cf Ep
   1433:16–20. The most direct evidence of action by Clement vii to silence the
   Louvain theologians is the letter written at the pope's direction by his chancellor, Albert Pigge, to the faculty of theology on 12 July 1525, Ep 1589; this letter
   also shows that the pope and the papal datary Gian Matteo Giberti personally
   instructed Theodoricus Hezius, who had supported Erasmus at the curia under Adrian vi, to go to Louvain and silence Erasmus' critics (Epp 1589:19–23
   and 1589A). Once he reached Louvain, however, Hezius turned his coat and
   undermined the pope's wishes (cf Ep 1717).
7 Cf Ep 1690 n11 on the difficulty of silencing Erasmus' critics at Louvain. See
   also Ep 1731, a letter of praise from Charles v himself to Erasmus, Epp 1700
   and 1747, in which Erasmus complains to Mercurino Gattinara that the emperor's order was ignored, or rather nullified by a legalistic subterfuge, 1784A,
   in which Gattinara obliquely but unmistakably warns the university that continued obstruction will lead to reprisals, and 1785, in which he encloses a copy
   of Ep 1784A for Erasmus.
8 The *Colloquies*, which had begun as a set of simple dialogues composed for
   the instruction of Erasmus' pupils at Paris in the 1490s and had first been
   printed in an unauthorized edition of 1518, drew criticism from Louvain conservatives like Nicolaas Baechem soon after the much-enlarged edition prepared by Erasmus himself appeared in 1522. The collection had been transformed from a simple manual of Latin conversation into genuine dialogues
   dealing with topics of current interest and controversy. As it grew in size, literary power, and boldness, many colloquies became targets for conservative

enemies of the humanities, and so my bitter enemies too, live there. I strongly approve of using remedies of every kind to attack a disease that is daily growing worse and worse. But the princes should use their influence and 30 good sense to ensure that when we pull up the tares, we do not injure the wheat, and that when we employ the knife and the iron,[9] we do no harm to those parts of the body that are sound. Among the monks and theologians who involve themselves in this business there are many stupid people with such bad judgment that they almost seem devoid of common sense. 35 And there are those who hate the humanities (which are flourishing everywhere at present) with a passion exceeding anything they feel for Luther and all his works. Some have no qualms about seeking fame and profit from the misfortunes of the innocent. Some, under the admirable pretext of defending the church, give vent to private spite and malice. They are obsessed 40 with an almost universal hatred of mankind and so, because of the kind

* * * * *

Catholic critics. See Epp 1299:59–79, 1301. On the gradual emergence of the *Colloquies* as a major work of literature and social criticism, see Ep 1341A:285–301; Craig R. Thompson's introduction to his translation of the *Colloquies* in CWE 39; the introduction to the modern critical edition of the Latin text in ASD I-3; and Franz Bierlaire *Erasme et ses Colloques* (Geneva 1977) and *Les Colloques d'Erasme* (Paris 1978). Although Erasmus' statement that no one had attempted to ban the *Colloquies* at Louvain or Paris was true at the date of this letter, his critics at both places had already attacked the work as heretical or at least scandalous. On 1 May the faculty of theology undertook a review of Erasmus' publications, appointing a faculty committee to review the *Colloquies*. On 16 May the faculty formally censured the *Colloquies* and urged the Parlement of Paris to ban their use, especially in the schools. Only repeated intervention by King Francis I, stimulated by a letter of complaint sent directly to the king by Erasmus (Ep 1723), prevented a formal and public condemnation of the *Colloquies* and other works. On 23 June 1528, the rector of the university ruled that the university as a whole joined in the theologians' censure. Various causes, but chiefly the opposition of the king, delayed publication of the censures of the *Colloquies* and other Erasmian works until 1531. See Farge *Orthodoxy* 190–6. There is no evidence of any official attempt to condemn the *Colloquies* in England, though Erasmus also had individual critics there, and even a friendly figure such as Cuthbert Tunstall, bishop of London, found certain passages dangerous and urged Erasmus to correct those passages in future editions, especially Ἰχθυοφαγία 'A Fish Diet' (see Ep 2226:56–62). Allen (23n) notes that although the report is probably unfounded, it may reflect action taken by Tunstall as bishop of London, by Thomas More, and by Wolsey himself to crack down on importation of Lutheran books from Germany.

9 A reference to surgical instruments used in the sixteenth-century for amputation and cautery

of people they are, they thwart the cause they pretend to serve. Nothing is
less likely to settle the present trouble than to allow the cause of the humanities and of good literature to become entangled in the Lutheran affair.
For the humanities bring pleasure to everyone except to those who are de-   45
void of ordinary feelings. How much they benefit and embellish the state is
clear from history. The number of those who have enrolled in Luther's cause
is great enough without pushing innocent people into his camp. There are
more than enough who openly and genuinely profess that proscribed doctrine without thrusting the waverers into Luther's arms or alienating those   50
whose condition could be cured.

I am told that the task has been assigned to the man who took violent
exception to my *In principio erat sermo*.[10] If the outcome is to depend on the
judgment of such men, no book of mine will escape the flames, nor would
a book written by Augustine if it had Erasmus' name on the title page! As   55
a result anything that has to do with polite letters or sound learning will be
removed from public use and we shall have thrust on us again Eberhard,
Uguccio, Florista, and the *Catholicon*,[11] unless wise and moderate men like

* * * * *

10 Probably the Franciscan theologian and bishop of St Asaph, Henry Standish,
   whom Erasmus had identified as early as 1515 as a narrow-minded scholastic
   opponent of humanistic patristic and biblical scholarship. The 'task' assigned
   to Standish was that of 'using remedies of every kind to attack a disease that
   is daily growing worse and worse' (lines 29–30 above) – that is, the exercise
   of his recently granted authority as member of a commission of bishops appointed by Cardinal Wolsey to examine heretics and burn dangerous books.
   Acquisition of such power by such a man made Erasmus concerned about his
   own reputation in England, a country he had always regarded as favourable
   to his studies. Erasmus had disliked Standish from the time he met him (probably in 1515), and as early as 1516 his friend More ridiculed Standish as the
   leader of a group of Franciscans who conspired to attack Erasmus; see Ep
   481. Erasmus made sport of him and of other conservative Franciscans in one
   of his *Adagia* (II v 98), which he called to More's attention (Ep 829). Several
   letters describe an incident in which (according to Erasmus) Standish made
   a fool of himself at court by vehemently pleading that the king and queen
   should do something to suppress the 'heresies' of Erasmus; see Epp 1126:15–
   193, 1127A:10–44, 1162:167–78, 1581:382–8. Erasmus also defended his use of
   the word *sermo* in the translation of John 1:1 in his *Novum Testamentum* against
   attacks by Standish; see *Apologia de 'In principio erat sermo'* LB IX 111E–112C.
11 Some of the obsolete medieval textbooks and reference works that northern humanists in the late fifteenth and early sixteenth century (that is, during Erasmus' youth) had struggled to replace with more recent works by
   humanist scholars. By the time of this letter, the struggle had been largely
   successful, at least in the arts faculties of German universities. Erasmus'

you, who are compelled to use the services of such people, can check the
violence of their passions. If there was nothing at all in my books that was   60
open to criticism, I would be more fortunate than all the Jeromes and Au-
gustines who ever wrote, especially since my enemies have so many head-
ings under which to ensnare me, and to which they add new ones every
day, so that no work could be written in such a pious and careful spirit that
it could not be criticized on some point or other if it failed to please them.   65
And it will fail to please some of them, if only because it contains Greek or
shows elegance of style.

There is nothing in my *Colloquies* that is offensive or irreligious or
seditious. The work contains much that is important for young people to
know: I tell them not to tumble headlong into a manner of life from which   70
they will be unable to extricate themselves[12] or to run off to Compostela,

* * * * *

earliest surviving letters denounce the same (and additional) old-fashioned
authors at a time when they still dominated the classrooms of northern grammar schools and universities – for example, Ep 26:99–100, where he calls them
'ringleaders of barbarism,' and 31:54–5. On Eberhard of Béthune (d 1212),
the principal author of a versified Latin grammar which typified the kind
of logical or speculative grammar that humanists had struggled to replace
with simpler humanistic grammars, see Ep 26:100n. On Uguccio of Pisa (d
1210), Ep 26:99n. Allen Ep 31:48n suggests that *Florista* was another of the
despised medieval grammars, either the work of John of Garland (c 1180–c
1258), who is listed among the 'ringleaders of barbarism' in Ep 26 and whose
works included *Floretus*, a poem on faith and morality, as well as grammatical textbooks; or alternatively, the work of Ludolph of Luchow (d c 1317),
author of *Flores artis grammaticae, alias Florista* (Cologne: Quentell 1507). The
Catholicon, by the Dominican Giovanni Balbi of Genoa (d 1298), was an encyclopedic work devoted to the three arts of the medieval *trivium* (grammar, rhetoric, and dialectic). Completed about 1286, it circulated widely in
manuscript and was first printed at Mainz in 1460 (probably by Gutenberg
himself) and often reprinted. The published portion of the *Gesamtkatalog der
Wiegendrucke* III (1928) 278–91 lists 23 editions before 1500, and the work was
still being reprinted after that. On the origins of the humanist campaign to
abolish use of these medieval textbooks and encyclopedic works, and for
a good description of many of them, see Paul F. Grendler *Schooling in Renaissance Italy* (Baltimore 1989), especially 111–17. On the largely successful
struggle of the humanists to reform the arts curriculum of German universities in the second and third decades of the sixteenth century, see James
H. Overfield *Humanism and Scholasticism in Late Medieval Germany* (Princeton 1984), especially 27–44, 61–158, 208–35, and for the humanist successes,
298–330.

12 The problem of premature decisions on religious vocation taken by youths
   not experienced enough to know themselves and often acting under pressure

leaving wife and children whom they ought to be looking after;[13] and
the book has countless other pieces of advice that my opponents ought
to be giving the people in their sermons. Perhaps, such being the diver-
sity of human temperament, there will always be some crabbed fellow   75
who will be upset by a showy passage or some censorious judge who
will find an idea suspect. Against the misrepresentations of such men
there is no defence. Some will say that it is unbecoming for an old man
to waste time on such trifles. But we praise old schoolmasters who ac-
commodate themselves to the halting language of children in order to   80
teach them to write. Your Eminence should give my *Colloquies* to someone to read who knows both Greek and Latin – I shall not suggest Thomas

* * * * *

from family and from monastic spiritual advisers was personally meaningful
for Erasmus, who believed that he himself had been hurried into a monastic commitment that he was not mature enough or experienced enough to
make. This claim was the basis on which he successfully sought a papal
dispensation releasing him from the obligation to observe his own monastic vows. See the thinly veiled autobiographical account, probably composed
in 1516 and related to his petition for release from the monastic life, his letter to a fictitious 'Lambertus Grunnius, a papal scribe,' published as CWE
Ep 447; its introduction discusses its probable relation to Erasmus' successful petition to Pope Leo X. The problem of premature commitment to irre-
versible vows also appears in the autobiographical *Compendium vitae* that he
composed for Conradus Goclenius in 1524 for eventual use in a posthumous
biography; see CWE IV 400–10, especially lines 61–105. The same concerns and
the consequent hostility to monastic vows taken under external pressure and
'in the ignorance of youth' are prominent in Erasmus' account of the life of
Jean Vitrier, a Franciscan friar who exercised a powerful influence on his
early spiritual development; see Ep 1211:34–48. Erasmus' hostility to permanent and binding vows (vows of marriage or secular professional commitment as well as vows related to ordination to the priesthood or entry into a
monastery or religious order) also found expression in his *Colloquia*, for example *Confabulatio pia* 'The Whole Duty of Youth' (1522) CWE 39 98:15–27; see
nn74–6.

13 In one of the most recent colloquies, *Peregrinatio religionis ergo* 'A Pilgrimage for
   Religion's Sake' (CWE 40 619–74), first published in the Basel edition of February 1526, Erasmus criticizes the character Ogygius for mindlessly running off
   on pilgrimage to the famous shrine of Santiago de Compostela in Spain and
   to the English shrine of Our Lady of Walsingham, contrasting the materialistic
   and superficial piety expressed in such popular pilgrimages with the sound
   and practical piety of the other participant, Menedemus, who expresses his
   faith through responsible behaviour in the actions of daily life and the fulfilment of his responsibilities as head of a household. On the Compostela and
   Walsingham shrines, see CWE 40 651 nn5, 6, 7.

More[14] or Cuthbert Tunstall,[15] for they are friends of mine, though both are the sort of friends who put the truth first.[16] But give the book to somebody who is not obviously biased in my favour or against me. If he finds passages   85

* * * * *

14 More had been a friend since he and Erasmus first met in 1499. They published translations of Lucian jointly in 1506, and More had already vigorously defended Erasmus' biblical and patristic scholarship against criticisms from Edward Lee and Maarten van Dorp. Although they had no direct personal contact after their brief meetings in 1520 and 1521 when More was in the Netherlands on diplomatic missions, scattered survivals from their later correspondence prove that they remained in touch even after More's rise to high government office prevented him from actively pursuing his interest in classical and patristic learning. Cf Ep 1666 n6, which also shows that More had defended Erasmus against conservative critics. More is generally regarded as the closest of Erasmus' English friends and as his only intellectual peer among his English acquaintances.

15 Although Erasmus had several supporters among the English bishops, including not only Wolsey but also Archbishop Warham of Canterbury and Bishop John Fisher of Rochester, Bishop Tunstall of London, a skilled Hellenist and Hebraist and holder of a doctorate in civil and canon law from Padua, probably shared his intellectual interests most closely. In 1516–17, while in the Netherlands on a diplomatic mission, Tunstall had given both advice and assistance on the revision of Erasmus' Greek New Testament in preparation for the second edition.

16 The Latin reads: 'Amici sunt; quamquam uterque sic est amicus Erasmo, ut veritatem anteponat.' In his life of Aristotle, pseudo-Ammonius of Alexandria records two relevant sayings: 'Amicus quidem Socrates, sed magis amica veritas,' and 'Socrates quidem parum curandus, at veritas plurimum.' Both of these sayings are attributed to Plato, whose example therefore Aristotle follows when he criticizes his teacher Plato. See Diogenes Laertius *De clarorum philosophorum vitis* ed C.G. Cobet and others, 2 vols in 1 (Paris 1878) II 10–11. It is by no means certain that Erasmus could have known this obscure work of Ammonius, which in any case was written in Greek but is here quoted in Latin. A similar point is made in Aristotle *Nichomachean Ethics* 1.6 1096a11, a text that Erasmus and most of his readers would have known (and known in Latin) since it was widely used in university courses. Both More and Tunstall were friends in this sense; each could be critical of Erasmus, but in a supportive way. They had exerted pressure on Erasmus to break openly with Luther, and Tunstall in his last surviving letter to Erasmus (Ep 2226, dated 24 October 1529) was mildly critical of Erasmus' high evaluation of the Greek patristic author Origen and urged that he revise the *Colloquies* to remove certain passages that were offensive. Yet both men remained loyal admirers of Erasmus' writings, and thus despite their frankness and honesty would never be accepted by his critics as impartial witnesses to his orthodoxy. Tunstall's desire to see an expurgated edition of the *Colloquies* was not voiced until more than three years after the date of the present letter.

in the work that are injurious to religion, then you will have my support for withdrawing it from the young. If there are lesser faults, these can be corrected on the advice of honest men; in this way the value of the work for the young will not be lost.

Recently a Dominican brought into England on his back some vol- 90 umes containing a scurrilous attack on me. They were written pseudony- mously by four buffoons from the same order and are filled with the most outrageous lies.[17] They found a purchaser, while my *Colloquies* are banned from the bookshops. An edition of my *Colloquies* by a fool called Lambertus Campester is on sale;[18] recently, after fleecing his patron, he decamped from 95 Lyon in disguise. My critics turn a blind eye to such things. What may we not expect from them if you, with your sense of justice, do not check their insolence? This does not matter to me as much as it affects the great issue that is now the centre of debate. I began a book on the Eucharist but gave it up,[19] not because of a change of purpose, but because I am afraid that the 100 turmoil we witnessed last year[20] may flare up again. Oecolampadius[21] has most of the people on his side and not a few from the council.[22]

* * * * *

17 The identity of the Dominican who imported these volumes into England is unknown, but the reference is clearly to an attack on Erasmus published by four Dominican friars in 1525 under the name Godefridus Ruysius Taxander. See Ep 1674 n13. Erasmus' complaint here is that his Dominican enemies are free to import and circulate a pseudonymous and slanderous attack on him while his own essentially harmless *Colloquies* had been banned from England (or so he believed, incorrectly).
18 On Campester and this forged and bowdlerized edition of the *Colloquies*, of which no copy survives but the existence of which can be demonstrated, see Ep 1581 nn59, 60.
19 See Ep 1679 n22; cf Ep 1679 n4.
20 A reference to the German Peasants' War, which reached its speak in the spring of 1525 and involved districts very close to Basel. See Ep 1686 n4 and CWE 11 xi–xiii. The disorders in the neighbouring parts of Germany are frequently mentioned in the correspondence of 1525.
21 Johannes Oecolampadius, a skilled Hebraist and Hellenist, had been a major collaborator in Erasmus' scholarly editions for the Froben press, but from late 1522 or early 1523 had gradually emerged as the leader of the Reformation in Basel. He also became one of the principal theological defenders of the symbolic or Sacramentarian interpretation of the Eucharist associated with his friend Zwingli. See Epp 224:30n, 1538 introduction and nn1, 3, 4, 1539:78–81, 1621 n13, 1636, 1670 n6, 1679 nn4, 22.
22 As early as 1523 the city council of Basel (in Erasmus' Latin, *senatus*) appointed Oecolampadius professor of theology at the university. As in most cities of Switzerland and southwestern Germany, the Reformation movement pitted

I am most grateful for all your promises of generous treatment if I
return to England,[23] but my poor body is so fragile that a change of bed
or a draft or any other trivial mishap exposes me to risk. Otherwise, there   105
have been many things to encourage me to remove myself from this place.
Pope Adrian offered me many inducements to go to Italy.[24] I have received
many invitations from France, where even a fortune is ready for me and
there is much evidence testifying to the king's special affection for me.[25]
Those who want me to go to Spain assure me there is no place where the   110
name of Erasmus is more respected, whether among kings or princes of the
church or the high priests of letters.[26] The most illustrious prince Ferdinand,
for whose person I have a very special affection, has already sent me one
or two kind letters, accompanied by a gift, and invited me to find with him
a safe haven from my present dangers.[27] Andrzej Krzycki, the bishop of   115

* * * * *

the wealthier citizens, the senior university faculty, and the cathedral clergy
against a few pro-Reformation clergy and monks (most of them humanists)
and the great majority of the artisans. The majority of the city councillors
opposed radical and violent changes but was willing to make concessions in
an effort to maintain control in the face of growing popular pressure. See
Hans Guggisberg *Basel in the Sixteenth Century* (St Louis, MO 1982) 24–5, and
Lee Palmer Wandel *Voracious Idols and Violent Hands: Iconoclasm in Reformation
Zurich, Strasbourg, and Basel* (Cambridge 1995) 163–74. On Erasmus' uneasiness
about residing in a city where the Reformation was clearly becoming more
and more powerful, see the preface xii above.
23 Although Erasmus often praised England and had many close and highly influential friends there, his effort to secure a rich benefice that would enable
him to live and work comfortably in England without involving court or academic duties failed to win clear guarantees from King Henry or Cardinal
Wolsey and so led nowhere. At the present date, Wolsey was planning the
foundation of a well-endowed new college at Oxford and probably had been
trying to recruit Erasmus as the most eminent humanistic scholar of the age.
24 See Epp 1324, 1324A, 1339.
25 See Epp 1439 and 1446 from Guillaume Budé, Ep 1375 from King Francis I
himself, and several additional letters of the period 1523–4, cited in Ep 1553
n3.
26 See Ep 1431 and n25 for Erasmus' own list of his supporters and would-be
patrons in Spain.
27 Archduke Ferdinand, younger brother of the emperor Charles V, was consistently helpful to Erasmus. See Epp 1545 n5, 1603 n7, and Ferdinand's letters of
1523–4 to Erasmus, Epp 1343, 1505. In Ep 2000 (17 June 1528) Johannes Fabri
laid out specific details of Ferdinand's offer of an annual income and full
freedom to pursue scholarly work if Erasmus would settle in Vienna. While
Erasmus did not accept the offer, he appreciated receiving it and frequently
referred to it as evidence of Ferdinand's endorsement of his scholarship.

Płock, a man of exquisite learning, wrote me on behalf of the king and the princes of the realm and gave me an invitation, along with most generous promises, to enjoy the quiet retirement there which my years have earned.[28] Other Poles have done the same thing, even sending wonderful gifts as a mark of honour.[29] I do not tell you this out of conceit, for I do not boast   120 of my own merits. But I want to acknowledge the kindness of these men, whose generous support I cannot enjoy because of my poor health. And yet I may have to slip away from here to some place or other.

With regard to what I said about the *Colloquies*, perhaps Karl misinformed me.[30] It will do no harm, however, to have alerted your Eminence   125 on this matter. For there is a great tendency among some people to involve

* * * * *

28 Ep 1652:111–32; on Krzycki see Ep 1629 introduction and nn2, 3, 1660 nn14, 15, 1683 n14. The attribution of the bishopric of Płock to Krzycki creates an anomaly, since he was not translated from his previous bishopric of Przemyśl until 27 April 1527 and his predecessor at Płock did not die until 24 March 1527. This discrepancy might suggest that the year-date of this letter should be changed to 1528 or later. But all of the other references in the letter make a date later than 1526 unlikely: for example, mention of Luther's (lost) letter written to Erasmus after publication of *De servo arbitrio* (see Ep 1688 introduction) and the reference to part 1 (but not to part 2) of *Hyperaspistes* in line 19. The most likely explanation of the discrepancy is that when Erasmus published this letter in his *Opus epistolarum*, he or an editor for Froben changed the text to attribute to Krzycki his current title.

29 For example, three brothers from the powerful Thurzo family, Alexius, a political adviser to the kings of Poland and Hungary (Ep 1572 introduction), Johannes, bishop of Wrocław (Ep 850 introduction), now deceased, and Stanislaus, bishop of Olomouc in Moravia (Epp 1242 introduction, 1544 introduction); also Krzysztof Szydłowiecki, chancellor of Poland (Ep 1593); Jan Antonin, personal physician to King Sigismund I (Ep 1602); Piotr Tomicki, bishop of Cracow and vice-chancellor of the kingdom (Ep 1919); and several members of the influential Łaski family: Hieronym (Ep 1242 n5), Stanisław (Epp 1341A n310, 1502), and above all, Jan (Ep 1593 n18), who had resided and studied in Erasmus' home at Basel for six months in 1525. A year later, the encouragement of these Polish friends led to direct correspondence between Erasmus and King Sigismund I (Epp 1819, 1952), and to a substantial gift of money from the king.

30 Karl Harst, Erasmus' courier, had just returned. The reference to Harst as the source of the false rumour about the banning of the *Colloquies* in England (n8 above) serves further to confirm the date of the present letter as 1526 despite the incorrect title attributed to Bishop Krzycki (see n28 above), for Harst's mission to England and the Netherlands is repeatedly discussed in the correspondence for late 1525 and early 1526, and he left the service of Erasmus in June 1526. Cf n2 above and Ep 1666 n2.

all good literature in the present raging conflagration. Any book that has elegance of style or is seasoned with Greek will be arraigned as suspect and haled before a court of inquiry, which will drag out the proceedings to the discomfiture of both buyer and seller. But with your singular good sense 130 you will always be on guard against the scheming of such men, even without being prompted by someone else. The study of the humanities will find a stout defence in your own humanity. For your generosity is showered on all, especially on those who are commended by their learning or uprightness of character, and so, by the excellence of your virtue, you have dis- 135 pelled all that envy which is the usual accompaniment of great success. May God preserve you for us for many long years to come.

Basel, St Mark's day 1526

1698 / To Jan Antonin Basel, 28 April 1526

A reply to Ep 1660. On this young physician, now settled in Cracow as physician to King Sigismund I, see Ep 1602 introduction. Erasmus' regret over Antonin's decision to leave Basel was heightened by his conviction that he had benefitted from Antonin's remedies during the period of several months in 1524 when he resided there (Epp 1512, 1564). Erasmus published this letter as a preface to his Latin translation of three treatises from the Aldine edition of Galen, *Galeni exhortatio ad bonas arteis, praesertim medicinam, De optimo docendi genere,* and *Qualem oporteat esse medicum* (Basel: Froben, May 1526).

TO THE MOST HONOURABLE JAN ANTONIN OF KOŠICE, PHYSICIAN, FROM ERASMUS OF ROTTERDAM, GREETING

A letter from the honourable Johann Henckel[1] removed all hope of your return, but, my dearest Antonin, the pain of missing a friend was greatly eased when I learned that you are kept at home by the high favour and 5 handsome rewards of princes, and also that you have married a young wife who is as distinguished for piety as for beauty, and who will not allow you to escape but holds you fast in happy bondage.[2] So all that is left for us is to communicate with one another in the only way we can.

The whole of Galen has now come out, speaking to us in his own 10 tongue.[3] I am sending you a translation of the first part, which I have done

* * * * *

1698
1 See Ep 1672 introduction.
2 Horace *Odes* 4.11.23–4
3 On this *editio princeps* of the works of Galen in Greek, see Ep 1594 nn3, 4.

to inspire young people with an interest in medicine. It cost me more trouble than you would imagine. I shall not go into the reasons, but if you will take the time to compare my version with the Greek, you will see at once that translation was the lesser part of the problem.[4]   15

The pearl you sent me will keep me in mind of the dazzling purity of your snow-white character.[5] I understand the symbolism of the 'Sebastian' which the preacher gave me:[6] it means that Erasmus is exposed to the arrows of slanderous critics.[7] I also received from the illustrious Krzysztof, palatine of Cracow,[8] such valuable gifts[9] as even a king would not be ashamed to   20 give or to receive. I shall write to them individually, but there is a chance that this book, which has just been published, will reach your part of the world more quickly than my letters. Best wishes, dear Antonin, to you and your charming wife. My prayer is that she will grow old with you in happy contentment.   25

Basel, 28 April 1526

* * * * *

4 The main reason was the poor quality of the Aldine edition. See Epp 1707:6–11, 1713:29–31.
5 This pearl sent from Antonin to Erasmus may be the present 'not as valuable as your kindness to me deserved' mentioned in Antonin's postscript to Ep 1660.
6 For 'significance,' Erasmus uses the Greek word αἰνίττεται.
7 Cf Ep 1660:14–15. Allen's note there suggests that the gift from Henckel must have been the gilt silver spoon bearing the figure of St Sebastian (traditionally portrayed as martyred by being shot with arrows) that is mentioned in Erasmus' first will (see 540 below). Henckel was at this period chaplain – and presumably court preacher – to Queen Mary of Hungary. In Ep 1660:25–6 Antonin, who had recently spent time at her court, specifically refers to the admiration for Erasmus reflected in Henckel's sermons.
8 Krzysztof Szydłowiecki, to whom Erasmus had dedicated his Lingua in 1525. See Ep 1593 introduction.
9 Erasmus uses a phrase from Greek poetry, ἀπερείσια δῶρα, here. Although the phrase may imply great value rather than number, the literal meaning of the passage alluded to, Apollonius Rhodius 1.419, is 'countless' (in the Loeb translation by R.C. Seaton, 'gifts in countless number'; in the French version by Émile Delage published by the Association Guillaume Budé, it is 'offrandes sans nombre'). Szydłowiecki's intention to send a valuable gift at the time of the Lenten fair at Frankfurt am Main is mentioned in Ep 1660:45–6. The delivery of gifts sent from Poland by the Nürnberg publisher Anton Koberger is mentioned in Ep 1728:15–16. Erasmus' letter of thanks to Szydłowiecki, Ep 1752, describes three gifts. Although not quite 'without number,' they were objects of elegance and significant value.

1699 / To [Jan Oem]   Basel, 29 April 1526

A reply to Ep 1668. Unlike that letter, this one appeared in Erasmus' own publication of his correspondence, *Opus epistolarum*.

ERASMUS OF ROTTERDAM TO A CERTAIN PERSON, GREETING
My dearest son, it is about two years now since I received a little book written, anonymously, in Dutch, which I suspected was the work of your father.[1] I deliberately did not reply, thinking that no good could come to the reader from our disagreement and that it would reflect badly on myself and even more on your father. Moreover, it seemed foolish to reply in Latin to someone who wrote in the vernacular – about as silly as for someone who stood accused before the people to defend himself in the senate. Let him begin a friendship with me under better auspices and he will find me very ready to assist in all the business of the Graces. The fact that, as you say in your letter, he is fond of Greek literature will endear him to me. I offer my congratulations to your brother;[2] and I congratulate you too, not so much for the priestly honour you have received as for the sound intelligence and promise of things to come that I detect in your letter. Please tell your father I reciprocate his greetings. Farewell.
Basel, 29 April 1526

1700 / To Mercurino Gattinara   Basel, 29 April 1526

The autograph of this letter of appreciation to the imperial chancellor survived at Madrid and forms the textual foundation for Allen's edition, though there were also nineteenth-century editions by Helfferich in 1859 and by Eduard

* * * * *

1699
1 See Ep 1668 n1; cf Ep 1469 introduction.
2 This younger brother had been sent at about age thirteen to study Latin and Greek at the municipal school at Rotterdam under its rector Jan Arentszoon Beren, a friend of Erasmus' early friend (and possible teacher) Cornelis Gerard (Ep 1668:16–18), but his given name is not recorded. De Vocht in CTL I 7 and II 345–6 cites evidence that Jan Oem had a brother who was probably the Cornelius Oem whose daughter married a son of the humanist Frans van Cranevelt. C.G. van Leijenhorst in CEBR III 27 also suggests that another brother named Herman matriculated at Louvain in 1523, but whether the brother here mentioned was either of these, or another whose name is not documented, remains uncertain.

Böcking in 1861. On Gattinara's sympathy for Erasmus' scholarly and religious programme, see the introductions to Epp 1150 and 1643.

Cordial greetings. Your Highness' letter, dated 28 October,[1] reached me towards the end of April. I am most grateful to his imperial Majesty and to you for your kindness in sending the official letter that I requested.[2] Nothing, however, has come of all this except that the hornets have been stirred up and are buzzing more furiously than ever. There seems no 5 prospect of getting my pension unless I return,[3] and even then it is most uncertain. But if illness is not a satisfactory excuse for my absence, surely events in Germany ought to have saved me from having to pay the penalty.

* * * * *

1700
1 Ep 1643
2 This imperial letter ordering the Louvain theologians to desist from their attacks on Erasmus is missing, but it is referred to in Ep 1643:17. The attacks continued despite the emperor's command; see Epp 1690:130–3, 1747:11–53, 1784A, Allen Ep 1815:24–31.
3 Erasmus received the honorary title of councillor to the ruler of the Netherlands, the future Emperor Charles v, in 1516. This appointment included the promise of an annual pension. Like many imperial and royal pensioners throughout Europe, Erasmus always had difficulty in securing payment and frequently called on friends at court to bring pressure on the treasury officials. After he left Louvain for Basel in October 1521, he never again received payment despite his frequent appeals for intervention by friends at Brussels and at the imperial court in Spain. Even a direct request for payment from Charles v to his aunt Margaret of Austria, his governor in the Netherlands (Ep 1380), was unavailing. Since the pension was charged against the revenues of the emperor's Netherlandish provinces, both the governor and her councillors (some of them quite favourably disposed to Erasmus) insisted that Erasmus must return to the Netherlands before he would be paid. Erasmus was fully aware of this policy but was unwilling to comply. In letters to his patrons he argued in vain that since his imperial service consisted of his scholarly work, which could be conducted more satisfactorily at Basel than in the Netherlands, payment should not be conditional on place of residence. For a summary of his problem, see Ep 1380 introduction. On his awareness of Margaret's policy and his fruitless efforts to circumvent it, see Epp 1408:11–12, 1434:9–13 and introduction, 1545:7–15 and n3, 1553:22–34, introduction and n6; 1554:12–20 and n2, 1585:10–18 and nn1–3, 1643:15–16 and n2, 1645:6–8. The insistence on his return before payment became even more explicit as time passed; see Allen Ep 1871:11–17. The pension is a frequent issue in the letters found in this volume; see especially Epp 1747 n5, 1757 and n3, 1790A n1, 1792 n6.

The angry noises that the Lutherans are making about me show the ab- 10
solute truth of what I am saying. Among others Hutten,[4] Otto Brunfels,[5] and
recently Luther himself have made their opposition clear by publishing savage attacks upon me. Luther replied to my *Diatribe* in a full-length volume,
revealing greater animosity than he has shown towards anyone before;[6] he
says that no one has been a greater obstacle than I to the spread of the gospel 15
(for that is the name they give to their heresy). All intelligent observers admit that no one has done more to break the spirit of the Lutherans than I, to
say nothing of the many defectors I have brought back to the fold by private letters and private conversations or the waverers I have held fast; and
I brave these dangers in a part of Germany around which the Lutheran fac- 20
tion reigns supreme. I only wish the emperor knew the whole story. If he
did, not only would he think it a disgrace to deprive me of my pension, but
he would offer me far larger rewards for the battle I am fighting against a
powerful sect at great danger to my life.

It is enough for me, as you say in your wise and pious way, to have 25
a good conscience and the blessing of Christ, who bestows upon us the rewards we deserve. At present, however, because I am stabbed in the back by
men of my own party, I am unable to withstand the violent onslaught of my
foes. Latomus[7] has long suffered from an implacable hatred both of me and
of the humanities. He is inciting the dean and others against me, the monks 30

* * * * *

4 Erasmus' refusal to endorse Luther's doctrines and reforms led to the alienation of this former admirer, the German knight and humanist Ulrich von
Hutten; see Epp 1331 n24, 1356 introduction. Hutten in 1523 published an *Ex-
postulatio* attacking Erasmus for alleged lack of constancy and courage because
he refused to endorse Luther. Erasmus published a sharp reply, *Spongia adversus aspergines Hutteni* (Basel: Froben, September 1523) despite his own and
others' discomfort about publishing an attack on a man who had died. See Ep
1378, Erasmus' preface to the first edition of *Spongia*, addressed to Huldrych
Zwingli, and also Epp 1384 (also to Zwingli) and 1389, the preface to the second edition of *Spongia*, addressed 'to the reader'; cf the summary of the affair
in Cornelis Augustijn's preface to his edition of *Spongia* in ASD IX-1 93–114.
5 Although a former admirer of Erasmus, Brunfels had become a supporter of
Luther and a close friend of Hutten. Since Hutten was dead and could not defend himself against Erasmus' *Spongia*, Brunfels early in 1524 published *Pro
Ulricho Hutteno defuncto ... responsio* (Strasbourg: Johann Schott, no date). Erasmus reacted angrily; see Ep 1405 introduction and Ep 1406. Although Brunfels tried to re-establish friendly relations in a letter now lost, Erasmus' reply
was formally civil but cool. See Ep 1614.
6 *De servo arbitrio*; see Ep 1667 introduction.
7 On this Louvain theologian see Ep 1674 n12.

above all. Unless the kings in their wisdom check the reckless passions of these men, they will take aim at languages and letters to destroy them and trump up some specious excuse for harming the innocent. Such behaviour, apart from being completely immoral, only serves to strengthen Luther's party. Whoever is now fighting against Erasmus is fighting for Luther. Our 35 leaders should take care that the glory of crushing that faction redounds to the general good of the church and not to the advantage of those who serve their own ends. We shall help the church only if we correct the faults that are responsible for the present turmoil.

I can claim for myself that I created a new interest in the study of 40 languages and good literature – that is something which cannot be denied. Through my efforts the theology of the schools, which had degenerated into the discussion of hair-splitting sophistries, has been brought back to its biblical sources and to the study of the old authorities.[8] I have tried to awaken a world that has fallen asleep over its pharisaical ceremonials and to bring 45 it back to true religion. I have never joined any faction or gathered a clique around myself. In all my many writings it is impossible to point to a single doctrine that is condemned by the church – though there are people who twist and distort some passages to make false charges and arouse suspicion. But there is no time for such cavils now, given the condition of the present 50 age, when new doctrines are arising constantly (for example, recently the notion that there is nothing in the Eucharist except a symbol of our Lord's body has suddenly found champions everywhere).[9] Even in the letters of St Paul it would be possible to find something to cavil at, given a sufficiently hostile exegesis. 55

But I am adding to your Highness' burdens when you are already occupied with matters of the greatest consequence. I thought it important, however, that his imperial Majesty and your Excellency should not be unaware of these things. I dedicate myself entirely to your service and I pray

* * * * *

8 A clear declaration of Erasmus' desire to shift the emphasis of university instruction in theology from the abstract and theoretical approach of traditional scholasticism to a textually oriented positive theology based on study of the Bible and the church Fathers. Cf Epp 1581:121–54, addressed to his French critic Béda, 1672 n14, 1679 n5, 1687 nn17, 19.
9 A reference to the Sacramentarian or Zwinglian interpretation of the Eucharist, which Erasmus (inaccurately, for the most part) attributed to the influence of Andreas Karlstadt, especially during his travels in Switzerland after he was expelled from Saxony in 1524, and (more accurately) to the writings and preaching of Erasmus' own former associates Johannes Oecolampadius and Conradus Pellicanus. See Ep 1670 n6 and the references given there.

that he who is the only giver of true felicity may grant you perpetual   60
happiness.

Basel, 29 April 1526

Your lordship's humble servant, Erasmus of Rotterdam (written in his
own hand)

To the right honourable Mercurino di Gattinara, grand chancellor to   65
his imperial Majesty. In Spain

1701 / To Felipe Nicola   Basel, 29 April 1526

The recipient had been a secretary in the imperial chancery in Spain and was
one of the growing body of Spanish admirers of Erasmus. Occasional documents dated from 1522 to 1530 reflect his activities in Spain and Italy. There
is little likelihood that Erasmus knew that an attempt at suicide in early January 1526 had led to his dismissal from his chancery position. See Bataillon
(1991) I 348; cf I 240, 447*. Although this is Nicola's only appearance in Erasmus' correspondence, Erasmus included the letter in his *Opus epistolarum*. On
Nicola see also Henry de Vocht *John Dantiscus and His Netherlandish Friends*
(Louvain 1961) 59, which cites a letter of 1530 in which Nicola criticizes the
German Lutherans. De Vocht describes Nicola as 'of Cremona,' but this may
mean only that he was then staying at that city.

ERASMUS OF ROTTERDAM TO NICOLA THE SPANIARD, GREETING
My distinguished young friend, I am most gratified and delighted to know
of your love of good literature and of the warm feelings you have for me;
and although I know that I am, as the saying goes, cheering on a runner,[1] I
urge you most strongly to press on as you have begun, so that you restore to   5
your native Spain its ancient splendour and add to the distinguished record
of your ancestors the undying glory of letters. In his dithyrambs Pindar
seeks to remove by the elegance of his verse the old insult commonly hurled
against Boeotians: 'We are escaping,' he says, 'from the Boeotian pig.'[2] How
much easier it will be for you to restore to Spain its former reputation for   10
wit, learning, and eloquence, in which at one time it did not take second
place to Italy, and to remove whatever faults of style may have come with
the invasion of Goths and Saracens. One can learn even from Pliny about

* * * * *

1701
1 *Adagia* I ii 46; cf III viii 322; 'to cheer on a runner' is to urge someone to do
   something he is already doing.
2 *Olympians* 6.90; cf *Adagia* I x 6.

the fertility of the region and its moderate climate.[3] Every day I am given
more abundant evidence of the kindness of its people. But while my mind   15
can pass swiftly over all the lands of the earth, my poor body is suffering,
not just from exhaustion, but from total collapse. Yet despite my sixty years
and my poor health, I am compelled to take up a new career as a gladiator
and to enter the arena with my sword to kill or be killed myself, though
I was born for the Graces and the grassy banks of the Muses, not for the   20
gladiatorial arena.

    I wish I had to deal only with men like Hutten[4] and Luther.[5] But
I have more trouble with those whose cause I have offered to champion
as best I can. Some people would like to see the death of languages and
letters, even if it meant that Luther was left unharmed. Such an outra-   25
geous attitude is disguised as zeal for defending the Christian faith. Italy
has now given us a third sect. There are people in that land who contend in a most belligerent way that all who do not adopt the style of
Cicero should be struck off the register of scholars. I admit that Cicero's
style is unsurpassed; but I cannot approve of those who have become its   30
slave.[6]

* * * * *

3 In *Naturalis historia* 37.201–3 Pliny places Spain second only to Italy in natural
   endowment.
4 Cf Ep 1700 n4.
5 For Erasmus' most recent clash with Luther, see Epp 1667, 1688.
6 Erasmus' criticism of those who slavishly imitate Cicero's Latin style (and by
   implication are critical of modern authors like himself, who write Latin in
   a more free and eclectic manner) is aimed at a largely Italian group of humanists centred mainly at Bologna, Padua, and the papal curia in Rome; his
   criticism also aims at the recently-deceased disciple of the Italian 'Ciceronians,' the Franco-Belgian scholar Christophe de Longueil. Cf Thomas Lupset's
   letter of 23 August 1525 from Padua (Ep 1595:138–44 and nn22, 23) and Ep
   1675 nn7, 12. Behind Erasmus' criticism of Ciceronian linguistic purism lay
   both his resentment of Italian humanists' tendency to belittle the works of
   'barbarians' like himself and a conviction that most of those humanists, especially the curial group, were pagan and anti-Christian. The eventual product
   of this criticism was his satirical dialogue *Ciceronianus* (Basel: Froben, March
   1528). In it he associates the Ciceronian purism typical of a closely-knit group
   of curial humanists (some of whom he regarded as dangerous enemies, such
   as Girolamo Aleandro and Alberto Pio, but a few of whom he respected as
   able scholars and sincere Christians, such as Pietro Bembo and Jacopo Sadoleto) not only with a ridiculous refusal to use the post-Ciceronian terminology needed to deal with Christian religion (CWE 28 388–92) but also with
   a lack of genuine Christian faith, thinly veiled behind their stylistic purism
   (CWE 28 394, 396, 447). On this attribution of a 'pagan' outlook to Italian and

Sancho Carranza[7] has been strongly recommended to me by Alonso of Olmedo.[8] So when you press me to befriend a man who is endowed with every quality, it is clearly a case of urging the proverbial horse to the plain.[9] So let this letter, written in my own hand, be a pledge and token of the 35 bond between us, which began under the auspices of the Graces and the Muses and which will never be destroyed by any evil spirit or by, what is more dangerous, an evil tongue. Let this be our wall of brass.[10] Please give Carranza my affectionate and respectful greetings and put it to him diplomatically that he may love me as much as he pleases but should be 40 more sparing in his praises because of the danger from malicious tongues. In a contest of affection I shall not yield him second place. Give my regards to Morillon,[11] Beat Arnold,[12] and Jean Lalemand.[13] I have no time to write to them now. Farewell, my dearest Nicola.

Basel, 29 April 1526   45

* * * * *

especially curial humanists, see Epp 1581:121–6, 1717 n2, Allen Ep 1805:64–92. On *Ciceronianus* and its background see the introduction by Betty I. Knott to her English translation (CWE 28 324–36); the introduction to the modern edition of the Latin text by Pierre Mesnard in ASD I-2 583–96; and Rummel II 139–46.

7 On this humanist theologian see Ep 1277 n8. His criticism of Erasmus' New Testament scholarship annoyed Erasmus (Ep 1312), in spite of its moderate tone and open-mindedness, but as a result of the energetic mediation of their mutual friend Juan de Vergara, Erasmus' *Apologia* was relatively mild and friendly relations were established, as reflected here and in Ep 1805. In 1527 Carranza was one of those who generally favoured Erasmus during the discussion of his orthodoxy at the conference of theologians held at Valladolid (Allen Ep 1814:489–94).

8 On this Spanish Erasmian, Alonso Ruiz de Virués, see Ep 1684 introduction.

9 The original phrase, expressed in Greek, is proverbial for urging someone to do something he enjoys doing. See *Adagia* I viii 82, citing Plato *Theaetetus* 183D, Lucian *Piscator* 9, and Synesius *Epistulae* 155.293C. Cf *Adagia* I ii 46, cited at n1 above, for another proverbial way of phrasing the same idea.

10 Horace *Epistles* 1.1.60

11 Guy Morillon, one of the Burgundian officials of the imperial court at Madrid and at this period apparently one of the emperor's secretaries. For his early career see Ep 532 introduction. He was a frequent correspondent of Erasmus and promoted his interests at court.

12 Another imperial secretary (also known as Batt Arnold), a native of Sélestat, who operated out of the imperial court at Madrid but was frequently used as a courier and hence was often in the Netherlands and Germany. He visited Erasmus at Basel in 1516, 1524, and 1525. See Ep 399:7n.

13 On this influential Burgundian, the emperor' principal secretary, see Ep 1554 introduction.

1702 / To Polidoro Virgilio   Basel, 30 April 1526

This is an answer to Ep 1666, though the dissatisfaction here attributed to
Virgilio with the work done by the Froben press in its edition of two of his
works (a publication reported to him by Erasmus in Ep 1606) is not made
clear in that letter. Perhaps his dissatisfaction was orally communicated by
Erasmus' courier Karl Harst, who in Ep 1666 is shown to have conveyed ver-
bally information about the duplicity of the bookseller Franz Birckmann from
Erasmus to Virgilio. Otherwise, there must have been some intervening letter or orally transmitted message. Erasmus published the letter in his *Opus
epistolarum*.

ERASMUS OF ROTTERDAM TO POLIDORO VIRGILIO, GREETING
Both Froben and I are dreadfully sorry that you are not satisfied with the
printing of your distinguished work. For we were both very anxious to
please you. Your letter seemed to rule out any departure from the text. So
I urged them to be most scrupulous in this matter and I stressed the same   5
point again and again during the progress of the work. They assured me
that they were doing so except where there was an obvious slip of the pen.
Sigismundus Gelenius, a man of great integrity with a considerable knowledge of both languages, was in charge of corrections.[1] I told him to follow

* * * * *

1702
1 Gelenius (c 1498–1554), born into a family of Bohemian nobility and the
  son of a man who translated Erasmus' *Praise of Folly* and works by Pe-
  trarch and Cicero, studied at Prague and in 1509 continued his studies at
  Bologna. Later he studied Greek under the Cretan-born Hellenist Marcus
  Musurus, probably at Venice, where Musurus had returned after resigning his professorship of Greek at Padua in 1509. After extensive travels
  through Sicily, Corsica, Sardinia, and France, he returned to Prague at an
  uncertain date and lectured privately on Greek authors. By July 1523 he
  was in correspondence with Philippus Melanchthon, and probably in 1524
  he moved to Basel, where he lived for a time in Erasmus' household and began working at the Froben press as scholar, editor, proofreader, and translator from Greek. He continued working for Froben for the rest of his
  life. A skilled classical scholar, he produced and published Latin translations of several Greek authors, edited Greek and Latin authors, and participated in a number of editions for which Erasmus was the principal editor. As this letter shows, Erasmus regarded his editorial and linguistic skills
  highly. Although he never became so famous as other collaborators of Erasmus at the Froben press, Gelenius quietly contributed to most of the important scholarly texts published by Froben and his heirs during his long

your copy carefully. You had not appointed me your agent, and I was re-   10
luctant to take liberties with another man's work. I should not have shrunk
from taking on the task for so dear a friend, even if it involved considerable
effort.

So Basel is my safe haven![2] That is the way the monks talk. Let one
of them come here and see if he has the courage to attack Luther as I am   15
doing. These men, sheltering behind the ramparts, hurl their insults against
the enemy from a distance, while I am locked in battle with them in the very
midst of the enemy camp. Your generosity heaps kindness upon kindness
and increases my obligation to you, although I have long been much in your
debt. You have given me money to procure a horse: I only wish you could   20
give me something to cure the horseman! You fill me with joy every time
you promise to come here. I wish you would find it possible sometime to
do what you promise. It is enough if you are aware of that clever rogue so
that he cannot cheat you; but you may make use of him in the meantime.[3]
Farewell.   25

Basel, 30 April 1526

There are many rumours of peace here,[4] but I see no one excited about
it. So the rumours must be false or the peace is not something to cheer
about.

* * * * *

career as an editor. He also published a *Lexicum symphonum* (1537, 1544),
an early attempt at comparative study of the classical, German, and Slavic
languages.

2 Virgilio had reported (Ep 1666) that Erasmus' enemies in England and elsewhere were claiming that he was a refugee at Basel, fearful of returning to
the Netherlands or France because he would be prosecuted as a heretic. Virgilio's advice was that Erasmus should give the lie to those reports and uphold his reputation by relocating to France or the Netherlands, where he had
many friends able to shelter him from prosecution.

3 Probably the bookseller Franz Birckmann; see Epp 1606, 1665 n1, 1666:26–7.

4 Presumably, peace between the king of France and the emperor. Although the
Treaty of Madrid had been signed on 14 January 1526 and King Francis had
been released at the Franco-Spanish border on 17 March, Erasmus may not
have received news of the release by the date of this letter. In any case, it soon
became obvious that King Francis was deliberately delaying formal ratifica-
tion of the treaty since he had no intention of dismembering his kingdom by
surrendering to Charles v the duchy of Burgundy as stipulated in the treaty.
Although this reference could also be to lingering pockets of peasant resistance in imperial lands north and east of Basel, the passage as it stands with no
explicit references to German conditions is unlikely to refer to the peasants,
especially in a letter addressed to someone at the English court.

1703 / To Jean (II) de Carondelet   Basel, 30 April 1526

Although given the archbishopric of Palermo by Charles v in 1519, Jean de Carondelet never visited his see and spent his career as a servant of the Hapsburg dynasty. After accompanying Charles to Spain in 1517, he returned to the Netherlands in 1519 and was one of the most influential advisors to the imperial governor, Margaret of Austria, and also to her successor, Mary of Hungary. He was favourable to Erasmus, who in 1523 dedicated to him his edition of the works of St Hilary. Erasmus repeatedly relied on his influence at court in his vain efforts to secure payment of his imperial pension (see Epp 1276, 1434, 1534 n6, 1806, 2055), even though Carondelet seems to have shared Margaret's opinion that Erasmus should not receive his pension unless he returned to the duchy of Brabant, the province whose revenues were obligated for its payment. Cf also Ep 803:12n for the earlier phase of Erasmus' relationship with him. The letter was first printed in Erasmus' *Opus epistolarum*.

ERASMUS OF ROTTERDAM TO JEAN DE CARONDELET,
ARCHBISHOP OF PALERMO, GREETING

I confess, my lord archbishop, that I am no less obliged to you than if I had obtained everything I wanted. If the emperor knew all the circumstances of this present business,[1] he would not only think it a shame for me to be   5
deprived of my pension but would go out of his way to offer me the most generous rewards. This is clear from the hue and cry of the Lutherans and from their writings; above all Luther himself frankly admits that no one has done more to break the spirit of that clique and check their violence than my poor self, a sick old man, living in that part of Germany where their   10
movement has won its greatest success. My critics are well aware of this. But so great is their jealousy and hatred that they would rather see me depart for the Lutheran camp, presumably because they are looking for a weapon with which to do harm both to myself and to the humanities. We read how pagan statesmen laid aside an old quarrel for a time until they completed their   15
term as joint magistrates so that their private hostility would not interfere with the good of the state.[2] But these men stab me in the back when I am

* * * * *

1703
1 On the unpaid pension see Ep 1700 n3.
2 Erasmus may have in mind the willingness of Pompey and Crassus to share the dual magistracy as consuls of the Roman republic despite the hostility between them. See Plutarch *Life of Crassus* 12.1–4 and *Life of Pompey* 22.1–3 and 23.1–2.

fighting, at great danger to my life, against well-equipped forces, and in the midst of the enemy camp.

I think it will not have escaped a man of your good sense how disin- 20
genuous X and Y are;[3] if this were not the case, I should have to paint a
brief portrait of them for you. But whatever we think of them, they ought
to have been on my side when I was straining every nerve in this perilous affair instead of making a fiercer attack on me than on Luther himself. Will there be any limit to the calumnies of these people, who have 25
tried to turn your sympathies away from me by citing a passage from my
Catalogus? The followers of Luther, in words and books and drawings,[4]
have spread the rumour through the whole of Germany that powerful men
have bribed me to write in their interest and that I am putting the word
of God up for sale. In this way they hoped to discredit me and dimin- 30
ish my influence before I could write anything in opposition to the teachings of Luther. To refute such a rumour was not so important to me personally as it was to the common interests of the church. For what good
would I have done by attacking people who were convinced that I was
bribed to write? Moreover, I did not accuse your lordship of miserliness. 35
When it was necessary for me to mention the many people who had given
me nothing, I began as follows: 'As for princes, let me say at the outset that to some who have not rewarded me, my debt is no less than to
those who have,' and after mentioning your name I immediately added,
'He gave me all I was seeking, his support and his good will.'[5] Surely this 40
is not the language of an antagonist? Moreover, it was only out of necessity that I said these things. And it was for the same reason that I mentioned the cardinal of Liège.[6] Finally, to remove all suspicion, I added, 'I do

* * * * *

3 Jacobus Latomus (Jacques Masson), probably the ablest of Erasmus' critics at
Louvain, and Nicolas Coppin, chancellor of that university and also holder of
a chair of theology. On Latomus, see Ep 1674 n12. On Coppin, who had formerly been favourable to Erasmus but had turned against him, see Ep 1719
n8. Erasmus' problem with them was not only that they were hostile and challenged his orthodoxy but also (especially in the case of Latomus) that their attacks were ostensibly directed against other people (such as Petrus Mosellanus
in 1519 and Oecolampadius in 1525), never mentioning Erasmus by name but
still recognizably attacking him. Such indirect, 'disingenuous' attacks were
especially hard for Erasmus to rebut.
4 Cf Ep 1693 n3.
5 Cf Ep 1341A:1703–6.
6 Erard de la Marck was prince-bishop of Liège. On him see Ep 738 introduction. He had been friendly to Erasmus, and this attitude even survived
Erasmus' indiscreet remark in a letter of 1519 to Martin Luther (Ep 980),

not recall these things because I have any complaints of the generosity of
princes. I reckon any profit that accrues to humane studies as though it were   45
money in my own purse; it is for their sake that I have wooed the favour of
princes.'[7]

A man of your shrewd intelligence does not need anyone to advise
him. But since I have had experience of the incredible cunning and untiring zeal with which some people blacken reputations, I thought I should   50
draw the matter to your attention.[8] If I had received reasonable assurances of having my pension paid, I would have tried to undertake the
journey.[9] But no firm promises were made. I am weary of the denunciations of which my critics never tire. If my poor body were stronger, I
would have all the pension I needed. I receive invitations from the great-   55
est kings in every quarter of the world; some even offer gifts as an earnest
of things to come. But I make my excuses to all and continue to be the
emperor's man, and though I am sick and far from his court, I endeavour to serve his wishes in that sphere in which I have some competence
and in which he is most anxious that I serve. Some day the emperor will   60
know my mind more fully; he will then recognize the twisted motives

* * * * *

promptly published by the Lutherans, that the bishop was one of several influential people in the Netherlands who favoured Luther's views. But from
about 1521, after Erasmus had moved from Louvain to Basel and the bishop
had attained his long-desired cardinal's hat and had come under the anti-
Erasmian influence of Girolamo Aleandro (see Epp 1548 n5, 1553 n9), a gradual though not total alienation developed. This situation was exacerbated by
Erasmus' remark in his long autobiographical letter to Johannes Botzheim,
published by Froben in April 1523, that in response to the dedication of his
Paraphrase on Paul's Epistles to the Corinthians (cf Ep 916) and the gift of
two elegant illuminated copies of his edition of the New Testament, the cardinal had responded with 'splendid promises' but not 'a single farthing.' See
Ep 1341A:1716–24.
7 Cf Ep 1341A:1754–7.
8 The literal meaning of the Latin is 'pluck you by the ear.' For this proverbial
expression see Adagia I vii 40.
9 The French translator, Aloïs Gerlo, emends Allen's reading of the verb adrepere
to adripere (see Gerlo VI 403 n8), but there seems little point in Erasmus' saying
'I would have tried to seize it' [that is, the hope of getting my pension].' The
present translator prefers to keep Allen's text. Adrepere must mean something
like 'creep there,' 'make my way there,' that is, 'undertake the journey' back
to Brabant, perhaps even 'come crawling back.' The reference would be to the
condition that Erasmus must return to Brabant in order to get his pension.
See the introduction to this letter. Although occasionally Erasmus did talk of
returning to the Netherlands, he never did so.

of those who are trying to change his generous attitude towards me. But even if that does not happen, I shall continue none the less in my loyalty, relying on Christ to be my judge. I pray he may keep you safe and well.

Basel, 30 April 1526

1704 / To John Longland   Basel, 30 April 1526

On Bishop Longland of Lincoln, a rather conservative prelate but one friendly to Erasmus, see Epp 1535 introduction, 1570. Erasmus published this letter in *Opus epistolarum*.

ERASMUS OF ROTTERDAM TO JOHN, BISHOP OF LINCOLN, GREETING
Reverend bishop, all the generous gifts you decided to lavish on me have been duly delivered. I received the ten angels through More and got another ten last year.[1] So much I can determine from your letters,[2] although it is not your practice to add the date. The gift you gave to Lieven[3] was delivered by   5
the man who brought you the *Letters* of Jerome.[4] I also received the sum

* * * * *

1704
1 On Longland's frequent gifts of cash to Erasmus over a long period of years, see Ep 1535 introduction and the letters there cited, and cf Ep 1386 n20. Other evidence of regular and friendly communication down to the end of Erasmus' life appears in Allen Epp 1874:59–60, 2961:31–2. Thus the reservations of Longland about the *Colloquies* implied here and still more clearly in Allen Ep 2037 did not upset either their friendship or the bishop's generous and wholly voluntary gifts to Erasmus. On the value of the English angel or angel-noble, see Epp 1681 n3, 1758 n6.
2 Only two letters from Longland to Erasmus survive, Epp 1570 and 2227.
3 Lieven Algoet, who had been a *famulus* of Erasmus at both Louvain and Basel from 1519 to 1525 and a courier bearing letters between Basel and the Netherlands and England. By the summer of 1525, he had left Erasmus' service, but he still occasionally carried letters for him, and the wording here implies that he had recently been in England and had received from Bishop Longland a gift that he forwarded to Erasmus. On him see Ep 1091 introduction and cf Ep 1716, where Erasmus solicited for him the favour of the papal datary, Gian Matteo Giberti.
4 The person who delivered a gift copy of Erasmus' edition of the letters of St Jerome to Archbishop Warham in September 1524 is not identifiable from the accompanying letter (Ep 1488), but the other letters written to England and the Netherlands at about the same time, and presumably carried by the same person (Epp 1486–1494), indicate that Algoet carried letters and presentation copies to England.

you recently gave to Karl,[5] namely five pounds sterling. You acknowledge
also in your letters that I wrote to your lordship several times. But it is still
possible that some of my letters were intercepted, or at least not delivered.
That would be nothing new these days. It is good that no one can intercept   10
my feelings of gratitude and indebtedness towards you. I would have been
glad to send you the whole of Jerome,[6] but when Karl Harst was leaving
for England, the work was not yet complete, and suitable couriers are not
always available to whom I may entrust such things.

　　If you read the book that Luther wrote against me and my partial   15
response, you will understand the vipers with which I have to deal.[7] But
what is harder to bear is the fact that, while I fight against a sect that is fully
equipped not just with numbers, swords, and pens but also with poisoned
barbs, I am stabbed in the back by those whose side I am defending. And yet
I could endure even this if I were not afraid that evil monks who want the   20
old tyranny restored will turn a victory won for Christ to their own ends. If
they succeed, woe betide the humanities and those who practise them, and
Erasmus above all!

　　Your Reverence's remarks about the *Colloquies* are most welcome.[8]
People's opinions differ. I have some wise and learned friends in England   25
who are greatly delighted by this work, regarding it as helpful in gaining a
good command of Latin and in correcting the wrongheaded ideas of ordinary people. On the other hand, there are those sober-minded readers who
dislike anything that is light-hearted and humorous. If your lordship has
time to read the book, you will realize that, in addition to its educational   30
value, it contains much that is relevant to the proper training of youth.
There is the added lure of pleasure, for young readers are more easily won

* * * * *

5 Karl Harst, more clearly identified below at line 12. On him see Epp 1215
　introduction, 1575 n2, 1666 n2.
6 The Froben press published the nine volumes of a second, revised edition
　of the complete works of St Jerome between 1524 and 1526. Evidently what
　Erasmus sent was the first three of the nine volumes, the *Epistolae*, the portion
　for which he had personally performed the bulk of the editorial work. Other
　parts of the complete set were still in production. His courier, Karl Harst, left
　Basel for the Netherlands and England late in 1525.
7 A reference to Luther's *De servo arbitrio*, published at the very end of 1525, and
　to Erasmus' *Hyperaspistes 1*, published early in 1526. See Ep 1667 introduction.
8 Both this passage and (more openly) Ep 2037 show that despite his friendship
　and general approval of Erasmus' scholarship, Bishop Longland had reserva-
　tions about the propriety of some of the *Colloquies* and other works critical of
　traditional religious practice.

by what is appealing than by something that is good for them. There is nothing offensive in the work or irreligious or destructive of public order. 'But,' they say, 'such trifles are not appropriate to men of my age.' On the contrary, when old men lisp the words along with children to encourage them to learn their letters, that is judged an excellent thing. What upsets these pseudo-monks is that the young are told not to rush prematurely into the labyrinth of the monastic life and are given other advice, which, though conducive to the welfare of the young, threatens the profits of these sham monks.[9] Nevertheless, I shall obey your orders and work no more on the *Colloquies* and, if anything seems in need of correction, I shall follow your advice and make the necessary changes. In these days nothing can be written that is not liable to be misinterpreted, and it is often the case that when you are most circumspect, you offend both parties, since both have their share of madmen.

Nothing will be done with Ambrose this year. The matter does not rest with me, but with Froben's associates.[10] But I shall produce an edition of the ancient text of Irenaeus,[11] which has never been published before, and some other things, if God gives me strength. May the Lord preserve you, excellent bishop.

Basel, 30 April 1526

1705 / To Leonard Casembroot   Basel, 1 May 1526

> On this young Flemish friend of Erasmus, currently studying in Padua, see Ep 1594 introduction and n10. Cf Ep 1650, to which this letter is a reply. Casembroot's reply is Ep 1720. Erasmus included this letter in *Opus epistolarum*.

ERASMUS OF ROTTERDAM TO LEONARD CASEMBROOT, GREETING
I imagine the danger of starvation about which you complained in your last letter is long past. Certainly it must be less of a threat, now that the season

* * * * *

9 On the problem of monks who exert pressure on youths to take religious vows before they are mature enough to understand the obligations, see Ep 1697 n12.
10 Erasmus had undertaken an edition of the works of St Ambrose, but (according to this letter, at least) financial and scheduling decisions by the publisher (Froben) dictated that its publication be deferred. The *Omnia opera* of Ambrose appeared in four folio volumes in 1527.
11 Published as *Divi Irenaei opus in quinque libros digestum* (Basel: Froben, August 1526)

of watermelons and cantaloupes has arrived.[1] I received a note from the
Polish baron,[2] informing me that you were in touch with a courier who was 5
getting ready to come this way. I have not received the second letter that he
says he sent.

The bearer of this letter is Froben's son Hieronymus,[3] a nice, unas-
suming young man. He has gone to your part of the world in search of
old manuscripts, which he is prepared to purchase, beg, borrow, or steal. 10
You could assist him greatly in this, and I strongly urge you to do so. Not
only will you help the cause of learning, but you will be doing a service to
people on whose gratitude you can count. I expect you to send back with
Hieronymus not just a letter, but a whole volume.

I have lost all of two months answering the letters I receive. I want to 15
know what you are doing. If you happen to know of anyone who is going to
Poland, please give him the enclosed brief note;[4] if anything happens to it, it
will be no great loss. If you are interested in discovering the advantages of
working in a printing press, here is someone with whom you can discuss it.
Farewell, my dearest Leonard. Give my good wishes to the German count.[5] 20
I sent him a letter by Karl.

Basel, 1 May 1526

* * * * *

1705
1 Cf Ep 1594:43, where Casembroot lists melons and other fruit among the advantages of living in Italy.
2 Jan (II) Łaski, who went to Italy with letters of introduction from Erasmus at
  the end of his six months' residence as a paying guest in Erasmus' home at
  Basel. He had returned to Poland from Italy at the beginning of April 1526.
  On him see Ep 1674 introduction.
3 Hieronymus Froben (1501–63), eldest son of the great Basel printer, active in
  his father's business from an early age. On his earlier years, see Ep 903 n3.
  Although deeply involved in the business side of the firm, Hieronymus was
  well educated and had a genuine grasp of the scholarly activity that had made
  the firm famous. Thus his task of obtaining the texts of classical and patristic
  authors while in Italy was suited to his abilities and interests. Cf Epp 1707,
  1720. Despite the lack of success reported by Casembroot in Ep 1720, young
  Froben did return to Basel with manuscripts that Erasmus used in his important edition of St John Chrysostom in 1530. See Ep 1661 nn2, 6. He carried not
  only the present letter but also Epp 1706–7 to Italy.
4 Not extant, but probably addressed to Jan Łaski, who had left for Poland about
  a month before
5 Christoph Truchsess, who like Casembroot was studying in Padua. See Ep
  1625 introduction.

1706 / To Andrea Alciati   Basel, [c 6 May 1526]

On this famous Milanese jurist, the outstanding leader of the effort to apply
humanistic textual criticism to the reform of jurisprudence (*mos gallicus*), see
Ep 1250 introduction. Although they never met, Erasmus and Alciati admired
each other's learning and wit, and they exchanged letters over a long period,
beginning in 1521; their principal contact was through Bonifacius Amerbach
of Basel, who had studied law under Alciati during the earlier (1518–21) of
his two periods of teaching at the papal university in Avignon and who became a close friend of both men. Alciati resettled at Milan in 1520 and lived
there, engaged in classical and literary studies, until 1527, when he returned to
his professorship at Avignon. In 1529 he accepted a professorship at Bourges,
where he had great success as a teacher until his return to Italy to accept a
chair of law at Pavia. His Italian students were far less favourable than the
northern Europeans to his untraditional approach to the study of Roman law.
Alciati became even more famous as the author of the *Emblemata*, a collection
of epigrams and woodcut illustrations, first published in 1531 and reprinted
in more than forty editions by the time of his death in 1550. Allen based his
estimate of the date of this letter on its similarity to others carried to Italy by
Hieronymus Froben and on a letter of Bonifacius Amerbach sent by the same
courier (AK III 163 Ep 1119). Erasmus published it in *Opus epistolarum*, where it
is misdated 1529, the year of publication rather than the year of composition.

ERASMUS OF ROTTERDAM TO ANDREA ALCIATI, GREETING
It makes me very happy, dear Alciati, if, amid all the tumults of Bellona,[1]
you have come through safely thanks to the protection of the Muses.
    I was deeply saddened by Longueil's untimely death.[2] Whatever his
attitude towards me, I hoped he would be spared for the advancement of   5
learning. In his letters he shoots little angry barbs at me, now criticizing

* * * * *

1706
1 Bellona was the goddess of war, and northern Italy was ravaged by the war
  between Francis I and Charles V. In 1523 French soldiers had entered Alciati's
  house when they occupied Milan; and in the summer following this letter
  (12 August 1526) Spanish troops occupied his house and prevented him even
  from having access to his books (AK III 177 Ep 1132).
2 Christophe de Longueil, a promising young humanist, born in Mechelen and
  educated in France and Italy, died in the home of Reginald Pole at Padua
  on 11 September 1522. Hence this reference is not to a recent event and is
  doubtless explained by Erasmus' emerging criticism of Italian 'Ciceronians.'
  On Longueil, see Epp 1675 nn7, 12; 1701 n6.

my *Folly* and now making snide remarks about Dutch rhetoric, as though he himself were Athenian bred and born.[3] But I always had the most sincere appreciation of his abilities. When he visited me at Louvain, I looked after him as courteously as my work allowed.[4] I cannot imagine why he felt such   10 resentment against me – I can only suggest two possible reasons. When he asked for a private meeting with me, I agreed. He began a long-winded account of how he pleaded his case in the Capitol in Rome at great danger to his life;[5] during this I think I did not appear sufficiently attentive, especially when he kept repeating himself with a solemn face and urging me to   15 mention the case somewhere in my writings. I made the sort of reply that I generally make when I am not particularly interested. I think this annoyed him.

Then he argued with me over a letter of his which had been printed with some of my own. In the letter he compared me to Budé. I liked every-   20 thing in it except a remark he added at the end, that he wondered why the

* * * * *

3 Nepos *Atticus* 4.1; cf n6 below.
4 After his dramatic but conflict-plagued visit to the Roman curia in 1516–19 (see next note) and subsequent travel through France and England, Longueil went to Louvain in order to meet Erasmus, a rather tense and cool encounter as Erasmus describes it. It occurred on 13–15 October 1519; cf Epp 1011, 1023, 1024, 1026, 1187.
5 Erasmus seems to be saying that during their meeting at Louvain in 1519 Longueil claimed to have pleaded in person before the curial assembly convened on 16 June to hear charges that his glorification of France in earlier orations had been an offence against the honour of Rome that should disqualify him for the honorary Roman citizenship for which he had been nominated. In reality, Longueil decided that it would be inappropriate for him to attend the public hearing and had already returned to France. He had composed his *Orationes duae* in his own defence and had circulated them at Rome, but he never delivered them orally in the Capitol or anywhere else. Apparently these orations were first printed in Venice in 1518 for distribution at Rome the following year, but what is commonly cited as the first edition and used as the basis for later reprints appeared in 1524, after his death (Florence: Giunta, December 1524; repr Farnborough, Hants 1967). The Capitol here mentioned is not the Capitoline hill of classical times, which was mostly covered by ruins and by postclassical structures, but a simple medieval building on that hill, the Palazzo Senatorio or Palazzo della Ratione, which was used by the civic administration of contemporary Rome and by lawyers. Presumably the 'trial' or public debate on Longueil's fitness for Roman citizenship occurred there. See Betty I. Knott's note to the account of Longueil's stormy (and in Erasmus' opinion farcical) experience at Rome in *Ciceronianus*, CWE 28 432 n778 (page 597).

king preferred a foreigner to one of his own citizens.[6] Although this was
a gratuitous remark, it did not prevent me from publishing the letter out
of respect for him.[7] He pointed out a number of misprints in the text and
while doing so made several improvements, which he wanted to pass off as 25
corrections. He had determined to spend the whole day on this and would
have done so if I had not wearied of it and broken off our conversation in
my blunt and honest way.

He left his sting in you too with a biting allegory. But he acted clev-
erly: for (as the saying goes) he 'planted the dart and ran.'[8] What I found 30
particularly wanting in him was any warmth or naturalness.[9] I could pardon
the desire for glory in someone of his age, if it had not been excessive – but
time would have corrected that fault or at least diminished it. During the
three days he spent with me I never saw the man smile even a tiny smile,
not even at the dinner table, which surprised me greatly. In his letters, it is 35

* * * * *

6 See Ep 914. Although Erasmus was probably offended by Longueil's implied
  conclusion that on balance the French humanist Guillaume Budé was the better
  Latin stylist, what irritated him most was the remark expressing surprise that
  King Francis had courted the services of the foreigner Erasmus rather than
  those of his native-born subject Budé. Cf Ep 935, Erasmus' reply (his only surviving letter to Longueil), and his comment on Longueil in Ep 1026:7–8: 'He
  is too much the Frenchman, considering that he is my fellow-countryman.'
  (Longueil was born in the Netherlands; cf *Ciceronianus* CWE 28 430.) Erasmus
  clearly thought that Longueil, who aspired to be a Roman citizen and a Ciceronian, was confused about his own identity.
7 Erasmus published Longueil's rather critical assessment in his *Farrago nova
  epistolarum* (Basel: Froben, October 1519).
8 Cf *Adagia* I i 5.
9 The Latin phrase, 'in illo desidero candorem [animi],' Erasmus' final definition of what he finds wanting in Longueil's character, presents nuances of
  meaning that are difficult to reproduce in translation. The translator of *Ciceronianus*, Betty I. Knott, in her introductory note (CWE 28 326) refers to this
  letter and concludes that Erasmus found Longueil 'lacking in openness and
  totally humourless.' But while Erasmus obviously thought Longueil 'humourless,' there seems to be no implication that his lack of *candor* implied devious-
  ness. Indeed in his only known letter to Longueil (Ep 935), Erasmus praises
  him precisely for his *candor*, a word which that translator (Sir Roger Mynors)
  phrased as 'your fair-minded way.' *Candidus* is one of Erasmus' favourite
  words of praise, and the Latin term has multiple and subtly shaded senses. In
  the present context, it seems that what Erasmus found wanting was a 'warmth,'
  and 'naturalness'; in other words, Longueil was so full of himself that he had
  no sensitivity (or openness, in that sense) to the opinions and feelings of others. Cf Ep 1713:7 where Erasmus' *candorem animi* is translated 'naturalness of
  temperament.'

true, he sometimes tries to be amusing so as not to seem too un-Ciceronian, but it goes against the grain,[10] or so it seems to me.

We now have a new sect, the Ciceronians,[11] who seem as fanatical in your part of the world as the Lutherans are among us. From now on it will not be permissible to call a bishop 'reverend father' or to write at the end   40 of a letter 'in the ... year since Christ's birth' because Cicero nowhere does that. But in an age that has seen a revolution in religion, government, public offices, place names, buildings, dress, and manners, could anything be more absurd than to be afraid to express oneself differently than Cicero? If Cicero himself were to come back to life, he would laugh at this band of Ciceronians.   45

But we shall laugh about it at another time. Please let me know how you are getting on. I imagine you will write and let Bonifacius know.[12] He is most assiduous in promoting your good name. Farewell.

Basel, [1529]

1707 / To Giambattista Egnazio   Basel, 6 May 1526

On this eminent Venetian humanist, see Epp 269:56n, 648, 1594 n20, 1626 n18. Erasmus regarded his abilities highly, and he was the only Italian recipient designated to receive a gift copy of the complete edition of Erasmus' works provided for in his first will (1527); see 545 below. Erasmus published this letter in *Opus epistolarum*.

ERASMUS OF ROTTERDAM TO GIAMBATTISTA EGNAZIO OF VENICE, GREETING

With regard to the terms *loedorophagoi* and *seneciae*,[1] Giambattista, I have accepted your authority, for I respect your learning as highly as I respect your other fine qualities. I translated several pages from the earlier sections   5

* * * * *

10 Literally, 'Minerva being unwilling.' Cf *Adagia* i i 42.
11 Cf Ep 1719:37, 54–6, where Erasmus refers to the hostility of 'that pagan fraternity of savants' led by Girolamo Aleandro and Alberto Pio and to 'a new
   party of Ciceronians ... revived by Longueil'; see also Epp 1660 n9, 1701 n6,
   1717 n2. On Longueil, see also Ep 1675 nn7, 9, 11, 12.
12 Bonifacius Amerbach; see the introduction to this letter.

1707
 1 These words in Jerome's preface to Ezekiel had puzzled Erasmus; see Epp
   372:5–21, 1623:19–22. The apparently abrupt opening phrase suggests that Egnazio may have sent Erasmus an explanation of the puzzling terms, perhaps
   in the missing letter postulated in n4.

of Galen.[2] I have never encountered anything more riddled with errors. This
vexes me three times over: I am embarrassed first for scholars who will read
it, then for the distinguished author,[3] and finally for Asulanus himself, who
has done nothing in this affair to promote his own interests, even if he cares
little for his reputation. The person responsible for correcting the text hardly   10
seems to know the first thing about the Greek language. I am very grateful
for the kindness you showed the Polish baron and my man Karl, although
when, in your letter to me, you praise Karl's refinement, I think you must
have got the wrong person. The Pole is a cultivated man, but I have never
noticed any refinement in the style of my friend Karl.[4]   15

The bearer of this letter is Hieronymus Froben,[5] the son of Johann
Froben. Besides attending to other business, he would like to bring back
with him any old manuscripts whose publication would be useful to scholars. I should not want to put you under an obligation, but your advice could
be very helpful to a young man whom you will find both courteous and ap-   20
preciative. I am saddened by the loss of Longueil to the world of learning,
although he seems to have had some sort of animus against me, which I did
nothing to deserve; not only did I think very highly of him, but I said so
openly.[6]

* * * * *

2 See Epp 1594 nn3, 4, 1698 introduction. Ep 1698 is Erasmus' preface to his
   Latin translation of three short treatises of Galen from the *editio princeps* of the
   original Greek text published at Venice by Andrea Torresani of Asola (Asulanus), the partner and then the successor of Aldo Manuzio, in 1525. As the
   following lines make clear, Erasmus' work as translator of these texts had left
   him with a low opinion of the quality of that edition.
3 Presumably the reference is to the physician Giambattista Oppizoni, who
   headed the team of editors who prepared the Greek text for publication; cf Ep
   1594 n4. Despite his harsh criticism of the edition, Erasmus had a favourable
   opinion of Oppizoni, certainly higher than his opinion of the publisher, Andrea Torresani, whom Erasmus and many contemporaries regarded as a crass
   businessman interested only in profit rather than in the excellent scholarship
   prized by his deceased partner, Aldo Manuzio. See Epp 1592 introduction,
   1594 n2, 1628.
4 The Polish baron is young Jan Łaski, who had travelled from Basel to Italy in
   1525 with Erasmus' courier, Karl Harst, before returning to his native Poland.
   The comparison between Łaski and Harst indicates that the present letter is a
   reply to a letter from Egnazio that is not extant. Allen (9n) surmises that this
   lost letter must have been contemporary with Epp 1648–50, all of which were
   sent from Padua to Basel in late November 1525.
5 See Ep 1705 n3.
6 See Epp 1675 nn7, 12, 1706 nn2, 4, 5, 6, 9, and the earlier correspondence cited
   in these references.

It is clear that what Homer wrote about Atê and the Litae[7] is no old   25
wives' tale.[8] How rapidly has Atê taken hold of the minds of kings and
peoples, involving almost the whole of Europe in the madness of war! And
how very slow is the progress the Litae make! The discussion about the terms
of the treaty has gone on for ages, and still everything seems uncertain. We
hear of peace, but we see no results. The crisis of the Lutheran fever is   30
passing, but the other side is reaching a paroxysm again. One faction has
split into five or six parts. I only wish I could have grown old amid the
grassy lawns of the Muses. Now, at sixty years of age, I am being thrust
into the gladiatorial arena and instead of a lyre I have a net in my hand.[9]
Farewell.   35
      Basel, 6 May 1526

1708 / To the Swiss Confederation   Basel, 15 May 1526

From 1525 to early 1526 the Swiss Confederation, under pressure by the conservative central cantons (Uri, Schwyz, Unterwalden, and Luzern) and stimulated by pamphlets and letters from the aggressive Catholic theologian Johann Maier of Eck, insisted on the need for a formal debate on religion to
cope with the emerging religious division within the confederation caused by
Zürich's formal adoption of a Reformed church system in 1525 and the activity of Lutheran and Zwinglian preachers in many parts of the confederation. Since it was clear that Eck, Johannes Fabri, and the conservative cantons that supported the assembling of a conference on religion would impose
ground rules for the debate at least as one-sided as those the Reformers had
defined for the religious debates at Zürich in 1523, the city of Zürich declined
to attend. Both the city and Zwingli himself also decided that Zwingli should
not attend, since they were not confident that promises of personal safety
for Zwingli would be kept. Thus the assembly that convened at the strongly
Catholic town of Baden on 16 May 1526 was dominated by Eck, Fabri, and
their junior associate, the Franciscan controversialist Thomas Murner. Thus

* * * * *

7 *Iliad* 9.502–12. Ate ('infatuation') is swift and strong, while the Litae ('prayers')
   move slowly.
8 Latin *anile somnium*. Cf 1 Tim 4:7 (Vulgate): 'Ineptas autem et aniles fabulas
   devita,' translated 'old wives' fables' in AV, 'profane myths and old wives'
   tales' in NRSV, but 'godless and silly myths' in RSV. The Greek text reads: τοὺς
   δὲ βεβήλους καὶ γραώδεις μύθους παραιτοῦ.
9 Equipment carried by the class of lightly armed gladiators known as *retiarii*.
   On the gladiatorial figures Erasmus used to describe his reluctant involvement
   in controversies; see Ep 1674 n8.

also it had a clearly Catholic agenda on major topics: issues to be discussed (such as the Eucharist and the veneration of the Virgin and the saints), authority (rejection of the Reformers' insistence that the text of the Bible be accepted as the sole decisive authority), and procedure (debate in Latin rather than in German, the opening of each day's proceedings with the celebration of mass). The principal burden of defending the Reformed cause fell upon Johannes Oecolampadius of Basel (present because in 1526 the canton was still officially Catholic) with some assistance from Berchtold Haller of Bern (another city that was still officially Catholic but was moving towards its later adoption of the Reformation). Under the rules established, and in the absence of Zwingli, their most articulate figure, the Reformed theologians were no match for the Catholic spokesmen, especially the articulate Eck, who so successfully played on the growing disharmony between Lutherans and Zwinglians on eucharistic doctrine that on the final vote on 8 June on that issue, all four avowed Lutherans present voted with the Catholic majority. The theological disputation began on 19 May, the fourth day after the conference opened, and ended with an overwhelming vote in favour of the propositions moved by Eck. The city of Zürich and Zwingli himself were thus formally isolated within the confederation, though in fact only nine small and politically unimportant states (of the total of thirteen) agreed to regard Zürich as an outlaw state and Zwingli as a heretic, Schaffhausen and the two powerful cities of Basel and Bern held aloof, and Glarus soon reversed its commitment to exclude Zürich.

Erasmus had received a formal invitation to participate in the disputation, and this letter is his polite notice declining the invitation. But the letter does reassert his rejection of the Zwinglian or Sacramentarian interpretation of the Eucharist and sets forth clearly what James McConica has defined as the underlying principle on which Erasmus' continuing loyalty to the Roman Catholic church was based, despite his many disagreements with its present condition and practices. This is the principle of *consensus omnium*, here translated (lines 42–3) as 'with general consent' – the Latin is *magno consensu*. On the role of this principle in Erasmus' theology and its sources in patristic thought, see Cornelis Augustijn *Erasmus: His Life, Works, and Influence*, trans J.C. Grayson (Toronto 1991) 152; James D. Tracy 'Erasmus and the Arians: Remarks on the *Consensus ecclesiae*' in *Catholic Historical Review* 67 (1981) 1–10; and James Kelsey McConica 'Erasmus and the Grammar of Consent' in *Scrinium Erasmianum* II 77–99. Other references to this concept by Erasmus at this period are Epp 1717:61–2, 1729:28–30. On the Baden Disputation in general, see *Dictionnaire d'histoire et de géographie ecclésiastiques* (Paris 1912–) VI 129–31; Augustijn (as above) 152–3; Potter 228–39; and in much greater detail Irena Backus *The Disputations of Baden, 1526, and Berne, 1528: Neutralizing the Early Church*, Studies in Reformed Theology and History 1 no 1 (Princeton 1993). For a good brief account of Erasmus' involvement in the eucharistic controversy and consequent conflict with Oecolampadius and Leo Jud see Tracy *Erasmus* 161–2.

Allen's introduction traces in detail the publication history of this letter. When he published it in 1926, the original Latin manuscript appeared to be lost, but a secretary's copy, with a heading written by Erasmus himself, which was sent to Duke George of Saxony (cf Ep 1728:8), survived in the Saxon archives at Dresden. This copy was the foundation of Allen's Latin text. Since the letter was addressed to the leaders of the Swiss Confederation, a group of laymen, Erasmus also had a secretary prepare a German text, which was the form in which the letter was sent to the confederation, bearing Erasmus' signature. This original letter survived in the archive at Bern, where Allen used it for his German text of the letter, published along with the Latin. The final German form was also read to the Basel city council (Ep 1723:24–5), which the preceding year had twice consulted Erasmus and a handful of other Catholic scholars on how it should deal with the Sacramentarian theology of the city's most prominent preacher, Johannes Oecolampadius; see Epp 1539, 1636. Allen also notes the existence at Basel of three manuscript copies of the Latin text, all in the hand of Erasmus' friend Basilius Amerbach, and one German manuscript, also in Amerbach's hand, which appears to be an earlier draft of the German text sent to Baden. In the next volume of his edition, published in 1928 (VII xxi Addenda), Allen records the discovery of the original manuscript of the Latin letter and the readings (none of them of great significance) which differ from his printed text in volume VI. The first edition of the Latin text was in an annex to Thomas Murner's publication of the acts of the Baden Disputation, *Die Disputacion vor den xii Orten einer loblichen Eidtgenoschaft* (Luzern: 18 May 1527), almost a year after the event. Erasmus included this letter in his *Opus epistolarum*.

TO THE BRAVE SWISS PEOPLE AT THE ASSEMBLY IN BADEN
FROM ERASMUS OF ROTTERDAM, GREETING
Worthy and respected friends, there was no lack of eagerness or enthusiasm on my part to accept your invitation, which both the unanimity of your request and the sacred nature of the business itself commended to me – 5
especially since the distinguished council of this city, to which I owe so much, has also sent me a most friendly and pressing invitation. I wish the confederation well in its efforts; but even if nothing else stood in the way, my health, which is more fragile than glass and is put in peril by even the slightest disturbance, has provided me with a better excuse than I would 10
wish to have for not being present at your meeting.

M. LEO IUD PASTOR ECCLESIÆ TIGURINÆ
AD D. PETRI AB AÑO 1522 AD 1542

Leo Jud (1482–1542)
Portrait by a contemporary artist
Zentralbibliothek, Zürich

No words from me are needed, for the spirit of Jesus will inspire your hearts with sound counsel, urging you to stand together in the true doctrines of the Catholic church. There is one point, however, which I thought proper, good sirs, to draw to your attention by letter, since it affects all of you no less 15 than myself. A few days ago a book was published with the title 'The views of Erasmus and Luther on the Lord's Supper.'[1] It is difficult to say of this work whether its silliness exceeds its malice. Although the name of Erasmus is mentioned once or twice on every page, the writer himself nowhere had the courage to put his own name on it, except at the end, where a fictitious 20 name is given – which is itself a sure sign of a bad conscience. Then he heaps lavish praise upon me, that is to say, he commits an outrage upon me in the form of a eulogy, praising my good sense and erudition in an attempt to persuade the reader that I agree with a view long ago condemned by the Catholic church – as if agreement in error could count against the truth. He tries to 25 convince us with the silliest of arguments that I hold a different view secretly in my heart from that which I am willing to profess publicly. The reason for this, he wishes to suggest, is timidity on my part. Then he collects a number of passages in my writings, which he impudently distorts or misconstrues

* * * * *

1708
1 Erasmus refers to the anonymous tract *Des hochgelerten Erasmi von Roterdam vnnd Doctor Martin Luthers maynung vom Nachtmal vnnsers herren Ihesu Christi.* This work took the form of a letter dated 18 April 1526 to 'Caspar Nagolt, burger zu Norlingen,' from 'Ludouicus Leopoldi, pfarrer zu Leberaw.' Both names are fictitious, but the latter is a disguised clue to the name of the real author, Leo Jud. On Jud see Ep 1737 n1. Erasmus was (or soon became) aware of the identity of the author; cf Epp 1737:1, 1741, 1744:9–10. As the present letter shows, Erasmus particularly resented the intimation by Jud and other Sacramentarian theologians that he privately agreed with their views on the Eucharist but lacked the courage to declare his belief openly – a charge that he thought especially offensive coming from an author who concealed his own identity. The publisher of Jud's anonymous *Maynung vom Nachtmal,* also anonymous, was Christoph Froschauer of Zürich. See E. Camillo Rudolphi *Die Buchdrucker-Familie Froschauer in Zürich* (Zürich 1869; repr Nieuwkoop 1963) 17 no 136. Jud openly identified himself as the author of *Maynung vom Nachtmal* in a rebuttal of Erasmus' *Detectio praestigiarum* (see next note), *Vf entdeckung Doctor Erasmi von Roterdam, der dückischen arglisten, eines tütschen büchlins, antwurt vnd entschuldigung Leonis Jud,* probably published in August 1526, without place or name of publisher but in fact by Froschauer at Zürich (Rudolphi *Froschauer* 17 no 135), and also in a letter to Erasmus, now lost but mentioned in Erasmus' letter of late August to Conradus Pellicanus (Ep 1737:1), whom he initially suspected of being the author of *Maynung* and still regarded as its chief instigator. See Augustijn's introduction in ASD IX-1 224–5, 229–30.

so as to arouse suspicion against me. I shall issue, perhaps within six days,   30
a short pamphlet in which I shall expose this writer's folly and stupidity.[2]

I do not want anyone to be harmed by the false glamour[3] of my name,
with which this cunning rogue has tried to blind the innocent. So please be
assured, good sirs, that you may call me the greatest of heretics if in all the
many books I have written even a single passage can be found that contains   35
a different view of the Eucharist from that which the Catholic church has so
far laid down for us on the authority of Holy Scripture or if any mortal man
has heard me supporting the opinion of the Wycliffites,[4] which some people

* * * * *

2 Erasmus' promised pamphlet took the form of a letter addressed 'to my
  beloved brothers in Christ,' published as *Detectio praestigiarum cuiusdam libelli Germanice scripti ficti autoris titulo, cum hac inscriptione 'Erasmi et Lutheri
  opiniones de coena Domini'* (Basel: Froben, June 1526) LB X 1557–72; ASD IX-1
  213–62. Here he refutes one by one the arguments used by the anonymous
  author. Froben also published quite promptly a German translation of Erasmus' pamphlet, *Entdeckung Doctor Erasmi von Roterdam der dückischen arglistenn
  eines Büchlin inn teutsch vnder einen erdichten titel, mit diser vberschrifft, Erasmi
  vnd Luthers meinung vom nachtmal vnsers herren, kurtzlich hievor vff den xviii tag
  Aprels vszgangen.* This translation is usually attributed to the Basel Carthusian
  monk Georg Carpentarii, since in a letter of 2 June he offered to Bonifacius
  Amerbach a translation of Erasmus' *Detectio* (AK III 168–9 Ep 1125). Leo Jud
  himself thought that Carpentarii was the translator. Augustijn in ASD IX-1 228
  nn143–4 is not so sure and thinks that the published translation either was
  the work of another person or that Carpentarii had to revise his work before
  publication, with the former being the more likely conclusion. The chief foundation of Augustijn's doubts about the translation of *Detectio* is the part of
  Carpentarii's letter where he describes and explains his introduction of some
  changes and some omissions in the text, whereas the published German translation varied from the original Latin in only a few places and had no significant omissions. Thus Augustijn thought it probable that the text he offered
  to Amerbach was rejected, or at least had to be revised extensively, and he
  classes the German text as unattributed (ASD IX-1 228–9). Alfred Hartmann in
  AK III 169 n3 notes the discrepancy between the letter's discussion of textual
  change and the close correspondence between Erasmus' Latin and the published German text, and he also suggests that the translator may have been
  some third party not now identifiable. For a sketch of Carpentarii's life see
  Hartmann's introduction to the letter of 2 June to Amerbach.
3 The Latin is *fumus* 'smoke.' For this meaning see *Adagia* IV viii 83.
4 John Wycliffe's eucharistic teaching clearly rejected transubstantiation and developed into a doctrine of 'remanence,' according to which the body of Christ
  is present 'in the nature of the bread' while 'the continuance of the bread as
  bread was affirmed,' according to Jaroslav Pelikan *The Christian Tradition: A
  History of the Development of Doctrine* 5 vols (Chicago 1984) IV 58. A good brief
  discussion of Wycliffe, including his eucharistic teaching, is the article by Anne

are now reviving. This is enough for me in the eyes of men. But I call God
as my witness, for he alone knows the hearts of men,[5] and I pray that his   40
anger may descend on me if any opinion has ever lodged in my mind that
is in conflict with that which the Catholic church has hitherto defended with
general consent. Others must examine for themselves whatever revelation
they have received. For myself, no arguments have thus far been able to
persuade me to depart from the doctrine laid down by the church. Nor is   45
it fear of men that makes me say this, but fear and dread of the divine
wrath. My opponents have the effrontery to criticize me for timidity when
they do not have the courage to put their names on their own books. They
think themselves brave because they sow discord in the world with their
defamatory and hysterical writings and their ever-changing opinions. 'If he   50
disagrees,' they say, 'why does he not say so in his writings?' Do they really
mean to say that anyone who does not write in opposition to a particular
view must be in agreement with it? Or can they really believe that there is
any shortage of critics to answer back?

There are those in your council who saw the work that I began to write   55
against the views of Karlstadt[6] and who know the reason why I stopped

* * * * *

Hudson in *Dictionary of the Middle Ages* ed Joseph R. Strayer, 13 vols (New York
1982–9) XII 706–11. Among Hussites who followed Wycliffe's position, a sharp
division occurred, with some radicals interpreting this as a purely symbolic
explanation of the eucharistic presence while some conservatives rejected the
concept of 'figurative language' and even the doctrine of 'remanence.' How
much Erasmus would have known about Wycliffite doctrine is debatable. He
probably would have known something of the condemnation of forty-five articles attributed to Wycliffe by the Council of Constance in 1415, of which the
first three rejected the doctrine of transubstantiation. See J.D. Mansi *Sacrorum
conciliorum collectio* (Paris 1903; repr Graz n d) 28 57–156 and Norman P. Tanner *Decrees of the Ecumenical Councils* 2 vols (London 1990) I 411–16 (Sessio 8, 4
May 1415) and I 421–6 (selections from the condemnation of 260 articles at Sessio 15, 6 July 1415). The acts of the Council of Constance were first published
in 1500 (Haguenau: Jerome of Croaria) according to an introductory note by
Tanner (I 403). Hence Erasmus could have known at least what eucharistic doctrines had been attributed to Wycliffe and condemned by the council. At this
point he probably had in mind a radically symbolic eucharistic doctrine such
as he attributed to Andreas Karlstadt, Huldrych Zwingli, Johannes Oecolampadius, and Conradus Pellicanus (see Ep 1670 n6 and the references given
there). Erasmus again refers to Wycliffe at Ep 1721:76.
5 Cf 2 Chron 6:30.
6 This claim that others (perhaps his Basel friend and theological adviser Ludwig Baer, who was one of the four theologians who took turns presiding at
the Baden Disputation) had actually seen the work against the Sacramentarian

what I had begun. Nor is the man who wrote, or inspired, this book ignorant of the reason. Those who release such libellous works without indicating place of publication, press, or author – works which are not just libellous but which spread dissension and heresy – were punished even in pagan   60
times with death. What was then a capital offence is now regarded as a joke by these self-styled champions of evangelical teaching.

This is my position, distinguished sirs, which I have set forth in good faith. So if anyone comes to grief as a result of this infamous book, he will not be able to blame it on me. I have done my duty. It is up to you to act justly   65
and to see that the silly nonentities who indulge in this sort of nonsense, endangering the life and reputation of others and imperilling the state, do not go unpunished. I pray that the Lord Jesus may prosper your actions, good sirs; I shall always consider you worthy of my undying regard.

Basel, 15 May 1526   70

Your lordships' devoted servant, Erasmus of Rotterdam (signed with my own hand)

1709 / From Lukas Klett   Tübingen, 7 May 1526

On Klett (also known under his Latin name, Paliurus), chancellor to Erasmus' friend Christoph von Utenheim, bishop of Basel, see Epp 316 introduction, 1690 n14. As a doctor of both laws, Klett was an appropriate person to help Erasmus' unfortunate friend, the bearer of this letter, Heinrich Schürer, by putting him in touch with the prominent Tübingen jurist Georg Simler. The original autograph letter survived at Leipzig, where Joseph Förstemann and Otto Günther discovered it and published it in 1904.

Greetings. My affection for you, dear Erasmus, most erudite of men, or rather my sincere (and justified) devotion, makes it impossible for me to let you out of my mind despite the many activities in which I am embroiled. I want you to be sure of this, even if I cannot be with you; so

* * * * *

eucharistic views of Oecolampadius is a rare (but not decisive) piece of evidence that Erasmus actually did begin writing, rather than merely thinking about, a treatise on the Eucharist, a project first mentioned in Ep 1616 (cf n2) and again mentioned in Ep 1618, also indirectly referred to in Epp 1620:97–9, 1650A. But no such work was ever published or in all likelihood even brought to completion. In Ep 1679:100–1, writing to Noël Béda, he reports that he had put the project aside; cf n22. Allen conjectures that his abandonment of the tract was the result of a private agreement with the leaders of the Reformation in Basel to avoid open attacks; see Ep 1616 n2.

putting aside all modesty (which ought to hold me back), I am writing   5
you this letter, though it is a case of an ignoramus addressing an eminent
scholar. It is my love for you which makes me do this. So forgive me, for
one must make allowances for love. Believe me, it has been my earnest
wish to make at least some return for the great kindness and generosity
that you showed long ago to a humble ten-cents fellow like myself. If ever   10
an opportunity arises to do you a service, do let me know and you will
soon discover what my feelings for you are; they are no less than you deserve. I am at your disposal, dear Erasmus, and I shall remain so as long as
I live.

Not infrequently your name is mentioned at the court of my most   15
serene prince,[1] always with the greatest acclaim; and your name comes up
no less often among the leading men in the university here.[2] Heinrich, the
bearer of this letter,[3] whom I assisted as much as I could out of regard for
you, has now been able to discover the truth of this for himself from the
conversations between myself and the eminent legal expert Georg Simler,[4]   20
a very close friend of mine. All men admire the genius of Erasmus, and I
myself, who saw you in the flesh and often think that you are still before
my eyes, do what I can to increase that admiration. Many men wish to see
you, and naturally so, for they would like to be able to boast that they had
looked upon someone whose knowledge is without bounds.   25

I write this from my heart, dear Erasmus. I could write more, but
the constraints of time make it impossible; I am also deterred by a deep

* * * * *

1709
1 Archduke Ferdinand of Hapsburg, with whom Klett was probably engaged in
 discussions about the election of a successor to his employer, Christoph von
 Utenheim, bishop of Basel, who intended to resign the see.
2 That is, the University of Tübingen
3 Heinrich Schürer; see Ep 1689 n3 and 1690:164.
4 Simler (d 1535/6) was a native of Wimpfen on the Neckar river. He studied under Ludwig Dringenberg at the famous humanistic school at Sélestat
 and then at Cologne before becoming rector of the Latin school at Pforzheim,
 where the humanist Johann Reuchlin (a native of the city) became his friend
 and where the youthful Philippus Melanchthon, Reuchlin's great-nephew, was
 one of his pupils. He matriculated at Tübingen in 1510, received the MA degree just two weeks later, and ultimately became a prominent professor of
 civil (Roman) law there. In Tübingen Melanchthon again became his pupil
 and junior colleague, and at Pforzheim and Tübingen he became a collaborator of the printer Thomas Anshelm, contributing verses to several publications,
 editing a text of Hrabanus Maurus, and publishing his own *Rationarium evan-*
 gelistarum (1502) and *Observationes de arte grammatica* (1512), a book on Latin
 and Greek grammar.

embarrassment about detaining a man of your refinement with my uncouth
and barbarous chatter. So farewell and may you flourish always! If it is not
too much trouble, give my greetings to Baer,[5] a generous and learned man   30
and an old patron of mine.

In haste. Tübingen, 7 May 1526

Lukas Klett, doctor of laws

To that eminent scholar, Erasmus of Rotterdam, his master and most
respected benefactor   35

1710 / From Bernhard von Cles   Stuttgart, 15 May 1526

A reply to Ep 1689. On the recipient, see the introduction to that letter. The
original of this letter survived among the Rehdiger manuscripts at Wrocław,
where L.K. Enthoven found and published it in 1906.

Venerable and noble sir, my dearly beloved friend in Christ, greeting.

It is my wish, indeed my most earnest wish, that I might be of such
service to you as would justly earn your gratitude; although, even if I did
so, I might appear in the role of recipient rather than donor, since one who
confers a benefit on a deserving person receives a benefit by the very act of   5
giving. But since I realize that I have never been of service to you in any
matter, there was no need for you to thank me, as you did in that handsome
letter you sent me recently with its most courteous expressions of respect.
But perhaps your intentions were different: just as the recipient of a good
turn who is not able to show his gratitude in some practical way but is grate- 10
ful in his heart is considered to have paid some part of his obligation, so you
wanted to say that anyone who is anxious to assist another if the opportunity
arises does indeed confer a benefit on him, at least by virtue of his intention. This last case, I want you to know, applies to me. For there is nothing I
desire more than to have the opportunity (and I hope there will be many op-   15
portunities) to fulfil my promises to you and make my actions fit my words.

With regard to the young man whom you commended to me,[1] I have
done what I could to win support for him with our most serene prince;[2]
I have commended his case most assiduously and have done everything in

* * * * *

5 Ludwig Baer, Basel theologian and friend of Erasmus. See Ep 1674 n17.

1710
1 Heinrich Schürer; see Epp 1689 n3 and 1690:164.
2 Archduke Ferdinand of Hapsburg. Bernhard von Cles was his closest adviser.

my power to settle his affairs as soon as possible and to his satisfaction.   20
How much my support has achieved for him you will be able to learn from
the man himself when you meet. If there is any other matter on which you
think I could be helpful, I hope you will use me as you see fit.

Stuttgart, 15 May 1526

B., bishop of Trent   25

To our dearly beloved friend in Christ, the excellent and venerable
Master Erasmus of Rotterdam. In Basel

1711 / To François Du Moulin   Basel, 16 May 1526

On the recipient, bishop-designate of Condom, who was closely linked to
Louise of Savoy, mother of King Francis I, see Epp 1426 introduction, 1719
introduction. Erasmus included this letter in *Opus epistolarum*.

ERASMUS OF ROTTERDAM TO FRANÇOIS DU MOULIN, GREETING

I am being urged in letters from certain people[1] to write something to congratulate his most Christian Majesty on his safe return to his people. For
myself, I am most willing to seize any occasion to oblige the king, who has
always had such friendly feelings towards me. But I am not yet certain in   5
my mind about the appropriateness of the suggestion; would it be proper
for me to broach this subject, which can scarcely be raised without offending
someone? Then I am not sure how welcome such an act on my part would
be to the king. But if it is your wise counsel that I should undertake it, I shall
tread cautiously over the fires hidden beneath the treacherous ash.[2] Before   10
I do so, I should like you to acquaint me with the whole situation, perhaps
by letter. It is not safe to put on paper anything that originates in the idle
gossip of the people.

If Hilarius Bertholf[3] is with you, you could send him to me so that, if
you like, he can take back the book, which has already been printed.[4] This   15

* * * * *

1711

1 One of these was Louis de Berquin (Ep 1692:98-102), a name to which Erasmus
   prudently makes no reference here.
2 An apt quotation from Horace *Odes* 2.1.7-8. Horace is describing Pollio's
   courage in writing a history of his own troubled times.
3 See Ep 1712 introduction.
4 The book that Erasmus had been urged to dedicate to Francis I as a congratulatory tribute to his release from captivity as a prisoner of war in Spain. The precise book under consideration for this suggested dedication is not made clear.
   Of Erasmus' new publications at Basel during 1526 (assuming that reprints

would be quicker and easier than to have a copy prepared by hand. The earlier it is done, the more welcome it will be. Forgive me, but I do not have time to write more at present. I wish you every success.

Basel, 16 May 1526

1712 / To Hilarius Bertholf   Basel, 16 May 1526

Hilarius Bertholf (d August 1533), a native of Ledeberg near Ghent, had studied at Ghent and had been a fellow student of Juan Luis Vives at Paris and a teacher 'for a long time' at Toulouse (Ep 1403:29) before becoming Erasmus' servant and courier (1522–4), service that may have begun as early as 1521, shortly before Erasmus moved from Louvain to Basel. In December 1523 he

* * * * *

and even revised editions of works previously dedicated to others would not have been considered, and also assuming that polemical works like his *Detectio praestigiarum* and his *Supputatio calumniarum Natalis Bedae* would have seemed inappropriate), the most likely candidate would have been his edition of *Adversus haereses* by the patristic author St Irenaeus, bishop of Lyon. Even the Irenaeus text was not a clear choice, and since it was not published until late August (cf Ep 1738 introduction), it probably was not 'already printed.' At this date Erasmus was still trying to get his hands on a Vatican manuscript that he wanted to consult before completing work on the text, and he was under obligation to Johannes Fabri, his source for this manuscript, to dedicate his edition to Fabri's patron Bernhard von Cles, bishop of Trent (see Ep 1715 introduction and n1). His *Institutio christiani matrimonii* was already intended for Queen Catherine of England (cf Ep 1727), and his edition of the Greek text of six sermons of St John Chrysostom, *Conciunculae sex de fato et providentia Dei*, and of three short treatises of Galen, *Exhortatio ad bonas arteis, praesertim medicinam, De optimo docendi genere, & Qualem oporteat esse medicum* were works too small and insignificant for a royal dedication, especially the Galen. And the *Conciunculae* had already been published in February (Ep 1661), while one other publication of 1526, the first part of his *Hyperaspistes* against Luther, although important enough for a royal dedication, had also been published much earlier in the year, probably very early in March. Perhaps Erasmus considered adding a dedication and reissuing this work, but it had already been put on the market at the Frankfurt fair. He had deliberately avoided including a dedication in *De libero arbitrio*, and there was none in *Hyperaspistes 1* when it went on sale at Frankfurt in March, only a preface addressed to the reader (Ep 1667); similarly, *Hyperaspistes 2* appeared in August 1527 with only a preface to the reader (Ep 1853). Erasmus avoided dedicating these works to a patron because he did not want his criticisms of Luther to appear to be motivated by a desire to curry favour with a ruler or prelate; see Epp 1419 introduction, 1486:9–12 on his decision that *De libero arbitrtio* would appear without a dedication.

carried the presentation copy of Erasmus' *Paraphrasis in Marcum*, along with Ep 1403, to King Francis I at Blois and subsequently spent some time at Lyon, where he edited an edition of Elio Antonio de Nebrija's Latin grammar (1523) and visited Geneva before returning to Basel. In 1524 Erasmus sent him back to France in connection with King Francis' offer of employment to Erasmus, and at the end of this mission he promptly returned to France, where he entered the service of Margaret of Angoulême, the king's sister. He remained in this employment until some date in 1526 later than the date of the present letter. During that same year he spent some time in Italy but by September of 1527 was living in Ghent, where he married (Allen Ep 2049:52–5). No later than 1531 (Ep 2570) he entered the service of Johannes Dantiscus, the Polish ambassador to the imperial court, who at that period was residing in Brussels. Erasmus, who had remained in touch with him, admonished him (Ep 2581) to abandon the restless, peripatetic life of the court and to settle in Lyon as a teacher and editor for the printers. Bertholf took this advice, probably after Dantiscus was recalled to Poland in February 1532. At Lyon he was associated with François Rabelais (Ep 2743) as well as the printer Sebastianus Gryphius. But in the summer of 1533 he, his wife, and their three children died of the plague (Ep 2865). Erasmus published this letter in *Opus epistolarum*.

ERASMUS OF ROTTERDAM TO HILARIUS BERTHOLF, GREETING
I invited you in my last letter[1] to come and visit me. But if you cannot tear yourself away from the lotus-land of France,[2] at least write me a letter and let me know how I should congratulate Francis, the best of kings, on his return to his people, and do it as soon as possible. You can easily find out 5 from members of the court what it would be appropriate to write. Many consider the terms of the treaty rather severe; but God will bring it all to a happy conclusion. Tell me, procrastinator, what do you mean by the 'Latin kalends'?[3] Farewell.

Basel, 16 May 1526   10

* * * * *

1712
1 Not extant, but clearly written while Bertholf was in France in the service of Margaret of Angoulême
2 The fruit of the lotus was believed to cause forgetfulness.
3 Presumably Bertholf had used this phrase in his missing letter, on the analogy of, or in error for, the 'Greek Kalends.' To postpone something to the Greek Kalends is to put it off forever; cf Suetonius *Augustus* 87.1 and *Adagia* I v 84: *Ad Graecas calendas*. There is no ancient parallel for the phrase 'the Latin Kalends.'

1713 / To Jacques Toussain   Basel, 16 May 1526

On Toussain, cf Ep 810:497n. Educated at Paris (MA 1521), Toussain had lived
there as a private teacher, had been (together with Christophe de Longueil)
one of the young humanists patronized by Louis Ruzé, and had become a
pupil of Erasmus' close friend Fausto Andrelini. He became particularly close
to Guillaume Budé, who promoted his career and in 1530 secured for him
appointment as the first royal reader (*lecteur royal*) in Greek, one of the four
scholars (soon increased to six) appointed by Francis I to lecture on humanistic subjects at Paris, a project for which a decade earlier Budé and the king
had tried to recruit Erasmus. The king's appointments are commonly (but not
accurately) regarded as the formal creation of the later Collège Royal. James
K. Farge in an unpublished paper, 'The University of Paris and the Collège de
France' (Renaissance Society of America, Los Angeles, 27 March 1999), demonstrates that at this early period the so-called 'Collège Royal' had no corporate
existence and that the 'royal readers' were simply a group of individual scholars appointed to lecture at Paris and promised salaries from the royal treasury (salaries that often went unpaid). Documentary evidence presented in
Farge *Parti conservateur* 38–9 supports this conclusion and also shows that in
the 1530s and 1540s the *lecteurs royaux* were regularly regarded as members
of the University of Paris, though their exact status was not clearly defined.
Farge's documents show that they lectured within the university in the colleges with which they already had connections; the king provided no lecture
halls. Cf the introduction by Marc Fumaroli to Farge's monograph (*Parti conservateur* 20). As the list of greetings near the end of this letter shows, Toussain
was in touch not only with Budé but also with the circle of Paris humanists with whom Erasmus still maintained friendly but not intimate relations.
Erasmus published this letter in *Opus epistolarum*.

ERASMUS OF ROTTERDAM TO JACQUES TOUSSAIN, GREETING
It is a great thing, most learned Toussain, to be the bringer of welcome news.
So I owe that kind young man, Nicolaus Episcopius,[1] no small debt of gratitude for writing to me about your wide knowledge of both languages, rivalling that of Budé;[2] he also mentioned your generous and supportive atti-   5

* * * * *

1713
1 See Ep 1714 introduction. The letter from Episcopius here mentioned is not
   extant.
2 Since Guillaume Budé had now become the most famous French humanist,

tude towards my work, such as it is. In these days one can congratulate many men on their erudition, but when it comes to naturalness of temperament, not everyone passes the test. Certainly this is a quality that I sometimes missed in Longueil, although I was always a great admirer of his scholarship and abilities and no grudging singer of his praises.[3] Whatever the cause of his hostility towards me, I am sorry that the man has been snatched before his time from the adornment and advancement of liberal studies. As if the world were short of factions, a new faction of Ciceronians has come to life again;[4] they hope, it seems, to strike the names of Budé and Erasmus from the roster of scholars and remove their works from circulation. I am ready to admit that Cicero deserves the highest praise for his style, but I think it silly to do nothing all one's life but copy Cicero and nobody but Cicero. In fact, not even those who think no one but Cicero worth reading qualify as Ciceronians.

When Lefèvre d'Etaples passed through here,[5] he filled me with dismay by announcing that Budé, the glory of France and the delight of scholars, had died. I infer that the rumour is untrue from the fact that Nicolaus Episcopius mentions him in his letter to me[6] but says nothing about his death.

I intend this letter, brief and carelessly written though it is, to be a pledge between us of undying friendship. At present it is not possible to write a longer or a different sort of letter. Give my greetings to Brie,[7]

* * * * *

highly regarded for his mastery of Greek and for his knowledge of the material remains as well as the literary works of classical antiquity, Erasmus' comparison of Toussain with him is high praise. On Budé see Ep 403 introduction, Marie-Madeleine de la Garanderie's article in CEBR I 212–17 (with extensive bibliography), and her book *Christianisme et lettres profanes: essai sur l'humanisme français (1515–1535) et sur la pensée de Guillaume Budé* 2nd ed (Paris 1995).

3 On this controversial humanist see Epp 1675 nn7, 9, 11, 12, 1701 n6, 1706 nn2, 4, 5, 6, 9.

4 Cf Epp 1701 n6, 1706 n11.

5 Lefèvre passed through Basel on his way back to France from his temporary exile in Strasbourg during the captivity of his protector, King Francis I. See Ep 1674 n27.

6 Not extant

7 On Germain de Brie's early association with Erasmus at Venice, see Ep 212:2n, and for their later association, Epp 569 introduction, 1597. He was one of several French humanists who wrote verses commemorating the death of Christophe de Longueil (Ep 1597 n5).

Bérault,[8] François Dubois,[9] Cyprianus,[10] and Bade.[11] I am sending you my translation of the opening sections of Galen; a complete Greek text has now come out from the Aldine press.[12] Please compare the versions and see if   30 any of my emendations are right. Emendation was certainly necessary. I have never seen a work more corrupt. Farewell.

Basel, 16 May 1526

1714 / To Nicolaus Episcopius   Basel, 16 May 1526

Allen located the original autograph letter in Parma, though he reports the existence of a previous edition published in 1836 in a German periodical, *Der Gesellschafter*, which neither he nor the present annotator has seen. Episcopius (1501–64), whose vernacular name was Bischoff, was a native of Rittershoffen in Lower Alsace. He entered the University of Basel in the spring term of 1518, became a citizen of Basel in 1520, and was employed by the Froben press. Although his period of formal academic study was brief and he and his close friend Hieronymus Froben travelled to Chur in 1520 to have the MA degree conferred on them by the papal legate rather than earning the degree through normal academic procedures, he seems to have had a sound education. At the time of this letter he was in Paris, perhaps on a business trip. In any event, he later was active in the merchandising as well as the publishing side of the Froben firm. In 1529 he married Justina, daughter of Johann Froben, and became a partner of Hieronymus Froben, spending the rest of his life in that business. In his will of 1527 Erasmus made him one of his executors and bequeathed gifts to him and his wife.

* * * * *

8 Nicolas Bérault was one of Erasmus' most influential French friends (see Epp 925 introduction, 1571:75 and n15, 1687 n13) and in the mid-1520s acted as an intermediary in the transmission of letters and documents between Erasmus and his Paris critic Noël Béda. Cf Epp 1579:132–5 and n28, 1581:16–17 and n2.
9 On this Paris humanist and editor see Epp 1407 n26, 1600 introduction.
10 This rather shadowy figure seems to be a Venetian humanist also known as Taleus or Talea, whose presence in Paris by 10 December 1510 is documented by a record of payment for a book of Lucian (see *Le carnet de voyage de Jérôme Aléandre en France et à Liège (1510–1516)* ed Jean Hoyoux, Bibliothèque de l'Institut historique belge de Rome 48 [Brussels 1969] 55 and n1), and who in a letter of 1530 is described as principal of the Collège des Lombards at Paris (Ep 2311; cf Ep 768:5n).
11 The famous Paris scholar-printer Josse Bade; see Ep 183 introduction.
12 Cf Ep 1594 nn3, 4. Erasmus had already expressed his low opinion of the textual quality of the Aldine-Asolano edition of Galen in a letter to the Venetian humanist Giambattista Egnazio, Ep 1707:6–11.

Cordial greetings. You beg forgiveness for your impertinence, but you could do nothing that would please me more than to interrupt me with lots of letters, especially if anything is going on where you are that you think important for me to know. I believe that Cousturier's *Antapologia* has been on sale for some time.[1] I am most anxious to have a copy sent to me as soon as possible. I was very pleased to be told about Jacques Toussain.[2] I wrote him a letter, but my situation being what it was, I could only manage a few lines. I believe that the rumour circulating about the death of Budé is false.

Farewell, dearest Nicolaus. See that you return enriched with the commerce of letters.[3]

Basel, 16 May 1526

Your friend, Erasmus of Rotterdam, wrote this with his own hand, as you will recognize.

To Nicolaus Episcopius

1715 / From Johannes Fabri   Baden, 19 May 1526

On Fabri, a close adviser of Ferdinand of Hapsburg, see Ep 1690 introduction. The original of this letter survived at Leipzig and was first published in 1904 in Förstemann/Günther. Erasmus had written to him in mid-April (Ep

* * * * *

1714
1 The work *Adversus insanam Erasmi apologiam Petri Sutoris antapologia*, the second of Cousturier's direct attacks on Erasmus' biblical scholarship and the first to attack him by name, had been speedily approved by the Paris faculty of theology for publication on 15 February 1526 without even the pretence of a formal review and report by a committee as was normally required, and it was published at Paris in June 1526. See Farge *Orthodoxy* 190; Farge *Registre* 127; Rummel II 69. Thus it was not yet on sale at Paris, as Erasmus supposes. On Cousturier see Epp 1571 n10, 1658 n7, 1687 n12.
2 See Ep 1713.
3 Literally, 'very rich with literary merchandise.' What exactly the phrase means depends on the primary purpose of Episcopius' trip to Paris. If the purpose was to purchase books for resale in Basel or to acquire new texts for publication or reprinting by Froben, then the literal meaning of Erasmus' Latin, 'literary merchandise,' would be the best translation. But Episcopius was an active salesman of Froben's books in Alsace, the Breisgau, and southeastern France, so that the purpose of this 'commerce of letters' may have been financial gain rather than delivery of precious books to Basel, and Episcopius would have hoped to return to Basel 'enriched' not with literary treasures but with cash. Erasmus' Latin is vague at this point, and the translator has deliberately chosen to make the English wording comparably imprecise.

1690), but the reference to his repeated request for a manuscript of St Irenaeus suggests that there may have been a more recent letter that is now lost.
Fabri wrote from Baden in the Aargau, where he was preparing to take part
in the Baden Disputation against Oecolampadius and other defenders of the
Swiss Reformation. Cf Ep 1708 introduction.

Cordial greetings. You ask again for the Irenaeus,[1] in which we share a common interest and which you urgently requested once or twice before. I expect you to do such good work in restoring the text that I would never dare
to refuse you; for with your industry and erudition, I know you will work
wonders in freeing the text of error. So keep your hopes up; you and Froben   5
will soon have what you want. You know what I am engaged on at present,
and you understand how valuable and important it is for the task that I have
undertaken to support one's interpretation of Scripture with the authority of
the ancient Fathers. As soon as I have completed my work,[2] I shall make the

* * * * *

1715
1 Erasmus was about to complete work on his edition of the *Adversus haereses*
  of St Irenaeus, the only work of that author then available, and was seeking the loan of a manuscript through the help of Fabri. The edition came off
  Froben's press in late August 1526; and in his dedicatory epistle to Bernhard
  von Cles, bishop of Trent, Erasmus acknowledged Fabri's help in securing
  one of his manuscript sources from Rome. See Ep 1738:111–13. (On the other
  manuscripts available to him, see Ep 1738 n24.) On this manuscript, which
  Erasmus could have used only in the final stages of his work on Irenaeus, see
  José Ruysschaert 'Le manuscrit "Romae descriptum" de l'édition érasmienne
  d'Irénée de Lyon' in *Scrinium Erasmianum* i 263–76. The manuscript itself does
  not survive. Ruysschaert 268–71 demonstrates that Fabri's original intention
  was to edit Irenaeus on his own, using the manuscript he had acquired in
  Rome; also that by October 1524, long before Erasmus came into possession
  of Fabri's manuscript, Archduke Ferdinand was anticipating an Irenaeus edition by him; and finally that the emphasis on the use of this manuscript expressed in the dedicatory epistle to the edition (Ep 1738) was a concession
  to Fabri's eagerness for the publication to be dedicated to his own patron,
  Bernhard von Cles, in recognition of Fabri's somewhat reluctant agreement
  to lend the manuscript and relinquish his own ambition to edit the work. A
  letter of 7 April 1522 from Fabri to Beatus Rhenanus shows that the editors
  working for the Froben press had already been seeking to acquire the text of
  this Vatican manuscript for their planned edition of *Adversus haereses* (BRE 305
  Ep 221).
2 A reference to Fabri's role in the Baden Disputation, which was to begin
  on 19 May, the date of this letter (cf Ep 1708 introduction). Fabri's reliance

manuscript available to you. In the meantime don't be cross with me; and   10
please believe that it is because I am occupied with a mountain of business
that this reply is shorter than is decent. All good wishes.

From Baden in Switzerland, 19 May 1526

I gave Eck[3] your greetings; he says he is very pleased. Also I am about
to send on your letter to Rome.   15

Your friend (for what little he is worth), Fabri

To the distinguished scholar, Master Erasmus of Rotterdam, his special
friend

1716 / To Gian Matteo Giberti   Basel, 21 May 1526

On Giberti, the influential papal datary under Pope Clement VII and one of
Erasmus' most influential supporters at Rome, see Epp 1443A, 1481, 1506, 1509,
1589, 1589A. Erasmus published this letter in *Opus epistolarum.*

TO GIAN MATTEO GIBERTI, BISHOP OF VERONA, DATARY
OF THE POPE, FROM ERASMUS OF ROTTERDAM, GREETING
The Collegium Trilingue acknowledges how much it owes to your lordship, whose support won for it, generously and without cost, all that it desired.[1] The college wishes to associate me with this success, thinking that   5

* * * * *

on patristic authority in preparation for his defence of the Catholic cause at
Baden is his excuse for delay in sending the requested manuscript, though
as n1 above suggests, his own ambition to publish the *editio princeps* of this
important patristic text may have contributed to the delay.
3 The Catholic theologian and controversialist Johann Maier of Eck had been the
prime mover behind the holding of a theological disputation at the meeting
of the delegates of the Swiss Confederation in Baden, and Fabri was Eck's
principal colleague in the debate. Both Eck and Fabri had arrived in Baden on
18 May (Potter 234).

1716
1 Despite the hostile attitude of many members of the University of Louvain, especially several influential theologians, towards him, Erasmus had interceded
with Giberti, the papal datary (and hence indirectly with Pope Clement VII) in
the university's favour when the unexpected death of Pope Adrian VI occurred
before he had completed execution of a papal bull confirming the right of the
faculty of arts to nominate its scholars to certain ecclesiastical benefices as a
means of supporting their university study. Nicolas Wary of Marville, a leading member of the faculty who had presented the university's request to Pope

my recommendation was not entirely without effect. But here too I gladly acknowledge my debt to you, to whom I owe everything.

My sense of decency has been telling me for some time that I should stop troubling you with begging letters. But there is one thing more that I want to ask of you; loyalty to a friend convinced me that I must ask it, and   10
your kindness encourages my boldness. There is a young man here called Lieven, whose surname is Algoet.[2] I enclose a petition from him. He has served me for almost seven years. He has sufficient ability and has made sufficient progress in literary studies to allow us to have hopes for him beyond the common run. He was born of a good family, but in poor circum-   15
stances because of his mother's frequent pregnancies. I took him in some time ago and treated him as a son. I would not have the face to ask that he gain his request free of charge, though I would not protest if the whole amount were charged to me. I am quite certain that, out of the goodness of your heart, you will make sure that he is treated fairly in his dealings with   20
those who are in charge of matters of this kind. He wants the business settled under papal seal. Pope Clement is in the happy position of being able to assist all who come to him and has the generosity of spirit to wish to do so.

An agreement has at last been patched up between the kings. I hope that the God of peace will make it last for ever. That other scourge[3] has   25
abated somewhat, partly because the leaders themselves are destroying one another with their internal feuds, and partly because princes and magistrates, along with the best of the citizenry, are coming to grips with the problem, no longer simply out of piety, but because they have learned from experience where that hypocritical claim to evangelical freedom leads. As   30
for my own contribution, I would rather you learned of it from others. If

* * * * *

Adrian in 1522 and had stayed in Rome to press his case, solicited Erasmus' intervention with Giberti when it seemed that the new pope might heed the opposition of the bishop of Liège, Erard de la Marck, and other opponents by abandoning the confirmation of benefices. In Ep 1481 Erasmus supported the merit of the university's cause (see nn17, 18). In Ep 1509 Giberti assured Erasmus that Pope Clement had granted the confirmation of the faculty's financial privileges.

2 Algoet had left Erasmus' service in 1525 but still occasionally carried letters for him. (Epp 1585 n7, 1627 n7, 1704 n3). In the present recommendation to Giberti, Erasmus was probably supporting Algoet's effort to secure appointment to a benefice; and at a later period Erasmus helped him secure an appointment in the household of Mary of Hungary, governor of the Netherlands (see Epp 2866, 2915).

3 That is, the Reformation

the book that Luther wrote against me has reached your part of the world, it will tell you part of the story. I realize what a nest of vipers I have stirred up against me. I could disregard that, if there were not people on the other side who, in their determination to ruin me, are more obstinate than any of the opposing faction. My relations with kings and princes and bishops are not just peaceful, but exceptionally cordial, as is evident not only from the friendly tone of their letters but also from the unsolicited gifts that come my way. There are certain people, especially from the old-fashioned sort of monks and theologians, who have long been the sworn enemies of the humanities; they use every trick and argument to link the humanities to the Lutheran affair and thus, under cover of religion, pander to their private animosities. This was where the tragedy began: the plot returns full circle to its opening scene.

In my opinion the better course to follow in this business was not to involve languages and polite letters, which are popular with many, or to provoke with false accusations innocent people whose love for these studies does not make them any less ready to detest impiety; nor should we push the waverers over the brink or alienate those whose loyalty could be retained. There are plenty of people who profess these schismatic ideas frankly and openly, so there is no need to trump up charges against the innocent or resort to accusations based on suspicion. At Louvain there are men whose profession it is to teach languages[4] and who conduct their lives in such a way that not even Momus[5] could find fault with them. This very fact greatly annoys some people. They would rather such men went over to Luther, so that they would have an excuse for pinning the blame on the humanities. They are angry because I am attacking Luther; they would prefer to see me writing in his defence, for this would hand them a weapon with which to destroy me. That violent and abusive book that Luther recently fired off against me is read more avidly by none of the Lutherans than by men who want to be seen as mighty Atlases, the staunch upholders of a tottering church. No scurrilous clown publishes an attack on me that fails to win their approval, however slanderous and outrageous it may be, while there is nothing I could write that would be pious enough to escape their calumnies.

* * * * *

4 Teachers of the humanistic studies such as Latin grammar, rhetoric, and Greek, all of them members of the faculty of arts, which Giberti had just helped by supporting papal confirmation of the faculty's privileges. Some of the leading individuals involved were members of the Collegium Trilingue.
5 The proverbial fault-finder; cf *Adagia* i v 74.

Those on whom the pope imposed a ban of silence[6] act as though he had ordered them to rave more furiously than before. They say things like this: 'We know what the pope means, whatever he writes.' What gives them this assurance, I do not know. The emperor issued a grim and threatening edict,[7] which my friends had requested without my knowledge. My opponents twist and turn: they would more readily make up with Luther than with me. I wrote much before Luther was heard of, and so far no one can point to a single issue on which I agree with him. All my opponents can do is to raise suspicions and distort my meaning: most of their attack is plain calumny. But even if some careless error had slipped into my work, it would have been better to put off criticism to another time and concentrate on the problem now before us. You could hardly imagine how detested these men are by all decent people; the fear that they inspire in others gives them all the more reason to fear themselves. There was no need for them to invite hatred, either by attacking me, who, though I belong to no party, have many supporters, especially among men of rank, or by striking at the humanities, since everyone loves the humanities except pigs who cannot stand marjoram.[8]

I imagine this sorry tale falls harshly on your ears. But what is unpleasant for you to hear is much more unpleasant for me to endure – although I have mentioned scarcely a hundredth part of their schemes. I hope all will turn out well; but I am afraid we shall learn our lesson too late, that in this matter too we should have been on our guard lest those who aim to cure the public sickness make it worse by their private conduct and personal animosities. As for me, through good and ill repute, through glory and dishonour, through life and death, I shall continue to keep a clear conscience before Christ my Lord and his bride the church. He, who alone is able, will

* * * * *

6 On Erasmus' efforts to secure orders from three successive popes imposing silence on his conservative critics (both those at Louvain and others such as Diego López Zúñiga), see Epp 1433, 1581 n19, 1589 and introduction, 1589A and introduction. As the last two letters cited demonstrate, Giberti himself was involved in the effort to use papal authority to silence the conservatives at Louvain, but like all previous and subsequent attempts to bring either papal or imperial authority to bear, the effort had no lasting success.

7 Cf Epp 1690 n11, 1747 (showing how his critics immediately worked on the Conseil d'Etat at Mechelen to nullify the emperor's order). Likewise the blunt and menacing letter from the emperor's most powerful adviser, the chancellor Mercurino Gattinara (Epp 1784A, 1785), was brushed aside by Erasmus' enemies at Louvain (Allen Ep 1815:26–31), though they may have become somewhat more circumspect.

8 Cf Adagia i iv 38, quoting Lucretius 6.973 and Gellius pref 19: 'A pig has nothing to do with marjoram' to stupid people the best things are unpleasant.

grant me the victory and the prize. May the omnipotent protector of all keep your lordship safe and well.

Basel, the day following Pentecost 1526

1717 / To Willibald Pirckheimer   Basel, 6 June 1526

On this influential Nürnberg patrician and humanist, see Ep 318 introduction. Though he and Erasmus never met, their correspondence went back to 1515 (Ep 322) and continued until Pirckheimer's death in 1530, sustained by their interest in classical and patristic literature and also by a somewhat parallel evolution of their attitudes to Luther and the other leaders of the Reformation (though Erasmus never shared the warm sympathy for Luther expressed by Pirckheimer in the opening years of the Reformation). By the time of this letter, Pirckheimer was in the process of joining the ranks of the opponents of the Reformers, though he still retained a sympathy for Luther (but not for the more radical Swiss leaders) that Erasmus here judges to be excessive. This letter was first published in Melchior Goldast's edition of Pirckheimer's *Opera* (Frankfurt 1610).

Cordial greetings, distinguished sir. Several times I began reading your *De eucharistia*,[1] but so far I have never managed to read it through, so great

* * * * *

1717
1 Pirckheimer's *De vera Christi carne et vero eius sanguine* (Nürnberg: J. Petreius 1526) was a refutation of the 'Sacramentarian' eucharistic doctrine enunciated by the Basel reformer Oecolampadius in his *De genuina verborum Domini 'Hoc est corpus meum' iuxta vetustissimos authores expositione liber* (1525). On this controversy see Ep 1792A introduction and n14. Although Pirckheimer criticized the Sacramentarians, his treatise did not embrace the official Catholic doctrine of transubstantiation but rather inclined to the doctrine of the real presence upheld by Luther and his followers, which is sometimes labelled 'consubstantiation.' Indeed, for his explicit defence of a 'Lutheran' eucharistic position he was scolded by his correspondent Johannes Cochlaeus and even (more mildly) by Erasmus in the present letter. In his second eucharistic treatise against Oecolampadius, Pirckheimer distanced himself from Luther and moved closer to the position endorsed by the community of the faithful through the centuries, and in his third tract against Oecolampadius, his move back to acceptance of transubstantiation and the authority of Rome was quite clear. See Paul Drews *Wilibald Pirckheimers Stellung zur Reformation* (Leipzig 1887) 98–110; and more recently, Niklas Holzberg *Willibald Pirckheimer: Griechischer Humanismus in Deutschland* (Munich 1981) 281–2 and Lewis W. Spitz *The Religious Renaissance of the German Humanists* (Cambridge, MA 1963) 189–92. On Pirckheimer's

are the troubles that crowd in on me from every side. The slaughter of the
peasants has encouraged everyone to believe that victory is possible. There
are certain pagans at Rome[2] who abhor all Germans. But two in particular   5

* * * * *

clashes with Andreas Osiander, the leading Lutheran pastor and theologian at
Nürnberg, see Gottfried Seebass *Das reformatorische Werk des Andreas Osiander*
(Nürnberg 1967) 115–16, 209–11.

2 A charge he made rather frequently against Italian humanists (cf Epp 1660
n9, 1701 n6, 1706 n11, 1719:36–7, 1753:24–5, Allen Ep 2465:40–6), especially
the members of the Roman Academy, a loose association of humanists active at the Roman curia, many of them employed as papal secretaries. Although this informal group was in some sense descended from the Roman
Academy founded in the late 1450s by Julius Pomponius Laetus to encourage
devotion to ancient Roman culture among curial scholars, that association had
been dissolved by Pope Paul II in 1468 when he arrested several of its leaders
on charges of political conspiracy and efforts to restore pagan religious ceremonies. It was revived under later popes, two of whom, Julius II and Leo
X, had been members before being elected pope. After the sack of Rome in
1527, Clement VII permanently suppressed the Academy. In Erasmus' time
the leaders of this group of curial 'Ciceronians' were Angelo Colocci (see Ep
1479 nn12–13 and lines 22–185, and cf Epp 1341A n115, 1482:34–63) and Battista Casali, author of an unpublished work attacking his orthodoxy (see Epp
1270A, 1597 n4, 1660 n9). Erasmus charged that their excessive adoration of
pagan literature was a cover for neopagan religious beliefs and also a major
cause of the alleged spiritual decline of the Holy See, and he associated their
'neopaganism' with attacks, both overt and covert, on himself; cf Ep 1660 n9.
The reputation of these curial insiders for excessive devotion to Roman paganism, even covert repudiation of Christian faith, goes back at least as far as
the suppression of the earlier Academy by Paul II in 1468; and while Erasmus
respected certain individuals at the curia, such as Pietro Bembo and Jacopo
Sadoleto, he fully shared the widespread belief among non-Italians in the existence of a malevolent and irreligious group of insiders within the curial establishment. He often expressed this opinion, even in letters to unsympathetic
(but non-Italian) figures like Noël Béda (Ep 1581:124–6) and to some of his
Spanish admirers (Allen Epp 1805:64–92, 1885:121–61). Far more dangerous
to Erasmus than narrow classical purists like Colocci and Casali were Girolamo Aleandro and Alberto Pio, prince of Carpi (on them see nn3, 17, and 18
below), for they (especially Aleandro) had significant influence on papal policy and possessed great personal ability and outstanding humanistic learning.
The hostility expressed in the present letter is also related to his troubles with
the Flemish-born Ciceronian humanist Christophe de Longueil (see Ep 1675
n7 and the references given there). The attacks in his letters on Italian 'neo-
pagans' and his objections to the linguistic purism known as Ciceronianism
(see, for example, Ep 1701:26–9 and n6, Allen Epp 1805:64–92, 1885:121–61)
were the prelude to his composition and publication of an attack on the whole
Ciceronian movement, *Ciceronianus* (1528; see the English translation and in-

are especially hostile towards me;[3] they are once again plotting desperate things – though they have never ceased to do that.

* * * * *

troduction by Betty I. Knott in CWE 28), in which both Longueil and Casali come under criticism, though the latter is mentioned only in passing.

The older literature on the 'pagan' current in curial humanism is dominated by Pastor VIII chapters 5 and 6, especially 184–255, and Ferdinand Gregorovius *Geschichte der Stadt Rom im Mittelalter* rev ed by Waldemar Kampf, 14 vols in 3 (Basel 1957) III 485–527. A translation by Annie Hamilton of an earlier edition is available: *History of the City of Rome in the Middle Ages* VIII-1 (London 1912) 289–388. Though written from very different perspectives, Pastor and Gregorovius offer similar (and similarly censorious) portraits of a frivolous and dechristianized curial society. On the curial culture of this time, cf E[mmanuel] Rodocanachi *Histoire de Rome: le pontificat de Léon X, 1513–1526* (Paris 1931) chapters 12 and 13, especially 205–10, 'Le paganisme.' He describes the bizarre mixture of pagan and Christian terms and ideas fashionable among curial humanists, poets, and artists, but is not quite so shocked by it as Pastor and Gregorovius were. The best recent discussion of curial culture in this age (which, however, focuses on problems other than alleged literary paganism) is John F. D'Amico *Renaissance Humanism in Papal Rome* (Baltimore 1983). The picture of curial culture under Leo X presented by Domenico Gnoli *La Roma di Leon X* (Milan 1938) Appendix 1, 'Secolo di Leon X?' 341–84, especially 373–8, emphasizes not so much the 'paganism' of curial society as its flippant, insouciant concentration on its own amusements, and depicts a society in which the more talented and serious figures, such as Bembo, Sadoleto, and Filippo Beroaldo the younger, received far less attention and favour than the comic poets and buffoons whom the inner circle and the Medici pope himself found amusing. For a thoughtful popular assessment of the character of the popes in this period and of the classicizing or 'pagan' tone of curial society, written without the religiously-coloured hand-wringing of older authorities like Pastor and Gregorovius, see also Bonner Mitchell *Rome in the High Renaissance: The Age of Leo X* (Norman, OK 1973) 11–20 (on the popes) and 87–103 (on curial literary culture).

3 Erasmus was convinced, apparently correctly, that Girolamo Aleandro, formerly his friend, was conducting a covert but persistent campaign against him within the curial establishment, accusing him of being the source of Luther's heresies and (despite his open break with Luther in 1524) a secret sympathizer with the German reformer. See n2 above, n18 below and Epp 1548 n5, 1553 n9, 1621 n6, 1660 n9. Since 1524 Erasmus had also heard troubling reports from informants in Italy that Alberto Pio, prince of Carpi, was slandering him at Rome. In this case, the attack eventually produced a book denouncing Erasmus and led to open conflict. See Epp 1634 introduction, 1660 n9, 1744 n22. Both critics were highly influential at the curia. In the case of Pio, the attack was all the more dangerous because of his high social rank and his personal connections as a nephew of Giovanni Pico della Mirandola and a former pupil of the great humanist-printer of Venice, Aldo Manuzio.

The pope twice sent a brief to the University of Louvain,[4] ordering them to control their troublemakers, and they had begun to put this into effect through the rector[5] acting on behalf of the whole university. But on his return Latomus,[6] aided by his colleague,[7] stopped all progress in the matter. Meanwhile the man to whom the execution of the order had been committed (he is a theologian)[8] was persuaded by Latomus's colleague, the biggest scoundrel alive, to write secretly to the datary and request that his excuses be made to the pope for contravening his wishes. The datary in a secret letter approved the man's action, commented favourably on his good sense, and promised silence. A stern edict arrived from the emperor;[9] this too they have managed to evade. They asked the court for an interpretation of the edict, that is, they are seeking a way to render it void. They have Joost on their side, the president of the council at Mechelen, a man whose hatred of the humanities passes all bounds.[10]

* * * * *

4 In fact Clement VII seems not to have sent a formal brief but rather indirect and informal communications directed to the Louvain faculty through his chamberlain, Albert Pigge, and his datary, Gian Matteo Giberti. He also dispatched a personal emissary, Theodoricus Hezius, to urge the theologians to stop their attacks on Erasmus. Hezius, however, though formerly favourable to Erasmus, seems to have been won over by Erasmus' critics and to have played a double game when he reached the Netherlands, formally delivering the pope's admonition but privately attacking Erasmus' reputation both at Louvain and in his letters to friends in Rome. See Epp 1589, 1589A, and 1747:31–9 and n9.

5 Allen (8n) observes that the rector under whom this papal intervention began must have been Jan Scarley of 's Hertogenbosch, but that a theologian, Willem of Vianen, took office on 31 August and was rector during the period when the papal mandate was in effect nullified. Yet the role of the rector may not have been crucial; Peter G. Bietenholz in CEBR III 390–1 cites evidence that Vianen was not among the group whom Erasmus (who was well informed about events at Louvain) regarded as his enemies.

6 On Latomus' persistent attacks on Erasmus, see Ep 1674 n12.

7 Nicolaas Baechem, commonly known as Egmondanus, the head of the Carmelite house of studies at Louvain and a graduate of the faculty of theology, an early, persistent, and vehement enemy of Erasmus. On him see Epp 878:15n, 1254 n6, 1553 n4, 1581 nn27, 46, 1582 n7, 1589 introduction, 1603 n11, 1608 n4.

8 Theodoricus Hezius; see n4 above.

9 See Ep 1690 n11 and introductions to Epp 1747 and 1784A.

10 Joost Lauwereyns, president of the Grand Council (supreme judicial court of the Hapsburg Netherlands) at Mechelen and also, as superintendent of the Inquisition, directly involved in the suppression of heresy. In 1522 Erasmus had written to him (Ep 1299) defending his own orthodoxy against Baechem's attacks, but he seems to have favoured the theologians and to have been hostile,

Béda sent me more than 200 articles collected from my writings that he
thought should be condemned, none of any consequence.[11] Louis de Berquin,
prefect and councillor to the king, has been thrown into prison a second
time for no other reason than that he translated a few of my works into   25
French.[12] The queen mother had written twice to ask them to wait for the
return of the king, but the judges delegate went ahead just the same and
pronounced him a heretic.[13] The articles, sent to me, reveal nothing but
the crass stupidity and impudent chicanery of these people. I wrote a reply.[14] When the king returned and found out what had happened, he sent   30
a representative to inform them that he wished to take cognizance of the
case.[15] And he sent a letter by another messenger to say that, if anything
happened, he would hold them responsible for Berquin's life or death. I
do not know how the case turned out. Jacques Lefèvre, who had gone
into exile out of fear, although the only reason for his alarm was that he   35
had translated the Gospels into French, has been summoned back to the
court.[16]

* * * * *

or at least cool, to Erasmus. Despite Erasmus' assertion that he hated humanistic studies, there is considerable evidence to the contrary.
11 Cf Ep 1664 introduction and n1.
12 For the troubles of this rash French admirer of Erasmus, see Ep 1692 introduction and n1. Although Berquin was of noble rank and held a degree in law from the University of Orléans, Erasmus' description of him
as 'prefect and councillor to the king' attributes to him titles not otherwise
documented.
13 On this mixed group of two members of the Parlement of Paris and two members of the Paris theological faculty, created during the captivity of Francis I
in Spain specifically to investigate and repress heresy and jointly authorized
by the regent, Louise of Savoy, and Pope Clement VII, see Farge *Orthodoxy*
257–60.
14 On this reply, addressed directly to the faculty of theology and responding to
the two sets of articles extracted from Erasmus' Paraphrases by Béda and laid
before the faculty for formal censure, see Ep 1664 introduction and n1.
15 This narrative is based on Berquin's report in Ep 1692. The Latin used by
Erasmus, *cognitorem illius causae fieri*, is a technical legal term meaning 'to act
as an attorney/defender/judge of the case.' Here, in reference to the king, it
probably implies 'to become [officially] cognizant of,' implying not that Francis
would actually judge the case but that as the fount of all judicial authority,
the person ultimately responsible for the equity of all court proceedings, he
would investigate the proceeding and take any action needed to ensure that
justice truly was done.
16 On Lefèvre's flight to Strasbourg, where he stayed until his protector, King
Francis, had returned from captivity in Spain, see Ep 1674 n27.

At Rome there is a real circumcised Jew (you know whom I mean),[17]
a man who is dreadfully jealous of all German scholars. He has made public part of a polemical attack on me, which had been written some time   40
ago but has now been furnished with outrageous additions to reflect the
present situation.[18] He does not reveal his name. Among other things he
says he is surprised that, when so many have been killed in Germany, I,
who was Germany's teacher, am still alive. Then he says that the Lutherans, heretical though they may be, attack me in their writings because they 45
cannot bear my godlessness, since I deny the virginity of the Virgin Mary
and the divinity of Christ; and to these he adds other charges that are sillier
still. In Spain a monk has addressed a book to me that is full of praise,
but scattered throughout are venemous barbs.[19] Luther in his book has
adopted such a tone that he has left no room for friendship between us;   50

* * * * *

17 Literally, 'circumcised man.' The reference is to Girolamo Aleandro, Erasmus'
   former friend at Venice in 1508, whom Erasmus had come to regard as his
   most dangerous enemy at the papal curia. See Ep 1553 n9 and nn2, 3 above.
   The claim that Aleandro was of Jewish descent, advanced here by Erasmus
   and used also by German Protestants and other antagonists who both shared
   and exploited the general anti-semitism of the age, was vehemently denied
   by Aleandro himself, who was the son of a physician resident in Friuli and
   claimed descent from noble families of both Friuli and Istria on his father's
   side and from a family of Venetian nobility on his mother's side. See DBI II
   128–35.
18 A reference to the anonymous and unprinted work *Racha*, which was circulating among anti-Erasmians at the papal curia. The title of the anonymous tract
   presumably comes from the warning spoken by Jesus in Matt 5:22: '. . . and
   whosoever shall say to his brother, "Raca," shall be in danger of the council.'
   The word (ῥακά in the Greek text of Matthew) is of Aramaic origin and means
   'worthless.' The exact reason for its use as the title remains obscure. Erasmus
   had received reports about this attack on his orthodoxy and attributed its authorship to Aleandro, probably correctly. See Ep 1553 n9. See also Ep 1719
   n16, Allen Ep 1987:6–10.
19 A reference to a work by Alonso Ruiz de Virués, a Spanish Benedictine, which
   suggested that certain specific passages in Erasmus' works might have been
   worded more cautiously so as not to incite the wrath of the monks, but which
   in general was sympathetic to Erasmus' scholarly work. Erasmus, who knew
   virtually nothing about the internal workings of Spanish religious and intellectual life and who in any case was habitually thin-skinned in the face of
   criticism, regarded Virués' sending him this work (which was never printed)
   as an act of hostility. It took more than a year of reassurances by his other
   Spanish sympathizers before he conceded that Virués' manuscript was a bit of
   advice from a friend rather than part of a monkish plot to slander his good
   name. See Ep 1684 introduction.

in spite of this he is under the impression that he has kept a firm grip on his temper.[20] While I battle against Luther, I am aware that some of those whose side I am supporting would rather see me dead than Luther himself.

Your *De eucharistia* is greatly liked by the anti-Lutherans, but it is very   55
unpopular with the followers of Oecolampadius.[21] If this controversy hurt only the guilty, it would be more tolerable, but while the disputants argue, certain people are raising their heads who wish no decent person any good.[22] I would much rather this topic had been postponed until another time or at least that there had been a genuine concord[23] among them. Oecolampadius'   60
opinion[24] would not offend me if it did not run counter to the consensus of the church. For if there is spiritual grace in the elements, I do not see what need there is for a body that is 'imperceptible' and could do no good if it were perceptible. Nevertheless, I cannot depart from the consensus of

* * * * *

20 A reference to Luther's harsh treatise *De servo arbitrio* and perhaps also to his lost letter of early spring 1526, to which Erasmus' Ep 1688 is a chilly and embittered reply. See Ep 1688 introduction.

21 See n1 above.

22 Erasmus feared that behind the dispute over the Eucharist between Luther and Zwingli there lurked the malevolent and destructive influence of Andreas Karlstadt, whom he mistakenly regarded as one of the radical fanatics who had stirred up the German Peasant War in 1524–5. Erasmus (like Luther) exaggerated both Karlstadt's sympathy for social revolution and his influence on the eucharistic teaching of Zwingli and Oecolampadius. See Epp 1616 nn5, 6, 1620 nn13, 14.

23 Although the precise meaning of Erasmus' Latin expression, *in vero concordes*, is elusive, the general sense is clear. He wishes that the Evangelicals at Wittenberg (Luther and his followers) and Zürich (Zwingli and his followers) had never raised the question of how to define the manner of Christ's presence in the Eucharist, an issue that further agitated and divided the Christian community and hence increased the danger of social upheaval.

24 For other indications that Erasmus found Oecolampadius' 'spiritual' interpretation of the Eucharist plausible and rejected it on the basis of the long-established consensus of the church to the contrary, see Epp 1618:9–13 and n4; 1620:94–9 (this in a letter to Noël Béda!); 1624:38–40; 1636 and introduction (his memorandum to the city council of Basel, advising them not to let Oecolampadius' *De genuina verborum Domini* circulate in the city); 1637 introduction. What disturbed Erasmus even more than the 'error' of Oecolampadius and disciples like Conradus Pellicanus was their claim that their Sacramentarian doctrine was the product of their following Erasmus' scholarly methods and their hints that he privately agreed with them but refused to admit it openly. See Epp 1538 (to Oecolampadius), 1637 (to Pellicanus), 1670 n6, 1674 n16.

The Four Horsemen of the Apocalypse
Woodcut by Albrecht Dürer, c 1498. Dürer is said to have modelled the third
horseman (carrying the scales) on his friend Willibald Pirckheimer.
Museen der Stadt Nürnberg, Graphische Sammlung

the church, nor have I ever done so.[25] In disagreeing with Oecolampadius, 65
you give the impression of siding with Luther rather than with the church.
On occasion you quote him with more respect than is necessary, when you
could have brought in other authorities.[26] As soon as I get free from my
present entanglements, I shall read the whole book through; then you will
see my position more clearly – that is, if you allow me to express an opinion 70
on your work.

I hope that, with your good sense, you will not share this letter with
everyone you meet. Please let me know what is going on in your part of the
world. Farewell.

Basel, 6 June 1526 75

Erasmus

George, duke of Saxony, in a stream of letters, urged me to send him
a successor to Mosellanus.[27] I sent Jacobus Ceratinus, who has an excellent
command of both Greek and Latin. The arrangement did not work out well.
Perhaps he began to suspect that Ceratinus was not sufficiently antipathetic 80
to Luther's views.[28] If the teaching position is still vacant there, let me know.

* * * * *

25 Cf Ep 1729:28–30 and n13. For the role of consensus in Erasmus' theology see
Ep 1708 introduction.

26 Erasmus refers to Pirckheimer's explicit preference for Luther's eucharistic
doctrine of the real presence, in preference not only to the Sacramentarian
views of Oecolampadius but also to the traditional medieval Catholic doctrine
which explained that real presence, the doctrine of transubstantiation, a doctrine that Luther rejected just as completely as the Sacramentarians did. See
Pirckheimer *De vera Christi carne et vero eius sanguine* (n1 above) fols F1v, H2r-
v, H5r, H5v, H8r, H8v, where he endorses Luther's arguments in favour of
the real presence. Pirckheimer's citation of Luther as an authority is all the
more striking because he is the only post-patristic author quoted in the whole
work except the authors against whom Pirckheimer is writing (Oecolampadius himself, Karlstadt, Zwingli, and, among the scholastics, Duns Scotus). On
Pirckheimer's subsequent shift back to the medieval Catholic doctrine, see n1
above.

27 Peter Schade, commonly known as Mosellanus, was an admirer of Erasmus.
He became professor of Greek at Leipzig in 1517 and died on 14 April 1524.
In May 1524, Duke George, as patron of the territorial university (and careful
supervisor of the orthodoxy of its teachers and students), asked Erasmus to
suggest a successor, 'who must however be entirely free from all taint of the
Lutheran faction' (Ep 1448:72–3). Cf Ep 1520:47–9, a reminder that Erasmus
had not responded to this request.

28 For Erasmus' nomination of Jacobus Ceratinus for the chair of Greek at Leipzig,
and for the ill success of the resulting appointment, see Epp 1561 and n3,
1564–8. These letters of nomination and introduction for Ceratinus were writ-

Sigismundus has determined not to leave here.[29] Many thanks for your Ptolemy[30] and the book of Dürer's.[31] I am waiting now for my portrait.[32]

To the distinguished Willibald Pirckheimer, city councillor[33]

1718 / To Martin Hune   [Basel, c 6 June 1526]

This is a fragment of a lost letter from Erasmus to Martin Hune, quoted in a letter written by Eobanus Hessus to Willibald Pirckheimer, Nürnberg, 7 July 1526. The manuscript of Eobanus' letter survived at Nürnberg and was first published in Johann Heumann von Teutschbrunn *Documenta literaria varii argumenti in lucem prolata cura Iohannis Heumanni* (Altdorf 1758) 114. On the physician Martin Hune, the recipient of the letter from which this text is quoted, see Ep 1462 introduction. After leaving the University of Erfurt in the autumn of 1525, Hune spent the summer of 1526 in Annaberg and Vienna and eventually proceeded to Italy, where he studied medicine at Padua.

I am happy about our friend Eobanus,[1] both because he is going to teach literature at a very good salary in a thriving city and also because it will

* * * * *

ten in March and April 1526, but already by September, Erasmus was expressing regret that Ceratinus had resigned and left Leipzig because of suspicions (apparently unjustified) by Duke George and others that he was a renegade priest and a sympathizer with Luther. See Ep 1611 and n2.

29 See Ep 1702 n1.
30 Cf Ep 1603 n23. Evidently Pirckheimer had sent Erasmus a copy of his translation of Ptolemy and of Dürer's book sometime after receiving that letter, which is dated 28 August 1525, and Erasmus had not yet received these gifts (or at least did not acknowledge them) by 20 September, the date of Ep 1611.
31 Albrecht Dürer's *Underweyssung der Messung mit dem Zirkel und Richtscheyt* (Nürnberg: Johannes Petreius 1525), a technical manual addressed to young artists, was published with a dedication to Pirckheimer.
32 On Dürer's engraving of Erasmus, see Ep 1729:12–13 and n9
33 The Latin is *senator*, which Erasmus frequently uses to designate city councillors. Pirckheimer had ceased to be a councillor in 1523, but Erasmus probably continued to use the term as a courtesy title. Or it is quite possible that he simply was unaware that his friend was no longer a member of the council of Nürnberg.

1718
1 On the highly regarded humanist poet Helius Eobanus Hessus, see Ep 874 introduction. Eobanus was a close friend and correspondent of Martin Hune and from 1526 to 1533 taught in the new city school at Nürnberg, where he was in touch with Pirckheimer, the city's most eminent humanist.

be easier from now on for letters to pass between us. Willibald, you know, writes to me often.

1719 / To François Du Moulin   Basel, [c 6 June] 1526

> This letter was printed in *Opus epistolarum* bearing the same date as the ob-
> viously earlier Ep 1711 addressed to the same person. Allen's estimate of its
> date is based on the similarity in content to Ep 1717 and also on the awareness
> of the death of Du Moulin shown in Ep 1722, dated 16 June 1526.

ERASMUS OF ROTTERDAM TO FRANÇOIS DU MOULIN, GREETING
I was greatly perturbed when Francis, the best of kings, set out for Milan
as winter was approaching, for I had a presentiment that an awful disaster
would overtake him. When I found out how the war ended, I was as upset
as if I had shared his fate and been exposed to the same peril. Few men,   5
I observe, are happy with the peace, presumably because the terms of the
treaty seem rather harsh and this makes them fear it will not last. But I
hope that God, the great ruler of the affairs of men, will turn all to good.
He knows what is expedient for us, and under his guidance failure often
turns out better than success. From now on the king will be more eager for   10
peace and less ready to think of war.[1] I only wish this insight had cost him
less. His goodness certainly deserves continuing success – I can only hope
his present misfortunes will prove a blessing in disguise. I am delighted
that he has arrived as a deus ex machina[2] to check those madmen who are

* * * * *

1719
1 A fine example of Erasmus' lack of understanding of political reality and the
  minds of rulers. Upon his release from nearly thirteen months of captivity,
  during which he had been compelled to agree to harsh conditions imposed by
  the emperor Charles v in the Treaty of Madrid (14 January 1526), the French
  king almost immediately took steps to repudiate the concessions he had made
  and to renew his struggle not only to preserve the territorial integrity of France
  but also to reassert his territorial claims in Italy. In fact, on 22 May he had
  already signed a treaty of alliance with Pope Clement vii and several Italian
  powers, looking ahead to eventual military action if the emperor did not renounce some of his gains from the treaty. Cf Knecht *Renaissance Warrior* 253–
  6. The principal impediment (other than lack of money) to repudiation of the
  Treaty of Madrid and open resumption of war against the emperor was that
  at the time of the king's release his sons François and Henri had been sur-
  rendered as hostages to be held in Spain until their father had fulfilled his
  obligations under the treaty. Cf Ep 1686 n3.
2 Erasmus uses the Greek equivalent of this Latin phrase; cf *Adagia* i i 68. The

conspiring to undermine the humanities and the power of the gospel. For   15
nothing could be cruel enough to satisfy those Pharisees and Romanizers.[3]

I, who have always been a lover of peace, must now fight single-handed
against a multitude of foes. For some time now I have been waging a bloody
war against the enemies of good literature. This has brought me into conflict
with not a few monks and theologians who consider it an affront to their   20
dignity if someone knows something they do not know. Luther, egged on
by others (though they disagree with him over the Eucharist) has produced
such an attack on me as to leave no room for friendship.[4] Karlstadt's followers,[5] first through rumours and then in a book written in the German

* * * * *

reference is to Francis' rapid intervention, once he was back in Paris, to rescue evangelical humanists like Louis de Berquin, Jacques Lefèvre d'Etaples,
Gérard Roussel, and Pierre Caroli from measures taken against them by the
Parlement of Paris. See Knecht *Renaissance Warrior* 260–1. Lefèvre and Roussel had fled to Strasbourg in October 1525, fearing arrest and prosecution on
charges of heresy, and they did not return to France until the spring of 1526,
when the king was back from captivity and able to ensure their safety.
 3 The pejorative form *Romanenses*. Cf Pirckheimer's use of the term in earlier letters, at a time when he was still rather sympathetic to Luther and certainly hostile to the actions of papal representatives and supporters in Germany (Allen
Epp 1344:73, 1480:34 / CWE Epp 1344:82, 1430:35, translated 'the Roman party'
and 'the Romans'). In the present instance, the 'Pharisees and Romanizers' are
obviously the conservative *parlementaires* and theologians who had led the attack on Bishop Guillaume Briçonnet and the evangelical humanists associated
with his abortive attempt to reform his diocese of Meaux (Epp 1579 nn39–41,
1650 n4). The term 'Romanizers' may reflect the fact that Erasmus is addressing a highly placed clergyman in a nation where the tradition of 'Gallican liberties' had for centuries implied resistance to the centralizing efforts of the
Roman curia, though ironically, after the Concordat of 1516, officials close to
the crown like Du Moulin had opposed the Gallican tradition. The institutional centres of hostility to the humanist reformers, the Parlement of Paris
and the University of Paris, however, had doggedly resisted the concordat as
an intrusion of 'Roman tyranny' into the 'Gallican liberties' of their national
church. On the Gallican tradition, see Pierre Blet 'Gallicanism' in *The Oxford
Encyclopedia of the Reformation* II 154–6.
 4 A reference to Luther's *De servo arbitrio*; cf Ep 1667 introduction.
 5 Erasmus consistently but mistakenly regarded the Swiss Sacramentarian reformers (Zwingli, Oecolampadius, Pellicanus, Capito) as followers of Karlstadt, and their eucharistic doctrine as a direct result of his influence. On Erasmus' growing alienation from these individuals, nearly all of whom had been
his admirers and several of whom (Oecolampadius, Pellicanus, Capito) had
been his associates and assistants in the biblical and patristic editions he published with the Froben press at Basel, see Epp 1538 (to Oecolampadius), 1637,

language,[6] allege that I am in agreement with Karlstadt. If in defiance of my   25
conscience I accept their point of view, I shall be professing a doctrine of
which I have never yet been able to convince myself; if I do not, I shall have
to confront their line of battle.

The Franciscan Standish has been charged with the investigation of
heresy in England.[7] You can guess what that means. At Louvain the same   30
office is held by the theologian Nicolas of Mons,[8] a close associate of Egmondanus, who could not be restrained from hurling abuse at me either by a
twice-issued edict from the pope or by a carefully worded letter from the
emperor.[9] His outbursts, however, do not carry much weight – he simply

* * * * *

1638, 1639, 1640, 1737, 1792A (to and from Pellicanus). Cf Epp 1670 n6, 1674
nn15, 16, 1679 nn4, 15, 1717 n22. As he admitted in a letter to his French critic
Noël Béda (Ep 1581:254–7), his earlier association with these men was a source
of embarrassment now that they had become supporters of the Reformation;
and he was especially sensitive to the claims they made that their Sacramentarian doctrines were the result of his own influence and even that he privately agreed with those doctrines but refused to avow it publicly. He bitterly
resented their published hints that this was so, and the issue led to an especially bitter break between Erasmus and Pellicanus, of whom he had been
especially fond. See Ep 1637 introduction. At least unconsciously, Erasmus'
exaggeration of Karlstadt's influence on the radical eucharistic doctrines of his
former friends may have been an attempt to refute the claim that he was indeed the source of their heretical doctrines, since he had never been close to
Karlstadt, whose origins lay in the theological faculty at Wittenberg, where
he began his religious deviation as a faculty colleague and radical follower of
Martin Luther.

6 On this book written by Leo Jud, see Ep 1708 n1. It repeated the allegation
that Erasmus secretly supported the Sacramentarian opinion but was afraid
to avow it publicly.

7 See Ep 1697 n10.

8 Nicolas Coppin of Mons, professor of theology and former principal of the
College of the Falcon at Louvain, was chancellor of the university by virtue of
his position as dean of the chapter of St Peter's and had become inquisitor in
1526. He had originally been favourable to Erasmus and still pretended to be
neutral, but Erasmus learned from his best friend in the faculty of theology,
Maarten van Dorp, that he had turned against Erasmus (see Ep 1585:52–5).
On Coppin see Epp 1162 n18, 1608 and introduction, 1703 n3, 1747:17–20.

9 The Carmelite Nicolaas Baechem of Egmond was one of the most virulent and
persistent of Erasmus' critics among the Louvain theologians. See Epp 878:15n,
1254 n6, 1581 n27, 1608 n4, and many other letters of the mid-1520s. On his bitter opposition to the humanistic Collegium Trilingue at Louvain, in the formation of which Erasmus had played an active role, see Ep 1556 n1; on the vain
attempt of Pope Adrian VI (himself a distinguished member of the Louvain

Alberto Pio
Portrait by Bernardino Loschi
National Gallery, London

keeps calling me a heretic. Nor has the viper of Paris been any gentler. [10] 35
Spain is well disposed towards me, the monks excepted.[11] At Rome that
pagan fraternity of savants has been growling about me for a long time,[12]
led, they say, by Aleandro and a certain Alberto, prince of Carpi.[13]

A book full of violent abuse of me has been shown to Clement; the author's name is not known for certain, but I am pretty sure who he is.[14] The 40
book divulges certain mysteries from the sacred Talmud which ought not to
be cast before swine. In the course of explaining the word 'Racha,' which he
does in almost the same terms as I used following the authority of Augustine and Chrysostom,[15] except that he wants to interpret it as a noun, while
they call it an 'interjection,' he suddenly returns to that old story, that al- 45
though Germany put thousands of men to death for heresy, Erasmus, who
was Germany's tutor, is, surprisingly, still alive. He adds that the Lutherans, heretics though they may be, are now attacking me because they cannot
stand my heresies;[16] for I have robbed Mary, the mother of Jesus, of her

* * * * *

theological faculty before he entered the service of Charles v and then was
elected pope) to silence Baechem's attacks, see Ep 1359 n2; cf Rummel I 135–
43; on the emperor's efforts to stop the attacks by Baechem and other Louvain
theologians, see Epp 1690 n10, 1697 n7, 1716 n7, 1747 and introduction.

10 Possibly Erasmus' critic Noël Béda, but more likely the Carthusian monk (and
Paris doctor of theology) Pierre Cousturier, whom Erasmus regarded as the
most despicable and most grossly incompetent of his French antagonists. On
Cousturier see Epp 1571 n10, 1658 n7.

11 For Erasmus' own list of his supporters in Spain, see Ep 1431:31–5 (but here
he disregards the critical stance taken towards his New Testament scholarship
by Spain's most distinguished biblical humanist, Elio Antonio de Nebrija; see
n19). Cf Epp 1277 and introduction, 1684 introduction, 1748 and introduction.

12 On Erasmus' conviction that the curial secretariat was not only hostile to him
but also only nominally Christian and essentially pagan in faith and morals,
see Ep 1717 n2.

13 On the hostility of both Girolamo Aleandro and Alberto Pio to Erasmus, see
Ep 1717 n3 and the earlier letters cited there, especially Ep 1634 introduction.

14 A reference to the work known as *Racha*, never printed but privately circulated at the papal curia and attributed by Erasmus to Aleandro, probably correctly. See Epp 1553 n9, 1717 nn3, 18, and Allen Ep 1987, a letter of 1528 from
Erasmus to Pope Clement VII himself, blunt to the point of indiscretion. Cf
also n16 below.

15 Erasmus' reference to Augustine and Chrysostom is from his notes on Matt
5:22; see LB VI 27.

16 In other words, Erasmus claims that the anonymous manuscript tract attributes
to him heresies so shocking that even the Lutheran heretics are attacking him,
not because he published his books against Luther, but because his religious
doctrines were allegedly so blasphemous that even the heretics were offended.

virginity and stolen from the Son of God his divinity, I have had the audac-   50
ity to interpret the Scriptures without reference to the Talmud, and I have
called the bishop of Rome a whoremonger, a procurer, and Antichrist. You
would imagine the man was possessed, so ready is he to blurt out whatever
his 'gleaming bile'[17] suggests to him. On top of all this, a new party of Ciceronians has arisen, which is no less fierce than the Lutherans. It is an old   55
movement, but it has been revived by Longueil.[18]

I must do battle on so many fronts, alone and unarmed, since the
support I receive from the court is not worth the proverbial fig.[19] Someone else has recently published three volumes in which he has paved the
road to theological tyranny;[20] he has gone so far as to state that all kings   60
through baptism have come under the control of the church and can be
removed from office by the church, that is, by the monks and bishops,
though they would not sanction this in the case of a pope, however ob-
noxious he might be. Such is the point their audacity has reached. But
since both sides have their madmen, great caution is necessary lest, in re-   65
straining one side, we slacken the reins on the other more than is wise.
Farewell.

Basel [16 May] 1526

1720 / From Leonard Casembroot   Padua, 6 June 1526

A reply to Ep 1705. The autograph of the original letter survived at Wrocław
as MS Rehdiger 254.47 and was first published by Enthoven in 1906. An ex-
cerpt from this letter appears as no 337 of the *Appendix epistolarum* in LB III-2
1715. In a note on the Rehdiger collection Allen III xxiv concludes that the textual source for a number of letters printed in LB, many of them abridged, is Johann Fecht *Historiae ecclesiasticae seculi A.N.C. XVI supplementum* book 8 (Frankfurt
1684). This letter is one of them.

* * * * *

Whether Erasmus ever actually saw the text and therefore knew its contents
   in detail, or whether he is depending on second-hand reports from friends at
   the curia, is an unresolved question.
17 The Latin, *splendida bilis*, is from Horace *Satires* 2.3.141. Black bile, which has
   a shining appearance, was believed to be responsible for madness.
18 See Epp 1701 n6, 1706 n11, 1717 n2; on Longueil, see Ep 1706 nn2–9 and the
   earlier letters cited there.
19 Cf *Adagia* I vii 85. The wood of the fig tree is proverbially weak and useless.
20 No doubt a reference to the Louvain theologian Jacobus Latomus; see Ep 1674
   n12.

Cordial greetings, my dearest Erasmus. My impatient longing for news of you was in some way satisfied by your friend Hieronymus Froben, who, besides the pleasure which he always brings wherever he goes, brought us the special delight of a packet of letters from you for your friends. I did what I could, as you requested, to help him in his hunt for old manuscripts. But Diana was uncooperative.[1] The result distresses me as much as it disappoints him.[2]

Master Reginald Pole was much more helpful (for he is in a position to help).[3] Thanks to him, you will be able to examine excellent copies of certain catalogues, those, for example, from the library in Rome, the Florentine library, and the library in Venice.[4] The monks at Padua, who are rather secretive about their holdings, were impregnable from every angle, although we attacked them with all the methods you suggested, that is, we were ready to offer money and to beg, borrow, or steal.[5] How Froben has fared in Venice I do not know. For he has buried himself there almost continuously since he left us. When he did return from Venice, he made an appearance here for only a few short hours; his departure was hastened, I imagine, by the offer of company for the journey. This is the reason you are not receiving a longer and more finished letter. I was holding back my pen in the hope of finding out what success or fortune attended the hunt.

Now there is nothing else for me to write about except to give you news of myself. The pangs of hunger have been dispelled even without the help of cantaloupes and watermelons (I am delighted to see the pleasure you take in recalling these little jokes of ours), for Hunger encountered some stout opponents from Germany;[6] but how long this will continue I do not

* * * * *

1720
1 The Latin is *Delia invita*; cf Ovid *Metamorphoses* 8.395. Diana, the Delian goddess, presides over the hunt, in this case the hunt for manuscripts of classical and patristic authors.
2 But Froben was not unsuccessful. See Ep 1705 n3.
3 See Ep 1675 introduction.
4 The Roman library would be the Vatican; the Florentine, the Laurentian; and the Venetian, the library of St Mark's.
5 Allen (12n) suggests that the monastery from which no information could be acquired was the Benedictine community of Santa Giustina.
6 The reference is to Casembroot's success in finding German students to tutor at Padua, remedying the financial hardship he faced after the father of two Netherlandish students he was tutoring removed them from his care, leaving him unemployed. See Ep 1650.

know, since they seem to be planning to return to their own country sooner
than I would wish. I should like to have a more reliable means of support,
either here or in France, since in one of these regions I would hope to make
progress in the study of civil law. This has been my steadfast goal for some
time, and I could not abandon it now without considerable embarrassment.   30

I have just heard from Flanders, to my great sorrow, of the death of
my saintly mother. No one could understand how greatly this affected me
unless he had witnessed the deep and extraordinary love which we felt for
one another. But I must not grieve now; I only pray that she is enjoying the
blessed reward of the Christian hope.   35

In my absence Master Marcus Laurinus is most generously acting for
me in securing my modest inheritance, or rather he took the initiative and
wrote asking to be appointed as my agent (you see what a kind and loyal
friend he is).[7] So there has been no need for me to alter course or abandon
my marvellous perseverance; and I shall now be able to proceed with fewer   40
worries along the path I have chosen. However, I must continue to place my
greatest hope in you, that on your recommendation I shall somewhere find
a place where a diligent worker may at length reap the fruits of his efforts.

You know what I would like, and I am well aware of what you can do.
But the complaints of decent men are, alas! only too just, that huge obstacles 45
prevent you from performing the useful services you could perform since
you are forced to defend yourself against the sputtering attacks of one critic
after another. As for your protest against Luther's unbridled spirit, you have
done well by muzzling the seditious.[8]

One thing remains to be done, which I understand was Froben's idea: 50
the world must be made aware of the foolishness and *amour propre* of some
Italians who will allow no one the least credit as a stylist except Cicero.[9] This
view has led many people to despise you and other authors of considerable

* * * * *

7 See Ep 1695 n6.
8 Casembroot's lively but eccentric Latin is punctuated by occasional Greek
phrases, equally eccentric and strange.
9 Evidence that Casembroot shared Erasmus' hostility to the Ciceronian stylistic
purism typical of many Italian humanists. The reference at line 50 to 'Froben's
idea' suggests that Casembroot already knew of Erasmus' intention to write
the work that became his *Ciceronianus* (1528), which was sharply critical of the
Ciceronianism of his Italian critics. The Greek expression translated 'by muzzling the seditious' above may have been used for reasons of discretion, since
it involves Erasmus' reaction to Luther, but here Casembroot's combination of
Greek and Latin in the phrase φίλαυτα *iudicia* was probably used for stylistic
reasons.

merit. The problem is especially acute at Bologna, where Lazzaro[10] holds
sway as a veritable Aristarchus,[11] not to say an Erasmiomastix.[12] Your friend   55
Froben will give you the rest of my news. I must finish now.

    Farewell, dear Erasmus, and may your humble servant, whom nothing
could rob of his devotion to you, continue to have a place somewhere among
your friends!

    Padua, 6 June 1526   60
    Yours truly, Leonard Casperotus (for that is his new surname)
    To that truly great man, Master Erasmus of Rotterdam. In Basel

1721 / To the Parlement of Paris   Basel, 14 June 1526

The present letter marks the continuing deterioration of relations between
Erasmus and the Paris faculty of theology, especially its syndic Noël Béda,
which was already evident in Erasmus' letter of 6 February 1526 to the faculty
itself (Ep 1664) and also in the increasingly hostile tone of the letters exchanged
between Béda and Erasmus during 1525 (listed in Ep 1664 introduction; cf also
Epp 1679 and 1685, the most recent and most hostile exchange). In Ep 1685
Béda reported that his *Annotationes* were in press. Here Erasmus appeals for
fair treatment to the supreme French judicial body and in the following letter
to the king himself. Ep 1664 had no effect. The faculty, led by Béda, continued
its investigation of Erasmus' publications and formally initiated an inquiry into
his *Colloquia familiaria* on 1 May, continued to discuss the *Colloquies* on 4 May
and 6 May, and at the latter session approved a resolution forbidding the reading of the *Colloquies*, especially by young people, and calling for suppression

* * * * *

10 Lazzaro Bonamico (1497/8–1552), a native of Bassano in the Veneto and a student of Latin under Giovanni Calfurnio and Raffaele Regio, Greek under Niccolò Leoniceno and Marcus Musurus, and philosophy under Pietro Pompo-
   nazzi, was active as a private tutor at Bologna in this period and later (1530)
   became lecturer on Latin and Greek at the University of Padua. He was a
   highly successful teacher, an outspoken defender of Ciceronian style, and a
   defender of writing in Latin and Greek rather than in Italian, which he dis-
   dained as a degenerate form of Latin. Despite Casembroot's mention of him
   here as a Ciceronian critic of Erasmus, he and Erasmus seem to have held each
   other in high regard, a point made clear by Thomas B. Deutscher in CEBR I
   166; see also R. Avesano in DBI XI 533–40.
11 Head of the great library at Alexandria in the second century BC, and a critic of
   Homer and other Greek poets. His name is synonymous with severity of criticism. But cf the preceding note, since, despite his commitment to Ciceronian
   Latin, Bonamico seems to have held Erasmus in high regard.
12 Literally, 'a Scourge of Erasmus'; see Ep 1658 n8.

of the book. At the session on 6 May (Farge *Registre* 134) it also authorized publication of Béda's book against both Lefèvre d'Etaples and Erasmus, *Annota-*
tionum Natalis Bedae ... in Jacobum Fabrum Stapulensem libri duo, et in Desiderium
Erasmum Roterodamum liber unus (Paris: Josse Bade, 25 May 1526). Béda had reported completion of this work to Erasmus in a letter of the preceding October
(Ep 1642), and its preface was dated 3 May 1526. As Farge has shown from repeated examples, the Parlement was generally respectful of the faculty of theology and worked in close collaboration with it for the suppression of heresy
and the prohibition of dangerous books (Farge *Orthodoxy*, especially 214–19,
251–70). Allen's introduction to this letter prints excerpts from the records of
the Parlement showing that the judges heard Erasmus' letter on 5 July, conferred with the dean and doctors of the faculty of theology the following day,
and referred to them Erasmus' *Elenchus*, his brief rebuttal of the censures that
Béda's book recorded against select passages from Erasmus' Paraphrases (see
n14 below). At its meeting on 9 July the faculty discussed the *Elenchus* but decided to enlarge the committee appointed to deal with it. Further independent
action by the faculty was forestalled by direct action of the king to prohibit
Béda's book and confiscate all unsold copies (of which, in fact, very few were
left). On 16 August the faculty discussed the matter in a spirit critical of Erasmus' letter to the king and appointed a committee (which included Béda) to
write a letter of protest to the king (Farge *Registre* 142–3). On this entire phase
of Erasmus' conflict with the faculty, see Farge *Orthodoxy* 190–3 and Rummel II
33–7. Erasmus published the present letter in his *Opus epistolarum*, but Allen's
Latin text is based primarily on a contemporary manuscript copy in the records
of the Parlement (now in the Archives Nationales), though he also consulted a
printed edition containing the text of Epp 1721–3, *D. Erasmi Rotherodami Epis-*
tolae tres nuper in apertum prolatae (no place or date, but probably 1526) which
he seems to attribute to an unknown Paris press. He also refers to a sixteenth-
century manuscript in the Stadtbibliothek at Bern which he judges, despite its
many textual flaws, to be indirectly derived from the manuscript in the records
of the Parlement. This Bern manuscript also contains Ep 1722, and Allen conjectures that it may have been made for Erasmus' friend Nicolas Bérault.

TO THE MOST VENERABLE PARLEMENT OF PARIS, GREETING
Distinguished sirs, champions of justice, I beg leave for a moment to intrude
upon your grave and serious business. When François Deloynes was still
alive,[1] Noël Béda marked certain passages in my Paraphrase on Luke at

* * * * *

1721
1 Deloynes (d July 1524) had been a distinguished jurist, a member of the Parlement of Paris since 1500, and *Président aux enquêtes* from 1522; he was a re-

which he took offence. Although he did not communicate them to me but   5
circulated them among others, I thanked him for his efforts and asked him
to do the same for the other volumes; I assured him he would never find me
wanting in the proper courtesy of a Christian. Then he sent me a number of
other passages, but without comment. I thanked him, expressing the hope
that the discussion could continue between us with due Christian sobriety.   10
I replied to several of his objections in the most temperate language. Soon,
when I realized from his letters the jaundiced nature of the man, I directed
my replies to the venerable faculty of theology, so that they could hand
them over to be read by people whose judgment would not be biased by
enmity or jealousy, and I requested that, if they judged anything there to   15
be injurious to true Christian teaching or to pious conduct, they advise me
of it in a friendly spirit.[2] I promised either to amend the passage or to add
an explanation, so that no one would be misled by it. Although my reply
was free from rancour, Béda was offended that I dared to reply, albeit in a
private communication; he published an attack on me and Lefèvre,[3] having   20
feigned the consent of the faculty or bullied it into agreeing.

I do not know what kind of case Lefèvre has. I answer only for myself,
and I affirm that in the criticisms that Béda makes of my Paraphrases there
are more than a hundred lying statements and false accusations, so palpable
that even smiths and cobblers could, as the saying goes, feel them with their   25
fingers.[4] At the very least he ought to have waited for the judgment of his
faculty[5] and not forestalled it. But he plunged ahead out of hatred and published his calumnies, bringing discredit on a famous university and upon

* * * * *

spected figure within the Parlement. He had also been a friend of Erasmus
since 1500 and the centre of a group of humanists that also included Erasmus'
friend (and frequent informant about developments in Paris) Nicolas Bérault.
He had privately sent Erasmus a copy of Béda's censures criticizing Erasmus'
Paraphrases on Luke and Exposition of the Lord's Prayer, a document that
Béda had given to him in connection with his duties in the Parlement. See
Epp 1571 introduction and n1, 1664 introduction.
2 See Ep 1664.
3 His *Annotationes* (1526). See the introduction to the present letter and Ep 1685,
  where Béda recounts his decision to append an attack on Erasmus' Paraphrases
  to a work attacking Lefèvre d'Etaples which was already being printed by
  Josse Bade.
4 Lucian *Demonax* 4; Cicero *Pro Caelio* 28
5 At the early stage (1523) of the quarrel over Erasmus' Paraphrases, Béda, whatever one may think of the soundness of his judgment, was acting appropri-
  ately in noting down passages that he found dangerous or questionable. On
  the background of Béda's actions and the conflict that resulted, see Ep 1664
  introduction and n1, 1666 n5.

the profession of theology, to say nothing of his own reputation, and giving commensurate delight to the Lutherans and those who are worse than Lutherans. I was fighting in the forefront of the battle with those whom the theologians condemn, as my writings testify; and while I conducted this campaign – under orders, too, from the emperor, the pope, and other princes, and not without danger to my life – Cousturier and Béda were attacking me in the rear with their hysterical writings.[6] This is certainly the way to give real support to the Lutherans!

I had issued the first part of my reply to Luther[7] and was working on the rest, which is unlikely to be completed now before the next fair. What will the Lutherans say when they read the wild jeremiads of Cousturier and the censures of Béda, so full of shameless lies? 'Are these the men,' they will say, 'who condemned the teaching of Luther? Is it men like these whose verdict sends others to the stake? Is it on such mighty Atlases that the Roman church relies?' For this is the way men think: those who publish books, especially books that have received official approval, set the standard by which others are commonly judged. If these men are inspired by religious zeal, why am I, who fight for true piety, the target of more virulent attacks than Luther himself?

I do not deny that it is possible to find instances of human error in my books, but so far no one has been able to point to an error condemned by the church. Those who, out of prejudice, have tried to find such errors can bring forward nothing except suspicions and slanders. Certainly, if I said anything inadvertently that might be injurious to faith or morals, I was ready to make corrections, and that has always been my attitude. Up to now I have followed this practice assiduously when my attention was drawn to something significant. I have always held theologians in the greatest respect. Genuine monks I cherish and respect; there are none among whom I would rather pass my life than such men if my poor health did not make this impossible. In my books I have said things respecting certain monks and theologians that I thought important for the dignity of the order and the salvation of all men. And because of that these people cry schism and scandal. If I were interested in schism and faction, I would not have suffered so much,

* * * * *

6 The Carthusian Pierre Cousturier, who held a doctorate in theology, published an open attack on Erasmus and Lefèvre well ahead of Béda. Erasmus' decision to publish a rebuttal set off a lengthy pamphlet controversy. See Epp 1571 n10, 1658 n7.
7 *Hyperaspistes 1*, published in early March 1526 as a hasty preliminary reply to Luther's sharp attack on Erasmus in *De servo arbitrio*. See Ep 1667 introduction.

and would not be suffering now, to keep myself clear of such things. For I chose to stand alone and be torn apart by imbeciles from both sides rather than seek security in a party that is condemned by the church.

What will become of us if the sort of books that Cousturier and Béda 65 write are published in Paris, while the writings of others are banned? Are they to be allowed to pour out their poison, while we cannot provide the antidote? The young converge on Paris in the hope of returning home more learned and virtuous, but what benefit will they reap from books like that, which contain nothing but bitterness and shameless falsehoods? I know that 70 among Paris theologians those who delight in the malevolence of Cousturier and Béda are few in number.[8] Is anything less likely to lead to victory than to drive into Luther's camp those who now disagree with him but could start up the whole tragedy afresh if they came to agree with him? It was animosity of this sort that made Arius a heresiarch,[9] drove Tertullian from 75 the church,[10] and turned Wycliffe into the church's enemy.[11] The job of a

* * * * *

8 A hopeful rather than an accurate statement, but it became obvious during later stages of the effort that eventually led to a formal condemnation of Eras-mus' books in October 1527 that a good many members of the faculty did not share Béda's eagerness to press on towards formal condemnation, and also that Erasmus did have friends inside the faculty who may not have been will-ing or able to oppose Béda openly but who did keep him informed about what was going on there. The lack of enthusiasm for a formal censure was reflected in poor attendance at sessions devoted to discussion of Erasmus' works, so that the faculty voted to increase the stipend paid to its members for atten-dance and to schedule such special meetings at fixed intervals in order to make progress in the case. See Farge *Orthodoxy* 176–7 for the early period, in 1524, and 194–5 for the period leading directly up to the formal condemnation of Erasmus' works, which was not made public until 1531. See also Rummel II 46–9.

9 Christian priest of Alexandria (c 250–336) whose opinions on the nature of Christ's divinity subordinated the Son to God the Father and precipitated a bitter theological conflict. The opposition was led by St Athanasius. The Coun-cil of Nicaea in 325 condemned Arius and his theological position, and artic-ulated the orthodox Trinitarian definition of the divine nature.

10 Priest of Carthage (c 155–c 220), one of the earliest figures in the develop-ment of Christian theology in the Latin-speaking part of the Roman world. His writings in many respects laid the foundations for all subsequent Latin theology, but his discontent with the laxity of religious observance and morals among most Christians had led him by 210 to reject the orthodox church and embrace the rigorist heresy known as Montanism.

11 John Wycliffe (c 1330–1384), Oxford theologian eventually condemned as a heretic. His career beyond the university began as a defender of the rights of the English monarchy against the papacy on questions of taxation and collation to

theologian is to minister to heretics or to prove them wrong. But behaviour like this turns men into heretics; it does not prove them wrong. It does nothing to quench the fire that Luther lit; instead it pours oil on the flames and makes them burn more fiercely.[12] The clearest proof of Béda's unmitigated spleen is the fact that, when I dealt in a private letter with the passages he had criticized,[13] and he read my answers, he did not wait for the theologians to give their judgment but rushed to produce his censures; what is more, in my reply to several of his points, I showed that in the latest edition I had corrected a number of passages that, in any case, were mistakes of the printers, not mine; moreover, in several places I demolished his argument so thoroughly that nothing was left to him except manifest distortions.

I thought it proper to advise your most august assembly of these matters so that you may be aware of the danger and use your wisdom and authority and sense of justice to protect the dignity of this university and the reputation of theology, and to look to the salvation of the young and maintain tranquillity in the world of learning. Rabid malevolence, the fount of sedition, has gone far enough. I have marked certain passages in Béda's criticisms;[14] If they are clearly misguided and slanderous (as they are), then either prevent such poisonous stuff from being published there or allow the antidote I have provided to be brought in. If they wish to produce genuine arguments to confute those who have defected from the truth of the Christian faith, they will find me a comrade in the battle. But if they are blinded by hatred and want only to hurt by any means at their command, I think

* * * * *

benefices. He proceeded to endorse moderate church reform, but after the origin of the papal schism in 1378 he raised the issue of authority over the church and increasingly put forward theological positions incompatible with established doctrines. Cf Ep 1708 n4 for Erasmus' views on his eucharistic doctrine.

12 *Adagia* I ii 9

13 Presumably Erasmus has in mind Ep 1581, especially lines 771–872, though most of this letter deals with other questions, in particular the high rank and intellectual and moral excellence of those ecclesiastical authorities who have (in general terms, not on specific issues) endorsed his writings.

14 A reference to Erasmus' *Elenchus*, a summary of his response to the charges against his Paraphrases that were published in Béda's *Annotationes*. He sent a copy of this summary as an enclosure with this letter, and the Parlement referred it to the faculty of theology. Erasmus published the *Elenchus* and several other replies to Béda and Cousturier under the general title *Prologus Erasmi Roterodami in supputationem calumniarum Natalis Bedae. Responsiunculae ad propositiones a Beda notatas. Appendix de antapologia Petri Sutoris & scriptis Iodoci Clithovei. Quibus addatur Elenchus erratorum in censuris Bedae, iampridem excusus* (Basel: Froben, August 1526). The text of the *Elenchus* is in LB IX 495–514.

it a more sober course to appeal for help to your Parlement, which stands   100
pre-eminent in matters of law and justice, than to join in the rancour. These
remarks apply only to men like Cousturier and Béda, not to the rest of the
theologians. May the Lord Jesus keep and preserve your venerable court.
　　Basel, 14 June 1526
　　Erasmus of Rotterdam   105
　　I signed this with my own hand.

1722 / To Francis I   Basel, 16 June 1526

This direct and blunt appeal to King Francis I for royal intervention to restrain the attacks of Noël Béda and Pierre Cousturier on Erasmus, but also on
Lefèvre d'Etaples and Louis de Berquin, closely parallels in sentiments and
even in wording the letter of 14 June to the Parlement of Paris. The conservatives' attacks on reform-minded humanists had been stimulated by the extended captivity of the French king in Spain after his defeat at Pavia (24 February 1525), leaving the government in the hands of the queen mother, Louise of
Savoy, who was more conservative than her son and also, as a woman and a
regent, less able to dominate the Parlement and the faculty of theology. Erasmus here takes advantage of the king's release from captivity (17 March 1526)
in order to plead for direct royal action to bring the theologians to heel. In
fact the king moved very slowly on most policies except his careful preparations to repudiate the treaty he had been forced to sign at Madrid in order
to secure his release. Erasmus knew that the king was generally favourable to
himself as well as to the other humanists, especially as Francis in 1523-5 had
made a major effort to persuade Erasmus to settle in France under royal patronage. See Epp 1375, 1400:3-13, 1434, 1439, 1446, 1484, 1487. The text of this
letter as published by Erasmus himself in 1529 (*Opus epistolarum*) omitted the
sentences near the end that explicitly endorse Berquin's good character (lines
87-8). The textual sources for this letter are identical to those for Ep 1721. The
letter got fairly prompt results. On 4 August the king, then at Amboise, wrote
to the Parlement, ordering them to stop further sale of Béda's *Annotationes* (cf
Farge *Orthodoxy* 193, 260; Rummel II 36-7; Farge *Registre* 142-3 and nn51-2,
session of 18 August 1526); but only fifty of the 650 copies of Béda's *Annotationes* remained unsold and hence exposed to the confiscation ordered by the
Parlement. In any case, a second edition of the *Annotationes* was published that
same month in Cologne, where the king's order had no effect.

THE LETTER OF DESIDERIUS ERASMUS TO THE KING OF FRANCE
The more bitter and prolonged the agony I suffered over the tragedy of
these past months, Francis, most Christian of kings, the greater my joy at

the long-delayed return of peace. The sorrow that gripped my heart had
more than one cause: for politically, it grieved me to see the two leading   5
monarchs of Christendom locked in battle, with the gravest consequences
for all mankind, for the world feels threatened when the moon does battle
with the sun; and personally, I was distressed to see a king of whose good
will I have had clear and evident proof on many occasions suffer a fate
that his intelligence and great virtues did not warrant.[1] But just as there   10
was more than one cause for my distress, so I have many reasons to be
filled with joy, for by the favour of heaven France has recovered its king,
the world has found peace, and the chorus of good and learned men has
regained a patron. Because of the generosity of your nature, the honesty of
your character, and the truly regal elevation of your mind, you deserved   15
to be blessed in everything you do, for your Majesty's good fortune would
have brought good fortune to the world in general and, on the personal
level, to many learned and virtuous men. Although some people think the
terms of the peace harsh,[2] not to say unfair, yet I trust that he who guides
all human affairs will bring about a happy outcome through his hidden and   20
inscrutable purposes. He, and he alone, knows what is expedient for us. He
alone, by his heavenly power, can bring happiness and blessing out of the
ill-considered actions of men. If Christian kings are united in a strong bond,
the Turks will be less venturesome, and men who flatter now one king and
now another, as they see an advantage for themselves, will be brought to   25
heel – for it is your disagreements, more than anything else, that give them
their power. Thus you will be able to bring relief to the cause of learning
and to the church, which has been labouring too long under an intolerable

* * * * *

1722
1 An oblique reference to the king's military disaster at Pavia (24 February 1525)
  and his subsequent year of captivity in Spain
2 Again, an oblique reference to a delicate matter, especially coming from Erasmus, a natural-born subject of the emperor and still officially an imperial councillor. Charles v had adamantly insisted that the French cede to him the duchy
  of Burgundy, which had been confiscated by Louis xi in 1477 at the death of
  Charles' ancestor Charles the Bold on the grounds that the French Salic law
  forbade inheritance of a fief by a female, Charles' Burgundian grandmother
  Mary of Burgundy, or by any male claiming through the female line. The
  Hapsburgs had never recognized the legality of this confiscation even though
  in the opinion of Francis and French lawyers Burgundy was an integral part
  of France and could never be severed from it. Francis had begun laying the
  legal groundwork for repudiating the harsh treaty of Madrid even before he
  signed it on 14 January in order to gain his release from imprisonment (Knecht
  Renaissance Warrior 243–7).

burden. Now both sides have their fiery and mindless partisans, who keep
the fire burning with their clamour and their ferocious pamphlets.   30

There are in Paris some godforsaken souls who were born to hate
good literature and the public peace. Chief among these are Noël Béda[3] and
Pierre Cousturier, a Carthusian monk.[4] These men by their writings, which
are as ignorant as they are venomous, make themselves the laughing-stock
of the world by the scurrillity and abusiveness of their attacks upon Jacques   35
Lefèvre and myself. They are despised by learned and intelligent men, but
they succeed in damaging our reputation among simple and uneducated
people and cheat us of the fruits of our labours, on which we have spent so
many long and wakeful hours. Lefèvre will answer for himself. But as for
me, I can point to a hundred manifest lies[5] and distortions in Béda's criti-   40
cisms which are so gross that, if the work had been published in the vernacular, cobblers and vegetable-growers would recognize that the fellow is out
of his mind. I am sending you a few passages with brief annotations. And
these are the men who lay down the law about heresy, on whose testimony
good men are dragged off to prison or tossed on the flames. They prefer   45
to see good men destroyed by one means or another rather than be proved
guilty of slander themselves. If they are to be permitted to lie openly about
us, and in works placed before the public too, and we on the other hand
are not to be allowed to refute their calumnies, will that once-celebrated
university be anything but a den of thieves?[6] If the outrageous behaviour   50
of these Pharisees goes unpunished, no good man will feel safe in future.
They justify themselves as defenders of the faith, but there is nothing further from their thoughts; their aim is tyranny, and they threaten even the
person of princes. They burrow away in secret to achieve this.[7] Unless the

* * * * *

3 Syndic of the faculty of theology and Erasmus' most persistent and most
   dangerous enemy at Paris. See Epp 1571 introduction, 1664 n1, and 1721
   introduction.
4 Paris doctor of theology and author of an attack on Erasmus and Lefèvre
   d'Etaples that led to a protracted pamphlet war. See Epp 1571 n10, 1591 introduction, 1658 n7, 1687 nn12–13.
5 Perhaps intended as a reference to the *Elenchus*, the first of Erasmus' point-
   by-point rebuttals of the charges levelled against his Paraphrases in Béda's
   recently published *Annotationes*. A copy of this rebuttal accompanied Ep 1721,
   addressed to the Parlement of Paris. The phrase itself is reminiscent of the title
   of an unpublished work of Erasmus replying to an attack on him by a group
   of Netherlandish Dominican friars writing anonymously; see Ep 1581A n1.
6 Mark 11:17
7 Erasmus' Latin is 'Huc tendunt per cuniculos.' Cf *Adagia* IV vii 61: *Cuniculis*
   oppugnare, which means literally to oppose through use of rabbit warrens,

prince meets their wishes in every particular, he will be branded a sup-   55
porter of heretics and is liable to be abandoned by the church – if we define
the church as a small cabal of monks and theologians. That they are working towards this goal by underground means is clear from their writings.
So it would be wise to nip the evil in the bud.[8]

I am not speaking about all monks and theologians, only certain ones   60
whose ignorance and depravity have more effect than the learning and moderation of the others. I was sent a list of disputed doctrines, chosen by some
agents of theirs from works of mine which Louis de Berquin had translated.
They are hardly much more sensible than the criticisms of Noël Béda. Because of this that excellent man is now in danger.[9] Papillon is dead and   65
there is grave suspicion that he was poisoned.[10] François Du Moulin[11] and
Du Blet[12] are gone. The life of Michel d'Arande is in danger.[13] They have

* * * * *

that is, by devious, secretive, and underhanded methods. Erasmus accuses the
mendicant orders and the theologians of using the pretext of religion to justify claims to public authority that threaten the authority of secular rulers – a
useful theme to sound in a letter to a king.

8 Cf *Adagia* I ii 40, where the figure of speech is medical but the underlying
idea, that it is better to act sooner rather than later against an ailment, is the
same.

9 See Ep 1692.

10 On Antoine Papillon, see Ep 1599 n2. The present letter seems to be the only
evidence suggesting that he was poisoned.

11 On this man, bishop-designate of Condom and a supporter of Erasmus, see Ep
1426 introduction, the earlier letters there cited, and the introductions to Epp
1711 and 1719. Evidently between the dates of Epp 1711 and 1719 (16 May
and about 6 June), Erasmus had received word of his death.

12 On Antoine Du Blet, a Lyonese banker and friend of the Reformer Guillaume
Farel (whom Erasmus detested), see Epp 1341A nn305–7, 1510 n7. Despite his
ties to Farel and the wounding taunt reported in Ep 1510, Erasmus seems to
have regarded him as a friendly person.

13 Arande (d March or April 1529) was a native of Tournai and probably of Spanish descent. He had been an Augustinian friar and early in the sixteenth century became a student of theology at Paris, where he may have come under the
influence of the reform-minded humanist and theologian Martial Mazurier,
head of the Collège de Saint-Michel. In the spring of 1521 he joined Mazurier,
Lefèvre d'Etaples, and others at Meaux to participate in the reform effort of
Bishop Guillaume Briçonnet. Shortly afterwards he moved to the royal court at
Paris, where he became a protégé of the king's sister, Margaret of Angoulême,
and an influential preacher for the ladies of her circle. In 1523 Guillaume Petit,
Dominican confessor to the king, accused Arande of preaching heresy, but the
king blocked efforts to prosecute him. Further preaching in other places led to
renewed complaints of heresy, but Margaret and the king sheltered him, and

attacked Berquin twice. Now they are striking out against Lefèvre and Erasmus. The passages they collect from my books provide material for nothing
but suspicion and calumny; so far they have not been able to find a single   70
passage that contains an idea contrary to the Christian faith. It is holy work
to rid the church of schism and impious doctrines, but there is nothing holy
about charging the defenders of gospel truth with impiety and driving into
the enemy camp those whom they see battling on their own side against the
enemy.   .   75

How the tyranny of these men can be controlled, I shall explain at another time, if your most Christian Majesty wishes me to do so in confidence;
for by acting confidentially, the prospects of success will be greater. In the
meantime I ask your Majesty to use your authority either to restrain madmen like Cousturier and Béda from defaming good men with their lies or   80
to ensure that our rejoinders are permitted to be printed and read in Paris.
For it would be most unfair to allow them to scatter their poison around
and not allow us to supply the antidote.

I have written frankly because many people have told me that your
Highness welcomes straightforward and unvarnished speech. What I have   85
written I can prove to be the absolute truth; even if I keep silent, the plain
facts of the case will speak for themselves. Louis de Berquin, because of his
pious nature, deserves to be freed from these false charges without delay.
May the Omnipotent Lord keep your most Christian Majesty safe and well.

Basel, 16 June 1526   90

1723 / To the Faculty of Theology at Paris   Basel, 23 June 1526

Having in the two preceding letters appealed over the head of the faculty of
theology to the Parlement of Paris and the king of France, Erasmus here adopts
a more severe and admonitory tone than in his previous letter of complaint to
the faculty, written on 6 February (Ep 1664). While he still presents Noël Béda
and Pierre Cousturier as fomentors of discord, here he openly faces the fact
that the faculty as a body has tolerated their attacks on him, has taken corpo-

* * * * *

Margaret named him her almoner. During the king's captivity in Spain, when
her protection was less effective, he joined her other protégés, Gérard Roussel and Lefèvre d'Etaples, in exile at Strasbourg, where he remained for six
months, until the king had returned from captivity. By May 1526 he not only
had rejoined Margaret at Cognac but had been named bishop of Saint-Paul-
Trois-Châteaux, a position that he held, and whose duties he carried out, to
the end of his life, despite his continued profession of evangelical sympathies.

rate action critical of him, and by licensing the anti-Erasmian books of Béda and Cousturier for publication has at least indirectly endorsed their accusations. According to this letter, the faculty shares the responsibility of Béda and Cousturier for stabbing him in the back while he was engaged in resisting the real heretics, such as Luther, Zwingli, and their supporters. He also repeats his charges, made previously in Ep 1679 to Béda, that the Paris theologians are functioning in an unreal and isolated academic world, totally ignorant of the depth and violence of the religious upheaval going on in Germany and Switzerland. Erasmus never published this blunt, accusatory letter, but it was printed not long after its delivery in Paris in a scarce pamphlet, *Epistolae tres* (no place, no date, but probably Paris 1526), which also contains Epp 1721 and 1722. See Ep 1721 introduction. Allen also drew on two manuscripts now at the Zürich Staatsarchiv, the first of which is probably a copy sent to Zwingli from Paris by Gaspar Mosager, and the second, a copy made for Zwingli and sent to Berchtold Haller at Bern. A third sixteenth-century manuscript survives in the Kirchenarchiv at Basel, probably based mainly on the two manuscripts now at Zürich. The letter is not in the Basel *Opera* of 1540 or in LB, but it has been printed several times, with the first of the Zürich manuscripts being the likely source. The earliest edition was by Johann Heinrich Hottinger *Historiae ecclesiasticae Novi Testamenti* 8 vols (Zürich 1651–67) *Seculi xvi* II 605; it was reprinted by Johann Konrad Füssli *Epistolae ab ecclesiae helveticae reformatoribus vel ad eos scriptae* (Zürich 1742) 39 and then by John Jortin *The Life of Erasmus* rev ed (London 1808) III 181–3 (in the first edition of Jortin [2 vols, London 1758–60], according to Allen, the letter is on II 492).

ERASMUS OF ROTTERDAM TO THE FACULTY OF THEOLOGY,
GREETING

Eminent doctors and respected brothers, I always hoped that if I faltered in my battle against Luther, you would be there to sustain me, and if I was driven out of this place by the clique that opposes me, I would find among you a peaceful haven and a safe refuge. But instead you are responsible for more stinging attacks on me than any of you has ever made on Luther. I refused to forsake the fellowship of the church, and as a result I have become the most hated man in Germany, where I was once held in the highest regard. I threw down the gauntlet to Luther, and what a venomous creature he is will be clear from the book I am sending you, of which he is the author.[1] For a long time now I have endured the noisy attacks of this whole faction (which is more powerful than anyone could imagine and is

* * * * *

1723
1 Presumably a copy of *De servo arbitrio*; see Ep 1667 introduction.

gathering strength every day) and suffered its threats and insults and its violent and slanderous writings. I have taken on a task that is too great for my   15
strength, but I did it to please the pope and the emperor and the princes; it
was a bold thing to do, especially in this part of Germany. How far I have
succeeded is shown by those who maintain that no one has done more than
Erasmus to thwart the spread of the gospel. And as if it were no great matter
to withstand the onslaught of the Lutherans, I have had to wage war against   20
the followers of Zwingli, who differ from the Lutherans on the question of
the Eucharist. In this connection I played no small part in the meeting recently held at Baden in Switzerland. The book and letter that I am enclosing will show you what I did.[2] My letter was translated into German and
read before the whole assembly and also at the council of this city. In the   25
midst of all these strenuous efforts, when I ought to have been supported
by your learned faculty, I was attacked in the rear with exceptional bitterness by men like Béda[3] and Cousturier.[4] It is hardly possible to estimate the
encouragement that their books gave to the followers of Luther and Zwingli.

No one has ever become disloyal or schismatic as a result of my books;   30
and if error has crept in (for we are all human), at least my intentions are
pure; anything that has given offence could easily be corrected. So what
is the point of raising such a fuss? Obviously private animosity lies at the
root of it. But in the present situation, where the dangers are so great, it
would have been better to put aside private grudges until peace returned   35
to the earth. What does Cousturier want to achieve? My translation of the
New Testament has been disseminated by the printers in more than 100,000
copies.[5] He ought to have put his views on paper at the proper time. Moreover, when I replied to Béda's criticisms and made it clear that in many of
the passages there was no cause to worry, what possessed the man to publish   40

* * * * *

2 The letter enclosed must be a copy of Ep 1708, addressed to the delegates of
  the Swiss Confederation assembled at Baden. The accompanying book would
  be his pamphlet *Detectio praestigiarum*, refuting an anonymous pamphlet that
  suggested that he privately agreed with the Eucharistic views of Zwingli and
  other Swiss Reformers. See Ep 1708 introduction and nn1, 2.
3 See Epp 1571 introduction, 1664 introduction and n1, 1679, 1685, 1721 introduction.
4 See Epp 1571 n10, 1658 n7.
5 Erasmus' Latin translation of the New Testament appeared in the first edition
  of his Greek text, the *Novum instrumentum*, in 1516 and was published separately (without the Greek) in 1519 (Louvain: Dirk Martens 1519; NK 335). It
  was frequently reprinted. See introductions to Epp 373, 384, 1010. For more
  detail on editions of the Latin text, see Allen Ep 1010 introduction and Ferdinand Vander Haeghen *Bibliotheca Erasmiana* II (Ghent 1893; repr Nieuwkoop
  1961) 57–66.

his objections,[6] which contained so many evident falsehoods and manifest lies[7] that anyone could recognize them, even if no one uttered a word in rebuttal? What jubilation there is among the Lutherans when they read such books! He had a better case for fulminating against Lefèvre,[8] and yet he is milder in his attacks on him. When it came to me, he took on the role of censor, and his talk was all of heresies and blasphemy. But I know very well what gnaws at the man's mind: one of my *Colloquies* contains a passing reference to his college, with a joke about rotten eggs.[9] This was surely reason enough for raising the roof![10] If we snap at one another in this way and tear one another apart, is it not inevitable that we shall both perish by mutually inflicted wounds, as Paul has said?[11]

*****

6 A reference to Béda's *Annotationum Natalis Bedae ... in Jacobum Fabrum Stapulensem libri duo, et in Desiderium Erasmum Roterodamum liber unus*, published at Paris a month before the date of this letter. Cf Ep 1721 introduction.

7 On the phrase 'manifest lies' see Ep 1581An9 and cf Ep 1722 n5.

8 Erasmus provides no argument in support of this judgment, but it is true that Lefèvre never made a direct attack on Luther's theological views comparable to Erasmus' *De libero arbitrio*, and also true that during the conservative attack on Bishop Guillaume Briçonnet and his reformers in the diocese of Meaux in 1525, Lefèvre was one of three reformers who fled over the border to Strasbourg and lived as guests in the home of Wolfgang Faber Capito, one of the leading Evangelical preachers in a city that had already formally adhered to the Reformation. Cf Philip Edgcumbe Hughes *Lefèvre: Pioneer of Ecclesiastical Reform in France* (Grand Rapids, MI 1984) 171–3.

9 In fact the *Colloquies* contain two disdainful, humorous, and unmistakable references to the Collège de Montaigu at Paris, of which Béda was director from 1504 to 1535. In the unauthorized first edition of 1518, *Percontandi forma in primo congressu* 'Form of Inquiry on First Meeting' characterizes Montaigu as a place noted for inadequate food and lice rather than for learning, and it puns on the names of Béda (Latin *Beta*, translated 'a beet') and another conservative theologian, Guillaume Duchesne (*Quercus*, translated 'an oak'); see ASD I-3 131–1 / CWE 39 112 and nn34–7. The references would have been obvious to any Latin-reading contemporary who knew the leading personalities of the Paris theological faculty. The more famous reference, first published this very year (Basel: Froben, February 1526), was in Ἰχθυοφαγία 'A Fish Diet,' where Erasmus repeated the charges about harsh diet (including feeding students rotten eggs), filthy living conditions, and brutal floggings. He explicitly blames Jan Standonck, the refounder of the college and Béda's mentor and immediate predecessor as director, for these inhumane conditions which (in Erasmus' opinion) transformed a charitable refuge for poor scholars into a house of degradation. See ASD I-3 531–2 / CWE 40 715–17 and nn284–95.

10 Literally, 'mixing earth with heaven'; cf *Adagia* I iii 81.

11 Gal 5:15

If it were only my reputation that they were injuring, the damage would be tolerable. But Luther's cause is strengthened, and the antipathy towards theology is intensified. Among theologians Béda treats me with lordly contempt, and he does so safely because I am not the sort of person he imagines I am. If I were, events themselves would show what a stir Erasmus could raise in the world. But if you allow such books to appear as Béda and Cousturier send us (I speak in particular of works aimed at me), and if my writings are banned, of course they are sure to win.[12] This is not to refute an argument but to crush it with the ferocity of a tyrant. You have nothing to fear from me; but I am afraid these men will discover what the Gospel means when it says 'He that smites with the sword shall perish with the sword.'[13] Béda is dreaming when he thinks the Lutheran faction has been destroyed. Would that this were so! What we see is only the beginning, and if we deal with the matter as we are doing, I do not know where it will end. You are sensible men; if you knew how things stand throughout Germany, you would judge that I deserve more respect than Béda and Cousturier show me. The Lutherans boast that there is no man living who can refute the arguments that Luther has piled up on the freedom of the will. I am sending you my preliminary statement, which I composed in haste.[14] I have been sweating over the rest, which I was expecting to complete by the first of August, had not books by Béda and Cousturier interrupted my progress. If these are the only reinforcements that Paris has to send me despite the fact that we share a common enemy, I shall keep my mouth shut in future. I commend the work of the church to you and to Christ and I pray you may be strengthened for the task. May he keep you all safe and well and may he grant to Béda and Cousturier a more Christian mind in the days to come.

Basel, 23 June 1526

* * * * *

12 Erasmus was doubly offended because the Paris faculty so rapidly censured his *Colloquies* in April and so readily approved publication of Béda's *Annotationes* in May. Even more offensive was its decision in February to approve publication of Cousturier's *Antapologia* directed against Erasmus without the usual formalities of appointing a committee and without full consideration of the recommendation of Jacques Berthélemy that publication be approved (Farge *Registre* 127, session of 15 February 1526; cf n13 on the unusual rapidity of this action) and Ep 1687 n12. See also Rummel II 33 on Béda and II 69 on Cousturier; she also notes the almost unprecedented rapidity of the faculty's action in approving Cousturier's book.
13 Matt 26:52
14 Part 1 of *Hyperaspistes*; see Ep 1667 introduction.

1724 / To Frans van Cranevelt   Basel, 24 June 1526

> Allen based his Latin text on the autograph letter at Louvain, first published
> by Henry de Vocht in his edition of Cranevelt's *Epistolae* (Louvain 1928). On
> Cranevelt's ability (remarked on by Erasmus in line 3) to continue his activity
> as a poet and classical scholar despite his duties as a member of the supreme
> judicial body, the Grand Council, at Mechelen, see Ep 1145 introduction. Allen
> confirms the year of this letter from the discussion of the marriage plans of
> Karl Harst. The apparent discrepancy caused by Allen's citation of the de Vocht
> edition of Cranevelt's *Epistolae*, a book published in 1928, in his own volume
> VI of the Erasmus correspondence, published in 1926, results from his having
> pre-publication access to de Vocht's manuscript. In the preface to his edition,
> de Vocht acknowledges Allen's support and interest and states that he has
> voluntarily released to Allen his own materials on letters to or from Erasmus.
> In his introduction to Ep 1724, Allen cites the Cranevelt edition but gives no
> page reference; and in his list of abbreviations for sources, he cites that edition
> with the indication 'Louvain 1926,' whereas it actually did not appear until
> two years later.

Cordial greetings. You have indeed a happy touch in your poetry in both
languages. Your Greek epitaph has something of Homer's spirit about it.[1] I
wonder how you have time for the Muses with all your responsibilities and
varied interests. Karl Harst,[2] following the precept of the gospel, is eager to
leave his father and mother and cleave to his wife.[3] He thinks every delay   5
an eternity. He wants to be commended to your good self. Best wishes to
you and to all you love.

* * * * *

1724
1 Neither this epitaph nor the vaguer reference to Greek and Latin poetry in
  the preceding sentence can be identified with certainty, but Allen (1n) conjectures that the epitaph might be for their mutual friend Paludanus (Jean Desmarez), professor of eloquence at the University of Louvain, who had died
  on 20 February 1526 and had been promptly succeeded by another mutual
  friend, Adrianus Barlandus. Cf Ep 1694 introduction.
2 On Karl Harst see Epp 1215, 1575 n2, 1666 n2. This letter is intended to secure for him the favour of the influential Cranevelt as he returns to his native
  country. Harst had intended eventually to get married even before he entered
  Erasmus' service, and evidently his recent mission to the Netherlands had reinforced this intention. He returned to Basel in April 1526. By autumn 1526 he
  was settled in Louvain and had found a bride (Ep 1768:79–81 and nn12–13),
  whom he married in January 1527 (Epp 1778, 1788).
3 Matt 19:5; Mark 10:7

Basel, 24 June 1526
Erasmus of Rotterdam
To the honourable Frans van Cranevelt, councillor.[4] In Mechelen   10

1725 / To the Reader   [Basel, c June 1526]

An address to the reader printed at the end (perhaps merely as a filler to oc-
cupy a blank page) of a new edition of the *Disticha moralia* attributed in the
Middle Ages to the famous Roman moralist M. Porcius Cato but actually written by an unknown author of the third century AD. Now generally known as
Disticha Catonis, this collection of Latin prose maxims and hexameter verses
dealing with moral topics was widely used in medieval and Renaissance grammar schools. Erasmus had published it along with several other short texts in
September 1514 (Louvain: Dirk Martens; NK 534). His edition was frequently
reprinted. The present edition (Basel: Froben, June 1526) was the first since
the Froben edition of October 1520 that Erasmus had supervised personally;
it seems to have been occasioned by the inaccuracy of many of the unauthorized reprints. Erasmus was fully aware that the author (or authors) was not
Cato, remarking in his dedication of the 1514 edition that the only possible
justification for attaching Cato's name to the verses is that 'the sentiments are
not unworthy of a Cato' (Ep 298:14).

ERASMUS OF ROTTERDAM TO THE LEARNED READER, GREETING
I admit that we owe a very great debt of gratitude to those who rescue fine
authors from oblivion, or remove corruptions from the text, or elucidate the
obscure. But we should have sufficient respect for an author's work, and
especially for the writings of dead authors, not to defile them by contami-   5
nation with the work of others.[1] This is something that has begun to happen
to dictionaries, both Greek and Latin. There seemed some excuse in the case
of the Greek lexicon, because the one that appeared first from the Aldine
press did not bear the name of any specific author.[2] Even so, it would have

* * * * *

4 Erasmus addresses Cranevelt as *senator*, that is, *conseilleur* in the Grand Council, the supreme judicial body of the Hapsburg-ruled Netherlands.

   1725
1 Perhaps evidence that Erasmus believed that selections from several different
   authors had been interpolated into the *Disticha*
2 Aldus' Greek lexicon appeared at Venice in 1497. Allen Ep 1460 introduction discusses the early Greek lexicons and notes that each successor freely
   incorporated the materials of its predecessors, adding its own contributions

been more honest to distinguish the additions with a special sign so that no 10
one would be cheated of his share of the credit, and those who were adding
material would be more careful, knowing that their actions involved some
risk to their own reputation. I hear that the same thing has been done to
Calepino[3] – with less excuse. In the case of Perotti[4] such a procedure would
be scarcely tolerable; and it would be sacrilege to take such liberties with 15
other authors. For example, if someone were to defile the *De asse* of Guillaume Budé[5] by stitching additional material on to it at every point, would
the author not bring the vandal to court as guilty of a capital offence and
prosecute him on a charge of fraud?

* * * * *

to the growing lexical resources for study of the language. Erasmus' point is
that the largely anonymous character of these Greek lexicons made the un-
acknowledged use of their materials by later lexicographers somewhat less
reprehensible than plagiarism from an identifiable single author might be.

3 Ambrogio Calepino or Calepio (c 1435–c 1510), an Augustinian hermit who
devoted his career to scholarship. His *Dictionarium* of classical Latin, first published in 1502 (Reggio in Lombardy: Dionigi Bertocchi), was so frequently
reprinted in both Italy and transalpine Europe that 'Calepino' became a word
meaning 'dictionary.' The work was based on the *Cornucopia* of Niccolò Perotti
and the *Elegantiae linguae Latinae* of Lorenzo Valla.

4 Niccolò Perotti (1429–80), one of the ablest classical scholars of fifteenth-
century Italy, produced one of the most successful new Latin grammars, *Rudi-
menta grammatices*, but became even more famous for his *Cornucopia, sive com-
mentaria linguae Latinae*, a lengthy commentary on the Roman epigrammatist
Martial, a landmark in the humanistic study of classical Latin literature and
language that was especially important for its grammatical, stylistic, and lexical materials. It was a major source for Calepino. On Perotti see Frank-Rutger
Hausmann 'Martialis, Marcus Valerius' in *Catalogus translationum et commentariorum* ed Paul Oskar Kristeller and others IV (Washington DC 1980) 252–4,
266–71.

5 On Budé see Ep 403 introduction. With the possible exception of Lefèvre
d'Etaples, he was the only French humanist of his generation who could be
seriously regarded as Erasmus' peer in classical scholarship, and especially in
Greek. He and Erasmus corresponded over a long period after their first letters in 1516, and both in 1517 and in 1524, Budé as a royal councillor played a
leading role in the effort of Francis I to persuade Erasmus to settle in France.
Yet although each publicly (and actually) respected the other's erudition, there
was always a certain coolness, and at times a somewhat veiled hostility, between them. *De asse et partibus eius* (1515; second edition 1516) was Budé's first
major publication outside the special field of law. Although nominally a study
of Roman coinage, weights, and measures, it was in reality a landmark study
of Roman material culture, based on a remarkable mastery of ancient sources
and of great importance to a society that idolized antiquity.

But the crime will be worse when Libitina[6] has set her sacred seal upon   20
the work, and the author is no longer able to purge what has been defiled.
Perhaps the offence seems less serious because it is now being committed
by good scholars; but once a precedent is established, it will soon be used
by everyone against everyone. So while this serves the interests of the printers, the great works of the past will be thrown into disarray, and books on   25
which learned men have spent many sleepless hours will be treated as public property. If, in a matter so fraught with danger, the laws are asleep and
princes have shut their eyes, at least the Senate and People of the Muses[7]
must do what they can to restrain and limit such shameless conduct, and
if no other course is open, to subject the transgressors to public execration   30
and run them through with the points of their pens.

It is better to treat an illness at the start than at the last moment.[8] In the
case of my little edition of Cato, where they changed the order, the damage
is slight. So in these remarks it is not my own case that I am pleading so
much as that of all scholars who by their labours serve the general cause of   35
learning. There is nothing too dreadful that greed will not attempt; it lays
its hands on the property of the gods and does not spare the caskets of the
dead. Farewell, and be on your guard before it is too late.

1726 / From Cuthbert Tunstall to Pieter Gillis   London, 1 July [1526]

Cuthbert Tunstall, bishop of London since 1522, was one of Erasmus' most reliable and most influential English friends, a Padua-educated doctor of civil and
canon law, a student of both Greek and Hebrew, and a supporter of humanistic
studies. His friendship with Erasmus went back to 1505 or 1506 and was never
seriously threatened by his generally more conservative outlook on theological
and ecclesiastical issues. On Tunstall's earlier career and public career, see Ep
207:25n. Although he opposed Henry VIII's divorce and the acknowledgment
of the king as supreme head of the church in 1531, he submitted to the royal
supremacy in 1535 and was one of the conservative Henrician bishops for the

* * * * *

6 Roman goddess of death and burial. Erasmus' point is that to plagiarize or
   corrupt the text of a deceased author who cannot defend himself is even worse
   than to victimize the living.
7 Latin *senatus populusque musarum*, a play on the official corporate title of the ancient Roman state, SPQR, or *Senatus Populusque Romanus* 'the Senate and Roman
   People.' The reference here is to the world of learning, or of devotees of the
   Muses.
8 *Adagia* I ii 40 (from Suidas A4098), here quoted in Greek, which in conventional
   opinion was a more learned language

rest of Henry's reign. The original letter survives in the British Library and
was first published in Allen VI in 1926. Allen notes that Tunstall's uncertainty
about how to transfer funds to Erasmus in Basel confirms the conjectural year-
date of 1526, since in November 1526 Erasmus Schets sent Tunstall instructions
on how best to make such transfers in the future (Ep 1764:4–6), and Ep 1866
shows that in the summer of 1527 Tunstall was aware how to use Schets and
his London correspondents for the transfer of funds. Gillis had been Erasmus'
financial agent for such transfers until Schets took over during the year 1525.

Cordial greetings. The day before yesterday I sent you a letter.[1] I very much
hope it will be passed on to Erasmus as quickly and safely as possible. Now I
am writing a second time, not because I have any doubt about your devotion
to him or because I want to spur the sluggard on, since I know there is no
need for that, but I wish to set my mind at rest, because there are things   5
in the letter that it is important for Erasmus to know. It also contains the
news that a friend[2] is sending him money, but, as I discovered later, the
man could think of no way of conveying the money to him without your
assistance. So I am enclosing a letter of exchange[3] (which people now refer
to by the word *excambium*) with the request that, as a token of your affection   10
for him, you will see that the money is delivered to him safely or, if that
cannot be done without change of currency, that the exchange be made with
the least possible loss. His friend entrusted me with sending the money. But
I have no one to whom I can assign the task except yourself, and I know
that in devotion to Erasmus you take second place to none of his friends.   15
So when I thought of the affection that you feel for him, I realized that
you were the one person who would be able and willing to see the matter
through for us. I ask you most earnestly to do this as soon as possible.

* * * * *

1726
1 Not extant
2 The identity of this friend is not certain, but it probably was Archbishop
  William Warham or his secretary Thomas Bedyll. Warham had arranged for
  Erasmus to receive a pension based on the revenues of the parish of Aldington
  in Kent (cf Ep 1583 n1) and from time to time intervened personally to ensure payment and safe transmission of the funds through Erasmus' agents in
  the Netherlands. See Allen Epp 1866:4–7 and 1965:30–4 (Bishop Tunstall was
  also directly involved in the latter case). On Bedyll, who regularly handled
  financial details for the archbishop, see Ep 1647 n3.
3 Latin *permutationum literae*, evidently a financial document such as a bill of
  exchange

Farewell. London, 1 July

In haste by the hand of your brother and friend, Cuthbert, servant of   20
the church in London

To the honourable Master Pieter Gillis, citizen and clerk of the city of
Antwerp. In Antwerp

1727 / To Catherine of Aragon   Basel, 15 July 1526

Although Erasmus had frequently praised the queen of England in his correspondence with others, this letter of dedication for his *Institutio christiani matrimonii* (Basel: Froben, August 1526) is the first to be addressed to her. For reasons not entirely clear, Queen Catherine did not reply promptly to this dedication, and in a letter of 30 March 1527 to Thomas More (Allen Ep 1804:285–7),
Erasmus speculated that because of the royal divorce, the reference in his book
to cases in which marriage could be lawfully terminated had given offence.
Shortly afterwards, a letter from his friend and former pupil, William Blount,
Lord Mountjoy, who was chamberlain to the queen and who in 1525 had asked
Erasmus in her name to write a book on marriage (n1 below), assured him
that his book had pleased the queen and that she thanked him for it (Allen Ep
1816:13–16). In December 1526 More reassured him that the queen did value
his treatise highly and expressed his own hope that she would send him a
tangible reward (Ep 1770:22–3). Eventually, in 1528, Erasmus had to send her
a polite reminder (Allen Ep 1960:68–71) before she responded by sending a
gift (cf Allen Ep 2040:43–9 and nn). Although he feared that his reference to
divorce might have offended the queen, in a letter of 1528 he seems to have
attributed the embarrassing delay to the dilatory habits of his friend in her
household, Lord Mountjoy; see Allen Ep 1966:9–11. Certainly Erasmus never
fully realized that the queen had more urgent matters to think about than
prompt acknowledgment of his dedication. When he composed the original
dedication on 15 July 1526, he probably did not know of the crisis facing the
queen. Henry VIII and his advisers kept their preparations to terminate the
royal marriage secret in the early months of 1526. The suit for divorce opened
in May 1526, when Cardinal Wolsey issued a secret summons citing the king
to appear before him to answer charges that he was living contrary to law
with his brother's widow. Not until June did the king himself inform Catherine of his intention to end the marriage, and only in July did his intention become a matter of common knowledge at court. Cf Garrett Mattingly *Catherine
of Aragon* (Boston 1941) 236–8. David Loades *The Politics of Marriage: Henry VIII
and His Queens* (Dover, NH 1994) 46 dates Henry's confrontation of Catherine
as 22 June.

TO THE ILLUSTRIOUS QUEEN CATHERINE OF ENGLAND,
GLORY OF MATRONS, FROM DESIDERIUS ERASMUS OF ROTTERDAM,
GREETING

It is now more than two years, illustrious queen, since I promised the honourable Master William Mountjoy, chamberlain of your court, that I would   5
write something on the institution of Christian marriage.[1] Although I never
lacked the will to fulfil my promise, I was constantly interrupted and prevented from performing the task by so many other obligations, vexations,
and bouts of illness that I am beginning to fear that Mountjoy will think me
wanting in good faith. I am now discharging my debt, late though it is, but   10
whether I am discharging it in full, I do not know. For those who pay their
debts in the correct amount but with coins that are deficient in weight and
debased in alloy may be forgiven by easy-going creditors, but they face serious difficulties with less flexible lenders. I might fear the same fate, except
that I am dealing with the kindest and most accommodating of creditors.   15
Moreover, if one's writing is to have life and spirit and to hold together,
it is of the utmost importance to maintain, if one can, the fire and inspiration of the moment. But I have never been able to continue on my task for
two days together. I shall be surprised, therefore, if you are not offended by
the flat and disjointed character of the piece. But if in my picture of matri-   20
mony I have shown myself a poor artist, in the saintliness of your character
one can find the perfect model of a most holy and blessed marriage. Do not
suspect me here of flattery. What we admire and praise in you does not belong to you, but is a gift from God. The valiant qualities of your mother
Isabella, the former queen of Spain, were celebrated throughout the world.[2]   25
Her spotless character was truly the sweet savour of God in every place.[3]
Your qualities are known to us from closer at hand; from them we can form
some idea of her virtues also, just as we recognize the skill of a painter from
his picture. We expect a work no less perfect in your daughter Mary.[4] For

* * * * *

1727
1 See Ep 1624:68–72.
2 Isabella (1451–1504) became queen of Castile in 1474, and the accession of her
  husband Ferdinand II to the throne of Aragon in 1479 made the royal pair
  the first rulers of a united Spanish crown. The queen was an active ruler, and
  Erasmus praised her piety and patronage of learning in several of his works
  and letters.
3 Cf 2 Cor 2:14–15.
4 Mary Tudor, daughter of Catherine by Henry VIII and subsequently queen
  of England (1553–8), had been born on 18 February 1516. As Erasmus

what should we not expect from a girl who is born of the most devout of 30
parents and brought up under the care of such a mother? I pray the Lord
may preserve this happy state to the benefit of the whole Christian world.
Farewell.

Basel, 15 July 1526

1728 / To Duke George of Saxony   Basel, 30 July 1526

> This letter is a reply to Ep 1691. For years Duke George had prodded Erasmus
> to attack Luther. He had been pleased by the publication of *De libero arbitrio*
> and positively delighted by Erasmus' alacrity in writing and publishing *Hy-*
> *peraspistes 1* as a preliminary rebuttal of Luther's *De servo arbitrio*; see Ep 1691
> introduction. The original letter survived at Dresden, where Allen consulted
> it; Erasmus himself published it in *Opus epistolarum*.

Cordial greetings, most illustrious prince. I received your Highness' letter
along with the material you had translated for me,[1] all of which was most

* * * * *

surmised (and probably learned from his friends at the English court),
she was being carefully educated not only in traditionally female subjects like needlework and music but also in the humanistic subjects then
deemed essential for a ruler or the close adviser of a ruler, with the advice of humanists like Thomas Linacre and Juan Luis Vives, and under
the watchful eye of her own well-educated mother. Cf Mattingly *Cather-*
ine of Aragon (introduction above) 174, 177–9. More recently, D.M. Loades
Mary Tudor: A Life (Oxford 1989) 28–35, 42–4 is more doubtful about
Queen Catherine's ability to exercise close supervision over the education
of the princess or her conscious intention to train her to rule in her own
right.

1728
1 On Duke George's repeated efforts to make Erasmus refute each of Luther's
  books, see Ep 1691 introduction. Erasmus had claimed (falsely, in all probability) that he could not read Luther's High German language (Epp 1313
  and n16, 1499), though Duke George did not take his claim seriously. Encouraged by Erasmus' *De libero arbitrio*, the duke in October 1524 sent him one of
  Luther's Latin works, *De votis monasticis*, for refutation (Ep 1503 and n2), and
  the translated material here mentioned was probably something derived from
  vernacular works of Luther or his supporters, sent in the hope that Erasmus
  would write a refutation. But Erasmus, who doubted the efficacy of opposing Luther by refuting his works one by one (Ep 1499:32–4) and who in any
  case did not intend to set aside all his other work in order to become an anti-

welcome. I shall write about it later when I have leisure. In the meantime, I thought I should give your illustrious Highness what news I have.

Before the beginning of June I gave a letter to the public courier of this city, whom I had hired specially for the purpose, and asked him to deliver it to the assembly at Baden, where the disputation lately took place.[2] The letter, a copy of which I am enclosing, will explain the reason. The messenger returned from Baden and brought back letters and the pages I just mentioned, but nothing else. When I heard nothing about the cup that your illustrious Highness told me you had sent (though I neither deserved nor expected anything of the kind),[3] I began to question the messenger about the person who gave him the letter. He said he received it from a man, apparently a scholar, who had come to the meeting but was otherwise completely unknown. I suspected the present would arrive through Koberger.[4] A few days earlier he had sent me some gifts that had come from Poland, but made no mention of a cup in his letter. If by any chance the cup is still with you, that is fine, for I have already enjoyed the best part of it, that is, the evidence of your kindly feelings towards me. But if it was sent, we must not allow it to disappear, for that would be a loss both to yourself and to me. If this letter is delivered in time, you will be able to indicate at the Frankfurt fair to whom you entrusted the cup.

This is all I can write at present since I am overwhelmed by illness and work. I pray the Lord will prosper your illustrious Highness in everything.

Basel, 30 July 1526

Your Highness' most devoted servant, Erasmus of Rotterdam (signed with my own hand)

* * * * *

Lutheran pamphleteer, here merely calls the translations 'most welcome' and makes no promise to take action on them. Similarly, in 1524 his response to the duke's sending of *De votis monasticis* merely referred to it as 'a very long-winded book' and contained no promise to produce a rebuttal (Ep 1526:244–6), observing that the Paris theologian Josse Clichtove had written a reply (ibid n48).

2 See Ep 1708 and introduction. Erasmus declined to attend the religious disputation at Baden, alleging his fragile health and other unspecified causes, but did explicitly declare his rejection of the Sacramentarian doctrine on the Eucharist. Sending Duke George a copy of this intervention on behalf of the Catholic side at Baden was a way of reassuring the duke that he was still actively engaged in defence of the faith.

3 See Ep 1691:22 and n4.

4 On this important publisher and bookseller of Nürnberg, with whom Erasmus and his publisher Johann Froben had frequent dealings, see Epp 581:23n, 1560 n5.

1729 / To Willibald Pirckheimer   Basel, 30 July 1526

On Pirckheimer, see Ep 1717 introduction and the many earlier letters. This
letter was first printed in Pirckheimer's *Opera* (Frankfurt 1610), edited by Melchior Goldast.

Cordial greetings. With regard to Philippus, I am ready to accept his explanation.[1] Nesen was a close and constant friend, but most unlucky for me.[2]
It was he, I suspect, who was responsible for Luther's attack on Cochlaeus[3]

* * * * *

1729
1 Melanchthon spent much of the month of May in Nürnberg, preached at the
   opening of the city's new Latin school, and advised the city council on the introduction of liturgical changes. He had been complaining that Erasmus had
   mistreated him and Wilhelm Nesen in *Hyperaspistes 1*, according to a letter
   of 20 May 1526 from Michael Hummelberg to Beatus Rhenanus (BRE 367 Ep
   257). The bitter conflict between Erasmus and Luther had affected but not destroyed the mutual admiration between Erasmus and Melanchthon, a situation reflected here in Erasmus' evident willingness to be reconciled. It may
   seem strange that this willingness should be expressed in words that imply
   an 'explanation' (apology?) by Melanchthon when the issue seems to be Erasmus' excessively harsh criticism of him and Nesen in *Hyperaspistes 1*, but the
   point may be that Erasmus pardons Melanchthon's excessive sensitivity to
   words that were not meant to be hostile. In any case, the unexpected harsh-
   ness of Luther's attack on Erasmus after Melanchthon's initial assurances that
   De libero arbitrio had been received at Wittenberg with equanimity must have
   put Melanchthon in a rather awkward position with respect to Erasmus. Cf
   Ep 1667 introduction on their relations during this difficult period.
2 On Wilhelm Nesen, whom Erasmus blamed for losing materials he had entrusted to him for an edition of the *Lucubrationes* of Seneca (Basel: Froben
   1515), see Epp 1257:7–10 and nn3, 5; 1341A:449–63 and nn101, 104; 1479:99–
   102; 1656 n1. Despite this incident and his judgment in Ep 1257 that Nesen
   was indiscreet and generally ineffectual, the two humanists enjoyed cordial
   relations which, however, cooled when Nesen became an outspoken adherent of Luther and moved to Wittenberg. Nesen drowned in a boating accident near Wittenberg in 1524. In his response to Melanchthon's report of this
   event (Ep 1500:66–7), Erasmus acknowledged Nesen as a faithful friend but
   concluded that the friendship had turned out unfortunately for himself (Ep
   1523:216–17).
3 Nesen had been an aggressive controversialist. His open support of Luther
   in 1521 had led to a published attack on him by Johannes Cochlaeus, dean
   of St Mary's church in Frankfurt am Main, who was beginning to emerge as
   an energetic Catholic pamphleteer against the Reformers. Cochlaeus' *De gratia sacramentorum* (Strasbourg 1522) was written after his personal clash with
   Luther at Worms. Erasmus may not be fully correct in assigning responsibility

and the king of England.[4] I made sure that your letter was delivered to
Oecolampadius without delay.[5] What he has in mind, I do not know. 5

* * * * *

for Luther's counterattack to Nesen, but Nesen had sent Cochlaeus' book to
Luther, and Luther's reply, *Adversus armatum virum Cokleum* (Wittenberg 1523),
had the form of a letter addressed to Nesen (WA 11 292–306). Luther himself
declares (295) that Cochlaeus had forced him to reply – presumably by sending him a copy of *De gratia sacramentorum*, in which he claimed that Luther
had lacked the courage to debate him at Worms. Cochlaeus replied to Luther's
attack with *Adversus cucullatum Minotaurum Wittenbergensem* (Cologne? July
1523), which was also addressed to Nesen; Luther made no further reply and
simply ignored Cochlaeus. On Cochlaeus see Allen Ep 1863 introduction and
NDB III 304–6; on his emergence as a Catholic controversialist, see David V.N.
Bagchi *Luther's Earliest Opponents* (Minneapolis 1991).
4 Henry VIII had published against Luther a book upholding the medieval doctrine of the sacraments, *Assertio septem sacramentorum* (London: R. Pynson, 11
July 1521; STC 13078); the following year, Luther replied with a tract that he
himself described as somewhat sharp (WA 10 part 2 177), published first in
German, probably about 1 August, as *Antworrt deutsch Mart. Luthers auff König
Heinrichs von Engelland buch* (Wittenberg 1522) and then in Latin, probably in
late October, as *Contra Henricum regem Angliae* (Wittenberg 1522). See WA 10
part 2 175–9, 223–7; Latin text 180–222; German text 227–62. Erasmus deplored
the abusive, disrespectful tone of Luther's attack on King Henry (Epp 1348,
1352:79–82, addressed respectively to Georgius Spalatinus and Pope Adrian
VI); cf an earlier letter of Wolfgang Capito to Erasmus, Ep 1308. But there is no
obvious reason, other than Nesen's presence in Wittenberg and his habit of engaging in verbal abuse, why Erasmus in 1526 thought that he incited Luther's
attack on the king.
5 Although Pirckheimer still had great personal respect for Luther despite his
gradual alienation from the Reformation in general, he was sharply opposed
to the Sacramentarian doctrine of the Eucharist put forward in Oecolampadius' *De genuina verborum Domini* and published his own work, *De vera Christi
carne et vero eius sanguine* earlier in 1526, adopting a eucharistic position similar to Luther's. See Ep 1717. On Oecolampadius' doctrines and publications
see Epp 1616 n4, 1636 introduction, 1637 introduction, 1792A introduction and
n14. Oecolampadius was the leading Reformer in Basel at this period, and
both his activities in this position and his eucharistic doctrine had chilled the
formerly close relations between him and Erasmus. Cf Epp 1538 introduction,
1574 n3, 1679 n4, 1697 nn21, 22; hence the rather distant tone Erasmus adopts
in reporting the delivery of Pirckheimer's letter to Oecolampadius. The nature
of that letter is not clear, but it probably replied to Oecolampadius' letter of
13 April, where he reaffirmed his opinion, stated his regret that Pirckheimer
had turned into a hostile critic, and expressed uncertainty whether he would
write a reply to Pirckheimer's book. For Oecolampadius' letter see Pirckheimer
Opera politica, historica, philologica et epistolica, ed Melchior Goldast (Frankfurt
1610) 320–1.

Erasmus
Copperplate engraving by Albrecht Dürer, 1526
Cabinet des Estampes, Bibliothèque Royale Albert 1, Brussels

You mention a letter and a gift from Duke George; the letter was delivered some time ago from Baden, where the disputation took place. But I have
no news of the gift.[6] Koberger sent me two sable skins.[7] But a letter to Bonifacius mentions a bundle of ermine. Perhaps our Polish friend has changed
his mind and held back the ermine to be delivered by someone else.[8]   10

I am wondering how I can thank Albrecht Dürer. He is someone who
deserves to be remembered for ever. It is not surprising if the picture is
not a good likeness, for I am not the man I was five years ago.[9] It is now
almost two years[10] since I had an attack of the stone, near the beginning of
February, and was so shaken by fits of vomiting that from that time on my   15
health has gone downhill; before that I usually recovered after an attack.
For some months I had felt fairly well. But suddenly I was ambushed, as it
were, by a new malady.[11] It caused an extraordinary flow of urine, at first

* * * * *

6 On the missing gold cup cf Epp 1691 n4, 1728:10–22. On the Baden disputation
  of May 1526, see Ep 1708 introduction.
7 Cf Ep 1728 n5.
8 Erasmus' young Polish admirer Jan Łaski wrote to Bonifacius Amerbach on 8
  April that he was sending to Erasmus and Amerbach two pelts of sable and
  two bundles of ermine (AK III 145 Ep 1110) through the agency of Koberger. Because of a merchant's error the ermine was sold at Nürnberg and hence Łaski
  promised to send two more bundles (Łaski to Amerbach, Gniezno, 1 July;
  AK III 174 Ep 1130). On Łaski see Ep 1593 n18.
9 On the origin of this engraving of Erasmus, which goes back to Dürer's trip to
  the Netherlands in 1520–1, see Epp 1376 and nn1–3, 1536 n6; cf introductions
  to Epp 1132, 1136, 1199. Dürer made a sketch of Erasmus at Antwerp and another when they met again in Brussels. One of these survived (reproduced
  in CWE 8 28), and either it or the sketch now lost must have been the basis
  for the engraving mentioned. For the engraving, see Campbell Dodgson *Albrecht Dürer, Engravings and Etchings* (London 1926; repr New York 1967) 104
  and Musée du Petit-Palais [Paris], 4 avril–21 juillet 1996 *Albrecht Dürer: Oeuvre
  gravé* (Paris 1996) 235–6. Erasmus' judgment that the engraving is 'not a good
  likeness' has been widely shared by later critics, who (like him) attribute the
  defects in part to the lapse of several years between Dürer's sketch and the
  making of the engraving. Cf Karl-Adolf Knappe *Dürer: Das graphische Werk*
  (Paris 1964) 32, 107.
10 More accurately, about a year and a half. See Ep 1543, also to Pirckheimer,
  dated 5 February 1525.
11 This ailment, briefly mentioned in Epp 1728, 1743, 1749, and described at some
  length in Epp 1735 and 1759, was related, as Erasmus himself realized, to
  his chronic and recurrently disabling problem with kidney stones – perhaps
  an infection in the bladder or elsewhere in the urinary tract. Erasmus' close
  friend Bonifacius Amerbach, in a letter of 9 September to Jan Łaski, described
  the ailment as an 'inflammation of the bladder' and expressed concern that it
  might prove to be fatal (AK III 189 Ep 1141).

painless, but then sheer torture. It looks like a case of ulceration, with a great   20
flux of matter of a chalky nature. The doctors are no more helpful than a
swarm of flies. Either the stone in the bladder or this ulceration will be the
death of me. May the Lord grant me the strength to endure! I hope I shall
be remembered by all of you who are my friends. I shall write at greater
length later. This is all I can manage now. Farewell.   25

Basel, 30 July 1526

There are some points in the doctrine of the Eucharist that, in my ignorance, I would be inclined to doubt if the authority of the church did not
give me support.[12] By the church I mean the consensus of Christ's people
throughout the world.[13] I would like the letter I wrote to Duke George to   30
be delivered to him as quickly as possible.

To the honourable Master Willibald Pirckheimer, city councillor

1730 / From Bernhard von Cles   Speyer, 1 August 1526

On this powerful bishop of Trent, a trusted adviser of Archduke Ferdinand of
Hapsburg, see the introductions to Epp 1357, 1689. The bishop was at Speyer
for the meeting of the imperial diet, which opened on 14 June and adopted its
last major act on 27 August. The original letter survived at Leipzig and was
first published in 1904 in Förstemann/Günther.

My venerable and distinguished friend and dearly beloved brother, we were
greatly delighted by your recent letter,[1] both because of its eloquence and
because it seemed to overflow with affection and good will towards us. We
were much distressed to learn that you are tormented by illness and by a

* * * * *

12 Erasmus found the orthodox doctrine of transubstantiation, given dogmatic
   status by the Fourth Lateran Council in 1215, difficult, even incomprehensible,
   and admitted publicly that if the church had not clearly determined otherwise,
   even the Sacramentarian doctrine of his former friend Oecolampadius might
   sound plausible. For examples, see Epp 1616 and nn2, 4, 5; 1618 and nn3, 4;
   1636; 1637; 1620 and n14; 1621; 1624.
13 On the concept of the consensus of the church, see Ep 1708 introduction. Erasmus' trust in the 'consensus of the church,' as he defined it, was the reason for
   his dissatisfaction with the basically 'Lutheran' eucharistic doctrine currently
   being upheld by Pirckheimer against Oecolampadius in *De vera Christi carne*;
   cf Ep 1717 n1.

1730
 1 Evidently a letter from Erasmus has been lost, since Bishop Bernhard's letter
   of 15 May (Ep 1710) replies to Erasmus' letter of 16 April (Ep 1689), and no
   intervening letter is known.

conspiracy of vicious men. But this latter trouble should bring you nothing 5
but delight, since, as you know, all excellence is subject to envy. So be strong
and brave, rely on your good sense and patience, and recognize that great
and outstanding virtue can, in the end, lack nothing in honour or reward.
Be sure to take the greatest care of your health. We want you to live as long
as possible, not just for yourself, but for us too, who cherish you dearly for 10
your learning and your signal virtues. Make whatever use you wish of our
assistance, which we are most ready to offer, both for your material benefit
and for the furthering of your reputation.

> Speyer, 1 August 1526
> Bernhard, bishop of Trent   15

1731 / From Charles V   Granada, 4 August 1526

In response to Erasmus' complaints about the malevolent attacks on himself
by the Louvain theologians (cf Ep 1554, addressed to the emperor's secretary,
Jean Lalemand), Charles v in October 1525 had sent to Louvain a stern mandate ordering the theologians to stop attacking Erasmus at a time when he was
engaged in opposing Luther (that letter is lost, but see Ep 1643 from the imperial chancellor, Mercurino Gattinara). This intervention had not silenced the
critics at Louvain (cf Epp 1690 n11, 1700 n2), but Lalemand, Gattinara, and
other close advisers kept the emperor informed about Erasmus' merits. The
present imperial letter, probably occasioned by news of the publication of *Hyperaspistes 1*, is a manifestation of the ruler's favour but did not stop the sniping from Louvain. A draft of this letter survived in the Spanish archives at
Simancas, where Allen found it.

CHARLES ETC
My honourable and devoted friend, nothing could have given me greater
pleasure or delight than to learn that you have publicly declared yourself
an enemy of the Lutheran heresy. Not that I ever believed you were sympathetic to Luther, but I was waiting with eager anticipation for the gesture 5
you are now making. Although you can expect greater rewards from him
from whom the true blessings of piety proceed, yet we, for our part, shall
not fail to make it clear to everyone, by our treatment of you, how highly we
esteem you for your abilities and your truly religious spirit; in this way we
hope that your detractors,[1] who stubbornly oppose all those who are inter- 10

* * * * *

1731
1 See the introduction to this letter. The phrase probably refers exclusively to
the detractors at Louvain, though there were also critics in Spain, as Erasmus

ested in good literature and genuine piety, will cease at last to yelp at your heels and learn that the emperor stands by you as a man strong in every branch of learning and in true piety, and that he will defend your honour and reputation as he does his own.

Please, amid all your labours, look after your health – for we were sorry to hear that you have been very ill and in great pain. You can expect from us all the favours of an excellent prince. 15

Granada, 4 August 1526

To our honourable, loyal, and beloved Erasmus of Rotterdam, our councillor 20

1732 / From Juan Luis Vives   Bruges, 6 August 1526

On Vives see Epp 1665 introduction, 927 introduction, 1531, 1613. At this period Vives, who had married a wife who continued to live in Bruges, divided his time between England and Bruges. He had been in London, where he was favoured by Queen Catherine, from February to May but then remained in the Netherlands until April 1527 (Carlos Noreña *Juan Luis Vives* [Madrid 1978] 124–8). It is possible that at this date, despite his ties to the English court, he still knew nothing about Henry VIII's intention to secure a divorce from the queen, even though the queen herself learned of it on 22 June and it became common knowledge at court during this summer. In any case, this letter contains no hint of that news, which would have been useful to Erasmus, who had dedicated *Institutio christiani matrimonii* to the English queen (Ep 1727) less than a month earlier. This letter was first published in Vives' *Opera* (1555).

VIVES TO ERASMUS

I sent you a letter from Britain;[1] it was long and, in my usual manner, dealt with many subjects. I should be distressed to think it had not reached you, but I have received no word from you for a long time. I put this down to the fact that you are busy with so many things, for as you move ahead along a 5 straight path, the dogs bark[2] from the alleyways, forcing you to step aside and remove the obstacles that block your way. I could tell you many fine

* * * * *

already knew and would soon discover in more detail. On the attacks from Louvain at this period, chiefly from Jacobus Latomus (Jacques Masson), see Rummel II 6–14.

1732
1 Not extant
2 Vives uses Greek here: κύνες ὑλακτοῦσι.

tales about that man,[3] but I would prefer to see the two of you discussing ideas rather than personalities. We await the rest of your response to Luther.[4]

I had determined to write to you some time ago (I don't know how it slipped my memory) to propose that you arrange for all your books to be organized in several volumes and printed during your lifetime.[5] I am sure that something similar occurred to you long ago and that you are working on it with the same plan in mind; but you will proceed more rapidly when you realize that others are very interested in it too. There are many editions and printings of your works. Some day you and all of us must depart this life; if you die before you have collected all your writings and made clear your definitive judgment on each point, so that we can be sure of the position you have taken and which you would like others who will share your views to follow, I am much afraid of the confusion and disarray that is bound to ensue in your works. If this happens, your reputation is likely to suffer (although perhaps that is of little concern to you). Certainly you risk losing the fruits of your labour, for the reader will be perplexed, not knowing what precisely you approved and what you rejected. At present those who can distinguish the various editions get some idea of your intentions, but later generations, who will not be able to unravel the different editions (for the printers leave everything in a muddle), will be robbed of much of the value of your work. Moreover, since different volumes have been of-

* * * * *

3 Allen (6n) assumes that Luther is meant and links this phrase to the following mention of Erasmus' controversy with him, but it is questionable whether Vives, writing from Brussels, would have many tales about the Wittenberg reformer. If this letter is a reply to Ep 1665, replacing the lost letter mentioned in the first line, the reference could be to the bookseller Franz Birckmann, who was discussed (and denounced) at some length in Ep 1665 and with whom both correspondents had extensive and highly unsatisfactory experience.

4 On Erasmus' haste in writing *Hyperaspistes 1* and his promise to bring out a more thorough second part, see Ep 1667 introduction. Vives expressed most of this sentence, including Luther's name, in Greek.

5 A plan for the arrangement of his works is set out in Erasmus' first will, dated 22 January 1527 and translated at 540–50 below. In a long letter to Johann von Botzheim dated 30 January 1523 and published the following April, subsequently expanded and republished in September 1524, Erasmus not only listed his writings up to that time but also set forth in great detail how his works should be grouped into ten volumes if after his death his friends should judge them worth collecting and republishing (Ep 1341A, especially lines 1500–1639). See also Ep 2283 for a later scheme of organization. The scheme set forth in 1524 provided the basis for the Basel (1540) and Leiden (1703–6) editions of his *Opera omnia*.

fered for sale in different places, there are many of your books whose titles
are not even known to those who are most solicitous for your reputation   30
and who are aware, and ready to acknowledge, how much they have gained
from your writings.

Some of your admirers keep asking me what I thought you had in
mind when you wrote 'A Fish Diet'[6] and the dialogue 'On the Vow,'[7] and
what you meant by the 'four commandments' in the work entitled *Puerilis*.[8]   35
The *Puerilis* seems to have been written for children, but they are not likely
to understand such a serious subject. I offered a few suggestions. I don't
know if my response satisfies them, but it certainly does not satisfy me, for
the discussion seems quite inappropriate both to the dramatic setting and
to the characters; so it seems to me that you have not observed the laws of   40
propriety.[9] In my opinion you should not have written it, especially since it
has caused offence to many (you know who some of these people are); but I
have no doubt you had the best of reasons for doing what you did. Perhaps

* * * * *

6 The colloquy Ἰχθυοφαγία, which expressed Erasmus' views on mandatory fasting and which many of his critics interpreted as an attack on the disciplinary
   authority of the church, had first been published in Froben's new edition of
   the *Colloquies* in February 1526; see CWE 40 675–762.
7 This colloquy, *De votis temere susceptis* 'Rash Vows,' criticizes vows to go on
   pilgrimages as foolish and even harmful and describes a fictitious pilgrimage to Rome and Santiago de Compostela as the result of a vow taken by a
   group of men at a drunken party. The colloquy also criticized indulgences.
   First published in 1522, it was denounced by Erasmus' Louvain critic Nicolaas
   Baechem. See CWE 39 35–43; on Baechem's criticisms, nn14, 24.
8 Cf the colloquy *Confabulatio pia* 'The Whole Duty of Youth' CWE 39 91:18–30.
   Erasmus in a subsequent letter to Vives (Ep 1830) dismissed the objections
   (which Vives' words here imply that he shares) as nonsense.
9 Vives writes much of this passage in Greek rather than Latin. The use of Greek
   words here seems to be motivated less by an effort to be stylish by using the
   'more learned' Greek than by a desire to make a critical remark in a language
   that most educated readers could not understand. The parenthetical phrase in
   the next sentence also is in Greek, perhaps again used as a sort of semi-private
   code. Cf n4 above on the use of Greek letters to write Luther's name. Although
   concealment may not be a motive in this letter, it probably is significant that
   Vives, the son of *converso* parents, knew that his father had been executed by
   the Spanish Inquisition in 1524 on charges of Judaizing and that his deceased
   mother had also been accused of the same offence (her body was later ex-
   humed and burned after a trial by the Inquisition). Although he was offered
   a choice university appointment at Alcalá in 1522, by 1523 he had declined the
   opportunity and in fact never returned to Spain. Even in the Netherlands at
   this period, it would have been wise to be prudent, though his Jewish ancestry
   would not have been quite so dangerous there as back home in Spain.

you would be kind enough to add a word or two in your next letter to clear
up the difficulty that my friends and I share.   45

De Corte arrived yesterday from Louvain.[10] He tells me that Godschalk[11] and your friend Vincentius[12] are nearing their end and that Egmondanus[13] is suffering from choking spells, which bode no good and become
more ominous every day. I am afraid he may not be able to hold out. I also
hear from De Corte that Latomus is living at Cambrai.[14] What a great loss   50
to the university to have so many of its strong pillars crumble![15]

* * * * *

10 At this period Pieter de Corte, a humanist and long-time friend of Erasmus,
   was regent of the College of the Lily at Louvain. See Epp 1357 n66, 1537.
   Since de Corte was also linked to the Louvain faculty of theology (bachelor of
   divinity in 1518, master in 1530) and later (1531) became professor of theology,
   his report on the Louvain theologians came from a friend inside that faculty.
11 The theologian Godschalk Rosemondt of Eindhoven died on 5 December of
   this same year. Erasmus respected him as an essentially fair and somewhat
   sympathetic person who tried, especially during his term as rector in 1520, to
   promote civility and mutual respect among members of the Louvain faculty
   of theology. Erasmus sought his intervention at that time to silence attacks on
   himself by Nicolaas Baechem of Egmond and Laurens Laurensen, conservative
   members of the Louvain faculty who had been making public attacks on Erasmus and trying to link his name with Luther. See Epp 1153 and introduction,
   1162, 1164, 1166 and n6; 1172; 1571 nn49, 50; 1582 n21.
12 Vincentius Theoderici (or Dierckx) of Beverwijk, a Dominican theologian and
   one of Erasmus' most unrelenting critics at Louvain, had died two days before
   this letter was written. Many letters of the period 1520–5 contain complaints
   about his malevolent hostility and especially about his leading role in the compilation of a pseudonymous *Apologia* attacking Erasmus that was published at
   Antwerp in March 1525. On Erasmus' conflict with him see Epp 1196 and
   introduction; on the pseudonymous *Apologia*, see Ep 1674 n13.
13 On the conservative Carmelite monk and theologian Nicolaas Baechem of
   Egmond see Epp 878:15n; 1254 n6; 1553; 1581: 263–9, 392–422 and nn4, 45–6,
   48; 1608 nn4, 5. Cf Rummel I 135–43, II 4–7. He died at Louvain on 23 or 24
   August.
14 Although Latomus (Jacques Masson) was a vehement opponent of Lutheran
   heresy and was highly suspicious of some of Erasmus' works, Erasmus recognized him as a competent theologian and did not regard him with the same
   contempt he felt for Baechem and Theoderici, though he resented Latomus'
   opposition to the teaching of Greek and Hebrew and his increasingly frequent
   though veiled criticisms of Erasmus in works ostensibly directed against others. See Ep 1674 n12. Vives was misinformed about Latomus' departure from
   Louvain. Although he became a canon of Cambrai in 1526, he did not move
   to Cambrai until 1529 and returned to Louvain in 1535 when he received one
   of the major chairs of theology and a canonry in St Peter's church there.
15 Vives probably means to be ironic, since he and Erasmus thought men like
   Theoderici and Baechem to be incompetent and poorly educated fools, and

My best wishes to Rhenanus[16] and your friend Froben;[17] also to Cantiuncula,[18] if he is with you. Laurinus[19] sends his greetings. Do look after your health, dear master, and continue to hold me in your affection.

6 August. Bruges, 1526   55

1733 / From Germain de Brie   Gentilly, 11 August 1526

> The French humanist Germain de Brie, who had met Erasmus at Venice in 1508 and had corresponded with him from time to time since 1517, had been inspired by the preface of Erasmus' edition of St John Chrysostom's *De sacerdotio*

* * * * *

Latomus was a foe of humanistic studies and a sharp critic of Erasmus. The theologians at Louvain whom Erasmus regarded as more reasonable and more competent were Nicolas Coppin (who, however, seems to have become less favourable to him from about 1525), Willem of Vianen, Godschalk Rosemondt, and Jan Driedo. Cf Ep 1582:125–8 and nn19–22. Vives, of course, having his own personal experience of Louvain, may have differed from Erasmus somewhat in his own assessment of these individuals.

16 At this period of his life, Erasmus' friend and editorial collaborator Beatus Rhenanus divided his time between Basel and his native city of Sélestat. He seems to have been resident in Basel during the spring of 1526: the Froben press published his commentary on the *Naturalis historia* of Pliny the Elder in March; his friend Paul Volz wrote from Sélestat on 5 April, scolding him for his delay in returning there (BRE 363 Ep 255); his friend Michael Hummelberg addressed letters to him at Basel in April and May. A letter from Bonifacius Amerbach at Basel to Claudius Cantiuncula dated 29 July 1527 seems to indicate that Beatus was not in Basel at that date (AK III 256–8:90–1 Ep 1197). By 25 August he had moved to Sélestat, from where he wrote to Bonifacius Amerbach at Basel on 25 August (BRE 369 Ep 259).

17 The printer Johann Froben had published Vives' edition of Augustine's *De civitate Dei* in 1522, but it had not been an entirely satisfactory experience, in part because the edition did not sell well (cf Ep 1531). In addition, Vives had hoped to employ Erasmus' close connection with Froben to persuade the printer to bring out a Basel edition of some of his collected works, but Froben was unwilling to do so. See Ep 1613 and nn2, 3. These efforts at collaboration had placed some strain on Erasmus' friendship with Vives himself, though the two men remained on reasonably good terms.

18 At this period Claudius Cantiuncula had left his native city of Metz and was residing at Vic-sur-Seille as an administrative official (and from 1527 as chancellor) to Cardinal Jean de Lorraine, bishop of Metz. He remained in close touch with his friends in Basel, including Erasmus and his fellow jurist Bonifacius Amerbach. In a letter written later this same year to Amerbach, Cantiuncula expressed his regret at having moved away from Basel; see AK III 225 Ep 1168. On Cantiuncula see Epp 852:85n, 1616 introduction, 1636 introduction.

19 See Ep 1695 n6.

(Basel: Froben, May 1525), and especially by Erasmus' letter of dedication addressed to Willibald Pirckheimer (Ep 1558), to improve on the quality of the ancient Latin translation by Anianus with the new translation here discussed. His version had already been published in France, *Divi Joannis Chrysostomi quod multae quidem dignitatis sed difficile sit episcopum agere dialogus* (Paris: Josse Bade, 5 August 1525), but (as the present letter shows) he was so disappointed by the many typographical errors that he wrote this letter not only as an apology for the defects of the book (which he enclosed as a gift) but also as a plea for Erasmus to use his influence with Johann Froben to secure publication of a revised edition by the Basel printer. Erasmus' reply is Ep 1736, in which he did not endorse Brie's hope for a reprint of his edition but did co-opt him into his own ongoing work on Chrysostom. He incorporated Brie's text in his edition of selected works, *Chrysostomi lucubrationes* (Basel: Froben, March 1527) and later included both it and another of Brie's translations in the edition of the saint's *Opera* (5 vols, Basel: Froben 1530). On the *Lucubrationes* see Ep 1800. On Brie see also Epp 212:2n, 569 and introduction, and Allen Ep 2359, the dedicatory preface of the 1530 *Opera*. The original of this letter, written by a secretary but signed by Brie, survived among the Rehdiger manuscripts at Wrocław and was first published in 1906 by L.K. Enthoven. On Brie see now Marie-Madeleine de la Garanderie *Christianisme & lettres profanes: essai sur l'humanisme français (1515–1535) et sur la pensée de Guillaume Budé* (Paris 1995) 133–60.

GERMAIN DE BRIE TO ERASMUS OF ROTTERDAM

I remember writing to you last year,[1] most learned Erasmus, to say that, as soon as I dipped into your text of Chrysostom's *De sacerdotio*, which had just been produced by the Froben press as the first edition of the work in Greek, I was so taken by its elegance that I could not be torn away from   5
it for a moment. For several months I devoted myself entirely to it, to the total neglect of all other authors, both Greek and Latin. I soon realized the effect that was made on me by this engaging, elegant, and important work, in which Chrysostom, a truly golden author,[2] discusses the subject with his

* * * * *

1733
1 No such letter survives, but Erasmus' letter of 25 August 1525 (Ep 1597) to Brie suggests that he had received recent news from his French friend.
2 Few Renaissance authors could resist punning on the epithet that since the sixth century had become attached to the name of John, who became patriarch of Constantinople in 398; he was called *chrysostomus*, or golden-voiced, on account of his eloquent preaching. *De sacerdotio* was one of his most highly regarded works. On its importance see Quasten *Patrology* III 459–63.

friend Basil.[3] The book was always in my hands: it became so familiar, so   10
much a part of me, that no treatise by any author, either Greek or Latin,
was better known to me. As a result of all this, it took my fancy (I am not
sure why) to spend several nights translating the dialogue into Latin. I did
not intend my nightly labours to see the light of day – for what light or
brilliance could I expect in something laboriously worked over by me? My   15
only aim was to exercise my wits and improve and enrich my style by this
mating of Greek and Latin; this was to be the first fruits of the peace and
quiet[4] of my *Gentilliacum*[5] – for that is the name of the small estate, about
a mile from Paris, that I bought this year so that I would have a place to
which to invite my friends and where, in Cicero's words, I might pass my   20
time agreeably without interruption.[6]

Certain friends of mine were more impressed by my nocturnal efforts
than I was myself – for some people are quite uncritical where friendship is involved and are ready to overlook the blemishes of a friend.
And so, at their prompting, I decided to risk my reputation by publish-   25
ing my midnight labours (or should I describe them as 'my bagatelles'?).
I handed them over to Ascensius[7] to be printed. As usual, the presses
and the workmen were to be under the direction of Ascensius' eldest

* * * * *

3 Chrysostom's *De sacerdotio* has the form of a dialogue between the author and
his intimate friend Basil, a former fellow student with whom he shared a religious calling that eventually led both men into the priesthood. Although some
later writers identified this friend with Basil the Great, bishop of Caesarea, and
others identified him with Bishop Basil of Seleucia, both suggestions are in-
validated by chronology: the first Basil was too old and the second too young
to have been a classmate and companion of John Chrysostom. Even the identification of the friend with Bishop Basil of Raphnea in Syria, though chrono-
logically plausible, is purely conjectural. See the introduction by Anne-Marie
Malingrey to her edition *Jean Chrysostome sur le sacerdoce* (Paris 1980) 7–10.
4 Cf Cicero *De oratore* 1.224.
5 Cicero called his estate *Tusculanum* 'my place at Tusculum'; likewise Brie calls
his country estate *Gentilliacum* 'my place at Gentilly.' His excellent connections
with powerful patrons, which had earlier won for him appointment as secretary to Anne of Britanny and almoner to her husband King Louis XII, predecessor of Francis I, as well as a long succession of appointments to well-endowed
benefices at Albi, Auxerre, Paris, and several other places, had enabled him
to establish a prosperous residence at Paris and earlier in 1526 to acquire an
estate in the country near the capital where he could live in scholarly leisure
and pursue his study of Greek.
6 *De officiis* 3:58
7 The Paris printer Josse Bade of Assche (Jodocus Badius Ascensius); see the
introduction to this letter.

son,[8] a young man whose learning belied his years and surpassed that of
all his contemporaries. He had gained great respect for the care with which   30
he spotted and corrected the printing errors in a text. But when no more
than a page or two had been set, the young man's sudden death plunged
Ascensius' shop into such grief and caused such distress and confusion that
the father was unable to pay proper attention to correcting the proofs of my
work, so recent and natural was his bereavement over the death of his son.   35
In the meantime the beauty of these gardens was restoring and relaxing my
mind, which had been wearied by the strain of the work. I did not think it
necessary to lower my spirits by putting up with the trouble and indignity
of proofreading.[9] I felt I had done enough when I presented the press with
a clean copy.   40
    The consequence was that there were serious and shocking errors in
several pages, particularly in those which had been handed to the workmen
first. For they are never willing to take a break or interrupt a job, once it
has begun, except at the appointed times. So in their haste, they refused to
wait for the sheets to be reviewed and corrected (after a fashion) by the   45
chief printer of the Ascensian Press[10] – it would be more accurate to call

* * * * *

8 The name of this son seems to be unrecorded. Allen (29n) notes evidence suggesting that the young man's death had not yet occurred by 8 July 1526, the
  date of Brie's preface to the edition, but is lamented in a note on the *errata*
  sheet, which must have been composed just before 5 August, the date when
  printing was completed. The only identified son of Josse Bade is Conrad (1510–
  62), who also became a noted printer at Paris and later at Geneva. See M. Pre-
  vost, 'Bade (Josse)' and 'Bade (Conrad)' in *Dictionnaire de biographie française*
  (Paris 1931–   ) IV 1138–41 and 1136–7. Cf Philippe Renouard *Bibliographie des
  impressions et des oeuvres de Josse Badius Ascensius, imprimeur et humaniste, 1462–
  1535* 3 vols (Paris 1908; repr New York, no date) II 529, where the text of Bade's
  note on the *errata* sheet explaining the many errors is reprinted; but the son's
  name is not given in the note. Likewise the article on Josse Bade's publications
  by Albert Labarre and Sylvie Postel in *Imprimeurs & libraires Parisiens du XVIe
  siècle* II (Paris 1969) 14 and item no 558 (page 230) does not record this son's
  name, but only that he worked for his father as a proofreader.
9 As Allen (40n) justly observes, 'This whole passage shows clearly the indiffer-
  ence with which authors and publishers regarded the work of proof-correcting;
  also the independent attitude adopted by compositors.' In this case, Brie clearly
  regards himself as above the laborious task of proofreading.
10 Not identifiable. In 1527, a Netherlander named Jean Loys (Lodoicus Tiletanus)
   of Thielt was in charge of compiling and proofreading the index of an edition
   of the *Opera* of Priscian (Labarre and Postel *Imprimeurs & libraires* [n8 above] II
   14, 237 item no 576, 467 [index]); but there is no evidence that he was the person who took charge of the proofreading of Brie's translation of *De sacerdotio*
   in the summer of 1526.

him the 'chief misprinter' – who had recently been appointed to take the place of the deceased. Ascensius himself, far from accepting responsibility for the work of reading and correcting the proofs (which amounted in the event to the disfigurement and distortion of the text), put the blame squarely 50 on the shoulders of his deputy, a charming fellow to be sure, but a bad omen as far as I was concerned. Ascensius had nothing to offer me by way of consolation or remedy except to tell me to excuse and put up with the carelessness, ignorance, stupidity, impudence, and folly of his workman and deputy. My friends Nicolas Bérault,[11] Jacques Toussain,[12] and Pierre Danès[13] 55 were sympathetic to my plight and understood my unwillingness to put up with it. For who could be so long-suffering as not to be deeply upset by such shameful and improper treatment? In these circumstances anger is not a sufficient response – such behaviour deserves the stick!

This fool (whoever he was), who laid his filthy and accursed hands 60 on the sacred writings of Chrysostom and on my translation while examining and correcting the proofs, actually arrogated to himself the right to remove expressions from my text that he did not understand and substitute others singularly unsuited to the context; he also spoilt good Roman figures of speech and good Latin tropes and replaced them with utterly barbarous, 65 Gothic expressions.[14] One might imagine his sole aim and purpose was to publish his own feeble and amateurish efforts at the expense of my reputation. My manuscript can prove the truth of this. I recovered it from Ascensius' workmen and I keep it by me, in case some spiteful persons (and there is no lack of them) should criticize me for making mistakes in my origi- 70 nal text and then later, when the work was being printed, erasing them on the advice of others. But I am sure that any fair-minded reader, particularly anyone who will take the time to investigate and examine my style without prejudice, will soon ferret out the truth: that these blemishes originated

* * * * *

11 A friend of Erasmus as well as of Brie. See Epp 925 introduction, 1571 n15, 1579 n28, 1581 n2, 1591 introduction; 1598:2, 1687 n13.
12 See Epp 810:497n, 1713 introduction.
13 On this young humanist, a pupil of Budé and a close associate of Josse Bade, and later (from 1530) a *lecteur royal* (along with Toussain) in Greek at Paris, see Ep 1713 introduction.
14 Brie here employs the term 'Gothic' in the pejorative sense (which is related to Lorenzo Valla's suggestion that the invading Goths were responsible for the decline of good Latin) that had become conventional among humanists. It reached its peak in the works of the sixteenth-century art historian Giorgio Vasari and continued to dominate learned usage until the revival of medieval studies in the nineteenth and early twentieth centuries. See Wayne Dynes 'Concept of Gothic' in *Dictionary of the History of Ideas* II 366–74.

in the printer's shop and not in the study of the author, who, unless I am   75
mistaken, is no mere novice.

But it is time to get a grip on my feelings. So I am sending you a
copy of the work itself. Although, as I have said, it was badly handled in
Ascensius' shop, I removed all the misprints while the subject was still fresh
in my mind; in fact, before the book was sent out, I noted all the errors and   80
made corrections, though some perhaps may have escaped my notice. In
sending you the volume, I have two objects in mind. First, I would like you
to oblige your friend Brie by devoting the time needed for a quick reading
of the work itself. Secondly, if you think the book has merit enough to be
circulated in your part of the world too, will you please hand it over at the   85
earliest opportunity to your friend Froben for printing, after you have made
whatever corrections you think fit.[15] I trust your judgment and so give you
complete authority to criticize, correct, delete, or add anything you wish.
Also please ask Froben to send me fifty copies from the run – if, that is,
he agrees to publish. They will be paid for handsomely from my account   90
to whoever delivers them to me. I am delighted by the work of the Froben
press; I am not alone in this: my pleasure is shared by all who are interested
in good literature. Farewell. Please continue to be my friend.

From my estate at Gentilly

11 August 1526   95

A duplicate copy of this letter has been sent to you by the servant of
the bookseller Konrad.[16]

My friend Janus Lascaris has returned.[17] Today he is at my home in
Paris and plans to stay with me for several months.

* * * * *

15 Brie seems to assume that Froben would print anything that Erasmus recommended. Both Erasmus and Froben probably judged that there would be no
   market for an immediate reprinting of *De sacerdotio*, an economic consideration that a wealthy clerical pluralist like Brie was unlikely to think of. See the
   introduction to this letter and Ep 1736:8–12.
16 Konrad Resch, a German-born bookseller with close family and commercial
   ties to the Basel book trade. He had managed the Paris bookstore belonging
   to his uncle Johann Schabler, Ecu de Bâle, and since 1523 had been one of
   the official booksellers to the University of Paris. On 1 August 1526 – that
   is, less than two weeks before the date of this letter – he sold the Paris shop
   to Chrétien Wechel and soon afterward moved to Basel, where he again became an associate of Schabler. Cf Ep 331:15n. The double dispatch of letters
   described here, intended to improve the chances of eventual delivery of a letter in an age when there was no public postal service, was not uncommon; cf
   Ep 1585:2.
17 On this Greek-born scholar, see Ep 269:55n. Brie studied Greek with him at
   Venice. Lascaris joined the French court after the fall of his Medici patrons

To Erasmus of Rotterdam, prince of scholars in Greek and Latin   100
literature

1734 / To Polidoro Virgilio   Basel, 19 August 1526

The preface to Erasmus' Latin translation of two of St John Chrysostom's homilies on the Epistle to the Philippians, followed by the Greek texts of these homilies and by a third text attributed to Chrysostom, presented only in Greek.
This third text is Σύγκρισις βασιλικῆς δυναστείας καὶ πλούτου καὶ ὑπεροχῆς πρὸς
μοναχὸν συζῶντα τῇ ἀληθεστάτῃ καὶ κατὰ Χριστὸν φιλοσοφίᾳ. In PG 47 387 the title of the Latin translation (not by Erasmus) is *Comparatio potentiae, divitiarum et
excellentiae regis, cum monacho in verissima et christiana philosophia vivente*. Erasmus' publication is *In epistolam ad Philippenses homiliae duae, versae per Erasmum roterodamum additis graecis. Eiusdem Chrysostomi libellus elegans graecus, in
quo confert verum monachum, cum principibus, divitibus ac nobilibus huius mundi*
(Basel: Froben, August 1526). The Latin text was reprinted in the edition of
selected works of Chrysostom published by the same press in March 1527 (Ep
1800). The two homilies and this dedication were not included, however, in
the 1530 Latin edition of Chrysostom's *Opera* (Basel: Froben), or in Chevallon's
edition (Paris 1536), or in the 1540 *Opera* of Erasmus himself, apparently because of Erasmus' doubts about their authenticity. On the homilies, see also Ep
1736 n10. On Virgilio, who at this period was royal historiographer to Henry
VIII of England, see Epp 531:456n, 1175 introduction, 1666 introduction, 1702
introduction.

TO THE MOST HONOURABLE AND ERUDITE PATRON OF LETTERS,
POLIDORO VIRGILIO OF URBINO, FROM ERASMUS OF ROTTERDAM,
GREETING
Lately, dear Polidoro, my learned friend, when I received from Italy sev-
eral works of St John Chrysostom,[1] I thought I had acquired the treasury   5
of Croesus.[2] Since time is too short to permit me to send you a complete

* * * * *

from power at Florence in 1494 and was in Venice as French ambassador when
both Erasmus and Brie met him there in 1508. He lived mostly at Rome in
his later years, but he visited Paris (and also visited Brie's country estate just
outside the city) in 1526–7; cf Ep 1794:7–10.

1734
1 See Ep 1733 and cf Epp 1623 and n3, 1675 and n4, 1705 n3, all of which reflect
   Erasmus' efforts to obtain manuscripts of Chrysostom's works from Italy. Cf
   also Allen Ep 1705:6n on the manuscripts of Chrysostom.
2 A king of Lydia, legendary for his wealth

volume of his works, I have selected some choice pieces to serve as a souvenir of your friend, who has the sincerest affection and regard for you, as you deserve. This I did all the more eagerly because I know that in your own earlier studies you combined an interest in Greek with a knowledge of the Holy Scriptures. Here is an easy way to combine the two – by beginning a conversation with Chrysostom in Greek. I have translated two of the *Homilies*; the third I leave for you to translate.[3]

I strongly support your attitude in such matters: this is indeed the proper sequence, to progress from the human level to the divine. Still, I should regret it if you abandoned your support of the Muses. By some malign fate they seem to be languishing these days amid the squabbles that divide the world – understandably enough, I suppose, since they are the children of peace.[4] As long as my years allowed, I was one of their most energetic supporters. Now I can adopt those lines of Horace to myself:

> Lately my life was useful to the Muses,
> Not without honour did I serve their cause.
> Now on this wall I place my arms and lyre,
> No longer needed in the war.[5]

However, I have abandoned the Muses only to take on the role of gladiator.[6] All that is left to me now is to encourage others in the defence of literature. You, I feel sure, will make an important contribution to this cause because of your exceptional learning and the influence that your distinction and integrity have won for you in the eyes of all. So I beg you, on behalf of the whole world of learning, to continue to do even more zealously in the future what you have done so assiduously in the past. By such service you will bind all the brightest minds in friendship to yourself. Farewell.

Basel, 19 August 1526

* * * * *

3 On the untranslated Greek text, which appears at the end of the volume on folios β6–γ4, see the introduction to this letter. Dr. Georgianna Ziegler, Head of Reference, Folger Shakespeare Library, kindly provided a description of the volume and a copy of the first page of the untranslated text.
4 Cicero *Phil* 7.8
5 *Odes* 3.26.1–4, but Horace begins: 'Lately my life was useful to the girls.'
6 Erasmus frequently lamented that he had been forced to become a gladiator – that is, had been driven against his will into a combative role. Cf Ep 1674 n8.

1735 / To Guillaume Cop   Basel, 27 August 1526

At this time Guillaume Cop (Wilhelm Kopp) of Basel was one of the physicians
of the king of France and was highly regarded for his medical knowledge as
well as for his humanistic learning and his publication of Latin translations
of Greek medical authors. Erasmus had known him since 1497 and over the
years mentioned him in many letters. On him see Ep 124:18n.

Although Erasmus had suffered for many years from kidney stones, he
seems to have been free from acute symptoms through the spring and early
summer of 1526, a conclusion warranted by his failure to mention his health
at all in his letter of 28 April to Jan Antonin (Ep 1698), a physician who had
treated him with great success when he was living in Basel for several months
in 1524 (cf Ep 1602 introduction). But at the end of July, in a letter to Willibald
Pirckheimer (Ep 1729), Erasmus complained of the acute symptoms here described in greater detail. Erasmus' problems with calculus were chronic, but
his description of his condition at this time suggests something more, probably an infection of the urinary tract in addition to accumulation of stones (calcium granules) that he had been unable to void. Erasmus published this letter
in *Opus epistolarum*.

ERASMUS OF ROTTERDAM TO GUILLAUME COP, PHYSICIAN
How fervently I wish you were here, dear Cop, most eloquent of physicians,
now that my health has taken a turn for the worse. Ever since I began to
dilute my wine with water boiled with liquorice root, the stone had been
kinder to me; and my friends were already congratulating me on being free   5
of the trouble. Then suddenly last July I began to have a great discharge of
urine, accompanied by lesions in the passage. At first there was not much
pain, but after a day or two it was torture. It felt as though a stone had
stuck in the bladder and could not be expelled. During all this time I excreted great quantities of chalky urine resembling pus. Alarmed, I consulted   10
the doctors here, who are just what the people deserve, since they do not live
very healthy lives and drink immoderately.[1] The doctors gave no grounds
for hope. One recommended the baths at Baden,[2] others suggested differ-

* * * * *

1735
1 Erasmus' low opinion of the medical profession in Basel is also reflected in
   Ep 1564:40–1.
2 Allen (12n) observes that the context does not make it clear which of the neighbouring medical springs was meant: Baden-Baden, Baden in the Swiss Aargau,
   or even Wildbad in the Black Forest; from Basel, the curative baths at Baden

ent things. So I dismissed them and committed myself to the Lord. Then the
pain became less severe, and the discharge of matter diminished consider-   15
ably. It seems, however, that there is ulceration and scarring in the urinary
tract. They tell me that Thomas Linacre died of this complaint.[3] Since I cannot visit you because of my health and the threats of war, I beg you most
urgently to write to me and give me your advice.

It seems that the monks and a number of theologians of the monkish   20
sort have entered into a conspiracy to remove Erasmus' books from circulation,[4] so that from now on we shall be forced to read the works of Béda[5]
and Cousturier[6] and others of their ilk. People suspect that Lee, both in your
country and during his visit to Spain on a diplomatic mission, is giving energetic support to these madmen.[7] Nor is your friend Aleandro idle, unless   25

* * * * *

in the Aargau would have been the closest and most easily accessible.
3 This distinguished English physician and humanist died on 24 October 1524,
  and his death was attributed to calculus – that is, complications arising from
  calcium deposits in the bladder, according to DNB XI 1147. Cf Epp 118:27n,
  862:22–9 1513 nn13–15, 1558:88–91 and n13, 1587 n46.
4 The charge of a conspiracy intended to destroy his reputation and to prohibit
  study of his books is a commonplace in Erasmus' letters, and it was not entirely a figment of his imagination. See Pieter de Corte's letter of 1525 reporting efforts to ban his books at Louvain: Ep 1538:29–31 and n4; cf Epp 1697:26
  and n8, 1747:69–72.
5 On this sharp critic of Erasmus, see Epp 1571 introduction, 1664 introduction
  and n1.
6 Another conservative, anti-humanistic theologian. See Epp 1571 n10, 1658 n7.
7 Erasmus wrote 'on a diplomatic mission' in Greek. His controversy with Edward Lee reached back to the period immediately after publication of his
  Novum instrumentum in 1516 and reached its peak in 1519–20; despite the efforts of mutual friends (Bishop John Fisher, Thomas More, Richard Pace, John
  Colet) to restore good relations, it was never resolved. Although Erasmus regarded Lee as an intellectual lightweight, he was alarmed by Lee's steady rise
  to influence at the English court, and at this time specifically by Lee's appointment as ambassador to the emperor Charles V in Spain, where he suspected that Lee was a source of attacks on his books by Spanish theologians
  and monks. On Lee see Epp 765 and introduction, 1579 n24, 1581 nn16, 18;
  1606 n6. Cf Epp 1744:133–4 (and n19) and 1747:79–82, both of which express
  Erasmus' belief that Lee is about to publish a second book attacking his orthodoxy. In Ep 1785:32–5, the imperial chancellor, Gattinara, assures Erasmus
  that Lee will not be allowed to publish anything in Spain unless it is carefully examined beforehand. In 1527 Juan de Vergara, reporting to Erasmus
  on the charges brought against his publications by a group of Spanish monks,
  surmised that the whole attack was hatched 'in Lee's workshop': Allen Ep
  1814:285; cf Rummel II 84–6. Lee's treatise against Erasmus, if it ever existed,

a lot of people are telling me lies.[8] Where all this fuss will end I do not
know. I cannot fight on alone against a host of demons unless the princes
intervene and exercise their authority. The pope had imposed a ban of silence on the babbling idiots at Louvain.[9] They secretly obtained permission
from the datary[10] not to do their duty – though on condition that I would   30
not be harmed. The emperor issued a stern edict.[11] As soon as it was made
known, they rushed off to Mechelen and demanded an interpretation of it
from the court, which completely nullified what the emperor had written.[12]

Papillon[13] and Du Moulin[14] are dead. Berquin is in prison and locked
in argument with the theologians.[15] The king has his hands full with his   35
own affairs.[16] I pray God will make all things turn out for the best.

* * * * *

was never published and seems not to have survived. But he had previously
published his criticisms of Erasmus' edition of the New Testament, *Annotationes Edouardi Leei in annotationes Novi Testamenti Desiderii Erasmi* with several
associated texts, in *Annotationum libri duo* (Paris: Gilles de Gourmont for Konrad Resch 1520). Lee had had difficulty finding a printer in the Netherlands
who was willing to print his book; hence he turned to the publisher at Paris.
8 Erasmus had identified his former friend Girolamo Aleandro as a secret enemy constantly at work trying to bring him into disrepute among orthodox
Catholics, especially at the papal curia. See Ep 1553 n9, and cf Epp 1549, 1582
n8, 1605 n2, 1621 n6, 1660 n9, 1717 nn3, 17, 18. On first learning of Alberto
Pio's attack on himself, Erasmus initially suspected Aleandro as the true author (Ep 1553 n9), just as in this letter he saw the hand of his old enemy
Lee behind the Valladolid articles presented against him by the Spanish religious orders. On Erasmus' concern about Lee's influence in Spain while he
was English Ambassador there, see also Ep 1744 n19.
9 See Ep 1716 n6.
10 On the datary Gian Matteo Giberti see Ep 1716 introduction.
11 See Epp 1643, 1690 n11, 1700 n2, 1716 n7, 1747 introduction and nn8, 9; and
the emperor's own reassuring letter to Erasmus, Ep 1731.
12 See Ep 1690 n11 and the later letters there cited, especially Epp 1716 n7,
1747:22–9, 40–9.
13 On Antoine Papillon see Epp 1599 n2, 1722 n10.
14 On François Du Moulin see Epp 523:9n, 1426 introduction and, concerning his
death on a date before 16 June 1526, Epp 1719 introduction, 1722 n11.
15 On this combative evangelical humanist, see Epp 1599 introduction and n1,
1692.
16 Erasmus' Latin is *satagit rerum suarum*, for which cf Terence *Heautontimorumenos* 225. In fact the king did intervene vigorously to prevent the execution of Berquin in the spring of 1526. When the Parlement refused his orders
to release Berquin, in November he compelled the Parlement to deliver the
prisoner into the custody of his own officer, the provost of Paris (cf Ep 1692
n9), thus securing *de facto* his release from prison but not from the formal

Claude, queen of France
Bibliothèque nationale de France, Paris
MS Nouv. acq. lat. 82 folio 100

The bearer of this letter [17] wants very much to be commended to you. He can better explain what his business is. He is a merchant, one of Mercury's men and a terrible windbag. You may listen to him by all means, but don't be taken in.[18] I shall be very grateful if you will send me a cure; and   40 if there is any news from court that I ought to know about, please pass it on.[19] My best wishes to yourself and to your wife and children.

Basel, 27 August 1526

1736 / To Germain de Brie   Basel, [c 27 August 1526]

A reply to Ep 1733, probably written at the same time as Ep 1735 and dispatched by the same courier, since Ep 1735 was also addressed to Paris. Erasmus gently rejects Brie's request that he persuade Froben to reprint immediately his new Latin translation of Chrysostom's *De sacerdotio*, which the Ascensian press at Paris had printed so badly. At the same time Erasmus recruits

* * * * *

condemnation for heresy. This standing conviction made it possible for a special judicial commission to rearrest him suddenly in April 1529 while the king was away from Paris, declare him to be an unrepentant heretic, and speedily execute him on 17 April 1529 before any further royal intervention was possible. But Erasmus was correct in stating that King Francis had his hands full as he prepared to repudiate the Treaty of Madrid and to reopen the war with the emperor.
17 Not identified
18 That is, he was a merchant; Mercury was, among other things, god of profit. Two unflattering phrases used to describe the bearer ('a terrible windbag' and 'but don't be taken in') are in Greek, which Cop could read but the unreliable courier (if he happened to peek at the letter) probably could not.
19 The court was in the vicinity of Paris for the funeral of Queen Claude in November. The queen had died on 26 July 1524, shortly after the king had left Paris to repel the invasion of Provence by an imperial army led by the rebellious duke of Bourbon (Knecht *Renaissance Warrior* 213–15). After driving Bourbon's army out of France, King Francis crossed into Italy on 17 October, thus launching the disastrous campaign that led to his defeat and capture at Pavia on 25 February 1525, which was followed by more than a year of captivity. The funeral for the deceased queen was deferred until after his return, though Francis did not attend the service. Instead, he remained at various places near the capital: at Vincennes for a time, then at Saint-Denis, at Ecouen (which belonged to Duke Anne de Montmorency, grand master of France), and finally at Saint-Germain-en-Laye, where he seems to have spent the last two months of 1526. See *Journal d'un bourgeois de Paris sous le règne de François premier (1515–1536)* ed Ludovic Lalanne (Paris 1854; repr New York 1965) 296–301.

Brie into his own plans for editing and translating the works of Chrysostom.
He included this letter in his *Opus epistolarum*.

ERASMUS OF ROTTERDAM TO GERMAIN DE BRIE, GREETING

In your translation of Chrysostom[1] I think you have proved yourself a wonderful artist and have surpassed his eloquence with your own. So even if
I were to show little interest in your reputation (which, on the contrary, is
very important to me, as indeed it ought to be), I should certainly be inter-   5
ested in a writer like Chrysostom and in a valuable work such as you have
chosen. Two copies of the translation and of your letter were delivered to
me. But in the daybooks of a printer profit has the first entry; and as I am
sure you know, the work you translated has been translated before after a
fashion.[2] Moreover, the whole of Chrysostom has recently been printed in   10
a stylish edition.[3] To speak plainly, I do not think this is the right moment
to push your name forward. Yet I know you have within you, my learned
friend, all the qualities that are needed not only to increase your own reputation (for you already have a fine reputation), but to raise others from
obscurity to fame. At any rate, I shall show you that I have not failed to take   15
advantage of this opportunity.

That will happen (if you are agreeable) when I finish the Annotations,
which is the treadmill round which I go at present again and again.[4] I propose, with Christ's help, to translate some of Chrysostom's works that no
one has yet published or translated.[5] To these I shall add the work you sent   20
me and I shall not forget to pay proper tribute to your merits. Later the

* * * * *

1736
1 Of *De sacerdotio*. See Ep 1733 introduction.
2 By Anianus of Celeda. See Ep 1558 n22.
3 Another Basel printer, Andreas Cratander, published a five-volume edition
 of Chrysostom's *Opera latina* in 1522, a work edited by Erasmus' former
 colleague at the Froben press, Johannes Oecolampadius. In 1525 the same
 translator published a sixth volume, containing *In totum Geneseos librum homiliae* LXVI (Basel: Andreas Cratander, January 1525). See Ernst Staehelin
 Oekolampad-Bibliographie in *Basler Zeitschrift für Geschichte und Altertumskunde*
 17 part 1 (1918) 50–1 no 104. G.W.F. Panzer *Annales typographici* 11 vols
 (Nürnberg 1793–1803; repr Hildesheim 1963–4) VI 252 no 598 records an edition of Chrysostom in seven volumes (Basel: Andreas Cratander, 1525), but
 this description is probably an error caused by counting the sixth volume
 twice.
4 A reference to the fourth edition of the New Testament, which was published
 in March 1527
5 See Ep 1733 introduction on this collection, *Chrysostomi lucubrationes*, published
 in March 1527. The dedicatory letter is Ep 1800.

opportunity will come for a complete Chrysostom to be printed in a splendid edition by Froben.[6] Here we can ensure that your labours do not go for
nothing. The business I mentioned just now will, if I am spared, be finished
before Easter. With regard to the other project, you could be useful both   25
to me and to Froben. Much of Chrysostom has been poorly translated by
others. Much has not yet appeared. I have acquired the following works: a
commentary on the Acts of the Apostles (clearly spurious);[7] a commentary
on the Epistle to the Romans (genuine);[8] a commentary, in translation, on the
Epistle to the Hebrews (also spurious);[9] two homilies on the Epistle to the   30
Philippians, which, unless I am mistaken, are spurious (I have already published these in a Latin translation);[10] a work *Against the Jews*;[11] about twelve
homilies that no one has touched;[12] finally, a commentary on the Second

* * * * *

6 On this edition, incorporating Brie's version of *De sacerdotio* and of one additional work, see Epp 1661 n2, 1733 introduction.
7 On Erasmus' Greek manuscript, see Ep 1623 n3. No formal commentary exists, but there is a series of fifty-five genuine sermons that Quasten (III 440)
   calls 'the only complete commentary on Acts that has survived from the first
   ten centuries.' Quasten (III 441) also mentions four homilies on the beginning
   of Acts and four on the change of names by Paul and other biblical person-
   ages. The literary form of these works 'is less finished than we are accustomed
   to expect from him (III 440),' perhaps because the text came from stenographic
   notes and was never revised by Chrysostom himself. Quasten seems to regard
   the authenticity of these homilies as certain. Perhaps the deficient literary style
   of these eight homilies is the reason why Erasmus regards all of the homilies
   on Acts as spurious. Or it may be that his manuscript contained some entirely different work, a true commentary that he realized could not have been
   Chrysostom's work.
8 See Ep 1795 n2. Erasmus clearly has in mind not a formal commentary but
   Chrysostom's thirty-two homilies on Romans. Cf Quasten III 442–5.
9 Again, the text is probably not a formal commentary but Chrysostom's thirty-
   four homilies on Hebrews, which Erasmus may have found suspect because
   they were published posthumously from rough stenographic notes. According to Cassiodorus, the thirty-four homilies were translated into Latin by Mutianus. See Quasten III 450, who adds that Chrysostom never wrote commentaries on the Catholic epistles (that is, epistles addressed not to a particular
   individual or local church but to the church in general), and that nearly half
   of the *catenae* fragments edited under Chrysostom's name are actually extracts
   taken from his other works.
10 See Ep 1734 introduction. In all, fifteen of Chrysostom's homilies on Philippians are known; see Quasten III 447.
11 Cf Ep 1800:96 and n15, 113. Quasten III 452–5 identifies eight homilies on this
   topic.
12 Cf Ep 1705 n3 on Erasmus' acquisition of a manuscript of Chrysostom's homilies that he prized highly.

Epistle to the Corinthians.[13] If you come across anything else that has not   35
yet been translated, translate it; or if you find a piece that has been translated, examine it and add notes pointing out the mistakes of the translator
or the copyists.[14] This will make the work more marketable.

    This, then, is my proposal. If you can think of anything better, I am
ready to agree. Let me know as soon as possible what you think. I continue   40
my work on behalf of literature, although I see the age is degenerating into
a state of Scythian barbarity to the point where there is no health anywhere.
I congratulate the distinguished Janus Lascaris first on his good health and
secondly on finding a place in your home[15] – though perhaps it is you I
should congratulate on having him. If you don't write, I shall press on, with   45
God's help, just the same. As for your lament about the printers,[16] I think it
is better to say nothing, however justified the complaint; it is an old problem
that many of us share. I wish, dear Brie, we could meet sometime and talk
together. My best wishes to you and to your dear companion.[17] I wonder if
that friend of ours is still arguing in his cage.[18]   50

    Basel, [1525]

    * * * * *

13 Quasten III 445 records thirty homilies on 2 Corinthians.
14 The Latin, *librariorum*, could refer to either copyists or printers.
15 See Ep 1733 n17.
16 See Ep 1733:31–5, 41–76, also introduction and nn7, 10, 15.
17 Allen (42n) suggests that this companion was Girolamo Fondulo of Cremona
    (documented 1518–40), who had studied Greek under Marcus Musurus, had
    come to France by 1520 as a protégé of Louise of Savoy, and was currently
    living at Gentilly as Brie's guest and tutor in Greek. In his introduction to Ep
    1733, Allen notes Brie's acknowledgment of Fondulo's assistance with his clas-
    sical and patristic studies, an acknowledgment expressed also in the preface
    to his Latin translation of Chrysostom's *De sacerdotio*. Possibly the reference
    could indicate Lascaris, who is mentioned a few lines above.
18 Allen (42–3n) plausibly identifies this 'friend of ours' as a reference, stim-
    ulated by the probable reference to Fondulo immediately preceding, to the
    close personal association between Brie and Erasmus in Venice while the
    former was studying Greek and residing with Janus Lascaris and the lat-
    ter was associated with the press of Aldo Manuzio and living in the house
    of Aldo's business partner and father-in-law Andrea Torresani of Asola.
    The 'friend' in that case may be Andrea Torresani of Asola (in Latin An-
    dreas Torresanus Asulanus), a conjecture supported by Erasmus' rather crit-
    ical attitude towards Torresani. On his judgment that unlike Aldo, Torresani
    was a profit-seeking businessman rather than a real lover of scholarship, re-
    cently reinforced by Torresani's rather brusque rejection of an offer to let
    him publish a new, expanded edition of the *Adagia*, see Ep 1592 introduction.
    As Allen notes, Erasmus later caricatured Torresani harshly in his colloquy

1737 / To Conradus Pellicanus   [Basel, c 27 August 1526]

On the humanist Pellicanus, a well-known Hebraist and a major collaborator in the editorial work on Erasmus' editions of St Jerome and other patristic authors, see Epp 1637, 1638, 1639, 1640, 1792A. The cause of the growing
alienation between him and Erasmus was not only his adherence to the Reformation but, far more, Erasmus' belief that both Pellicanus and another former
associate, Johannes Oecolampadius, were insinuating that Erasmus privately
supported their Sacramentarian position on the Eucharist; see Ep 1674:44–5. In
February 1526 Pellicanus left Basel for Zürich, where he taught Hebrew and
Greek and was closely associated with Huldrych Zwingli. The occasion for the
present letter was Erasmus' receipt of a vernacular letter from another Zürich
Reformer and scholar, Leo Jud, together with a vernacular pamphlet upholding his Sacramentarian views against Erasmus' criticisms; see Ep 1708 n1. As
this letter clearly shows, Erasmus suspected that his former friend Pellicanus,
rather than Jud, was the real author of the pamphlet. Except for one additional angry letter to Pellicanus, now redated to 1527 and renumbered from
Ep 1644 to Ep 1792A, there was no further communication between them until
Pellicanus visited Erasmus at Basel in 1536 just a few days before the latter's
death; cf Ep 3072. The approximate date of this letter is confirmed both by
references to Erasmus' acute illness in the late summer of 1526 and by references to Leo Jud's recent vernacular publication. Allen edited this letter from
the autograph original preserved at Zürich; it had previously been published
in Salomon Hess *Erasmus von Rotterdam nach seinem Leben und Schriften* 2 vols
(Zürich 1790) II 602. Kenneth A. Smith of the Reference Department, Regen-
stein Library, University of Chicago, kindly verified Allen's citation of this
scarce publication.

Cordial greetings. I have not yet had time to read Leo's letter or his book,[1]
for I am so swamped with work and my health has been utterly wretched.

* * * * *

Opulentia sordida 'Penny-Pinching' (cwe 40 979–95), where the printer appears
under the easily recognized name 'Antronius.' Cf also *Adagia* II v 68, 'Antronius asinus' ('Antronian ass'). But the real Torresani would better fit the character in the colloquy, who is a shrewd, stingy, hard-driving money-grubber,
than the 'Antronius' in the adage, who is stupid and grossly fat.

1737
1 The letter from Leo Jud (1482–1542), a colleague of Zwingli among the Reformed clergy at Zürich, is lost, but its sharp criticism of Erasmus is reflected

The stone has been followed by a more serious complaint, for which there is no cure.

You have much to say about our friendship, and yet you do things 5 which not even my enemies would do. Capito, [2] in a letter that was intercepted, points to you as the author of the book that you disown in your letter.[3] Such behaviour I find wanting not just in honesty and civility but even in prudence. If I had strangled your father, could you find anything more threatening to do to me than to stir up a fuss like this? I count you 10 plainly responsible, since neither in your presence nor in the presence of any other living creature have I ever professed the views you now profess. In a situation fraught with danger you behave as though you were acting in a comedy.

What is your object in all this? To make people believe that I am on 15 your side? Suppose I were – would that bring you an immediate victory? In the intercepted letter Capito writes that, whether I like it or not, I shall come eventually to your point of view.[4] But not even a thousand Capitos would

* * * * *

in Epp 1741, 1744:9–12, and Allen Ep 1804:148–51. On the background of this controversy, which is linked to Erasmus' opposition to the Sacramentarians of Zürich and Basel, see Ep 1708 introduction and nn1–2. Jud's book, *Vf entdeckung Doctor Erasmi ... antwurt vnd entschuldigung*, excused his own earlier anonymous publication (*Maynung vom Nachtmal*) by charging that Erasmus himself had published books anonymously, among which he lists not only *Julius exclusus* but also the sharp attack on the Louvain theologians, *Dialogus bilinguium ac trilinguium* (Paris 1519). In a letter to Thomas More, Erasmus mentions the charge concerning his authorship of *Julius exclusus* in carefully chosen words that deny only that he had published an anonymous work, studiously avoiding the question whether he had ever written it (Allen Ep 1804:154–9; 154n quotes illustrative passages from Jud's extremely rare publication). The *Dialogus*, published under the name of Konrad Nesen, was often attributed to Erasmus at the time but was probably the work of Wilhelm Nesen; it has been translated in CWE 7 329–47.

2 On this former Benedictine, humanist, and professor of theology at Basel, whose mastery of Hebrew and far-ranging erudition Erasmus formerly had praised warmly, see Ep 1674 n24. Since 1523, when he moved to Strasbourg, Capito had become one of the principal leaders of the Reformation in that city. The intercepted letter from Capito is not extant, but Erasmus for a time was firmly convinced that it suggested that Pellicanus himself was the author of the anonymous *Maynung vom Nachtmal*, which upheld Sacramentarian eucharistic doctrine and was mentioned in Ep 1708, addressed to the Basel city council.

3 Not extant

4 That is, the Sacramentarian understanding of the Eucharist. Throughout this period, Erasmus repeatedly expressed his dismay that former close associates at Basel, such as Pellicanus, Oecolampadius, and Capito, intimated that their

make me profess a doctrine of whose truth I have not yet found convincing
proof. My end is not far off; I want at least to have a clear conscience to   20
present to Christ. If you people trust in the spirit within you, show it by your
deeds. These tricks and quarrels destroy any hope I had of a happy outcome.
You seem to me completely changed[5] – I only wish it were for the better!
I fear truly for the salvation of your soul. What words your soul speaks in
the presence of Christ I do not know. If you wish to attract me into your   25
party, you should show fruits of a different kind. I am engaged in a fight to
the death with the whole league of theologians. And yet I would rather be
torn limb from limb than profess a belief contrary to my conscience. I leave
you and your friends to your consciences. It is only fair that you leave me
to mine. So if you wish our friendship to continue, give up these games and   30
find something else to write about. Farewell.

You will recognize the hand of one who remains a friend, if you still
wish it so.

To Conradus Pellicanus. In Zürich

1738 / To Bernhard von Cles   Basel, 27 August 1526

This letter is the preface to the first edition of a major patristic publication of
Erasmus, *Adversus haereses* (Basel: Froben, August 1526), by St Irenaeus, bishop
of Lyon, one of the earliest patristic theologians; the work is especially important for study of Gnostic heresies in the early church. It was originally written in Greek but survived in its entirety only in a Latin translation (probably
from the late fourth century) which Quasten judges (presumably on the basis of fragments of the Greek text found in some *catenae* and papyri and in
quotations by other patristic authors) to be 'very literal' (I 288).

Erasmus addressed the preface as a dedication to Bernhard von Cles, prince-
bishop of Trent, who was a close adviser to the emperor's brother, Archduke
Ferdinand, and a generous patron of arts and humanistic learning; see Epp
1357 and 1689 introductions. His delight at being honoured by the dedication
of this major patristic edition is reflected in Ep 1793, which mentions a 'little

* * * * *

own eucharistic doctrines were natural consequences of ideas they had learned
from Erasmus, or even that Erasmus privately agreed with their opinions but
hesitated to affirm his belief publicly.
5 Erasmus implies not only, primarily, that formerly trustworthy friends like
Pellicanus were now deceitfully attributing to him beliefs that he did not hold
and had never professed to them, but also, secondarily, that Pellicanus and
his associates had abandoned the religious faith that he and they had shared
in earlier years.

gift of money' sent to express his admiration of Erasmus (actually, the substantial sum of 100 pieces of gold; Ep 1771 and n1). The present letter was
printed in the 1527 edition of Irenaeus, which the Froben press reprinted in
1528 and 1534, and also in the third volume of Erasmus' *Opera* (Basel 1540).

TO THE RIGHT REVEREND FATHER IN CHRIST, BERNHARD,
LORD BISHOP OF TRENT, FROM DESIDERIUS ERASMUS
OF ROTTERDAM, GREETING

Here under your auspices, my lord bishop, I am ushering into the light of
day that great champion of the church Irenaeus,[1] who fulfilled the promise   5
of his name and became a stout defender of peace in the church. For εἰρήνη
is the Greek for 'peace,' and in the Gospel our Lord says 'Blessed are the
εἰρηνοποιοί' (that is, 'the peace-makers') 'for they shall be called the children
of God.'[2] God is not the author of discord but of peace, and through his
Son he brought peace to all that is in heaven or on earth. Those, on the   10
other hand, who trouble the world with their quarrels act like their father,
who was the first to sow discord between God and man and to destroy the
saving harvest of the gospel by secretly planting tares among the wheat –
a job for the darkness of the night and apt for the prince of darkness.[3] It is
my hope that in the present troubles in the church – and we read in history   15

* * * * *

1738
1 Irenaeus (born sometime between 140 and 160 in Asia Minor, probably at
  Smyrna, bishop of Lyon in Gaul from about 177–8, date of death unknown but
  probably early third century) was an influential opponent of the many Gnostic heresies of the late second century. He wrote in Greek. Only two of his
  many works survive intact (though not in Greek). A Latin translation of *Adversus haereses* was known in Erasmus' time (cf n11 below); an Armenian translation of books 4 and 5 was discovered and published in 1910. An Armenian
  translation of Ἐπίδειξις τοῦ ἀποστολικοῦ κηρύγματος / *The Demonstration of the
  Apostolic Preaching*, unknown in the sixteenth century, was first published in
  1907.
2 Matt 5:9. Erasmus' point here is that even Irenaeus' name ('Peaceful') symbolized his loyalty to Christ's message of peace, as reported by the evangelist.
3 Satan is traditionally the father of lies, a sower of discord between man and
  God, and the prince of darkness. This is a not-very-subtle blow at the religious zealots and dogmatists on both sides, whose controversial books were
  destroying the peace and unity of the church. The echo of Matt 13:25 in the
  English translation is not in Erasmus' Latin; he did, however, use this biblical
  reference himself in warning against reckless use of force to suppress heresy.
  See Tracy *Erasmus* chapter 12, especially 165–6, citing Ep 1422, addressed to
  Cardinal Campeggi.

of no graver or more widespread crisis than this (although the Arian heresy spread its influence far and wide) – new men like Irenaeus will arise to restore peace to the world through the spirit of the gospel. For the books that are now flying like weapons in both directions are more likely to start a new fire than put out an old. But the Lord will put out the fire with the help   20
of Christian princes; for when we have changed our ways for the better, he will put aside his anger and begin to show mercy.

But I return to my Irenaeus – and why should I not call him 'mine,' since I found him almost buried[4] and have done my best to clear away the dust of ages and restore him to the light? Certainly he did not deserve to   25
languish in perpetual darkness, for his writings breathe the ancient power of the gospel, and his style reveals a soul prepared for martyrdom. For martyrs have their own way of speaking – serious, strong, and manly. He was close to the age of the apostles, when the church still flourished with the triumph of the martyrs. As a boy he heard Polycarp in Asia (and Polycarp was a   30
disciple of John the Evangelist, who appointed him bishop of Smyrna, and was well known to other apostles and disciples who had seen and heard the Lord; he would often tell many of the stories he had heard from them that have not been preserved in the written record).[5] As a boy Irenaeus listened avidly to what Polycarp had to say about Christ and the disciples. What he   35
heard was etched so deeply in his heart that, even as an old man, he retained a clear and vivid memory of everything that was said, as he himself amply testifies in his letter to Florinus. This is also recorded in the fifth book of the *Ecclesiastical History*, chapter 20. That age still showed evident traces of the gifts of grace given to the church in those early days. Irenaeus himself tells   40
in the fifth book how he heard many brothers who had the gift of prophecy, who could expound the mysteries of God, speak in tongues, and bring out

* * * * *

4 Irenaeus' work had never been printed. Earlier in the year Erasmus had requested the loan of a manuscript (probably based on a manuscript of the Vatican library) that was transmitted to him by his friend Johannes Fabri (like Bernhard von Cles a close adviser to Archduke Ferdinand of Hapsburg). See Ep 1715, especially n1.

5 In the letter to Florinus cited below, which survives in the form of a quotation in Eusebius *Historia ecclesiastica* 5.20 (cf lines 95–6 below), Irenaeus describes his upbringing in the household of Polycarp, bishop of Smyrna. Since Polycarp (martyred in 156) had been a disciple of St John and thus represented a direct link with the apostolic age, this connection gave Irenaeus' writings great authority in the early church and in the opinion of Erasmus. See Quasten I 287 and, on the importance of Polycarp as a surviving link to the apostles, I 76–7.

the secrets of men, not for show, but for the general good.[6] Elsewhere he tells us of men who, by invoking the name of Jesus, could cure diseases and cast out devils.[7]   45

So you see, Irenaeus is important because of his great antiquity. Let me now set out the evidence for his piety and goodness. The record is all the more impressive because he earned it in an age when such distinction had generally to be bought at the price of suffering and death. There is no discomfort now in professing the name of Christ since there is no danger   50
of legal action against either one's property or one's life. Irenaeus, when he was a presbyter of the church at Lyon and Eleutherus was pope,[8] was sent to Rome to settle a dispute within the church. He set out on his mission highly commended in letters from the martyrs both for his great zeal for the gospel and for the probity of his character, which matched the dig-   55
nity of his office as presbyter. As a result, he was thought worthy to succeed the bishop of Lyon, one Photinus or Pothinus (for the manuscripts vary in the spelling of his name), who suffered martyrdom when he had almost reached his ninetieth year. Irenaeus was so zealous for the peace of the church that when Victor, the Roman pontiff, excommunicated a num-   60
ber of churches because they differed from Rome on the date of Easter and the practice of fasting, he went so far as to criticize the pope for setting aside the example of his predecessors and showing himself too ready to cut off churches that differed, not in faith, but only in matters of observance. The story is told at length in the *Ecclesiastical History*, book 5, chapter 24.[9]   65
This was the way the peace-loving Irenaeus acted. Now we have our belligerent Ptolemies,[10] who on the flimsiest of pretexts are quick to raise false charges of heresy and schism. But where should I look for better evidence of Irenaeus' piety than in the writings of the man himself, which breathe the spirit of the gospel and reveal, if I may put it so, the future candidate   70
for martyrdom?

* * * * *

6 *Adversus haereses* 5.6.1: 'prophetica habentes charismata'; cf 1 Cor 12:4–11, cataloguing the works of the Spirit, which the Greek text calls χαρίσματα.
7 *Adversus haereses* 2.32.4
8 The translator here and elsewhere in this letter has followed Erasmus' traditional Latin preferences in spelling Greek patristic names: Eleutherus instead of Eleutherius, Abraxas instead of Abrasax, Basiliscus instead of Basilicus, Syrenus instead of Synerus, and Calistio instead of Callistio.
9 5.24.9–18
10 The apparently untoward reference to the Macedonian kings of Egypt at this point has a verbal explanation. The name *Irenaeus* ('man of peace') contrasts with the Greek *ptolemos*, which means 'war.'

Now let me say a few words about his education. He himself admits, in the preface to the first book, that he had no pretensions to style or skill as a writer. I am ready to believe that he did not strive for eloquence; but the idea that he ignored it is belied by the flow of his language, which, in a 75 subject that is so complex and tangled (not to say wearisome), is lucid, well ordered, and logical. I am not yet certain whether he wrote in Greek or in Latin.[11] I am inclined to think that he wrote in Latin, but was more at home in Greek. This explains why in his Latin he makes free use of Greek idioms; for example, he puts *noceri* for *laedi* ['to be injured'] on the analogy of the 80 Greek βλάπτεσθαι and uses *habentes* ['having'] for *ualentes* ['being able'] on the analogy of ἔχοντες.[12] I have noted several instances of this in the margins to prevent the reader from being tripped up. There is no doubt that he was familiar with all the liberal arts. In the book he wrote *Against the Valentinians*, Tertullian numbers among his sources 'Justin the philosopher and mar- 85 tyr, Miltiades the sophist of the churches, Irenaeus the most diligent inquirer into every kind of learning . . .'[13] Likewise Eusebius of Caesarea, in the catalogue of distinguished writers who by their lives and writings brought glory to the church around the time of Soter, says this of Irenaeus: 'Irenaeus was chief among those who have left us distinguished works on sound doctrine 90 and the apostolic faith.'[14] He was active mainly in the reign of Commodus.[15]

* * * * *

11 Allen (74n) points out that by 1570, when Nicolaus Gallasius published his edition of Irenaeus, this question had been resolved. Gallasius printed fragments of the Greek text found in Epiphanius *Panarion* and reported in his dedicatory epistle to Edmund Grindal, bishop of London, that a complete Greek manuscript was said to exist either at Venice or in the Vatican Library. No such manuscript is known, although substantial fragments of the Greek text are embedded in Epiphanius and Hippolytus.

12 Unlike its Greek equivalent, *noceo* 'to injure' in Latin is not usually found in the passive voice. The Greek equivalent of *habere*, ἔχειν, can mean both 'to have' and 'to be able.'

13 *Adversus Valentinianos* 5.1. Jean-Claude Fredouille, in his Latin-French edition *Contre les Valentiniens* 2 vols (Paris 1980–1) II 213, notes that *sophista* is the equivalent of *philosophus* and has no pejorative connotation. Cf the discussion of the phrase in Timothy David Barnes *Tertullian: A Historical and Literary Study* (Oxford 1971) 104, 232, and more broadly chapter 14, 'The Christian Sophist.'

14 *Historia ecclesiastica* 4.21. The following chapters, 4.22–4.29, further catalogue the writings of these champions of orthodoxy and some of their heretical opponents.

15 Emperor 161–92 AD. According to Quasten II 287–8, Irenaeus became bishop of Lyons in 177 or 178. The date of his death is unknown. The report that he was martyred in 202 is very late, unrecorded until Gregory of Tours (538–94)

Now that the time has come to say something about the writings of this remarkable man, I feel a stab of pain in my heart, because it seems that of all his admirable works this alone has come down to us intact. But we know that he wrote a book to Blastus *On Schism*,[16] and another to Florinus, 95 a presbyter who had defected from the church, entitled *On Sole Sovereignty or That God Is Not the Source of Evil*.[17] Blastus seems to have fallen into the same error as Florinus; he had once been a disciple of Polycarp, but later slipped into the Valentinian heresy.[18] Irenaeus also produced a work *On the Ogdoad*,[19] which St Jerome esteems very highly.[20] It was to this book that 100 Irenaeus added his *Entreaty to the Copyists*, which I have also prefixed to the present volume.[21] These were the only works that Eusebius had seen. Jerome also mentions a short volume *Against the Heathen* and another *On Discipline* and also a work addressed to his brother Martianus *On Apostolic Preaching*, and finally a volume of various tracts.[22] 105

* * * * *

HistoriaFrancorum 1.27 and *In gloria martyrum* 50, according to Berthold Altaner *Patrology* trans Hilda C. Graef (New York 1960) 150.

16 A letter addressed to a Roman heretic, known only from the citation of its title in Eusebius *Historia ecclesiastica* 5.20.1.

17 Only one fragment of this work survives, quoted in Eusebius *Historia ecclesiastica* 5.20.4–8; cf Quasten I 293.

18 The followers of Valentinus (d c 165) constituted the most widespread of the many Gnostic heretical groups of the late second century. Irenaeus *Adversus haereses* 1, especially 1.11.1 and 3.4.4, provides one of the earliest orthodox attacks on the Valentinians and remains a major source for study of this and other Gnostic groups. Tertullian *Adversus Valentinianos* 1.1 calls this sect 'the most numerous group of heretics.' See also Ep 1232 and n18.

19 The only part of this anti-Gnostic treatise of Irenaeus to survive is a passage at the end (see n21 just below), quoted in Eusebius *Historia ecclesiastica* 5.20.2. Cf Quasten I 293. As understood by Irenaeus, the dualism underlying the Gnostics' conception of the divine nature led them to conceive of God as an ogdoad, or eightfold nature.

20 *De viris inlustribus* 35 ed Carl Albrecht Bernoulli (Freiburg im Breisgau 1895; repr Frankfurt 1968) 25 / PL 23 683

21 Cf n19 above. This plea for painstaking accuracy by scribes must have been especially meaningful to an editor of classical and patristic texts like Erasmus: 'If, dear reader, you should transcribe this little book, I adjure you by the Lord Jesus Christ and by His glorious advent, when He comes to judge the living and the dead, to compare your transcript and correct it carefully with this copy, from which you have made your transcript. This adjuration likewise you must transcribe and include in your copy'; Eusebius *The History of the Church from Christ to Constantine* trans G.A. Williamson (Baltimore, MD 1965) 227.

22 *De viris inlustribus* 35 (as in n20 above)

Of all his many works only this present volume has been spared by the envious hand of time. I only wish I could offer it to you as it left his pen. The first and second books, since they consist mainly of a survey of the strange language and ideas of the heretics, caused me from time to time a lot of pain. No one, unless possessed of uncommon patience, will be able   110 to read these books without boredom. I made use of three manuscripts: one was copied in Rome and sent to me from there by that excellent patron of learning, Johannes Fabri;[23] the other two were provided on loan from the monasteries.[24] Tertullian was not much help for restoring the text, since there is even greater corruption in the language of that author.[25] In not a few   115 places I have resorted to conjecture; when a conjecture seemed uncertain, I merely noted it in the margin.

Relying only on the help of Scripture, Irenaeus fought against a multitude of heretics,[26] chief among whom was the famous Simon of Samaria,[27] a practised sorcerer, who dared to proclaim himself the most high god and   120

* * * * *

23 Cf Ep 1715.
24 Like the manuscript borrowed from Johannes Fabri (Ep 1715 n1), the two monastic manuscripts here mentioned, which must have been the principal textual sources for Erasmus' edition, cannot be identified with any surviving manuscript of Irenaeus. According to José Ruysschaert 'Le manuscrit "Romae descriptum" de l'édition Erasmienne d'Irénée de Lyon' in *Scrinium Erasmianum* I 265–6, a marginal note in Erasmus' edition identifies one of these manuscripts as coming from the abbey of Hirsau in Württemberg. Ruysschaert surmises that it may have perished in the fire at that monastery in 1692. The source of the second monastic manuscript has not been identified, but Ruysschaert concludes that comparison of textual variants suggests that it was the hypothetical unknown manuscript that the editor B. Hemmerdinger in the introduction to his edition of Irenaeus *Contre les hérésies* book 4 (Paris 1965) 21–37 labels *Codex Helvetius* and regards as the source of the existing *Codex Salmanticensis lat. 202*, which entered the library of the University of Salamanca in 1457 and is written on paper that watermark evidence connects with the region of Sion in Switzerland about 1444. Sion was the location of another medieval abbey known for its collection of manuscripts, and it is at least plausible that Erasmus borrowed this second monastic manuscript from that source.
25 Jean-Claude Fredouille in *Contre les Valentiniens* (n13 above) I 46 also remarks on 'the wretched state of the manuscript tradition.'
26 *Adversus haereses* alternates between description of the erroneous doctrines of the Gnostic heretics, in general and individually, and defence of the opposing orthodox doctrines on the basis of Scripture and the apostolic tradition handed down in direct succession from bishop to bishop.
27 Irenaeus *Adversus haereses* 1.23.1–4. This is the Simon Magus of Acts 8:9–13, 18–24; Irenaeus presents him as the first source of all subsequent Gnostic and magical heresies.

convinced people that his harlot Selene was the Supreme Mind.[28] This impostor earned a statue in Rome with the inscription 'In honour of Simon,
the sacred deity.'[29] His disciple Menander baptized, not in the name of Jesus, but in his own name; like Simon, he held that the world was not created
by God but by angels,[30] a misconception he seems to have borrowed from   125
Plato.[31] After Menander, Saturninus of Antioch said that this world was not
created by the supreme deity but by seven angels.[32]

After these came Basilides of Alexandria, who suffered from a worse
case of lunacy. Besides other strange doctrines he introduced his own
'supreme deity,' and to this fantastic creature he gave the equally fantas-   130
tic name of 'Abraxas.'[33] He seems to have sown the seed for the mad notions of Valentinus, for what Basilides called the 'heavenly ones' Valenti-

* * * * *

28 According to Irenaeus *Adversus haereses* 1.23.2 her name was Helen. Why Erasmus chose to call her Selene instead of keeping the name used by Irenaeus is
uncertain. Other patristic sources also used the name Helen. But patristic accounts of Simon's precursor (and subsequent disciple) Dositheos show that he
presented his wife (also named Helen) as the moon-goddess (Selene or Mene
in Greek, Luna in Latin), foreshadowing Simon's claim that his Helen (whom
he had freed from a life of prostitution and from a chain of reincarnations
that included Helen of Troy) was his First Thought (*Ennoia*), or even the Holy
Spirit. See O. Gruppe in PW V-2 1612–13. In Pseudo-Clement *Recognitiones* 2.8
(the text survives only in the Latin translation by Rufinus of Aquileia), the
woman associated with Dositheos is Luna (PG 1 1251–2); in Pseudo-Clement
Homiliae 2.23, for which the text (PG 2 91, 92) is in Greek, she is called Helen.
Both pseudo-Clementine references present Simon and Dositheos as disciples
of John the Baptist.
29 Irenaeus *Adversus haereses* 1.23.1
30 According to Irenaeus *Adversus haereses* 1.25, this successor and disciple of
Simon also came from Samaria and also practiced the magical arts. Irenaeus
attributes to him the doctrine that the world was created by angels.
31 Obviously, Plato knew nothing about angels. What Erasmus has in mind is
probably Plato's account of God's creative activity in the *Timaeus* 41A–42D,
69B–73A, where the creator (the demiurge) called into existence the immortal lesser deities (*daemones*) but commanded the latter to create mortal things
since these would be immortal and equal to the gods if created directly by the
supreme creator himself. This account of an indirect creation of spiritual and
material beings became even more prominent in Middle Platonism and Neoplatonism and is a common characteristic of the Gnostic systems denounced
by Irenaeus.
32 According to Irenaeus *Adversus haereses* 1.24.1–2, he was a disciple of Menander
and Simon and founder of a Gnostic group in Syria.
33 Irenaeus *Adversus haereses* 1.24.3–1.24.7 presents Basilides as a Gnostic teacher
at Alexandria. Cf n59 below and Ep 1232 n14.

nus called the 'aeons.'[34] Then Nicolas,[35] a master of depravity, joined his
predecessors in denying that the world was created by God. The Ophites[36]
advanced some strange and fantastic ideas about the aeons and about the 135
principal aeon, called 'Ialdaboth.' They were succeeded by Carpocrates, the
founder of Gnosticism,[37] who openly practised sorcery and boasted of his
familiar spirits, which reminds us of Socrates' *daimon.*[38] Cerinthus, who
came next, denied that the world was created by God and expounded the
false doctrine that Jesus was born of the seed of Joseph and that the Law 140
was given us by angels, not by God.[39] Ebion, on the other hand, made
so much of the Law that he undermined the gospel.[40] These strange ec-
centrics were followed by the strangest of all, Valentinus, a student of
Platonic philosophy and a man, despite his shortcomings, of some considerable learning and eloquence. He had ambitions to reach the rank 145
of bishop, but when a man who had professed the name of the Lord
under torture was preferred to himself, he took it badly and turned
his abilities to spreading confusion in the church by reducing all Christian doctrine to fantastic language and complicated myths.[41] Ptolemaeus[42]

* * * * *

34 On the thirty aeons which constitute the *pleroma*, or fullness of being, in his
Gnostic system, see Irenaeus *Adversus haereses* 1.10.3. Cf n18 above.
35 One of the first seven deacons consecrated by the apostles; Irenaeus *Adversus
haereses* 1.26.3. His followers supposedly led morally profligate lives, teaching
that fornication and the consumption of meat sacrificed to idols were indifferent acts. Irenaeus identifies this Gnostic sect with the Nicolaitans (*Nicolaitae*)
denounced in Rev 2:6.
36 On this Gnostic sect and on the *aeon* named by Erasmus Ialdaboth, born of the
divine Mother or Holy Spirit, see Irenaeus *Adversus haereses* 1.30.1-14.
37 Irenaeus *Adversus haereses* 1.25. Whether he was 'the founder of Gnosticism' depends on the definition of Gnosticism. Irenaeus does not call him
that, but Eusebius *Historia ecclesiastica*, a work well known to Erasmus, 4.3.9
does.
38 Plato *Apology* 31D, 40B
39 Irenaeus *Adversus haereses* 1.26.1. See also Ep 1333 n22.
40 Irenaeus *Adversus haereses* 1.26.2 describes the Ebionites as a sect who rejected
the apostle Paul on account of his 'apostasy' from observance of Jewish law.
See also Ep 1333 n22.
41 See n18 above. The story that Valentinus became a heretic only after his hopes
of being elected bishop of Rome were disappointed is not in Irenaeus but
appears in Tertullian *Adversus Valentinianos* 4.1.
42 An Italian follower of Valentinianus. His *Letter to Flora*, which is one of the
most important early Gnostic texts, divides the Mosaic law into three parts,
of which only the Ten Commandments came from the true God and remain
binding under the Christian dispensation. The text of the *Letter* survives in

and Secundus[43] made their contribution to these blasphemous inventions by   150
increasing the number of the aeons, dissenting from Valentinus on several
points. Heracleon taught the same doctrine as Valentinus, but tried hard to
appear different by innovations in language.[44] After him came Marcus and
Colarbasus, who were worthy disciples of Valentinus except for their ridiculous theory that all the mysteries of the faith could be related to the Greek   155
alphabet.[45]

Their successor was Cerdo,[46] who brought with him a witches' brew
of heresies.[47] He conceived the notion that there are two gods, one good, the
other cruel, and that the world was created by the cruel god. He rejected the
Law in its entirety and accepted only the Gospel of Luke, and not all of that.   160
As for the letters of the apostle Paul, he rejected some of them and parts of
others. He regarded the Acts of the Apostles and the Apocalypse as spurious

* * * * *

Epiphanius *Panarion* 33.3–33.7. Epiphanius was bishop of Constantia (Salamis)
in Cyprus. See Quasten I 261.

43 Irenaeus *Adversus haereses* 1.11.2

44 Quasten I 262 describes him as the most esteemed disciple of Valentinus, a
member of the Italian school of Valentinian heretics. On him cf Clement of
Alexandria *Stromata* 4.9 (PG 8 1281–2).

45 See Irenaeus *Adversus haereses* 1.13–1.21.5. Marcus is described as a magician
active in Asia who is notorious for the financial and sexual seduction of women
and whose followers had seduced women even as far west as the Rhone valley
– that is, in Irenaeus' own diocese. Cf Quasten I 266.

46 On this Syrian Gnostic, who resided at Rome, see Irenaeus *Adversus haereses*
1.27.1, where he is described as the predecessor of the heretic Marcion. Cf
Quasten I 268. Erasmus provides much more detail than is found on Cerdo
in Irenaeus, attributing to him many of the heresies that Irenaeus presents
as doctrines of his successor Marcion. This opinion is seconded by pseudo-
Tertullian *Adversus omnes haereses* 6.1. This text was included in the *Opera* of
Tertullian edited at Basel by Erasmus' friend and editorial collaborator Beatus
Rhenanus and so is a probable source of the details about Cerdo not found
in Irenaeus. See Erasmus' warm praise of Beatus' edition in Ep 1232. As the
introduction to that letter notes, Beatus' edition was published as a 'companion
volume' to Erasmus' own edition of Cyprian. Thus Erasmus certainly knew it,
and very likely this text as well. Whether Erasmus knew that *Adversus omnes
haereses* was spurious is unclear. Ep 1232 n13 suggests that he used it as if it
were genuine; cf n63 below.

47 Literally, 'a Lerna of heresies,' a variant on the proverb *Lerna malorum*, *Adagia* I iii 27. Lerna was a lake associated in mythology with the seven-headed
hydra. The image was frequently employed by writers on heresy. Irenaeus
Adversus haereses 1.30.15 uses it of the Ophites, and Hippolytus *Refutatio omnium haeresium* 5.11, in writing of the Naasenes (but the Hippolytus text was
not published until 1851).

and taught that Christ was the son of the good god and that he came down
to earth only in the form of a phantom and never truly suffered nor, in the
true meaning of the term, was he born. He believed in the resurrection of   165
the soul, but not of the body. From time to time he confessed his error, then
resumed his blasphemous teaching, sometimes secretly, sometimes openly.
In the end he was convicted and cut off from communion with the brethren
as someone beyond hope of cure. Next in the line of heresies came Marcion,
whose family belonged to the Pontus, a devoted adherent to the Stoic phi-   170
losophy and the son of a bishop. He was expelled from the church for raping
a girl, but, ironically, went on to deny marriage to Christians.[48] The blasphemous teachings of Cerdo and Marcion were carried on by a certain Lucanus, who remains a shadowy figure, since he deviated in no way from the
doctrine of his predecessors.[49] But Apelles, a pupil of Marcion's, wishing   175
to establish himself as the founder of a new school, criticized many points
in the teachings of his master, though without putting anything more sensible in their place.[50] He employed as an intermediary a girl called Philumena,[51] who, he claimed, was possessed of prophetic powers. Augustine

* * * * *

48 Irenaeus *Adversus haereses* 1.27.2–1.28.1 emphasizes Marcion's suppression of
   all parts of the New Testament that identify the God of Jesus with the creator
   of the universe as presented in the Old Testament, and also emphasizes his
   total prohibition of marriage, but Irenaeus is not the source for Erasmus' claim
   that Marcion was expelled from the church for raping a girl. This story does
   appear, however, in pseudo-Tertullian *Adversus omnes haereses* 6.2; on this text
   see n46 above.
49 According to Epiphanius *Panarion* 43.1, Lucian (Lucanus, in Erasmus' Latin)
   was a follower of Marcion and was succeeded by his fellow student Apelles.
   Pseudo-Tertullian *Adversus omnes haereses* 6.3 also mentions him as a follower
   of Marcion.
50 On this follower of Marcion, who seems to have abandoned the dualistic conception of God held by Marcion and by most Gnostics, but in a very indecisive way, see Quasten I 272–3. He is not discussed in Irenaeus, but Erasmus
   would have known references to him in Eusebius *Historia ecclesiastica* 5.13.2–7
   and in several anti-heretical works of Tertullian: *De carne Christi* 1.30–4; 6.1–3;
   8.1–3; 24.2; *Adversus Marcionem* 3.11.2; 4.17.11; *De praescriptione haereticorum* 6.6;
   10.8; 33.4–6; 34.4; 37.3; and in the spurious work attributed to Tertullian *Adversus omnes haereses* 6.4–6. All of these texts were included in Tertullian's *Opera*
   (Basel: Froben 1521) edited by Beatus Rhenanus and well known to Erasmus;
   see n46 above.
51 Mentioned by Apelles' opponent Rhodon, in a passage quoted by Eusebius *Historia ecclesiastica* 5.13.2. There is a brief reference to this prophetess in pseudo-
   Tertullian *Adversus omnes haereses* 6.6 and also in the genuine works of Tertullian mentioned in the preceding note.

said, on what authority I do not know, that she was the protégé of a certain   180
Severus.[52] But Eusebius and Tertullian agree on the version I have given.
Somewhere among these strange individuals we should place Potitus and
Basiliscus, who followed Marcion in supposing that two fundamental principles operate in the world.[53] Syrenus, advancing an even madder theory, introduced three principles, or three natures.[54] After all of these came Tatian,[55]   185
who, though a pupil of Justin,[56] turned heretic and revived the pernicious
ideas of Valentinus and Marcion. He had Calistio as his pupil.[57]

The abominable filth that flowed from Simon Magus had a long history and proved remarkably difficult to stop. Even when the name of Valentinus had already been forgotten, there was still no shortage of Valentinians.   190
I doubt if the end would have come at all had not Montanus appeared
on the scene, for he robbed all the others of their influence by proclaim-
ing himself the Holy Spirit promised by Christ to lead us into all truth.[58]

* * * * *

52 *De haeresibus* 24. The text in PL 42 30 confines the passage on Philumena to a
note, since the editor found the passage in the printed editions but not in the
manuscripts. Allen (172n) observes that Erasmus included this passage in his
edition of 1529 but that the Louvain editors of 1576 already bracketed it as
doubtful.

53 Both Potitus and Basiliscus are briefly mentioned by Eusebius *Historia ecclesiastica* 5.13.2–4 as followers of Marcion's belief in two opposed divine principles.

54 Eusebius *Historia ecclesiastica* 5.13.2–4, as quoted by Quasten I 273, but Quasten
has the name as Syneros.

55 Irenaeus *Adversus haereses* 1.27.1 describes him as a former disciple of Justin
Martyr who fell away from true doctrine after Justin's martyrdom and was
the first to deny that the first man (Adam) had attained salvation. He became
the founder of a sect known as the Encratites. See Quasten I 220–8, 274. Two of
his writings, perhaps written before he became a heretic, survive. His *Oratio
ad Graecos* was not published until 1546. A Latin version of his *Diatessaron*, a
harmony of the Gospels, which presents a continuous narrative of Christ's life
drawn from the four canonical Gospels, was known in the West since the sixth
century and was widely used during the Middle Ages, though it was not used
in the Greek East, and no Greek text has been identified. An edition of it was
published by J. Schoeffer at Mainz in 1524.

56 The most important Greek apologist of the second century and the teacher of
Tatian. He was martyred in 165. See Quasten I 196–219. His works were not
published until after Erasmus' death.

57 References to this Gnostic heretic cannot be located in the works of Irenaeus
or any of the other sources that Erasmus commonly used, such as Eusebius,
Epiphanius, and Jerome, nor in the modern patristic handbooks of Quasten
and Altaner.

58 Montanus, a Phrygian convert to Christianity, active from about the middle
of the second century, emphasized the presence of the Holy Spirit in believers

Manichaeus, however, seems to have borrowed some of his erroneous ideas
from Basilides.[59] The situation had much in common with a stubborn fever,   195
now mild, now severe, taking on different forms, but never ceasing until
it turns into delirium or some other serious illness. Works were written to
refute these fiends by Justin, whom Irenaeus cites several times,[60] and by
Miltiades,[61] Proculus,[62] and Tertullian. If you take the trouble to read the
erudite books that Tertullian wrote *Against Marcion* and *Against the Valen-*   200
tinians or his work *On Heresies*[63] or *On the Prescript against the Heretics*, you
will understand the writings of Irenaeus better.

* * * * *

and founded a movement whose leading figures, many of them women, experienced religious raptures, spoke in tongues, and uttered prophecies. The
Montanist movement demanded extremely strict moral discipline and attracted
many followers in the late second and third centuries, of whom the most famous was a former defender of orthodoxy, Tertullian (c 160–c 225), the first
major Latin theologian. Irenaeus focuses his attention on Gnostic and Judaizing heresies, especially the former, and does not deal with the type of ecstatic,
Spirit-related heresies represented by Montanus and his followers.

59 Manichaeus or Mani (c 216–276) founded a dualistic religion that borrowed its
conception of God from Persian Zoroastrianism but also incorporated Christian elements. Although regarded as illegal, Manichaeism spread rapidly into
the Roman empire, where it attracted the young Augustine. Later it was considered to be a Christian heresy and eventually suppressed. Mani's belief
that an eternal struggle goes on between light (identified with spirit and the
good) and darkness (identified with matter and evil) is sometimes, though not
accurately, associated with the Gnostic heresy of Basilides. Cf Quasten 1 259.

60 Cf *Adversus haereses* 4.6.2, where Irenaeus cites a work by Justin, *Against Mar-*
cion, which is known only from this citation and one by Eusebius *Historia*
ecclesiastica 4.11.8–10.

61 Greek apologist of the second half of the second century, probably a pupil of
Justin Martyr. He is known to have written a treatise against the Montanists,
but all of his works are lost and are known only from citations by later patristic authors. See Quasten 1 228. Tertullian *Adversus Valentinianos* 5.1 refers to
Miltiades, 'the sophist of the churches' [that is, a professional rhetorician], as
one of his sources. On the use of the term 'sophist' in patristic literature see
n13 above.

62 Tertullian *Adversus Valentinianos* 5.1 refers to 'our Proculus' as one of his
sources, evidently citing a lost work by that author.

63 If Erasmus here is referring to the work *Adversus omnes haereses*, he has in mind
a work falsely attributed to Tertullian. His reference immediately following to
a genuine work, *De praescriptione haereticorum*, makes it likely that he did accept
the attribution to Tertullian, a conclusion made more likely by the inclusion
of the work in the *Opera* of Tertullian edited by his friend Beatus Rhenanus.
See n46 above.

I think I have gone on long enough, my lord bishop, to explain the nature of this work, and the time has come to bring this preface to an end. But first I want to tell you in a few words the thoughts that came 205 into my head when I was working on this subject. No language can express my wonder at the inscrutable purposes of God, who in a marvellous way has defended his bride the church, purified her, instructed her, raised her up, and glorified her; and in all his actions there was nothing that was not totally foreign to the ways of men, as he himself tells us through 210 the mouth of Isaiah: 'For my thoughts are not your thoughts, neither are your ways my ways, saith the Lord. For as the heavens are higher than the earth, so are my ways higher than your ways, and my thoughts than your thoughts.'[64] Just as the Lord himself by coming down from heaven opened up the way to heaven and in taking on the form of a slave prepared for 215 himself dominion over all that is in heaven and on earth; just as by bearing the deepest shame he obtained eternal glory, by suffering he overcame the enemy, and by his death won eternal life; so he helped his small and feeble flock to advance by means completely alien to the ways of this world. By the innocent he confounded the wisdom of the world, by the few he con- 220 quered all the nations of the earth, by the weak he brought low the might of tyrants, by the unwarlike he destroyed every force that rose against God, and by the humble and meek he eclipsed the whole pomp of the world; with the help of sheep he tamed the lions, and with doves he banished the serpents.   225

He allowed the world and the devil to invade his little sheepfold with all their wiles and all their might, but in some mysterious way he turned all that was evil to good for his elect. For he alone, the King of Kings, knows how to use what is good and turn what is wicked to his glory and the salvation of his church. The tiny band of Christ's humble followers had to face 230 the fanaticism of the Jews, the arrogance of the Pharisees, the power of the priests, the hocus-pocus of the sorcerers, the learning of philosophers, the betrayal of heretics, and the might of kings armed with laws and the sword. But the sheepfold of Christ destroyed the power of Satan with all its wiles. The Lord guided the plans and actions of men, and out of persecution and 235 martyrdom the church prospered and grew strong. The philosophy of the gospel gathered strength from the yapping of godless philosophers. The chicanery of the sorcerers showed up the divine power of Christ working among his disciples. The exertions of schismatics brought the faithful into a

* * * * *

64 Isa 55:8–9

closer harmony, created, so to speak, a common battleline, and the ungodly   240
teaching of heretics forced them to study the holy mysteries of Scripture.
And so it came about that while the Jews fought against the gospel with
all their zeal for the Law but without true understanding, we became more
certain that the darkness of the Law had been superseded, and the glory of
the gospel shone with a new light; again, when the oppressor tried to ex-   245
tinguish the Christian faith with insults, torture, and death, he deepened
faith, kindled the flames of charity, strengthened hope; and while he put the
courage of the faithful to the test, he crowned it with glory. Finally, truth,
when challenged by the sophistries of heretics, learned to put on the armour
of sacred Scripture and grew stronger under attack.   250

The first battle of the church was with the Jews – I only wish that
a remnant of this faith did not survive even to this day![65] Here the apostle Paul proved a strong champion of the liberty of the gospel. Peter vanquished the prince of sorcery. The second battle was with philosophers and
heretics, who as a rule used the weapons of philosophy to make war on   255
the gospel. Their attacks were borne, after the apostles, by men of great
learning and eloquence. We must not, however, condemn the sober study of
philosophy on the ground that almost all heresies began with the philosophers, for it was also through the efforts of philosophers that these heresies were stamped out. Valentinus the philosopher attacked the church, but   260
it was the philosopher Justin and the philosopher Irenaeus who defended
it. Marcion the philosopher declared war on the truth, but the philosopher
Tertullian destroyed the enemy.[66] Celsus the philosopher spewed out blas-

* * * * *

65 Erasmus fully shared his contemporaries' hostility to the Jews of his own time,
though he nevertheless conceded that they had certain rights, those that Johann Reuchlin had tried to defend. See Ep 1006:146–50 (addressed to Reuchlin's antagonist Jacob of Hoogstraten).

66 Although he was learned in Greek philosophy, Tertullian might have been
surprised or even displeased to be labelled 'the philosopher.' One of his major assumptions is that pagan philosophy and religious faith have no common ground and are in fact inevitably opposed, a view summarized in his famous rhetorical question in *De praescriptione haereticorum* 7: 'What indeed has
Athens to do with Jerusalem?' a question that he immediately answered by
denouncing 'all attempts to produce a mottled Christianity of Stoic, Platonic
and dialectic composition' (translation by Peter Holmes in *The Ante-Nicene Fathers* ed Alexander Roberts and James Donaldson, 10 vols [New York 1911–26;
repr Grand Rapids MI 1950–8] III). Cf Quasten I 320–1. Tertullian is now regarded as a rhetorician and a legist, for his works show clear traces of training
in the law, a subject that he seems to have practised professionally until his
conversion about 193.

phemies against Christ,[67] but Origen, a better philosopher, turned his blasphemies to the glory of Christ.[68] Libanius the sophist defended idolatry,[69] 265
but Chrysostom, a better writer than he, championed the true worship of
God.[70] Symmachus the orator did the same as Libanius,[71] but Prudentius, a
better orator, cut him to pieces.[72] And so I have good hopes that the Lord, in
his unsearchable wisdom, will bring good out of the present turmoil in the
church and that he will raise up men like Irenaeus to settle our differences 270
and restore peace to the world.

* * * * *

67 Platonic philosopher who in the years 175–81 AD wrote a philosophical attack
on Christianity, *The True Doctrine*, which elicited the important rebuttal *Contra
Celsum* by the first major Christian theologian, Origen (c 184–c 254)
68 Origen (c 185–c 254), a native of Alexandria, learned in the philosophy of the
Middle Platonists and a student of philosophy and literature under the traditional founder of Neoplatonism, Ammonius Saccas. Although some of his
ideas, or ideas attributed to him, were later condemned as heretical, he was one
of the creative figures of early Christian theology. Erasmus recognized and
admired the theological power of Origen even in the face of criticism from
conservative theologians who suspected his authority because doctrines attributed to him were condemned long after his death. In 1527 Erasmus edited
a Latin translation of a fragment from Origen's commentary on St Matthew,
and he was the general editor of the *Opera* of Origen published by the Froben
press in September 1536, two months after his own death.
69 Greek rhetorician (314–93), an influential literary figure and teacher of rhetoric
whose pupils included important Christian theologians like John Chrysostom
and Theodore of Mopsuestia but whose own intellectual and religious position strongly favoured old classical values, including traditional pagan cults,
at a time when Christianity was gaining the upper hand. Erasmus had published the Greek text of three declamations of Libanius, *Aliquot declamatiunculae graecae*, with Latin translations, at the press of Dirk Martens (Louvain 1519;
NK 1367), and after he settled at Basel, the Froben press reprinted it in 1522.
Cf Ep 1341A n57.
70 On this famous patristic bishop, preacher, and theologian see Ep 1661 n2.
71 Quintus Aurelius Symmachus (340–402), Gallo-Roman orator and imperial administrator, an outspoken defender of the old Roman cults, known especially
for his unsuccessful attempt (384/5), while prefect of the city (of Rome), to
persuade the emperor Valentinian II to restore the pagan Altar of Victory to
the Roman senate-house.
72 Aurelius Clemens Prudentius (348–c 410) was the greatest Christian Latin poet
of the late empire. Among his writings was a poem in Latin hexameters, *Contra orationem Symmachi*, opposing Symmachus on the issue of restoring the Altar of Victory. He also wrote a treatise against the heretic Marcion. Erasmus
published a commentary on two hymns of Prudentius as an annex to his commentary on the *Nux* of Ovid in 1524 (see Epp 1402, 1404); they are translated
in CWE 29.

Meanwhile, excellent bishop, I hope you will be pleased to accept this *Irenaeus* of mine and give it the favourable omen of your approval, for it sees the light of day under the good auspices of your name. What has persuaded me to send it to you is not so much your esteem for me (which is as constant   275 as it is undeserved) as the probity of your character, which is celebrated by all, and your wonderful good sense and admirable courtesy. But no praise I could give you is more fitting for a bishop than this, that you are ever striving for peace and concord among the people of Christ. What makes these qualities all the more remarkable is the fact that while still in the   280 prime of life you are filling the role of Nestor[73] both for our illustrious prince Ferdinand[74] and for the church of Christ. I have said nothing that is not known to everyone. Nor am I praising you for your abilities, but giving thanks to God, and congratulating myself, for the gifts with which he has endowed you. May he from whom alone true happiness proceeds   285 bless your Lordship with all good things.

Basel, 27 August 1526

1739 / From Johannes Fabri   Speyer, 28 August 1526

On the writer see Epp 386 introduction, 1690 introduction. By this time he was suffragan bishop of Constance, and since 1523 he had been a close adviser of Archduke Ferdinand and hence also a close associate of Bernhard von Cles, prince-bishop of Trent. He was sympathetic to humanism and to humanistic ideas of church reform and a persistent admirer of Erasmus. For a time he felt some sympathy for both Luther and Zwingli but from the early 1520s became openly hostile to the Reformation while still favouring moderate Catholic reform. As an official of the diocese of Constance and of the Hapsburg court, he took an active role in the Baden disputation of May and June 1526, at which the majority of Catholic cantons of Switzerland overwhelmingly upheld the traditional Catholic faith against the Reformation. See Ep 1708 introduction. Fabri had also helped Erasmus' edition of St Irenaeus by providing him the text of a Vatican manuscript that Erasmus used in the final stages of his work

* * * * *

73 The aged counsellor of the Greeks in Homer
74 Archduke Ferdinand of Hapsburg, younger brother of the emperor and since 1522 regent of the hereditary Hapsburg lands in Germany, who was still quite young (born in 1503). Although he already showed signs of being an astute political figure, he relied on a circle of loyal and more experienced advisers. Bernhard von Cles, prince-bishop of Trent, the addressee of this letter, was the most influential of these.

on the edition (see Ep 1715 n1). Erasmus had already complied with Fabri's request that he dedicate his edition of St Irenaeus to Bishop Bernhard; see Ep 1738, dated at Basel on the preceding day. Fabri was currently in Speyer in connection with the imperial diet, which sat between 25 June and 27 August. The original manuscript of this letter survives at Leipzig. It was published in Förstemann/Günther in 1904.

Greetings. I wish you were so sure of my good faith, which has now been tested so many times, that you would never feel the slightest inclination to doubt it. I have such respect for your erudition and your way of life that I would judge it quite wrong to urge upon you any course that would be out of line with your merits. You will always have in Fabri a true and faithful   5
friend, quite unlike those people we see nowadays whose only aim is to flatter.

You would perhaps have preferred, dear Erasmus, to dedicate your Irenaeus to someone else, because you do not yet fully appreciate that man's mind and qualities. But if you continue as you have begun along the path I   10
have recommended, neither he nor you will ever have cause to regret it. The bishop of Trent is delighted with the prospect of having his name handed down to posterity in your writings.[1] As a recompense, not only will you receive from him a most elegant and valuable gift, but you will also have something from his most serene Highness the prince that will do full justice   15
to his princely dignity and to the unparalleled learning and reputation of Erasmus. So as soon as the work is finished, get a copy ready for the bishop of Trent. You will soon discover that your suspicions were quite unfounded, since he is all set to demonstrate his generosity.

The assembly, which seemed at first blush to threaten unimaginable   20
ruin both to religion and to our other interests, reached a fairly happy and satisfactory conclusion for everyone.[2] As for the other matters, act with due prudence and as you judge best. Farewell.

Speyer, 28 August 1526

Your friend, Fabri   25

To the eminent and erudite Master Erasmus of Rotterdam, his very dear friend

* * * * *

1739
1 At Fabri's urging, Erasmus had dedicated his edition of Irenaeus *Adversus haereses* to Bernhard von Cles, the bishop of Trent; see the preceding letter.
2 The just-completed imperial diet. See the introduction to this letter.

1739A / From Matthias Pistor   [Speyer? 1526?]

Although the manuscript of this letter survived into the twentieth century in the Rehdiger collection at Wrocław, L.K. Enthoven omitted it from his collection of Erasmus' correspondence (1906), 'perhaps because of its singular Latinity, which is difficult to translate satisfactorily,' according to P.S. Allen in the headnote for his edition of it (Allen VIII, unpaginated fol d2), a judgment seconded by the present translator. Almost nothing is known about Pistor except that he matriculated at the University of Heidelberg on 11 January 1501; in this letter he claimed an MA degree and identified Leiningen (near Worms) as his place of origin or residence. The contents seem to indicate that he wrote from Speyer, and that he was (or had been) there during the imperial diet in the summer of 1526. The circumstances of what he calls his 'exile' and the contents of two earlier begging letters that he sent to Erasmus remain totally unknown, but his connections (desired in one case and apparently actual in the second) with Henry, count Palatine and bishop of Worms, and Johannes Fabri, as well as his desire to take refuge with the rector of Überlingen, Johann Schlupf, all closely linked to the Hapsburg dynasty and all defenders of Catholicism, suggest that Pistor might have been ejected from a benefice or some other public office for opposition to the Reformation. One other possible motive for his desire to reach Überlingen, in view of the serious illness mentioned in his letter, is that this region on the Bodensee (Lake Constance) has a mild climate and was noted for its production of apples, grapes, and other agricultural products. Pistor's appeal to Erasmus, whom he obviously knew only by reputation, may be explained by sixteenth-century travel routes. A traveller headed from Speyer to the Bodensee, especially one who had been seriously ill, would likely proceed up the Rhine to Basel and then would follow the regular trade route leading from Basel towards Constance.

Greetings. It was because of my exile, most learned Erasmus, that in the past you have received two begging letters from me written in times of need, and this will be the third. Since one cannot approach anyone one wishes, I am proposing to address your Excellency[1] with these letters, both open and sealed, enclosing testimonial letters (from my native region) with information about myself and my family.

* * * * *

1739A
1 Latin *praestantiam*, apparently short for *tuam praestantiam*

I set out for Worms, then travelled on to Speyer at the time of the imperial diet and awaited (to take my leave)[2] the arrival of our most illustrious prince, the most reverend Henry, count Palatine of the Rhine, duke of Bavaria, bishop of Utrecht, and bishop-elect of Worms,[3] and hap- 10 pily[4] I reached both places. I shall tell you about them, if you would be interested.

At Speyer, for almost the space of a month, I was greatly shaken by recurring attacks of a burning fever. But thanks to the goodness of God and his abundant grace,[5] I began to recover. Armed with a letter of ref- 15 erence from Dr Johannes Fabri[6] for Johann Schlupf, the eminent doctor of

* * * * *

2 The Latin is *dimissorii ex parte*; the English translation is a guess at what Pistor may have meant. *Litterae dimissoriae* were letters from a bishop authorizing a priest of his diocese to move to another diocese: 'dimissory letters' in English. The adjective *dimissorii* can also refer to leave-taking, but in this case the word seems to be used as a noun. The present translator suggests that the phrase may mean, 'I waited for the bishop in the role of leave-taker.'
3 On Henry, a younger brother of the Palatine elector whose family and political connections ensured him a rich accumulation of ecclesiastical benefices and incomes, see Ep 612:15n. Henry had been bishop of Worms and simultaneously of Utrecht from 1524 but resigned the latter bishopric in 1529. He later (1540) received the diocese of Freising while retaining the see of Worms until his death there in 1552. For his acquisition of the humanistic library of Johann von Dalberg, see Ep 1774. Why Henry is called bishop-elect rather than bishop of a diocese he had held for more than two years is uncertain. It may be that his formal consecration as bishop of a second diocese was deferred, either because possessing the revenues was more important than taking up the duties of the office or because such blatant pluralism at the episcopal level required the prior acquisition of a dispensation from Rome, even for a member of an electoral family. (Such a dispensation had been necessary in the notorious case of Albert of Brandenburg. His acquisition of the archbishopric of Mainz had required complicated political and financial negotiations with Rome, which led to the preaching of the indulgence that provided the occasion for Martin Luther's criticism of indulgences in 1517, the event that set off the Protestant Reformation).
4 Latin *gratiose*. The word really means 'showing favour,' which does not make sense here. Perhaps Pistor misused it for *gratis* or *gratuito* 'to no purpose,' that is, he got no help at either place.
5 Another puzzling phrase (Latin *proulterioris gratiae*). The obscure compound *proulterior*, typical of Pistor's strange Latin style, seems to mean 'going beyond.'
6 See Ep 1739. Evidently Pistor's presence in Speyer during the imperial diet gave him an opportunity to gain a letter of reference addressed to Johann

sacred theology and parish priest in Überlingen,[7] I am planning to make my way there. I go about seeking bodily sustenance and aid for the journey in order to find a remedy for my present trouble, and I move from place to place driven by the genuineness of my need, never settling in 20 any one spot. I believe that great men are attracted by all that pertains to genuine integrity. Inspired by this confident belief and with reason as my guide, I make my suppliant prayer for the blessings of health and request that you be gracious enough to relieve me from starvation by supporting my travel at least as far as Constance and by any other assistance 25 which it may please you to offer out of the goodness of your heart and in the inestimable joy[8] of charity. I have no doubt that, in return, God in his might and majesty will reward you richly. In a word I am begging for health.

Signed personally by me, Matthias Pistor of Leiningen, Master of Arts, 30 the writer and author of this letter

Let this be delivered to Dr Erasmus of Rotterdam at his home in Basel or to his accustomed residence.

1740 / To Pieter Gillis   Basel, 29 August 1526

On this trusted friend, city clerk of Antwerp, see Epp 1671 n6, 1696 introduction. As this letter shows, Gillis continued to manage some of Erasmus' financial affairs in the Netherlands even though the merchant-banker Erasmus Schets had become Erasmus' principal financial agent there in 1525. Erasmus published this letter in his *Opus epistolarum.*

* * * * *

Schlupf. In addition, Fabri was on friendly terms with Erasmus and hence a good name to drop when writing this request for financial help.
7 Schlupf, probably born at Bittelbrunn near Lake Constance, was schooled at Engen near his birthplace and already had an MA degree from some university when he matriculated at the University of Freiburg in 1503. He obtained a licence in theology and became a member of the faculty of theology there. He had received the parish of Überlingen, a small city located on an arm of the Bodensee, even before he went to Freiburg, and from 1506 he resided there and discharged the duties of his priestly office. From at least 1521 he was a leader of the struggle to prevent the spread of the Reformation in the area, preaching against the Reform-minded clergy of Constance; and in May 1526 he was one of the clergy who represented the bishop of Constance at the Baden Disputation.
8 Latin *inestimabili ... tripudio*; cf Esther 8:16.

The young man who brought your letter to me[1] told me as a fact that your wife Cornelia had passed away.[2] I did not want to believe such sad news, though he insisted it was true. If it is true, I am sure you will wish to marry again and I am not going to dissuade you. But this I do ask, if you will permit me the liberty, that in the meantime you avoid all the follies of youth.   5
I understand your nature and I realize you are young. You are not yet of an age when such behaviour would be thought unbecoming, though you are not far away from your fortieth year. But remember you are the father of a large family, that the dignity of your office imposes certain obligations upon you, and, above all, that God (unless I am mistaken) has marked you out   10
for better things. In saying this (to be quite frank with you), I am thinking

* * * * *

1740
1 Allen (1n) suggests that this may have been Quirinus Talesius of Haarlem (Quirijn Dirckszoon van Lipsen), who is first mentioned by name in Ep 1890 but had probably been in Erasmus' service since 1524, employed as his *famulus* (secretary, confidential messenger, financial agent, and sometimes valet), a position which he retained until 1531, demonstrating outstanding loyalty and concern for Erasmus' interests. Talesius (1505–73) matriculated at Cologne in 1523 and studied at Louvain with Conradus Goclenius, who probably recommended him to Erasmus as a successor to Lieven Algoet. As was his custom, Erasmus recommended him for employment when he was ready to adopt a more settled existence, and Talesius returned to Haarlem, where he obtained the position of pensionary, married, and eventually left government service to become a clothmaker like his father. He prospered and was repeatedly elected burgomaster between 1543 and 1570. He died during the wars of religion in 1573, when, as a prominent local Catholic, he was lynched by a mob in reprisal for the execution of prisoners by the Spanish army that was then besieging the city. See Allen Ep 1966 introduction. Erasmus' will of 1527 leaves him a bequest; see 548 and n55 below.
2 Gillis had married Cornelia Sandrien in 1514, and they had nine children. Cornelia is mentioned in Erasmus' colloquy 'Epithalamium of Pieter Gillis,' which includes a poem honouring the couple (CWE 39 520–30). Erasmus began his *Epithalamium* in the year of their marriage and stayed in their home on several visits between 1515 and 1517, but he did not publish the *Epithalamium* until 1524. Gillis did remarry later in 1526 and after the death of his second wife in 1529 or 1530 took a third wife. In 1530 Erasmus also wrote two Latin epitaphs commemorating Cornelia, whom he knew, and one for the second wife, whom he never met (CWE 85–6 nos 83–4, 85 pages 162–5, 164–5, 554–5 [notes] / *The Poems of Desiderius Erasmus* ed C. Reedyk [Leiden 1956] nos 126–7, 128). He sent all of these to Gillis along with Allen Ep 2260, dated from Freiburg on 28 January 1530. The poems show that Erasmus believed that Cornelia was the mother of eight children and the second wife, Maria Denys, the mother of one daughter by Gillis.

of my own interests; for I would rather lose half my property than such
a friend. And I have a case before my eyes. As soon as X^3 ceased to be a
husband and became a suitor, he changed so much you would not believe
he is the same man. He forgets his old friends and his old pursuits.   15

I believe you have taken care of preparing the Jerome[4] and sending it
to the archbishop of Canterbury.[5] I have seen nothing yet of the linen that

* * * * *

3 Allen (13n) surmises that Erasmus may be referring to his old friend, patron,
and former pupil William Blount, Lord Mountjoy, who was widowed (for the
third time) in 1521 and remarried in 1523. After a letter (missing) from Mountjoy in 1521 (answered by Ep 1219), the only trace of correspondence between
them is a letter that Mountjoy wrote in 1525 in his capacity as chamberlain
to Queen Catherine asking Erasmus to dedicate to the queen a work on the
obligations of marriage. This letter from Mountjoy is also missing, but Erasmus refers to it in Ep 1624. Erasmus' response to the request was his *Institutio
christiani matrimonii*, published by Froben in August 1526 and dedicated to the
queen. Even then, he was left without a reply from either the queen or Mountjoy. On his efforts to obtain acknowledgment and a gift from the queen, and
his speculation about the reasons for her failure to reply and for Mountjoy's silence, see Ep 1727 introduction. Only at the beginning of May 1527 did Mountjoy resume direct communication (Allen Ep 1816), acknowledging receipt of
two letters (now missing) to which he had not previously replied, admitting
his negligence in not replying sooner, and assuring Erasmus of his continued
devotion. Probably Mountjoy's awkward position as chamberlain to the queen
whom King Henry wished to divorce, not any domestic change related to his
own remarriage (as Erasmus here surmises) was the principal cause of the decline in direct communication – assuming, of course, that Mountjoy really was
the anonymous inattentive friend referred to in the letter.
4 The first three volumes (the correspondence) of the revised second edition of
St Jerome's *Lucubrationes omnes* had begun coming off Froben's press in the
summer of 1524. Cf Epp 1465, the dedication to Archbishop William Warham
(to whom the first edition of 1516 also was dedicated), and 1488. The present
letter marks the publication of the last of the nine volumes of the revised
edition.
5 Erasmus relied on his learned friend Gillis to make sure that a full set of his
new edition of the works of Jerome was properly bound and sent to William
Warham, the most generous of his many English patrons. On Warham see
Ep 188 introduction. The persistence and generosity of Warham's support of
Erasmus is reflected throughout the correspondence and is warmly acknowledged in Erasmus' preface to the reader in Chevallon's edition of Jerome's
Opera (Paris 1533). Despite his habitual opposition to burdening the revenues
of parishes with payments to non-residents who did not perform the duties
of pastoral care of souls, Warham granted Erasmus a pension charged against
the revenues of the parish of Aldington in Kent, explicitly declaring that he
made this exception to his policy because of the value of Erasmus' scholarship

Dilft is sending and that you purchased.[6] I am expecting your brother[7] to
deliver it along with the Prudentius and the Seneca[8] and whatever balance
there is in my account. The bearer of this letter is the man who painted   20
my portrait.[9] I shall not bother you with a recital of his merits, but he is
a distinguished artist. If he wants to visit Quinten[10] and you do not have
the time to take him yourself, you can get a servant to show him the house.
The arts are not appreciated here, so he is off to England in the hope of
scraping together a few angels. He will take any letters you care to write.   25
Farewell.

    Basel, 29 August 1526
    Give my regards to the cantor[11]

   * * * * *

to the church at large. This benefice supplied a significant portion of Erasmus'
regular income from the time it was granted in 1512 until the end of his life.
See Epp 255 introduction, 1583 n1.

6 Erasmus' *famulus* Frans van der Dilft was in the Netherlands, making preparations to settle either in his native land or at the imperial court in Spain but
still remaining sporadically in Erasmus' service through 1527–8 and again in
1529. At this time he was purchasing cloth at Antwerp for Erasmus' use. On
Dilft see Epp 1545 n12, 1663 introduction.

7 Frans Gillis seems to have been a merchant, and his attendance at the Frankfurt fair the preceding spring had already created the opportunity for transfer
of money that Pieter Gillis had held for Erasmus. See Epp 1654, 1681, 1682,
1696. On the present occasion Frans carried letters as well as books and money
for Erasmus, probably again travelling to the autumn Frankfurt fair and ex-
changing packets of letters and other goods with Johann Froben, whose business regularly took him to this important book-distribution market. For an
earlier reference to plans for this transfer of money, see Ep 1696 n2.

8 These are probably manuscripts that Erasmus desired for his editorial work,
since he reissued an edition of two poems of the early Christian poet Prudentius in 1528 and published the *Opera* of Lucius Annaeus Seneca in 1529
(Basel: Froben and Herwagen, March 1529). In Ep 1758 he asked Pieter Gillis
to send a Seneca (probably a manuscript) and a manuscript of St Augustine's
De civitate Dei to the Basel [*sic*] fair; clearly a slip for the Frankfurt fair.

9 Hans Holbein the Younger; cf Epp 1397 n1, 1452 n25. His arrival in England
is mentioned in a letter of 18 December 1526 from Thomas More to Erasmus;
see Ep 1770:77–9 and n11.

10 The painter Quinten Metsys, though born at Louvain, spent most of his career
at Antwerp, where Gillis lived, and was a highly regarded and prosperous
artist. On his twin portraits of Erasmus and Gillis, see Epp 584:8n, 616:10n,
654 introduction.

11 The identity of this person, presumably a clergyman having charge of the music in a collegiate church at Antwerp, could not be determined. Erasmus had

1741 / From Ludwig Baer   [Basel, c August 1526]

Erasmus had recently received a copy of a book by Leo Jud, *Vf entdeckung doc-tor Erasmi von Roterdam der dückischen arglisten eynes tütschen büchlins, antwurt vnd entschuldigung,* which was a sharp reply to the German version of Eras-mus' *Detectio praestigiarum,* in which Erasmus had attacked the anonymous au-thor (actually Jud) of a book that tried to show that Erasmus' eucharistic doc-trine agreed with Luther's. See Epp 1708 nn1 and 2, 1737 introduction and n1. Jud had been living since 1523 at Zürich, where he was minister of the parish of St Peter and one of the closest associates of Huldrych Zwingli. Since Eras-mus found involvement in such intricate theological questions repugnant and was too busy to read and analyse Jud's book closely, he sent it to his close friend Baer, professor of theology at Basel, whose judgment on theological questions he trusted. On Baer see Ep 1674 n17. The original letter survived in the library of the Société de l'histoire du protestantisme français in Paris, with a copy in the City and University Library at Basel. It was first published by Allen in 1926.

Greetings. When that Zoilus[1] of yours from Zürich says on the third page of the book he sent your Excellency that in his earlier volume his role was that of translator and paraphrast, it is clear from the letter[2] he wrote in Latin that this remark must be understood to apply, not to the book as a whole, but only to the excerpts from your works and the works of Luther. In the   5 letter he insists strongly on his own authorship of the earlier publication, while claiming that only one other person was aware of it. Farewell.

Your friend, Ludwig Baer

To the Reverend Master Erasmus of Rotterdam

* * * * *

many long-standing acquaintances with canons of collegiate chapters in his native land – for example, with Nicolaas de Beuckelaer, canon of Notre Dame at Antwerp, and from 1512 to 1534 treasurer of that chapter (see Ep 1594 n12).

1741
1 Cynic philosopher of the fourth century BC notorious for his bitter attacks on respected authorities such as Isocrates, Plato, and especially Homer. Cf Ep 1658 n8.
2 This letter from Jud is lost, but Erasmus in Allen Ep 1804:154–9 implies that it may have been even more aggressive than his book in defending Jud's first, anonymous publication by accusing Erasmus of being the anonymous author of the infamous satire *Julius exclusus* (as he was).

1742 / From Juan Maldonado   Burgos, 1 September 1526

The purpose of this letter is twofold. First, the writer wanted to inform Erasmus of the overwhelmingly favourable reception of his publications and his ideas among those Spaniards who were truly learned (that is, the humanists) and even among pious individuals who could not read Latin but who had heard reports about him or had an opportunity to read recent Spanish translations of the *Enchiridion* and some of the *Colloquies*. The second aim is to inform him that there were others, chiefly scholastic theologians and monks, who disliked his publications, and to suggest, ever so gently, that Erasmus should be cautious and should moderate some of his bold statements in order not to frighten the unlearned and undecided into the arms of the foes of humanistic learning. In the near term, the result of this clash of opinions was the lodging of formal charges of heresy against Erasmus by several Spanish monks, leading to a conference of theologians at Valladolid in the summer of 1527 that allowed the opponents to ventilate their charges but ended without an official judgment either for or against him. On the background of the Valladolid conference, see Ep 1786 n5. This letter only hints at the contending forces while emphasizing the positive elements. Despite the manifestation of determined opposition, the fashion for Erasmus and his writings continued to flourish into the early 1530s. It was then followed by an increasingly severe reaction that within a decade had destroyed or silenced the Spanish Erasmians and made open support or citation of Erasmus in Spain dangerous, a situation that continued into the following century. Even Maldonado abandoned his sympathy for Erasmus. His turning against Erasmus, evident by 1534 even at a time when he was fully engaged in teaching humanistic literature, was a sign of the shift away from Erasmus' approach to church reform and spiritual life on the part of educated Spanish humanists. By 1541 he had published a book in which he rejected the *Colloquies* as subversive and endorsed only the Paraphrases on the New Testament as useful to Catholic readers.

The classic modern work on the rise and fall of the Spanish Erasmians is Marcel Bataillon *Erasme et l'Espagne*, first edition 1937; the definitive revised edition (1991), which is cited here, includes two additional volumes of corrections, commentaries, bibliography, and reprinted essays by Bataillon on related topics. There were also two editions of the original one-volume study in Spanish, revised by Bataillon (Mexico City 1950; 2nd ed Mexico City and Buenos Aires 1965/6). His interpretation of Spanish Erasmianism has not been without critics, who included Bataillon himself. Most recently the origins and outcome of the Valladolid Conference of 1527 have been reconsidered, with careful attention to the records of the conference, by Homza. She warns against Bataillon's tendency to interpret the conference as a simple encounter between

Title-page of the second edition of the Spanish translation of Erasmus' *Enchiridion*
(Alcalá: Miguel de Eguía, September 1526)
This title-page refers to the report of a special inquisitorial commission,
appointed in late summer 1526, that examined the *Enchiridion*
and recommended it as a pious and useful book. Biblioteca Nacional, Madrid

'progressive' and 'reactionary' forces, demonstrating from archival sources that even the 'defenders' of Erasmus at Valladolid regarded some of his statements as open to valid criticism. A striking feature of the incident is that, however oppressive the Spanish Inquisition may seem when judged by modern standards, the system functioned in an orderly and 'just' way – the rules were followed so scrupulously that not even the fact that the inquisitor-general himself, Alonso Manrique de Lara, was broadly sympathetic to Erasmus could prevent those who lodged the complaint from receiving full opportunity to make their case.

Maldonado (c 1485–c 1554) of Bonilla (Cuenca) studied at Salamanca under the most talented Spanish humanist of the early sixteenth century, Antonio de Nebrija, and also under the Belgian humanist Christophe de Longueil. After his ordination as a priest, he settled at Burgos, where he received administrative appointments from Bishop Juan de Fonseca and was a member of a group of well-placed Erasmians. From 1532 he also taught humanistic subjects at the local Latin school. Maldonado compiled an anthology of selections from classical authors, published a Latin comedy, *Hispaniola* (Valladolid 1525), and became a student of the history of contemporary Spain. He wrote an account of the Comuneros rebellion of 1522, *De motu Hispaniae*, and presented a manuscript of it to Prince Philip in 1545, though the book was not printed until 1572, long after the author's death. He also wrote a history of the reign of Ferdinand and Isabella, first rulers of a united Spain, that survived in manuscript until as late as 1783 but is now lost. Several of his later books on classical and religious topics were published, some of them critical of Erasmus but also critical of corrupt clergymen.

Erasmus' reply to this letter (Ep 1805) was so indiscreet that Alfonso de Valdés, Latin secretary to the emperor Charles v, through whom it was transmitted and who was named as an alternative addressee, withheld it from Maldonado for fear that if the text and the other letters enclosed with it somehow became public, their disclosure would compromise the whole group of Spanish Erasmians, including the inexperienced and untested Maldonado. In fact Ep 1839 written to Erasmus by Valdés contains at least a hint that he was offended by Erasmus' willingness to favour the obscure Maldonado with such a warm and lengthy letter while sending to Valdés himself only a very brief note (Ep 1807) acknowledging his role in securing the strongly worded letters (Epp 1731, 1757) that the emperor himself and the imperial chancellor, Gattinara, had written in order to silence attacks on Erasmus by the Louvain theologians.

The present letter was first published by Jean Leclerc in LB III-2 1715–18 *Appendix epistolarum* no 338, and the original manuscript survived in the Rehdiger collection at Wrocław, where it was consulted by P.S. Allen for his edition.

JUAN MALDONADO TO DESIDERIUS ERASMUS OF ROTTERDAM,
CORDIAL GREETINGS

I know, most learned Erasmus, that you are bothered repeatedly by letters
from every quarter of the globe from those who know Latin, or think they
know it, and that you are kept from serious business by unreasonable in- 5
terruptions. Some reckon they will immediately be taken for great men if
they can say that they actually made contact with Erasmus; others are seized
with a burning desire to be named in your writings or to be honoured by
some sort of reply; both certainly realize that even to be mentioned by you
will compensate for the transience of life by bringing them the eternal fame 10
that is promised by your works – and not just those that deal with serious
subjects, but even the light and amusing pieces. But although I envy those
who can enjoy a learned skirmish with you at close quarters or even those
who can draw you into debate only by letter, thinking that even if they are
defeated, there is great glory in a contest with you, I must tell you that my 15
reason for writing is of a very different kind.

My aim is to acquaint you with the attitude of my fellow Spaniards
towards yourself and your prodigious learning and to describe the good
will you have earned from everyone here without distinction of class or sex
for the light you have shed on literature both sacred and profane. I would 20
not have you think that all Spaniards are to be judged by one or two.[1] Your
name stands high among us, and there is enormous admiration for your
learning – some even see in you a kind of divinity.

There are four classes of men who make judgments about you and
your sacred labours.[2] First, there are those who revere good literature and 25

* * * * *

1742
1 No names are mentioned, but Maldonado is probably referring to earlier Spanish critics such as Diego López Zúñiga and Sancho Carranza de Miranda. One
purpose of this letter is to demonstrate that such men were not typical of all
well-educated Spanish scholars (cf lines 182–6 below). Maldonado probably
did not know that his own master at Salamanca, Elio Antonio de Nebrija, had
supported some of López Zúñiga's criticisms of Erasmus' biblical scholarship.
Nebrija never published his critical remarks, which were rediscovered only in
the twentieth century, though Erasmus himself was aware of his tract and was
disappointed by it. See Rummel I 145–61.
2 This division of opinion into four classes is conventional among Erasmus and
his admirers: 1/ the virtuous and enlightened, who praise Erasmus for reviving the humanities after centuries of darkness; 2/ the sophists (that is, scholastic philosophers and theologians), who detest Erasmus because his work exposes their own shallowness and uselessness and who scrutinize his every
word for evidence of heresy; 3/ the great mass of plain, uneducated folk, who

are devoted to the holy Muses; they have a burning desire to restore the glories of antiquity; they are drawn by the splendour of its language and the majesty of its thought and want to quench their thirst in those limpid pools. These are all on your side. They credit you with the revival of the humanities; it is because of you, they say, that even the indolent are filled with eagerness to learn, that a path is open by which one may climb to the summit, that a light has begun to shine upon the eyes of the blind, that after so many centuries eloquence and true wisdom are joined again, that impostors, who are to be found everywhere in positions of power, have had their tricks exposed and are now driven out and left to starve or hang themselves.

Blessings upon you, dear Erasmus! May heaven be kind to you and smile upon you, for you have done such wonders for our age and served the Christian commonwealth so well. Throughout the world those who are truly wise look up to you as the best of models,[3] recognizing you as their leader and sharing a deep and heartfelt desire, however distant they may be, to see you face to face and hear you speak. You will not find an exception to this rule anywhere: that if a theologian knows Latin and has understood the teaching of those great figures on whom the church mainly depends, and if he wishes to be useful and not merely a poseur, he will have the name of Erasmus constantly on his lips, will cite him frequently, and will openly proclaim Erasmus as the theologians' guide and standard-bearer. And if this is true of theologians, need I say anything about teachers and literary men? I can claim at any rate, Erasmus, that you hold sway in our schools. Your supremacy is freely recognized, especially by those who are best able to judge; so much so that you have cast almost all previous authorities into the shade.

There is a second class of men, who are interested only in sophistries and teasing enigmas and appear to have got nothing from their unending labours except an empty pretentiousness; they jabber away about things of no consequence, but when it comes to serious questions or moral progress they are as inarticulate as children. These are the people who detest you and attack you viciously wherever they go without ever letting up. They do everything they can to damage your reputation, for they believe (and in this

* * * * *

know nothing about Erasmus but often mention his name because they hear of conflicts between the first two groups; and 4/ the monks, who vainly try to destroy Erasmus because his writings threaten their livelihood, which is based on their ability to exploit the ignorance of the common people.

3 The Latin is *scopus* 'target'; cf *Adagia* I x 30; III v 45.

they are not mistaken) that you were born for their ruin. In a long series of   60
distinguished books, which everyone is eager to read for their marvellous
style and exceptional learning, you argue that those who are conscientious
about instructing the people and preaching the gospel must find another
way that is very different from the sophistries those people deal in. When
they waste the time of the ignorant masses on frivolous questions and fu-   65
tile trifles, they only make whatever hearers and spectators they have managed to attract more uncertain and perplexed about the subject they came
to learn about than they were before the sermon began. Such people, you
rightly believe, should be banished from human society. So I am sure it is
no surprise to you that these men are your implacable enemies. They scruti-   70
nize your writings line by line (as far as their intelligence allows) and boldly
pronounce you guilty of treason against God and a defector to the enemies
of the true faith.

The third class consists of the general mass of ordinary people, men
and women without any education. Although they know nothing about you,   75
your name is often on their lips. They say great things about you and imagine you deserve much more. Should we not expect both high and low alike
to be intrigued and impressed by someone over whom battles are waged
every day among the learned and the seemingly learned, whose praises are
sung by friends and scholars, on whose head insults are heaped by enemies   80
and captious fools, who is the main subject of conversation among boys at
the grammar schools, whom those who are considered learned are eager
to emulate, and whose writings are perused in the secret watches of the
night by his worst enemies (who, if they subsequently say anything that is
sensible, are said to have stolen it from him)?   85

The fourth class of men is drawn from the other three – if men they
can be called who have no desire to look like men and who try hard to prevent external appearances from revealing their humanity. I refer of course
to the monks. They have tried every trick to destroy you, but so far they
have had no success since good men support you and turn back against your   90
accusers the charges those men unjustly bring against you. There are, to be
sure, monks who are rightly commended by their considerable learning and
whose lives are admirable, since they live out in reality what one would expect from their habit and the expression on their faces. If you question them
privately, there is no compliment too great for Erasmus, no eulogy they do   95
not heap upon him. They commend his brilliance and his remarkable energy; they praise his incomparable style, they call him another Cicero, but a
Cicero no longer worried by the 'nature of the gods' but holding firmly in
his hand the truth that was sought so long and describing it in the most polished prose. They admire, one might almost say revere, his wide and var-   100

ied learning and his untiring labours. But these same people, when they are among their own kind and are reminded of the cowl they wear, necessarily sing a different tune and are easily turned around. They realize that in striving everywhere to defend the truth you are threatening their way of life; worse still, you are destroying their whole source of income and rob- 105 bing them of their profit. This is why even the most learned of the monks form up against you with their comrades in arms and declare war on you and on all who are dear to you.

But those who have taken up arms under compulsion and cannot bring themselves to hate something they find very attractive and persuasive could 110 easily be won over and induced to change sides if only you would tone down the severity of your criticism, find some words of praise for their way of life or their 'order' (as they call it), distinguish the eloquent and learned among them from the fractious, and see that appropriate honour is paid to the original founders of their communities. On the other hand, those who 115 covet the title of 'Master,' who maintain that only in their syllogisms is true knowledge to be found, and who profess a kind of philosophy that is full of thorns and prickles – these people lord it over their brethren and exercise within the monastery a tyranny pure and simple; outside the monastery they stop at nothing, leave no course untried to maintain their monopoly over 120 wisdom and have an excuse for meddling in everyone's affairs. Under the pretext of religion they court the favour of distinguished ladies from good families and try to persuade them that they cannot clear their consciences and lay aside the burden of their sins unless they fall at the knees of some sophistical monk; no one, they hold, can distinguish the various categories 125 and types of sin unless he knows how to trap a colleague in a syllogism.

Why say more? The point is clear enough. No one from the humblest journeyman to the emperor is judged a true Christian by these people unless he acknowledges some monk as what they call his 'spiritual father' – although women have many shocking stories to tell about the shameless be- 130 haviour of these sham philosophers. So don't be surprised if you are hated by these ogres for ripping the mask from their faces and doing everything you can to foil and upset and thwart their schemes by pointing out over and over again what mischief their machinations have wrought in the world and how, by their never-ending debates, they have held back those who are 135 interested in true knowledge and made a tangled mess out of the plain and simple teaching of the gospel. One could hardly describe the bitterness with which they pronounce their awful curses on your head, how often they consign you to the world below, what pains they take, what lengths they are prepared to go to in order to persuade princes and magistrates and even 140 bishops to prevent your books from being sold in the bookshops.

Then just when they thought they had made some progress, the highest
court, which had been established for the defence of the faith, forbade anyone from speaking ill of Erasmus and issued threats against those who condemned his writings for lack of piety unless they publicly recanted.[4] This   145
injunction shocked the 'scourges of Erasmus,'[5] who feared their widespread
influence would be decisively broken. So they attempted to retain control
at least over noble women, who never acted without their advice, and also
over the houses of nuns and the convents, which are very numerous and
wealthy in Spain; they did everything in their power to prevent any men-   150
tion of your name or of your teaching from reaching them. These brethren
of the cowl know full well that your counsel is a direct challenge to their
hypocrisy and that your books point a simple path to blessedness and the
understanding of Christ's teaching. They know they cannot maintain their
influence even over women, an influence they have gradually built up by   155
the specious appeal of a solemn face, flattering words, and the monastic
cowl, unless your writings are suppressed and your name buried in oblivion. So they have tried to persuade the women not to admit anyone to
their company who might mention the name of 'that dogmatist Erasmus'
(to use the milder term),[6] much less anyone who might communicate his   160
ideas.

* * * * *

4 Allen (134–5n) suggests that this is a reference to Alonso Manrique de Lara's
  support for Erasmus in the face of complaints from some members of the religious orders. On the circumstances leading up to the Valladolid Conference
  of the following summer, see the introduction to this letter and Ep 1786 n5.
  Allen cites his own introduction to Ep 1791. But at this date these events, even
  the private conference of the monks with the inquisitor, lay many months in
  the future. A more likely instance of the inquisitor's support was his action
  in ordering an examination of the Spanish translation of Erasmus' *Enchiridion* made by Alonso Fernández de Madrid before publication of the second
  edition, probably in September 1526. As a result of the formal inquisitorial
  review of the first edition (date unknown; no copy survives), the new edition appeared bearing the inquisitor-general's official coat of arms, and it was
  dedicated to Manrique with a declaration that his examiners had found the
  book 'very profitable and highly edifying.' Presumably the book itself was not
  published until after the date of the present letter, but word of the inquisitorial declaration may well have spread among interested and well-connected
  Erasmians like Maldonado.
5 Latin *Erasmomastiges*; see Ep 1658 n8.
6 Milder, that is, than 'heretic.' For the usage see Erasmus' lengthy and frank
  reply to the present letter, Allen Ep 1805:94, 344; and cf Jerome *Letters* 49.14.2,
  where Jerome claims to be writing as an interpreter and commentator on the
  apostle Paul, rather than as a *dogmatiste*.

But human nature being what it is, as soon as the most sensible of the women heard of the ban, they immediately suspected that you had something important to say that did not please the monks; so they were most anxious to find someone to translate Erasmus in confidence and to explain   165 to them why the monks were upset. So while the monks were plotting your ruin and working to ban your writings, all they succeeded in doing was to make your name familiar to everyone; in fact, not only are those who know some Latin falling in love with your brilliant books and purchasing copies but the ordinary masses, who are familiar only with the vernacular,   170 are clamouring to hear about you and want to become acquainted with your ideas. And this is true not only of men, spurred on, as they are, by the natural interests of their sex; even weak and ignorant women burn with desire to find out about the teachings of this Erasmus whose fame is blazoned abroad throughout the learned world. Nor is it only those women who live in the   175 world and in the broad light of day who want access to Erasmus' writings; the same desire is to be found among those who are shut behind bars and within convent walls and who may not speak unless someone is present; and when they cannot get their wish because of the opposition of the monks, they contrive a way in secret by tricking the guards or inducing them to help.   180

So here is where you stand today. To please the women and all who are ignorant of Latin, a bevy of scholars are busy translating your works into our language. Already the *Enchiridion* has come out in Spanish,[7] and the printers cannot meet the demand, although they have run off thousands of copies.[8] Several of the dialogues in your *Colloquies* are now in Spanish   185 and are circulating rapidly among men and women.[9]

* * * * *

7 The translator of Erasmus' *Enchiridion* into Spanish was Alonso Fernández de Madrid (c 1475–1559), canon of Palencia and archdeacon of Alcor, a highly regarded preacher with close ties to several influential bishops, two of whom he served as vicar-general during his career. His translation of the *Enchiridion* was 'by far the most important translation of any work by Erasmus to appear in Spain' (R.W. Truman in CEBR II 24). On him and his translation see Bataillon (1991) I 205–20. Truman notes that the biographical information on him in Allen VII 243–4 (Ep 1904) is inaccurate at several points and cites instead J. Galán *Diccionario de historia eclesiástica de España* II 919 and *El Enquiridión o manual del caballero cristiano* ed Dámaso Alonso (Madrid 1932; repr 1971) 18–22, and Bataillon (Mexico City and Buenos Aires 1965/6).

8 The first edition, of which no copy is known to have survived, can be dated only as earlier than the second (Alcalá: Miguel de Eguía), which probably appeared in September 1526, bearing the coat of arms and endorsement of the inquisitor-general of Spain; cf n4 above.

9 Bataillon (1991) I 711 n2 cites a manuscript work of unspecified date, which includes an unpublished Spanish translation of the colloquy 'Charon.' The

I have touched briefly on these matters to let you see that my Spanish compatriots are not ill disposed towards you, if you make an exception for the one or two people you have wounded with your pen and disregard as of little account the great horde of monks who hound you everywhere to 190 their own dishonour and your not inconsiderable renown. It is true (not to conceal my own feelings) that I am most anxious for you to be reconciled with the monks. I should like to see you take up your pen and explain what you had in mind; then those of the monks who stand out both in character and learning – and there are very many whose excellence should redeem the 195 reputation of the rest – will understand that you were guided not by a spiteful temperament, but by a desire to instruct. It will become clear to them that what you criticize in every order is the fact that the majority have abandoned the path of their predecessors and are rushing headlong to satisfy their desires, thinking they have met the requirements of the rule to which 200 they have given their allegiance if they imitate their masters in matters of dress. But you will stand by your judgments, for you weigh all sides carefully and will not be influenced by the hostility of a few unless you yourself decide that a retraction is necessary. Time itself, if nothing else, will show up their hostility for what it is and lessen its effect, and will make it clear 205 that there is nothing high and noble that escapes the assaults of jealousy and the attempts of the envious to pull it down.

Please pardon my impertinence for daring to break in upon your serious and godly labours with my silly chatter and for calling you away from your holy task and forcing you to interrupt your work. It is because of 210 my love for you and your incomparable learning that I feel compelled to warn and urge you, in whatever words I can find, to take no notice of your enemies, whose carping does more for your reputation than the eulogy of

* * * * *

first known translation of any colloquy to be printed was *Coniugium*, which later editions called *Uxor* μεμψίγαμος 'The Wife Complaining of Marriage.' This colloquy was translated by Diego Morejón and published at Medina del Campo late in 1527 (no copy survives), and soon reprinted under the title *Coloquio de Erasmo intitulado Institución del matrimonio christiano* (Valencia: Juan Joffre, 21 April 1528); two revised editions followed in 1528, one without known place of publication and the second published at Caragoça (Saragossa). Another colloquy, *Proci et puellae* 'Courtship,' translated by Luis Mexía (Valladolid: Nicolás Tierry?), was published in 1528. From 1528 several editions of selected colloquies were published in Spanish, some of them translated by Mexía and by Erasmus' Benedictine admirer Alonso Ruiz de Virués, and some of them the work of translators who have remained anonymous. On the influence of the *Colloquies* in Spain, see Bataillon (1991) I 309–35, II 399–401 (Bibliographie).

your friends. It is because of them that your name is better known in Spain
than it is in Rotterdam.   215

Farewell. Keep a warm place in your heart for these friends of yours
whose names you may not know but who are deeply devoted to you. Here
at Burgos you have many admirers who are sincerely attached to you and
show, whenever the chance arises, that they are as dedicated to your interests
as to their own.   220

Burgos, 1 September 1526
To Desiderius Erasmus of Rotterdam, imperial councillor

1743 / To Duke George of Saxony   Basel, 2 September 1526

On George, duke of Saxony, see Epp 514, 1691 introduction. He was favourable
to humanistic studies and reform programmes, but since hearing Luther at the
Leipzig disputation of 1519 had become a determined foe of Luther and his
supporters. He had repeatedly pressed Erasmus to oppose Luther. Erasmus'
Hyperaspistes 1 had pleased him greatly, and he looked forward to publication
of the promised second part and sent valuable gifts both to reward Erasmus
and to encourage him to further efforts. The original letter survived at Dresden. Erasmus published the text in *Opus epistolarum*, where, however, it was
misdated.

Cordial greetings, illustrious prince. When I was preparing this reply, I
searched far and wide for your lordship's letter,[1] but it refuses to come to
hand. This is always the way: the harder one looks for something, the less
likely it is to turn up; and sometimes by putting an object carefully away,
we mislay the very thing we are particularly anxious to keep within easy   5
reach. So I shall reply to your letter from what I can remember.

I wrote several days ago to tell you that your letter had been delivered,
but not the cup.[2] Shortly afterwards, a citizen of Basel brought it on the
instructions of an Augsburg merchant,[3] as I acknowledged in my receipt. It
is a magnificent and elegant gift, but I was not so delighted by the gift itself 10

* * * * *

1743
1 Ep 1691, to which Erasmus wrote only a very brief reply (Ep 1728) on 30 July,
  promising to write at greater length when he had leisure to do so.
2 On this valuable gift see Ep 1691 n4. When he wrote Ep 1728, Erasmus had
  not received the cup.
3 Neither the Augsburg merchant nor the citizen of Basel to whom he entrusted
  the gold cup for final delivery can be identified.

as by the clear evidence it brought me of your good will and the assurance
that your mind is now purged of all suspicion about me. Your Highness'
letter, so friendly, so lively, so good-natured, gave me no ordinary comfort
in these fateful and troubled times. I also read, and more than once, the letter
you wrote in answer to Luther's challenge[4] – it was a wonderfully witty and   15
honest and clever letter, firm enough, but more tolerant than firm, as befits
a Christian prince. Would that the Lord might change Luther's mind so that
he would accept the helpful advice with which you end your letter! I never
cease to be puzzled by the spirit and temper of the man. If he is guided by
a perverse and evil spirit, then the threat he poses to the Catholic church   20
is without parallel. But if the spirit that guides him is good, then why, I
wonder, does he fail, in so many of his actions (if not in all), to manifest the
fruits of the spirit of the gospel?[5] If his spirit is both good and bad, how can
two spirits within the same breast act with such energy?

I am well aware that many faults have crept into the practice of Chris-   25
tians that can no longer be tolerated. Some have become so habitual as to be
taken for virtues. There is much that pious men find upsetting and would
like to see changed, if it could be done without causing turmoil in the world.
I know that the emperor too is of this mind. But Luther is dissatisfied with
everything. That faction, however, even if no one wrote a word against it,   30
even if the pope and the emperor looked the other way, would fracture
of its own accord, so great is the dissension among its members; and I say
nothing of the behaviour which this new gospel has produced – although it
has little of the gospel about it. All that can be done now is for the princes
to use their good judgment and authority to check the rebellious licence of   35
the Lutherans in case a more dangerous fire breaks out on the other side.
I refer to evil monks and to some theologians of the same stamp. I do not
know what they are like in your part of the world, but in Spain, Hungary,
Poland, England, Brabant, and above all in France, they have conspired to
raise a fearful song and dance over the humanities and against myself, for   40
they consider me the originator or promoter of these studies. They would
have won the day by the sheer noise of their protests and the slanderous
character of their writings – for these are their favourite weapons – had not
the princes and bishops used their authority[6] to quell the reckless agitation

* * * * *

4 See Ep 1693 n8.
5 Gal 5:22
6 Whereas a few lines earlier Erasmus had referred to use of the princes' authority to control rebellious outbreaks stirred up by the Lutherans' preaching,
  just as they had already done in suppressing the peasant uprisings of 1524–5,

of these centaurs.[7] A few days earlier the most Christian king of France had   45
acted similarly in that country.[8] If your Highness wishes to learn something
of that story, you can do so from a letter I wrote to your protégé Hieronymus Emser;[9] for I have not dared to intrude upon your illustrious Highness'
time with such a silly tale when you are so busy with affairs of state.

How fit I am to deal with Luther or what we can hope to gain from   50
my writings, I do not know. For what has my *Diatribe* accomplished except
to fortify the man more firmly in his own beliefs? Certainly, I shall not fail
to use what little powers I have to promote the peace of the Catholic church,
to which I owe even my life. The second part of my *Hyperaspistes* would
already have appeared, but the conspiracy that was stirred up in every part   55
of the world by the people I have just mentioned forced me to put the task
aside and confront this new evil in books and letters.[10] This summer Paris
sent me five volumes full of wild and calumnious attacks upon myself.[11]

* * * * *

here he has in mind the need for princes and bishops to silence the agitation of
conservative monks and theologians who were continually attacking him: the
efforts of the imperial court in Spain to silence the attacks on himself at Louvain (cf Epp 1643, 1700, 1731, 1747, 1784A, 1785); of the French royal court to
silence similar attacks by the theologians of Paris (Epp 1591, 1598, 1678, 1721,
1722); and of at least three successive popes to silence attacks by the Louvain
theologians and by his persistent Spanish critic López Zúñiga (see Ep 1716 n6).

7 Wild, beast-like creatures of Greek mythology noted for their drunkenness
and animal behaviour, ordinarily conceived as having the upper part of a
human being and the lower part of a horse. They seem to have symbolized
the antisocial and violent behaviour that challenges the restraints imposed by
civilization.

8 King Francis I, who upon his release from captivity in Spain intervened to stop
the prosecution of Louis de Berquin by the Parlement of Paris and the judges
delegate, an attack that in the opinion of both Berquin and Erasmus was aimed
at Erasmus as well. See Epp 1692 (especially lines 46–9, 64–76) and 1717:23–33.

9 See Ep 1683 introduction and the earlier letters there cited. The letter to him
mentioned here (probably dispatched concurrently with this letter to Duke
George) is not extant, but he replied with Ep 1773.

10 Completion and publication were delayed until September of 1527 (Epp 1667
introduction, Allen Ep 1853), and Erasmus frequently excused this delay by
referring to his need to spend time and energy defending himself from his
Catholic critics.

11 Although some of these books must have reached him long before the summer
of 1526, he probably has in mind hostile French publications such as a forged
and bowdlerized edition of his *Colloquies* compiled by Lambertus Campester
(see Epp 1581 n59, 1591:19–22), two or three of the attacks on Erasmus and
biblical humanism in general published by his Carthusian critic Pierre Cousturier in 1525–6 (listed in Farge *Biographical Register* 121), and Noël Béda's

The same has been happening in other regions also. I might have dealt with both matters, if my poor body, which was weak enough to begin with, had 60 not been seized during the month of June with so serious an illness that the doctors could do nothing and were reluctant to hold out any hope.[12] So I put my trust in God alone and am still alive, and will live as long as it is his will. I am now ready to resume the work I had begun. If the Lord gives me strength, I shall finish it soon.   65

I sent to the English court a copy of Luther's letter to your Highness and of your Highness' letter to him.[13] About the professor I sent you[14] – I gave all the details to Emser. Nothing gives me greater satisfaction than to see your generous and enthusiastic support of languages and letters. My earnest prayer is that you will continue what you have begun. May the om- 70 nipotent Lord keep your illustrious Highness safe and give you success in all good works; and when these present conflicts have been settled with your help, may he be pleased to restore peace and tranquillity to his church.

Basel, 2 September 1526

Your illustrious Highness' humble servant, Erasmus of Rotterdam   75

To the most illustrious Prince George, duke of Saxony, landgrave of Thuringia and margrave of Meissen

1744 / To Simon Pistoris   Basel, [c 2 September] 1526

A reply to Ep 1693 and evidently also to the earlier letter from Pistoris mentioned there (lines 38–9), which is lost. It is evident that Pistoris, like

* * * * *

attack, *Annotationum Natalis Bedae ... in Jacobum Fabrum Stapulensem libri duo, et in Desiderium Erasmum Roterodamum liber unus* (Paris: Josse Bade, 25 May 1526). Cf Epp 1744:127–8, 1753:42–3 for similar complaints, and Epp 1658 n7 (on Cousturier), 1664 introduction and n1 (on Béda).

12 Although Erasmus was a valetudinarian by temperament and suffered frequently from chronic and painful kidney stones, he does seem to have suffered from an acute and virtually incapacitating ailment, perhaps an infection of the bladder or urinary tract, in the summer of 1526. See Epp 1729 and n11, 1735 and introduction.

13 On the exchange of letters between Luther and Duke George, see Ep 1693 n4. The person at the English court to whom Erasmus sent these letters is not identified.

14 The humanist Jacobus Teyng of Hoorn, known as Ceratinus, whom Erasmus at Duke George's request had nominated for the professorship of Greek at Leipzig in 1525. See Ep 1683 n15 and the earlier letters there cited. Although he was appointed on Erasmus' recommendation, Ceratinus did not please the Saxon ruler and left his position there after only a few weeks.

his master Duke George, was eager not only for Erasmus to finish the second part of *Hyperaspistes* against Luther but also for him to undertake an extensive series of works directed against a host of Luther's doctrines – a task that Erasmus had no intention of accepting. The catalogue of his recent editorial projects and his promise to focus his remaining energies on completing the second part of his reply to Luther (lines 146–50) is an indirect but obvious refusal to undertake the role of full-time pamphleteer against Luther, a decision further excused by his embittered reference to the determination of some of his Catholic critics to convert him against his will into a Lutheran. Erasmus included this letter in his *Opus epistolarum*.

ERASMUS OF ROTTERDAM TO SIMON PISTORIS, GREETING
In this foul and festering age I am beset by so many suspicions and complaints from all sides that I have neither time nor inclination to answer them all. I am, however, most anxious to justify myself against all charges before someone so devout and sensible as the prince.[1] So although I am swamped 5
with work, I shall reply briefly to your letter. If I omit anything, I know you will be kind enough to supply it with all your customary eloquence.

My letter to Baden[2] found favour with all pious men, but it deeply offended Leo Jud of Zürich.[3] In a work written in German and circulated by the publishers, he confessed to being the author of the book I denounced 10
in my letter. He also sent me a letter in his own hand,[4] which was much more virulent than the book, challenging me to a gladiatorial contest. But I kept my mouth shut.

* * * * *

1744
1 Duke George of Saxony, whom Pistoris served as chancellor. See Ep 1743 and the earlier correspondence cited there, especially Ep 1691. This letter would have been dispatched concurrently with Ep 1743, as Erasmus habitually paired letters to a ruler like Duke George with letters to one or more of his acquaintances in the ruler's entourage.
2 Erasmus' letter to the diet of the Swiss Confederation that met the preceding May and June to consider (among other topics) the problems raised by the spread of the Reformation to Zürich and other parts of the Confederation. See Ep 1708. Erasmus sent a fair copy of this letter to Duke George.
3 See Ep 1737 n1 on Jud's vernacular book replying sharply to Erasmus' criticism for publishing anonymously his pamphlet upholding Sacramentarian eucharistic doctrines against both Luther and Erasmus. Jud's lost letter to Erasmus seems to have been even more aggressive.
4 Jud's letter is not extant, but it accompanied his pamphlet criticizing Erasmus; see Ep 1737 n1.

I do not understand what you meant when, in pleading my case before the prince, you said that I had never willingly departed from the decrees 15 of the church.[5] I have never departed from the decrees of the church either willingly or unwillingly. In any case, it is important to distinguish different kinds of church decrees. Some come from a general council, some from rescripts, some belong to the bishops, some to the Roman pontiff but have the character of a ruling, like the constitutions of the Camera.[6] Again, some 20 of the decrees of synods are permanent, some temporary. Similarly, some are inviolable – those, for example, that rest on Holy Scripture; some can be altered to suit the circumstances. So whenever I suggest changing a decree, I am thinking of those that can be changed without damage to true religion. Nor do I ever urge that changes be made except on the authority of 25 the hierarchy. To be frank, when the present deadly conflict was becoming increasingly serious, I certainly felt that if some decrees were changed, the storm would abate and we might have some measure of peace. And I say nothing about the vices that crept into the church under the guise of religion and established themselves so firmly that they almost extinguished the 30 spark of evangelical fire.

* * * * *

5 In this whole section Erasmus points out that many different types of declaration, issued by various authorities and having varying degrees of applicability and permanence, are hidden behind the vague phrase 'decrees of the church.' The implied questions are 'which decrees?' 'issued by which source of authority?' and 'for what purposes?' Thus he raises the difficult, in his time still vaguely defined and hotly disputed, issue of the ultimate source of authority in the church, a question not finally resolved (even as regards the Roman Catholic version of the total Christian community) until the Vatican decrees of 1870. He points out that Catholic authority has been widely attributed to a general council, to bishops, to the pope as sovereign authority, and to the pope acting in concert with the consistory of cardinals or other agencies of the papacy conceived as an institution. When the discussion resumes in lines 66–75, he notes that certain monks and theologians, especially Italian ones, attribute total and unlimited authority to the Roman pontiff while most northern Europeans (by clear implication including most Catholics and probably himself as well) do not attribute quite such an absolute power to the supreme pontiff.
6 The Camera Apostolica, as developed in the medieval church, was the institutional expression of papal authority in its financial and administrative side, including judicial authority, and during a vacancy of the Holy See it had principal responsibility for administering and preserving the temporalities of the Holy See. Thus its constitutions, though they normally dealt only with fiscal and administrative rather than spiritual matters, were also expressions of church authority, 'decrees of the church,' and in some cases could be backed up by spiritual as well as temporal penalties.

Not everyone understands what the problem is. It is the proper duty of princes to see that the fabric of the state does not disintegrate. But the issue is one of conscience. Now that I realize that neither side is willing to concede to the other, I can only pray that the Lord will bring about a happy 35 outcome, for I do not see how else this can come to pass. Many believe that the problem could be settled by legislation and penalties – and perhaps it could, but only for a time; and even if it could be solved permanently, this would not put an end to secret murmurings and arguments over matters of conscience. The authority of the church would not be diminished if for good 40 reason some changes were made by the hierarchy. This has happened many times in the past.

I come now to the letter of advice that I provided for the town council here.[7] I enclose a copy from the original in case those who published it added something of their own. I am also sending a letter I wrote to Glare- 45 anus asking him to make my excuses to the council before the magistrates could approach me.[8] It was no use. I suspect a plot of certain Lutherans, who thought that if my advice were favourable to them, they would have me at their mercy, and if it were not, I would rouse the deepest hostility towards myself in this city. For there was a faction here at the time that was 50 doing everything in its power to create the same situation in this city as we

* * * * *

7 See Ep 1539. Evidently, Pistoris' missing letter had criticized Erasmus' letter on the grounds that it was insufficiently firm in rejecting the Reformers' demands and too ready to endorse concessions on the printing of religious tracts, on changes in the external forms of worship, on relaxation of disciplinary rules governing fasting, and on permitting the marriage of clergymen. Despite assurances given by those who sought his written advice, the letter was published, without name of place or printer, in 1526.
8 The influential Swiss humanist Henricus Glareanus was at this time living in Basel as a successful schoolmaster; see Ep 440 introduction, 1595 n17, 1619 n1. Evidently Erasmus, who admired him and knew that he had political skills and connections in the city that a non-Swiss like Erasmus himself lacked, had attempted (but in vain) to use Glareanus' influence on certain city councillors (predominantly the moderate Catholic ones) to prevent the ruling magistrates from formally requesting the advice on religious policy given in Ep 1539. Such a request would have put Erasmus, as a resident alien who opposed the steady drift of the city government towards adopting the Reformation, in an awkward position. When the Reformers gained full control at Basel in 1529, Glareanus moved to Freiburg im Breisgau (as did Erasmus, Baer, and every member of the local cathedral chapter) and continued to work as a successful private teacher and as a lecturer on poetry at the local university until his death in 1563.

now see in Zürich. I was given a perpetual pledge of confidentiality. So I
tempered my advice to suit the conditions in the city (my letter applied to
one jurisdiction only); I did not want to cause a commotion that would have
dangers for more than myself, and at the same time I could not hand over   55
the authority of the church to the first person who came along. How much
the burgomaster appreciated my counsel, moderate though it was, you can
see from the fact that he suppressed it for three months and would not have
made it public had not some members of the church party repeatedly demanded to see it.[9] Certainly my advice brought about no change of policy   60
here, though everything went on in a more temperate spirit than before.

   As for your reference to Ludwig Baer, you have surely got the name
wrong.[10] Baer is a pious and scholarly man, who disagrees with everything
those people teach, especially on the subject of the Eucharist. He presided
over the meeting at Baden on behalf of the church party. I think you meant   65

* * * * *

9 Adelbert Meyer (1474–1548), a member of a prominent Basel family active in
   the cloth trade, became an influential political figure in the city. He was a city
   councillor from 1514, and he was elected burgomaster every second year from
   1521 until his death. He was sympathetic to humanism and a religious moderate, but unlike Erasmus he favoured a measured, gradual adoption of the
   Reformation. Erasmus seems to be saying that having secured the letter containing Erasmus' reluctantly given advice on religious policy, Meyer withheld
   it from the council because it was too much opposed to his own preference for
   gradual religious change. Only after three months did the Catholic members
   of the city council force him to make the letter public. Erasmus' point here is
   that his letter gave no impetus to a pro-Reformation policy but did moderate
   the drive towards such a policy.
10 Evidently Pistoris' lost letter had mistakenly identified the Basel theologian
   Ludwig Baer as a supporter of the Reformation. In fact, before Erasmus completed his *De libero arbitrio* opposing Luther, he submitted it to Baer (a high-
   ranking graduate of the Paris faculty of theology who remained a scholastic
   theologian despite his positive attitude towards Erasmus) for his criticism of
   the first draft (Epp 1419, 1420, 1422). Baer also examined other works of Erasmus that dealt with theological topics and sometimes judged them critically.
   He had attempted unsuccessfully to prevent publication of Luther's works in
   Basel and in 1525 (along with Erasmus) was one of the theological experts who
   successfully advised the city council to prohibit circulation of Oecolampadius'
   Sacramentarian book on the Eucharist in the city (Ep 1636 introduction). See
   also Ep 1674 n17 and the letters there cited. Just a few days previously, Baer
   had counselled Erasmus on the theological content of a vernacular attack on
   him by the Zürich pastor Leo Jud (see Ep 1741). So Pistoris was indeed misinformed about Baer's religious views. When the Reformation gained full control of Basel in 1529, Baer joined the other cathedral canons in going into exile
   in Freiburg.

Capito,[11] who receives no plaudits in that letter. When I wrote that neither party seemed to me to be acting responsibly, this was not an attack upon the church but upon those who push more doctrine down our throats than it is necessary to believe. My words were aimed at certain theologians and monks, not at the church. For example, those on the other side of the Alps   70 want us to believe that the Roman pontiff has more authority in himself than all the churches together and the whole people of Christ; and those on this side of the Alps hold certain articles of belief several of which I would be reluctant to defend, and yet if I did not do so, there would be an outcry. So I did not say I belonged to neither party, only that I was bound to neither,   75 for to be bound is to be a slave in everything. Moreover, it would not be enough to submit to their opinions; I should also have to defend their way of life and their character; but some of them, who think that if they make a loud enough noise they will be seen to be doing the church's work, lead lives that I find totally corrupt.   80

As for the suggestion that Luther's books should not be banned completely here, that seemed appropriate at the time, considering the mood in the city. If the church allowed the use of the sacrament in both kinds, I do not see how the least harm would result, for this practice was permitted for a while in Bohemia. At the same time, I do not approve of anyone getting   85 Christian people excited over this matter. I do not accept the marriage of priests or the release of monks from their vows unless this is done on the authority of the bishops and with the intention of building up the church, not tearing it down. I consider it inhuman to force boys and girls into the monastic life and charitable to rescue those who have been deceived. It is   90 to be hoped above all else that priests and monks practise chastity and embrace the spiritual life. But things have now sunk so low that perhaps we must choose the lesser evil. If this opinion is unacceptable to the leaders of the church, let them treat it as an aberration.

You speak in your letter of the godless licence of certain people, but   95 no man has been led by me to act this way, and I have restrained a fair number. You are worried about paganism; I, on the other hand, see a Jewish legalism taking over almost everywhere.[12] If all of us – clergy and people,

* * * * *

11 A humanist admirer of Erasmus whose full commitment to Luther's teachings in 1523 led to an enduring break; see Ep 1764 n24 and cf Ep 1737:17–20 and n2.
12 From the time of the apostles, one of the principal complaints of Christians against Judaism was the charge that it conceived religion as a set of external acts regulated by Mosaic law and rabbinical interpretation, to the neglect of faith in God and the inner spirit. The most famous examples

great and small – turned with pure hearts to Christ, the author of our faith, and if each of us confessed our sins and joined in prayer to beg his mercy, we would soon see a happy release from our present turmoil. But now most men are devoted to their own interests, and no proper thought is given even to the public good.

The prejudice you seem to feel towards Greek because of the short-comings of one or two men is out of character with your usual good sense and kindly nature. By the same argument you would have to dismiss all good literature. The fact that several devotees of the subject were initially sympathetic to Luther was caused in part by the unscrupulous behaviour of certain people: they fought against such studies, which were beginning to revive among us, and waged an unremitting war by land and sea for many years. It's a long story. You recall Reuchlin.[13] I have seen much more. As for our friend,[14] I cannot think what got into the man's head. I have never encountered anything that surprised me more. But what has this to do with Greek, without which all our learning gropes in the dark?

I think you received the letters I sent at the last fair. I wrote to our most illustrious prince and to Emser and yourself.[15] The cup pleased me greatly, though I was even more delighted by what it showed me of our esteemed

* * * * *

are in Paul's Epistle to the Romans, for example 2:17–3:28, 4:1–15, 7:1–8:4. At the end of the Middle Ages, critics of the emphasis on external rit-ual and the pious acts that had become typical of popular religious obser-vance charged that a similar, 'pharisaical' and 'legalistic' emphasis on ex-ternals had grown up within Christianity, leading to neglect of inner spir-itual life. Erasmus was one of the principal exponents of this view, and his ideal of a 'philosophy of Christ' contrasted the inwardness of genuine religion with the 'Jewish legalism' that had come to dominate contemporary Catholic observance.

13 Pistoris' missing letter seems to have accused the famous humanist and He-braist Johann Reuchlin of sympathy for Luther (quite contrary to Reuchlin's real opinion), whereas Erasmus regards him as a good Catholic unjustly per-secuted by religious bigots. See, for example, Erasmus' private letters in be-half of Reuchlin to two influential friends at the Roman curia, Epp 333:112–47, 334:187–218.

14 Ceratinus; see Ep 1743 n14. Erasmus here seems to share Pistoris' and Duke George's suspicion that Ceratinus sympathized with Luther (suspicions that were almost certainly unfounded; cf Epp 1611 n2, 1693 n7); but his main point is that even if the suspicions about Ceratinus' Lutheran sympathies were true, the failings of this one individual do not affect the value of the Greek language and do not justify Pistoris' apparent prejudice against the study of Greek.

15 Of these three contemporaneous letters, those to Duke George and Pistoris are lost; only the letter to Emser (Ep 1683) survives.

prince's feelings. You wish me a long life, but, my good Pistoris, I have already had your wish. I have lived a long time, if it can really be called living. The doctors promised me no relief, and if they had, I would certainly 120 not have believed them. So I gave them up and committed myself to Christ. Whether he wishes the rest of my life to be long or short, I shall submit and be content. Even if there were any serious prospect of restraining Luther, even if I were really equal to the task, even if I had the will and the time to carry it out, it would still be impossible because of the conspiracies I see 125 forming against me.

Paris sent me four books this year that were absolutely libellous and obviously mad.[16] People suspect that this does not happen without the consent of the faculty of theology. It is not that all of them support this sort of thing, but, as generally happens, the good are no match for the wicked. 130 To produce this farce they have co-opted a number of ambitious fools without a vestige of common sense, in particular the Carthusian Cousturier[17] and Béda.[18] Someone, while on a diplomatic mission to the emperor, wrote a most scurrilous attack on me and, unless I am mistaken, has already published it, although, while he was in Britain, he gave no hint of his intentions.[19] 135

* * * * *

16 Cf Ep 1743:57–8, where he counts them as five.
17 See Epp 1571 n10, 1658 n7.
18 Epp 1571 introduction, 1664 introduction and n1, and the ensuing (and increasingly acrimonious) correspondence between him and Erasmus, most recently Epp 1679, 1685.
19 Erasmus' use of Greek in the phrase translated 'on a diplomatic mission' probably would not have concealed the identity of the attacker from any well-informed reader. The 'someone' who supposedly wrote this 'scurrilous attack' on Erasmus was Edward Lee, who was currently (1525–30) English ambassador to the court of Charles v in Spain. Although no such work was ever published and no manuscript has been found, Erasmus saw the hand of Lee, who had been a hostile and persistent critic of his biblical scholarship since 1518, behind the growing criticism of himself by Spanish monks; see Ep 1735 n7. The outcome of the new wave of criticism discussed here was a formal inquisitorial investigation of charges that his books were heretical; see Ep 1742 introduction. There is no proof that Lee was actually circulating a manuscript book against Erasmus in Spain. While it is possible that Lee's published *Annotationum libri duo* (Paris: Gilles de Gourmont for Konrad Resch, 1520) or even his unpublished notes criticizing Erasmus' New Testament scholarship were used by the Spanish monks who early in 1527 compiled a series of charges against Erasmus that became the focus of the Valladolid Conference, the Spanish articles were organized on an entirely different basis than any of the earlier attacks. Thus it is unlikely that Lee's role was so active or so central as Erasmus suspected (Rummel II 85–6; Homza 84–5).

The monks of Salamanca have raised a fuss there too.[20] There are also others at Rome besides Zúñiga and his ilk who write against me.[21] One work was sent me by its author, Alberto Pio;[22] another, which was anonymous, reached me through friends – it has not yet been published, but is being circulated in the papal court.[23] Not even Orestes, when pursued by the Furies, 140 could have written anything so mad.[24] I can guess who the author is: the style fits the character of the man, for I know the fellow intimately. There are other Zúñigas in Spain,[25] to say nothing of Louvain.[26] When it comes to obloquy and abuse, they are none of them ever at a loss for words.

* * * * *

20 At this point Erasmus did not know that his critics among the Spanish regular clergy were taking steps that would produce formal charges of heresy and would lead in the summer of 1527 to an inquisitorial conference of theologians at Valladolid; see Ep 1742 introduction. But he knew that publication of a Spanish translation of his *Enchiridion* had produced objections from at least one critic whom he identified as a Dominican. See Ep 1581 nn104–5.

21 This Spanish theologian was one of the earliest and most persistent of Erasmus' Spanish critics. See CWE 8 336 and Rummel II 145–77, also Ep 1579 n25. He had moved to Rome in 1520 and continued to write and publish attacks on Erasmus there despite action by both Pope Adrian VI and Pope Clement VII to impose silence on him. After 1524 he continued compiling critical notes on Erasmus' editions of the New Testament and the works of St Jerome but refrained from publishing this material; before his death at Naples in 1531 he arranged for these notes to be sent to Erasmus (Epp 2637, 2701, 2705, 2905, 2951).

22 On this Italian prince and humanist, highly influential at the papal curia, see Epp 1634 introduction, 1717 nn2, 3. Pio did send a manuscript copy of his attack to Erasmus, as documented in this letter; and the work circulated in manuscript but was not printed until 1529 (Paris: Josse Bade, 7 January 1529).

23 The anonymous denunciation of Erasmus as a dangerous heretic that was being handed around at the papal curia was called *Racha*. Erasmus attributed its authorship to his former friend Girolamo Aleandro, and apparently he was correct. See Epp 1553 n9, 1717 n18.

24 In Greek mythology, as reflected in fifth-century tragedy, the Furies (Erinyes) relentlessly pursue Orestes because he had murdered his mother Clytemnestra in order to avenge her part in the murder of his father Agamemnon.

25 Erasmus probably has in mind not only the Spanish theologian Sancho Carranza de Miranda (Ep 1277 n8, 1701 n7), who in 1522 published a book critical of Erasmus, with the declared hope that Erasmus would modify and clarify certain points in order to forestall attacks, but also far more hostile critics, the monks and theologians of Salamanca, about whose hostility he was beginning to learn.

26 Erasmus had encountered the hostility of conservative Louvain theologians even before the first publication of his edition of the Greek New Testament in 1516, and despite his assiduous efforts to win over some of these critics by

In preparation for the book fair I took on a heavier load of work than   145
my health could stand. Among other things I reprinted the New Testament
and made substantial additions to the Annotations. I think I have now given
perhaps enough attention to Jerome, the *Proverbs*, and the New Testament.[27]
If the little strength I have left in this poor body is up to it, I shall finish my
reply to Luther,[28] though nothing I write could be holy enough or cautious   150
enough to escape the malicious onslaught of those who are determined that
no reader will profit from my books and whose one object is to smother me
with insults and drive me into the Lutheran camp. But in this they will never
succeed, so long as the Lord in his mercy suffers me to keep my present
frame of mind.   155

You can confidently assure your prince of this, dear Pistoris, that, as I
said at the beginning, I have never been, and never will be, either willingly
or unwillingly, a member of any proscribed sect; that in all my writings
I have had no other aims than these: to join the study of languages and
letters to more serious disciplines; to bring scholastic theology, which had   160
often degenerated into mere sophistic wrangling, back to its roots in Holy
Scripture; to have less ceremony in our practice, more piety in our hearts; to
encourage bishops and priests to remember their office and urge monks to
be true to what they are claimed to be; and, finally, to rid the minds of men
of many wrong-headed and misguided ideas that have now plunged the   165
world into confusion. Anyone who reads my works carefully and without
prejudice will see that this is what I am doing. If these people read the

* * * * *

personal discussion or to silence them through papal and imperial intervention, he never succeeded in ending these public attacks. The letters of Erasmus
repeatedly reflect these controversies with Louvain theologians. For a good
survey see Rummel I 2–13, 59–60, 63–93, 131–43; II 1–22.

27 Erasmus expresses a sense of finality (though not a claim of perfection) for
these three great editorial achievements. On Jerome, see Epp 396, 1623 n5,
1675 n6, and especially 1465, all of which express Erasmus' sense that the revised edition of Jerome's *Opera* (in this case, the letters, the part for which he
assumed direct editorial responsibility) represented the fruition of his labour
to produce the best text possible. In the case of his *Proverbs* (the *Adagia*), the
preface of his revised edition of early 1526 (Ep 1659) also expresses a sense
of completion, even in a work which by its nature could be expanded and revised almost *ad infinitum*. In fact Erasmus continued to publish expanded editions until his death. Cf Ep 1659 introduction. The fourth edition of the Greek
New Testament was published in March 1527, and it was the last edition to
which Erasmus devoted a major scholarly effort. The final edition of the New
Testament published in his lifetime (1535) introduced only minor changes.

28 The second part of *Hyperaspistes*, not published until September 1527

writings of Chrysostom and Jerome in the spirit in which they read mine, they would find more to criticize in them than in anything from my pen. Farewell.   170

Basel, 1526

1745 / To Stephen Gardiner   Basel, 3 September 1526

A reply to Ep 1669. Erasmus published it in his *Opus epistolarum*.

ERASMUS OF ROTTERDAM TO STEPHEN GARDINER, GREETING

I was delighted, my dear Stephen, to have my memory of you revived by your letter. There was no need for all the documentation. The image I formed of you in Paris has stuck so firmly in my mind that I could almost paint a picture of you now. In your letter and in the manner in which you deal with   5
more serious issues I recognize the same intelligence that you showed in Paris in the business of the kitchen.[1] My spirits were as refreshed by your letter as my palate was by the lettuce you prepared with such skill on that occasion. I am glad we have a patron in common,[2] and I rejoice with you in the knowledge that you have a special place in his regard.   10

At the moment I have to get letters ready for the couriers to take to Saxony, Poland, Hungary, Italy, Spain, Brabant, and England. So I must be brief. Since I could hardly find the time even for a short note, I must put the burden on you of giving my greetings to everyone: Francis the physician,[3] Toneys,[4] Burbank,[5] Pietro della Rena,[6] and all my other well-wishers.   15

* * * * *

1745
1 As a young student at Paris Gardiner had prepared salads that Erasmus had enjoyed. See Ep 1669:13, 26–9.
2 Gardiner was secretary to Cardinal Thomas Wolsey, archbishop of York and principal minister to King Henry VIII. Wolsey was a 'patron' of Erasmus in the sense that he expressed sympathetic interest in Erasmus' scholarship and generally favoured humanistic studies, but there is no evidence that he ever followed through on his vague promises and became a true patron, as Archbishop William Warham of Canterbury, Bishop John Fisher of Rochester, and several other English prelates did. Cf Ep 1697 introduction.
3 John Francis, an old friend and currently physician to Cardinal Wolsey. See Epp 1138:23–4 and n6, 1532, 1759.
4 Robert Toneys, another English friend who was then in Cardinal Wolsey's service. See Epp 1138 n4, 1492.
5 On William Burbank, chaplain and secretary to Cardinal Wolsey, see Ep 1138.
6 Pietro Vannes of Lucca, also known as Pietro Ammonio, a kinsman of Erasmus' Italian friend Andrea Ammonio and currently Latin secretary to Cardinal

Farewell. Live up to the promise of your name[7] and work hard to win the crown of an eternal reward.

Basel, 3 September 1526

1746 / To Gianfrancesco Torresani   Basel, 3 September 1526

The addressee was the son of the Venetian printer-publisher Andrea Torresani of Asola, who had been Aldo Manuzio's partner and took full control of the firm after Aldo's death in 1515. See Ep 1592 introduction. Allen observes that there is no clear evidence to confirm the year-date that Erasmus assigned when he published the letter in his *Opus epistolarum* in 1529, which is not particularly reliable in its dating of letters. But because of the publication date of the edition of Galen mentioned in this letter and the evidence in Ep 1628 that Erasmus had not yet seen it in October 1525, Allen plausibly concludes that 1526 is the correct year.

ERASMUS OF ROTTERDAM TO FRANCESCO ASOLANO, GREETING
My dearest Francesco, nothing has happened to me for a long time that brought me greater pleasure than your most generous gift of a complete Galen.[1] The author is welcome on his own account, but he is a particular

* * * * *

Wolsey. In 1517–18, Erasmus had been gravely dissatisfied with his dilatory efforts to help him recover or destroy his private correspondence with Ammonio, which included documents dealing with Erasmus' illegitimate birth and his successful pursuit of a papal dispensation (see Epp 655–6, 822, 828); but by this period, friendly relations seem to have been restored and old grievances forgotten. The Latin name used by Erasmus, Petrus ab Arenis, is probably a reference to the *Arena*, the district of Lucca around the marketplace of the medieval city, which stood outside the walls of the Roman colony (cf PW XIII 1540).
7 The name Stephen comes from the Greek *stephanos*, which means 'crown.' In addition, St Stephen was the first Christian to receive the 'crown of martyrdom' (Acts 6:8–7:60).

1746
1 On this important first edition of the Greek text of Galen by the Aldine/Asolano press in 1525, see Ep 1594 nn2, 3. Although Erasmus recognized the importance of this edition and was obviously delighted to receive the five volumes as a gift from the publisher, his work in translating and publishing three of the Galenic treatises using the Aldine Greek text as his source had made him critical of the poor quality of the Greek text, an opinion implied in his prefatory letter (Ep 1698:14–15 and n4) and repeated in Epp 1707 (cf nn2–3) and 1713 (cf n12), both to competent Hellenists, Giambattista Egnazio and Jacques Toussain.

favourite of mine, appealing both to my personal taste and my critical judg-   5
ment. Nor do I reject altogether that saying of the philosopher, that to receive
a gift is a delight indeed.[2] Nevertheless, what pleased me most was not the
gift itself or my enthusiasm for the author, but what it told me about your
feelings towards me and your remembrance of our old friendship. Either I
am no prophet, or this edition will bring you no small fame and profit. You   10
need not fear competitors: even if someone wished to challenge you, there
is no one in a position to do so. How I would like to be able to return the
favour! For I would rather repay a debt than simply acknowledge it. In the
meantime I shall do what I can to see that whatever comes from your press
is given a special welcome, although everything you produce is welcomed   15
by men of learning. How lucky the young are to have been born into this
age! I wish I were young again! But that is impossible.

   You could make my name more marketable in your country, if you did
me the honour of bringing out my works from your press[3] – I am thinking
particularly of some of my religious works. You might consider, for exam-   20
ple, *De misericordia Domini*,[4] *De modo orandi*,[5] my little commentaries on four

* * * * *

2 Thales; cf Erasmus *Apophthegmata* LB IV 323A; Diogenes Laertius 1.36. Both the
   Latin and the Greek sources define the most delightful thing as literally 'to get
   what you want.'
3 In 1525 Erasmus had offered Torresani an expanded text of his highly successful *Adagia*, of which the same press under Aldo Manuzio had produced
   the decisive edition of 1508, which transformed the *Adagia* from a limited
   and minor collection of sayings from classical (mainly Roman) sources into
   a treasure-trove of classical erudition drawn heavily from Greek as well as
   Latin sources. But both Gianfrancesco and his father Andrea, whether because
   they were fully committed to other projects like the Greek edition of Galen
   or because of crass calculations of profit, showed no interest and were even
   rude to the friends of Erasmus who urged them to undertake the new edition.
   See Epp 1592, 1594, 1595. The works which Erasmus now wished the Aldine
   press to reprint were, as he says here, religious in nature; and since he (unlike his conservative critics) regarded them as expressions of his own piety
   and orthodoxy, his desire to have them diffused by the great Venetian publishing firm was probably motivated less by commercial considerations than
   by a desire to establish a strong expression of his religious identity in Italy at
   a time when he knew that enemies at the Roman curia were accusing him of
   heresy.
4 Erasmus' *Concio de immensa Dei misericordia* (Basel: Froben, September 1524)
   rapidly became popular and so might have been a commercially attractive
   item for republication at Venice. See Ep 1474 introduction.
5 Erasmus' *Modus orandi Deum* (Basel: Froben, October 1524) had the form of a
   long letter addressed to the Polish diplomat and courtier Hieronim Łaski.

of the Psalms,[6] and my Paraphrases on the New Testament.[7] I would not want you, however, to touch the Paraphrases until you got from me a list of corrections. I shall send them to you as soon as I know your mind. Give my kind regards to your father and your brother and the rest of the family.[8]   25
Farewell.

Basel, 3 September 1526

1747 / To Mercurino Gattinara   Basel, 3 September 1526

On Gattinara, the imperial chancellor, a man warmly sympathetic to Erasmus' programme of scriptural scholarship and spiritual renewal, see the introductions to Epp 1150 and 1643. The text of the imperial order of October 1525 (here called an interdict) commanding the Louvain theologians to desist from their attacks on Erasmus is missing (see Ep 1643 n3), but Erasmus' complaints about the legalistic subterfuges used to render it ineffectual are already evident in a letter of April 1526 (Ep 1690 n11; cf Ep 1716 n7). He complained again of the theologians' subterfuges in a letter of April 1527, also addressed to Gattinara (Ep 1815). Erasmus had not yet received, and did not yet know of, the strongly favourable letter (Ep 1731) already on its way from the emperor himself, which not only praised Erasmus' orthodoxy but also denounced his detractors and promised to defend his reputation. Subsequently Gattinara followed through with a stern letter (Ep 1784A) addressed to the University of

* * * * *

6 On the four commentaries on individual Psalms published by this date (Pss 1–4) see Ep 1581 n12. These commentaries are meditative and contemplative rather than textual in nature. They are now available in the English translation by Michael J. Heath, with introduction by Dominic Baker-Smith, in CWE 63 (Toronto 1997).

7 Erasmus had published separately his Paraphrases on all four Gospels between 1522 and 1524; see Ep 1672 n25. Even earlier, he had published a Paraphrase on St Paul's Epistle to the Romans (1517) and then on all of the epistles attributed to specific apostles (1519–21). He concluded with a Paraphrase on the Acts of the Apostles, published in 1524 and dedicated to Pope Clement VII (Ep 1414). These publications were very successful, and most of them were frequently reprinted from an early date. Erasmus knew that the earlier editions had defects and wished to correct the errors; see Ep 1672:156–61. Several of his paraphrases have already appeared in English translation: CWE 42 (Romans), 44 (the Epistles to Timothy, Titus, and Philemon, the Epistles of Peter, Jude, James, and John, and the Epistle to the Hebrews), 46 (the Gospel of John), 49 (Mark), and 50 (Acts).

8 Andrea Torresani was head of the printing firm. The brother mentioned here was Frederico Torresani. Erasmus knew the family well; in fact, he had lodged in Andrea's house while living at Venice in 1508. See Ep 1592 introduction.

Louvain itself, denouncing the theologians' disregard of the emperor's command and directly threatening to take punitive action against the university.
But all in vain; the attacks continued, though perhaps with some greater degree of caution. There is a striking similarity between the themes outlined
by Erasmus towards the end of the present letter (lines 127–51) and the topics covered in Gattinara's stern letter of February 1527 to the Louvain faculty
(Ep 1784A), though the peremptory and menacing tone of Gattinara's letter reflects the mental habits of a powerful man accustomed to giving commands
and being obeyed rather than those of a scholar accustomed to pleading for
fair treatment.

Erasmus did not publish this letter, but the original manuscript survived at
Madrid and provided the text for Allen's edition.

Cordial greetings, distinguished sir. The wonderful and continued success
of our truly invincible emperor, which I am sure could not have come about
without the intervention of a merciful providence, gives me cause for hope
that God will use him as his instrument to better the affairs of men, which
have steadily been going from bad to worse. May God add this (and soon)   5
to the emperor's many blessings, that he may be able to restore the peace
we pray for and calm the storm that, for a long time now, has not only been
causing havoc and confusion in government and learning, but has almost
toppled from its foundations the citadel of the Christian faith. I would leave
this world a happier man if I could see that day.   10

I am most grateful for the interdict that was sent to curb the insolence of certain theologians at Louvain; I thank you most sincerely for your
concern and the emperor for his kindness. But the guile and dishonesty of
these people have more effect than the authority of the emperor. Even children laugh at Nicolaas of Egmond, the Carmelite, as someone who is unbal-   15
anced.[1] Latomus, who is of French nationality, never ceases to sow discord
in that university.[2] Nicolas of Mons, who has been assigned the chief role as

* * * * *

1747
1 Nicolaas Baechem of Egmond (Egmondanus), one of the most relentless of
  Erasmus' critics at Louvain, was consistently presented in Erasmus' letters, including this one, as so ridiculously incompetent that he seemed mentally de-
  ranged. On him see Ep 878:15n and, for more recent complaints by Erasmus,
  Epp 1581 n27, 1608 n4. Baechem had died on 23 or 24 August (cf Ep 1732:47–9
  and n13), but Erasmus had not received word of this event. He learned of it in a
  letter of 12 November from a friend at Louvain, Conradus Goclenius (Ep 1765).
2 On Jacobus Latomus see Ep 1674 n12. Erasmus' mention of Latomus' French
  nationality in connection with his alleged role as a constant sower of discord in the university (lines 16–17) is surely not accidental in this letter to the

inquisitor, is a remarkably crafty man.[3] Both are unable to conceal, however much they try, their implacable hatred of good literature and therefore of me. It bursts out against their will. And these two exploit the stupidity and effrontery of Egmondanus.

As soon as the emperor's edict was published, Montanus and Latomus rushed off to Mechelen, threatening to resign from their responsibilities if their authority was undermined by interdicts of this sort.[4] The most reverend the archbishop of Palermo took my side.[5] The opposite side was supported by Joost, president of the Grand Council of Mechelen, whom I always considered a good man and pretty able in his own field, but, as you know, a professed enemy of the humanities.[6] Need I say more? With Joost's help a request was forwarded for an interpretation of the emperor's edict. This has simply encouraged them to even bolder action.

By similar devises they have twice got round an interdict from the pope.[7] On both occasions they kept quiet about it, and then wrote secretly

* * * * *

imperial chancellor, one of the principal leaders in the anti-French policy of Charles v.

3 Nicolas Coppin of Mons was not only dean of the chapter of St Peter's in Louvain but also chancellor of the university. He became inquisitor in 1526. On him see Ep 1719 n8.

4 Mechelen was the seat of the Grand Council, the chief judicial court of the Netherlands. It was therefore the natural place to which Coppin (Montanus) as inquisitor and Latomus as a theologian active in combatting heresy would carry their complaint that the emperor's order to desist from their attacks on Erasmus would undermine their efforts to stamp out heresy.

5 Jean (ii) de Carondelet, a leading member of the Grand Council at Mechelen and a wholly absentee archbishop of Palermo in Sicily. He was one of Erasmus' most reliable and most influential supporters in the Hapsburg administration of the Netherlands and was involved not only in this matter of enforcing the imperial mandate to silence the theologians but also in Erasmus' repeated efforts to secure payment of his pension as an imperial councillor. See Epp 803, 1700 n3.

6 Joost Lauwereyns of Bruges (d 1527) became imperial councillor as a member of the supreme judicial court, the Grand Council, in 1515 and was its president from 1522, concurrently becoming superintendent of the Inquisition in the Netherlands. He seems not to have been very favourable to Erasmus, though there is evidence that he was not so totally hostile to humanistic learning as Erasmus alleges.

7 On Erasmus' success in obtaining an informal papal order imposing silence on the Louvain theologians who attacked him and on their success in evading it, see Epp 1589, 1589A, 1717 n4.

Jean (II) Carondelet
Portrait by Jan Cornelisz Vermeyen, before 1525
The Brooklyn Museum, gift of Horace Havemeyer

to the datary, asking him to show understanding.[8] They said that it was important for the Catholic faith that nothing diminish their influence with the people, and that they meant Erasmus no harm; the datary should keep 35 their communication secret and try to set Clement's mind at rest. I am not telling you a fairy tale, good sir. I have a note from the datary added in his own hand to a letter written by his secretary. A friend copied it from the datary's actual letter and sent it to me.[9]

* * * * *

8 Cf Epp 1589 n1, 1589A. The datary at this period was Gian Matteo Giberti, who later became a distinguished Catholic reformer as bishop of Verona. See Epp 1443A, 1589 n2.

9 In his letter of 21 July to Theodericus Hezius, the datary Giberti firmly reminded Hezius of the task entrusted to him by Pope Clement 'to rescue our friend Erasmus from his detractors at Louvain' (Ep 1589A:2–3) by demanding that the theologians stop making public accusations that Erasmus favoured Luther's heresy. The friend who copied Giberti's letter and sent it to Erasmus must have been Erasmus' trusted courier Karl Harst, who was in Rome on business for Erasmus in the summer of 1525. But Erasmus, who had many friends at Louvain and was usually well informed about developments there, soon concluded that Hezius and even Giberti had conspired with the Louvain faculty to nullify the pope's intervention. This letter shows awareness of Hezius' complicity with the theologians, though Giberti seems still to be regarded as a friendly person. The same conclusion about Hezius' betrayal of his own mission appears in Erasmus' letter to Willibald Pirckheimer, Ep 1717:12–17; cf n4. The evidence that Hezius went over to the side of Erasmus' critics after (perhaps even before) he reached Louvain is conclusive. His own letter of 26 October 1525 to Blosius Palladius, secretary to the pope, reveals that Nicolaas Baechem and Vincent Theoderici, the two theologians most directly affected by the pope's admonition, replied to his message by insisting that the need to repress heresy outweighed their duty to obey papal commands, and also that they maintained as an indisputable fact that Erasmus had favoured Luther and that many of his works subverted orthodox religion. It reveals that Hezius himself, despite his responsibility as a messenger for the pope, totally embraced the theologians' position and consciously acted to nullify his mission. His letter to Blosius explicitly urges the recipient not to inform Erasmus' friend Albert Pigge of its contents. It also shows that in the Netherlands Hezius took pains to confine knowledge of the pope's commands to a handful of conservative theologians and to keep all knowledge of the affair from the general public and especially from Erasmus, despite the explicit instructions from Giberti (Ep 1589A:13–14) that he should write directly to Erasmus and inform him of the pope's orders and of the measures taken to silence the Louvain theologians. The following day, 27 October, Hezius wrote in the same vein to the datary, informing him that he had decided not to carry out Pope Clement's orders and urging him to keep the whole affair confidential, even claiming the secrecy of the confessional for his account

But to get back to the emperor's edict: they returned to Louvain with   40
the interpretation. Far from being chastened, they were in an uglier mood
and launched even more virulent attacks upon me than before. Not only
did Egmondanus not obey the edict, but acting as agent for the dean, he
publicly burned my New Testament at 's Hertogenbosch. When someone
challenged the dean and asked on what authority Egmondanus ventured to   45
act in this way in opposition to the edicts of the emperor and the pope, the
wily fellow replied that this was not part of the instructions he had given
him. When a second person pressed him more strongly on the point, he
let all the venom in his heart pour out.[10] Latomus gave a public reading
of three tracts directed against me, which he subsequently published.[11] He   50

* * * * *

of what he had done. These two letters are published in *Monumenta Reformationis Lutheranae ex tabulariis secretioribus S. Sedis, 1521–1525* ed Petrus Balan (Regensburg 1884) 552–63. No documents survive to prove that Giberti approved Hezius' decision to subvert his own mission, but the lack of any further action by him or other papal officials confirms the conclusion of Henry de Vocht *History of the Foundation and the Rise of the Collegium Trilingue Lovaniense* 4 vols (Louvain 1951–5) II 277 that the datary consulted Erasmus' most dangerous enemy at the curia, Aleandro, as Hezius recommended, and then sent a secret reply endorsing Hezius' decision. For a detailed narrative of the whole affair, see De Vocht II 266–81. Erasmus soon learned of Giberti's change of heart. There is no evidence of further appeals to him after a fruitless effort in the spring of 1526 (Ep 1716:66–8). De Vocht II 281 notes that by 1530, in a letter to Germain de Brie, Erasmus even affected vagueness about the name of the datary (Allen Ep 2379:9–14). Although awareness of Pope Clement's orders may have caused the conservatives at Louvain to moderate their direct attacks on Erasmus for a time, the cooperation of Hezius, and probably of Giberti, spared them the embarrassment of letting Erasmus and the whole world know that they had been admonished by the pope. Erasmus gained access to some of the letters relevant to this affair, but he seems to have been totally unaware of Pigge's letter (Ep 1589) commanding the Louvain faculty of theology in the pope's name to stop their attacks on Erasmus, for he never mentions it, even though it was the kind of proof of Clement's favour that he surely would have cited in his own defence if he had been aware of it (De Vocht II 277).

10 If it really happened, the burning of Erasmus' Greek New Testament at 's Hertogenbosch by Baechem as if it were a heretical book would have been a measure so extreme that the dean, Nicolas Coppin, might well have denied that he had ordered it when he authorized Baechem to go to 's Hertogenbosch. But the report that when pressed further on this point, Coppin poured forth his hostility to Erasmus confirms the report that he had turned against Erasmus (cf Ep 1719 n8).

11 On three tracts see Ep 1674 n12.

was preparing a fourth[12] and was planning to continue in the same way had the emperor's edict not arrived in the meantime. He had conceived the idea of ridiculing me in a constant stream of new publications. Now he has been equipping the Parisians with weapons from his armoury, for he was a chicken from the nest at Montaigu before he crawled out to live 55 among us.[13] Pierre Cousturier, a theologian at the Sorbonne and a Carthusian monk, with his friend Noël Béda have published three books against me, stuffed with manifest lies and palpable falsehoods and filled with insults for which the word 'scurrilous' is inadequate.[14] They are all the more hostile to me because I am the emperor's man. The shameless be- 60 haviour of this cabal of monks and theologians reached such a point that the king and the Parlement had to issue an edict forbidding the writing of such books and the sale of those that had been written. No polemic is written against me, however tasteless and defamatory it may be, not even one issued under a false name, without the tacit support of Latomus 65

* * * * *

12 The tract that Erasmus had in mind is uncertain. Latomus' *Pro dialogo de tribus linguis apologia* was printed only several years after his death in 1544. Perhaps Erasmus thought that his recent book on papal primacy against Luther, *De primatu Romani pontificis adversus Lutherum* (Antwerp: M. Hillen 1526) was aimed at himself as well as at Luther; cf Ep 1674 n12. Or some otherwise unknown and unpublished work may be meant; Erasmus had friends at Louvain who kept him informed about people, events, and rumours there.

13 Erasmus himself had resided in the Collège de Montaigu during his first year of residence in Paris and always remembered it as a place marked by intellectual narrowness, inhumane discipline and living conditions, and food so foul that he blamed his own chronic ill health on the year he spent there; cf Ep 1723 n9. Latomus was a resident there during his undergraduate studies at Paris and then moved to Louvain in 1502 to head a similar residence for poor students founded by Jan Standonck, the same person who had reformed Montaigu and invented the austere discipline that Erasmus remembered with such distaste. In addition, his most dangerous enemy at Paris, Noël Béda, had studied there, had succeeded Standonck as principal of the college (1504–14), and (even though he resigned the position of principal after becoming a member of the faculty of theology) remained its director until 1535.

14 These attacks on Erasmus by his most unrelenting foes at Paris were Cousturier's *De tralatione Bibliae* and *Antapologia* and Béda's *Annotationes*. On Cousturier, the Carthusian monk and theologian, see Epp 1571 n10, 1658 n7, 1685 n3, 1714 n1. On Béda see Epp 1571 introduction, 1642 n5, 1664 introduction and n1, 1666 n5, 1679:44–50, 1685:62–4 and n5, 1721 introduction and n14. Erasmus' direct appeal to King Francis I (Ep 1722) produced an order of the Parlement prohibiting sale of Béda's *Annotationes*; for this success and its limitations see Ep 1763.

and the dean,[15] an open invitation to impudent fools to act in the same manner.

With this sort of chicanery they get round the edicts of the emperor and the pope and fancy themselves very clever. This plan hatched by certain monks and by theologians of the same stamp to remove all my books 70 from circulation in the belief that only in this way can the humanities be crushed is not new; on the contrary, they had given it birth long ago. After the defeat of the peasants they decided to move in with all their forces in England, Hungary, Poland, and Spain (for they are not yet strong enough in Germany). But the authority of princes and bishops blocked their disor- 75 derly campaigns. So I owe a great deal especially to you for your kindness and also to the archbishop of Toledo[16] and to all the others whose names and favourable interest in me I have heard about from friends. From their letters I have learned that Edward Lee, who is on a diplomatic mission to your country on behalf of the king, is preparing to publish a book that will 80 treat me in the most insulting manner – perhaps he has already published it.[17] If this is true, he is doing in Spain what he would not dare to do in his native Britain, for in that country I have the enthusiastic support of the king, the cardinal, the queen, the archbishop of Canterbury, and nearly all the bishops. 85

You will sensibly ask: How then does all this opposition come about? There are three causes. They believe that their authority and prestige will collapse unless they can destroy the study of languages and letters. The truth is that, if they embraced these studies generously, which are flourishing everywhere, they would even gain in prestige and have something of 90 value as well. Instead, they wage an endless battle against polite learning and, as a result, stir up a lot of animosity against themselves. They blame it all on me, for I am thought to have made some contribution by my industry to the advancement of these studies. This is one reason for their hostility.

Secondly, in various places in my writings I am critical of theologians 95 who ignore both Holy Scripture and the writings of the old commentators and wear themselves out over sophistical wrangles. My advice had the effect of persuading a great number of theologians to return to the sources and enlist the help of the humanities, and thus treat the mysteries of divine wisdom in a more sensible way. They were furious and blamed me. 100

* * * * *

15 Nicolas Coppin, dean of St Peter's at Louvain. See Ep 1719 n8.
16 Alonso de Fonseca. See Ep 1748 introduction.
17 See Ep 1744 n19 for Erasmus' belief that this old enemy was encouraging Spanish monks and theologians to attack him.

The third reason is similar: the fact that in my writings I sometimes disagree with Scotus, Thomas, Lyra, and Hugo,[18] and that I repeatedly stress the nature of true religion. That irks the monks, to see their favourite authors ignored. Yet I nowhere condemn them totally, though I place them second to better men. Then they protest noisily that young men are being   105 discouraged from entering the monastic life. But it was supremely important for the young to know what true religion is and how it differs from superstition, so that they are not deceived by an empty pretence of piety and plunge headlong into a way of life from which they may later want in vain to escape. If they took this advice, we would perhaps have fewer   110 monks, but they would be more sincere. Now we might quote the words of the prophet: 'Thou hast multiplied the nation, but not increased the joy.'[19]

This is the source of all the trouble. But it will cease at once if the princes and men like you use your authority to end their attacks. If this does not happen, there is danger that they will stir up a worse storm than that caused   115 by the Lutherans. For what can come of these conspiracies, protests, insults, savage libels, and malicious calumnies except discord throughout the world? Nothing is gained by issuing edicts.[20] It would be more helpful if his imperial Majesty gave a clear signal of his support for genuine learning. He could do this by honouring teachers of languages in Spain and at Louvain   120 and Tournai[21] with generous rewards, or special privileges, or some other

* * * * *

18 In other words, he disagrees sometimes with four of the principal authorities of medieval scholastic theology, John Duns Scotus, Thomas Aquinas, Nicholas of Lyra, and Hugo of St Cher. For an earlier exchange between Erasmus and Noël Béda on the authority of the earlier scholastic theologians, see Epp 1571:45–7, 1579:28–31, 1581:90–8, 134–6, 587–92, 643–57. Cf also Epp 1672 n14, 1679 n5, 1687 nn17, 19.

19 Isaiah 9:3; for Erasmus' concern about the practice of encouraging youths to take monastic vows at an early age, see Ep 1697 n12.

20 Erasmus suggests that prohibitions and warnings such as the emperor and Gattinara himself had issued were no real solution to the problem of attacks by the scholastic conservatives but that generous acts of imperial patronage to encourage the growth of humanistic studies would produce far more positive and more durable results.

21 Louvain was the seat of the only university in the Hapsburg-ruled Netherlands. It already had the *Collegium Trilingue* (Trilingual College), founded as a centre for humanism by a bequest from Erasmus' friend Jérôme de Busleyden, and humanists held influential positions in several of the colleges. In addition, since 1521 Pierre Cotrel, vicar-general of the diocese of Tournai, with the assistance of Erasmus' friend Robert de Keysere, tried to transform an existing classical school into a new university that would be a centre of humanistic

form of recognition. As for my own case, it would help if your Highness on behalf of the emperor, or someone else on your behalf or the emperor's (Jean Lalemand,[22] for example, or Cornelis de Schepper[23]) sent a private letter to Nicolas of Mons, chancellor of the University of Louvain,[24] and the rest of the theologians to the following effect (or in whatever terms you may, in your wise judgment, prefer): 'Do not teach others by your example to flout the emperor's edicts; instead make a serious effort to curb your tongue and stop issuing offensive tracts that can produce nothing but discord. Remember there is enough dissension in the world at present without adding new causes of friction; there are enough people ready to come forward and defend the teachings of Luther without driving into his faction, by false charges, those who wish to remain, and have thus far remained, within the fellowship of the Catholic church – and not just remained, but are struggling with all their might against the enemies of the church. Do you not realize how unfair it is for a man standing in the front line of the battle and locked in combat with Luther to be stabbed in the back by the very people he is defending? Surely it is enough to be the constant target of the Lutherans in books written in Latin and German. It would be better to call deserters back to the church's camp rather than to expel its friends.

125

130

135

140

* * * * *

studies. This new university actually came into being in 1525 as a *Collegium Bilingue* (Bilingual College, for Greek and Latin), despite bitter opposition by the Louvain faculty, but it was forced to close permanently in 1530, largely because of the hostile influence of Louvain. See Ep 1237 n8.

22 Secretary to the emperor Charles v from 1519 to 1528. See Ep 1554 introduction.

23 Schepper, also known as Cornelis de Dobbele (1502/3–1555), was a native of Nieuwpoort in Flanders and a descendant of a family of Flemish nobles. He studied at Paris under the humanist Gérard Roussel and then at the University of Louvain, where he matriculated in 1522, studied languages at the Collegium Trilingue, and became a close friend of the humanist Conradus Goclenius. He published a book against astrology in 1523, but he made his career in the service of rulers, including the exiled King Christian ii of Denmark (brother-in-law of the emperor Charles v), and from 1526, the emperor himself. He became councillor and secretary to the imperial court in Spain and was especially close to Gattinara. He was also active as an imperial diplomat and administrator. It is not known whether or when Erasmus met Schepper in person, but the latter's ties to Louvain (especially to the Collegium Trilingue) and to the pro-Erasmian group of imperial councillors headed by Gattinara probably explain why Erasmus here regards him as an influential friend. There were also many mutual friends, of whom Erasmus' former *famulus* Lieven Algoet and Schepper's former teacher Goclenius were probably the most important in maintaining contact. See CEBR iii 218–20

24 That is, Nicolas Coppin. See n3 above.

For even if something could be found in the writings of Erasmus that had been put down without due care (and no author is able to avoid such faults), there is no need to make an issue of it in these dangerous times and amid such general turmoil, especially since the author gives clear evidence of a devout and pious mind, and has always submitted his work to the judg-   145
ment of the church, and is ready, moreover, to correct or explain anything that justly gives offence to good and honest men. Nothing will ever satisfy those whose minds are filled with hate. The judgments of love are blind, but blinder still are the judgments of hate. Then you should also take some account of the long hours Erasmus has spent, and is still spending every day,   150
for the advancement of theology and the humanities.'

But it is foolish of me to put words into the mouth of so wise a person as yourself. I can say at any rate that there is nothing here that is not the absolute truth. If you have some other plan that you think more effective in controlling the commotion caused by these people, then, I beg you, come to   155
the aid of sound learning and assist Erasmus and all honest scholars. May the Lord Jesus keep your Highness safe and well.

Basel, 3 September 1526

Your illustrious Highness' humble and devoted servant, Erasmus of Rotterdam   160

Signed by my own hand

To the right worshipful Master Mercurino Gattinara, chancellor to his imperial Majesty. In Spain

1748 / To Alonso de Fonseca   Basel, 3 September 1526

Although Erasmus had only a limited understanding of personalities, factions, and issues in the imperial court and ecclesiastical hierarchy of Spain (a fact ev-idenced by his suspicious misinterpretation of the manuscript *Collationes* sent to him by his Benedictine admirer Alonso Ruiz de Virués) he had known since 1524 that both Alonso de Fonseca (cf Ep 1431), archbishop of Toledo and pri-mate of Spain, and his secretary, Juan de Vergara (cf Epp 1277, 1684), admired his scholarly and religious publications and supported him against conser-vative monks and theologians in Spain. Hence reports of the effort to bring charges of unorthodoxy against him naturally led him to appeal directly to Archbishop Fonseca as the highest-ranking prelate of the Spanish church. On these reports see Epp 1742, 1744 nn19, 20. Fonseca (1475–1534) was far from a model prelate. The illegitimate son of an archbishop of Santiago de Com-postela, he was supported by valuable ecclesiastical benefices from an early age. In 1506 his father secured for him the succession to his own archbishopric. He was active in court politics and himself fathered a son, for whom he cre-ated a hereditary estate. But as archbishop of Santiago he founded colleges at the University of Salamanca, where he had studied, and in Santiago itself. At the end of 1523 he was elected to the primatial see of Toledo, which under his predecessor Guillaume (II) de Croy had already become a centre of Erasmian influence. Vergara confirmed his respect for Erasmus' scholarship, and he became an active supporter of the new University of Alcalá, where Vergara had been an influential figure, and of the printer Miguel de Eguía, who published many of the editions of Erasmus' works that stimulated the wave of enthusiasm for Erasmus that swept through Spanish intellectual life in the late 1520s and early 1530s. As a councillor of state from 1526, he supported the policies of the imperial chancellor Mercurino de Gattinara, who was the most powerful supporter of Erasmus at court. For assurances that Fonseca would support Erasmus against the inquisitorial investigation launched against him by Spanish monks, see the letter of 13 March 1527 to Erasmus from Pedro Juan Olivar (Ep 1791). In April 1527 Fonseca offered Erasmus a pension of four hundred ducats a year if he would settle in Spain (Epp 1813, 1814). A manuscript copy of the present letter in Vergara's hand survives in the Biblioteca Nacional at Madrid. It was first published by Adolfo Bonilla y San Martín in *Revue hispanique* 17 (1907) 526–7.

Cordial greetings, most reverend archbishop. I learn in letters from my friends[1] of the plots that certain desperate individuals are hatching in your part of the world against the humanities and against my own writings, and of the sterling efforts your lordship has made, not just on my behalf, but also for the cause of liberal studies. These are flourishing now in every cor- 5
ner of the world, but nowhere more than in Spain, once the most celebrated cradle of learning, whose men of genius have shed their light even on Italy. I have no time to write more now; so I am enclosing a copy of a letter I sent to Master Mercurino Gattinara, chancellor to his imperial Majesty, from which you will learn what is happening.[2] At another time I shall prove to you that 10
these services of yours were not rendered to an ungrateful wretch. May Christ keep your lordship safe and well.

Basel, 3 September 1526
Your lordship's most devoted servant, Erasmus of Rotterdam
In his own hand 15

* * * * *

1748
1 Not identified, but doubtless Juan de Vergara, Archbishop Fonseca's secretary, was one of them. Juan Luis Vives and Erasmus Schets were other frequent correspondents who had strong connections with Spain and might have provided Erasmus with word of Fonseca's interest in him.
2 Ep 1747

Ferry de Carondelet
Portrait by Sebastiano del Piombo, 1511
Sammlung Thyssen-Bornemisza, Lugano-Castagnola

1749 / To Ferry de Carondelet   Basel, 7 September 1526

On this aristocratic friend of Erasmus, born and reared in the Netherlands
of an old Burgundian family, see Ep 1350 n6. After studying at Dôle and
Bologna and receiving a doctorate of law, he became a member of the Grand
Council at Mechelen and a trusted adviser of the governor of the Netherlands,
Margaret of Austria. Although he was never ordained a priest, from 1504 he
was canon and archdeacon of the cathedral at Besançon in the Franche-Comté.
In 1511 he became commendatory (and absentee) abbot of Montbenoît in the
Franche-Comté. He settled at Besançon in 1520 and was active in the affairs
of the chapter; Erasmus visited him there in 1524 (Ep 1610). He also carried
out an ambitious programme of repair and new construction at Montbenoît.
This letter was first printed in Erasmus' *Opus epistolarum* (1529).

ERASMUS OF ROTTERDAM TO FERRY DE CARONDELET, GREETING
Most honoured sir, several of my friends have written to tell me of the
favourable regard in which I am held by your brother, the archbishop of
Palermo.[1] But the chicanery and unscrupulousness of certain people there
count for more than the merits of a few. I derived much comfort from your   5
letter,[2] which was couched in such affectionate language. But my poor health
makes me unfit for company, and I am ashamed of the trouble I caused you
by my illness. The stone has developed into another problem, for which
there is no cure. Familiar maladies are easier to bear: this one is all the more
distressing because it is unknown. Then I am bound to the treadmill of the   10
printing shop, so that I cannot move a step from here.
      Froben has begun another edition of my New Testament.[3] If your li-
brary[4] contains any old manuscripts, especially of the Gospels and apostolic
letters, please send them, and you will make me very grateful. That will
give me an excuse for honouring your chapter and yourself properly.   15
      Now can I ask a favour of you? I had three casks of Burgundy, enough,
I thought, to last the winter. The one I am drinking at present is going flat;

* * * * *

1749
1 This was Jean (ii) de Carondelet, elder brother of Ferry, a councillor to Charles
   v who was rewarded with the archbishopric of Palermo but became an adviser
   to the Hapsburg government in the Netherlands and never visited his diocese.
   Cf Ep 1703.
2 Not extant
3 The fourth edition, published by Froben at Basel in March 1527. Cf Ep 1571 n9.
4 Erasmus means the chapter library at Besançon. There is no evidence that this
   collection contained anything useful for Erasmus' textual revision.

when I open the second one, I find it is completely flat. You will save your friend's life if you send him a small cask of wine, a light ruby in colour, not too fiery, but of good quality, though it should be well aged.[5] I have given instructions about this to our friend Biétry,[6] who will see that it is delivered here at my expense. If there is any way in which I can return the favour, there is nothing I shall refuse. May God keep you safe and well.

Basel, the eve of the Nativity of the Virgin Mother, 1526

1750 / From Erasmus Schets   Antwerp, 8 September 1526

This is business correspondence from Erasmus' financial agent in Antwerp. On Schets see Ep 1541 introduction. Like nearly all of this correspondence, Erasmus carefully preserved it but never published it. The original survives at Basel, and Allen was the first to edit it, in 1926.

Cordial greetings. I told you in my last letter how much money I received on your behalf from the bishop of London,[1] namely 120 crowns,[2] which

* * * * *

5 Erasmus was convinced that a supply of good Burgundy wine was necessary to keep his chronic problem with kidney stones under control. Cf Epp 1316 n7, 1359 n5, 1510:109–12. Not the least of Basel's advantages as a place of residence was its easy communication with the source of this wine. The French translator of Erasmus' letters, Aloïs Gerlo (vi 489), rendered Erasmus' descriptive adjective, *subrubri,* as 'rosé,' but the letters cited above make it clear that Erasmus is talking about 'light red' or 'light ruby,' not 'pink' or 'rosé.'

6 On Thiébaut Biétry, parish priest at Porrentruy in the Jura, a place on the route from Besançon to Basel, see Epp 1391 introduction, 1573, and 1610. He was a personal friend of Erasmus and probably also of Ferry de Carondelet, and he accompanied Erasmus on his visit to Besançon in the spring of 1524. He forwarded this letter to the addressee, a mutual friend; cf Ep 1760:9.

1750

1 On the generosity regularly shown to Erasmus by Cuthbert Tunstall, bishop of London, see Ep 1726, which enclosed a bill of exchange intended as a monetary gift to Erasmus and which the bishop addressed to Pieter Gillis in Antwerp, evidently because he did not know that Erasmus Schets had replaced Gillis in the management of Erasmus' financial affairs. Schets' 'last letter' to Erasmus is lost.

2 The reference to 'crowns' and 'florins' in this sentence may be confusing (see also the following note). The 120 'crowns' (*coronatos*) received from the bishop of London are not the familiar French coins but the newly introduced English 'crown of the rose.' This was struck from 22 August 1526 at 23.875 carats fineness (117.333 to the Troy pound of 373.242g), with 3.164g fine gold (worth 4s 6d sterling), and thus it was similar in form and value to the French écu

is the equivalent in current money of 252 florins.[3] Then after much delay
Pieter Gillis handed me the money to settle his account with you;[4] I en-

* * * * *

au soleil (which, however, contained 3.296g fine gold). Thus 120 crowns were
worth £27 sterling: 1,080 days' wages for a master carpenter at Oxford. The
ordinance introducing this new coin also provided that all English and foreign
gold coins of legal tender were to be increased in value by 10 percent, 'because
[gold] money is enhanced and is leaving the kingdom,' that is, the value of
these coins was increased to accord with rising continental gold values. The
French 'gold crown soleil' was raised to 4s 6d [= 54d]; the Venetian ducat and
Florentine florin to 4s 8d [= 56d]; the English gold sovereign to 22s 0d sterling;
the ryal or rose-noble to 11s 0d; and the angel-noble to 7s 4d [= 88d] sterling.
See *Tudor and Stuart Proclamations 1485–1714* I *England and Wales* ed Robert
Steele (Oxford 1910) 11 no 104 and n3.

3 Latin *qui conficiunt monete currentis summam ii^c lii florenis*: In Antwerp, those
'florins' whose value is equated with that of the new English crowns (see
the preceding note) are neither the Rhenish (Rheingulden) nor the Florentine
florins, but the Burgundian-Hapsburg money-of-account, formerly based on
the Rheingulden, as noted below, consisting of 40d groot Flemish – that is,
$^1/_6$ of the pound groot Flemish (CWE 1 347). If the new English rose crown
enjoyed the same value as the French *écu au soleil* in the Hapsburg Netherlands, and if the former gold rates of August 1521 were still holding valid,
then 120 crowns at 76d groot should have been worth £38 groot Flemish or
228 Burgundian-Hapsburg florins of account (that is, 120 × 76/240 = 38; 38
× 240/40 = 228). But Schets tells us that they were worth instead 252 such
florins, thus indicating that the value of both 'crowns,' English and French,
was now about 84d groot Flemish (252 florins/120 crowns × 40d groot = 84d).
This accords with our independent knowledge of rising gold values during
this era. On 5 November 1526, Henry VIII increased the official value of gold
coins once more, for an overall increase of 12.5 per cent, and introduced a new
gold crown, the 'double rose' crown of just 22 carats fineness, but with a heavier weight (100.5 to the Troy pound), containing 3.404g fine gold, and worth
5s 0d sterling; he also reduced the silver coinage in weight and thus the silver
content of the pound sterling by 11.11 per cent, thereby adjusting the bimetallic mint ratio more in favour of gold. The same ordinance also again denied legal tender to ducats and other foreign gold coins, declaring them to be bullion
(that is, requiring them to be sold to the King's Exchanger and the Tower Mint
for the value of their gold contents only). See Steele (n2 above) I 12 no 105; *A
New History of the Royal Mint* ed Christopher Challis (Cambridge 1992) 720; and
also n5 below. The Latin term *monete currentis* used by Schets, was commonly
used in documents at this time to distinguish sums expressed in money-of-
account (that is, sums recorded in money reckoned according to the value of
the currently circulating silver penny) from those reckoned in the actual gold
coins. Needless to say, it is often crucial to distinguish between the different
types of florins so frequently mentioned in Erasmus' correspondence.

4 On Gillis see Ep 1671 n6 and the references given there. This payment to
Schets completed the rather awkward business of closing Erasmus' account

close a copy of the account with this letter. The total has been properly and   5
accurately calculated; you will be pleased to see from the statement that
the total of your receipts amounts to 445 florins and 12 stuivers in current
money.[5] Everything received and paid to your account has been estimated
in this currency. This was precisely the sum that Pieter Gillis paid over to
me himself.   10

So I have in your name 697 florins and 12 stuivers in current money,
which, when changed into gold florins, comes to a total of 436.[6] I have given

* * * * *

with Gillis and completing the transfer of full responsibility for Erasmus' financial affairs from Gillis to Schets. There had been an earlier transfer of
funds by Gillis the previous spring, using the spring session of the Frankfurt fair and employing Pieter's brother Frans Gillis as the one who transferred money destined for Erasmus to Johann Froben, but that payment
had not satisfied the full amount owed by Pieter Gillis. See Epp 1681, 1682,
1696.

5 Latin *ad summam iiii^c xlv florenorum et xii stuferorum monete currentis*. The stuiver
was originally a silver coin worth 2d groot (also known as the double groot
or patard) and had become the 'shilling' in the Burgundian-Hapsburg money-
of-account. By 1459–60, the actual circulating Rhenish gold florin had risen
in value to 40d groot Flemish (= 60d groot Brabant), thus equalling in value
the old money-of-account known as the *livre d'Artois*, or more commonly the
livre de quarante gros (Stadsarchief Leuven, Stadsrekening 1459–60 nos 5087–8).
From this time the name 'florin' superseded the other terms for this silver-
based money-of-account, which was always tied to the currently circulating
Flemish silver groot – not to the Rhenish florin itself. Just as the pound contained 20 shillings, so this florin money-of-account contained 20 stuivers (that
is, 2d × 20 = 40d). In this money-of-account, the sum recorded on this financial
statement (445.6/6 florins) was worth £74 5s 4d groot Flemish; or, in equivalent silver values, £48 14s 11d sterling or £466 10s 9d tournois. As for the actual Rhenish gold florin itself, its value in terms of the Flemish silver coinage
had continued to rise, from 40d groot Flemish in 1460 to 59d groot in 1521
and possibly to 64d groot by 1526 (see nn2, 3 above). See also n6 just below
and CWE 1 331, 347; but note two serious and related typographical errors in
the latter: the second and third lines of Appendix E no 3 should read: '£1 10s
od groot of Brabant (from 1434) = £6 os od Artois, or livres de quarante gros
= £12 os od parisis.'

6 Latin *tuarum pecuniarum vi^c lxxxxvii florenos cum xii stuferis monete currentis; qui reducti in florenos aureos valent iiii^c xxxvi floreni aurei*. The sum of
697 florins of account and 12 stuivers (see nn 3, 5 above) was worth £116
5s 4d groot Flemish, at 40d per account florin. At the official rate of exchange of 59d groot per Rhenish gold florin, this sum should have represented 473 florins; but since Erasmus tells us that it was worth only 436
Rhenish florins, we may deduce that with the recent and sharp rise in
gold values – the result of a rising influx of South-German and Bohemian

orders for this sum to be handed over to Froben for you at the next Frankfurt fair.[7] I hope this will work out, and that the money will reach you.
Please inform me when it arrives.   15

This packet of letters comes from Spain;[8] I was instructed to take the
greatest care in passing it on to you. I am sending it to Frankfurt so that
Froben can take it on from there to Basel. I could not find a more reliable
messenger; they told me to make sure that I had a note from you acknowledging receipt of the packet. Please let me have it as soon as possible so that 20
I can do what my friend requested.

My sincerest good wishes, dear Erasmus, and please don't forget to
write to Portugal.[9]

Antwerp, 8 September 1526
Your devoted friend, Erasmus Schets   25
To the eminent scholar, Master Erasmus of Rotterdam. In Basel

* * * * *

silver into the Antwerp market – the actual market value of the Rhenish florin had now risen to about 64d groot Flemish; that is, as silver became cheaper because of its increasing supply, gold became more expensive when priced in relation to that cheaper silver. The rate of 64d represents a 12.5 per cent rise in gold values, corresponding to the increased
rates proclaimed in England in November 1526. See nn2, 3, 5 above, Ep
1758 n2, and John Munro 'The Central European Mining Boom, Mint Outputs, and Prices in the Low Countries and England, 1450–1550' in *Money,
Coins, and Commerce: Essays in the Monetary History of Asia and Europe (From
Antiquity to Modern Times)* ed Eddy H.G. Van Cauwenberghe (Louvain 1991)
119–83.

7 For an example of the reliance of Schets on the semi-annual commercial fair
at Frankfurt, regularly attended by Johann Froben because it was the major
centre for distribution of books throughout Germany and much of western
Europe, see Ep 1654 nn5–6. The fair facilitated the transfer of books, other
merchandise, and money between Antwerp and Basel because merchants from
both places went there to do business. See also Ep 1660 n4.

8 The packet of letters from Spain must have included Ep 1731 from the emperor Charles v. In Ep 1781 (31 January 1527), Erasmus reported to Schets
that he had already received the Spanish letters, including one from the emperor, through Maximilianus Transsilvanus, an official at the imperial court
in the Netherlands. It had been dispatched in duplicate, following two different routes, a common practice of royal and papal chanceries on account of the
dangers and uncertainties of travel even for official couriers in the sixteenth
century. As of 20 December 1526 Schets had not received word that the letters
had reached Basel safely (Ep 1772).

9 For Schets' eagerness to have Erasmus gain the patronage of King John III of
Portugal, see Epp 1681 introduction, lines 34–47 and nn8, 10; 1682 introduction
and lines 18–24.

1751 / To Hieronim Łaski   Basel, 9 September 1526

The recipient of this letter, a Polish baron, was the elder brother of Erasmus'
young friend and disciple Jan Łaski; see Epp 1242 n5, 1443 introduction, 1593
n18, 1622 n3. In 1524 Erasmus dedicated to him his *Modus orandi Deum* (Ep
1502). On the present occasion, he is sending a gift copy of his *Institutio christiani matrimonii*, which he published in August, dedicated to Queen Catherine
of England (Ep 1727). Erasmus included this letter in *Opus epistolarum*.

ERASMUS OF ROTTERDAM TO HIERONIM ŁASKI,
VOIVODE OF SIERADZ, IN POLAND, GREETING

Distinguished sir, here is the latest product of my modest wits, the *Matrimo-*
nium christianum. I am not sending it to your brother, since he has espoused
the celibate life,[1] but to you, who have chosen to ensure that the human race   5
does not die out! In doing so, it is not my aim to teach you how you ought
to conduct yourself in marriage – for I have no doubt that you live most vir-
tuously in holy matrimony; rather I want you to let me know if I have omitted anything or treated some aspect of the subject otherwise than I ought.
Perhaps you will think that in laying down rules for marriage I am just as   10
silly as that celebrated philosopher whom Hannibal judged mad for holding
forth about war, of which he had no personal experience.[2] So I shall await
your verdict before preparing a second edition. I would like to carry on this
chat a little longer, but my other obligations call me away. I pray that you
and yours may continue to prosper.   15
    Basel, the morrow of the Feast of the Nativity of the Virgin Mary AD
1526

1752 / To Krzysztof Szydłowiecki   Basel, 9 September 1526

In 1525 Erasmus had dedicated his *Lingua* to this influential Polish political
figure and patron of literature and art (cf Ep 1593) and had already received
Szydłowiecki's thanks in a letter (now lost) from their mutual friend Hieronim
Łaski (see Ep 1622). The young physician Jan Antonin, who had settled in
Cracow, had already informed Erasmus of Szydłowiecki's promise to reward

* * * * *

1751
1 Jan Łaski was being groomed to become the successor to his uncle and name-
  sake Jan Łaski, archbishop of Gniezno, the primate's seat of Poland. He already
  held several benefices, though later in his life he became a leading figure of
  Reformed Protestantism. See Ep 1674 introduction.
2 Cicero *De oratore* 2.75–6

the literary dedication with valuable gifts, including gold work produced by Antonin's father-in-law, a skilled goldsmith patronized by the royal court (Ep 1660:45–7. Erasmus acknowledged receipt of these gifts in a letter of 28 April 1526 to Antonin (Ep 1698:16–21) and in this letter expresses his thanks to the donor himself. Several of these objects are identical with items given to specific individuals under the terms of Erasmus' first will, dated 22 January 1527 (540–50 below). Erasmus published this letter in *Opus epistolarum* (1529).

ERASMUS OF ROTTERDAM TO KRZYSTOF SZYDŁOWIECKI,
CHANCELLOR TO THE KING OF POLAND, GREETING

For the first time I am beginning to be less displeased with my *Lingua*, now that I see how much you think of it. If a man like you, endowed with every kind of virtue and accomplishment, had merely expressed his opinion in a   5
letter, that would have answered all my prayers. But with your extraordinary generosity you were not content with that. You corroborated the verdict of your letter with the further evidence of some remarkable gifts. Everything arrived safely, the gold hourglass[1] and the gold fork and spoon. Something made of clay would have suited me, but these gifts were appropriate   10
to your golden nature and your bright and shining character. Now I have

* * * * *

1752
1 Erasmus' word, *horologium*, could refer either to an hourglass or to a watch. The spring-driven watch (often worn on a chain about the neck) had been developed during the fifteenth century, perhaps initially in Italy; and by the first decade of the sixteenth century, it had come into regular production as a luxury item at Nürnberg and perhaps at other German cities active in the metal trades. By the 1520s watches were being purchased by kings and nobles as luxury items. The city of Nürnberg on several occasions in the 1520s presented watches as gifts to foreign ambassadors, and a group of admirers at Nürnberg gave Philippus Melanchthon a watch in 1530. See Eric Bruton *Clocks & Watches* (Feltham, Middlesex 1968) 34–7, 46; Gerhard Dohrn-van Rossum *History of the Hour: Clocks and Modern Temporal Orders* (Chicago 1996) 120–3; Samuel Guye and Henri Michel *Time and Space: Measuring Instruments from the 15th to the 19th Century* (New York 1971) 66–81; and David S. Landes *Revolution in Time: Clocks and the Making of the Modern World* (Cambridge, MA 1983) 83–7. But careful study of the will that Erasmus made in 1527 and of the inventory of Erasmus' possessions drawn up in 1534 by his secretary Gilbert Cousin shows that Szydłowiecki's gift was not one of the new pocket watches but a costly hourglass (a timepiece using sand). Erasmus left to his friend Ludwig Baer his *horologium arenarium ex puro auro* 'sand timepiece made of pure gold,' and the inventory lists an *horologium* 'of pure gold, with case,' as a gift from Szydłowiecki. Furthermore, Bonifacius Amerbach, acting as executor of Erasmus' estate, wrote on Cousin's inventory a note that he had delivered this item to Baer; see Allen (7n) and Erasmus' First Will 541 below.

something to show off; for I imagine there are people who will argue that
a compliment paid in a letter means little. But there is nothing commonplace about such gifts as these. I am most grateful for them, distinguished
sir, as indeed I ought to be, but I owe you even more for using your influ-   15
ence to defend my reputation against the slanderous cackle of my critics. It
is not just myself whom you have put under an obligation by this action,
but everyone who loves good literature. Those who wish me ill direct their
fire against the humanities.

The *Lingua* has done well under your auspices. Froben has had a most   20
successful sale. The book has already gone into a third printing and has
been issued simultaneously by several other presses.[2] This would not have
happened unless a lot of people had liked the work. Farewell.

Basel, the morrow of the Feast of the Nativity of the Virgin Mother
1526   25

1753 / To Andrzej Krzycki   Basel, 9 September 1526

A reply to Ep 1652. On the addressee, bishop of Przemyśl from 1522 and (by
exchange) of Płock from 1527, see Ep 1629 introduction. Since Allen's Latin
text was based on only the printed texts, of which the earliest is Erasmus' own
Opus epistolarum (1529), the chronological discrepancy between the date of this
letter and the attribution of the see of Płock to Krzycki in the address probably
results from a 'correction' made by Erasmus or someone else at the Froben
press in order to give Krzycki his correct title as of the date of the printed
edition. As this letter suggests, Krzycki was a skilled and prolific Latin poet.

ERASMUS OF ROTTERDAM TO ANDRZEJ KRZYCKI,
BISHOP OF PŁOCK, GREETING

My lord bishop, when chance offered me the services of a courier, I reread
your long autograph letter,[1] not so much with the intention of replying,
since I did not have the time, but to experience again the pleasure I felt   5

* * * * *

2 The original edition was printed in August 1525; the second, in February
  1526; and the third, in July 1526. In addition, the delighted Szydłowiecki had
  arranged for an edition to be produced in Poland (Cracow: Hieronymus Vietor, January 1526). On these editions and a great many additional, unauthorized, editions, see Elaine Fantham's introduction to the translation in CWE 29
  253; cf the introduction by J.H. Waszink in ASD IV-1A (1989) 9–10, 16–17.

1753
1 Ep 1652

Andrezj Krzycki
Portrait sculpture on his tombstone in the cathedral of Gniezno, Poland
Polska Akademia Nauk Instytut Sztuki, Warszawa

when I first read it, and also to find relief from ill health, hard work, and
the storms that beat upon our world. For your letter is learned, lively, and
warm-hearted. In it one feels that the Muses have joined forces with the
Graces. Not even Cicero was lucky enough to be praised in both prose and
verse. You write poetry as though this were your only *métier*, and your care-   10
fully crafted prose, while it can rise to the grand manner of the historian,
never aspires to the licence of poetry.[2] The more you regret the fact that
episcopal office and public obligations have kept you from literature, for
which you feel a natural aptitude, the more reason we have to congratulate
the Christian world; for none are more useful to Christendom than those   15
who are most reluctant to leave the sweet study of philosophy to serve their
country. And yet, even amid the rushing waters of your busy life, you will
be able from time to time to carve out for yourself a little leisure for the
Muses.

To the generous compliments you were kind enough to pay me I have   20
nothing to say except that I am less conscious of the merits you see in me
than of what I owe to your good will. I have worked hard to smooth the
rough corners of my Dutch nature by contact with the humanities.[3] But that
was not my only aim; I wanted above all to make the humanities speak about
Christ, for hitherto in Italy, as you are aware, they were largely pagan.[4]   25
My efforts brought me great unpopularity, but they would have turned out

* * * * *

2 It was a cardinal doctrine of ancient rhetoric that prose should not aspire to
the freedom of poetry; see, for example, Cicero *De oratore* 3.153. Historians,
however, were accorded greater licence than orators.
3 Erasmus from time to time used reference to his Dutch origins as a way to
express his modesty and to disclaim any title to elegance and sophistication,
presenting the Dutch character as rather crude and unpolished but essentially
good-hearted. See Epp 1629:11–12 (also to Krzycki), 1635:9–10 (to Benedetto
Giovio), and cf Krzycki's response indicating that Erasmus is excessively modest, Ep 1652:13–16. A well-known passage from the *Colloquies* where Erasmus
describes the good traits of his fellow Dutchmen (in this case, Hollanders) appears at the end of *Naufragium* 'The Shipwreck'; see CWE 39 360:11–16 and n32.
4 On Erasmus' opinion that most of the fashionable Italian humanists of his
time, especially those at the papal curia, had little or no Christian belief, see
Ep 1717:4–5 and n2, and cf Epp 1479:133–6, 176–85, and 195–9, 1581:8–14, and,
much later, his tart response to the criticism of Germans by Agostino Steuco,
Allen Ep 2465:470–6, where he recalls the irreverent and blasphemous things
he had heard and seen while visiting Rome in 1509. In his *Ciceronianus* (1528)
he flatly charged that the 'Ciceronians' were so captivated by pagan mythology
that their treatment of Christian themes lacked any true religious spirit; see
CWE 28 436–9, 447.

tolerably well had it not been for the deadly storm that is now turning the Christian world upside down.[5]

Some time ago I published my *Diatribe*,[6] realizing that there was no other way in which I could free myself from the persistent suspicions that 30 my enemies had planted firmly in the minds of the princes. I confined myself to rational argument. Luther replied with unprecedented bitterness.[7] This charming fellow wrote to me after the publication of his book, swearing that he had the warmest regard for me.[8] He came close to demanding that I thank him for treating me so civilly, since he would have written in a very different 35 spirit had he been dealing with an enemy. All this time, while I was locked in battle with a gladiator like this, some theologians and monks (especially the latter) formed a solid phalanx against me. So obsessive is their hatred that they are beginning to side with Luther because he has raved so violently against me. It is clear that this is a deliberate plot, for they have begun 40 the same nonsense simultaneously in Spain, Italy, England, Brabant, France, Hungary, and Poland. Four books have appeared in Paris, attacking me in the strongest terms.[9] To say no more, the king will find it difficult to suppress them. These people get round the edicts of the emperor and those of the king and the Parlement. They have no shame, no respect for law. Whatever pleases 45 them is right. Unless the princes use their authority to control their excesses, they will ignite a more dangerous blaze in the world than ever Luther did.

As for your kind invitation to escape the stormy waters of Germany and seek a quiet harbour with you, even supposing that this were permitted by my health and the demands of the arena I have just entered as a 50 new combatant, I am afraid I would not find everything in your country as tranquil as I would like – if only for your sake. To your excellent king and queen,[10] of whose good will I learn in letters from other friends, I feel as

* * * * *

5 That is, the outbreak of the Reformation
6 *De libero arbitrio* διατριβή (1524), his work directly challenging Luther's theology
7 In his *De servo arbitrio* (1525), a savage attack impugning not only Erasmus' theological competence but also his spiritual and moral integrity. Cf Ep 1667.
8 This letter, which Erasmus regarded as representing the height of arrogance and ill temper, is lost, but the tone of Erasmus' reply (Ep 1688) shows that he found it at least as offensive and patronizing as the published treatise. Erasmus' friend Thomas More agreed that Luther's letter was offensive; see Ep 1770:63–5.
9 Cf Epp 1743:54–5 (where he counts five such books) and n11, 1744:127–8.
10 On Sigismund I (1467–1548, king from 1506), see Epp 1652 n5, 1819. The queen was Bona Sforza (1494–1557), daughter of Giangaleazzo Sforza, duke of Milan, Sigismund's second wife. Well educated and politically influential,

deeply obliged as though I had accepted all the kind offers they made. But
what vexes me most is the difficulty of maintaining even this literary kind   55
of friendship, given the distances that separate us and the burden of my
work, which is enough to wear out even a Milo.[11] So, my excellent friend,
please don't judge my feelings towards you from this flat and clumsy letter; perhaps I shall have an opportunity to express what I feel at another
time. Meanwhile, I count myself lucky to have such a friend and patron. I   60
preserve your letters among the things I treasure most as an expression of
your undying good will. May the Lord Jesus keep your lordship safe and
well and guide you always to ever greater and better things.

    Basel, the morrow of the feast of the Nativity of the Blessed Virgin
Mary 1526   65

1754 / To Jacobus Piso   Basel, 9 September 1526

> A reply to Ep 1662. On Piso, a prominent Hungarian humanist and courtier,
> see Ep 1662 introduction. The letter was first published in Erasmus' collection
> *Opus epistolarum*.

ERASMUS OF ROTTERDAM TO THE HUNGARIAN JACOBUS PISO,
PROVOST ETC, GREETING
Dear Piso, my learned friend, you do indeed observe the ancient custom,[1]
for you have been most generous (or should I say compassionate?) towards
your old friend. I received two letters from you[2] and two coins, one in gold   5
bearing the image of the emperor Gratian,[3] and the other in silver with the

* * * * *

    she patronized the arts actively and showed some (but not much) interest in
    literature and scholarship.
11 An athlete of the sixth century BC who was reputed to be strong enough to
    carry a heifer on his shoulders

    1754
 1 Evidently a reference to something Piso wrote, but the exact meaning remains
    obscure. It may simply refer to Ep 1662:103–6, where Piso says that he is send-
    ing the two coins Erasmus speaks of here as a New Year's gift. The Romans
    sent such gifts (*strenae*) and this may be the 'ancient custom' mentioned.
 2 Piso in Ep 1662 admits with embarrassment that after writing Ep 1297 as much
    as four years earlier, he misplaced it; after rediscovering it, he dispatched it
    on 1 February 1526 along with his letter of that date. Hence Erasmus got the
    two letters in the same packet.
 3 Flavius Gratianus, Roman emperor (367–83). See Ep 1662 n16. From the time
    of Augustus, the image of the reigning emperor was the usual figure on the
    obverse of imperial coins.

image of Hercules[4] – agreeable evidence of your feelings towards me. But nothing could have brought me more delight or been more charming or enjoyable than your letters. I read them often to myself and to my friends when I want to rid myself of depression, which inevitably creeps over me   10 because of the burden of my work and the tumult of the times, and especially on account of my ill health (to say nothing of the problems that come with old age). I never doubted your good will, even when you did not write. For Piso will always act like Piso. I am glad, however, to be reminded by your letters of the magnitude and extent of my indebtedness to   15 you, an indebtedness I am glad to acknowledge.

Velius[5] chides me repeatedly in his letters for my slowness in writing something for the bishop of Olomouc. I dedicated my Pliny to the bishop, but now he is demanding a work of my own.[6] I have just published the *Institutio matrimonii*, but this is a subject the queen of Britain commissioned   20 a year ago.[7] I intend to avoid such subjects altogether in the future. In any case, it would perhaps be inappropriate to dedicate a secular work to such a pious bishop. I have procured some Greek manuscripts of Chrysostom.[8] I shall translate some of these and dedicate them to the bishop if Velius thinks it a good idea. I have published an edition of Irenaeus. But Johannes   25 Fabri, who supplied a manuscript, would not hear of my dedicating it to anyone but the bishop of Trent.[9] So please ask Velius to let me know what will please the bishop best. I want to satisfy his repeated requests and at

* * * * *

4 Roman name for the deified Greek hero Herakles. His image, generally depicted performing one of his legendary exploits, appears frequently on coins of the Roman empire.
5 On Caspar Ursinus Velius, commonly known as Ursinus, a Silesian-born humanist and friend of Piso who visited Erasmus at Basel in 1521–2, see Epp 548:5–6nn, 1280 introduction. At this period he held the chair of rhetoric in the University of Vienna, and in 1527 he became historian to Archduke Ferdinand, later (1532) becoming tutor to Ferdinand's children. He disappeared from his home in Vienna in 1539 and was thought to have been a suicide.
6 On Stanislaus Thurzo, bishop of Olomouc in Moravia, see Ep 1242 introduction. Erasmus' dedication of his edition of Pliny *Naturalis historia* to him is Ep 1544. Eventually Erasmus did dedicate an original work to him in response to his requests, but only a minor one, *Enarratio psalmi trigesimi octavi* (Basel: Froben, March 1532). See Epp 2608 (the dedication) and 2699 (the bishop's letter of acknowledgment and thanks).
7 See Ep 1727.
8 See Ep 1705 n3.
9 See Ep 1715 n1 for Fabri's dispatch of a manuscript requested by Erasmus, and Ep 1738 for Erasmus' letter dedicating his edition of Irenaeus to Bernhard von Cles, prince-bishop of Trent.

the same time honour the memory of his distinguished brother,[10] something
I am most eager to do. If he would be happy with something like the *De*   30
modo orandi or the *De misericordiis Domini*,[11] I shall choose a subject that is
as free as possible from controversy. If he prefers Greek, I shall send him a
fair-sized volume.

I am sorry to hear of the trouble in your part of the world[12] – this
explains why I am not writing at greater length. I shall answer the rest of   35
your letter when I find a reliable courier and know where in the world you
are. Give my best wishes to Ursinus,[13] who is a good friend like yourself.
Perhaps the Frankfurt fair will bring something from you in the way of a
letter. Farewell.

Basel, 9 September 1526   40

1755 / To Bernhard von Cles   Basel, 26 September 1526

This letter accompanied a copy of Erasmus' edition of the *Adversus haereses*
of St Irenaeus, still too freshly printed to be properly bound, which Erasmus
had already dedicated to this influential bishop of Trent a month earlier (Ep

* * * * *

10 Johannes (II) Thurzo (1464/5–1520), bishop of Wrocław, had shared his
   brother's interest in humanism. Cf Ep 850.
11 Erasmus dedicated his *Modus orandi Deum* to Hieronim Łaski in October 1524
   (Ep 1502); his dedication of *De immensa Dei misericordia concio* to Christoph von
   Utenheim, bishop of Basel, is dated 29 July 1524 (Ep 1474).
12 'Trouble' (*res ... turbatas*) was hardly adequate to describe the situation that
   Piso and his patroness Queen Mary of Hungary faced. The defeat of the Hungarian army and the death of King Louis II in the battle of Mohács on 29 August 1526 led to the disintegration of the Hungarian monarchy, and the resulting chaos lasted for at least fifteen years. The native aristocrat John (János)
   Zápolyai claimed election to the royal title, the Turks raided freely and controlled most of the country, and the widowed Queen Mary fled from the in-
   secure capital at Buda and settled her household at Bratislava in the northern part of the country (now in Slovakia), while supporting the claim of her
   brother Archduke Ferdinand to the Hungarian throne. Eventually Ferdinand
   established himself as king, but he held control over only the western and
   northern districts. The Ottoman Sultan Suleiman annexed the central part of
   the country and established a strong garrison at Buda. Zápolyai and later his
   son János were recognized by the Turks as kings of Hungary but in practice were allowed to rule only the province of Transylvania under Ottoman
   suzerainty. See *A History of Hungary* ed Peter F. Sugar and others (Blooming-
   ton, IN 1990) 80–5; Denis Sinor *History of Hungary* (New York 1959) 144–59;
   C.A. Macartney *Hungary: A Short History* (Edinburgh 1962) 63–7. Cf Ep 1762
   introduction and n5.
13 Velius; see n5 above.

1738). It is also a reply to Bishop Bernhard's letter of 1 August written from the Diet of Speyer (Ep 1730). The bishop was delighted with the dedication and reciprocated with a substantial gift of money (Epp 1771, 1793). Erasmus published the letter in *Opus epistolarum*. On Bernhard see Ep 1689 introduction.

ERASMUS OF ROTTERDAM TO BERNHARD VON CLES,
BISHOP OF TRENT, GREETING

Right reverend bishop, from the earlier services your lordship did me I recognized the remarkable kindness of your nature; but now in your recent letter, in which you offer me such friendly consolation, I see also your loyal 5 devotion. I only wish we lived in happier times more suited to your kind nature and my labours.

I hesitated to dedicate my Irenaeus to you, although he is an excellent author, for this is a gesture that is not welcomed by everyone, and there is nothing I am more anxious to avoid than the reputation of a money-grubber; 10 but Johannes Fabri's advice and his influence won me over.[1] I am sending the book with him, though in a plain copy, for it came out too recently to be properly bound. If you approve what I have done, I shall be delighted; if not, I hope you will not be too cross with me, since I acted as I did to humour my distinguished friend. I wish you continued happiness in the 15 future, most illustrious bishop.

As you will see, the enormous burden of my studies is teaching me brevity. I am now revising for the fourth time my Annotations on the New Testament.[2]

Basel, the Wednesday before Michaelmas 1526 20

* * * * *

1755
1 Fabri, like Bishop Bernhard a trusted adviser to Archduke Ferdinand, had assisted Erasmus' editorial work by securing for him the loan of a manuscript of Irenaeus (Epp 1715 introduction and n1, 1738:111–13) and had urged him to dedicate the edition to Bernhard. Indeed, he had been distressed by Erasmus' tardiness in sending a copy of the edition and seems to have obtained one on his own in an attempt to placate the bishop's desire for a properly bound gift copy from Erasmus. Hence he was relieved to learn that the copy sent with the present letter had reached Bernhard at Esslingen; see Ep 1771. In his introduction to this letter Allen prints a letter Fabri wrote on 20 December to his protégé Johannes Alexander Brassicanus in which he grumbles about Erasmus' failure to look after his own interests by sending the gift copy promptly.
2 Erasmus was working on the text and notes for the fourth edition of the Greek New Testament, which, except for a few minor changes made in the fifth edition of 1535, was the definitive edition prepared by Erasmus himself; it was published by Froben in March 1527. See Ep 1571 n9 and cf Ep 1789, the preface to a set of supplementary notes appended to the fourth edition.

1756 / To Nicolas Wary   Basel, 26 September 1526

Nicolas Wary (Varius) of Marville was a friend from Erasmus' years at Louvain. From the very beginning of the Collegium Trilingue there, he had been
associated with the new humanistic institute. He became its second president on 21 January 1526. On him, see Epp 1481 nn17, 18 and 1716 n1 (these
letters show Erasmus' continuing concern for the college he had helped to
found, which embodied his educational ideals). The main subject of this letter is a violent explosion of gunpowder stored in one of the towers of the
Basel city walls, which provided Erasmus an opportunity to bemoan both the
general condition and the warlike habits of European society. In the course
of this story he also reminisces on a disastrous storm he experienced while
staying at Florence in 1506, and he comments unfavourably on the custom
of using warlike instruments like drums at weddings, at public festivals,
and even in church ceremonies. Erasmus included this letter in his *Opus
epistolarum*.

ERASMUS OF ROTTERDAM TO NICOLAS WARY OF MARVILLE,
GREETING

We are like Africa, my dearest Nicolas: every day we produce a host of marvels; some, I think, you would not want to read about, nor would it be safe
for me to describe them.[1] But here is something that happened recently. On   5
20 September I was inspired by the beauty of the weather to retreat to the
large and splendid garden that Johann Froben purchased with my encouragement.[2] Whenever the weather is inviting, I like to spend several hours

* * * * *

1756
1 Africa was understood to be a place of marvels and surprises (see *Adagia* III
  vii 10), though the 'marvels' (*nova*) that he has in mind but prudently chooses
  not to describe in detail were no doubt the religious changes and social upheavals going on all around him in southwestern Germany, Switzerland, and
  even in Basel itself.
2 The great Basel printer and publisher had early recognized the value of Erasmus' growing reputation for the quality and marketability of his publications
  and from their initial meeting in 1514 (Ep 305:192–9) had taken pains to make
  him welcome. When Erasmus came to Basel in 1521 and in effect made it his
  permanent residence, Froben welcomed him into his own home for the first
  ten months (though Erasmus insisted on paying for room and board) and then
  purchased a house which he made available as Erasmus' residence (Ep 1316
  n10); it had the advantage of having an open fireplace, since Erasmus detested
  the German custom of heating with stoves and was convinced that it was bad
  for his health (Ep 1422:28–31). Likewise when Froben in June 1526 purchased a
  garden set against the city wall and easily accessible from his house, Erasmus

there in the afternoon to fend off the approach of sleep and relieve the tedium of my interminable labours. After a short walk, I had made my way   10
up to the little garden house and had just begun to translate Chrysostom[3]
when a flash struck the windows; it was not very bright and there was no
noise. At first I thought my eyes had deceived me, but when it was repeated
once or twice, I was puzzled and looked up to see if the sky had changed
and clouds had come over threatening a rainstorm. When I saw there was   15
no danger of this, I returned to my book. Shortly afterwards I heard a dull
muffled sound. It was the sort of sound that, according to the poets, Jupiter
makes when he is in merry mood,[4] quite unlike the thunderbolt with which
he shattered the mighty construction of the Giants[5] or hurled Salmoneus[6]
and Ixion[7] into Tartarus. A little later there was a brighter flash and I heard 20
a terrific bang, like the noise made by a thunderbolt when it strikes violently
against something hard.

When I was staying in Florence at the time when Pope Julius, our
earthly Jupiter, was hurling his thunderbolts against Bologna,[8] there was a

* * * * *

had ready access to it for relaxing afternoon visits such as the one described
in this letter.
3 On Erasmus' continuing interest in the works of St John Chrysostom, see Epp
1558, 1661 n2.
4 Jupiter originated as a sky-god and was commonly conceived as a god of
storms, thunder, and lightning; he was often depicted brandishing a lightning
bolt or a flint from which fire could be struck. But he was also conceived in
gentler roles, as the god of rain (Iuppiter Elicius), of calm weather and sun-
shine (Iuppiter Serenus), of the wine harvest, and as the presiding deity at the
most solemn and formal type of Roman wedding, confarreatio. In addition, as
Iuppiter Optimus Maximus he was supreme over all other gods and the special patron of the Roman republic and of all political obligations and actions,
including popular assemblies, oaths, and treaties. Erasmus' reference to 'the
poets' here is not very clear, but he must have in mind the transformation of
Jupiter from the personification of a violent storm to a gentler, even 'merry'
persona as the storm recedes and the crash of thunder recedes into a distant
and less threatening rumble. Cf H.J. Rose A Handbook of Greek Mythology 6th
ed (London 1958) 47–8.
5 The Giants piled Pelion on Ossa in an attempt to scale heaven; see Apollodorus
1.6.1 and cf Rose Handbook (preceding note) 56–8.
6 Son of Aeolus, the mythical ruler of the winds. According to Virgil Aeneid
6.585–94, he was king of Elis and impersonated Zeus by hurling torches that
were supposed to be lightning and by making a thundering noise with his
chariot. For this offence Zeus struck him with a real thunderbolt.
7 Ixion attempted to rape Juno; Pindar Pythia 2.21–48.
8 As Erasmus explains in Epp 200 and 203, the military campaign of Julius II
against Bologna forced Erasmus to detour from that famous university town

violent thunderstorm lasting most of the day accompanied by a heavy down-   25
pour of rain. I was sitting in the privy to relieve my bowels, when I heard
a dreadful crash. I was terrified and fled to join the others. 'If I am not mistaken,' I said, 'after this blast you will hear some unpleasant news.' And
sure enough not long afterwards a surgeon arrived with the news that three
nuns had been struck in their convent. One of them died soon after, the sec-   30
ond was near death, and the third was so badly hurt that he thought there
was no hope she would live.

So since this was a similar sound, I got up to see what the sky was like.
To my left all was clear, but on my right I saw a peculiar cloud, rising from
the ground into the air. It was almost ashen in colour, and its top, which was   35
roughly round in shape, was gradually subsiding. You would have thought it
was a huge rock with its top sinking into the sea. The closer I examined it, the
less it looked like a cloud. While I was looking at the sight in stunned amaze-
ment, one of my servants, whom I had left behind in the house, ran up, out
of breath, and told me to return to the house at once, for there were armed   40
men around and confusion everywhere. This is the usual practice in the city:
when a fire breaks out, immediately the militia rush out to protect the gates
and the walls. It is not very safe to encounter these men, for the possession of
a sword makes people reckless, especially when there is no danger present.
The garden in which I was working lay behind the walls. I ran home, meeting   45
many armed men on the way. Some time later, we learned the whole story.

A few days before, several barrels of gunpowder had been carried
into one of the towers that reinforce the walls at fixed intervals. The authorities had given orders for the gunpowder to be placed on the top floor, but
through someone's carelessness it had been left at the bottom of the tower.   50
Had the force of the explosion been confined to the top floor, it would only
have blown the roof into the air with no damage to the rest. But by an extraordinary accident lightning entered through the peepholes in the tower
and struck the gunpowder; before long all the barrels had caught fire. At
first the fire tested its strength to see if it could lift the whole structure into   55
the air. According to the report of eyewitnesses, once or twice the tower rose
and left an opening at the bottom, but settled back again into its original

* * * * *

and spend several weeks of November 1506 at Florence until the pope's successful conquest of Bologna made it safe for him and the boys he was tutoring to proceed to their studies at the university. Erasmus' dislike of the pope's
militarism finds expression in the image of him as an earthly Jupiter, hurling
thunderbolts; this image leads to his reminiscence about the storm at Florence
and then to his account of the explosion at Basel.

position. When the fire realized that the structure was too heavy to be raised as a whole, it abandoned the attempt and split the tower apart into four pieces with an enormous bang, but so neatly that you might have thought it 60 had been measured with a surveyor's rule. The various sections were tossed through the air in different directions. The gunpowder that had been ignited rose into the air, and when the flames had gone out, it looked like a cloud of ash. You could have seen great pieces of the tower flying through the air like birds. Some, where there was open space, were carried two hundred 65 yards; others cut a long swath through the homes of the townsfolk.

Not far from the tower the council had built small houses for women who prefer to sell their bodies rather than work at the spindle or the loom.[9] These buildings took the force of the explosion on one side. So loud and unexpected was the bang that those who were in the neighbourhood thought 70 the sky had burst and the world would collapse into chaos. The common saying about the 'sky falling'[10] did not seem at all ridiculous. In the fields many were crushed by falling debris, many lost a limb or were so badly injured that they presented a piteous sight to all who met them. They say twelve lost their lives and fourteen suffered serious injuries. Some believe 75 that this occurrence portends something for the future. I, being less of a 'fore-teller' than an 'after-teller,'[11] think it simply means that people were careless and did not take precautions against an eventuality that is not all that rare. Nor should we be surprised that gunpowder, which is very light, tore apart a building made of stone; even if the tower had been surrounded 80 by a two hundred-foot wall, the sudden and violent force of the fire would have carried everything in its path. For what is gentler than the wind? And yet when Boreas[12] is shut up in the hollows of the earth, can it not shake whole mountains, cause fissures in the earth, and sometimes push up a wide expanse of flat ground to form a hill?   85

*****

9 Basel, like many cities of the time, tolerated prostitution but tried to control it by supervising the women involved and confining their activities to a designated district. On prostitution in German and Swiss cities at this period, see Merry E. Wiesner *Women and Gender in Early Modern Europe* (Cambridge 1993) 100–2 and, in greater detail, Wiesner's *Gender, Church, and State in Early Modern Germany* (London 1998) 102–13.
10 Terence *Heautontimorumenos* 719
11 Erasmus uses two Greek words, προφήτης and ἐπιφήτης, the second being his own invention.
12 The north wind. According to one ancient theory, earthquakes were caused by the pressure of wind in the caverns of the earth; see Lucretius *De rerum natura* 6.535–607.

Who was it who invented this kind of device? Antiquity attributed to the gods the discovery of the arts that are needful to sustain human life: medicine, for example, was attributed to Apollo,[13] agriculture to Ceres,[14] viticulture to Bacchus,[15] and the art of stealing to Mercury.[16] Whoever deserves the credit for this invention must, I think, be some highly ingenious, 90 but equally malevolent, devil.[17] If Salmoneus had discovered something like this, he could have given the finger even to Jupiter.[18] And yet this is now

* * * * *

13 This major Greek deity had medicine (as well as music, archery, and prophecy) among his functions, and according to the myths, one of his love affairs, that with Coronis, produced Asclepius, a deified hero who became the god of healing; Hesiod 'Catalogue of Women' (κατάλογος γυναικῶν) 63 and Pindar *Pythia* 3. In his Roman manifestations, Apollo was primarily a god of healing, and the Vestal Virgins invoked him as *Apollo medice, Apollo paean* (Macrobius *Saturnalia* 1.17.15). He remained, of course, a god of prophecy.

14 Roman goddess of grain, evidently a very ancient Roman deity with a special priest (*flamen Cerialis*) and a well-established festival (19 April), conventionally identified with the Greek goddess Demeter; see Rose *Handbook* (n4 above) 92–6.

15 Roman god of wine, identified with the Greek Dionysus, who was primarily the god of an ecstatic popular cult that stood somewhat apart from the more aristocratic and formal worship of the Olympian deities, though of course he was integrated into the syncretic pantheon of classical Greek and Roman religion.

16 Roman equivalent of the Greek Hermes. The Roman cult is often seen as an example of Hellenizing influence, and the Latin name suggests one of his principal functions as the god of merchants and trading (*merx, mercari*). Although he is also regularly depicted as the messenger of the gods and as a herald, Greek mythology depicts him as cunning and thievish. The association between his thieving habits and mercantile activity is suggestive of the low social esteem in which merchants were held, not only in Antiquity but also in the opinion of Erasmus; see Rose *Handbook* (n4 above) 145–9.

17 Erasmus, whose Latin expression is *cacodaemoni*, here contrasts the invention of the useful, life-sustaining arts (even merchandising) by the (good) classical gods with the invention of gunpowder and firearms, a life-destroying device. The devil was normally conceived as the source of destructive forces and was traditionally associated with fire and sulphurous odours. The legendary inventor of gunpowder, a German Franciscan of the fourteenth century named Berthold Schwarz (that is, Black, a colour associated with the devil), was supposedly a servant of Satan; and literary texts of the sixteenth and seventeenth centuries (among them Milton *Paradise Lost* 6.470–506) treat the diabolical origin of gunpowder and firearms as a conventional story if not necessarily as a historical fact. See Maximilian Rudwin *The Devil in Legend and Literature* (Chicago 1931; repr New York 1970) 251.

18 Literally, 'show the middle fingernail,' an ancient expression of contempt; see *Adagia* II iv 68. On Salmoneus, see n6 above.

the plaything of Christians and even of children.[19] To such an extent has civilization declined among us and barbarism increased.

Long ago the Corybantes drove men into a frenzy by the noise of drums and flutes,[20] for such music can work powerfully on human emotions. But our drums make a more frightful sound with their deafening rat-tat's and rat-tat-*tat*'s.[21] Nowadays we Christians use these instruments in war instead of trumpets,[22] as though it were not enough to be brave in battle without also working oneself up into a frenzy. But why did I mention war? We use these instruments at weddings and festivals and in church. To that maddening sound young women rush out into public, and the new bride does her dance.[23] It is the same when we celebrate a feast day, which is only regarded as successful if the streets are filled from morning till night with a riotous uproar, worse than anything the Corybantes ever thought of. If there are feast days in hell, I am sure these are the instruments with which they are celebrated. Plato thought that the kind of music adopted by the state was a matter of the utmost importance.[24] What would he think if he heard the music in use these days among Christians? Furthermore, the

* * * * *

19 Fireworks using gunpowder were probably first developed in China no later than the first half of the eleventh century and had spread by way of the Arab world to Europe by the thirteenth century. Roger Bacon in *Opus tertium* (1267) ed A.G. Little (Aberdeen 1912) 51 clearly describes a firecracker and its use as a toy by children. The relevant passage is quoted in English in Hugh B.C. Pollard *Pollard's History of Firearms* rev ed, edited and rewritten by Claude Blair and others (New York 1983) 26. On the history of fireworks in sixteenth-century Europe, see Alan St.H. Brock *A History of Fireworks* (London 1949) 29–38.

20 Priests of Cybele whose music drove men mad; cf Euripides *Hippolytus* 141–7; Horace *Odes* 1.16.8.

21 Literally 'in anapaestic and pyrrhic rhythms,' but the present translator has reversed the order of the two rhythms for the sake of the rhythm of the English sentence. Anapaestic rhythms are easy enough to understand: rat-tat-*tat*. But in metre a pyrrhic is two shorts, and a series of such rhythms would simply amount to a repetition of the same dynamics. Probably Erasmus did not intend the terms to be taken literally. Perhaps he chose the term *pyrichiis* because of its relation to *pyrricha*, which means 'war dance.' He has a long note on this dance in *Adagia* III vii 71.

22 He refers to the European practice of organizing troops into formation and moving them forward into battle to the beat of drums.

23 In *Institutio Christiani matrimonii* LB V 677F–679C Erasmus criticizes the lascivious dancing that a modest bride is expected to engage in with men of every sort, but he does not specifically criticize the style of music or the type of instruments used on these occasions.

24 *Republic* 3.400–412B

sort of music we hear frequently in church,[25] which is produced by blowing 110
and banging at the same time, is acceptable to some only if it is louder than
a military trumpet; and this frightful racket penetrates to the ears of nuns
during the saying of the holy office. Nor is that all: these days celebrants
use their voices like a peal of thunder – certain German princes will have
nothing else. The truth is that nothing is acceptable to modern taste unless 115
it smacks of war. But enough of this raillery![26] Farewell.

Basel, 26 September 1526

1757 / From Mercurino Gattinara   Granada, 1 October 1526

> This reply to Ep 1700 expresses the imperial chancellor's high regard for Eras-
> mus and his sympathy for Erasmus' exposure to attacks from conservative
> Catholics as well as Lutherans. Of particular interest is Gattinara's conviction
> that Christendom is divided into three (rather than two) contending religious
> camps: the first totally opposed to all reform, which he comes close to labelling
> 'papist'; the second, those who stubbornly follow 'the Lutheran party'; and the
> third, with which he identifies Erasmus, himself, and (implicitly) the policy of
> the emperor, an 'Erasmian third force' of moderate reformers, still Catholic
> but wanting reform and hence exposed to attack from both extremes. Eras-
> mus did not publish this favourable but very candid (even indiscreet) and very
> personal letter. A contemporary copy survived at Sélestat, presumably sent by
> Erasmus to his friend Beatus Rhenanus. It was first published in Hermann
> Baumgarten Geschichte Karls v 3 vols (Stuttgart 1885–92) II 714–15.

Cordial greetings, distinguished sir. I can only thank you for wanting to
write to me despite your busy involvement in such taxing, indeed godly,
labours. I wish I could express my gratitude not just in words, but in some
practical way. You would then see what my feelings towards you are, though
they are no more than you have earned by your piety and godlike erudition. 5
These have so impressed me that, if ever I could escape this tiresome burden of worldly affairs, I would find my greatest satisfaction in immersing
myself in your writings. I now see beyond doubt that you have enemies in
both camps.

* * * * *

25 The use of secular tunes in the elaborate church music of the later Middle Ages
   was often criticized by reformers of the sixteenth century, and one aspect of
   the Catholic liturgical reforms after the Council of Trent was a return to the
   simpler musical idiom of the early medieval church.
26 Erasmus uses the Greek term σατυρίζειν.

I wonder, however, why a man of your standing is so upset by insults   10
from men like that. As I see it, the Christian world in our day is divided into
three parts. One, with its ears blocked and its mental vision blinded, sticks
to the pope whether his judgments and decrees are good or bad. A second
clings tenaciously to the Lutheran party. The men of both these factions,
wrapped up, as they are, in their own concerns, cannot be impartial on any   15
issue and will not suffer anyone to dissent from their views. The praises of
such people are really a humiliation; likewise their insults should properly
be regarded as true praise.

But let us consider a third group, which is the exact antithesis of the
other two, those who seek only the glory of God and the well-being of the   20
state. Not wanting evil to go unrebuked or virtue unpraised, and refusing
to bind themselves body and soul, as the saying is,[1] to any faction, they can
hardly escape the biting tongue of criticism whenever they feel called upon
to speak the truth. So if you have both sides against you, that certainly is
something to be deplored for the sake of the country, but for you it should   25
be a source of satisfaction to know that you have this third group entirely
on your side and always singing your praises. Their acclaim is glory indeed.
As for the Lutheran faction, I wanted to see the pressure kept up until it
disappeared altogether and all those other evils were corrected. It is my
hope that this will happen under the auspices of our emperor.   30

Nothing has been done so far about your annuity.[2] But I am sure something will be done, and it will turn out better than perhaps you expected.
Meanwhile, I think you should stay where you are until the present turmoil settles down.[3] And please count me among your friends and accept my
renewed affection. Farewell.   35

Granada, 1 October 1526

Your good friend, Mercurino Gattinara, whose friendship is everything
you could desire

* * * * *

1757
1 The Latin is *toto pede* 'with the whole foot,' a variant on *toto corpore* 'with the
  whole body,' *Adagia* I iv 23, and also on *manibus pedibusque* 'with hands and
  feet,' *Adagia* I iv 15.
2 Cf Ep 1700 n3 and the further references given there.
3 The sympathetic Gattinara gives this (probably welcome) advice even though
  he knew that his master's officials in the Netherlands were insisting that Erasmus must return to the Netherlands before they would consider payment of
  his annual pension as an imperial councillor; cf Ep 1700 n3. The disturbances
  of the Peasant War were not completely over by this time, even though most
  of the organized rebel bands had been put down.

1758 / To Erasmus Schets   [Basel, 2 October 1526]

A reply to Ep 1750 from Erasmus' trusted financial agent in the Netherlands acknowledging receipt of a large sum of money. This letter was unpublished until Allen found it in the British Museum and edited it in 1926. Schets' answer is Ep 1764 and establishes a firm date for this letter.

Cordial greetings. My dearest Schets, I received from Hieronymus Froben[1] the 436 gold florins. [2] I want to thank you for relieving Pieter Gillis and myself of the trouble of making up the account. I enclose a receipt to satisfy your obligations in England.[3] As for the king of Portugal, I shall remember him as soon as I have the time.[4] The bishop of Lincoln[5] promises me fifteen angels every year.[6] I shall write and ask him to pass on the money to Juan   5

* * * * *

1758
1 On Hieronymus Froben see Ep 1705 n3. Evidently he had attended the autumn fair at Frankfurt in lieu of (or accompanying) his father and had received from Schets or an agent the sum of money mentioned here. See Ep 1750 n4; on the importance of the Frankfurt fairs for Erasmus' financial transactions, see Ep 1660 n4.
2 Latin *florenos aureos quadrigentos triginta sex*, 436 Rhenish gold florins. Schets had arranged for the transfer of this money to Erasmus at the Frankfurt fair. This sum was then officially worth £107 3s 8d groot Flemish, but according to Erasmus it was worth 697 florins and 12 stuivers of account, or £116 5s 4d groot (40d per florin of account), a value evidently based upon a current exchange rate of 64d groot, instead of the official rate of 59d. See Ep 1750:11–12 and n6. This sum was equivalent to 2,790 days' wages or 12 years and 7 months' wage income for an Antwerp master carpenter; or £72 13s 4d sterling, equivalent to 2,907 days' wages or 13 years and 3 months' wage income for an Oxford master carpenter; or £654 tournois (or, with rising gold values, as much as £717 tournois. See Ep 1796 n5).
3 See Ep 1750 n4. Schets had requested a receipt; Ep 1750:19–20
4 Schets, who had business connections in Portugal as well as Spain and also some kind of personal connection with the Portuguese court under the previous king, Manuel I, repeatedly encouraged Erasmus to seek the favour of John III, the young Portuguese king, by dedicating a publication to him. See Epp 1681, 1682, 1750. Despite his somewhat brusque reference to the matter in this letter, Erasmus did dedicate his *Chrysostomi lucubrationes* to King John in March 1527 (Ep 1800), although the effort failed to attract the king as his patron.
5 John Longland; on his patronage of Erasmus see Epp 1386 n20, 1704.
6 Latin *quindecim angelatos*. As noted in Ep 1750 nn2, 3, the English gold angel-noble, originally worth 6s 8d sterling, was officially raised in value to 7s 4d

de Castro, Alvaro's brother.[7] Give my regards to Pieter Gillis and ask him to
send to the Basel fair the Seneca he promised me,[8] if this is possible; also, if
he happens to have the manuscript of Augustine's *City of God* in Lombardic
script,[9] he should send it too. And ask him to explain what happened to the   10
seven copies of Tertullian that are owed to me.[10] Best wishes to you and to
all who are dear to you.

To the honourable Erasmus Schets. In Antwerp

1759 / To John Francis   [Basel, October 1526]

Allen establishes an approximate date for this letter by associating it with Erasmus' letter of 27 August (Ep 1735) to the Paris physician Guillaume Cop, which
describes the same illness. He argues that it must be later than Ep 1745, dated 3

* * * * *

[= 88d] on 22 August 1526, and then to 7s 6d [= 90d] sterling on 5 November
1526. Thus by November this sum would have been worth £5 12s 6d sterling
(the equivalent of 225 days' wages or about a year's wage income for an Oxford master carpenter, whose nominal money wages had not risen since the
1360s), or officially £7 8s 9d groot Flemish (and, with rising gold values, more
probably £8 3s 2d groot, equivalent to 196 days' wages for an Antwerp master carpenter), or £45 15s 0d tournois (or, for the same reason, as much as £50
3s 2d; see Ep 1796 n5).

 7 Apparently Erasmus has in mind Luis de Castro, brother of Alvaro, but he was
   not very good at names, especially the Christian names of people he knew
   primarily by their family names. On the Castro brothers, Spanish merchants
   from Burgos settled in London and commercial correspondents of Schets, see
   Epp 1590 n2, 1647, 1658 n5, 1772 n3.
 8 See Ep 1740 n8. No doubt Erasmus means the Frankfurt fair; on its importance
   in the transmission of books, letters, and money to Erasmus, see Ep 1660 n4.
 9 Probably the early manuscript of *De civitate Dei* that Erasmus had borrowed for
   use by Vives in preparing his edition of that work for the Froben press, published in 1522. See Ep 1309 introduction. But in Ep 1778, through Conradus Goclenius, Vives informs (or more likely reminds) Erasmus that he had returned
   the manuscript to its owner, the convent of Benedictines at Cologne named
   Maccabean (because it possessed the supposed relics of the Maccabees); see
   Epp 842 introduction, 1346 introduction. If the manuscript was really written
   in Lombardic script, it would indeed be an early textual authority.
10 Probably a reference to Beatus Rhenanus's edition (Basel: Froben, July 1521).
   Erasmus claimed these copies were owed to him (along with a sum of
   money) by the bookseller Franz Birckmann, whom he regarded as a dishonest scoundrel. See Ep 1507:14–19. Evidently Erasmus now believed that these
   books had come into the possession of Gillis during the time when he was
   acting as Erasmus' financial agent in the Netherlands.

September, in which Erasmus includes Francis among a list of friends in London whom he wants to be greeted by the recipient, Stephen Gardiner; it must also be earlier than 20 December, when Erasmus Schets reported that his correspondent in London had duly delivered several letters that Erasmus had written to English friends about the time of Ep 1745. Allen assumes that news of Erasmus' illness prompted Francis' decision to send the unsolicited medical advice gratefully acknowledged here at lines 78–9, and he would assign it a date early in October 1526. On Erasmus' illness see Ep 1735 introduction. The annotator acknowledges with thanks the help of two historians of medicine, Nancy G. Siraisi of the City University of New York and Michael McVaugh of North Carolina State University, in his efforts to understand and explain the medical aspects of Erasmus' letter. Erasmus published this letter in *Opus epistolarum* (1529).

ERASMUS OF ROTTERDAM TO FRANCIS, PHYSICIAN, GREETING
What a priest is to our souls, a doctor is to our poor bodies. Whoever expects a remedy should not hide his symptoms, and I have no doubt that a good doctor like yourself always keeps the pledge of confidentiality that Hippocrates requires all practitioners of the art to observe scrupulously.[1]   5

It is several years now since I first suffered the torment of kidney stone, and since then, there has been no let-up in the cycle of conception, pregnancy, and delivery; indeed, I wonder how my poor body has stood up to such constant battering. Often the excruciating pain would bring on vomiting; then for sixteen days on end my stomach would tolerate no food   10
at all except a light broth. Each day the agony would get worse; finally becoming so bad that I began to despair, so painful was the effort to pass the stone. After a time I changed to a light wine, lighter than the local varieties

* * * * *

1759
1 Hippocrates of Cos was a famous Greek physician of the fifth century BC, commonly regarded as the founder of rational, scientific medicine. Although he may have written medical treatises, the consensus of modern scholars (and even of many ancient textual critics) is that none of the so-called Hippocratic books was written by him, at least not in its entirety. The reference to the physician's obligation to preserve the confidentiality of secrets learned while treating patients is from the so-called Hippocratic Oath; see *Hippocrates* trans W.H.S. Jones and others, Loeb Classical Library, 7 vols (Cambridge, MA 1923–96) I 300–1:29–32; cf Jones' introduction to the text (I 291–7). See also Ludwig Edelstein *The Hippocratic Oath* (Baltimore 1943) 2–3 (Greek and English), reprinted in his *Ancient Medicine* (Baltimore 1967) 3–63, especially 5–6 (text of the oath); and John Chadwick and W.N. Mann *The Medical Works of Hippocrates* (Oxford 1950) 4, reprinted in *Hippocratic Writings* ed G.E.R. Lloyd, Penguin Books (Harmondsworth, Middlesex 1983) 67.

here; I drank it diluted with water boiled with liquorice root, and in modest
quantities too. For several months I was free of the agony.   15

But lately I felt on the tip of my penis the sort of sensation we often
experience as children when exposed to the wind. It is generally known as
'chilly urine.'[2] I suspect the trouble began when I stayed out too long after
sunset talking in the open air. I applied camomile oil to the belly below the
navel – that is usually effective – and I felt no discomfort after that. Then   20
one day, when I was having a cheerful dinner with my friends, I drank, contrary to my usual custom, half a pint of Burgundy mixed with water in the
manner described above. As I discovered later, the wine had been hung up
but had not settled. After my first sleep I passed water in a great burst; the
passage was badly swollen and the pain was excruciating. I did not feel it in   25
the side, where it is usually most severe, but in the bladder and the muscles
of the penis. A great quantity of stones, both big and small, and a lot of matter came out with the urine, causing lesions in the passage. This happened
more than ten times during the night, though there was no pain in the stomach. I did not preserve the urine, which I now regret. I kept what I passed   30
in the morning – it looks like milk mixed with bits of stone. The matter was
like chalk. All this time the pain in the bladder was most disagreeable.

I consulted the doctors, first one, then another, then a third – such doctors at least as we have here. They were puzzled. I was afraid the matter
in the bladder would solidify, for the pain lasted several days. Finally, it   35
became less severe, though it did not depart altogether but was more bear-
able. So I dismissed the doctors and as a last resort decided on a moderate
regime. I drink Burgundy, but in small quantities and only when it is old,
and I compensate for its age by adding a lot of sugar and liquorice boiled
in water. My stomach has now improved and so has my brain, which was   40
exhausted by the frequent vomiting. My urine is still clouded and chalky
and there are stones in it, but too small to cause the usual torture. I prefer
this chronic discomfort to the sort of pain that is intermittent but unbear-
able. If the disease had not taken this new form, I would have been in my

* * * * *

2 Erasmus probably has in mind the burning sensation caused by the voiding
of urine by a person suffering an infection of the urinary tract. Evidently
the sensation reminded him of what he felt as a child when he urinated out-
doors and the chilling effect of the wind and the passing of the urine combined to produce a chilling or stinging sensation. Professors Siraisi and Mc-
Vaugh kindly inspected this passage and advised the annotator that, to the
best of their knowledge, there was no distinctive medical symptom or condition known as 'chilly urine,' and that this phrase is probably a simile to explain
the discomfort he felt as a result of his ailment.

grave long ago. At times the pain is mild, at other times severe. I feel worse   45
when the weather is overcast; and I cannot depart from my moderate regime
without immediately paying the price. I have adopted the practice of passing water frequently for fear of coagulation in the bladder. My first sleep is
regular and peaceful, but the second is fitful and frequently broken by periods of wakefulness, although this does not bother me much. There is no   50
gonorrhoea,[3] no flux from the brain nor problem with the spinal marrow;[4]
for these would leave me very weak, whereas I am in fact fairly active.

    I think I know the origin of the problem. For more than twenty years
now I have been accustomed to write standing up. I almost never sit down
except when eating lunch or dinner or when I doze off after lunch, as I   55
sometimes do, especially when worn out with work. Often pressure from
the printing press or, more particularly, the demands of a voluminous correspondence force me to rush off immediately after lunch to the writing
desk. After dinner I have to take it easy because of the strain; either I enjoy a relaxed conversation or walk around listening to my servant reading   60
something that might prove useful to me later. One day when I was particularly busy, a messenger arrived from a friend who was in danger of his
life.[5] I wrote a number of letters to assist him without taking any thought

                    * * * * *

3 Erasmus is probably not referring to the venereal infection in any specific way
   but, in his case, to the absence of any discharge of yellowish pus. The Latin
   word *gonorrhoea* in general refers to seminal fluid, voluntarily or involuntarily
   discharged. The venereal disease in male patients often manifests itself by a
   discharge of pus from the urethra resulting from inflammation of the mucous
   membranes caused by the bacteria associated with the disease.
4 The prevalent Hippocratic medicine held that sperm was a fluid originating
   in the brain and passed through the spinal marrow to the kidneys and thence
   to the testicles and the penis. See [pseudo-]Hippocrates *On Generation* in *The
   Hippocratic Treatises 'On Generation,' 'On the Nature of the Child,' 'Diseases IV,'* Ars
   Medica, II. Abteilung, Band 7, ed Gerhard Baader and others (Berlin 1981) 1.
5 Allen (58n) remarks, 'Clearly Berquin.' It is true that in Ep 1692, dated from
   Paris on 17 April, Berquin does make an urgent appeal for support, and the
   present letter refers to a second urgent appeal sent 'a few days later,' a message
   which (if sent in written form) is not extant. In his introduction to Ep 1692 Allen
   suggests that Epp 1721–3, addressed to the Parlement of Paris, to Francis I, and
   to the faculty of theology, were the results of this second appeal. This conclusion is not certain, since Erasmus dealt with complaints of his own in these letters, but the passage in the letter to the king (Ep 1722) that directly appeals for
   help for Berquin does increase the plausibility of Allen's conjecture (Erasmus
   omitted this one sentence when he printed Ep 1722 in 1529). If Allen's conjecture is valid, Erasmus is here blaming the special exertions he made in behalf of
   Berquin for his severe illness. The dating of these letters is compatible with the
   probable interval needed for transmission of letters between Paris and Basel.

of my health, something I had done frequently in the past. A few days later
he sent a second messenger. I was anxious to oblige him again, but this was   65
the start of the trouble I have just described. Anyone who writes standing
up must necessarily bend slightly at the stomach; I suspect that, as a consequence, my stomach expels the food in a half-digested state, and that the
spirits are driven off to another part of the body.[6] This explains why the
stone does not grow large. Perhaps nature has also opened up some of the   70
passages so that the stone may pass more easily.

    This, then, is the nature of my illness. The Lord only knows how it will
end. I worry that a sudden movement or something of that sort will take the
lining off the bladder. Nothing could be more excruciating than that. They
say that Thomas Linacre died from that painful complaint.[7] Now you have   75
the whole story. If medical science has any way of relieving the distress –
for I do not expect a cure – it would be characteristic of your good nature to
pass it on. The remedy you sent me unsolicited is evidence enough of your
long-standing devotion to me. It touches me all the more deeply because I
have never done you even the slightest service. I wish there were some way   80
in which I could show you how much I appreciate your kindness and how
eager I am to repay it. Farewell.

     * * * * *

6 The medical terminology is somewhat puzzling. Erasmus seems to think that
  one physiological effect of the extended time he spent standing at his writing-
  desk to compose letters was to interrupt the proper digestion of his food and
  to displace the intestinal 'spirits' from their normal course, thereby upsetting
  his system. Although the modern French translator, Aloïs Gerlo (VI 504:83),
  translates Erasmus' word for 'spirits' by 'sécrétions,' in fact Erasmus may be
  thinking of intestinal gas or flatulence as part of the mechanism that precipitated his acute spell of urinary-tract disease. In medieval medicine, *pneuma*
  or *spiritus* is an extremely refined material substance derived from inhaled air
  and necessary for transmission of the vital force, on which life itself depends,
  from the heart throughout the body. Some part of the *spiritus* went to the liver
  and there aided in nutrition, including digestion. On the role of *spiritus* in
  late medieval physiology, see Nancy G. Siraisi *Medieval and Early Renaissance
  Medicine* (Chicago 1990) 101, 107–9. According to Meno, a pupil of Aristotle
  (one of the few reasonably contemporary ancient sources), Hippocrates associated disease with air in the body: the general cause of disease is that if food
  is not properly digested, air is excreted from the remnants in the gastric tract
  and invades various parts of the body, causing illness (J.T. Vallance in *Oxford
  Classical Dictionary* 3rd ed [1996] 710–11). The degree to which Erasmus had
  in mind specific details of Hippocratic physiology is uncertain, but it is obvious that he thought that poor digestion of food, probably brought on by his
  urgent work at the writing-table, caused *spiritus* (perhaps intestinal gases) to
  exacerbate his chronic urinary ailment and bring on a near-fatal illness.
7 See Ep 1735 n3.

1760 / From Thiébaut Biétry   Porrentruy, 11 October 1526

Erasmus had dedicated his mass in honour of the Virgin of Loreto to Thiébaut
Biétry in 1523 (Ep 1391), and had revised it for a second edition in 1525 (Ep
1573). In an exchange of letters now lost, Biétry must have asked Erasmus to
write for him another tract of spiritual edification. No known work of Erasmus can be identified with the unspecified 'divine subject' he suggested. The
autograph letter survived in the Rehdiger collection at Wrocław. The text was
first published by L.K. Enthoven in 1906.

Cordial greetings, my distinguished benefactor. The affectionate way in
which you are always ready to meet my requests makes me realize how
dear I am to you. I owe you a great debt of gratitude, but it is not within my
powers to repay it. I am delighted with the divine subject you suggested; it
would even be suitable for reading in schools. I know you need no advice   5
from me since, as my friend Iussellus[1] says, all things are possible with you.
So do as you wish; but if it could be printed before the next fair at Basel,
that would make me particularly happy.

I sent your letter to the archdeacon.[2] I also wrote right away to our
friend Iussellus. You are too generous to the couriers and coachmen. That   10
is why they like you so much. I never cease to wonder at the insanity of
those Rabbis and Jews.[3] No matter what they bring forward, you and the
church will come out on top (and I know you have no quarrel with the
church). I believe that God has permitted Lutheranism to emerge because
of the wickedness of men like these.   15

* * * * *

1760
1 This person is known only from references in this letter and in Ep 1354. The
  context makes it likely that he was a resident of the Franche-Comté.
2 Biétry forwarded Ep 1749 to their mutual friend Ferry de Carondelet, archdeacon of Besançon.
3 In this habitually anti-Semitic society, Biétry, like Erasmus, uses 'Rabbis' and
  'Jews' as labels of reproach and, again like Erasmus, uses these terms to
  refer to the professors of theology and the monks, on the assumption that
  such persons had imported into Christian practice an arid ceremonial legalism that Christians since apostolic times had associated with Jewish religious observance. Though less explicitly, Biétry divides the Christian world
  into three camps much as Mercurino Gattinara had done in Ep 1757: the
  Lutherans, who may have meant well in the beginning but have fallen into
  heresy and schism; the conservative, anti-reform Catholics (scholastic theologians and monks); and reform-minded Catholic humanists like himself and
  Erasmus.

In conclusion, I feel some embarrassment, even perhaps trepidation, at
constantly badgering you with these letters of mine. But I have acted with
the purest and best of motives. Now that you are being buffeted with such
a dreadful illness,[4] I see it as an obligation of friendship to comfort you
with pious consolations until your health and energy gradually return and   20
my prayers for you are answered. May God, the ruler of all, smile upon my
prayer and bless you and Froben and the rest of our friends.

Porrentruy, 11 October 1526
You will recognize your friend Biétry's hand.
To the most eloquent master of the Latin tongue, Erasmus of Rotter-   25
dam, his much respected friend

1761 / From Johann von Botzheim   Constance, 22 October 1526

> Erasmus' close friend Botzheim was a canon of the cathedral at Constance.
> Erasmus visited him there in 1522 and assisted with letters of endorse-
> ment when he faced charges of Lutheran heresy in 1524–5. On Botzheim's
> earlier life and connection with Erasmus see Epp 1103, 1285, 1316 and
> 1342 (accounts of Erasmus' visit to Constance), 1519, 1540, 1555, 1574. At
> Botzheim's request Erasmus addressed to him a catalogue of all his writ-
> ings, which was published in 1523 and again in an expanded edition in 1524;
> see Ep 1341A. Botzheim had felt some sympathy for Luther at the begin-
> ning of the Reformation (even writing a favourable letter to him in 1520),
> but he gradually became alienated from the Reformers because of the vi-
> olence and disunity associated with the religious upheaval. At Constance
> he was an active patron of humanism, and his home was a natural place
> for foreign humanists like Thomas Lupset and Reginald Pole to visit while
> stopping in Constance on their way home from Italy. The original of this
> letter survived at Leipzig and was first published in Förstemann/Günther
> in 1904.

The Englishman Thomas Lupset,[1] a good friend of both of us, called in
at Constance on his way back from Italy in the company of your splendid

* * * * *

4 On Erasmus' serious illness of summer 1526, see Epp 1729, 1735, 1759.

1761
1 Lupset had been studying and teaching at Padua and had resided in the house-
    hold of Reginald Pole there. On his early connection with Erasmus see Epp
    270:69n, 271; and for his recent career see Epp 1594 n3, 1595, 1624. He had

friend Pole.[2] He did me the honour of bringing Pole to my house so that I might increase the number of my friends. Pole left me, however, without knowing that I was aware of his identity. You see, he was taking great care 5 that no one should know who he was. I parted from him without revealing what I knew. He was a most agreeable guest, reminding me somewhat of our Polish friend, Jan Łaski,[3] for whose generosity no words of praise are adequate.

I showed Pole and Thomas the manuscript of the Gospels,[4] especially 10 the passage at the end of John. They were delighted to see it. They will be able to assure you that the reading in both verses is *si eum volo manere* ['if I will that he tarry']; the lettering is clear and distinct.[5] I am sending you two manuscripts of the apostolic Epistles;[6] the courier is an old man whom I engaged for the purpose, but he asked to be excused from proceeding 15 further after he had delivered the manuscripts.[7]

* * * * *

made Erasmus acquainted with the wealth, ancestry, and humanistic interests of Reginald Pole (Ep 1595 introduction and n10), with whom he was now travelling on the way home to England.

2 Reginald Pole, who a generation later became archbishop of Canterbury under Queen Mary Tudor, was deeply involved in both humanistic studies and the movement for spiritual renewal during his period of study in Padua (1521–6), where his well-financed household was a refuge for English and other foreign humanists. On him see Epp 1595 n10 (showing his kinship to Henry VIII), 1627 introduction.

3 Erasmus had commended this aristocratic Polish humanist to Pole in Ep 1627 when Łaski travelled to Italy after his residence with Erasmus in Basel and before his return to Poland. On him see Epp 1593 n18, 1604 n1, 1615 n3.

4 According to Allen (10n), there is good evidence that Erasmus used one or perhaps two New Testament manuscripts from Constance in the revision of the Gospel of St John for the fourth edition of the Greek New Testament, which was published the following spring. In his annotations to the passage here discussed (see next note) he refers to one manuscript that Botzheim made available to him; in Allen Ep 1858:82–5 he refers to his use of two manuscripts 'recently acquired' from the cathedral library of Constance. It is possible that he first saw one or more New Testament manuscripts while visiting Botzheim at Constance in September 1522.

5 John 21:22–3; the standard Vulgate text in each of these two verses has *sic* instead of *si*. Here Erasmus is depending on early manuscripts of the Latin (not the Greek) New Testament.

6 Allen Ep 373 introduction notes three places in the *Annotationes* to the fourth edition of the New Testament where Erasmus refers to his use of two manuscripts of the Epistles from Constance, presumably the ones now sent on loan from the chapter library by Botzheim.

7 Evidently this unidentified old man did not intend to return (or to return promptly) to Constance and so could not be employed for dispatch of return

I like your *Matrimonium christianum*[8] very much. There are Lutherans, however, who accept nothing of Erasmus' if it departs at all from their own point of view or is critical of their fatuous and ill-considered ideas. Troops are being got ready for service in Italy.[9] There is much discussion about the   20 Turks.[10]

* * * * *

letters from Basel to Constance as would normally have been expected when a courier was hired.

8 The *Institutio christiani matrimonii*, dedicated to Catherine of Aragon. See Ep 1727.

9 Allen (18n) speculates plausibly that these troops might have been Swiss mercenaries being dispatched to enlarge the pope's Swiss Guard. The disastrous defeat of the French at Pavia on 24 February 1525 and the capture of the king had put the Medici pope Clement VII, who had followed a pro-French, anti-Spanish policy, at the mercy of Charles V and the jubilant pro-Spanish, anti-Medicean faction of the Roman aristocracy, the Colonna, who were engaged in fighting in and near the city against the pro-French faction, the Orsini. Although Pope Clement tried to negotiate terms with the emperor by sending a special embassy to Spain, he was soon engaged in secret negotiations with Venice, other anti-Spanish Italian governments, and the French regent, Louise of Savoy. Gian Matteo Giberti, the most anti-Spanish of the pope's advisers, urged him to recruit from eight to ten thousand Swiss mercenaries so that he would be ready to fight if war broke out again. In the autumn of 1525 Clement ordered the recruitment of additional troops, probably including Swiss mercenaries. Such preparations for renewed war accelerated once Francis I was safely back in France in March 1526 and it became clear that he would repudiate the harsh Treaty of Madrid and renew his struggle. On 22 May 1526 Clement VII, Francis I, Venice, and Francesco Sforza, duke of Milan signed the League of Cognac; its terms called for war if the emperor did not moderate his political demands on France and Italy. There were disorders in Rome at the end of June 1526, incited by Spanish agents, and on 8 July the pope publicly proclaimed his adherence to the League of Cognac. But decisive military action against Spanish troops in Lombardy was delayed pending arrival of additional Swiss troops, for whose pay a French subsidy would be necessary. Indecisive fighting in Lombardy, Tuscany, and near Genoa went on through the summer, and in September the leaders of the Colonna faction, after months of feinting and negotiation, led a force reported at five thousand men into Rome, action that resulted in the plundering of the papal palace, several churches including St Peter's, and the households of many curial officials. See Pastor IX 274–340. English documents from this period refer frequently to efforts by the pope and his allies to finance and recruit Swiss troops to fight in Italy. See for example LP IV-2, nos 2556, 2557, 2613, 2629.

10 The decisive victory of the Ottoman army over King Louis II of Hungary at Mohács on 29 August 1526, which took the life of the king and left Hungary in political chaos, exposed not only Hungary but also Austria to Turkish attack. It was viewed with alarm throughout Christian Europe, although not to such

If you wish to write to me, you can make free use of Benoît,[11] who will be looking after the transfer of several bundles of books from Basel to Constance. Leodegarius has not been seen anywhere,[12] nor has anyone appeared on his behalf. So please excuse me; you know I shall never fail 25 your friends, if there is anything I can do. Farewell.

Constance, 22 October 1526

To the greatest of all scholars, Master Erasmus of Rotterdam, his dearly beloved teacher

1762 / From Justus Diemus   Speyer, 22 October 1526

Diemus had recently been in Rome staying with his cousin Jacobus Apocellus, an apostolic protonotary at the papal curia; see Ep 1630. He had left Rome for Germany, carrying letters through the perils of war-torn northern Italy and the disorders in the German countryside, and had entered the service of Johannes Fabri at the court of Archduke Ferdinand of Hapsburg. His experience in having all the letters he was carrying, including some addressed to Erasmus, opened and inspected by the Venetians at Verona illustrates the difficulties of communication in the sixteenth century, especially in wartime. No doubt the Venetians, engaged in war against the emperor, were trying to intercept communications between pro-Spanish individuals at the curia and the court of the emperor's brother, Archduke Ferdinand, in Germany. Allen suggests that Diemus may be identical with the Jodocus Dymer of Heilbronn who received a BA degree at Heidelberg in 1521. Enthoven published this letter from the original manuscript in the Rehdiger collection at Breslau (now Wrocław).

* * * * *

a degree as to cause the powers to put aside their own conflicts and unite to oppose Turkish expansion.

11 Benoît Vaugris operated a bookstore at Constance and travelled frequently to Basel on business. See Ep 1395 introduction.
12 As Allen (22n) notes, the initial editors of this letter suggest that this may be Léger Duchesne (d 1588), humanist and professor of Latin eloquence at the French Collège Royal from 1561 to 1586 (Förstemann/Günther 381). But there is nothing in Duchesne's known career to explain why he would have had any connection with Basel or with Botzheim at Constance. The dates of his tenure as royal reader in Latin eloquence make it unlikely that he was the person mentioned here, as (perhaps) does his extreme opposition not only to the French Calvinists but also to moderate Catholics who attempted a policy of accommodation with them, which culminated in a tract written to glorify the St Bartholomew's Day Massacre of 1572 (cf R. Limouzin-Lamoth in *Dictionnaire de biographie française* [Paris 1931–　] xi 1241). It is a barely possible but not a likely identification.

Greetings. I was expecting to be the bearer of the enclosed if my journey had taken me to Basel.[1] But when that did not happen, the opportunity was missed. The Venetians searched me at Verona and opened all my letters. So don't be surprised that the letter from Hovius,[2] which I am forwarding, has been opened. I left Rome because the climate did not suit me. Dr Johannes 5 Fabri[3] will be with us shortly; I intend travelling to Spain with him. Hovius suffers badly from the stone. He would have liked to come with me to Germany, but there was no chance of his getting away.

The Turks are pressing Hungary in full force; they seize any place they have a mind to.[4] The sister of his imperial Majesty had a hard time reaching 10 the archduke, even though she was travelling in disguise.[5] The Turks are leading their army into Styria. They have occupied almost the whole of Croatia.

There is a story that the pope has been besieged in Castel Sant' Angelo by the most reverend Cardinal Colonna.[6] The pope had invited him to come

* * * * *

1762
1 Diemus had intended to deliver in person letters addressed to Erasmus but was forced to forward them as enclosures to the present letter when he found that his duties in the service of Johannes Fabri prevented him from including Basel on his itinerary.
2 Johannes Hovius, Erasmus' secretary from 1518 to about 1523, had settled in Rome after leaving Erasmus' service, helped along by letters of recommendation from Erasmus to people with influence at the curia, such as Felix Trophinus, bishop of Chieti (Ep 1575). On Hovius cf Epp 867:189n, 1387 n3, 1605 n5.
3 See introductions to Epp 386, 1690, 1739.
4 Although the military threat of Turkish expansion after their victory at Mohács on 29 August worried many political and intellectual figures at this time, Diemus' association with Fabri and with Archduke Ferdinand made him especially concerned, since Ferdinand administered the Hapsburg lands in Austria most immediately threatened by Turkish expansion and was also claiming the Hungarian throne in succession to his brother-in-law King Louis II, who perished in the battle.
5 Mary of Hapsburg, widow of the slain Hungarian king, had hurriedly relocated her household to Bratislava in Slovakia after the military disaster at Mohács. Since Hungary was internally divided between pro-Hapsburg partisans of her brother Ferdinand's claim to the throne and the partisans of the native noble, John Zápolyai, who was favoured by most of the country's magnates, and since not only Croatia and Styria but also the central Hungarian plain was exposed to Turkish raids and occupation, her ability to rejoin her brother Ferdinand was in jeopardy. She acted as regent in behalf of his claim to the throne for about a year. See Ep 1754 n12.
6 In fact he had not taken refuge in Castel Sant'Angelo at this time but was engaged in a struggle to assert his control of Rome in the face of conspiracies and a large military incursion in September 1526 led by the anti-Medicean, anti-

and see him privately. Not wishing to be rude, the cardinal came after an 15
interval – and ransacked the papal palace. But the story has not yet been confirmed. Perhaps you people are better informed about events in Italy than we
are. If I hear of anything that I think you should know, I shall write as soon as
possible. Please continue to think well of me; remember I would do anything
for you that conscience would allow,[7] if only you expressed the wish. 20

In haste, Speyer, 22 October in the year 1526 from the delivery of the
Virgin

My slowness in writing is explained by the fact that there was no one
here to whom I could entrust a letter; and I was detained in several places
in the course of my journey.[8] 25

Justus Diemus of Bruchsal, at your service

To the eminent Desiderius Erasmus of Rotterdam, his most worthy
master and patron. In Basel

1763 / From Levinus Ammonius to Johannes de Molendino

St Maartensbos, 6 November 1526

As Erasmus had always insisted when making statements critical of them,
not all monks were opposed to 'good letters' (that is, humanistic studies) and
to his own writings. Ammonius, a native of Ghent, became a Carthusian in
1506. Despite his isolated existence in a strictly cloistered community near
Bruges, he eagerly studied Latin and Greek and coped with his intellectual
isolation and loneliness by conducting an active correspondence with other
scholars. In 1524 he sent Erasmus a long letter expressing his admiration (Ep
1463); this effort did not elicit a reply, but a second attempt in 1528 (Ep 2016)
brought a response from Erasmus (Ep 2062) and opened a correspondence that
continued, of which several letters survive. Despite his monastic isolation, and
presumably because of his active correspondence, Ammonius got news of the
suppression of the published *Annotationes* in which the Paris theologian Noël
Béda attacked Erasmus and Lefèvre d'Etaples. An order from the Parlement of

* * * * *

French faction-chief among the Roman nobility, Cardinal Pompeo Colonna.
See the description of these disorders in Rome and throughout Italy in Pastor
IX 274–340, and cf Ep 1761 n9.
7 Diemus' Latin expression is *ad aras usque*, literally 'up to the altars.' Cf *Adagia*
III ii 10.
8 Presumably either by bands of armed peasants left over from the Peasant War,
which was not totally suppressed in some regions of southern Germany, or by
troops supposedly engaged in that suppression and suspicious of travellers

Paris, acting under pressure from King Francis I, mandated this suppression (see Ep 1722; cf Ep 1721 introduction).

In this letter, which the translator has described in a note to the annotator as marked by 'a most lively style with a remarkably elegant use of Latin idiom,' Ammonius exultantly passes on the details of Béda's judicial defeat and public humiliation to his kinsman Johannes de Molendino, another admirer of Erasmus. Molendino studied with Lefèvre d'Etaples at Paris, taught there in the Collège de Bourgogne and the Collège du Cardinal Lemoine for two decades before becoming a canon at Tournai, and himself served a term as rector of the University of Paris in 1501. Allen was the first to edit this (and the other surviving letters of Ammonius) from a manuscript in the Bibliothèque municipale at Besançon.

For a modern account of the incident reported by Ammonius, see Rummel II 35–7, who notes that Erasmus' triumph over Béda was not quite so complete as Ammonius thought; most copies of the banned publication had already been sold before the order for its confiscation from the Paris bookstores was published, and the French king's authority could not prevent publication of a second edition of Béda's *Annotationes* beyond the French border, at Cologne, in August. In fact, Farge *Orthodoxy* 192–3 and *Registre* 143 n52 notes that there is no evidence from Paris confirming this detailed story of Béda's public humiliation. Thus the evidentiary value of this letter is open to question. On Béda see Epp 1571 introduction, 1664 introduction and n1.

LEVINUS AMMONIUS TO JOHANNES DE MOLENDINO, GREETING

Do you want to hear a story, my dear kinsman, that will make you laugh? Not so many days ago our friend Erasmus scored a triumph in Paris, and – what makes it all the more astonishing – he was not even there! 'What triumph?' you will ask. A splendid triumph, which, with your natural sympathy for Erasmus, I know you will be delighted to hear about. Béda was on the point of publishing his *censurae*, a list of foolish criticisms of the beautiful writings of Erasmus. He was like a spider gathering poison from the sweetest flowers, not a poison that he found there, but one he introduced from his own nature; or, to put it more precisely, he poisoned those sweet and fragrant juices with the venom from his own mind. Well, as I was saying, he had gathered a lot of poison, or what he thought was poison, and was about to publish it, when Erasmus heard of it and dashed off letters to the most Christian king of France[1] and

* * * * *

1763
1 Ep 1722

to the senate of Paris (they call it the 'Parlement'),[2] and finally, (for he   15
had nothing to fear) to the faculty of theology itself,[3] protesting that they
should either not allow this buffoon to publish his silly volume, or, if
that could not be stopped in the event that he had already rushed the
work into print, that they should at least permit himself to provide the
antidote.   20

At this point, dear kinsman, to quote the poet,[4] 'such a proof was
sought, such a battle fought' to determine who would emerge the winner:
would it be Erasmus, the greatest of all theologians in the general opinion of the whole Christian community, the man who first broke the ice and
called all students of theology to forsake those muddied pools and turn to   25
the fountains of purest water? Or would it be Béda, an upstart whose name
before this was scarcely known beyond his own front door, who realized
that, if he were not to languish in obscurity for ever, there was only one way
by which he could make a name for himself – by launching an attack on the
work of others.[5] But thanks be to God, the truth prevailed. And how could   30
it not prevail? For even if it were suppressed, it could not be vanquished
utterly. The Parlement, on receiving Erasmus' letter, and after hearing (we
may suppose) from the king, took upon itself a review of the whole matter. Everything was scrupulously examined in the most careful detail, and
a decree was passed and openly proclaimed[6] that Béda's unholy 'censures,'   35
on which he had laboured in vain, be suppressed. Was that not a glorious
triumph indeed?

* * * * *

2 Ep 1721
3 Ep 1723
4 Plautus *Casina* 516; *Bacchides* 399
5 According to Farge *Biographical Register* 32–3, Béda was not very active in the
   business of the Paris faculty of theology until his concern that the critical ex-
   egetical methods of the biblical humanists were undermining the unity of the
   church led him in 1520 to propose the restoration of the lapsed office of syndic of the faculty and then to transform it into a position that allowed him
   to dominate the business of the faculty for more than a decade. This sudden
   emergence into a leading role after an early career of no particular distinction
   may be what Ammonius, who seems well informed on the inner business of
   the Paris faculty (as his friend Molendino certainly was), has in mind when
   he calls Béda an upstart.
6 Literally, 'passed, as it were, on the third market day.' According to Macrobius
   Saturnalia 1.16.35, Roman laws were promulgated on the third market day. On
   market days the city would be crowded, offering an opportunity to publicize
   new laws.

But this is not the end of the story. 'Is there more to it, then?' you will ask. Just be patient and I shall tell you the rest, for we have not yet reached the climax. So far I have said nothing to make Crassus laugh; but unless he has become too fond of his nickname 'Agelastos,' he will have no choice but to laugh! We are told by Cicero on the authority of Lucilius and by St Jerome in a letter to Chromatius that Crassus laughed only once in his life: it was over a witticism about a donkey eating thistles, 'like lips, like lettuce.'[7] If this story is true, then he will surely have to laugh, even perhaps split his sides, at the sight of this other donkey devouring not lettuce, but his very own, first-born, only-begotten offspring, to which he was so desperately and hopelessly attached. You might say that one ass was eating another.[8]

Listen, now, to the rest of the story. When the Parlement decided to suppress the work, Béda was assigned a companion, so that our great theologian would not have to go out alone, for that, of course, would have been beneath his dignity. The companion was selected from the king's attendants (they are known as his *clientes*),[9] and an order was issued in the king's name that Béda, the celebrated critic of Erasmus, should go with his companion to every bookshop, of which, as you know, there are many in Paris, and announce in his own name and in the name of the king that no one should henceforth offer for sale his 'censures,' which were now under a ban; everyone was to be informed that it was illegal to palm off on anyone these vile and lying calumnies against the innocent Erasmus. You can imagine, my dear kinsman, with what enthusiasm Béda carried out these orders! Was this not a marvellous triumph? Is it not a story that deserves to be recorded by learned men and passed on to posterity?

* * * * *

7 Ammonius gives Licinius Crassus' nickname in Greek ἀγέλαστος 'one who never laughs'). The point is that his account of Béda's public humiliation would make even the solemn Crassus laugh. Erasmus tells the story of Crassus in *Adagia* I x 71 (*Similes habent labra lactucas* 'Like lips like lettuce'); cf Cicero *De finibus* 5.92, *Tusculanae disputationes* 3.31; Jerome *Letters* 130.13. For other references to Cicero and Jerome, see CWE 32:382–3, nn3–5, 7.
8 In other words, the asinine Béda was compelled to 'devour' (that is, confiscate) his own asinine book. The editor of the French translation of Erasmus' correspondence, Gerlo VI 509 n4, regards this passage as a modification of the proverb *asinus asinum fricat*; see *Adagia* I vii 99 and Suidas T 767.
9 That is, the Gentlemen of the Chamber who attended on the king personally

When Béda was carrying out his assignment, as luck would have it, he ran into Merlin,[10] a man of shrewd judgment,[11] who also has the title of 'theologian,' but with more claim to it than ten Bédas. When he came upon Béda doing his rounds and saw him looking as cheerful as you may well imagine, he said testily, 'So Béda, you fool, this is the reward you have got   70 for your "censures" and for presuming to write against Erasmus. The wild calumnies that you rained down on Erasmus' head have been condemned both for brutishness and for heresy. Yes, there are heresies in your own work that you failed to notice,[12] though you were sharp-eyed enough in

* * * * *

10 On the Paris theologian Jacques Merlin and his controversy with Béda over his edition of Origen's works (1512) and Béda's support of a publication by Christian Masseeuw attacking Merlin, see Ep 1609 nn10, 14; cf Ep 1579 n1. This controversy lasted for years and led to litigation before the Parlement of Paris; see n15 below. Hence it is not surprising that Merlin would have been pleased to see Béda being paraded about to effect the confiscation of his *Annotationes* from the booksellers, and he may even have taunted him as here described. For a sense of the personal hostility that developed between Merlin and Béda, see Farge *Biographical Register* 327–8.

11 Ammonius' Latin phrase is *emunctae naris*, literally 'with well-wiped nose'; see *Adagia* II viii 59, which cites Horace *Satires* 1.4.8. Undoubtedly Ammonius regarded Merlin as having shrewd judgment both because (unlike Béda) he had some appreciation of the central role of Origen in the development of early Christian theology and because he had the spirit to defend himself aggressively within the faculty of theology and before the law courts against Béda's attack.

12 Whether or not one believes that Ammonius (or the unidentified source of his information) has closely reproduced words said to Béda by Merlin, it is likely that another theologian being attacked by Béda would have known that early in Béda's career (in fact, in his Sorbonic disputations as a degree candidate), he had asserted doctrines that the faculty regarded as erroneous and imprudent (though not heretical) and was forced to make a formal public recantation. See Farge *Biographical Register* 31–2. Hence the story that during their chance encounter Merlin accused him of maintaining heresies in his own work is plausible if the encounter itself actually happened. Walter F. Bense 'Noël Beda and the Humanist Reformation at Paris, 1504–1534' (unpublished PhD dissertation, Harvard University 1967) 422 n179, and Farge *Parti conservateur* 90 n101 have suggested that the accusation against Béda reflected in this letter may have been a reference to an anonymous tract printed in 1527 that attributed heretical doctrines to Béda: *Duodecim articuli infidelitatis magistri Natalis Bedae ex libro suarum Annotationum excerpti, reprobantur et confutantur* (Paris: [Josse Bade 1527]). Both Bense and Farge also suggest that Merlin himself, rather than Berquin, who is the usual suspect, may have been the anonymous author of this work. As corroborative evidence, Farge prints the record of a hearing held before the Parlement on 18 January 1527 in which Merlin's lawyer of-

dealing with the work of others, seeing even things that were not there!' He   75
went on in this strain, saying whatever sprang to his lips – and he is not a
man who is ever at a loss for words.

Then the valiant Béda, the one and only defender of the truth (this
at least is how he saw himself!), was not taken aback; rather, he was like a
grasshopper held by the wing.[13] He seemed to forget what he was doing and   80
to lose sight of the mission on which he had been sent; he even forgot, or
perhaps had not yet heard, what the Parlement had decided about him. He
rounded on his tormentor with a flood of invective such as rabble-rousers of
his sort always carry about with them as ready cash. In the end tempers on
both sides became so heated that they nearly came to blows. Béda, fearing he   85
might be forced to give ground[14] and that in the end he was likely to come
off second best, summoned Merlin to court,[15] placing his hopes, I suppose,
in the syllogisms and inferences he had been preparing for just such an
event.

Merlin did not refuse the challenge. The matter came before the Par-   90
lement and each pleaded his case. Both were given leave to speak, and Béda
began a long emotional tirade, counting on his fingers all the verbal buffet-
ings that Merlin had inflicted on him, which – so he claimed – he had suffered for the faith and in the cause of the Crucified One. Merlin, in reply,
having a better case and superior learning, defended himself with consid-   95
erable skill, and while the whole court sat in hushed silence, repeated the
charges he had previously levelled against Béda, calling him a barbarian
and a heretic. When Béda realized that there was no one with any sympathy for his predicament, no one, as he kept repeating, who was ready to

* * * * *

fered to show the court 'a large number of erroneous propositions, suspicious
vis-à-vis the faith, drawn and excerpted from the books of Béda' (translation
by Farge in a letter to the editors).
13 *Adagia* I ix 28. The grasshopper when caught was thought to make an even
louder noise.
14 Literally, 'give grass to the stronger,' a reference to the ancient practice of
acknowledging defeat by offering a wreath of grass to the victor; cf *Adagia* I
ix 78.
15 Merlin had appealed to the Parlement of Paris for action to stop Béda's efforts to forbid republication of his work on Origen (including his introductory *Apologia*, in which he defended Origen's orthodoxy against the condemnation of him as a heretic by a council in 553, some three centuries after his
death). At the same period, Béda had sought permission to publish an attack
on Merlin. On this conflict see Farge *Registre* 327. The present letter suggests
a counter-suit by Béda based on Merlin's public taunting of him.

take up the cause of the faith and the Crucified One, he began to look for   100
help from a higher power. He happened to notice a picture of the crucifix-
ion on the wall. He turned to this, and baring his head and stretching out
his hand, cried out in a loud voice: 'O holy cross and thou, O Crucified One,
it is thy case, not mine, that is before this court. I implore and entreat thee
to take upon thyself the defence of thy own cause and not permit the truth   105
to be trampled under foot and the perpetrators to go unpunished.' But neither the cross nor the Crucified One answered Béda's prayer; for he does
not listen to slanderers. The Slanderer and all who stand with him are the
enemies of God.[16]

When no one spoke up for Béda, he lost all hope of support from that   110
quarter, and decided on a different approach. Like a wolf encircled by dogs,
he looked around for some avenue of escape. He approached the royal advocate, a man called Lizet,[17] who happened to be present. He addressed this
man by name and said, 'You are here as advocate for the king's interests, but
you have a greater obligation to plead the cause of Christ the king, which,   115
as you see, is now in the gravest danger. So step forward and do your duty
boldly. There is no need to be afraid; you will have God's help, I promise
you, provided you do not desert this noble cause.' The advocate, along with

* * * * *

16 Ammonius uses the Greek word, διάβολος, which has the sense 'slanderer.'
   The Septuagint uses that word to translate the Hebrew 'Satan,' meaning 'enemy.' Ammonius plays on the various associations of the Word: the 'devil' is
   a 'slanderer' and an 'enemy' of God.
17 Pierre Lizet (c 1482–1554), here referred to as *regius orator* and at lines 105 and
   109 as *advocatus*, had become a councillor in the Parlement in 1514 and royal
   advocate in 1517. He had conducted several politically sensitive cases for the
   crown before the Parlement. He was a native of Salers in the Auvergne and
   presumably had training in law, though there is no record of his educational
   background. The favour of the chancellor Antoine Duprat and an advanta-
   geous marriage to a daughter of the paymaster of the Parlement facilitated
   his rise to high office. Although at this period he opposed Béda on the condemnation of Erasmus and on the debate over the legality of Henry VIII's divorce, he later supported the efforts of the faculty of theology to publish its
   condemnation of Erasmus (Allen Ep 2587:7n). Indeed, despite his position as
   king's counsel in the Parlement, he was a conservative in religion, hostile to
   humanists and reformers. This is shown by his long speech in the Parlement
   in August 1525 supporting Béda against the Meaux reformers (Bishop Guillaume Briçonnet, Lefèvre d'Etaples, and Martial Mazurier), summarized in the
   record printed in Farge *Parti conservateur* 67–78. That record makes this report
   of his open ridicule of Béda surprising if not incredible and suggests either
   that Ammonius misunderstood his source, or that the source was untrue, or
   even that Ammonius fabricated the story.

all the members of the Parlement and everyone else who was present, burst
out laughing, amazed at the man's shameless temerity in promising to an-   120
other what he had been unable to obtain for himself. And so Béda was hissed
out of the Parlement, followed, as he departed, by the jeers[18] of all. One of the
advocates[19] said, 'So these are the theologians to whom we assign power and
authority to destroy learned and pious men, though their proper duty is the
defence of our Christian faith! Is this what our doctors of divinity are like?   125
    And so the story ended. I could wish a similar fate for all those other
'scourges of Erasmus'[20] who dare to lay their sacrilegious hands upon his
brilliant writings. Upon my word, I am delighted the business turned out
so well for Erasmus. It almost seems that he is now beyond the reach of
envy, and that God himself is fighting on his side. A while ago the pit   130
of hell claimed 'the Camel.'[21] Vincentius[22] too has gone down to perdi-
tion, though Christian piety is merciful even to its enemies and always
hopes and prays they may have a happier destiny. These two were the
worst enemies of good literature and true theology. As for Cousturier,
who is more fit for stitching shoes than writing books, there is no dan-   135
ger now from him, or from Béda either.[23] Béda won a splendid victory, to

* * * * *

18 The Latin is *posticis sannis* 'sneers behind one's back,' an elegant phrase from
   Persius 1.62.
19 Ammonius' Latin expression, 'quidam ex oratoribus,' seems not to distinguish clearly between the *avocats*, lawyers accredited to argue cases before the
   Parlement, and the *conseillers*, the real members of the Parlement who acted
   as judges. The identity of the person who made the remark cannot be determined, but Ammonius implies that it expressed the consensus of those present
   at the hearing.
20 On the Latin term *Erasmomastix* see Ep 1658 n8.
21 A dismissive nickname (*camelita*, 'camel,' a pun on the Latin word for a member of the Carmelite order, *Carmelita*), often also used by Erasmus for one of
   his harshest critics at Louvain, Nicolaas Baechem of Egmond, also known as
   Egmondanus. He had died at Louvain on 24 or 25 August. Erasmus did not yet
   know of his death on 3 September (Ep 1747:14–16). On him see Epp 879:15n,
   1254 n6, 1553 nn4–5, 1581 nn27, 46; 1603 n11, 1608 n4.
22 Vincentius Theoderici (Dierckx), a Dominican friar and professor of theology
   at Louvain, died on 4 August. Erasmus regarded him as one of his enemies
   at Louvain and correctly concluded that he was one (probably the leader) of a
   group of Dominicans who published an anonymous attack on him under the
   pseudonym 'Taxander.' See Epp 1571 n14, 1581A introduction, 1674 n13.
23 On this Carthusian theologian, whom Erasmus regarded as the most unrelenting but also the most incompetent of his Paris critics, see Epp 1571 n10,
   1658 n7. If Ammonius really thought that the royal action against Béda's *Annotationes* would overawe either Cousturier or Béda, however, he did not

be sure, but he scored in his own goal. I am told that Cousturier's lips are now stitched tight and restrained with a strong bridle; neither of them, I think, will ever sing that old song again. It is a law of nature that a cock once beaten crows no more. As for the rest of them (if there are any oth-   140
ers still around), they will take warning from these examples and come to their senses if they are not utterly beyond hope; at any rate they will be less ready to attack, now that they have seen the reception that these men received and so richly deserved. I thought I ought to tell you all this, since I know you are always glad to hear of anything good that happens to   145
Erasmus.

Farewell, my good kinsman, and goodbye to all the Bédas and Cousturiers and cobblers everywhere! Please give my best wishes to our mutual friend, Jacobus Ceratinus,[24] and to all in your circle.

St Maartensbos, 6 November 1526   150

1764 / From Erasmus Schets   Antwerp, 9 November 1526

A reply to Ep 1758. The original manuscript survives at Basel and was first published in Allen VI in 1926.

Cordial greetings, Master Erasmus, my respected friend. I received your letter, dated 2 October, along with a receipt for the money I sent to Froben on your behalf. I was pleased to have news of this.

* * * * *

know his men. Both of them pressed ahead with their attack on what they regarded as the 'Lutheran heresies' in Erasmus' publications, bringing out additional books against him and in Béda's case working persistently to- wards the formal censure of Erasmus' books voted by the faculty of the- ology on 16 December 1527. On the delay in publication of this censure until July 1531, see Ep 1687 n13. The references to stitching (shoes and lips) and to 'Cousturiers and cobblers' in the following lines are based on a pun that Erasmus also used regularly: both the French name Cous- turier and the Latinized equivalent *Sutor* mean 'stitcher of shoes,' 'cobbler,' 'shoemaker.'

24 Erasmus' humanist friend Ceratinus, whom he had recommended for the chair of Greek at Leipzig in 1525 but who had been forced out of the job by suspi- cions (unjustified, apparently) that he favoured Luther, had returned to his na- tive Netherlands and had been teaching Greek in the new humanistic college at Tournai, where Molendino lived, though he may already have moved on. In a letter of 10 December (Ep 1768:89–91) Conradus Goclenius reports that Cera- tinus had left Tournai for his home town of Hoorn in North Holland 'several months' earlier. On Ceratinus see Epp 622:34n, 1611 n2, 1683 n15, 1693 nn6–7,

I wrote to the bishop of London in England[1] to tell him that, if it pleased his lordship to send you any money, he should give it in my name to Luis 5 de Castro (he is Alvaro's brother).[2] I shall see to it that any gift of his will reach you with no charge for exchange – or at least with the smallest possible loss to you. I also sent on the letters you gave me for forwarding to the same destination.

The letters for Spain, which you sent to the Frankfurt fair, I put aboard 10 a ship that came along opportunely. It weighed anchor shortly afterwards and sailed away. I have no reason to doubt it has reached port by now.

I passed on your message to Pieter Gillis.[3] He replied that he would attend to the matter and would dutifully carry out the wishes of his friend.

The whole world thinks you deserve to be congratulated on the *De in-* 15 *stitutione Christiani matrimonii.*[4] It is a truly divine and pious work. I too, dear Erasmus, offer my congratulations. You have shown us the true pattern of a virtuous life and the way to nourish a chaste love; you have demonstrated that the holy estate of matrimony, which was instituted by God but has now degenerated almost to the level of a pagan ritual, is purified by the 20 practice of Catholic teaching. Farewell.

Antwerp, 9 November 1526

Your devoted servant, Erasmus Schets

To that incomparable scholar, Master Erasmus of Rotterdam. In Basel

1765 / From Conradus Goclenius   Louvain, 12 November 1526

On Goclenius, professor of Latin at the Collegium Trilingue in Louvain, whom Erasmus respected as a scholar and trusted as a friend, see the introductions to Epp 1209, 1641. The manuscript of this letter survived at Basel and was first published in Allen VI.

* * * * *

1717 n28. On the new college, part of an attempt to found a new university at Tournai, see Ep 1558 n28, 1747 n21.

1764
1 See Epp 1726 introduction, 1750 n1.
2 Schets corrects Erasmus' error in Ep 1758, where he mistakenly refers to Alvaro's brother as Juan. Alvaro was Schets' commercial correspondent at London in matters relating to Erasmus' English revenues.
3 Though no longer Erasmus' financial agent in the Netherlands (having been replaced by Schets), Gillis remained a close friend. See Ep 1671 n6.
4 Ep 1729 is Erasmus' dedication of this book to Catherine of Aragon, queen of England.

Cordial greetings. The fact that on this occasion you are receiving a letter only from me should be blamed on the courier who is delivering it to you.[1] He reached Louvain on 12 November about six o'clock and refused my request to stay over even for an extra day. He said his companions were in a hurry and that he had to leave before dawn; if I wanted to send a letter, he 5 would have to receive it that night, otherwise I would be wasting my time. I did not get this message until seven, since I was not at home, having been called out on business. I would like you to know first of all that the courier carried no letter from you. The bundle brought by Pieter Gillis' brother has been distributed in accordance with your instructions,[2] as you will find out 10 in due course from your friends' replies.

I read your long letter[3] with mixed feelings. I was greatly pained to hear that an innocent person like yourself should be the target of attack by evil men who conspire to destroy you. Yet at the same time, when I thought how bravely, and with what evident signs of divine support, you have stood 15 up for the truth against falsehood, I began to hope that the wickedness of your enemies would cast your goodness in a brighter light, and that the more they tried to bury the name of Erasmus in obscurity, the greater your renown would be. I was quite delighted that you approve my decision with regard to the offers from England and Denmark.[4] Your opinion has always 20 meant more to me than anyone else's. The golden rule for those contemplat-

* * * * *

1765
1 Because of the unidentified courier's haste to depart, Goclenius did not have time to inform other people in and near Louvain that a courier to Basel was available; he had time only to produce his own letter before the courier left.
2 This shipment of letters was brought to the Netherlands by Frans Gillis, who had been expected in Basel in August; cf Ep 1740:18–20 and n7. No existing letter can be clearly identified as part of this bundle.
3 Allen (14n) suggests that this may be Erasmus' letter of 3 September to the imperial chancellor, Mercurino Gattinara (Ep 1747), 'which seems to have been intended for circulation.' He notes that in Ep 1748 to Alonso de Fonseca, Erasmus says that he has enclosed a copy of the letter to Gattinara.
4 Goclenius had been offered the chair of humanities at Corpus Christi College, Oxford, a chair founded by Cardinal Wolsey in preparation for carrying out his plan to establish an entirely new college, to be called Cardinal College. The professorship had recently been vacated by Juan Luis Vives. The exiled king of Denmark, Christian II, brother-in-law of the emperor, had also sought to employ Goclenius as tutor to his son. But Goclenius had decided to remain at the Collegium Trilingue, where his skill at teaching Latin had attracted many students, even though he found his salary from the Trilingue inadequate.

ing responsibilities of this sort was laid down long ago: *festina lente* [make
haste slowly].[5]

The month of August dealt a fairly severe blow to the theologians.
They have suffered a heavy loss, while our studies, I think, have been made   25
a lot more peaceful by the death of two of our most implacable foes, Vincentius and Egmondanus.[6] Vincentius died on 4 August from a type of dropsy
that the doctors call by the Greek name *tympanitês*.[7] Egmondanus passed
away on 23 August, though what caused his death I do not know. Some say
he was poisoned by the Lutherans in 's Hertogenbosch. He himself, while   30
he was alive, refused to believe this sort of thing and rebuked those who
tried to make him share their suspicions. After his death his friends in the
university were discouraged from disseminating the rumour by the following circumstance. A few of the monks had gone out in search of surgeons to
examine the body for poison, hoping, I suppose, to find better reasons for   35
his being numbered among the saints.[8] They were met by a clever fellow
who enquired after Egmondanus' health. On being told that he had passed
away and that they were looking for a doctor because they suspected poisoning, the man said, 'What makes you think he was given aconite? Do you
have any evidence for this?' They replied, 'Nothing definite, except the hos-   40
tility the Lutherans felt towards him.' 'If,' said he, 'that is all the reason you
have for your suspicions, watch out that you are not suspected of poisoning
him yourselves. For no one hated him as much as you did and no one had
more opportunity to administer the dose than those who shared with him
the familiar intercourse of daily life. So be careful that your actions don't   45
have the unintended effect of bringing down trouble on your own heads.'
They took his advice and went no further.

We do not know how he died: we can only conjecture. At four o'clock
on the day before he died, he took some medicine, as prescribed by his
doctors. When he saw it had no effect on his stomach and that the disease   50
would not yield to medication, he walked about in his room for several
hours, as was his custom. Near noon he asked the nurse who was looking

* * * * *

5 Goclenius cites this famous maxim in Greek. It was a favourite of the emperor Augustus, who commended it to military commanders; Suetonius *Divus
  Augustus* 25.4, Aulus Gellius *Noctes Atticae* 10.11.5. Cf *Adagia* II i 1.
6 See Ep 1763 nn22, 21.
7 Celsus 3.21.2
8 Presumably if it could be shown that Lutherans had poisoned him at 's Hertogenbosch, where according to Erasmus' report in Ep 1747 he had publicly
  burned a copy of Erasmus' New Testament as if it were a heretical book, he
  could at least be regarded as a martyr for the Catholic faith.

after him to leave the room, for (according to her statement) he intended to recite the hours. What happened then is unclear. But when the nurse returned, she found he had choked on his own vomit. He had met his end in a manner that he himself had characterized, in speaking of Neve's death, as the most horrible of all.[9] This is how the story ended.

His body was taken to Mechelen and buried there with the Carmelites. Yesterday Godschalk was again given extreme unction.[10]

If anything else happens that is worth mentioning, I shall write you a longer letter as soon as I find a courier.

Farewell. From the Collegium Trilingue, 1526

To Master Erasmus of Rotterdam. In Basel

1766 / From Robert Aldridge   [Cambridge, c December 1526]

In connection with the revision of his 1515 edition of the works of the Roman philosopher Seneca, which he regarded as very defective, Erasmus wrote his former pupil Aldridge at the end of 1525 (Ep 1656), asking him to collate the printed text of 1515 with manuscripts that Erasmus remembered using at King's College and at Peterhouse during his own residence in Cambridge. This letter from Aldridge is both an apology for his tardiness and a report that he had been only partly successful in finding the manuscripts that Erasmus had in mind. In his reply (Ep 1797), Erasmus explained that there was another manuscript at King's and urged Aldridge to try again. This exchange is a good example of how Erasmus worked through friends to obtain variant readings from manuscripts in distant places, and his reply in Ep 1797 shows that he retained a vivid memory of a manuscript that he had not seen in more

* * * * *

9 Jan de Neve of Hondschoote was regent of the College of the Lily at Louvain for much of his career and welcomed Erasmus as a resident of that college during his longest period of residence in Louvain from 1517 to 1521. He was partially disabled by a stroke in 1521 and died of a second stroke on 22 April 1522. He was the subject of an extended letter of condolence from Erasmus to Joost Vroye that was also published as a meditation on sudden and unexpected death (Ep 1347; see also Ep 298 introduction). Presumably Nicolaas Baechem had preached on the horrors and dangers of sudden death, using Neve as an example. Erasmus' opinion on this topic, expressed in his letter to Vroye, was quite different.
10 Godschalk Rosemondt of Eindhoven, professor of theology at Louvain, regarded by Erasmus as one of the most friendly and most fair of the Louvain theologians, lived until 5 December. He had been seriously ill for several months. On him see Ep 1153. Cf Ep 1732 and n11, and for Goclenius' report of his death and praise of his character, Ep 1768:46–56.

than a decade but that was important for his textual scholarship. His revised edition of the *Opera* of Seneca was published by Froben in 1529. The original manuscript letter survived at Wrocław and was first published by Enthoven in 1906.

Erasmus, my good and learned friend, you may well wonder why someone who was once your pupil and whom you treated much more kindly than he deserved is so slow to do the only thing you asked of him, though it was not a huge task or difficult to accomplish. You have good reason to doubt whether he really wants to do it or has made up his mind to 5 refuse. But perish the thought that I am planning to refuse or that you should think me unwilling to perform the one service my distinguished master has asked of his undistinguished pupil. For to tell you the truth, when you invited me to join you as your secretary, those six months I spent reading with you, when, among other things, I experienced every day the 10 delights of the learned jest, were worth more to me than many years of study.[1]

So don't think that I have refused your request; I have simply put it off. And don't imagine that I put it off when I might have done it. Day after day my hand was poised to seize the manuscript; but what could I do when 15 there was no one here, or available, to read it with me? To mention only one problem: from the beginning of March the plague ravaged our university so mercilessly that almost the whole student body fled to the country to protect their health.[2] So when I was ready to turn my attention to the text, there was no one here whom I could engage at any price. But eventually I found 20 competent and reliable assistants, and since then I have let no day slip by without making as much progress as I could.

* * * * *

1766
1 These six months of experience as Erasmus' amanuensis at Cambridge were a remarkable opportunity for young Aldridge. On him see Ep 1656 introduction. The date of their association must have included the summer of 1512, since in Ep 262, dated 9 May 1512, Erasmus mentions his plan to make the pilgrimage to the shrine of Our Lady of Walsingham, an experience which is reflected in his colloquy *Peregrinatio religionis ergo* 'A Pilgrimage for Religion's Sake,' in which Aldridge appears as 'a smooth-tongued young man' who acted as his interpreter (see CWE 40 633:25–6).
2 Allen (15n) cites C.H. Cooper *Annals of Cambridge* 1 (1842) 324 for a record showing that in 1526, Easter term was prorogued until 28 May because of the plague. It was quite common for sixteenth-century universities to disperse if plague struck the university town.

Here was my plan of action. The copy that is kept in our library at King's College[3] has the *Letters to Lucilius*[4] and nothing else. These letters are also to be found in the manuscript in Peterhouse. I suppose it was as a par- 25 ticular favour to Erasmus that I was permitted to borrow this manuscript from the Peterhouse library despite their serious concern for the protection of the books, an obligation imposed on them by special regulations. So in working through the *Letters to Lucilius*, I collated these two old manuscripts with the text printed by Froben. I marked the variants in the margin, distin- 30 guishing the two manuscripts by different signs. When the King's College manuscript had a different reading, I indicated this with a θ; I used the following sign :? for distinctive variants in the Peterhouse manuscript. When the two codices agreed against Froben's text, I wrote down the variant without a distinguishing mark. I have never failed to record a discrepancy if it 35 made sense at all. Even when I thought the printed text of Froben much superior, I recorded the variants, first because I gathered from your letter that this was what you wanted, and secondly to give your sharp wits something to work on, to enable you to recognize the lion by its claw.[5] For you possess the sort of mind that can restore broken and mutilated words, dis- 40 entangle a jumbled passage, replace what is false and spurious with the true and proper reading, and bring sense out of nonsense.

I discovered the quickness of your judgment when I read some Seneca and Jerome with you at Queen's College, Cambridge[6] – though perhaps I should speak rather of your powers of divination, which surpass those of 45

* * * * *

3 Aldridge was a member of King's College and so had more ready access to its library than to the books of Peterhouse, to which he had access only as a special favour.
4 Seneca's *Ad Lucilium epistulae morales* were among the most highly regarded examples of ancient moral philosophy in the Renaissance. As they have come down to us, they consist of 124 letters divided into twenty books. Additional letters of Seneca were known in antiquity but are lost. In his *Moral Letters* the fiction of the epistolary form is often abandoned; they are really short essays on various topics. Seneca's prose works are an important source for the history of Stoicism.
5 *Adagia* i ix 3
6 Erasmus was at work on editions of both authors, as well as on the New Testament, during his years of residence in Cambridge (1511–14), a period which (despite his complaints about the university's isolation and the difficulty of finding good wine) provided him an opportunity for significant progress towards completion of his editions of the works of Seneca (1515) and Jerome (1516) and also the Greek New Testament (1516), all of them published at Basel by Froben.

Apollo and the Sibyl.[7] Anyone whom jealousy has not deprived of sight and hearing will find evidence every day of this ability of yours if, with honest eyes and unbiased ears, he examines the notes and emendations you have made both in many passages of Scripture and in a host of excellent authors. But how ungrateful people are today – unless we count their ignorance an excuse! And what a pitiful age we live in, when men who lack judgment pass sentence on the greatest judges of literature, and (what is harder to bear) have their verdict widely approved. But, then, is there any reason for surprise that a vulgar judgment should please the vulgar mob? At noisy public meetings, in the buzz of conversation, at the table, even from the pulpit one hears that Erasmus is ruining good and holy books, because he is replacing old and ingrained errors with something new and apt. I can think of only one explanation for this: that some people are so blind and look upon the world with eyes so full of spite (I speak here of the inner eye, meaning the disposition of one's mind) that they cannot, or will not, see how much they have gained by having filth and dung replaced with gold and precious stones. If nothing else can move them to spare Erasmus and respect his name (and if they do not want to be more stony-hearted than the rocks of Marpessus),[8] then at least they should be touched by all the intolerable hardships he has suffered on their behalf and for the good of all.

Let me assure you, Erasmus, my distinguished friend, that even from here I have some appreciation of what that busy sweatshop is like in which you spend your days; for you get through so many works, not just skimming them as I do, but revising and correcting them. When I simply read, and collate with the help of others, a single work of Seneca, and not even that in its entirety, although I may not be utterly exhausted myself, I often

* * * * *

7 The god Apollo was closely identified with prophecy, especially at his principal oracular shrine at Delphi but in other locations as well. The Sibyl was thought to be a single prophetic woman, but as the prophecies arose from various localities, the Sibyl came to be conceived as a plurality of prophetesses, each associated with a particular place, so that by the time of Varro in the late Roman republic, ten Sibyls were generally recognized. Sayings and prophecies attributed to them were written down, normally in Greek hexameters, and were collected. At Rome there was from an early date an official collection which could be consulted only at the command of the Senate. Sibylline books, of heterogeneous nature and often contaminated with Jewish and Christian interpolations, survived throughout the Middle Ages and into modern times.
8 Marpessus is a mountain on the island of Paros, famous for its marble quarries; a well-known literary reference is Virgil *Aeneid* 6.471.

have to encourage my weary helpers, urging them to stay the course and
overcome their tedium by calling to mind a happy memory. This is what
I say to myself and how I try to cheer the others: 'Just think,' I say, 'how 75
much work Erasmus gets through, how much weariness he overcomes, and
what a treadmill he endures! He reads so many authors, but he is not content simply to read – he examines every line for errors and corruptions,
and whatever faults he finds are put right. Whether it is a problem of language or of sense, he knows what effort it will take to restore a passage 80
devoid of meaning. If, I say, we are bothered and bored by our superficial reading, think what troubles must be borne by this prince of letters,
who has so many other torments to endure and is nailed in truth to his
own cross. Moreover, he receives no gratitude from those he serves at such
cost to himself. Is this the tragedy of Erasmus or of literature in general? 85
That question should be pondered by those who, by their attacks on men of
letters, would slow down the progress of the humanities, if literary scholars were not too stout of heart to cave in before malicious tongues.' And
you, Erasmus, must match your accomplishments as a scholar with a determination to carry on through thick and thin. All of us who love liter- 90
ature and learning beg you to persevere in the cause of the humanities.
Keep yourself well, have regard for your years, and call upon us when you
wish. All men of learning and all who love learning stand ready at your
command.

I, the least of scholars, am now carrying out your orders. I have col- 95
lated the volumes you asked for. There were two exemplars for the *Letters*, as you indicated. For the other works for which I entered my collations
there was only the Peterhouse manuscript.[9] The rest were not collated, since
there was no copy available in the places you mentioned, nor could I find
one elsewhere. As you requested, I sent the book with the collations to Mas- 100
ter Thomas More on 11 May and pressed him to forward it as rapidly as
possible.[10] He had promised to do so when I visited him at Easter, when

* * * * *

9 But Erasmus was still convinced that the librarians at King's College had misinformed Aldridge and that he himself had seen another manuscript there.
See Ep 1797:3–9.
10 In his letter (Ep 1656) requesting Aldridge to collate the Cambridge manuscripts of Seneca, Erasmus instructed him to transmit his notes using Thomas
More as intermediary. This passage shows that even though few letters survive
from this period (only Epp 1770 and 1804), Erasmus and More remained on
friendly terms and were in touch with each other.

he received me most graciously, as you would expect from someone of his kindly and obliging nature. I realize of course that my reception owed much to you, for he was aware that you and I have long been on close and familiar terms. Please commend me to him when next you write. That would please me very much.

Even if I had been reluctant to take this trouble on your behalf – though in fact I was ready to repay more than I owed – the weighty Seneca, as you call him, was well worth the effort. His ethical teaching forms an excellent basis for character and his natural philosophy, unless I am mistaken, holds the first place in that discipline – if indeed there is anyone else in Latin besides him worth reading. If he takes first place for the brilliance of his exposition of the secrets of nature and for the attractiveness of his moral teaching, then you must have second place for emending his work so that we can study both departments of philosophy in good texts.

You write in your letter that I owe a debt to scholarship but nothing to you except the obligation to return your affection; but the truth is that I owe everything to you on account of that very scholarship which you have done so much to foster and advance. I am entirely in your debt, and especially because you thought fit to number me among your friends and to remind me of our long friendship. I shall forget my own name before I cease to remember that. There is no need to think of compensating me for my work and expenses – it is enough if you continue to treat me as a friend.

I gave your greetings to the booksellers, Nicolaas, Garret, and Siberch. Fawne is ensconced in the palace of the bishop of Winchester and is now, I hear, very happy. Fate took Vaughan away from us shortly after you left, to what destination I do not know. Death has returned Humphrey to the bosom of our common mother.[11] Greetings and best wishes for a long and happy life to you and to my friend Froben.

Robert Aldridge

This letter is to be delivered to Master Erasmus, mighty prince of letters.

* * * * *

11 On these acquaintances from Erasmus' years at Cambridge, whom he had enumerated and asked to be greeted in his earlier letter to Aldridge; see Ep 1656:21–3 and n4. John Fawne had left Cambridge in the intervening year and was living in the household of his patron Richard Foxe, bishop of Winchester. John Vaughan had also left, and C.S. Knighton in CEBR III 380 notes that he probably was the bachelor of divinity by the same name who unsuccessfully claimed a rectory in Cambridgeshire in 1526.

1767 / To Theobald Fettich   Basel, 5 December 1526

Fettich is documented for the period 1510–34. He seems to have studied at
Cologne but is first clearly recorded by his matriculation at Heidelberg on 30
September 1510. In the second part of *Epistolae obscurorum virorum* (ed and
trans Francis Griffin Stokes [London 1909] II 9 152 [Latin] and 416 [English],
and II 12 159 [Latin] and 422 [English]), he is described as a doctor of medicine,
one of a circle of humanists, most of them jurists and assessors at the imperial court (*Reichskammergericht*) at Frankfurt, and as the most outspoken of the
group who defended Reuchlin and (despite his previous study in the Bursa
Montis at Cologne) who opposed the Cologne theologians who were pros-
ecuting him. During the Diet of Worms in 1521, the humanist Hermannus
Buschius stayed in his home at Worms. He was the physician of Wolfgang
von Affenstein (see Ep 1774), who administered the library left to the diocese by Johann von Dalberg (1455–1505), bishop of Worms and chancellor of
the Palatinate (a major patron of early German humanists, including the famous Rodolphus Agricola); hence Fettich was Erasmus' contact in an attempt
to investigate the resources of that collection of manuscripts and early printed
books. The library was in the castle of Ladenburg on the Neckar, where Affenstein resided. In 1526, as a result of intervention by Fettich, Affenstein lent
to Johann Sichard, a jurist and humanist who taught Roman law at Basel and
also acted as editorial adviser to several Basel printers, a manuscript of the
late classical medical author Caelius Aurelianus for publication (Basel: Henricus Petri, August 1529). Although Erasmus was not close to Sichard (who
worked with other Basel printers but not Froben and also was a supporter
of the Reformation), he knew enough about the local book trade to hear of
that manuscript discovery and decided to use the same contacts (Fettich and
Affenstein) to inquire about other old manuscripts that might be available at
Ladenburg. Affenstein responded by supplying from Ladenburg a manuscript
that Erasmus subsequently used for his edition (the *editio princeps* of the Greek
text) of Ptolemy's *De geographia* (Basel: Froben and Episcopius 1533), which he
dedicated to Fettich. Fettich, who was also physician to the electoral prince
of the Palatinate, was friendly with other humanists, including Otto Brunfels,
who praised his knowledge of Hebrew language and history in dedicating
to him his *Catalogus illustrium medicorum* (Strasbourg: J. Schott 1530). Erasmus
published this letter in *Opus epistolarum*.

ERASMUS OF ROTTERDAM TO THEOBALD FETTICH, GREETING
The greater the threat to the humanities in this most turbulent age, the
greater the challenge for those who know and understand that without the

seasoning of languages and polite letters all other disciplines lose their
savour and become speechless and almost blind; that states cannot flour- 5
ish or civilized life continue; in short, that a man can scarcely be a man at
all. I am told that where you live there is a rare collection of old manuscripts. The strong support that you and the honourable Wolfgang von Affenstein give to the cause of learning has long been known to me both from
the voice of hearsay and from my correspondence with learned friends, and 10
I know also of the generosity that both of you show towards men of letters.
It is for this reason that Hieronymus Froben did not hesitate to visit you,[1]
and I have not scrupled to address you by letter. My instinct tells me that
our temerity (or should I call it our confidence in your kindness?) will turn
out well for us. 15

No one can have failed to observe how long Johann Froben has
laboured, how much effort and time and money he has expended, to present
the best authors in attractive form – and all for a cause that brought him
much more fame than profit. He has in his household someone who is an
accomplished scholar in Greek and Latin;[2] he is also as dependable as he is 20
learned (and that is something I consider by no means unimportant). As for
myself, I shall be happy to devote myself to this service till my last breath
– for I regard it as both valuable and helpful to the faith. In my opinion
no one deserves your favour more than Froben and no other press will do
more for outstanding authors. Nor will you find anyone more grateful and 25
appreciative of your support. Besides, 'If anything my works avail' (so far
I can go with Virgil; I only wish I could add), 'no day will ever take you
from remembering time.'[3] Certainly, I shall do everything in my power to
see that posterity will not forget to whom it owes this contribution to the
literature of the past. Best wishes to you and to the illustrious lord deputy 30
Wolfgang von Affenstein.

Basel, 5 December 1526

* * * * *

1767
1 This son and eventual successor of the Basel printer Johann Froben had already
sought manuscripts for Erasmus in Italy (Ep 1705).
2 Allen (17n) suggests plausibly that Erasmus means the Bohemian humanist
Sigismundus Gelenius, whom in Ep 1717:81–2 he described as well qualified
for the unfilled chair of Greek at Leipzig but unwilling to leave his employment as editor for Froben. On Gelenius see Ep 1702 n1.
3 Virgil *Aeneid* 9.446–7. Erasmus adapts the first half-line, changing Virgil's *si
quid mea carmina possunt* 'if anything my songs avail' to *si quid mea scripta
valebunt*.

1768 / From Conradus Goclenius   Louvain, 10 December [1526]

> The Louvain humanist sends additional news as part of a shipment of letters
> for Erasmus, following up on his letter of about a month earlier, Ep 1765.
> Allen's edition (1926) was the first publication of this letter, drawn from the
> same Basel manuscript as Ep 1765.

Cordial greetings. My recent prediction that, with the disappearance of our
enemies,[1] the study of the humanities would enjoy a more tranquil existence
has so far turned out very much as I thought, although I imagine this is due
less to any good will on the part of the survivors than to their discouragement. All their efforts have proved vain or have had the opposite to the in-   5
tended effect, and many people have turned back on them the hatred they
tried so hard to heap on us. I pray that God will further our success and
that he will strengthen in the minds of the emperor and the other princes
that resolve which was evident in the emperor's letter.[2] I was sure the letter would not displease you and I felt it important for the commonwealth   10
of letters that you be roused by this clarion call to finish the fight against
barbarians and heretics. So I decided to send you a trusted messenger at
my own expense, who would acquaint you with all these matters. To make
my letter more welcome, I thought I should inquire from Pieter Gillis if he
had anything for Erasmus.[3] The letter he sent me in reply persuaded me to   15
abandon my former plan, for he told me that a merchant at Antwerp would
shortly be leaving for Basel and that I could safely entrust anything to him.
    So I followed Gillis' advice and sent the merchant a packet of various
letters, as you will see. On receiving them, he was to be responsible for delivering them to you. Among the letters from Spain were some written in   20
Spanish.[4] Since I was afraid you might have trouble with these through lack

* * * * *

1768
1 Nicolaas Baechem and Vincentius Theoderici, among the most hostile of the
  Louvain theologians; he had reported their deaths in Ep 1765.
2 Probably Ep 1731, the emperor's letter of 4 August 1526 to Erasmus praising
  his scholarly work, but the missing letter of October 1525 from the emperor to
  the Louvain theological faculty ordering them to stop their attacks on Erasmus
  could also be meant, since it may have had more effect at Louvain now that
  the two most irrepressible anti-Erasmians were dead. On that missing letter
  see Epp 1643 n3 and 1747 introduction.
3 Erasmus' friend and former financial agent at Antwerp. See Epp 1696 and
  1740 for their most recent letters.
4 Of this group of letters, only Epp 1731 (from the emperor), 1742 (from Juan

of a translator, I took the liberty (if you want to call it that) of engaging a Spaniard called Honoratus,[5] a great admirer of yours and of your writings, to translate them into Latin. There is no need, however, for me to think up excuses for my action, since the letters contained nothing that could not be shouted from the housetops. The letter from Juan Maldonado reached me without a seal, exactly as I am passing it on to you.[6] I kept a copy for myself, for, quite apart from its remarkable erudition, it shows a mind that is as lofty and noble as it is acute and judicious. I shall make sure that no one but my friends is allowed to see it – although secrecy does not appear to have troubled the author, since he took no steps to keep the letter confidential, which he could easily have accomplished by sealing it. Those who know the man say he carries great weight among his own people.

I cannot conceal my delight at the progress our studies are making. You too, more than anyone else, must be very happy at the growing interest in religion and the humanities, to which you have given new life and spirit. You have now achieved the one goal you set yourself. Other things, which a noble mind need not despise, have been added as a bonus – you have won an immortal name and much greater glory during your lifetime than many famous men have won after their death. I have no doubt (such being the spirit of the age) that, now that the envious and the jealous have been vanquished, you will reap a richer harvest for your hard work and perseverance. You see, I am beginning to babble; but I know you will pardon me, since it is a mark of my affection for you.

I believe you have had a full account of developments here from others. So I shall say nothing myself. Godschalk Rosemondt passed away on

* * * * *

Maldonado), and perhaps 1757 (from Gattinara, the imperial chancellor) survived; none of the letters that Goclenius had translated from Spanish into Latin seems to have been preserved. On the transmission of the packet via Antwerp see Ep 1750 n8. Erasmus reports receiving the letters in Ep 1781 but also reports that he had already received duplicate copies sent by an alternative route.

5 Honoratus Joannius of Valencia (1507–66), a Spanish student at Louvain, had studied under Vives and remained there when Vives left for England in 1523. He moved to Paris by 1529 and returned to Valencia by 1531. Many years later, he was a tutor to Philip II's son Don Carlos and to Don Juan of Austria, and this service was rewarded by his appointment as bishop of Osma in 1564.

6 See Ep 1742. Had he seen it earlier, Goclenius' positive evaluation of Maldonado and his reputation might have altered Erasmus' initial reaction to Maldonado's letter. Except for a handful of people linked to the imperial court, most of them non-Spaniards, Erasmus knew virtually nothing about either his enemies or his friends in Spain; and his first impressions were therefore sometimes mistaken.

the eve of St Nicholas' day, leaving a fine reputation behind him.[7] He was regarded as a great lover of peace – or if at times he acted a different part on the world's stage, people attribute this to the influence of others. One thing will always be remembered about him, something quite unusual for 50 a theologian: during his lifetime he sold everything he inherited from his family, and having no close relatives, he gave the money to the poor. The sum provided for this purpose was in excess of 2,000 florins. He also left a living allowance for two theology students (the theologians call this a 'bursary'), but they say that this was less a matter of conviction than a gesture 55 to convention or a response to pressure from others.

Visitors arriving from France say that the king[8] and the emperor[9] are of one mind about the encouragement of learning and about the ban recently imposed on Bade to prevent him from selling that rubbish of Béda's. This action of the king's, although it shows what he thinks of you, does more 60 harm than good, for nothing could benefit you more than for Béda to betray the ignorance of his profession and thus build up your reputation among men of sense. And since these are the people whose approval you seek, why bother with the rest, who are nothing but jackasses?

Things are going well here, except that we are all upset at the depar- 65 ture of our colleague Rutgerus Rescius from the college.[10] I urged Nicolas

* * * * *

7 Goclenius had reported him near death in his letter of 12 November; see Ep 1765 n10.
8 Francis I, who after his release from captivity in Spain had resumed his role of protecting reform-minded humanists like Lefèvre d'Etaples and even the indiscreet Louis de Berquin. His intervention in behalf of Erasmus, including the order for the confiscation of unsold copies of Noël Béda's *Annotationes* attacking Lefèvre and Erasmus, was a direct response to Erasmus' complaint to him in Ep 1722. Cf Ep 1763 for Levinus Ammonius' exultant account of Béda's public humiliation (for which there is no independent evidence; see the introduction to that letter).
9 Goclenius clearly knew of the Emperor Charles v's letter to Erasmus (Ep 1731) and, being in Louvain, may also have seen, or at least known of, the emperor's letter to the Louvain faculty of theology. See n2 above.
10 Rescius became the first professor of Greek at the new Collegium Trilingue in Louvain. In 1525 he married a local woman and moved into a house owned by her or her family. In the opinion of the executors of the founder's will and perhaps also of the president of the college, Nicolas Wary, his new domestic arrangements were unacceptable. Previously he had lived and taken his meals in the college and thus was more accessible to students and colleagues and in general for supervisory duties that would fall upon a resident master. The executors considered dismissing him and may even have done so (Allen [65n] says so, but De Vocht CTL II 318–19 thinks that there was never an actual dis-

Wary,[11] who says he acts in all matters in the name of the trustees, not to be overhasty. I told him it would be easier to find another than a better man, and that no one should be appointed to this position whose learning was not demonstrably superior to that of our colleague. I pointed out that even if there are candidates who appear more promising, yet when put to the test, they may prove a disappointment to the trustees and even to their auditors. Certainly, Rescius should not be sent packing because of his marriage. Marriage in the past, far from incurring penalties, brought with it certain privileges. In reply to all these points Wary cited the evidence of the will. If he writes to you on this subject, tell him what you judge best to do.

I have heard nothing of Karl.[12] I am not writing to him now because in his last letter, dated 7 October, he indicated that he was planning to leave Basel within ten days. I would like to know what happened to the girl. She was left in a wretched state of uncertainty, although she more than deserves to have her heart's desire.[13]

Farewell, great and mighty prince of letters. I wish you every success. Berquin, about whom you wrote recently, has been freed in Paris by the king.[14]

* * * * *

missal, only the threat of one). Erasmus wrote to Wary on 30 March 1527 (Ep 1806A), urging him to tolerate the inconveniences arising from Rescius' marriage and warning that it would be difficult to find a successor so competent. In October 1527 he wrote to Rescius (Ep 1882) pointing out that the executors' dissatisfaction was not entirely unreasonable and urging him to strive to give satisfaction to them and to his colleagues and so to continue his successful teaching in Louvain. He also advised Rescius not to accept the offer he had received from the king of France, an offer related to Francis I's plan to establish what eventually became the Collège Royal. On Rescius see Ep 546. The problem of inadequate attention to his responsibilities to the college arose again when he became directly involved in the printing business as a second occupation; despite other administrative troubles later in his career he remained on the faculty until his death in 1545.

11 Wary became president of the Collegium Trilingue on 21 January 1526. See Ep 1756 introduction.

12 Karl Harst, Erasmus' former secretary and courier, who had left his service in June 1526 because he wanted to get married and settle in his native Netherlands. See Epp 1666 n2, 1724 n2.

13 Evidently the delay in Harst's return from a trip to Basel was causing anxiety on the part of his intended bride, Katharina van der Klusen. Cf Epp 1778, which reports on the wedding, and 1788, which reports on the happiness of the newlyweds.

14 On his release from imprisonment in the Conciergerie see Ep 1692 n1 and Farge *Orthodoxy* 259–60. In fact the Parlement flatly refused the king's order

Louvain, 10 December 85

I enclose a letter from Lips,[15] though I have held on to his notes, which would have added considerably to the bulk of this packet. You will have them when I find a suitable courier. The letter Melchior promised did not arrive in time.[16] Ceratinus[17] has been away from Tournai for several months on a visit to his native region. I think he has gone to collect the income from 90 a small inheritance.

To Master Erasmus of Rotterdam. In Basel

1769 / To Erasmus Schets [Basel, c December 1526]

Like others in the correspondence with Schets, this letter deals with the collection and transfer of Erasmus' income in England and the Netherlands. Erasmus also informs Schets that he plans to dedicate a publication to the king of Portugal, John III, as Schets had recommended more than once (see nn11, 12). The original letter, in Erasmus' own hand except for the address, survived among the Neve manuscripts in the British Library and was first published in Allen VI (1926). None of the letters to other individuals mentioned here is extant.

Cordial greetings. A sum of money was deposited for me some time ago in Bruges with Marcus Laurinus, dean of St Donatian's.[1] I have written to ask him to hand it over to you. I think it amounts to 130 Rhenish florins.[2] The

* * * * *

to release him, and finally, on 19 November, the provost of Paris came with a force of archers and took custody, transferring him to the Louvre, where technically he was a prisoner in the custody of the king.

15 This letter is missing. On Maarten Lips, an Augustinian canon of Louvain with humanistic interests and a friend of Erasmus and Goclenius, see Ep 750 introduction. He was assisting Erasmus with the edition of the works of St Augustine, and the notes that Goclenius mentions probably dealt with that project.

16 If, as seems likely, this is Melchior of Vianden (cf Ep 1427), his letter would have had to reach Goclenius from Tournai, where he was teaching classical languages in the new humanistic college being organized under the patronage of Pierre Cotrel. He was a close friend of both Goclenius and Maarten Lips.

17 See Ep 1763 n24.

1769
1 See Ep 1695 n6.
2 Latin *centum ac triginta florenos Renenses*. This sum was officially still worth £31 19s 2d groot, but by current market rates, more likely worth £34 13s 4d groot

same sum will come due on the Feast of the Purification from my Courtrai
annuity. I have asked that it too be given to you. It is paid by Jan de Hondt, an 5
excellent man and most friendly. He will make no difficulties about handing
over the money.[3] I enclose a blank receipt, this being the usual way in which
honourable men deal with such things. Pierre Barbier retained six months of
my annuity in addition to the sums I told you about.[4] If he pays, accept. If
not, don't press him; he is a friend of mine and perhaps in need of money. 10

The reverend Father John, bishop of Lincoln in England,[5] has been
kind enough to give me fifteen angels every year.[6] I wrote to say that he
should either pay this sum to Luis Alvaro[7] or pass it over to Cuthbert, bishop
of London.[8] I have written to this effect to Cuthbert and likewise to the
archbishop of Canterbury.[9] If the money comes in time, you will be able to 15
arrange to have it paid to Froben's son, Hieronymus,[10] at the next fair – the

* * * * *

Flemish, the equivalent of 832 days' wages or 3 years and nine months' wage
income for an Antwerp master mason (see Ep 1750 n6; Ep 1758 n2). And even
though foreign gold coins were denied legal tender in England, it was also
worth £21 13s 4d sterling, the equivalent of 867 days' wages or 3 years and
11 months' wage income for an Oxford master carpenter; or £195 tournois (or
as much as £213 15s 11d tournois; see Ep 1796 n5). See also Ep 1750 nn3, 5, 6.
3 De Hondt was the actual holder of the prebend at Courtrai from which Erasmus received an annual pension. He seems to have been prompt and reliable
in his payments. Erasmus' receipt of this income was complicated by the resid-
ual rights of the previous holder, Pierre Barbier, who seems to have been less
reliable, and also by the problems of transferring money safely and promptly
from the Netherlands to Basel. See Epp 436:6n, 751 introduction, 1094, 1433
introduction, 1458, 1470; cf the following note.
4 On Barbier's role in the payment of Erasmus' pension from the prebend at
Courtrai, see preceding note and Epp 1605 n1, 1621 nn3–6.
5 See Ep 1704 n1 on his frequent gifts of money to Erasmus; cf Ep 1386 n20.
6 Latin *singulis annis quindecim angelatos*. For these angel-nobles, see Epp 1750
nn2, 3, 1758 n6.
7 Another example of Erasmus' vagueness about the names of Schets' helpful
commercial correspondents in London, the Spanish merchant-bankers Alvaro
and Luis de Castro. See Ep 1658 n5, and cf Ep 1758, where Erasmus has the
surname right but refers to Luis as Juan.
8 Cuthbert Tunstall, another of Erasmus' patrons among the English bishops.
See Epp 207:25n, 1697 n15, 1726 introduction.
9 William Warham, probably the most generous of Erasmus' English patrons.
See Ep 188 introduction and, on his crucial role in granting Erasmus his substantial English pension, Ep 1583 n1; cf also Ep 1740 n5 on his generosity over
a period of many years.
10 Johann Froben's son and business associate who succeeded to the management
of the press after his father's death in October 1527. Like his father, while

father, I think, will not be going back to the fair. If this is not possible, at
least write and let me know what you have received, and send the money
when you have a chance to do so. If you incur any expenses as a result of
these transactions, deduct it from the total. I should not want you to oblige   20
a friend at a loss to yourself.

I have obtained a work of John Chrysostom that has not yet been translated.[11] I have decided to translate it and dedicate it to the king of Portugal.[12] Tell me about the man's character and background so that I can write
a more appropriate dedication. I hope to have a printed copy to send you   25
before the fair.

I want you to know, my dear Schets, how much I appreciate your good
offices. If there is anything I can do for you in return, don't hesitate to ask;
you have earned the right to do so. If the bearer of this letter, Hans the
Dane,[13] is planning to return, you can safely trust him with anything you   30
wish to write. Best wishes to you and your good wife and children.

The blank receipt is for Jan de Hondt.

To the honourable Master Erasmus Schets, merchant of Antwerp. In
Antwerp

1770 / From Thomas More   Greenwich, 18 December [1526]

Reference in this letter to Erasmus' serious illness in the summer of 1526 and
to the trip of Hans Holbein the Younger to England in the autumn of 1526

* * * * *

attending the semi-annual fair he received letters, gifts, and money sent to
Erasmus by Schets and others and brought them back to Basel. See Ep 1705
n3. For his attendance at the previous autumn fair and his receiving money
sent from Antwerp by Schets, see Ep 1758 n1.
11 See Epp 1661 n2, 1705 n3.
12 Schets had been urging Erasmus to seek the patronage of King John III since
the previous March (Ep 1681) and had repeatedly reminded Erasmus of this
opportunity to win the favour of a wealthy young king (see for example Epp
1681, especially nn8–10, 1682, 1750, 1758); cf Ep 1758 n4.
13 Probably Hans Bogbinder of Copenhagen (d circa 1564), whom Erasmus may
have met at Louvain. He had been brought up with King Christian II of Denmark, and after the king's exile in 1523, he accompanied him to the Netherlands
and spent many years working in vain for his restoration, travelling widely
on diplomatic missions but apparently also for commercial ends. He often carried letters to and from Erasmus, and Erasmus mentions him favourably in
Ep 1780 and in his only surviving letter to him, Ep 1883. Late in life he received amnesty from King Christian III and returned to Denmark, where he
entered the service of the new king.

(see n11) makes it clear that 1526 is the correct date, rather than 1525, the date given in LB, where it was first published. Although there are no surviving letters between the summer of 1521 (Ep 1220) and this letter, there is strong evidence that Erasmus and More remained in touch; see Ep 1666 n6. The original manuscript in More's hand survived in the Rehdiger manuscript collection at Wrocław.

Cordial greetings. I received two letters from you, dearest Erasmus, first one and then a second,[1] and I have also read the letter you sent to the reverend Father the bishop of London.[2] We are very distressed to hear that the torments of the stone, which have troubled you for so long, have now been followed by the illness that proved fatal to Linacre;[3] and although, through   5
the benevolence of God and your own courage, you draw good out of such misfortunes, we, your dear friends, can never rejoice in the riches of your spirit without at the same time feeling anxious for the human frailty of your body. Our concern is not just for you (although we hope and pray that you will have all the blessings we would wish for ourselves); rather our spe-   10
cial concern is for the whole of Christendom, for we worry that your illness will interrupt that brilliant series of works by which you are nurturing the Christian faith. I pray God you will be able to bring these to a happy conclusion, especially the remaining volume of the *Hyperaspistes*.[4] You could not produce anything more useful to the world at large, more gratifying   15
to your friends, or more glorious and important for yourself. You could hardly credit the eager anticipation with which good men await that work. The wicked, on the other hand, either from partiality for Luther or jealousy at your success, are puffed up and exultant at the tardiness of your reply. I

* * * * *

1770
1 Both letters to More are lost, but one was probably contemporary with Ep 1740 and was carried to England by Holbein (see introduction), and the other, carrying news of Erasmus' serious illness, accompanied Ep 1759, addressed to the English physician John Francis.
2 This letter from Erasmus to Bishop Tunstall is also lost. See Ep 1769 n8 and the earlier references given there.
3 Erasmus was aware that the death of the great English physician Thomas Linacre was attributed to calculus. See Epp 1735 n3, 1759:74–5.
4 Part 1 of *Hyperaspistes*, published in early March of 1526, concluded with a commitment to publish a more systematic and thorough second part (LB X 1336 / CWE 76 297), but the appearance of this second volume was delayed until September 1527. More's evident concern that Erasmus might have abandoned the project was shared by other Catholic friends as well.

am content to accept the delay if you have put the work aside for the time   20
being in order to complete other things – your *Institutio christiani matrimonii*,
for example, which her serene Majesty rightly values most highly, as, I hope,
you will soon discover in some tangible way.[5] And if you want to take time
to go into the subject more thoroughly, that too I am happy to accept, for I
am anxious that this part of the work be treated with the greatest care. But   25
if, as some people say, fear of the consequences has driven all thought of the
project from your mind, so that you lack the courage to go further, then I
cannot tell you how surprised and disappointed I am. God forbid, my dearest Erasmus, that you, who have faced such hardships, run such risks, taken
upon yourself such Herculean tasks, and spent the best years of your life in   30
unremitting toil and sleepless vigils for the benefit of all mankind, should
now become so wretchedly attached to a life made miserable by sickness
that you are ready to desert the work of God rather than face the possibility
of defeat.[6]

I have no fears you will throw back at me those lines from the comedy,   35
'All of us when we are well etc' and 'If you were in my shoes, you would
think differently.'[7] True, I cannot promise, nor would anyone expect me,
to equal the brilliance that all men expect of you after the manifest proofs
you have given of a heart that finds its strength and confidence in God. I
have no doubt that you will continue to demonstrate this same firmness of   40
purpose up to the last act of your life, even if the final scenes are filled with
turmoil, for nothing could make you lose faith that in the end a merciful
God will arrive *ex machina* to unravel the tragic tangle of events. This is
not the moment to be crushed by fear, since, so far as I can see, there is
little cause for worry. If the Lutherans had been planning to attack you   45
over this business, I am sure they would have acted before you produced
anything in reply, for by doing so they might have prevented you from
writing. If, on the other hand, they had wanted to pay you back for what
you had written, they would have poured out all their fury as soon as your
first volume appeared; for in that volume you drew such a vivid picture of   50
the beast and pointed your finger so precisely at the harsh spirit that drives
him on that you unveiled for everyone to see a portrait of a fuming fiend
from hell, a sort of Cerberus dragged up from the underworld.

* * * * *

5 On Queen Catherine's slowness to acknowledge and reward his dedication of
  this work, see Ep 1727 introduction.
6 The Latin is *perdas calculum*, literally 'lose the vote.'
7 Terence *Andria* 309–10; line 309 reads in full, 'All of us, when we are well, are
  only too ready to give advice to the sick.'

I see no danger ahead that you would not have to face just the same even if you never put another word on paper. You have already replied to   55 Luther's insults and you have let him feel the sharp edge of your pen. All that remains now is the discussion of Scripture. By issuing a thousand copies of the first part, like so many affidavits, you have bound yourself before the world to do all in your power to finish the work. Surely, in view of all this, Luther cannot be so foolish as to expect, or so brazen as to demand,   60 that you, who have pleaded your own cause, should now betray the cause of Christ and abandon a promise publicly given – and it is not as though the task were beyond your powers. I am sure Luther would like you to be silent despite his feigning a lordly contempt for you in that remarkable letter, of which it would be hard to judge between its arrogance and its stupidity.[8]   65 But the man knows in his heart that when you examine those glosses of his by which he seeks to obscure the bright clarity of Scripture, you will show them up for the anaemic things they are[9] – though, God knows, they look feeble enough as they stand.

But you are on the scene of action and I am far away. So if a reply   70 would involve you in a danger which you could not escape and which I cannot foresee, let me at least make this request: why not produce your reply in secret and send it here by a servant whom you trust? You can be confident that neither I nor the bishop of London,[10] who, as you know, is a man of the utmost integrity and a great friend of yours, will permit your   75 work to be made public unless this could be done safely.

Your painter friend, my dear Erasmus, is a wonderful artist.[11] I fear he will not find English soil as rich and fertile as he hoped. But I shall do my best to make sure it is not completely barren. I very much approve of

* * * * *

8 Luther's letter to Erasmus (now lost), sent after he had published *De servo arbitrio*, was apparently even more insulting and condescending than the book. See Ep 1688, Erasmus' reply, and cf Ep 1667 introduction. More's remark about the letter shows that someone – probably Erasmus himself – had sent him a copy.
9 This is not a literal translation of More's Latin. He uses a different metaphor, describing Luther's glosses as 'pure ice,' although they look 'frigid' (that is, 'feeble') enough as they stand.
10 Cuthbert Tunstall
11 Hans Holbein the Younger, who visited England in the autumn of 1526; see Ep 1740 n9. More was mistaken about the market for Holbein's services in England. He stayed until the summer of 1528, then returned to his home in Basel for a few years, but left Basel permanently in 1532 and spent the rest of his career in England, becoming the leading painter at the English court until his death in 1543.

IOANNES HOLPENIVS BA· SILEENSIS
SVI IPSIVS EFFIGIATOR Æ: XLV.

Hans Holbein the Younger
Self-portrait, 1542/3
Uffizi, Florence

the pamphlet you published elegantly demolishing the rumour, spread by   80
unprincipled people, that you are sympathetic to the heresy of Karlstadt;
at the same time it neatly foiled the tricks of that worthless wretch who
planted that story in a book written in German.[12] Some day, if God gives
you time and leisure, I should like to see a treatise on that subject emerge
from your mind to buttress the faith, for that mind of yours is a powerful   85
instrument for the defence of truth. Meantime, however, I am so anxious
about the *Hyperaspistes* that I would not want you to concern yourself with
anything that might turn your thoughts and interests elsewhere and prevent
you from finishing that work as soon as possible.

Farewell, Erasmus, dearest of men.   90
From the court at Greenwich, 18 December
Your sincere and most devoted friend, Thomas More
To the excellent and erudite Master Erasmus of Rotterdam

1771 / From Johannes Fabri   Esslingen, 20 December 1526

> Fabri, having renounced his own ambition to edit a manuscript of the *Adversus
> haereses* of St Irenaeus that he had obtained from the Vatican Library, and hav-
> ing after some delay provided the manuscript to Erasmus (see Epp 1715 and
> n1, 1739 introduction), expected at the very least that Erasmus would not only
> dedicate the edition to his patron Bishop Bernhard von Cles (as he did; see Ep
> 1738) but would also send an appropriately bound copy for presentation to
> the bishop. He was dismayed that after sending Bernhard a preliminary un-
> bound copy fresh from the press (cf Ep 1755), Erasmus did not follow up with
> a bound copy suitable for formal presentation to such an important prelate.
> Here he describes how the bishop saw through his own effort to contrive a
> presentation copy on his own and present it as if it came from Erasmus. He as-
> sures Erasmus that he will receive a large monetary reward if only he meets the
> bishop's reasonable expectation, as indeed he did in February or March 1527
> (Ep 1793). Never published in the lifetime of either Erasmus or Fabri, the origi-
> nal manuscript of this letter, written in a secretary's hand and signed by Fabri,
> survived at Leipzig and was first published by Förstemann/Günther (1904).

* * * * *

12 The *Detectio praestigiarum*, directed against an anonymous vernacular pamphlet
   (which Erasmus later learned was the work of Leo Jud of Zürich) that seemed
   to associate him with the Sacramentarian (or Zwinglian) interpretation of the
   Eucharist. See Ep 1708, especially n2. Like Erasmus himself, More seems to
   share the mistaken belief that the radical reformer Andreas Karlstadt was the
   principal source of this doctrine.

Greetings. For some time now, dear Erasmus, my learned friend, I have
been worried on your behalf. I was greatly afraid you would neglect your
own best interests by delaying to send the bishop of Trent a copy of the
book that is dedicated to him. He is most eager to receive it and looks for it
every day. A present is ready and has been waiting for you for some time. I   5
have tried one expedient after another to help you. I made a presentation in
your name; there was nothing I left untried, for I was afraid you were not
as anxious about this as the bishop. But my efforts had little success. Being
the astute man he is, he sniffed out the whole thing at once. What he wanted
and what would give him pleasure was something fresh from the pen of   10
Erasmus. I have now received a letter here at Esslingen, in which he tells
me that you have sent the book. He was delighted and gave me 100 gold
florins[1] as a gift for your Excellency. I hope it will reach you soon. He would
like you to move to Trent and pay your respects to the Muses there in peace
and quiet. He will pay your expenses and give you 600 gold florins[2] each   15
year. This shows the regard he has for you. The offer does justice both to
Erasmus and to the prince who makes it. Farewell.

Esslingen, 20 December 1526
Your friend, Fabri
To the honourable Master Erasmus of Rotterdam, his dearest friend   20

1772 / From Erasmus Schets   Antwerp, 20 December 1526

Schets' letter of 9 November (Ep 1764) evidently accompanied a packet of letters from Spain being forwarded to Erasmus, and in this letter, having received no acknowledgment of their safe delivery, he seeks assurance that they
did reach their destination. The autograph original survives among Erasmus'
papers at Basel and was first published by Allen in 1926.

* * * * *

1771
1 Latin *centum aureos*, undoubtedly 100 gold Rhenish florins, which would have
  been worth about £26 13s 4d groot Flemish (but officially only £24 10s 0d
  groot), or £16 13s 4d sterling, or £150 tournois (or, with rising gold values, as
  much as £164 9s 2d; see Ep 1796 n5).
2 Latin *sexcentos aureos*, undoubtedly 600 gold Rhenish florins, which would
  have been worth £100 sterling (the equivalent of 4,000 days' wages for an Oxford master carpenter – almost 20 years' wage income), or officially £147 10s
  0d groot, but more likely, at current market rates, £160 groot Flemish (equivalent to 3,840 days' wages or 17 years and 4 months' income for an Antwerp
  master carpenter), or £900 tournois (or, with rising gold values, as much as
  £988 15s 0d); see Ep 1796 n5.

Cordial greetings, Master Erasmus, my respected friend. I wrote you most recently in November; since then I have heard nothing from you. I also sent you several letters that I received from Spain.[1] I am being pressed to confirm that you received them. I hope they reached you, even though you did not mention it in your letters. I have now received another letter from the same   5
friends,[2] which I enclose. If you will acknowledge receipt of this and of my earlier letter, I shall not fail to pass on the information to Spain.

Several days ago Luis de Castro wrote to me from England.[3] He tells me that the letters I sent him to be passed on to your friends there have been duly delivered, and he assures me that if they give him any money on   10
your behalf, he will let me know immediately on receiving it. I shall see to it that whatever sums are sent from England will always get to you safely and without deductions. Remember I am more than willing to serve you in other ways too, if only you will say the word and the matter is within my power. Farewell.   15

Antwerp, 20 December 1526

Yours sincerely, Erasmus Schets

To the incomparable and learned Master Erasmus of Rotterdam. In Basel

1773 / From Hieronymus Emser   Dresden, 25 December 1526

On this secretary and chaplain to the strongly Catholic Duke George of Saxony, see Epp 553, 1551, and most recently, 1683. Duke George had been nagging Erasmus for years to devote his talents to the task of refuting Luther. See Ep 1691 introduction. Since Erasmus had no intention of becoming a full-time controversialist, he seems to have sent the duke a bundle of his letters and books (unrecorded except for their mention here) demonstrating that in his own way he had published much work opposing the Reformation. This tactic seems finally to have convinced the duke that Erasmus had not shirked his duty to defend the orthodox faith and to have persuaded him of the unfairness

* * * * *

1772

1 See Ep 1750 n8.

2 Allen (444n) suggests that this may be the sympathetic letter dated 1 October from the imperial chancellor, Mercurino Gattinara (Ep 1757), which was written after the dispatch of the packet mentioned in Schets' letter of 8 September (Ep 1750).

3 Luis and his brother Alvaro were Schets' business correspondents in London. See Epp 1590 n2, 1658 n5.

of the attacks on Erasmus by conservatives like Noël Béda. On Duke George's previous impatience with Erasmus, see Ep 1691 introduction; cf Ep 1743 intro- duction. The original autograph letter was preserved at Leipzig and was first published in Förstemann/Günther (1904).

Greetings thrice-mighty Erasmus. I was handed by my most illustrious prince a bundle of your letters with some sheets attached. I was asked to read all of them to his Highness before leaving his presence. His first re- action was astonishment that you could have produced so many tomes and volumes – it would have been an extraordinary feat even if you had never   5 stopped writing. Then when we came to your account of the tricks and machinations of your rivals, his face became set in a grim expression. But the stern frown dissolved into laughter at the fable of the ass's hide,[1] with which you thought Béda's book[2] should be bound. There was another burst of laughter at the man who married a young woman in accordance with the   10 rule laid down in the Mosaic law,[3] but shared her with many of his brothers in Christ, following perhaps the Platonic or the Lutheran law.[4] These two witticisms softened the impact of the rest, a sorry tale indeed.

The chancellor, Dr Simon Pistoris, is totally devoted to you. He believes you have never been in error in anything you have written,[5] nor would he   15

* * * * *

1773
1 Probably a story contained in the letter (now lost) mentioned in Ep 1743:47–
8, as Allen (8n) suggests, referring also to the discussion of an amusing story
about Noël Béda mentioned by Jan Antonin in Allen Ep 1810:32–5. The Latin
word for 'hide' (*corium*) is related to *coriarius* 'leatherworker,' which is suggestive of *sutor* 'cobbler,' the Latin form of the surname of Erasmus' other
obstreperous Paris critic, Pierre Cousturier.
2 Béda's *Annotationes*. In Ep 1743 to Duke George (and probably in greater detail
in his accompanying letter to Emser, now lost) Erasmus had mentioned the
actions of Francis I to silence the Paris theologians who were attacking him.
3 The requirement that in certain circumstances a man should marry the widow
of his childless brother and raise up children for his brother; Deut 25:5–10.
4 The guardians in Plato's *Republic* (457C–464B) share wives and children. Emser
refers to the common slander that the Lutherans (or some Lutherans) encouraged or permitted sexual promiscuity.
5 Emser's assurance that Pistoris 'believes you have never been in error in anything you have written' is an indirect and apologetic response to Erasmus'
challenge to a statement by Pistoris that he was confident that Erasmus had
'never *willingly* [our emphasis] departed from the decrees of the church.' Erasmus' tart reaction was to state flatly, 'I have never departed from the decrees
of the church either willingly or unwillingly' Ep 1744:16–17, after which he
launched into a lengthy demonstration that the phrase 'decrees of the church'
is dangerously ambiguous.

believe it even if a thousand Cousturiers and Cerdos and Bédas rose up in anger against you.[6] You will receive from the prince, dear Erasmus, the reply to Luther written by the king of England.[7] Luther is never consistent ex-

* * * * *

6 The reference to the two conservative French theologians who attacked Erasmus is obvious. The meaning of 'Cerdos' is puzzling at first sight. Cerdo was a well-known Gnostic heretic of the early church, and Erasmus referred to him (as to many other Gnostic heretics) in the dedicatory epistle for his recent edition of St Irenaeus *Adversus haereses* (Ep 1738:157; cf n46). He uses the name here because *cerdo* is Latin for 'tradesman' and is used by Martial (3.16.1) as equivalent to *sutor* 'cobbler,' the Latin equivalent for Cousturier's surname. Since the Latin text, based on the autograph letter preserved at Leipzig, capitalizes the first letter of 'Cerdo,' a proper name rather than a common noun must be intended. In the Latin text, Erasmus uses *Sutor* for the name translated here as 'Cousturier' and then makes the two following plural names rhyme: *Cerdones aut Bedones*, a deliberate distortion of Béda's name not only for the sake of the rhyme but probably also intending another verbal pun: the vulgar French *bedon* means *gros ventre*; even in standard modern French, the adjective *bedonnant* means 'stout' or 'pot-bellied.'

7 In response to Henry VIII's *Assertio septem sacramentorum* (London: Richard Pynson 1521; STC 13078) against Luther, Luther had published a sharply worded reply in both Latin and German: *Contra Henricum regem Angliae* (Wittenberg: Johann Grunenberg, November 1522) and *Antwortt deutsch Mart. Luthers auff König Henrichs von Engelland buch* (Wittenberg: Nickell Schyrlentz, August 1522), which many readers judged to be disrespectful of Henry's royal status; cf Ep 1776 n2. On 1 September 1525, Luther addressed to the king a somewhat apologetic letter justifying his criticisms (WA-Br III 562–5 Ep 914; cf Ep 1776 n3); this letter did not reach Henry until 20 March 1526. By September or October the king had produced a reply, which was published, with the text of Luther's letter, in December: *Literarum quibus invictissimus princeps, Henricus octavus, respondit, ad quandam epistolam M. Lutheri, et ipsius Lutheranae quoque epistolae exemplum* (London: Richard Pynson, 2 December 1526; STC 13084). The editors of the Weimar edition of Luther's works, however, located an undated edition in the Austrian National Library in Vienna that they thought to be earlier than the Pynson edition. This, they argue, was printed specifically for private distribution by the king to important rulers and prelates abroad – including of course Duke George, the most active defender of Catholicism among the German princes, who had corresponded with Henry about the religious situation in Germany (see WA-Br III 562, IV 125–6, and also WA XXIII 18). The king probably sent Duke George several copies (presumably the undated private edition) in addition to one intended for Luther. Duke George dispatched the book to Luther (see WA-Br IV 142–3 Ep 1058, dated 21 December 1526), and he fulfilled Emser's promise to send Erasmus this publication with Ep 1776. Duke George also saw to it that an edition was promptly produced in Germany (Dresden: Wolfgang Stöckel [1527]); it is possible but not likely that this reprint of the Latin edition was ready by 1 January and was the one sent to Erasmus. He also had a German translation prepared (by Emser) and published (Dresden:

cept in his hostility towards you; if the fellow had had any sense, he would
have benefited more from you than from any king. This makes me suspect   20
he is a fool, driven crazy perhaps by your Folly; for if he were sensible and
not fatally handicapped by his own stupidity, he would realize that he owes
more to Erasmus than to any other human being.[8] As it is, he gives in to
almost everyone else but sticks stubbornly and arrogantly to his opposition
to you. But, to be frank, you are making us suspect you by your procrasti-   25
nation. So do keep your promise about the conclusion of your work on free
will.[9] For you have found a powerful supporter in the king; and he is now
pressing hard on Luther, by saying, 'Now there is only one question: are we
to believe you or Christ etc'?

When you ask for a list of my books in return for yours,[10] you are   30
making fun of me again, as you love to do; for what use would such a list

* * * * *

Wolfgang Stöckel; preface dated 7 January 1527). Luther himself thought that
Erasmus had contributed to Henry VIII's reply (cf WA-Br IV 165–6 Ep 1079,
168–9 Ep 1082), but there is no evidence of this; neither the present letter nor
Duke George's letter to Erasmus (Ep 1776) assumes that Erasmus had prior
knowledge of it. The duke probably would have known if it had been so, for
he and his advisers were well informed on such matters.

8 Although there is much truth in what Emser says, and at the outset of the
Reformation Luther himself acknowledged the value of Erasmus' work on
the Greek New Testament to his own theological development, this statement
(though presumably meant as a compliment) could hardly have delighted Erasmus since, with different implications, it was precisely what conservative theologians were charging against him: that he was the source of Luther's heresies. Despite Emser's insistence in this passage that Luther was now more hostile to Erasmus than to anyone else, there is an (unintentional?) undercurrent
of menace here, reflected in the ensuing complaint about Erasmus' slowness
in finishing part 2 of *Hyperaspistes*.

9 In voicing suspicions about Erasmus' devotion to this task, and by implication
about his loyalty to the Catholic faith, Emser is trying to exert pressure on
Erasmus to complete and publish the second part of *Hyperaspistes*, his detailed
reply to Luther's *De servo arbitrio*, as he had promised when he brought out
the hastily composed first part in March 1526 (see Ep 1667); cf Ep 1770 n4.
The efforts of Duke George and his servants such as Emser and Pistoris to
make Erasmus into an anti-Lutheran pamphleteer are evident in many of their
letters, but see especially Epp 1691 introduction and 1728:2–3 and n1. Erasmus
in Ep 1743:50–3 to Duke George even questioned the usefulness of his own
attacks on Luther.

10 Emser had recently published a number of works against Luther and Karlstadt,
but his role was more that of controversialist than theologian, and much of his
publication was in German, a language that Erasmus could not (or at least did
not) read. A good bit of Emser's polemical work was as a translator, and at this

be to you? Since Luther uses the vernacular to corrupt the people, I am compelled to answer him in the vernacular too. Were I not concerned for ordinary, uneducated people, I might perhaps have won greater favour among
the learned by writing in Latin. I might even have drawn compliments on   35
my abilities from yourself despite the gaps in my learning. But when our
muddy little streams flow on beside the golden river of your eloquence, this
brings new glory to your name. For it makes it easier to see what a difference there is between the limpid pools of Erasmus and the muddy waters of
our Phlegethon.[11] But the courier is already dressed for the road and won't   40
let me write a longer letter. Farewell Erasmus, the glory of our age.

Dresden, 25 December 1526

Your most devoted servant, Emser

To that great prince of letters, both sacred and humane, Desiderius
Erasmus of Rotterdam, theologian, and my most respected teacher   45

1774 / From Wolfgang von Affenstein   Ladenburg, 28 December 1526

Affenstein (d 1556) came from a family of Rhenish nobles and about 1517
married the duchess of Zimmern, a woman of even higher rank than himself. Although the nature and place of his professional training in law are
not known, he did conduct litigation in the imperial court of justice (*Reichskammergericht*) and for some years was officially listed as an advocate at that
court. He was an official of the bishop of Worms, Henry, count Palatine, whom
he served for some time in his second diocese at Utrecht and for whom he was
currently administering the temporalities of the diocese of Worms. He represented the bishop at several imperial diets. He was also a councillor of the
Palatine electoral prince. His importance for Erasmus, however, was that his
service to the bishop of Worms put him in control of the library left by an earlier bishop of Worms, Johann von Dalberg, who had acquired a valuable collection of manuscripts and early printed books. See Ep 1767 for Erasmus' letter
to Theobald Fettich, Affenstein's physician, through whom Erasmus sought
permission for Hieronymus Froben to inspect the contents of the Dalberg
library in the castle at Ladenburg in search of manuscripts useful for Erasmus'
editions of scriptural, patristic, and classical texts. The original manuscript
letter survived at Leipzig and was first published in Förstemann/Günther
(1904).

* * * * *

very time he was working on a translation of Henry VIII's reply to Luther's
letter of September 1525 for the German-reading public; see n7 above.
11 One of the fabled rivers of the underworld

The library of that excellent man Johann von Dalberg, bishop of Worms,[1] although filled with a fine collection of writers of every kind, has long been
left to gather dust. Because of the neglect of the bishop's successors, the library was practically closed to everyone, whether scholar or not, except to
the gnawing teeth of mice, until the illustrious prince Henry, count Pala-   5
tine, duke of Bavaria, etc,[2] took over the reins of the diocese. When I was appointed to take charge in the bishop's absence, I decided it would be worth
while making some renovations in the library and restoring the books, some
of which were half eaten away, while others had deteriorated and decayed
through mould and age. Until now I have not dared to lend a volume or   10
two to anyone without the consent and express command of my master, the
aforementioned prince. However, when I was shown the letter from your
learned self, brought here by my physician Theobald Fettich, I was eager
to satisfy your wishes.[3] So I immediately opened the door of the library,
which had been locked for so many years, and gave Hieronymus (who is   15
the bearer of this present letter) complete freedom to look around and bor-

* * * * *

1774
1 Dalberg (1455–1503), like Affenstein more than a generation later, belonged to
  a family of Rhenish nobles associated with service to the electoral princes of
  the Rhenish Palatinate. Educated at Erfurt and then in law at Pavia, he rose to
  power and wealth both through the church and through service to the Palatine elector and became bishop of Worms. As bishop and as chancellor of the
  Palatinate, he made both Worms and Heidelberg active centres of early German humanism. He was associated with Konrad Celtis in founding one of the
  early humanistic sodalities at Heidelberg and was a patron of the ablest of the
  early German humanists, Rodolphus Agricola. His valuable library, preserved
  by the bishops of Worms, served not only Erasmus but many other scholars
  during the sixteenth century as a source of classical and patristic manuscripts.
2 Henry (1487–1552) was a younger brother of the Palatine elector Louis v. He
  had studied at Heidelberg, but his family connections to the Palatine dynasty
  and to the Hapsburgs explain his rich accumulation of ecclesiastical benefices.
  In 1524 he became bishop of both Worms and Utrecht. At this time he was
  in Utrecht, the more valuable of the two bishoprics, trying to establish stable control over an area repeatedly torn by war. In 1529 he resigned the see
  of Utrecht because of the continuing military incursions, transferred the temporalities (the political sovereignty) to the Emperor Charles v, and retired
  to Worms; but he later acquired another valuable diocese at Freising, though
  Worms remained his residence. On him see also Ep 612:15n.
3 A request originating in Ep 1767 to Theobald Fettich, the personal physician
  of Affenstein. Since Bishop Henry was away in Utrecht, Affenstein was administering the temporalities of the diocese of Worms for him, including the
  library at Ladenburg, where he resided.

row any manuscripts he wished on condition that they be returned in good faith.[4] May this loan prove useful to your Excellency and win favour for my poor inarticulate self!

In haste. Ladenberg, 28 December 1526   20

Wolfgang von Affenstein, German knight, lord deputy to the bishop of Worms and your Excellency's most devoted servant

Signed by Wolfgang von Affenstein in his own hand

To Erasmus of Rotterdam, a man of great learning and eloquence, and my revered friend   25

1775 / From Jacobus Sobius   [Cologne,] 28 December 1526

Sobius (in German, Sob, Sobbe, d 1528) was from a prominent Cologne family, matriculated at the local university on 10 June 1508, and received his BA in 1509. Together with the Swiss student Henricus Glareanus, he became a pupil of the well-known humanist Johannes Caesarius. Sobius spent the years 1512–16 travelling in various parts of Germany, visiting the influential humanist Mutianus Rufus in Gotha and teaching in the school at Freiberg in Saxony founded by Johannes Aesticampianus, a prominent humanist who also had connections with Cologne. Sobius returned to his native city to take his MA degree in 1516 and a doctorate of laws in 1519. By then Caesarius, Sobius, and Count Hermann von Neuenahr had become the three leading Cologne humanists. Also in 1519 he joined Neuenahr in attending the imperial diet that elected Charles V as emperor. He and his associates were among the 'patriotic' Germans who supported the Hapsburg prince against his electoral rival, King Francis I of France; and on 30 June he delivered an oration hailing the new emperor in the name of the German nobility, a work later published as *Oratio Germaniae nobilium ad Carolum Caesarem* (Sélestat: L. Schürer 1519).

Sobius taught at the Bursa Corneliana in Cologne until it was dissolved for lack of funds in 1523. The city council then appointed him *orator*, a position in which he represented the city on public occasions and also taught humanistic subjects in the university. Faced with student complaints about the inferior position given to the humanities in the arts curriculum and about inadequate opportunities for study of classical languages and literature, Sobius became an advocate of university reform and was authorized by the council to pursue it. But the difficult financial condition of the university and the city, together with resistance within the arts and theological faculties to any sig-

* * * * *

4 Allen Ep 1767:11n observes that in BRE 373 Ep 264 Johann Huttich complained that Froben's search of the library had left the manuscripts in disarray.

nificant change made his efforts fruitless, and only a handful of largely cos-
metic reforms was enacted and actually carried out. Sobius' feeble health in
the last years of his life also contributed to his failure in this endeavour. It
is likely that he and Neuenahr, both of whom admired Erasmus, hoped that
attracting him to the city would revive the movement. If he is the author of
the anonymous dialogue *Henno Rusticus* (no place or date, but probably Basel:
Andreas Cratander 1520), published under the pseudonym 'Philalethes civis
Utopiensis' but commonly attributed to Sobius, he must have been for a time
not simply a moderate Catholic reformer; the dialogue is a savage attack on
the papacy and its exploitation of Germans through its legates and the sale of
indulgences. This attribution, which is based on a remark in a letter of Henricus Cornelius Agrippa of Nettesheim, has, however, been challenged. Whatever his opinions may have been in 1520, by this period he seems to have
become committed to a vaguely reformist rather than an explicitly Lutheran
religious programme. On his failed effort at university reform, see Charles
G. Nauert 'Humanists, Scholastics, and the Struggle to Reform the University of Cologne, 1523–1525' in *Humanismus in Köln / Humanism in Cologne* ed
James V. Mehl, Studien zur Geschichte der Universität zu Köln 10 (Cologne
1991) 39–76. The original letter was preserved at Leipzig and first published
by Förstemann/Günther (1904).

Cordial greetings. Your Danish friend[1] came to see me and brought your
good wishes. Since he could not conveniently find Count Hermann,[2] he left
your letter with me and I undertook to see that it was duly delivered. Heresbach[3] too lives some distance from his route; so since he could not reach him,

* * * * *

1775
1 Hans Bogbinder, who travelled widely on both commercial and diplomatic
  business; see Ep 1769 n13.
2 Hermann von Neuenahr, son of a noble family from the Cologne region,
  thoroughly imbued with humanism during his studies at the University of
  Cologne, and influential both within the local university (of which he was
  chancellor) and among the beneficed clergy of the city. See Ep 442, and cf
  Charles G. Nauert 'Graf Hermann von Neuenahr and the Limits of Humanism in Cologne' in *Culture, Society and Religion in Early Modern Europe* ed Ellery
  Schalk, special issue of *Historical Reflections / Réflections Historiques* 15 no 1
  (1988) 65–79.
3 Konrad Heresbach, a young Cologne humanist whose career Erasmus had
  aided, had been tutor to young Duke William of Cleves since 1523 and later
  (1535) became a privy councillor and an important influence on the moderate 'Erasmian' religious reforms carried out in that principality. See Ep 1316
  introduction.

he left that letter also with me. I shall make sure that it is delivered. We fell to   5
talking, your Danish friend and I, about something Provost Neuenahr once
told me, that you might easily be prevailed upon to move here.[4] I could see
about a suitable house and make arrangements with the council to ensure
that you could live here in peace and quiet without interference from our
people. When the Dane heard this, he assured me that you had not changed   10
your mind, always providing there would be no trouble from people like
Hoogstraten[5] and Noviomagus[6] and the rest of that scum. That will pose no

* * * * *

4 Despite its reputation as a centre of ultra-conservative Catholicism and hostility to humanism, Cologne had a significant group of humanists securely
   placed in the beneficed clergy, the university, and the wealthy patriciate that
   controlled the local government. What Sobius (no doubt backed by Neuenahr,
   the most influential of the Cologne humanists) here offers is that the city council would ensure that Erasmus was sheltered from attack by conservatives like
   Jacob of Hoogstraten if he settled in the city.
5 Jacob of Hoogstraten OP (d 1527), notorious among humanists as the principal
   figure among the Cologne monks and theologians who had prosecuted Johann
   Reuchlin a decade earlier, was not in fact quite so hostile a figure as Sobius'
   words imply; and while Erasmus had disapproved of his attacks on Reuchlin
   and made this opinion known, he seems to have held Hoogstraten in higher
   regard than he felt towards many other conservative Dominican theologians
   (cf Ep 856:28–39). Hoogstraten was the Inquisitor for all three German arch-
   dioceses and an aggressive foe of Luther and for a time seems to have suspected Erasmus of complicity in Luther's cause. Gilbert Tournoy and Peter G.
   Bietenholz provide a judicious survey of their relationship in CEBR II 200–2.
6 A puzzling reference. Noviomagus (Gerard Geldenhouwer, 1482–1542) had
   strong humanist connections and was particularly close to Erasmus' good
   friend Frans van Cranevelt, who had been his fellow student in boyhood
   (see Ep 487 introduction). Far from being anti-humanist or fanatically anti-
   Lutheran, Noviomagus was an intimate friend of most of the leading Netherlandish humanists, Erasmus included. Between 1519 and 1524, the two seem
   to have been very close friends. Far from being a fanatical heresy-hunter like
   Hoogstraten, Noviomagus became strongly attracted to the Reformation; he
   went to Wittenberg and attended lectures by Luther and Melanchthon in 1525–
   6, visited the Reformers Bucer and Capito at Strasbourg, and then married in
   November 1526 at Worms despite his vows as a member of the order of Crosier
   Canons (known in England as the Crutched, or cross-bearing, Friars). Goclenius reported this marriage to Erasmus in Ep 1778. Furthermore, although
   Noviomagus did spend the years after his return from Wittenberg residing in
   a number of cities in the Rhineland, there is nothing in the record to suggest
   that he settled in Cologne at any time. In 1532 he became professor of his-
   tory, and from 1534 professor of theology, in the new Protestant university at
   Marburg. If this reference is not just an error on Sobius' part, it may reflect
   Geldenhouwer's move from humanistic and reformist Catholicism into full

problem: these hornets have already lost their sting. The house about which
I wrote before is still free and would do you proud. Just let me know what
you want. I would have arranged for your Danish friend to look over the   15
house, but eye trouble made this impossible. Farewell.

28 December 1526

Jacobus Sobius

If you move here, you will be able to count on the influence and support of two princes, the archbishop of Cologne[7] and the duke of Jülich.[8]   20

* * * * *

adherence to the Reformation. There does seem to have been an estrangement
between him and Erasmus from the mid-1520s, probably due to his association with the Reformers and his repudiation of his vow of celibacy. The real
issue may have been Noviomagus' effort to link Erasmus' name with the Reformation, an effort that culminated in publication of *D. Erasmi Annotationes
in leges pontificias ac Caesareas de hereticis* together with his *Epistolae aliquot de
re evangelica et haereticorum poenis* (Strasbourg: C. Egenolf 1529). Erasmus was
very distressed by this publication. He was no more willing to let Protestants
link his name with the Reformation than to let conservative Catholics do the
same, and he protested to the magistrates of Strasbourg (Allen Ep 2293 and
several other letters of 1530–1). He also protested publicly in his *Epistola contra pseudevangelicos* (Freiburg: Joannes Faber Emmeus, January 1530). See the
introduction by Cornelis Augustijn to his edition of *Contra pseudevangelicos* in
ASD IX-1 263–309. Even so, it still seems strange for Sobius to link him with
Hoogstraten as someone from whom Erasmus might need to be protected if
he settled in Cologne.
7 Hermann von Wied (1477–1552), archbishop of Cologne since 1515. Although
he gained his many ecclesiastical promotions because of his aristocratic birth
rather than his personal accomplishments and although (despite his matriculation at the University of Cologne in 1493) he had only a rudimentary knowledge of Latin, he seems to have been favourable towards both humanistic studies and a programme of moderate (though vaguely defined) reform. Through
the influence of his friend, the equally aristocratic Neuenahr, he became a
supporter of Erasmus; and in 1529, after Erasmus left Basel on account of
the Reformation there, he authorized Neuenahr to renew the invitation to settle in Cologne. At this period he firmly opposed the Protestants, but in the
late 1530s and 1540s he attempted to promulgate a largely Protestant reform
programme. Faced with the opposition of the university, most of the higher
clergy, and the aristocracy, he was compelled to resign his office in 1547 and
spent the rest of his life in retirement at his estate at Wied.
8 John III, duke of Cleves-Mark-Jülich-Berg (1490–1539) brought together,
through inheritance and marriage, an important secular principality in close
proximity to Cologne between 1511 and 1521. Although he rejected Lutheran
doctrine, in the 1530s he carried through a moderate program of church reforms along lines strongly influenced by Erasmian advisers such as Heresbach.
In 1533 he granted Erasmus an annual pension.

Hermann von Wied, archbishop of Cologne 1515–47
Unsigned and undated painting
Stadtmuseum, Cologne

1776 / From Duke George of Saxony   Dresden, 1 January 1527

Although Duke George was mollified by Erasmus' publication of *De libero arbitrio* against Luther in 1524 and absolutely delighted by the obvious anger reflected in *Hyperaspistes 1*, he was far more hostile to Luther and Luther's movement than Erasmus ever became; see Ep 1691 introduction. Here he scolds Erasmus for what he regards as continued ambivalence about Luther and at the end calls on him to complete the more detailed second part of *Hyperaspistes*. His secretary and chaplain Hieronymus Emser had given much the same message a few days earlier in Ep 1773. The manuscript letter is preserved at Hamburg and was first published by Allen in 1926.

GEORGE BY THE GRACE OF GOD DUKE OF SAXONY ETC
Cordial greetings. I have noticed, dear Erasmus my learned friend, that for some time now, since the publication of your unassailable *Hyperaspistes*, you seem quite unable to decide what kind of guiding spirit drives your implacable enemy Luther in his attacks upon the decrees of our most holy church.   5
You seem to labour under the same misapprehension that I and many good men suffered from. For has there ever existed on this earth anything more volatile and Protean than this fiendish creature? Is there anyone who has not been taken in by the fellow's unparalleled depravity and his clever pretence of virtue? At first he professed many of the principles of true doc-   10
trine, not in so many words but hinted at by vague suggestion. Claiming the privileges of a theologian, he took on the role of stern critic of the corrupt morals of the Christian world. He would have gained considerable respect if he had acted with the sobriety and gentleness set forth in the gospel. But since this was not in the man's nature, he could not avoid betraying from   15
time to time his real character. He gathered into his slimy fellowship all the miscreants and madcaps from every quarter of the world; he infected the common people, that many-headed monster, with his poisonous paradoxes; he played on their emotions, turning fools into raving madmen; and he subjected every decent man to the most scurrilous abuse imaginable, harassing   20
them and holding them up to universal contempt. It has now reached the point where he is subverting and destroying the ordinances of our Christian faith, the laws of public morality, and every kind of civilized behaviour, while all the time this egregious fellow is duping the world with his grand and specious language, calling his ungovernable tongue 'the spirit of Chris-   25
tian freedom' and his contempt for every mark of decency and courtesy 'the simplicity of the gospel.'
Every day he reveals his true self ever more clearly. Yet in spite of this he has managed to drive great numbers of men into such a state of

madness that, consciously and deliberately and with their eyes open, they 30
prefer to continue in the error into which they have fallen and to accept the
fatal consequences rather than listen to the pleas of honest men and come
to their senses. For, I ask you, could you have imagined anything more
shocking and insolent than the behaviour of this vile impostor, during these
past few years, towards that great defender and champion of the Chris- 35
tian faith, his serene Majesty, the king of England?[1] That one small volume of his could have told us what a mad spirit drives him on?[2] How few
of his turbulent followers have been willing to take even a tiny step back
towards the right path? On the contrary, have they not stubbornly hoped
that we will excuse his dangerous insolence, although he himself could no 40
longer hide it? His private demons have not destroyed his conscience to that
extent.

Consider, my dear Erasmus, how true to form (God help us!) is the latest move of this strange new preacher! What a clever palinode he has composed![3] How evangelical (or should I say hypocritical) his trick of evading 45
blame! I have decided to send the work to you along with the king's reply,
which he himself gave me to pass on to Luther.[4] I want you to be convinced
at last, as I have long been convinced, that the man is possessed by a mad
and perverse spirit,[5] if not by something worse. I also want you to realize that you were not mistaken when you wrote that it was to curry favour 50

* * * * *

1776
1 See Ep 1773 n7.
2 Luther's reply to Henry VIII's *Assertio septem sacramentorum* was so aggressive,
even rude, that it shocked even many people well disposed to Luther; in the
sixteenth century, one just did not address crowned heads in such a way. See
Ep 1773 n7 on this reply, which was published first in German and then in
Latin.
3 Realizing that his sharp response to King Henry's *Assertio* had offended many
people, Luther wrote a letter of partial apology to the king (WA-Br III 562–5 Ep
914), admitting that he had gone too far because he had not realized that the
book had been contrived by sophists who misused the king's name rather than
by the king himself. This letter laid principal blame on the cardinal-archbishop
of York, Thomas Wolsey, whom Luther called 'that plague of your kingdom.'
This letter only gave further offence, and Henry replied with a letter of his
own which he caused to be printed along with Luther's and circulated to
rulers, high prelates, and other recipients abroad, especially in Germany. See
Ep 1773 n7.
4 This fulfils the promise already made in the duke's name by Emser; Ep 1773
n7.
5 Isa 19:14: 'the spirit of giddiness' (Douay); 'perverse spirit' (AV)

with another that he crossed swords with the king.[6] I believe you will be
serving the interests of the Christian community if you follow the example
of this great king and, with courage and a pure heart, bring out what you
have long been promising to bring out, an answer to the teachings of this
arch-heretic.[7] Farewell.   55

Dresden, 1 January 1527

To the most learned and eloquent theologian, Master Erasmus of Rotterdam, my devoted friend

1777 / To Pierre de Mornieu   Basel, 11 January 1527

Little information is available about Mornieu except that his aristocratic family connections had already made him abbot of the Cistercian abbey of Saint-
Sulpice near Chambéry in Savoy. He had recently been in Basel, perhaps just
on a visit but perhaps as a student, probably in the company of his private
tutor Hieronymus Gemuseus of Mulhouse (cf Ep 2162), who, after attending
the famous humanistic school conducted by Johannes Sapidus (Johann Witz)
at Sélestat, had studied at Basel between 1522 and 1525, receiving the MA
degree. Mornieu and Gemuseus next went to study at Avignon, where the
famous Andrea Alciati was teaching law in the papal university. They may
have proceeded from there to Turin, though Mornieu may have returned to his
abbey instead. He certainly was residing there somewhat later, and Erasmus

* * * * *

6 At the beginning of *Hyperaspistes 1* (LB X 1250A–C / CWE 76 99–100), Erasmus
  stated that Luther wrote *De servo arbitrio*, with its savage attack on Erasmus'
  character, in order to satisfy the prejudices of those who surrounded him,
  many of whom, he claimed, have moral habits far removed from the gospel
  whose title they claim for themselves when they call themselves 'Evangelicals.' But he seems to have believed that Luther's sharp attacks on Henry VIII
  of England and the German Catholic apologist Johannes Cochlaeus were produced in order to please his own former friend Wilhelm Nesen, who had become a follower of Luther; cf *Hyperaspistes 1* CWE 76 99–100 nn18, 23. Why
  Erasmus thought that Luther wrote these works 'to curry favour' with this
  talented but youthful German humanist is not clear, and his claim here is all
  the more surprising since Nesen had drowned in a boating accident near Wittenberg on 6 July 1524, before Erasmus had finished writing *De libero arbitrio*.
  Erasmus was not unaware of this accident: he had learned of Nesen's death
  in a letter from Philipp Melanchthon (Ep 1500:67) and expressed his regret in
  Epp 1523:216–17, 1524:48.
7 In other words, he is demanding that Erasmus complete the second part of
  Hyperaspistes. At the very end of *Hyperaspistes 1* (LB X 1336 / CWE 76 297),
  Erasmus had promised speedy completion of a longer and more thorough
  response to Luther.

continued to correspond with him there during the period 1529–31 (Epp 2084, 2162, 2473). Mornieu's tutor Gemuseus was a protégé of Bonifacius Amerbach, and after he had completed a doctorate in medicine at Turin in 1533, Amerbach helped him secure appointment as professor of physics at Basel, though he did not take up the position until 1537, after Erasmus' death. Although Mornieu seems to have remained just an aristocratic abbot with humanistic interests, Gemuseus became a noted editor of Greek and Latin texts, chiefly medical and scientific, in the late 1530s and 1540s. Erasmus published this letter in *Opus epistolarum*.

ERASMUS OF ROTTERDAM TO PIERRE DE MORNIEU,
ABBOT OF SAINT-SULPICE, GREETING

The pain I felt at your departure was greatly softened by the thought of the many advantages to yourself. First, you snatched yourself in good time from the flames, for the plague has spared no one here and has been dancing 5 around my house for days,[1] only stopping short of the threshold. Then, you are off to a celebrated university that has won distinction in every branch of learning.[2] I have no doubt you will now devote yourself heart and soul to a course of serious study and amply compensate for any previous idleness to which you may have been tempted by the frivolity of youth. If you do, 10 you will return home, like an eager merchant, rich in the profits of humane learning. Your city, I hear, has its Sirens as well as its Muses. I would be urging you to block your ears against the music of the Sirens and attach yourself to the virgin Muses, had I not observed your remarkable self-control. I have written this letter when half-dead with work. I only wanted to let you 15 know that you have not slipped from my mind.

 Basel, 11 January 1527

  * * * * *

1777
1 An outbreak of plague at Basel is mentioned in a letter probably written 9 October 1526 from Michael Hummelberg at Ravensburg to Johann von Botzheim at Constance, published in 'Analecten zur Geschichte der Reformation und des Humanismus in Schwaben' ed Adalbert Horawitz in [Vienna] Kaiserliche Akademie der Wissenschaften *Sitzungsberichte, philosophisch-historische Klasse* 89 part 1 (1878) 176–8 Ep 66; also in letters from Beatus Rhenanus in Sélestat to Bonifacius Amerbach at Basel dated 8 November and 29 November 1526 in BRE 369–71 Epp 260, 261; also in other correspondence of Amerbach, AK III Ep 1151 (28 October 1526), Ep 1154 (5 November), Ep 1157 (16 November); the last of these letters reports that the outbreak seems to be waning. In Ep 1780:25–6, dated 26 January 1527, Erasmus remarks that he is not certain whether the plague has died out, but that people no longer talk about it.
2 The papal university at Avignon; see introduction to this letter.

1778 / From Conradus Goclenius   Louvain, 13 January [1527]

> Goclenius was Erasmus' chief source of news from Louvain at this period. See,
> for example Epp 1765, 1768. This letter remained an unpublished manuscript
> at Nantes until Allen edited it in 1926; the contents justify Allen's determina-
> tion of the year-date.

Cordial greetings. When Franz Birckmann instructed the bearer of this letter
to call here, although I had no news it would be important for you to know
(and if I had, I would prefer to keep it until Hans the Dane leaves),[1] yet
knowing your interest in your Danish friend, I thought you would like to
be informed of his safe arrival here; so I did not let the courier set out   5
without a letter from me.

How long the Dane spent on the journey was not clear from your letter, since it did not have a date. But he reached us on the eve of Epiphany.[2]
Three days later, Karl Harst, who had returned here before Christmas,[3] was
due to celebrate his marriage and 'openly and in the sight of this congre-   10
gation' (as the formula goes)[4] to wed the woman whom he had bedded so

* * * * *

1778
1 Although Erasmus and many of his friends regarded Birckmann as untrust-
  worthy and even dishonest, his important role in bookselling throughout
  northwestern Europe forced them to rely on him and his couriers at times.
  Goclenius' remark that if he had any important news, he would hold it until Hans Bogbinder (a reliable courier; see Ep 1769 n13) made his next trip
  to Basel reflects that mistrust and extends it to include an assumption that
  Birckmann's couriers would also be dishonest; Goclenius expresses the same
  mistrust of a courier engaged by Birckmann in Ep 1788:5–7. Birckmann's bad
  reputation is a frequent topic in the correspondence; see Ep 1665 n1.
2 5 January
3 Erasmus' former confidential secretary and courier, who had decided to return
  to his native Netherlands. On him see Epp 1666 n2; on his marriage, cf Epp
  1724 n2, 1768 nn12, 13, 1788:17–18.
4 Although the medieval Latin church did not require the participation of a
  priest for a canonically valid marriage, which rested entirely on the present
  consent of the two people who were marrying, a formal ceremony of some
  kind in the presence of witnesses (especially the families and friends of the
  couple) was customary, though not legally necessary. Such ceremonies were
  conducted in different ways in different parts of Europe. In northern Europe,
  the ceremony itself was often conducted at the church door in the presence of
  family and friends; it might be, but did not have to be, followed by the couple's entering the church for a celebration of mass. But the phrase used by Goclenius, here given in its traditional English form from the Book of Common
  Prayer, is very ancient. The presence of witnesses certainly strengthened the

often before. To help on the celebrations, the Dane stayed with us for four days. He promises to return to you soon or send a reliable messenger who will give you a full report. At that time I shall write at greater length and urge my friends to do likewise. There is no time for this now, since the   15
courier is in an inordinate hurry.

I think you received the emperor's letter that I sent.[5] Gerard of Nijmegen, about whom you had asked the Dane to inquire, has abandoned his earlier way of life and married a wife.[6] He is now living in Worms. I got this information from a certain Lambertus,[7] secretary to the bishop of Utrecht,[8]   20
whom he invited to the banquet.

* * * * *

legal credibility of a marriage, and there were many complaints about clandestine marriages contracted by an exchange of vows by a man and a woman in private, without any witnesses. At the Reformation, the Protestant reformers acted to outlaw clandestine marriages and require a certain degree of publicity in the exchange of vows. In post-Reformation Catholicism, there was no change until 1563, when the decree *Tametsi* of the Council of Trent required the presence of a priest, though even then, this decree did not become legally binding until the local diocesan bishop made it so. Obviously, having the exchange of vows witnessed in some formal way made it more likely that the existence of a marriage, once contracted, could be legally established if conflict arose.
Since marriage was a sacrament of the church and all members of the medieval community were Christians, those who assembled to witness the exchange of consent were, in a sense, 'the church.' This concept was reflected in the liturgies that were customary (though not legally necessary) for the making of a marriage; for example, in an old Sarum Manual, the couple married each other *coram Deo, et angelis, et omnibus Sanctis ejus, in facie ecclesiae*; see *Manuale ad usum percelebris ecclesie Sarisburiensis* ed A. Jefferies Collins, Henry Bradshaw Society 91 (London 1960) 45. The corresponding English version at York says 'before God and his angels, and all his halowes, in the face and presence of our moder holy Chyrche.' The York Latin text is identical to the Sarum rite. See *Manuale et processionale ad usum insignis ecclesiae Eboracensis* ed W.G. Henderson, Publications of the Surtees Society 63 (Edinburgh 1875) 24 for both Latin and English texts.
5 Ep 1731, which Goclenius had forwarded with Ep 1768
6 Gerard Geldenhouwer of Nijmegen, commonly known as Noviomagus. He had been a Crozier Canon, subject to a vow of celibacy. Thus his marriage marked the completion of his drift towards Protestantism. See Ep 1775 n6.
7 This secretary of Henry, count Palatine, bishop of both Worms and Utrecht, has never been fully identified. Presumably he was not the exiled French Lutheran (and Franciscan friar) François Lambert, who had entered the service of Duke Philip of Hesse in 1526 and in October of that year had been a leading figure in the Synod of Homberg, which began the transformation of Hesse into an Evangelical principality.
8 See Ep 1774 n2.

The copy of the *De Trinitate* with annotations by Dorp,[9] which you asked the Dane to recover from Pieter de Corte,[10] has been in my possession for some time. I remember telling you this in an earlier letter. Pieter Gillis says that the old manuscript of the *De civitate Dei* was sent back to the   25
Maccabeans at Cologne and that you are aware of this.[11]

Farewell. Louvain, 13 January

Your friend, Conradus Goclenius, for what little he is worth

To Master Erasmus of Rotterdam, the incomparable ornament of our age. In Basel   30

1779 / From Johann Hornburg   Vienna, 18 January 1527

As this letter of self-introduction shows, Johann Hornburg (Hornburgius) was at this time secretary to Bernhard von Cles, bishop of Trent, and had been an admirer of Erasmus since early youth. In his only other surviving letter to Erasmus (Ep 1935), written more than a year later from Buda, he describes his homeland as *Francia Orientalis* 'Eastern Franconia.' On the assumption that this was a learned reference to the region south and west of Saxony proper, Ilse Guenther in CEBR II 205–6 suggests that he may be identified with the second son of Ludeke, burgomaster of Brunswick, who matriculated at Wittenberg in 1504, at Leipzig in 1507 (BA 1508), and at Bologna in 1515, and who by 1520 claimed a doctorate in both laws. By 1530 he was a canon of Hildesheim, by

* * * * *

9 Erasmus had been trying since at least February 1525 to regain possession of his own manuscript of Augustine's *De Trinitate*, on which Maarten van Dorp had entered variant readings from a manuscript at Gembloux. Erasmus needed this material for his planned edition of Augustine's *Opera omnia*, which was finally completed and published in ten volumes two years later (Basel: Froben 1528–9). After Dorp's death (31 May 1525), Goclenius retrieved the manuscript from the Carthusian monastery in which Dorp had stayed during his final illness; but he then had difficulty finding a courier willing to carry such a bulky object from Louvain to Basel. Finally Erasmus sent an employee of Froben, Burchardus, to carry the manuscript back to Basel. See Ep 1547:11–14, Allen Epp 1890:9–12, 1899:14–26. According to Ep 1890, lack of the manuscript had caused work in the print shop to be held up.
10 Regent of the College of the Lily at Louvain and one of Erasmus' most influential friends in the university. See Epp 1347 n66, 1537. According to Allen Ep 1899:21–2, he had helped Goclenius regain possession of the manuscript from the Carthusian monastery where Dorp was buried, which apparently had custody of Dorp's personal effects.
11 Cf Ep 1758:8–10, where Erasmus had asked Schets to inquire of Gillis about this manuscript.

1535 councillor to Cardinal Albert of Brandenburg. He held many ecclesiastical offices, culminating in the bishopric of Lebus. He died in 1565. Although a convinced Catholic, he was tolerant and a patron of learning. This identification is much more plausible than Allen's very tentative suggestion that he might be Johann Hornburg of Rothenburg, a considerably younger man (MA at Wittenberg in 1520) and an enthusiastic disciple of Luther, who was described in 1525 as an exile for the Evangelical faith. As Allen himself notes, while the dates and Franconian origin of this man make it possible that he is the author of the letter, it is unlikely that so pronounced a Lutheran would have returned to Catholicism so quickly and would have won acceptance so rapidly that by early 1527 he had become secretary to the bishop of Trent, the most confidential adviser of Archduke Ferdinand. This letter was first printed in Förstemann/Günther, based on the original manuscript preserved at Leipzig.

Cordial greetings. Even from my boyhood, from the time when my education began, I have always honoured and revered the name of Erasmus, to whom I owe whatever progress my poor wits have allowed me to make. So I thought it would be unpardonable if, while staying with the right reverend the bishop of Trent, I did not take the opportunity that was offered 5
me to write you a letter and send my greetings. My only object in doing so is to have you recognize me as one of your admirers, even as the humblest among them. Etiquette would demand that I introduce myself with a more formal and complimentary address, but when I reflected that for one who is occupied with serious business unnecessary letters are nothing but a 10
nuisance and a distraction, I deliberately decided to abandon any such idea and present myself in these few words as your Excellency's most devoted servant.

Vienna, 18 January 1527

I am, dear sir, your most willing and humble servant, Johann Horn 15
burg, secretary to the right reverend the bishop of Trent

To the most learned and distinguished Master Erasmus of Rotterdam, his respected mentor and teacher

1780 / To Ludwig Baer   Basel, 26 January 1527

On Baer, professor of theology at Basel, see Epp 488 introduction, 1571 n6, 1674 n17. The preceding August, he had obliged Erasmus by scanning a vernacular pamphlet by Leo Jud of Zürich and advising Erasmus of its contents (see Ep 1741). At the time of this letter, Baer seems to have been away from Basel; Allen (1n) suggests that he may have been visiting Nikolaus von Diesbach, who had been coadjutor-bishop and designated successor to the diocese of Basel but had become alienated from the bishop and was negotiating terms for his resignation from these appointments. The original letter survived in the Dreer collection of the Historical Society of Pennsylvania in Philadelphia and was first printed in *Luther's Correspondence and Other Contemporary Letters* ed Preserved Smith 2 vols (Philadelphia 1913–18) II 532–3 Appendix 2, with an English translation at II 393–5 (no 752).

Cordial greetings. Your letter,[1] which was as learned as it was pious, swept much of the depression from my mind. It was not so much the miseries of ill health or the shameless behaviour of certain persons that troubled me as the sorry state of the world, for I see Christendom moving in the direction I would least wish it to take. But wondrous is the power of the Lord to guide 5
and transform the affairs of men! So I shall not abandon hope of a better outcome, provided we realize that the present turmoil is calling us to the philosophy of Christ. Let us not be more foolish than the man who, after a shipwreck, gave thanks to Fortune for calling him, even by such means, to the study of philosophy. I too, I must confess, have plucked some good 10
from these great disasters.

There are people here who want to make this city another Zürich.[2] They cannot tolerate your preacher,[3] although, in my opinion, he is a born

* * * * *

1780
1 Not extant
2 That is, to commit Basel to a sweeping religious change such as the one carried out between 1522 and 1525 in Zürich under the leadership of Huldrych Zwingli, culminating in the abolition of the mass by the city council. From the year 1525 Zwingli's leadership had been challenged by the Anabaptist movement, which demanded an even more radical religious reform; the first Anabaptist martyr of the Reformation at Zürich, Felix Mantz, had recently been executed by drowning (on 5 January 1526).
3 As provost of St Peter's church in Basel, Baer was expected to preach, and apparently the preacher who took his place during his absence irritated the leaders of the Reformation party, which was growing larger and more aggressive throughout this period. Preserved Smith in *Luther's Correspondence* (see the introduction above) II 394 n1 suggests that this preacher may have been Augustine Marius. The basis of this suggestion is a complaint made about this time concerning Marius' 'unscriptural' preaching. See the letter of 23 December 1526 from Johannes Oecolampadius, leader of the pro-Reformation clergy in Basel, to Zwingli, complaining that the suffragan bishop of Freising (Marius) was upholding the authority of the institutional church in his sermons and refusing either to preach the plain gospel or to listen to the complaints of the Reformation preachers; Ep 561 in *Huldreich Zwinglis sämtliche Werke* ed Emil Egli and others (Leipzig 1914; repr Zürich 1982) VIII 814–16; on Marius

teacher and not the sort of person to cause trouble. His great crime is that
he speaks to large congregations! I imagine the news has reached you of   15
Damian's latest schemes.[4] If such behaviour goes unpunished, what use are
the laws? He cannot be excused on the ground that this is his first offence.
However, the event is not so serious in itself as the ominous precedent it
sets for the future.

My stomach (thank the Lord!) has been fairly well for some months,   20
but lately a pain has developed in my right side.[5] What it means I do not
know, but I have committed my poor body unconditionally to Christ. I have
at last made a will. Things have now reached the point where even people
with nothing make a will. A priest at Louvain made his will in the following
terms: 'I have nothing, I owe much, the rest I leave to the poor'![6] I am not   25

* * * * *

see 815 n4. Marius (1485–1543) studied at Vienna, received a doctorate in theology at Padua in 1520 and then taught briefly as professor of theology at Vienna before becoming cathedral preacher (*Domprediger*) at Regensburg in 1521
and auxiliary bishop of Freising in 1522; he came to Basel as a canon of St Peter's church in 1526. When the Reformers gained control of Basel in 1529, he
joined Baer and all the other cathedral canons (and Erasmus) in voluntary exile
at Freiburg im Breisgau and later moved to Würzburg as cathedral preacher.
He became auxiliary bishop of Würzburg in 1536 and died on 25 November
1543.

4 Damian Irmi, a Basel merchant who provided financial support for the city's
Reformers. On 27 December 1526 Oecolampadius wrote to Guillaume Farel,
reporting that 'our Damian ... yesterday was marked with a blow for the sake
of Christ'; see *Correspondance des Réformateurs dans les pays de langue française*
ed Aimé-Louis Herminjard, 9 vols (Geneva 1866–97; repr Nieuwkoop 1965)
I 468 (Ep 187). Allen reports, on the authority of a letter from the historian
Preserved Smith, that in 1527 Irmi was supplying Pellicanus, and later also
his pupils, with books in Hebrew, a subject that Pellicanus taught at Zürich;
see Allen VII xxii (Addenda).

5 Following his painful and unusually severe trouble with an infection of the
bladder and urinary tract in the preceding summer, Erasmus seems to have
suffered severe stomach pain. When his will of 22 January 1527 was formally
registered, his failure to appear in person was excused on the grounds that he
was too ill to come before the magistrate. In a letter of 25 December 1526 from
Bonifacius Amerbach to the Avignon physician Hieronymus Lopis, Amerbach
thanked him on Erasmus' behalf for sending medical advice that had brought
some relief from pain. He described Erasmus at this time as one 'than whom
you have never seen a man more emaciated [*subtilius*] or more feeble' (AK
III 228:40–1 Ep 1170). There were rumours in Poland the following June that
Erasmus had died. No doubt this new health crisis, following so closely upon
the one in late summer, led him to make his will.

6 The priest is probably the fictitious subject of a humorous saying.

sure if the plague has died down, but talk about it certainly has.[7] I wish you were here – but only if it was for your own good.

I still feel some uneasiness about the Athanasius, for I am afraid that, in the present state of things, the dedication will cause embarrassment, not for myself (for that would have no effect on me), but for the man 30 I wish to please.[8] So do give this matter the benefit of your good judgment. No decision need be taken for fourteen days. There is a flood of new books attacking Luther and Oecolampadius;[9] they come from the bishop of Rochester,[10] Jacobus Latomus,[11] Jacob of Hoogstraten,[12] and others. What

* * * * *

7 See Ep 1777 n1.
8 Erasmus' forthcoming edition of Chrysostom contained an appendix (pages 307–445) of Latin translations of some works by St Athanasius, patriarch of Alexandria. These *Lucubrationes aliquot* of Athanasius were dedicated to John Longland, bishop of Lincoln; see Ep 1790 introduction. Erasmus' uneasiness about the dedication probably comes from the fact that the edition dedicated to Longland was not an independent publication but an annex to an edition dedicated to some one else (King John III of Portugal; see Ep 1800) Erasmus probably feared that Bishop Longland might feel slighted, or would be regarded by others as having been slighted, by a dedication that Erasmus certainly wanted to please and honour him.
9 Although there were indeed many books defending the Catholic faith against Luther, published especially but not exclusively in Germany, the consensus of those who have studied the apologetic publications of the period is that the Lutheran publications were far more numerous, more widely diffused, and generally more successful. Two recent studies are David V.N. Bagchi *Luther's Earliest Opponents: Catholic Controversialists, 1518–1525* (Minneapolis 1991) and Mark U. Edwards *Printing, Propaganda, and Martin Luther* (Berkeley 1994).
10 John Fisher had published *Assertionis Lutheranae confutatio* (Antwerp: Michaël Hillen, 2 January 1523; NK 939), followed more recently by *Defensio regiae assertionis contra Babylonicam captivitatem* (Cologne: Petrus Quentel 1525) and *Sacri sacerdotii defensio contra Lutherum* (same publisher and year). He now had in press a work attacking the Sacramentarian opinions of Oecolampadius on the Eucharist, *De veritate corporis et sanguinis Christi in Eucharistia adversus Iohannem Oecolampadium* (Cologne: Petrus Quentel 1527).
11 On Latomus' works attacking Luther and Oecolampadius but also obviously critical of Erasmus without mentioning his name, see Ep 1674 n12.
12 See Ep 1775 n5. He was a prolific author of treatises against Luther and his followers, producing six tracts and pamphlets (one of them in two parts) between 1521 and 1526, four of them in 1525–6. For their titles, dates, and publishers, see Hans Peterse *Jacobus Hoogstraeten gegen Johannes Reuchlin* (Mainz 1995).

France is bringing forth, I have not yet heard. I fear the whole cause of the   35
church may be undermined by the passion and ambition of these scribes.
We have seen the example set by Béda and Cousturier,[13] and there is not
much more sense in Clichtove.[14] Everyone is writing now. I think it will
turn out the way it does in war, that in struggling for the rewards of glory
we shall let victory slip through our hands. It is the old story of private   40
passions betraying and ruining the public interest. I have not yet decided
if I want to reply to men like Béda and Clichtove, although I promised
to do so in my latest books. I shall make up my mind when my Danish
friend[15] returns. In the meantime let me know what you think about the
Athanasius.   45

I shall not pester his lordship, the coadjutor-bishop,[16] with a letter from
me. This does not mean that I was unappreciative of his kind greetings. So
please commend me to a man who is himself commendable in so many ways.
The rest must wait till you are here. I hope that will be soon, but only if it
is for your own good. May the Lord keep you safe.   50

Basel, the morrow of the feast of St Paul 1527
Your friend, Erasmus of Rotterdam
To the accomplished theologian, Ludwig Baer, provost etc

1781 / To Erasmus Schets   Basel, 31 January [1527]

Like nearly all of Erasmus' correspondence with his financial agent at Antwerp,
this letter remained unpublished until the twentieth century. It came into the
custody of the Royal Academy of Science and Letters at Brussels, where P.S.
Allen found it; he published it in 1926, assigning a year-date on the basis of
the contents.

* * * * *

13 The attacks of these two critics of Erasmus in the Paris faculty of theology are
   mentioned repeatedly in the letters for 1525 and 1526; see, for example, Ep
   1571 introduction and n10, 1642 n5, 1658 n7 (on Cousturier), 1664 introduction
   and n1 (on Béda).
14 His principal publications against the Reformers were *De veneratione sanctorum*
   (Paris: Simon de Colines 1523), *Antilutherus* (Paris: Simon de Colines 1524),
   and *Propugnaculum ecclesiae* (Cologne: Petrus Quentel, 1526). The latter work
   was directly critical of Erasmus, a point that Béda was careful to point out
   to Erasmus in Ep 1642. In 1527 he published *De sacramento Eucharistiae contra
   Oecolampadium* (Paris: Simon de Colines 1527).
15 See Ep 1769 n13.
16 Probably Nikolaus von Diesbach; see the introduction to this letter.

Cordial greetings. Cuthbert, bishop of London,[1] sent me a statement concerning the fifty crowns[2] which, unless I am mistaken, he paid to Luis de Castro.[3] If it is not convenient to send the money to the forthcoming fair, hold on to it till the next occasion. But if you can send it, I shall be most grateful. I gave Hans the Dane[4] a letter for you. Your calculation of the moneys deposited with Pieter Gillis is approved by the accountants and I am very happy with it too.[5] You are sensible enough to understand Pieter Gillis. He has his failings, but is a loyal friend just the same. Sometimes, however, his good nature is taken advantage of by Franz Birckmann, the worst scoundrel the sun has shone on for many a year.[6] I enclose a receipt for Luis de Castro,[7] although I think you already have one.

I received a packet of letters from Spain.[8] The same letters, however, had been delivered to me earlier by Maximilianus Transsilvanus, secretary to the imperial court.[9] And now another letter has arrived. A Benedictine

* * * * *

1781
1 Cuthbert Tunstall; see Epp 1726 introduction, 1769 n8.
2 Latin *quinquaginta coronatorum*. These are English and not French crowns, presumably the new gold 'double rose' or 'crowned rose' crowns struck from 5 November 1526, at 5s sterling each; see Ep 1750 n2. If so, this was a sum worth £12 10s 0d sterling (the equivalent of 500 days' wages for an Oxford master carpenter), or £100 0s 0d tournois, or about £15 16s 8d groot Flemish (or, with rising gold values at Antwerp, as much as £17 18s 6d groot). The earlier, lighter English crowns, struck in August 1526, with a rose in the middle of the cross, were still circulating in France, where they were currently valued at 37s 6d tournois, while the heavier new crown was officially valued at 40s 0d tournois. See Richet 380.
3 One of Schets' commercial correspondents in London; see Epp 1590 n2, 1658 n5.
4 See Ep 1769 n13.
5 See Ep 1750 n4.
6 Frequently mentioned, usually as a dishonest scoundrel, in Erasmus' correspondence; see Ep 1665 n1 and the references given there.
7 The Latin wording could mean either a receipt for Castro or a receipt issued by him, but the context of the relationship shows that the former is meant, since Castro would need a receipt to show to Bishop Tunstall proving that Erasmus had actually received the money sent via Castro in London and Schets in Antwerp.
8 See Ep 1750 n8.
9 As an influential official in the administration of the Hapsburg governor of the Netherlands (Margaret of Austria) and as a known supporter of Erasmus, he was a natural choice for relaying letters from the imperial court in Spain to Erasmus in Basel. See Ep 1553 introduction.

theologian called Alonso is causing trouble.[10] I did not reply directly to him, 15
but wrote to Francisco Vergara.[11] Perhaps my reply has not yet got to Spain.
I shall answer Alonso by the next fair. I cannot always find the time to reply
– so many letters and pamphlets flow in from every corner of the world.

There is no better man in England than the bishop of London. He is
aware that I want you and Luis de Castro to look after my affairs. If ever the 20
opportunity arises for me to be of use to you, you will find in me a second
self. I send my best wishes to your good wife and to all the members of
your household.

Basel, the last day of January
Erasmus of Rotterdam, in my own hand 25
To the honourable Erasmus Schets, merchant. In Antwerp

1782 / From Johann von Botzheim   Constance, 2 February 1527

On Botzheim's relationship with Erasmus, see Ep 1761 introduction. He had
been strongly attracted to the movement for church reform, but as he witnessed the social and religious upheavals at first hand in a city where the
city council and a group of Evangelical preachers were pressing for whole-
sale adoption of the Reformation from 1524, he became 'a hundred times
cooler' than formerly. He was even more strongly opposed to the Sacramentarian eucharistic theology of Zwingli and Oecolampadius, towards which
local Reformers like Ambrosius Blarer and Johannes Zwick were sympathetic. He still found Luther's eucharistic position, which rejected the me-

* * * * *

10 Erasmus, who knew very little about the politics of contemporary Spanish in-
    tellectual life, completely misunderstood the intentions of the Benedictine hu-
    manist Alonso de Virués in sending him a list of passages from his works that
    others less favourably inclined than himself might find objectionable. At this
    period, Virués was an enthusiastic supporter of Erasmian humanism. See Ep
    1684 introduction and the subsequent letters there cited, especially Ep 1786
    from Virués himself.
11 Evidently Erasmus has once again forgotten the Christian name of a friendly
    individual and remembered only the surname of Juan de Vergara, who as sec-
    retary to the primate of Spain, Alonso de Fonseca, archbishop of Toledo, was
    one of the most influential prelates in the Spanish church. Vergara used his in-
    fluence to promote both humanistic studies and the reputation of Erasmus in
    Spain. In the case of Vergara, Erasmus (who had met him in the Netherlands
    in 1520) knew his man, if not his man's Christian name. Vergara, who did not
    know Virués, took pains to inquire about him and eventually to meet him. In
    Ep 1814 he assured Erasmus that Virués had the best of intentions and was an
    admirer of his work. On Vergara see Ep 1277 introduction.

dieval dogma of transubstantiation but upheld the real presence of Christ in and with the consecrated bread and wine, to be convincing. For a brief summary of the religious conflict in Constance at this time, see the article by Mary Jane Haemig in *The Oxford Encyclopedia of the Reformation* 4 vols (Oxford 1996) 1 417–18. By 1526 the city council had begun seizing control of church institutions and properties and forcing all clergy except the bishop and the canons of the cathedral chapter to take an oath of loyalty as citizens and to accept the obligations of citizenship. The bishop left Constance in 1526, and by the spring of 1527 all of the canons and other clergy who remained Catholic were doing likewise. Botzheim was one of the last to go, in April 1527. He joined the other members of the chapter, who had established a new residence in the nearby town of Überlingen, and remained there until his death in 1535.

This letter survived in manuscript at Leipzig and was first published in Förstemann/Günther (1904). Two lines at the head of the letter are damaged, with some loss of text at the very beginning and at the top of the verso.

... Luther's sermon on the sacrament[1] ... which I took up again in translation. I did so to fortify myself against those who deny the presence of the body and blood of our Lord in the Eucharist. My views and my faith are different from theirs, not just in regard to the Eucharist but in many other matters as well. It is not that I am particularly fond of the author. My feelings 5 towards him are a hundred times cooler now than they were some years ago. But I liked what he has to say in defence of the Lord's body and blood in the Eucharist. And since I know that in several letters you have professed the same opinion, I am anxious to have my ideas confirmed and supported by your judgment. No great effort was wasted on the task, as is clear from 10 the results and from the barbarity of the style (as I have acknowledged).

* * * * *

1782

1 In opposition to Zwingli's eucharistic opinions, Luther had preached a series of three sermons in late March 1526 on the Lord's Supper and confession. They were published in a single volume, probably in late September or very early October, under the title *Sermon von dem Sacrament des leibs vnd bluts Christi, widder die Schwarmgeister* (Wittenberg: Hans Lufft 1526). A Latin translation, which also included a letter of Luther opposing the ideas of Martin Bucer, a sermon of Johannes Bugenhagen, and a tract by Vincentius Obsopoeus, was also published very early in 1527 as *Martini Lutheri Sermo elegantissimus, super Sacramento Corporis & Sanguinis Christi* (Haguenau: Johannes Secerius 1527). This is the translation read by Botzheim. Both the German and Latin texts are in WA 19 474–523.

The Oecolampadians and the Zwinglians[2] argue interminably against our position or, as I should prefer to call it, the position of the gospel. Ambrosius Blarer, God's gift to Constance, says it is up to the individual to decide whether to believe the doctrine or not; there is no need to believe it, and a man is not a heretic whichever side he takes. Such doctrine is not to everyone's liking. Blarer's sympathies are completely with Oecolampadius and Zwingli.[3] He is running with full sail[4] against the mass. He received a commission from the council to take charge of some nuns from an enclosed order; when he had them in his care, he forbade any observance of their ecclesiastical rule. He has banned the mass absolutely from the cloister. The money previously paid to the monks is now given to the poor. The monks have all been thrown out; they are not allowed even to set foot in the place. Nuns are forbidden to talk to the bishop or to the monks without the consent of the council. Every day our traditions are being turned upside down through the influence of Lutheran preachers like this. Every day priests are thrown into prison contrary to the terms of our agreements. Our church treasury has been locked by the council, ostensibly to prevent us from moving its contents out of the city. The leading nobles are on our side. They are asking the emperor, or agents appointed by him, to act as mediators in the dispute. But <in so controversial a matter> the council is dragging its feet.

<As for myself, I am still living here in peace,> thanks (if the truth be told) to support from members of the council. But if things take a serious turn, I shall not leave the cathedral chapter.

If I misunderstood what you said in your letter[5] about coming here, put it down to carelessness rather than ignorance – although I suffer from ignorance badly enough too. I thought you had definitely decided on leaving Basel and that you would take the first opportunity that presented itself to

* * * * *

2 That is, the defenders of the Sacramentarian interpretation of the Eucharist. The real argument was over the meaning of *is* in Christ's words at the Last Supper, 'This is my body' as reported in the Gospels (Matt 26:26; Mk 14:22; Luke 22:19).
3 See Ep 1341A n430. In the years since he left his Benedictine monastery in 1522 and was appointed as a preacher by the city council of Constance, he had become one of the most noted defenders of Zwinglian or Sacramentarian eucharistic doctrine; and this conception of religious reform is reflected in the city's policies towards communities of nuns, celebration of mass, dissolution of monasteries of men, and administration of ecclesiastical incomes and properties.
4 *Adagia* IV vi 1
5 Missing. It may have been a reply to Ep 1761.

come to us. But when I read your letter carefully, as you advised me to
do, I saw that you meant that if circumstances allowed I should go to visit   40
you. I shall try my best to arrange that; I hope it will happen soon. Our
mutual friend Glareanus[6] has been very encouraging. He seems genuinely
concerned about your health and about the immense burden of work you
have undertaken.

You mentioned books by Latomus, the bishop of Rochester, and oth-   45
ers;[7] I hope they enjoy great success. Once more you have made me ashamed
of my loose tongue, although I do not recall saying anything except for your
ears alone.[8] But I shall see that it does not happen again. Fabri will be Fabri,
but he is not, I am told, the sort of man he appears to be from his words.[9] You
should take Hummelberg[10] to your bosom; he is an honest man through and   50
through and very fond of you. I shall pass on your greetings. Best wishes,
my dearest master.

Constance, on the feast of the Purification of Mary, 1527

You have no reason to doubt my good faith with regard to the letters
you have addressed to me.[11] I want to keep them as evidence of your affec-   55
tion and as a remembrance of my beloved patron. From time to time I take
them out and enjoy them, as we often do with things that are very precious
to us. I do not think I have given you reason to suspect me of anything
dishonest.

* * * * *

6 See Ep 1744 n8.
7 See Epp 1674 n12 (Latomus), 1780 n10 (Fisher).
8 Literally 'into your bosom'; see *Adagia* I iii 13, and cf n11 below.
9 Both in Ep 1519:67–9 and in Ep 1530:10–11, Botzheim writes in terms that
  suggest that he and Erasmus agreed that Johannes Fabri, though friendly, was
  a very self-important man. In addition, Erasmus, and probably Botzheim as
  well, did not fully approve of the harsh and repressive policies towards the
  Reformation that Fabri actively supported in the Hapsburg court at Vienna.
  Ep 1690 shows Erasmus writing to him as to a friend (and a powerful one) but
  still trying to maintain a certain distance and to discourage him from using
  Erasmus' name in his own anti-Lutheran writings.
10 Michael Hummelberg was currently living and teaching as chaplain of St
   Michael's church in Ravensburg and was a frequent visitor to Constance,
   where one of his kinsmen was a physician and where he became a close
   friend of Botzheim and an admirer of Erasmus. See Epp 263:26n, 1253 n6,
   1454 n1.
11 The published correspondence between Erasmus and Botzheim makes it clear
   that many other letters were exchanged between them that are now lost, and
   also that (like the present letter) their letters often expressed opinions on religion, politics, and people that would be embarrassing if not kept confidential.
   Note that just above (at lines 46–9) Botzheim is apologetic about some incident
   of indiscreet talk on his own part.

Your devoted friend, Johann von Botzheim   60
    To the most learned theologian and incomparable champion of the
best literature, Master Erasmus of Rotterdam, his greatly revered guide and
mentor

1783 / From Erasmus Schets   Antwerp, 4 February 1527

As usual, Schets writes about the financial affairs that he manages for Erasmus, but he also continues to encourage Erasmus to seek the patronage of the
king of Portugal by dedicating one of his publications to him. The original
letter is among Erasmus' papers at Basel; Allen published it in 1926.

Cordial greetings. Hans the Dane[1] brought me your letter, which was very
welcome indeed. There was a rumour here that you were in mortal danger and had already gone to the next world. I have already had your letter delivered to the dean of St Donatian's.[2] I have also sent him the letter
for Master Jan de Hondt, who pays your Courtrai annuity.[3] I told the dean   5
what you said in your letter about the portion of your pension that is still
in de Hondt's hands; I also asked him to intercede with Master de Hondt,
at his earliest convenience, concerning payment of the annuity that is ow-
ing. When he informs me of the amount and of the sum which the dean
himself owes you, and has handed it over to a merchant friend of mine   10
at Bruges, whom I have named, I shall follow my usual practice, that is, I
shall see that the money is safely transferred to you in Basel or given to
Froben's son Hieronymus at the next fair.[4] The day before yesterday I had a
letter from Luis de Castro in London,[5] confirming that he had received fifty
crowns on your behalf from the bishop of London.[6] This too I shall send to   15
the Frankfurt fair.

* * * * *

1783
1 See Ep 1769 n13.
2 Marcus Laurinus, dean of the chapter at Bruges, a friend of long standing. See
   Ep 1695 n6.
3 See Ep 1769 n3. He was the actual holder of the prebend at Courtrai from
   which Erasmus' pension was paid.
4 Hieronymus Froben; see Ep 1769 n10. As this letter shows, he had joined the
   Basel publishing firm headed by his father Johann Froben and now represented the publisher at the major German book market, the semi-annual fair
   held each spring and autumn at Frankfurt.
5 See Epp 1590 n2, 1658 n5.
6 Latin *coronatos quynquaginta*: For the 50 English rose crowns from Cuthbert
   Tunstall, see Epp 1750 n2, 1781 n2.

I am glad you have decided to dedicate one of your works to the king of Portugal.[7] It will not be wasted effort, for his royal Highness deserves great praise. With regard to his background and character, anything complimentary you choose to say will be justified. There is a medical doctor   20
here, of Portuguese nationality,[8] who on being approached by myself and by Dom Rui Fernandes,[9] his Highness' agent in these parts, has produced an account of his royal Highness' family and of the exploits of his ancestors. Hans the Dane will send you a copy. Among other things you could praise his country for its serious interest in the humanities, its respect for the fac-   25
ulty of theology, and its loyal adherence to the Christian faith. Portugal is a small kingdom, but it has sovereignty over large areas occupied by barbarians, Mohammedans, and pagans, in lands as far away as India and the Moluccan islands; by sailing around the world and establishing colonies, it has spread the faith of Christ almost across the globe. With your eloquence   30
and broad learning, you will know how to fill out the details. Farewell.

Antwerp, 4 February 1527

Your friend, Erasmus Schets

To the incomparable and most learned Master Erasmus of Rotterdam etc. In Basel   35

1784 / From Nicolaus Vesuvius   Mussy, 8 February [1527]

Vesuvius was chaplain to Michel Boudet, bishop of Langres, who was closely linked to the French court and was a friend of Guillaume Budé and a supporter of humanism, especially its patristic researches. On him see Ep 1612 introduction. Vesuvius is documented only in Erasmus' correspondence for

* * * * *

7 Schets had been urging Erasmus since early in 1526 (Ep 1681) to seek the patronage of John III of Portugal by dedicating a book to him. Erasmus had been rather noncommittal but in December 1526 informed Schets that he would dedicate his forthcoming edition of some works of St John Chrysostom (Chrysostomi lucubrationes) to the king; see Epp 1769 n12, 1800.

8 Not further identified, but evidently a physician who served the community of Portuguese merchants and government representatives living in Antwerp and engaged in the distribution of products of the Indies throughout northern Europe.

9 See Ep 1681 n13; Marcel Bataillon 'Érasme et la cour du Portugal' in his Études sur le Portugal au temps de l'humanisme (Coimbra 1952) 95–8 suggests that Fernandes was far less interested in Erasmus than in the paintings of his friend Albrecht Dürer, who had visited Antwerp in 1520–1 while Erasmus still lived in the Netherlands.

the years 1527–8. The original letter survived in the Rehdiger manuscripts at Wrocław and was first published by Enthoven in 1906. Enthoven's year-date of 1527 is confirmed by the contents.

Greetings, Erasmus, my honoured friend. It was Anton's fault that my letter did not reach you earlier.[1] When he left these parts for Basel, he chose to shorten his journey by three or four miles rather than visit us and give pleasure to his friends. Had he come, I would have written what you must by now have learned from others, that certain works of Erasmus, the *Collo-* 5 *quies*, the *Folly*, and the *Parabolae*, have been banned by the faculty of theology as dangerous to faith and morals.[2] But I am sure you do not need advice as to what should be done in this situation. My bishop,[3] who always thinks and speaks well of you, is distressed that you have to suffer such unpleasantness; he denounces these people for their shameless and malevolent 10 behaviour; they should be sitting at your feet and studying your marvellous writings, not trying to distract you from greater and loftier things by petty controversies. But you must not turn aside from your work. I know what serious-minded people say and think about you – and I meet many such people in Paris and at the court. You must not believe for a moment 15 that all theologians are against you. In fact there are some – and they are

* * * * *

1784
1 Anton Bletz of Zug was a professional courier who regularly carried messages between Basel, Freiburg, and Paris; he is documented from the date of this letter until July 1533 and also mentioned in the correspondence of Bonifacius Amerbach (AK III 366–7 Ep 1303) between 1528 and 1533.
2 Although royal opposition impeded publication of this decision, the faculty had in fact decreed on 16 May 1526 that Erasmus' *Colloquies* threatened the faith and morals of readers and that the reading of that book should be forbidden generally, especially to young readers who would be easily corrupted because the book was used in the schools under the pretext of its eloquent style. See Ep 1697 n8. Erasmus received reports of this action from friends but found them hard to believe (Allen Ep 1875:83–7), observing that the book had recently been published at Paris without difficulty; but in a letter of 16 July 1528 to Johannes Faber (Ep 2006) he admitted that the Paris faculty had condemned the *Colloquies* even though, he insisted, they could not show a single article to be impious. Vesuvius, who admitted that he was 'not too well informed about what is happening in Paris now,' was mistaken about a censure of the *Praise of Folly* and the *Parabolae* at this period. See James K. Farge 'Texts and Context of a *Mentalité*: The Parisian University Milieu in the Age of Erasmus' in *Editing Texts from the Age of Erasmus* ed Erika Rummel (Toronto 1996) 20–1 n59.
3 Michel Boudet, bishop of Langres

numerous – who see Erasmus as the very model of humane learning; but they are afraid to say so, for if they do not acquiesce in the motions of censure proposed by their seniors, they are immediately suspected of Lutheran sympathies. I am not too well informed about what is happening in Paris now, since I have been away for some time, but I am confident that your good and loyal friends have seen to it that justice has been done to you. Farewell, chief glory of the learned world.

Mussy, 8 February

Your friend for always, Nicolaus Vesuvius

To the eminent Master Erasmus of Rotterdam. In Basel

1784A / From Mercurino Gattinara to the University of Louvain
[Valladolid, c 10 February 1527]

In late October 1525, at the request of Erasmus, the emperor Charles v sent to the University of Louvain a letter commanding the faculty of theology to desist from its attacks on Erasmus (see Ep 1747 introduction). Having learned from Erasmus (Ep 1747) that the theologians had effectively nullified the imperial edict through legalistic manoeuvres, Gattinara, the imperial chancellor, wrote this stern and threatening letter to the faculty in his own name, warning them indirectly but unmistakably that the continuation of his own intervention at court in behalf of the university would depend on their willingness to obey the imperial mandate in favour of Erasmus. A rough draft of this letter, in the hand of Alfonso de Valdés, imperial secretary and a leading Spanish Erasmian, survived in the archives at Simancas and was first published by Marcel Bataillon in *Bulletin Hispanique* 26 (1924) 29–30. The points covered in Gattinara's letter correspond closely to the topics suggested by Erasmus in Ep 1747. Allen quotes a letter from Maximilianus Transsilvanus to Valdés reporting that Gattinara's letter had greater impact on the faculty than earlier letters from the emperor and the governor of the Netherlands, Margaret of Austria, and that the theologians had become more circumspect. The date of Valdés' manuscript draft must be very close or identical to that of the following letter.

Cordial greetings, distinguished sirs. Many reasons move me to write this letter to you. First, my duty to the emperor, by which I am bound to promote the authority of his Majesty everywhere, especially in times like these, when we see the whole world plunged into turmoil by a malign fate. Then, there is my sympathy for the humanities and for liberal studies and my good will towards you and your university. It is for these reasons that I have taken upon myself the responsibility of writing to you. As soon as I heard that some of you were daily forming new conspiracies to discredit the name of

Erasmus,[1] in total disregard of the emperor's edict, which was sent to you
to deal with this very matter, I decided not to inform the emperor, for I   10
knew how upset he would be if he heard that his edict was being flouted.
Instead, I thought it best to write this letter and give you a friendly warning
against allowing such a thing to happen again, for this would dishonour the
emperor, your university, and all of you. The last thing we need in these
troubled times is for the emperor's edicts to be ignored everywhere by his   15
own people.

Everyone knows how well Erasmus has served the Christian commonwealth. Here in Spain, in this remote corner of the world, no one has a
name so universally celebrated as his. What you are doing, perhaps in good
faith, is interpreted in this country as evidence of jealousy. People here do   20
not have a good word for you. Erasmus is a distinguished countryman of
yours, and for that reason you might be expected to hold him in the highest
esteem; but you allow him to be pursued with relentless hostility, and some
of you are trying to blot out his name altogether. To speak frankly, this sort
of behaviour is quite inappropriate – indeed it is an offence against religion.   25
So, gentlemen, keep your tongues in check and curb your insolent writings,
for these cause nothing but trouble. The world suffers more than enough
from the canker of discord without adding new causes of friction. There are
already too many people openly defending the teachings of Luther without
driving into his camp, by false accusations, those who wish to remain, and   30
thus far have remained, within the fellowship of the Catholic church; and
in fact, they have done more than remain in the church, they are fighting
with all their might against its enemies. Do you not realize how unfair it is
that Erasmus, who is standing in the forefront of the battle and is locked in
conflict with Luther, should be stabbed in the back by the very people he is   35
defending? Surely it is enough that this fine man is maligned, in both Latin
and German, in the vicious writings of the Lutherans. We would be better
employed recalling deserters to the ranks of the church than repelling those
who are its friends.

Even if there were something in Erasmus' books that seemed to have   40
been introduced without due reflection (and no author has yet been able to
avoid such careless errors), why make an issue of it in these perilous times
and in such an explosive manner, especially since the author gives clear
evidence of a devout and pious mind? He has always submitted his work

* * * * *

1784A
1 In Ep 1747 Erasmus had described several specific actions taken by hostile
  Louvain theologians to attack his reputation as an orthodox Catholic.

to the judgment of the church, and is ready to correct or explain anything   45
that justly gives offence to good and honest men. Nothing will ever satisfy
those whose minds are filled with hate. The judgments of love are blind, but
blinder still are the judgments of hate. Moreover, it is only fair to take some
account of the long hours Erasmus has spent, and is still spending every
day, for the advancement of theology and the humanities.   50

I thought these things needed to be said to you. My hope, now that you
have received this sincere and confidential admonition, is that you will take
thought for the dignity of the emperor, the peace of the community[2] (and
especially of your own province),[3] and the honour of the faith and of your
celebrated university. If I find that these considerations have carried some   55
weight with you, I shall count it a great favour, and I shall use whatever
influence I have to promote your interests and those of your university.

Farewell, from

1785 / From Mercurino Gattinara   Valladolid, 10 February 1527

This letter was written to accompany a copy of the preceding letter from Gattinara to the University of Louvain. It was first published as one of the letters
annexed to Erasmus' *De puritate tabernaculi sive ecclesiae christianae* (Antwerp:
Michael Hillen 1536; NK 859).

MERCURINO GATTINARA, CHANCELLOR TO EMPEROR CHARLES,
TO DESIDERIUS ERASMUS OF ROTTERDAM, GREETING
I have good reason now to be pleased with myself, for I see I have something
in common with so great a man as yourself. You write, most excellent sir,
that you will leave this life a happier man if you live to see the present   5
turmoil in the world give way to peace, a peace for which we all pray.[1] O
how I wish I too could see that day! There is nothing I desire more fervently,
nothing for which I strive more earnestly. If every Christian prince and

* * * * *

2 The Latin is *reipublicae ... tranquillitatis*, and the 'republic' meant is the whole
  community of Christendom, identified in Gattinara's mind with the Hapsburg
  imperial lands.
3 Gattinara might mean the duchy of Brabant, in which Louvain was located; the
  term might also apply to the entire Hapsburg Netherlands, since Louvain was
  the only established university in those provinces (even though there was now
  a fledgling but ultimately abortive college at Tournai that aspired to become
  a second university in that region).

1785
1 Ep 1747:5–9

bishop were as concerned about this as the emperor is, Christendom would
lack nothing to make its happiness complete. But we are victims of a malign   10
fate: while every man stubbornly seeks his own private gain (if gain it can
be called), we see the public interest crumbling everywhere. But I am not
yet ready to despair. For I hope that the day will soon dawn when not only
will our quarrels be settled but the evils that produced our present troubles
will be put right. As for yourself, I know how great is the jealousy that   15
racks the world and how ancient is that conspiracy of the wicked against
the righteous and of the ignorant against the learned. But you seek nothing
except the glory of God and the public good; so what harm can evil tongues
do you as long as you keep on doing what you are doing, that is, working
constantly for the advancement of the humanities, sound learning, and true   20
piety? I wish I could show you, by some special gesture, what my feelings
towards you are. You would then see how true and sincere is my good will.
I shall do my best to make you understand that.

I am writing to the University of Louvain. You can read what I have
written in the enclosed copy of my letter. I am astonished at the gall and   25
impudence of these great men. But I am happy to see that you have now
experienced something that happened to me on more than one occasion in
the past, for many men who pursued me with implacable hatred and wanted
me removed from the emperor's court have now been removed themselves
from the land of the living. The same fate, I hear, has befallen two of your   30
enemies.[2] Thus it is that God looks after his own.

I have heard nothing so far about Edward Lee's book,[3] although I am
aware that the fellow has been planning a libellous attack on you for some
time. Whatever it is, he will not be allowed to publish it in Spain without
having it looked at and examined carefully. In Spain we have taken steps   35
to prevent anyone from publishing the first nonsense that comes into his
head.[4] I wish the same practice was followed in Germany.

* * * * *

2 Two of Erasmus' most extreme critics at Louvain, Vincentius Theoderici and
  Nicolaas Baechem, had died the preceding August. See Ep 1763 nn22, 21; cf
  Epp 1732 nn12, 13, 1765:27–9.
3 Erasmus was convinced that Lee was the source, or at least one of the sources,
  of the criticisms by Spanish monks and theologians of which he had been receiving reports; and in Ep 1747 he reported to Gattinara that Lee was preparing to publish in Spain (where he was present as ambassador from Henry VIII)
  a book that would slander Erasmus (see Ep 1744 n19 and cf 1747:79–82). Cf
  Rummel II 84–5.
4 Although several German dioceses had instituted censorship in the 1480s and
  the papacy had endorsed pre-publication censorship for Germany in 1501
  and throughout the universal church by a constitution of the Fifth Lateran

Keep your courage up and look after your health. And write often.
Valladolid, 10 February 1527

1786 / From Alonso Ruiz de Virués   Burgos, 23 February 1527

Knowing little about Spanish intellectual life and being suspicious of conspiracies (especially by monks), Erasmus had misinterpreted the comments about
his publications that Virués compiled in 1525–6 and sent to him. He regarded
these manuscript *Collationes ad Erasmum* (which do not survive) as possibly
the beginning of another series of attacks on his orthodoxy and did not reply. In reality, Virués was an admirer who merely wanted to alert Erasmus to
statements in his writings that might stir up avoidable attacks. Eventually (Ep
1968) Erasmus was convinced by repeated assurances from friends in Spain
that Virués was a devoted admirer, not a duplicitous critic. On Virués and

* * * * *

Council confirmed by Leo x in 1515, Spain preferred to create its own system of press control, just as it had created its own Inquisition. A decree of
Ferdinand and Isabella issued on 8 July 1502 established prior censorship of
books published in Spain and required booksellers to obtain a licence for
importing books. Imported books had to be inspected before they were exposed for sale, and every printer was required to obtain a printing licence.
A limited number of civil and ecclesiastical officials designated in the law
had authority to license books: the presidents of the *audiencias* of Valladolid
and Granada, the archbishops of Toledo and Seville, and the bishops of Burgos and Salamanca. Those who violated the law faced confiscation of their
books and their profits, plus a fine (divided between the informant, the judge,
and the royal treasury). In addition, they were excluded from engaging in
the occupation of printer or merchant. The actual examination was to be conducted by officials who received an adequate salary, and criteria for approval
were set. All books judged to be apocryphal, superstitious, condemned, useless, or dangerous were to be denied a licence. Once a manuscript had been
printed, the edition had to be collated with the manuscript viewed by the
censors. Thus Spain had created a state-sponsored and state-controlled ma-
chinery of censorship, even though some of the officials in charge were members of the clergy. These regulations of 1502 governed the printing and sale
of books throughout the earlier part of the sixteenth century. In 1554, the
royal council, deploring the laxity with which licences were being granted,
decreed that henceforth the licence to print should be obtainable only from
the president of the royal council and that the originals of texts submitted
for censorship should be retained by the council. See J.H. Elliott *Imperial
Spain, 1469–1716* (London 1963) 222–3, and for greater detail, *Index des livres
interdits* vol 5 *Index de l'Inquisition espagnole* ed J.M. De Bujanda and others
(Sherbrooke, Quebec 1984) 33–5 and, for the text of the law of 1502, 121–2
(Document 1).

on the background, see Ep 1684 introduction; cf Ep 1717 n19. The autograph
of this letter was preserved among the Rehdiger manuscripts at Wrocław and
was first published by Enthoven in 1906.

TO THE MOST HONOURABLE AND LEARNED MASTER
DESIDERIUS ERASMUS OF ROTTERDAM
FROM BROTHER ALONSO VIRUÉS OF OLMEDO
Cordial greetings. Perhaps, most learned Erasmus, you had your mind on
higher things and so forgot that last year I sent you a little book, in the form   5
of a letter, in which I sought your wise judgment on certain passages in your
work. I pointed to things that appealed to me as an unbiased reader (for so
I consider myself to be) and to other readers like myself, and I drew your
attention both to points that might offend simple folk and to passages that
slanderous critics would attempt to impugn. I wanted you to examine all   10
these passages and make a simple reply that would (if possible) set everyone's mind at rest. If you did not wish to do this, at least you could express
your support for me for attempting your defence and make it clear that you
do not hold the views which certain of those 'scourges of Erasmus'[1] suspect
you of holding. For you say nothing, and this silence on your part gives the   15
impression that you accept the construction which these men put upon your
work; as a result, however hard I work on your behalf, no one believes me.
I know from your letter to the excellent Juan Vergara[2] that my little book
got into your hands, for Vergara recently sent me a copy of your letter along
with a letter of his own,[3] in which (if I may put it this way) he protests   20
to me over your protests to him. As soon as I received these, although the
courier was in a pressing hurry to return, I took up my laboured pen and
wrote a reply, and enclosed a copy of the response that I had decided to

* * * * *

1786
1 Virués' Latin term is *Erasmomastiges*. See Ep 1658 n8.
2 Only the fragment of this letter (Ep 1684) that deals with Virués is preserved.
  Vergara was secretary of Alonso de Fonseca, archbishop of Toledo, and was
  one of the most strategically placed of Erasmus' Spanish admirers. Erasmus
  had met him in the Netherlands in 1520, and he was one of the few native
  Spaniards whom Erasmus trusted sufficiently to write candidly about his relations with Spain and individual Spaniards. Vergara himself at first knew nothing about Virués but made inquiries about him and eventually met him, finding him to be a supporter of Erasmus, a conclusion that he reported to the
  suspicious Erasmus in April 1527 (Ep 1814).
3 For Vergara's letter to Virués and Virués' reply see The Letters of Juan de
  Vergara and Others, Letters 2 and 4, 522–6 and 529–33 below.

send you.[4] I hoped that if you did not receive my letter from the hands of
the merchants whose good offices I was using, the second copy would even-   25
tually reach you through Vergara. Whether this actually happened, that is,
whether you got a copy of my letter either from the merchants or from the
imperial couriers, I still do not know. So far I have not been able to discover
the fate of the letters, since I have not had even a few lines from you or
from my friend Vergara, whom you have chosen as your oracle in this coun-   30
try. Perhaps, given the hazards of the long journey, both copies have gone
astray. So I am now sending you, for the third time, a copy of Dr Vergara's
letter of protest, of my reply to him, and of the letter I addressed to you.
These will give you proof of my feelings towards you and of the warmth
of my affection. I hope this will be the last act of the drama and the end of   35
this whole imbroglio.

I want to add one point as a sort of postscript, namely that new attacks
upon you from certain monks are emerging every day, but they are also being submerged under the weighty authority of judges and the impressive
learning of scholars.[5] In the pulpit these men will babble away about any-   40
thing, for they feel they are on home ground – 'crowing from their own
dunghill,'[6] as we say in this country; when, however, they are called to defend their views in debate, they have nothing to say, yet have not the good

*****

4 Not extant
5 The inquisitor-general of Spain, Alonso Manrique de Lara, who was sympathetic to Erasmus' scholarship, had summoned the heads of the principal religious orders and warned them to restrain those among their members who
had been publicly denouncing Erasmus in their sermons, especially after the
publication of a vernacular translation of the *Enchiridion*. He instructed them
that if they had serious concerns about Erasmus' publications, they should put
them in writing, and he assured them that he would bring any serious allegations before a conference of qualified theologians for study. This instruction
was given at a meeting held before the council (*Suprema*) of the Inquisition
about 1 March 1527. At another meeting on 28 March, finding that the representatives appeared with lists from each of the orders that duplicated each
other, he ordered them to combine their charges into a single list; and on 12
April he promised that this list would be referred to a conference of theologians that would meet at Valladolid. The principal contemporary account of
these negotiations is Vergara's letter of 24 April 1527 to Erasmus (Ep 1814).
See Bataillon (1991) I 253–6 and, for a revisionist view focused more directly
on the Valladolid conference of summer 1527 and its immediate background
and based on surviving documents of the Inquisition, see Homza 82–4. On
Manrique see also Ep 1742 n4.
6 Seneca *Apocolocyntosis* 7.3

sense to keep quiet. For all that, their furtive sniping is upsetting to ordinary people. I am afraid this hydra, which grows seventy heads for every 45 one it loses, will win in the end. For, as you know, however long you live, you must leave this world some day, but monastic communities never die.[7] It is true they have many good and honest men among them who cherish true wisdom and strive to emulate the simplicity of the gospel; but all of us, whatever kind of men we are, are prejudiced in favour of our own order 50 and want to safeguard its honour. This explains how it is that the majority, who err through malice or a shabby piety, easily gain the upper hand or, rather, draw the better part over to their own opinion.[8] We think we are promoting the glory of Christ Jesus, but all the while we are fighting with you for our own glory. So driven on by a double goad, we outrun those who 55 support you, though only when it is consistent with their desire to support the gospel. Alas, the stronger this emulation, the more likely it is to fade and die in the hearts of mortal men.

Unless I am mistaken, you have it in your power to overcome this problem. You have published several apologies on specific issues in the past; now 60 you should write what I might call a general and comprehensive apology. It would not cost you much effort. In such a work you could respond to some of the issues I have raised and to other criticisms that, as you are aware, are matters of public concern. It would be useful (at least this is how I see it), if you explained in a thorough and comprehensive manner what you feel 65 about these issues and what you think we ought to feel. But if you do not like this filial advice of mine, this short letter will be the last time I shall lecture you. Farewell.

Burgos, 23 February AD 1526

Your friend Virués of Olmedo (written in his own hand) 70

To the most honourable and learned Master Desiderius Erasmus of Rotterdam. In Basel

1787 / From Jan Becker   Louvain, 27 February 1527

Jan Becker of Borssele was a friend of long standing, and he and Erasmus had corresponded frequently since 1514. On him see Epp 291 introduction, 1321 introduction. The latter, dating from November 1522, appears to have been their most recent piece of correspondence; hence the reference here to the long

* * * * *

7 Sage advice, especially coming as it does from a monk who was by no means uncritical of his fellow monks.
8 Livy 21.4.1; cf *Adagia* I vi 28, IV iii 44.

break in contact. Erasmus had, however, sent greetings to Becker in a letter
of July 1525 (Ep 1584, cf n4) addressed to Adrianus Barlandus, professor of
Latin in the Collegium Trilingue at Louvain. Erasmus must have replied to the
present letter. That reply is lost, but Becker refers to it in Ep 1851. The original letter survived at Leipzig and was first published in Förstemann/Günther
(1904).

Cordial greetings. It has been a long time since I last wrote to you, my
honoured and most respected master. But I have not forgotten you or your
kindnesses to me, and in the many wonderful and helpful books you have
written I still hear you teaching and explaining. I had several reasons for not
writing, but one was not altogether frivolous and silly: I thought it would   5
be inconsiderate to interrupt you with some trivial communication when
you were busy with serious religious issues and forced, it seems, every day
to respond to Lutherans and anti-Lutherans alike. I realized that you are
now an old man, almost worn out with long hours of study and the labours
of many years. However, when I found out that you had been convinced   10
by a letter from a friend or by a story that someone had told you that last
summer I had succumbed to illness and had departed this life, I felt I had to
write – even if only a few lines. The illness was real enough. It was so severe
and prolonged that my poor body was robbed of its natural powers, and the
spirit that inhabits the body had almost left it. So I want to tell you first of all   15
that, by the mercy of God, I pulled through; secondly I must thank you (as I
do from the bottom of my heart) for the flattering things you wrote about me
to our friend Barlandus when you thought I had already passed away. But
in addition to these reasons for writing I have a third, a small matter to be
sure, as perhaps it will appear to you, but something, in my judgment, that   20
should not be dismissed out of hand. Here is the sort of thing I have in mind.
    Everyone has a copy of your splendid and distinguished corpus of
letters.[1] I hear you are now about to publish a new edition, which (as

* * * * *

1787
1 A reference to the most recently published collection of Erasmus' correspondence, *Epistolae ad diversos* (Basel: Froben, 31 August 1521). Erasmus' missing
  reply to this letter must have confirmed the report of his plan to issue an enlarged collection of his letters (see Allen Ep 1851:29–31); but the pressure of
  other work and then the personal disruption involved in his leaving Basel in
  1529 and settling in Freiburg meant not only that the revised collection (*Opus
  epistolarum Erasmi* [Basel: Froben, Herwagen, and Episcopius 1529]) was delayed but also that it was not so carefully revised as Erasmus seems to have
  intended.

one might imagine) will be greatly enlarged. In the new edition, if my
advice does not arrive too late, I would like you to preserve the actual   25
order in which the letters were written, that is to say, you should follow the sequence of years, months, and even days (if that could be done
without too much trouble). Some writers, whose letters are entirely personal and of no great significance or importance, observe this principle
scrupulously, but I see that you have completely disregarded it in the one   30
edition I have been able to examine so far, where several recent letters
to friends come at the very front, while not a few written long ago to
classmates and others are in the middle of the volume. I am convinced
that the order I propose has great advantages both for you and for the
reader. First of all, if you arrange the letters in this way, the sequence   35
of events in your life and work and in everything else you have done
will immediately be clear. Then you will provide future writers with a
sort of catalogue of dates for the events of which you write, the friendships you enjoyed with the leading figures of Christendom, and the many
controversies you were forced to take part in against your will; all this   40
and more you will make clear, and everyone will be very grateful. Please
don't take this recommendation of mine amiss; and if it is still possible to
comply, I hope you will treat it more seriously than you treated the advice I gave you eight years ago, that you should write on the theory of
preaching.[2]   45

I am now living at Louvain at the home of Master Robertus Virulus[3]
along with the eldest surviving son of the lord of Beveren.[4] But I have been
away for a year and a half since I first moved here four years ago. All good
wishes.

* * * * *

2 Erasmus had talked and written about a plan to produce a treatise on preaching since at least 1519, and many other friends shared Becker's desire for such
a work; but his *Ecclesiastes* was not completed and published until 1535. See
Ep 1660 n10.
3 Virulus, or Manneken (d after 1527), was the son of a widely respected regent
of the College of the Lily, Carolus Virulus (1413–93), who in his day was regarded as a humanist. The younger Virulus seems to have accepted well-to-do
students into his house as boarders. In the present case, he lodged both the
student and Becker, his tutor. Virulus would have been an elderly man at this
time, older than Erasmus, since he matriculated at Louvain in 1476 and had
studied law at Pavia sometime before 1484.
4 Becker's private pupil at the home of Virulus was Maximilian II of Burgundy
(1514–58), son of Adolph of Burgundy, lord of Veere and Beveren, a member
of an aristocratic family in which the young Erasmus had found patrons many
years earlier.

Louvain, 27 February 1527   50
Jan van Borssele, dean of Zanddijk, your affectionate friend
To the eminent theologian, Desiderius Erasmus of Rotterdam, high
priest of learning and his most respected teacher. In Basel

1788 / From Conradus Goclenius   Louvain, 28 February 1527

> The original manuscript letter remained unpublished among Erasmus' papers
> at Basel until it was edited by Allen in 1926. Goclenius is writing mainly to
> inquire whether Erasmus has received earlier letters forwarded to him from
> Louvain. On him, see Epp 1765, 1768, 1778.

Cordial greetings. I have been wondering for some time if you got the
packet of letters from Spain. It included one for you from the emperor himself[1] along with other letters that, I am sure, would have given you much
pleasure. I also wondered if you ever received a letter of mine that I sent
you shortly after Epiphany;[2] I gave it to a courier from Antwerp who had   5
been commissioned by Franz Birckmann to go to Basel.[3] To add to the uncertainty, I have been waiting all this time for your Danish friend[4] to appear,
but he has not come. When he left here, he did everything but swear an
oath that he would not stay in Brabant for more than two weeks and that, if
some important business turned up to require a change of plan, he would   10
send you a reliable messenger, who, after first informing me, would assure
you on all those matters you had entrusted to his care. What he has done
or decided to do, I do not know. If he comes here on his way back to you,
or sends someone reliable, I shall write at greater length. I do not propose
to entrust a letter about present events to this courier.[5] However, there is   15
practically nothing happening here at present that would interest you.

* * * * *

1788
1 Ep 1731, transmitted as part of a shipment of letters from Spain forwarded to
   Erasmus by Goclenius. See Ep 1768.
2 Ep 1778, dated 13 January 1527
3 Goclenius' distrust of Birckmann extended to the courier he commissioned;
   cf Ep 1778:1–3 and n1. On Birckmann's reputation, see Ep 1665 n1 and the
   further references given there.
4 Hans Bogbinder, often referred to as Hans the Dane. See Ep 1769 n13.
5 Goclenius expresses the phrase 'about present events' – that is, current political and religious events – in Greek, probably to prevent a possibly unreliable
   courier from understanding the reference to himself if he opened the letter
   and read it.

Karl Harst has managed to disentangle all the knots and is now happily in possession of his beloved Philomela.[6] He is grateful for your many kindnesses and wishes you every blessing. Frans van der Dilft has now been away from here for more than three months.[7] He is so secretive about his plans that I can report nothing for certain about him. Some say that he is preparing to go to Spain and that his many influential friends are holding out rosy prospects for him at the emperor's court. Others maintain that he is busy hunting for a wife and is already on the slippery slope that will end in submission to the yoke. If he does not write to you, you can conclude that he has his hands full with his own affairs.

Matters in the college are still where they were.[8] We are wearing down our enemies by patience. Dr van Paesschen has taken Egmondanus' place and is beginning to raise a fuss.[9] We are weaving our ivy-clusters[10] and will continue to do so until these Codruses are bored stiff or burst their loins with envy.[11] Hoogstraten, that old enemy of literature and the source of all

* * * * *

6 A romantic name from legend; the bride's real name was Katharina van der Klusen. Goclenius had kept Erasmus apprised of the engagement of his former secretary Harst and in Ep 1778:9–13 had reported on the wedding.
7 On him see Ep 1663 introduction. Goclenius is correct in writing that since his return from Basel to the Netherlands in 1525, Dilft had been casting about for the right career opportunity and that seeking patronage at the imperial court in Spain was one possibility he pursued. After an abortive attempt in 1528, he did secure a position in Spain in 1530, in the retinue of Alonso de Fonseca, archbishop of Toledo.
8 The Collegium Trilingue, where Goclenius was professor of Latin. As this letter implies, the new humanistic college remained an unwelcome innovation in the opinion of some conservative theologians and older masters of arts at Louvain.
9 Nicolaas Baechem of Egmond, Erasmus' most vociferous critic at Louvain, had died in August 1526. See Ep 1763 (from Levinus Ammonius to Johannes Molendino) lines 130–2 and n22 and Goclenius' detailed report of the circumstances of his death in Ep 1765:26–30. Jan van Paesschen of Brussels, a Louvain doctor of theology and from 1505 prior of the Carmelite monastery at Mechelen, where Baechem had been received as a novice in 1506, had supported Baechem's repeated public attacks on Erasmus' and now evidently had begun to denounce Erasmus and the Collegium Trilingue on his own.
10 That is, giving vague answers which have nothing to do with the question, evidently a reference to the tactics used by the members of the Collegium Trilingue when they came under attack. The expression is clarified by *Adagia* III ii 96, though in fact the example cited there by Erasmus does not come from ancient Greek comedy but from some Byzantine source that has not been identified; see R.A.B. Mynors' note in CWE 34 404.
11 In Virgil Codrus is the type of an inferior writer. For his envy see *Eclogue* 7.26.

of Germany's troubles, died recently at Cologne to the great sorrow of those who found his effrontery a great support.[12] The rest of my news must wait for your Danish friend or a more reliable courier. Farewell.

From Busleyden's college, Louvain, 28 February AD 1527   35

Yours affectionately, Conradus Goclenius

To Master Erasmus of Rotterdam, peerless champion of literature and true religion. In Basel

1789 / To the Pious Reader   [Basel, March 1527]

This letter is prefixed to four sheets of supplementary material added to the fourth edition of Erasmus' *Annotationes* on the New Testament and must be dated shortly after the colophon of the revised New Testament had been put in place in February 1527. The printing of the entire volume was completed in early March; hence this epistle must date from the very end of February or the first few days of March.

ERASMUS OF ROTTERDAM TO THE PIOUS READER, GREETING

When I was working on this fourth edition, there came into my possession some Greek manuscripts of Chrysostom[1] and Athanasius,[2] in which I observe that their citations of Scripture generally agree with my edition. All previous translators of the Greek commentaries have chosen for some rea-   5
son to give the reading of the Vulgate rather than to translate what was in the Greek manuscripts. As a result, the commentary frequently does not correspond to the text as it has been translated. The problem is particularly evident in the Latin translation of Theophylact's commentaries on the

* * * * *

12 Jacob van Hoogstraten, the Dominican theologian and inquisitor, best known
   for his prosecution of Johann Reuchlin, died on 21 January 1527. For Erasmus'
   opinion of him, which was not entirely hostile, see Epp 1775 n5, 1780 n12.

1789
1 Erasmus had been working on Latin and Greek texts of St John Chrysostom for
   a number of years and would soon publish a volume of his own translations,
   Chrysostomi lucubrationes; see Ep 1661 n2.
2 Erasmus' dedication of the works of Athanasius for which he had found a
   manuscript source is Ep 1790, addressed to John Longland, bishop of Lincoln.
   This edition was appended to his *Chrysostomi lucubrationes* despite some doubts
   on his part whether such a dedication would offend Bishop Longland; cf Ep
   1780 n8.

Cardinal Francisco Jiménez de Cisneros
Wall painting in the chapter house of Toledo Cathedral
by Juan de Borgoña, 1509–11
Ampliaciones y reproducciones MAS, Barcelona

Epistles of Paul.[3] But even greater confusion faces the reader who exam- 10
ines citations or notes in the translations of commentaries on the Old Testament, for discrepancies in the Old Testament are much greater than in
the New. It is extremely important, if only to make the Greek commentaries more accessible, to have a Latin translation of both Testaments that
is based on the reading of the Greek. I attempted this in my New Testa- 15
ment, being the first to do so, and met with considerable hostility. His Eminence Francisco, cardinal of Spain, met with more success and less hostility
when, with much effort and expense, he performed the same task for both
the Old and the New Testaments.[4] I thought I should mention this; it might

* * * * *

3 On Erasmus' awareness that the Greek commentaries traditionally attributed
  to Athanasius were really the work of a medieval Bulgarian commentator
  who wrote in Greek, Theophylact, archbishop of Ochrida, see Ep 1680 n3;
  cf Ep 1790:10–24 and the lengthy historical demonstration that he, and not
  Athanasius, must be the author of the commentaries on Paul's Epistles. Theophylact's use of the Greek biblical texts in his references caused confusion
  among Latin commentators who tried to match his biblical references with
  their own Latin Vulgate text.
4 Francisco Jiménez (or Ximénes) de Cisneros (1436–1517), archbishop of Toledo,
  inquisitor-general of Spain, and cardinal, was an important patron of learning, including humanistic learning, and founded the University of Alcalá de
  Henares as a centre for scholarship on the biblical text. Of particular importance to Erasmus in the present context, he assembled and sustained the team
  of textual scholars who produced the famous Complutensian Polyglot Bible,
  which included not only the Latin text but also the Hebrew text of the Old
  Testament and the Greek text of both the Old Testament (the Septuagint) and
  the New Testament. Indeed, the Greek New Testament produced by the editors of this project was printed in 1514, earlier than Erasmus' famous Greek
  New Testament of 1516, but was not supposed to be released for publication
  until the whole Bible was completed in 1517. In fact, none of the volumes of
  the Complutensian Polyglot could be circulated until the whole edition was licensed for publication in 1520. Erasmus saw Jiménez' work as an authoritative
  parallel to his own biblical scholarship. In reality, however, the Complutensian editors took an exceedingly cautious approach and rarely introduced any
  changes into the Vulgate text on the basis of the Greek manuscripts. They
  were so conservative in their attitude towards traditional readings and interpretations that their decisions now appear to be arbitrary and lacking in any
  consistent editorial principles. Antonio de Nebrija, Spain's ablest humanist,
  whom Cardinal Jiménez had recruited into the project in 1513, got along very
  well with the cardinal but had little influence when he challenged the excessively cautious editorial decisions of the other editors. When he found that
  Jiménez supported the traditionalist majority, he resigned from the project.
  On the textual limitations of the Complutensian edition, see Jerry H. Bentley
  Humanists and Holy Writ (Princeton 1983) 88–110.

quieten the barking from certain quarters, which would be a great blessing 20
to Christendom.

1790 / To John Longland   Basel, 3 March 1527

The dedication of several works of St Athanasius, *Athanasii lucubrationes aliquot*,
printed in Latin translation as an annex at the end of Erasmus' *Chrysostomi lucubrationes* (Basel: Froben, March 1527), also in Latin. It is addressed to Longland, bishop of Lincoln, one of Erasmus' most loyal and most generous English patrons. For his concern that publication of this edition as an annex to a
longer work dedicated to another person (see Ep 1800) might offend Bishop
Longland, see Ep 1780 n8. The autograph letter survives in Copenhagen (MS
Thottske s.73), a source not known to Allen, who relied on the first edition
and subsequent editions for his text.

TO THE REVEREND FATHER IN CHRIST, JOHN, LORD BISHOP OF
LINCOLN IN ENGLAND, FROM ERASMUS OF ROTTERDAM, GREETING
Every hunter, reverend bishop, has his favourite quarry. I count myself the
luckiest of men, because recently I tracked down a manuscript containing
many of the writings of St Athanasius. I think it is of the greatest importance 5
for the well-being of Christendom that we lose none of the writings left us
by that eloquent champion of the church. This great man deserved not just to
have an immortal name, but to live on, immortal in a mortal world, and to
survive entire. Up to the present we have only a few of Athanasius' writings,
translated after a fashion. I wonder who it was who ascribed to Athanasius 10
those not unimportant commentaries on the letters of Paul, since the Greek
manuscripts bear the name Theophylact, archbishop of Bulgaria, and the
style differs radically from that of Athanasius.[1] If this is not enough to convince you on the question of authorship, let me offer you another argument.
In the commentaries of which we have just spoken there are frequent 15
citations from John Chrysostom and Basil, both of whom lived about forty
years later than Athanasius.[2] The author took so much from Chrysostom

* * * * *

1790
1 On Theophylact's authorship, see Epp 1680 n3, 1789 n2.
2 John Chrysostom was born between 344 and 354, became a deacon in 381,
a priest and preacher at Antioch in 386, and patriarch of Constantinople in
398. He died in 407. Basil the Great was born about 330, ordained priest about
364, became bishop of Caesarea in 370, and died in 373. Erasmus' point is that
citations from Chrysostom and Basil in these commentaries show that they
must have been the work of an author of later date than Athanasius.

that he often quotes several lines from him word for word, while suppressing the name of his source; more often he reproduces the sense of the original, changing a few words here and there. It seems, then, that this Theophylact belonged to a later age; he was known neither to Jerome nor to Gennadius[3] nor to those from whose works the *Historia tripartita* was compiled.[4] He appears to have done for the Greeks what Bede,[5] Remigius,[6] Claudian,[7] and other similar commentators did for speakers of Latin. These writers avoided the digressions that Augustine indulges in, often at considerable length, when addressing the people; they also omitted anything that seemed irrelevant to the matter at hand. The result was a précis of what had been treated more extensively by others. Chrysostom too has frequent lengthy di-

* * * * *

3 Jerome wrote a catalogue of outstanding Christian writers, *De viris inlustribus*. Gennadius (fl 490), a priest of Marseilles, wrote a continuation of it, extending it into the latter part of the fifth century. On him see Ep 676:21n. Erasmus assumes that this work would have mentioned the biblical commentaries in its list of Athanasius' works (as it does not) if they had been in existence and had been regarded as genuine in the time of Jerome and Gennadius. See Hieronymus and Gennadius *De viris inlustribus* ed Carl Albrecht Bernoulli (Freiburg im Breisgau 1895; repr Frankfurt 1968) 46. The texts are also in PL 23 631–760.

4 The *Historia ecclesiastica tripartita*, covering the history of the church from 306 to 439, was compiled in the sixth century by the monk Epiphanius at the direction of the founder of his monastery, Cassiodorus. It was based on the works of the earlier Greek church historians Socrates, Sozomen, and Theodoret and was modelled on a similar Greek-language compilation from the same sources made by Theodore Anagnostes. It was one of the most important sources on early church history and was known throughout the Middle Ages. The first printed edition was edited by Erasmus' collaborator Beatus Rhenanus under the title *Auctores historiae ecclesiasticae* (Basel: Froben 1523), a volume that also contained the earlier *Historia ecclesiastica* written by Eusebius and continued by Rufinus.

5 Erasmus thinks of Bede (673–735) as a biblical commentator (cf Ep 1112:37–8), though in modern times his *Ecclesiastical History of the English People* has been the most influential of his works. His commentaries on both the Old and New Testaments constitute the largest part of his work and draw explicitly on a wide reading of all patristic interpreters he could find available in Latin. On him see M.L.W. Laistner *Thought and Letters in Western Europe, AD 500 to 900* (London 1931; repr London 1957) 156–66.

6 Remigius, a ninth-century monk of Auxerre, expounded both Christian and classical pagan authors and several books of the Bible, including the Epistles of St Paul. See Laistner *Thought and Letters* (preceding note) 260.

7 Allen (23n) suggests that Erasmus has in mind Claudius, bishop of Turin (d 830), a biblical commentator from the time of Charlemagne. See Laistner *Thought and Letters* (n5 above) 290, 300–3.

gressions in which he deals with moral questions, but these generally come
near the end of a homily. From various writings of Chrysostom and others   30
Theophylact wove together his commentaries on the four Gospels and on
all the letters of Paul.

Among works written by Athanasius St Jerome mentions the following:[8] two books *Against the Heathen*, of which we have only one;[9] *On the*
Titles of the Psalms, part of which we have in translation;[10] *On the Arian Per-*   35
secution, in many books, several of which I am now offering;[11] *On Virgin-*
ity (although it is not clear if this is the same as the work I found under the title περὶ παρθενίας ἢ περὶ ἀσκήσεως. If it is by Athanasius, then
he has modified his style to suit the unsophisticated girl to whom he is

* * * * *

8 *De viris inlustribus* 87 ed Bernoulli (n3 above) 46 / PL 23 693–4. Erasmus' list
  is carelessly compiled. It does not present the works in the order found in the
  printed texts of Jerome, though it does include all of the titles mentioned there
  and adds two letters to Serapion (out of a total of four) that deal with the doctrine of the Holy Spirit. Except for *De virginitate* and perhaps the Festal Letters,
  Erasmus' own *Athanasii lucubrationes* does not include the works that appear
  on Jerome's list, though Jerome explicitly states that his list is not complete.
  Erasmus' table of contents (on the verso of the title page) lists the following
  titles: De S. Spiritu ad Serapionem epistolae duae; Quod Nicena synodus . . .
  Arianam haeresim decreta; Apologeticus contra eos qui calumniabantur . . .;
  Apologeticus secundus; De passione domini ac de cruce (see n15 below); De
  hoc quod scriptum est, Euntes in vicum . . . (see n15 below); De virginitate sive
  de exercitatione (see n12 below); De hoc quod dictum est in Evangelio: Qui-
  cunque dixerit; De spiritu sancto (see n15 below). Jill Rosenshield, associate
  curator, Department of Special Collections, Memorial Library, University of
  Wisconsin-Madison, kindly inspected this volume and provided information
  on its contents.
9 Athanasius' works include 'two books *Against the Heathen*,' but the second
  of these books was also known under the separate title *Oratio de incarnatione*
  Verbi / *On the Incarnation of the Word*, and Erasmus seems unfamiliar with it
  (PG 25 1–94).
10 Erasmus' citation of '*On the Titles of the Psalms*, part of which we have in
   translation' could also mean 'part of which we [Erasmus] have translated.'
11 The reference to *De persecutione Arianorum* / *On the Arian Persecution* probably
   means 'On the Persecution by [rather than of] the Arians.' This title does not
   conform exactly to the title of any known work by Athanasius, but his *Apologia*
   contra Arianos is an account of the Arian controversy, in which he was a central
   figure, and it does cover the first two periods of exile (out of a total of five) to
   which he was subjected because of his firm opposition to politically devised
   compromises on the Trinitarian controversy of the fourth century. His work
   Historia Arianorum is another possibility for this reference, but as with much
   of the list, the reference remains vague. Cf Quasten III 347.

writing);[12] *Against Valens and Ursacius*, one book;[13] *Life of Antony, the Monk;*[14]   40
Festal Letters, that is, letters concerning the celebration of feast days (we have
none of these, unless we include certain works under this heading, a few of
which I have translated: 'On the Passion of Christ,' 'On the Foal of an Ass,'
'On Blaspheming against the Holy Ghost').[15] Jerome cited these works by
name, but added that there were 'many others too numerous to mention.'   45

* * * * *

12 *De virginitate / On Virginity* was highly influential on Christian ascetic thought.
   Most modern scholars have rejected the attribution to Athanasius on the basis
   of its style and vocabulary, precisely the grounds that Erasmus cites here for
   his own doubts. Cf Quasten III 45.
13 'Against Valens and Ursacius' is not the title of any known work of Athanasius,
   and the Migne editor (PG 25 xxvi) says that the work is not extant. Chapters
   51–8 of Athanasius' *Apology Against the Arians* contain letters from Valens and
   Ursacius but no work against them. Hilary of Poitiers wrote a book by this title, and Jerome knew of it; *De viris inlustribus* 100 ed Bernoulli (n3 above) 49 /
   PL 23 740. Perhaps Jerome mistakenly transferred Hilary's title to Athanasius'
   De synodis (PG 26 678–794), which deals with the same events.
14 Athanasius' *Life of Anthony* is a known work (PG 26 823–978) and was highly
   influential as an authoritative patristic biography of the major figure in early
   Christian monasticism.
15 The Festal Letters were pastoral letters sent to all their dependent churches by
   early patriarchs of Alexandria, including Athanasius, every year shortly after
   Epiphany to notify the churches of the correct date for the beginning of Lent
   and the celebration of Easter in the new year. But they also contained pastoral
   advice, spiritual exhortations, and discussion of problems faced by the church.
   Only fragments of those issued by Athanasius survive in Greek, and thirteen
   complete Festal Letters survive in Syriac but would not have been known to
   Erasmus. Migne (PG 26 14, 21–44) publishes some of the Greek fragments, but
   others have not yet been collected and edited. The fact that Erasmus does not
   call attention to letter 39, for the year 367, confirms his own suspicion that the
   letters he had in hand were not the ones described as Festal Letters by Jerome,
   for that letter is the earliest known document that lists all twenty-seven books
   of the present New Testament, and no others; hence it is of great importance in
   tracing the emergence of the canon of the New Testament, the books that the
   church recognized as divinely inspired revelation. It seems unlikely that Erasmus would have failed to mention this letter if he had known it. The three
   titles he does list here are vague, but it might be conjectured that they are
   the homilies *In passionem et crucem Domini* 'On the Passion of Christ,' classed
   among the *dubia* in PG 28 185–250; *In illud Evangelii secundum Matthaeum. Ite
   in castellum quod contra vos est* ... 'On the Foal of an Ass,' classed among the
   spuria in PG 28 1023–48, a homily on Matt 21:2 on fetching the ass and foal
   for Christ's entry into Jerusalem on Palm Sunday; and *Epistola ad Serapionem
   Contra illos qui blasphemant et dicunt Spiritum Sanctum rem creatam esse* 'On Blaspheming against the Holy Spirit' (PG 26 525–607). The Benedictine editors of
   the congregation of St Maur rejected Erasmus' challenge to the authenticity of

Knowing how eager you are for such delights, I have translated a small sample of the works that came into my possession. I would have sent more, but at the time I was faced with a mountain of work; in fact, I had to dictate most of these in the afternoons ('dictating' is an impressive word for a wretched business), and I am well aware of the difference there is between 50 what is written with one's own pen and what is spoken to an amanuensis. But I was forced to submit to this dictatorship, contrary to my usual practice, partly because of the daily worsening of my health, and partly on account of the persistent demands that are made on me. If I discover that you like these, I shall find some free time and send you more.   55

There is a proverb that says: 'Honey's all tinged with gall; rich soil, crops spoil.'[16] The almost excessive delight that I felt at my discovery was tempered by its accompanying pain. Besides the trouble that the copyist caused by his careless writing, I discovered a number of false attributions; for (not to mention doubtful cases) works were attributed to Athanasius 60 that one would scarcely believe had come from a sane man.[17] I wasted much time and effort over this, for the further I proceeded with my translation, the more absurdities I found; in the end I was forced to put the project aside. I have included, however, a few fragments from this class. 'Why?' you may well ask. And I answer 'To point out the flippant and cavalier manner in 65 which Greek copyists have dealt with the writings of great men, where to alter even a syllable would be sacrilege.' In Latin, too, we have the same reckless irresponsibility, falsifying, truncating, augmenting, and corrupting the commentaries of sound theologians.

Let me tell you what I recently discovered. Some of Clement's writings 70 and several letters of the early popes had just been published.[18] I asked my

* * * * *

the last-named letter (cf n17 below), calling that judgment 'rash and unjust.' But even if it is genuine, it is not one of the Festal Letters. On the genuine Festal Letters and the textual problems associated with them, see Quasten III 52–5.

16 Apuleius *Florida* 18
17 In his introduction to this letter Allen observes that at the end of the volume Erasmus prints a Latin translation of Athanasius' *First Letter to Serapion*, which (unlike recent scholars) he rejects as spurious on stylistic grounds and describes as the work of 'an idle man endowed with no intelligence who wanted to imitate Athanasius' letters to Serapion.' He then adds at the very end of the book a fragment of a treatise *Adversus omnes haereses*, 'which you would judge to be the work of a madman.' He breaks off this text abruptly after about half a page, with the remark 'I think this is enough to give you a taste.'
18 This is pseudo-Clement, edited by Johannes Sichardus as *Recognitionum libri x ad Iacobum fratrem Domini, Rufino Torano Aquileiense interprete. Cui accessit non poenitenda epistolarum pars vetustissimorum episcoporum, hactenus non visa, eorum*

servant to read them to me, for I find this a pleasant way in which to beguile
the interval between dinner and sleep. After a time we came on a letter of
pope Anterus.[19] I discovered that an interpolator had stitched several lines
on to it that he had taken, almost word for word, partly from Jerome's letter   75
to Heliodorus[20] and partly from the same author's letter to Nepotianus.[21] I
have no doubt that the work contained several other cases of the same sort,
for it was only by chance that I noticed this example. The substance of the
letter seems to have been taken from material in the *Catalogue of the Roman
Popes*, which records Anterus' ruling that bishops could move to another   80
church if the interests of their flock required it.[22] If I chose to examine every

* * * * *

qui ab hinc an. M.CC. Romanae ecclesiae praefuerunt ... Quibus vetustissimorum
episcoporum adiecimus epistolas perquam eruditas, annotatiunculis & argumentis a
Ioanne Sichardo illustratas ... (Basel: J. Bebelius 1526). Allen (74n) reports that
part 2 page 74 of this volume includes a letter ascribed to Anterus, pope for
only a month at the end of 235. At page 76D are sentences taken from two
letters of Jerome; see nn19–21 below.

19 The spurious letter of Pope Anterus is part of the False (or Pseudo-Isidorean)
Decretals (Ep 36 PL 130 148–9). Near the middle of the letter, the forger inserted two passages from the letters of Jerome, which Erasmus, whose own
edition of the letters of Jerome was one of his greatest achievements in the
field of patristic scholarship, easily recognized. The False Decretals, supposedly a collection of decretals issued by early popes but now believed to have
been forged in France during the mid-ninth century, are part of a collection
of texts attributed to Isidorus Mercator, who was incorrectly identified with
Isidore of Seville. This collection had recently been edited for the first time
by the Paris theologian Jacques Merlin *Tomus primus [Secundus tomus] quatuor
Conciliorum generalium* 2 vols (Paris: Jean Cornillau for Galiot du Pré 1524).
The genuineness of these texts was first seriously challenged in a general way
by the Lutheran historian Flacius Illyricus in the *Magdeburg Centuries* (1559).

20 Pseudo-Isidore PL 130 149B quotes from Jerome Ep 14.8 (cf CWE 61 113).
21 Pseudo-Isidore PL 130 148D–149A quotes from Jerome Ep 52.14 (cf CWE 61 143).
22 There are several lists of the names of the Roman popes, some of them going back to very early times; some of these also attempt to determine their
dates in office and to record a few events associated with each of them. Irenaeus *Adversus haereses* 3.3.2–3 traces the succession of the Roman bishops
from Linus to his own contemporary Eleutherus, but Irenaeus himself (bishop
of Lyon from about 177–8) predates Anterus (pope 235–6). Erasmus himself
edited Irenaeus' work in 1526; the dedicatory letter is Ep 1738. Eusebius *Historia ecclesiastica* provides no catalogue in list form but does trace the careers
of the Roman bishops. He briefly mentions Anterus, merely recording that he
succeeded Pontianus, held office for only a month before his death, and was
succeeded by Fabian (4.22.3). Other lists of the early popes were known in
the early sixteenth century. The oldest and best-known list goes from Peter

passage, there would be no end to my litany of complaints. I wish that, even at this late hour, the bishops, as a public duty, would concern themselves with this matter.[23]

Now back to Athanasius. You will recognize from his writings that the world in which he lived was not very different from our own. I only wish that he who rules the winds and the waves and scatters the unclean spirits of the air would bring a happy ending to our present turmoil.[24] Athanasius deserved to live in an age of peace and tranquillity; he would then have given us the marvellous fruit of his mind and of his eloquence, for he possessed that quality which Paul thought essential in a bishop – the ability to teach.[25] He speaks plainly, he is intelligent, sensible, and conscientious, in a word, he is ideally qualified to be a teacher. He has none of the heaviness that offends in Tertullian; there is nothing flashy as in Jerome; nothing laboured as in Hilary, nothing redundant as there is in Augustine and even in Chrysostom, nothing that smacks of the cadences of Isocrates or the

* * * * *

to Liberius (pope 352–66) and is often called the Liberian Catalogue. It survives in many manuscripts, none of which is complete. Erasmus could not have known a printed edition, and must have used a manuscript that contained the Anterus passage. The list of popes itself, without the related materials, seems to have been first edited by Petrus Crabbe in *Concilia omnia, tam generalia, quam particularia, ab apostolorum temporibus in hunc usque diem ...* 2 vols (Cologne: Petrus Quentel 1538). Another version was not printed until Johannes Cuspinianus included it in his *De consulibus Romanorum commentarii* (Basel: Johannes Oporinus 1553). The first relatively full edition was edited by A. Bucherius (Antwerp 1636) and this collection was subsequently sometimes known as the 'Bucherian Catalogue.' The fragments were first assembled into a complete text by Theodor Mommsen, who attributed the compilation to an anonymous 'Chronographer of 354': see 'Über den Chronographen vom Jahre 354' in *Abhandlungen der philologisch-historischen Klasse der königlich sächsischen Akademie der Wissenschaften* I (1850) 547–693; repr *Monumenta Germaniae Historica, Auctores Antiquissimi* IX-1 (1892) 13–196. The list was also edited by Louis Duchesne in *Le Liber pontificalis* (1886) rev ed, 3 vols (Paris 1955–7) I 1–9.

23 That is, with scholarly investigation of the question of forged documents (not Anterus' ruling on the translation of bishops).

24 Erasmus seems to bring together the Gospel accounts of Jesus' casting out of unclean spirits (Mark 5:8, Luke 4:36) with the notion that the devil is 'the prince of the power of the air' (Eph 2:2), ending with the wish that Christ will cast out the demons of conflict who are rending the church apart.

25 1 Tim 3:2; Titus 1:9. Erasmus used the Greek διδακτικόν for 'ability to teach.' His motive here was neither stylistic nor a concern to keep his meaning concealed but to repeat the precise word used in Paul's Epistle to Timothy.

studied artistry[26] of Lysias such as one finds in Gregory of Nazianzus. Instead he concentrates wholly on making his meaning clear. Please sample his work and give me your opinion. There is no one whose lead I would rather follow. May the Lord keep you safe and well.   100

Basel, 3 March AD 1527

1790A / From [Mercurino Gattinara]   [Valladolid, c 12 March 1527]

The imperial chancellor Gattinara was one of Erasmus' most influential admirers and intervened directly (Ep 1784A) to impose silence, or at least a certain discretion, on Erasmus' critics at Louvain. Nevertheless, while the two men agreed on many issues, Erasmus did not support the programme of a Hapsburg world monarchy that Gattinara favoured as the basis of the policy of Charles V, since he thought that its anti-French bias and its stark opposition to the temporal interests of the papacy in Italy would inevitably lead to a worsening of the wars and suspicions that already divided Christian Europe. Hence he did not take up Gattinara's proposal that he prepare an edition of Dante's pro-imperialist, anti-papal treatise *Monarchia*. A letter of 1529 to Alfonso de Valdés, imperial secretary for Latin correspondence and a close associate of Gattinara, makes it clear that Erasmus did not favour the idea of a universal monarchy of the sort upheld in Dante's political treatise, regarding it as contrary to the realities of his own time (Allen Ep 2126:21–40). Indeed, despite his great admiration for the Romans and his tendency to favour monarchical constitutions and to be suspicious of popular regimes, Erasmus had a generally negative view of the record of the ancient Roman emperors, whom he associated with tyranny and violence. See the long prefatory letter (Ep 586) to his edition of *Historiae Augustae scriptores* (Basel: Froben, June 1518), which he dedicated to the two Saxon dukes, the Elector Frederick and Duke George. Thus his coolness towards imperial world-monarchy was already on record. In some way, probably in a lost letter to Gattinara or to a close associate, he must have rejected the plan for him to publish *Monarchia*, for it is not mentioned again in any subsequent letter. A draft of this letter survived in the Spanish archives at Simancas and was first published by Marcel Bataillon in *Bulletin Hispanique* 26 (1924) 33. He based his attribution to Gattinara partly on the contents, partly on the fact that the manuscript is in the hand of Alfonso de Valdés, Latin secretary to the emperor, and partly on the mention of such a letter from Gattinara to Erasmus in Ep 1791:21. Allen's introduction

* * * * *

26 The Latin word is *compositio*. For this term see A.D. Leeman *Orationis ratio* (Amsterdam 1963) 32, 149–55, 307–9.

quotes from a letter of 12 March 1527 from Valdés to Maximilianus as further evidence of the letter's authorship, approximate date, and place of origin.

Cordial greetings. There are many things, dear Erasmus, that I would like you to know, but Valdés[1] will write about them. Recently I obtained a little work of Dante's, to which he gave the title *Monarchy*.[2] It was suppressed, I hear, by people who wished to seize monarchic rule for themselves. It was because of this that I first became interested in the work. Then when I   5 had sampled a few passages, I was deeply impressed by the author's talent. I would like to see the book published, since it would be helpful to the

* * * * *

1790A
1 Alfonso de Valdés (c 1500–32), who may have been privately tutored by the prominent Italian humanist Pietro Martire d'Anghiera, was the son of a Spanish noble family and accompanied the court of Charles v to Germany in 1520–1 as a member of the emperor's secretarial staff. He continued in service when the court returned to Spain and in February 1526 was appointed to the influential position of secretary for Latin correspondence. He became the most active partisan of Erasmus' interests at the imperial court. For example, he was the official who drafted Ep 1731, the emperor's letter warmly praising Erasmus. He also did what he could (but without success) to bring pressure on the emperor's officials in the Netherlands to pay Erasmus' pension as an imperial councillor. During the inquisitorial investigation in Spain into the orthodoxy of Erasmus' books in the spring of 1527, Valdés informed Erasmus of the proceedings that led to the Valladolid conference the following summer (Ep 1839). There are references in the correspondence (including in the present letter) to letters written to Erasmus that have not survived. Erasmus' first letter to Valdés is Allen Ep 1807.
2 Dante's political treatise *Monarchia*, written in 1312 or 1313, was a defence of the ideal of a universal monarchy as the promoter of peace, social justice, and true religion. It hailed the German emperor Henry vii (1308–13) as the contemporary embodiment of the Roman ideal and harshly criticized the medieval popes for attempting to extend their proper spiritual authority into a claim to supreme political authority as well. On its importance see *Monarchia* ed and trans Prue Shaw (Cambridge 1995), with Latin and English texts and a helpful introduction and bibliography; another recent version is by Richard Kay (Toronto: Pontifical Institute of Mediaeval Studies 1998). On Dante's political theories, see also several chapters in *Dante and Governance* ed John Woodhouse (Oxford 1997) and Quentin Skinner *The Foundations of Modern Political Thought* 2 vols (Cambridge 1978) I 16–18. After Erasmus' refusal to edit the work, it remained unpublished until 1559, when it was included in a collection of tracts concerning the Roman empire compiled by Andrea Alciati, *De formula Romani imperii* (Basel: Johannes Oporinus, October 1559), though in the interval it continued to circulate in manuscript among critics of papal policy.

emperor's cause. However, the copyists have left it in a corrupt state, so I thought it would be worth while sending it to you and asking you to read it when you have a spare moment. Then if you think it worth while, you   10 might correct it and have it printed. There is no one alive today to whom I would rather entrust this task. It will be up to you to publish or bury the book. I leave the decision in your hands. Farewell.

1791 / From Pedro Juan Olivar   Valladolid, 13 March [1527]

The opening page (or pages) of this letter, which may have contained a summary of the articles that the Spanish religious orders presented to the Inquisition as charges against Erasmus (cf lines 1–8), is missing from both the original manuscript at Wrocław and the earliest printed version (LB III-2 1858–9 *Appendix epistolarum* no 469). Erasmus had known for some time that in spite of (or because of) the growing interest in his books, which were being printed in both Latin and Castilian in Spain, some theologians and members of religious orders in that country were denouncing him. On this background see Ep 1742 introduction and the works of Bataillon and Homza cited there. In a letter of 2 September 1526 to his Saxon correspondent Simon Pistoris, Erasmus shows awareness of at least one attack on the Spanish translation of his *Enchiridion* (see Ep 1744 n20). A long letter (Ep 1814, dated 2 September 1528) from his admirer Juan de Vergara, secretary to Archbishop Alonso de Fonseca of Toledo, primate of Spain, informed Erasmus of the series of events that had led to the lodging of formal complaints by representatives of four religious orders. See Epp 1742 introduction, 1786 n5. Many letters of the spring and summer of 1527 trace the course of these events.

  Olivar (d 1533) was a native of Valencia. He studied Greek first at Alcalá and then at Paris with a nephew of the famous Hellenist Marcus Musurus. One of his other teachers at Paris was Lefèvre d'Etaples. He accompanied Charles v to the Netherlands in 1520 and matriculated at Louvain, where he met Erasmus. Next he spent three years in England before returning to Spain. At the time of this letter, he was close to the imperial chancellor, Mercurino Gattinara, the most powerful of Erasmus' sympathizers at the imperial court. He moved back to his native city of Valencia for a time but (perhaps because of the increasingly serious attacks on Erasmians in Spain) in 1535 moved to France. He made another visit to England in 1542, spent three years in the service of the prince-bishop of Liège, and died in 1553, probably not long after he dedicated a defence of the doctrine of the real presence of Christ in the Eucharist to the archbishop of Cologne.

... I am sending you, dear Erasmus, the twenty-one articles, all of them ridiculous, which those stalwart fellows have dreamed up among them-

selves.[1] The fools are attributing to you ideas that it would be wrong for a
Jew or a Turk to hold. They quote from the *Colloquies*, in which you speak
only through the mouth of fictional characters. One of the charges they make 5
against you is that you say in the *Colloquies* that there is no more sacred duty
than to support heretics, but they fail to notice that this was said by a character who is himself a heretic.[2] The letter you appended to the *Colloquies*
answers these people quite adequately.[3] I shall show it to the archbishop of
Seville[4] when they present their articles. They promise to do this on the third 10
Sunday in Lent, a date which they have set themselves and for which our
side is not prepared. In the meantime Valdés[5] and Coronel[6] are busy trying
to influence Toledo and Seville.[7] Toledo has promised you every support
and thinks you should keep your courage up. Seville takes the same position. The chancellor, Mercurino Gattinara, speaks of you often with hushed 15
reverence.[8] Recently, when I paid him a visit (he was suffering from gout),
he asked me if I had ever been a friend of yours; when I replied that I had,
though for a brief period, he burst out: 'Then, make no mistake, you enjoyed the friendship of a very great Christian and a very fine scholar, who

* * * * *

1791
1 The precise number seems uncertain. Erasmus' own *Apologia adversus monachos* (Basel: Froben 1528) seems to respond to twenty-two charges, but twenty
is the number specified by the authoritative recent article on the Valladolid
Conference; see Homza 84.
2 *Inquisitio de fide* 'An Examination concerning the Faith' CWE 39 431:7
3 His letter addressed to the reader, *De utilitate colloquiorum* 'The Usefulness of
the *Colloquies*,' added to the new edition of the *Colloquies* published in June
1526 and dated 21 May 1526; see CWE 40 1095–1117. He makes many of the
same arguments more briefly in Ep 1704.
4 Alonso Manrique de Lara, the inquisitor-general, who was generally favourable
to Erasmus' scholarly work and on friendly terms with the leading Spanish
Erasmians. On his decisive action in favour of the Spanish translation of Erasmus' *Enchiridion* in 1526, see Ep 1742 n4.
5 Alfonso de Valdés was the emperor's secretary for Latin correspondence and
the most energetic supporter of Erasmus at the imperial court. See Ep 1790A n1.
6 Luis Núñez Coronel was secretary to the inquisitor-general Manrique (n4
above), and therefore strategically placed to support Erasmus against the
charges lodged by representatives of the Spanish monastic orders and discussed by the theologians at Valladolid during the summer of 1527. On him
see Ep 1274 introduction.
7 That is, Alonso de Fonseca, who as archbishop of Toledo was primate of Spain,
to whom Valdés was close, and Manrique, archbishop of Seville and inquisitor-
general of Spain, whom Coronel served as secretary.
8 On the imperial chancellor's fervent admiration and support of Erasmus, see
Epp 1757, 1784A, 1785.

has always been a good friend of mine.' Valdés and Schepper[9] were present   20
at the time. The chancellor is writing you a letter now.

Coronel, Valdés, and Vergara[10] feel that you would help our cause if
you wrote to the very reverend Alonso Manrique, archbishop of Seville and
inquisitor-general. You should make clear the sincerity of your purpose –
and do so without delay, at the earliest possible moment.[11] I am surprised   25
you have not written to Coronel, for he is your staunchest supporter and
has great influence with the archbishop of Seville. Morillon sends his best
wishes; he too is writing to you.[12] Valdés sent me a letter of entreaty,[13] written in the vernacular in his most elegant style. He wants me to send him
the articles that have been compiled against you. He refers in the course of   30
the letter to your deeply Christian spirit and to the approval your writings
have won in every land and from the supreme pontiff and the college of
cardinals. I shall translate his letter into Latin and attach it, along with the
articles, to this account of our troubles.[14] You will then be able to appreciate

* * * * *

9 Like Valdés, Cornelis de Schepper was an imperial councillor and secretary
  and was very close to Gattinara. See Ep 1747 n23.
10 As secretary to the archbishop of Toledo, Juan de Vergara was one of the most
  strategically placed of Erasmus' Spanish admirers. See Ep 1786 n2.
11 Erasmus delayed in following this advice but did so on 26 August 1527 (Ep
  1864).
12 Guy Morillon (d 1548), a Burgundian who may have met Erasmus while studying and teaching in Paris early in the century, had settled at Brussels by 1515
  and had then moved to Spain, probably as secretary to the chancellor, Jean Le
  Sauvage. After the death of Le Sauvage in 1518, he became one of the secretaries to Charles v, accompanying him back to the Netherlands in 1522 and
  then remaining in Spain until 1531, when he moved to Louvain, where he
  spent most of the rest of his life. He corresponded frequently with Erasmus
  over a long period, though many of his letters are known only from references
  in other correspondence. He was helpful to Erasmus in the financial transactions arising from the latter's annuity at Courtrai. See Ep 532 introduction.
  The letter mentioned here, if it was in fact written, is lost.
13 Apparently this letter and the Latin translation that Olivar enclosed in the
  present letter are lost. The Latin phrase is *litteras petitorias*. Letters of entreaty
  are one of the classes of letters defined by ancient grammarians and also by
  medieval authorities on the *ars dictaminis*. Erasmus treats this topic in his *De
  conscribendis epistolis* 52 (CWE 25 172–82).
14 Olivar's Latin phrase is *in fine tragoediae* 'at the end of the tragedy,' by which
  he apparently means 'at the end of my account' of the melodrama. This phrase
  might mean at the end of this whole affair of the monastic orders' attack on
  Erasmus' orthodoxy, but his own words indicate that he plans to enclose the
  translation with this letter.

the man's modesty and the high value he attaches to everything you do. I   35
would venture to say that Valdés is more Erasmian than Erasmus (if I may
put it that way). He is writing to you – although all your correspondents are
referring you to this letter of mine on the ground that their style is more
barbarous or more wordy.[15]

Count Baldesar Castiglione, the papal nuncio, a man of some learn-   40
ing,[16] the Venetian scholar Navagero,[17] who has a fine command of both
Greek and Latin, and Andrea of Naples[18] are all constantly ranting about
your literary style. Italians cannot bear the thought that a single German has
humbled their pride. I never meet them without their immediately bringing
up the subject of Erasmus' style. 'Your friend Erasmus,' they say, 'has turned   45
from a Latin to a barbarian.' 'Your friend' is intended as an insult, because
my only boast is that I have you as my friend. They praise the artistry of
the *Moria*, calling it 'Lucianic.' They put you in the ring against Giovanni
Pontano,[19] who, so far as I can see from his writings, is an excellent scholar

* * * * *

15 Allen (35n) observes that this letter from Valdés, like all of the other letters
   which referred Erasmus to Olivar's account for details of the charges drawn
   up by the monastic orders, is lost.
16 The famous Mantuan humanist and diplomat (1478–1529), best known now for
   his *Book of the Courtier*, had been papal nuncio to the imperial court in Spain
   since 1525. He subsequently became involved in a bitter personal controversy
   with Valdés because of his sharp objection (both as a papal diplomat and as
   a Catholic) to Valdés' dialogue *Lactancio* which justified the imperial policies
   and denounced the papal policies that led to the infamous sack of Rome by the
   imperial army in May 1527. Castiglione wrote a denunciatory *Risposta a Valdés*.
   Valdés' own account of this conflict appears in a letter to Erasmus, Ep 2163.
   Here Olivar identifies him as one of the Italian critics who habitually carped
   at Erasmus' literary style. Stylistic preferences were one of the major points
   of dispute between Erasmus and the curial critics criticized in his dialogue
   Ciceronianus (1528).
17 Andrea Navagero (1483–1527), Venetian humanist and patrician, was historiographer and librarian at Venice from 1516 to 1523, a period during which
   he made important editorial contributions to Aldine editions of several major
   Latin authors. In 1523 the republic sent him as ambassador to the emperor, and
   in 1526 he became ambassador to France, though apparently he did not leave
   for France for some time; he died of plague in July 1527, soon after arriving
   at the French court.
18 Alessandro d'Andrea of Naples (documented 1527–57) was present at the imperial court (in what capacity is not made clear) and joined his fellow Italians
   in belittling Erasmus' literary achievement.
19 Pontano (1429–1503) was a highly regarded humanistic poet and satirist at
   Naples in the second half of the fifteenth century, especially admired for his
   love poems and his satirical prose dialogues written in a Lucianic spirit. He

Baldesar Castiglione
Portrait by Raphael, 1516
Louvre, Paris

but whose language is dreadfully affected. They claim that Erasmus' style   50
is nothing in comparison with his. I disagree: I contend that Erasmus is by
far the more eloquent, while Pontano is simply affected. Over the wine I
remarked on the pedantry of Pontano's *Actius*, a work in which he gives
a most pedantic account of the rhythmic patterns in Virgil's writing. They
admit that the man is more pedantic than he ought to be, but insist on his   55
learning. Whether they want to or not, they are compelled by my argument
to acknowledge your command of language and the fluency of your style.

You are being called a 'Dutchman'[20] by Benedetto Tagliacarne,[21] tutor to the sons of the king of France, a pretentious fellow like all Italians,
a mere Greek and Latin schoolmaster, devoid of learning, strong on impu-   60
dence, but totally lacking in judgment, although he is very knowledgeable
about the Tuscan language.[22] I took up the cudgels on your behalf and at-

* * * * *

was commonly regarded as a master of the Ciceronian style against which
Italian critics frequently measured Erasmus' Latin. See Ep 337:355n. Erasmus
referred to him from time to time, often criticizing him on the grounds that
he had an artificial Ciceronian style (Ep 531:496–8) and also because those
who praised him made him seem more 'Ciceronian' than Christian (Allen Ep
1885:122–41). His *Actius* (referred to below) is a work on the principles of
poetry, posthumously published in a collection of his prose works, *Opera omnia*
3 vols (Venice: Aldus 1518–19). In *Ciceronianus* Erasmus praised his style as
elegant but objected that one would hardly know from his works whether he
was a Christian; ASD I-2 699–700 / CWE 28 436–7.

20 The Latin is *Batavus*. Erasmus himself liked to play on the connotation of
Batavus as 'barbarous' or at least 'unrefined' or 'inelegant.' Cf Epp 996:45,
1629:11–12, 1635:9, 1652:13–15 (the last of these is a response by a Polish correspondent to Erasmus' diffident characterization of his own works as 'typi-
cally Dutch'). But he resented it when Christophe de Longueil (himself born
at Mechelen and reared in the Netherlands) made 'snide remarks about Dutch
rhetoric' when discussing Erasmus' works; see Ep 1706:7–8.

21 Italian humanist (d 1536) born at Sarzana near La Spezia. He served as secretary to the city of Genoa (1514–22) and then settled in France, where in 1524
he became tutor to the sons of the king of France. When the princes were sent
to Spain as hostages in 1526, Tagliacarne accompanied them and continued
as their tutor until their release in 1530. The king rewarded him with several
benefices, including in 1535 the bishopric of Grasse. In 1536 he published a
book of his *Poemata*.

22 The Latin phrase, *Hetrusca lingua*, could refer to the ancient Etruscan language,
but although a few Etruscan inscriptions had been known since the preceding
century, no one at this period knew much about the ancient language. Almost
certainly, Olivar is referring to a reputation for mastery of the Tuscan language, an attribute that would be important for the reputation of an Italian
poet.

tacked this impudent fellow vigorously. They are now saying (God help us!)
that Longueil (you know whom I mean) is the most eloquent of the 'Tramon-
tanes,' as they call them.[23] But surely everyone knows that Longueil, in his   65
ambition to be a Ciceronian, developed a number of affected mannerisms.
They will not allow that any 'Tramontane' can have success in poetry. To
this I have countered with an epigram or two of Thomas More's.[24]

Now, dear Erasmus, you have been brought up to date on the begin-
nings of our melodrama and also on the jealousy of the Italians. You will   70
get the whole story later. In the meantime do not permit the philosophy of
Christ, which has gained so much ground under your guidance, to suffer
decline. Rather, let these battles inspire you to loftier heights. Farewell, Erasmus, the pride of theologians everywhere. May God preserve you in your
old age to serve the Christian commonwealth.   75

Valladolid, 13 March

Signed by your devoted friend, Pedro Juan Olivar

The general of the Order for the Redemption of Captives,[25] an honest
and scholarly man who wields considerable influence, is a great supporter
of yours. Farewell again.   80

1792 / From Juan Luis Vives   Bruges, 18 March [1527]

On Vives see Epp 927, 1613, 1665, 1732. Erasmus' most recent surviving letter
to him is Ep 1531, dated 27 December 1524. There must have been one letter

* * * * *

23 Christophe de Longueil was frequently identified as the ideal 'Ciceronian' humanist, or at least the best of the non-Italian Ciceronian stylists.
24 Like Erasmus, his friend More had a taste for the concise and witty classical epigram and wrote or translated (from Greek into Latin) many of them.
   Erasmus took on the task of arranging publication, and they first appeared
   in print in a single volume containing three sections, each with its own title-
   page but with pagination consecutive throughout the volume: a reprinting of
   Utopia, More's epigrams (*Epigrammata clarissimi disertissimique viri Thomae Mori
   Britanni*), and the epigrams of Erasmus (Basel: Froben, March 1518). This volume was reprinted in December 1518 and again, with two of the poems by
   More dropped and eleven new ones added, by the same publisher in December 1520. See More CW III-2 3–9 (introduction); the texts, with Latin (or Greek)
   and English on facing pages, appear on pp 78–305; commentary follows.
25 Benet Safont (d 1535) of Barcelona had been general of the Trinitarian order
   (officially known as the Order of the Most Holy Trinity for the Redemption of
   Captives) since 1520. The special purpose of this order was to ransom Christians who had become prisoners of the Muslims as a result of war or piracy.
   It was important in Spain because of the frequent loss of Christian captives
   to the Barbary states of western North Africa.

in early 1526, for Vives refers to it in Ep 1665, written from Bruges on 14 February 1526. That letter indicates that the missing letter contained the usual complaints about the dishonesty of the bookseller Franz Birckmann and that it confirmed the bad news that for financial reasons Froben had refused to publish a collection of Vives' works that the author had submitted to the press with the aid of Erasmus (see Ep 1613). In Ep 1732, written to Erasmus on 6 August 1526, Vives refers to a long letter (not extant) that he had sent from Britain and complains that he has received no reply and he has had 'no word from you for a long time.' Erasmus replied to this letter on 29 May (Ep 1830), and it was first published in Vives' *Opera* (1555).

VIVES TO ERASMUS

While I was waiting every day for a letter from you, almost an age has gone by, and while hoping for something from you to which I could reply, I have missed many an opportunity to write. In fact, I have already written two or three times and am now beginning to feel uneasy about your silence; either 5 my letters have not been delivered or you are overwhelmed with work. This or something else must be the reason you did not write. But none of that matters if you are in good health and have not forgotten me entirely. If you remember me and keep a place for me in your heart, that is enough for me. That you should demonstrate your feelings by sending me a letter as a sort 10 of affidavit, that does not matter to me at all.

I do not know what news you have from Paris about your affairs. The dean says he got a letter from you,[1] in which you bewail what is happening here.[2] But all the university people who come here from Paris testify to the great esteem in which you are held by everyone, even by those who 15 used to hate you most bitterly. In Spain your *Enchiridion* has begun to speak our language[3] and with the full approval of the people whom the brothers[4]

* * * * *

1792
1 Marcus Laurinus, dean of St Donatian's at Bruges. See Epp 1695 n6, 1769. Erasmus' letter to him is not extant.
2 Vives uses a Greek phrase in order to ensure privacy in case anyone might open and read the letter in transit. The reference is to Erasmus' complaints about events in Paris, probably about the continuing attacks on his orthodoxy by members of the faculty of theology.
3 A reference to the publication of a Spanish translation of this work, which became one of the principal sources for the growth of enthusiasm for Erasmus' works, especially those dealing with spiritual life, in Spain during the 1520s. See Ep 1742 introduction and nn4, 7, 8.
4 Vives' text uses the Greek word for 'brothers.' Representatives of the monastic orders were the ones who formulated and officially brought before the

used to keep under their thumb. There is talk now of doing the same for the
Paraphrases.[5]

Some people cannot understand why you don't move to this country,[6]   20
or at least to France, where your life could be more pleasant. You know why
I say this:[7] I want you to have peace and quiet in your old age. For if you
are happy and content, religion and letters will have much to gain from
what remains of your life, but if you are worried and anxious, very little
will come of it.   25

If you see any of the books I have published in your absence,[8] please,
dear master, write and give me your opinion of them, or rather, act like a

* * * * *

Inquisition the charges against Erasmus' orthodoxy that led to the hearing
and debate about his works at the Valladolid conference in the summer of
1527.

5 The printer Miguel de Eguía of Alcalá published Latin editions of each of Erasmus' paraphrases on the four Gospels between 30 June and 24 November and
(apparently shortly afterwards) also an edition (of which no copy survives) of
the paraphrases on the Epistles. Despite what Vives writes here, none of Erasmus' paraphrases on books of the New Testament was translated into Spanish
at this period; see Bataillon (1991) I 175–6, 304.

6 A number of Erasmus' friends in the Netherlands urged Erasmus move back
to his native region, and the imperial government in the provinces stubbornly
refused to consider making payments on his pension as an imperial councillor
unless he returned. This issue is a frequent topic in the correspondence; see
Epp 1380 introduction, 1700 n3.

7 Vives' use of two phrases in Greek appears to derive from stylistic considerations and humanist fashion rather than from the usual concern that anyone
who intercepted the letter would be able to read sensitive material.

8 Vives was a prolific author. Since Erasmus' departure from the Netherlands in
October 1521, and excluding works published by Froben at Basel (which Erasmus would have seen while arranging for their publication), first editions of
Vives' works up to the date of this letter included: *In sapientem praelectio* (Louvain 1522), *De Europae statu ac tumultibus* (Louvain 1522), *Veritas fucata sive de
licentia poetica* (Louvain: Dirk Martens, January 1523; NK 2175), *Satellitium animi* (Louvain 1524), *Institutio feminae christianae* (Antwerp: Michael Hillen 1524;
NK 2167), *Introductio ad sapientiam* (Louvain: Petrus Martens 1524; NK 2168), *De
conditione vitae christianorum sub Turca* (Ypres 1526), *De Europae dissidiis et bello
Turcico* (Bruges: Hubertus de Croock, December 1526; NK 2164), *De subventione
pauperum* (Bruges: Hubertus de Croock, 17 March 1526; NK 4066). The bibliography of Vives' publications seems rather muddled. The preceding list is
based partly on the two lists of his works in Carlos Noreña *Juan Luis Vives* trans
(from English) Antonio Pintor-Ramos (Madrid 1978) 347–56 and partly on entries in Wouter Nijhoff and M.E. Kronenberg eds *Nederlandsche bibliographie van
1500 tot 1540* 3 vols in 7 (The Hague 1923–61). The Nijhoff-Kronenberg entries,

teacher or a father and send me your criticisms and advice, for I can think of nothing more helpful than criticism from a wise friend. Indeed, even criticism from a foolish or hostile person does no harm. I wish you were 30 closer at hand, so that I could consult you as an oracle.

If it is the Lord's will, I shall leave shortly for Britain.[9] If there is anything you would like me to do, just say so and it will be done. If you have nothing specific to request, I have a general idea about what you want – there is no need to explain. Look after your health and do not cease to love me. 35 Sincere and respectful greetings from your friends Laurinus and Fevijn.[10] Farewell.

Bruges, 18 March [1517]

1792A / To Conradus Pellicanus   Basel, [c 18 March 1527]

This letter has been redated on the basis of internal evidence and moved from Ep 1644, where Allen placed it because of its apparent connection with the angry exchange of letters between Pellicanus and Erasmus, who believed that Pellicanus was one of several former friends who not only had embraced the Reformation but also claimed his authority in support of the Sacramentarian eucharistic theology of Zwingli and Oecolampadius. See Epp 1637–40. Allen's evidence for the date 'early November 1525' is based on what seemed to be a reference in lines 4–5 to the circulation of the very private Ep 1637, which Erasmus wrote entirely in his own hand and in which he poured forth his anger against his former associate. But Allen's date is incompatible with lines 29–30, where Erasmus refers to a work by Oecolampadius that he calls *De Eucharistia* and describes as 'a reply to Willibald.' Allen assumed that this is a reference to Oecolampadius' first and most influential eucharistic tract, *De genuina Verborum Domini, Hoc est corpus meum ... expositione* [Strasbourg: no publisher, mid-September 1525?]. It is possible that Erasmus might have referred to that

* * * * *

which assign a serial number to each edition and rest on actual inspection of a copy of the book, are more certain. The list includes two highly influential books, *Institutio feminae christianae* and *De subventione pauperum*.
9 Vives did not actually make his intended trip to England until April 1527. For a time he became tutor to Princess Mary, but he lost favour with the king and Cardinal Wolsey on account of his support for Queen Catherine in the matter of the royal divorce and was held under house arrest from 25 February to 1 April 1528, when he was released and allowed to return to Bruges.
10 On Laurinus, see n1 above. Jan van Fevijn was canon of St Donatian's and from about 1523 scholaster of the chapter, the person in charge of the chapter's highly regarded grammar school; see Ep 1012 introduction.

publication as *De eucharistia*, since its subject is indeed the Eucharist; but the phrase *de eucharistia* does not appear in the title, *Genuina expositio* would be a more likely short title for the work, and Willibald Pirckheimer is not its target. Oecolampadius published another work, however, in two parts, as a result of a controversy with his former friend Willibald Pirckheimer, who had responded to *Genuina expositio* (see Ep 1717 n1). The first part of Oecolampadius' reply to Pirckheimer is *Ioannis Oecolampadii ad Billibaldum Pyrkaimerum de re Eucharistiae responsio* (Zürich: Christoph Froschauer 1526); the second is *Ad Bilibaldum Pykraimerum [sic] de Eucharistia, Ioannis Husschin, cui ab aequalibus a prima adolescentia Oecolampadio nomen obuenit, Responsio posterior* (Basel: Andreas Cratander, March 1527). The first of the works against Pirckheimer was completed by 20 June 1526, printed by 11 August, and actually released for sale in September. Its title contains the phrase *de re eucharistiae*. Oecolampadius' second reply to Pirckheimer, which is actually called *De Eucharistia* on its title-page, was published in March 1527 (no later than 18 March). Furthermore, it was printed at Basel, where Erasmus, closely linked to the rival printing firm of Froben, must have had good intelligence of local publications on topics that concerned him. Thus the present letter is probably a direct and prompt reaction to Oecolampadius' most recent publication. On these publications see Ernst Staehelin 'Oekolampad-Bibliographie' *Basler Zeitschrift für Geschichte und Altertumskunde* 17 (1918) 1–119, items 131, 140 and *Das theologische Lebenswerk Johannes Oekolampads* (Leipzig 1939) 276–7, 301–7.

A date as late as 1527 would also harmonize with the last paragraph of this letter, where Erasmus expresses his expectation (or hope) that the Basel city council 'will not be silly enough to expel everyone who disagrees with Oecolampadius.' In 1525 the city council, after taking advice from Erasmus himself and his close friends Ludwig Baer, Bonifacius Amerbach, and Claudius Cantiuncula (Ep 1636), created a system of press censorship in order to suppress Sacramentarian books. Probably for this reason, Oecolampadius chose to publish both his *Genuina expositio* of 1525 and the earlier of his two works against Pirckheimer abroad in order to evade the censorship. His second work against Pirckheimer, however, could be published in Basel in March of 1527 because by that date the council had lifted its censorship and had become increasingly favourable to Sacramentarian views. Thus by March 1527, the most likely date of the present letter, Erasmus might well wonder whether the city council would be 'silly enough' to expel persons who disagreed with Oecolampadius, the most influential preacher in the city.

As is the case with Epp 1637 and 1640, Erasmus published this letter in his *Opus epistolarum* (1529), no doubt because it clearly documented his rejection of the Sacramentarian position on the nature of Christ's presence in the Eucharist.

ERASMUS OF ROTTERDAM TO CONRADUS PELLICANUS, GREETING
I thank you a hundredfold for the gift of five figs.[1] I hope for your sake
that all your friends are still safe. For myself, it is enough if I give no one
just cause for growling at me. I would be happy if that letter had not been
circulated;[2] I assure you, I had nothing to do with it. Yet one way or an-   5
other a false and dangerous rumour had to be scotched. Some people are
angry at the four counsellors;[3] and now, I hear, a letter is going the rounds

* * * * *

1792A
1 This worthless 'gift' could have been a printed pamphlet containing Epp 1637–
  9, a sharp and intensely personal exchange of letters, in the first of which Erasmus denounced Pellicanus for telling Jan Łaski and others that Pellicanus'
  own eucharistic doctrine stemmed directly from what Erasmus had taught
  him and that Erasmus privately agreed with his opinion, while in the second and third letters Pellicanus defended both his own integrity and the correctness of his theology of the Eucharist. Erasmus suspected that Pellicanus
  was responsible for one or both of these pamphlets (published without date
  or name of place or publisher, but probably in 1526) that made their correspondence public. See Ep 1637 introduction. But in view of the redating
  of the present letter to 1527, the 'gift of five figs' seems more likely to refer to a copy of the vernacular pamphlet opposing Erasmus on eucharistic
  doctrine that had been published by Leo Jud of Zürich in the summer of
  1526. Erasmus had received a copy sometime in August of that year. Pellicanus and Jud were living in Zürich and working together as leaders of
  the Reformation there, and Pellicanus may have played a role in transmitting to Erasmus a copy of Jud's book and of his sharply critical letter (now
  lost); see Epp 1737 introduction and n1, 1741 introduction and n2, 1744 n3.
  It is also possible that in some way Erasmus connected Pellicanus with the
  appearance of Oecolampadius' just-published second pamphlet on eucharistic doctrine against Pirckheimer. This, however, is not very likely, since Pellicanus was living in Zürich while Oecolampadius himself lived in Basel and
  had published the pamphlet with a Basel publisher; so a middleman living
  in another city was not needed in order to communicate this publication to
  Erasmus.
2 This might refer to Erasmus' Ep 1637 to Pellicanus and Pellicanus' two replies
  (Epp 1638, 1639). More likely, however, 'that letter' is a letter (not extant) from
  Leo Jud to Erasmus, even more harshly critical of him than Jud's printed vernacular pamphlet. See the preceding note. Erasmus suspected (though without justification) that Pellicanus, not Jud, was the real author of the pamphlet
  and perhaps also of the even harsher letter. The letter was never published
  and is now lost, but that does not prove that Jud (or Pellicanus, as Erasmus
  suspected) did not circulate it in manuscript among select friends.
3 Apparently the four experts consulted by the Basel city council in 1525 about
  the first major tract on the Eucharist published by Johannes Oecolampadius,
  De genuina verborum Domini, concerning whether the work should be allowed

that is weakening their influence[4] (people suspect that Capito is responsible).[5] I hear too that a defamatory pamphlet is being prepared against them.[6]
Such is the fine work of the Evangelicals! I have not been consulted about   10
anything except whether there was any reason why Oecolampadius' book
should not be sold in public. I gave my reply,[7] without saying anything
derogatory about Oecolampadius. In presenting his views, he did not follow my advice. In fact, he treated me with complete contempt. So if he has
offended some people or is afraid, I see no reason why I should struggle   15
with my conscience on his behalf.

What is all this threatening talk about having me banished? Is it because I refuse to abandon the official position and general consensus of the
church, since no one has persuaded me to think differently? You fight like
gladiators among yourselves: Zwingli and Oecolampadius against Luther   20
and Bugenhagen,[8] Balthasar against all of them,[9] and Farel against you.[10]
Do you want me to join such a fractious clique at the risk of my life, or
rather of my soul? If any harm comes to you, you will have no one to blame
but yourselves. I have always prophesied that a drama of this sort could not

* * * * *

to be sold within the city. See the introduction to this letter and Ep 1636
  introduction.
4 This appears to be a rebuttal of Erasmus' letter of about 15 October (Ep 1637),
  criticizing the Sacramentarian opinions of Conradus Pellicanus; see Ep 1674
  n25.
5 On Capito see Ep 1674 n24.
6 The defamatory pamphlet mentioned in Ep 1674:78–9 (where Capito is named
  as the probable author) is probably the anonymous *Maynung von Nachtmal
  Christi*, which was written by Leo Jud; see n26 there. Erasmus refers here to a
  rumour that a pamphlet directed against those who had advised the Catholic
  members of the Basel city council on religious policy (probably chiefly concerning the Eucharist) was under preparation. No such pamphlet is known.
7 See Ep 1636, addressed in 1525 to the city council of Basel.
8 Erasmus frequently made critical reference to the bitter sectarian divisions
  among the Reformers, especially between the Reformed (Sacramentarian) and
  Lutheran leaders whose names he mentions.
9 Balthasar Hubmaier, the Anabaptist leader at Waldshut. See Ep 1540 n4.
10 Unlike the preceding disputes, a quarrel between two supporters of the Sacramentarian viewpoint like Pellicanus and Farel was not to be expected. Farel's
   collective biographers, the Comité Farel list no tract against Pellicanus among
   his works; see *Guillaume Farel, 1489–1565: Biographie nouvelle* (Neuchâtel 1930;
   repr Geneva 1978) 37–9. Farel was, however, a very combative individual,
   and perhaps Erasmus had heard gossip of some discord between him and
   Pellicanus.

hope to have a happy ending. Zwingli somewhere cites a passage from a   25
Paraphrase of mine.[11] Does he now think well of me, this man who previously described me as an ignoramus?[12] I am told that in a sermon Oecolampadius made some disparaging remarks about 'the orator,' meaning me, or so
people generally understand the reference.[13] He criticizes me also in his *De
eucharistia*, which is a reply to Willibald.[14] In his preface to Isaiah he smoth-   30
ers me with invidious compliments.[15] He takes me to task in his commentary on the Epistle of John,[16] suppressing my name but quoting my actual
words, though I had altered the passage in question. Moreover, his interpretation of my words is somewhat disingenuous: I had written 'How many
"worlds" we have here!' meaning to imply that the letter was John's since he   35
is fond of this kind of repetition. He understands the remark as a criticism
of the writer's excessive prolixity. A fine friend he is! Is it to please him that
I am supposed to profess a doctrine that Luther considered heretical? How
neatly Zwingli quotes the passage in which I use the word 'consecrate'![17]
And yet he implies that I mean something different from what I say.   40

* * * * *

11 Allen Ep 1644:23n refers to Zwingli *Subsidium de Eucharistia* (Zürich: Christoph
   Froschauer 1525), which discusses 1 Cor 10:16.
12 Allen Ep 1644:24n observes that such a description of Erasmus is highly unlikely, since Zwingli's references to Erasmus at this period 'are uniformly
   polite and sincere.'
13 The specific sermon seems not to be identifiable, but Oecolampadius had already criticized Erasmus' *De libero arbitrio* in sermons. See Ep 1526:231.
14 Allen Ep 1644 introduction and line 26n interprets this as a reference to Oecolampadius' first treatise on the Eucharist, *De genuina Verborum Domini ... expositione*, probably published at Strasbourg in September 1525. But it seems certain that Erasmus has in mind two later works directed against Pirckheimer,
   probably the second one, *Ad Bilibaldum Pykraimerum [sic] de Eucharistia*, since
   the precise phrase used here by Erasmus, *de eucharistia*, appears on the title
   page. See the introduction to this letter.
15 Cf Ep 1538 n1.
16 *In epistolam Ioannis apostoli catholicam primam, Ioannis Oecolampadii demegoriae,
   hoc est homiliae una et xx* (Basel: Andreas Cratander 1524), reprinted by the
   same printer in 1525 and also at Nürnberg by Johannes Petreius in 1524.
17 Zwingli published several tracts on the Eucharist. Erasmus may have had in
   mind his *Subsidium sive coronis de eucharistia* (Zürich: Christoph Froschauer
   1525), where the author refers to Erasmus' *Paraphrasis in omneis epistolas apostolicas* in support of his non-literal way of interpreting biblical passages relevant to eucharistic theology. See *Huldreich Zwinglis sämtliche Werke* ed Emil
   Egli and others, Corpus Reformatorum vol 91, IV (Berlin 1927; repr Zürich
   1982) 489.

I think the council here will not be silly enough to expel everyone who disagrees with Oecolampadius. There was nothing in your letter that I did not find deeply offensive. Farewell.

Basel, [1526]

1793 / From Bernhard von Cles   Prague, 20 March 1527

> Erasmus had dedicated his edition of St Irenaeus *Adversus haereses* to Bernhard von Cles, prince-bishop of Trent, the preceding August (Ep 1738) and on 26 September had sent him a letter enclosing a copy so freshly printed that it could not be bound for formal presentation (Ep 1755). The bishop was delighted, but his associate Johannes Fabri, who had encouraged the dedication (Ep 1739), had become distressed when by 20 December Erasmus still had not followed up with a copy suitably bound for presentation to a patron of high rank. Apparently Fabri had tried to make up for this failure by having the preliminary copy bound and presenting it to Bernhard, but the bishop had seen through the deception, and there was no letter from the author to accompany it (see Fabri's letter of complaint to Erasmus, Ep 1771). Evidently in the letter from Erasmus that is mentioned here but is now lost, Erasmus had informed the bishop that a properly bound and gilt copy was on its way. At the date of the present letter, only his letter, not the presentation copy itself, had reached Prague, where Fabri and Bishop Bernhard were attending the court of Archduke Ferdinand. In spite of this, Bishop Bernhard was delighted that Erasmus had dedicated an important patristic edition to him, and he had already sent, not a 'little gift of money,' as he describes it here, but a substantial cash gift. See Ep 1738 introduction. His manuscript letter remained unpublished until Förstemann and Günther discovered it at Leipzig and published it in their collection of Erasmus letters in 1904. On Bernhard see also Epp 1357, 1689.

Venerable father in Christ, distinguished sir, dearly beloved friend, etc. We received your letter and were pleased to learn that our letter reached you with the little gift of money. The money was not intended as a reward, but as an expression of our sincere affection for you. The book you dedicated to us was duly presented by Johannes Fabri and we value it highly. We have 5 not yet seen the gilt copy which you say you sent at the same time as the letter, but we expect it will come soon. We shall always be ready to do your pleasure so far as it lies within our power. I am delighted at the letter you received from his imperial Majesty. I am sure his sacred Majesty will be better than his word and will go beyond what he has promised. 10

Prague, 20 March 1527

Bernhard, by the grace of God bishop of Trent

To the venerable father in Christ, Erasmus of Rotterdam, his distinguished and dearly beloved friend, doctor of sacred theology. In Basel

1794 / To Guillaume Budé   Basel, 23 March 1527

> The most recent surviving letter between Erasmus and Budé is Erasmus' Ep 1619, dated 2 October 1525, though there may have been intervening letters of which no trace survives. Quite typical of the polite but not entirely trusting relationship between Erasmus and the great French humanist is Erasmus' request here that in some of his books that he judges to be most significant, Budé should 'find a place, not for a compliment to me, but for some indication of your good will.' This request is justified by reference to reports that some (unspecified) persons suspect that Budé harbours 'less than friendly' feelings towards Erasmus. In fact their previous correspondence seems to reflect a certain reserve on Budé's part. This was somewhat evident when he tried to calm the open quarrel between Erasmus and Lefèvre d'Etaples in 1518–19, and even more obvious when at the order of King Francis I he tried in 1523–4 to persuade Erasmus to settle in France under the king's patronage (Epp 1439, 1446). This letter was included in Erasmus' *Opus epistolarum*; obviously he did not object to publication of his request for a friendly statement from Budé. Erasmus also published Budé's reply, Ep 1812.

ERASMUS OF ROTTERDAM TO GUILLAUME BUDÉ, GREETING

Jacques Toussain's letter[1] brought me news that delighted me greatly, for I learned from it that you have at last begun to do what I have long wanted you to do, namely to give to the world your observations on the Greek and Latin languages,[2] which you have gathered from your long and careful 5

* * * * *

1794
1 Toussain, a disciple and close friend of Budé, probably never met Erasmus but had become an admirer of his. With Budé's encouragement (Ep 810) he opened a correspondence with Erasmus in 1518, of which Ep 1713, from Erasmus to Toussain, is the earliest surviving example. The letter to which Erasmus refers is not extant.
2 Budé pointed out in his reply that his planned philological work dealt almost exclusively with Greek words, not with both languages (Allen Ep 1812:3). He suggested that because of friendship Toussain had exaggerated the scope and importance of his work. Budé wrote that he was already at work on the book when he was called into the king's service in 1519 (Allen Ep 1812:31–2). It was finally published as *Commentarii linguae graecae* in 1529 (Paris: Josse Bade).

Guillaume Budé
Portrait drawing by Jean Clouet, c 1535
Musée Condé, Chantilly
Photo Giraudon

reading of the best authors. I have no doubt the work will prove useful to students of both languages. I am pleased to hear that Janus Lascaris is now staying with you.[3] I could wish that the chains that tie him to your house were more pleasant:[4] now that old age approaches, I hear he has to battle with the gout.   10

I have just published the fourth edition of my New Testament with the Annotations.[5] On looking it over, I see that I have made highly complimentary references to yourself in several places.[6] I know that you deserve more praise than this and that the sun of your glory needs nothing from the light of my little lamp. In fact, I shall not deny that my writings have been made   15 somewhat brighter by the splendour of your name. So I have no reason to beg a favour in return, and yet I wish that in some of your writings, especially in those that you expect to live on and enjoy a wide circulation, you would find a place, not for a compliment to me, but for some indication of your good will, for there are people who suspect you of less than friendly   20 feelings towards me. I should like this suspicion to be dispelled completely, not just for our sake, but for the general reputation of learning. It matters greatly for the advancement of scholarship that those who are engaged in this enterprise be united in mutual good will.

I hear that the most Christian king is giving his backing to liberal   25 studies.[7] If you people 'cheer on the runner' (as the saying goes),[8] I am sure things will turn out well. Believe me, nothing dims the lustre of your university more than the fact that young people have scarcely had their first taste of grammar before they are whisked off to the study of sophistic and of those

* * * * *

3 See Ep 1733 n17.
4 Horace *Odes* 4.11.23–4. Horace writes 'bound with pleasant chains,' *grata compede vinctum*; Erasmus uses the comparative form of the adjective, *gratiore compede vinctum*, which could also mean 'rather pleasant,' much the same as Horace's original word.
5 This edition of the New Testament was published by Froben in March 1527; on its textual importance see Ep 1571 n9.
6 In his notes on Luke 1:4 and 16:26 LB VI 299 n25.
7 See the report in Ep 1795 that King Francis had commissioned Lefèvre and Gérard Roussel to translate Chrysostom's commentaries on the Acts of the Apostles into Latin. The reference could also apply more generally to the king's long-discussed plan to create a centre for humanistic studies in Paris, partially realized in 1530 with the appointment of two *lecteurs royaux* for Greek (one of them being Jacques Toussain) and two for Hebrew. Toussain had already received a promise of his appointment by 1526; see his letter of 29 June 1527, Allen Ep 1842:26–8.
8 *Adagia* I ii 46

subjects that arm them for the arena of the schoolmen. Such studies, it is true,   30
help to develop powers of judgment. But knowledge of languages is simply indispensable. Many people, with no knowledge of logic, make correct
judgments. But without a familiarity with languages no one can understand
what he hears or reads. There will be protests at the start, but soon the fuss
will die down. The young are all eager. Older people who protest in public   35
secretly aspire to this new learning. We can observe this in the writings of
Hoogstraten, whose style improves with every publication. The same can be
said of Cousturier and Béda. Even Clichtove is much more polished than he
used to be. And Latomus is not contemptuous of every elegance of style.[9]

Longueil was taken from us before his time.[10] He left behind a great   40
reputation in Italy as a Ciceronian.[11] But I see no one emerging there who
really resembles Cicero except superficially and by the use of a few chosen expressions. The man who makes me feel the whole spirit of Cicero,
he is the real Ciceronian. At Rome there is a whole coterie of savants who
can scarcely tolerate hearing a German or a Frenchman mentioned.[12] Their   45
director and cheerleader is someone not unknown to you;[13] and just as no
homage is too great to satisfy him, so he cannot abide anyone being praised,
either god or man, except himself. These people have become more hostile towards me since, somewhere in a letter I wrote you, I said that you
can stand comparison with men like Ermolao Barbaro or even Pliny. But   50
the greater their hostility, the more tightly we should wrap ourselves in the
bonds of friendship. Farewell.

Basel, 23 March 1527

* * * * *

9 Erasmus here attributes to his most severe scholastic critics (even Cousturier,
   whom he usually presents as a totally incompetent fool) a tendency to exercise
   greater care to write a good Latin style than they had shown in earlier years.
   Of the group, Hoogstraten was the only one with whom Erasmus seems to
   have established a reasonably civil relationship; see Ep 1775 n5.
10 The leading non-Italian representative of the 'Ciceronian' tendency within humanism had died in September 1522. On him, see Epp 1675 nn7, 12, 1706 nn2,
   4, 5, 6, 9. Budé had enjoyed better relations with him than Erasmus had.
11 On Erasmus' dislike for the Italian 'Ciceronians' see Epp 1701 n6, 1717 n2.
12 Like many other non-Italian humanists, Erasmus resented the casual assumption of superiority expressed by many Italian humanists.
13 Erasmus clearly had Girolamo Aleandro in mind, though Allen (46n) observes
   that Budé mistook the reference and assumed that Erasmus meant the professor of Greek at the curial university, Pietro Alcionio, to whose criticism of
   French and German humanists Budé had responded in print; see Allen Ep
   1812:120n. On Erasmus' alienation from his former friend Aleandro, see Epp
   1553 n9, 1660 n9, 1717 nn3, 17, 18.

1795 / To Jacques Lefèvre d'Etaples Basel, 24 March 1527

Relations between Erasmus and this leading French humanist always remained
somewhat distant after their nasty public quarrel in 1517–18 over the interpretation of a passage in the Epistle to the Hebrews (Epp 597:37n, 607:2–14, 724,
778:59–381, 810, 813). Despite this incident, Erasmus continued to hold Lefèvre
in high regard. In this letter, he offers encouragement and support for a plan
to translate and publish some of Chrysostom's works, a plan he had learned
about in a letter (now lost) from Germain de Brie. There seems to be no evidence that the proposed translation was made or that if made, it was ever
published. Erasmus published this letter in *Opus epistolarum* and probably dispatched it together with Ep 1794 to Budé. Erasmus' *Apologia ad Iacobum Fabrum
Stapulensem* (Louvain: Dick Martens, 1517) is available in a critical edition, ASD
IX-3, and there is an English translation by Howard Jones in CWE 83:1–107.

ERASMUS OF ROTTERDAM TO JACQUES LEFÈVRE, GREETING
I hear that the most Christian king has charged you and your friend Gérard
Roussel[1] with the task of translating into Latin the commentaries of Chrysostom on the Acts of the Apostles.[2] Some time ago I acquired from Venice a
manuscript of that work written in an elegant script.[3] There is also another 5
in England. A year has now passed since I started to translate it. But I began
to doubt the authenticity of the ascription and so set it aside. Now when I
was publishing some other translations from Chrysostom, I added three of
the homilies that I had translated earlier.[4] My idea was to provide scholars

* * * * *

1795
1 On this disciple of Lefèvre, now serving as confessor and almoner to Margaret
  of Angoulême, see Ep 1407 n22.
2 Allen (1n) plausibly suggests that this translation project had been proposed
  to the king in hopes of gaining financial support. Though Francis I may have
  given his approval, no publication resulted, probably because the king's money
  at this time was more committed to preparations for renewed war against the
  emperor than to subsidizing patristic scholarship. The source of Erasmus' information, the humanist Germain de Brie, had himself recently published a
  new Latin translation of Chrysostom's *De sacerdotio*; see Ep 1733 introduction
  and Erasmus' reply, Ep 1736. Erasmus was about to publish an edition of several works of the patristic saint, *Chrysostomi lucubrationes* (see the dedicatory
  epistle, Ep 1800) and in 1530 brought out a full edition of Chrysostom's *Opera*
  in five volumes.
3 On this manuscript see Epp 1661 nn2, 6; 1705 n3.
4 This reference to his publication of other collections of the works of Chrysostom probably does not concern three short works published together in

with a sample; I would then decide on the basis of their reaction whether 10
to complete the work or abandon it. I had already done this when I learned
from Brie's letter[5] what I have just mentioned. If the letter had come a month
earlier, I would have sent you what I had translated and willingly resigned
to you all interest in the matter. As it is, if you would like, I shall make
what I have published available to you. I should not want this coincidence 15
to hold you back from your fine project. In addition to the homilies that I
have just published, I also have Chrysostom's commentaries on the Epistle
to the Romans, on both Epistles to the Corinthians, and on the Epistle to the
Galatians. These, however, will prove less interesting, since almost everything in Chrysostom, except his digressions, is in Theophylact.[6] I pray your 20
old age may be blessed with peace and quiet. Give my very best wishes
to your friend Roussel; and commend me most cordially to your excellent
bishop.[7]

Basel, 24 March 1527

1796 / To Polidoro Virgilio   Basel, 24 March 1527

On this prominent Italian humanist, historiographer to the English royal court,
see Epp 1666, 1702. Virgilio's dissatisfaction with the quality of the work
of the Froben press in its edition of two of his works caused some strain
in their relations, but in general he and Erasmus remained good friends.
Erasmus had dedicated to Virgilio a Greek-Latin edition of two homilies of
St John Chrysostom on the Epistle to the Philippians in August 1526 (Ep

* * * * *

August 1526, since only two of these are homilies and in the case of the third,
the Greek text is unaccompanied by a Latin translation; see Ep 1734 introduction. He may have in mind the *Lucubrationes* (see n2 above) or possibly an already printed Latin edition of six homilies, *Conciunculae perquam elegantes sex
de fato et providentia Dei* (Basel: Froben, February 1526).
5 Not extant; perhaps a reply to Ep 1736
6 On this commentator, whom Erasmus had identified as a medieval Bulgarian
patriarch rather than a patristic commentator, see Ep 1789 n3.
7 Presumably Erasmus refers to Guillaume (II) Briçonnet, still bishop of Meaux
but, on account of the judicial charges he faced before the Parlement of
Paris in 1525, no longer involved in efforts to reform his diocese, though
still a favoured preacher at the royal court. He assumes that Lefèvre was
closely in touch with him. Lefèvre, however, avoided both Meaux and
Paris after his return from exile at Strasbourg (cf Epp 1650A n4, 1674
n27).

1734). In this letter he seems to regard the reprinting of those homilies as part of a larger collection of Chrysostom's works that he was about to publish with a dedication to the king of Portugal (Ep 1800) as somehow a public reaffirmation of their friendship. Erasmus published the letter in *Opus epistolarum.*

ERASMUS OF ROTTERDAM TO POLIDORO VIRGILIO, GREETING

Is there no limit to what evil tongues will say? But, my dear Polidoro, if we seek revenge, there is no better way than to maintain the friendship that they want to destroy and hold it fast with the strongest bonds. You will see that the homilies I dedicated to you have now been reprinted in a 5 handsome edition. Those who suffer agony at the thought of our intimacy will be nettled even more by this.

As for your zealous work as peacemaker between Lee and myself,[1] Christ will reward your good intentions with that blessedness he promised.[2] But Lee lays down terms that are anything but fair: that he 10 would show where I have wronged him in my writings and I in turn would show him where he has wronged me; then after a double recantation our friendship could be renewed. But this would not be a reconciliation but a renewal of the quarrel. The best course would be to forget all past wrongs and, with the help of that *amnestia* which the Greeks talk 15 about, to blot out the memory of all our old injuries.[3] Then we could draw up a friendly document and testify that our quarrel is settled and that our hearts are joined in Christian amity. This is what happened between Lefèvre and me.

As for the battles I must fight against a host of demons, I know my 20 fate and I accept it. I am on good terms with men of the highest rank.

* * * * *

1796

1 Erasmus' old controversy with Edward Lee in 1518–20 had been smoothed over through the efforts of mutual friends in England but never really resolved. When news of attacks on him by Spanish monks and theologians reached Erasmus in 1526, he at once assumed that Lee, who had become English ambassador to the Spanish court in 1525, was the instigator (Epp 1735 n7, 1744 n19). Virgilio had written to Lee on 19 October 1526 suggesting terms for finally resolving the disagreement with Erasmus; his letter is in John Jortin *The Life of Erasmus* rev ed, 3 vols (London 1808) III 46–7.

2 Matt 5:9

3 Erasmus wrote 'to forget all past injuries' and *amnestia* in Greek; see *Adagia* II i 94.

Clement VII twice[4] sent me 200 florins and made all sorts of promises.[5] The emperor recently wrote me a most friendly letter,[6] as did his chancellor.[7] I have boxes full of the most flattering letters from kings, cardinals, dukes, and bishops. Many also send gifts of uncommon generosity. Yet out of the dark come these shady creatures, who bite like bugs and lice;[8] for neither the emperor nor the pope can silence them. They are safe in their own obscurity. All they accomplish is to blacken their own reputations. As for myself, I shall hold the tiller straight[9] to the last hour of my life. Let Christ, who directs this play, take charge of its final scene.

* * * * *

4 On first gift, see Ep 1414 introduction and Clement's letter to Erasmus, Ep 1443B. Allen (18n) suggests that the second gift (which seems not to be recorded in the surviving correspondence) may have occurred in July 1525. Certainly at that period the pope and his circle took several steps favourable to Erasmus. Pope Clement granted a brief authorizing him to dispose of his property by drawing a will (Ep 1588), the papal chamberlain Albert Pigge wrote to admonish the Louvain theologians for allowing their members to make public attacks on him (Ep 1589), and the papal datary, Gian Matteo Giberti, wrote to remind Theodoricus Hezius that the pope had instructed him, at the time of his return to the Netherlands, 'to rescue our friend Erasmus from his detractors at Louvain' (Ep 1589A).

5 Latin *ducentos florenos*. Since they were sent by Pope Clement VII, these were presumably Florentine gold florins, which had the same value as the Venetian ducat, though weighing marginally less (3.51g versus 3.56g). If so, this sum amounted to about £46 13s 4d sterling (the equivalent of 1,867 days' wages or about 8 years and 6 months' income for an Oxford master carpenter); or officially £66 13s 4d groot Flemish (and more likely, with rising gold values, £75 groot, the equivalent of 1,800 days' wages or 8 years and 2 months' wage income for an Antwerp master carpenter); and officially £415 tournois, but, with rising gold rates, more likely £455 tournois. Florins and ducats, which had been tariffed at 41s 6d tournois in 1516, were valued at 45s 6d tournois in 1533; and this higher rate was probably also valid for 1526, for the reasons given in Ep 1750 nn2–3; see also Richet 377–96.

6 Ep 1731

7 Mercurino Gattinara. Three letters, in fact, Epp 1757, 1785, 1790A, but perhaps only the first of these had reached Erasmus by this time; the third could not possibly have arrived in Basel, and the second probably not.

8 That is, the anti-Erasmian theologians and monks at Paris and Louvain, whom not even repeated imperial and papal commands had been able to silence for long

9 *Adagia* III i 28

I discussed with Froben the printing of your book.[10] He says he is
prepared to undertake it on the same conditions that applied to the *Adagia*.
Farewell, my great protector.

Basel, 24 March 1527   35

1797 / To Robert Aldridge   Basel, 24 March 1527

> A reply to Ep 1766, in which Aldridge reported only limited success in his
> search for manuscripts of the philosophical works of Seneca that Erasmus re-
> membered using at Cambridge. See also Ep 1656 (and introduction), Erasmus'
> letter requesting Aldridge's help. Erasmus included the present letter in *Opus
> epistolarum*.

ERASMUS OF ROTTERDAM TO ROBERT ALDRIDGE, GREETING
Your Seneca reached me finally just before Lent.[1] It was not necessary to
send the whole book; everything could have been copied on sheets of paper.
The librarians at King's College have misled you. In the smaller library[2] they
have another manuscript, on parchment. You could have recognized it by   5
the alphabetical arrangement of the maxims and by the fact that, in the space
between, the same maxim is repeated in the form of a couplet, though of
the most amateurish kind.[3] The initial letters have been decorated in gold

* * * * *

10 Allen (28n) suggests that this is Virgilio's *De prodigiis* but that the negotiations
   with Froben fell through. The book was not printed until 1531, and then by
   another Basel printer, Johann Bebel.

1797
1 Aldridge had sent a copy of the first edition (1515) of Erasmus' edition of
   Seneca with the variant manuscript readings he had succeeded in finding
   written into the margins.
2 The description of the college library by Montague Rhodes James *A Descriptive
   Catalogue of the Manuscripts Other Than Oriental in the Library of King's College,
   Cambridge* (Cambridge 1895) 69–71 does not mention a division of the collection into two parts. The inventory itself, however, which was made in 1452,
   does list *Epistolae Senecae* and two copies of *Tragediae Senecae* among its holdings (81–2). James (70–1) indicates that there is reason to believe that many
   of the books in that inventory, which includes both classical and Italian humanistic texts, had belonged to the famous patron of early English humanism,
   Duke Humphrey of Gloucester, who died in 1447.
3 Apparently the manuscript that Erasmus wanted Aldridge to find had a commentary and a 'barbarous distich' after each of the alphabetically arranged

and various colours. I had made a large number of emendations in the *De beata vita*. If you have time, you could indicate the variants by noting the line numbers of Froben's text[4] and writing down the reading of the codex. The rest would be up to me. I am sorry that you put yourself to so much trouble with little result. I knew that the manuscript containing the *Letters* was worthless. I have not the heart to impose on your good nature further, but if you could face the drudgery, you would do me a great favour. If you would suggest how I might repay you, your kindness would not be lost on a thankless creature. I have commended you most warmly to Thomas More.[5]

As for the ingratitude of certain persons, that is an old complaint. To be cursed when you have acted well is to suffer the fate of kings.[6] Posterity will see things more clearly, though even now, all the highest in the land – the emperor, Ferdinand,[7] the pope, cardinals, kings, dukes, and bishops – acknowledge my services with flattering letters and generous gifts. It is only a few shady individuals who snarl at me, but they will achieve nothing except to bring discredit on their own heads. The story will have a different ending from what many people imagine. But whatever the ending, I shall continue to give true and loyal service to Christ and to the cause of learning. Farewell.

Basel, 24 March 1527

1798 / To Valentin Furster   Basel, 24 March 1527

This is a letter of encouragement and scholarly advice to a young man, son of the chancellor of the archbishop of Trier and a student at Koblenz under

* * * * *

maxims and thus should have been easily recognizable because of this un-usual page layout.

4 That is, the first Erasmian edition of Seneca's complete works, *Lucubrationes omnes* (Basel: Froben 1515). Aldridge had transcribed variant readings into a copy of this edition and had sent the whole volume, but Erasmus suggests that it would have been simpler to record the variants by page and line number.

5 This letter to More is not extant, but the reference is further evidence that Erasmus and More corresponded more frequently in this period than the small number of surviving letters would indicate.

6 *Apophthegmata* book 4 Alexander Magnus no 32 LB IV 199E and book 7 Antisthenes Atheniensis no 7 LB IV 325C; cf Plutarch *Alexander* 41. The same expression occurs in Ep 1578:37–8.

7 The archduke Ferdinand, brother of the emperor and a reliable friend; see Epp 1545 n5, 1553 n13, 1697 n27.

the humanist Ludovicus Carinus (see next letter), who seems to have been a successful private tutor to wealthy youths at this stage of his career. This letter is Furster's only appearance in Erasmus' correspondence. He later entered the service of Duke Philip of Hesse and died, probably at Kassel, in 1555. Erasmus included this letter in *Opus epistolarum*.

ERASMUS OF ROTTERDAM TO VALENTIN FURSTER, GREETING
If you fulfil the promise that your letter[1] suggests, you will do well for yourself and for all your friends. Remember that no time is better than the palmy days of youth for acquiring sound morals and sound learning, and this will stand you in good stead throughout your life. But although the youthful years are the best, they are also the most fleeting, and once they have slipped away, they never return. Pay most attention to historians and moralists. For the former you have Titus Livius, the *Lives* of Plutarch, and Cornelius Tacitus; for the latter there is Cicero's *De officiis*, *De amicitia*, *De senectute*, the *Tusculan Disputations*, and the *Moralia* of Plutarch. From these in particular you will gain the knowledge that best suits a man in public life. Moreover, reading them is as pleasurable as it is useful. Give my best wishes to your friend, my dear Erasmius.[2] Farewell.
Basel, 24 March 1527   15

1799 / To Ludovicus Carinus   Basel, 24 March 1527

At the date of this letter, Erasmus was still friendly with Carinus, whom he had met while visiting Froben at Basel between 1514 and 1516 (Ep 630) and had known again at Louvain in 1519–20 as a fellow resident of the College of the Lily. At the time of this letter, Carinus was working as a private tutor at Koblenz. On him see Epp 920, 1034, 1798. For some reason not now known, the two men had a bitter and permanent falling-out in the summer of 1528 (see Allen Epp 2048:49–53, 2063). Probably because of their quarrel, Erasmus did not publish this letter. The manuscript survived in the City and University Library at Hamburg and was first printed in Johann Christoph Wolf *Conspectus supellectilis epistolicae et literariae* (Hamburg 1736).

* * * * *

1798
1 Not extant
2 Erasmius Froben, son of the Basel printer and godson of Erasmus, was a fellow-student with Furster under the tutelage of Ludovicus Carinus at this period.

Ludovicus Carinus
Zentral- und Hochschulbibliothek, Luzern

ERASMUS OF ROTTERDAM TO LUDOVICUS CARINUS, GREETING

Cordial greetings. If you are well, I shall forgive Jupiter for treating you so roughly, for he wanted to make a man out of you instead of a weakling. You give in to the doctors more than you should. If you became a courier, you would feel better.   5

I have seen nothing of Leodegarius.[1] What a risk we run when we do a good turn to certain people! I am not yet reconciled to accepting the six crowns you thrust upon me[2] – you took no thought of my character and wishes, dreadful bully that you are! I replied to your friend Furster, though briefly.[3] Do let me know what you are doing and how you are.   10

Basel, 24 March 1527

Your friend, Erasmus of Rotterdam

I would have replied to the chancellor,[4] but his letter does not come to hand, being buried beneath great piles of paper. You will have to take the place of a letter – you are eloquent enough.   15

To Ludovicus Carinus. At Koblenz

1800 / To John III   Basel, 24 March 1527

This is the dedicatory epistle of Erasmus' edition of Latin translations of several works of St John Chrysostom, *Chrysostomi lucubrationes* (Basel: Froben,

* * * * *

1799

1 See Ep 1761 n12 on the problem of identifying this person.

2 Latin *sex coronatos*. From the context, one cannot say with certainty whether these are French crowns, that is, *écus au soleil*, or English rose crowns; but since they were of the same approximate value, the difference is immaterial for such a small sum. If the latter, this amount was officially worth about 30s 0d sterling or 38s groot Flemish or £12 tournois. See Ep 1750 nn2–3.

3 Ep 1798

4 Allen (10n) suggests that Matthias von Saarburg is meant. He was vice-chancellor and rector of the University of Trier and dean of the chapter of St Simon's church there from 1515. Erasmus had visited him at Koblenz in 1518 (Ep 867:64n) and again while on his way to Basel in 1521 (Ep 1342:185–9). In Allen Ep 1946 Justin Gobler reported that he had written to Matthias at Trier seeking help for Erasmus' effort to discover manuscripts of Tertullian's treatise *De spectaculis*. But a more likely identification of this chancellor is Ludwig Furster, father of Carinus' student Valentin. He was chancellor of the electoral principality in the service of the archbishop and is also mentioned in the same letter from Justin Gobler, which reports that Ludwig Furster and Carinus had come to him seeking the location of a manuscript of Tertullian that had been inherited by Gobler's wife from her first husband.

March 1527), addressed to John III, king of Portugal. Erasmus' financial agent Erasmus Schets had been urging Erasmus for more than a year to dedicate a book to the young king, whom he described as highly favourable to humanistic learning and as a wealthy and potentially generous new patron; see Ep 1681 introduction and nn8–9. In subsequent letters, while repeatedly urging Erasmus to make a dedication to the king, Schets also provided information on the overseas conquests and missionary work of the king and his father (Ep 1682) and even arranged (Ep 1783) for a Portuguese medical doctor resident in Antwerp to write for Erasmus an account of the royal family's history, support for learning, religious zeal, overseas conquests and empire, and successful missionary work 'among the barbarians,' so that Erasmus would have useful material for his dedication. Erasmus had been somewhat cool to the enterprise, informing Schets in October 1526 that he would do something for the king when he found time (Ep 1758); but in December 1526 he informed Schets that he planned to dedicate to the king his forthcoming edition of Chrysostom (Ep 1769). In the event, hopes of finding a rich new patron came to nothing. In a letter of 29 August 1530, Erasmus informed Schets that he had learned from a Portuguese visitor that his references to monopoly and profiteering in the dedication (lines 41–7) had made the Portuguese courtiers fearful that it would offend the king, and so they never presented the dedication and gift copy to him (Ep 2370).

TO HIS SERENE MAJESTY, JOHN, KING OF PORTUGAL,
THE THIRD OF THIS NAME, SON OF MANUEL,
FROM DESIDERIUS ERASMUS OF ROTTERDAM, GREETING
Your Majesty, in past times men who tilled the fields and wanted to be known for their piety and gratitude used to acknowledge the bounty of the 5 gods by offering to each of them a part of their harvest, believing that they owed it to divine generosity. Thus they offered a crown made from ears of wheat to Ceres, a garland of vine leaves to Bacchus, one of poplar to Hercules, and a chaplet of roses to Venus. They thought they would reap a better harvest if they pleased the authors of this bounty with a little gift. If 10 pagans, with their superstitious beliefs, did this, is there not greater reason for us, who till fields that yield a better harvest, to show our gratitude to Christian monarchs by whose favour and generosity literary studies are nourished, protected, and adorned by offering something from those very studies that we enjoy through their support? 15
In the past I have often been intrigued by stories of the glorious deeds of your father, the invincible King Manuel,[1] whose fame is celebrated around

* * * * *

1800
1 See Ep 1681 nn9–10 on Manuel I and his patronage of learning and the arts.

the world as though proclaimed on the ringing notes of the trumpet. Among his countless virtues let me mention those that have won him particular acclaim throughout the Christian world. First, he showed by his actions that he was the equal of King John, the first of that name and tenth in order of the kings of Portugal, who was the founder of his line and is remembered by an honourable title; [2] he inherited a kingdom that was not by itself very large, more like the proverbial Sparta,[3] and extended it by clever policies until there is scarcely a country in the world to which it takes second place in the fame and glory of its name. Secondly, by force of arms he pacified that vast sea which stretches from the town of Ceuta[4] near the Pillars of Hercules to the Chinese people in the state of India,[5] and which, because

* * * * *

2 Literally, 'with a cognomen of blessed memory.' John I (1383–1433), called 'the Great,' was the founder of the Aviz dynasty from which Manuel I and his son John III derived their title to the Portuguese throne. It had become customary for Portuguese kings since the late thirteenth century to be accorded some laudatory epithet as a title of honour: John I, 'the Great'; Afonso V, 'the African'; John II, 'the Perfect Prince'; Manuel I, 'the Great' or (more accurately) 'the Fortunate.' John III came to be known as 'the Pious.' Erasmus' numbering of the Portuguese kings here is wrong. John III's father Manuel was the fourteenth, not the tenth, since the first king of an independent Portugal, Afonso I (1143–85), and the fifth since John I founded the dynasty in 1383. But surely Erasmus knew nothing personally about this; the source of his information or misinformation was probably the historical sketch about the royal family produced for him by a Portuguese physician resident at Antwerp who wrote at the request of Erasmus Schets; see Ep 1783.

3 *Adagia* II v 1

4 Seaport located at the Mediterranean entrance to the Strait of Gibraltar. An important stronghold of the Muslim rulers of Morocco, it was conquered in 1415 by an expedition led by Prince Henry of Portugal ('the Navigator') and became the first of a chain of fortified outposts held by the Portuguese on the Atlantic coast of Morocco, useful both for the developing West Africa trade and as a defence against Moorish raids on the coasts of Spain and Portugal.

5 Although obviously Erasmus' grasp of the geography and demography of Southern and Eastern Asia was shaky, the Portuguese admiral in the Indian Ocean, Afonso de Albuquerque, had conquered Goa and established a base there in 1510 and in 1511 conquered the Muslim port of Malacca, the key to economic expansion towards the spice islands (the Moluccas) and China. Allen (23n) reminds readers that medieval Europeans thought of the Chinese of South China and their diaspora in Malaysia, Indo-China, and Indonesia as *Sinae* (the word used here by Erasmus), while the Chinese of North China who had been reached by the overland route in the thirteenth and fourteenth centuries were thought of as a different people and in Latin were called *Seres*. This distinction was already established in ancient times; see Ptolemy 7.3.1. The Portuguese naval victory over the Egyptian fleet in 1509 at Diu off the

of barbarian attacks, had previously been unnavigable. He thus brought a huge territory under Christian control. As a result, there is hardly any ocean 30 in which it is safer for our mariners to sail. And while he pursued these aims, he went about spreading the Christian faith and sowing the seeds of Catholic piety in many different lands.

To ensure that nothing would impede the successful propagation of the faith, this wise man took steps to prevent any suspicion of self-interest 35 from spoiling his victory over the barbarians. There are eight great cities of Africa that your ancestors brought under their control because they were used by pirates as a base and place of retreat, thus making the passage to India unsafe for everyone.[6] It is said that nothing returns to your coffers from these cities except what was spent on protecting your sovereignty. I 40 only wish that this remarkable record of generosity was not being spoilt by the monopolies held by certain people.[7] Admittedly, it is easier now to import things, but people tell me that thanks to these monopolies, prices, far from dropping, have actually increased, and some items, sugar for example, have not just gone up in price but now reach us in a more adulterated state.[8] 45

* * * * *

coast of India opened a long period in which the Portuguese held control of the Indian Ocean, though not (as Erasmus here claims) of the mainland areas except for a few fortified bases held for commercial and naval use.

6 The concept in Erasmus' mind must have been vague, but his Portuguese source at Antwerp almost certainly had in mind the eight outposts held by the Portuguese on the Atlantic coast of Morocco: Ceuta (conquered in 1415), Tangier (1471), and far lesser places such as Santa Cruz de Guer, Mazagão, Safi, Azammur, Alcácer-Seguir, and Arzila. Only Ceuta and Tangier were cities of any economic consequence, and only they were economically useful and financially viable colonies. In the middle of the sixteenth century, between 1542 and 1550, in the face of the pressure created by unification of the Muslim states of the Magrib into a single state, the Portuguese abandoned the last four outposts listed. See Livermore 149.

7 Although the failure of the Portuguese attempt to control the entrance to the Red Sea by attacking Aden in 1513 meant that the ancient spice route used by the Arabs, by way of the Red Sea and Egypt, recovered and became an alternative source of supply, the Portuguese naval victories in the Indian Ocean did establish a hegemony, if not quite a true monopoly, in the spice trade, so that the Portuguese were able to manipulate the supply and price of pepper, cloves, and other spices for most of the century, just as Erasmus complains in this letter. But his remarks gave offence, and as a result this dedication was never presented to the king. For a brief discussion of the Portuguese near-monopoly of spices, see Livermore 142–3.

8 That is, mixed with cheaper ingredients to produce greater profit. Erasmus' Latin word is *corruptiora*, which usually means 'more spoiled.' But it is hard

Perhaps some day princes will use their authority to put a stop to such avarice. In the meantime there is no reason to rob your pious endeavours of their due recognition.

These glorious deeds are praised by all who honour the name of Christ. They touch me more particularly because Manuel took such a kindly inter- 50 est in scholars in every branch of sound learning, especially in theology. The piety of his mind, a piety worthy of a Christian king, was often evident in those letters of his that were made public. As I said, my interest was kindled by these reports of his excellence, but it was further excited when certain people pressed me, on behalf of scholars everywhere, to honour this 55 great patron of learning with some token of our regard. While I was casting around for a subject that would not seem utterly unworthy of him, this distinguished man, who deserved a place in heaven, was snatched from this world and translated to the more peaceful abode of the saints.

My interest, however, was rekindled, as soon as I learned that your il- 60 lustrious Majesty has so completely taken your father's place that it seems he is not dead but has come to life again in you, a young man scarcely twenty-six years old.[9] What your father began with such distinction, you have completed; what he completed, you have reinforced; what he achieved so brilliantly, you have enhanced; and what he left undone, you have un- 65 dertaken. As soon as you began your reign, you reformed the administration of justice, which had been perverted by the venality of lawyers, you

* * * * *

to spoil sugar, the commodity specified here, though it would be ruined if contaminated by salt water. The comparative degree expressed in the form of the Latin word does not fit well with that meaning: things are generally either spoiled or not spoiled. In the case of some of the oriental spices, as well as of sugar, it is possible that some cheap adulterant was added to increase profit. In any case, sugar (unlike pepper and other spices) did not come from the Indian Ocean but from the newly discovered and rediscovered islands of the eastern Atlantic: the Canary Islands, where Spanish control had been established, the Madeiras, and the Azores, which came under Portuguese control. Colonization of these islands began in the first half of the fifteenth century, and the cultivation of sugar cane was introduced early – by 1433 on the island of Madeira. Sugar cane, which was produced for export in Sicily both before and after the Christian reconquest of that island in the eleventh century, had been introduced to the Portuguese and Spanish mainlands early in the fifteenth century. Long before 1500, the Atlantic islands had become major centres for production of sugar, and sugar remained an important product there. In the sixteenth century, sugar cane was introduced from the Atlantic islands into the West Indies, where it has remained of major economic importance.

9 John III was born in 1502 and succeeded his father Manuel in 1521.

raised the stipends of those who pursue the learned disciplines, you increased your maritime strength by building a strong fleet, and you cleared your land of all the tares that choked the rich harvest of true piety. Nor 70 were you content to foster and support teachers and students, especially teachers and students of theology, but from a tender age you yourself studied both Greek and Latin under men of great distinction, one of whom was Luis de Teixeira (with whom, unless I am utterly mistaken in the name, I enjoyed in Italy a friendship which was as delightful as it was close and 75 which I count among my happiest experiences);[10] you were also trained in mathematics, astrology, geography, and history (which more than any other subject is the philosophy of kings), and in all these you achieved such success that your example inspires the lazy and indifferent with the love of learning.   80

And what am I to say of your brother Fernando?[11] Like all your brothers he is very dear to you, but he is especially dear, because in his attachment to learning and his support of it, he has shown himself a man after your own heart. For just as you cherish the most honourable studies, so you are cherished by all devoted to them, into whose company I should like to be 85 admitted, if only at the humblest rank. So I formed the confident, or perhaps I should say presumptuous, decision to make the dedication I had planned for your father to his blessed memory and to yourself.

While I was planning how to carry out my decision, God, I believe, provided me with the means. I was sent from Venice a very old manuscript 90 in Greek script,[12] in which I found several homilies of John Chrysostom

* * * * *

10 This son of João Texeira, chancellor of King John II, had attended lectures on Latin and Greek at Florence under Angelo Poliziano (in 1481 according to Diogo Barbosa Machado *Bibliotheca Lusitana* 4 vols [Lisbon 1741–59; repr Coimbra 1965–7] III 155–6, but in 1489 according to Joaquim de Carvalho in *História de Portugal* ed Damião Peres and others, 9 vols [Barcelos 1928–54] IV 251). Subsequently, he studied law at Siena and Bologna, received his doctorate, and taught for a time at Ferrara. His commentary on a section of the Digest, *De rebus dubiis,* was twice published (Venice: Gregorius de Gregoriis 1507; 2nd ed Siena 1515). In 1519 Manuel I appointed him tutor to Prince John, and later he became chancellor to John III. Erasmus could have met him either at Bologna in 1506–7 or at Siena in 1509.
11 See Ep 1681 n11.
12 The manuscript of Chrysostom's work obtained for Erasmus by Hieronymus Froben during his trip to Italy in the summer of 1526; see Epp 1661 n2, 1705 n3. Allen (82n) adds that in addition to the works enumerated in lines 112–17 below, the manuscript contained Chrysostom's sermons to the people of Antioch and his homilies on Job.

that no one had previously translated.[13] They did not deserve such neglect. On the contrary, I believe it is vital for Christendom that they be made widely available. In my opinion, hardly any other works of his demonstrate so clearly his golden voice[14] and honeyed eloquence. It turned out to be 95 a lucky find, for we are told that his work *Against the Jews*[15] was the first he wrote, while he was still a lector at Antioch. His book *On the Priestly Function*,[16] which was written when he was a deacon, was considered by the Greeks to take first place for eloquence among all his writings. This is the only book of his that Jerome testifies to having read,[17] presumably because 100 it was the most celebrated. Two years ago I published a Greek text of it. With my encouragement it has now been turned into Latin by Germain de Brie of Auxerre,[18] a man of such exceptional eloquence in both Greek and

* * * * *

13 On this important Greek church Father and Erasmus' interest in him, see Epp 1558 introduction, 1661 n2, 1675 n4, 1736 nn3, 5, 7–13, 1789 n1, 1790 n2.
14 Here as elsewhere, Erasmus plays on the literal meaning of Chrysostom's name; cf Ep 1733 n2.
15 Chrysostom's eight homilies *Against the Jews* were preached at Antioch in 386–7, early in his career. The texts are in PG 48 843–942. Erasmus translated five of these (nos 4–8), and the Latin text in the Migne edition is his, with some corrections. It is not clear whether Erasmus knew that kings John II, Manuel I, and John III, under pressure from the religious orders and the Spanish monarchs, had gradually withdrawn the laws granting toleration to Jews and protecting nominally converted Jews from molestation by ecclesiastical courts for a period of twenty years. The population affected included some sixty thousand Jews who had fled from Spain in 1494 and had paid either high fees (60,000 cruzados per family) for the right to settle permanently in Portugal, or much lower fees (8 cruzados a head) for the right of temporary residence and transit to some other country; on the cruzado see CWE 1 313. Although the monarchs sometimes resisted the pressures to revoke Jewish liberties because they found it useful to exploit the Jews financially, the rights of Jews were being gradually narrowed, culminating in the papal bull of May 1536 founding an Inquisition to pursue both heretics and those who relapsed into Jewish religious observances. See Livermore 125–7, 149.
16 Erasmus followed the church historian Socrates *Historia ecclesiastica* 6.3 in attributing Chrysostom's *De sacerdotio* to his period as a deacon (381–6), before he became a priest. Erasmus edited the Greek text in 1525. See Epp 1558 introduction, 1661 n2.
17 In *De viris inlustribus* 129 ed Albrecht Bernoulli (Freiburg im Breisgau 1895; repr Frankfurt 1968) 55 / PL 23 754, where he refers to him as 'John, priest of the church at Antioch,' rather than by the popular nickname Chrysostom or by his title as patriarch of Constantinople
18 See Epp 1733, 1736. Brie's translation was inspired by Erasmus' complaint about the inadequacy of the ancient Latin translation; see the dedication of

Latin that the exuberance of his language has nearly surpassed that of his
golden-voiced original. I could imagine I was listening to Chrysostom him-   105
self, almost as though there was no other person acting as intermediary. It
was fortunate indeed that the most polished work that has come down to
us from this Doctor of the church fell into the hands of an artist comparable to himself. The texts that have fallen to my lot are equally useful, but
they are less polished, since they were intended for the ears of the general   110
public, while the book translated by Brie was written for the learned Basil.[19]
The other works which, under your auspices, I am offering the Latin reader
are as follows: five homilies against the Jews, four concerning Lazarus, four
on the vision of Isaiah and King Uzziah, one in praise of Philogonius and
on worthily receiving the sacrament. I have given no more than a sample   115
of the commentaries on the Acts, since I have doubts about their authenticity.[20] I propose to await the verdict of the scholarly world and then decide
whether to publish the rest or abandon them.

I had other works of Chrysostom in addition to these,[21] but they were
too long to be dealt with on this occasion, since my energies were divided   120
over many other literary projects; in fact, I was forced sometimes to resort
to dictation as a short cut. But with Christ's help I shall publish them soon.
For there is no one I would rather read either for business or for pleasure.
More than any other ecclesiastical writer he 'won every point by joining
the useful with the sweet.'[22] I can think of no one who is more vivid in   125

* * * * *

Erasmus' Greek edition of *De sacerdotio* to Willibald Pirckheimer, Ep 1558,
especially n22.

19 Not Basil the Great, bishop of Caesarea, as Erasmus may intend to imply, but
an unknown friend of Chrysostom, one of the two interlocutors in the work,
which has the form of a dialogue. See Ep 1733 n3.

20 On the homilies *Against the Jews* see n15 above. On the homilies (not truly commentaries) on Acts, see Ep 1675 n4. The other works can generally be identified with works in the Migne collection: the four homilies concerning Lazarus
are PG 48 963–1044; on Isaiah and Uzziah, PG 56 107–35 (but only one of these,
columns 112–20, is relevant here); on Philogonius (*In beatum Philogonium*), PG
48 747–56 (a work which discusses the life of Philogonius and ends with a
sermon on the Eucharist).

21 Erasmus had published other short works of Chrysostom: *De orando Deum* in
1525 (Ep 1563 introduction), *Conciunculae perquam elegantes sex de fato et providentia Dei* in 1526 (Ep 1661 introduction and n2), and *In epistolam ad Philippenses homiliae duae*, also in 1526 (Ep 1734 introduction). In 1530 he edited the
Opera in five volumes. All of these editions were first published by Froben at
Basel, but *De orando Deum* was speedily reprinted in several other cities.

22 Horace *Ars poetica* 343

his teaching, more shrewd in refuting heretics, no one who speaks out on moral issues more frequently or more boldly and yet in a manner that is accessible to ordinary people. Even subjects that are by their nature sour he makes agreeable by the sweetness of his charity. There are people whose compliments we can scarcely bear, but you could love Chrysostom even if he rebuked you. Think, moreover, of his care and thoughtfulness for the poor, his passionate exhortations to kindliness, his earnest commendation of the religious life, for in those days, I believe, the world was blessed with monks of the highest character. 130

I say nothing of his exceptionally prolific output – and remember that he never tackled any subject not concerned with the Christian faith. Our Augustine, who can perhaps compete in the number of his writings, devoted much of his energies to grammar, logic, music, and problems of secular philosophy. Although Chrysostom was well trained in these disciplines (as a boy he is said to have studied rhetoric under the orator Libanius and philosophy under Andragathius),[23] he nowhere parades his learning but makes all his secular knowledge serve the Christian faith, bringing the two into harmony. It is like diluting a fine wine with a little water: there is no evidence of the taste or colour of water, but you are aware that the wine is sweeter. And yet, for all his learning and eloquence, so great was his concern to serve humanity that he accommodated almost everything he wrote to the understanding of the people. Just as a teacher slows down his speech to keep pace with his young pupil, so Chrysostom brought down the level of his discourse to the comprehension of his hearers. Were all his homilies delivered before the people in their present form and style? If so, then I do not know which should surprise me more, the stamina of the author who stood up to such a heavy burden of preaching or the eagerness of the people to learn the lessons of true religion. It is a debatable point whether he allowed his words to be written down as he delivered them,[24] as clearly happened with several of Augustine's works, or (since this first hypothesis is not very likely) if he first wrote out what he was going to say or wrote down later what he had said. In any case, it is evident from his writings that he did not speak from a script, for there are many references to situations that chance or occasion offered unexpectedly: comments, for example, on an unusually large or excited congregation, references to an unseemly outburst, and other accidental happenings of this sort. Perhaps he wrote some of his works with an 135 140 145 150 155 160

* * * * *

23 Socrates *Historia ecclesiastica* 6.3
24 Socrates *Historia ecclesiastica* 6.4 suggests that his homilies were taken down by 'shorthand writers' (*notarii*, ὀξυγράφοι).

imaginary audience in mind, like much of Isocrates.[25] We can hardly suppose that as a mere lector he would have been permitted to preach to the
people – and he was no more than that when he wrote *Against the Jews* –
unless, being the kind of lector he was, he was given special permission to   165
deliver his work in public.

There is nothing in Holy Scripture so obscure that in his hands does
not (so to speak) take on the drama of a play and become appealing to ordinary people. He uncovers and explicates the hidden meanings of a passage,
sets them before our eyes so vividly that you would say, 'Here is a man   170
who holds the spectators spellbound with a picture of exceptional artistry;
the longer and more closely you inspect it, the more you see in it something
new that had escaped you before, and each new discovery gives it fresh
life.' Holy Scripture is like such a painting, created for us with a heavenly
brush by the incomparable artistry of the Holy Spirit. When we spend our   175
days contemplating it, we escape the tedium of this world and never fail to
derive some new pleasure from its eternal truths. No one can be a fit guide
to such a picture unless he is himself a brilliant artist and endowed with
a keen insight. Consider, for example, how our author brings the rich man
and Lazarus onto the stage.[26] Would anyone else have seen what he shows   180
us in that story? And when the spectator is ready to leave, believing there
is nothing left to be said, he calls him back. 'Wait a minute,' he says, 'there
is something else here that is worth commenting on.' Then he makes one
point after another and keeps your attention fastened on the picture. Finally
he lets you go, eager and panting for more.   185

He makes frequent use of metaphors and illustrations, since these contribute greatly to clarity and attractiveness of style. He is skilful at finding
apt comparisons, but even more remarkable is the way in which he devel-
ops them. He chooses examples from situations that are similar, or grander,
or humbler than the thing compared. He can thus introduce a remarkable   190
range of effects to lower or build up a subject. He is constantly urging on his
listeners, at one time praising them for their eagerness to learn, then scolding them for their laziness or, if he finds them eager and attentive, holding

* * * * *

25 The famous Athenian orator (436–338 BC) lacked the voice and self-confidence
needed for success in addressing large audiences but won his earliest fame
by writing speeches for others to use in the law courts. Many of his later
speeches were addressed to imaginary audiences; they were really tracts on
political questions and other topics of concern to him.
26 Luke 16:19–31. Chrysostom's sermons explore the story's spiritual meaning in
many directions, especially its significance for the life of a sincere Christian.

out the prospect of something worth knowing, then suggesting one reason
after another for the importance of the subject he is about to treat, sometimes   195
repeating what he had said the day before, occasionally repeating himself
within the same sermon. Such were the concessions made to simple and un-
retentive minds by this most eloquent of men; for ordinary people do not
grasp the point unless you put it clearly and bluntly, and they remember
nothing unless you hammer it home with constant repetition.   200

I have mentioned this so that no one will criticize for long-windedness
what is in fact a concession to the weakness of ordinary people; this is the
mark of the man's charity, which seeks only to edify.[27] Paul too, when speaking to the Thessalonians, accommodated himself to their weakness and became a little child in their midst, as a nurse cherishes her children.[28] Chry-   205
sostom never goes in for witty aphorisms or striking epigrams,[29] which
speakers often introduce to win the applause of an audience (Jerome and
Ambrose were fond of such devices), nor did he employ jokes (as Tertullian
often does, sometimes to excess, and Jerome more frequently still); rather
he holds the attention of his hearers with the charm and fluency of his style,   210
delighting by his piety, not by his wit. A preacher will quickly learn how to
win over an audience if he has made the people understand and love what
they are learning. There is enough in the mysteries of Scripture to delight
and comfort pious minds without having recourse to the meretricious at-
tractions of poetry and the comic stage. If the preacher is on fire, he will   215
soon kindle a flame in others. If he delights in what he teaches, that feeling will quickly be transmitted to the hearts of his listeners. Such were the
mind and golden voice of Chrysostom, once destined for the secular courts
till Christ took them over and used them for the proclamation of the gospel.

How I wish we had such fine speakers today in every part of the Chris-   220
tian world, for it is on these that the education of the people in large measure depends. If we understand nothing of the philosophy of the gospel, if
we flag in doing the work of charity, if our faith is weak where it should
be strongest, it is because the people rarely hear preachers of the gospel,
and competent gospel preachers are rarer still. And yet the situation for the   225

* * * * *

27 Cf 1 Cor 8:1.
28 Erasmus follows the Vulgate text of 1 Thess 2:7. The Greek manuscripts varied
   between νήπιοι 'children' and ἤπιοι 'gentle.' The Vulgate reading is *parvuli*
   'little children.' AV follows the other reading and translates 'we were gentle
   among you, even as a nurse cherisheth her children.'
29 The Latin is *epiphonemata*. An 'epiphoneme' is an exclamatory or striking sentence that concludes or sums up a narrative or argument.

speaker is more favourable today than it was for Chrysostom. For then the influence of paganism was still felt: gladiatorial contests, horse races, athletes, and boxers, as well as other kinds of competition in the theatre, competed with the sacred homily for the attention of the people, and bishops had no authority except the authority of their own words. Moreover, even 230 during sermons, preachers had to put up with the manners of the theatre: catcalls, clapping, shouts, and gestures that were often rude. Such behaviour could spoil a speaker's fervour or temporarily put him off. Yet Chrysostom spoke to packed congregations, even though he addressed the people every day. And who would not rather listen to such a man speaking so attractively 235 about holy things than watch gladiators or go to horse races or play dice? Today these public distractions have been removed. People are submissive and quiet and listen reverently, never interrupting even when a fatuous remark is uttered from the pulpit. Yet there is a great scarcity of suitable preachers, although there is no shortage anywhere of bishops, priests, and monks. 240 So, illustrious sovereign, it is not the least commendable of your benefactions that here too your pious mind has been at work, ensuring a supply of suitable preachers to present to the people the teachings of the gospel.[30]

Constantinople was at the height of its brilliance, adorned with beauty and riches of every kind. But the emperor Arcadius did not think his city 245 and the seat of his empire splendid enough unless it also had an eminent preacher of the gospel.[31] So he called John Chrysostom from Antioch to Constantinople to fill the sacerdotal office left vacant by the death of Nectarius.[32] I wish, your Majesty, that all our princes would follow the example set by you and Arcadius! I wish a great multitude of priests would strive to emu- 250 late Chrysostom. If that happened, the world would not be shaken by so much war and controversy, and we would have moved much further from Judaic and pagan ways. Christ would reign in us, and under his banner we would enjoy peace and felicity. Finally, the boundaries of Christ's kingdom

* * * * *

30 Erasmus may have in mind John III's decision in 1526 to provide funds for the maintenance of fifty students at the Collège de Sainte-Barbe in the University of Paris (see Livermore 148), though there seems to be no proof that the primary purpose of the new endowment was the education of preachers.
31 Socrates *Historia ecclesiastica* 6.3
32 The succession is described in Socrates *Historia ecclesiastica* 6.2. Chrysostom's reputation as a preacher was the reason why the emperor favoured his election. Sozomen *Historia ecclesiastica* 8.2 describes how the reluctant Chrysostom was brought to Constantinople by a combination of force and deception and how the patriarch of Alexandria, who had opposed his selection, was compelled to consecrate him.

would be extended far and wide. For I fear that our conduct is part of the   255
reason why Turks, Mohammedans, Saracens, Muscovites, Greeks, and all
those other nations who are semi-Christian or schismatic do not join Christ's
fold. This is why the Jews do not recover from that blindness in which they
have lived for so many centuries. I should be surprised if the lucid arguments of Chrysostom and the persuasive evidence of Scripture did not at   260
the very least make the Jews feel shame and regret for the miseries they
have so long endured.

This unhappy people owes it to the apostle Paul that it survives to this
day, that the seed remains from which it may grow again.[33] For in the Epistle
to the Romans, chapter 11, he gave us hope that one day the Jews would   265
come to their senses and acknowledge with us the true Messiah, that there
would be one shepherd and one sheepfold.[34] It is with this hope that they
are watched over by us. 'For,' says Paul, 'lest you should be exalted in your
own eyes, I want you, brethren, to understand this mystery, that blindness
has fallen upon part of Israel, until the full number of the gentiles has come   270
in; and so all Israel will be saved, as it is written, "And there shall come from
Zion a deliverer, who shall turn away all ungodliness from Jacob."'[35] A little
later Paul says, 'For just as you once did not believe in God but have now
obtained mercy through their unbelief, so also these do not believe because
of the mercy shown to you so that they too may obtain mercy.'[36] Again in   275
the same chapter Paul shows that the calamity of the Jewish people need not

* * * * *

33 The survival and eventual conversion of the Jews to Christianity had remained
   a goal of the Christian church from its origins, expressed as early as Paul's discussion in Rom 9–11, especially in Rom 11:25–31. Erasmus assumes that Paul
   is responsible for the preservation of the Jewish people because he assigned
   to them a crucial role in the salvation of humankind. He certainly knew that
   Spain and Portugal had large Jewish communities; whether he also knew the
   extent to which in both countries in his own time they were being converted
   (more by force than by persuasion) is uncertain.
34 John 10:16
35 Rom 11:26, citing Isa 59:20. Erasmus uses his own translation in this paragraph
   (see LB VI 626). The present translator has rendered the Latin text as Erasmus
   interpreted it in the Paraphrase on Romans (LB VII 815–16 / CWE 42 67).
36 Rom 11:30–1. In his Annotations on the Epistle to the Romans, Erasmus explains this difficult passage as follows: 'For when the gentiles persisted in their
   unbelief, the Jews were called to the Law; afterwards, when the gentiles were
   called to the gospel, the Jews fell away, persevering in unbelief; but they were
   once more, through the example of the gentiles, to be recalled to faith. Thus
   by a sort of reciprocal succession, each was saved through the other' (CWE 56
   313).

make us despair. He says, 'Have they stumbled that they should fall? God forbid! Rather through their fall salvation came to the gentiles, so that the Jews might be inspired to emulation. Now if their fall means riches for the world and if their humiliation means riches to the gentiles, how much more will their full inclusion mean? For I speak to you gentiles, inasmuch as I am the apostle of the gentiles; I magnify my ministry so that I may inspire the men of my own race to emulation; in this way I hope to save some of them.'[37]

If after the Jews rebelled against Christ we were received so that in turn we might call them to follow our example, we must strive to let the truth and purity of the gospel shine forth in all its fullness as long as we live. Let us glorify this gospel that is ours. It is true that this is the special duty of bishops and priests, who are called the messengers of the Lord,[38] and it is from their mouths that the people seek to know God's law. Yet every Christian, to the measure of his ability, can glorify the gospel if he rejects the things of this world and has his citizenship in heaven.[39] For thus it will come to pass that Turks and Jews will see our good works and glorify our father who is in heaven,[40] and will be eager to be members of such a company.

You have made no small contribution to the glorification of the gospel by your devoted encouragement and support of those who are scattering the seeds of the Catholic faith in barren soil. The more closely these missionaries follow the example of Chrysostom, the more converts they will win to share our faith. I pray, great king, that the supreme ruler of the world, who guides us by his secret and inscrutable will and steers the ship of the church through storm and tempest, will bless and prosper all that you are doing with such zeal and singular devotion. You have in Charles, our invincible emperor, one who is as close to you in his zeal for the revival and promotion of the Christian faith as he is bound to you by ties of marriage.[41]

I was about to take leave of your Majesty, but first there is one thing I must mention in case some reader should trip up through ignorance. I have rendered passages of Scripture in accordance with the Greek text as I found it in the manuscript. The Greek text, however, does not seem to

* * * * *

37 Rom 11:11–14
38 Mal 2:7
39 Phil 3:20
40 Matt 5:16
41 In 1525 John III had married Catherine, the sister of Charles v, and in 1526 Charles had married Isabel, sister of John.

be simply that of the Septuagint, but is modified by the editions of Aquila,   310
Symmachus, and Theodotion.[42] I could not therefore substitute the Vulgate
reading, since in many cases the tenor of the argument does not square
with our text.[43] This problem arises often with the New Testament, but in
the Old Testament textual variations are much more frequent and significant. In their citations from Scripture there is general agreement among   315
the Greek Doctors of the church: Gregory of Nazianzus, Basil, Chrysostom, Athanasius, Theophylact, Cyril, and all those others whose learned
writings have brilliantly illuminated the philosophy of Christ. This in itself is enough to justify a Latin translation of the New Testament based
on the reading of the Greeks.[44] I provided such a translation to howls of   320
protest from my critics and the considerable profit of the scholarly world.
Others have done the same for the books of the Old Testament, where
the need was even greater. Those who have given us Latin translations
of Cyril, Chrysostom, and Theophylact have preferred to substitute the
reading of the Vulgate, often with ridiculous results, since the text sings   325
one tune and the accompanying commentary another. It would be folly for
someone to emend the text of Cyprian, Tertullian, Ambrose, and Augustine to make it conform to our translation[45] where their commentaries cry
out in protest; by the same token it would be even less appropriate to do

* * * * *

42 Erasmus is explaining that the biblical text in his Greek source does not always
   follow the Septuagint, the traditional Greek version of the Hebrew Scripture,
   but has been modified in places to follow three more recent Greek translations.
   Aquila was a Jew who about 150 AD produced a Greek text that was intended
   to be more literal than the Septuagint. Symmachus about 200 AD produced
   a more idiomatic Greek translation. Theodotion, a Christian of Ephesus, in
   the late second century made a quite free translation. All three versions were
   incorporated into Origen's *Hexapla*, but only fragments of them survive.
43 That is, the Vulgate text, the one that normally would be cited in a Latin
   translation of a patristic work at this period
44 As he points out just below, such a translation is precisely what Erasmus produced, along with his edition of the Greek text, cautiously in the first edition
   of his New Testament (1516), then more boldly in the second (1519).
45 Here again, he means the Vulgate text, not his own Latin version, though his
   Latin words could be understood in either sense. His point is that the early
   patristic commentaries on the Bible could not have used the Vulgate because
   it was not yet available. (Augustine, for example, used the Old Latin text until
   400 AD.) For Erasmus to use the Vulgate readings in translating works written
   before the Vulgate had become the standard Latin version, or even before
   it existed, would be misleading. Clearly Erasmus is fortifying his edition of
   Chrysostom against possible complaints that some of his biblical quotations
   did not conform to the Vulgate.

this in translating the Greeks, among whom Jerome's translation was never   330
accepted.

I hope, great king, you will be graciously pleased to accept this garland woven from the flowers of Chrysostom, which I offer in the name of all scholars. May the Lord Jesus guard and prosper your Majesty.

Basel, 24 March 1527   335

1801 / To the Reader   [Basel, March 1527]

This is the editor's preface addressed to the reader of *Chrysostomi lucubrationes* (see Ep 1800) and must be dated at a time shortly before the publication of the volume. In it Erasmus focuses on the question of authorship of the homilies on Acts. This collection was preparatory to a more complete publication, the five-volume *Opera* (Basel: Froben 1530), a project already conceived when he tried to persuade Germain de Brie to become a collaborator in the work; see Ep 1736.

ERASMUS OF ROTTERDAM TO THE READER, GREETING

From the moment that I began translating the commentaries on the Acts of the Apostles, I had doubts about their authenticity. It was not that the work was unattractive, but there was something clipped and abrupt about the writing that seemed out of keeping with the style of Chrysostom. On the   5
other hand, there was much that fitted the attribution: the frequent questions, the passages of dialogue, the constant appeal to the reader to pay attention with 'Look' and 'You see,' and the digressions on commonplace themes, especially at the end of a homily. Clearly, if this is not Chrysostom, it must be someone who has aped his manner very well. But on this point   10
I have not wanted to trust my own judgment. So I have given a few of the homilies as a sample. I shall complete the rest, God willing, if scholars think the work worthy of Chrysostom. I shall rely on their judgment and gladly lay aside whatever suspicions I may have had. But these were not lightly formed, for so often in the past I have been sadly led astray by false claims   15
on the title-page. Farewell.

LETTERS FROM JUAN DE VERGARA
AND OTHERS CONCERNING ERASMUS

September 1522–August 1527

The six letters translated here from Appendix 18 of Allen VI were exchanged between Spanish admirers of Erasmus. The first, written in 1522, is a selection by Allen from a letter from Juan de Vergara at Valladolid to Juan Luis Vives, then living in Antwerp. In it Vergara urges Vives to make sure that books by two Spanish critics of Erasmus, Sancho Carranza and Diego López Zúñiga, reached Erasmus at Basel. The letter deals with the early criticisms of Erasmus by conservative Spanish scholars and is therefore closely linked to the five letters appended to CWE 8 (pages 336–46) as 'The Vergara-Zúñiga Correspondence.'

The other letters in this appendix date from 1526–7. They reflect the flowering of Erasmus' reputation in Spain, marked by the publication and translation of several of his works, especially the *Enchiridion* and some of the *Colloquies*. Thus they demonstrate the beginning of the great enthusiasm for Erasmus among certain humanistic and spiritual groups in Spain. But they also reveal the first concerted efforts by conservative monks and theologians to bring formal charges of heresy against him and so to block the circulation of his books. The same developments are evident in some of the letters in the main body of this volume, written by some of the same people: Epp 1684 (Erasmus to Juan de Vergara), 1742 (Juan Maldonado to Erasmus), 1748 (Erasmus to Alonso de Fonseca, archbishop of Toledo), 1786 (Alonso Ruiz de Virués to Erasmus), and 1791 (Pedro Juan Olivar to Erasmus). The next volume of letters in CWE will reflect the continuing growth of Erasmus' reputation in Spain and the climax of this first concerted effort to obtain a formal condemnation of his publications at the conference of theologians convened at Valladolid in the summer of 1527 on orders of the inquisitor-general of Spain, Alonso Manrique de Lara, archbishop of Seville, who personally favoured Erasmus but felt obliged to give the critics an opportunity to ventilate their charges. Bataillon (1991) traces the rise and fall of Spanish Erasmianism; Homza provides a significant revision of his account of the Valladolid conference.

CGN

1 / From Juan de Vergara to Juan Luis Vives
Valladolid, 6 September 1522

The first of the six letters exchanged between Spanish friends of Erasmus printed in Allen VI Appendix 18 is a paragraph extracted from a manuscript preserved at Madrid. It formed part of the so-called Heine collection formed by a German physician from Munich who travelled in Spain during the nineteenth century. On that collection, see CWE 8 336. The entire letter, most of which deals with the invitation of Vives to succeed the recently deceased humanist Antonio de Nebrija in the chair of eloquence at the University of Alcalá, was edited by Adolfo Bonilla y San Martín in *Clarorum Hispaniensium epistolae ineditae* (Paris 1901) 76, also issued under the same title in *Revue Hispanique* 8 (1901) 250. The portion extracted by Allen is the final paragraph, with a few irrelevant words omitted at the end. On Vergara see Epp 1277 introduction, 1684 introduction. On Vives see Ep 927 introduction and, for more recent developments, Epp 1362 introduction, 1613 introduction, 1665 introduction, 1732 introduction, 1792 introduction and nn8–9.

... Please give my sincerest greetings to our friend Erasmus, or if he is not with you, then convey my good wishes by letter. He is very popular with everyone in Spain, both learned and unlearned, religious and secular. At Bruges, when I was about to set out for Spain, I gave you a packet of letters, including one from me for Erasmus and a book published at Rome by a   5 Spanish theologian, in which he attacked the *Apologia* that Erasmus wrote in answer to Zúñiga.[1] Later, at the port of Southampton in England, when I was on the point of sailing for Spain,[2] I gave you a second packet of letters with another one for Erasmus[3] and a book of Zúñiga's to which he had given

* * * * *

1

1 Sancho Carranza of Miranda's reply to Erasmus' *Apologia contra Stunicam*. See Ep 1277, nn1, 8.
2 The Emperor Charles V left the Netherlands on 24 May, was at Calais on 25 May, landed at Dover on the twenty-sixth, and spent the whole month of June on a state visit to Henry VIII of England, ending at Southampton on 4 July; he sailed from that port two days later for Santander in Spain, where he landed on 16 July. Thus he was at Southampton on 4–6 July, and Vergara accompanied him as a member of his retinue. For the emperor's itinerary at this time, see *Collection des voyages des souverains des Pays-Bas* ed Louis-Prosper Gachard (Brussels 1874) II 32.
3 Not extant

the title *De Erasmi impietatibus et blasphemiis*.[4] I have no doubt that someone   10
as reliable and efficient as you will have made sure that everything reached
Erasmus, but I should like to be informed of this by a letter from the man
himself.[5] Would you be kind enough to arrange this? Farewell.

Valladolid, 6 September 1522

To the most learned Master Luis Vives, my special friend. In Louvain   15

2 / From [Juan de Vergara] to [Alonso Ruiz de Virués]

Granada, 31 July 1526

Erasmus had been puzzled early in 1526 when he received a letter from Alonso
of Olmedo, a man totally unknown to him, accompanied by the manuscript of
a commentary on his writings that claimed to be offered in a spirit of friendship but that he took to be too critical and possibly an underhanded beginning
of a new line of attack on himself. Neither the letter nor the suggestions (which
advised Erasmus to modify some of his statements in order to avoid stirring
up the hostility of the Spanish monks) has survived, but the author seems to
have claimed (evidently with no justification) that Vergara and his two brothers had encouraged him to write. Hence Erasmus wrote to Vergara (Ep 1684)
to express his fear that 'tricksters' would misinterpret the criticisms and make
them the occasion for another round of attacks. Since by that time he regarded
Vergara as someone he could trust, he asked him to persuade the author to be
more cautious about what he wrote. The present letter describes Vergara's successful identification of Alonso as Alonso Ruiz de Virués. Although Vergara
accepts Virués' statement of his friendly intentions, he complains about the
unjustified claim in his letter to Erasmus that Vergara and his brothers had en-

* * * * *

4 On López Zúñiga, see Ep 1128 n2 and Rummel I 145–77. The book mentioned
  here is his *Erasmi Roterodami blasphemiae et impietates* (Rome: A. Bladus 1522).
5 When he first met Vergara in 1520, Erasmus was suspicious that despite Vergara's declarations of friendship, his personal connections with López Zúñiga
  and Sancho Carranza meant that he tacitly supported their attacks. But Vergara's letter of 24 April 1522 to Erasmus (Ep 1277), describing López Zúñiga
  as irrevocably hostile but assuring him that Carranza was not, seems to have
  convinced Erasmus that he could be trusted. Erasmus' reply (Ep 1312), written on 2 September, acknowledged both the sincerity of his friendship and
  the excellence of his learning. Although it was not a response to this present
  request, sent by way of Vives, for a letter from Erasmus, Ep 1312 cemented
  the friendship between Erasmus and Vergara. Whether Erasmus did send a
  letter acknowledging receipt of López Zúñiga's book is uncertain; the next
  surviving letter in their correspondence is Ep 1684, dated 29 March 1526.

couraged him to send his critical notes to Erasmus. As Erasmus had urged in Ep 1684, Vergara advises Virués that it would be better to write refutations of Erasmus' Spanish critics than to compose even restrained and moderate criticisms of Erasmus' publications. A contemporary manuscript in the hand of Vergara's secretary was the source of the first edition of this letter, which appeared in 1901, like the preceding one, in Bonilla y San Martín's collection of sixteenth-century letters, pages 255–7 (Ep 11); see the introduction to Letter 1 above.

Recently I received a letter from Erasmus, written in response to a little book by a certain Alonso of Olmedo.[1] The author claims to have written it to admonish Erasmus (if you please) and not only that, but to have done so with my encouragement. I was utterly perplexed: who was this man from Olmedo and what did Erasmus mean by 'his book' and 'my encouragement'?   5
I had never read a line of any such book, nor had the author's shadow[2] ever crossed my path. So I pondered the matter carefully and thought about it and canvassed various possibilities in my mind. I could scarcely trust my eyes or believe I was looking at Erasmus' handwriting; I almost suspected a trick: could some malevolent persons be trying to provoke a fight between   10
Erasmus and myself by making it appear that I was secretly encouraging critics to deliver magisterial verdicts on his writings? Such people would know that, although he has a host of enemies, I am a great supporter of his. So after I had let my imagination loose on the matter for a long time without being able to find an answer, I turned for help to my friends, not just   15
to learned acquaintances who live here, but also to absent friends whom I consulted by letter. I was like a new Sphinx posing my riddle to everyone,[3] but there was no one to play the part of Oedipus – until I heard from my brother Bernardino.[4]

* * * * *

2
1 Alonso Ruiz de Virués of Olmedo. On him see Epp 1684, 1717 n19, 1781, 1786, and Vergara's subsequent report to Erasmus on his identity in Ep 1814.
2 *Adagia* 1 ix 86
3 The monster in Greek mythology who stopped passers-by at Thebes, posed a riddle to them, and then devoured them when they failed to solve it. Oedipus was the one who solved the riddle of the Sphinx, causing her to destroy herself; and for this service the Thebans accepted him as their king. The story is recounted in Sophocles' *Oedipus Tyrannus* and in more detail in Apollodorus *Bibliotheca* 3.5.8.
4 Bernardino Tovar (c 1490–c 1545) was a half-brother of Juan, Francisco, and Isabel de Vergara. He was educated in law at Alcalá and Salamanca and at

He replied to my questions in a letter from Alcalá, identifying you as   20
the Alonso in question, a Benedictine monk known as Alonso Virués. He
described you as a learned and serious theologian, a long-time resident of
Burgos, and one of Erasmus' most ardent supporters; and he added many
other touches to this portrait of you as a fine and learned man. All this, it
seems, he had discovered from conversation with various people and from   25
an exchange of letters, for he had never had any direct contact with you
apart from a brief meeting at Alcalá. As for the book, Bernardino told me
that up to that point he had not read it, nor had you given him a copy except
for the preface and the peroration, in which you conveyed my greetings to
Erasmus and those of my brothers, Francisco[5] and Bernardino himself. He   30
went on to say that you claimed to have begun your work as a result of
our encouragement (though it was not clear whether you were referring to
me or to my brothers – Erasmus certainly thought you were referring to
me.) All this was a great surprise to Bernardino, for nothing of the sort had
ever occurred to him, much less to Francisco; both were well aware what it   35
means to take on the role of critic of Erasmus. All that Bernardino wrote to
you was that, since you are so sincerely devoted to Erasmus that you suffer
countless rebuffs for his sake every day, you should not hesitate to send him
a letter and take whatever opportunity offers to work your way into favour
with so excellent a man.[6] But he never suspected you had any thought of   40
criticism.

When I received this report from my brother, I was delighted to know
that you are one of Erasmus' supporters; nevertheless (and I don't want to
be too hard on you), it would have been better if you had omitted those

* * * * *

this period was the central figure of the Erasmian circle at Alcalá. His earlier
involvement with followers of the female mystic Francisca Hernández led to
his being questioned by the Inquisition in 1529; he was imprisoned and tried
on charges of heresy in 1531. After a decade of hearings, he seems to have
been required to abjure and to do penance. His arrest led to the dissolution of
the Alcalá circle of 'Erasmians' and eventually involved his half-brother Juan
de Vergara, who was charged with heresy in 1533, an event which, despite the
intervention of powerful patrons, destroyed his public career. On Tovar see
Bataillon (1991) I 191–4, 228, 472–3, 484, 514. Cf Allen Ep 1814:57n.
5 Francisco de Vergara (d 1545) was a full brother of Juan and was professor of
   Greek at Alcalá from 1522. Like the other members of his family, he admired
   Erasmus; but unlike them he seems not to have had trouble with the Inquisition during the wave of persecutions that broke up the Spanish Erasmian
   movement in the years following 1529.
6 As he did the following February; see Ep 1786, which refers to an earlier letter
   that is now lost.

remarks about my encouragement and refrained from sending greetings in   45
my name without my knowledge and against my wishes. You have given
Erasmus some reason for thinking that there was a compact between us
and that I was assisting you in your role as critic. This is how Homer's Ate
causes a rift among good men.[7] And this is how Eris stirs up strife;[8] for
when we are not satisfied with showing our cleverness at the expense of   50
another man's work, but must also, like a great flood,[9] sweep along in our
path friend and stranger alike and smear with the same suspicion those
who have never entertained any such thoughts – that is Eris at work! Yet
my brother's eulogy of your integrity has convinced me that you are far
from being that sort of person; so I prefer to overlook whatever it was that   55
drove you to write as you did and to believe that you acted out of courtesy,
imagining that this would please my brother, who thinks and speaks so
highly of you.

With regard to the book, since I have not yet had a chance to see it, I
can say nothing about it one way or the other; and as for Erasmus' feelings   60
on the subject and the message he wants me to pass on to you, I would
rather you found these things out from his own letter, a copy of which I
am attaching. In it he pleads his case before me, but he is really responding
to you. It ought not to surprise you that your admonition, however well
intentioned and courteous it may have been (as I am sure it was), must   65
perhaps be viewed by Erasmus in the light of other criticisms that also began
in a courteous and engaging manner but ended bitterly. He is an old veteran
of the ring, hardened by many blows of this kind. He cannot but be worried
by your zeal, for in such encounters in the past no one has come up wagging
his tail without in the end leaving the mark of his teeth.[10] I realize he has   70
nothing to fear from you, but it is ordained by nature that good men fall
victim to suspicion because of sins committed by the wicked.

So act in a way that is worthy of you: show the sincerity of your purpose by modifying the vehemence of your pen or (as Erasmus puts it) changing the tone of your writing, and turn your dialectical skill against those who   75
interpret Erasmus' words in a perverse manner. If you do so, not only will
your efforts not be wasted, but you will earn Erasmus' heartfelt gratitude

* * * * *

7 Moral blindness, in Homer, daughter of Zeus; *Iliad* 19.90–4. Vergara writes the
   names of Ate and Eris in Greek letters.
8 The personification of strife; Homer *Iliad* 4.440–3
9 Vergara wrote this expression in Greek. The image of a river in flood carrying
   all before it goes back to Homer *Iliad* 5.87–92.
10 *Adagia* IV i 32

and that of all learned men. How I wish that my present barbarous duties allowed me to approach the shrine of the Muses as once I could! I would have brought to the task, if not perhaps the greatest competence, at least great 80 dedication. You have the advantage of peace and quiet and of a rich store of learning, so since the task will be easier for you, scholars everywhere will be disappointed if you do nothing. Meanwhile, try to make Erasmus understand that you have a gentle disposition with no taste for controversy. From now on consider me as someone whom your learning and integrity 85 have made a devoted friend. Farewell.

Granada, 31 July 1526

3 / From Alonso Fernández to Luis Núñez Coronel

Palencia, 10 September [1526]

Alonso Fernández de Madrid, archdeacon of Alcor at Palencia, where he was a popular preacher, was the translator of Erasmus' *Enchiridion* into Spanish. The book was probably first published in or before the summer of 1526 in an edition of which no copy survives. A second edition (Alcalá: Miguel de Eguía, no date, but probably September 1526) appeared shortly thereafter. This second edition had been officially examined by the Inquisition at the behest of the inquisitor-general of Castile, Alonso Manrique de Lara, archbishop of Seville, and appeared bearing his official coat of arms and containing an introduction that quoted the endorsement of the book by the inquisitor's examiners. See Ep 1742 n4. There is a modern edition of this translation by Dámaso Alonso, with introduction by Marcel Bataillon, in a yearbook annexed to *Revista de filologia española*, *Añejo* 6 (1932; repr Madrid 1971); cf Bataillon (1991) I 205–7. The recipient of this letter, Luis Núñez Coronel, had studied and taught at Salamanca and at the Collège de Montaigu in Paris. He held a doctorate in theology from Paris (1514), but unlike Noël Béda and most other members of Montaigu, he had become an admirer of Erasmus (Epp 1274, 1281) by 1522 and kept in touch with him (at least indirectly through mutual friends). He became secretary to Archbishop Manrique, the inquisitor-general, a position from which he could do much in favour of Erasmus. According to Erasmus' letter of June 1525 to Béda, he had written 'a most elegant reply' to the attacks by an unidentified Dominican friar on the Spanish *Enchiridion* (Ep 1581 nn104, 105); but that reply does not survive. Fernández' remark at the beginning of this letter about Coronel's lending his 'favour and good will' to the publication of the *Enchiridion* in Spanish suggests that as secretary to Archbishop Manrique, Coronel played a helpful role in the inquisitor-general's decision to inspect and publicly endorse the publication. The contemporary manuscript of the present letter is in Spanish and was first printed by Eduard Boehmer in *Jahrbücher für romanische und englische Literatur* 4 (1862) 159. Boehmer also reported the presence of a Latin version, but Allen was unable to locate it. Charles Fantazzi translated the letter from Spanish.

Most reverend and noble sir, after the publication of Erasmus' *Enchiridion* in Spanish, to which your Grace lent his favour and good will, I instructed the printer in Alcalá[1] to send you, along with my letter, two well-bound copies, one for the most reverend lord Archbishop[2] and the other for your Grace. I believe this commission has been accomplished. Now it is well for   5 your Grace to know that a Franciscan priest in this city, Fray Juan de San Vicente,[3] more of a ranter than a scholar, has tried to inflame the city by his public preaching as he did once before at the time of the Comunidades.[4] On the feast day of St Antoninus,[5] when clergy and townsfolk and people from the province meet at the cathedral church, he uttered countless blasphemies   10 against the book, saying that it contained a thousand heresies. Moreover, he drew a resolution from the folds of his garment and fixed it with pins to

* * * * *

3
1 Miguel Eguía had succeeded Arnao Guillen de Brocar as printer to the University of Alcalá in 1523 and printed a number of works by the Erasmian humanists there, including Fernández' translation of the *Enchiridion*.
2 Manrique, the inquisitor-general, to whom Coronel was secretary
3 On this public denunciation of the *Enchiridion*, see Bataillon (1991) I 241, who also discusses Fernández' open challenge to Fray Juan at a public discussion; but Bataillon's account is based on this letter.
4 The uprising of the Castilian municipalities known as the Comuneros rebellion began in May 1520 and was put down by force in April 1521. It was directed against the non-Spanish ambitions of Charles v and especially against the levying of taxes for what most Spaniards regarded as the pursuit of Hapsburg ambitions in Germany and the Netherlands. One major reason for its failure was that it turned socially radical. Popular agitation among the lower classes of the kind described here alienated the nobility and caused them to give decisive military support to the monarch despite their own coolness to his policies in other parts of Europe. Palencia itself was one of the radical comunero cities, though the major thrust of the local agitation was not against the royal government but against the bishop, who held the lordship of the city. The radical agitators wanted to end the lordship of the bishop and make Palencia a royal city, and some of the opposition to the bishop came from the clergy, though there is no mention of a prominent role for mendicant preachers in stirring up the local insurrection. See Juan Ignacio Gutierrez Nieto *Las comunidades como movimiento antiseñorial: La formación del bando realista en la guerra civil castellano de 1520–1521* (Barcelona 1973) 145–52.
5 2 September

the canopy of the pulpit.[6] I believe a copy of this has been sent from Alcalá, but I am enclosing one so that your Grace may see it.

On the following day I went to the public discussion, but no one got up   15
to engage in debate, since they are all friars; moreover, the resolution did not contain any specific matter for discussion. Then he brandished a document with about thirty articles that he had collected from the *Enchiridion*, as well as from a letter of Erasmus that usually goes with it,[7] and from the *Paraclesis*, etc.[8] I tell you (as God is my witness) that of the thirty articles there were   20
not ten that the priest understood; nor did Erasmus say what is attributed to him – indeed, in some sections he said the very opposite. In the end I decided to oppose him face to face, with good arguments, and without the use of sophisms. When all had heard my case, and understood what was going on, and learned of the diligence exerted by your Reverence in submitting   25
the book to investigation, when they saw that you had authorized its publication and that the book bore your coat of arms, etc, when they realized that the truth was on my side, while on his was nothing but abuse and bad manners, he was hissed and derided by all present, and made his exit from the stage. But he has not ceased his wrangling and even enters the houses of all   30
the nobles here, rousing them up publicly and privately against Erasmus and against the authority of the lord archbishop and the lords of the council.[9] He has dared to say that they were wrong in approving the book for publication.

* * * * *

6 This list of propositions or articles extracted from the Spanish editions of the *Enchiridion* and the *Paraclesis* (presumably the same as the thirty articles mentioned at line 19 below) was part of the background for the conference of theologians held at Valladolid in the summer of 1527 to discuss charges made by the monastic orders against Erasmus. See Ep 1786 n5.

7 Ep 858, addressed to Paul Volz, the preface to an edition of the *Enchiridion* published by Froben in August 1518. The letter was an important statement of Erasmus' conception of church and society. That separate edition of the *Enchiridion* (previously published only as part of volumes containing several works) marks the beginning of the book's career as a religious best-seller, leading to its popularity in Spain and to the Spanish translation by Fernández.

8 The preface to Erasmus' 1516 edition of the Greek New Testament was printed separately from February 1519 on, often with *Ratio verae theologiae*, a more extended explanation of his principles of biblical scholarship. The latter appeared with the prefatory material in the 1519 edition of the New Testament but also was published separately (from November 1518 on). See Epp 1253 n1, 1341A n217.

9 That is, the members of the Suprema, or council of the Inquisition, which had endorsed reprinting of the Spanish translation of the *Enchiridion* (cf Ep 1742 n4) and subsequently would refer the complaints against Erasmus to a special conference of theologians that met at Valladolid in the summer of 1527 (cf Ep 1786 n5).

The truth is that, since all of us hanker after what is forbidden,[10] the only thing the priest accomplished was to ensure that those who did not know   35 who Erasmus was now never put his book down, and nothing else is read but the *Enchiridion*, which was so censured and defamed by the reverend father. Although I live here, I am not the one principally affected by this affair: it is God and his church who are most affected; it affects the author who harms himself in denigrating a doctrine that can be of benefit to many Christians;   40 and it injures a man of great learning and piety, who has done such service to the Christian religion and to good letters. It also concerns your Reverence and the members of the council that a lowly friar, little more than an idiot, dares to condemn for heresy in the church one whom the protectors of the Christian religion approve as a good man. And it concerns no less your Grace,   45 through whose approval and recommendation this book was published.

Certainly, if this man were to speak ill of the *Folly* or some of the *Colloquies* written for children, although it would still be presumptuous, it would have to be tolerated.[11] But to have directed such virulent language against the *Enchiridion*, to this day never challenged by anyone, is something that   50 must not be hushed up. I write to your Grace to beg you to apprise the archbishop of this as well as the members of the council, so that his lordship will have him punished or at least have him make a recantation from the pulpit and restore honour to those whom he has defamed. In this way I think a great service will be done to our Lord, by silencing blabberers of this sort   55 and seeing that true doctrine is not scorned and vilified. May your Grace for the love of our Lord pardon my discourtesy and importunity. May our Lord keep your Reverence as you would wish.

From Palencia, 10 September

Kissing the hand of your Grace   60

Your servant, the archdeacon of Alcor

4 / From Alonso Ruiz de Virués to Juan de Vergara

Burgos, 9 October 1526

A reply to Vergara's letter of 31 July (Letter 2 above). The original, in Virués' hand, survived in the Burscher collection at Leipzig and was first printed in

* * * * *

10 Ovid *Amores* 3.4.17
11 The distinction drawn here is between Erasmus' satirical and humorous works, which might be open to some criticism because of their frank and outwardly irreverent discussion of problems of corruption in the church, and his works of scholarship and spiritual exhortation, which Fernández (and the Spanish Erasmians in general) regarded as valuable expressions of genuinely Catholic piety.

Allen VI, though two short extracts had appeared in Eduard Boehmer *Franziska Hernandez* (Leipzig 1865) 55, according to Allen's introductory note.

TO THE MOST DISTINGUISHED AND LEARNED MASTER
JUAN DE VERGARA, DOCTOR OF THEOLOGY

Cordial greetings. Your letter and the pages from our friend Erasmus brought me the greatest pleasure (how could it be otherwise?). I had been warned to expect them by Bernardino Tovar, whose noble generosity of spirit 5 and remarkable probity of character have bound me to him in a friendship of uncommon closeness.[1] Such joy and delight were only to be expected from receiving a letter from you, a man whose evident mastery in every branch of learning is a miracle (to use no more exalted term). I had not earned this honour by any previous letter of mine, or any service to you, or any ac- 10 tion on my part that might advance your interests. Then there was the additional delight of receiving a copy of a letter Erasmus had written to you.[2] Nothing could have delighted or pleased me more, for I am always eager for a literary banquet of this kind. But you did not want me to be carried away by the magnitude of the favour you had done me; so running almost 15 through the whole of your letter is a note of reproach: you complain that I sent greetings to Erasmus in your name and in the name of your brothers without your knowledge or permission. As a consequence, Erasmus thought himself justified in taking (or should I say 'snatching'?) the opportunity to complain to you about my helpful offer of advice.[3] Since I must beg for- 20 giveness from both of you for what is almost the identical offence, please consider what you read in my letter to Erasmus (a copy of which I enclose)[4] as a reply to you too. For where the truth is simple and straightforward it needs no variation or specious justification. If I were to repeat in a letter to you exactly what I am writing to Erasmus, I fear the length and barbarous 25 style of my letter would bore you to tears. A short time ago, however, I did write you a fairly long letter in Spanish on much the same subject.[5] If you do not approve of it or do not find it satisfactory, then think of me as an-

* * * * *

4
1 Vergara's half-brother. See Letter 2 n4 above; cf Allen Ep 1814:56–72.
2 Ep 1684; see Letter 2:62–4 above.
3 The set of critical notes on Erasmus' publications sent to him by Virués. These notes are lost, but Erasmus' negative reaction is expressed in Ep 1684 to Vergara; cf Letter 2:35–41 above.
4 Not extant
5 Not extant

other Dinocrates,[6] with some grand and useful project in mind, dressed in
a lion's skin and with my club and poplar chaplet; when I burst upon the   30
theatre in this garb, I caused you and Erasmus to sit up and take notice, as
you make quite clear in your perceptive and brilliant reply.

What charge can you bring against me except that I chose to use your
name, like the accoutrements of Hercules, to attract the attention of Erasmus? Was this to act like a flooding river, carrying before me friend and   35
stranger alike? Does this make me Homer's Ate?[7] Do I seem to you like Virgil's Iris?[8] I do not have so high an opinion of this troublesome book of mine
that I expect people will think me clever at the expense of another man's
work. I did not publish it to show off, but to give advice in the spirit of the
gospel. I do not see the book as a showcase for my talents; rather it will at-   40
tract the barking of slanderous critics. 'Barking'? Heavens! it is not barking,
but savage bites that I suffer every day from these enemies of the gospel,
men who under the cloak of piety pursue their own ends, corrupting the
word of God[9] and thinking godliness a means to profit,[10] or at least (if that
is too grave a sin to suspect of Christians who have taken a vow to follow   45
the apostles) having a zeal for God, but not according to knowledge.[11]

But it is better not to provoke some of these fools, who have such tender ears that you must be careful not to harm them with the bite of truth.[12]
Moreover, it is not safe to entrust anything to a letter, since there are spies[13]
everywhere with an ear cocked for anything that is said or written. Although   50
I need even an Amyclaean informer[14] to tell of all the suffering I have en-

* * * * *

6 An architect who dressed himself like Hercules in order to attract the attention
of Alexander the Great and thus get a commission; Vitruvius 2 pref 1–2
7 See Letter 2 n7 above.
8 A confusion of Iris, the goddess of the rainbow (who does appear in Virgil)
with Eris, the personification of strife (who does not)
9 2 Cor 2:17
10 1 Tim 6:5
11 Rom 10:2
12 Persius 1.10.107–8. Conservative clergymen in this period often denounced
statements that they disliked but that were not quite heretical as 'offensive to
pious ears.'
13 Literally, 'there is a Corycaean.' The people who lived on the coast beneath
Mt Corycus were celebrated in antiquity for their habit of spying on shipping
and seizing the cargoes of passing vessels. See Adagia I ii 44 and Cicero Ad
Atticum 10.18.
14 On several occasions false news of enemy attack had caused panic among
the people of Amyclae. As a result, they passed a law forbidding anyone to
bring such news. The 'silence' of Amyclae became proverbial; see Adagia I ix 1.

dured thus far, someone to break the silence with the relentless voice of
Stentor[15] and rouse Erasmus' friends who slumber on, indifferent to the
danger,[16] yet it is you more than anyone else whose help I want because
of your influence with the emperor and with bishops and laymen in high   55
places, for men speak ill of me everywhere simply because I am a supporter of Erasmus. I wish this vilification were confined to out-of-the-way
places and to private conversation. But it goes beyond that: in courts, the-
atres, and crowded gatherings I am reviled, snubbed, and hissed at. The
charge, believe it or not, is heresy, and it is made in sermons and delivered   60
from the pulpit, where one should teach and practise the piety and moderation of the gospel. Since I am denied all human help, I pray that Christ,
our good and mighty Lord, will aid me in this task, which I began under
his inspiration and which I plan to carry forward if it is his will. May he
make my forehead strong, stronger than the forehead of my enemies, as he   65
tells us he did for his prophet Ezekiel.[17] Even today Israel, which lives according to the flesh, still preserves a brazen forehead and a stiff neck, and
refuses to bear the yoke of Christ, in which alone it could find true peace,
although it does not shrink from living in bondage under the elements of
this world.[18]   70

But what sort of person am I, when the courier is in a hurry, to turn
my letter into a declamation! My constant obligations as a preacher have
had such an effect on me that I cannot speak in any other way than in the
rhetoric of the pulpit. So I must try to moderate my language and not give
free rein to the hurt and bitterness of my mind. Here then, most learned sir,   75

* * * * *

Virués means that Erasmus' friends are similarly unwilling to hear bad news
of impending attacks on him, and there is no one to inform them.
15 A shadowy figure in ancient literature. The reference here seems to be to *Iliad*
5.785, where Hera rouses the Greeks to action in the loud voice of Stentor.
Cf *Adagia* II iii 37: *Stentore clamosior* 'Noisier than Stentor,' which presents the
proverbially loud voice of Stentor and cites the passage from the *Iliad* but does
not otherwise match very closely the figure presented by Virués.
16 Literally, 'sleep on either ear,' a proverbial expression for sleeping soundly,
unaware of imminent danger; see *Adagia* I viii 19.
17 Ezek 3:8
18 This sentence is a remarkable cento of biblical phrases: Rom 8:1, 8, 9; 9:3, 5
(according to the flesh); Matt 11:29 (yoke, peace); Ezek 3:7 (a brazen forehead);
Exod 32:9 and elsewhere (a stiff neck); Gal 4:3 (bondage under the elements
of the world). The connection of thought is somewhat elliptical. It depends on
Ezek 3:7, where the Lord addresses the prophet: 'But the house of Israel will
not listen to you; for they are not willing to listen to me; because all the house
of Israel are of a hard forehead and of a stubborn heart.'

is a letter which must serve as a reply to that brilliant and charming letter of yours. It is brief, to be sure, but in every word it shows a lack of polish; what it reveals all too clearly is the illiteracy and inarticulateness of its author. You have also my reply to Erasmus, in which I show, as you asked me to, that my mind is as big a stranger to calumny and controversy as it 80 could be. Your brother Bernardino Tovar has a copy of my little book.[19] If you think it worth your while to read it, you will understand that, while my treatment of the issue may be thin and barbarous in style, it was fair-minded with nothing of the obsequiousness of the parasite about it.[20] If you are offended by the lack of substance and the barbarity of my style, remem- 85 ber that nothing more could be expected of an Arevacian,[21] worse still a man from Olmedo. But whatever I am, please consider me henceforth your willing servant; and perhaps you would be kind enough to count me among your friends, if only at the lowest rank. Farewell.

Burgos, 9 October 1526   90

5 / From Juan de Vergara to Juan Luis Vives   Valladolid, 12 April 1527

> This is an extract from a letter of Vergara to Vives, informing him of the actions by the monastic orders (the 'conspiracy' mentioned in line 1) to bring formal charges of heresy and impiety against Erasmus. These efforts led to the conference of theologians that met at Valladolid in the summer of 1527 on orders of the Inquisition to discuss the charges. See Ep 1786 n5 and Ep 1814, where Vergara gives Erasmus a summary narrative of the events that led to the Valladolid conference. In Ep 1847 to Erasmus, Vives quoted verbatim the entire first paragraph of the extract translated here. The full letter survived in two manuscripts at the Biblioteca Nacional in Madrid, one a rough draft by Vergara and the other a copy made by his secretary with corrections and the Greek words added by Vergara. It was first edited by Bonilla y San Martín (see Letter 1 introduction above), page 80 of the separate edition, or *Revue Hispanique* 255–7.

... Recently our monks have launched a conspiracy against Erasmus, not all of them of course, but the majority. The less a monastic order depends on

* * * * *

19 See n3 above.
20 Literally, 'in the manner of a Gnatho,' the name of a parasite in Terence's *Eunuchus*, and subsequently used to refer to parasites in general
21 A member of the ancient Arevaci (Pliny *Naturalis historia* 3.3.19 and 27), still reflected in the name of Arevalo, a town located between Olmedo and Avila. In other words, an unpolished provincial.

begging, the less hostile it is to him. The case has been referred to the commission.[1] So far at least, the results have been most favourable to Erasmus. My prince[2] has undertaken to do his utmost to protect him. The emperor is openly favourable; the commissioners themselves are also on his side, as are all good men. Since his enemies see they will gain nothing from this controversy except general unpopularity, they are now beginning to lose interest, and in my opinion would gladly undo what has been done if this could be accomplished to the general satisfaction of everyone.

I intended to write a letter to Erasmus himself and give it to my man Jacobus,[3] who is delivering this to you. I was also hoping, when I wrote to Erasmus, to enclose the list of charges that his critics were compiling against his writings.[4] Every day I expected the document to arrive. So I held Jacobus here for several days. But he is in a hurry, and I do not wish to detain him any longer. So I am sending him off with this one letter. I shall write to Erasmus as soon as I obtain a copy of the charges. Farewell.

Valladolid, 12 April 1527

6 / From Juan Luis Vives to Juan de Vergara   Bruges, 14 August 1527

Extracted from a reply to the preceding letter. The text is found in the same Madrid manuscript as that letter and also was first printed by Bonilla y San Martín (see Letter 1 introduction above), page 92 of the separate edition, or *Revue Hispanique* 266.

... You will do me a great favour if you write and give me the latest news of Erasmus. I have been informed, particularly in letters from Spain, that the Erasmians have lodged an indictment against Thomas and Scotus and

* * * * *

5
1 See Letter 3 n9 above.
2 Alonso de Fonseca, archbishop of Toledo and primate of Spain, to whom Vergara was secretary. Influenced by Vergara, Archbishop Fonseca (like Archbishop Manrique, the inquisitor-general) was sympathetic to Erasmus. As Vergara notes just below, the emperor himself and his councillors, including his secretary, Alfonso de Valdés, and the chancellor, Mercurino Gattinara, also favoured Erasmus.
3 The full name and identity of this servant of Vergara remain unknown.
4 The missing initial page or pages of Ep 1791, written to Erasmus by Pedro Juan Olivar on 13 March, probably contained the list of charges or at least a summary.

are demanding that an inquiry be made into them too.[1] How could that idea have got into their heads? I could never have imagined that such a thing were even possible. Clearly, if we subjected the great works that those men have left us to the same sort of scrutiny as his critics apply to Erasmus, even more intolerable things would appear there – except that familiarity softens much that is harsh and unpleasant. There would be no shortage of doctrines that no one could hold or defend except by advancing such specious interpretations and subtle distinctions as would make it easy to defend a heretic of any sort.

Recently I had a letter from Alonso Virués,[2] a Benedictine, apparently a great partisan of Erasmus, and a lover of those arts and letters in which we also take delight. Could you tell me who this man is? He seems not to lack wit or learning. Farewell.

Bruges, 14 August 1527

To Juan de Vergara, theologian, and secretary to the most reverend the archbishop of Toledo

* * * * *

6

1 Most of this sentence is written in Greek, probably from a desire to discuss sensitive matters (reports of Spanish humanists' counter-attack against their scholastic critics, the mendicant orders) in a form that only a handful of humanists could read. This letter is the only known source to suggest that the Spanish defenders of Erasmus dared to mount an attack on the orthodoxy of Thomas Aquinas and Duns Scotus, though Bataillon (1991) I 284 n1 speculates that some Erasmian pamphleteer may have suggested such an inquiry into the orthodoxy of Thomas and Scotus, since the anti-Erasmian Franciscan theologian Luis de Carvajal in one of his publications complained of an anonymous author who claimed that one could find heresies in the works of St Jerome as easily as in the works of Erasmus. Erasmus himself (in Ep 1581 to Noël Béda, for example) had argued that censorious scholastic theologians could find heresy in any statement and also that errors could be found even in the writings of the great scholastic doctors. In the present letter, however, Vives obviously regards such a line of argument, at least in Spain and in the face of formal charges of heresy, as unwise and even potentially risky, though like Erasmus he also says that a dishonest critic can make any passage sound heretical.

2 On him see Letter 2 n1 above.

ERASMUS' FIRST WILL

The earliest of Erasmus' three wills, which was sealed in the presence of witnesses in Basel on 22 January 1527, survives at Basel in a copy written in the hand of the heir or trustee (that is, the person selected to take charge of administering the estate), Bonifacius Amerbach, who as a jurist may well have advised Erasmus on its form. Ludwig Sieber was the first to edit it: *Das Testament des Erasmus vom 22. Januar 1527* (Basel 1889). The will was never formally put into effect, since Erasmus drew up a second will (of which no copy survives) in 1533 while living at Freiburg and a third, drawn up at Basel on 12 February 1536 (Allen xi 362–5). The third will was the one actually executed after Erasmus' death. Nevertheless, Amerbach as trustee seems to have carried out the bequests made in the first will whenever possible; above all, he proceeded with the plan for a full edition of the collected works of Erasmus, a plan outlined in this document but missing from the final will of 1536. For a brief discussion of Erasmus' three wills, see Schoeck (1993) 384–6 Appendix D.

Erasmus had considered making a will as early as 1518, when he described to Antonio Pucci (Ep 860) an illness so severe that he felt he should take steps to dispose of his properties, but he seems not to have proceeded further. In the intervening years, he continued to suffer from various ailments, especially painful calculus, with some periods of remission but other periods of prostrating pain. No doubt his acute illness in the late summer of 1526, when his calculus was aggravated by what seems to have been a serious infection of the urinary tract (see Epp 1729, 1735), made him think again of making a will, and in the autumn or early winter of that year he experienced another period of illness, this time marked by acute stomach pain. On 25 December 1526 Bonifacius Amerbach in a letter described his condition as very feeble (cf Ep 1780 n5). Since by the mid-1520s Erasmus had accumulated rather substantial wealth, he concluded that he must provide for its orderly disposition after his death.

He had taken the most essential step towards this end in July 1525, when he obtained a papal brief from Pope Clement vii (Ep 1588) authorizing him to dispose of his property by will. Although he was very reticent about it, his illegitimate birth had made him ineligible to hold benefices or even to be ordained to the priesthood except under the sponsorship of a religious order. Under Pope Julius ii and again under Pope Leo x, he had obtained dispensations granting several privileges, including the right to live outside any monastery of his order, the right to lay aside the garb of the Augustinian canons and dress like a secular priest, and the right to hold ecclesiastical benefices or to receive incomes arising from ecclesiastical benefices. Nevertheless, he was still legally a monk of the Augustinian monastery at Steyn, which he had entered as a youth, and there was a possibility that upon his death the abbot of his home monastery might have a legal claim to ownership of all his property. The papal brief of 8 July 1525 solved that problem by specifically authorizing him to dispose of his property by drawing a will. He had sent his most trusted confidential courier, Karl Harst, to Rome that summer with several tasks, but the most important of these was completing the arrangements for this papal brief and acquiring possession of the document, which Erasmus carefully retained among his private papers.

CGN

ERASMUS' FIRST WILL

In the name of the Lord, Amen. In the year of our Lord one thousand, five hundred, and twenty-seven, on the morrow of St Agnes' day, at Basel, I, Erasmus of Rotterdam, doctor of theology and priest of the diocese of Utrecht,[1] being, by the grace of God, of sound and healthy mind, have set down in this document, written by my own hand, my final wishes concerning all the   5 property which I shall leave behind. I appoint as my heir or trustee Dr Bonifacius Amerbach[2] and as my executors Beatus Rhenanus of Sélestat, Basilius Amerbach, and Hieronymus Froben.[3] It is my wish and intention:

First, that my heir take for himself from my property all my rings,[4] which he will find listed in the inventory, also a solid gold spoon[5] and a gilded   10 double cup, the gift of Duke George,[6] as well as 100 crowns;[7]

* * * * *

1 Here Erasmus assumes the two professional titles on which his work as a biblical and patristic scholar and as a critic of abuses in the church was based. On his doctorate, a genuine academic degree even though conferred somewhat irregularly (*per saltum*), see Ep 1687 n15. Even though he usually did not emphasize his possession of a doctorate in theology, he did firmly uphold his right to discuss theological issues when it was challenged by his scholastic critics, notably in his second letter to Noël Béda (Ep 1581:21–30), where he asserts his status both as priest and as theologian. Although Erasmus never undertook a parish ministry, he did receive pensions from the revenues of two parishes (at Aldington in Kent and Courtrai in Flanders) by virtue of his status as a priest. After he received a papal dispensation allowing him to abandon the habit of his religious order, the Augustinian canons, he dressed 'in the reputable garb of a secular priest,' precisely as specified in the dispensation granted by Pope Leo x in January 1517. See Epp 517, 518, 519. On his ordination and the importance of his priestly status in his view of his own religious vocation, see Germain Marc'hadour 'Erasmus as Priest: Holy Orders in His Vision and Practice' in *Erasmus' Vision of the Church* ed Hilmar M. Pabel, Sixteenth Century Essays and Studies 33 (Kirksville, MO 1995) 115–49.
2 He was probably Erasmus' closest friend at Basel, a doctor of civil and canon law and professor in the faculty of law at the University of Basel.
3 Three of Erasmus' closest friends at Basel, who were also associates in his work as scholarly editor for the Froben press. Rhenanus had recently moved back to his native city of Sélestat but remained in close touch with his friends and the publishers in Basel.
4 Allen VI 503:10n notes that these rings are listed in the inventory of Erasmus' property compiled in 1534 by his secretary Gilbert Cousin. See *Bodleian Quarterly Record* 2 (1918) 143.
5 A gift from Krzysztof Szydłowiecki; see Ep 1752:9.
6 See Epp 1691 n4, 1743 n2.
7 Latin *coronatos centum*. These are probably French crowns, that is, *écus au soleil,*

that he give:

> to Henricus Glareanus[8] all my household linens with my two best cloaks, one dark purple, the other black and lined with sable fur (now commonly known as 'martens'),[9] and fifty crowns;[10]   15

> to Ludwig Baer,[11] who, as the truest of friends, will not refuse to help my trustee and assist with the will, an hourglass of pure gold;[12]

> to Basilius Amerbach two silver trenchers with a silver flask and a silver cup with a cover bearing the image of St Jerome;

> to Beatus Rhenanus two forks, one gold, the other silver;[13]   20

> to Hieronymus Froben two purses, one with a silver ring and the other a ring of silver gilt;

> to Johann Froben my bed curtains with two tapestry hangings;

> to Sigismundus, Froben's corrector,[14] the rest of my clothes and twenty-six common ducats[15] with a gilt spoon;   25

* * * * *

whose value, as noted in Ep 1799 n2, was about the same as that for the new English crowns. If so, this was a sum worth about £23 6s 8d sterling (£25, if English crowns) or officially £31 13s 4d groot Flemish (or as much as £35 12s 6d groot, at current market rates), and £200 tournois (or as much as £219 5s 0d, with rising gold rates; see Ep 1796 n5).

8 The most famous Swiss humanist of this time; teacher of Greek at Basel, 1522–9. See Epp 440, 1619 n1.

9 Allen (15n) observes that the black cape lined (or trimmed – the Latin can mean either) with fur appears on Cousin's inventory of 1534 (see n4 above).

10 Latin *coronatos quinquaginta*. Probably these were French *écus au soleil*, and if so, a sum which would be worth about £11 6s 8d sterling, or officially £15 16s 8d groot Flemish (or as much as £17 16s 4d groot, with rising gold rates), or officially £100 tournois (or as much as £109 12s 8d tournois; see Ep 1796 n5).

11 On Baer, see Ep 1674 n17.

12 On this gift from Krzysztof Szydłowiecki, see Ep 1752 n1.

13 The gold fork was probably another gift from Szydłowiecki (Ep 1752:9).

14 Sigismundus Gelenius, a Bohemian humanist, worked as an editor and proof-reader for the Froben press and was himself a textual scholar of great ability. See Epp 1702 n1, 1767 n2.

15 Latin *ducatos communes viginti sex*. These were Venetian ducats, or Florentine or other Italian gold florins, all of the same value; this sum was worth £6 1s 4d sterling, or officially £8 13s 4d groot Flemish (or as much as £9 15s 0d groot, with rising gold rates), and officially £53 19s 0d tournois (or as much as £59 3s 0d tournois; see Ep 1796 n5).

to Johann von Botzeim,[16] canon of Constance, as a remembrance of me, a silver spoon having the figure of Sebastian on it;

to Conradus Goclenius[17] all my gold and silver medals and six silver cups, now in his possession.

The rest of my silver and gilt vessels shall be used to defray the cost 30 of printing my works,[18] as my heir decides and the executors advise.

Some time ago I sold all my library to the distinguished Polish count, Jan Łaski,[19] for 400 gold pieces, 200 of which he has already paid.[20] My Greek manuscripts on parchment and paper are not included. If he wishes to have these, he will pay separately, as the documents will show. 35

With regard to the edition of my works, this is what I wish my heir and executors to do:

To arrange for the printing of all my works, if possible by Johann Froben, otherwise by someone else, in an elegant and appropriate edition, divided into volumes as I described in the *Catalogus*.[21] As an incentive to the printer, 40 I desire that, immediately on beginning the task, he be paid at the rate of 300 florins per year[22] if he completes the work within four years, and at the

* * * * *

16 On this humanistic canon of Constance, see Epp 1761, 1782 and n11.
17 Professor of Latin in the Collegium Trilingue at Louvain, a friend of long standing, and a regular source of valuable information on people and events at Louvain. See Epp 1209 introduction, 1641 introduction.
18 See Ep 1341A:1500–1639, which shows that Erasmus was already planning a complete edition of his works in 1523–4, and Ep 1732 n5, where Vives urges Erasmus to take steps to produce such a collection. See his instructions below (lines 36–76) regarding this proposed edition, which actually was published by the Froben firm in 1540.
19 On Łaski, who lived in Erasmus' household at Basel for six months in 1525, see Ep 1593 n18. Erasmus' Latin word for his title of nobility was *baro*.
20 Latin *quadringentis aureis*. These were probably Rhenish gold florins; if so, this sum was then worth about £66 13s 4d (the equivalent of 2,667 days' wages or 12 years and 1 month's income for an Oxford master carpenter), or officially £98 6s 8d groot Flemish, but more likely, with rising gold rates, £106 13s 4d groot (the equivalent to 2,560 days' wages or 11 years and 7 months' wage income for an Antwerp master carpenter), or £600 tournois (or as much as £657 16s 8d, with rising gold values; see Ep 1796 n5).
21 See Ep 1341A, his *Catalogus lucubrationum*, drawn up (and soon printed) in response to a request from Botzheim (Ep 1285).
22 Latin *trecentos florenos*, probably Rhenish gold florins; if so, this sum was then worth about £50 sterling, or officially £73 15s 0d groot Flemish, but with rising

rate of 400 florins[23] if he completes it within three years. My work on St Jerome[24] and Hilary[25] and any other similar editions will not be included in this calculation, unless it is to the advantage of the printer to publish   45 them; this, however, is something I should like to see happen, if it could be accomplished at a reasonable price.

I do not wish the correctors to add anything of their own to my works; only errors caused by my carelessness or the carelessness of the typesetters should be corrected, and only if the case is clear and the change can be made   50 in a very few words, and only after consulting among themselves. Special care should be taken with references to authors, books, and chapters. For this task my particular wish is to have the services of Henricus Glareanus, Beatus Rhenanus, Bonifacius Amerbach, Basilius Amerbach, and Sigismundus. If they refuse, I authorize my heir to find suitable substitutes. If Conradus   55 Goclenius agrees to move to Basel to oversee this business, I wish him to be paid 100 crowns[26] each year for up to four years in addition to anything the printer may choose to give him. Glareanus should receive sixty gold florins[27] each year for the same period and Sigismundus forty.[28] If my heir and his brother wish to participate in this project, my heir shall use his own judg-   60 ment in estimating the value of their contribution. Since the function each person will assume cannot now be clearly foreseen, I give my heir authority, in accordance with his own judgment and the advice of the executors,

* * * * *

gold rates, probably as much as £80 groot, or £450 tournois (or as much as £493 7s 6d; see Ep 1796 n5).

23 Latin *quadringentos*; see nn20 and 22 above.

24 Froben had completed publication of the revised second edition of Jerome's *Opera*, of which Erasmus was general editor, in February 1526; see Epp 1623 n5, 1675 n6.

25 Erasmus had published the works of St Hilary of Poitiers with Froben in February 1523; Ep 1334 is the dedication, addressed to Jean de Carondelet.

26 Latin *coronatos centum*, probably French *écus au soleil*; if so, this sum was worth about £23 6s 8d sterling; or officially £31 13s 4d groot, but as much as £35 12s 6d groot Flemish, with rising gold values; or £200 tournois (or as much as £219 5s 6d; see Ep 1796 n5).

27 Latin *aureos florenos sexaginta*, probably Rhenish gold florins once more; if so, this sum was worth £10 sterling, or officially £14 15s 0d groot Flemish, but, with rising gold values, probably about £16 groot, or £90 tournois (or as much as £98 13s 6d; see Ep 1796 n5).

28 If these were Rhenish gold florins (see the preceding note), this was a sum amounting to £6 6s 8d sterling, or officially £9 16s 8d groot Flemish, but with rising gold values, probably about £10 13s 9d groot, or £60 tournois (or as much as £65 15s 8d; see Ep 1796 n5).

to increase or decrease the emoluments in proportion to the responsibilities assumed by each. I should not wish, however, more than three, or at the most four, correctors to be employed. If two can do the work, by compensating for their numbers by their industry, let their remuneration be increased accordingly.

With regard to the contract with the printers,[29] I authorize my heir, in conjunction with the executors, to adjust the payment in relation to the quality of the edition and the number of copies printed. I should not want a run of less than 1500. I should like Froben, or anyone who succeeds to his business, to be treated generously. If, however, he is reluctant to undertake the work, let them seek out someone else. If either my heir or my executors incur any expense in this matter, I desire that they be paid from the residue of the estate, so that their individual legacies are not diminished.

Let them prepare twenty carefully bound sets made up of individual volumes (or 'parts'),[30] and when the work is complete, send:

one set to the archbishop of Canterbury;[31]

the second to Cuthbert Tunstall, bishop of London;[32]

the third to Thomas More, English baron;[33]

the fourth to John, bishop of Lincoln;[34]

* * * * *

29 Erasmus knew from personal experience the importance of the publication contract, especially for an edition of the scope he had in mind, but he also knew from experience that revisions in the contract might be needed as an extensive project went forward. His clear preference for Froben rested both on his opinion of the high quality of his work as a printer and on his record of fair dealing. Froben himself died before the year was out (26 October 1527), but his heirs and successors did become the publishers of the 1540 edition of Erasmus' *Opera*.

30 For discussion of the distribution of these sets to the individuals named below, see Charles G. Nauert 'Erasmus' Spiritual Homeland: The Evidence of His 1527 Will' in *Habent sua fata libelli / Books Have Their Own Destiny: Essays in Honor of Robert V. Schnucker* ed Robin B. Barnes, Robert A. Kolb, and Paula L. Presley, Sixteenth Century Essays and Studies 50 (Kirksville, MO 1998) 103–10.

31 William Warham, one of Erasmus' most generous patrons

32 One of Erasmus' most reliable patrons among the English bishops; see Epp 1697 n15, 1726 introduction.

33 This provision is further proof that even though few letters between More and Erasmus survive from the mid-1520s, their friendship remained strong.

34 John Longland, another of his English patrons

the fifth to Cambridge, to be deposited in Queen's College, in the public library of that college;[35]

the sixth to John, bishop of Rochester;[36]   85

the seventh to Spain, to be deposited in the imperial library;[37]

the eighth to the bishop of Toledo;[38]

the ninth to Ferdinand, brother of the emperor Charles;[39]

the tenth to Bernhard, bishop of Trent;[40]

the eleventh to Giambattista Egnazio;[41]   90

* * * * *

35 Recognition of the hospitality that Erasmus received during his period teaching at Cambridge (1511–14), when he resided in Queen's

36 John Fisher, whom Erasmus respected both as a friend and as an especially learned theologian. Erasmus frequently defended his own biblical and patristic scholarship, especially when facing criticism from conservative theologians, by citing Fisher's approval of his work; for example, Epp 1571:16 (and see n8), 1581:332–3, both addressed to Noël Béda.

37 Although directed to Spain, this gift was really intended for Charles v in his role as emperor and hereditary ruler of the Netherlands; despite his difficulty in receiving his pension, Erasmus was still a member of Charles' council.

38 This is the only copy actually intended for a Spanish recipient. As archbishop of Toledo, Alonso de Fonseca was primate of Spain. Encouraged by his secretary, Juan de Vergara, he was the most powerful native Spanish supporter of Erasmus against the attacks on his orthodoxy by the monastic orders. Many of Erasmus' other supporters at the imperial court were Netherlanders and Burgundians. See Ep 1748. Knowing that he was being denounced by some monks and theologians, Erasmus had identified Archbishop Fonseca as a crucial figure in the defence of his reputation in Spain.

39 Ferdinand of Hapsburg, archduke of Austria and brother of the emperor, had long demonstrated sympathetic support for Erasmus' scholarship and his ideas of moderate religious reform. See Epp 1545 n5, 1697 n27.

40 Bernhard von Cles, the most influential of Archduke Ferdinand's advisers and himself a would-be patron of Erasmus. See Epp 1357, 1689, 1738, 1755, 1771, 1793.

41 Erasmus had met him while living in Venice and seems to have regarded him as the most competent, and the most reliably friendly, of all Italian humanists. See Ep 1707 introduction and the earlier correspondence there cited. This copy of the Opera would have been the only one presented to any Italian recipient; not even the papal library is on Erasmus' list.

the twelfth to Busleyden's College in Louvain, to be deposited in its library;[42]

the thirteenth to be deposited in the College of the Lily;[43]

the fourteenth to Tournai, to be deposited in the college founded by Pierre Cotrel for languages and letters;[44]   95

the fifteenth to Frans van Cranevelt, member of the Council of Mechelen;[45]

the sixteenth to Hugenoys of Ghent, abbot of St Bavo's;[46]

the seventeenth to Marcus Laurinus, dean of St Donatian's, to be deposited in the chapter library;[47]   100

the eighteenth to Nicolaas Everaerts, president of Holland,[48] or to his successor;

the nineteenth to Herman Lethmaet, theologian;[49]

* * * * *

42 The famous Collegium Trilingue, founded to be the major centre of humanistic studies at Louvain. Erasmus was one of the trustees designated by the founder's will to bring the new institution into being, and he took an active role in the foundation of the college. He retained a lifelong sympathy for it and had many friends there.
43 The college in which Erasmus resided during most of his time in Louvain, known as a centre for humanistic studies. He also had many friends there.
44 On the attempt of Cotrel to found a new university in the Netherlands at Tournai, beginning with a college devoted to humanistic studies, see Ep 1747 n21.
45 A humanist and friend of Erasmus, formerly pensionary of the city of Bruges but now a member of the Grand Council of Mechelen, the supreme judicial court of the Hapsburg Netherlands. See Epp 1145, 1582 n8.
46 Lieven Hugenoys, abbot of the Benedictine abbey of St Bavo in Ghent, had made manuscripts from the monastery's library available to Erasmus for his scholarly work. On him see Ep 1214.
47 Another old friend in the Netherlands; see Ep 1695 n6.
48 Lord President of the Council of Holland, another old friend. See Epp 1092 introduction, 1653 introduction.
49 A native of Gouda, doctor of theology, and canon of St Mary's at Utrecht. See Epp 1320, 1345, 1350, 1360. Although no letters between him and Erasmus survive after 1523, Erasmus continued to regard him highly as a theologian and in a letter to Noël Béda (Ep 1581:335-7) defended his editions of the New Testament by pointing out that he had consulted three Paris graduates in theology, Lethmaet being one of them. The point was strengthened by the fact that Lethmaet (like Ludwig Baer of Basel, one of the others) had ranked at the

the twentieth to the monastery of Egmond, to be deposited in its
library.[50]   105

If any of these persons shall have died,[51] let my heir appoint others
of his own choosing in their place. The contract with the printers shall be
negotiated secretly to prevent any ill-disposed person from causing delay
in the work. I desire my editions of Jerome and Hilary to be included with
the sets of my work when they are sent out.   110

When the work is finished, or the costs have been calculated, let the
residue of the estate be used for worthy causes, in particular for the support
of young men of promise and for the provision of dowries for young women
of good character.[52]

* * * * *

head of his class when he received the licentiate in theology at Paris; see Farge
Biographical Register 278–9 (no 307).

50 This was the oldest Benedictine abbey in Erasmus' native county of Holland,
founded by the counts of Frisia in the tenth century; it was also noted for
its rich library of manuscripts. See A.C.F. Koch in *Dictionnaire d'histoire et de
géographie ecclésiastiques* xv 23–7. Erasmus knew the man who had been abbot
since 1510, Meynard Man (who had died on 4 December 1526, though it is unlikely that Erasmus would have known this by the date of the will). Man was
related to Erasmus' servant-pupil Quirinus Talesius (who is mentioned in the
will; cf also Ep 1740 n1) and to his humanist friend Alaard of Amsterdam; he
was also devoted both to spiritual reform and to the promotion of learning
and had been a patron of Erasmus' best friend among the Louvain theologians, Maarten van Dorp. He and Erasmus regarded each other highly (see
Epp 304:178n, 676, 1044). Yet the correspondence does not indicate that he and
Erasmus were especially close, and the gift (which is to the abbey, not to the
individual) was probably intended as a courtesy to an ancient monastery in
Erasmus' native county, especially as it was noted for the riches of its library.

51 Allen (112n) observes that of the thirteen individuals named to receive gift
copies, six (Archbishop Warham, Thomas More, Bishop John Fisher, Archbishop Alonso de Fonseca, Abbot Hugenoys, and Nicolaas Everaerts) died
before Erasmus did, and that Bishop Bernhard von Cles died before the edition of Erasmus' *Opera* was published in 1540.

52 The two charities which Erasmus designated for the residue of his estate after
expenses were paid and individual legacies were distributed, scholarship support for promising young men and dowries for young women of good character who were too poor to make a respectable marriage, are compatible with
Erasmus' own conception of 'good' works and also with the terms of Clement
vii's brief (Ep 1588) authorizing the will, which recommended legacies for pious purposes and specifically mentioned support of colleges and universities.
In the event, Amerbach used much of the residue to found scholarships for
students at the University of Basel.

Let my heir take charge of my funeral. It should be neither mean nor pre-   115
tentious and should be carried out according to the rites of the church and
in such a manner that no one can find fault.[53] I owe nothing to anyone; I
have no natural heir; I was given the right to make a will in a letter from
the apostolic see,[54] which covers also ecclesiastical benefactions.

If my servant Quirinus is still with me at the time of my death,[55] I wish him   120
to be given 200 gold florins[56] for his long and faithful service.

These appointments I have made, being sound of mind and body, in the year
and on the day indicated above, and for greater certainty I have written both
copies in my own hand and affixed thereto my personal seal, namely the
'Terminus,'[57] always reserving the right to add or delete anything, or alter   125
my will completely if I so wish, as the law provides.

Signed with the seal of the Terminus encircled with the words 'Cedo nulli.'

* * * * *

53 The specification of a funeral according to the rites of the church was of some
   importance, since in 1527 Basel was a religiously divided city and several
   churches were already in the hands of Protestant preachers.
54 Ep 1588, from Clement VII
55 Quirinus Talesius of Haarlem probably had been Erasmus' servant-pupil since
   1524, although he is not mentioned in any surviving letter until later in 1527
   (Allen Ep 1890). See Ep 1740 n1.
56 Latin *florenos ducentos aureos*, presumably Rhenish gold florins; this sum was
   worth £33 6s 8d sterling (the equivalent of 1,333 days' wages or 6 years and
   3 months' income for an Oxford master carpenter), or officially £49 3s 4d
   groot Flemish, but more likely, at current market rates, £53 6s 8d groot (the
   equivalent of 1,280 days' wages or 5 years and 9 months' wage income for an
   Antwerp master carpenter), or £300 tournois (or as much as £328 18s 4d, with
   rising gold values; see Ep 1796 n5).
57 Erasmus' silver seal, bearing an image of the Roman god Terminus and his
   own personal motto *Cedo nulli* 'I yield to none,' was made at Antwerp in 1517–
   18 (Epp 712:40n, 736, 754) and was inspired by an antique gem depicting Terminus given to Erasmus by Alexander Stewart (c 1493–1513), illegitimate son
   of King James IV of Scotland and (from age eleven) archbishop of St Andrews,
   just before his return to Scotland after being tutored by Erasmus at Padua and
   Siena (Ep 604:4n). Both the gem, set into a ring, and the seal inspired by it,
   which Erasmus used for sealing letters, survive in the Historisches Museum
   at Basel; they are reproduced in CWE 11 150. The Terminus theme and image
   also appeared on a medal designed for Erasmus by the Flemish artist Quinten
   Metsys in 1519 (Ep 1092 n2; reproduced in CWE VII 260). Having been criticized for the allegedly pagan origin and spirit of the image and the apparent

Also, before the Tribunal he was granted permission to make a will in accordance with his wishes, provided that he did so in the presence of notaries and likewise if he wished to make any alterations.[58] Heintzmann was 130 the notary who wrote on the front of the document that it was sealed in the presence of witnesses,[59] namely Peter Bitterlin,[60] Sixt Birk,[61] and Clemens Rechberger,[62] in the year etc 27, on the thirteenth day of the month of June at Erasmus' house near St Peter's.

* * * * *

arrogance of its (and his own) motto, Erasmus in a letter of 1528 to Juan de Vergara interpreted it in a Christian sense, as a reminder that every person must be constantly aware of the imminence and inevitability of death (Ep 2018). On the Terminus theme, see James K. McConica 'The Riddle of "Terminus"' *Erasmus in English* 2 (1971) 2–7; he also traces its influence on drawings of Erasmus by Hans Holbein the Younger, including the famous woodcut (1535) of Erasmus with the figure of Terminus (but not the motto). For a brief account of the gift and Erasmus' intentions in adopting the image and the motto, see Roland H. Bainton *Erasmus of Christendom* (New York 1969) 86–7, who at n26 (page 99) is even more reserved than McConica about accepting the interpretation of Edgar Wind '*Aenigma Termini*: the Emblem of Erasmus' *Journal of the Warburg Institute* 1 (1937–8) 66–9, who discounts Erasmus' pious interpretation and associates the theme with classical and pagan ideas current among the humanists among whom Erasmus worked at the Aldine press in Venice in 1508.

58 This concluding passage is the notarial attestation that Erasmus executed his will in conformity with the authorization granted by the Basel court. Hence it refers to Erasmus, the testator, in the third person. The surviving manuscript copy is in the hand of the trustee of Erasmus' estate, Bonifacius Amerbach. See the introduction to this will. The court had authorized Erasmus to make his will and to have it officially registered without appearing in person because illness made him unable to leave his house. Allen Ep 1780:3n quotes the court record as published by Ludwig Sieber *Das Testament des Erasmus vom 22. Januar 1527* (Basel 1889) 13.

59 Johann Heinzmann (d before 1533) was a notary employed by the bishop of Basel and hence was qualified to verify the signature of legal documents. The concluding authentication is written in his hand.

60 Peter Bitterlin of Ehingen (d 1544) was a graduate of the University of Basel and master of the Latin school attached to the cathedral chapter. His presence at the signing of Erasmus' will may have been in an official capacity, since he was (as the paragraph added by Heinzmann notes) diocesan collator of wills. Subsequently he studied law at Basel and probably also at Freiburg.

61 Birk was a humanist (1501–54) and schoolmaster, educated at Erfurt and Tübingen and then at Basel (MA 1536).

62 Rechberger (d 1545) matriculated at Basel in the autumn of 1525. He was probably a relative of Bonifacius Amerbach's brother-in-law, Jakob Rechberger, and probably witnessed the signing because he was Amerbach's *famulus* at this time.

Then he recorded the name of Bonifacius Amerbach and publicly des-   135
ignated him as his heir on the first day of July in the presence of the officials and of the notary Heintzmann in his customary residence near St
Peter's, having summoned as witnesses Master Peter Bitterlin and Georg
Hoffisscher,[63] collators of wills for the diocese of Basel.

All this was written on the outside of the will in several copies by the   140
hand of the notary Heintzmann.

* * * * *

63 A notary active in the bishop's court at Basel; see AK III 96 n3 (Ep 1069). In medieval and early modern Europe, wills and probate were under the jurisdiction
of ecclesiastical courts.

MONEY, WAGES, AND REAL INCOMES IN THE AGE OF ERASMUS: THE PURCHASING POWER OF COINS AND OF BUILDING CRAFTSMEN'S WAGES IN ENGLAND AND THE LOW COUNTRIES FROM 1500 TO 1540

Historical introduction

The mint outputs and coinages of Renaissance England, France, and the Hapsburg Low Countries

The purchasing power of coins and wages in the Hapsburg Low Countries

The purchasing power of coins and wages in southern England

Price changes and the purchasing power of coins

Building craftsmen and the purchasing power of wages

The income of Erasmus in 1526

JOHN H. MUNRO

I
HISTORICAL INTRODUCTION

The comparative purchasing powers of coins and wages and the data sources

Those reading the voluminous correspondence of Erasmus (1466–1536), in particular from the 1490s, soon become aware of the wide variety of coins and other forms of money that he used on his far-ranging travels, from his homeland in the Burgundian-Hapsburg Netherlands to England, France, the Rhineland, Southern Germany, Switzerland, and Italy. Three major questions come to mind. What were the values of these coins – what was their purchasing power in terms of everyday commodities? What was the real value of the various benefices and stipends that Erasmus received from his benefactors: was he really so ill paid, as he frequently intimated? How would his 'standard of living' compare with that of a skilled master building craftsman – a mason or carpenter – at least in so far as the purchasing power of their money income may be deduced?

An initial attempt to answer some of these questions was presented more than twenty-five years ago, at the very outset of the project to present Erasmus' correspondence in English, in appendixes for the first two volumes of correspondence in *The Collected Works of Erasmus* (CWE), which covered the years 1484 to 1514.[1] The present study extends this inquiry to 1540, four years beyond the death of Erasmus. It also revisits the evidence for the first fifteen years of the sixteenth century by offering an expanded range of price and wage data, chiefly for urban centres in the southern Low Countries and southern England, in the tables that follow. For each region, the tables have been organized to provide more precise responses to two questions. First, what quantity of various common commodities, chiefly foodstuffs and textiles, could have been purchased, each year, with the primary silver and gold coinages of the region? Second, what quantity of these same commodities could masters in the building trades – masons and carpenters – have acquired with their daily wages, and also (for the Low Countries), with their estimated annual wage income? These tables differ most markedly from those in the prior appendixes by presenting the data entirely in metric, rather than in local (indigenous), or modern imperial, measures.

* * * * *

1 See John Munro 'Money and Coinage of the Age of Erasmus' CWE 1 311–47, 'The Purchasing Power of Coins and of Wages in England and the Low Countries from 1500 to 1514' CWE 2 307–45, 'Money and Coinage of the Age of Erasmus' CWE 8 347–50.

The principal source for the Low Countries' price and wage data – for Antwerp, Lier, Brussels – is, again, Herman Van der Wee's richly detailed study *The Growth of the Antwerp Market*, supplemented by my own archival research data on textile prices for Ghent and Mechelen. For southern England, chiefly the Oxford and Cambridge regions, the primary source is the often criticized but absolutely indispensable multi-volumed publication of James E. Thorold Rogers, *A History of Agriculture and Prices in England*.[2] The defence offered in CWE 2 for using Thorold Rogers' data still seems perfectly valid a quarter century later, since there are no comparable data available for these regions in this period, certainly not on such a continuous annual basis.[3]

Analysis of wage data and 'wage stickiness' during the Price Revolution

The wages of master craftsmen and their purchasing power are the central concern of this study, as they were in the appendix in CWE 2, all the more so since the early sixteenth century marked the very end of the so-called 'golden age of the labourer,' when real-wage incomes in northwestern Europe had reached an unprecedented peak. That 'golden age' was brought to an abrupt halt and then dramatically reversed by the inflationary forces of the ensuing period, known as the Price Revolution (c 1520–c 1650). Even after the Price Revolution came to an end, allowing some recovery in the real wages of English master craftsmen during the next century (c 1650–c 1750), and even after the subsequent Industrial Revolution achieved a momentous increase in per capita output, those 'golden age' real wages would not again be equalled, according to most indexes, until the late nineteenth century (1886).[4]

* * * * *

2 Herman Van der Wee *The Growth of the Antwerp Market and the European Economy, Fourteenth–Sixteenth Centuries* 3 vols (The Hague 1963), I Statistics, II *Interpretation*, III *Graphs*; James E. Thorold Rogers *A History of Agriculture and Prices in England, from the Year after the Oxford Parliament (1259) to the Commencement of the Continental War (1793), Compiled Entirely From Original and Contemporaneous Records* 7 vols (Oxford 1866–1902), especially IV (*1401–1582*)
3 CWE 2 308–9. See 623 below.
4 E.H. Phelps Brown and Sheila V. Hopkins 'Seven Centuries of the Prices of Consumables Compared with Builders' Wage-Rates' *Economica* 23/92 (November 1956) 296–314, repr in *Essays in Economic History* ed E.M. Carus-Wilson II (London 1962) 179–96 and in E.H. Phelps Brown and Sheila V. Hopkins *A Perspective of Wages and Prices* (London 1981) 13–59, containing additional statistical appendixes not provided in the original publication or in earlier reprints

CWE 2 presented the wage data that Thorold Rogers extracted from the accounts of Cambridge and Oxford colleges. This study has substituted the data that Sir Henry Phelps Brown and Sheila Hopkins used in their well-known index of real wages for a much longer period and a much wider area of southwestern England. While the Thorold Rogers wage data frequently show minor fluctuations from year to year, the Phelps Brown and Hopkins series reveal a remarkable uniformity – so much so that the prevailing daily wage of a master building craftsman in southwestern England (excepting London) was an unvarying 6d sterling per day for an astoundingly long period, from 1408 to 1535. Indeed, in the Oxford and Cambridge college accounts, that rate had prevailed as the standard wage from as early as 1363.[5] As we now know, that uniformity is not an indication of faulty data. On the contrary, it reflects the general behaviour of European wages in the pre-industrial era, which economists call 'wage stickiness.' This is evident, for example, in the Low Countries, which had a much less stable monetary structure than England. The prevailing daily (summer) wage of master masons and carpenters in Mechelen was an unvarying 12d *groot* Brabant (= 8d *groot* Flemish) from the Burgundian monetary unification of 1434–5 to 1490, and from 1490 to 1540 it was an unvarying 13.5d per day (= 9d *groot* Flemish).[6] In the nearby Antwerp region, the prevailing daily summer wage for carpenters was 8d *groot* Brabant from 1404–5 to 1431–2; it rose to 12d *groot* by 1442, remained at that fixed rate until 1513 (except for a temporary rise to 13.5d in the tumultuous revolt years of 1486–7), and from 1515 to 1536 that daily summer rate was fixed at 15d (= 10d *groot* Flemish).[7]

The decision to choose the more uniform Phelps Brown and Hopkins wage series is not meant as a challenge to the validity of Thorold Rogers' data. He was perfectly accurate in compiling his wage data, but not necessarily so well advised in his methods of presenting them. A quarter-century of research in the late-medieval, early modern Low Countries and England

* * * * *

5 E.H. Phelps Brown and Sheila V. Hopkins 'Seven Centuries of Building Wages' *Economica* 22/87 (August 1955) 195–206, repr in *Essays in Economic History* ed Carus-Wilson (n4 above) II 168–78 and in Phelps Brown and Hopkins *Perspective* (n4 above) 1–12. See also Thorold Rogers *History of Agriculture and Prices* (n2 above) I (1259–1400) 318–19, IV (1401–1582) 514–20.
6 *Dokumenten voor de geschiedenis van prijzen en lonen in Vlaanderen en Brabant / Documents pour l'histoire des prix et des salaires en Flandre et en Brabant* ed Charles Verlinden, E. Scholliers and others, 4 vols (Bruges 1959–65) II. For a discussion of the differences between summer and winter wages, see 630 and n98 below.
7 Van der Wee *Antwerp Market* (n2 above) I 360–3 Appendix 28/4, 457–61 Appendix 39

has convinced me that the Phelps Brown and Hopkins method of presenting wage data is the better one. In any given location, wages for building craftsmen – that is, for master masons and carpenters, chiefly – vary both within the year and from year to year according to the composition or mix of the labour force employed for the tasks for which such payments were tabulated. Not all masons and carpenters were paid the same wage, which varied by levels of skill and seniority or the difficulty of the tasks. But a prosopographical approach, which relates wages year by year to names of specific craftsmen, reveals that – apart from anomalies of unusual tasks – the same mason, once he reached a senior level in his status as master, was usually paid the same wage year after year, for long periods of time.[8]

The task of research scholars therefore is to ascertain the *prevailing and standard* wage for senior master craftsmen (and for their labourers) for each location, year after year. Such research shows that the historical pattern of wage payments throughout late-medieval and early modern western Europe was one of wage stickiness, often for extraordinarily long periods of time. Indeed, even in the eighteenth century, the father of the modern science of economics, Adam Smith, commented as follows on this phenomenon in his classic *Wealth of Nations*:

> The wages of labour do not in Great Britain fluctuate with the price of provisions. These vary every-where from year to year, frequently from month to month. But in many places the money price of labour remains uniformly the same, sometimes for half a century together ... The high price of provisions

* * * * *

8 Wage-data research in the London Guildhall Library Archives; the Corporation of London Record Office; the Archives of the British Library of Political and Economic Science; the Algemeen Rijksarchief België, Rekenkamer (various town accounts); the *Stadsarchieven* of Bruges, Ghent, Mechelen, and Leuven. As an example of a 'compositional error' in tabulating such wage data, consider a building project or manorial repairs employing fourteen carpenters in a given year, with three senior master carpenters earning 7d sterling per day, eight ordinary master carpenters earning 6d per day, and three junior, less experienced master carpenters, two earning 5d and the other 5¹/₂d per day. Their mean wage would then be 5.875d unweighted and 6.036d weighted. If, in the following year, only ten carpenters were employed, with only one senior carpenter earning 7d per day, six ordinary carpenters earning 6d per day, and three junior carpenters earning 5¹/₂d per day, the weighted mean would now be 5.950d and the unweighted mean, 6.167d. An examination of these accounts year after year would reveal that for each class or status of master carpenters the wage rates were in fact unchanging – and thus very 'sticky' – with a standard or predominant wage of 6d per day.

during these ten years past [1765–75] has not in many parts of the kingdom been accompanied with any sensible rise in the money price of labour.[9]

Similar wage stickiness is readily apparent in the tables that follow illustrating craftsmen's wages and their purchasing power in Brabant and southern England for the first four decades of the sixteenth century; in the latter, money wages began to rise only in the final decade.[10] As suggested earlier, they did so, as the tables reveal, because the inflation that marked the onset of the Price Revolution meant, certainly by the 1530s, a steep rise in the real cost of living in both England and the Low Countries.

Price and wage changes during the sixteenth-century Price Revolution: monetary and demographic (real) factors in inflation

The onset of the Price Revolution is the pivotal feature of the western European economy in the age of Erasmus. Most economists contend – justifiably – that the Price Revolution was essentially a monetary phenomenon. Indeed so are all long-term inflations: continuous and sustained rises in price levels as opposed to momentary, temporary price shocks. They are brought about by increases in the stock of money circulating in the economy, or by an increased velocity or flow of such money, or, most commonly, by some combination of increased stocks and flows. If, however, these monetary forces, perhaps in combination with other so-called 'real' factors, help to stimulate economic growth, the consequent expansion in the output of goods and services usually moderates the degree of inflation, or even fully counteracts it, so that few prices would rise under these circumstances.[11]

* * * * *

9 Adam Smith *An Inquiry Into the Nature and Causes of the Wealth of Nations* (London 1776) ed with introduction and notes by Edwin Cannan (New York 1937) 74. In fact, the prevailing daily wage for a master building craftsman in southwestern England had been 24d per day – that is, quadruple the money wage rate of the fifteenth and early sixteenth centuries – from 1736 to 1773, just before the publication of the *Wealth of Nations*. By its publication date, that prevailing wage rate had risen to 29d, where it would remain until 1792; with the onset of severe inflation during the French Revolutionary-Napoleonic Wars, it rose to 36d by 1796. See Phelps Brown and Hopkins 'Seven Centuries of Building Wages' (n5 above) 11.

10 For a discussion of the problems and forms of 'wage stickiness' in this period, see John Munro 'Wage Stickiness, Monetary Changes, and Real Incomes in Late-Medieval England and the Low Countries, 1300–1470: Did Money Matter?' *Research in Economic History* 21 (2002) 187–97.

11 The formal expression of this relationship is a variant of the so-called Fisher Identity: $M \cdot V = P.y$. In this equation, M stands for the total stock of money

Many historians strongly disagree, contending that the inflations that constituted the Price Revolution were instead fundamentally due to demographic factors: in particular, to an inexorable rise in population.[12] This view is, however, quite mistaken, for two reasons. The first is simpler to put forth: the late-medieval demographic crises had, in fact, continued to depress the populations of both England and the Low Countries until well into the first quarter of the sixteenth century. England's population, which may have been as high as 7.5 million in the 1290s (though more likely about 4.5 million), was only 2.25 million in the early 1520s, according to the Tudor muster

* * * * *

in circulation; V, for its income velocity, or the average rate of flow for a unit of that money; P for an index of the price level (for example the consumer price index or CPI); y, for the real Net National Income (NNI); and $P.y$ for the NNI in current money. If y expands at the same rate as the combined increase in M and V, there should be no inflation; if y does not expand at the same rate as does $M.V.$, then inflation will inevitably follow. On this question, see John Munro 'Mint Outputs, Money, and Prices in Late-Medieval England and the Low Countries' in *Münzprägung, Geldumlauf und Wechselkurse / Minting, Monetary Circulation and Exchange Rates* ed Eddy Van Cauwenberghe and Franz Irsigler, Trierer Historische Forschungen 7, *Akten des 8th International Economic History Congress, Section c-7, Budapest 1982* (Trier 1984) 31–122, 'The Central European Mining Boom, Mint Outputs, and Prices in the Low Countries and England, 1450–1550,' in *Money, Coins, and Commerce: Essays in the Monetary History of Asia and Europe (From Antiquity to Modern Times)* ed Eddy H.G. Van Cauwenberghe, Studies in Social and Economic History 2 (Leuven 1991) 119–83, 'Patterns of Trade, Money, and Credit' in *Handbook of European History in the Later Middle Ages, Renaissance and Reformation, 1400–1600* ed James Tracy, Thomas Brady jr, and Heiko Oberman 1 *Structures and Assertions* (Leiden 1994) 147–95, 'Precious Metals and the Origins of the Price Revolution Reconsidered: The *Conjuncture* of Monetary and Real Forces in the European Inflation of the Early to Mid-Sixteenth Century' in *Monetary History in Global Perspective, 1500–1808* ed Clara Eugenia Nuñez, Proceedings of the Twelfth International Economic History Congress at Madrid, August 1998 (Seville 1998) 35–50, and 'The Monetary Origins of the "Price Revolution" Before the Influx of Spanish-American Treasure: The South German Silver-Copper Trades, Merchant-Banking, and Venetian Commerce, 1470–1540' in *Global Connections and Monetary History, 1470–1800* ed Dennis Flynn, Arturo Giráldez, and Richard von Glahn (Aldershot 2003) forthcoming.

12 For contrary views, see R.B. Outhwaite *Inflation in Tudor and Early Stuart England* 2d ed (London 1982) 39–60; *The Price Revolution in Sixteenth-Century England* ed Peter Ramsey, Debates in Economic History series (London 1971); David Hackett Fischer *The Great Wave: Price Revolutions and the Rhythm of History* (Oxford and New York 1996); and my critical review of this book for *EH Net Review* 24 February 1999.

rolls and lay subsidies.[13] Similarly, most economic historians now agree that after the economic depredations that the Low Countries suffered during the revolts against Archduke Maximilian (1487–96), demographic recovery did not begin in this region until c 1510–20. Statistical evidence for the continued slump can be found in the census of hearths (family homes) conducted in Brabant: the number fell from 92,738 hearths in 1437 to 75,343 hearths in 1496.[14] If population was indeed growing in both England and the Low Countries during the second quarter of the sixteenth century, that demographic growth, from such a very low level earlier in the century, could hardly have exerted enough pressure by itself to induce any major rise in prices.

Nevertheless, the economics of the subsequent demographic expansion must be examined more fully, since it embraced the better part of the Price Revolution period. Stated simply, a steady, prolonged rise in population that was not accompanied by a proportional expansion in the amount and quality of land and capital employed productively, or by significant technological changes, or by other forces that promoted economic growth would almost inevitably have resulted in 'diminishing returns,' particularly in agriculture or other land/resource-based occupations, and thus in rising marginal costs and prices. That may also explain the perceived fall in real wages, because most economists believe that such wages were determined

* * * * *

13 See John Hatcher *Plague, Population, and the English Economy, 1348–1530* (London 1977) 11–73 and 'Mortality in the Fifteenth Century: Some New Evidence' *Economic History Review* 2d series 39 (February 1986) 19–38; Julian Cornwall 'English Population in the Early Sixteenth Century' *Economic History Review* 2d series 23/1 (April 1970) 32–44; Ian Blanchard 'Population Change, Enclosure, and the Early Tudor Economy' *Economic History Review* 2d series 23/4 (December 1970) 427–45; Bruce Campbell 'The Population of Early Tudor England: A Re-evaluation of the 1522 Muster Returns and the 1524 and 1525 Lay Subsidies' *Journal of Historical Geography* 7 (1981) 145–54; Pamela Nightingale 'The Growth of London in the Medieval English Economy' in *Progress and Problems in Medieval England* ed Richard Britnell and John Hatcher (Cambridge and New York 1996) 89–106.

14 Joseph Cuvelier *Les dénombrements de foyers en Brabant, xive–xvie siècle* 2 vols (Brussels 1912–13) I cxxxv, clxxviii, ccxxiii, ccxxvii, 432–3, 446–7, 462–77, 484–7; Van der Wee *Antwerp Market* (n2 above) I 546–8 Appendix 49/1–3; John Munro 'Economic Depression and the Arts in the Fifteenth-Century Low Countries' *Renaissance and Reformation* 19 (1983) 235–50, repr in John Munro *Textiles, Towns, and Trade: Essays in the Economic History of Late-Medieval England and the Low Countries* Variorum Collected Studies series CS 442 (Aldershot 1994) XI 235–50

by the marginal productivity of labour, which presumably fell sharply during the sixteenth and early seventeenth centuries.[15] But, even though such a demographic model can explain the rise in individual relative prices and wages – why wheat prices rose more than, say, linen prices – such a model cannot be used in this simplistic fashion to explain a general rise in prices, a rise in the *average price level*, as measured by some form of a consumer price index (CPI).[16]

A rise in prices in general would have occurred in this situation only if population growth had stimulated an increase in the stock and/or flow of circulating money, since inflation is indeed essentially a monetary phenomenon. Three leading economic historians have in fact contended that population growth in sixteenth-century England did lead to a more than proportional increase in money flows, in what economists call 'a rise in the income velocity of money.' As the population grew, especially from the 1520s, it became more and more urbanized. The growth of towns with expanding industrial and financial sectors in turn promoted a more rapid expansion of commercialized agriculture, and those developments in turn led to much more complex commercial and financial networks. At the same time, changing demographic structures (changes in 'the age pyramid') and a higher dependency ratio forced many more families to draw upon their cash savings and to 'dishoard' by converting plate into coin in order to meet their growing financial obligations.[17] Apart from the changing demographic structures, the other

* * * * *

15 The classic statement that the real wage of labour equals its marginal product (*MP*) is a gross oversimplification. The true equation is $W_L = MRP_L$ – the real wage for labour is equal to its marginal revenue product; that is, the (extra) market value of the extra unit of output that it produces. If those forces that supposedly depressed wages also increased the relative prices for agricultural products and the profits from commercial faming, they would have provided a counterbalancing force to increase the *MRP* of labour.

16 The best known is the Phelps Brown and Hopkins 'basket of consumables'; this index, and the one that Herman Van der Wee constructed for Brabant on the same model, are used in this study. See 553 and n4 above, 594-7 and n52, 618-22 and nn84-7 below.

17 See Harry Miskimin 'Population Growth and the Price Revolution in England' *Journal of European Economic History* 4 (1975) 179-85, repr in his *Cash, Credit and Crisis in Europe, 1300-1600* Variorum Reprints CS 289 (London 1989); Jack Goldstone 'Urbanization and Inflation: Lessons from the English Price Revolution of the Sixteenth and Seventeenth Centuries' *American Journal of Sociology* 89 (1984) 1122-60; Peter Lindert 'English Population, Wages, and Prices: 1541-1913' *The Journal of Interdisciplinary History* 15 (Spring 1985) 609-34; see also n13 above.

economic circumstances portrayed in these models pertain largely to England alone and thus they fail to explain the very similar inflationary patterns of prices in the Low Countries, which had undergone urbanization and most of the other structural economic changes much earlier. Nevertheless, most economic historians agree that sixteenth-century western Europe did experience a rise in the income velocity of money. Such a rise in velocity would seem to contradict the views of the famous John Maynard Keynes and many other economists after him, namely, that increases in the stock of money, which undeniably did occur in sixteenth-century Europe, should have led to a decline in the income velocity of money, because of a reduced need to economize on its use and because of an expected fall in interest rates.[18]

The traditional monetary explanations for the European Price Revolution, theories first enunciated by the Spanish cleric Azpilcueta Navarra and then by the French philosopher Jean Bodin in publications from 1556 to

* * * * *

18 See John Maynard Keynes *The General Theory of Employment, Interest and Money* (London 1936) 165–85. For compelling evidence on the sharp rise in the income velocity of money during the sixteenth and early seventeenth centuries, see not only the articles cited in the previous note, but also Nicholas Mayhew 'Population, Money Supply, and the Velocity of Circulation in England, 1300–1700' *Economic History Review* 2d series 48/2 (May 1995) 238–57. An increase in the income velocity of money is the same as a reduction in the quantity of hoarded money or of idle cash balances. A mathematical representation of such hoarding in holding cash balances can be found in the Cambridge Cash Balances equation, which most economists prefer to the better known Fisher Identity (see n11 above). With almost identical symbols, it is presented as $M = k.P.y$. The symbol k stands for the proportion of real Net National Income (NNI $= P.y$) that the public chooses to hold in real cash balances, that is, in M, in a form often called 'high powered money.' This symbol k also represents the constituent elements of the Keynesian concept of 'liquidity preference' (which explains why people prefer holding idle cash balances to spending or investing them): precautionary motives ('savings for a rainy day'); speculative motives (to take advantage of future investment opportunities); and the more general anticipation of future spending or 'transactions.' In this equation k is simply the reciprocal of the income velocity of money, that is, $k = 1/V$. If the conditions of 'liquidity preference' and in general the demand for money remain unchanged, then an increased stock of money should – by the law of supply and demand – lead to a fall in interest rates (the price of money, in lending or borrowing it). A fall in interest rates would thus reduce the 'opportunity cost' of holding idle, non-invested cash balances and thus should lead to a rise in k, which therefore means a fall in the income velocity of money. Opportunity cost is one of the most important concepts in economics: the cost of doing A is foregoing the benefits to be derived from doing the alternative B, in this case, investing money to yield interest or dividend income.

1578, focused on increases in the stock of money and above all on the influx of Spanish American treasure.[19] As opponents of the monetary explanation have noted more recently, however, the inflation that marked the onset of the Price Revolution had begun just before 1520, and thus long before any significant quantities of Spanish American silver reached Europe. This influx began only in the 1530s (with a mean annual import of 12,148 kg in 1536–40). No truly large imports of silver are recorded before the early 1560s (with a mean of 83,374 kg in 1561–5), just after the mercury amalgamation process had begun to effect a technological revolution in Spanish-American mining.[20] Even if such Spanish-American silver imports clearly served to augment and aggravate the monetary expansion that fuelled the inflation of the Price Revolution from the 1560s on, they did not instigate it. We must seek elsewhere for the fundamental monetary causes that sparked the onset of this inflation, which lasted over 130 years.

The initial and least important monetary factor was the Portuguese export of gold from West Africa (São Jorge): beginning as a trickle in the 1460s, it rose to 170 kg a year by the early 1480s, to peak at about 680 kg per year in the late 1490s.[21] Far more important, since almost all European money-of-account or pricing systems were based on silver coinages, was the central European mining boom in silver and copper, which had begun in the 1460s, a time of severe coin scarcity and of even more severe deflation throughout western Europe. Generally low silver-based prices meant an increase in the purchasing power of silver, ounce for ounce, which thus provided a profit incentive for the development of new methods to produce silver. A remarkable technological revolution in mining and metallurgy ensued. The first revolution was in mechanical engineering: the invention of mechanical, water-powered pumps to remove excess water, via specially drilled adits, from much deeper mine shafts in the mountainous regions of Saxony, the Tyrol, and Bohemia. The second was the *Saigerhütten* process in chemical engineering: a new method of smelting with lead to separate silver from argentiferous-cupric ores, by far the most plentiful source of silver

* * * * *

19 See 583–4 and n48 below for the debate between Bodin and Malestroit on the cause of inflation.
20 See John TePaske 'New World Silver, Castile, and the Philippines, 1590–1800 A.D.' in *Precious Metals in the Medieval and Early Modern Worlds* ed John F. Richards (Durham, NC 1983) 424–46; Earl Hamilton *American Treasure and the Price Revolution in Spain, 1501–1650* (Cambridge, MA 1934; repr 1965).
21 Ivor Wilks 'Wangara, Akan, and the Portuguese in the Fifteenth and Sixteenth Centuries' in *Forests of Gold: Essays on the Akan and the Kingdom of Asante* ed Ivor Wilks (Athens, OH 1993) 1–39

in western Europe. According to John Nef, Europe's output of mined silver rose more than fivefold by the 1530s, when this German-based mining boom reached its peak, with an annual production that ranged from a minimum of 84,200 kg to a maximum of 91,200 kg fine silver – well in excess of any amounts imported into Seville before the mid-1560s. My own statistical compilations, limited to the major German and Hungarian-Bohemian mines and thus only partial estimates of total outputs, indicate that the central European production of mined silver rose from a quinquennial mean of 12,973 kg in 1471–5 to one of 55,704 kg in 1536–40. The increased output of copper from the mining boom was also economically very important, for two reasons: copper was an essential ingredient as the alloy in all silver and gold coinages, and it was used in the production of bronze artillery pieces, which were safer and more effective than iron cannons.[22]

Comparative coinage statistics for England and the Burgundian-Hapsburg Low Countries

After the 1460s, as several recent publications have sought to demonstrate, the competitive monetary and commercial policies of England and the Burgundian-Hapsburg Netherlands, along with other factors that propelled the

* * * * *

22 See John Nef 'Silver Production in Central Europe, 1450–1618' *Journal of Political Economy* 49 (1941) 575–91 and 'Mining and Metallurgy in Medieval Civilisation' in *The Cambridge Economic History of Europe* II *Trade and Industry in the Middle Ages* (1952) 2d ed rev M.M. Postan and E.E. Rich (Cambridge 1987) 691–761; Philippe Braunstein 'Innovations in Mining and Metal Production in Europe in the Late Middle Ages' *The Journal of European Economic History* 12 (1983) 573–91; Michael North *Geldumlauf und Wirtschaftskonjunktur im südlichen Ostseeraum an der Wende zur Neuzeit (1440–1570)* Kieler Historische Studien 35 (Sigmaringen 1990); Ekkehard Westermann *Das Eislebener Garkupfer und seine Bedeutung für den europäischen Kupfermarkt, 1460–1560* (Vienna 1971), 'Die Bedeutung des Thüringer Saigerhandels für den mitteleuropäischen Handel an der Wende vom 15. zum 16. Jahrhundert' *Jahrbuch für die Geschichte Mittel- und Ostdeutschlands* 21 (1972) 68–92, and 'Tendencies in the European Copper Market in the 15th and 16th Centuries' in *Precious Metals in the Age of Expansion* ed Hermann Kellenbenz (Stuttgart 1981) 79–86; John Hatcher 'The Great Slump of the Mid-Fifteenth Century' in *Progress and Problems in Medieval England: Essays in Honour of Edward Miller* ed Richard Britnell and John Hatcher (Cambridge and New York 1996) 237–72; Pamela Nightingale 'England and the European Depression of the Mid-Fifteenth Century' *The Journal of European Economic History* 26/3 (Winter 1997) 631–56; Munro 'Central European Mining Boom' (n11 above); and other sources cited in n11 above.

rapid expansion of the Brabant trade fairs of Antwerp and Bergen op Zoom, succeeded in attracting more and more South-German silver and copper to these fairs, and thus away from Venice, historically the more natural outlet for them. At the Brabant fairs, these metals and other German commodities were used to purchase textiles from England and the Netherlands for re-export to Germany, Central Europe, and Italy.[23] This burgeoning commerce is reflected in the mint accounts for the Burgundian Low Countries and, to a lesser extent, in the English mint accounts. Thus, in the Antwerp and Bruges mints, the quinquennial mean production of coined silver rose from just 101.8 kg in 1451–5 to 7,314.0 kg in 1471–5, with an overall quarter-century mean of 2,386.0 kg in 1451–75; in the next quarter century, 1476–1500, that mean more than doubled to 5,374.0 kg, and, though it declined in 1501–25, it rose again to peak at 11,403.9 kg of fine silver in 1551–75. In the London Tower Mint, the quarter-century mean of minted silver coinage rose from 1,303.7 kg in 1476–1500 to 2,452.6 kg in 1501–25, then to 9,456.5 kg in 1526–50, and peaked at 11,549.7 kg in 1551–75. Despite the absence of further coinage changes in England, the mean output in 1576–1600 was virtually identical, at 11,329.7 kg, while the mean output of coined silver fell drastically in the Low Countries during this final quarter-century to a mean of 6,214.5 kg because of the revolt against Spanish rule (from 1568 to 1609).

Equally significant are the changes in the overall composition of the coined money supply. In England, silver accounted for only 22.5 per cent of the total value of the coinage in 1501–26 but 84.2 per cent in 1576–1600. In the southern Low Countries, silver coinage rose from 27.6 per cent of the total in 1451–75 to 74.9 per cent during the German silver-mining boom, fell to 28.4 per cent in 1501–25, but rose again to 48.3 per cent in 1526–50, and then soared to 72.3 per cent in 1576–1600. But since merchants and consumers made their expenditures in current coin, not in bullion, the more appropriate statistics to cite are the aggregate values of the combined outputs of the

* * * * *

23 Van der Wee *Antwerp Market* (n2 above) I 523 Appendix 44/1: Hungarian copper trade; John Munro *Wool, Cloth, and Gold: The Struggle for Bullion in Anglo-Burgundian Trade, ca. 1340–1478* (Brussels and Toronto 1973) 127–54, 'Anglo-Flemish Competition in the International Cloth Trade, 1340–1520' *Publication du centre européen d'études bourguignonnes* 35 (1995) 37–60, *Rencontres d'Oxford (septembre 1994): L'Angleterre et les pays bas bourguignonnes: relations et comparaisons, xve–xvie siècle* ed Jean-Marie Cauchies, 'The Low Countries' Export Trade in Textiles with the Mediterranean Basin, 1200–1600: A Cost-Benefit Analysis of Comparative Advantages in Overland and Maritime Trade Routes' *International Journal of Maritime History* 11/2 (December 1999) 1–30, and 'Central European Mining Boom' (n11 above).

gold and silver mints, in current money-of-account, for both countries. In England, the quarter-century mean of those aggregate mint outputs more than doubled, from £24,378.6 sterling (per annum) in 1476–1500, to £64,885.5 in 1501–25, and then more than tripled, to £199,540.6 in 1526–50, a quarter-century that includes, of course, the 'great debasement' of Henry VIII and his successors (1542–52). Yet even the ensuing period of restored and stable coinages produced a respectable mint output with a mean annual value of £127,821.8 sterling in 1551–75. In the Burgundian-Hapsburg Netherlands (Flanders and Brabant), the comparable quarter-century mean values of the combined gold and silver coinages were: £31,499.4 *groot* Flemish in 1451–75, £65,650.9 in 1476–1500, £64,460.0 in 1501–25, £58,750.7 in 1526–50, and £162,859.7 in 1551–75.[24]

The financial revolution in the Hapsburg Low Countries during the Price Revolution

An equally important factor that contributed to the increasing rate of western European monetary expansion during and from the second quarter of the sixteenth century was a financial revolution whose origins lay partly in late-medieval England, but chiefly in the early sixteenth-century Low Countries. In 1507, Antwerp's civic law merchant court, apparently relying on a 1436 precedent from London's law merchant court, issued a formal legal *turba*, which, when copied by other civic courts (Bruges in 1529, for example), and then enshrined in parliamentary legislation by the Haps-

* * * * *

24 The data for England were calculated from tables and other references in Christopher E. Challis 'Lord Hastings to the Great Silver Recoinage, 1464–1699' and his Appendix 1, Mint Output, 1220–1985, in *A New History of the Royal Mint* ed C.E. Challis (Cambridge 1992) 179–397, 673–98. The English mint output data for 1526–50 include, of course, the recycled silver coinages of the 'great debasement' (1542–52); and those for 1551–75 include the Elizabethan Recoinage of 1560–1 (when the Tower Mint called in and restruck all of the currently circulating silver money into stronger coins whose fineness had been restored to the former sterling standard). Thereafter there were no further monetary changes to explain the very high rates of coinage outputs, especially of silver. Data for Flanders and Brabant during the fifteenth and sixteenth centuries were computed from the archival mint accounts for Bruges, Ghent, Mechelen, and Antwerp in the Algemeen Rijksarchief, Rekenkamer; see Eddy H.G. Van Cauwenberghe, Rainer Metz, Franz Irisgler, and John Munro *Coinage in the Low Countries (14th–18th Centuries)* 1 *Antwerp-Bruges-Brussels-Ghent* (Leuven 1988) 1–292.

burg Estates General in 1537 and 1541, established the virtually complete legal and judicial foundations for negotiability in early modern Europe. In essence, these legal measures provided full protection for third-party cred- itors, including 'bearers,' in all commercial bills (bills of exchange and bills obligatory). Those holding such bills at maturity, after they had circulated from hand to hand over several transactions, were thus permitted to sue and claim full damages from defaulting debtors (and others who had signed or endorsed their names in transferring such bills in payment). Furthermore, the Estates General of 1541, for the first time in European legal and finan- cial history, broke with the long medieval tradition of usury laws to permit interest payments up to 12 per cent (so that only rates above that would be considered usury); and this provision at least implicitly permitted commer- cial discounting (that is, selling a bill before maturity for some value less than, 'discounted from,' the stipulated face value). Along with the establish- ment of the Antwerp *Bourse* in 1531 as a secondary market for commercial bills and bonds, these changes prompted a rapid expansion in the use of credit, both private and public. For example, the annual volume of Spanish government annuities (*rentes* or *juros*), much of it marketed on the Antwerp *Bourse*, rose from 5 million ducats (of 375 maravedis) in 1515 to 83 million ducats in the 1590s.[25]

* * * * *

25 See Herman Van der Wee 'Monetary, Credit, and Banking Systems' in *The Cam- bridge Economic History of Europe* v *The Economic Organization of Early Modern Europe* ed E.E. Rich and Charles Wilson (Cambridge 1977) 290–393 and 'Anvers et les innovations de la technique financière aux xvie et xviie siècles' *Annales: Économies, Sociétés, Civilisations* 22 (1967) 1067–89, republished as 'Antwerp and the New Financial Methods of the 16th and 17th Centuries' in his *The Low Countries in the Early Modern World* trans Lizabeth Fackelman, Variorum Collected Studies (Aldershot 1993) 145–66; John Munro 'The International Law Merchant and the Evolution of Negotiable Credit in Late-Medieval Eng- land and the Low Countries' in *Banchi pubblici, banchi privati e monti di pietà nell'Europa preindustriale: amministrazione, tecniche operative e ruoli economici, Atti della Società Ligure di Storia Patria* nuova serie 31 ed Dino Puncuh (Genoa 1991) 49–80, repr in Munro *Textiles, Towns, and Trade* (n14 above) x 49–80, and 'Eng- lish "Backwardness" and Financial Innovations in Commerce with the Low Countries, 14th to 16th Centuries' in *International Trade in the Low Countries (14th–16th Centuries): Merchants, Organisation, Infrastructure* Studies in Urban, Social, Economic, and Political History of the Medieval and Early Modern Low Countries 10 ed Peter Stabel, Bruno Blondé, and Anke Greve (Leuven- Apeldoorn 2000) 105–67. Note that 'usury' originally meant any amount of interest (payment beyond the stipulated principal) on any loan (*mutuum*); and

Clearly, therefore, the common and once persuasive argument that there had been no significant monetary expansion in Europe before the influx of Spanish-American silver that began in the 1560s can no longer stand scrutiny. Then why did the Price Revolution begin so late, with the onset of sustained inflation in the 1520s, rather than so early? That is much too complex a question to examine in this study. In brief, the answer may be twofold. First, as a consequence of a pronounced depression and population decline in the mid-fifteenth century, the European economy enjoyed so much 'slack' in underutilized resources that it could readily respond to a large expansion in newly monetized demand by increasing outputs without incurring rising costs. Second, Venice succeeded in retaining an important share of the South-German silver and copper flows until c 1515–20, when its commerce suffered a series of ruinous disasters at the hands of the expanding Ottoman Turks; only at that point were more of these metals, and the international trade based upon them, diverted to the Antwerp market.[26]

II
THE MINT OUTPUTS AND COINAGES OF RENAISSANCE ENGLAND, FRANCE, AND THE HAPSBURG LOW COUNTRIES (TABLES 1–4)

The mechanics of minting and the economics of debasement

Any study of medieval and early modern money and prices requires a detailed knowledge of the coinage systems then in use and of the relationship between those coinages and the money-of-account systems used to record prices, wages, and rents. For any given period, all changes in the precious metal contents of the gold and silver coins – in both fineness and weight – and thus of the money-of-account values of these coins must be carefully documented. As demonstrated in greater detail in the appendixes for CWE 1 and 2, most of western Europe, in the millennium from Charlemagne to the French Revolution, used a silver-based money-of-account consisting of pounds, shillings, and pence. Charlemagne's original 'pound' (libra, and thus livre) was intended to be worth one and a half of the Roman pound

* * * * *

that the amount of discount on a bill cashed before maturity represents foregone interest.

26 See Munro 'Monetary Origins of the Price Revolution' and the other sources cited in nn11, 22–3, 25 above.

weight of pure silver, a weight that became the French *livre* of 489.506 g (subdivided into two *marcs*, each weighing 244.753 g).[27]

No silver coins of that pound weight were ever struck, but only pennies or deniers (based on the Roman silver *denarius*) at 240d to the pound. To simplify accounting procedures, the 'pound' value was divided into 20 shillings or *solidi* (from the Roman gold *solidus*) or *sous* (*schelling* in Dutch). Thus each shilling contained 12d, to produce an accounting system that combined the Celtic manner of counting in twenties (*quatre-vingt* = 80) and the Graeco-Roman heritage of counting in twelves. The relationship between the actual coin and this almost universal money-of-account system was simply that the silver penny was always worth 1d, and 12 pence were always worth one shilling.[28]

Subsequently, over the ensuing centuries, the monetary pound deviated more and more from the original pound weight because of the virtually universal fiscal policy known as 'debasement,' more accurately represented by the French term *affaiblissement* and the Italian *indebolimento*. Debasement was, quite simply, the reduction of the amount of a coin's fine precious metal, silver or gold, represented in the unit of the money-of-account (that is, in 1d, in 1s, and in £1); consequently the 'pound' in the money-of-account came to contain far less silver than the original pound weight of silver. In England, for example, the pound sterling, which following the Norman Conquest consisted of a full Tower pound weight of sterling silver (12 Tower ounces = 349.914 g; see CWE 1 332), from 1464 to 1526 contained

* * * * *

27 The Roman pound supposedly weighed 327.5 g. See Edouard Fournial *Histoire monétaire de l'Occident médiéval* (Paris 1970), whose arguments justifying the weight for the French *livre* are quite complex. This weight has been challenged by other numismatists (by even more complex arguments), who offer various alternative gram weights for the *livre*: 408.0, 411.36, 459.36, and 483.33. The last is based on the recent supposition that the Roman pound in fact weighed only 322.2 g. See in particular Willem Blockmans 'Le poids des deniers carolingiens' *Revue belge de numismatique et de sigillographie* 119 (1973) 179–81. None of the critics explains, however, the origin or evolution of the Parisian pound of 489.506 g, nor why its weight, readily verifiable from the surviving official metallic weights, was virtually identical to that ascribed to the Carolingian pound by Fournial.

28 See n1 above. In some few exceptions in later medieval debasements, discussed below (580–2 and n44), the subdivisions of the penny were more drastically reduced in their silver contents than was the penny itself. That had the effect of raising the money-of-account value of the penny, no longer deemed to be a penny; and these subdivisions then became the 'link money' with the money-of-account.

only 6.4 oz or 186.72 g of sterling silver. Thus, over these four centuries, the number of silver pence struck from the Tower pound rose from 240 (just 242 in the reign of Henry III, 1216–72) to 450, worth 37s 6d sterling.

There were two basic methods of reducing the precious metal contents of a coin: by reducing its fineness (that is, by increasing the relative proportion of the base metal alloy, usually copper, in the coin), and by reducing its weight (by increasing the number struck from the mint-weight unit). Some princes also employed a third technique, leaving the coin physically untouched while decreasing the quantity of precious metal represented in the unit of money-of-account by issuing a decree to raise the face value of the coin in money-of-account. Such decrees were often necessary when the ruler, in undertaking a debasement of the silver coins, wished to maintain the same bimetallic ratio, that is, the mint's official ratio of the values of gold and silver (generally 11 : 1 or 12 : 1 in the later fifteenth and early sixteenth centuries). To do so necessarily meant a proportional debasement of the gold coinage. In late-medieval Europe, continental princes frequently used a combination of the first two techniques, with often quite subtle changes in fineness and weight, the better to disguise changes that in fact represented an 'inflation tax' on the public at large. England was then virtually unique in altering its coinages, gold and silver, by weight reductions alone – until the 'great debasement' of Henry VIII and his successors (1542–52), which ultimately reduced the fineness of the silver coinage to just 25 per cent of the traditional sterling standard (see 574, 583 below). Hence the inadequacy of the term 'debasement' when applied to English coinage.

The fineness of gold, in both England and the Low Countries, and indeed almost universally, was expressed in terms of a maximum of 24 carats (with 4 grains to a carat in England and 12 grains in the Low Countries). The traditional fineness of the English gold coinage, as well as that of Italian florins and ducats, was the effective maximum of 23.875 carats, because at least one-eighth carat of copper was always required to provide the hardness and durability necessary to permit the coin's effective circulation.

For silver, the effective maximum fineness in France and the Low Countries (the latter until 1520) was known as *argent-le-roi* (AR), with a maximum of 12 *deniers argent-le-roi*, with 24 grains per *denier*; this meant 23/24 or 95.833 per cent pure silver, with the remainder in copper alloy. In England, from shortly after the Conquest, the traditional standard of 'sterling silver' consisted of 11 ounces and 2 pennyweight (dwt) silver and the necessary 18 dwt copper for hardness; thus, with 20 dwt per ounce, it was only 92.50 per cent pure silver.

The weight of the coin was specified by the *taille* or the number cut from the fixed mint-weight unit. In England, as just noted, it was the Tower pound (11.25 Troy ounces) from the Norman conquest until 1526, when it was displaced by the Troy pound (12.00 Troy ounces = 240 dwt = 5,760 grains), weighing 373.242 g. In France and the Low Countries, the corresponding unit was the *marc de Troyes*, with 8 *onces de Paris* (or one-half *livre* of 16 *onces*), weighing 244.753 g (CWE 1 324, 328, 332).

The consequence of using any combination of the methods described to reduce the precious metal content of the coins was to increase the number that could be minted from the pound weight or *marc* weight of fine metal and thus the total money-of-account value of the coins so minted, which, in medieval documents, is called the *traite* value of the *marc* or the pound. Because coinage debasements augmented the coined money supply, they were almost always inflationary, with one significant exception in this period, to be noted below. For reasons enunciated earlier (see 556–60 above), with unpredictable changes in coinage velocity and in the economy's real output, such increases in the money supply almost never produced a proportional degree of inflation.

Furthermore, the mathematical law of reciprocal values must be called upon to explain why debasements cannot produce proportional changes in prices. The theoretical relationship between a reduction in a debased coin's silver content and the consequent increase in the price of a *marc* (or pound) of fine silver is expressed by the equation $\Delta T = [1/(1 - x)] - 1$. Here ΔT stands for the percentage change in the *traite* or coined value of that silver *marc*. That *traite* value can be readily calculated by multiplying the number of coins struck from the *marc* (the *taille*) by the coin's face value, and then by dividing that amount (the product) by the percentage fineness (alloy) of the minted metal, to obtain the quotient T. Thus, *traite* = *taille* × coin value / fineness; or, more simply, $T = (t.v)/f$. Finally, in this equation, the letter x represents the percentage reduction in the silver content of the penny, or other 'link money' to the money-of-account. As the following example of a fifteenth-century English debasement demonstrates, the consequent percentage increase in the *traite* value of silver was not the same as the percentage reduction in the penny's silver content, but instead the reciprocal value of that reduction, as indicated in the equation given above.

In 1464–5, Edward IV reduced the weight of the penny from 0.972 g to 0.778 g – without altering its sterling fineness (92.5 per cent fine) – producing a new silver coinage that would remain unaltered for over sixty years, until 1526. In so doing, he increased the number of pence struck per Tower pound from 300 to 360, thus increasing its *traite* value from 30s 0d to 37s 6d sterling. While the weight reduction in the silver coinage was exactly 20.0 per cent, the increase in the official value of silver was – exactly as predicted by this formula – 25.0 per cent.[29] The subsequent rise in other commodity prices was, however, far less than that. The Phelps Brown and Hopkins composite index (1451–75 = 100) rose by only 3.5 per cent in the next quinquennium, from a mean of 102.8 in 1461–5 to one of 106.4 in 1466–70. Then, with stronger countervailing deflationary forces at work, the price level resumed its decline, so that the composite index fell to a mean of 97.8 in 1471–5 and then to a fifteenth-century nadir of 91.0 in 1476–80.[30]

The objective of a well-designed medieval debasement was to attract more silver or gold bullion to the mints by offering merchants and bankers more *debased* coins and thus a greater money-of-account value for their bullion than before – and greater than that offered by competing mints. The merchants or bankers supplying the bullion would profit, but only if they spent the increased number of coins before the ensuing increase in the money supply produced some inflation, and also before the public became aware of these changes and responded by raising prices. The mint and the prince profited from the increased volume of minting, and often also from an increase in the mint fees of *brassage* (for the mint) and *seigniorage* (for the prince), fees levied as a percentage of the fine bullion coined. (This is a classic case of gains to be derived from 'asymmetric information,' a concept for whose elaboration three scholars won the 2001 Nobel Prize in Economics.)

So long as the changes in weight and fineness were relatively small, they were exceptionally difficult to detect, essentially because of the crudity of medieval and early modern minting techniques of 'hammered coinages.' From thin sheets of alloyed metal, the mint-master cut small round circular 'blanks,' which were then placed between coin dyes: the lower one acted as the anvil and the upper as the hammer. The resulting coins, even when carefully trimmed, were rarely identical to each other in weight, so that a 'debasement' could be detected only weighing a large number of such coins with finely tuned scales, which were generally unavailable to the public and most merchants. Even more difficult to detect were changes in the alloy or fineness, since the so-called 'touchstone' on which the merchant marked or scratched the coin was rarely accurate within 5 per cent, even for those highly skilled in detecting the differences in the colours of the coin residue left on it. Not until the nineteenth century, with steam-powered milling ma-

* * * * *

29 Thus: $[1/(1-0.20)]-1 = 0.25$ or 25.0 per cent
30 See Phelps Brown and Hopkins 'Seven Centuries of the Prices of Consumables' (n4 above) 29, 48–9. For the deflationary forces at work in the mid-fifteenth century European economy, see 561–2 and nn11, 22 above.

chines and improved chemical techniques of deduction, would the universal menace of public debasement and private counterfeiting – much the same thing for the victimized public – be finally discouraged.[31]

Gold coins were much less frequently subjected to physical debasements, that is, to reductions in their weights and/or fineness, though certainly some did occur, especially in the medieval Low Countries and France. But because gold coins were so much more highly valued than silver coins and because they were therefore largely reserved for banking, finance, and international trade, the merchants who used them were much more likely to have the incentive, knowledge, and facilities to test gold coins for proper weight and fineness. As noted earlier however (568), a prince who, in debasing his silver coins, wished to retain the same bimetallic mint ratio was compelled to increase the face value of his gold coins, by the same degree, in the silver-based money-of-account; and for the reasons just elaborated (569), that change had to be the reciprocal of the percentage reduction in the fine metal content of the silver coins $[1/(1 - x) - 1]$. He could also achieve the same objective by issuing new coins, bearing a different design and name, with a smaller quantity of gold represented in the unit of money-of-account. Technically, as also noted earlier, these changes constituted a debasement. Such coinage alterations and new issues can be seen in the monetary history of England, France, and the Hapsburg Low Countries (Netherlands) during the later medieval and early modern periods.

Coinage and monetary changes in late-medieval, early modern England (1344–1526)

In August 1344, Edward III inaugurated England's era of bimetallism in issuing the gold noble, containing 7.776 g of virtually pure metal (23.875 carats), with a value of one-third of a pound, that is, 6s 8d or 80d; for over

* * * * *

31 See Philip Grierson *Numismatics* (London 1975) 146–52, who states (151) that 'when carried out by an expert, this "touching" is said to give results accurate to half a carat; but much practice is required to ensure that the strike of the needle and that of the object being tested are equally firmly made.' See also Grierson 'Medieval Numismatics' in *Medieval Studies: An Introduction* ed James M. Powell (Syracuse, NY 1976) 124–7, 'Coin Wear and the Frequency Table' *Numismatic Chronicle* 7th series 3 (1963) i–xiv, and 'Weight and Coinage' *Numismatic Chronicle* 7th series 4 (1964) iii–xvii, all reprinted in his *Later-Medieval Numismatics (11th–16th Centuries): Selected Studies* Variorum Reprints cs 98 (London 1979) nos 1, 19, and 20; Angela Redish *Bimetallism: An Economic and Historical Analysis* (Cambridge 2000).

two centuries, it served as an international medium of exchange. Almost seventy years later (1411–12), Henry IV undertook a purely defensive debasement by reducing the noble's weight to 6.998 g; this coin then remained unchanged in both weight and traditional fineness until Edward IV's debasement of 1464–5. Edward IV's mint alterations involved striking two new gold coins: the *Ryal* (Royal) or *rose-noble*, in effect a reissue of Edward III's noble but now valued at 10s 0d; and the *angel-noble*, significantly reduced in weight to 5.184 g, but with the noble's historic fineness and its value of 6s 8d sterling. With these new issues, Edward IV 'debased' the gold coinage by 25.92 per cent and thus by a greater extent than the 20.00 per cent debasement that he imposed on the silver coinage (see 569–70 above). Consequently the English bimetallic mint ratio rose from 10.332 : 1 to 11.158 : 1, thereby 'overvaluing' gold and 'undervaluing' silver in competition with the mints of the Burgundian-Hapsburg Low Countries. In the 1490s, their bimetallic mint ratio was only 10.537 : 1, and in 1500 (see 581–2 below) it was reduced again to 10.176. Such a difference in the bimetallic ratios helps to explain why the English mints generally proved to be generally less successful than those in the Low Countries in coining silver but relatively more successful in coining gold during the later fifteenth and early sixteenth centuries.

The comparative performance of the mints in England and the Low Countries in coining both metals during this period can be seen in Table 1 (see also the comparison of these two countries' mint outputs during the 1520s and early 1530s, 573, 582–3 below). The columns of this table present the following information, for England (Table 1A) and the southern Low Countries (Flanders and Brabant, Table 1B):

1   the quinquennial means from 1481–5 to 1546–50
2   the quinquennial mean outputs of silver coinage, in kilograms of pure metal
3   the quinquennial mean values of the silver coinage outputs, in English pounds sterling and in Flemish pounds *groot* (current moneys), respectively
4   the quinquennial mean outputs of the gold coinages, in kilograms of pure metal
5   the quinquennial mean values of the gold coinages, in English pounds sterling and in Flemish pounds *groot* (current moneys), respectively
6   the quinquennial mean values of each country's total coinage outputs, gold and silver combined, in English pounds sterling and in Flemish pounds *groot*, respectively
7   the percentage of each country's total mint outputs by value in silver coinage, for each quinquennium

8   the percentage of each country's total mint outputs by value in gold
      coinage, for each quinquennium

From 1481 to 1500, the English mints coined only about one-third as
much (32.4 per cent) silver as did those in the Low Countries: a twenty-
year total output of 28,418.98 kg of fine metal, compared to an output of
87,641.62 kg of fine silver from the Low Countries' mints. To be sure, the
much higher output from the latter's mints reflects coinage debasements and
then a recoinage *renforcement* (see 581–3 below) during these two decades. It
also reflects the other economic factors, discussed above (566), that directed
the expanding flow of silver from the South-German mining boom down the
Rhine to Antwerp and the Brabant fairs. Conversely, with a more favourable
mint ratio for gold, the English mints coined substantially more of that metal
– 36.00 per cent more – than did the mints in the Low Countries during
this twenty-year period: a total of 4,485.53 kg of fine gold compared to a
total output of 3,298.49 kg of fine gold produced by the mints of the Low
Countries.

      Between 1500 and 1520, however, the influence of the bimetallic ratios,
which remained unchanged in both countries, seems to have weakened in
determining whether a country's mints coined relatively more gold or more
silver. From 1501 to 1510, as Table 1 indicates, the English mints coined more
kilograms of fine silver than did the mints of the Low Countries, only to
fall behind the latter in the following decade, 1511 to 1520, in outputs of
silver coinage. Nevertheless, from 1481 to 1525, as Table 1 also indicates,
gold coinage consistently continued to account for well more than half of
the total value of English mint outputs, ranging from a low of 61 per cent
(1486–90, 1521–5) to a high of 99 per cent (1511–15).

      During this entire period, indeed for the sixty years from Edward
IV's debasements of 1464–5 to Henry VIII's recoinage of 1526, both the English silver and gold coinages remained perfectly stable. The only significant
monetary innovations to be noted during this interim period are those of
Henry VII: he issued the gold *sovereign*, worth a full pound sterling, in 1489,
and then the *teston*, a sterling silver shilling coin (proportional in weight
and value to the penny), in 1504.[32]

      Henry VIII's coinage alterations of November 1526 pale in compari-
son with those of his later 'great debasement' (commencing in 1542; see
574 below), and consequently they have unfairly received little attention

* * * * *

32 Christopher Challis *The Tudor Coinage* (Manchester and New York 1978) 44–67

from economic historians. The latter was clearly an aggressive measure, designed to maximize mint outputs and seigniorage revenues, while the 1526 recoinage was no more than a purely defensive measure. Since the precious-metal content of the circulating coins had, in general, diminished from both wear and fraudulent clipping over these six decades, the mint officials evidently advised the crown to adjust the two coinages so that newly issued coins would match the weight of the currently circulating coins. To achieve this goal, the crown implemented a relatively minor debasement of 11.18 per cent (for silver, a weight reduction from 0.778 g to 0.691 g).[33] Both coinages were altered by the same degree (in the reciprocal manner explained 569 above) to leave the bimetallic ratio virtually unchanged at 11.16 : 1. The value of the *angel-noble*, whose weight and fineness were unaltered, was now raised by 12.5 per cent, from 6s 8d (80d) to 7s 6d (90d) sterling, while two new gold coins were introduced: the *St George noble* (4.608 g of traditional fineness of 23 carats 3.5 grains), worth the traditional 6s 8d; and the far more popular and better known gold *rose crown* (3.456 g), with the lesser fineness of 22 carats and a value of 5s 0d (60d, that is, one quarter of the pound sterling). Half crowns of 2s 6d were also issued, and coins of that name and value continued to circulate (but as silver coins) until England's adoption of metric coinage in 1972.[34] An equally significant change, already noted (568–9 above), was the substitution of the heavier 12 ounce Troy pound (373.242 g) to replace the Tower pound (349.914 g). These coinages remained unaltered until the beginning of the 'great debasement' in 1542, which is beyond the scope of this study (see Tables 2 and 3).[35]

* * * * *

33 For an explanation of the mechanics and economics of this monetary situation, see Sir Albert Feaveryear *The Pound Sterling: A History of English Money* 2d ed rev E. Victor Morgan (Oxford 1963) 231–45; Munro *Wool, Cloth, and Gold* (n23 above) 25–35.

34 The first attempt to issue the crown, with a value of 4s 6d sterling, took place in August 1526; see the complete text in *Tudor Royal Proclamations* ed Paul L. Hughes and James F. Larkin 3 vols (New Haven and London 1964–9) I *The Early Tudors (1485–1553)* (London 1964) 158–63 no 112 (5 November 1526). According to the previously discussed formula for reciprocal relationships (see 569 above), the silver debasement of 11.127 per cent meant an increase of 12.51 per cent in the coined value of the Troy pound of sterling silver, from £2.000 to £2.500; the gold debasement, of 11.111 per cent, similarly, meant an increase in the coined value of the Troy pound of fine gold of 12.50 per cent, from £24.000 sterling to £27.000 sterling: $\Delta T = [1/(1 - 0.1111)] - 1 = 0.125$ or 12.50 per cent.

35 On English coinage in this period and the Henrician 'great debasement,' see Challis *Tudor Coinage* (n32 above) 68–72, 81–111; Feaveryear *Pound Sterling* (n33 above) 48–50, 435–9 Appendixes I–III; Challis 'Lord Hastings to the Great

TOP Crown of the double rose
struck by Henry VIII from 1526 at 22 carats, 54.0 grains Troy, or 3.456 grams

BOTTOM The *réal d'or* of Charles V
struck from 1521 with a theoretical weight of 5.32 grams, 992/1000 gold,
that is, almost 24 carats

The University of Oxford
Ashmolean Museum, Heberden Coin Room
The coins on this page are reproduced at 138 per cent of size.

Coinage and monetary changes in early modern France

Across the Channel in France, the coinage changes, though they appear from the tables to have been more complex, were, like the English alterations, relatively minor, and they were implemented only many years after the previous set of changes, in the late fifteenth century. As was explained in CWE 1 (328, 331–2, 340–1), the predominant money-of-account used in late medieval and early modern France was the *livre tournois*, which was composed of 20 *sous* (*sols*), each of which contained 12 *deniers* (240d per *livre tournois*). The older and more rarely used *livre parisis* was worth 1.25 *livres tournois* (see CWE 1 326–7). The original 'link money' with the actual silver coinage was the silver *denier* or penny, though by the late fifteenth century it was largely copper (just 8.0 per cent fine silver). The primary French silver coin was now the *blanc à la couronne* or *douzain*; when it was first issued in April 1488, it was worth 12d *tournois* (that is, a *sol* or shilling) and about 2d *groot* Flemish. It remained unchanged with a fineness of 4 *deniers* 12 *grains argent-le-roi*, and a *taille* per *marc de Troyes* of 86 (2.846 g, and 1.023 g pure silver) until the next coinage issue, in July 1519. Then its fineness was very subtly changed by just 6 *grains* AR, and its *taille* marginally increased to 92 per marc (2.660 g), thus reducing the fine silver content by 11.73 per cent (to 0.903 g) and raising the value of the silver *traite* per marc correspondingly by 13.27 per cent (from £48.887 to £55.375 *tournois* per marc of fine silver).

The changes made in the same year in the primary French gold coin, the *écu au soleil à la couronne* (the French 'crown'), were even more subtle than those for the silver coinage. The fineness was reduced from 23 carats 1.5 grains, set in 1494, to 23 carats, and the *taille* was very slightly raised from 70.000 to 71.167 per fine marc, thus reducing the gold content by just 3.68 per cent. But the *écu*'s value was raised from 36s 3d to 40s 0d *tournois* (that is, £2), to effect an overall debasement of 11.34 per cent, thus correspondingly raising the value of the gold *traite* per fine marc by 12.77 per cent (from £537.994 to £606.823 *tournois*). These changes also reduced the bimetallic ratio from 11.684:1 to 10.959:1 and thus 'favoured' silver in relation to gold. Once established in their new format, the gold and silver coinages of France remained unaltered for more than twenty years, until

* * * * *

Silver Recoinage' (n24 above) 189–217, 228–44, and 720 Appendix 2. See also Philip Grierson 'The Monetary Pattern of Sixteenth-Century Coinage' *Transactions of the Royal Historical Society* 5th series 21 (1971) 45–60, repr in his *Later-Medieval Numismatics* (n31 above) no 16.

1541, just a year before Henry VIII embarked on his 'great debasement' (see Tables 3-4).[36]

Coinage and monetary changes in the Hapsburg Low Countries during the early sixteenth century

These changes in the French coinages may have prompted the similarly minor alterations in the coinage of the Burgundian-Hapsburg Netherlands that took place just two years later, after more than twenty years of perfect monetary stability. From February 1500, the two primary gold coins had been the *toison d'or*, struck at 23 carats 9.5 grains and a *taille* of 54.5 per *marc de Troyes* (4.452 g pure gold), with an official value of 8s 4d *groot* Flemish (100d), and the *Philippus* florin, struck at 15 carats 11 grains and a *taille* of 74 per marc (2.194 g fine gold), with an official value of 4s 2d (50d) *groot* Flemish.[37] The first Hapsburg monetary ordinance, which the government of Charles V proclaimed on 20 February 1521, proved to be abortive for the gold coins, by undervaluing them; but, as will be noted later (578-9), the government subsequently sought to resurrect this ordinance. The initial problem about gold coinage rates was remedied in the revised ordinance

* * * * *

36 Adrien Blanchet and Adolphe E. Dieudonné *Manuel de numismatique française* 4 vols (Paris 1912-36) II Adolphe E. Dieudonné *Monnaies royales françaises depuis Hugues Capet jusqu'à la Révolution* (Paris 1916) 314-21, for Francis I (1515-47); for the preceding eras of Charles VIII (1483-98) and Louis XII (1498-1515), see 303-13.

37 These coinages of Archduke Philip the Fair were, in fact, first introduced by the ordinance of 10 April 1496: the *toison d'or*, of the fineness and weight just specified but with an official value of just 8s 0d *groot* (96d); and the *Philippus* florin, with a fineness of 16 carats and the same *taille* of 74 per *marc*, and with half the value of the *toison d'or*, that is, 4s 0d (48d) *groot* Flemish. For the text of this ordinance, see Louis Deschamps de Pas 'Essai sur l'histoire monétaire des comtes de Flandre de la Maison d'Autriche et classement de leurs monnaies (1482-1556): Philippe-le-Beau (1482-1506): Suite' *Revue numismatique* nouvelle série 15 (1874-77), 89-93. Minting commenced on 20 May 1496. The subsequent changes to reduce the fineness of the *Philippus* florin and to raise the official exchange values of both gold coins proclaimed on 20 February 1500 are not provided in any ordinance or text published by Deschamps de Pas, though he does cite a subsequent ordinance of 2 July 1504 confirming these changes and values (98-105). These changes are, however, perfectly evident, and with the February 1500 dating, in the mint accounts for Bruges from 2 May 1499 to 5 September 1500, and for Antwerp from 3 June 1499 to 8 August 1500, in Algemeen Rijksarchief van België, Rekenkamer, registers nos 18,122-4 and 17,822:11-13, respectively. See 598 below.

of 15 August 1521, which introduced three new gold coins: the *réal d'or*, of virtually pure gold (23 carats 9.5 grains; 46 struck to the *marc de Troyes*, each with 5.275 g fine gold), valued at 10s 7d (127d) *groot* Flemish; the *demi-réal*, with only 18 carats (70.125 per *marc*, each with 2.618 g fine gold), valued at 5s 3d (63d) *groot*; and the famous *Carolus* florin, named after Charles V, with just 14 carats (84 per marc, each with 1.700 g fine gold), valued at 3s 6d (42d) *groot*. In accepting certain foreign gold coins, the government raised the exchange value of the French *écu au soleil* to 76d *groot* (from 72d in the February ordinance) and of Italian ducats and florins to 80d *groot*.[38] The issue of the *Carolus* florin, the only new gold coin henceforth to have any widespread circulation, in effect meant a 7.75 per cent *affaiblissement* of the gold coinage (in relation to the *Philippus* florin, now worth 54d *groot*), which correspondingly raised the value of the gold *traite* per marc by 8.40 per cent (from £23.246 to £25.200 *groot* Flemish per *marc de Troyes*).

The gold coin values proclaimed in the August 1521 ordinance were confirmed in Hapsburg ordinances of 1522 and 1524, but then, with a decree dated 25 November 1525, they were increased by 10 per cent. The following year, on 10 December 1526 (amended on 1 January 1527), the Hapsburg government in Brussels decreed that the former rates – not those of 15 August 1521, but the original rates of 20 February 1521 (see CWE 8 350 Table B) – were to be restored from 1 March 1527, so that the gold *carolus* should then circulate at 40d *groot* Flemish.[39] In *The Growth of the Antwerp Market*, Van der Wee lists these changes in the gold rates in an appendix and suggests that the restored lower rates, those of February 1521, remained in force

* * * * *

38 For the text of the two 1521 ordinances see Louis Deschamps de Pas 'Essai sur l'histoire monétaire des comtes de Flandre de la Maison d'Autriche et classement de leurs monnaies (1482–1556): Charles-Quint (1506–1556)' *Revue belge de numismatique* 32 (1876) 73–9, 82–3. The term *Carolus* had, however, been used earlier as a new alternative name for the *Philippus* florin in an ordinance of 2 January 1517: '... ung autre denier d'or qui se nommera carolus, ou lieu du philippus d'or, de tel poix, alloy et sur le mesme piet et instructions que ledit philippus a esté forgé jusques à present; et vauldra icellui carolus iiii s. et ii d. gros [de Flandres]' (ibidem 68).

39 Deschamps de Pas 'Histoire monétaire: Charles Quint (n38 above)' 82–6. From November 1525 to 10 December 1526 the gold *réal* was supposed to circulate at 132d *groot* (raised from 127d) and the gold *Carolus* at 44d (raised from 42d). From 10 December 1526 to 1 March 1527 the gold *réal* was to circulate at 136d, and thereafter for only 120d *groot*; the gold *Carolus*, for 45d and thereafter for only 40d *groot*.

from 1527 until the end of Charles v's reign.[40] His data, along with commercial statistics from other tables in his book and gold values extracted from monetary ordinances and mint indentures, are tabulated in Table 2. It presents the annual market prices for fine gold bullion at the Antwerp fairs from 1500 to 1540 and compares them with the official values of fine gold contained in the Burgundian-Hapsburg coinage. The columns present the following information:

1   years, from 1500 to 1540 inclusive
2   the annual market value of one kilogram of fine gold, at the Antwerp fairs, in pounds *groot* Flemish (£1.5 *pond groot* Brabant = £1.0 *pond groot* Flemish)
3   the official value of one kilogram of fine gold in the Hapsburg coinage, each year, according to monetary ordinances and official mint indentures (see Table 3c, 649 below)
4   the market value of fine gold as a percentage of the official value of gold when coined

As this table indicates, there is no compelling evidence that the reduced exchange rates for gold, those from the 1527 decree restoring the February 1521 ordinance, remained in force or were ever observed. Indeed, had these gold coinage rates prevailed, they would have been substantially below the free-market rates for gold bullion at the Antwerp fairs – as much as 10 per cent below in 1536–7. Table 2 indicates, however, that the official gold coinage rates decreed on 15 August 1521 were usually very close to, though just above, the free-market rates. Normally, gold coins commanded a premium or *agio* over bullion (ingots) that reflected the lower transaction costs associated with their use, because the coin's official stamp was a guarantee of its value, while the value of bullion ingots had to be determined by using scales and touchstones.[41]

* * * * *

40 Van der Wee *Antwerp Market* (n2 above) I 128–34 Tables xv–xvi
41 The added costs in minting, those of *brassage* and *seigniorage*, accounted for the difference between the mint's price in purchasing bullion per *marc* and the coined or *traite* value of the *marc* of fine metal, silver or gold. See Munro *Wool, Cloth, and Gold* (n23 above) 25–6 and 'Deflation and the Petty Coinage Problem in the Late-Medieval Economy: The Case of Flanders, 1334–1484' *Explorations in Economic History* 25 (October 1988) 387–423, repr in John Munro *Bullion Flows and Monetary Policies in England and the Low Countries, 1350 – 1500* Variorum Collected Studies series cs 355 (Aldershot 1992) VIII 387–423.

Table 2 also shows why the government of Charles v felt compelled to change both the gold and silver coinages in 1521, albeit reluctantly, in the February and August ordinances, in order to alter the bimetallic ratio in favour of gold. For the free-market price of gold had been rising from 1516, when the French government had authorized a rise in the value of the *écu au soleil* from 36s 3d *tournois* to 40s 0d *tournois*.[42] The need for the subsequent monetary ordinances of 1525, 1526, and 1527 can be seen in the further rise in gold prices on the Antwerp market. After 1526–7, however, the free-market rates fell to just 92.1 per cent of the gold rates decreed in August 1521, then rose slowly to peak again at 101.4 per cent in 1536–7. (For that reason the rates decreed in the August 1521 ordinance have been used for the years 1521–40 in Tables 5 and 6; see 658–72 below).

The two Hapsburg monetary ordinances of February and August 1521 were virtually identical for silver and made only slight changes in that coinage (see CWE 8 349–50). These changes appear to be more complex than they really were, because the ordinance had also instituted a new standard for silver fineness: *argent fin* (AF) or 100 per cent pure silver, to displace the very old and traditional French-based system of *argent-le-roi* (95.833 per cent pure), even though the French monetary authorities themselves continued to use the AR standard. To add to the confusion, the new Hapsburg mint standard employed the same subdivisions: 12 deniers, with 24 grains per denier.[43] Two new silver coins were introduced to match the gold: the

* * * * *

42 Denis Richet 'Le cours officiel des monnaies étrangères circulant en France au XVIe siècle' *Revue historique* 225 (1961) 377; Frank Spooner *The International Economy and Monetary Movements in France, 1493–1725* (Cambridge 1972) 121

43 See the 20 February 1521 monetary ordinance in Deschamps de Pas 'Charles Quint' (n38 above): 'ung denier d'argent qui se nommera double karolus, et aura cours pour six gros de Flandres ... tenant unze deniers cincq grains de fin argent en alloy ...' The first indication of this change comes in the Bruges mint account for 17 May 1503 to 25 May 1504, which specified the fineness of the double patard: 7 deniers 16 grains *argent fin* or 8 deniers *argent-le-roi*; and that for the single patard: 3 deniers 20 grains *argent fin*, or 4 deniers *argent-le-roi*. (Algemeen Rijksarchief België, Rekenkamer, register no 18,127). But the official ordinances had continued to use the *argent-le-roi* standard up to 1520, though usually just specifying that the previous ordinances were to remain in force. For the text of the April 1496 ordinance specifying the silver fineness in *argent-le-roi*, see n37 above. According to Dieudonné *Monnaies royales françaises* (n36 above) 34: 'Pour l'argent, les évaluations, soi-disant rapportées "au fin," partaient de ce qu'on appelait l'argent-le-roi (A.R.), c'est-à-dire d'un métal préalablement allié, ou supposé allié, aux 23/24 d'argent et 1/24 cuivre (0,958). On ne sait pas toujours, quand les textes parlent d'argent pur, s'ils

single *Carolus* or *demi-réal* of 5 deniers 12 grains *argent fin* (45.833 per cent pure), with 78.5 struck to the *marc* AF (thus with 1.429 g pure silver); and the double *Carolus* or *réal*, at 11 *deniers* 5 *grains* AF, slightly finer than sterling silver, at 93.40 per cent purity, with 80 struck to the *marc* AF (2.858 g pure silver). Very few of these high-value silver coins were struck, but even fewer of the small denomination coins were struck, in part because their high base-metal (copper) contents gave them greater durability in circulation, but mainly because the combination of high-base metal content and low value was a strong disincentive against either hoarding or exporting these coins abroad.[44]

The most important and most widely circulated coin in the Low Countries was now the double *groot* (2d), more commonly known as the *patard* or *stuiver*; from the proclamation of the April 1496 Hapsburg monetary ordinance, it displaced the single *groot* as the standard coin and 'link money.' According to that ordinance and the subsequent mint accounts (to 1499), the *patard* was struck with a *taille* of 79 per *marc de Troyes* with a fineness of 4 *deniers argent-le-roi* (AR); it thus contained 0.990 g of pure silver (see CWE 1 340). The next monetary ordinance, issued on 20 February 1500, retained the same fineness for the *patard* but raised its *taille* to 80 per marc, thus reducing the pure silver content to 0.977 g.[45] The *patard* remained unchanged until the monetary ordinance of 20 February 1521, which retained its *taille* (weight) of

* * * * *

visent l'argent fin ou l'argent-le-roi. L'usage de l'A.R. aurait été abandonné, d'après Abbot de Bazinghen, vers le milieu du XVIIe siècle.'

44 The only difference to be found in the two 1521 ordinances was that the first (February) had given the silver *réal* a value of 6d *groot*, and the second (August) raised its value to 6½d. See CWE 8 349–50 and Table 4c below on silver coinage, for the relative weights and fineness of the petty coins: the single groot, the demi-groot, the quarter-groot (*gigot*), and the quadruple and double mites (with 24 mites per denier or penny *groot*). Note that the lower the denomination, the greater the *taille* (that is, the lower the weight) and the higher the base-metal content, the more expensive it was to mint such petty coins; and thus the higher *brassage* fee required necessarily meant a higher *traite* or coined value of the *marc argent-le-roi*. See the Bruges mint accounts from 17 September 1505 to 28 July 1507, for examples of and precise data on their very rare issues, in Algemeen Rijksarchief, Rekenkamer, registers nos 18,129–30. For the economics of using such coins, see Munro 'Deflation and the Petty Coinage Problem' (n41 above).

45 The mint accounts of Bruges and Antwerp indicate that the weight reduction (increase in the *taille*) of the silver *patard* had begun as early as May 1499. Algemeen Rijksarchief, Rekenkamer, registers nos 18,124–5, 17,882:13, and CWE 1 340 Appendix B. See also nn37–8 above and Table 4c below.

80 per marc while slightly reducing its fineness to 3 *deniers* 21 *grains argent-le-roi* (AR), which, according to the ordinance, was now to be expressed as 3 *deniers* 17 *grains argent fin* (AF). Thus the pure silver content of the *patard* was reduced to 0.945 g, for a relatively minor debasement of 3.26 per cent. That correspondingly raised the value of the silver *traite* per *marc fin* by 3.37 per cent: from a *traite* of £2.087 *groot* Flemish (£2.000 *groot* for the *marc argent-le-roi*) to one of £2.157 *groot* Flemish. Consequently, these changes 'favoured' gold, if only slightly, over silver, so that the mint's bimetallic ratio rose from 11.139:1 to 11.681:1, and thus above the current English bimetallic ratio of 11.157:1. These monetary ordinances of 1521 effected the only major changes in the silver coinage undertaken during the reign of Charles v. Apart from the adjustments in gold rates in 1525–7 (see 578–9 above), and the even more minor alterations in silver (July 1548) and gold (March 1553), the silver and gold coinages of the Hapsburg Low Countries remained essentially unchanged until Charles' abdication in September 1555.[46]

The coinage changes and consequent alterations in the bimetallic ratio imposed by the 1521 monetary ordinances help to explain why the mints in the Hapsburg Low Countries fared relatively less well than did those in England in coining silver during the 1520s and early 1530s. As Table 1 (see 573 above) shows, the mean annual outputs of English silver coinage, just a meagre 79.15 kg of fine metal in 1516–20, rose to a mean of 3,148.21 kg in 1521–5, and then soared to a mean of 9,244.70 kg in 1526–30. To be sure, some considerable if immeasurable part of that large silver output was due to the recoinage that Henry VIII implemented in 1526, but the mean annual outputs achieved a very impressive level of 5,150.46 kg in the two following quinquennia, from 1531 to 1540 (before the 'great debasement'). As Table 1

* * * * *

46 For the 1521 silver debasement, note that the formula for the reciprocal relationship between debasement and increased coinage values, that is, the increase in the *traite*, still holds true: $\Delta T = [1/(1 - 0.032609)] - 1 = 0.033707$ or an increase of 3.37 per cent. For subsequent changes, see nn37–8 above and Table 4C. For a comparison of mint outputs in England and the southern Low Countries in this period, see Munro 'Central European Mining Boom' and 'Precious Metals and the Origins of the Price Revolution' (n11 above). In England, the mean annual output of coined silver rose from 79.145 kg of pure metal in 1516–20 to a mean of 9,244.701 kg in 1526–30; in the southern Low Countries (Antwerp and Bruges), the mean annual output of coined silver rose from 705.122 kg of pure metal in 1516–20 to 2,979.875 kg in 1526–30. Both countries were of course benefiting from the current South-German silver mining boom (n11 above). Conversely, the mean annual gold outputs from English mints were: 743.656 kg in 1516–20, 442.135 kg in 1521–5, and 736.421 kg in 1526–30. In the Low Countries, the mean annual mint outputs of gold were: 145.094 kg in 1516–20, 1,306.588 kg in 1521–5, and 240.990 kg in 1526–30.

also shows, the value of silver coinage outputs never exceeded 45 per cent of the total from 1481 to 1520 (and were just 0.94 per cent in 1516–20); but silver's share of the total value of English coinage outputs suddenly rose from 1521–5 to peak at 68.41 per cent of the total in 1536–40, and continued to account for over half (55 per cent) of the total value of coinage outputs over the next decade. In the southern Low Countries (Flanders and Brabant) the outputs of silver coinage were always quite respectable in the six quinquennia following the 1521 monetary ordinances; obviously both countries' mints were benefiting from the now rapidly expanding South-German silver-mining boom, which reached its peak in the 1530s (see 561–2 above). Nevertheless the silver coinage output in the first quinquennium, 1521–5, which amounted to an annual mean of 1,904.20 kg of fine metal, accounted for only 11.63 per cent of the total value of coinage struck in these Hapsburg mints (and thus the 1,306.59 kg in fine gold accounted for 88.37 per cent). During the next three quinquennia, from 1526 to 1540, the volume of silver coinage outputs from the mints of the southern Low Countries rose considerably, peaking at 5,364.00 kg of fine metal per year in 1536–40; in none of these three quinquennia did their mean annual outputs quite match those of the English mints. Finally, one may observe that the truly gigantic mean annual output of 22,029.73 kg of fine silver in the quinquennium 1546–50 reflects the great success of Henry VIII's 'great debasement' in drawing silver into the English mints; and perhaps some of that silver was coming from the Low Countries, as the fall in their mints' silver coinage outputs in that same quinquennium may suggest.

Coinage and the Price Revolution: the Bodin-Malestroit debates.

Although coinage debasements played a major role in the inflations and oscillating price levels of the chaotic later Middle Ages, especially after the Black Death, they had virtually nothing to do with the onset of the sixteenth-century Price Revolution. The only one that subsequently did play a significant, if purely temporary and regional, role was Henry VIII's 'great debasement' of 1542–52.[47] Many contemporary observers in the sixteenth century and earlier, however, viewed coinage debasements as the chief culprit

* * * * *

47 See n32 above and J.D. Gould *The Great Debasement: Currency and the Economy in Mid-Tudor England* (Oxford 1970) 34–86. For the late-medieval debasement-induced inflations, see the collected essays in John Day *The Medieval Market Economy* (Oxford 1987); Munro *Bullion Flows and Monetary Policies in England and the Low Countries* (n41 above) and 'Mint Outputs, Money, and Prices' (n11 above).

(along with greedy 'monopolists') to be blamed for rising prices. Certainly for much of the later medieval period, in the Low Countries and France especially, silver debasements were the principal cause of periodic, if temporary, inflations. In the 1560s, the French economist Malestroit reiterated that traditional view to explain the now readily apparent Price Revolution. But his chief opponent, the philosopher-economist Jean Bodin, proposed an alternative monetary explanation – increases in the stock of money from the growing imports of 'Spanish treasure.' He won a major victory over Malestroit in establishing what now may be regarded as the modern foundations of the Quantity Theory of Money, even if he was in error concerning the *initial* causes of the inflation that began in 1520s, and thus well before the influx of Spanish-American silver, for reasons already elaborated.[48]

The coinage tables for England, France, and the southern Low Countries

Because many of the tables in this study concern the purchasing power of coins, in which the changes were so complex, some analysis of the tables on

* * * * *

48 See *The Response of Jean Bodin to the Paradoxes of Malestroit and The Paradoxes, translated from the French Second Edition, Paris 1578* ed George Moore (Washington 1946). See also *Écrits notables sur la monnaie, XVIe siècle: de Copernic à Davanzati reproduits, traduits, d'après les éditions originales et les manuscrits, avec une introduction, des notices et des notes* ed Jean-Yves Le Branchu, Collection des principaux économistes, nouvelle édition, 2 vols (Paris 1934): *Les paradoxes du Seigneur de Malestroict, conseiller du Roy, et Maistre ordinaire de ses comptes, sur le faict des monnoyes, presentez à sa Majesté, au mois de mars* MDLXVI (Paris 1566); *La response de maistre Jean Bodin advocat en la cour au paradoxe de monsieur de Malestroit touchant l'enchérissement de toutes choses et le moyen d'y remedier* (Paris 1568). Some modern economists would give priority to some contemporary Spanish economists, but their writings never had the impact of those produced by Jean Bodin; see Marjorie Grice-Hutchison *The School of Salamanca: Readings in Spanish Monetary Theory, 1544–1605* (Oxford 1952). For modern views on the role of Spanish silver in the Price Revolution, see Georg Wiebe *Zur Geschichte der Preisrevolution des XVI. und XVII. Jahrhunderts* Staats- und sozialwissenschaftliche Beiträge II/2 (Leipzig 1895); Earl Hamilton 'American Treasure and Andalusian Prices, 1503–1660: A Study in the Spanish Price Revolution' *Journal of Economic and Business History* 1 (1928), repr in *The Price Revolution in Sixteenth-Century England* ed P.H. Ramsey (London 1971) 147–81, 'American Treasure and the Rise of Capitalism, 1500–1700' *Economica* 27 (November 1929) 338–57, and *American Treasure and the Price Revolution* (n20 above). For contemporary English Tudor views, see Outhwaite *Inflation in Tudor and Early Stuart England* (n12 above) 17–25. See also 560–1 and n11 above.

coinage may be helpful. There are eight tables, in two groups of four; Tables 3A–D on gold coins and their official values or exchange rates; and Tables 4A–D on silver coins and their official values or exchange rates. Most values have been rounded to three decimal places, but the calculated totals (though rounded) are those produced by the computer using *unrounded* values.

In Table 3A, on the gold coinages of England from 1464 to 1526, the columns present the following data:

1   the date of the mint ordinance prescribing changes in the coins (in weight and/or fineness and/or value) or issuing new coins and the name of the gold coin struck; the ordinances remained in force until the next date provided in this column, and those for 1526 remained valid until the 'great debasement' that began in 1542

2   the fineness of the gold coin in carats, with a maximum of 24 carats

3   the fineness expressed in grains, as a subdivision of a carat, with a maximum of 4 grains per carat

4   the percentage fineness: 23 carats and 3.5 grains = 23.875 carats = 99.479 per cent fine

5   the number of gold coins struck to the Tower pound of fine gold, with a mint-weight of 349.914 g, in use until 1526 (at the Tower of London)

6   the number of gold coins struck to the Troy pound of fine gold, with a mint-weight of 373.242 g, in use from 1526

7   the prescribed or theoretical weight of the gold coin in grams, that is, the weight of the Tower pound and then of the Troy pound in grams divided by the number of coins cut from that weight of fine gold

8   the grams of pure gold in the coin; that is, the weight of the gold coin multiplied by its percentage fineness

9   the grams of pure gold in the coin represented in the English pound sterling money-of-account, calculated by dividing the gram weight of the Tower or Troy pound by the *traite* or total money-of-account value of the coins struck from that pound weight of gold, with the standard fineness of 23.875 carats (given in column 12), multiplied by its percentage fineness (see 569 above); for example, in August 1464, for the angel-noble: $349.914/22.500 \times 0.995 = 15.471$ g

10   the official exchange value of the coins, in shillings and pence sterling

11   the value of the coins in decimal pound sterling: 6s 8d = £0.333

12   the coined, money-of-account value of the Tower pound of fine gold, with 23.875 carats, the effective maximum fineness attainable; this is the *traite* value, as explained above (569)

13   the coined, money-of-account value of the Troy pound of commercially fine gold, with 23.875 carats

14   the value of one kilogram of pure gold (24 carats) in current pounds sterling

15   the value of one kilogram of pure silver in current pounds sterling

16   the official bimetallic or gold : silver ratio, that is, the ratio of the values in columns 14 and 15

In Table 3B, on the gold coinages of France from 1494 to 1550, the columns present the following data:

1   the date of the mint ordinance prescribing changes in the coins (in weight and/or fineness and/or value) or issuing new coins and the official name of the coin; the ordinances remained in force until the next date provided in this column

2   the fineness of the gold coin in carats, with a theoretical maximum of 24 carats

3   the fineness expressed in grains, as a subdivision of a carat, with a maximum of 12 grains per carat

4   the percentage fineness: 23 carats and 1.5 grains = 23.125 carats = 96.354 per cent fine

5   the *taille* or the number of coins struck to the mint-weight unit, the *marc de Troyes*, containing 244.753 g

6   the weight of the coin in grams

7   the amount of pure gold in the coin in grams; that is, the weight of the gold coin multiplied by its percentage fineness

8   the grams of pure gold in the coin represented in the French money-of-account, the *livre tournois*, calculated by dividing the gram weight of the *marc de Troyes* by the *traite* or total money-of-account value of the coins struck from the marc of pure gold (in column 11; for example, in 1494, for the *écu au soleil*: 244.753/131.678 = 1.859 g)

9   the official value of the gold coin in shillings and pence *tournois*

10   the value of the coin in decimal *livres tournois*, for example: 36s 3d = 36.25s = £1.813 *tournois*

11   the *traite* (see 569 above) or the coined, money-of-account value of the *marc de Troyes* of pure gold, in *livres tournois*

12   the value of one kilogram of pure gold in *livres tournois*

13   the value of one kilogram of pure silver in *livres tournois*

14   the official bimetallic or gold:silver ratio, that is, the ratio of the values in columns 12 and 13

In Table 3C, for gold coins in the Burgundian-Hapsburg Low Countries from 1496 to 1556, the columns present the following data:

1   the date of the mint ordinance prescribing changes in the coins (in weight and/or fineness and/or value) or issuing new coins and the official name of the coin; the ordinances remained in force until the next date provided in this column
2   the fineness of the gold coin in carats, with maximum of 24 carats
3   the fineness expressed in grains, as a subdivision of a carat, to a maximum of 12 grains per carat
4   the percentage fineness, for example, the *toison d'or* in 1496: 23 carats and 9.5 grains = 23.792 carats = 99.132 per cent fine
5   the *taille* or the number of coins struck to the mint-weight unit, the *marc de Troyes*, containing 244.753 g
6   the weight of the coin in grams
7   the amount of pure gold in the coin in grams, that is, the weight of the gold coin multiplied by its percentage fineness
8   the grams of pure gold in the coin represented in the Flemish money-of-account, for the Hapsburg Low Countries, the *pond groot* or *livre gros*, calculated by dividing the gram weight of the *marc de Troyes* by the *traite* or total money-of-account value of the coins struck from the marc of pure gold (in column 11); for example, in 1496, for the *toison d'or*: 244.753/21.991 = 11.130 g
9   the official value of the gold coin in shillings and pence *groot* (*gros*)
10   the value of the coin in decimal *livre gros* (*pond groot*), for example (*toison d'or*): 8s 0d = £0.400
11   the *traite* (see 569 above) or the coined money-of-account value of the *marc de Troyes* of pure gold, in *livres gros*
12   the value of one kilogram of pure gold in *livres gros*
13   the value of one kilogram of pure silver in *livres gros*
14   the official bimetallic or gold:silver ratio, that is, the ratio of the values in columns 12 and 13

In Table 3D, on the official values of or exchange rates for the principal gold coins in this study, from 1500 to 1540, the columns present the following data:

1   the name of the country or principality issuing the coin and the official name of the coin
2   the years for which the exchange rates for each coin were in force

3   the value of the coin in pence or d *groot* (*gros*) of Flanders (Hapsburg Low Countries)
4   the value of the coin in *deniers tournois* of France
5   the value of the coin in *livres tournois* of France
6   the value of the coin in pence sterling of England

The notes for this table provide the references in CWE 1 and 12 that discuss these gold coins.

In Table 4A, on the silver coins of England from 1464 to 1526, the columns present the following data:

1   the date of the mint ordinance prescribing changes in the coins (in weight and/or fineness and/or value) or issuing new coins and the official name of the coin; the ordinances remained in force until the next date provided in this column; and those for 1526 remained valid until the 'great debasement' that began in 1542
2   the value of the coin in pence sterling
3   the number of coins struck from the Tower pound, of sterling silver fineness (92.50 per cent pure), weighing 349.914 g, in use until 1526
4   the number of coins struck from the Troy pound, of sterling silver fineness, weighing 373.242 g, in use from 1526
5   the fineness of the coin in ounces, to a maximum of 12 ounces
6   the fineness of the coin in pennyweight (dwt), as a subdivision of the ounce, with 20 dwt per ounce
7   the percentage fineness; for example, a penny of sterling silver fineness: 11 oz 2 dwt = 11.10 = 0.925 fine
8   the weight of the coin in Troy grains, with 5,760 grains to the Troy pound (24 grains to the pennyweight): the 1464 penny, with 480 to the Troy pound, contained $5760/480 = 12$ Troy grains
9   the weight of the coin in grams: the 1464 penny, with 450 to the Tower pound, weighed $349.914/450 = 0.778$ g (and $373.242/480 = 0.778$ g)
10   grams of pure silver in the coin, and thus the number of grams of pure silver in the unit (1d) of the sterling money-of-account, calculated by multiplying the weight of the coin by its percentage fineness
11   the *traite* or money-of-account value of the Tower pound struck into these coins, valued in shillings and pence sterling
12   the *traite* value of the Tower pound expressed as a decimal pound sterling
13   the *traite* or money-of-account value of the Troy pound struck into these coins, valued in shillings

14   the *traite* value of the Troy pound in decimal pounds sterling
15   the value of one kilogram of pure silver in decimal pounds sterling

Table 4B, for silver coins in France from 1488 to 1541, and Table 4C, for silver coins in the Hapsburg Low Countries from 1496 to 1556, use essentially the same format and, therefore, will be discussed together. Their columns present the following data:

1   the date of the mint ordinance prescribing changes in the coins (in weight and/or fineness and/or value) or issuing new coins and the official name of the coin; the ordinances remained in force until the next date provided in this column
2   the value of the coin in *deniers* (d) *tournois* for France and in pence (d) *groot* (or *gros*) for the Hapsburg Low Countries
3   the *taille* or number of coins cut from the *marc de Troyes* of the specified fineness, weighing 244.753 g
4   the weight of the coin in grams; that is, 244.753 divided by the *taille*
      – the 1488 French *blanc couronne* (*douzain*, worth 12d *tournois*) weighed
        244.753/86 = 2.846 g
      – the 1496 *patard* (*stuiver* or double *groot*) of the Low Countries weighed
        244.753/79 = 3.098 g
5   the *titre* or degree of fineness in deniers *argent-le-roi* (see 568 above), with a maximum of 12 deniers
6   the *titre* measured in grains, with a maximum of 24 grains to a denier (288 grains total for *argent-le-roi*)
7   the type of fineness: AR or AF
      – AR = *argent-le-roi* = 23/24 = 95.833 per cent pure (commercially fine silver); this type was used exclusively by late-medieval and early modern France, and by the Burgundian-Hapsburg Low Countries, until 1521 (see 568, 580 above)
      – AF = *argent fin* = 100.00 per cent pure; this type displaced AR in the Burgundian-Hapsburg Low Countries in 1521 (see 580 above), but was not used in France
8   the percentage fineness in *argent-le-roi*
      – the 1488 French *blanc couronne* (*douzain*), with 4 deniers and 12 grains AR, had a fineness of 4.5/12 = 37.50 per cent AR
      – the 1496 *patard* in the Low Countries, with 4 deniers (no grains), had a fineness of 4/12 = 33.33 per cent AR
9   percentage purity (pure silver, or, in the Low Countries, *argent fin*): column 8 multiplied by 23/24 (0.95833)

- the 1488 French *blanc couronne* (*douzain*) had a pure silver fineness of 0.375×0.9583 = 35.94 per cent pure
- the 1496 *patard* in the Low Countries had a pure silver fineness (AF) of 0.333×0.9583 = 31.94 per cent pure

10   grams of pure silver in the coin: its weight (column 4) multiplied by its percentage purity (column 9)
- the 1488 French *blanc couronne* (*douzain*) contained 2.846×0.359 = 1.023 grams pure silver
- the 1496 *patard* in the Low Countries contained 3.098×0.319 = 0.990 grams pure silver

11   grams of pure silver represented in the unit of money-of-account, calculated by dividing the weight of *marc de Troyes* (244.753 g) by the *traite* value of the pure silver marc, or marc AF (column 13), expressed in pence (that is, the value in *livres* or *ponden* multiplied by 240)
- in 1488 the French d *tournois* (money-of-account) contained 244.753/ (11.965×240) = 244.753/2871.60 = 0.085 g pure silver
- in 1496, the d *groot* (*denier gros*) contained 244.753/(2.061×240) = 244.753/494.64 = 0.495 g pure silver

12   the *traite* or coined money-of-account value of the *marc de Troyes argent-le-roi*, calculated by multiplying the official value (column 2) of the coin by its *taille* per marc (column 3) and dividing that sum by its percentage fineness AR (column 8)
- in France, in 1488, the *traite* value of the marc AR, when coined into *blancs couronne*, was 12×86/0.375 = 2,752d or £11.467 *tournois*
- in the Hapsburg Low Countries, in 1496, the *traite* value of the marc AR, when coined into *patards*, was 2×79/0.333 = 474.00d = £1.975 *groot* Flemish

13   the *traite* or coined money-of-account value of the pure silver marc (AF), which is calculated by dividing the *traite* value in column 12 by 0.95833 (that is, the marc AR = 23/24 = 0.95833)
- in France, in 1488, that value for the pure silver marc coined into *blancs couronne* was 11.467/0.95833 = £11.965 *tournois*
- in the Hapsburg Low Countries, in 1496, that value for the pure silver marc (AF) coined into *patards* was £2.061 *groot* Flemish; from 1521 it was calculated by multiplying the official value of the coin by its *traite* per marc and dividing that sum by the percentage of pure fineness (column 9)

14   the values of one kilogram of pure silver in the official money-of-account, calculated by multiplying the *traite* value of the pure silver marc (column 13) by the ratio of the gram weight of the kilogram and marc (1000/244.753)

- in France, in 1488, that value for one kilogram of pure silver coined into *blancs couronne* was $11.965 \times (1000/244.753) = 11.965 \times 4.086 = £48.887$ *tournois*
- in the Hapsburg Low Countries, in 1496, that value for one kilogram of pure silver coined into *patards* was $2.061 \times (1000/244.753) = 2.061 \times 4.086 = £8.420$ *groot* Flemish

Finally, Table 4D compares the relative values of the primary silver coins circulating in the Hapsburg Low Countries, France, and England; its columns present the following information, largely taken from Tables 4A–C:

1   the year in which these values first came into effect, for any of the coins in the list; for each coin, these data remain in effect until the next year indicated in the column
2   the grams of pure silver in the English penny (1d sterling)
3   the percentage change in the fine silver content of the sterling silver penny from the previous coinage issue
4   the grams of pure silver in the French *blanc couronne* (*douzain*), worth 12d *tournois*
5   the percentage change in the fine silver content of the *blanc couronne* from the previous coinage issue
6   the grams of pure silver in the Flemish *patard* (Hapsburg Low Countries), worth 2d *groot*
7   the percentage change in the fine silver content of the *patard* from the previous coinage issue
8   the value of the English sterling silver penny in pence *groot* Flemish
9   the value of the French *blanc couronne* (*douzain*) in pence *groot* Flemish
10   the value of one kilogram of fine silver in pounds sterling of England
11   the value of one kilogram of fine silver in *livres tournois* of France
12   the value of one kilogram of fine silver in *ponden groot* (*livres gros*) of Flanders
13   the ratio of the English and French values for coined silver (per kilogram of fine metal)
14   the ratio of the Flemish and French values for coined silver (per kilogram of fine metal)
15   the ratio of the English and Flemish values for coined silver (per kilogram of fine metal)
16   the ratio of the Flemish and English values for coined silver (per kilogram of fine metal)

III

THE PURCHASING POWER OF COINS AND WAGES
IN THE HAPSBURG LOW COUNTRIES (TABLES 5–9)

Tables of commodity prices and wages in quinquennial means (arithmetic and harmonic)

The inflation that occurred during the first two decades of the Price Revolution (see 556–62 above) is clearly evident in the tables on commodity prices and the related purchasing power of coins and wages in the southern Low Countries and southern England that accompany this essay. The tables are so numerous that considerations of space, and the reader's patience, do not permit the presentation of annual data for the first four decades of the sixteenth century. Price and wage data are presented in quinquennial (five-year) means that begin with years 1 and 6 in each decade.[49] For years with missing commodity-price and/or wage data, an interpolated estimate was made by taking the simple arithmetic mean of the values for the two adjacent years or by estimating the proportional differences for two or more years of missing data.[50]

While the five-year averages for commodity prices and wages are all calculated by taking simple *arithmetic* means, the averages of *quantities* that could be purchased by the various coins or by daily and annual wages have been computed as *harmonic* means, that is, 'the reciprocal of the arithmetic mean of the reciprocals of the individual numbers in a given series.'[51] The mathematical expression for this harmonic mean (HM) is:

* * * * *

49 In the appendix on coinage in CWE 2 (see n1 above) I had – regrettably in retrospect – followed the then prevalent but erroneous custom of commencing the quinquennia with the years 0 and 5. Decades, centuries, and millennia all begin with the year 1.

50 If data were missing for two or more years the interpolation involved calculating proportional differences in values between the year before and the year after the missing data. Thus, if the commodity price for the year 1516 was 10d and that for the year 1519 was 12d, the estimate made for year 1517 would be: $10 + 1/3 \times (12 - 10) = 10.667$d; and that for year 1518 would be: $10d + 2/3 \times (12 - 10) = 11.333$d. The algebraic formula to interpolate the missing data, year by year, is $X + n/Y \times (Z - X)$, in which X is the value for the year before the missing data, Z is the value for the year after the missing data, Y is the number of years from year X to year Z, and n is the number of the year after year X.

51 F.C. Mills *Introduction to Statistics* (New York 1956) 108–12, 401

$$1/[\sum(1/r_1 + 1/r_2 + 1/r_3 + \ldots 1/r_n)]/N$$

This can be rewritten in a two-part equation, for each quinquennium (five-year period):

$$\text{HM} = 1/x, \text{ when}$$
$$x = \sum(1/r_1 + 1/r_2 + 1/r_3 + 1/r_4 + 1/r_5)/5$$

First the reciprocal value of each item in the series is computed ($1/r$); then the sum ($\sum$) of the reciprocals of the total number of items in each five-year period is divided by the total number of the items in the series ($N = 5$) to produce the 'quotient' value x. The reciprocal of this quotient x is then computed to obtain the harmonic mean, that is, HM equals $1/x$. The harmonic mean must be used because of the method required to compute the quantities purchased, that is, by taking the reciprocal of the price per unit, and then multiplying that result by the face-value of the coin or by the daily money wage in current coin.

Economists call the money wage the 'nominal' wage to distinguish it from the 'real' wage, which indicates the purchasing power of that nominal, money wage. Normally, the real wage (RW) is computed by dividing the nominal wage index (NWI) by the current consumer price index (CPI). If, for example, inflationary forces drove the consumer price index up by 12 per cent over a five-year period, and if the craftsman's nominal money wage rose by only 10 per cent over that period, he would be slightly worse off, despite the increased pay. A chief purpose of the tables that follow is to ascertain the course of real wages – to see to what extent money wages kept pace with or fell behind the consumer price index, as a measure of inflation, in the Low Countries and England during the first four decades of the sixteenth century.

To illustrate the computation of the harmonic mean, for each quinquennium in these tables, consider the following example. In Brussels, in 1501, eggs cost 10.191d *groot* Flemish per hundred and thus 0.102d *groot* per egg. With a single Flemish penny or 1d *groot*, one could thus purchase 1/0.1019 = 9.812 eggs; and with the Burgundian silver *patard* (the *stuiver* or double groot, worth 2d *groot* Flemish and 3d *groot* of Brabant) one could acquire double that amount, or 19.625 eggs. The procedure for calculating the quinquennial means – arithmetic means for the prices but harmonic means for quantities purchased – can be seen in Table A (p 594). In this table, the average prices given in the two price columns are the simple arithmetic means of the prices for each of the five years, but the averages in the three quantity columns – the five-year average of the quantities of eggs acquired in

Table A Prices of eggs in Brussels in d *groot* Flemish and quantities purchased with silver coinage, 1501–5

| year | price of eggs in d groot Flemish | | quantity bought with | | |
	for 100	for one	1d groot	2d groot	master mason's daily wage: 8.333d groot
1501	10.191	0.102	9.812	19.625	81.771
1502	10.947	0.105	9.527	19.054	79.39
1503	10.802	0.108	9.257	18.515	77.145
1504	11.108	0.111	9.003	18.005	75.023
1505	11.413	0.114	8.762	17.523	73.014
1501–5 mean	10.802	0.108	9.257	18.515	77.145

SOURCE

See Table 6E below.

each of these five years – are the harmonic means, as explained above. One can test the validity of this method by calculating the means of the price-relatives or index numbers: those for the quantities purchased agree only with the independently calculated harmonic means, not with the arithmetic means.

In the sources used for the tables for the Low Countries, the actual prices were recorded in the standard money-of-account for the duchy of Brabant (in *ponden* or pounds, shillings, and pence *groot* of Brabant). After the Burgundian monetary unification and reform of 1434–5, this money-of-account remained tied to the *pond groot* of the adjacent (and economically more advanced) county Flanders by the fixed ratio of 1.5 : 1, that is: 30s *groot* Brabant = 20s *groot* Flemish; 3d *groot* Brabant = 2d *groot* Flemish. In many of the tables in this study, prices and values recorded at Antwerp and other towns in Brabant have been expressed in both moneys-of-account, with this same ratio.

The Van der Wee 'basket of consumables'

Annual changes in all the commodity prices are demonstrated by using price-relatives in what is more commonly known as a consumer price index and in this study as a 'basket of consumables' price index. For the southern Low Countries, chiefly for the Antwerp-Lier-Mechelen-Brussels region of southern Brabant, the price-index employed is the one that Herman Van der Wee constructed on the model of the well known Phelps Brown and Hopkins 'basket of consumables' price index, using as far as possible their selection and weighting of the commodities.[52] Van der Wee's basket, presented in detail in Table 5A for the years 1501–5, contains the prices, in d *groot* Brabant, for ten commodities: rye, barley, beef, herrings, cheese, butter, charcoal, tallow candles, cheap woollen cloth, and cheap linen cloth. The specific units and quantities of each of these ten commodities in the basket are indicated in the top row of the column: in litres, kilograms, metres, or number, respectively. These commodity-weights were chosen to correspond as closely as possible to those used in the Phelps Brown and Hopkins index for the period 1500 to 1750.

In his set of tables, Van der Wee provided the annual values for each of the ten components in the 'basket of consumables' – that is, the specified quantity unit multiplied by the commodity price for each year – over the three-century period from 1400 to 1700. For those years when prices were missing for any commodity, he estimated or interpolated them, usually by computing a mean value from the commodity prices for adjacent years. The values so calculated represent each commodity's share of the total annual value of the basket; the total value of his basket, for each year, was therefore the sum of those ten annual commodity values (actual or estimated). The next column of Table 5A presents that value, in d *groot* Brabant, for each year from 1501 to 1505. For each of these ten commodities, the sum of the annual values and of the total value of the basket was computed and then divided by five to provide the quinquennial mean for 1501–5. This table also groups these commodity values in three categories: grains (rye and barley, both of which were more important in the Low Countries than wheat); meat-fish-dairy (beef, herrings, cheese, and butter); and industrial goods (charcoal, candles, woollen and linen cloth).

This five-year period or 'quinquennium' has been chosen as the *base* period for this study in order to present the index numbers or the relative prices and wages for both the Low Countries and England; the mean

* * * * *

52 Herman Van der Wee 'Prijzen en lonen als ontwikkelingsvariabelen: Een vergelijkend onderzoek tussen Engeland en de Zuidelijke Nederlanden, 1400–1700' in *Album offert à Charles Verlinden à l'occasion de ses trente ans de professoriat* (Ghent 1975) 413–35, republished in English translation as 'Prices and Wages as Development Variables: A Comparison between England and the Southern Netherlands, 1400–1700' *Acta Historiae Neerlandicae* 10 (1978) 58–78 and 'Nutrition and Diet in the Ancien Régime' in his *The Low Countries in the Early Modern World* (n25 above) 279–87; Phelps Brown and Hopkins 'Seven Centuries of the Prices of Consumables' (n4 above) 179–96. See 618–21 and n85 for a further detailed discussion and comparison of the Van der Wee and the Phelps Brown and Hopkins price indexes.

for that base is expressed as: 1501–5 = 100. In each table, the mean commodity values, prices, and wages for each quinquennium, from 1501–5 to 1536–40, were divided by the mean calculated for 1501–5 (and the same number divided by itself equals 100). The resulting index numbers, often known as price relatives, thus express the percentage that each quinquennial mean value, price, or wage has in relation to the base value for 1501–5. For example (see Table 5B), an index number of 147.981 for the quinquennium 1536–40 is 47.98 per cent greater than the base index number (1501–5 = 100).

Both Van der Wee and Phelps Brown and Hopkins, however, chose another period for their base, 1451–75 = 100, the one recommended in 1929 by the International Scientific Committee on Price History as the ideal period of relatively stable prices that could serve as an anchor for both medieval and early-modern surveys of European prices. This period also happens to be, as noted above (560–2), a strongly deflationary era, one with unusually low prices. Because of the widespread prominence of price indexes with the base 1451–75 in the historical literature, I have presented the index-number values for both base periods in Tables 5A and 5B, along with the index numbers computed from prices in both d *groot* Brabant and d *groot* Flemish. The values expressed in d *groot* Flemish are those in d *groot* Brabant divided by 1.5, according to the fixed ratio of the two currencies (594 above).

One may wonder if the weights that Van der Wee selected were valid for the period from the middle of the fifteenth century to the early sixteenth. If the weights did not reflect consumption patterns over this period, we would expect to find that the percentage of the basket's total value that each commodity commanded would vary between the two base periods. For the original base period of 1451–75, for which the entire basket had a value of 155.02d *groot* Flemish, the grain subindex accounted for 35.32 per cent of the total basket, by value; the meat-fish-dairy products subindex accounted for 38.87 per cent of the basket; and the industrial products subindex, for the remaining 25.81 per cent. In the subsequent base period of 1501–5, for which the entire basket had the significantly higher total value of 194.47d *groot* Flemish (higher by 25.45 per cent), grains accounted for 38.31 per cent (reflecting the slightly higher relative value of grains in this period); meat-fish-dairy products, for 36.94 per cent; and industrial products, for 24.75 per cent. Nor, for most of the individual commodities, are the differences in these percentage shares significant. Thus, for example, rye accounted for 18.24 per cent of the basket in 1451–75 and for 18.76 per cent in 1501–5; beef, for 23.53 per cent in 1451–75 and for 22.23 per cent in 1501–5; woollen cloth, for 10.68 per cent in 1451–75 and for 10.18 per cent in 1501–5. The commodity whose values show the most significant relative difference, but hardly significant in terms of its minimal weight, is herring, which accounted for 4.30 per cent of the basket's value in 1451–75 but 'only' 3.83 per cent in 1501–5 (see 627–8 below for one explanation).

Table 5B continues the presentation of the commodity values and index numbers for the Van der Wee 'basket of consumables,' in five-year means, for the eight quinquennia from 1501–5 to 1536–40, with the base 1501–5 = 100. While the data presented in Van der Wee's tables are values and not prices, nevertheless they may be used to calculate price indexes, because the quantities used in computing the values are fixed every year (so that only the prices change). Van der Wee himself, it should also be noted, did not present his data in either quinquennial or decennial means, nor did he group the commodity values in the categories chosen for this table. The eleven columns are set out as follows:

1   years of the eight quinquennia from 1501–5 to 1536–40
2   mean values of the grain components (rye and barley) in d *groot* Brabant for each quinquennium
3   price-index numbers for the grain subindex (based on the mean 1501–5 = 100)
4   mean values of the meat-fish-dairy products components (beef, herrings, cheese, butter) in d *groot* Brabant for each quinquennium
5   price-index numbers for the meat-fish-dairy products subindex
6   mean values of the industrial goods components (charcoal, candles, woollen and linen cloth) in d *groot* Brabant for each quinquennium
7   price-index numbers for the industrial goods subindex
8   total values of the entire basket in d *groot* Brabant (the sum of columns 2, 4, and 6) for each quinquennium
9   total values of the entire basket in d *groot* Flemish (values in d *groot* Brabant divided by 1.5)
10   price-index numbers for the entire basket, in terms of the base period 1451–75 = 100 (based on the values in d *groot* Flemish)
11   price index numbers for the entire basket, in terms of the base period 1501–5 = 100 (based on the values in d *groot* Flemish)

Tables 6A–K present the actual market prices for eleven commodities in the region of Antwerp, Lier, Mechelen, and Brussels in the duchy of Brabant in the southern Low Countries. The commodities are not, however, the same as those in Van der Wee's 'basket of consumables.' The set of tables in this study does not contain prices for rye, barley, cheese, cheap woollen cloth, and linens, but along with prices for four of the commodities in the Van der Wee 'basket' – beef, herring, butter, and tallow candles – it also contains prices for red wine, eggs, wheat, peas, sugar, high-quality woollens, and cheap worsteds, chiefly in order to provide a more effective comparison with the English prices chosen for this study (616–29, 678–89 below) and the earlier appendix in CWE 2. Also for comparison, these tables contain the quinquennial mean values of the Van der Wee 'basket of consumables' (which are repeated in each of the tables).

In tables 6A–I (Tables 6J–K will be considered separately), the columns are as follows:

1   years of the eight quinquennia from 1501–5 to 1536–40
2   mean commodity price per metric unit (litre, kilogram) or number in d *groot* Flemish (in pence) for each of these eight quinquennia
3   *harmonic* mean number of units (in litres, kilograms, numbers) that might have been purchased with the Burgundian-Hapsburg silver *patard* or double *groot* (2d)
4   *harmonic* mean number of these units purchased with the French silver *blanc à la couronne* or *douzain*, worth 12d *tournois*
5   *harmonic* mean number of these units purchased with the English silver sterling penny (1d)
6   *harmonic* mean number of these units purchased with the Burgundian-Hapsburg gold florin *St Philip* or *Philippus*, worth 50d *groot* Flemish from 1500 to 1520 and (officially) 54d *groot* from 1521 to 1540
7   *harmonic* mean number of these units purchased with the Burgundian-Hapsburg gold *Carolus* florin, first issued in February 1521 with an official value of 40d *groot* Flemish (60d *groot* Brabant) but raised to 42d *groot* Flemish in August 1521 (the value used throughout these tables)
8   *harmonic* mean number of these units purchased with the French gold *écu au soleil à la couronne*, worth 71d *groot* from 1500 to 1518, 72d in 1519–20, and 76d *groot* from 1521 to 1540
9   *harmonic* mean number of these units purchased with Italian gold ducats and florins, worth 79d *groot* Flemish from 1500 to 1520 and 80d *groot* from 1521 to 1540
10 *harmonic* mean number of these units purchased with English gold angel-nobles, worth 116d (9s 8d) *groot* Flemish from 1500 to 1520 and 119d (9s 11d) *groot* from 1521 to 1540, in each of these quinquennia
11 arithmetic mean of the daily summer wage of a master mason in Antwerp, in d *groot* Flemish, in each of these quinquennia

12 *harmonic* mean number of these commodity units (litres, kilograms, numbers) that could have been purchased with that mason's daily summer wage, in each quinquennium

13 index numbers for the quantity purchased with the silver *patard*, with the base 1501–5 = 100, in each quinquennium (quantity index as a *harmonic* mean)

14 arithmetic mean index numbers or price-relatives for the price of this commodity, with the same base, 1501–5 = 100 (as constructed and shown in Table 5), for each quinquennium

15 Van der Wee commodity-price index: the index numbers or price-relatives for this 'basket of consumables,' with the same base, 1501–5 = 100

The values, for each column, for the eight quinquennia from 1501–5 to 1536–40, are presented in the rows.

The commodity-price tables

The nature or composition, origin, and units of measurement of the commodities priced in these tables can be briefly summarized.[53]

6A Red Rhine wine: young, good quality red wines, purchased by various ecclesiastical institutions, hospitals, and the Lier Poor Relief, in quantities measured by the *gelte* = 2.50 imperial quarts = 2.840 litres. The recorded prices usually centred on the Easter season.

6B Butter: fresh, salted local butter, purchased by various ecclesiastical institutions, especially the Béguinage of Brussels, throughout the calendar year, by the 100-*pond* weight of Brussels = 103.103 lb avoirdupois = 46.767 kg

6C Salted beef: purchased by hospitals and ecclesiastical institutions in Mechelen, during the November season for slaughtering cattle, by the 100-*pond* weight of Mechelen = 103.451 lb avoirdupois = 46.925 kg

6D Herrings, Flemish red: dry smoked red herrings, chiefly from the adjacent North Sea coast of Flanders and Zeeland, purchased in both Brussels and Mechelen during the Lenten season, by hospitals, the Poor Relief, and various ecclesiastical institutions, by the *stroo* = 500 red herrings

* * * * *

53 The sources of the data are given in each table.

6E   Eggs: local, fresh eggs that the Brussels Béguinage purchased from the
      Brussels region, throughout the calendar year, by the hundred

6F   Wheat: from 1427 to 1509, as purchased by the Lier Poor Relief on
      the Lier market, excluding taxes, as the unweighted arithmetic means
      of quarterly prices; from 1509 to 1540, the prices are those recalcu-
      lated from the 'official weekly bread weights,' again as an unweighted
      annual mean price. For all price series, the unit is the *viertel* of Lier
      = 86.606 litres; and note that the bushel = 36.369 litres (that is, 2.381
      bushels per *viertel*). Though wheat prices were not included in the pre-
      vious study in CWE 2 or in Van der Wee's composite price index, they
      are included here for the sake of comparison with wheat prices in
      southern England (Table 11D).

6G   Peas: dried peas, purchased on the Mechelen market, again by the Lier
      Poor Relief and various other institutions (especially hospitals in both
      Lier and Mechelen), by the *viertel* of Mechelen = 86.499 litres (that
      is, 2.378 bushels). Prices are the unweighted arithmetic mean of sales
      from December to March of each year. This price series, also not in-
      cluded in CWE 2, is provided to offer a comparison with the price series
      for peas in southern England (Table 11E).

6H   Loaf sugar: chiefly fresh cane sugar imported from the Portuguese
      islands of Madeira, the Azores, and the Spanish Canaries, as sold on
      the St Bavo or Bamis market of the Antwerp fairs, in October of each
      year, priced by the Antwerp pound of 470.156 g. As noted in CWE 2,
      sugar products experienced one of the most striking declines in price
      over the half century, because colonization and the rapid development
      of sugar plantations on these Atlantic islands dramatically increased
      the supply of this formerly luxury commodity.[54]

6I   Tallow candles: purchased by various ecclesiastical institutions in Brus-
      sels, Antwerp, Lier, and Mechelen, during the autumn and winter
      months, by the *steen* (stone) of 8 lb = 8.272 lb avoirdupois (as the
      average weight of these towns' *steen* weights) = 3,752.194 g

    The prices of various textiles made and sold in the sixteenth-century
Low Countries are presented in Tables 6J and 6K. While Table 6J presents
prices of fine woollen broadcloths from Ghent and Mechelen in the form of
the quinquennial means used in the preceding tables (1501–5 to 1536–40),
Table 6K presents the prices of Hondschoote says (and of Ghent woollens)

* * * * *

54 Van der Wee *Antwerp Market* (n2 above) I 306–8, 318–24 Appendix 26; cf CWE
   2 314.

as annual data and only for the years 1535 to 1544. Textile prices are useful only if they come from the same archival source each year; if the composition, dimensions, and weights of the cloths are fully documented; if the cloths are sold by the same or similar manufacturer each year to the same class of consumers; if the cloths appear to be very closely similar, if not absolutely identical, year after year; and if the prices can be compared with other commodity prices and daily wages in the same location each year. Indeed, most of these cloths were sold under the same 'brand name,' indicated by their lead seals, to the same group of civic officials in Ghent and Mechelen.

6J   Woollen broadcloths from Ghent and Mechelen. The columns in this table are as follows:

1   the eight quinquennia from 1501–5 to 1536–40
2   the quinquennial arithmetic mean prices of Ghent's *dickedinnen* broadcloths, priced in pounds *groot* Flemish. The most renowned of Ghent's medieval and Renaissance textiles, the *dickedinnen* was produced in the format (wool composition, dimensions, weight, finishing) indicated in Table 7 from about the mid-fourteenth to the mid-sixteenth centuries. Its descriptive name means literally 'thick and thin' and evidently had its origin in the double-twilled nature of the weave (two wefts over and under individual warp yarns).[55]
3   the quinquennial arithmetic mean prices, in Flemish pounds *groot*, of Ghent's next most famous woollen cloth, the *strijpte laken*, or rayed cloth, a cloth whose warp yarns were dyed in colours, often varying colours, that were different from those of the weft yarns, to produce the desired striped effect. Some historians, regrettably, have incorrectly referred to these as 'cheap cloths,' a description clearly contradicted by the comparative prices in this table.

* * * * *

55 The warp yarns, about 30 or so metres in length, are those that are wound on the warp-roller beam at the rear of the broadloom and then stretched through heddles to be wound on the cloth-beam in the front of the loom. Foot-powered treadles raise and lower sets of heddle harnesses to separate the warps, and thus to allow the passage of the weft yarns (carried by a wooden shuttle) between alternating warps; the wefts are then 'beaten up into the fell of the cloth' by a laysword. For a description and analysis of these cloth-making processes, see John Munro 'Textile Technology in the Middle Ages' in *Dictionary of the Middle Ages* ed Joseph R. Strayer and others, 13 vols, 11 *Scandinavian Languages to Textiles, Islamic* (New York 1988) 693–711, repr in Munro *Textiles, Towns, and Trade* (n14 above) I 1–27.

4   the quinquennial arithmetic means prices of Mechelen's fashionable woollen broadcloth, the *rooslaken*, which was normally dyed black, at least in this period; again the prices are given in Flemish pounds *groot*, converted from the actual prices in Brabant pounds *groot*. This *rooslaken* was probably similar in dimensions, composition, and weight to the Mechelen *gulden aeren* (see Table 7 below), though it was evidently of lower value; as will be noted, these unquestionably very fine woollens were relatively cheaper than those from Ghent.

5   the quinquennial mean values of the Brabant 'basket of consumables' that appear in the previous tables, priced in d *groot* Flemish

6   the relative prices or price indexes of this 'basket of consumables,' with the mean for the first quinquennium 1501–5 serving as the base 100 (so that price indexes that follow are, in effect, percentages of this mean value)

7   the daily summer wage of a master mason in Antwerp, also in d *groot* Flemish

8   the quinquennial mean number of these daily wages (that is, the sum of a master's summer wages for that number of days) that would have been required to purchase a single Ghent *dickedinnen* of the composition, dimensions, and weight indicated in Table 7 below. To have applied the previously used method of computing the purchasing power of wages would have been absurd, for in 1535, for example, an Antwerp mason's daily summer wage earnings would have allowed him to purchase only 0.003 Ghent *dickedinnen*, or about 0.064 metre of cloth (were that possible, with 21.0 metres for the full-sized cloth).[56]

9   the quinquennial mean number of daily wages required to purchase a single Ghent *strijpte laken* (rayed cloth)

10   the quinquennial mean number of daily wages required to purchase a single Mechelen *rooslaken*

11   the quinquennial mean value of a single Ghent *dickedinnen* in terms of the number of the Van der Wee 'basket of consumables,' that is, how many of these baskets would equal the value of this broadcloth, on average, for each five-year period

12   the quinquennial mean value of a single Ghent *strijpte laken* in terms of the Van der Wee 'basket of consumables'

13   the equivalent quinquennial mean value of a single Mechelen *rooslaken*, in terms of the number of Van der Wee 'baskets of consumables'

* * * * *

56 The daily summer wage was 10.333d and the full-sized *dickedinnen* was then worth £14.150 or 3,396d *groot* Flemish; thus $10.333/3396 = 0.0030427 \times 21.0 = 0.064$ metre.

The cloth prices are taken from the annual civic treasurers' accounts for Ghent and for Mechelen, which list the specific woollen cloths, with their prices (often also with their finishing costs, included in these prices), which the town government purchased, from various named drapers, to be given on festive occasions to the leading town government officials. These specific cloths were purchased annually for the town's *burgermeesters* and *schepenen* (*échevins*, or aldermen), and about three full dress suits could be made from a full woollen broadcloth.[57]

6K   A comparison of the values of Hondschoote says and Ghent *dickedinnen* woollens. As the preceding table makes abundantly clear, these woollens from Ghent and Mechelen were very costly luxury articles. Their purchase would have required more than a master mason's annual money-wage income (wages for about 210–20 days); indeed in 1501–5 a Ghent *dickedinnen* would have cost an Antwerp mason about two years' wages. This table therefore compares the value of these cloths with that of textiles of much more popular consumption, the far cheaper worsted-style textiles whose purchase would have cost an Antwerp mason less than three weeks' daily wages. As one may also see from Table 7, these worsted-style says (*sayes*) were far lighter and much less durable textiles than the true woollens. The difference between the values of these two textiles – a much greater difference from that to be found in the mid-fourteenth century, when woollens were less 'luxurious' – is too striking to require any further comment.[58] For their composition and dimensions see 606–8 below and Table 7. The columns of Table 6K present the following data:

1   individual years, without any quinquennial means, from 1535 to 1544, since data on Hondschoote say prices are available only for these few years
2   the annual prices of Hondschoote single says, in pounds *groot* (decimal) Flemish
3   the annual prices of Hondschoote double says (twice the length; see Table 7) again in pounds *groot* Flemish
4   the annual prices of Ghent's *dickedinnen* woollen broadcloths, in pounds *groot* Flemish

        * * * * *

57 See CWE 2 323–6, especially n34, and 344–5 Table F.
58 See John Munro 'Textiles as Articles of Consumption in Flemish Towns, 1330–1575' *Bijdragen tot de geschiedenis* 81/1–3 (1998) 275–88.

5   the daily summer wage, year by year, of an Antwerp master mason, in
     d *groot* Flemish
6   the number of this mason's daily summer wages that would have been
     required to purchase a single Hondschoote 'single say'
7   the number of these daily wages required to purchase a single Ghent
     dickedinnen
8   the value, year by year, of the Van der Wee 'basket of consumables,' in
     d *groot* Flemish
9   the equivalent value of the Hondschoote single say in terms of the
     number of such 'baskets of consumables' whose total cost would equal
     the price of the say
10   for comparison, the equivalent mean value of a Ghent *dickedinnen* in
     terms of the number of such 'baskets of consumables'

Woollen and worsted (say) textiles in the economies of late-medieval and Renaissance England and the Low Countries

A full understanding of textiles and textile prices depends upon some basic knowledge of the quite different natures of woollens and worsteds and of the technical processes involved in their manufacture. Unfortunately, the literature in economic history has rarely defined the distinctions between woollens, worsted, and hybrid or mixed fabrics. Virtually all wool-based textiles worn today are of the worsted type, while true woollens are now found only in the robes adorning the cardinals in the papal curia.

The essential differences between these two medieval and early modern textiles lay in the quality of their wools and the ways by which they were processed. The woollen broadcloths listed in these tables were all woven from very fine, short-stapled, curly-fibred wools, chiefly English wools from the Welsh Marches (Herefordshire and Shropshire), the Cotswolds (Worcestershire, Gloucestershire, Oxfordshire), and (a distant third) from Lincolnshire (Lindsay and Kesteven regions).[59] Before the mid- to late sixteenth century, when Spanish *merino* wools finally reached their level of true

* * * * *

59 John Munro 'Wool-Price Schedules and the Qualities of English Wools in the Later Middle Ages, ca. 1270–1499' *Textile History* 9 (1978) 118–69 and 'The Medieval Scarlet and the Economics of Sartorial Splendour' in *Cloth and Clothing in Medieval Europe: Essays in Memory of Professor E.M. Carus-Wilson* ed Negley B. Harte and Kenneth G. Ponting, Pasold Studies in Textile History 2 (London 1983) 13–70, both repr in Munro *Textiles, Towns, and Trade* (n14 above) III 118–69, V 13–70.

perfection, these English wools were unrivalled for their fineness, quality, and thus price.[60] So fine and delicate were these wools, which had to be greased with butter to prevent damage in the spinning and weaving processes, that cloths woven from their yarns could acquire cohesion, strength, and durability only through the arduous and complex processes of fulling and felting. The traditional method of foot-fulling, which best ensured the quality of the final product, required two or three men to trample upon the full-sized woven cloth for about three days in a stone vat containing water, soap, and 'fullers earth' (*floridin*, with hydrous aluminum silicates). The combination of heat, pressure, water, and chemicals forced the curly, scaly wool fibres to intermesh or interlock, which condensed the cloth and shrank its final area by 50 per cent or more. This explains its exceptionally heavy weight – heavier indeed than a modern overcoat, as indicated in Table 7.[61] English woollen broadcloths were just as heavy as the more luxurious ones manufactured in the Low Countries.

In sharp contrast, the worsted cloths of this period were woven from much cheaper, much coarser, but also much stronger, tightly-twisted, long-

* * * * *

60 The gradual improvements in the quality of Spanish merino wools were essentially the product of advances in sheep management, cross-breeding, and adaptations to environmental factors during the annual *transhumance* sheep migrations. The world's best wools today, found chiefly in Australia, are those produced by sheep that are descendants of the Spanish *merinos*. See Carla Rahn Phillips and William D. Phillips *Spain's Golden Fleece: Wool Production and the Wool Trade from the Middle Ages to the Nineteenth Century* (Baltimore and London 1997); Robert Lopez 'The Origin of the Merino Sheep' *The Joshua Starr Memorial Volume: Studies in History and Philology*, Jewish Social Studies 5 (New York 1953) 161–8; Peter J. Bowden *The Wool Trade in Tudor and Stuart England* (London 1962) 1–76. See also the sources cited in nn58 and 59 above.

61 While this method of foot-fulling prevailed in the luxury-oriented draperies of the Low Countries, most English draperies adopted mechanical fulling, with water-powered mills to power a pair of heavy, oaken fulling 'hammers' or stocks, a method that many rightly considered to be injurious to the quality of finer fabrics. See John Munro 'Industrial Entrepreneurship in the Late-Medieval Low Countries: Urban Draperies, Fullers, and the Art of Survival' in *Entrepreneurship and the Transformation of the Economy (10th–20th Centuries): Essays in Honour of Herman Van der Wee* ed Paul Klep and Eddy Van Cauwenberghe (Leuven 1994) 377–88 and 'Anglo-Flemish Competition (n23 above) 37–60; Raymond Van Uytven 'De volmollen: motor van de omwenteling in de industrielle mentaliteit' *Tijdschrift van de kring der alumni van de wetenschappelijke stichtigen* 38 (1968) 61–76, republished as 'The Fulling Mill: Dynamic of the Revolution in Industrial Attitudes' *Acta Historiae Neerlandica* 5 (1971) 1–14; see also nn55, 58, 59 above.

stapled yarns. When woven, usually on a narrow rather than on a broad-loom, such yarns, warp and weft, provided this worsted cloth with suffi-cient cohesion and strength that it did not require the fulling and felting processes requisite for true woollens. Consequently, even apart from differ-ences in the wools themselves, a worsted was much lighter, a third or even less of the broadcloth's weight. In Hondschoote, some says were a hybrid textile, with a long-stapled dry worsted warp and a shorter-stapled greased woollen weft. These hybrids underwent at least some cursory fulling, if only to degrease the cloths. True worsted says – those of Bergues-Saint-Winoc, for example – were fully worsted in both warp and weft. They were distin-guishable from a woollen not only by their relative thinness and light weight but also by their readily visible weave. In the true woollens of this era, the weave was completely obliterated by both the fulling and the subsequent processes of napping or teaseling, alternated with cropping or shearing, which gave the cloth a texture rivalling that of silk.

Table 7 summarizes the differences in the dimensions and compositions of selected woollens and says in sixteenth- century England and the southern Low Countries: Essex and Suffolk broadcloths, Ghent broadcloths (*dickedin-nen*), Mechelen broadcloths, Hondschoote says, Bergues-Saint-Winoc says, and Essex says. The columns of this table present the following data:

1   dimensions and composition of the cloths, including
     – dimensions on the loom: length in ells/yards and in metres; width in ells/yards and metres; weights in the local pound units and in kilograms[62]
     – final dimensions of the cloth, after fulling and tentering or stretching (if any), with both length and width again given in ells/yards and metres[63]

* * * * *

62 The table also provides the documentary sources of all the data. Notes to this table indicate the metric conversion values of the various local pounds, ells, and yards. A Flemish ell was about 27 inches or about 0.7 metre; and the Eng-lish cloth yard was often reckoned at 37 rather than 36 inches, evidently to take account of the selvages along the edges of the cloth. In this and the other tables, however, both the yard and the ell, for all materials, have been reck-oned at the standard 36 inches, partly for reasons explained in the following note.

63 In medieval and early modern England, there was no difference between the ell and the yard, either for woollens or for linens. See Thorold Rogers *History of Agriculture and Prices* (n2 above) IV 554: 'The commonest measure, and in the

- the number of warp yarns in the loom (measured by the width); the number of warps per centimetre in the fulled or finished cloth; and the final area of the finished cloth, in square metres
- the final weight of the cloth in the local pound units and in kilograms; and finally the weight per square metre, in grams

2   Essex and Suffolk (in East Anglia): standard woollen broadcloths, popularly known as 'shortcloths,' 24 yards long by 'seven-quarter' yards wide, to distinguish them from the 'long cloths' (30 yards), of which very few were produced at this time. Such woollens had become England's primary and most lucrative export, displacing wool, by the early sixteenth century, and by that time they had gained primacy over most of England's continental textile rivals in European cloth markets.

3   Ghent: the *dickedinnen* broadcloth, slightly smaller and lighter than the English broadcloths. This cloth was the city's best known and its finest luxury broadcloth, one that still enjoyed a niche in the upper echelons of European markets.

4   Mechelen: its finest woollen, the *gulden aeren* (golden eagle), made from the world's then finest wools, 'Lemster Ore' from Herefordshire (Welsh Marches), whose warp-yarn count and cloth weight were significantly greater than those of the Ghent *dickedinnen*. Mechelen's luxury-woollen drapery had fared rather better than had Ghent's drapery in the first half of the sixteenth century.

5   Hondschoote: the small double say (longer than the short say), probably woven with a dry worsted 'say' warp and a greased, short-stapled

* * * * *

early part of the period the almost universal measure, is the ell. I stated, as I believe with good reason, that there did not appear to be any practical difference (1 571) between the ell and the yard in early times, the later difference of nine inches not having been recognised. Nor does it appear that there was any substantial difference between the two quantities in the fifteenth, and hardly in the sixteenth century. Linen is generally sold by the ell, woollen cloth by the yard, and the exceptions are few. When they do occur for linen simultaneously they seem to be used indifferently.' On the equality of the yard and ell, and their use as synonyms for each other, in thirteenth-century England, see John Munro 'The "Industrial Crisis" of the English Textile Towns, 1290–1330' *Thirteenth-Century England* VII ed Michael Prestwich, Richard Britnell, and Robin Frame (Woodbridge 1999) 103–41, especially nn22, 26, 35, 46. Indeed, the *Compositio ulnarum et perticarum*, written between 1266 and 1303, stipulated that all linear measures, including those for textiles, were to be based on the iron *ulna* of 36 inches (see n35), and the texts of this era use the two terms ell and yard interchangeably.

woollen weft. This was the best representative of what had now become the southern Low Countries' leading textile industry.

6   Bergues-Saint-Winoc (a rural neighbour of Hondschoote): true light worsteds, in both warp and weft yarns

7   Essex, one of East Anglia's post-1560 'New Draperies': a very light broad say, closely imitating those produced in Flanders. Its weight (grams per square metre) was the lightest: only 18.0 per cent of that of an Essex broadcloth.

By the time of Erasmus' death (1536), the primary focus of the cloth manufacturing industries in the southern Low Countries had shifted from the heavy-weight luxury woollens, the predominant West European textile during the late-medieval period, to the much cheaper, coarser, and lighter worsted fabrics of the *sayetteries* and related *draperies légères*. Much earlier, however, from the early twelfth to the early fourteenth century, similar *draperies légères* had played a very significant role in the economies of France, the Low Countries, and England. In the thirteenth century, Hondschoote itself had been one of northern Europe's leading say exporters to the Mediterranean, and collectively the *sayetteries* and other *draperies légères* had surpassed the northern woollen draperies in both the volume and value of aggregate production. Subsequently, however, from the very late thirteenth or early fourteenth century, most of these northern *draperies légères* disappeared with the onset of sustained and ever more widespread warfare throughout the entire Mediterranean basin and western Europe; the chronic, ever more debilitating strife lasted until the end of the Hundred Years' War (1337–1453). Warfare, the economic nationalism that it bred, and the accompanying national fiscal, monetary, and commercial policies put in place in order to conduct it led to frequent and often serious disruptions in international trade, with severe economic contractions (especially, of course, after the Black Death in 1348) and periodic depressions. For the cheap, northern textile industries, the most serious consequence of these adverse conditions was the continuous rise in transport and transaction costs, which discouraged or even prohibited long-distance trade in cheap products and thus favoured an international commerce in the luxury-oriented woollen draperies, whose higher-priced products were better able to sustain and 'bear the freight' of rising costs.[64]

* * * * *

64 See John Munro 'Industrial Transformations in the North-West European Textile Trades, c. 1290–c. 1340: Economic Progress or Economic Crisis?' in *Before*

During these dark days for the northern textile producers, Hond-schoote, despite the loss of its Mediterranean markets, was one of the very few northern *sayetteries* to survive, and it became the undisputed leader of the Flemish *draperies légères* from the mid fifteenth century, when they be-gan to revive as a result of increasing political stability, the central European silver-mining boom, and then demographic revival, which together fostered a renewed expansion of the western European economy. Those more pro-pitious economic forces and the development of new, more secure overland continental trade routes between Italy and the Low Countries, a develop-ment that also flowed from the South-German mining boom, led in particu-lar to a sustained expansion in international and especially Mediterranean-oriented trade. That in turn propelled the dramatic growth of the Brabant fairs, linked to Italy by these overland trans-Alpine trade routes, thus allow-ing Antwerp to become the commercial and financial capital of Renaissance Europe.[65]

The extent to which those economic forces also boosted the fortunes of the Flemish *sayetteries* and other *draperies légères* during the second half of the fifteenth century and first quarter of the sixteenth century can be seen in Table 8, on the outputs of the Hondschoote sayetterie. The production of

* * * * *

the *Black Death: Studies in the 'Crisis' of the Early Fourteenth Century* ed Bruce M.S. Campbell (Manchester 1991) 110–48, repr in Munro *Textiles, Towns, and Trade* (n14 above), 'The Symbiosis of Towns and Textiles: Urban Institutions and the Changing Fortunes of Cloth Manufacturing in the Low Countries and England, 1270–1570' *The Journal of Early Modern History: Contacts, Comparisons, Contrasts* 3/1 (February 1999) 1–74, 'The "New Institutional Economics" and the Changing Fortunes of Fairs in Medieval and Early Modern Europe: the Textile Trades, Warfare, and Transaction Costs' *Vierteljahrschrift für Sozial- und Wirtschaftsgeschichte* 88/1 (2001) 1–47, 'Industrial Crisis of the English Textile Towns' (n63 above) , 'Economic Depression and the Arts' (n14 above); Hatcher 'Great Slump of the Mid-Fifteenth Century' (n22 above); Nightingale 'England and the European Depression' (n22 above); Robert Lopez and Harry Miskimin 'The Economic Depression of the Renaissance' *Economic History Review* 2d se-ries 14 (1962) 408–26; Robert Lopez, Harry Miskimin, and Carlo Cipolla 'Eco-nomic Depression of the Renaissance: Rejoinder and Reply' *Economic History Review* 2d series 16 (1964) 519–29; Robert Lopez 'Hard Times and Investment in Culture' in *The Renaissance* ed Wallace Ferguson and others (New York 1962) 29–52.

65 See n22 above and n69 below; Van der Wee *Antwerp Market* (n2 above) II 113–244, 333–68; Munro 'The "New Institutional Economics" and the Changing Fortunes of Fairs' (n64 above) 1–30.

its says, as measured by the 8d excise tax, rose from 5,400 says in 1441–5 to 17,640 says in 1501–5; and then it shot up a further 2.45 times to 43,176 says in 1536–40.[66] While excise-tax indexes are often a very imperfect indicator, their validity here seems vindicated by data on cloth sales beginning in 1526, which closely parallels these output data, with mean sales of 42,761 says in 1536–40. As in the thirteenth century, so in the early sixteenth century these *draperies légères* found their major markets in the Mediterranean basin, via the German and trans-Alpine overland routes, and, via Spain, in the Americas as well, to become quite decisively the leading textile industry of the southern Low Countries.[67] According to recent estimates of this region's industrial production in the 1550s, they were then producing about 3.64 million metres of the light worsted-type fabrics, while the various woollens draperies, in both traditional and newer forms, were collectively manufacturing only about 2.07 million metres of cloth.[68] As Table 9 indicates, in this

* * * * *

66 See Emile Coornaert *La draperie-sayetterie d'Hondschoote, XIVe–XVIIIe siècles* (Paris 1930) 485–90 Appendix IV.
67 See John Munro 'The Origins of the English "New Draperies": The Resurrection of an Old Flemish Industry, 1270–1570' in *The New Draperies in the Low Countries and England, 1300–1800* ed Negley B. Harte, Pasold Studies in Textile History 10 (Oxford and New York 1997) 35–127, 'Symbiosis of Towns and Textiles' (n64 above) and 'The Low Countries' Export Trade' (n23 above).
68 Statistics from Hugo Soly and Alfons Thijs 'Nijverheid in de Zuidelijke Nederlanden' *Algemene geschiedenis der Nederlanden* 6 (Haarlem 1979) 27–57. See also Emile Coornaert *La draperie-sayetterie d'Hondschoote* (n66 above) 22–43, 236–53, 'Draperies rurales, draperies urbaines: l'évolution de l'industrie flamande au moyen âge et au XVI siècle' *Revue belge de philologie et d'histoire* 28 (1950) 60–96, and *Une industrie urbaine du XIVe au XVIIe siècle: l'industrie de la laine à Bergues-Saint-Winoc* (Paris 1930); E. Maugis 'La saietterie à Amiens, 1480–1587' *Vierteljahrschrift für Sozial-und Wirtschaftsgeschichte* 5 (1907) 1–115; Maurice Van Haeck *Histoire de la sayetterie à Lille* 2 vols (Lille 1910); Robert S. DuPlessis and Martha C. Howell 'Reconsidering the Early Modern Urban Economy: The Cases of Leiden and Lille' *Past and Present* 94 (February 1982) 49–84; Florence Edler 'Le commerce d'exportation des sayes d'Hondschoote vers Italie d'après la correspondance d'une firme anversoise, entre 1538 et 1544' *Revue du Nord* 22 (1936) 249–65; Donald C. Coleman 'An Innovation and its Diffusion: The "New Draperies"' *Economic History Review* 2d series 12 (1969) 417–29; Van der Wee *Antwerp Market* (n2 above) II 133–208 (especially 186–91); Robert DuPlessis 'The Light Woollens of Tournai in the Sixteenth and Seventeenth Century' and Alfons Thijs 'Les textiles au marché anversois au XVIe siècle' in *Textiles of the Low Countries in European Economic History* ed Erik Aerts and John Munro (Leuven 1990) 66–75, 76–86; Robert S. DuPlessis 'One Theory, Two Draperies, Three Provinces, and a Multitude of Fabrics: the New

same period (c 1560), these *says* and similar worsted or semi-worsted products accounted for 15.6 per cent of total exports, by value, from the Brabant fairs, or 21.6 per cent of total textile exports, by value, as did the similarly priced, light-weight linens, while the share for the heavier-weight woollens from the other draperies in the Netherlands was only 8.75 per cent, or 12.1 per cent of textile exports. But the largest share of textile exports was claimed by the re-export of dyed and finished English woollens: 27.00 per cent of total textile exports and 19.50 per cent of aggregate exports, by value.

Indeed, the English cloth trade boom, which began in the 1460s (Table 8) and would endure until the early 1550s, along with the South-German mining boom in silver and copper (see 561–4 above), together provided the first two legs of the tripod on which the commercial supremacy of Antwerp would rest for virtually a century, from c 1460 to c 1560. The great success of the English cloth industry was fundamentally based upon its ready access to tax-free wools that were still Europe's finest, while their continental rivals faced increasingly high English wool-export taxes, other rising costs, and various commercial restrictions in obtaining them. Furthermore, to worsen the plight of the Netherlands' traditional luxury woollen draperies, the English cloth trade came to be increasingly funnelled upon the Antwerp market, as the only available continental outlet that remained to English merchants. From the 1460s on, cloth merchants from England (English and Hanseatic German) met the South-German merchants, with their growing flood of silver and copper, in Antwerp, providing them with their chief return cargo, to be marketed throughout Germany and Central Europe, in the form of English woollens dyed and finished in Dutch and

* * * * *

Drapery of French Flanders, Hainaut, and the Tournaisis, c. 1500–c. 1800' in *The New Draperies in the Low Countries and England, 1300–1800* ed Negley Harte (n67 above) 129–72; Patrick Chorley 'The "Draperies Légères" of Lille, Arras, Tournai, Valenciennes: New Materials for New Markets?' in *Drapery Production in the Late Medieval Low Countries: Markets and Strategies for Survival* ed Marc Boone and Walter Prevenier (Leuven 1993) 151–65; Herman Van der Wee 'Structural Changes and Specialization in the Industry of the Southern Netherlands, 1100–1600' *Economic History Review* 2d series 28 (1975) 203–21 and 'Industrial Dynamics and the Process of Urbanization and De-Urbanization in the Low Countries from the Late Middle Ages to the Eighteenth Century: A Synthesis' in *The Rise and Decline of Urban Industries in Italy and in the Low Countries: Late Middle Ages–Early Modern Times* ed Herman Van der Wee (Leuven 1988) 307–81.

Brabantine drapery towns. This blossoming commerce attracted more and more merchants from all over Europe and finally lured the Portuguese, who had only recently gained temporary mastery of the commerce and trade routes in the Indian Ocean, to establish their European spice-staple at Antwerp in 1501 – the third leg of the tripod supporting Antwerp's commercial dominance. They did so chiefly in order to gain access to South-German silver, copper, fustians, and other cheap textiles for their African and Asian commerce, and also to the South-German banking houses recently established there (Fuggers, Höchstetters, Welsers, Imhofs, Herwarts, Tuchers).[69]

The overall significance of the various textile industries for the economy of the southern Low Countries can be seen in their ability to command almost three-quarters of the region's total export values in the mid sixteenth century, as indicated in Table 9. We owe these data to the keen-eyed Italian merchant and writer Luigi (Ludovico) Guicciardini, who published his observations in *Description de la cité d'Anvers*.[70] By the time that he did so, however, both the South-German mining boom, the English cloth trade, and the Brabant fairs had all passed their peak, though this table does seem to be representative of Antwerp's economy at its peak.

* * * * *

69 Jan A. Van Houtte 'La genèse du grand marché international d'Anvers à la fin du moyen âge' *Revue belge de philologie et d'histoire* 19 (1940) 87–126, 'Bruges et Anvers: marchés 'nationaux' ou 'internationaux' du xive au xvie siècle?' *Revue du Nord* 24 (1952) 89–108, 'Anvers aux xve et xvie siècles' *Annales: Economies, Sociétés, Civilisations* 16 (1961) 248–78, and 'The Rise and Decline of the Market of Bruges' *Economic History Review* 2d series 19 (1966) 29–47; Oskar De Smedt *De engelse natie te Antwerpen in de 16e eeuw* 2 vols (Antwerp 1950); Van der Wee *Antwerp Market* (n2 above) II 34–120; John Munro 'Bruges and the Abortive Staple in English Cloth: An Incident in the Shift of Commerce from Bruges to Antwerp in the Late Fifteenth Century' *Revue belge de philologie et d'histoire/Belgisch tijdschrift voor filologie en geschiedenis* 44 (1966) 1137–59, repr in Munro *Textiles, Towns, and Trade* (n14 above), 'Anglo-Flemish Competition' (n23 above), 'Symbiosis of Towns and Textiles' (n64 above), and 'Patterns of Trade' (n11 above).
70 Ludovico Guicciardini *Description de la cité d'Anvers, 1560* trans François de Belleforest (1582; published in Antwerp, 1920). The table is based upon his data, as collated and presented by Wilfrid Brulez 'Le commerce international des Pays-Bas au xvie siècle: essai d'appréciation quantitative' *Revue belge de philologie et d'histoire* 46 (1968) 1205–21, reissued in English translation as 'The Balance of Trade in the Netherlands in the Middle of the Sixteenth Century' *Acta Historiae Neerlandica* 4 (1970) 20–48 and further modified by Jan De Vries and Ad Van der Woude in *The First Modern Economy: Success, Failure, and Perseverance of the Dutch Economy, 1500–1815* (Cambridge 1996) 360 Table 9/1

Table 8 shows the dramatic growth in the exports of English woollens during the first four decades of the sixteenth century. This growth of
broadcloth exports, which dominated the cloth markets of the Brabant fairs
and of western Europe generally, was at the expense of England's still very
heavily-taxed wool exports and thus also at the expense of the draperies
in the Netherlands that had so long remained dependent on the finer English wools, especially those of Ghent, Mechelen, and Leiden. As the table
indicates, English wool exports, whose volume in 1500 was only half that
of 1400, fell again by another half during these four decades. Nevertheless, when converted into equivalent broadcloths (a ratio of 4.333 cloths per
wool-sack), their early sixteenth-century exports still represented a considerable volume of potential cloth production. The traditional Flemish woollen
draperies, led by the triumvirate of Ghent, Bruges, and Ypres (the *drie ste-
den*), had been the first to succumb to the growing English competition, with
its flood of cloth imports, compared by a Hanseatic observer in 1487 to an
inundacionis maris immensis.[71] As Table 8 indicates, the indexes of Ghent's
cloth production, having fallen dramatically from the 1420s, fell even more
sharply during the early sixteenth century. The industrial indexes for Mechelen's drapery, especially the cloth outputs calculated from the *clergiegeld* tax,
indicate a rather greater resilience and success in withstanding the growing
English competition, in part thanks to its rule as the judicial capital of the
Hapsburg Netherlands and to its location on the Germanic trade routes leading to the Brabant fairs. But the Mechelen drapery's Indian summer of relative prosperity, fading by the 1530s, was followed by a very precipitous
decline.[72] As Table 8 also demonstrates, the early sixteenth-century cloth output of Mechelen's drapery was far smaller than that of its Dutch neighbour
to the north in Leiden, which was then by far the Netherlands' most successful producer of traditional woollens, one still largely based on English

* * * * *

71 For the quotation, see *Hanserecesse, 1477–1530* ed Dietrich Schäfer 3d series, 9
   vols (Leipzig 1881–1913) III 105.
72 Raymond Van Uytven 'De Omvang van de Mechelse lakenproductie vanaf de
   14e tot de 16e eeuw' *Noordgouw: Cultureel tijdschrift van de Provincie Antwerpen* 5/3 (1965) 1–22 and 'La draperie brabançonne et malinoise du xiie au
   xviie siècles: grandeur éphémère et décadence' in *Produzione, commercio e con-
   sumo dei panni di lana* ed Marco Spallanzani (Florence 1976) 85–97; Wenceslaus
   Mertens 'Changes in the Production and Export of Mechelen Cloth, 1330–1530'
   in *Textiles of the Low Countries in European Economic History* ed Erik Aerts and
   John Munro (Leuven 1990) 114–23 and 'Toenemende economische welvaart'
   in *De geschiedenis van Mechelen: van heerlijkheid tot stadsgewest* ed Raymond Van
   Uytven (Lannoo 1991) 83–93

wools. The Leiden drapery's prosperity fundamentally rested upon the aggressive expansion of the Dutch merchant marine in marketing its woollens, especially in the North Sea-Baltic region, and also on its ability to produce very good quality woollens that were less expensive than those of its Flemish and Brabantine competitors.[73] But its output peaked in 1516–20, with a mean production of 26,245 half-cloths (*halvelakenen*), and with a continuing rise in English wool prices, the Leiden drapery then (1522) authorized a switch to the much cheaper – cheaper by 25 per cent – but still inferior Spanish *merino* wools. This experiment ultimately failed, and when the Leiden drapery restored the regulations stipulating the exclusive use of English wools, to safeguard its now shaky reputation for high quality, the *volte-face* proved to be too little and too late. As Table 8 shows, Leiden's cloth production continued its precipitous decline in the face of the now overwhelming English competition.[74]

* * * * *

73 See Marian Malowist 'L'expansion économique des Hollandais dans le bassin de la Baltique aux xive et xve siècles' *Studia z dziejow rzemiosla w okresie kryzysu feudalizmu w Europie Zachodniej w xiv i xv wieku* (Warsaw 1954), republished in his *Croissance et regression en Europe, xive–xviie siècles* (Paris 1972) 91–138; Dick E.H. De Boer *Graaf en Grafiek: sociale en economische ontwikkelingen in het middeleeuwse 'Noordholland' tussen 1345 en 1415* (Leiden 1978) 211–32; T.S. Jansma 'Philippe le Bon et la guerre hollando-wende 1438–1441' *Revue du Nord* 42 (1960) 5–18; Hanno Brand 'Urban Policy or Personal Government: The Involvement of the Urban Elite in the Economy of Leiden at the End of the Middle Ages' in *Economic Policy in Europe Since the Late Middle Ages: The Visible Hand and the Fortune of Cities* ed Herman Diederiks, Paul Hohenberg, and Michael Wagenaar (Leicester 1992) 17–34; De Vries and Van der Woude *The First Modern Economy* (n70 above) 350–62; and especially Dieter Seifert *Holland und die Hanse* (Cologne 1997).

74 See *Bronnen tot de geschiedenis van de leidsche textielnijverheid, 1333–1795* ed Nicholas Posthumus 3 vols (The Hague 1910–22) ii 316–17 no 903 and *Geschiedenis van de Leidsche lakenindustrie* 3 vols (The Hague 1908–39) i *De Middeleeuwen, veertiende tot zestiende eeuw* (1908) 182–235, 368–408; Hanno Brand 'Crisis, beleid en differentiatie in de laat-middeleeuwse Leidse lakkennijverheid' in *Stof uit het Leidse verleden: zeven eeuwen textielnijverheid* ed J.K.S. Moes and B.M.A. De Vries (Leiden 1991) 52–65, 201–5 (notes) and 'A Medieval Industry in Decline: The Leiden Drapery in the First Half of the Sixteenth Century' in *La draperie ancienne des Pays Bas: débouchés et stratégies de survie (14e–16e siècles) / Drapery Production in the Late Medieval Low Countries: Markets and Strategies for Survival (14th–16th Centuries)* ed Marc Boone and Walter Prevenier, Studies in Urban Social, Economic and Political History of the Medieval and Modern Low Countries (Leuven-Appeldorn 1993) 121–49. On this question and the relative qualities of Spanish wools, see also Munro 'Symbiosis of Towns and Textiles' (n64 above); and also the sources cited in n60 above. In 1535 the English

Meanwhile, in the southern Low Countries, the various *draperies légères* continued to flourish until the very eve of the Revolt of the Netherlands against Spanish rule (1568–1609). Hondschoote's production peaked in the quinquennium 1566–70, with average annual sales of 93,057 says.[75] The devastation wreaked upon the southern Low Countries over the ensuing years by Spain's massive military retaliation, the sack of Antwerp in 1576 by mutinous unpaid soldiers ('The Spanish Fury'), subsequent interventions by other foreign troops – German, French, and English – and continuous civil strife combined to bring about the irredeemable decline of the Brabant fairs and of the textile industries, the *sayetteries* above all, in the southern Low Countries.[76] As early as the 1560s, a flood of Flemish refugee artisans began to pour northwards to seek sanctuary in Holland and westwards across the Channel into East Anglia, where they transplanted these *sayetteries* as the so-called 'New Draperies.'[77]

* * * * *

writer Clement Armstrong contended that 'the wolles of Spayn are of such kynds [that] withowt the wolles of England be myxed with, it can no make no clothe of itself for no durable weryng, to be nother reisid nor dressid, by cause it hath no staple'; see *Tudor Economic Documents* ed R.H. Tawney and Eileen Power 3 vols (London 1924) III 102 section II.2, 'A Treatise Concerninge the Staple and the Commodities of this Realme.' Indeed many of the leading so-called *nouvelles draperies*, such as Armentières, which produced cheaper imitations of the finest Flemish luxury woollens by resorting to cheaper raw materials, still used a mixture of two-thirds Spanish and one-third English wools. See *Recueil de documents relatifs à l'histoire de l'industrie drapière en Flandre* ed Henri De Sagher and others IIe partie: *le sud-ouest de la Flandre depuis l'époque bourguignonne* 3 vols (Brussels 1951–66) I 102–17 no 36 (Armentières drapery *keure*); Munro 'New Draperies' (n67 above) 36–48.

75 See nn66, 68 above and the sources in Table 8 below.

76 Hondschoote's sales fell to a low of 12,128 says in 1586–90 (mean) and recovered to a mean of only 25,007 says in 1601–5, on the eve of the Truce of 1609, which ended the Revolt; but sales rose to a seventeenth-century peak of 54,761 says in 1626–30, before declining again, this time permanently, in the face of competition from the English 'New Draperies.' See nn65, 75, and the next note; and also Van der Wee *Antwerp Market* (n2 above) II 245–82.

77 See Munro 'New Draperies' (n67 above); K.J. Allison 'The Norfolk Worsted Industry in the Sixteenth and Seventeenth Centuries, 2: The New Draperies' *Yorkshire Bulletin of Economic and Social Research* 13 (1961) 61–77; J.E. Pilgrim 'The Rise of the "New Draperies" in Essex' *University of Birmingham Historical Journal* 7 (1959–60) 36–59; Ursula Priestley *The Fabric of Stuffs: The Norwich Textile Industry from 1565* Centre of East Anglian Studies, University of East Anglia (Norwich 1990); and also Leo Noordegraaf 'The New Draperies in the Northern Netherlands, 1500–1800,' B.A. Holderness 'The Reception and Distribution of the New Draperies in England,' Luc Martin

Subsequently, after England's Old Draperies, those producing the true heavy-weight woollens (see Table 7), suffered a severe export decline during the Thirty Years War (1618–48), the East-Anglian New Draperies superseded them as the primary manufacturing industry, ultimately spelling the doom of the *sayetteries* and other *draperies légères* in the Netherlands as well.[78]

IV
THE PURCHASING POWER OF COINS AND WAGES
IN SOUTHERN ENGLAND (TABLES 10–11)

Tables of commodity prices and wages in quinquennial means (arithmetic and harmonic)

The method used to establish index numbers for prices and wages in arithmetic and harmonic quinquennial means has already been described (592–4 above). In the tables for England, unlike those for the Low Countries, no foreign coins have been used to illustrate purchasing power, for the simple reason that no foreign coins really enjoyed the status of legal tender in insular England before 1522. In May and November of that year, Henry VIII grudgingly permitted the circulation of a few foreign gold (no silver) coins, but at specified exchange rates set below their intrinsic bullion values. Italian ducats and florins were rated at 4s 6d sterling; the French *écus au soleil à la couronne*, at 4s 4d; older French *écus*, at 4s 0d; the Rhenish florin, at 3s 3d; and the new Burgundian-Hapsburg *Carolus* florin, at 2s 1d sterling.[79]

* * * * *

'The Rise of the New Draperies in Norwich, 1550–1622,' Ursula Priestley 'Norwich Stuffs, 1600–1700,' all in *The New Draperies in the Low Countries and England, 1300–1800* (n67 above) 275–88, 173–96, 217–44, 245–74, respectively.

78 See the sources cited in nn67, 77; and also George D. Ramsay *The Wiltshire Woollen Industry in the Sixteenth and Seventeenth Centuries* (London 1943; 2d ed London 1965) and *The English Woollen Industry, 1500–1750* Studies in Economic and Social History (London 1982).

79 See Hughes and Larkin *Tudor Royal Proclamations* (n34 above) I 136 no 88 (25 May 1522), 141 no 95 (24 November 1522), 145 no 102 (6 July 1525), 146 no 103 (8 July 1525); Feavearyear *Pound Sterling* (n33 above) 48; Challis *Tudor Coinage* (n32 above) 68–9. See also CWE 2 311–12. These ordinances also stated that 'every piece of fine gold named a carolus keeping weight' should circulate at 6s 10 sterling. But this could not possibly be the recently issued Burgundian-Hapsburg *Carolus* florin, which contained only 1.700 g fine gold. The ordinance might have meant the *réal d'or*, also first issued in August 1521, with 5.275 g

Subsequently, on 22 August 1526, with sharply rising market prices for gold in northwestern Europe, Henry VIII permitted very modest, undoubtedly ineffective increases in the rates for Italian ducats from 4s 6d to 4s 8d (to 56d, a 3.70 per cent rise); and for French *écus au soleil* from 4s 4d to 4s 6d (to 54d, a 3.85 per cent increase).[80] Shortly after, on 5 November 1526, as noted earlier (573–4 and n34 above), Henry VIII's government undertook a general debasement of both silver and gold coinages, which effectively raised the values of English gold coins by a far more substantial 12.5 per cent (the angel-noble, for example, from 80d to 90d). But this same ordinance maintained the same unduly low rates that the ducats and *écus* had received in the August ordinance.[81] In view of the political nature of the 1522 monetary ordinances on foreign gold coins, adopted to secure Emperor Charles v's alliance against France, and in view of this serious undervaluation of foreign gold coins, one may doubt that many did circulate thereafter in England,

* * * * *

fine gold. If the Italian ducats and florins, with 3.60 g fine gold, were rated at 4s 6d (54d), then the proportional value for the *réal d'or* should have been 79d (= 5.275/3.600×54), which is still less than 6s 10d sterling. The proportional value of the new *Carolus* florin should have been 25d or 25.5d sterling; and thus the 'pieces of base gold, also named florins' rated at 2s 1d probably did refer to these *Carolus* florins.

80 By this ordinance, Henry VIII also issued the first rose crown, with the initial value of 4s 6d sterling; see Hughes and Larkin *Tudor Royal Proclamations* (n34 above) I 156–8 no 111. The explanation given for these coinage changes was a rendition of Gresham's Law (that 'cheap money drives out dear,' to places abroad where it commands a higher value): 'Forasmuch as now of late in outward parts beyond the sea, as well in Flanders and France, the price of money and gold, not only coined in those countries but also gold of the King our sovereign lord's coin of this realm, is so much enhanced in the valuation thereof that not only strange golds, as crowns and ducats, but also the gold of this realm, as nobles, half nobles, and royals [*Ryals*], by merchants as well strangers resorting hither as the King's subjects repairing into those parts, for the great gain and lucre that they find thereby daily, be transported and carried out of this realm to no little impoverishing thereof, and finally to the total exhausting and drawing out of all the coins out of the same, unless speedy remedy be provided in that behalf.' On this see Raymond De Roover *Gresham on Foreign Exchange* (Cambridge, MA 1949); George Selgin 'Salvaging Gresham's Law: The Good, the Bad, and the Illegal' *Journal of Money, Credit, and Banking* 28/4 (November 1996) 637–49.

81 See 574 above; Hughes and Larkin *Tudor Royal Proclamations* (n34 above) I 158 no 112; Challis *Tudor Coinage* (n32 above) 68, who incorrectly indicates that both foreign and English gold coins enjoyed proportional increases in their silver-exchange values.

and certainly not at these low rates.[82] In any event, including such coins in the tables for England would provide no additional information on purchasing power, nothing more than already indicated in the tables for commodity prices in the southern Low Countries, where florins, ducats, *écus*, and English nobles certainly circulated much more freely in this period.

The Phelps Brown and Hopkins 'basket of consumables'

The set of tables (10A–B, 11A–J) for southern England (chiefly the Oxford-Cambridge region) are based on the 'basket of consumables' that E. Henry Phelps Brown and his associate Sheila V. Hopkins constructed and published in *Economica* in 1956.[83] The price indexes in their tables have, however, been amended. In analysing their original work sheets, now deposited in the Archives of the British Library of Political and Economic Science, I have corrected many compilation and calculation errors.[84]

Phelps Brown and Hopkins also produced a separate table that shows the composition of four baskets, 'around four dates': 1275, 1500, 1725, and 1950. Obviously the 1500 basket has been used for this study. But while their table, and the entire article, give the impression that the composition of the baskets was changed only in those years, a study of their working papers reveals that Phelps Brown introduced subtle changes in many more years, but fortunately none for the years 1501 to 1540. For this entire period, therefore, their basket has the following weights for the following five major subindex groups (Table 10A):

1   farinaceous: 20.0 per cent, with 1.25 bushels of wheat (45.461 litres), 1.00 bushel of rye (36.369 litres), 0.50 bushel of barley (18.184 litres), and 0.667 bushel of peas (24.243 litres)

2   meat and fish: 37.5 per cent, with 1.5 sheep, 15 white herrings, and 25 red herrings

3   drink: 22.5 per cent, with 4.5 bushels of barley malt (163.659 litres)

* * * * *

82 The next ordinance permitting and prescribing official rates for foreign gold coins was issued on 27 July 1538: the rate for ducats was raised to 5s 0d; for *écus au soleil*, to 4s 8d. See Hughes and Larkin *Tudor Royal Proclamations* (n34 above) I 264 no 180.

83 See nn4–5 and 16 above.

84 The box numbers of the Phelps Brown and Hopkins papers in the Archives of the British Library of Political and Economic Science (BLPES, in the London School of Economics) are: 1a.324 (comprising most of the commodity-price lists), J.III.2a, and J.IV.2a.

4   fuel and light: 7.5 per cent, with 4.25 bushels of charcoal (154.567 litres), 2.75 lb of tallow candles (1.247 kg), and 0.50 pint of oil (0.284 litre)

5   textiles: 12.5 per cent, with 0.667 yard of canvas (0.610 metre); 0.50 yard linen shirting (0.457 metre); and 0.333 yard of cheap woollen cloth (0.305 metre)

In more general terms, foodstuffs thus account for 80 per cent of the basket and industrial products for the remaining 20 per cent. The other three baskets (those for 1275, 1725, 1950) contain another group, butter and cheese, with an unvarying 10 lb or 4.536 kg in each basket, and a weight of 12.5 per cent. The virtually complete absence of price data for both butter and cheese in the early sixteenth century has, unfortunately, meant the elimination of this category and thus the transfer of its basket weight to the meat-fish group, whose weight consequently rises from 25.0 per cent to 37.5 per cent.

Phelps Brown and Hopkins justified these weights, especially for the two medieval baskets (1275 and 1500), by citing evidence from the expenditure account-books for the Savernak household in Dorsetshire during the years 1453–60: with 20 per cent for grains, 35 per cent for meat and fish, 23 per cent for drink, though only 2 per cent for butter and cheese, but still totalling 80 per cent for foodstuffs. Textile expenditures are, however, not indicated in the Savernak household accounts.[85]

As noted earlier (594–7), the Phelps Brown and Hopkins basket served as the model for Van der Wee's Brabant 'basket of consumables' price index (Tables 5A and 5B). There are, however, some important differences between the indexes presented in Tables 5A–B and 10. Of lesser importance is the difference in the commodities in each basket. The Van der Wee basket contains only two farinaceous products, rye and barley (no wheat or peas), and no barley malt, but it does contain the butter and cheese missing from the Phelps Brown and Hopkins index. Of much greater importance is the method of presenting the data. First, the Phelps Brown and Hopkins index provides only annual index numbers for each commodity, and not their actual money-of-account values in pence sterling; and second, their index uses the fixed proportions or percentages noted above.[86]

* * * * *

85 Phelps Brown and Hopkins 'Seven Centuries of the Prices of Consumables' (n4 above) 180 Table 1; K.L. Wood-Legh *A Small Household of the Fifteenth Century* (Manchester 1956)

86 Their worksheets, however, did provide an estimated value of the basket for 1500 at 104d sterling, which has been incorporated into this table. Using their original worksheets, I have provided annual prices for all the commodities in

The Van der Wee index, on the other hand, presents the actual money-of-account prices (in Brabant pence *groot*) for each commodity, and thus the total value of the basket, for each year. As a consequence, the percentage shares for each major subgroup in the basket change from year to year with changes in relative prices. Indeed, as has been mentioned (596 above), the rise in the *relative* prices of grains from the original base period of 1451–75 to the base period for this study, 1501–5, meant that the proportional share for the farinaceous index rose from 35.32 per cent to 38.31 per cent, while the shares for the meat-dairy-fish and industrial product indexes fell from 38.87 to 36.94 per cent and from 25.81 to 24.75 per cent, respectively. By the final quinquennium of 1536–40, the share for farinaceous products had again risen to 43.81 per cent, that for meat-dairy-fish had also risen, though much less dramatically, to 38.97 per cent, while the share for the industrial product index had necessarily fallen to 17.22 per cent by 1536–40.

Van der Wee's presentation of the data, which shows relative price changes, is much superior to that of Phelps Brown and Hopkins, with its fixed proportions, since rising food prices would have forced all but the very rich to curb their expenditures on industrial goods. That relative shift in demand would have ied to a *relative* fall in industrial prices (even though nominal prices, in current-money-of account, were rising with general inflation).

Table 10B provides the revised price-relatives or index numbers of the Phelps Brown and Hopkins index, based upon their mean values for 1451–75, for each of the years 1501 to 1505, and thus the mean of that quinquennium 1501–5, for the five commodity groups just listed, and for the total composite index, in columns 2–7. In columns 8–10, the commodities have been re-grouped into the three major subindexes: farinaceous (with drink); meat-fish; and industrial products. Column 11 again presents the Phelps Brown and Hopkins composite price index numbers for the years 1501–5 and their quinquennial mean; columns 12–17 provide wage indexes for master building craftsmen (chiefly masons and carpenters) in southern England for these years, as follows:

12   the nominal daily wage in pence for a master (6d)
13   the nominal daily wage in pence for a craftsman's labourer (4d)
14   the nominal wage index for a master (1451–75 = 100)

* * * * *

their basket from 1264 up to 1830, and I am currently compiling the annual values of these baskets in pence sterling and decimal-pounds sterling. From these values I shall compute a new index and publish the comparative results in a forthcoming journal article.

15   the nominal wage index for a labourer (1451–75 = 100)
16   the real wage index for a master (1451–75 = 100)
17   the real wage index for a labourer (1451–75 = 100)

The real wage indexes (columns 16 and 17) have been calculated by dividing, year by year, the nominal wage index number by the commodity price
index number. The quinquennial means so calculated then serve as the new
base 1501–5 = 100; and thus the mean composite price index for 1501–5,
based on the values for 1451–75 = 100, with a value of 106.79, becomes the
new base 100.00 for 1501–5, used in the commodity-price tables (11A–J). In
other words, in these tables, the composite price index numbers (that is, the
composite of weighted prices for these five groups of commodities) represent the percentage, in each quinquennium, of the base value for 1501–5 (as
explained 594–9 above, for the tables on the Low Countries).

Each of Tables 11A–J for commodity prices in southern England
presents, for each commodity, the following data:

1   the eight quinquennia from 1501–5 to 1536–40
2   the commodity price per unit (litre, kilogram, or number) in pence (d)
      sterling
3   the number of commodity units that could have been purchased with
      the English silver penny
4   the number of units purchased with the gold angel-noble (5.157 g fine
      gold), valued at 6s 8d (80d) from 1464 to 1526 and at 7s 6d (90d) there-
      after
5   the number of units purchased with the gold crown (3.438 g fine gold),
      after its introduction in August 1526, with the revised value of 5s 0d
      (60d) set on 5 November (elevated from the original 4s 6d, set in Au-
      gust 1526)
6   the nominal daily wage of a master building craftsman, which was
      consistently 6d per day for all quinquennia except the final one, when
      it rose to 6.5d per day (1536–40), as noted earlier[87]
7   the number of commodity units (litres, kilograms, etc) that could have
      been purchased with a craftsman's daily wage
8   the quantity index, with the base 1501–5 = 100, based upon the pur-
      chasing power of the sterling silver penny
9   the commodity-price index for the specific commodity, with the base
      1501–5 = 100

* * * * *

87 On the reasons for using the Phelps Brown and Hopkins wage data in preference to those in Thorold Rogers, see 553–6 above.

10   the Phelps Brown and Hopkins composite price index, with the revised base 1501–5 = 100

The values for each quinquennium are presented in the rows.

The commodity-price tables

The nature or composition, origin, and units of the measurement of the commodities priced in the tables on the purchasing power of coins and wages are as follows: [88]

11A   Red wine: usually Bordeaux (claret), purchased by various ecclesiastical institutions and colleges at both Cambridge and Oxford, by the dozen gallons = 55.550 litres; 1 gallon = 4.546 litres or cubic decimetres

11B   Herrings: North Sea smoked red herrings, possibly supplied by Flemish and Dutch as well as by English fishermen, purchased at Cambridge and Oxford by the cade, or kemp, which evidently contained 500 fish, as did the Flemish *stroo*[89]

11C   Codfish (mores): cod caught from the waters off the Orkney and Shetland Islands and Iceland, purchased at Cambridge by the 'short hundred,' that is, 100

11D   Wheat: purchased from local producers in the Cambridge-Oxford region, by the quarter = 8 bushels = 64 gallons = 290.935 litres; 1 bushel = 36.369 litres. Wheat prices were not included in the comparable set of

* * * * *

88 For more information see Thorold Rogers *History of Agriculture and Prices* (n2 above). The precise sources of the data are given in each of the tables.

89 See Thorold Rogers *History of Agriculture and Prices* (n2 above) I 1259–1400 608–9: '... reckoned by the cade and the barrel; it would seem then that the cade contained between 500 and 600 fish' and IV 1400–1582 526–37: 'The cade of red herrings, however, and the barrel of white are the commonest quantities. I have assumed that the cade, the mase, and the kympfe or kemp of red herrings were identical in quantity, as they are nearly the same price at the localities where these terms are found. The barrel of white herrings is nearly double the price of the cade of red on an average.' See also *The Shorter Oxford English Dictionary on Historical Principles* I 264: 'Cade: 2. *spec.* A barrel of herrings, holding six great hundreds, i.e. 720; afterwards 500.' In their working papers, Phelps Brown and Hopkins (see n84 above) stated prices for 'the red herrings in shillings and pence per cade, which is not defined,' but then noted that 'the *Economist* table of measures (contemporary) gives the barrel [cade?] of herrings as 500.' They evidently ascribed 500 herrings to the cade as well. See also Van der Wee *Antwerp Market* (n2 above) I 277–86 Appendix 22.

commodity-price tables in CWE 2,[90] although they were presented there in another table, with prices drawn from a much different region, the Exeter series that William Beveridge had published in 1929.[91] In retrospect, however, the commonly cited arguments for the superiority of the Beveridge data are not compelling, especially since they contain far more lacunae than do Thorold Rogers' price series. It seems more logical to present Thorold Rogers' price data, all drawn from the same, comparably selected Cambridge and Oxford accounts, than to interject the Beveridge data, drawn from a distant source in Devonshire.[92]

11E   Peas: fresh garden peas, purchased from local producers at Cambridge, by the quarter = 8 bushels = 64 gallons = 290.935 litres; 1 bushel = 36.369 litres

11F   Sugar: loaf or cane sugar, variously from the Mediterranean, Madeira, the Canaries, and the Azores, purchased at Cambridge and Oxford, by the dozen pounds avoirdupois = 5.443 kg; 453.493 g = 1 lb

11G   Tallow candles: English and French tallow candles made from mutton fat, purchased at Cambridge and Oxford, by the dozen pounds avoirdupois = 5.443 kg

11H   Paper: good quality linen paper (made from linen rags), probably imported from the Low Countries, averaging in size 12 inches by 8.5 inches = 30.48 cm by 21.59 cm = 658.063 cm^2

11I   Linen: table linen, medium to good quality, with a width of 1.0 to 1.5 ells or yards, priced by the dozen ells = 10.973 metres; 1 ell/yard = 36

* * * * *

90 CWE 2 342 Table E: The Standard of Living of the English Mason 1500 to 1514
91 CWE 2 321 Table 3: A comparison of the purchasing power of the daily summer wages of masons at Cambridge and Oxford and at Antwerp, 1501–1514; William Beveridge 'A Statistical Crime of the Seventeenth Century' *Journal of Economic and Business History* (1929), data republished in *Abstract of British Historical Statistics*, ed B.R. Mitchell and Phyllis Deane (Cambridge 1962) 484–6
92 See Thorold Rogers *History of Agriculture and Prices* (n2 above), IV 280–92 Table I: Averages of Grain (wheat, barley, drage, oats, rye, beans, peas, vetches, pulse, malt, oatmeal). The wheat prices are drawn from 1363 localities over the period 1401–1582. There is no indication, in any of the volumes of this series, that the unit employed was the Winchester quarter that Beveridge used for his grain price data; see in particular I chapter 10 'Weights and Measures' 166–8, on gallons, bushels, and quarters. The Winchester bushel contains 96.945 per cent of the volume of the imperial bushel. See William Beveridge *Prices and Wages in England from the Twelfth to the Nineteenth Centuries* I *Price Tables: Mercantile Era* (London 1939; repr London 1965) lix. (No more volumes were published.)

inches = 0.914 metre;[93] imported from the Low Countries, Normandy, and Ireland, but also purchased from suppliers in the West of England, Lancashire, and within the Oxford-Cambridge region. This is the one commodity whose price series lacked the desired consistency, because of the varying provenance and price variations, with possible variations as well in the width of the cloth. Nevertheless, the mean prices are surprisingly stable over this long period, varying from a low of 7.364d per metre in 1506–10 to a high of 9.446d per metre in 1531–5.

11J　Woollen cloth: first-quality English broadcloths, priced by the *pannus* of statutory dimensions: 24 yards/ells (21.945 metres) by 1.75 yards (1.600 metres), purchased by New College, Oxford, and King's College, Cambridge. Though Thorold Rogers provided price data for second and third quality woollens, only those for the best quality have been used in this table.[94] Because these woollens were so much cheaper than the Flemish broadcloths, this table follows the format for the preceding tables on English prices and includes the number of metres of these English woollens that a master mason could purchase with both his daily and weekly wage (that is, for six days). For comparison with the cost of woollens in the Low Countries (Tables 6J–K), the alternative estimate of the number of days' wages that such a mason would have had to spend in purchasing one of these woollens each year is also included. These tabulated data indicate that while the English woollens were indeed substantially cheaper than the Flemish and Brabantine woollens, they were still luxury items that few craftsmen could or would have afforded to purchase in this era – not when they would have cost a master mason or carpenter from 130 to 193 days' wages. As in the Low Countries, worsteds (says) and linen fabrics were the more obvious choice for even the best-paid master craftsman.

V

AN OVERVIEW OF PRICE CHANGES AND
THE PURCHASING POWERS OF COINS
IN THE LOW COUNTRIES AND ENGLAND
DURING THE AGE OF ERASMUS

Detailed analysis of all of these commodity-price tables for the southern Low Countries and southern England is hardly necessary, for they should

* * * * *

93 See n63 above.
94 See Thorold Rogers *History of Agriculture and Prices* (n2 above) IV 563–5; on ells and yards see n63 above.

be self-explanatory. One can readily see that in both countries, virtually all commodities were affected by the inflationary forces of the Price Revolution, even as early as the quinquennium 1516–20. As the commodity-price tables for the southern Low Countries (Tables 6A–K) indicate, the average price level, as measured by the Van der Wee 'basket of consumables' index (Tables 5A–B), rose by almost 48 per cent from the initial quinquennium 1501–6 to the final one, 1536–40; and as the similar tables for England indicate (Tables 10A–B, 11A–J), the Phelps Brown and Hopkins 'basket of consumables' index rose by almost 43 per cent over this same forty-year period (indeed, in a shorter period, rising by 47 per cent in 1526–30, before declining slightly and then sharply rising once more). As the synoptic tables for these two regional price indexes indicate, over the forty-year period the subindex for grain prices rose the most (at least in Brabant), followed by the index for meat-dairy-fish products, with the smallest rise, though still a substantial rise, in the industrial products index.

These differences in the behaviour of the price indexes are fully to be expected, and are quite typical of the behaviour of prices during expansionary eras in early modern and modern European economic history. This in no way contradicts the previously expressed view that the Price Revolution was fundamentally monetary in its origins and nature. Indeed the commonly expressed view that if the causes of inflation were essentially monetary, then all prices should have moved together in tandem, and also necessarily in proportion to the increased stock of money, is completely false.[95] Obviously, during any inflation, the continual fluctuations of a myriad of *real* forces in the economy and the individual reactions of producers and consumers continued to play their usual role, along with monetary expansion, in effecting numerous changes in *relative* individual prices and wages within the economy.

As noted earlier (556–60 above), the capacity of the early modern economy to respond to large increases in aggregate demand largely determined the degree of inflation that would ensue, with a continuous monetary expansion in coinage stocks and/or flows. Thus, the more that various economic sectors enjoyed access to underutilized resources (in land, capital, and labour), allowing them to be fairly flexible or elastic in their individual responses to large increases in effective demand, the less would be the over-

* * * * *

95 Anna Jacobson Schwartz, in a review of Spooner's *International Economy and Monetary Movements in France* in *The Journal of European Economic History* 3/1 (Spring 1974) 253, comments that 'the author subscribes to a familiar fallacy, namely that a monetary explanation to be valid requires that all prices move in unison.' See the following note.

all extent of inflation. At any given time, some sectors were more flexible or had more elastic supply schedules than others. Historically, the arable agricultural sector tended to have the least elastic supply schedules, especially since population growth and economic development led to a greater and greater use of existing resources, and to what economists would call 'full employment.' Indeed, in the short run, once village farming communities or estate owners had used up their available supplies of arable land, decided upon the division of resources between arable and pastoral agriculture, and established the crop rotations to be pursued, their ability to respond quickly to changes in demand were rather limited. In the longer run, during periods of economic growth agricultural producers were usually able to increase their outputs only by resorting to less fertile, less productive, and thus more costly 'marginal' lands.[96]

* * * * *

96 During such inflationary periods, prices for individual commodities can change for 'real' reasons as well as for purely 'monetary' reasons. Those commodity-price changes can and usually do differ from each other, and that is why economists speak about changes in 'relative prices.' These relative price changes may reflect the various micro-economic factors concerning differences in the 'elasticity' of supply and demand, for both producers and consumers. In general elasticity is calculated as the ratio between a given percentage change in price or in real income and the consequent percentage change in the quantity of goods demanded or supplied. A numerical result greater than 1.0 is said to be 'elastic' and a result less than 1.0 is said to be 'inelastic'; a result that equals 1.0 is said to have unitary elasticity (because the percentage changes are equal). The 'elasticity of supply' measures the extent to which producers can increase their outputs, and merchants can increase the supply of their goods on the market, in response to growing demand and/or rising prices; in particular it measures the extent to which producers can increase output without encountering rising 'marginal costs' (the extra costs, in producing one additional unit of output) that would lead to further price increases. Supply is deemed to be 'elastic' when output rises without a significant increase in production costs. The 'price elasticity of demand' measures the extent to which a rise in prices leads consumers in general to reduce the quantity of each of the goods that they regularly consume (demand), while they seek substitute products or decide to do without such goods. The 'income elasticity of demand' measures the extent to which those who enjoy rising real incomes will increase the quantity of each of the goods that they choose to consume (the 'quantity demanded'). The choices that consumers make will be influenced by the availability and cost of substitute products, by the changes in and extent of their purchasing power, and by the relative priorities that they assign to various goods when they are faced with a limited budget ('budget constraints'). For example, a small rise in the price of salt or a small decrease in consumers' real income will not likely result in a proportional or even significant reduc-

In many areas of the manufacturing sector (apart from the extraction of natural resources), producers enjoyed a much more elastic supply of inputs, especially labour – usually the key resource, particularly during periods of population growth. In response to changes in demand, producers could readily hire or dismiss workers (few of whom ever had guaranteed full-time employment) and increase or decrease their orders for raw materials (flax, wool, leather, metals, wood, etc), usually without incurring much higher costs. For such reasons, therefore, we would expect that during inflationary periods costs and prices tended to rise less in the labour-intensive manufacturing sector than in the agricultural sector (and there, less in livestock husbandry than in arable farming).

Of course, these relationships did not remain fixed in this fashion over time. The exploitation of newly acquired land resources, changes in capital formation, and technological or institutional changes continually altered 'production functions' in the various sectors and industries, and thus production costs and the relative prices of the products so produced also changed. Yet the extent and impact of such changes were, in historical perspective, relatively small and limited in scope before the modern Industrial Revolution.

Factors related to demand also played a role in the annual and longer-term behaviour of commodity prices (see n96 above). First, the impact of increased stocks and/or flows of money could not be general throughout the entire economy and society. Their impact would have depended upon how those who received the additional money incomes chose to spend the portions not saved on various commodities, domestic and imported. Thus differences in consumer demand and their choices within the economy would also be reflected in differential price changes.

Second, even if man lives not by bread alone, most people did require a basic supply of bread grains as their first necessity. As grain prices rose, without any substantial diminution in per capita consumption, those with relatively fixed incomes were forced to reduce their expenditures on other commodities (as noted earlier, 596 and 620), and thus the demand for them, reducing the pressure to increase their prices. But conversely, as prices for

* * * * *

tion in the quantity demanded ('inelastic demand'); but a small decrease in the price of worsted textiles or a rise in the real incomes of the lower and middle classes may well result in a more than proportional increase in the quantity demanded ('elastic demand'). The supply of wheat – generally fixed once the crop is sown – is far less elastic than is the supply of worsted textiles (for which labour rather than land is the chief factor of production).

grains and similar commodities rose much more swiftly than others in re-sponse to differing supply and demand conditions, most consumers would have responded by switching to acceptable substitutes whose prices were rising more slowly, especially if they were ranked on a lower scale in the consumer hierarchy of demand. Such substitutions would then have con-tributed to a rise in these commodity prices, while reducing the rate of price increases for the 'first choice' commodities.

These continual, fluctuating substitutions in consumer choice reveal, of course, one of the most serious faults in these consumer price indexes, a weighted average of prices. The individual components in these 'baskets' must remain fixed, without accounting for substitutions – at least in the shorter run, and certainly for the period of this study. For this reason such price indexes tend to overstate the consequences of inflation for the typical consumer.

All of the tables on the purchasing power of wages, therefore, chart both the price increases for each commodity from 1501 to 1540 and the rise in the overall CPI for these two regions. In the southern Low Countries, principally the Antwerp region, as already noted (625 above), the Van der Wee 'basket of consumables' index rose by 47.98 per cent (Tables 6A–J; cf Ta-ble 12). Of the individual commodity prices, those that rose the most, and thus more than the overall rise in the CPI, were salted beef (64.49 per cent), herrings (54.65 per cent), wheat (68.30 per cent), and – heading the list – loaf sugar (100.94 per cent). The three main subindexes rose in a quite pre-dictable fashion: grains (farinaceous) by 69.2 per cent; meat-dairy-fish prod-ucts, by 56.1 per cent; and industrial goods, by just 3.0 per cent (though it had risen by 29.6 per cent in 1526–30, only to fall sharply over the next decade).

In southern England, over the same forty-year period, the Phelps Brown and Hopkins 'basket of consumables' index rose by 42.64 per cent, slightly less than the Van der Wee index for Brabant (Tables 11A–J; cf Ta-ble 14). The two English price leaders, rising more than the overall CPI, were peas (though just barely) and – again by a very wide margin – sugar, which rose by 162.1 per cent. Very surprisingly, and contrary to all ex-pectations, not only did the price of wheat rise less than did the CPI (by only 10.07 per cent), but so did the subindex for farinaceous products (wheat, rye, barley, peas, with a weight of 20.0 in the index); it rose by just 25.47 per cent. Had demographic forces been the primary motor of the English inflation, we would have expected the contrary. The subindex for meat and fish, however, did rise much more than did the CPI: by 68.20 per cent; conversely, and not surprisingly, the industrial-goods index rose by substantially less than did the CPI: by only 22.21 per cent, though by considerably more than did the similar index for Brabant over the same period.

VI
BUILDING CRAFTSMEN AND THE PURCHASING POWER OF WAGES IN THE EARLY SIXTEENTH-CENTURY LOW COUNTRIES AND ENGLAND (TABLES 12–16)

Tables 12–16 provide some answers to the questions raised at the beginning of this study about real incomes and living standards in the age of Erasmus by presenting the purchasing power of a craftsman's daily wages in the southern Low Countries and England.

Work and wages in the Hapsburg Low Countries

In Table 12 (Price and wage indexes for southern Brabant, 1501–5 to 1536–40), the real wages for master masons and carpenters in the Antwerp-Lier-Brussels region – that is, the purchasing power of their nominal money wages – have been calculated in relation to the Van der Wee 'basket of consumables' consumer price index (see Table 5). The columns present the following data:

1 the years of the eight quinquennia from 1501–5 to 1536–40
2 the quinquennial mean value, in d *groot* Brabant, of the Van der Wee composite 'basket of consumables'
3 the equivalent current values of the baskets in the preceding column, expressed in d *groot* Flemish
4 the Van der Wee price index (basket of consumables) with the original base 1451–75 = 100 (= 232.524d *groot* Brabant or 155.016 d *groot* Flemish, for the entire basket)
5 the Van der Wee price index (basket of consumables) with the new base 1501–5 = 100 (= 291.700d *groot* Brabant or 194.467d *groot* Flemish for the entire basket)
6 the nominal wage index for master building craftsmen in Antwerp, with the base 1501–5 = 100 (= 12.250d *groot* Brabant or 8.167d *groot* Flemish). The craftsmen's wages are the annual means of the money wages, in d *groot* Flemish, paid to master masons and master carpenters, and thus the annual means of those two sets of money wages.

7   the real wage index for these two sets of building craftsmen, with the
      same base 1501–5 = 100, calculated as the quotient of the nominal wage
      index divided by the consumer price index and adjusted as required[97]

For each set of quinquennial index numbers in this table, the values for
the subsequent quinquennia are expressed, in effect, as a percentage of the
values calculated for the initial base period 1501–5.

The price and wage indexes of Table 12 are repeated in Table 13, 'The
purchasing power of daily money wages for building craftsmen in Brabant,'
which provides more complex information about the wages of masons and
carpenters in Antwerp, in particular on the seasonal nature of wages. An
often marked difference between summer and winter time-work wages, if
not in piece-work wages, was common in continental western Europe until
the eighteenth century. Time-wages were normally paid by the day (sometimes by the week of six working days). Before the Industrial Revolution,
the only effective limitation on the number of hours to be worked each day
was the number of hours of sunlight, reduced by the time necessarily taken
for meals and some rest. Indeed, most men worked literally 'from sun to
sun.' That meant that in the months of spring, summer, and early fall the
normal working day was at least twelve, sometimes fourteen hours; in the
late fall and winter months, it was about eight hours to nine hours. Consequently, the winter wage – despite the much higher cost of living (food, fuel,
clothing) – was usually only about two-thirds to three-quarters of the summer wage, as is clearly evident in this table. Thus seasonality in wages indicates that the wage was implicitly hourly rather than daily.[98] The columns
of Table 13 present the following data:

* * * * *

97 For each year, the RWI (real wage index) is calculated in this fashion: NWI/CPI
   (nominal wage index divided by the consumer price index). But, for mathematical reasons too complicated to discuss here, the calculation of the mean values for the RWI for this base-period quinquennium does not produce a value
   equal to 100.00, as one might expect, but a slightly different value: 100.219.
   If we also calculate the mean value of the indexes for the number of Van der
   Wee 'basket of consumables' that could be purchased with the annual wage
   income (discussed 632 below), we arrive at the same value: 100.219. The RWI
   index numbers for each year, so calculated (NWI/CPI), are then multiplied by
   this value (100.219) to produce a new set of index numbers, whose mean now
   provides the true base for the actual quinquennial real wage indexes in this
   table, so that the mean of 1501–5 = 100.
98 See John Munro 'Urban Wage Structures in Late-Medieval England and the
   Low Countries: Work-Time and Seasonal Wages' in *Labour and Leisure in Historical Perspective, Thirteenth to Twentieth Centuries* ed Ian Blanchard, Vierteljahrschrift für Sozial- und Wirtschaftsgeschichte Beiheft series 116 (Stuttgart

1   the quinquennial means from 1501–5 to 1536–40
2   the quinquennial mean values of an Antwerp master mason's daily
     summer wage, in d *groot* Flemish
3   the quinquennial mean values of that same wage in d *groot* Brabant
     (that is, 1.5 times as much)
4   the quinquennial mean values of the master carpenter's daily summer
     wage in d *groot* Brabant
5   the quinquennial mean values of these two sets of masters' wages (ma-
     sons and carpenters) in d *groot* Brabant
6   the quinquennial mean values of masters' winter wages in d *groot* Bra-
     bant
7   the quinquennial mean values of the winter wage as percentages of
     the summer wage
8   the quinquennial mean values of summer wages of a mason's labourer,
     in d *groot* Brabant
9   the quinquennial mean values of that wage as a percentage of a master
     mason's daily summer wage
10   the quinquennial mean number of days that craftsmen worked in the
     Antwerp-Lier region of Brabant

The remaining columns in this table on wages of Antwerp craftsmen
provides some alternative means of estimating the purchasing power of
those wages, for each quinquennium. Columns 11 to 18 present the following data:

11   the quinquennial mean values of Van der Wee's 'basket of consum-
     ables' in d *groot* Brabant
12   the quinquennial mean values of Van der Wee's 'basket of consum-
     ables' in d *groot* Flemish
13   the quinquennial mean values of Van der Wee's 'basket of consum-
     ables' price index (consumer price index or CPI), with the base mean

* * * * *

1994) 65–78; Jan De Vries 'An Inquiry into the Behaviour of Wages in the
Dutch Republic and the Southern Netherlands, 1580–1800' *Acta Historiae Neerlandicae* 10 (1978) 79–97, repr in *Dutch Capitalism and World Capitalism* ed Maurice Aymard (Cambridge 1982) 37–62 and 'An Employer's Guide to Wages
and Working Conditions in the Netherlands, 1450-1850' in *Hours of Work and
Means of Payment: The Evolution of Conventions in Pre-Industrial Europe* ed Carol
S. Leonard and Boris N. Mironov, Proceedings of the Eleventh International
Economic History Congress, Milan, September 1994, Session B3b (Milan 1994)
47–63.

1501–5 = 100 (= 194.467d *groot* Flemish, but obviously identical for both sets of prices in Flemish and Brabant moneys-of-account, tied together by the 1.5:1 ratio)

14   the quinquennial mean index numbers of the nominal wage index (NWI, same base), based on the mean daily summer wages for masons and carpenters (1501–5 = 100 = 12.250d *groot* Brabant or 8.167d *groot* Flemish)

15   the quinquennial mean index numbers of their real-wage index computed by the formula NWI/CPI, adjusted as required[99]

16   an alternative measure of real wages: the quinquennial mean number of Van der Wee's 'baskets of consumables,' computed by the *harmonic mean*, that a master mason or carpenter might have purchased with his annual money-wage income if he had been employed for 210 days a year at the summer wage. A second real-wage index, constructed in a similar fashion, demonstrates that this method produces the same results as does the first real-wage index.[100] Although 210 days of employment was the mean number computed for the century 1450–1550, the average number of days of employment in 1501–40 was slightly more: 217.15 days.

17   the quinquennial mean index numbers for the number of Van der Wee's 'baskets of consumables' acquired, with the base 1501–5 = 100 (that is, 8.819 baskets for 1501–5)

18   the quinquennial mean number of baskets acquired with the mean number of days of employment for this period: 217.15 days

19   the quinquennial mean number of Van der Wee's 'baskets of consumables,' calculated by combining an estimate of the value of the summer and of the winter wages. In these calculations, 70 per cent of the time employed was allocated to the summer wage and 30 per cent to the winter wage.

20   the quinquennial mean index numbers for the number of Van der Wee's 'baskets of consumables' acquired (summer and winter wages earned), with the base 1501–5 = 100 (= 8.212 baskets)

* * * * *

99 See n97 above.

100 The numerical value of the harmonic mean of the number of such commodity baskets for 1501–5, 8.819 baskets, was used to compute the first set of index numbers for this quinquennium (= each year's number of baskets divided by 8.819), and the mean of this sum of index numbers was taken, providing the same result of 100.219 (see n97 above). That result was used to compute the second set, to produce the mean 1501–5 = 100.00 and quinquennial index numbers identical to those produced in computing the first real wage index.

For purposes of comparison, the last three columns give the price and wage index numbers for the original base period, 1451–75 = 100, the traditional base period for medieval and early modern price history mandated by the International Scientific Committee on Price History (see 596 above).

21   quinquennial mean values for Van der Wee's 'baskets of consumables' (serving as the consumer price index or CPI)
22   the quinquennial mean index numbers of the nominal wage (NWI) index of Antwerp craftsmen
23   the quinquennial mean index numbers of their real wage index (RWI)

If we take as our true base the initial quinquennium 1501–5, we see that the real-wage income of Antwerp building craftsmen deteriorated by only 1.5 to 3.5 per cent (according to the index used), from 1501 to 1540, although there was a temporary dip in real income during the early 1520s. On the other hand, if the traditional base of 1451–75 = 100 is used, a quarter century that coincidentally marks the so-called 'golden age' of the artisan and labourer in northwest Europe, a major deterioration in real income, about 19.5 per cent, had already taken place before the beginning of the sixteenth century. By 1540, the real-wage index of these Antwerp craftsmen was only about 77 per cent of the level achieved in 1451–75. One should also remember, however, that this so-called 'golden age' in the third quarter of the fifteenth century was one of continued plague and depopulation, sporadic warfare (civil and foreign), and economic depression, quite unlike the far more buoyant and propitious economic circumstances of the expansionary age of Erasmus.[101]

Work and wages in England

For England, comparable price and wage data for 1501–40 can be found in Tables 14 and 15. The Phelps Brown and Hopkins 'basket of consumables' index is presented in Table 14, with its five subindexes and the composite price index (CPI). Their original index numbers, with the base 1451–75 = 100, have been converted to accord with the new base, 1501–5 = 100 (see Tables 10A and 10B). The columns present the following data:

* * * * *

101 See Munro 'Economic Depression and the Arts' (n14 above) and 'Symbiosis of Towns and Textiles (n64 above); Hatcher 'Great Slump of the Mid-Fifteenth Century' (n22 above); Nightingale 'England and the European Depression' (n22 above); Van der Wee *Antwerp Market* (n2 above) II 61–142.

1   the eight quinquennia from 1501–5 to 1536–40
2   the quinquennial mean index numbers for the farinaceous sub-index (wheat, rye, barley, peas), with a weight of 20.0 per cent
3   the quinquennial mean index numbers for the meat and fish subindex (sheep, white and red herrings), with a weight of 37.5 per cent, because, in the complete absence of prices for butter and cheese, there is no dairy products subindex for this period
4   the quinquennial mean index numbers for the drink subindex (barley malt), with a weight of 22.5 per cent
5   the quinquennial mean index numbers for the fuel and light subindex (charcoal, candles, oil), with a weight of 7.5 per cent
6   the quinquennial mean index numbers for the textiles subindex (canvas, linen shirting, cheap woollen cloths), with a weight of 12.5 per cent
7   the quinquennial mean index numbers for the Phelps Brown and Hopkins composite price index, as the weighted sum of these subindexes (that is, = 100)
8   the quinquennial mean index numbers for the combined farinaceous and drink index, with a weight of 42.5 per cent
9   the quinquennial mean index numbers for the combined meat-fish-dairy index, with a weight of 37.5 per cent
10   the quinquennial mean index numbers for the combined industrial index, with a weight of 20.0 per cent
11   the quinquennial mean index numbers for the composite Phelps Brown and Hopkins 'basket of consumables' index, for the base period 1501–5 = 100
12   the quinquennial mean index numbers for the composite Phelps Brown and Hopkins 'basket of consumables' index, for the original base period 1451–75 = 100

Table 15 continues with the calculations of the real wages – the purchasing power of nominal money wages – for master building craftsmen (masons and carpenters) in southern England, principally the Oxford-Cambridge region, with the following columns:

1   the years of the quinquennia from 1501–5 to 1536–40
2   the quinquennial mean nominal daily wage for master building craftsmen (masons and carpenters), in pence sterling, for each quinquennium (6d for all but the last quinquennium)
3   the quinquennial mean nominal wage index, with the base 1451–75 = 100 (= 6d daily)

4   the quinquennial mean index numbers for the Phelps Brown and Hop-
     kins composite price index, with the same base, 1451–75 = 100
5   the quinquennial mean index numbers for the real wage index for these
     master building craftsmen, with the same 1451–75 base, calculated as
     the quotient of NWI/CPI
6   the quinquennial mean index numbers for the nominal wage index
     with the new base, 1501–5 = 100 (but also equal to 6d daily)
7   the quinquennial mean index numbers for the Phelps Brown and Hop-
     kins composite price index with the new base, 1501–5 = 100
8   the quinquennial mean index numbers for the real wage index for
     these building craftsmen with the 1501–5 base, unadjusted
9   the quinquennial mean index numbers for the real wage index, ad-
     justed as required[102]

As this table indicates, the real-income trends for southern England's
master building craftsmen (masons and carpenters) are rather different from
those just examined in the Antwerp-Lier region in Brabant. In the first place,
we find no evident seasonal wages in the data. Although the payment of
lower winter wages had indeed been common before the Black Death, it was
rarely observed thereafter, at least in the extant records; and if and when a
reduced winter wage was imposed, it was usually about 5/6 (83.33 per cent)
of the summer wage. The payment of a higher winter wage was, perhaps,
one way that post-Plague employers could circumvent the overly severe
limitations (on summer wages) imposed by the Ordinance and Statute of
Labourers (1349–51), the crown's injudicious response to labour scarcities.[103]
Nevertheless, as in the Low Countries, a working day of twelve hours or
more for most of the year remained standard in England, until 1847, when
Parliament, by Fielden's Act, mandated a maximum ten-hour day for all
factory workers.[104]

* * * * *

102 See n97 above.
103 The Ordinance of Labourers, decreed on 14 June 1349, is restated and reissued
     in *The Statutes of the Realm* ed T.E. Tomlins and J. Raithby, Record Commission,
     6 vols (London 1810–22) I 307–8; for the Statute of Labourers, 25 Edwardi III
     stat 2.c.3 see I 311–12. Yet seasonal wages evidently did continue in England
     well into modern times. Cf Smith *Wealth of Nations* (n9 above) 74: 'First, in
     almost every part of Great Britain there is a distinction, even in the lowest
     species of labour, between summer and winter wages. Summer wages are
     always highest.'
104 See Munro 'Urban Wage Structures' (n98 above). In Great Britain, the 1833 Fac-
     tory Act stipulated a maximum working day of 9 hours for children aged nine

Second, the daily nominal money wage (summer and winter) still remained fixed, as it had been from the early fifteenth century (and from 1363 in the Oxford and Cambridge colleges) at 6d sterling; only in 1536 was that wage raised, to 6¹/₂d per day (an 8.33 per cent rise). Third, therefore, because of the inflation that began around 1516–20 and raised the price level (composite price index) by 42.6 per cent, building craftsmen suffered a significant decline in their real wage the years 1501–40. By the late 1520s (when the CPI was even higher, at 147.3), it had fallen to just about two-thirds of the level prevailing at the beginning of the century (which was 93.7 per cent of the 'golden age' real-wage level for 1451–75). By 1536–40, building craftsmen had regained some of that loss, achieving a real wage that was about three-quarters of that for the base period 1501–5. Since the extent of inflation was about the same in both countries, the losses that the English craftsmen suffered in their real wages must be attributed to continuous 'wage stickiness' (see 553–6 above), the failure to achieve a proportional raise in nominal money wages during this inflation.

Changes in the absolute and relative levels of wages in England and the Low Countries

Table 16 presents a comparison of the purchasing power of master craftsmen's wages in England and the Low Countries in relation to the individual commodities that were common to both regions. Such a table permits us to compare the relative and absolute levels of real wages in both regions and to ascertain whether these labour and commodity markets were truly

* * * * *

to thirteen, and for those aged thirteen to eighteen, a maximum of 69 hours a week, with no more than 12 hours per day. The 1844 Factory Act limited the working day for women to 12 hours per day, and for children aged eight to thirteen, to 6.5 hours. Fielden's Act was passed at a time of great labour unrest, on the eve of the 1848 Chartists' Revolt. See John H. Clapham *An Economic History of Modern Britain* II *The Early Railway Age, 1820–1850* (Cambridge 1964) 572–8; S.G. Checkland *The Rise of Industrial Society in England, 1815–1885* (London 1964) 244–9; John Derry *A Short History of Nineteenth-Century England* (New York 1963) 124–37, 151–4. In the United States, New Hampshire's state legislature also enacted a maximum ten-hour day in 1847, but the legislation applied only to women. It proved to be unenforceable, and the effective state legislation dates only from 1887. See Claudia Goldin *Understanding the Gender Gap: An Economic History of American Women* (New York 1990) 189–92 and Table 7/1; Jeremy Atack and Peter Passell *A New Economic View of American History: From Colonial Times to 1940* 2d ed (New York 1994) 542–3.

'efficient.' If they were fairly 'efficient,' we should expect to find that relative commodity values and relative real wages were comparable in the two regions. What we do find is that, although they were not closely comparable, they did correspond to each other, in many commodities and in real wages, rather more than most historians would expect for this 'pre-modern' era.

There are three sets of columns in Table 16: the first set of columns for Antwerp, the second set for southern England, and the third set for both. The first two sets present the following data:

1   the years of the eight quinquennia from 1501-5 to 1536-40
2   the quinquennial mean values of the mean daily summer wage for a master mason at Antwerp in d *groot* Flemish
3   the quinquennial mean number (harmonic mean) of litres of red Rhenish wine purchased with that daily wage by an Antwerp master mason
4   the quinquennial mean number (harmonic mean) of North Sea herrings so purchased
5   the quinquennial mean number (harmonic mean) of litres of peas so purchased
6   the quinquennial mean number (harmonic mean) of litres of wheat so purchased
7   the quinquennial mean number (harmonic mean) of kilograms of sugar so purchased
8   the quinquennial mean daily wage (summer and winter) for a master mason in southern England (Oxford-Cambridge), in d sterling
9   the quinquennial mean number (harmonic mean) of litres of red Bordeaux wine (claret) purchased with that daily wage by an English master mason (Oxford-Cambridge)
10   the quinquennial mean number (harmonic mean) of litres of North Sea herrings so purchased
11   the quinquennial mean number (harmonic mean) of litres of peas so purchased
12   the quinquennial mean number (harmonic mean) of litres of wheat so purchased
13   the quinquennial mean number (harmonic mean) of kilograms of sugar so purchased

The final set of columns, 14 to 18, compares the purchasing powers of wages in the two regions by estimating the percentage advantage or disadvantage that the English master mason enjoyed in purchasing wine, herrings, peas, wheat, and sugar, during each quinquennium, over his Antwerp counterpart during this period. In purchasing wine, the English mason enjoyed an advantage of 10 to 16 per cent until 1516–20, but by the final quinquennium the disadvantage was almost one-third. In purchasing herrings, he enjoyed an advantage only in the years 1506–15, and a major one in 1521–5, but significant disadvantages in the other quinquennia. Peas were the only commodity for which the English mason enjoyed a consistent advantage in every quinquennium. In purchasing wheat, he enjoyed a very significant advantage in 1506–10 and in 1521–5, and a relatively minor disadvantage in 1511–20 and 1526–30. Finally, in purchasing sugar, which had become a very important item in Iberian trade with the Antwerp market, the English master mason suffered a disadvantage in each quinquennium, and a major disadvantage in 1516–20 and in 1536–40, the final quinquennium in this survey.[105]

Thus Tables 14–16 indicate a relative decline in the purchasing power of the nominal money wage for English building craftsmen over this period because of wage stickiness during sustained inflation. In contrast, the Antwerp building craftsmen enjoyed earlier and steeper rises in their nominal money wage (Table 13) and maintained a better ability to protect their real wage, which declined by only five per cent over this period. Nevertheless their purchasing power in absolute terms was not necessarily higher, certainly not consistently higher for all commodities, than that of their English counterparts over these four decades.

VII
A NEW PERSPECTIVE ON THE INCOME
OF ERASMUS IN 1526 (TABLE 17)

The information presented in Tables 12–16 on the purchasing power of craftsmen's wages in the Low Countries and England permits new insights into and thus a better assessment than was previously possible of Erasmus' standard of living. His correspondence during the calendar year 1526 contains many references to his receipt of various forms of income. Table 17 lists twelve specific references in eight letters and its columns present the following information for each of them:

1   the letter number
2   the date, the coins or currency designated, and an indication as to how the sum was transmitted to Erasmus, if known

* * * * *

105 See Van der Wee *Antwerp Market* (n2 above) I 306–18, 317–24 Appendix 26.

3   the value of the coin or currency unit in d *groot* Flemish (that is, the exchange rate)
4   the value of the coin or currency unit in £ *tournois* (the exchange rate)
5   the value of the coin or currency unit in d sterling English (the exchange rate)
6   the amount (number) of coins or currency units
7   the value of the specified sum in £ *groot* Flemish
8   the value of the specified sum in £ *tournois*
9   the value of the specified sum in £ sterling English
10   the equivalent value of this sum in terms of the number of days' wages for an Oxford master mason in 1526 (6d sterling per day)
11   the equivalent value of this sum in terms of the number of days' wages for an Antwerp master mason in 1526 (mean of 10d *groot* Flemish = 15d *groot* Brabant per day)
12   the number of years' wage income for an Antwerp mason that this sum represented

According to Van der Wee's tabulated data on annual employment in the Antwerp-Lier region, building craftsmen were employed for 230 days in 1526.[106] Thus a master mason in Antwerp might have earned, that year, £9 11s 8d *groot* Flemish (summer wage of 11d for nine months and winter wage of 7d for three months). If the Oxford master mason had been similarly employed for 230 days, his annual wage income would have been £5 15s 0d sterling.

When we consider the data in this table with those figures in mind, we can readily see that Erasmus was far from being poor. Indeed, since many of his stipends and benefices (especially those from the Low Countries) are not mentioned in these letters, Erasmus was even richer than these data indicate. Care was taken to avoid duplicate references in this table; but the letters do not always clearly distinguish between specific gifts, annual income (from a variety of sources), and reimbursements for expenses incurred. The exchange rates used here are the official rates (or calculated rates), rather than the possibly higher market rates indicated in the letters, and thus the total sums may be understated. Since the record of Erasmus' finances discerned from these letters is incomplete, it is astonishing to find that the total payments for the calendar year 1526 amount to £534.420 sterling (or £789.206 *groot* Flemish), an amount equivalent to at least the annual

* * * * *

106 Van der Wee *Antwerp Market* (n2 above) I 542 Appendix 48

wage income of eighty-two Antwerp master masons or ninety-three Oxford master masons, and very likely more.

Some specific examples of annuities and gifts may more effectively establish the high level of Erasmus' standard of living in this year. In Ep 1750, dated 8 September 1526, we learn that Erasmus was receiving an annuity of 120 English gold rose crowns from the bishop of London. With the revaluation of those crowns in November 1526, that annuity was worth £30 sterling (£42 *groot* Flemish), equivalent to 1,200 days' income for an Oxford master mason and 1,008 days' income for an Antwerp master mason. In Ep 1769, dated December 1526, we find that Erasmus was also receiving another English annuity, this one from the bishop of Lincoln, worth 15 gold angel-nobles or £5 12s 6d, the equivalent of 225 days' wages for an Oxford mason. The same letter indicates an even more important annuity from Courtrai (Kortrijk), paid in Bruges at Candlemas (2 February): 130 Rhenish gold florins, worth £34 13s 4d *groot* Flemish or £23 16 8d sterling, the equivalent of 832 days' wages for an Antwerp master mason or 953 days' wages for an Oxford master mason. Most impressive of all was the offer of a benefice from the bishop of Trent in December 1526: 600 Rhenish gold florins a year, then worth £110 sterling or £160 *groot* Flemish, an amount equal to 4,400 days' wages for an Oxford mason or 3,840 days' wages for an Antwerp master mason (that is, virtually 17 years' wage income). Indeed, in the same letter Johannes Fabri also informed Erasmus that he would be receiving a gift of 100 Rhenish florins from the bishop as a reward for the recent book that Erasmus had dedicated to him.[107] In March 1527 Erasmus informs his good friend Polidoro Vergilio that Pope Clement VII 'twice sent me 200 [Florentine] florins and made all sorts of promises'; *each* of those gifts was then worth the equivalent of 1,660 days' wages for an Antwerp master mason and 1,867 days' wages for an Oxford master mason.[108]

Such income disparities are not unknown today, when chief executive officers of many large multi-national corporations command combined salaries and benefits that are sometimes more than a hundred times those earned by still well paid steel- or auto-workers. But certainly not even the most renowned academic scholars (let alone clerics) would today receive an income so much higher than those in the building trades. Senior professors at the University of Toronto may command almost two and one-half times

* * * * *

107 Ep 1771. The bishop's offer of this handsome annuity was evidently conditional upon Erasmus' agreement to move to Trent.
108 Ep 1796

the pre-tax money-wage incomes of senior carpenters; but no more.[109] The
age of Erasmus was, however, entirely different, and for this most eminent
scholar (one-time professor of divinity and of Greek at Cambridge) a truly
golden age.

* * * * *

109 At the University of Toronto, a senior full professor (aged about 60) would
currently (2002) earn about $125,000 CAD per annum (gross pay, but before
benefits). The highest hourly rate for skilled carpenters in Toronto, equivalent
to the Renaissance master carpenters, is currently $28.79 per hour. Working
37.5 hours per week, and about 49 weeks a year, they would expect to receive
an annual income of about $52,900.00 CAD (apart from benefits; with benefits,
$38.36 per hour). The difference in after-tax incomes would be, of course, sig-
nificantly less, with marginal tax rates of 43.4 per cent in the top tax bracket
(in Ontario, Canada).

TABLE 1

AGGREGATE MINT OUTPUTS OF ENGLAND AND THE SOUTHERN LOW COUNTRIES
IN QUINQUENNIAL MEANS FROM 1481–5 TO 1546–50
Gold and silver coinages in kilograms of fine metal, with values in English pounds sterling
and Flemish pounds groot

A   THE MINTS OF ENGLAND

	silver		gold		total value of gold and silver coinages in £ sterling	per cent in	
years	total kilograms coined	value of coinage in £ sterling	total kilograms coined	value of coinage in £ sterling		silver coinage	gold coinage
1481–5	995.231	5,765.296	219.449	14,184.753	19,950.049	28.90	71.10
1486–90	926.785	5,368.794	129.749	8,386.730	13,755.524	39.03	60.97
1491–5	1,270.840	7,361.876	268.983	17,386.525	24,748.402	29.75	70.25
1496–1500	2,490.940	14,429.823	278.926	18,029.238	32,459.060	44.46	55.54
1501–5	4,313.544	24,988.026	516.604	33,392.271	58,380.297	42.80	57.20
1506–10	3,633.212	21,046.916	1,523.115	98,451.267	119,498.183	17.61	82.39
1511–15	1,089.012	6,308.562	694.599	44,897.564	51,206.126	12.32	87.68
1516–20	79.145	458.481	743.656	48,068.530	48,527.011	0.94	99.06
1521–5	3,148.207	18,237.317	442.135	28,578.780	46,816.096	38.96	61.04
1526–30	9,244.701	60,248.025	736.421	54,079.255	114,327.280	52.70	47.30
1531–5	4,616.832	30,088.071	189.160	13,890.972	43,979.043	68.41	31.59
1536–40	5,684.094	37,043.459	406.719	29,826.052	66,869.511	55.40	44.60
1541–5	5,707.032	100,776.324	963.792	79,997.508	180,773.832	55.75	44.25
1546–50	22,029.731	402,892.436	1,992.083	188,860.922	591,753.358	68.08	31.92

TABLE 1 (continued)

B   THE MINTS OF THE SOUTHERN LOW COUNTRIES (FLANDERS AND BRABANT)

years	silver		gold		total value of gold and silver coinages in £ groot Flemish	per cent in	
	total kilograms coined	value of coinage in £ groot Flemish	total kilograms coined	value of coinage in £ groot Flemish		silver coinage	gold coinage
1481–5	5,577.466	48,426.678	52.818	4,735.692	53,162.370	91.09	8.91
1486–90	4,553.062	53,449.788	112.938	20,319.780	73,769.568	72.46	27.54
1491–5	2,524.833	17,996.158	19.308	1,273.661	19,269.819	93.39	6.61
1496–1500	4,872.964	40,743.791	474.633	44,464.280	85,208.071	47.82	52.18
1501–5	3,157.836	26,902.913	538.871	51,112.530	78,015.442	34.48	65.52
1506–10	1,383.730	11,892.196	311.480	29,575.609	41,467.805	28.68	71.32
1511–15	1,640.383	14,074.127	257.699	24,459.800	38,533.927	36.52	63.48
1516–20	705.122	6,152.620	145.094	13,779.872	19,932.492	30.87	69.13
1521–5	1,904.198	16,787.119	1,306.588	127,563.456	144,350.575	11.63	88.37
1526–30	2,979.875	26,198.479	240.990	24,562.665	50,761.144	51.61	48.39
1531–5	2,896.280	25,435.427	136.232	13,503.586	38,939.013	65.32	34.68
1536–40	5,364.987	47,297.893	138.663	13,443.702	60,741.595	77.87	22.13
1541–5	2,317.446	20,428.434	543.900	49,338.059	69,766.493	29.28	70.72
1546–50	1,458.283	12,887.662	731.630	60,657.466	73,545.128	17.52	82.48

SOURCES

England Christopher Challis 'Mint Output, 1220–1985' in *A New History of the Royal Mint* ed Christopher E. Challis (Cambridge 1992) 684–6 and *The Tudor Coinage* (Manchester 1978) 305–17; C. G. Brooke and E. Stokes 'Tables of Bullion Coined, 1337–1550' *The Numismatic Chronicle* 5th series 9 (1929) 27-69

Flanders and Brabant Algemeen Rijksarchief België, Rekenkamer, registers nos 17,881–2 (Antwerp), nos 18,116–30 (Bruges), 18,197–200 (Ghent); Eddy Van Cauwenberghe, Rainer Metz, Franz Irsigler, and John Munro *Coinage in the Low Countries, 14th–18th Centuries* 3 vols (Leuven 1988) 1 *Antwerp-Bruges-Brussels-Ghent* 4–20, 73–83, 163, 190–219

TABLE 2

MARKET PRICES FOR FINE GOLD BULLION
Prices for gold at the Antwerp fairs and the official values of fine gold in the coinage of the
Burgundian-Hapsburg Low Countries from 1500 to 1540, with values of one kilogram of fine
gold in pounds groot Flemish

year	value of 1 kg fine gold on the Antwerp market in £ groot Flemish	official value of 1 kg fine gold in the Hapsburg gold coinage in £ groot Flemish according to the mint ordinances	market price as percentage of the official value of fine gold in the coinage
1500	91.979	94.978	96.84
1501	91.979	94.978	96.84
1502	91.979	94.978	96.84
1503	91.979	94.978	96.84
1504	91.979	94.978	96.84
1505	91.979	94.978	96.84
1506	91.979	94.978	96.84
1507	91.979	94.978	96.84
1508	91.979	94.978	96.84
1509	91.979	94.978	96.84
1510	91.979	94.978	96.84
1511	91.979	94.978	96.84
1512	93.214	94.978	98.14
1513	93.214	94.978	98.14
1514	94.482	94.978	99.48
1515	94.482	94.978	99.48
1516	94.482	94.978	99.48
1517	95.785	94.978	100.85
1518	95.785	94.978	100.85
1519	95.785	94.978	100.85

TABLE 2 (continued)

year	value of 1 kg fine gold on the Antwerp market in £ groot Flemish	official value of 1 kg fine gold in the Hapsburg gold coinage in £ groot Flemish according to the mint ordinances	market price as percentage of the official value of fine gold in the coinage
1520	95.785	94.978	100.85
1521	102.124	102.961	99.19
1522	107.666	102.961	104.57
1523	108.507	102.961	105.39
1524	110.229	102.961	107.06
1525	112.461	102.961	109.23
1526	105.352	102.961	102.32
1527	94.805	102.961	92.08
1528	94.805	102.961	92.08
1529	96.451	102.961	93.68
1530	96.451	102.961	93.68
1531	98.155	102.961	95.33
1532	99.920	102.961	97.05
1533	101.379	102.961	98.46
1534	102.881	102.961	99.92
1535	102.881	102.961	99.92
1536	104.428	102.961	101.42
1537	104.428	102.961	101.42
1538	102.124	102.961	99.19
1539	94.805	102.961	92.08
1540	96.451	102.961	93.68

NOTE

The coinage changes of February 1521 initially tried to set gold values, with 0.0293 grams fine gold in the Brabant groot (0.04395 g in the Flemish groot), but the government was forced to adjust the rate in August to 0.0276 g fine gold in the Brabant groot. According to Van der Wee, in March 1527 the government restored the original rate of February 1521, but it is not clear that this lower exchange rate held.

SOURCE

Herman Van der Wee *The Growth of the Antwerp Market and the European Economy, Fourteenth–Sixteenth Centuries* 3 vols (The Hague 1963) I 133–4 Table XVI

TABLE 3

THE GOLD COINS STRUCK IN ENGLAND, FRANCE, AND THE BURGUNDIAN-
HAPSBURG LOW COUNTRIES, FROM THE LATE FIFTEENTH TO THE
MID-SIXTEENTH CENTURY

A   ENGLAND, 1464–1526

date name of coin	fineness			number cut to		weight in grams	grams pure gold in coin
	carats (max 24)	grains (max 4)	per cent	Tower pound (349.914 g)	Troy pound (373.242 g)		
August 1464							
angel-noble	23	3.500	99.479	67.500	72.000	5.184	5.157
ryal, rose-noble	23	3.500	99.479	45.000	48.000	7.776	7.735
October 1489							
sovereign	23	3.500	99.479	22.500	24.000	15.552	15.471
August 1526							
angel-noble	23	3.500	99.479	67.500	72.000	5.184	5.157
ryal, rose-noble	23	3.500	99.479	45.000	48.000	7.776	7.735
sovereign	23	3.500	99.479	22.500	24.000	15.552	15.471
rose crown	23	3.500	99.479	110.000	117.333	3.181	3.164
November 1526*							
angel-noble	23	3.500	99.479	67.500	72.000	5.184	5.157
St George noble	23	3.500	99.479	75.938	81.000	4.608	4.584
crown	22	0.000	91.667	101.250	108.000	3.456	3.438

date name of coin	grams pure gold in £ sterling	official value in shillings and pence sterling	value in decimal £ sterling	nominal value	
				Tower pound in £ sterling	Troy pound in £ sterling
August 1464					
angel-noble	15.471	6s 8d	0.333	22.500	24.000
ryal, rose-noble	15.471	10s 0d	0.500	22.500	24.000
October 1489					
sovereign	15.471	20s 0d	1.000	22.500	24.000
August 1526					
angel-noble	14.064	7s 4d	0.367	24.750	26.400
ryal, rose-noble	14.064	11s 0d	0.550	24.750	26.400
sovereign	14.064	22s 0d	1.100	24.750	26.400
rose crown	14.064	4s 6d	0.225	24.750	26.400
November 1526*					
angel-noble	13.752	7s 6d	0.375	25.313	27.000
St George noble	13.752	6s 8d	0.333	25.313	27.000
crown	13.752	5s 0d	0.250	25.313	27.000

TABLE 3 (continued)

date name of coin	value of 1 kilogram		bimetallic ratio (gold:silver)
	fine gold in £ sterling	fine silver in £ sterling	
August 1464			
angel-noble	64.638	5.793	11.158
ryal, rose-noble	64.638	5.793	11.158
October 1489			
sovereign	64.638	5.793	11.158
August 1526			
angel-noble	71.102	5.793	12.274
ryal, rose-noble	71.102	5.793	12.274
sovereign	71.102	5.793	12.274
rose crown	71.102	5.793	12.274
November 1526*			
angel-noble	72.718	6.518	11.157
St George noble	72.718	6.518	11.157
crown	72.718	6.518	11.157

* In November 1526, the English mints switched the metrological unit from the Tower pound weighing 349.914 grams to the Troy pound of 373.242 g.

TABLE 3 (continued)

THE GOLD COINS STRUCK IN ENGLAND, FRANCE, AND THE BURGUNDIAN-
HAPSBURG LOW COUNTRIES, FROM THE LATE FIFTEENTH TO THE
MID-SIXTEENTH CENTURY

B   FRANCE, 1494–1550

date name of coin	fineness			taille: number cut to marc (244.753 g)	weight in grams	grams pure gold	
	carats (max 24)	grains (max 12)	per cent			in coin	in £ tournois
August 1494 écu au soleil	23	1.500	96.354	70.000	3.496	3.369	1.859
November 1507 écu épic	23	1.500	96.354	70.000	3.496	3.369	1.859
January 1515 écu au soleil	23	1.500	96.354	70.000	3.496	3.369	1.859
May 1519 écu au soleil	22	9.000	94.792	71.500	3.423	3.245	1.790
July 1519 écu au soleil	23	0.000	95.833	71.167	3.439	3.296	1.648
March 1541 écu croisée	23	0.000	95.833	71.167	3.439	3.296	1.465
January 1550 Henri d'or	23	0.000	95.833	67.000	3.653	3.501	1.400

date name of coin	official value in shillings and pence tournois	value in decimal £ tournois	traite of marc fine gold in £ tournois	value of 1 kilogram		bimetallic ratio (gold:silver)
				fine gold in £ tournois	fine silver in £ tournois	
August 1494 écu au soleil	36s 3d	1.813	131.676	537.994	46.045	11.684
November 1507 écu épic	36s 3d	1.813	131.676	537.994	48.887	11.005
January 1515 écu au soleil	36s 3d	1.813	131.676	537.994	48.887	11.005
May 1519 écu au soleil	36s 3d	1.813	136.714	558.581	55.374	10.087
July 1519 écu au soleil	40s 0d	2.000	148.522	606.823	55.374	10.959
March 1541 écu croisée	45s 0d	2.250	167.087	682.676	57.982	11.774
January 1550 Henri d'or	50s 0d	2.500	174.783	714.119	63.486	11.248

TABLE 3 (continued)

C   THE BURGUNDIAN-HAPSBURG LOW COUNTRIES, 1496–1556

date name of coin	fineness			taille: number cut to marc (244.753 g)	weight in grams	grams pure gold	
	carats (max 24)	grains (max 12)	per cent			in coin	in £ groot Flemish
10 April 1496							
toison d'or	23	9.500	99.132	54.50	4.491	4.452	11.130
Philippus florin	16	0.000	66.667	74.00	3.308	2.205	11.025
20 February 1500							
toison d'or	23	9.500	99.132	54.50	4.491	4.452	10.685
Philippus florin	16	0.000	66.667	74.00	3.308	2.205	10.584
Philippus florin	15	11.000	66.319	74.00	3.308	2.194	10.529
15 August 1521							
Philippus florin	15	11.000	66.319	74.00	3.308	2.194	9.713
15 August 1521 to 1556							
réal d'or	23	9.500	99.132	46.00	5.321	5.275	9.968
demi-réal	18	0.000	75.000	70.13	3.490	2.618	9.972
Carolus florin	14	0.000	58.333	84.00	2.914	1.700	9.712

date name of coin	official value in shillings and pence groot	value in decimal £ groot Flemish	traite of marc fine gold in £ groot Flemish	value of 1 kilogram		bimetallic ratio (gold : silver)
				fine gold in £ groot Flemish	fine silver in £ groot Flemish	
10 April 1496						
toison d'or	8s 0d	0.400	21.991	89.849	8.527	10.537
Philippus florin	4s 0d	0.200	22.200	90.704	8.527	10.638
20 February 1500						
toison d'or	8s 4d	0.417	22.907	93.593	8.527	10.976
Philippus florin	4s 2d	0.208	23.125	94.483	8.527	11.081
Philippus florin	4s 2d	0.208	23.246	94.978	8.527	11.139
15 August 1521						
Philippus florin	4s 6.2d	0.226	25.199	102.956	8.814	11.681
15 August 1521 to 1556						
réal d'or	10s 7d	0.529	24.555	100.325	8.814	11.382
demi-réal	5s 3d	0.263	24.544	100.280	8.814	11.377
Carolus florin	3s 6d	0.175	25.200	102.961	8.814	11.681

TABLE 3 (continued)

THE GOLD COINS STRUCK IN ENGLAND, FRANCE, AND THE BURGUNDIAN-
HAPSBURG LOW COUNTRIES, FROM THE LATE FIFTEENTH TO THE
MID-SIXTEENTH CENTURY

D   OFFICIAL VALUES OF THE PRINCIPAL GOLD COINS CIRCULATING
IN THE HAPSBURG LOW COUNTRIES, 1500-56

		value of coin			
country of origin		in d	in d	in £	in d
name		groot	tournois	tournois	sterling
of coin	years	(Flanders)	(France)	(France)	(England)
Hapsburg Low Countries					
Philippus florin	1500-20	50	294	1.225	36
Carolus florin	1521-6	42	247	1.029	25
Carolus florin	1526-40	42	247	1.029	26
France					
écu au soleil	1500-19	74	435	1.813	51
écu au soleil	1521-6	76	960	4.000	52
écu au soleil	1526-40	76	960	4.000	56
England					
angel-noble	1500-20	116	682	2.842	80
angel-noble	1521-6	116	732	3.050	80
angel-noble	1526-40	119	732	3.050	90
rose crown	August 1526	70	450	1.875	54
rose crown	1526-40	76	480	2.000	60
Italy					
ducat, florin	1500-20	79	498	2.075	54
ducat, florin	1521-6	80	546	2.275	54
ducat, florin	1526-40	80	546	2.275	56
Four Imperial Electors					
Rhenish florin	1500-20	56	345	1.438	39
Rhenish florin	1521-6	59	360	1.500	39
Rhenish florin	1526-40	59	360	1.500	40

TABLE 3 (continued)

NOTE

For an explanation and analysis of the English rose crown and the Hapsburg Carolus florin, see 574, 577–8 above; for explanations the other coins, see CWE 1 327 (Philippus), 315 (écu au soleil), 312 (angel-noble), 314 (Venetian ducat), 316 (Florentine florin), 316–17 (florin of the Rhine; Rijnsgulden, florin of the Four Imperial Electors).

SOURCES

England Christopher Challis *The Tudor Coinage* (Manchester and New York 1978), 'Lord Hastings to the Great Silver Recoinage, 1464–1699' in *A New History of the Royal Mint* ed C.E. Challis (Cambridge and New York 1992) 179–397, and ibidem 673–98 Appendix 1: Mint Output, 1220–1985; Albert Feavearyear *The Pound Sterling: A History of English Money* 2d ed rev E. Victor Morgan (Oxford 1963); *Tudor Royal Proclamations* ed Paul Hughes and James F. Larkin 3 vols (New Haven and London 1964–9) I *The Early Tudors (1485–1553)* (London, 1964)

France Adrien Blanchet and Adolphe E. Dieudonné *Manuel de numismatique française* 4 vols (Paris 1912–36) II Adolphe E. Dieudonné *Monnaies royales françaises depuis Hugues Capet jusqu'à la Révolution* (Paris 1916); Denis Richet 'Le cours officiel des monnaies étrangères circulant en France au XVIe siècle' *Revue historique* 225 (1961) 377–96; Frank Spooner *The International Economy and Monetary Movements in France, 1493–1725* (Cambridge 1972)

Hapsburg Netherlands Algemeen Rijksarchief, Rekenkamer, registers nos 17,880–5 (Antwerp mint accounts), nos 18,123–56 (Bruges mint accounts); Louis Deschamps de Pas 'Essai sur l'histoire monétaire des comtes de Flandre de la Maison d'Autriche et classement de leurs monnaies (1482–1556): Philippe-le-Beau (1482–1506): Suite' *Revue numismatique* nouvelle série 15 (1874–77) 89–93 and 'Essai sur l'histoire monétaire des comtes de Flandre de la Maison d'Autriche et classement de leurs monnaies (1482–1556): Charles-Quint (1506–1556)' *Revue belge de numismatique* 32 (1876) 73–9, 82–3. See also: CWE 1, 316–17, 336–9; CWE 8 349–50.

TABLE 4

THE SILVER COINS STRUCK IN ENGLAND, FRANCE, AND THE
BURGUNDIAN-HAPSBURG LOW COUNTRIES FROM THE LATE FIFTEENTH
TO THE MID-SIXTEENTH CENTURY

A ENGLAND, 1464–1526

		number struck to		fineness		
date name of coin	value in d sterling	Tower pound (349.914 g)	Troy pound (373.242 g)	in ounces (out of 12 oz)	in penny- weight (out of 20 dwt)	per cent
August 1464						
penny	1	450.000	480.000	11	2	92.500
1504						
shilling	12	37.500	40.000	11	2	92.500
November 1526*						
penny	1	506.250	540.000	11	2	92.500
shilling	12	42.188	45.000	11	2	92.500

	weight of coin		grams pure silver in coin	value of Tower pound		value of Troy pound		value of 1 kg
date name of coin	in Troy grains	in grams		in shil- lings and pence	in deci- mal £ sterling	in shillings sterling	in deci- mal £ sterling	pure sil- ver in £ sterling
August 1464								
penny	12	0.778	0.719	37s 6d	1.875	40	2.000	5.793
1504								
shilling	144	9.331	8.631	37s 6d	1.875	40	2.000	5.793
November 1526*								
penny	10.667	0.691	0.639	42s 2d	2.108	45	2.250	6.517
shilling	128	8.294	7.672	42s 2d	2.108	45	2.250	6.517

SOURCES

See the sources for Table 3.

---

* In November 1526, the English mints switched the metrological unit from the Tower
  pound weighing 349.914 grams to the Troy pound of 373.242 g.

TABLE 4 (continued)

B FRANCE, 1488–1541

date / name of coin	value in d tournois	taille: number cut to marc (244.753 g)	weight in grams	fineness (titre) in deniers (max 12)	fineness (titre) in grains (max 24)	type
April 1488						
blanc couronne (douzain)	12	86.000	2.846	4	12	AR
November 1488						
karolus	10	92.000	2.660	4	0	AR
May 1489						
gros de roi	36	69.000	3.547	11	12	AR
April 1498						
blanc couronne (douzain)	12	86.000	2.846	4	12	AR
November 1507						
grand blanc (douzain)	12	86.000	2.846	4	12	AR
February 1512						
gros	30	45.000	5.439	6	0	AR
demi-gros	15	68.000	3.599	4	12	AR
Ludovicus	10	92.000	2.660	4	0	AR
April 1513						
teston	120	25.500	9.598	11	18	AR
January 1515						
teston	120	25.500	9.598	11	18	AR
blanc couronne (douzain)	12	86.000	2.846	4	12	AR
July 1519						
blanc couronne (douzain)	12	92.000	2.660	4	6	AR
dizain	10	98.000	2.497	3	18	AR
September 1521						
teston	120	25.500	9.598	11	6	AR
February 1540						
douzain	12	92.000	2.660	4	4	AR
March 1541						
douzain	12	91.000	2.690	3	16	AR

SOURCES

See the sources for Table 3.

TABLE 4 (continued)

THE SILVER COINS STRUCK IN ENGLAND, FRANCE, AND THE
BURGUNDIAN-HAPSBURG LOW COUNTRIES FROM THE LATE FIFTEENTH
TO THE MID-SIXTEENTH CENTURY

B   FRANCE, 1488–1541 (continued)

date name of coin	fineness (titre)		grams pure silver		traite per marc AR in £ tournois	traite per marc AF in £ tournois	value of 1 kg pure silver in £ tournois
	per cent AR	per cent AF	in coin	per d tournois			
April 1488							
blanc couronne (douzain)	37.50	35.94	1.023	0.085	11.467	11.965	48.887
November 1488							
karolus	33.33	31.94	0.850	0.085	11.500	12.000	49.029
May 1489							
gros de roi	95.83	91.84	3.258	0.090	10.800	11.270	46.045
April 1498							
blanc couronne (douzain)	37.50	35.94	1.023	0.085	11.467	11.965	48.887
November 1507							
grand blanc (douzain)	37.50	35.94	1.023	0.085	11.467	11.965	48.887
February 1512							
gros	50.00	47.92	2.606	0.087	11.250	11.739	47.963
demi-gros	37.50	35.94	1.294	0.086	11.333	11.826	48.318
Ludovicus	33.33	31.94	0.850	0.085	11.500	12.000	49.029
April 1513							
teston	97.92	93.84	9.007	0.075	13.021	13.587	55.515
January 1515							
teston	97.92	93.84	9.007	0.075	13.021	13.587	55.515
blanc couronne (douzain)	37.50	35.94	1.023	0.085	11.467	11.965	48.887
July 1519							
blanc couronne (douzain)	35.42	33.94	0.903	0.075	12.988	13.553	55.374
dizain	31.25	29.95	0.748	0.075	13.067	13.635	55.708
September 1521							
teston	93.75	89.84	8.623	0.072	13.600	14.191	57.982
February 1540							
douzain	34.72	32.28	0.885	0.074	13.248	13.824	56.481
March 1541							
douzain	30.56	29.28	0.788	0.066	14.891	15.538	63.486

SOURCES

See the sources for Table 3.

TABLE 4 (continued)

C THE HAPSBURG LOW COUNTRIES, 1496–1556

date name of coin	value in d groot Flemish	taille: number cut to marc (244.753 g)	weight in grams	fineness (titre) in deniers (max 12)	fineness (titre) in grains (max 24)	type
10 April 1496						
toison d'argent	6	72.00	3.399	11	0.00	AR
double patard	4	79.00	3.098	8	0.00	AR
patard, stuiver	2	79.00	3.098	4	0.00	AR
20 February 1500						
toison d'argent	6	72.00	3.399	11	0.00	AR
double patard	4	79.00	3.098	8	0.00	AR
patard, stuiver	2	80.00	3.059	4	0.00	AR
réal, royal d'Espaigne	6	71.25	3.435	11	5.00	AR
groot	1	134.00	1.827	3	6.00	AR
demi groot	1/2	224.00	1.093	2	16.00	AR
gigot, quart de gros	1/4	316.00	0.775	1	20.00	AR
quadruple mite	1/6	162.00	1.511	0	12.00	AR
double mite	1/12	226.00	1.083	0	7.50	AR
20 February 1521						
double Carolus, réal	6	80.00	3.059	11	5.00	AF
Carolus, demi-réal	3	78.50	3.118	5	12.00	AF
patard, stuiver	2	80.00	3.059	3	17.00	AF
23 August 1500 [to 1556]						
réal, royal d'Espaigne	6 1/2	71.25	3.435	11	5.00	AR

NOTE

By the monetary ordinance of February 1521, the monetary authorities of the Hapsburg Low Countries changed the standard of silver fineness from *argent-le-roi* (23/24 or 95.833 per cent pure) to the new standard of *argent fin* (100.00 per cent pure). See 580–1 above.

TABLE 4 (continued)

THE SILVER COINS STRUCK IN ENGLAND, FRANCE, AND THE
BURGUNDIAN-HAPSBURG LOW COUNTRIES FROM THE LATE FIFTEENTH
TO THE MID-SIXTEENTH CENTURY

C   THE HAPSBURG LOW COUNTRIES, 1496–1556 (continued)

date name of coin	fineness (titre) per cent AR	per cent AF	grams pure silver in coin	per d groot Flemish	traite per marc AR in £ groot Flemish	traite per marc AF in £ groot Flemish	value of 1 kg pure silver in £ groot Flemish
10 April 1496							
toison d'argent	91.67	87.85	2.986	0.498	1.964	2.049	8.372
double patard	66.67	63.89	1.979	0.495	1.975	2.061	8.420
patard, stuiver	33.33	31.94	0.990	0.495	1.975	2.061	8.420
20 February 1500							
toison d'argent	91.67	87.85	2.986	0.498	1.964	2.049	8.372
double patard	66.67	63.89	1.979	0.495	1.975	2.061	8.420
patard, stuiver	33.33	31.94	0.977	0.489	2.000	2.087	8.527
réal, royal d'Espaigne	93.40	89.51	3.075	0.473	2.066	2.156	8.808
groot	27.08	25.95	0.474	0.474	2.062	2.151	8.789
demi groot	22.22	21.30	0.233	0.466	2.100	2.191	8.953
gigot, quart de gros	15.28	14.64	0.113	0.454	2.155	2.248	9.186
quadruple mite	4.17	3.99	0.060	0.362	2.700	2.817	11.511
double mite	2.60	2.50	0.027	0.324	3.013	3.144	12.847
20 February 1521							
double Carolus, réal		93.40	2.858	0.476		2.141	8.749
Carolus, demi-réal		45.83	1.429	0.476		2.141	8.747
patard, stuiver		30.90	0.945	0.473		2.157	8.814
23 Aug 1500 [to 1556]							
réal, royal d'Espaigne							

NOTE

By the monetary ordinance of February 1521, the monetary authorities of the Hapsburg Low
Countries changed the standard of silver fineness from *argent-le-roi* (23/24 or 95.833 per cent
pure) to the new standard of *argent fin* (100.00 per cent pure). See 580–1 above.

SOURCES

See the sources for Table 3.

TABLE 4 (continued)

D　THE RELATIVE VALUES OF THE PRINCIPAL SILVER COINS FROM 1500 TO 1540 IN ENGLAND, FRANCE, AND THE HAPSBURG LOW COUNTRIES

year	England silver penny (1d sterling): grams pure silver	silver content per cent change from previous coin	France silver douzain (12d tournois): grams pure silver	silver content per cent change from previous coin	Hapsburg Low Countries patard/ stuiver (2d groot Flemish): grams pure silver	silver content per cent change from previous coin	England penny: value in d groot Flemish	France douzain: value in d groot Flemish
1499	0.719		1.023		0.977		1.472	2.093
1519	0.719	0.00	0.903	−11.71	0.977	0.00	1.472	1.848
1521	0.719	0.00	0.903	0.00	0.945	−3.26	1.522	1.910
1526	0.639	−11.12	0.903	0.00	0.945	0.00	1.352	1.910
1540	0.639	0.00	0.885	−1.96	0.945	0.00	1.352	1.873
1541	0.639	0.00	0.788	11.03	0.945	0.00	1.352	1.666

year	value of 1 kg fine silver in £ sterling (England)	in £ tournois (France)	in £ groot (Flanders)*	English: French ratio per kg silver	Flemish: French ratio per kg silver	English: Flemish ratio per kg silver	Flemish: English ratio per kg silver
1499	5.793	48.887	8.527	8.439	5.733	1.472	0.679
1519	5.793	55.374	8.527	9.559	6.494	1.472	0.679
1521	5.793	55.374	8.814	9.559	6.282	1.522	0.657
1526	6.518	55.374	8.814	8.496	6.282	1.352	0.739
1540	6.518	56.481	8.814	8.666	6.408	1.352	0.739
1541	6.518	63.486	8.814	9.741	7.203	1.352	0.739

SOURCES

See the sources for Tables 1 and 2.

* 1 pound groot of Flanders = 1.5 pound groot of Brabant

TABLE 5

A   THE VAN DER WEE BASKET OF CONSUMABLES PRICE INDEX, 1501–5
For the Antwerp-Lier-Brussels region, with the values of the ten commodities in the basket in deniers of the Brabant pond groot and the Flemish pond groot*
Index: mean 1501–5 = 100

years	rye 126.00 litres	barley 162.00 litres	beef 23.50 kg	her-rings 40.00 fish	cheese 4.70 kg	butter 4.80 kg	char-coal 162.00 litres	tallow candles 1.33 kg	woollen cloth 1.13 metres	linen cloth 1.80 metres	total in d groot Brabant
1501	54.80	53.00	56.30	11.50	7.30	23.40	11.40	8.20	25.40	23.40	274.700
1502	78.10	57.00	64.30	8.60	7.40	21.80	12.60	8.90	30.60	21.30	310.600
1503	48.70	57.00	64.30	8.60	9.50	24.60	10.20	9.00	30.10	22.40	284.400
1504	43.30	61.20	64.30	10.60	9.20	23.90	8.80	9.30	28.80	24.40	283.800
1505	48.70	57.00	75.00	16.60	7.60	23.90	7.80	9.30	33.60	25.50	305.000
1501–5											
Brab gr	54.72	57.04	64.84	11.18	8.20	23.52	10.16	8.94	29.70	23.40	291.700
Flem gr	36.48	38.03	43.23	7.45	5.47	15.68	6.77	5.96	19.80	15.60	194.467
per cent	18.76	19.55	22.23	3.83	2.81	8.06	3.48	3.06	10.18	8.02	100.000
1451–75											
Brab gr	42.40	39.71	54.70	9.99	5.97	19.73	10.57	7.61	24.84	17.00	232.524
Flem gr	28.27	26.47	36.47	6.66	3.98	13.15	7.05	5.07	16.56	11.33	155.016
per cent	18.24	17.08	23.53	4.30	2.57	8.48	4.54	3.27	10.68	7.31	100.000

	grains		meat-fish-dairy		industrial	
years	total value in d groot Brabant	price index 1451–75 = 100 = 82.116d	total value in d groot Brabant	price index 1451–75 = 100 = 90.388d	total value in d groot Brabant	price index 1451–75 = 100 = 60.02d
1501	107.800	131.278	98.500	108.975	68.400	113.962
1502	135.100	164.523	102.100	112.957	73.400	122.293
1503	105.700	128.720	107.000	118.379	71.700	119.460
1504	104.500	127.259	108.000	119.485	71.300	118.794
1505	105.700	128.720	123.100	136.191	76.200	126.958
1501–5						
Brab gr	111.760	136.100	107.740	119.197	72.200	120.293
Flem gr	74.507		71.827		48.133	
per cent	38.313		36.935		24.751	
1451–75						
Brab gr	82.116	100.000	90.388	100.000	60.020	100.000
Flem gr	54.744	100.000	60.259	100.000	40.010	100.000
per cent	35.315		38.873		25.812	

* Value = price times quantity

TABLE 5 (continued)

| years | basket of consumables | | | | |
	total value in d groot Brabant	price index 1451–75 = 100	total value in d groot Flemish	price index 1451–75 = 100	price index 1501–5 = 100
1501	274.700	118.138	183.133	118.138	94.172
1502	310.600	133.578	207.067	133.578	106.479
1503	284.400	122.310	189.600	122.310	97.497
1504	283.800	122.052	189.200	122.052	97.292
1505	305.000	131.169	203.333	131.169	104.559
1501–5					
Brab gr	291.700	125.449	194.467	125.449	100.000
Flem gr			194.467	125.449	
1451–75					
Brab gr	232.524	100.000			
Flem gr			155.016	100.000	

SOURCE

Herman Van der Wee 'Prijzen en lonen als ontwikkelingsvariabelen: Een vergelijkend onderzoek tussen Engeland en de Zuidelijke Nederlanden, 1400–1700,' in *Album offert à Charles Verlinden à l'occasion de ses trente ans de professoriat* (Ghent 1975) 413–35, republished in English translation as 'Prices and Wages as Development Variables: A Comparison between England and the Southern Netherlands, 1400–1700' *Acta Historiae Neerlandicae* 10 (1978) 58–78. Only the Dutch version, however, contains the specific annual data in tabular form.

TABLE 5 (continued)

COMMODITY PRICES IN SIXTEENTH-CENTURY BRABANT

B   THE VAN DER WEE 'BASKET OF CONSUMABLES' PRICE INDEX
IN QUINQUENNIAL MEANS FROM 1501–5 TO 1536–40
For the Antwerp-Lier-Brussels region, with the values of the main components (grains,
meat-fish-dairy, and industrial goods) in the basket in deniers of the Brabant pond groot
and the Flemish pond groot*
Index: mean 1501–5 = 100 (and a comparison with index 1451–75 = 100)

years	grains		meat-fish-dairy		industrial	
	total value in d groot Brabant	price index 1501–5 = 100 = 111.76d	total value in d groot Brabant	price index 1501–5 = 100 = 107.74d	total value in d groot Brabant	price index 1501–5 = 100 = 72.20d
1501–5	111.760	100.000	107.740	100.000	72.200	100.000
1506–10	88.560	79.241	101.800	94.487	76.580	106.066
1511–15	120.960	108.232	114.360	106.144	85.340	118.199
1516–20	133.160	119.148	131.520	122.072	84.720	117.341
1521–5	177.360	158.697	147.740	137.126	93.300	129.224
1526–30	166.120	148.640	155.440	144.273	93.540	129.557
1531–5	170.080	152.183	162.800	151.105	71.700	99.307
1536–40	189.120	169.220	168.200	156.117	74.340	102.964

year	basket of consumables total value		basket of consumables price index in d groot Flemish	
	in d groot Brabant	in d groot Flemish	1451–75 = 100 = 232.52d Brabant = 155.016d Flemish	1501–5 = 100 = 291.700d Brabant = 194.467d Flemish
1501–5	291.700	194.467	125.449	100.000
1506–10	266.940	177.960	114.801	91.512
1511–15	320.660	213.773	137.904	109.928
1516–20	349.400	232.933	150.264	119.781
1521–5	418.400	278.933	179.938	143.435
1526–30	415.100	276.733	178.519	142.304
1531–5	404.580	269.720	173.995	138.697
1536–40	431.660	287.773	185.641	147.981

SOURCE

Herman Van der Wee 'Prijzen en lonen als ontwikkelingsvariabelen: Een vergelijkend onderzoek tussen Engeland en de Zuidelijke Nederlanden, 1400–1700,' in *Album offert à Charles
Verlinden à l'occasion de ses trente ans de professoriat* (Ghent 1975) 413–35, republished in English
translation as 'Prices and Wages as Development Variables: A Comparison between England
and the Southern Netherlands, 1400–1700' *Acta Historiae Neerlandicae* 10 (1978) 58–78

* Value = price times quantity

TABLE 6

THE PURCHASING POWER OF COINS AND WAGES IN THE SOUTHERN LOW COUNTRIES, 1501–40

A   RED RHINE WINE
Priced by the gelte of Lier (= 2.840 litres)

		litres purchased with					
years (Easter)	price per litre in d groot Flemish	Burgundian-Hapsburg patard (= 2d groot)	French blanc or douzain (= 12d tournois)[a]	English penny (= 1d sterling)[b]	Burgundian-Hapsburg Philippus florin[c]	Burgundian-Hapsburg Carolus florin[d]	French écu au soleil[e]
1501–5	2.852	0.701	0.734	0.516	17.531		24.894
1506–10	2.923	0.684	0.716	0.504	17.108		24.294
1511–15	3.415	0.586	0.613	0.431	14.639		20.788
1516–20	3.310	0.604	0.632	0.445	15.106		21.502
1521–5	3.838	0.521	0.545	0.414	14.070	10.943	19.802
1526–30	3.451	0.580	0.607	0.409	15.649	12.171	22.024
1531–5	3.521	0.568	0.594	0.401	15.336	11.928	21.584
1536–40	3.468	0.577	0.604	0.407	15.571	12.110	21.914

	litres purchased with		master mason's daily wage in d groot Flemish	litres purchased with daily wage	index (1501–5 = 100)		
years (Easter)	Italian ducat, florin[f]	English angel-noble[g]			quantity	wine price	Van der Wee CPI
1501–5	27.699	40.672	8.333	2.922	100.00	100.00	100.000
1506–10	27.031	39.692	8.333	2.851	97.59	102.47	91.512
1511–15	23.130	33.963	9.333	2.720	83.51	119.75	109.928
1516–20	23.868	35.047	10.000	3.021	86.17	116.05	119.781
1521–5	20.844	31.006	10.267	2.676	74.31	134.57	143.435
1526–30	23.184	34.486	10.267	2.676	82.65	120.99	142.304
1531–5	22.720	33.796	10.067	2.858	81.00	123.46	138.697
1536–40	23.068	34.313	12.133	3.485	82.24	121.60	147.981

TABLE 6 (continued)

THE PURCHASING POWER OF COINS AND WAGES IN
THE SOUTHERN LOW COUNTRIES, 1501–40

A   RED RHINE WINE (continued)

NOTES ON COINAGE VALUES

a value of the French blanc or douzain in d groot Flemish
  1500–18   2.093
  1519-20   1.848
  1521-39   1.910
  1540-1   1.873
b value of the English sterling penny in d groot Flemish
  1500–20   1.472
  1521–5   1.522
  1526–40   1.352
c value of the Burgundian-Hapsburg Philippus florin in d groot Flemish, estimated only
  by relative gold contents
  1500–20   50.000
  1521–40   54.000
d value of the Burgundian-Hapsburg Carolus florin in d groot Flemish, originally issued
  February 1521 at 40d
  1521-48   42.000
e value of the French écu au soleil in d groot Flemish
  1500–18 (3.369 g fine gold)   71.000
  1519–20 (3.245 g fine gold)   72.000
  1521–48 (3.296 g fine gold)   76.000
f value of the Italian florin and ducat in d groot Flemish
  1500–20 (3.559 g fine gold)   79.000
  1521–48 (3.559 g fine gold)   80.000
g value of the English angel-noble in d groot Flemish
  1500–20 (5.157 g fine gold)   116.000
  1521–6 (5.157 g fine gold)   119.000
  1527–48 (5.157 g fine gold)   119.000

SOURCE

Herman Van der Wee *The Growth of the Antwerp Market and the European Economy, Fourteenth-Sixteenth Centuries* 3 vols (The Hague 1963) I 294–9 Appendix 24

TABLE 6 (continued)

B   BUTTER

From Brussels, priced per 100 lb weight of Brussels (1.0 lb of Brussels = 467.670 g)

years (from 1 May)	price per kilogram in d groot Flemish	kilograms purchased with					
		Burgundian-Hapsburg patard (= 2d groot)	French blanc or douzain (= 12d tournois)[a]	English penny (= 1d sterling)[b]	Burgundian-Hapsburg Philippus florin[c]	Burgundian-Hapsburg Carolus florin[d]	French écu au soleil[e]
1501–5	3.353	0.597	0.624	0.439	14.913		21.176
1506–10	3.443	0.581	0.608	0.428	14.524		20.624
1511–15	4.743	0.422	0.441	0.310	10.543		14.971
1516–20	4.811	0.416	0.415	0.306	10.393		14.834
1521–5	4.845	0.413	0.394	0.314	11.145	8.668	15.685
1526–30	4.738	0.422	0.403	0.285	11.396	8.864	16.039
1531–5	4.995	0.400	0.382	0.271	10.811	8.408	15.215
1536–40	4.892	0.409	0.389	0.276	11.038	8.585	15.534

years (from 1 May)	kilograms purchased with		master mason's daily wage in d groot Flemish	kilograms purchased with daily wage	index (1501–5 = 100)		
	Italian ducat, florin[f]	English angel-noble[g]			quantity	butter price	Van der Wee CPI
1501–5	23.562	34.598	8.333	2.485	100.000	100.000	100.000
1506–10	22.948	33.695	8.333	2.421	97.391	102.679	91.512
1511–15	16.657	24.459	9.333	1.959	70.694	141.454	109.928
1516–20	16.420	24.111	10.000	2.079	69.689	143.495	119.781
1521–5	16.511	24.560	10.267	2.114	69.197	144.515	143.435
1526–30	16.883	25.114	10.600	2.229	70.758	141.327	142.304
1531–5	16.016	23.824	10.067	2.015	67.123	148.980	138.697
1536–40	16.352	24.324	12.133	2.471	68.531	145.918	147.981

NOTES ON COINAGE VALUES

See the notes for Table 6A.

SOURCE

Van der Wee *Antwerp Market* (Table 6A above) I 210–15 Appendix 8

TABLE 6 (continued)

THE PURCHASING POWER OF COINS AND WAGES IN
THE SOUTHERN LOW COUNTRIES, 1501–40

C   SALTED BEEF

From Mechelen, priced per 100 lb weight of Mechelen (1.0 lb of Mechelen = 469.247 g)

years (Nov- ember)	price per kilogram in d groot Flemish	kilograms purchased with					
		Burgundian- Hapsburg patard (= 2d groot)	French blanc or douzain (= 12d tournois)[a]	English penny (= 1d sterling)[b]	Burgundian- Hapsburg Philippus florin[c]	Burgundian- Hapsburg Carolus florin[d]	French écu au soleil[e]
1501–5	1.842	1.086	1.136	0.799	27.140		38.539
1506–10	1.664	1.202	1.258	0.885	30.052		42.673
1511–15	1.615	1.238	1.296	0.911	30.951		43.950
1516–20	2.131	0.938	0.933	0.691	23.462		33.503
1521–5	2.370	0.844	0.806	0.642	22.787	17.723	32.071
1526–30	2.719	0.735	0.702	0.497	19.858	15.445	27.949
1531–5	2.941	0.680	0.650	0.460	18.362	14.281	25.843
1536–40	3.030	0.660	0.628	0.446	17.820	13.860	25.079

years (Nov- ember)	kilograms purchased with		master mason's daily wage in d groot Flemish	kilograms purchased with daily wage	index (1501–5 = 100)		
	Italian ducat, florin[f]	English angel- noble[g]			quan- tity	salted beef price	Van der Wee CPI
1501–5	42.882	62.966	8.333	4.523	100.000	100.000	100.000
1506–10	47.482	69.720	8.333	5.009	110.727	90.312	91.512
1511–15	48.902	71.806	9.333	5.768	114.039	87.689	109.928
1516–20	37.071	54.433	10.000	4.692	86.448	115.676	119.781
1521–5	33.759	50.216	10.267	4.340	77.741	128.632	143.435
1526–30	29.420	43.762	10.600	3.885	67.749	147.603	142.304
1531–5	27.203	40.464	10.067	3.422	62.643	159.634	138.697
1536–40	26.399	39.269	12.133	3.996	60.793	164.492	147.981

NOTES ON COINAGE VALUES

See the notes for Table 6A.

SOURCE

Van der Wee *Antwerp Market* (Table 6A above) I 225–6 Appendix 10

TABLE 6 (continued)

D   FLEMISH RED HERRINGS
Dry smoked red Flemish herrings, priced per stroo of 500 fish

years (Lent)	price per fish in d groot Flemish	Burgundian-Hapsburg patard (= 2d groot)	French blanc or douzain (= 12d tournois)[a]	English penny (= 1d sterling)[b]	Burgundian-Hapsburg Philippus florin[c]	Burgundian-Hapsburg Carolus florin[d]	French écu au soleil[e]
					number purchased with		
1501–5	0.172	11.628	12.169	8.558	290.698		412.791
1506–10	0.201	9.949	10.412	7.322	248.736		353.205
1511–15	0.243	8.234	8.617	6.060	205.847		292.303
1516–20	0.224	8.945	8.842	6.583	223.614		318.576
1521–5	0.328	6.090	5.816	4.633	164.434	127.893	231.425
1526–30	0.254	7.862	7.508	5.316	212.264	165.094	298.742
1531–5	0.230	8.681	8.290	5.870	234.375	182.292	329.861
1536–40	0.266	7.519	7.152	5.084	203.008	157.895	285.714

years (Lent)	Italian ducat, florin[f]	English angel-noble[g]	master mason's daily wage in d groot Flemish	number purchased with daily wage	quantity	herrings price	Van der Wee CPI
	number purchased with				index (1501–5 = 100)		
1501–5	459.302	674.419	8.333	48.450	100.000	100.000	100.000
1506–10	393.002	577.067	8.333	41.456	85.565	116.870	91.512
1511–15	325.239	477.565	9.333	38.341	70.811	141.220	109.928
1516–20	353.309	518.784	10.000	44.723	76.923	130.000	119.781
1521–5	243.605	362.363	10.267	31.296	52.375	190.930	143.435
1526–30	314.465	467.767	10.600	41.819	67.610	147.907	142.304
1531–5	347.222	516.493	10.067	43.642	74.653	133.953	138.697
1536–40	300.752	447.368	12.133	45.478	64.662	154.651	147.981

NOTES ON COINAGE VALUES

See the notes for Table 6A.

SOURCE

Van der Wee Antwerp Market (Table 6A above) I 277–85 Appendix 22

TABLE 6 (continued)

THE PURCHASING POWER OF COINS AND WAGES IN
THE SOUTHERN LOW COUNTRIES, 1501–40

E   EGGS
In Brussels, priced per hundred

years (from 1 May)	price per egg in d groot Flemish	number purchased with					
		Burgundian-Hapsburg patard (= 2d groot)	French blanc or douzain (= 12d tournois)[a]	English penny (= 1d sterling)[b]	Burgundian-Hapsburg Philippus florin[c]	Burgundian-Hapsburg Carolus florin[d]	French écu au soleil[e]
1501–5	0.108	18.515	19.376	13.626	462.868		657.272
1506–10	0.108	18.452	19.310	13.580	461.311		655.062
1511–15	0.111	18.001	18.838	13.248	450.018		639.026
1516–20	0.124	16.072	15.950	11.828	401.789		573.813
1521–5	0.127	15.700	14.994	11.944	423.902	329.701	596.603
1526–30	0.124	16.086	15.363	10.877	434.316	337.802	611.260
1531–5	0.139	14.388	13.742	9.729	388.489	302.158	546.763
1536–40	0.160	12.526	11.911	8.470	338.205	263.048	475.992

years (from 1 May)	number purchased with		master mason's daily wage in d groot Flemish	number purchased with daily wage	index (1501–5 = 100)		
	Italian ducat, florin[f]	English angel-noble[g]			quan-tity	eggs price	Van der Wee CPI
1501–5	731.331	1073.853	8.333	77.145	100.000	100.000	100.000
1506–10	728.872	1070.242	8.333	76.885	99.664	100.337	91.512
1511–15	711.029	1044.042	9.333	83.523	97.224	102.855	109.928
1516–20	634.826	932.150	10.000	80.358	86.804	115.202	119.781
1521–5	628.003	934.154	10.267	80.378	84.798	117.928	143.435
1526–30	643.432	957.105	10.600	85.008	86.881	115.100	142.304
1531–5	575.540	856.115	10.067	72.379	77.714	128.677	138.697
1536–40	501.044	745.303	12.133	75.809	67.655	147.809	147.981

NOTES ON COINAGE VALUES

See the notes for Table 6A.

SOURCE

Van der Wee *Antwerp Market* (Table 6A above) I 204–8 Appendix 7

TABLE 6 (continued)

F WHEAT

In Lier, priced per viertel of Lier (viertel = 86.606 litres; bushel = 36.369 litres)

		litres purchased with					
years (from harvest, average)	price per litre in d groot Flemish	Burgundian-Hapsburg patard (= 2d groot)	French blanc or douzain (= 12d tournois)[a]	English penny (= 1d sterling)[b]	Burgundian-Hapsburg Philippus florin[c]	Burgundian-Hapsburg Carolus florin[d]	French écu au soleil[e]
1501–5	0.420	4.762	4.984	3.505	119.052		169.053
1506–10	0.411	4.871	5.098	3.585	121.774		172.920
1511–15	0.413	4.846	5.071	3.566	121.143		172.023
1516–20	0.463	4.320	4.312	3.179	107.988		153.760
1521–5	0.718	2.787	2.662	2.120	75.256	58.533	105.916
1526–30	0.586	3.415	3.261	2.309	92.195	71.707	129.755
1531–5	0.656	3.049	2.912	2.062	82.323	64.029	115.862
1536–40	0.707	2.829	2.691	1.913	76.395	59.419	107.519

	litres purchased with		master mason's daily wage in d groot Flemish	litres purchased with daily wage	index (1501–5 = 100)		
years (from harvest, average)	Italian ducat, florin[f]	English angel-noble[g]			quantity	wheat price	Van der Wee CPI
1501–5	188.101	276.199	8.333	19.842	100.000	100.000	100.000
1506–10	192.404	282.517	8.333	20.296	102.287	97.764	91.512
1511–15	191.406	281.052	9.333	22.778	101.757	98.273	109.928
1516–20	170.620	250.531	10.000	21.598	90.707	110.246	119.781
1521–5	111.491	165.842	10.267	14.364	58.531	170.850	143.435
1526–30	136.585	203.170	10.600	17.975	71.705	139.461	142.304
1531–5	121.960	181.416	10.067	15.321	64.027	156.184	138.697
1536–40	113.178	168.353	12.133	17.154	59.417	168.303	147.981

NOTES ON COINAGE VALUES

See the notes for Table 6A.

SOURCE

Van der Wee *Antwerp Market* (Table 6A above) I 183–6 Appendix 3

TABLE 6 (continued)

THE PURCHASING POWER OF COINS AND WAGES IN
THE SOUTHERN LOW COUNTRIES, 1501–40

G PEAS

In Mechelen, priced by the viertel of Mechelen (= 86.499 litres)

years (from March)	price per litre in d groot Flemish	litres purchased with					
		Burgundian-Hapsburg patard (= 2d groot)	French blanc or douzain (= 12d tournois)[a]	English penny (= 1d sterling)[b]	Burgundian-Hapsburg Philippus florin[c]	Burgundian-Hapsburg Carolus florin[d]	French écu au soleil[e]
1501–5	0.423	4.727	4.947	3.479	118.168		167.799
1506–10	0.355	5.626	5.888	4.141	140.649		199.721
1511–15	0.458	4.369	4.572	3.215	109.216		155.087
1516–20	0.428	4.669	4.646	3.437	116.735		166.187
1521–5	0.541	3.698	3.532	2.813	99.844	77.656	140.521
1526–30	0.475	4.213	4.023	2.848	113.741	88.465	160.079
1531–5	0.639	3.128	2.988	2.115	84.466	65.695	118.877
1536–40	0.567	3.527	3.351	2.385	95.230	74.067	134.027

years (from March)	litres purchased with		master mason's daily wage in d groot Flemish	litres purchased with daily wage	index (1501–5 = 100)		
	Italian ducat, florin[f]	English angel-noble[g]			quan-tity	peas price	Van der Wee CPI
1501–5	186.705	274.150	8.333	19.695	103.925	100.000	100.000
1506–10	222.225	326.305	8.333	23.441	119.024	84.016	91.512
1511–15	172.561	253.381	9.333	20.595	92.424	108.197	109.928
1516–20	184.441	270.825	10.000	23.347	98.787	101.228	119.781
1521–5	147.916	220.026	10.267	19.004	78.234	127.821	143.435
1526–30	168.505	250.651	10.600	22.155	89.123	112.204	142.304
1531–5	125.134	186.137	10.067	15.729	66.184	151.093	138.697
1536–40	141.081	209.858	12.133	21.380	74.619	134.015	147.981

NOTES ON COINAGE VALUES

See the notes for Table 6A.

SOURCE

Van der Wee *Antwerp Market* (Table 6A above) I 199–203 Appendix 6

TABLE 6 (continued)

H LOAF SUGAR
In Antwerp, priced per pound (= 470.156 grams)

years (October)	price per kilogram in d groot Flemish	kilograms purchased with					
		Burgundian-Hapsburg patard (= 2d groot)	French blanc or douzain (= 12d tournois)[a]	English penny (= 1d sterling)[b]	Burgundian-Hapsburg Philippus florin[c]	Burgundian-Hapsburg Carolus florin[d]	French écu au soleil[e]
1501–5	8.150	0.245	0.257	0.181	6.135		8.711
1506–10	9.296	0.215	0.225	0.158	5.379		7.638
1511–15	15.952	0.125	0.131	0.092	3.134		4.451
1516–20	14.889	0.134	0.134	0.099	3.358		4.780
1521–5	16.199	0.123	0.118	0.094	3.334	2.593	4.692
1526–30	17.441	0.115	0.110	0.078	3.096	2.408	4.358
1531–5	12.016	0.166	0.159	0.113	4.494	3.495	6.325
1536–40	16.378	0.122	0.116	0.083	3.297	2.564	4.641

years (October)	kilograms purchased with		master mason's daily wage in d groot Flemish	kilograms purchased with daily wage	index (1501–5 = 100)		
	Italian ducat, florin[f]	English angel-noble[g]			quantity	sugar price	Van der Wee CPI
1501–5	9.693	14.232	8.333	1.022	100.000	100.000	100.000
1506–10	8.498	12.478	8.333	0.896	87.675	114.057	91.512
1511–15	4.952	7.272	9.333	0.582	51.093	195.720	109.928
1516–20	5.306	7.791	10.000	0.672	54.743	182.672	119.781
1521–5	4.939	7.346	10.267	0.635	50.315	198.747	143.435
1526–30	4.587	6.823	10.600	0.608	46.732	213.987	142.304
1531–5	6.658	9.904	10.067	0.838	67.831	147.425	138.697
1536–40	4.885	7.266	12.133	0.741	49.766	200.939	147.981

NOTES ON COINAGE VALUES

See the notes for Table 6A.

SOURCE

Van der Wee Antwerp Market (Table 6A above) I 306–24 Appendix 26

TABLE 6 (continued)

THE PURCHASING POWER OF COINS AND WAGES IN
THE SOUTHERN LOW COUNTRIES, 1501–40

I   TALLOW CANDLES

From Brussels, Lier, Antwerp, and Mechelen, purchased by the stone of 8 lb (= 3,752.194 g);
unweighted mean values

years (autumn) Flemish	price per kilogram in d groot	kilograms purchased with					
		Burgundian-Hapsburg patard (= 2d groot)	French blanc or douzain (= 12d tournois)[a]	English penny (= 1d sterling)[b]	Burgundian-Hapsburg Philippus florin[c]	Burgundian-Hapsburg Carolus florin[d]	French écu au soleil[e]
1501–5	4.224	0.473	0.496	0.348	11.837		16.809
1506–10	4.637	0.431	0.451	0.317	10.782		15.311
1511–15	4.685	0.427	0.447	0.314	10.673		15.156
1516–20	5.031	0.398	0.395	0.293	9.938		14.151
1521–5	5.677	0.352	0.336	0.268	9.513	7.399	13.388
1526–30	5.637	0.355	0.339	0.240	9.580	7.451	13.483
1531–5	5.450	0.367	0.350	0.248	9.908	7.706	13.945
1536–40	5.693	0.351	0.336	0.238	9.486	7.378	13.351

years (autumn)	kilograms purchased with		master mason's daily wage in d groot Flemish	kilograms purchased with daily wage	index (1501–5 = 100)		
	Italian ducat, florin[f]	English angel-noble[g]			quantity	candles price	Van der Wee CPI
1501–5	18.703	27.462	8.333	1.973	100.000	100.000	100.000
1506–10	17.036	25.015	8.333	1.797	91.088	109.784	91.512
1511–15	16.864	24.762	9.333	1.986	90.169	110.903	109.928
1516–20	15.703	23.057	10.000	1.988	83.960	119.105	119.781
1521–5	14.093	20.963	10.267	1.810	74.410	134.391	143.435
1526–30	14.193	21.112	10.600	1.880	74.940	133.440	142.304
1531–5	14.679	21.835	10.067	1.847	77.505	129.023	138.697
1536–40	14.053	20.904	12.133	2.124	74.201	134.769	147.981

NOTES ON COINAGE VALUES

See the notes for Table 6A.

SOURCE

Van der Wee *Antwerp Market* (Table 6A above) I 249-52 Appendix 16

TABLE 6 (continued)

J   WOOLLEN BROADCLOTHS FROM GHENT AND MECHELEN
Prices of woollen cloths from the Low Countries in pounds groot Flemish;
cloths of 30 ells (= 21.0 metres) in length

years	Ghent dickedinnen in £ groot Flemish	Ghent strijpte laken in £ groot Flemish	Mechelen rooslaken in £ groot Flemish	Brabant basket of consumables		master mason's daily wage in d groot Flemish
				value in d groot Flemish	price index (1501–05 = 100)	
1501–5	14.667	11.100	9.967	194.467	100.000	8.333
1506–10	14.130	11.701	10.000	177.960	91.512	8.333
1511–15	13.000	12.750	10.933	213.773	109.928	9.333
1516–20	13.143	13.500	11.200	232.933	119.781	10.000
1521–5	13.225	13.550	11.200	278.933	143.435	10.267
1526–30	13.580	13.833	11.333	276.733	142.304	10.600
1531–5	13.760	14.320	11.067	269.720	138.697	10.067
1536–40	13.950	14.440	11.067	287.773	147.981	12.133

years	number of days' wages of a master mason to buy			value of woollens in commodity baskets		
	1 Ghent dickedinnen	1 Ghent strijpte laken	1 Mechelen rooslaken	Ghent dickedinnen	Ghent strijpte laken	Mechelen rooslaken
1501–5	422.410	319.680	287.040	18.101	13.699	12.300
1506–10	406.950	336.979	288.000	19.056	15.780	13.486
1511–15	334.286	327.857	281.143	14.595	14.314	12.275
1516–20	315.438	324.000	268.800	13.542	13.910	11.540
1521–5	309.156	316.753	261.818	11.379	11.659	9.637
1526–30	307.472	313.208	256.604	11.777	11.997	9.829
1531–5	328.053	341.404	263.841	12.244	12.742	9.847
1536–40	275.934	285.626	218.901	11.634	12.043	9.229

SOURCE

Stadsarchief Gent, Stadsrekeningen 1499/1500–1539/40; Stadsarchief Mechelen, Stadsrekeningen M 175–215; Algemeen Rijksarchief België, Rekenkamer, registers nos 41,280–5; John Munro 'Mint Outputs, Money, and Prices in Late-Medieval England and the Low Countries' in *Münzprägung, Geldumlauf und Wechselkurse / Minting, Monetary Circulation and Exchange Rates* ed Eddy Van Cauwenberghe and Franz Irsigler, Trierer Historische Forschungen 7, *Akten des 8th International Economic History Congress, Section c-7, Budapest 1982* (Trier 1984) 31–122; Van der Wee *Antwerp Market* 46–61 Appendix 39: Synoptic Tables

TABLE 6 (continued)

THE PURCHASING POWER OF COINS AND WAGES IN
THE SOUTHERN LOW COUNTRIES, 1501–40

K   HONDSCHOOTE SAYS AND GHENT DICKEDINNEN WOOLLENS
Prices compared with the purchasing power of an Antwerp master mason's daily wages

years	Hondschoote says single: prices in £ groot Flemish	Hondschoote says double: prices in £ groot Flemish	Ghent dickedinnen woollens: prices in £ groot Flemish	Antwerp master mason's daily wage in d groot Flemish	number of days' wages of a master mason to buy a single say	number of days' wages of a master mason to buy a dickedinnen
1535			14.150	10.333		328.656
1536			14.250	11.000		310.909
1537			14.500	11.667		298.277
1538	0.967	2.278	14.500	12.667	18.322	274.730
1539	0.945	2.184	15.000	12.667	17.905	284.203
1540	0.835	1.961	15.000	12.667	15.821	284.203
1541	0.879	2.015	15.500	12.667	16.654	293.676
1542	0.838	2.005	14.500	12.667	15.877	274.730
1543	0.783	1.775	14.000	14.000	13.423	240.000
1544	0.908	1.942	14.000	14.000	15.566	240.000

years	Brabant basket of consumables value in d groot Flemish	value of textiles in commodity baskets a single say	value of textiles in commodity baskets a Ghent dickedinnen
1535	268.733		12.637
1536	297.467		11.497
1537	254.333		13.683
1538	295.533	0.785	11.775
1539	300.400	0.755	11.984
1540	291.133	0.688	12.365
1541	278.000	0.759	13.381
1542	293.600	0.685	11.853
1543	324.200	0.580	10.364
1544	351.067	0.621	9.571

SOURCE

Stadsarchief Gent, Stadsrekeningen, Reeks 400 nos 46–52 (1534/5–1544/5); Van der Wee *Antwerp Market* I 457–68 Appendix 39: Synoptic Table of Wages; *Recueil de documents relatifs à l'histoire de l'industrie drapière en Flandre* ed Henri De Sagher and others, IIe partie: *le sud-ouest de la Flandre depuis l'époque bourguignonne* 3 vols (Brussels 1951–66) II 342–6 no 287, 356–60 (30 April 1534); Florence Edler 'Le commerce d'exportation des sayes d'Hondschoote vers Italie d'après la correspondance d'une firme anversoise, entre 1538 et 1544' *Revue du Nord* 22 (1936) 249–65

TABLE 7

THE DIMENSIONS AND COMPOSITIONS OF SELECTED WOOLLENS AND SAYS
IN THE SIXTEENTH CENTURY

drapery: city/region	Essex/Sussex	Ghent	Mechelen
date of ordinance	1552	1546	1544
textile name	short broadcloth	dickedinnen	gulden aeren
additional names	Suffolk, Essex	five seals	five seals
origin of wools	England	England	England: Herefordshire
wool types	short-stapled	March, Cotswolds	Lemster Ore
on loom			
length in ells or yards (metres)	ns	42.500 (29.750)	48.000 (33.072)
width in ells (metres)	ns	3.625 (2.538)	4.000 (2.756)
weight in pounds (kilograms)	ns	88.000 (38.179)	ns
final			
length in ells or yards (metres)	24.000 (22.555)	30.000 (21.000)	30.000 (20.670)
width in ells or yards (metres)	1.750 (1.645)	2.375 (1.663)	2.500 (1.723)
number of warps	ns	2066	3120
warps per centimetre, fulled	ns	12.427	18.113
area in square metres	37.095	34.913	35.604
weight in pounds (kilograms)	64.000 (29.030)	51.000 (22.126)	58.000 (27.217)
weight per metre^2 in grams	782.575	633.766	764.421

drapery: city/region	Hondschoote	Bergues-St-Winoc	Essex
date of ordinance	1571	1537	1579
textile name	double say	narrow say	says
additional names	small	fine	broad
origin of wools	Flanders, Friesland	Flanders, Artois	England
wool types	Scotland, Pomerania	long-stapled	long-stapled
on loom			
length in ells or yards (metres)	40.000 (28.000)	ns	ns
width in ells (metres)	1.438 (1.006)	ns	ns
weight in pounds (kilograms)	ns	ns	ns
final			
length in ells or yards (metres)	36.750 (25.725)	40.000 (28.000)	10.000 (9.398)
width in ells or yards (metres)	1.250 (0.875)	1.000 (0.700)	1.000 (0.940)
number of warps	1800	1400	ns
warps per centimetre, fulled	20.571	20.000	ns
area in square metres	22.509	19.600	8.833
weight in pounds (kilograms)	16.000 (7.257)	11.000 (5.103)	2.750 (1.247)
weight per metre^2 in grams	322.421	260.352	141.193

NOTE ON WEIGHTS AND MEASURES

ns = not specified
Flemish ell = 0.700 metre
Ghent pound = 433.850 grams
Bruges pound = 463.900 grams
Mechelen ell = 0.689 metres

Mechelen pound = 469.250 grams
English pound avoirdupois = 453.593 grams
English cloth yard (37 in) = 0.940 metre

TABLE 7 (continued)

THE DIMENSIONS AND COMPOSITIONS OF SELECTED WOOLLENS AND SAYS
IN THE SIXTEENTH CENTURY

SOURCES

Ghent Recueil des ordonnances des Pays Bas deuxième série V *1506–1706* ed M.J. Lameere, H. Simont, and others (Brussels 1910) 272–83

England, woollens The Statutes of the Realm ed T.E. Tomlins and J. Raithby, Record Commission, 6 vols (London 1810–22) IV 1, 136–7 (statute 5–6 Edwardi VI c.6)

England, worsted says J.E. Pilgrim 'The Rise of the "New Draperies" in Essex' *University of Birmingham Historical Journal* 7 (1959–60) 36–59; A.P. Usher *The Industrial History of England* (Boston 1920) 200

Mechelen 'Le règlement général de la draperie malinoise de 1544' ed G.M. Willemsen *Bulletin du cercle archéologique de Malines* 20 (1910) 156–90

Hondschoote Recueil de documents relatifs à l'histoire de l'industrie drapière en Flandre ed Henri De Sagher and others IIe partie: *le sud-ouest de la Flandre depuis l'époque bourguignonne* 3 vols (Brussels 1951–66) II 362–9 no 290, 378–81 no 291, 415 no 299.

Bergues-Saint-Winoc Recueil ed De Sagher IIe partie I 530–1 no 163, 535–42 no 165, 561–9 nos 176–7

TABLE 8

ENGLISH TEXTILE EXPORTS AND TEXTILE PRODUCTION
IN FLANDERS, BRABANT, AND HOLLAND
English textile exports, in woolsacks and broadcloths, and indexes of textile production
in Flanders, Brabant, and Holland in quinquennial means, from 1501–5 to 1536–40

years	total English wool exports in sacks[a]	equivalent number of broadcloths[b]	total English broadcloth exports[b]	London broadcloth exports	London exports as per cent of total	Ghent drapery excise tax farms in d groot[c]
1501–5	7,806.80	33,829.44	77,270.80	46,610.80	60.32	132.00
1506–10	7,326.20	31,746.84	84,802.60	52,390.40	61.78	93.60
1511–15	7,087.20	30,711.18	86,592.00	62,257.00	71.90	97.20
1516–20	8,194.40	35,509.04	90,098.80	63,084.00	70.02	62.40
1521–5	5,131.60	22,236.92	82,268.80	61,854.40	75.19	
1526–30	4,834.80	20,950.78	93,534.40	72,350.00	77.35	
1531–5	3,005.20	13,022.52	94,086.80	75,502.60	80.25	
1536–40	3,951.40	17,122.72	109,278.00	91,730.60	83.94	

years	Mechelen drapery tax excise farms in £ groot[d]	Mechelen cloth output from the clergiegeld tax	Leiden outputs of halvelakenen	Hondschoote say outputs in the 8d tax	Hondschoote say sales
1501–5	224.30	2,155.05	25,148.20	17,640.00	
1506–10	224.33	1,912.00	23,782.80	20,016.00	
1511–15	185.16	1,796.00	24,673.20	22,728.00	
1516–20	190.05	2,394.00	26,244.90	29,400.00	
1521–5	181.21	2,307.00	24,334.60	32,148.00	
1526–30	143.71	2,402.00	23,094.20	34,896.00	31,583.44
1531–5	127.51	2,594.00	17,257.60	43,584.00	41,184.50
1536–40	94.97	1,660.00	16,646.20	43,176.00	42,761.40

NOTES

   a one English woolsack = 364 lb = 165.108 kg = 4.333 woollen broadcloths
   b one English broadcloth (24.0 yards by 1.75 yards = 21.947 m by 1.600 m) = 3 kerseys =
      4 straits or dozens
   c In Ghent, the sum of the excise taxes levied on the *Ramen* (cloths taxed on the tentering
      frames) and the *Nieuw Huusgeld in de Ramen* (a new tax on tentered cloths), which are
      the only ones in the series indisputably measuring cloth production. The *pond* or *livre*
      de paiement was worth 6d groot Flemish, and thus £1 groot Flemish = £40 *paiement*.
   d In Mechelen, total of the sale of the excise-tax farms for *Wolle* (wool), *Rocghewande* (raw
      woollen cloth), and *Ghereede Ghewande* (finished woollen cloth)

SOURCES

England England's Export Trade, 1275-1547 ed E.M. Carus-Wilson and Olive Coleman (Oxford
1963) 36–119; Anthony R. Bridbury *Medieval English Clothmaking: An Economic Survey* (London
1982) 118–22 Appendix F

Ghent Stadsarchief Gent, Stadsrekeningen, Reeks 400 nos 35–48 (1501–40)

TABLE 8 (continued)

ENGLISH TEXTILE EXPORTS AND TEXTILE PRODUCTION
IN FLANDERS, BRABANT, AND HOLLAND

SOURCES (continued)

Mechelen Stadsarchief Mechelen, Stadsrekeningen, series I: 214–55 (1501–40); Algemeen Rijks-archief België, Rekenkamer, registers nos 41,219–85; Raymond Van Uytven, 'De Omvang van de Mechelse lakenproductie vanaf de 14e tot de 16e eeuw' *Noordgouw: Cultureel tijdschrift van de Provincie Antwerpen* 5/3 (1965) 1–22

Leiden Bronnen tot de geschiedenis van de leidsche textielnijverheid, 1333–1795 ed Nicholas W. Posthumus 3 vols (The Hague 1910–22) II 317–20; Nicholas W. Posthumus, *Geschiedenis van de Leidsche lakenindustrie* 3 vols (The Hague 1908–39), I *De Middeleeuwen, veertiende tot zestiende eeuw* 370–425

Hondschoote Emile Coornaert *La draperie-sayetterie d'Hondschoote, XIVe-XVIIIe siècles* (Paris 1930), calculated from Appendix IV 485–90.

TABLE 9

THE INTERNATIONAL COMMERCE OF THE BRABANT FAIRS, C 1560
Estimated values of imports and exports in pounds groot Flemish

imports			exports		
commodity	value in £ groot Flemish	per cent of estimated total	commodity	value in £ groot Flemish	per cent of estimated total
textile products			*textile products*		
silks, fabrics and raw, Italian	666,667	17.78	says, worsteds, serges	416,667	15.63
			linens	416,667	15.63
woollens, English	540,000	14.40	woollens,		
fustians, German	40,000	1.07	Netherlander	233,333	8.75
wools, Spanish (via Bruges)	208,333	5.56	English (finished)	520,000	19.50
English	83,333	2.22	fustians, German	40,000	1.50
woad, French	66,667	1.78	silks, re-exports	83,333	3.13
alum, Italian	23,333	0.62	tapestries	116,667	4.38
Spanish	16,667	0.44	other textile exports	100,000	3.75
cochineal, Spanish-American	37,500	1.00			
sub-total textile products	1,682,500	44.87		1,926,667	72.25
foodstuffs					
grains, Baltic	500,000	13.33			
spices, Portuguese-Asian	333,333	8.89			
sugar, Portuguese	41,667	1.11			
wines, French	191,667	5.11			
Rhenish	120,000	3.20			
Italian	41,667	1.11			
Spanish and Portuguese	41,667	1.11			
salt, French	41,667	1.11			
Spanish	29,167	0.78			
olive oil, Spanish and Portuguese	33,333	0.89			
sub-total foodstuffs	1,374,167	36.64			
copper, German	26,667	0.71			
other commodities, estimated	666,667	17.78	other commodities	740,000	27.75
total value of commodities	3,750,000	100.00		2,666,667	100.00

SOURCES

Wilfrid Brulez 'Le commerce international des Pays-Bas au xvɪe siècle: essai d'appréciation quantitative' *Revue belge de philologie et d'histoire* 46 (1968) 1205–21, reissued in English translation as 'The Balance of Trade in the Netherlands in the Middle of the Sixteenth Century' *Acta Historiae Neerlandica* 4 (1970) 20–48, based upon Ludovico Guicciardini *Description de la cité d'Anvers, 1560* trans François de Belleforest (1582; published in Antwerp 1920); Jan De Vries and Ad Van der Woude *The First Modern Economy: Success, Failure, and Perseverance of the Dutch Economy, 1500–1815* (Cambridge 1996)

TABLE 10

COMMODITY PRICES IN SOUTHERN ENGLAND

A   THE PHELPS BROWN AND HOPKINS 'BASKET OF CONSUMABLES' INDEX
FOR ENGLAND: COMPONENTS OF THE INDEX AND THEIR WEIGHTS FOR 1500

commodity	units	quantity	weights (per cent)	cost in pence in 1500
farinaceous				
wheat	bushels (litres)	1.250 (45.461)	20.00	20.80
rye	bushels (litres)	1.000 (36.369)		
barley	bushels (litres)	0.500 (18.184)		
peas	bushels (litres)	0.667 (24.243)		
meat and fish				
sheep	number	1.500	37.50	39.00
white herrings	number	15.000	[25.00]	
red herrings	number	25.000		
butter and cheese				
cheese	nil		[12.50]	0.00
butter	nil			
drink				
malt	bushels (litres)	4.500 (163.659)	22.50	23.40
fuel and light				
charcoal	bushels (litres)	4.250 (154.567)	7.50	7.80
candles	pounds avoirdupois (kilograms)	2.750 (1.247)		
oil	pints (litres)	0.500 (0.284)		
textiles				
canvas	yards (metres)	0.667 (0.610)	12.50	13.00
shirting	yards (metres)	0.500 (0.457)		
woollen cloth	yards (metres)	0.333 (0.305)		
total			100.00	104.00

NOTE

1 quarter = 8 bushels = 64 gallons

TABLE 10 (continued)

B THE PHELPS BROWN AND HOPKINS PRICE AND WAGE INDEXES
FOR ENGLAND, 1501–5
In terms of the bases 1451–75 = 100 and 1501–5 = 100

years	farinaceous: wheat, rye, barley, peas	meat and fish	drink: malt	fuel and light	textiles: linens, woollens	composite price index	farinaceous (with drink)	meat and fish	fuel and textiles (industrial)
weights (per cent)	20.00	37.50	22.50	7.50	12.50	100.00	42.50	37.50	20.00
1501	127.00	91.75	99.00	91.00	107.00	102.28	112.18	91.75	101.00
1502	139.00	95.50	125.00	82.00	111.00	111.76	131.59	95.50	100.13
1503	130.00	99.25	102.00	98.00	126.00	109.27	115.18	99.25	115.50
1504	129.00	103.00	95.00	96.00	116.00	107.50	111.00	103.00	108.50
1505	111.00	99.00	107.00	90.00	104.00	103.15	108.88	99.00	98.75
1501–5 (1451–75 = 100)	127.20	97.70	105.60	91.40	112.80	106.79	115.76	97.70	104.78
1501–5	100.00	100.00	100.00	100.00	100.00	100.00	100.00	100.00	100.00

years	composite price index	nominal daily wage in pence		nominal wage index (1451–75 = 100)		real wage index (1451–75 = 100)	
		for a master	for a labourer	for a master (6d daily)	for a labourer (4d daily)	for a master	for a labourer
1501	102.28	6.00	4.00	100.00	100.00	97.77	97.77
1502	111.76	6.00	4.00	100.00	100.00	89.48	89.48
1503	109.27	6.00	4.00	100.00	100.00	91.52	91.52
1504	107.50	6.00	4.00	100.00	100.00	93.02	93.02
1505	103.15	6.00	4.00	100.00	100.00	96.95	96.95
1501–5 (1451–75 = 100)	106.79	6.00	4.00	100.00	100.00	93.75	93.75
1501–5	100.00	100.00	100.00	100.00	100.00	100.00	100.00

SOURCES

E. Henry Phelps Brown and Sheila V. Hopkins, 'Seven Centuries of Building Wages' *Economica* 22/87 (August 1955) 195–206, reprinted in *Essays in Economic History* ed E.M. Carus-Wilson II (London 1962) 168–78 and in E.H. Phelps Brown and Sheila V. Hopkins *A Perspective of Wages and Prices* (London 1981) 1–12; E.H. Phelps Brown and S.V. Hopkins 'Seven Centuries of the Prices of Consumables Compared with Builders' Wage-Rates' *Economica* 23/92 (November 1956) 296–314, reprinted in *Essays in Economic History* ed Carus-Wilson II 179-96 and in Phelps Brown and Hopkins *Perspective* 13–59, with additional statistical appendixes not provided in the original publication or in earlier reprints.

TABLE 11

THE PURCHASING POWER OF COINAGE AND WAGES IN ENGLAND, 1501–40

A BORDEAUX RED WINE (CLARET)
Purchased by the dozen gallons (1 gallon = 4.546 litres)

years	price per litre in d sterling	litres purchased with			master mason's daily wage in d sterling	litres pur- chased with daily wage	index (1501–5 = 100)		
		1d sterling	angel- noble[a]	crown[b]			quantity	wine price	PBH CPI
1501–5	1.730	0.578	46.231		6.00	3.467	100.000	100.000	100.000
1506–10	1.758	0.569	45.508		6.00	3.413	98.436	101.589	97.17
1511–15	1.848	0.541	43.296		6.00	3.247	93.651	106.780	101.62
1516–20	1.784	0.561	44.854		6.00	3.364	97.020	103.072	112.78
1521–5	2.830	0.353	28.266		6.00	2.120	61.140	163.559	136.76
1526–30	2.427	0.412	37.083	24.722	6.00	2.472	71.299	140.253	147.34
1531–5	2.321	0.431	38.782	25.855	6.00	2.585	74.566	134.110	145.74
1536–40	2.464	0.406	36.531	24.354	6.50	2.638	70.238	142.373	142.64

NOTES ON COINAGE VALUES

a angel-noble: 5.157 g fine gold; from 1464 to 1526 valued at 6s 8d or 80d and 7s 6d or 90d thereafter

b crown: 3.438 g fine gold; struck from November 1526 with a value of 5s 0d or 60d

SOURCE

James E. Thorold Rogers *History of Agriculture and Prices in England from the Year after the Oxford Parliament (1259) to the Commencement of the Continental War (1793), Compiled Entirely From Original and Contemporaneous Records* 7 vols (Oxford 1866–1902) IV *1401–1582* (1882) 684–6

TABLE 11 (continued)

B   HERRINGS

Smoked North Sea red herrings, priced by the cade of 500 fish

years	price per fish in d sterling	herrings purchased with			master mason's daily wage in d sterling	fish purchased with daily wage	index (1501–5 = 100)		
		1d sterling	angel-noble[a]	crown[b]			quantity	herring price	PBH CPI
1501–5	0.139	7.218	577.439		6.00	43.308	100.000	100.000	100.00
1506–10	0.140	7.141	571.312		6.00	42.848	98.939	101.072	97.17
1511–15	0.150	6.671	533.689		6.00	40.027	92.424	108.198	101.62
1516–20	0.141	7.077	566.171		6.00	42.463	98.049	101.990	112.78
1521–5	0.154	6.500	519.963		6.00	38.997	90.046	111.054	136.76
1526–30	0.157	6.361	559.789	381.679	6.00	38.168	88.132	113.467	147.34
1531–5	0.159	6.309	567.823	378.549	6.00	37.855	87.409	114.405	145.74
1536–40	0.170	5.872	528.479	352.319	6.50	38.168	81.352	122.922	142.64

NOTES ON COINAGE VALUES

See the notes for Table 11A.

SOURCE

Thorold Rogers *History of Agriculture and Prices* (Table 11A above) IV 608–10

TABLE 11 (continued)

THE PURCHASING POWER OF COINAGE AND WAGES IN ENGLAND, 1501–40

C   CODFISH

From the Orkney Islands and Iceland, priced by the short hundred (= 100)

years	price per fish in d sterling	codfish purchased with			master mason's daily wage in d sterling	fish pur-chased with daily wage	index (1501–5 = 100)		
		1d sterling	angel-noble[a]	crown[b]			quantity	cod price	PBH CPI
1501–5	3.946	0.253	20.274		6.00	1.521	100.000	100.000	100.00
1506–10	2.736	0.365	29.240		6.00	2.193	144.225	69.336	97.17
1511–15	5.008	0.200	15.974		6.00	1.198	78.794	126.913	101.62
1516–20	6.552	0.153	12.210		6.00	0.916	60.226	166.042	112.78
1521–5	6.080	0.164	13.158		6.00	0.987	64.901	154.080	136.76
1526–30	7.920	0.126	11.364	7.576	6.00	0.758	49.823	200.710	147.34
1531–5	5.832	0.171	15.432	10.288	6.00	1.029	67.661	147.795	145.74
1536–40	4.878	0.205	18.450	12.300	6.50	1.333	80.894	123.619	142.64

NOTES ON COINAGE VALUES

See the notes for Table 11A.

SOURCE

Thorold Rogers *History of Agriculture and Prices* (Table 11A above) IV 542–4

TABLE 11 (continued)

D   WHEAT

In the Oxford-Cambridge regions, purchased by the quarter (= 8 bushels = one-quarter hundredweight = 28 lb = 64 gallons = 290.935 litres; 1 bushel = 1/8 imperial quarter = 8 gallons = 36.369 litres)

years	price per litre in d sterling	litres purchased with			master mason's daily wage in d sterling	litres purchased with daily wage	index (1501–5 = 100)		
		1d sterling	angel-noble[a]	crown[b]			quantity	wheat price	PBH CPI
1501–5	0.270	3.709	296.698		6.00	22.252	100.000	100.000	100.00
1506–10	0.180	5.558	444.622		6.00	33.347	149.857	66.730	97.17
1511–15	0.272	3.674	293.889		6.00	22.042	99.053	100.956	101.62
1516–20	0.282	3.544	283.508		6.00	21.263	95.554	104.653	112.78
1521–5	0.246	4.072	325.766		6.00	24.432	109.797	91.077	136.76
1526–30	0.373	2.680	241.230	160.820	6.00	16.082	72.271	138.368	147.34
1531–5	0.340	2.945	265.035	176.690	6.00	17.669	79.403	125.940	145.74
1536–40	0.297	3.369	303.248	202.165	6.50	21.901	90.851	110.070	142.64

NOTES ON COINAGE VALUES

See the notes for Table 11A.

SOURCE

Thorold Rogers *History of Agriculture and Prices* (Table 11A above) IV 286–8

TABLE 11 (continued)

THE PURCHASING POWER OF COINAGE AND WAGES IN ENGLAND, 1501–40

E   PEAS

Priced by the quarter (= 8 bushels = 64 gallons = 290.935 litres; 1 bushel = 1/8 imperial quarter = 8 gallons = 36.369 litres)

years	price per litre in d sterling	litres purchased with			master mason's daily wage in d sterling	litres pur- chased with daily wage	index (1501–5 = 100)		
		1d sterling	angel- noble[a]	crown[b]			quantity	peas price	PBH CPI
1501–5	0.149	6.711	536.904		6.00	40.268	100.000	100.000	100.00
1506–10	0.161	6.223	497.857		6.00	37.339	92.727	107.843	97.17
1511–15	0.224	4.462	356.976		6.00	26.773	66.488	150.404	101.62
1516–20	0.182	5.505	440.435		6.00	33.033	82.032	121.903	112.78
1521–5	0.136	7.332	586.563		6.00	43.992	109.249	91.534	136.76
1526–30	0.257	3.895	350.524	233.683	6.00	23.368	58.032	172.318	147.34
1531–5	0.251	3.991	359.179	239.453	6.00	23.945	59.465	168.166	145.74
1536–40	0.213	4.693	422.325	281.550	6.50	30.501	69.919	143.022	142.64

NOTES ON COINAGE VALUES

See the notes for Table 11A.

SOURCE

Thorold Rogers *History of Agriculture and Prices* (Table 11A above) IV 287–9

TABLE 11 (continued)

F   SUGAR

Priced by the dozen pounds, the pound, and the kilogram (12 lb = 5443.116 g = 5.443 kg; 1 lb avoirdupois = 453.593 g)

years	price per kilogram in d sterling	kilograms purchased with			master mason's daily wage in d sterling	kilograms purchased with daily wage	index (1501–5 = 100)		
		1d sterling	angel-noble[a]	crown[b]			quantity	sugar price	PBH CPI
1501–5	6.393	0.156	12.513		6.00	0.938	100.000	100.000	100.00
1506–10	7.937	0.126	10.080		6.00	0.756	80.556	124.138	97.17
1511–15	12.346	0.081	6.480		6.00	0.486	51.786	193.103	101.62
1516–20	14.661	0.068	5.457		6.00	0.409	43.609	229.310	112.78
1521–5	13.001	0.077	6.153		6.00	0.461	49.176	203.352	136.76
1526–30	15.714	0.064	5.727	3.818	6.00	0.382	40.686	245.785	147.34
1531–5	16.039	0.062	5.611	3.741	6.00	0.374	39.863	250.862	145.74
1536–40	16.755	0.060	5.371	3.581	6.50	0.388	38.158	262.069	142.64

NOTES ON COINAGE VALUES

See the notes for Table 11A.

SOURCE

Thorold Rogers *History of Agriculture and Prices* (Table 11A above) IV 685–7

TABLE 11 (continued)

THE PURCHASING POWER OF COINAGE AND WAGES IN ENGLAND, 1501–40

G   TALLOW CANDLES

English and French tallow candles, made from mutton fat, purchased at Cambridge and Oxford by the dozen pounds (1 pound avoirdupois = 453.592 g)

years	price per kilogram in d sterling	kilograms purchased with			master mason's daily wage in d sterling	kilograms pur- chased with daily wage	index (1501–5 = 100)		
		1d sterling	angel- noble[a]	crown[b]			quantity	candles price	PBH CPI
1501–5	2.462	0.406	32.496		6.00	2.437	100.000	100.000	100.00
1506–10	2.370	0.422	33.756		6.00	2.532	103.876	96.269	97.17
1511–15	2.563	0.390	31.215		6.00	2.341	96.057	104.104	101.62
1516–20	2.728	0.367	29.323		6.00	2.199	90.236	110.821	112.78
1521–5	2.618	0.382	30.558		6.00	2.292	94.035	106.343	136.76
1526–30	2.627	0.381	34.257	22.838	6.00	2.284	93.706	106.716	147.34
1531–5	3.096	0.323	29.073	19.382	6.00	1.938	79.525	125.746	145.74
1536–40	2.903	0.345	31.005	20.670	6.50	2.239	84.810	117.910	142.64

NOTES ON COINAGE VALUES

See the notes for Table 11A.

SOURCE

Thorold Rogers *History of Agriculture and Prices* (Table 11A above) IV 378–80

TABLE 11 (continued)

H   PAPER

Good quality linen paper, probably imported from the Low Countries, purchased at Cambridge and Oxford by the ream (1 ream = 20 quires = 480 sheets)

years	price per sheet in d sterling	sheets purchased with			master mason's daily wage in d sterling	sheets pur-chased with daily wage	index (1501–5 = 100)		
		1d sterling	angel-noble[a]	crown[b]			quantity	paper price	PBH CPI
1501–5	0.079	12.698	1015.873		6.00	76.190	100.000	100.000	100.00
1506–10	0.069	14.436	1154.887		6.00	86.617	113.684	87.963	97.17
1511–15	0.064	15.534	1242.718		6.00	93.204	122.330	81.746	101.62
1516–20	0.057	17.647	1411.765		6.00	105.882	138.971	71.958	112.78
1521–5	0.080	12.565	1005.236		6.00	75.393	98.953	101.058	136.76
1526–30	0.071	14.035	1263.158	842.105	6.00	84.211	110.526	90.476	147.34
1531–5	0.085	11.794	1061.425	707.617	6.00	70.762	92.875	107.672	145.74
1536–40	0.098	10.213	919.149	612.766	6.50	66.383	80.426	124.339	142.64

NOTES ON COINAGE VALUES

See the notes for Table 11A.

SOURCE

Thorold Rogers *History of Agriculture and Prices* (Table 11A above) IV 605

TABLE 11 (continued)

THE PURCHASING POWER OF COINAGE AND WAGES IN ENGLAND, 1501–40

I   LINEN

Table linen, medium to good quality, with a width of 1.0 to 1.5 yards (ells); most imported from the Low Countries; priced by the dozen ells/yards (= 0.914 metre)

years	price per dozen ells in shillings	price per metre in d sterling	metres purchased with		
			1d sterling	angel-noble[a]	crown[b]
1501–5	7.225	7.901	0.127	10.125	
1506–10	6.733	7.364	0.136	10.864	
1511–15	7.550	8.257	0.121	9.689	
1516–20	7.125	7.792	0.128	10.267	
1521–5	8.000	8.749	0.114	9.144	
1526–30	7.275	7.956	0.126	11.312	7.541
1531–5	8.638	9.446	0.106	9.528	6.352
1536–40	7.575	8.284	0.121	10.864	7.243

years	master mason's daily wage in d sterling	metres purchased with daily wage	days' wages for master mason to buy 24 ells/yards	index (1501–5 = 100)		
				quantity	linen price	PBH CPI
1501–5	6.00	0.759	28.900	100.000	100.000	100.00
1506–10	6.00	0.815	26.933	107.302	93.195	97.17
1511–15	6.00	0.727	30.200	95.695	104.498	101.62
1516–20	6.00	0.770	28.500	101.404	98.616	112.78
1521–5	6.00	0.686	32.000	90.313	110.727	136.76
1526–30	6.00	0.754	29.100	99.313	100.692	147.34
1531–5	6.00	0.635	34.550	83.647	119.550	145.74
1536–40	6.50	0.785	27.969	95.380	104.844	142.64

NOTES ON COINAGE VALUES

See the notes for Table 11A.

SOURCE

Thorold Rogers *History of Agriculture and Prices* (Table 11A above) IV 586–8

TABLE 11 (continued)

J WOOLLEN BROADCLOTH

First quality cloth, sold by the pannus of 24 yards, priced by the pannus of 24 yards (ells) and the metre (1 yard = 0.914 metre; 1 metre = 1.094 yards)

years	price per piece in £ sterling	price per metre in d sterling	metres purchased with			master mason's daily wage in d sterling
			1d sterling	angel-noble[a]	crown[b]	
1501–5	3.243	35.460	0.028	2.256		6.000
1506–10	3.578	39.133	0.026	2.044		6.000
1511–15	3.940	43.088	0.023	1.857		6.000
1516–20	4.053	44.328	0.023	1.805		6.000
1521–5	3.200	34.996	0.029	2.286		6.000
1526–30	4.820	52.712	0.019	1.707	1.138	6.000
1531–5	3.373	36.891	0.027	2.440	1.626	6.000
1536–40	4.560	49.869	0.020	1.805	1.203	6.500

years	metres purchased with		days' wages for master mason to buy one woollen cloth	index (1501–5 = 100)		
	daily wage	weekly wage		quantity	woollens price	PBH CPI
1501–5	0.169	1.015	129.700	100.000	100.000	100.000
1506–10	0.153	0.920	143.133	90.615	110.357	97.172
1511–15	0.139	0.835	157.600	82.297	121.511	101.618
1516–20	0.135	0.812	162.133	79.996	125.006	112.777
1521–5	0.171	1.029	128.000	101.328	98.689	136.756
1526–30	0.114	0.683	192.800	67.272	148.651	147.337
1531–5	0.163	0.976	134.933	96.122	104.035	145.741
1536–40	0.130	0.782	168.369	71.107	140.632	142.641

NOTES ON COINAGE VALUES

See the notes for Table 11A.

SOURCE

Thorold Rogers *History of Agriculture and Prices* (Table 11A above) IV 586–8

TABLE 12

PRICE AND WAGE INDEXES FOR SOUTHERN BRABANT FROM 1501–5 TO 1536–40
The Van der Wee composite price index in deniers of the Brabant pond groot for the
Antwerp-Lier-Brussels region, and wage indexes for Antwerp master building craftsmen
Index: mean 1501–5 = 100 (and a comparison with index 1451–75 = 100)

			Brabant price index in d groot Flemish		wage index for a master mason/carpenter	
					nominal	real
years	basket of goods total value		1451–75 = 100 = 232.524d groot Brabant = 155.016d groot Flemish	1501–5 = 100 = 291.700d groot Brabant = 194.467d groot Flemish	1501–5 = 100 = 12.250d groot Brabant = 8.167d groot Flemish	1501–5 = 100 NWI/CPI adjusted*
	d groot Brabant	d groot Flemish				
1501–5	291.700	194.467	125.449	100.000	100.000	100.000
1506–10	266.940	177.960	114.801	91.512	100.000	109.368
1511–15	320.660	213.773	137.904	109.928	109.796	99.689
1516–20	349.400	232.933	150.264	119.781	122.449	102.226
1521–5	418.400	278.933	179.938	143.435	124.082	87.733
1526–30	415.100	276.733	178.519	142.304	126.122	88.666
1531–5	404.580	269.720	173.995	138.697	122.857	89.469
1536–40	431.660	287.773	185.641	147.981	140.408	95.011

SOURCE

Herman Van der Wee 'Prijzen en lonen als ontwikkelingsvariabelen: Een vergelijkend onderzoek tussen Engeland en de Zuidelijke Nederlanden, 1400–1700' in *Album offert à Charles
Verlinden à l'occasion de ses trente ans de professoriat* (Ghent 1975) 413–35, republished in English
translation as 'Prices and Wages as Development Variables: A Comparison between England
and the Southern Netherlands, 1400–1700' *Acta Historiae Neerlandicae* 10 (1978) 58–78. Only the
Dutch version, however, contains the specific annual data in tabular form.

* See 629–30 and n97 above.

TABLE 13

THE PURCHASING POWER OF DAILY MONEY WAGES
FOR BUILDING CRAFTSMEN IN BRABANT
Summer and winter wages for Antwerp masons and carpenters, in five-year means,
from 1501–5 to 1536–40, in d groot Flemish and d groot Brabant

| | daily summer wage | | | daily winter wage | | | summer wage of |
| | master mason in d groot | | master carpenter in d groot Brabant | master crafts-man (mason/ carpenter) in d groot Brabant | master crafts-man (mason/ carpenter) in d groot Brabant | as per cent of summer wage | mason's labourer in d groot Brabant |
years	Flemish	Brabant					
1501–5	8.333	12.500	12.000	12.250	9.000	73.47	7.700
1506–10	8.333	12.500	12.000	12.250	9.000	73.47	8.000
1511–15	9.333	14.000	12.900	13.450	9.600	71.46	8.200
1516–20	10.000	15.000	15.000	15.000	10.500	70.00	8.500
1521–5	10.267	15.400	15.000	15.200	11.250	73.99	9.400
1526–30	10.600	15.900	15.000	15.450	11.700	75.81	9.450
1531–5	10.067	15.100	15.000	15.050	12.000	79.74	9.000
1536–40	12.133	18.200	16.200	17.200	12.000	69.92	10.050
mean	9.883	14.825	14.138	14.481	10.631	73.48	8.788

| | mason's labourer's wage as per cent of master's wage | number of days employ-ment per year | basket of goods total value | | Brabant price index (1501–5 = 100 = 194.467d groot Flemish) | wage index for a master mason/carpenter (1501–5 = 100) | |
years			in d groot Brabant	in d groot Flemish		nominal	real (NWI/ CPI) adjusted*
1501–5	61.60	212.800	291.700	194.467	100.000	100.000	100.000
1506–10	64.00	215.200	266.940	177.960	91.512	100.000	109.368
1511–15	58.93	214.600	320.660	213.773	109.928	109.796	99.689
1516–20	56.67	226.600	349.400	232.933	119.781	122.449	102.226
1521–5	61.07	226.400	418.400	278.933	143.435	124.082	87.733
1526–30	59.45	216.400	415.100	276.733	142.304	126.122	88.666
1531–5	59.61	206.000	404.580	269.720	138.697	122.857	89.469
1536–40	55.21	219.200	431.660	287.773	147.981	140.408	95.011
mean	59.57	217.150	362.305	241.537	124.205	118.214	96.520

* See 629–30 and n97 above.

TABLE 13 (continued)

THE PURCHASING POWER OF DAILY MONEY WAGES
FOR BUILDING CRAFTSMEN IN BRABANT
Summer and winter wages for Antwerp masons and carpenters, in five-year means,
from 1501–5 to 1536–40, in d groot Flemish and d groot Brabant

years	for 210 days' earnings	index 1501–5 = 100	for 217.15 days' earnings	for summer and winter (annual employment)	for summer and winter (annual employment) index 1501–5 = 100 adjusted*
	master's wage in commodity basket units				
1501–5	8.819	100.000	9.119	8.212	100.000
1506–10	9.637	109.368	9.965	9.079	110.608
1511–15	8.781	99.689	9.080	8.204	99.793
1516–20	9.015	102.226	9.322	8.836	107.648
1521–5	7.623	87.733	7.883	7.560	93.602
1526–30	7.807	88.666	8.073	7.438	90.863
1531–5	7.811	89.469	8.077	7.197	88.318
1536–40	8.351	95.011	8.635	7.883	96.911
mean	8.430	96.520	8.717	8.004	98.468

years	Brabant price index (1451–75 = 100 = 155.016d groot Flemish)	wage index for master craftsmen (1451–75 = 100) nominal	real
1501–5	125.449	102.083	81.552
1506–10	114.801	102.083	89.192
1511–15	137.904	112.083	81.298
1516–20	150.264	125.000	83.368
1521–5	179.938	126.667	71.548
1526–30	178.519	128.750	72.309
1531–5	173.995	125.417	72.963
1536–40	185.641	143.333	77.484
mean	155.814	120.677	78.714

SOURCES

Herman Van der Wee 'Prijzen en lonen als ontwikkelingsvariabelen: Een vergelijkend onderzoek tussen Engeland en de Zuidelijke Nederlanden, 1400–1700' in *Album offert à Charles
Verlinden à l'occasion de ses trente ans de professoriat* (Ghent 1975) 413–35, republished in English
translation as 'Prices and Wages as Development Variables: A Comparison between England
and the Southern Netherlands, 1400–1700' *Acta Historiae Neerlandicae* 10 (1978) 58–78 and *The
Growth of the Antwerp Market and the European Economy, Fourteenth–Sixteenth Centuries* 3 vols
(The Hague 1963) I section ii (Wages) 333–4, 339–41, 457–61, 541–2 Appendix 48

* See 629–30 and n97 above.

TABLE 14

THE PHELPS BROWN AND HOPKINS PRICE INDEXES FOR SOUTHERN ENGLAND
Mean 1501–5 = 100 (converted from 1451–75 = 100)

years	farinaceous: wheat, rye, barley, peas	meat and fish	drink: barley malt	fuel and light	textiles: linens, woollens	PBH CPI
weights (per cent)	20.00	37.50	22.50	7.50	12.50	100.00
1501–5	100.00	100.00	100.00	100.00	100.00	100.00
1506–10	80.03	116.17	85.80	94.31	99.29	97.17
1511–15	91.82	116.00	87.69	102.84	104.79	101.62
1516–20	94.50	129.14	114.02	106.78	104.08	112.78
1521–5	106.76	178.71	128.79	104.81	110.82	136.76
1526–30	143.40	161.72	155.30	107.44	123.05	147.34
1531–5	127.04	168.07	155.68	107.66	123.23	145.74
1536–40	125.47	172.16	133.52	109.19	128.55	142.64

years	farinaceous (with drink)	meat-fish-dairy	industrial	PBH CPI (1501–5 = 100 revised)	(1451–75 = 100)
weights (per cent)	42.50	37.50	20.00	100.00	100.00
1501–5	100.00	100.00	100.00	100.00	106.79
1506–10	82.82	116.17	97.66	97.17	103.77
1511–15	89.83	116.00	104.15	101.62	108.52
1516–20	103.92	129.14	104.96	112.78	120.44
1521–5	117.40	178.71	108.85	136.76	146.05
1526–30	149.15	161.72	117.94	147.34	157.35
1531–5	140.87	168.07	118.13	145.74	155.64
1536–40	129.36	172.16	122.21	142.64	152.33

SOURCES

E. Henry Phelps Brown and Sheila V. Hopkins 'Seven Centuries of Building Wages' *Economica* 22/87 (August 1955) 195–206, reprinted in *Essays in Economic History* ed E.M. Carus-Wilson II (London 1962) 168–78 and in E.H. Phelps Brown and Sheila V. Hopkins *A Perspective of Wages and Prices* (London 1981) 1–12; E.H. Phelps Brown and S.V. Hopkins 'Seven Centuries of the Prices of Consumables Compared with Builders' Wage-Rates' *Economica* 23/92 (November 1956) 296–314, reprinted in *Essays in Economic History* ed Carus-Wilson II 179–96 and in Phelps Brown and Hopkins *Perspective* 13–59, with additional statistical appendixes not provided in the original publication or in earlier reprints. The price indexes have been amended by recalculations of the original price data recorded on their working sheets now deposited in the Phelps Brown Collection in the Archives of the British Library of Economic and Political Science (London School of Economics).

TABLE 15

INDEXES OF NOMINAL AND REAL WAGES OF MASTER BUILDING
CRAFTSMEN (MASONS AND CARPENTERS) IN SOUTHERN ENGLAND
FROM 1501–5 TO 1536–40
Means of 1451–75 = 100 and 1501–5 = 100

years	nominal daily wage for a master	nominal wage index for a master (6d daily)	PBH composite price index	real wage index for a master
			(1451–75 = 100)	
1501–5	6.0	100.000	106.793	93.746
1506–10	6.0	100.000	103.773	96.391
1511–15	6.0	100.000	108.520	92.528
1516–20	6.0	100.000	120.438	83.659
1521–5	6.0	100.000	146.045	69.128
1526–30	6.0	100.000	157.345	64.274
1531–5	6.0	100.000	155.640	65.008
1536–40	6.5	108.333	152.330	71.393

years	nominal wage index for a master (6d daily)	PBH composite price index	real wage index (NWI/CPI) for a master unadjusted	adjusted*
			(1501–5 = 100)	
1501–5	100.000	100.000	100.000	100.000
1506–10	100.000	97.172	102.910	102.821
1511–15	100.000	101.618	98.408	98.700
1516–20	100.000	112.777	88.670	89.240
1521–5	100.000	136.756	73.123	73.739
1526–30	100.000	147.337	67.872	68.562
1531–5	100.000	145.741	68.615	69.345
1536–40	108.333	142.641	75.948	76.156

SOURCES

See the sources for Table 14.

* See 629–30 and n97 and Table 13 above.

TABLE 16

A COMPARISON OF THE PURCHASING POWER OF A MASTER MASON'S
SUMMER WAGES IN THE ANTWERP REGION AND IN SOUTHERN ENGLAND
FROM 1501–5 TO 1536–40

	Antwerp					
	master mason's nominal daily summer wage in	amount purchased with daily wage				
years	d groot Flemish	Rhine wine: litres	herrings: number	peas: litres	wheat: litres	sugar: kilograms
1501–5	8.333	2.922	48.450	19.695	19.842	1.022
1506–10	8.333	2.851	41.456	23.441	20.296	0.896
1511–15	9.333	2.720	38.341	20.595	22.778	0.582
1516–20	10.000	3.021	44.723	23.347	21.598	0.672
1521–5	10.267	2.676	31.296	19.004	14.364	0.635
1526–30	10.267	2.676	41.819	22.155	17.975	0.608
1531–5	10.067	2.858	43.642	15.729	15.321	0.838
1536–40	12.133	3.485	45.478	21.380	17.154	0.741

	England					
	master mason's nominal daily summer wage	amount purchased with daily wage				
years	in d sterling	Bordeaux wine: litres	herrings: number	peas: litres	wheat: litres	sugar: kilograms
1501–5	6.000	3.467	43.308	40.268	22.252	0.938
1506–10	6.000	3.413	42.848	37.339	33.347	0.756
1511–15	6.000	3.247	40.027	26.773	22.042	0.486
1516–20	6.000	3.364	42.463	33.033	21.263	0.409
1521–5	6.000	2.120	38.997	43.992	24.432	0.461
1526–30	6.000	2.472	38.168	23.368	16.082	0.382
1531–5	6.000	2.585	37.855	23.945	17.669	0.374
1536–40	6.500	2.638	38.168	30.501	21.901	0.388

TABLE 16 (continued)

A COMPARISON OF THE PURCHASING POWER OF A MASTER MASON'S
SUMMER WAGES IN THE ANTWERP REGIONAND IN SOUTHERN ENGLAND
FROM 1501–5 TO 1536–40

	advantage or disadvantage of an English mason's purchasing power in percentages based on English wages and prices, in relation to specific commodities				
years	wine	herrings	peas	wheat	sugar
1501–5	15.73	−11.87	51.09	10.83	−8.95
1506–10	16.46	3.25	37.22	39.14	−18.58
1511–15	16.23	4.21	23.08	−3.34	−19.73
1516–20	10.19	−5.32	29.32	−1.57	−64.11
1521–5	−26.22	19.75	56.80	41.21	−37.61
1526–30	−8.23	−9.57	5.19	−11.77	−59.35
1531–5	−10.56	−15.29	34.31	13.29	−124.00
1536–40	−32.07	−19.15	29.91	21.68	−90.92

SOURCE

See the sources for Tables 6, 11–15.

TABLE 17

VALUES OF ERASMUS' RECEIPTS AND INCOMES IN 1526

letter number	date / coins or currency designated details of transmission	official value of coin			amount or number of coins	value of sum			value of sum in days' wages of a mason		number of years' wage income for an Antwerp mason
		in d groot Flanders	in £ tournois France	in d sterling England		in £ groot Flemish	in £ tournois	in £ sterling	Oxford (6d sterling)	Antwerp (10d groot Flemish)*	
1658	*16 January 1526* French gold écu au soleil from England via Martin Lompart of Basel	76.00	2.000	52.00	138.500	43.858	277.000	30.008	1,200.333	1,052.600	4.577
1671	*7 March 1526* English pounds sterling received via Alvaro de Castro	365.17	9.559	240.00	38.000	57.819	363.238	38.000	1,520.000	1,387.652	6.033
1681	*17 March 1526* Rhenish gold florins from Alvaro de Castro via 'your man Harst'	59.00	1.500	39.00	72.000	17.700	108.000	11.700	468.000	424.800	1.847
	Rhenish gold florins to come from Pieter Gillis via Frans Gillis	59.00	1.500	39.00	600.000	147.500	900.000	97.500	3,900.000	3,540.000	15.391
1696	*21 April 1526* French gold écu au soleil from Frans Gillis via Johann Froben	76.00	2.000	52.00	400.000	126.667	800.000	86.667	3,466.667	3,040.000	13.217
1750	*8 September 1526* English rose crowns from the bishop of London via Erasmus Schets	70.00	1.875	54.00	120.000	35.000	225.000	27.000	1,080.000	840.000	3.652

TABLE 17 (continued)

VALUES OF ERASMUS' RECEIPTS AND INCOMES IN 1526

letter num-ber	date / coins or currency designated details of transmission	official value of coin			amount or number of coins	value of sum			value of sum in days' wages of a mason		number of years' wage income for an Antwerp mason
		in d groot Flanders	in £ tournois France	in d sterling England		in £ groot Flemish	in £ tournois	in £ sterling	Oxford (6d sterling)	Antwerp (10d groot Flemish)*	
1750	*8 September 1526* (continued) Flemish florins of account from the bishop of London via Erasmus Schets, converted into florins in Antwerp	40.00	1.047	27.37	252.000	42.000	263.847	28.737	1,149.474	1,008.000	4.383
1758	*2 October 1526* Rhenish gold florins from Hieronymus Froben at the Frankfurt fair, converted from 687 florins 12 stuivers Flemish	59.00	1.500	39.00	436.000	107.183	654.000	70.850	2,834.000	2,572.400	11.184
1769	*15 December 1526* Rhenish gold florins Courtrai annuity, paid at Candlemas/Purification (2 February), deposited in Bruges with Marcus Laurinus	59.00	1.500	40.00	130.000	31.958	195.000	21.667	866.667	767.000	3.335
	English angel-nobles annual income from John, bishop of Lincoln, to be sent via Castro to Hieronymus Froben at the Frankfurt fair	119.00	3.050	90.00	15.000	7.438	45.750	5.625	225.000	178.500	0.776

TABLE 17 (continued)

letter number	date / coins or currency designated / details of transmission	official value of coin			amount or number of coins	value of sum			value of sum in days' wages of a mason		number of years' wage income for an Antwerp mason
		in d groot Flanders	in £ tournois France	in d sterling England		in £ groot Flemish	in £ tournois	in £ sterling	Oxford (6d sterling)	Antwerp (10d groot Flemish)*	
1771	*20 December 1526*										
	Rhenish gold florins gift from the bishop of Trent on receiving Erasmus' book	59.00	1.500	40.00	100.000	24.583	150.000	16.667	666.667	590.000	2.565
	Rhenish gold florins promised annuity from the bishop of Trent	59.00	1.500	40.00	600.000	147.500	900.000	100.000	4,000.000	3,540.000	15.391
annual totals						789.206	4,851.835	534.42	21,376.807	18,940.952	82.352

* 10d is the mean of the summer wage of 11d for nine months, or 172.5 days, and the winter wage of 7d for three months, or 57.5 days. The sum would be 2,300d for 230 days, or 10d per day. Similarly: (0.75 × 11.00) + (0.25 × 7.00) = 8.25 + 1.25 = 10d.

TABLE OF CORRESPONDENTS

WORKS FREQUENTLY CITED

SHORT-TITLE FORMS
FOR ERASMUS' WORKS

INDEX

TABLE OF CORRESPONDENTS

LETTERS OF JUAN DE VERGARA AND OTHERS CONCERNING ERASMUS

WORKS FREQUENTLY CITED

This list provides bibliographical information for works referred to in short-title form in this volume. For Erasmus' writings see the short-title list, pages 709–12. Editions of his letters are included in the list below.

AK	*Die Amerbachkorrespondenz* ed Alfred Hartmann and B.R. Jenny (Basel 1942–)
Allen	*Opus epistolarum Des. Erasmi Roterodami* ed P.S. Allen, H.M. Allen, and H.W. Garrod (Oxford 1906–58) 11 vols and index
ASD	*Opera omnia Desiderii Erasmi Roterodami* (Amsterdam 1969–)
Bataillon (1991)	Marcel Bataillon *Érasme et l'Espagne* rev ed, text by Daniel Devoto, ed Charles Amiel (Geneva 1991) 3 vols. This revised posthumous edition is now the standard text, replacing the original French edition (Paris 1937) and two editions of the Spanish translation (Mexico City 1950 and 1966).
BRE	*Briefwechsel des Beatus Rhenanus* ed Adalbert Horawitz and Karl Hartfelder (Leipzig 1886; repr Hildesheim 1966)
Brecht	Martin Brecht *Martin Luther* trans James L. Schaaf (Philadelphia 1985–93) 3 vols
CEBR	*Contemporaries of Erasmus: A Biographical Register of the Renaissance and the Reformation* ed Peter G. Bietenholz and Thomas B. Deutscher (Toronto 1985–7) 3 vols
CWE	*Collected Works of Erasmus* (Toronto 1974–)
DBI	*Dizionario biografico degli Italiani* (Rome 1960–)
Enthoven	*Briefe an Desiderius von Rotterdam* ed L.K. Enthoven (Strassburg 1906)
Farge *Biographical Register*	James K. Farge *Biographical Register of Paris Doctors of Theology, 1500–1536* Pontifical Institute of Mediaeval Studies, Subsidia Mediaevalia 10 (Toronto 1980)
Farge *Orthodoxy*	James K. Farge *Orthodoxy and Reform in Early Reformation France: The Faculty of Theology of Paris 1500–1543* Studies in Medieval and Reformation Thought 32 (Leiden 1985)
Farge *Parti conservateur*	James K. Farge *Le parti conservateur au XVIe siècle: Université et Parlement de Paris à l'époque de la Renaissance et de la Réforme* ([Paris] 1992)

Farge *Registre*	*Registre des procès-verbaux de la faculté de théologie de l'Université de Paris de janvier 1524 à novembre 1533* ed James K. Farge (Paris 1990)
Förstemann/ Günther	*Briefe an Desiderius Erasmus von Rotterdam* ed J[oseph] Förstemann and O[tto] Günther, XXVII. Beiheft zum *Zentralblatt für Bibliothekswesen* (Leipzig 1904; repr Wiesbaden 1968)
Gerlo	*La correspondance d'Erasme* ed Aloïs Gerlo 12 vols (Brussels 1967–84)
Homza	Lu Ann Homza 'Erasmus as Hero, or Heretic? Spanish Humanism and the Valladolid Assembly of 1527' *Renaissance Quarterly* 50 (1997) 78–118
Knecht *Renaissance*	R.J. Knecht *Renaissance Warrior and Patron: The Reign of Francis I* (Cambridge 1994) (a revision of his earlier *Francis I* [1982])
LB	*Desiderii Erasmi Roterodami opera omnia* ed J[acques] Leclerc (Leiden 1703–6; repr 1961–2) 10 vols
Livermore	H.V. Livermore *New History of Portugal* 2nd ed (Cambridge 1976)
LP	*Letters and Papers, Foreign and Domestic, of the Reign of Henry VIII* ed J.S. Brewer, J. Gairdner, and R.H. Brodie (London 1862–1932) 36 vols
More CW	*The Complete Works of Saint Thomas More* ed Louis L. Martz and others (New Haven 1963–97) 15 vols in 21
NK	*Nederlandsche bibliographie van 1500 tot 1540* ed Wouter Nijhoff and M.E. Kronenberg (The Hague 1923–61) 3 vols
OED2	*The Oxford English Dictionary* 2nd ed (Oxford 1989) 20 vols
Opus epistolarum	*Opus epistolarum Des. Erasmi Roterodami per autorem diligenter recognitum et adjectis innumeris novis fere ad trientem auctum* (Basel: Froben, Herwagen, and Episcopius 1529)
Opuscula	*Erasmi Opuscula: A Supplement to the Opera Omnia* ed Wallace K. Ferguson (The Hague 1933)
Pastor	Ludwig von Pastor *The History of the Popes from the Close of the Middle Ages* ed and trans R.F. Kerr and others, 6th ed (London 1938–53) 40 vols

PG	J.P. Migne ed *Patrologiae cursus completus ... series Graeca* (Paris 1857–91) 161 vols
PL	J.P. Migne ed *Patrologiae cursus completus ... series Latina* (Paris 1878–90) 222 vols
Phillips *Adages*	Margaret Mann Phillips *The 'Adages' of Erasmus* (Cambridge 1964)
Potter	G.R. Potter *Zwingli* (Cambridge 1976)
PW	*Paulys Real-Encyclopädie der classischen Altertumswissenschaft* ed Georg Wissowa (Stuttgart 1894–1963) 24 vols in 31
Quasten	Johannes Quasten *Patrology* (Utrecht 1950–86) 4 vols
Richet	Denis Richet 'Le cours officiel des monnaies étrangères circulant en France au XVIe siècle' *Revue historique* 225 (1961) 377–96
Rummel	Erika Rummel *Erasmus and His Catholic Critics* 2 vols (Nieuwkoop 1989)
Schoeck (1993)	R.J. Schoeck *Erasmus of Europe: The Prince of Humanists, 1501–1536* (Edinburgh 1993)
Scrinium Erasmianum	*Scrinium Erasmianum* ed J[oseph] Coppens (Leiden 1969) 2 vols
STC	*A Short-Title Catalogue of Books Printed in England, Scotland, and Ireland and of English Books Printed Abroad, 1475–1640,* comp A.W. Pollard, G.R. Redgrave and others, 2nd ed rev, 3 vols (London 1986–91)
Tracy *Erasmus*	James D. Tracy *Erasmus of the Low Countries* (Berkeley 1996)
de Vocht CTL	Henry de Vocht *History of the Foundation and Rise of the Collegium Trilingue Lovaniense 1517–1550* Humanistica Lovaniensia 10–13 (Louvain 1951–5) 4 vols
WA	*D. Martin Luthers Werke, Kritische Gesamtausgabe* (Weimar 1883–)
WA-Br	*D. Martin Luthers Werke: Briefwechsel* (Weimar 1930–78) 15 vols

Titles following colons are longer versions of the same, or are alternative titles. Items entirely enclosed in square brackets are of doubtful authorship. For abbreviations, see Works Frequently Cited.

Acta: Acta Academiae Lovaniensis contra Lutherum *Opuscula* / CWE 71

Adagia: Adagiorum chiliades 1508, etc (Adagiorum collectanea for the primitive form, when required) LB II / ASD II-1, 4, 5, 6 / CWE 30–6

Admonitio adversus mendacium: Admonitio adversus mendacium et obtrectationem LB X

Annotationes in Novum Testamentum LB VI / CWE 51–60

Antibarbari LB X / ASD I-1 / CWE 23

Apologia ad Caranzam: Apologia ad Sanctium Caranzam, or Apologia de tribus locis, or Responsio ad annotationem Stunicae ... a Sanctio Caranza defensam LB IX

Apologia ad Fabrum: Apologia ad Iacobum Fabrum Stapulensem LB IX / ASD IX-3 / CWE 83

Apologia adversus monachos: Apologia adversus monachos quosdam Hispanos LB IX

Apologia adversus Petrum Sutorem: Apologia adversus debacchationes Petri Sutoris LB IX

Apologia adversus rhapsodias Alberti Pii: Apologia ad viginti et quattuor libros A. Pii LB IX

Apologia contra Latomi dialogum: Apologia contra Iacobi Latomi dialogum de tribus linguis LB IX / CWE 71

Apologia de 'In principio erat sermo' LB IX

Apologia de laude matrimonii: Apologia pro declamatione de laude matrimonii LB IX / CWE 71

Apologia de loco 'Omnes quidem': Apologia de loco 'Omnes quidem resurgemus' LB IX

Apologiae contra Stunicam: Apologiae contra Lopidem Stunicam LB IX / ASD IX-2

Apologia qua respondet invectivis Lei: Apologia qua respondet duabus invectivis Eduardi Lei *Opuscula*

Apophthegmata LB IV

Appendix de scriptis Clithovei LB IX / CWE 83

Appendix respondens ad Sutorem LB IX

Argumenta: Argumenta in omnes epistolas apostolicas nova (with Paraphrases)

Axiomata pro causa Lutheri: Axiomata pro causa Martini Lutheri *Opuscula* / CWE 71

Carmina LB I, IV, V, VIII / ASD I-7 / CWE 85–6

Catalogus lucubrationum LB I / CWE 9 (Ep 1341A)

Ciceronianus: Dialogus Ciceronianus LB I / ASD I-2 / CWE 28

Colloquia LB I / ASD I-3 / CWE 39–40

Compendium vitae Allen I / CWE 4

Concionalis interpretatio (in Psalmi)

Conflictus: Conflictus Thaliae et Barbariei LB I

[Consilium: Consilium cuiusdam ex animo cupientis esse consultum] *Opuscula* / CWE 71

De bello Turcico: Consultatio de bello Turcico (in Psalmi)

De civilitate: De civilitate morum puerilium LB I / CWE 25

Declamatio de morte LB IV

Declamatiuncula LB IV

Declarationes ad censuras Lutetiae vulgatas: Declarationes ad censuras Lutetiae vulgatas sub nomine facultatis theologiae Parisiensis LB IX

De concordia: De sarcienda ecclesiae concordia, or De amabili ecclesiae concordia (in Psalmi)

De conscribendis epistolis LB I / ASD I-2 / CWE 25

De constructione: De constructione octo partium orationis, or Syntaxis LB I / ASD I-4

De contemptu mundi: Epistola de contemptu mundi LB V / ASD V-1 / CWE 66

De copia: De duplici copia verborum ac rerum LB I / ASD I-6 / CWE 24

De esu carnium: Epistola apologetica ad Christophorum episcopum Basiliensem de interdicto esu carnium LB IX / ASD IX-1

De immensa Dei misericordia: Concio de immensa Dei misericordia LB V / CWE 70

De libero arbitrio: De libero arbitrio diatribe LB IX / CWE 76

De praeparatione: De praeparatione ad mortem LB V / ASD V-1 / CWE 70

De pueris instituendis: De pueris statim ac liberaliter instituendis LB I / ASD I-2 / CWE 26

De puero Iesu: Concio de puero Iesu LB V / CWE 29

De puritate tabernaculi: De puritate tabernaculi sive ecclesiae christianae (in Psalmi)

De ratione studii LB I / ASD I-2 / CWE 24

De recta pronuntiatione: De recta latini graecique sermonis pronuntiatione LB I / ASD I-4 / CWE 26

De taedio Iesu: Disputatiuncula de taedio, pavore, tristicia Iesu LB V / CWE 70

Detectio praestigiarum: Detectio praestigiarum cuiusdam libelli germanice scripti LB X / ASD IX-1

De vidua christiana LB V / CWE 66

De virtute amplectenda: Oratio de virtute amplectenda LB V / CWE 29

[Dialogus bilinguium ac trilinguium: Chonradi Nastadiensis dialogus bilinguium ac trilinguium] Opuscula / CWE 7

Dilutio: Dilutio eorum quae Iodocus Clithoveus scripsit adversus declamationem suasoriam matrimonii / Dilutio eorum quae Iodocus Clithoveus scripsit ed Emile V. Telle (Paris 1968) / CWE 83

Divinationes ad notata Bedae LB IX

Ecclesiastes: Ecclesiastes sive de ratione concionandi LB V / ASD V-4, 5

Elenchus in N. Bedae censuras LB IX

Enchiridion: Enchiridion militis christiani LB V / CWE 66

Encomium matrimonii (in De conscribendis epistolis)

Encomium medicinae: Declamatio in laudem artis medicae LB I / ASD I-4 / CWE 29

Epistola ad Dorpium LB IX / CWE 3 / CWE 71

Epistola ad fratres Inferioris Germaniae: Responsio ad fratres Germaniae Inferioris ad epistolam apologeticam incerto autore proditam LB X / ASD IX-1

Epistola ad graculos: Epistola ad quosdam imprudentissimos graculos LB X

Epistola apologetica de Termino LB X

Epistola consolatoria: Epistola consolatoria virginibus sacris, or Epistola consolatoria in adversis LB V / CWE 69

Epistola contra pseudevangelicos: Epistola contra quosdam qui se falso iactant
  evangelicos LB X / ASD IX-1
Euripidis Hecuba LB I / ASD I-1
Euripidis Iphigenia in Aulide LB I / ASD I-1
Exomologesis: Exomologesis sive modus confitendi LB V
Explanatio symboli: Explanatio symboli apostolorum sive catechismus LB V /
  ASD V-1 / CWE 70
Ex Plutarcho versa LB IV / ASD IV-2

Formula: Conficiendarum epistolarum formula (see De conscribendis epistolis)

Hyperaspistes LB X / CWE 76–7

In Nucem Ovidii commentarius LB I / ASD I-1 / CWE 29
In Prudentium: Commentarius in duos hymnos Prudentii LB V / CWE 29
Institutio christiani matrimonii LB V / CWE 69
Institutio principis christiani LB IV / ASD IV-1 / CWE 27

[Julius exclusus: Dialogus Julius exclusus e coelis] *Opuscula* / CWE 27

Lingua LB IV / ASD IV-1A / CWE 29
Liturgia Virginis Matris: Virginis Matris apud Lauretum cultae liturgia LB V /
  ASD V-1 / CWE 69
Luciani dialogi LB I / ASD I-1

Manifesta mendacia CWE 71
Methodus (see Ratio)
Modus orandi Deum LB V / ASD V-1 / CWE 70
Moria: Moriae encomium LB IV / ASD IV-3 / CWE 27

Novum Testamentum: Novum Testamentum 1519 and later (Novum instrumentum
  for the first edition, 1516, when required) LB VI

Obsecratio ad Virginem Mariam: Obsecratio sive oratio ad Virginem Mariam in re-
  bus adversis, or Obsecratio ad Virginem Matrem Mariam in rebus adversis LB V /
  CWE 69
Oratio de pace: Oratio de pace et discordia LB VIII
Oratio funebris: Oratio funebris in funere Bertae de Heyen LB VIII / CWE 29

Paean Virgini Matri: Paean Virgini Matri dicendus LB V / CWE 69
Panegyricus: Panegyricus ad Philippum Austriae ducem LB IV / ASD IV-1 / CWE 27
Parabolae: Parabolae sive similia LB I / ASD I-5 / CWE 23
Paraclesis LB V, VI
Paraphrasis in Elegantias Vallae: Paraphrasis in Elegantias Laurentii Vallae LB I /
  ASD I-4
Paraphrasis in Matthaeum, etc (in Paraphrasis in Novum Testamentum)
Paraphrasis in Novum Testamentum LB VII / CWE 42–50
Peregrinatio apostolorum: Peregrinatio apostolorum Petri et Pauli LB VI, VII
Precatio ad Virginis filium Iesum LB V / CWE 69

Precatio dominica LB V / CWE 69
Precationes: Precationes aliquot novae LB V / CWE 69
Precatio pro pace ecclesiae: Precatio ad Dominum Iesum pro pace ecclesiae LB IV,
  V / CWE 69
Psalmi: Psalmi, or Enarrationes sive commentarii in psalmos LB V / ASD V-2, 3 /
  CWE 63–5
Purgatio adversus epistolam Lutheri: Purgatio adversus epistolam non sobriam
  Lutheri LB X / ASD IX-1

Querela pacis LB IV / ASD IV-2 / CWE 27

Ratio: Ratio seu Methodus compendio perveniendi ad veram theologiam (Methodus
  for the shorter version originally published in the Novum instrumentum of
  1516) LB V, VI
Responsio ad annotationes Lei: Liber quo respondet annotationibus Lei LB IX
Responsio ad collationes: Responsio ad collationes cuiusdam iuvenis gerontodidas-
  cali LB IX
Responsio ad disputationem de divortio: Responsio ad disputationem cuiusdam
  Phimostomi de divortio LB IX / CWE 83
Responsio ad epistolam Pii: Responsio ad epistolam paraeneticam Alberti Pii, or
  Responsio ad exhortationem Pii LB IX
Responsio ad notulas Bedaicas LB X
Responsio ad Petri Cursii defensionem: Epistola de apologia Cursii LB X / Allen
  Ep 3032
Responsio adversus febricitantis libellum: Apologia monasticae religionis LB X

Spongia: Spongia adversus aspergines Hutteni LB X / ASD IX-1
Supputatio: Supputatio calumniarum Natalis Bedae LB IX

Tyrannicida: Tyrannicida, declamatio Lucianicae respondens LB I / ASD I-1 / CWE 29

Virginis et martyris comparatio LB V / CWE 69
Vita Hieronymi: Vita divi Hieronymi Stridonensis Opuscula / CWE 61

Index

Adrian VI, pope: silences Zúñiga's attacks 5n; school friend of Floris Oem at Louvain 43; makes Jan Oem his successor as canon of Liège 44; rejects Erasmus' advice on response to Luther 143; invites Erasmus to Rome 150, 172; effort to silence Louvain theologians fails 165 and n, 231–3 and n; dies before confirming Louvain's privileges 215n

Aesticampianus, Johannes, German humanist 427

Affenstein, Wolfgang von, steward of bishop of Worms in Ladenburg 425; administers Dalberg library for bishop 406; greetings to 407
– letter from 425–7

Africa 368 and n; Moroccan cities conquered by Portuguese 506 and n

Agricola, Rodolphus: patronized by Bishop Dalberg of Worms 406, 426n

Agrippa von Nettesheim, German humanist and occultist 428

Alaard of Amsterdam, Louvain humanist 43n, 547n

Alber, Erasmus, Lutheran schoolteacher at Eisenach 88n

Albuquerque, Afonso de, Portuguese admiral 505n

Alcalá de Henares: Erasmian books published at 484n; Bernardino Tovar at centre of Erasmian circle 523–4n
– University of: founded 466n; Miguel Eguía becomes university printer 527n

Alciati, Andrea, Italian humanist and jurist 434; affected by war in northern Italy 192n; edits first edition of Dante's *Monarchia* 475n
– letter to 192–5

Alcionio, Pietro, professor of Greek at Rome 494n

Aldington, parish in Kent: Erasmus draws pension from 77n, 256n, 311–12n

Aldridge, Robert, Cambridge scholar 401n; collates manuscripts of Seneca 400–2, 403–4, 499 and nn
– letter from 400–4
– letter to 499–500

Aleandro, Girolamo, humanist, curial official and diplomat 160n; influential enemy of Erasmus at Roman curia 12n, 181n, 220n, 233, 280–1 and n; probable author of *Racha*, a clandestine attack on Erasmus 12n, 224n, 233n, 335n; influences Erard de la Marck against Erasmus 187n; Erasmus' indirect attack on 494 and n

Algoet, Lieven, of Ghent, Erasmus' courier and secretary: greeted by Jan Antonin 15; forwards gift from Bishop Longland 188 and n; Erasmus endorses his petition to papal curia 216 and n

Alvaro, Luis. *See* Castro, Alvaro de, and Castro, Luis de

Ambrose, St, bishop of Milan 132, 513; Erasmus' edition of 190 and n; sermons of 513

mus informs of Luther's marriage
79n; studies at Padua 383n; with
Pole, visits Botzheim at Constance
383
Luther, Hans, father of Martin 58n
Luther, Martin: Erasmus sometimes
charged with being source of heresies
of 9n, 424n; opinion of, at Polish
court 15; consulted by Duke John of
Saxony 48; and the Sacramentarians
51n, 84, 488; Erasmus explains initial
sympathy for 58–9 and nn, 137n;
opposition to, affects humanistic
studies 60 and n, 137; marriage
of 79 and n; Erasmus finds two
personalities in 83; and Cochlaeus
136 and n, 261–2n, 434n; exchange of
letters with Duke George of Saxony
157 and n; Erasmus' opposition to,
impeded by attacks on conservative
Catholic critics 240–2, 248–9, 326, 334;
attacked in many books 442
– *De servo arbitrio*: delayed response to
Erasmus *De libro arbitrio* 37; harsh-
ness of attack shocks Erasmus 37,
47, 68–9, 76, 79, 81, 90, 107, 109,
140 and n, 164, 178, 189, 215, 225,
230, 363; Erasmus suspects plot to
prevent timely reply to 40, 41, 81
and n, 108; translated into German
81 and n; circulation of 52 and n, 141
and n
– *Antwort deutsch Mart. Luthers auff
König Heinrichs von Engelland buch /
Contra regem Angliae*: reply to Henry
VIII *Assertio septem sacramentum* 262
and n, 423n, 433 and n
– letter from (lost) 40, 135, 142, 164,
363n, 417n
– letter to 135–8
Lyra, Nicholas of, OFM, medieval exegete: authority undermined by ignorance of Greek 99, 100; Erasmus' disagreement with, offends theologians
348
Lysias, Greek rhetorician: writing style
of 474

Macrobius *Saturnalia* 390

Maier von Eck, Johann. *See* Eck, Johann
Maier of
Maldonado, Juan, of Bonilla, Spanish
humanist: on Erasmus' popularity
in Spain 314, 317; turns against
Erasmus from 1534 314n; defines
four types of reaction to Erasmus'
publications 314, 317–20; former
student of Longueil 316n; urges
avoidance of language that might
shock the undecided 320; reports
many Spanish translations of Erasmus
322
– letter from 314–24; arrives unsealed
409 and n
Man, Meynard, abbot of Egmond 547n
Manetti, Giannozzo, Florentine humanist: defends humanist principles of
translation 93n
Manichaeus: heretic opposed by St
Irenaeus 301
Manrique de Lara, Alonso, archbishop
of Seville and inquisitor-general of
Spain: creates inquisitorial commission that endorses Spanish *Enchiridion*
321n, 526n; negotiates with monastic
opponents of Erasmus 458n; generally favourable to Erasmus 477n;
Erasmus urged to write to 478;
receives Spanish *Enchiridion* from
Alonso Fernández 527
Mantz, Felix, Anabaptist martyr 440n
Manuel I, king of Portugal: Schets
claims close friendship with 102
and n, 376 and n; famous for conquests, piety, and patronage of
learning 504–7
Manuzio, Aldo (Aldus Manutius),
director of Aldine press at Venice 8
and n; Alberto Pio his former pupil
221n; Greek lexicon of 253 and n;
business partner of Andrea Torresani
338n
Marcion: heretic opposed by St Irenaeus
and Tertullian 299, 301, 303
Marck, Erard de la, prince-bishop of
Liège 186; opposes papal confirmation of privileges of Louvain
216n

This book

was designed by

VAL COOKE

based on the series design by

ALLAN FLEMING

and was printed by

University

of Toronto

Press